American Government and Politics in the New Millennium

Ninth Edition

American Government and Politics in the New Millennium

Ninth Edition

Virginia Stowitts Traina
  Palo Alto College
  San Antonio, Texas

Karen Sunshine
  SUNY Rockland Community College
  Suffern, New York

Christine Schultz
  Santa Monica College
  Santa Monica, California

Abigail Press   Wheaton, IL 60189

Design and Production: Abigail Press
Typesetting: Abigail Press
Typeface: AGaramond
Cover Art: Sam Tolia

...an Government and Politics
... New Millennium

Ninth Edition, 2014
Printed in the United States of America
Translation rights reserved by the authors
ISBN 1-890919-13-6
     978-1-890919-13-9

Copyright @ by Abigail Press Inc., 2050 Middleton Dr., Wheaton, IL 60189

All rights reserved. No part of the material protected by the copyright notice may be reproduced or utilized in any form or by any means, electronic or mechanical, including photocopy, recording, or any information storage and retrieval system, without permission in writing from the publisher.

Contents in Brief

Introduction
    How Do Political Scientists Know What They Know?   1

Chapter One
    The Language of Political Science   25

Chapter Two
    Constitutional Government   43

Chapter Three
    Federalism   69

Chapter Four
    Public Opinion, Political Culture, and Political Socialization   97

Chapter Five
    Political Parties   113

Chapter Six
    Campaigns and Elections   143

Chapter Seven
    The Media   185

Chapter Eight
    Interest Groups   217

Chapter Nine
    The Congress   247

Chapter Ten
    The Bureaucracy   283

Chapter Eleven
    The Presidency and Leadership   309

Chapter Twelve
    The Federal Court System   355

Chapter Thirteen
    Civil Liberties   383

Chapter Fourteen
    Civil Rights   421

Chapter Fifteen
    Public Policy   471

Chapter Sixteen
    Social Services   507

Chapter Seventeen
    The Environment   539

Chapter Eighteen
    Foreign Policy   575

Appendix   613
Glossary   639
Index   670

Table of Contents

Introduction
How Do Political Scientists Know What They Know ... 1

   How Do They Know? ... 1
   Methods, Techniques, and Approaches: The Differences ... 5
      Methods and Techniques ... 5
         Nonpolitical Techniques ... 5
         Political Techniques ... 6
      Limitations of Political Techniques ... 12
      Approaches ... 13
      Two Broad Approaches ... 14
         Traditional Approaches ... 14
         Behavioral Approaches ... 14
      Reading the Matrix ... 17
      Why Government Leaders Play Games ... 17
      Why Political Scientists Take This Approach ... 18
      Micro and Macro Approaches ... 18
      Systems Analysis (S/A) ... 18
         A System ... 19
         A Political System ... 20
      Conclusion ... 22
   Chapter Notes ... 23
   Suggested Readings ... 23

Chapter One
The Language of Political Science ... 25

   Evolution, Concepts, Theories, and Definitions ... 26
      Evolution ... 26
      Concepts ... 27
      Theories ... 27
      Definitions ... 27
   American Government Terminology ... 28
      Politics ... 28
         Lasswell's Definition ... 29
         Easton's Definition ... 29

Political Science	29
Government/American Government	30
Political Institutions	30
The "People"	30
Democracy	32
Direct and Indirect Democracy	33
The Political Spectrum	33
Power	35
Group Theories	37
Elite Theory	38
Authority and Legitimacy	38
Conclusion	40
Chapter Notes	41
Suggested Readings	41

Chapter Two
Constitutional Government 43

Theories of Government and Constitutionalism	44
Is Government Necessary?	44
Is Government a Social Contract?	46
Democracy	47
Constitutionalism	49
The Framer's Challenge—Creating a Constitutional Government	51
The Seeds of Discontent	51
The Articles of Confederation	53
The Gathering at Philadelphia—The Convention Setting	56
The Gathering at Philadelphia—The Convention Charge	56
The Gathering at Philadelphia—Designing a New Government	59
Amending the Document	64
Ratification and Adoption	64
The Ratification Process	64
Federalists versus Anti-Federalists	65
Conclusions	65
Chapter Notes	66
Suggested Readings	67

Chapter Three
Federalism 69

Types of Intergovernmental Relationships	73
Why a Federal System?	74
Constitutionally Mandated Intergovernmental Relationships—Vertical Federalism	74
Constitutionally Mandated Intergovernmental Relationships—Horizontal Federalism	78

Federalism and the Federal Courts	79
States' Rights v National Power	82
The Changing Faces of Federalism	85
Federal Grant Programs	89
Rising Interstate Conflicts	91
The Future of Federalism	92
Chapter Notes	93
Suggested Readings	95

Chapter Four
Public Opinion, Political Culture, and Political Socialization — 97

Public Opinion	97
The Importance of Public Opinion	98
Limited Range Importance	98
Public Opinion and Democracy	99
Public Opinion and Political Culture	100
American Political Culture	100
A Few Selected Descriptions of U.S. Political Culture	101
Benjamin Franklin	101
Alexis de Tocqueville	101
Gabriel Almond and Sidney Verba	102
The Source of Political Culture	102
Political Socialization	103
Political Socialization and the Individual	103
Agents of Socialization	103
The Significance of Political Socialization	108
Conclusion	109
Chapter Notes	110
Suggested Readings	111

Chapter Five
Political Parties — 113

The Anatomy of a Political Party	115
Historical Development of Political Parties	116
Party Systems	117
The Political Spectrum	119
Conservatism—The Right of the Spectrum	119
Moderates—The Center of the Spectrum	120
Liberalism—The Left of the Spectrum	121
Ideological Versus Issue Base Parties	123
American Political Parties	124
Historical Development	124
The Modern Republican Party	125
The Modern Democratic Party	127

American Third Party Movements	129
Factions Within the American Party Organizations	130
Organizational Structure of American Political Parties	133
The National Party Organization	134
The State Party Organization	137
County/District Organization	138
Precincts	138
Conclusion	139
Chapter Notes	140
Suggested Readings	141

Chapter Six
Campaigns and Elections — 143

The Changing Face of American Campaigns and Elections	144
Nominating the Candidates	146
Historical Background	146
The Caucus System	147
The Primary System	147
The Entitlement Revolution	148
Special Interests and the Nominating Conventions	150
Independent and Third-Party Nominees	150
Nominations for Congress and State Offices	151
The General Elections	152
House Elections	153
Single-Member Plurality Elections	153
Criticisms of the Single-Member System	154
Senate Elections	155
Presidential Elections	156
The Electoral College	156
Abolish the Electoral College?	158
Campaigning in the General Election	159
The Political Context	159
Financing Campaigns	160
How Much Campaigns Cost	160
Regulating Campaign Finance	160
The Bipartisan Campaign Reform Act of 2002	161
Legal Challenges to BCRA	162
New Loopholes in the Wake of the 2002 Campaign Finance Reform	162
Soft Money to State Political Parties	162
The 527 Organizations and Independent Expenditures	162
Issue-Related Advertisements	164
Bundling	164
Effects of the American Campaign Finance System	166
The Incumbency Advantage	166
Selling Access and Influence	167

Weakening the Role of the Political Parties	168
A Weakening of the Public Finance System	168
Increased Number of Personally Wealthy Candidates	168
Raising Campaign Money: A Distraction	169
Abuse and Scandals: The Case of Enron	169
Money and Campaigns: Prognosis for the Future	170
Campaign Strategies and Tactics	171
Polling	171
Making the News	171
The Tabloids	172
Advertising	172
Internet and High Tech Campaigning	173
The Mechanics of Elections	173
Hanging Chads, Pregnant Chads	173
Political Participation in Elections: The Waxing and Waning of the American Electorate	174
The Waxing of the American Electorate	174
The Waning of the American Electorate	175
Explaining Turnout	175
Increasing Turnout	176
The Voters: Explaining Vote Choice	177
Long-Term Forces: Group and Party Identification	177
Short-Term Forces: Issues and Candidate Image	178
Issues	178
Candidate Image	178
The 2010 Midterm Elections: A Return to Divided Government	179
The 2012 Presidential Election	179
Conclusion	180
Chapter Notes	181
Suggest Readings	183

Chapter Seven
The Media — 185

Democracy and the Mass Media	187
The Structure of the Mass Media	187
Books	187
Magazines	187
Newspapers	187
Television	188
Radio	188
Records	189
Motion Pictures	189
The Internet	189
Social Media	189
Government Regulation of the Media	190

Technical and Ownership Regulation	191
Regulation of Content	192
Political Functions of the Mass Media	194
Entertainment	194
Surveillance	194
Interpretation	194
Watchdog	194
Socialization	195
Persuasion and Propaganda	195
Agenda Setting	195
The Increased Importance of the Modern Mass Media	195
A Pervasive News Media	195
An Autonomous Press	196
Phase I: The Early Partisan Press	196
Phase II: The Penny Press and Yellow Journalism	198
Phase III: Investigative Journalism	199
Phase IV: Conglomerate Ownership of the Press	199
Phase V: Atomization of the Media	201
The News Gathering Process	202
Personal Background and Values	202
Professional Values	202
Organizational Factors	203
The Content of the News: Informational Biases	203
The Bias Debate	203
Informational Biases	204
Infotainment	204
Negativity	204
Coverage of Campaigns	204
The Horserace	205
Gaffes	205
Coverage of the Incumbent	205
Coverage of the President	206
Coverage of Congress	206
The Politicians Respond: The Management of News Coverage	207
Shorter Campaign Speeches	207
Spin Control	207
Presidential Debates	208
Political Advertisements	209
The Effects of the Mass Media	210
What People Remember and Know	210
Influencing Public Opinion	211
Setting the Political Agenda	211
Cynicism, Alienation, and Declining Efficacy	211
Behavior	211
Conclusion	212
Chapter Notes	212
Suggested Readings	215

Chapter Eight
Interest Groups — 217

Defining Interest Groups — 218
Interest Groups versus Political Parties — 218
The Roles of Interest Groups — 218
Representation — 219
Political Participation — 219
Education — 219
Agenda Building — 219
Program Monitoring — 219
Who is Organized? — 220
Economic Interest Groups — 220
Business Groups — 220
Organized Labor — 221
Agriculture — 222
Professional Associations — 222
Citizen Groups — 222
Women's Groups — 222
Religious Groups — 223
Gays and Lesbians — 223
The Elderly — 224
Environmental Groups — 224
Single-Issue Groups — 225
Foreign Governments — 225
The Internet — 225
Government Interest Groups — 226
Common Features of Interest Groups — 226
Biases in Interest Group Formation and Maintenance — 227
Obstacles to Interest Group Formation — 227
Overcoming the Obstacles Through Interest Group Maintenance — 228
Interest Group Bias — 229
The Proliferation of Interest Groups — 230
Sources of Interest Group Proliferation — 231
Increased Government Regulation — 231
Postindustrial Changes and Public Interest Groups — 232
Interest Group Friendly Laws and Actions — 232
Cheaper Forms of Communication — 233
The Rise of Single-Issue Groups — 233
Interest Group Methods and Strategies — 233
Electioneering and Political Action Committees — 233
The Creation of Political Action Committees — 234
Super PACs — 234
The Effects of PACs and Campaign Contributions — 235
Direct, or Inside, Lobbying — 236
Providing Information — 236

   The Effects of Direct Lobbying
   Regulating Lobbying
   The Newest Trend in Lobbying: Supreme Court Nominations
   Grassroots, or Outside, Lobbying: Going Public
   Litigating
   Bribery
   Prospects for Reform   242
   Conclusion   242
  Chapter Notes   243
  Suggested Readings   245

Chapter Nine
The Congress   247

The Origin and Powers of Congress   248
 The Constitution and the Great Compromise   248
 The Powers of the House and Senate   249
  The Expressed Powers   249
  The Implicit Power   249
 The Ebb and Flow of Congressional Powers   250
 The Era of Divided Government   252

Representation in Congress   252
 Theories of Representation   252
  The Instructed-Delegate View of Representation   253
  The Trustee View of Representation   253
  The Politico View of Representation   253
 The Quality of Congressional Representation   254
  Descriptive Representation   254
  Constituent Ties   255
 Congressional Elections   256
  Congressional Reapportionment   256
  Redistricting and Gerrymandering   257
  Racial Gerrymandering and "Minority-Majority" Districts   258
  Candidates for Congress   258
  The Costs of Congressional Campaigns   258
  The Advantages of Incumbency   259
 The Role of Gerrymandering in House Incumbency   260
 Campaign Finance and Incumbency   260
 The Issue of Term Limits   261

The Organizational Structures of Congress   261
 The Formal Leadership of Congress: The Political Parties   261
  Leadership in the House   261
  Leadership in the Senate   263
 The Role of Money in Choosing Congressional Leadership   264
 Party Discipline   265

The Committee and Subcommittee System   267

Work of Committees: Legislation and Oversight	267
The Committee System in the Era of Divided Government	268
Types of Congressional Committees	268
Standing Committees	268
Select Committees	269
Joint Committees	269
Conference Committees	269
The House Rules Committee	269
Committee Membership	269
Committee and Subcommittee Chairs	270
The Staff System	270
The Caucuses	271
The Legislative Process	273
Step One: The Bill is Introduced	273
Step Two: The Bill is Assigned to Committee	273
Step Three: Floor Action	274
Step Four: The Conference Committee	275
Step Five: The President	276
Step Six: Oversight	277
Conclusion	278
Chapter Notes	279
Suggested Readings	281

Chapter Ten
The Bureaucracy   283

The Development of the Bureaucratic State	285
Constitutional Beginnings	285
The Progressive Movement	286
The New Deal and Social Welfare Legislation	286
World War II	287
The Great Society and the Entitlements Revolution	287
Lobbying by Administrators	287
Ronald Reagan and Deregulation	288
Privatization of the Bureaucracy	289
Budget Cuts and the Size of the Bureaucracy	290
The Expanding Functions of the Bureaucratic State	291
National Maintenance	291
Clientele Services	291
Regulation	291
Income Redistribution	292
The Organization of the Federal Bureaucracy	292
Cabinet Departments	292
The Fifteenth Department: The Department of Homeland Security	292
Independent Agencies	293
Regulatory Agencies or Commissions	293

   The Effects of Direct Lobbying
   Regulating Lobbying
   The Newest Trend in Lobbying: Supreme Court Nominations
   Grassroots, or Outside, Lobbying: Going Public   237
   Litigating   238
   Bribery
   Prospects for Reform   242
   Conclusion   242
 Chapter Notes   243
 Suggested Readings   245

Chapter Nine
The Congress   247

 The Origin and Powers of Congress   248
  The Constitution and the Great Compromise   248
  The Powers of the House and Senate   249
   The Expressed Powers   249
   The Implicit Power   249
  The Ebb and Flow of Congressional Powers   250
  The Era of Divided Government   252
 Representation in Congress   252
  Theories of Representation   252
   The Instructed-Delegate View of Representation   253
   The Trustee View of Representation   253
   The Politico View of Representation   253
  The Quality of Congressional Representation   254
   Descriptive Representation   254
   Constituent Ties   255
  Congressional Elections   256
   Congressional Reapportionment   256
   Redistricting and Gerrymandering   257
   Racial Gerrymandering and "Minority-Majority" Districts   258
   Candidates for Congress   258
   The Costs of Congressional Campaigns   258
   The Advantages of Incumbency   259
  The Role of Gerrymandering in House Incumbency   260
  Campaign Finance and Incumbency   260
  The Issue of Term Limits   261
 The Organizational Structures of Congress   261
  The Formal Leadership of Congress: The Political Parties   261
   Leadership in the House   261
   Leadership in the Senate   263
  The Role of Money in Choosing Congressional Leadership   264
  Party Discipline   265
 The Committee and Subcommittee System   267

Work of Committees: Legislation and Oversight	267
The Committee System in the Era of Divided Government	268
Types of Congressional Committees	268
Standing Committees	268
Select Committees	269
Joint Committees	269
Conference Committees	269
The House Rules Committee	269
Committee Membership	269
Committee and Subcommittee Chairs	270
The Staff System	270
The Caucuses	271
The Legislative Process	273
Step One: The Bill is Introduced	273
Step Two: The Bill is Assigned to Committee	273
Step Three: Floor Action	274
Step Four: The Conference Committee	275
Step Five: The President	276
Step Six: Oversight	277
Conclusion	278
Chapter Notes	279
Suggested Readings	281

Chapter Ten
The Bureaucracy   283

The Development of the Bureaucratic State	285
Constitutional Beginnings	285
The Progressive Movement	286
The New Deal and Social Welfare Legislation	286
World War II	287
The Great Society and the Entitlements Revolution	287
Lobbying by Administrators	287
Ronald Reagan and Deregulation	288
Privatization of the Bureaucracy	289
Budget Cuts and the Size of the Bureaucracy	290
The Expanding Functions of the Bureaucratic State	291
National Maintenance	291
Clientele Services	291
Regulation	291
Income Redistribution	292
The Organization of the Federal Bureaucracy	292
Cabinet Departments	292
The Fifteenth Department: The Department of Homeland Security	292
Independent Agencies	293
Regulatory Agencies or Commissions	293

The Effects of Direct Lobbying	237
Regulating Lobbying	238
The Newest Trend in Lobbying: Supreme Court Nominations	239
Grassroots, or Outside, Lobbying: Going Public	240
Litigating	241
Bribery	242
Prospects for Reform	242
Conclusion	242
Chapter Notes	243
Suggested Readings	245

Chapter Nine
The Congress — 247

The Origin and Powers of Congress	248
The Constitution and the Great Compromise	248
The Powers of the House and Senate	249
The Expressed Powers	249
The Implicit Power	249
The Ebb and Flow of Congressional Powers	250
The Era of Divided Government	252
Representation in Congress	252
Theories of Representation	252
The Instructed-Delegate View of Representation	253
The Trustee View of Representation	253
The Politico View of Representation	253
The Quality of Congressional Representation	254
Descriptive Representation	254
Constituent Ties	255
Congressional Elections	256
Congressional Reapportionment	256
Redistricting and Gerrymandering	257
Racial Gerrymandering and "Minority-Majority" Districts	258
Candidates for Congress	258
The Costs of Congressional Campaigns	258
The Advantages of Incumbency	259
The Role of Gerrymandering in House Incumbency	260
Campaign Finance and Incumbency	260
The Issue of Term Limits	261
The Organizational Structures of Congress	261
The Formal Leadership of Congress: The Political Parties	261
Leadership in the House	261
Leadership in the Senate	263
The Role of Money in Choosing Congressional Leadership	264
Party Discipline	265
The Committee and Subcommittee System	267

The Work of Committees: Legislation and Oversight	267
The Committee System in the Era of Divided Government	268
Types of Congressional Committees	268
Standing Committees	268
Select Committees	269
Joint Committees	269
Conference Committees	269
The House Rules Committee	269
Committee Membership	269
Committee and Subcommittee Chairs	270
The Staff System	270
The Caucuses	271
The Legislative Process	273
Step One: The Bill is Introduced	273
Step Two: The Bill is Assigned to Committee	273
Step Three: Floor Action	274
Step Four: The Conference Committee	275
Step Five: The President	276
Step Six: Oversight	277
Conclusion	278
Chapter Notes	279
Suggested Readings	281

Chapter Ten
The Bureaucracy   283

The Development of the Bureaucratic State	285
Constitutional Beginnings	285
The Progressive Movement	286
The New Deal and Social Welfare Legislation	286
World War II	287
The Great Society and the Entitlements Revolution	287
Lobbying by Administrators	287
Ronald Reagan and Deregulation	288
Privatization of the Bureaucracy	289
Budget Cuts and the Size of the Bureaucracy	290
The Expanding Functions of the Bureaucratic State	291
National Maintenance	291
Clientele Services	291
Regulation	291
Income Redistribution	292
The Organization of the Federal Bureaucracy	292
Cabinet Departments	292
The Fifteenth Department: The Department of Homeland Security	292
Independent Agencies	293
Regulatory Agencies or Commissions	293

Government Corporations	294
Who are the Bureaucrats?	294
A Bureaucracy of Gentlemen	294
The Spoils System	295
The Civil Service	295
Changes in the Demographic Composition of the Bureaucracy	295
Presidential Appointees	295
Where are the Bureaucrats?	296
What Bureaucracies Do	296
Policy Development	296
Rule Administration	297
Rule Making and Regulation	297
Rule Adjudication	297
Litigation	298
Program Evaluation	298
The Political Resources of the Federal Bureaucracy	298
Authority	298
Administrative Discretion	298
Rule Making	299
Expertise	299
Clientele Support	300
How Bureaucracies Make Decisions	300
The Rational-Comprehensive Model	300
The Incremental Model of Bureaucratic Decision-Making	301
Bureaucratic Accountability	301
Presidential Control over the Bureaucracy	302
Congressional Control over the Bureaucracy	302
Iron Triangles and Issue Networks	303
Reform and Reorganization	304
Benefits of Bureaucracy	305
Managing Complexity	305
Stability and Predictability	305
Conclusion	305
Chapter Notes	305
Suggested Readings	307

Chapter Eleven
The Presidency and Leadership — 309

The Presidency	310
Qualifications: Formal and Informal	310
Getting Elected: The Electoral College	311
Presidential Powers and Duties: Given and Assumed	312
Powers Given	312
Powers Assumed	313
Presidential Roles	314

Chief of State	314
Chief Executive: The Executive Office of the President, The White House Office, and The Cabinet	315
Commander in Chief	318
Chief Diplomat	320
Chief Legislator	323
Presidential Roles v. The Whole Picture	327
Leadership and Leaders	327
What is Leadership?	328
Leadership and Headship	328
Leadership Failures: Two Case Studies	329
The Case of Jimmy Carter	329
The Case of George Herbert Walker Bush	331
Presidential Types	333
Barber's Presidential Typology	334
Clinton Typed	337
George W. Bush Typed	342
Barack H. Obama Typed	345
Presidential Types and Leadership	348
Conclusion	349
Chapter Notes	350
Suggested Readings	353

Chapter Twelve
The Federal Court System   355

Law—The Guiding Principle of Justice	356
Codification of Law	357
The Terminology and Process of the Justice System	358
The Federal Justice System	363
The United States Attorney General	364
The Investigative Arm of the Department of Justice	364
The Litigation Arm of the Department of Justice	366
The Federal Court System	367
Constitutional Courts	367
Selection of Judges	367
Jurisdiction	369
Federal District Courts	370
Federal Appellate Courts	370
The Supreme Court	371
The Power of Judicial Review	372
Federal Courts—Territorial Courts	377
Federal Courts—United States Court of Appeals for Veterans Claims	377
Federal Courts—Court of International Trade	378
Federal Courts—The Court of Federal Claims	378
Federal Courts—Court of Appeals for the Federal Circuit	378

      Federal Courts—United States Court of Appeals for the Armed Forces   378
The Final Arm of Justice—The Federal Prison System   379
    Conclusion   379
  Chapter Notes   380
  Suggested Readings   381

Chapter Thirteen
Civil Liberties   383

  The Concept of Civil Liberties   384
    Due Process   389
    The Importance of the First Amendment   390
      Freedom of Religion   390
      Freedom of Speech   395
      Obscenity   399
      Freedom of the Press   400
      Assembly and Association   402
    The Right to Bear Arms   405
    Protecting the Rights of the Accused   406
    Protection of Property and Privacy   414
    Conclusion   416
  Chapter Notes   417
  Suggested Readings   419

Chapter Fourteen
Civil Rights   421

    Civil Rights and Racism   424
    Theories of Racism   425
    Racism in America   429
    Native Americans   430
    African Americans   435
    The Hispanic Experience   447
    Gender Issues   456
    The LGBT Community   463
    Disabled Americans   463
    Conclusion   465
  Chapter Notes   466
  Suggested Readings   469

Chapter Fifteen
Public Policy   471

  Public Policy Development   475
    Who Makes Public Policy?   477
    What is the Purpose of Public Policy?   483

The Public Policy Process	485
Problem Identification	486
Agenda Building	488
Formulation of Policy	490
Budgeting	494
Political Implications	498
Adoption/selling	498
Implementation	500
Evaluation	501
Conclusion	502
Chapter Notes	502
Suggested Readings	505

Chapter Sixteen
Social Services   507

The Vocabulary of Poverty	510
A Profile of America's Poor	513
The Philosophy and Politics of Poverty	518
The Historical Development of the Welfare State	521
The Programs of the Welfare State Entitlements:	
Social Security and Unemployment Compensation	526
Public Assistance Programs	528
The Reform Bandwagon	529
Welfare Reform—Is It Working?	530
Health-care Reform	531
Conclusion	535
Chapter Notes	535
Suggested Readings	537

Chapter Seventeen
The Environment   539

Federal and State Roles in Environmental Policies	542
The Air We Breathe	548
Global Warming	556
The Water We Drink	557
Oil Spills and Toxic Wastes	560
Superfund Programs	563
Forest and Wetland Conservation	563
Endangered Species	565
Policy Options and the Political Climate	566
Conclusion	570
Chapter Notes	570
Suggested Readings	573

Chapter Eighteen
Foreign Policy 575

    Foreign Policy Terminology 577
    Foreign Policy Options 581
    Foreign Policy Process 583
    Securing the Economy 589
    The Development of American Foreign Policy 590
        Constitutional Authority 590
            Commander-in-Chief and Warmaking 591
            The Power to Make Treaties 595
        The President's Foreign Policy Team 597
        Brief Overview of American Foreign Policy 599
    Current Foreign Policy Issues and Challenges Ahead 603
        The Far East: North Korea 603
        Far East: China 604
        Central and Latin America—Mexico and Cuba 605
        The Middle East 606
        International Terrorism and Afghanistan 608
        Conclusion 610
    Chapter Notes 610
    Suggested Readings 612

Appendix
    Appendix A: Declaration of Independence 613
    Appendix B: Constitution of the United States of America 616
    Appendix C: Presidential Elections 632
    Appendix D: Supreme Court Justices 636
Glossary 639
Index 670

INTRODUCTION

HOW DO POLITICAL SCIENTISTS KNOW WHAT THEY KNOW? A BRIEF LOOK AT APPROACHES AND METHODS

Most consumers are probably well aware of the dictum "let the buyer beware," which is a reminder to examine merchandise carefully before buying it. This adage is an important one for students to keep in mind for, although they are not often categorized as such, they too are consumers. Students are buyers of knowledge or information, and information, just as any other commodity, requires inspection and evaluation.

HOW DO THEY KNOW?

To evaluate information is to determine whether the knowledge that is presented, be it in a radio, online, or television report, a magazine, a journal, a newspaper, a lecture hall, or an academic text such as this one, is valid. That determination is made essentially by questioning how the information being conveyed was acquired. In short, "How do they know?" (which is another way of asking "Is this product worth buying?") is the question that all students, including those of American government and politics, should ask. The following nonpolitical but true story illustrates why.

The story begins on Sunday, October 30, 1938, at 8:00 P.M. when CBS went on the air with a radio program that was soon to make history.[1] The program, as *The New York Times* reported the next day, started with a weather report. Then:

> an announcer remarked that the program would be continued from a hotel, with dance music. For a few moments a dance program was given in the usual manner. Then there was a "break-in" with a "flash" about a professor at an observatory noting a series of gas explosions on the planet Mars.
>
> News bulletins and scene broadcasts followed, reporting, with the technique in which the radio had reported actual events, the landing of a "meteor" near Princeton, N. J., "killing" 1,500 persons, the discovery that the "meteor" was a "metal cylinder" containing strange creatures from Mars armed with "death rays" to open hostilities against the inhabitants of the earth

The casualties at the landing site in Grovers Mill, N. J., as reported by one of the radio announcers, were enormous. He broke the news to his listeners in graphic detail:

> Ladies and gentlemen, I have a grave announcement to make. Incredible as it may seem, both the observations of science and the evidence of our eyes lead to the inescapable assumption that those strange beings who landed in the Jersey farmlands tonight are the vanguard of an invading army from the planet Mars. The battle which took place tonight at Grovers Mill has ended in one of the most startling defeats ever suffered by an army in modern times; seven thousand men armed with rifles and machine guns pitted against a single fighting machine of the invaders from Mars. One hundred and twenty known survivors. The rest strewn over the battle area from Grovers Mill to Plainsboro crushed and trampled to death under the metal feet of the monster, or burned to cinders by its heat ray. The monster is now in control of the middle section of New Jersey and has effectively cut the state through its center. Communication lines are down from Pennsylvania to the Atlantic Ocean. Railroad tracks are torn and service from New York to Philadelphia discontinued except routing some of the trains through Allentown and Phoenixville. Highways to the north, south, and west are clogged with frantic human traffic. Police and army reserves are unable to control the mad flight. By morning the fugitives will have swelled Philadelphia, Camden and Trenton, it is estimated, to twice their normal population.
>
> At this time martial law prevails throughout New Jersey and eastern Pennsylvania. We take you now to Washington for a special broadcast on National Emergency . . . the Secretary of the Interior . . . .

The announcer of course was right. This was an incredible story. It was, in fact, as stated numerous times before, during and after the transmission, a work of fiction, a play, "Invasion From Mars," based on a classic novella by H. G. Wells entitled *The War of the Worlds*. However, many listeners did not seem to hear the disclaimers, or to question what one reporter called "a totally unreasonable, completely fantastic proposition." Instead, they joined the estimated 1,200,000 others who "took the program literally and reacted according to their natures and circumstances." The reactions, as can be seen in the samples reported by the Associated Press, can be summarized in a single word, "panic." (See "War's Over: How U. S. Met Mars.")

Without passing judgment on their behavior, it is reasonable, perhaps unavoidable, to ask why those individuals who panicked did not know the difference between fact and fiction. While there probably is no simple response to that question, nor single explanation for the mass hysteria, some understanding of what happened can be achieved by recognizing that people come to "know" things in a wide variety of ways.

If time permitted, a lot of space could be devoted to exploring the many ways of knowing. There is actually an entire field of study devoted to understanding how people know the world. The field, for those interested in exploring the subject more fully, is a branch of philosophy called **epistemology** (from the Greek word "epistéme" meaning knowledge).

According to experts in this area, knowledge may be based—and there is considerable overlap in this list—on: myths, superstitions, hunches, intuition, common sense, casual observations,

War's Over
How U. S. Met Mars

The radio's "end of the world," as some listeners understood it, produced repercussions throughout the United States. Samples, as reported by the Associated Press, follow:

Woman Tries Suicide

Pittsburg.—A man returned home in the midst of the broadcast and found his wife, a bottle of poison in her hand, screaming: "I'd rather die this way than like that."

Man Wants to Fight Mars

San Francisco.—An offer to volunteer in stopping an invasion from Mars came among hundreds of telephone inquiries to police and newspapers during the radio dramatization of H. G. Wells' story. One excited man called Oakland police and shouted: "My God! Where can I volunteer my services? We've got to stop this awful thing!"

Church Lets Out

Indianapolis.—A woman ran into a church screaming: "New York destroyed; it's the end of the world. You might as well go home to die. I just heard it on the radio." Services were dismissed immediately.

College Boys Faint

Brevard. N. C.—Five Brevard College students fainted and panic gripped the campus for a half hour with many students fighting for telephones to inform their parents to come and get them.

It's a Massacre

Providence, R. I.—Weeping and hysterical women swamped the switchboard of the Providence Journal for details of the "massacre." The electric company received scores of calls urging it to turn off all lights so that the city would be safe from the "enemy."

She Sees "the Fire"

Boston.—One woman declared she could "see the fire" and told the Boston Globe she and many others in her neighborhood were "getting out of here."

"Where Is It Safe?"

Kansas City.—One telephone informant said he had loaded all his children into his car, had filled it with gasoline, and was going somewhere. "Where it is safe?" he wanted to know. The Associated Press bureau received queries on the "meteors" from Los Angeles, Salt Lake City, Beaumont, Tex., and St. Joseph, Mo.

Prayers in Richmond

Richmond, Va.—The Times-Dispatch reported some of its telephone calls came from persons who said they were praying.

Atlanta's "Monsters"

Atlanta—Listeners throughout the Southeast called newspapers reporting that "a planet struck in New Jersey, with monsters and almost everything, and anywhere from 40 to 7,000 people were killed." Editors said responsible persons, known to them, were among the anxious information seekers.

unverified beliefs, opinions, imagination, custom, astrology, magic, dreams, faith, and so on. There is nothing wrong with any of these ways of knowing things. Most people, for example, have relied upon hunches and intuition when there is nothing else to base their actions upon. Students frequently do that when taking objective exams. Virtually everyone has acted on faith or what others have told them is true. Patients take the medicine the doctor prescribes not because they have tested the drugs in a laboratory but because they have confidence in the physician and in the medication that is recommended. At the very least, life would be a lot more complicated than it already is if all data received from others, such as that the earth is round or that broccoli and spinach are nutritious or even that one political party is superior to the other, was rejected.

In a similar way the panic of those individuals who believed the "information" being reported on the radio on the evening of October 30, 1938, can be understood in terms of their faith, intuition, and/or the reactions of those around them. As one analyst of the event explained, "We are ready to believe almost anything if it comes from a recognized authority. This man [the announcer] gave complete credibility to the "news bulletins.... He mentioned the 'Secretary of State' [by name] although it was actually the fictional Secretary of the Interior...whose voice came over the air. Instead of hearing what was actually said, the listener heard what accorded with his preconceptions."

Given this, why then was it that the majority of those who heard the broadcast, approximately 4,800,000 listeners, knew or very quickly learned that what they were hearing was not true? How did they know?

Perhaps they reasoned that what was being described—a large alien that emitted rays and had tentacles, serpent-like eyes, skin that glistened like wet leather, and a lipless, V-shaped mouth that dripped saliva—had never been seen before and therefore probably did not exist; or they might have been somewhat suspicious about the accelerated pace and illogical sequence in which events were said to have taken place. (Within minutes of announcing the monster's arrival, it was reported that three million people had already moved out of New York.) Or maybe the "facts" were checked, and it was found that the agency doing the reporting, the Intercontinental Radio News, was nonexistent; or, after changing the radio dial, it was discovered that no other station was reporting the catastrophic invasion of Martians; or, after consulting a published listing of radio programs, it was ascertained that a play based on *The War of the Worlds* had been scheduled. The individuals who used such logical reasoning and who made such direct observations had a particular way of "knowing" or explaining reality that is described as **empirical** (based on experience or observation) or scientific.

Sometimes, as it was in the case just examined, it is preferable to rely more on knowledge based on observation than on intuition. The answer to the "How do they know?" question, in other words, provides a sound basis for accepting or rejecting information.

As with most people, those who study and write about political phenomena come to know things in a variety of ways. Some, including two of the great political philosophers, Plato and Jean Jacques Rousseau, were rather mystical thinkers who relied more on subjective impressions than on objective experiences. Others, such as Aristotle and John Locke, are recognized as being systematic or scientific thinkers. The reader will probably find that although the full range of ways that knowledge may be derived is represented within the covers of this volume that scientific studies rather than intuitive or mystical speculations are the dominant sources of information.

The reason for the scientific slant, in this and in most current political science texts, is related to the fairly recent evolution of the study of politics. During the 1950s, in a period now referred to as the "behavioral revolution," a number of political scientists argued that the study of politics should become much more systematic and objective than it had been up to that point. By the mid-1960s the majority of political scientists had been persuaded, and their efforts to become more scientific led to the introduction of many new methods, techniques, and approaches.

METHODS, TECHNIQUES, AND APPROACHES: THE DIFFERENCES

Before beginning any discussion of methods, techniques, and approaches, which will be treated here as distinct but related concepts, it should be made clear that not all political scientists agree that there are any distinctions or, if they do think that they exist, about what the differences are. Disagreements about the meanings of terms, as will be more fully explained in Chapter 1, are not unusual among political scientists. However, most of them do recognize that "scientists" have to be quite specific about their meanings.

Methods and Techniques

A **method** refers to a generally accepted way of obtaining and explaining information. (Methodology is a subfield of epistemology.) As has been pointed out earlier, at present the generally accepted way for political scientists to obtain and analyze information is "empirically." That is to say that, to the extent it is possible to do so, the scientific method, which for political scientists consists of the systematic and objective investigation of political phenomena, is used.

A **technique** refers to the SPECIFIC empirical or scientific procedures used to obtain and analyze political information. To put it more plainly, a technique refers to how something (including empirical research) is explicitly "DONE."

Nonpolitical Techniques

If asked for some "nonpolitical" examples of techniques, the reader could probably list a large number. The procedures an automobile mechanic uses to tune an engine, a dentist's techniques for filling a cavity, the procedures that an architect uses to design a house or an apartment building, the techniques that a pastry chef uses to bake chocolate chip cookies, and the procedures a student follows to prepare for an exam in American government would all be good examples. To tune an engine, fill a tooth, design a house, bake cookies, or prepare for an exam, certain things will inevitably be done.

The chef, for instance, would probably begin by blending and mixing the appropriate quantities of butter, flour, sugar, and chips and would then shape the delectable morsels into portions of the desired size, place them on a cookie sheet, and, finally, would pop them into the oven and bake them at approximately 350 degrees for twenty minutes or until they were a golden color.

Each step in the process of preparation is physical and can be observed. The baker has DONE something, employed procedures or techniques that, in the case of the cookies, are set out precisely, step by step, in a recipe. Obviously, the recipe for chocolate chip cookies just given is not the only one there is. One might add nuts, raisins, or M & Ms, or might blend instead of mix, stir instead of blend, or bake for thirty minutes rather than twenty.

Political Techniques

Just as there is more than one method to bake cookies, tune engines, study for exams, fill teeth, and design houses, there is more than one way to investigate political phenomena. Political scientists who are interested in the field of American government could, for example, select from the following limited list of common empirical or scientific techniques: surveys, statistics and content analysis.

✴ **Surveys:** The survey, or opinion poll, in which individuals are asked to respond to mailed questionnaires or to answer questions in telephone, online, or personal interviews is probably the most widely used technique for obtaining and analyzing current information about the government and about the attitudes of American citizens.

Every incumbent politician such as Senator Schumer or Senator Warren; every candidate for public office such as Obama and Romney in 2012; every topical issue including terrorism, health care, welfare, taxes, crime, and immigration policy; every political process including judicial decisions, legislative vetoes, and the influence of lobbyists; and every political institution such as the presidency, the bureaucracy, and interest groups are grist for the pollster's mill.

Some readers may have at one time or another actually participated as respondents in a poll and, in the future, many more are likely to. Among those that regularly conduct or commission these polls are:
1. local, state, or federal governments
2. government agencies
3. politicians
4. college and university faculty
5. political parties
6. survey research centers (Inter-University Consortium for Political and Social Research, University of Michigan; National Opinion Research Center, University of Chicago; Roper Center, University of Connecticut)
7. polling agencies (Gallup, Yankelovich Clancy Shulman)
8. the communications media (The ABC television network collaborates with the *Washington Post* on polls; CBS works in conjunction with *The New York Times*; and NBC news polls are associated with the *Wall Street Journal*.)

Media journalists are convinced that most of their audience thoroughly enjoys the juicy bits of gossipy-type information about political personalities that some polls report. However, it is reasonable, given their pervasiveness in society and the vast amount of more serious information that is often received from them, to ask whether knowledge derived from surveys is valid.

Should an individual decide to run or not to run for political office based on the reported results of popularity in a public opinion poll? Should citizens change their opinions about an issue or a policy, as they sometimes do, to conform to the attitudes that polls show most other Americans have? In other words should polls be trusted? Do researchers and reporters who rely on survey data really know what they think they know?

One expert on the survey method provides a checklist of eighteen specific questions that he believes have to be answered to evaluate the validity of survey findings. (See "Guide to Reading Survey Reports" p. 8.) The questions on the "Guide" list indicate that it is important to examine the procedures that have been followed by those who design the polls, those who administer them, and those who interpret the data.

Such a task is less daunting than it may initially seem, because at least some of that information is often made readily available to average readers of surveys. A responsible polling agency will explain, along with its published findings, how the poll was conducted. (See below "How the Poll Was Conducted.") The next table, "Summary of Polling Methodology," (pp. 10-11) describes the polling techniques of the four major national polling organizations in their efforts to find representative samples of the population to question during one election year. It is important, as can now be appreciated, to look for these explanations and descriptions before deciding to accept or to reject survey results.

How the Poll Was Conducted

The latest *New York Times*/CBS News Poll is based on telephone interviews conducted Aug. 5 to 9 with 1,478 adults throughout the United States.

The sample of telephone exchanges called was randomly selected by a computer from a complete list of active residential exchanges in the country. The list of more than 36,000 residential exchanges is maintained by Marketing Systems Group of Philadelphia.

Within each exchange, random digits were added to form a complete telephone number, thus permitting access to both listed and unlisted numbers. Within each household, one adult was designated by a random procedure to be the respondent for the survey.

The results have been weighted to take account of household size and number of telephone lines into the residence and to adjust for variations in the sample relating to geographic region, race, sex, age and education.

Source: R. W. Apple Jr., "Poll Shows Disenchantment With Politicians and Politics," *The New York Times*, 13 August 1995, A(8).

Guide to Reading Survey Reports

1. What general topic does the researcher wish to examine?

2. What was his motivation in designing and executing the study?

3. Is the researcher's main purpose one of exploration, description, explanation, or a combination of these?

4. What general population are the findings meant to represent?

5. What was the sampling frame used for purposes of selecting a sample to represent that population?

6. How was the sample actually selected?

7. How many respondents were initially selected in the sample and how many actually participated?

8. To what extent is sampling error likely to affect the results of the survey?

9. How were the data collected? Was the data collection method appropriate to the population and the subject matter of the study?

10. When did the data collection take place and how long did it take?

11. How were specific variables measured in the analysis? How were questionnaire items worded and/or how were responses combined into composite measures of variables? Does a given response pattern—imagining the orientations of persons giving it—reflect our common sensible interpretation of the summary term associated with the response pattern (for example, "very religious")?

12. Have composite measures been validated in such a way as to further ensure their adequate representation of the variables under consideration?

13. Are the methods of analysis used in the report appropriate both to the subject matter and the form of the data collected?

14. How strong are the associations discovered among variables? What do associations of that strength mean in understanding the real world?

15. Has the researcher adequately presented the logic of associations discovered empirically? Has he presented plausible reasons for those associations?

16. Has the researcher adequately tested for alternative explanations? Has he tested the possible spuriousness of the relationships?

17. Do the empirical relationships suggest further analyses that the researcher has neglected?

18. Could an independent reader replicate the survey on the basis of information presented in the report?

While these questions will not provide an exhaustive critique of all survey reports, they indicate the kinds of questions that a critical reader should ask and that the conscientious researcher should anticipate in the framing of his report.

Source: Earl R. Babbie, *Survey Research Methods* (Belmont, CA: Wadsworth Publishing Company, Inc., 1973), 3645.

Statistics: Statistics refer to the mathematical procedures that are used to interpret **data** (information) such as that collected in surveys. As students who have taken a "stat" (or as some have been known to call it "sadistics") course realize, some of the procedures used by statisticians can be quite complex and therefore somewhat intimidating. However, it's important to keep in mind that the reason for doing statistics in the first place is to simplify, not to complicate, the way information is analyzed and communicated.

Anyone who has ever calculated a college grade point average already knows that. Such a calculation is made by summing up all earned numerical scores (4.0 + 3.5 + 4.0 + 3.0 + 3.5) and then dividing the total by the number of grades received (five). The resulting number is the **mean** or average (a 3.6 using the numbers above), which is a statistical measure of **central tendency**. Why do students take the time to calculate the mean? Probably because it is easier to describe their academic performances with this single number than it is to communicate a long list of five, or ten, or twenty, or more individual grades. In short, statistics are used to simplify the communication of this information to others.

There are many, many other descriptive and inferential statistical procedures that allow people to measure data, make projections, test the strength of the **relationship** (association, dependence, covariance) between and among **variables** (the objects being examined or tested), validate or invalidate **hypotheses** (educated guesses about what a researcher expects to find), and so on. It is not necessary for purposes of this text to know how to mathematically perform all the tasks. It is enough just to be aware that these procedures do exist and that knowledge of them allows an individual to go beyond mere hunches or intuition in interpreting information and acquiring knowledge about American government. At some point in their academic careers those students who decide to pursue a bachelors degree in political science, or economics, or criminal justice, or just about any of the social and physical sciences will probably be required to take a least one course in statistics to complete their degree requirements.

Content Analysis: The name of this technique, **content analysis**, is fairly self-explanatory. What political scientists and others who use this technique do is to analyze the written record of the news media or to examine and "analyze" the "contents" of written remarks (in autobiographies, diaries, letters, etc.) and oral statements (formal speeches, casual remarks and conversations, press conferences, etc.) of individuals such as the President of the United States or a member of Congress.

The procedures used in the analysis, which are quite sophisticated, include: sampling, categorizing, coding, quantifying, and statistically evaluating the content being studied. A content analyst (To enhance reliability more than one coder is generally used.) might, for instance, want to determine the frequency with which a political leader uses a particular word or expression or calculate its **salience** (importance) to the user. If the leader's remarks and statements are found to be filled with abundant, fist-pounding references to acts of "war" or "terrorism" or are saturated with frequent tearful predictions of "economic collapse" or "doom," the utterings may be deemed to be significant.

Summary of . . .

Designing a "perfect" poll is a bit like creating the "perfect" spaghetti sauce: all cooks start with tomatoes, but each uses his own favorite combination of seasonings—sometimes with widely varied results. Presented below are the ingredients that went into the survey designs of four major national polling organizations during an election year.

CBS/New York Times

Population sampled from: National adult population telephone survey.
Household selection: Random digit dialing. Up to four attempts to contact household.
Respondent selection: Random selection, appointment made if designated respondent not at home.
Weighting: To correct for household size and to reflect demographics.
Identification of electorate: "Likelihood weight" based on past voting behavior and current intention and reported behavior of similar groups in 1976.
Actual choice: Choice among three major candidates, labeled by party. Leaners included in reported distributions.
Adjustments: None.

Gallup

Population sampled from: Registered voters. In-person interviews.
Household selection: Households randomly selected from sample precincts. No callbacks.
Respondent selection: Systematic selection based on age and sex.
Weighting: To correct for "times at home" and to reflect demographics.
Identification of electorate: "Likely voters" identified based on past behavior, interest, and intention to vote, and expected turnout.
Actual choice: "Secret ballot" for tickets, labeled by party. Undecided asked to mark ballot based on leaning.
Adjustments: Undecideds allocated; figures corrected for deviation of sample precincts from national results in 1976.

ABC/Harris*

Population sampled from: Expected electorate (based on 1976). Series of telephone surveys.
Household selection: Random digit dialing. Households not reached retained for one more survey.
Respondent selection: Systematic selection by modified sex quota.
Weighting: To reflect demographics.
Identification of electorate: "Likely voters" identified based on past behavior and intention to vote, and expected turnout.
Actual choice: Choice among three major candidates, labeled by party. Leaners included in reported distributions.
Adjustments: Survey results from last 12 days combined. (No day-to-day differences noted). Undecided allocated evenly between Carter and Reagan.

... Polling Methodology

NBC/AP**

Population sampled from: National adult population. Telephone survey.
Household selection: Random digit dialing. No callbacks (except for "busies").
Respondent selection: Systematic selection based on sex quota.
Weighting: None. Sample deemed "self-weighting."
Identification of electorate: "Likely voters" identified based on past behavior, interest, and intention to vote.
Actual choice: Choice among three major candidates, labeled by party (following questions on open-ended preferences and whether respondents had made up minds).
Adjustments: None

Glossary

National adult population. The sample is designed to reflect the characteristics, including geographic distribution, of the entire adult population.
Registered voters. The same, but the population is registered voters, instead of all adults.
Electorate. The same, but the actual electorate—i.e., taking differential turnout on a geographic basis into account.
Random digit dialing. Procedures giving households (both listed and unlisted numbers) a fair chance to be reached.
Callbacks. Multiple attempts to reach a household.
Random selection. Procedures to give each potential respondent in a household a random chance to come into the sample.
Systematic selection. Selection according to same system, depriving the interviewer of the choice of respondent.
Likelihood weight. An estimate of how likely someone is to vote. Someone who is 80 percent likely will count twice as much in the final figures as someone only 40 percent.
Likely voters. An attempt to separate respondents into two groups: "likely voters" and "non-likely voters." Only the former enter into the reported distributions.
Allocation. Division of the undecided based on other information, such as their partisan preference, issue positions, or data from other surveys.

Note: This overview cannot capture the full details of procedures used—for example what precise "demographics" were used.
*ABC had conducted polls with Louis Harris and Associates at the time of this summary. **AP conducted a survey on its own after the last joint survey.

Source: C. Everett Ladd and G. Donald Ferree, "Were the Pollsters Really Wrong?" *Public Opinion*, vol. 3, no. 6 (December/January 1981): 18. Reprinted with permission of American Enterprise Institute.

Source: Herbert Asher, *Polling and the Public: What Every Citizen Should Know* (Washington, D. C. : CQ Press, 1988), 140-141.

One news correspondent, William Safire, who informally used the technique, found that in his second inaugural address President Ronald Reagan used the word "freedom" twelve times and the words "free" and "freely" an additional four times. Clearly, Safire states this president saw freedom (from excessive government at home and from tyranny abroad) "as the essence of his message and the mark of his administration."[2] An analysis of Mr. Safire's columns might reveal that his conclusions about President Reagan were either based on an objective analysis or were the product of Safire's personal bias.

Other analysts have found that the structure of a leader's communication, the syntax, whether she/he is subdued or ecstatic, stuttering or hesitating, speaking exceptionally rapidly or slowly, loudly or quietly, and so forth, may show emotional distress. Take a few moments and think about what, if anything, the following quotation taken from one of many secretly recorded presidential conversations might reveal about the emotional state of the speaker.

> The report was not frankly accurate. Well it was accurate but it was not full. And, he tells me the reason it wasn't full, was that he didn't know. Whether that is true or not, I don't know. Although it wasn't I'm told. But I'm satisfied with it.[3]

Although it is difficult, without formal training in psychology, to specify precisely what it is that is wrong here, it is likely that most readers did recognize that something seems to have been troubling the speaker of these words. Dr. Walter Weintraub, a psychiatrist who is an expert on verbal behavior, certainly thinks so. He argues that the statement, which is "full of vacillation and negative words," indicates that the president who spoke them, Richard Nixon, "may have been clinically depressed at the time the conversations were recorded" (during the Watergate investigations).[4]

Content analysis has also been used to predict the winner of presidential elections. In one study an examination of the nomination speeches made by candidates in every presidential election year from 1948 through 1988 was conducted. The analysts extracted expressions of "optimism" (defined as talking about global or personal problems as being temporary and correctable), and "pessimism" (marked by the taking of blame for the problems or by stating that they are intractable) from the speeches and found that with one exception (not named in the source), the most optimistic candidate won the election.[5]

Analyses, such as those described above, show that a careful examination of oral remarks or written records can provide interesting information about politicians. Such studies can also provide insight into the people who vote for and write about them.

Limitations of Political Techniques

It would not be right to leave the impression that each of the three techniques we have just briefly examined provides an infallible way of knowing about American government.

For example, statistics (including those used in content analysis) can intentionally or unintentionally be extremely misleading. A very short, humorous, classic book of "pretty little instances of [statistical] bumbling and chicanery," *How to Lie with Statistics* by Darrell Huff, provides excellent examples of how politicians (among others) can lead the unknowing and the unthinking astray.

Polls too have been wildly inaccurate. Both the infamous 1936 poll conducted by the *Literary Digest* that inaccurately predicted that the Republican presidential candidate, Alf Landon, would win a landslide victory over the Democratic challenger, Franklin Delano Roosevelt, and the notoriously wrong forecasts in 1948 of a sweeping victory for Republican candidate Thomas E. Dewey over the incumbent President Harry S. Truman are examples of such inaccuracies.

Having noted these limitations, it should also be pointed out that when the intentions of a researcher are not to mislead but to convey accurate information (and that is probably the case most of the time) and when research techniques are carefully and explicitly carried out, they yield valid, as well as interesting, knowledge. There is something else to keep in mind about research techniques and that is that they are related to "**approaches**."

Approaches

Rather than beginning with the customary definition, this segment will start with an example—a nonpolitical one—and work back to a definition of an approach. The example that follows is based on an actual conversation that took place between two students who were sitting and talking in the cafeteria at their college (and who weren't aware that their conversation was overheard by a professor who would soon immortalize it in a textbook).

Student 1. It's hard to believe that another semester has started but I'm glad to be back.
Student 2. You're kidding.
Student 1. No, I like it here. I'm taking really interesting courses, and my instructors are great.
Student 2. You're kidding. Wouldn't you rather be watching the soaps?
Student 1. Nope. I think that being a Student Senator and a member of the Political Science Association is a lot more interesting than "The Young and the Restless."
Student 2. You're kidding. Are you forgetting about reading assignments, term papers, and exams? I can't wait to get out of this place!
Student 1. It's true that there is a lot of work. But after all, this is college, not nursery school. Besides, some of that stuff we read and study is pretty amazing.
Student 2. You're kidding.

This conversation is not an unusual one. In fact, at least one of the authors of this text recalls engaging in a similar exchange many years ago. It's hardly a revelation to say that attitudes about school, work, or just about anything else may range anywhere from intense dislike to rapturous enjoyment. People simply "approach" life differently.

An **approach** then is a way of looking at something. It is an orientation or a perspective (as opposed to a method or technique, which is something that is done). Just as there are many ways of looking at or approaching life, there are many ways to approach or look at American government.

Two Broad Approaches

Traditional Approaches

Traditional approaches to government tend to focus on what "was" and on what "should be"; they look at governmental institutions and tend to be "normative" or value-laden. The historical approach, the constitutional/legal approach, and the philosophical approach are a few of the traditional ways to look at American government. There will be places throughout this text in which one or more of these approaches will be taken.

Behavioral Approaches

Behavioral approaches tend to focus on what "is." They look at people (behavior) and tend to be "empirical" or scientific. Game theory and systems analysis are two important behavioral ways to look at American government.

Game Theory: In many ways it's easier to understand what game theory is all about, and to appreciate its usefulness, by actually playing a "game" before any of the details about the approach are discussed. The following nonpolitical game is a simple one, but it does explain this particular way of looking at things.

The Game: To begin, the reader is asked to suspend reality for a while and pretend that she/he is on a railroad station platform getting ready to board a train. At that moment,

> you meet a friend you are trying to avoid; he is going to coax you onto some committee. Your reservations are in different cars, but he suggests meeting in the diner. When the steward comes through [to take reservations for lunch], you discover to your relief that there are two diners, first-class and buffet, and if you choose correctly, you may "innocently" miss your friend. You have to be careful; he can guess that you'll evade him if you can. Normally you'd dine first class and he knows it. For which car [first-class or buffet] do you make your lunch reservation?[6]

Characteristics of Games: A few of the important attributes of games are illustrated, or implied, in this dining car example. So, before explaining what a game theorist might do in this situation, three of these characteristics should be noted.

1. A game, like the dining car game, (or chess, trivial pursuit, monopoly, or one of the many computer-generated games) involves making a choice or decision (to dine first class or buffet) after anticipating what the opponent might do. If he thinks that since you always eat in the first class diner that he can meet up with you there, he is likely to make a first class reservation. But, since he knows that you will try to avoid him, perhaps he will choose the buffet. However, if you think that he knows that you know that he knows that you will try to avoid him, then making the choice appears to be more problematic.

2. It is assumed that the players (at least two in a game) are rational, meaning that they are playing to win (or, in situations where winning is not possible, that they are trying to minimize

losses and maximize gains). Irrational players cannot be anticipated, and hence the theory of gaming becomes irrelevant.

3. Each of the participants in the game has to have full information about the options or choices that are available. If, for example, the steward taking lunch reservations forgot to mention that the train had two restaurants, there is no game being played. Whether the two do or do not meet in a dining car would then be simply a matter of fate.

Political Games: Before explaining how a game theorist could use game theory to make the best possible lunch reservation decision, it should be noted that there is a very strong connection between the somewhat frivolous nonpolitical dining car game and the more serious political games associated with politics and American government. For instance, political decisions and actions such as declaring and fighting in a war or running for a political office are often conceptualized or looked at as games because they generally involve the same assumptions and characteristics as the three listed above; they involve two or more rational (if they are playing to win) players (countries like the United States and Syria or people like Obama and Biden) that formulate strategies and make decisions after anticipating the moves of an enemy or an opponent.

Both political and nonpolitical games then ultimately involve making calculations. Making calculations means following a procedure(s). A behavioral or scientific **approach**, such as Game Theory, may require the use of certain empirical **techniques**, such as mathematics. For purposes of explanation it is useful to separate the topics of approaches and techniques, but, in practice, they are closely associated.

Making the Decision: After considering the options in the dining car game, a decision or choice about where to eat must be made by each of the players. (Skipping lunch altogether may seem like a good idea, but that's not an option in this particular game.) Is it to be first class or buffet? How was the reader's decision reached? What might a game theorist do in this situation?

A game theorist would probably begin by calculating all the possible outcomes. In many decision-making situations such calculations are often highly complex, but the dining car game happens to be a relatively simple one. It is a game with only two players (you and your friend,) each having two choices (first class or buffet dining car).

These small numbers allow for a visual display of all the possible combinations of the choices the two players can make. This is done by constructing a **matrix** (a rectangular array of information). Two players with two choices result in a 2 x 2 matrix and looks like this.

FRIEND'S CHOICES

	First Class	Buffet
YOUR CHOICES ⇒ First Class		
⇒ Buffet		

It can be seen that this 2 x 2 matrix contains two rows that reflect the reader's possible choices (Rows go in this direction ⇒.) and two columns that reflect your friend's possible choices. (Columns go in this direction ⇓.) There are 4 squares, which are called **cells**, in a 2 x 2 matrix, and each cell reflects a different combination of the players' choices and indicates for each which player would win and which would lose the game if both players select the same option.

In the next matrix, letters are used to indicate the outcome or the results. From your point of view a successful outcome (indicated by the letter "S" in the lower left hand corner) is one in which you avoid your friend. Meeting with him results in a failure for you (indicated by the letter "F" in the lower left hand corner). The letters in the upper right corner of each cell indicate the outcome of the game (success [S] or failure [F]) from your friend's point of view. The matrix will then look like this.

FRIEND'S CHOICES

	First Class	Buffet
Y O U R C H O I C E S ⇒ First Class	S (upper right) / F (lower left)	F (upper right) / S (lower left)
⇒ Buffet	F (upper right) / S (lower left)	S (upper right) / F (lower left)

Possible Outcomes: A matrix is read by moving across the row (⇒) for the outcome of your decision and down (⇓) the column for your friend's. The four possible combinations are:

Possibility 1: You decide to dine, as always, in first class and so does your friend. This combination of choices is found in the cell in the upper left corner. This is a failure for you (F) and a success for him (S).

Possibility 2: You decide to dine in first class, but your friend, believing that you might try to avoid him, made his reservation where he expected to find you—in the buffet. This combination of choices is found in the cell in the upper right corner. These decisions result in a success for you (S) and a failure (F) for him.

Possibility 3: You decide to go to the buffet, and your friend decides to dine first class. This combination, a success (S) for you and a failure (F) for him is found in the cell in the lower left corner.

Possibility 4: The last combination of choices is displayed in the lower right corner. In this situation you have chosen to eat in the buffet dining car and so has your friend. This results in a failure (F) for you and a success (S) for him.

Since game theorists are more likely to use numbers than letters in calculating their options, the matrix will be adjusted accordingly by replacing each "S" with +1 and each "F" with -1. So the final matrix (sometimes referred to as a "payoff" matrix because the payoffs—the rewards and penalties for each player's decision—are given) will look like this.

FRIEND'S CHOICES

	First Class	Buffet
YOUR CHOICES First Class	+1 / -1	-1 / +1
YOUR CHOICES Buffet	-1 / +1	+1 / -1

Reading the Matrix

What the matrix clearly shows is that no matter where the reader decides to eat, in first class or buffet, half of the time that will be a winning choice (S or +1) and half of the time it will not (F or -1). Since this was a simple win/lose or "zero-sum" (if all the +1 and the -1 numbers are added the result is zero) game, a matrix might not even have been needed to figure out that there is a fifty-fifty chance of meeting. The advantage of knowing these odds before making a reservation is that a decision to dine, as the reader usually does, in first-class elegance would not cause undue emotional angst.

The matrix also shows that until both of the players of the game make their decisions, there is no "right" choice or "wrong" choice. Choosing to dine first class turns out to be right only if your friend chooses buffet. It turns out to be wrong if he also chooses first class. In short, a decision becomes right or wrong **after** both of the players have made their choices. All that game theory helps the decision-makers to do is to make the best possible choice given the information that they have.

Why Government Leaders Play Games

Government leaders have to make decisions that are virtually always more complex than the game just played. Usually there are more players and more choices, and their games can be "non zero-sum" (involve cooperation among the players) as well as "zero-sum" (win or lose games in which cooperation is not an option).

Furthermore, a leader's decision, for example a president's decision to use troops rather than diplomacy to settle a domestic or international problem, can be a matter of life and death. It is essential then for him to make a rational decision, to get as much information about the possible choices as he can, to look at all of his and his opponents' options, to think clearly about the payoffs, and then to make the best possible decision given the information that he has. Playing out the "game" before making the actual decision is one way for a president, just as it was for the players in the dining car game, to accomplish these objectives.

Why Political Scientists Take This Approach

One important task for many political scientists has always been to analyze both the decisions that are made by government officials and the processes by which they are made. That used to be a more difficult job than it is now because game theory was not invented until 1944 and because the pioneering work in the field was done by economists who used it to analyze economic decisions. (Fifty years later, in 1994, three of the early pioneers were awarded the Nobel prize for their efforts.) However, it didn't take long for political scientists to begin to appreciate how useful game theory could be for their work, and so they borrowed it. Today researchers use this approach because it helps them to understand what a leader thought he "knew," how he "knew" it, and whether the decision (be it to raise taxes or to send troops to Iraq) he ultimately made was the best possible one that could have been made at the time.

Micro and Macro Approaches

The game theory approach is sometimes referred to as a "micro" approach. The next approach to be examined is often referred to as a "macro" approach. The differences between the two, as the following nonpolitical example illustrates, are fairly easy to spot.

To simplify matters imagine that there are only two ways of looking at the geographical features of the forty-eight contiguous states that comprise the United States. The first way, or approach, is to get on an airplane and look down as the jet flies from the northern U.S. border shared with Canada to the southern border that separates the United States from Mexico and then from the eastern Atlantic coast to the western Pacific coast. This approach will provide an overall view, a view of the land masses and rivers, of the urban cities and the rural farmlands, and of the mountains and the plains. This broad, widespread perspective is the "macro" view.

But for someone who wants to see more than vague shapes and the general features of the U.S., this broad aerial view would simply not be sufficient. An individual who wants to see the faces of people, the details of buildings, the variation of plants, and the major tourist attractions between Santa Monica and New York, or between San Antonio and Kentucky, would be better advised to get into an automobile and drive from one destination to the other. This more restricted or narrowly defined perspective is the "micro" approach. Game theory is the equivalent of traveling by car. It is a micro approach. Its focus is limited to "rational" decision-making. The next approach to be examined is like the view from the plane. It is a broad way of looking at politics that provides an overall perspective. This macro approach is called "systems analysis" (S/A).

Systems Analysis (S/A)

Anyone who has ever engaged in a conversation about the sound "system" in a car (or its exhaust, steering, braking, and suspension systems) or about the inadequate heating or air conditioning "system" in an uncomfortably hot or cold classroom, or made a reference to the solar "system," or to the grading or registration "system" used in a college, or to a computer "system," or even to their own digestive "system" after having consumed an entire pineapple-pepperoni pizza already has some understanding of what a system is.

What is that understanding? Exactly what is meant when people talk about such different entities as CD players and stereo radios, oil heaters and air conditioners, stars and planets, computers and printers, and the internal organs and tissues of the human body as "systems"? These are not easy questions to answer.

A System

A **system** is made up of two related components: (1) a set of interdependent parts and (2) an environment(s). This can be seen by analyzing a few of the nonpolitical systems mentioned above.

1. The sound "system" in a car:
    Parts: AM/FM radio, CD player, speakers, etc.
    Environments: (1) The interior of the car (upholstery that can muffle the sounds)
    (2) The exterior of the car (competing sounds and noises that come from people and traffic outside the car)

A radio is just a radio. A CD player is just a CD player. But when the two are looked at as interdependent parts, and when these parts are looked at in terms of their relation to, or interaction with, their environments, then they are referred to as a system.

2. The heating system in a college:
    Parts: Furnace, thermostat, ducts, etc.
    Environments: (1) The weather (subfreezing v. moderate temperature)
    (2) The school building (insulation, number of windows, number of people in it)

The furnace in the basement of a classroom building is one of the many interdependent parts that collectively provide heat. When the relationship between these parts and the environments with which they interact are discussed, then it is more accurate to refer to them as a heating system.

3. The solar system:
    Parts: Sun, planets, comets, satellites, meteoroids, interplanetary dust and gas, etc.
    Environments: (1) gravitational forces
    (2) electromagnetic forces
    (3) "strong" and "weak" nuclear forces

There are other solar systems, such as the Earth's, within the Milky Way galaxy, and that galaxy is only one of many. (Telescopes have identified at least 1000 million others!) It would be possible then to think of the solar system as one part, or a subsystem, of other systems. This holds true for all types of systems; the sound system of a car and the heating system in a building, for example, can each be looked at as a subsystem of an electrical system.

4. A computer system :
    Parts: Control unit, monitor, keyboard, cables, printer, mouse, modem, programs, etc.
    Environments: (1) Paper to print on
    (2) People (programmers and users)

Many, if not most, college students can probably see how the many parts are interdependent and how they are related to (affect and are affected by) their environments. Those who can look at the monitor or printer as interdependent parts of a whole rather than as separate entities, and those who recognize that the related parts have an impact on the environment and vice-verse, understand the concept of a system.

As the examples above indicate, virtually anything can be looked at as a system. The question is why one would want to. Perhaps the best way to answer that question is to recall the old Indian fable, "The Blind Men and the Elephant."

> Six blind beggars sitting by a roadside as an elephant passed were told they might touch it so that they would know what an elephant was like. The first one touched only the elephant's side and said, "He is like a wall!" The second one felt only his tusk and said, "No, no, he is like a spear." The third one took hold of his trunk and said, "Surely he is like a snake." "No such thing," cried the fourth, grasping one of his legs, "he is like a tree." The fifth was a tall man and took hold of his ear and said, "All of you are wrong, he is like a fan." The sixth man happened to catch hold of his tail and cried, "O foolish fellows, he is not like a wall, nor a spear, nor a snake, nor a tree, nor a fan; he is exactly like a rope." So the elephant passed on while the six blind men stood there quarreling, each being sure he knew exactly how the elephant looked, and each calling the other hard names because the rest did not agree with him.

The point, or moral, of the story is that to understand the essence of an elephant one first has to know how all the parts are related. It has to be considered as an entity. And, it has to be seen as it relates to its environment. This is as true for CD players and radios, furnaces and thermostats, planets and comets, and modems and printers as it is for elephants. It is also true for politics.

A Political System

As in all systems, a political system is made up of interdependent parts and environments. These are:

Parts: Everything that constitutes **Government**, including
   a) **people**, such as the president, senators, representatives, and bureaucrats;
   b) **political institutions**, including the executive, legislative, and judicial branches of government, the bureaucracy, interest groups, and political parties;
   c) **political processes**, for instance the legislative and electoral processes;
   d) **interactions**, for example bargaining and negotiation.

These "parts" are interdependent. Just imagine how difficult it would be to make political decisions about "who gets what, when, how" if any one of these elements were missing!

Environments: Everything else! Something is either part of the government or it is in the government's environment. The U.S. government, as does every government, has two major environments:

   (1) a domestic environment: the people and events in the United States that are related to (affect and are affected by) the government;
   (2) an international environment: the people and events in another country(ies) that are related to (affect and are affected by) the United States government.

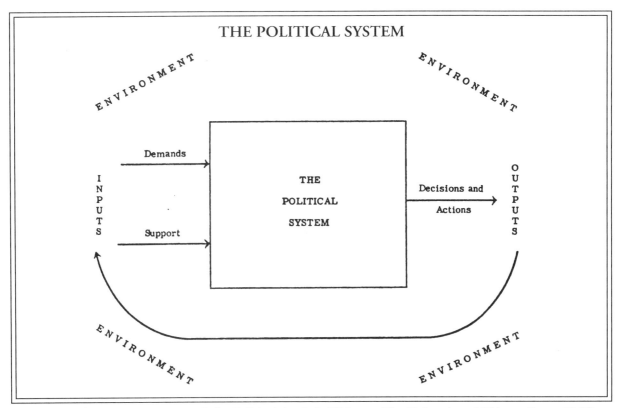

Source: David Easton, *A Framework for Political Analysis* (Chicago: The University of Chicago Press, 1965), p. 112.

The close relationship between a government and its environment[s] is sometimes illustrated in a figure that looks like "The Political System" on the following page.

Consider where in this diagram a class of American government students would be found. Most of them are probably located out in the environment, more specifically, in the U.S. domestic environment. If some of them feel strongly enough about a given political issue such as health care, women's rights, or welfare, they might decide to express their opinions and to request that government take some action. That may be done by texting a message to Congress, by voting on election day for new representatives with different and more compatible points of view, by joining with others in a protest march, or in a myriad of other ways.

In systems analytic terms the requests made to government by those American government students (and others in the environment) are called **demands**. Demands are one type of **input** (information that comes from the environment and goes into the government). As the diagram shows, there is another type of input called **support**. Support reflects the degree of satisfaction or dissatisfaction with how the government responds to demands. For instance, if Congress passes a health-care bill that many citizens approve of, that would probably be reflected in an increased level of support for the government. If, on the other hand, they find a Supreme Court decision on affirmative action or on abortion undesirable, that might be reflected in a withdrawal of support. A government that experiences the withdrawal of support from large numbers of its citizens, as the United States did during the Vietnam War in the 1960s, may be in serious trouble.

Laws, executive orders, judicial decisions, bureaucratic rules and regulations—everything that comes from the government and goes out into the environment—are called **outputs**. These outputs, or governmental decisions, may then have an **impact** on the individuals out in the domestic environment. Some of the readers of this text, for example, might have been among the numerous students that felt the impact of the government's decision in many states to cut back the availability of student loans during the past few years. If the response to this impact will be to cast a vote in the next election against the office holders who advocated the financial cutbacks, or to join with the thousands of students who have already protested in their state capitals, they will be giving or "feeding" new information (called **feedback**) to the government in the form of new inputs (demands and support). The hope is that government will respond with different outputs to which students would be likely to react with new inputs and to which government would respond with different outputs and so on. This never-ending cycle of government converting inputs into outputs, through what is simply referred to as the **conversion process**, is the overall view of how politics works in the United States (and in every other country as well). It is a view of the "whole elephant."

Systems analysis was first used in the physical sciences and was introduced in the discipline of political science by a series of works written during the 1950s and 60s by one of its most respected theorists, David Easton.[7] In the second of these works, *A Framework for Political Analysis*, Easton explains the utility of the systems approach. It, he states,

> is a way of unveiling the basic processes through which a political system, regardless of its generic or specific type ["democratic, dictatorial, bureaucratic, traditional, imperial or otherwise"], is able to persist as a system of behavior in a world either of stability or of change.[8]

What Easton is saying is that by introducing systems analysis to political scientists he has given them an approach, the only approach to date, which explains how politics (who gets what, when, how; or, the authoritative allocations of values) works anywhere and at any time. In other words, inputs are converted into outputs by all governments. Those which can not or do not meet the demands of their citizens are probably doomed while those governments that are successfully carrying out the conversion process are more likely to persist.

The U.S. government has, with one notable exception, the Civil War era, always been able to meet the demands of enough of its citizens to insure its continuity. Systems analysis, a macro approach to politics, clearly shows us that.

CONCLUSION

The importance for the consumer of every academic text, every television and radio news report, news magazine, newspaper, and academic journal to critique, evaluate, and question how the information being communicated was acquired and to accept or reject it on that basis was made at the start of this chapter. The authors of this text would now like to ask readers to keep just four general points in mind as they move on to examine the subsequent chapters in this book.

1. There are many approaches (traditional and behavioral, macro and micro) and many methods and techniques (empirical and non-empirical) that can be used to investigate American government.

2. It is preferable, when possible, for a researcher to use the scientific method, which is to empirically (objectively and systemically) examine American government using reliable and valid techniques.

3. The approach or way of looking at U.S. politics that is selected limits what the investigator finds and reports. Systems analysis is an approach that can yield information about various types of inputs but little, if any, data about how decisions are reached. The game theory approach gives some insight into the decision-making process but does not explain much about demands or supports.

4. While cynicism for the sake of being a cynic is not a particularly attractive quality, it is okay not only to question how political data or information is acquired but to accept or reject it on that basis. In fact, it is more than okay; it is expected. It is expected that as an educated citizen, the first reaction to all of what is read about American government, and seen and heard about it on the media and from friends and acquaintances (including instructors), is to ask "HOW DO THEY KNOW?" At the very least if this question is asked, the readers of this text are not likely to find themselves panicking in the streets of their hometowns because of a reported invasion by Martians!

CHAPTER NOTES

[1] All the data on the broadcast of "Invasion From Mars," the responses to it by the audience, the coverage by the news media, and the subsequent analysis of the events are taken from Howard Koch, *The Panic Broadcast: Portrait of an Event* (Boston: Little, Brown and Company, 1970).

[2] William Safire, "Grading the Speech," *The New York Times*, 24 January 1985, 25(A).

[3] Dava Sobel, "Language Patterns Reveal Problems in Personality," *The New York Times*, 27 November 1981, 1(C).

[4] Ibid.

[5] Daniel Goleman, "For Presidential Candidates, Optimism Appears a Winner," *The New York Times*, 8 May 1988, 1(A). The procedures used in the study are elaborated upon in this article; *The New York Times*, "Now That It's Over," 21 November 1988.

[6] T. C. Schelling, "What is Game Theory?" in *Contemporary Political Analysis*, ed. James C. Charlesworth (New York: The Free Press, 1967) 212. Thomas Schelling, an economist at the University of Maryland, is considered to be one of the founders of applied game theory.

[7] David Easton introduced systems theory in three works: *The Political System: An Inquiry into the State of Political Science* (New York: Alfred A. Knopf, 1953); *A Framework for Political Analysis*, (Chicago: The University of Chicago Press, 1965); *A Systems Analysis of Political Life* (Chicago: The University of Chicago Press, 1965). See also Easton's, "An Approach to the Analysis of Political Systems," *World Politics* 9 (1957): 383-400.

[8] Easton, *A Framework for Political Analysis*, Preface, xiv.

SUGGESTED READINGS

Crick, Bernard. *The American Science of Politics: Its Origins and Conditions.* Berkeley, CA: University of California Press, 1964.

Easton, David, John G. Gunnell, and Luigi Graziano, eds. *The Development of Political Science: A Comparative Survey*. New York: Routledge, 1991.

Katznelson, Ira and Helen Milner, eds. *Political Science: The State of the Discipline III*. Washington, D.C.: The American Political Science Association, 2002.

Hoover, Kenneth R. *The Elements of Social Scientific Thinking*. 7th ed. New York: Bedford/St. Martin's, 2001.

Chapter One

THE LANGUAGE OF POLITICAL SCIENCE

> The irresponsible use of language leads to the destruction of the social, moral, and political structure that is our society, our culture, our nation.
>
> William Lutz[1]

A glossary is generally found in the back of a volume or at the end of a chapter. This placement is a convenient one both for knowledgeable readers who are already somewhat familiar with the subject of the text, and the language or specific terms used in it, and also for casual readers who may not need to have more than a general understanding of the material or the vocabulary. However, for college students who are beginning their formal study of a field, such as American government, it is logical to discuss at least some of the key terminology that will be used repeatedly throughout the text at the beginning.

The logic of this arrangement is probably very clear to any individual who has had the unsettling experience of attending a lecture or reading an article in which some of the terms used by the speaker or writer were not understood. In such cases the spoken or written words may have seemed to be nothing more than meaningless babble. Those, for example, who are unfamiliar with expressions such as a "popped-up bunt attempt" or a "power-play rebound" or a "360-degree spin move on a driving layup" or a "birdie putt from a tough lie" would probably find much of the Sports Section of a daily newspaper rough going. And how much more confusing it would be for those without the appropriate vocabulary to comprehend the following statement, written by a professor of English, which appeared in an academic journal.

> Quintilian's uncertainty whether irony is included in allegory turns on whether antiphrasis is a sport of irony or its radical essence. If antiphrasis is irony's essence, then all

> forms of irony must threaten from their place on the inside of allegory the existence of what allegory cannot help affirming . . . the logocentric plurality of its meanings, grounded in the material unity of its signs—in a word, polysemy.[2]

The subject of inquiry for political scientists is, of course, politics. But just like their counterparts who write about "sports" or about "irony," they too have a unique language—one that may seem to be incomprehensible until it is learned. Until that language is learned, political dialogue or discourse between individuals is often quite difficult.

Complicating the matter of political discourse still further is the often highly subjective and emotional nature of much of what is discussed. Questions such as whether Republicans or Democrats make the best presidents and issues such as whether federal funds should be used for the development of military weapons or should be earmarked for social programs, including welfare and education, have sometimes brought those engaged in conversations about these matters almost to the point of physical combat.

There are, however, no absolute political "truths," and hence there is neither a "right" or a "wrong" response to such questions, nor a "good" or a "bad" side to take on such issues. And so, in the absence of universal political verities, it is not surprising that passionate feelings are aroused and that people—as was discussed in the introductory chapter of this text—rely heavily on myths, superstitions, hunches, intuition, stereotypes, and unverified beliefs to support those feelings. Perhaps this is why conventional wisdom has it that, as happens in the case of religion, which is largely based on faith, it is sometimes best to avoid talking about politics in polite company.

Nonetheless, in the "real," as well as in the academic, world it is frequently difficult, if not impossible, to avoid political discourse. And because it is, every attempt should be made to both use empirical data whenever feasible (See introductory chapter.) and to keep the language used in the discussion as clear and as precise as possible.

EVOLUTION, CONCEPTS, THEORIES, AND DEFINITIONS

Evolution

All political constructs occur within a particular time, place, and culture. Time, place, and culture, then, comprise the "context" within which political concepts, theories, and definitions emerge. It is important for students of politics to be aware of this for as time, place, and culture change so do political constructs. Political phenomena, for example, have been the subject of speculation and investigation in both the Eastern and the Western worlds for thousands of years. The very different nature of experiences in these two ancient worlds eventually led to two very different political traditions.

The roots of American political thought are found within the Western tradition and culture and are generally traced back in time and space to ancient Greece (c. 500 B.C.E.). Two of the early political philosophers from this era who wrote about and who influenced Western ideas about the nature of government were Plato and Aristotle. Plato (417-347 B.C.E.,) in his major work, *The*

Republic, discussed the attributes of an ideal or utopian government (which is the "republic" referred to in the title) while his student Aristotle (384-322 B.C.E.) described existing or actual governments in *The Politics*. Interestingly, neither of these great thinkers, who started what is sometimes referred to by current philosophers as "The Great Conversation," formally defined the term government.

Over the subsequent twenty-five hundred years many scholars, all viewing and writing about the political world from the unique perspective determined by their particular era, place, and culture, entered into this Conversation. As they did, the language of politics, which includes its concepts and theories as well as the definitions of its terms, gradually evolved, developed, and became much more precise.

Concepts

Concepts are simply the words or names used to symbolize or represent ideas. "Warmth," to use a nonpolitical example, is simply the concept or the name given to, among other things, the feeling or experience of the sun on the skin.

Among some of the more frequently used concepts in the field of American government are: government, politics, democracy, and power. Concepts such as these are sometimes referred to as the building blocks of political science because they are the components that are used to construct theories.

Theories

Theories are the attempts made to explain, rather than just name, political phenomena. Using the concept of democracy as a starting point, for instance, an investigator might try to find out why some countries are democratic and some are not or why some democracies are stable or long-lasting and others are unstable. In the process of trying to understand and explain the conditions that are conducive to or promote the democratic process, the researcher is developing a theory of democracy. However, without first defining the concept "democracy," the effort to explain it or to theorize about it would be an exercise in futility.

Definitions

There are different types of definitions. For the most part political scientists use **nominal definitions**, "which indicate how a concept is to be used. In other words, we specify that for our purposes something is this and not that." Democracy, for instance, is according to some "rule by the people" and not "rule for the people."[3] (See "What Constitutes a Democracy is Subjective" p. 28.)

Such definitions do not claim to describe all of a concept's important qualities. There is often much disagreement among experts on precisely what those qualities are and, for that reason, there are frequently many definitions of the same concept. Since concepts are used in constructing theories, it follows that there are often also many competing theories or different explanations for the same political phenomena.

Some of the definitional and theoretical disagreements will become rather evident as a sample of the more frequently used political terms, including the concepts of "politics," "political science," "government," "American government," "democracy," "power," "authority," and "legitimacy," are discussed in the remainder of this chapter.

AMERICAN GOVERNMENT TERMINOLOGY

Politics

[Politics is one of those concepts about which there is some disagreement.] Although most of the hundreds of definitions of the term do acknowledge that "**governmental decision-making**" is the essence of the concept of politics, some of those definitions stress the importance of the people who make the decisions while others focus on the people who are the recipients of the decisions made. A look at two of the most widely used definitions, Harold D. Lasswell's and David Easton's, reflect these different perspectives.

"WHAT CONSTITUTES A DEMOCRACY IS SUBJECTIVE"

It was a grand pronouncement tucked into a long inaugural speech, the kind of sweeping statement that most people lump with the likes of "The Internet is expanding by leaps and bounds."

But when President Clinton declared that, "And for the first time in all of history, more people on this planet live under democracy than dictatorship," it begged the question: Is that right? And if so, well, just how many people are free?

The answer, according to a very rough estimate by *The New York Times*, is yes, Mr. Clinton is correct. According to 1996 United Nations population data, an estimated 3.1 billion people live in democracies, and 2.66 billion do not. This is a margin of 53.82 percent to 46.18 percent, a difference of 7.6 percentage points, or nearly the same as that of Mr. Clinton's popular vote count over Bob Dole, his Republican challenger.

The biggest democracies are India, with 944.58 million people, and the United States, with 269.44 million. On the flip side are China, with 1.232 billion, and Indonesia, with 200.453 million.

Of course, deciding what constitutes a democracy is subjective. Do you include countries in which voting irregularities are common? Do you exclude places like Pakistan, Bangladesh and Kenya that ambassadors would likely call democracies? (We did, but this is not scientific.)

The reason Mr. Clinton even mentioned this, presumably, is that the pendulum has swung sharply in favor of the democratic nations in the last few years, due largely to the 280 million people in the nations that comprised the Soviet Union. Then again, the numbers are always subject to a coup here or a pro-democracy outbreak there.

One thing that is certain in this first year of Mr. Clinton's second term, though, is that the pro-democracy population will slip a fraction on July 1 [1997.] That is when Hong Kong, population 6.2 million, reverts to China from Britain.

Source: David W. Chen, "The Numbers Favor Those Living in Democracies," *The New York Times*, 21 January 1997, 14 (A).

Lasswell's Definition

In 1936 Lasswell's book, *Politics: Who Gets What, When, How*, was published.[4] The catchy sounding second part of the title, "who gets, what, when, how," soon became one of the most frequently used responses to the question "what is politics?" For Lasswell, whose definition focuses on the recipients, those who have the most (the elite) get the most of what government has to give: the most "deference," the most "income," and the most "safety."[5]

Easton's Definition

Easton has defined politics as "the authoritative allocation of values for a society."[6] This definition, just as Lasswell's, refers to the object of political decisions, which is the "society." However, unlike Lasswell's, Easton's definition places an emphasis on the idea that the things that the individuals in a society want or "value" are "allocated" (distributed) by those with authority. In most instances, the authority to make decisions or allocate values for an entire society resides with government.

An examination of some of the major issues debated during the 2012 presidential election reveals what it is that the American people have considered to be of value in recent times. Among these are: the economy (jobs and the deficit,) immigration, healthcare, and national security.

The two candidates, Barack Obama and Mitt Romney, disagreed not about what the values were but to whom they were to be allocated. The positions they took about taxes clearly show this. Romney proposed making the Bush tax cuts (2001 & 2003) permanent while the Obama proposal called for allowing those cuts to expire for individuals earning more than $250,000 a year.

Whether the executive branch is headed by Obama or Romney or by any other individual does not alter the fact that in the United States the "government" authoritatively allocates values for the entire society; it determines who gets what, when, how. Both Lasswell's and Easton's definitions accurately convey the essence of the concept of politics.

Political Science

Political science is the academic discipline or body of knowledge that is devoted to the study of politics ("who gets what" or the authoritative allocation of values"). It is classified, as are the disciplines of history, sociology, social psychology, economics, geography, and anthropology, as a "social" science. The social sciences share a common focus—a focus on human behavior—and for that reason they are sometimes referred to as "behavioral sciences."

Because they have a common subject, there is a lot of overlap in the material they examine. In fact, before political science emerged as a separate and distinct area of study, which was around the turn of the twentieth century, the study of politics was incorporated into the disciplines of sociology, economics, law, religion, and, particularly, history. Currently, however, each one of the social or behavioral sciences places its primary focus on a different aspect of human behavior, and for political science the emphasis is obviously on political conduct (everything related to the authoritative allocation of values).

It does not necessarily follow that because its focus is directed only to the subject of politics that the scope (fields and subjects) of political science is limited. Actually, as the number of fields

of specialization enumerated in the list prepared by the American Political Science Association (APSA) in 2010 shows [See "APSA Organized Sections" p. 31.], the scope is actually rather extensive. However, it is also true that students who major in political science in the United States generally select their courses from approximately five to eight principal fields. Among these are:
1. Comparative Government/Politics
2. International Relations/Politics
3. Political Philosophy/Theory
4. Public Administration
5. American Government

Of these, this text introduces the reader to the fifth field on the list, American Government.

Government/American Government

If politics is defined as "who gets what, when, how" then **government** can be described as the people and the institutions who decide who gets what or, in Eastonian terms, as the people and institutions who authoritatively allocate values. American government then refers to the people and institutions that allocate or make political decisions for the inhabitants of the United States.

Political Institutions

Among the political institutions that allocate values in the U.S. are the:
a. Congress   b. presidency
c. courts   d. bureaucracy

Political parties, the media, elites, interest groups and their lobbyists, and big businesses and corporations and their Political Action Committees (PACs) are also, as will be described in later chapters, institutions that play a significant role in the process of determining who gets what.

The "People"

The people who allocate values occupy positions in these institutions. Their titles may vary depending upon the level of government (national, state, or local government) for which they work. So, for instance, the president is the chief decision maker in the executive branch of government at the national level; the governor is responsible for allocating values in the executive branch at the state level; and mayors, who are among the many executives at the local level (cities, counties, school districts, and special districts) of government, are among those who decide who gets what in sub-state communities.

At each of these different levels, the "**regime**" or the "way of governing" is essentially democratic, which is to say that while there are different types of regimes including communism, socialism, and fascism, the people and institutions that allocate values in the United States are expected to do so according to the principles of democracy.

APSA ORGANIZED SECTIONS

1. Federalism and Intergovernmental Relations
2. Law and Courts
3. Legislative Studies
4. Public Policy
5. Political Organizations and Parties
6. Public Administration
7. Conflict Processes
8. Representation and Electoral Systems
9. Presidency Research
10. Political Methodology
11. Religion and Politics
12. Urban Politics
13. Science, Technology and Environmental Politics
14. Women and Politics Research
15. Foundations of Political Theory
16. Information Technology and Politics
17. International Security and Arms Control
18. Comparative Politics
19. European Politics and Society
20. State Politics and Policy
21. Political Communication
22. Politics and History
23. Political Economy
24. New Political Science
25. Political Psychology
26. Political Science Education
27. Politics, Literature, and Film
28. Foreign Policy
29. Elections, Public Opinion, and Voting Behavior
30. Race, Ethnicity and Politics
31. International History and Politics
32. Comparative Democratization
33. Human Rights
34. Qualitative and Multi-method Research
35. Sexuality and Politics
36. Health Politics and Policy
37. Canadian Politics
38. Political Networks
39. Experimental Research

Democracy

Although the term democracy was coined by the historian Herodotus in ancient Greece, it took, according to political scientist James David Barber, over two thousand years for a democratic government to come into existence. That government, he says, was in the United States—"the world's first true democracy."[7]

Perhaps it took so long because maintaining a democratic regime requires considerable effort and vigilance. At a minimum it entails following three basic principles or "essentials": [(a) holding regular elections; (b) creating a constitution; and (c) protecting citizens' rights.] As Barber explains,

a. Democracy is a **national government elected by the people.**

[The chief executive and the legislature make the rules of the nation, but the citizens decide, through elections, who will be the chief executive and who will serve in the legislature.] Those elections must be clear-cut, regular, and honest. When people vote for different candidates, the candidates who get the most votes must win the positions. The citizens need to know how to predict how the different candidates will operate once in office, so knowledge of candidates' political positions is essential. Thus democracy depends on citizens freely and knowledgeably selecting political governors who recognize that their power derives from popular election and may be removed in the next popular election.

b. Democracy requires a **constitution.**

The legislature makes laws, but the constitution is the law above all laws. Established at the birth of democracy, it sets forth procedures: how elections will be conducted and how the government must act. The constitution must be known to the public and truly implemented—not just asserted. The constitution can be changed, but only by a difficult procedure requiring far more discussion and votes than ordinary laws.

c. Democracy requires **human rights.**

The main constitution establishes rules of procedure, but a bill of rights gives the fundamental rights of the people, typically including freedom of religion, speech, and the press; the right of assembly; and equality of all citizens under the law. For example, the bill of rights should protect individuals from arrest and imprisonment because of their political beliefs. These rights are original and should be subject to change only by the same difficult procedure for changing the constitution.[8]

Besides adhering to these three principles, Barber continues, [a democratic government **must** also control police and military violence; provide freedom, equality, and justice under law; and promote a knowledgeable citizenry that participates in "frequent public discourse."[9]]

There is, of course, no guarantee that because the United States was the first country to meet all of these criteria or because it has continued to meet them for over two hundred years, that it will always do so. The fate of American democracy, in both its "direct" and "indirect" forms is, in short, dependent upon the will of an educated public to maintain it.

Direct and Indirect Democracy

As indicated earlier in this chapter, the term democracy, as it is translated from the original Greek, means government, or rule, by the people. In a **direct democracy**, or as it is sometimes referred to a **participatory democracy**, such as that which existed in ancient Athens, that definition is taken literally—the people (those who meet established criteria such as age, citizenship, etc.) actually make decisions about who gets what or allocate values for themselves.

Such an arrangement works well when the decisions to be made are for relatively small geographic areas, such as a Greek city-state, or more currently, in a Swiss canton or an American town or village. This is because the small size makes it possible for the resident voters of the community to get together to discuss, debate, and decide.

Direct democracy is also practiced in some U. S. states, which are considerably larger in size, through such processes as the:

a) direct initiative: registered voters, by following specified state procedures, may propose new legislation or an amendment to the state constitution
b) recall: registered voters, by following specified state procedures, may vote to remove an official during his/her term of office
c) popular referendum: registered voters may vote their approval or disapproval of existing, or proposed, legislation or constitutional changes

It is important to note, however, that at present not every state has provisions for these three processes. Furthermore, the Constitution of the United States makes no provision for the referendum, initiative, or recall at the national level of government.

It is unlikely that the framers of the Constitution, who had little faith in the people's ability to make rational decisions, would have provided for direct democracy even if the technology to do so had existed in the eighteenth century. What they devised instead was a plan where citizens elect representatives, representatives make political decisions for the people, and the citizens control their representatives through regularly scheduled elections. A country that adheres to this system of **indirect rule** by the people is called a **representative democracy** or more simply a **republic**.

Identifying a country as a democracy, either direct or indirect, is to locate it on a linear representation often referred to as the "political spectrum."

The Political Spectrum

As explained by James B. Whisker, the editor of a dictionary of American political concepts, "the **political spectrum** is often divided into right, center, and left."[10] Those on the **political right**, which according to Whisker include "those who tend toward **conservatism** or other protectionist or reactionary political ideas" generally are predisposed

34 / *Chapter One*

in varying degrees, to accept ideas of nationalism and traditionalism. The past is a general guide to present and future action and change is generally destructive of the political system in rightist views. [On the far end of the rightist side of the political spectrum are fascism and nazism.] In Europe rightists may support the restoration of traditional monarchies.[11]

Those on the **political left**, which as Whisker points out include liberals, socialists, communists, and radicals, hold

in varying degrees, to ideas of change and alteration in the political system. They generally favor, or pretend to favor, mass democracy and popular sovereignty. In Europe, the distinction is seen more clearly than in America. One might not speak of a "liberal" as a "leftist" here so frequently as one might in Europe.[12]

It is quite useful to place political parties along the linear spectrum described by Whisker especially if the reason for doing so is to make comparisons between and among the parties of different countries. Using the scale, for example, Whisker is able to communicate the idea that "Continental European parties tend more toward political extremes whereas American parties tend toward the political center."[13]

While American political parties and their members do tend toward the political center, there are both parties and people in the United States to be found at virtually each of the degrees along the spectrum. Furthermore, there are individuals who hold conservative views on some policy issues and take a liberal position on still others. Classifying or labeling an individual then is no easy matter. (See, "Who's A Liberal!" p. 36.) It may, therefore, be useful to think of the left and right positions not as isolated and rigid but as related and flexible categories. The following spectrum, a slight variation on the traditional left-center-right scale, is useful for examining and thinking about the relational ties that often exist.

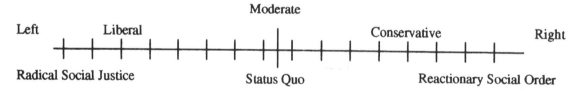

[The "**status quo**" position on the scale refers simply to what the official governmental policy on any issue, such as health care, is at a given time.] Health-care policy and hence the status quo may vary from country to country; Canada, for instance, currently has a national health-care system and the United States does not. And a policy may vary within a country over time; to say that the United States does not now have a national health-care system is not to say that it never will.

Political parties and individuals who are presently satisfied with the health-care policy of their country are situated squarely on the status quo line. Those that want to alter the policy would be located to the right of that line if they prefer a pre-existing or more conservative policy than that of the current one and to the left of that line if they prefer a more innovative or liberal policy. [The degree to which an individual is placed to the right or the left of the status quo line is determined by the **intensity** (how strongly the change is wanted) and the **preferred speed** (how fast or slow the change is wanted) of the desired policy change.] The further away from the status quo line, in either direction, that a person or party is located is also determined by the amount of change that is desired and the amount of resources, such as time and money, willing to be invested to cause that change.

The two amounts are usually highly correlated. Those individuals who are located at the extreme ends of the spectrum and who wish to drastically alter the status quo may, for example, even be willing to invest or sacrifice their lives to promote their causes (social justice, or political and economic equality, to the left of the spectrum and social order, or the adherence to traditional values and laws, to the right of the spectrum) and to bring about political change. However, in the U.S., as indicated earlier, the majority of people are not extremists. Today Americans, for the most part, neither desire profound changes in existing policies nor wish to invest very much time in facilitating those changes that they may want. As a consequence, policies do not tend to change dramatically in the United States.

That has not always been the case. It is an interesting mental exercise to look back in time to the founding of this country and to think about where on the political spectrum John Adams, John Hancock, Benjamin Franklin, Thomas Jefferson, and the other signers of the Declaration of Independence would have been placed in 1776 and where they would be placed today. A consideration of how yesterday's revolutionaries have become today's heroes might serve to both dispute stereotypical notions of extremism and to illustrate the importance of knowing the time, the place, and the cultural context within which political terms such as liberal, conservative, radical, and reactionary are used.

Power

It is frequently observed that the United States is the most "powerful" country in the world and that the president is the most "powerful" leader in both the domestic and international arenas. Such an observation implies that both the U. S. and the president are powerful because they are likely to get whatever it is they desire or want from another or others. It implies that the United States uses its great wealth and military strength to get what it wants from other countries and that the president uses the status of his office, his personal magnetism, and/or the force of the Constitution, among other things, to get his constituents, the Congress, and other world leaders to go along with his proposals.

These common-sense notions of power are actually pretty good descriptions of the term and are very much in keeping with the more formal definition proffered by the noted logician and moral philosopher Bertrand Russell. According to Russell, **power** is "the production of intended effects."[14] A country (or an individual), in other words, has power if it can get or "produce" what it wants or "intends" to get from another country (or another person).

As Russell goes on to explain, producing the intended effects usually involves the promise of rewards (such as economic, military, or humanitarian aid) or the threat of penalties (such as a trade embargo or a military action)—which he calls "sanctions." Clearly the more sanctions a country has at its disposal, the more powerful it is, and the more likely it is to get what it wants. Power, in short, is distinguished by the following qualities:

> ### Who's a Liberal! Is Clinton One? Was Nixon?
>
> How do you stump a liberal? Ask him or her whether President Clinton is one. The response will be momentary bewilderment and often a stammer, but almost never a definitive "yes."
>
> "It's in the eye of the beholder, but I think he's a pragmatic progressive," said Michael S. Dukakis, the 1988 Democratic Presidential nominee who proclaimed his liberalism on the eve of that election—and lost.
>
> "He's neither liberal or conservative—he is a progressive," agreed Harold M. Ickes, a deputy White House chief of staff and the most devoted liberal in Mr. Clinton's inner circle.
>
> "We would have an internal debate about that question, especially after his decision to sign the welfare bill," said Robert J. Carolla, communications director of Americans for Democratic Action, the nation's oldest liberal organization....
>
> Given [his] record, calling Mr. Clinton a liberal these days could be likened to calling Richard M. Nixon a liberal: a case can be made, but it does not easily stick. Despite his reputation as the hard-edged partisan who tried to weed out Communists, Mr. Nixon proposed universal health coverage and a guaranteed minimum income for all Americans, and he created the Environmental Protection Agency.
>
> "If you peeled away Nixon's paranoia, basically I'd say they're not so far apart," Walter Dean Burnham, a professor of government at the University of Texas at Austin, said of Mr. Clinton and Mr. Nixon. As for Mr. Clinton, he said, "He's an Eisenhower Republican, brought up to date, of course."
>
> Source: Richard L. Berke, "Who's a Liberal! Is Clinton One? Was Nixon?" *The New York Times*, 29 September 1996, Section 4, 1 (E) and 5 (E).

- **It is a relationship.** [To exercise power there must be at least two people or two countries, one of which gets what is desired from the other.] Power would be a meaningless concept in a world inhabited by only one individual or in which there was only one country. Clearly it would be foolish to call the U.S. powerful if there were no other country from which it could extract what it wanted. <u>Power then is a relationship that exists between two or more entities.</u>
- **It is predictable.** Because the **power base** or assets (wealth, a large military, abundant natural resources, status, etc.) possessed by one of the individuals or countries in a relationship are greater than that of the other, it can be predicted, with a "reasonable" degree of accuracy, that the one that has the most assets to use as sanctions (rewards/penalties) will be successful in producing the intended effects. However, as the Vietnam conflict, in which the United States did not succeed in stopping Hanoi from uniting its country under Communist rule, demonstrated—there are no guarantees. <u>Power does not always ensure victory.</u>
- **It costs.** Conflicts, such as that between the U.S. and North Vietnam, reveal another facet of power—that it "costs." In a military confrontation its costs may include the expenditure of money, raising taxes, the time and energy of political leaders, the loss of citizens' lives and possibly—as

it did the U.S. in the case of Vietnam—public support for the government. There is little doubt that President Lyndon Johnson's decision not to run for re-election in 1968 was largely based on the calculation that he had lost so much support that he could not win. As one of his biographers concluded

> forced to confront a precipitous drop in his public standing, a sharp shift in editorial reaction, and the loss of support from key-interest-group leaders, Johnson finally accepted the fact that he was in a situation he could no longer control and that further escalation would produce only more uncontrollability. Faced at the same time with loss of love and gratitude on what seemed an irretrievable scale, Johnson had no choice but to withdraw.[15]

All in all it appears that in the case of Vietnam, the cost of exercising power was very high. Some have argued that it was too high.

- **It is sometimes exercised by the people**. The "vote," as was just discussed, is clearly one of the most important assets that citizens possess for use as a sanction. It can be used as a reward when it is given to a candidate or as a penalty when it is withheld. This sanction is a major component of the power base of the American people.

The notion that power resides with the people or, more precisely, with the majority of the people is referred to as the "majoritarian theory" of democracy. This theory is one of three popular theories of who holds "**actual**"—or largely nonelected—as opposed to "**formal**"—or governmental—power in a democratic country such as the United States. The other two power theories are the "group" and the "elite" theories.

Group Theories

Arthur F. Bentley, one of the earliest group theorists and author of the classic study on the subject, *The Process of Government* (1908), set forth the basic argument in support of actual power residing with groups. It is theorized that

- the United States is a <u>pluralist</u> country, that is a country that consists of many different or diverse populations
- the numerous religious, ethnic, racial, occupational, and cultural differences lead to the formation of organized groups
- some of the groups are considered to be "political" in that they compete with one another in an attempt to get whatever it is that they want from the government
- the government provides multiple access points for the groups to participate in policy making
- policies benefiting the general public are made through compromise and coalition building.

[Some interest groups, including the tech companies that are discussed in Chapter 8, are so well organized and so wealthy that they have successfully pressured presidents, legislators, judges, bureaucrats, and other officials to shape governmental policies and to pass and enforce laws that suit their needs. These interest groups, then, according to group theorists, wield immense political power.]

[Some reject the optimistic vision of what has become known as the **pluralist theory**. Like Theodore Lowi, they argue that pluralism is out of control, that groups have become so powerful they can effectively dominate policy. This leads, according to these theorists, to **hyperpluralism** with conflicting sets of policies, stalemate, and gridlock.]

Elite Theory

[Those who have the **most** of whatever is valued in a society (wealth, education, power, etc.) are called the **elite**.] By definition then an elite consists of relatively few individuals as compared with the large memberships found in the powerful interest groups. Thomas Dye has calculated that America's national elite consists of individuals in just over 7,300 corporate, public interest, and governmental positions and adds

> these top positions, taken collectively, control almost three quarters of the nation's industrial assets; one half of all assets in communication and utilities; over one half of all U.S. banking assets; over three quarters of all insurance assets; and they direct Wall Street's largest investment firms. They control the television networks, the influential news agencies, and the major newspaper chains. They control nearly 40 percent of all the assets of private foundations and two thirds of all private university endowments. They direct the nation's largest and best-known New York and Washington law firms as well as the nation's major civic and cultural organizations. They occupy key federal governmental positions in the executive, legislative, and judicial branches. And they occupy all the top command positions in the Army, Navy, Air Force and Marines.[16]

Dye naturally concludes, that these figures "are important indicators of the concentration of authority and control in American society."[17] More recently Americans have referred to the elite as the 1%.

The three theories (majoritarian, group, and elite) briefly described above are competing theories. That means if one theory accurately describes the power reality in the U.S. then the other two can not. Which then provides the most accurate description? Unfortunately there is no definitive answer to that question. Scholars simply do not agree. However two observations can be made: (1) of these three contending theories, scholars generally adhere to either the group or the elite explanations of power and (2) while sociologists generally favor the elite theory, political scientists tend to support the group theory.

Authority and Legitimacy

Authority is a form of power. It is, more precisely, "**legitimate**" or **accepted** power. Although power, by definition, requires the promise or the threat of sanctions, it does not necessarily follow that those sanctions must be used to produce the intended effects.

When, for example, the government wants to conserve fuel or decrease traffic fatalities and attempts to do so by reducing highway speed limits, or when it raises taxes, or when it calls on Americans to fight in a war, voluntary citizen compliance indicates that the government has au-

"THE GOVERNMENT'S DOUBLESPEAK OF WAR"

In war the first casualty is language. And with the language goes the truth. It was the Vietnam "conflict," not the Vietnam War. It was the Korean "police action," not the Korean War....

The doublespeak of war consists, as Orwell wrote of all such language, 'of euphemism, question-begging, and sheer cloudy vagueness.' It is, fundamentally, the language of insincerity, where there is a gap between the speaker's real and declared aims. It is language as an instrument for concealing and preventing thought, not for expressing or extending thought. Such language silences dialogue and blocks communication.

During the Vietnam 'conflict' we learned that mercenaries paid by the U.S. government were 'civilian irregular defense soldiers,' refugees fleeing the war were 'ambient noncombatant personnel,' and enemy troops who survived bombing attacks were 'interdictional nonsuccumbers.' In Vietnam, American war planes conducted 'limited duration protective reaction strikes' during which they achieved an 'effective delivery of ordnance.' So it went too in the Persian Gulf.

Just as officially there was no war in Korea or Vietnam, so officially there was no war in the Persian Gulf. After all, Congress didn't declare war, it declared an authorization of the 'use of force,' a power clearly delegated to Congress in Article I, Section 8 of the Constitution, which now apparently reads: 'Congress shall have the power to authorize the use of force.' So now we have not war but Operation Desert Storm, or 'exercising the military option,' or, according to President Bush, an 'armed situation.'

During this 'armed situation' massive bombing attacks became 'efforts.' Thousands of war planes didn't drop tons of bombs; 'weapons systems' or 'force packages' 'visited a site.' These 'weapons systems' didn't drop their tons of bombs on buildings and human beings, they 'hit' 'hard' and 'soft targets.' During their 'visits,' these 'weapons systems' 'degraded,' 'attrited,' 'suppressed,' 'eliminated,' 'cleansed,' 'sanitized,' 'impacted,' 'decapitated,' or 'took out' targets, they didn't blow up planes, tanks, trucks, airfields, and the soldiers who were in them, nor did they blow up bridges, roads, factories, and other buildings and the people who happened to be there. A 'healthy day of bombing' was achieved when more enemy 'assets' were destroyed than expected.

If the 'weapons systems' didn't achieve 'effective results' (blow up their targets) during their first 'visit' (bombing attack), as determined by a 'damage assessment study' (figuring out if everything was completely destroyed), the 'weapons systems' will 'revisit the site' (bomb it again). Women, children, or other civilians killed or wounded during these 'visits,' and any schools, hospitals, museums, houses, or other 'nonmilitary' targets that were blown up were 'collateral damage,' which is the undesired damage or casualties produced by the effects from 'incontinent ordnance' or 'accidental delivery or ordnance equipment,' meaning the bombs and rockets that miss their targets.

To function as it should and as we expect it to, language must be an accurate reflection of that which it represents. The doublespeak of war is an instance of thought corrupting language, and language corrupting thought.

Source: Lutz, **The New Doublespeak**, 182-184.

thority. Their compliance does not mean that the people actually like the new legislation. It only indicates that they psychologically accept the right of the government to make such laws and thus no governmental sanctions, no force or physical coercion such as calling out the national guard, actually has to be used. As a popular couplet more succinctly explains the distinction between power and authority:

Power and might, Authority and right

Any government that has to rely on the use of sanctions because its people have not "internalized the social order," that is they do not accept its right to allocate values or to decide who gets what, is in trouble.[18] It is in trouble because its attempts to obtain compliance primarily by power are likely to be very costly and possibly unsustainable. Governmental authority, such as that which has long existed in the United States, hardly costs at all.

CONCLUSION

In an experiment conducted by Dr. J. Scott Armstrong, an actor was coached to deliver what was purported to be a scientific talk entitled "Mathematical Game Theory as Applied to Physician Education" to three separate groups of social workers, psychologists, psychiatrists, educators, and administrators. Far from being scientific, the lecture actually consisted entirely of "double talk, meaningless words, false logic, contradictory statements, irrelevant humor, and meaningless references to unrelated topics."[19] Surprisingly none of the knowledgeable listeners caught on to the hoax. In fact, most of the individuals in the three audiences who later responded to a poll taken by the experimenter went so far as to describe the lecture as being "clear and stimulating."[20]

One conclusion that can be drawn from Armstrong's rather amazing findings is that language can, intentionally or unintentionally, be used to deceive virtually everyone.

Politicians, for instance, seem quite adept at using language to obfuscate or befuddle the thinking of their constituents particularly about what they deem to be unpopular activities such as war and unpopular legislation such as raising taxes. (See, "The Government's Doublespeak of War" p. 39.) For example, rather than risk the wrath of the voters the term "tax increases" is sometimes simply replaced by legislators with such expressions as: "revenue enhancements," "receipts strengthening," "receipts proposals," "passenger facility charges," "user fees" and "wage-based premiums."[21] Students of American government, who have learned the language of politics, will not, however, be easily deceived.

CHAPTER NOTES

[1] William Lutz, *The New Doublespeak: Why No One Knows What Anyone's Saying Anymore* (New York: Harper Collins Publishers, 1996), xi.
[2] Stephen G. Bloom, and James L. Wunsch, "Prof Talk," *The New York Times Magazine*, 25 August 1996, 22.
[3] Alan S. Zuckerman, *Doing Political Science: An Introduction to Political Analysis* (Boulder, Colorado: Westview Press, 1991), 8.
[4] Harold D. Lasswell, *Politics: Who Gets What, When, How* (Cleveland, Ohio: The World Publishing Company, 1958.
[5] Ibid., 13.
[6] David Easton, *The Political System: An Inquiry into the State of Political Science* (New York: Alfred A. Knopf, 1971), 129.
[7] James David Barber, *The Book of Democracy* (Englewood Cliffs, New Jersey: Prentice Hall, Inc., 1995), 2.
[8] Ibid., 3.
[9] Ibid., 4-7.
[10] James B. Whisker, *A Dictionary of Concepts on American Politics* (New York: John Wiley & Sons, 1980), 9.
[11] Ibid., 16.
[12] Ibid., 9-10.
[13] Ibid., 10.
[14] Bertrand Russell, *Power: A New Social Analysis* (New York: W.W. Norton & Company, Inc., 1938), 35.
[15] Doris Kearns, *Lyndon Johnson and the American Dream* (New York: Harper & Row,
[16] Thomas R. Dye, *Who's Running America? The Clinton Years*. 6th ed. (Englewood Cliffs, New Jersey: Prentice Hall, 1995), 11.
[17] Ibid.
[18] Stanley Milgram, *Obedience to Authority: An Experimental View* (New York: Harper & Row, Publishers, 1974), 138.
[19] Malcolm W. Browne, "Wanted: Interpreters for the Frontiers of Science," *The New York Times*, 6 January 1987, 3.
[20] Ibid.
[21] Lutz, 13-14; 154-155; 185.

SUGGESTED READINGS

Elliot, Jeffrey M., and Sheikh R. Ali. *The Presidential-Congressional Political Dictionary.* Santa Barbara, Calif.: ABC-Clio Information Services, 1984.

Erickson, Paul D. *Reagan Speaks: The Making of an American Myth.* New York: New York University Press, 1985.

Hart, Roderick P. *The Sound of Leadership: Presidential Communication in the Modern Age.* Chicago, Ill.: The University of Chicago Press, 1987.

Lutz, William. *Doublespeak: From "Revenue Enhancement" to "Terminal Living": How Government, Business, Advertisers, and Others Use Language to Deceive You.* New York: Harper & Row Publishers, 1989.

Plano, Jack C., and Milton Greenberg. *The American Political Dictionary.* 10th ed. Fort Worth, Texas: Harcourt Brace Jovanovich College Publishers, 1996.

Safire, William. *The New Language of Politics: An Anecdotal Dictionary of Catchwords, Slogans and Political Usage.* New York: Random House, 1968.

Chapter Two

CONSTITUTIONAL GOVERNMENT

In a 1794 speech delivered in the House of Commons, British lawmaker Edmund Burke reminded his fellow lawmakers of the reverence and awe he held for his nation's supreme law of the land—its constitution:

> Our Constitution is like our island, which uses and restrains its subject sea, in vain the wave roar. In that Constitution, I know and exultingly I feel, both that I am free; and that I am not free dangerously to myself or to others. I know that no power on earth, acting as I ought to do, can touch my life, my liberty or my property. I have that inward and dignified consciousness of my own security and independence which constitutes, and it's the only thing which does constitute, the proud and comfortable sentiment of freedom in the human beast.[1]

Burke's message is simple. A constitution protects one's freedom while at the same time provides the parameters within which members of a social structure can legally exercise their own individual freedoms without impeding upon the rights of others. A constitution, guided by the principles of democracy, guarantees one's rights to own and use one's property without undo interference from government, as long as one follows the legal limits detailed in the document. Yet, a constitution is more than just a piece of paper. It is the one document that guides the governing arms of the nation state while at the same time, limits the power those governing arms exercise over those they govern. In particular, the United States Constitution is unique among her sister documents in that it definitively provides the means to prevent the usurpation of and the abuse of governing power through its application of the separation of powers doctrine coupled with a detailed system of checks and balances. This chapter analyzes the concept of constitutionalism and the impact the document has on all who govern as well as those who are governed.

As so eloquently articulated by Jean Jacques Rousseau, Charles de Montesquieu, David Hume, and, of course, John Locke, constitutions are social contracts negotiated among the members of a society or nation state to form a governing structure. They are unique documents giving one an insight into the guiding political philosophy, social structure, economic orientation, cultural perspectives, mores, folkways, and, in some instances, the religious perspectives of those who gathered at their respective tables to debate the issues and ultimately, to embody them into a constitution. Understanding the background of those who write the document, gives one an insight as to how they addressed the issues they were tasked to handle. Constitutions are themselves fragile documents that oftentimes do not survive the test of time. They are not etched on stone tablets. Consequently, many nation states and in the United States, state constitutions must be revised or even completely rewritten to address changing perspectives. Thomas Jefferson once wrote that:

> Some men look at constitutions with sanctimonious reverence, and deem them like the ark of the covenant, too sacred to be touched. They ascribe to the men of the preceding Age a wisdom more than human, and suppose what they did to be beyond amendment.... I am certainly not an advocate for frequent and untried changes in laws and constitutions.... But I know also, that laws and institutions must go hand and hand with the progress of the human mind.... We might as well require a man to wear still the coat which fitted him when a boy, as civilized society to remain ever under the regimen of their barbarous ancestors.[2]

As discussed in Chapter 3, the Framers of the United States government discovered that their original design for their governing institutions simply did not work. They boldly opted to void the existing document and write a totally new constitution that they believed would stand the test of time. Before casting his vote for the new constitution, Benjamin Franklin comment to his fellow Framers that:

> when you assemble a number of men to have the advantage of their joint wisdom, you inevitably assemble with those men, all their prejudices, their passions, their errors of opinion, their local interests and their selfish views. From such an assembly, can a perfect production be expected? It therefore astonishes me, Sir, to find this system approaching so near to perfect as it does; and I think it will astonish our enemies, who are waiting with confidence to hear that our councils are confounded like those of the Builders of Babel. Thus I consent, Sir, to this Constitution, because I expect no better, and because I am not sure that it is not the best."[3]

This chapter examines both the concepts of constitutionalism as well as the development and implementation of the governing principles outlined in the United States Constitution. In addition, this chapter analyzes the ability of the current constitution to survive the test of time that for at least over two hundred years, it has remained intact with only twenty-seven major changes, ten of which were adopted and added to the document in 1791.

THEORIES OF GOVERNMENT AND CONSTITUTIONALISM

Is Government Necessary?

The question of the necessity of government has plagued political philosophers since Plato and Aristotle. In particular, Aristotle believed "that the state is a creation of nature, and that man is by nature a political animal. And he who by nature and not by mere accident, is without a state, is either a bad man or above humanity; he is like the tribeless, lawless and heartless one."⁴ By his use of the phrase "political animal," Aristotle was referring to man's innate survival instincts to take care of his wants and needs first regardless of consequences to others. Just like the lion or the tiger, man's predatory nature seeks what he needs to survive, i.e., food, shelter, and clothing. What separates man from the beast is rational thinking and the need for emotional companionship with his fellow mankind. In his epic *The Politics*, Aristotle concluded that while beasts can live and survive in isolation from each other, man could not. Therefore,

> a social instinct is implanted on all men by nature. . . . For man, when perfected is the best of animals, but, when separated from law and justice, he is the worst of all; since armed injustice is the more dangerous and he is equipped at birth with arms meant to be used by intelligence and virtue, which he may use for the worst ends. Wherefore, if he have not virtue, he is the most unholy and the most savage of animals, and the must full of lust and gluttony. But justice is the bond of men in states, for the administration of justice, which is the determination of what is just, is the principle order in a political society.⁵

Consequently, both Aristotle and Plato agreed that once men left their nomadic individualist lifestyles behind and bounded together into a society, they would out of necessity develop rules and regulations to protect themselves from each other. In turn, the society would create a higher authority to implement and enforce those rules upon the citizenry. Thus, the evolution of **government** defined as "the formal institutional structure and processes of a society by which policies are developed and implemented in the form of law binding on all."⁶ Some form of government is a universal feature of any society whether it be a clan, tribe, city, nation state, or empire. Even the most rudimentary social structure had its own rules, regulations, codes, and laws enforced by some form of authority carried out either by a chieftain, a monarch, or a tribal council. The ancient civilizations of the Maya, Inca, Aztec, Egyptian, and Babylonian all had very sophisticated governing and religious institutions as well as structured social classes. A governing structure was necessary for they all realized that without it, there would be no means of providing for the common defense against internal and external attacks and no mechanism to maintain domestic order. Life would be chaotic.

Few, however, agreed that there was one preferred form or a single guiding political philosophy suitable for all. Both Plato and Aristotle wrestled with this dilemma. In *The Politics*, Aristotle employed a comparative study of different governing systems. He rationalized that while "every state is a community of some kind, and every community is established with a view to some good," it would be a mistake to conclude that there is only one accepted form of government since by necessity "governments differ in kind."⁷ He subsequently classified different governing formats as either good or bad. Aristotle determined that a monarchy or rule of one was a sound-governing format as long as the monarch ruled for the benefit of his/her people. But once the monarch began to initiate laws for the benefit of himself or herself, the government flipped to its bad form—tyranny. Likewise, he believed that the rule of the few, an aristocracy, was a good government that if left unchecked, could well developed into a corrupt oligarchy. For governing structures centered on the rule of many, Aristotle envisioned the good form as a polity but he concluded that democracy was a bad form of government.

After himself studying various forms of governing formats, Jean Jacques Rousseau wrote in his *Confessions*: "I had seen that everything is rooted in politics and that, whatever might be attempted, no people would ever be other than the nature of their government made them. So the great question of the best possible government seemed to me to reduce itself to this: 'What is the nature of the government best fitted to create the most virtuous, the most enlightened, the wisest, and in fact, the best people, taking the word 'best' in its highest sense?'"[8] Consequently, Rousseau entertained the concept of **self-determination**, that is, "the aspiration of some group—grounded in some existing sentiment of national or racial identity associated with common territory, language or religion—to form its own sovereign state and to govern itself."[9] It was, therefore, left up to the people of a given state to determine for themselves both the rules they wished to follow and the format of their governing institutions.

Plato focused more on the person or persons heading a government rather than on the form of the governing system. As a young man, he was disillusioned by Athens's defeat in the Peloponnesian War to their archenemies the Spartans. Consequently, Athenian democracy was replaced by a Spartan oligarchical government that was eventually overthrown and replaced by, once again, a democratic form. However, both the ruling oligarchy and the re-emergent democratic government failed the Athenian people. A frustrated Plato lamented, "I kept waiting for favorable moments, and finally saw clearly in regard to all states now existing that without exception their system of government is bad. Their constitutions are almost beyond redemption except through some miraculous plan accompanied by good luck."[10] He concluded that the problem with the Athenian government was not its format but the people running it. In *The Republic*, Plato wrote, "existing cities are hopelessly corrupt and must remain so unless they can be rescued from their plight by philosophic rulers, i.e., if their kings become philosophers, or philosophers became kings."[11] He concluded that "the human race will not see better days until either the stock of those who rightly and genuinely follow philosophy acquire political authority, or else the class who have political control be led by some dispensation of providence to become real philosophers."[12] However, Plato would echo the same distrust that James Madison and his contemporaries expressed in Philadelphia about the fear that if left unchecked, the statesman no matter how virtuous he may be could be easily swayed towards corruption. Plato's solution was to populate his "Just City" with three distinct classes—the rulers or philosopher kings, the auxiliaries or the military, and everyone else known as the productive class. Together, the philosopher kings and the auxiliaries would form the guardians who would watch over the people, but more importantly watch over each other. Perhaps, Plato should be renamed as the Father of Checks and Balances!

Is Government a Social Contract?

The Enlightenment philosophers including Charles de Montesquieu, John Locke, and Jean Jacques Rousseau collectively went a step further. They rationalized that in the state of nature, man had the absolute and fundamental right to life, liberty, and property. However, when men decided to collectively form a society, they had to give up their absolute natural rights to form a governing body that would indeed protect the rights to life, liberty and property for the benefit of the entire society, not just for the lone individual. "Thus in spite of the great advantage of living free under the law of nature, people will see that they would be better off in a civil society under government.

The main impediment to peace and safety in the state of nature is an absence of clear standards of conduct, which can be applied impartially, and effectively enforced. Each person will accordingly agree to surrender the right to enforce the law of nature. Though this is a renunciation, it actually increases everyone's rights. Without this renunciation, no rights are secure in a conflict-ridden, precarious state of nature."[13] The collectivity of the bond was a **social contract**. The contract oftentimes known as a constitution should not be taken lightly because it is the cement that holds a citizenry together to both each other and to their governing institutions. In his *Reflections on the Revolution in France*, Edmund Burke emphasized the importance of this relationship:

> Society is indeed a contract. Subordinate contracts for objects of mere occasional interest may be dissolved at pleasure—but the state ought not to be considered as nothing better than a partnership agreement in a trade of pepper and coffee, calico, or tobacco, or some other such low concern, to be taken up for a temporary interest, and to be dissolved by the fancy of the parties. It is to be looked on with other reverence, because it is not a partnership in things subservient only to the gross animal existence of a temporary and perishable nature. It is a partnership in all science; a partnership in all art; a partnership in every virtue and in all perfection. As the ends of such a partnership cannot be obtained in many generations, it becomes a partnership not between those who are living, those who are dead, and those who are to be born. Each contract of each particular state is but a clause in the great primeval contract of eternal society, linking the power with the higher natures, connecting the visible and invisible world, according to a fixed compact sanctioned by the inviolable oath which holds all physical and all moral natures, each in their appointed place.[14]

Experiencing the wrath of absolute monarchies, Locke advocated that a social contract has two purposes. The contract would specify the philosophy guiding the governing institutions as well as the structure and functions of those institutions. But most importantly, the contract had to demand limited government. "People surrender only some of their rights, and do so in order to protect the rest. In addition, the relationship between individuals and government is to enforce the law of nature and are obligated to obey government has long as it fulfills its function. For its part, government claims obedience only as long as it fulfills its function. If it violates people's rights, it loses it power and its claim to be obeyed."[15] Locke called the relationship between the governed and the governing a **fiduciary trust**. Thus, "[t]he Legislative being only a Fiduciary Power to act for certain ends; there remains still in the People a Supreme Power to remove or alter the Legislative, when they find the Legislative act contrary to the trust reposed in them."[16] The same notion was expressed by John Locke. A contract is only a binding document when all of the signees fulfill their obligations. If one or more signees fail to abide by this contractual agreement, then the aggrieved parties have the right to end the relationship.

Democracy

As a political ideology, **democracy** is basically "a system of government in which the ultimate political authority is vested in the people."[17] The initial experiment with democracy occurred in the Greek city-states with the development of the polis in approximately 8th Century B.C.E. A polis was "a small but autonomous political unit in which all major political, social and religious activities were carried out at one central location."[18] In Athens, the whole body of male citizens over twenty years of age would meet at least ten times a year as the Assembly of Ecclesia. The task of the Assembly was to pass laws governing the city-state as well as to make important foreign policy decisions including war making. Although the body was limited to only native born male Athenians, this Assembly is the best example of pure democracy whereby everyone had a voice in the policy making process. Leading Athens into its Golden Age, Pericles (495 BC to 429 BC) was an early advocate of democracy. In explaining the concept of the democratic ideal, Pericles emphasized that:

> our constitution is called a democracy because power is in the hands not of a minority but of the whole people. When it is a question of settling private disputes, everyone is equal before the law; when it is a question of putting oneself before another in positions of public responsibility, what counts is not membership of a particular class, but actual ability which the man possesses. No one, so long as he has it in him to be of service to the state, is kept in political obscurity because of poverty."[19]

Full participatory or pure democracy worked as long as the membership of the governing assembly was manageable. Once deemed unmanageable, the format shifted from a pure participatory body to a representative one. **Representative** or **indirect democracy** is "a form of governance in which the citizens rule through representatives, who are periodically elected in order to keep them accountable."[20] The success of any representative democratic government rests on one word—accountability. It is a shared responsibility for the governors are accountable to the people who elected them in the first place to adequately turn their issues and concerns into corrective legislative acts. In turn, the governed accomplish their responsibilities by ensuring that their elective representatives are fulfilling their responsibilities to them. The governed have options for rewarding those who are faithfully fulfilling their responsibilities by re-electing them or if they are deemed unrepresentative, then the governed can vote them out of office.

A democratic form of government is preferred for several reasons. First, the selection of the governing is determined by the people through mandated periodic election cycles. This assures that offices will become vacant at a specific time and subsequently filled by a specified process on a specific date. Under a constitutional monarchy such as Great Britain, the monarchy is a hereditary position. However, the monarch does not have any input to the crafting and implementation of legislation for that function belongs to an elected House of Commons with the hereditary House of Lords playing little or no role in the actual governing process. Second, a basic premise to a democratic government is the principle of seeking consultation from and the consent of the ruled. The democratic doctrine underscores the premise that people should get what they want regardless of how wrong it may be! The leadership of any successful democratic government must take into account the ever-changing fickle mood swings of the governed that can be supportive of their governors on one day but switch their allegiance the next day. In a democratic government, it is a wise ruler who knows that although the people do not govern themselves, they surely will create a commotion if they dislike the way they are being governed. Third, the personal freedoms granted under a democracy give people the unique opportunity to voice their concerns without the fear of retaliation from their government. Today, Americans see the news footage coming from Egypt, the

Ukraine, and other countries of the discontented forming mass demonstrations in protest of their governments. Unable, or perhaps unwilling, to meet their demands, their respective government leadership sends in their military with the orders to use whatever it takes to disperse the mob. These governments are not true democracies for if they were, the people would have the absolute right to question the actions of their governments without fear of reprisal. Non-violent protest is a tenet of democratic governments. Lastly, democratic governments incorporate the mechanisms to prevent abuse of the governing authority. In his *Spirit of the Laws*, Charles Montesquieu stressed that "all would be lost if the same man or the same body of principal men, either of nobles or of the people, exercised these three powers: that of making the laws, that of executing public resolutions, and that of judging the crimes or the disputes of individuals."[21] Therefore, the governing authority must be divided between the governing institutions.

Constitutionalism

In 1215, the concept of holding one's rulers accountable to those they ruled was conceived by a group of disgruntled nobles who demanded an audience with their king in a field called Runnymede. Throughout England and most of Europe, the nobility were bound to their king under feudalism, a contractual agreement between a vassal and his lord and, in turn, between the lords and their king. Each member of the nobility dutifully pledged their homage and loyalty to their king by taking a public oath to "become your man by mouth and hands, and I swear and promise to keep faith and loyalty to you against all others, and to guard your rights with all my strength."[22] The relationship was one of mutual dependency as the lords were dependent upon their king to protect their rights to hold their lands while the nobility, in turn, would perform services for the king. The relationship, however, turned sour when John assumed the throne upon the death of his brother, King Richard I. Constantly either quarreling or at war with France, John called upon his nobility to fight his wars and collect his taxes. The nobility finally decided to reign in John's misuse of power by forcing him to sign the **Magna Carta**. The agreement was basically a list of grievances against the King with the mild threat that if John did not comply, grave consequences would follow. Although John adhered to the agreement for only two weeks and his ally Pope Innocent III declared it null and void, the Magna Carta serves as the first legal document questioning a divine right of the monarch's authority over his/her people. Its importance to the development of the American constitution cannot be overlooked. This one document "eventually came to inspire the children of subsequent eras to stand up for some of the important rights contained within it. Over time, the Great Charter (Magna Carta) also took on a life and culture of its own, spawning numerous other legal documents and doctrines in the common law. Its cultural relevance in the twentieth and twenty-first centuries has solidified its importance."[23] In many respects, the Magna Carta or the Great Charter introduced a new 'ism' to political science. **Constitutionalism** is "the political principle of limited government under a written contract" and served as the blueprint for subsequent documents commonly known as constitutions.[24]

By definition, a **constitution** is "a fundamental or 'organic' law that establishes the framework of government of a state, assigns the powers and duties of governmental agencies, and establishes the relationship between the people and their government."[25] Whether a single document or several documents collectively known as a constitution, all constitutions have the exalted status as the organic law or supreme law over there established jurisdictions. In *The Rights of Man* (1792), Thomas Paine drew a direct connection between a constitution, a government, and the concept of the social contract by pointing out "a constitution is a thing antecedent to a government, and a government is only the creature of a constitution. The constitution of a country is not the act of its government, but of the people constituting a government."[26] Basically, a constitution has "four main purposes. First, it must provide the structure of the governmental system, the organs and institutions of public authority. Second, it must authorize the powers that the government is to possess, and allocate them among the various branches and organs. Third, it must state the limitations on governmental power, for the essence of constitutionalism is the maintenance of a balance between authority and liberty, between governmental power and individual rights. Fourth, it must provide for some means other than violent revolution by which the constitutional design can be adopted to future necessities."[27]

Embedded in the various provisions of a constitution is the state's ideological approach to its governing principles, the structure of its governing bodies, and the responsibilities placed on both the governing and the governed. An **ideology** is "the 'way of life' of a people, reflected in their collectively held ideas and beliefs concerning the nature of the ideal political system, economic order, social goals, and moral values."[28] For example, after securing their independence from the British, there was little debate that the appropriate political ideology for the United States would be a democratic one that would vest ultimate political authority with the people. **Democratic ideology** is based on the principles of:

- Individualism with the primary task of government enabling each individual to achieve his/her highest potential of development;
- Liberty that allows each individual the greatest degree of freedom consistent with societal order;
- Equality that maintains that all persons are created equal and have equal rights and opportunities; and
- Fraternity that underscores the belief those individuals will not misuse their freedom but will cooperate in creating a wholesome society.[29]

In order to be a meaningful and viable document, a constitution must be regarded as the organic law of its state. No ordinance from a city hall, no law issued by a legislative house, no decree issued by a president, and no decision issued by a court can run counter to the provisions detailed in that document. Both those who rule and those being ruled must respect the legitimacy of their state's constitution. Far too often nation states have adopted constitutions with the intention of selectively abiding by their dictates. For example, the majority of the constitutions governing the world's states call for periodic elections. While the United States conducts its election cycle according to the dictates of its constitution, many nations do not. Far too often, the frequency of the election cycle is determined by the political fortunes of the incumbent leadership who will hold elections when they know they will win and postpone them when they know they will probably lose. Constitutionally guaranteed civil rights and liberties must be consistently enforced, not selectively applied to those who favor the incumbent regime.

Envious of the respect Americans revere for their Constitution, Alexis de Tocqueville decried his own French government's inability to follow the democratic principles they detailed in the numerous constitutions and governments formed after a very violent and bloody revolution in 1789. After the defeat and exile of Napoleon, the French government installed Louis XVIII to the throne in 1814 only to be followed by Charles X in 1824, who was disposed six years later in another bloody revolution. France had a constitution but the governing bodies opted not to follow it. Instead the governing bodies wanted to change the constitution to fit their own needs. A frustrated de Tocqueville wrote:

> From what does the king derive his powers? From the Constitution. And the Peers? From the Constitution. The deputies? From the Constitution. How, then, can a king, peers, and deputies combine to change something in a law which is the sole source of their right to rule? They are nothing outside the Constitution, so on what ground could they stand in order to change the Constitution? There are just two alternatives: either their efforts are impotent against a charter which continues to be valid in spite of them, in which case they can continue to rule in its name; or they may succeed in changing the character, in which case the law from which their existence derives is gone, and they are nothing. By destroying the charter they have destroyed themselves.[30]

THE FRAMERS' CHALLENGE—CREATING A CONSTITUTIONAL GOVERNMENT

The Seeds of Discontent

Similar to her contemporaries, Great Britain's quest for colonial possessions fulfilled its objectives of providing the newly emerging British industrial machine with essential raw materials and natural resources as well as captured markets for the purchase of its finished products. After its initial colonization failure in Raleigh in 1585, the British launched a full-scale effort with the founding of Jamestown in 1607. As colony after colony was founded, the British government soon realized that governing such a vast territory would prove troublesome. Colonial governors were appointed by the Crown with the London-based Privy Council overseeing the majority of colonial affairs. The real day-to-day governing of the colonies was basically left up to the colonials themselves through their own legislative assemblies. Opening its doors in 1619, Virginia's House of Burgess was the first colonial assembly in the American colonies. As long as the colonists followed British laws, they exercised considerable local control over their affairs. However, the tide turned toward a more repressive presence from the British during the Seven Years' War or as Americans called it, the French and Indian War. The British military was tied up in a two-front war—one in Europe and the other in the colonies against the French. Lacking the full force of its military, the British government called upon local militiamen to join the war front. Faced with an ever-growing national debt, the British government then decided to impose a series of revenue generating taxes upon the American colonists. In 1764, the **Revenue Act** or as the colonials referred to it, the **Sugar Act,** placed a duty or tax on molasses and required American shippers to post bonds to guarantee compliance with British trade regulations. The **Currency Act** of 1751 prohibited colonials from issuing their own paper money as legal tender. The most objectionable law was the **Stamp Act** of 1765, requiring the purchase of a stamp for all commercial and legal documents, liquor licenses, all print media, playing cards, and dice. In addition, the British imposed the **Quartering Act** upon the colonists. This legislation mandated that colonials were to offer-up their houses to provide quarters for British soldiers. Although promised reimbursement, the act required the colonists to furnish everything from fuel, beer, rum and food to the soldiers, as well as to pay for their transportation costs. After protest riots broke out, the British retaliated by arresting the participants, confiscating firearms, and randomly searching homes and businesses at will without benefit of a warrant. Colonial discontent was widespread.

Yet, the question of what action the colonialists should take fell into three broad groups. Those who benefited from British rule really did not want to take part in any action that would jeopardize their cozy relationship with the British government. The middle-of-the-road group realized that there were serious complaints against Britain. Yet, they also believed the advantages to British rule far outweighed the disadvantages. They wanted a negotiated settlement that would enable the British government to appropriately address colonial grievances without ending British rule. The final group had had enough with the overbearing tactics of the British government. They truly believed that the door to compromise had closed and the only option left was complete separation from Britain. Thomas Paine lambasted the middle-of-the-road crowd by pointing out that "absolute governments have this advantage with them, they are simple; if the people suffer, they know the head from which their suffering springs; know likewise the remedy; and are not bewildered by a variety of causes and cures. But the constitution of England is so exceedingly complex, that the nation may suffer for years together without being able to discover in which part the fault lies . . . many strong and striking reasons may be given to show that nothing can settle our affairs so expeditiously as an open and determined declaration of independence."[31]

Not everyone in Parliament was supportive of their government's colonial policies. As a sitting member of the House of Commons, Edmund Burke expressed his views in speeches entitled *On American Taxation* delivered in 1774, and *On Conciliation with America* delivered in 1775, followed by a commentary entitled *A Letter to the Sheriffs in Bristol*. Burke argued that Parliament and King George should use restraint with the colonials simply because their issues were not radical or even revolutionary. All they wanted was to receive the rights and privileges guaranteed to all Englishmen for themselves. Rather than leveling an accusatory finger at the colonists, Burke viewed Parliament as allowing an incompetent home government to enact misguided and ill-conceived acts upon the colonials. In his *On American Taxation* speech he plainly posed the question:

> Will they [the colonies] be content in such a state of slavery? Reflect how you are to govern a people who think they ought to be free, and think they are not. Your scheme yields no revenue, it yields nothing but discontent, disorder, disobedience; and such is the state of America, that, after wading up to your eyes In blood, you could only end just where you begun . . .[32]

As Paine predicted, the British government opted to ignore colonial complaints. Realizing there was no other option available to them, fifty-six men met as the Continental Congress in 1775 in Philadelphia to consider their options. Writing the **Declaration of Independence** was a simple task. The Declaration enumerated the various grievances the colonials had against their mother country and leveled an accusatory finger at King George for his abuse of governing authority. However, actually signing the document was for many a very difficult personal decision. A signee, Benjamin Rush, noted that a "'pensive and awful silence pervaded the house as we were called up, one after another, to the table of the President of Congress' to sign 'what was believed by many at that time to be our own death warrants.'"[33] The document was written by John Adams, Roger Sherman, Robert Livingston, Thomas Jefferson and Benjamin Franklin. By signing this document, each man knew that if caught, they would be charged with the hanging offense of treason. Every now and then the sober atmosphere was peppered by humor. Overweight himself, Benjamin Harrison told a skinny Elbridge Gerry that "I shall have a great advantage over you, Mr. Gerry, when we are all hung for what we are now doing. From the size and weight of my body I shall die in a few minutes, but from the lightness of your body you will dance in the air an hour or two before you are dead."[34] Of course, the most notable signature on the document is John Hancock's who commented that he wanted his signature to be so large and bold that "fat King George can read it without his spectacles."[35] The Declaration of Independence is the embodiment of Locke, Montesquieu, Rousseau, Plato, and Aristotle. The document clearly states their case. "A government which fails to serve the ends for which it was set up has breached the contract under which it was established and forfeited the loyalty of its citizens. . . . Whenever any form of government becomes destructive of these ends, it is the right of the people to alter or to abolish it, and to institute new government, laying its foundation on such principles and organizing its power in such forms, as to them shall seem most likely to effect their safety and happiness."[36] The first shots of the inevitable revolution were fired in Massachusetts in 1775. Six years later, the war ended with the surrender of General Cornwallis at Yorktown.

The Articles of Confederation

As the war effort began, the same men who signed the Declaration gathered once again to plan a government just in case they happened to win the war. On June 20, 1776, shortly after they declared their independence from Britain, a special committee chaired by John Dickinson met to plan a government for their future country. By November 1777, the delegates sent the final draft of the **Article of Confederation** for ratification. It was not an easy process for "each of the ex-colonies had strong objections, but amid the pressures of wartime, they all swallowed their misgivings—except Maryland, holding out for four years, until March 1781. Meanwhile, the Continental Congress was forced to carry on the war effort without any constitutional authority."[37]

The Articles established a confederative form of government hoping to serve two purposes for the newly formed nation. First, it gave to the former colonies a sense of nationalism. Instead of being thirteen different entities taking action independent of each other, they were now the United States of America, one governing body on their own shores. Second, it enabled the former colonies, now states, to retain their sovereignty and independence to govern the residents of their particular states. Life under a constitutional government was not new to them for the majority of the states had their own legislative houses and had already drafted and adopted constitutions. So, the confederative system seemed to be the best option available to them.

Under the Articles, the traditional executive and legislative functions were merged into the National Congress, composed of representatives from each state. The elimination of a strong executive was a consequence of British colonial rule. "The royal governors had been the symbol of tyranny, and so the executive office in the new [state] constitutions was deliberately weakened, while the legislature, a symbol of resistance to foreign rule, was strengthened. In eight states, the governor was chosen by the legislature, he had only a one-year term in ten states, his appointing power was generally limited, and he had the veto power in only three states. The one-year rule was common for all officials, not only for governors, as John Adams said, 'Where annual elections end, there tyranny begins.'"38 Collectively, each state had one vote in the Congress regardless of the number of delegates selected to represent their state. Once a legislative act passed through Congress, the sovereignty of each state was preserved through the provision that nine of the thirteen state legislative bodies had to approve it before it could be implemented in any state. The National Congress was empowered to declare war, conduct foreign policy and make treaties. However, the National Congress did not have the powers to levy and collect taxes or regulate trade and commerce between the states. The Articles created a true confederative form of government whereby the member states controlled the national government, not the other way around.

It did not take long for the inherent weaknesses of the confederative system to surface. No sooner were the signatures affixed to the document, state legislative houses began arguing among themselves about boundary lines and tariffs. Without a nationally backed currency, states began to issue their own currencies and charged excessive tolls to merchants trying to haul their goods across state boundary lines. Unfortunately, the confederative format succeeded only to divide rather than to unite the American people. Basically, the counter-productive actions taken by the individual states against each other coupled with the inability of the National Congress to exert effective leadership to quell the growing controversies between the various states caused grave alarm. If the National Congress could not stop the states of Virginia and North Carolina from clashing with each other over a trade route, how could it stop a possible invasion from the British or some other hostile enemy? The economic viability and the security of the nation were in grave peril. A bearer of things to come, John Jay wrote in *Federalist #5*:

> Instead of their being "joined in affection" and free from all apprehension of different "interests," envy and jealously would soon extinguish confidence and affection, and the partial interests of each confederacy, instead of the general interests of all America, would be the only objects of their policy and pursuits. Hence, like most other bordering nations, they would always be either involved in disputes and war, or live in constant apprehension of them.... They who well consider the history of similar divisions and confederacies will find abundant reason to apprehend that those in contemplation would in no sense be neighbors than as they would be borderers; that they would neither love nor trust one another; but on the contrary would be prey to discord, jealousy, and mutual injuries; in short, that they would place us exactly in the situations in which some nations doubtless wish to see us, viz., formidable only to each other.39

As early as 1785, George Washington hosted a meeting of key political leaders from Virginia and Maryland at Mount Vernon. The discussion centered on their joint concerns over the navigation of commerce on both the Chesapeake Bay and the Potomac River. They purposively ignored a provision in the Articles requiring the prior consent of the National Congress for all interstate agreements. They instead developed their own plan calling for uniform import duties and standardized commercial regulations. When Maryland's legislature adopted the proposals, Pennsylvania and Delaware expressed their interests in a similar joint agreement. James Madison saw this as a prime opportunity to gather people together to meet in Annapolis in September 1786, for the sole purpose of discussing the problems with the Articles and to propose possible solutions. Although nine states were invited, only five sent a delegation. However, the meeting proved fruitful as their report was distributed to all thirteen state legislatures and the National Congress suggesting that another conference be held in Philadelphia in May 1787, for the sole purpose "to take into consideration the situation of the United States, to devise further provisions as shall appear to them necessary to render the Constitution of the Federal Government adequate to the exigencies of the Union."[40]

It was not just the economic and political elites that were disenchanted with their government. In 1783, a group of disgruntled former Revolutionary War soldiers surrounded the Pennsylvania State House where the National Congress was in session, holding its membership captive for a day. The delegates were further insulted when the governor of Pennsylvania refused to call out its state militia to rescue them. Consequently, the National Congress became a mobile group moving their sessions from Princeton, New Jersey, to Annapolis, Maryland and finally to New York City. "The *Boston Evening Post* mocked the politicians for not being stars of the first magnitude, but rather partaking of the nature of *inferior* luminaries, or *wandering* comets."[41] Attention was then drawn to Massachusetts in 1786, when a group of approximately 1,200 angry farmers and shopkeepers under the leadership of their former Revolutionary War commander Daniel Shays launched an ill-fated insurrection against the state government. Their complaints were similar to those heard across the country. With no national or even state banking system, people had to borrow from each other to pay their taxes and even plant their crops. Cities and towns defaulted on their tax obligations. Violent protests erupted in six other states. Few if any other state militias went to the aid of their sister states to quell the violence. Meanwhile, an inept National Congress left the door wide open for state legislative houses to fill the void by enacting their own commercial agreements,

Shays led a band of farmers in revolt against tax creditors attempting to repossess their farms.

treaties with foreign countries, etc. "Like most other Federalists, Madison through that the [state] legislatures were dominated by demagogues who sought office for reasons of 'ambition' and 'personal interest' rather than 'public good.'"[42] For Madison, Washington, Alexander Hamilton, and many other concerned individuals, enough was enough.

The Gathering at Philadelphia—The Convention Setting

Although every state was encouraged to send a delegation, only fifty-five delegates actually made the journey to Philadelphia to meet in Independence Hall. Of the group, six had signed the Declaration of Independence, fourteen were either landowners or property speculators, twenty-one were veterans of the Revolutionary War, fifteen were slave owners, twenty-four were either current members of or had served in the National Congress, and thirty-four were lawyers.[43] The notables were the "whose who" of the American political scene—Benjamin Franklin, George Washington, Alexander Hamilton, John Adams, and George Mason. This gathering was the intelligentsia of their time. All were well educated and well versed on the political perspectives held by Aristotle, Plato and the Enlightenment thinkers including Locke, Rousseau, Montesquieu, John Mill, and John Stuart Mill. Those invited but not in attendance were equally among the notables—Thomas Jefferson, John Adams, Samuel Adams, Thomas Paine, and Patrick Henry. Jefferson and John Adams were absent due to their respective assignments as American ministers to France and England. Rhode Island's legislature opted not to attend while the delegation from New Hampshire was two months late due to a lack of traveling funds. Although the session was to begin on May 14, 1787, it actually kicked off on May 25. To no surprise, George Washington was elected as the president of the Convention with James Madison serving as its secretary. Meeting six days a week, the session ended on September 17, 1787.

The Gathering at Philadelphia—The Convention's Charge

For Madison, the convention's charge was three-fold. The first item of business was to create a strong national government that would according to Madison provide:

1. Security against foreign danger;
2. Regulation of the intercourse with foreign nations;
3. Maintenance among the States;
4. Certain miscellaneous objects of general utility;
5. Restraint of the States from certain injurious acts; and
6. Provisions for giving due efficacy to all these powers."[44]

His was not the only voice advocating a stronger national government with enough teeth to keep the union together and end the strife between the various states. The Framers believed that "this country and this people seem to have been made for each other, and it appears as if it was the design of Providence, that an inheritance so proper and convenient for a band of brethren, united to each other by the strongest ties, should never split into a number of unsocial, jealous and alien sovereignties."[45] But they also did not want a national government so strong that the individual

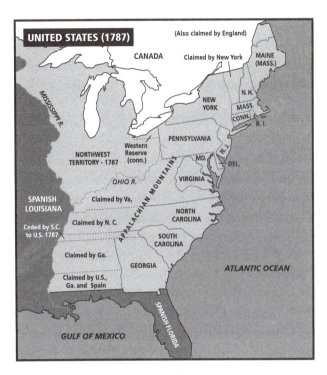

states would be stripped of their governing authority, and, ultimately, the people would become the victims of a repressive regime. Therefore, they wanted a document that specifically listed or enumerated what powers the government could exercise. This was to be a **limited** government. After a careful assessment of the Articles, the delegates believed it no longer suited the nation's need and unanimously voted to declare it null and void and to begin anew.

Second, Madison wanted a document that would both clearly delineate the duties of the governing and legally bind them to their charge so that they would not have any avenue to abuse their authority. In *Federalist No. 51* entitled "Internal Checks of the New Constitution," Madison wrote:

> Ambition must be made to counteract ambition. The interest of the man must be connected with the constitutional rights of the place. It may be a reflection on human nature, that such devices should be necessary to control the abuses of government. But what is government itself, but the greatest of all reflections on human nature? If men were angels, no government would be necessary. If angels were to govern men, neither external nor internal controls on government would be necessary. In framing a government that is to be administered by men over men, the great difficulty lies in this: you must first enable the government to control the governed; and in the next place, oblige it to control itself. A dependence on the people is, no doubt, the primary control on the government; but experience has taught mankind the necessity of auxiliary precautions.[46]

Madison's solution was to borrow from Plato the concept of checks and balances and from Montesquieu the separation of powers doctrine. Madison gained an important ally in Alexander Hamilton from New York. Hamilton aided Madison's unsuccessful efforts to strengthen the Articles of Confederation, wrote a large portion of the *Federalist Papers*, and would later play an essential role in securing ratification of the Constitution in both Virginia and New York. For Hamilton, the only way to fix the growing problems of the new nation was to implement a strong national government designed "to protect property and civil liberties from the state governments, to direct economic activities into the channels most conductive to the national welfare, and to re-establish public credit."⁴⁷ What emerged from the Convention was "the assumption that the greatest dangers to republic government are those of divisive power of faction and the threat of tyranny resulting from too great a concentration of political power. Madison's solution to those problems was to establish a powerful national government that could balance state and local units and maintain its own checks and balances to ensure moderation in the exercise of power."⁴⁸

Third, Madison truly believed that the appropriate format for governing this nation had to be a republican government guided by the principles of democracy. A **republic** is "a form of government in which sovereign power resides in the electorate and is exercised by elected representatives who are responsible to the people."⁴⁹ In *Federalist #10,* Madison drew a distinction between a democracy and a republic:

> It is that in a democracy, the people meet and exercise the government in person; in a republic, they assemble and administer it by their representatives and agents. A democracy, consequently, will be confined to a small spot. A republic may be extended over a large region. . . . Under the confusion of names, it has been an easy task to transfer to a republic observations applicable to a democracy only; and among others, the observation that it can never be established but among a small number of people, living within a small compass of territory. Such a fallacy may have been the less perceived, as most of the popular governments of antiquity were of democratic species; and even in modern Europe, to which we own the great principle of representation, no example is seen of a government wholly popular, and founded at the same time, wholly on that principle. If Europe has the merit of discovering this great mechanical power in government . . . American can claim the merit of making the discovery the basis of unmixed and extensive republics.⁵⁰

Peppered throughout Madison's desire for a republican government was also the fear many of the delegates held about the uncontrollable nature of democracy. When Aristotle classified his governments, he placed democracy as the bad form of the rule of the many. So the task before the Convention was how to craft a republican government capable of controlling the empowerment and zeal of democracy. The fear was that the masses, if left unchecked, would elect the wrong people to public office. Alexis de Tocqueville actually drew a distinction between the political knowledge of an aristocracy over the uneducated or ill-informed masses:

> An aristocracy is infinitely more skillful in the science of legislation than democracy can ever be. Being master of itself, it is not subject to transitory impulses; it has far-sighted plans and knows how to let them mature until the favorable opportunity offers. An Aristocracy moves forward intelligently; it knows how to make the collective force of all its laws converge on one point at a time. A democracy is not like that; its laws are almost always defective or untimely. Therefore the measures of democracy are most imperfect than those of an aristocracy; if often unintentionally works against itself; but its aim is more beneficial.⁵¹

Consequently, the delegates on purpose did not mention in the body of the Constitution the guarantees to universal suffrage or even specify the qualifications for casting a ballot. They left those details up to the individual state legislative houses. Initially, the majority of the states required some form of property ownership as a pre-requisite for voting privileges thus eliminating a large number of people from casting a ballot. Only members of the House of Representatives would be directly elected by the people, all others indirectly. It took subsequent amendments to the Constitution to broaden the scope of voting rights and truly move this nation to a republican government.

The Gathering at Philadelphia—Designing a New Government

The next order of business was to determine the format of the new government. The Framers decided upon a federal system to replace the confederative format. Whereas the confederative format places the states in charge with the national government playing a subservient role, the federal system reverses the relationship by elevating the national government's powers above those of the states.

One of the main problems with the Articles was that all governing authority was concentrated in just one body—the National Congress. They did not want to duplicate the British system whereby a constitutionally weak monarch was totally beholden to his/her Parliament. "The draftees of the Constitution were very familiar with Sr. William Blackstone's Commentaries on the Law of England (1973) which asserted that: 'In all tyrannical governments the supreme magistracy, or the right both of making and of enforcing the laws, is vested in one and the same man, or one and the same body of men; and wherever these two powers are united together, there can be no public liberty.'"[52] Madison pointed out "the accumulation of all powers, legislative, executive, and judiciary, in the same hands, whether of one, a few, or many, and whether hereditary, self-appointed, or elective, may justly be pronounced the very definition of tyranny."[53] Consequently, the Framers opted to divide or separate governing authority by creating three distinct branches of government and giving them specific duties and responsibilities. The **separation of powers** is "a major principle of American government whereby power is distributed among three branches of government—the legislative, the executive and the judicial. The officials of each branch are selected by different procedures, have different terms of office, and are independent of one another. The separation is not complete, in that each branch participates in the functions of the other through a system of checks and balances. The separation, however, serves to ensure that the same person or group will not make the law, enforce the law, and interpret and apply the law."[54] Thus, the legislative branch would make the laws (**Article I**) while the executive branch would be charged with the implementation of those laws (**Article II**), and if deemed necessary and as later detailed in the Judiciary Act of 1789, the judicial branch would interpret both the meaning and application of the law (**Article III**). The separation of powers doctrine was indeed challenged before the Supreme Court. In *Myers v United States* (1926), Justice Louis D. Brandies wrote in his official opinion document "the doctrine of separation of powers was adopted by the Convention of 1787, not to promote efficiency but to preclude the exercise of arbitrary power. The purpose was not to avoid friction, but, by means of the inevitable friction incident to the distribution of the governmental powers among three departments, to save the people from autocracy."[55]

Two plans emerged for the creation of a legislative body. Edmund Randolph introduced the **Virginia Plan**. This proposal called for a bicameral or two-house legislative congressional body.

Representatives to the lower house (House of Representatives) would be selected by the direct vote of the people in their respective states while the membership of the upper house (Senate) would be selected by the lower house from nominees proposed from state legislative houses. The plan also called upon the Congress to select the executive or president as well as to select members of the national judiciary and a special group called the Council of Revision whose main task would be to review the constitutionality of congressional acts. The contentious part of this plan was that the number of representatives from each state would be based on the population of that state, meaning that the most populated states would have the upper hand over the less populated states. Not pleased by that alternative, William Patterson introduced the **New Jersey Plan,** representing the interests of the smaller states. This plan called for revising the Articles simply because under the Articles, every state had the same number of representatives regardless of the population of their states. The plan addressed some of the major concerns levied against the Articles in that it called for giving the national government the power to tax, regulate interstate commerce, and oversee foreign relations. Although the delegates voted to accept the Virginia Plan, the protests from the smaller states cast a cloud about the future of both the convention and a new constitution. After months of protracted arguments, Robert Sherman proposed a compromise. The **Connecticut Plan** or as it is commonly known as the **Great Compromise**, combined the two proposals. From the Virginia Plan, the number of representatives from each state elected to the House of Representatives would be based on a state's population. The larger populated states would have more representatives in that chamber than the lesser-populated states. From the New Jersey Plan, each state would have an equal number of Senators—two from each state, regardless of the population of that state. The membership of the lower house would be directly elected from the representatives' respective states while Senators would be selected from their respective state legislative houses. (The Seventeenth Amendment adopted in 1913 mandates direct popular election of Senators.) The executive or president would be selected from a body separate from Congress—the Electoral College.

Before the ink was dry on the Great Compromise, another issue arose that nearly caused the demise of the convention. The southern states of Virginia, North Carolina, and South Carolina included in their calculation of state population their African-American slaves, which in many instances outnumbered Anglos three or four times to one. If slaves were to be counted as population for representational purposes, then the larger populated northern states of Pennsylvania and New York who had very few slaves would lose some of its power in the House to the southern states. The northern states simply did not want slaves to be counted at all. The southern states balked at the notion that since slaves were the private property of their owners, then the owners should pay taxes on that property just as they did for their real estate holdings. Once again, a compromise was reached. The **Three-fifths Compromise** called for 3/5's of a state's African-American slave population to count towards the population base for House representation districts and 3/5's of that same population would count in direct tax calculations.

It is interesting to note that the Framers did not believe that previous political or elective experience should be a pre-requisite for seeking elective office. The qualifications to hold the office of the president were age (thirty-five or older), native born, and a fourteen-year residency requirement prior to seeking the office. The native born and residency requirements were to prevent someone outside of the United States from seeking the office. There were no educational requirements or any mention of prior governing experience attached to qualifications for office. In an annual message to Congress, President Ulysses S. Grant comment on the lack of attaching job experience to the qualifications for the presidency: "It was my fortune or misfortune to be called to the Chief Magistracy without any prior political training. Under the circumstances, it is but reasonable to suppose that errors of judgment must have occurred."[56] The same holds true for Congress. To be a member of the Congress, the only requirements are age (twenty-five or older for the House, thirty or older for the Senate), citizenship, and residency in the state one is representing. One could speculate that the Framers did not want "professional' politicians but instead desired to see individuals from different walks of life, backgrounds, and credentials to seek public office.

The delegates did have some difficulty in assigning the various duties to the separate branches of government. Taking from their knowledge of the British Parliament, they were able to clearly see what duties should be assigned to the legislative branch. However, creating the executive branch proved to be problematic. Their only role model, if you can call him one, was George III, an hereditary monarch with a proven track record of abusing his royal powers. From the very beginning they agreed that the head of the executive branch would be elected not for life, but for a four-year term of office. If successful in his job, then it would be up to the voters through the Electoral College to grant him additional terms. In *Federalist No. 69*: Powers of the President, Alexander Hamilton justified his support of a limited term for the president:

> In these circumstances [four-year term of office], there is a total dissimilitude between him and a King of Great Britain, who is an hereditary monarch. . . . If we consider how much less time would be requisite for establishing a dangerous influence in a single State, than for establishing a like influence throughout the United States, we must conclude that a duration of four years for the Chief Magistrate of the Union is a degree of permanency far less to be dreaded in that office."[57]

throughout Article II, whatever power or duty is assigned to the president, there is a check upon that power in Article I. The Framers were skeptical about the office and the potential office holders.

The lack of details for the presidency would be filled in by the person who first held the office—George Washington. He pondered whether he should be called His Excellency or Mr. President, how he should greet foreign dignities, and so forth. Even he was unsure if he fit the bill for the presidency. "My movements to the chair of government will be accompanied by feelings not unlike those of a culprit, who is going to the place of his execution; so unwilling am I, in the evening of a life nearly consumed in public cares, to quit a peaceful abode for an ocean of difficulties, with that competency of political skill, abilities, and inclination which are necessary to manage the helm."[58] It was Washington who decided he needed a Cabinet of appointed experts to assist him. He subsequently formed his first Cabinet with Thomas Jefferson as Secretary of State, Alexander Hamilton as Secretary of the Treasury, Edmund Randolph as Attorney General and Henry Knox to serve as Secretary of War. Washington then formed the nation's bureaucratic structure of civil servants to run the executive branch of this government.

The Framers were sure that they needed to include in the document the provisions for a smooth transition of power if the president should die or leave office before the four-year term expired. Thus, the vice president would be the second most important person in the executive branch. The Framers simply did not know what a vice president should be doing while waiting, if necessary, to assume the vacated office of the presidency. The vice president is the presiding officer of the Senate. However, his only official duty is to cast the deciding vote needed to break a tie vote in the Senate. Himself a delegate and ultimately waiting to approve the Constitution, John Adams served as the nation's first vice president. He lamented "my country has, in its wisdom, contrived for me the most insignificant office [the vice presidency] that ever the invention of man contrived or his imagination conceived."[59] Thomas Jefferson complained that his stint in the vice presidency was "honorable and easy, the first is but a splendid misery."[60] The role a vice president plays is perhaps defined by the president he/she serves. For many a vice president, the primary duty was indeed to sit and wait to see whether they would become a president "by accident."

The shortest of the first three articles is Article III, providing for a national judiciary. The Articles of Confederation did not provide for a national court system. The Framers believed they needed one to act as a mediator or higher authority to decide disputes between the states. The Court's original jurisdiction was limited to cases involving ambassadors and other public ministers, cases of admiralty and maritime, controversies in which the United States was a party, controversies between states, impeachment, and treason. The Article did not specify the number of judges needed to sit on the Supreme Court or any of the inferior courts. The creation of additional federal courts was left up to Congress. There were no official qualifications for a federal judgeship. The only provision in Article III was that judges would hold their offices "during good behavior," meaning that these were lifetime appointments.

The next item of business was to merge the concept of separation of powers with a system of checks and balances that would provide an internal mechanism against any branch of the government or any person within a specific branch of government from abusing power. **Checks and balances** is "the notion that constitutional devises can prevent any power within a nation from becoming absolute by being balanced against, or checked by, another source of power within that same nation."[61] Each House of Congress was given specific duties. The House of Representative has the power of the purse as specified in Article I, Section 7: "all bills for raising revenue shall originate in the House of Representatives." However, the Senate can propose amendments to the legislation and must give its stamp of approval on House revenue bills. Both houses of Congress can propose legislation but both chambers must approve the bills before they are sent to the executive branch for the president's approval. If the president vetoes the legislation, both Houses must cast a 2/3's vote to overturn the veto. Neither House of Congress can adjourn without the consent of the other. The impeachment of elected officers, in particular the president, is a shared responsibility. The House of Representatives draws up the Articles of Impeachment or charges against the president. The Senate has the sole power to try impeachments with the Chief Justice of the Supreme Court acting as the presiding judge. The only exclusive powers given to the Senate are to ratify treaties and approve presidential appointments.

Each assigned task or duty given to one branch is also checked by a provision given to one or both of the other branches. The bulk of the legislative duties assigned to Congress are detailed in Article I, Section 8 of the Constitution. Although the president is designated as the commander-in-chief of the nation's military forces, only Congress can declare war. A president can send troops into a combat situation but Congress with its "power of the purse" can deny the funding for the military action. Presidents are empowered by Article II to make treaties with foreign nations. However, the Senate must consent or approve the treaty or it is not a binding agreement. As many presidents have discovered, they only have the authority to nominate to the Senate individuals to serve in their Cabinets and key government positions. It is the Senate that has the final approval over those nominations. Although presidents may appoint an individual when Congress is not in session, even his/her recess appointments are subject to Senate confirmation when the legislature reconvenes. Of course, the federal courts can declare a legislative act unconstitutional but Congress can ultimately retool that act into a constitutional amendment that once approved becomes a part of the Supreme Law of the Land. Congress can impeach a president; however, a president cannot impeach a member of Congress. The system of checks and balances, as well as the doctrine of separation of powers, has been frustrating for both members of Congress and occupants of the White House. But the system designed by the Framers forces the executive and legislative branch to work together. If not, nothing gets done.

Although the subject of slavery was discussed, many of the delegates were themselves southern slave owners. During the ratification process, questions arose as to why the delegates opted just to end the importation of slaves but not abolish slavery altogether. Madison addressed this concern in his *Federalist Paper No. 42: Powers Over Foreign and Interstate Affairs*:

> It was doubles to be wished, that the power of prohibiting the importation of slaves had not been postponed until the year 1808, or rather that it had been suffered to have immediate operation. But it is not difficult to account, either for this restriction on the general government, or for the manner in which the whole clause is expressed. It ought to be considered as a great point gained in favor of humanity, that a period of twenty years may terminate forever, within these States, a traffic which has so long and so loudly upbraided the barbarism of modern policy; that within that period, it will receive a considerable discouragement from the federal government, and may be totally abolished, by a concurrent of the few States which continue the unnatural traffic, in the prohibitory example which has been given by so

great a majority of the Union. Happy would it be for the unfortunate Africans, if an equal prospect lay before them of being redeemed from oppressions of their European brethren![62]

Amending the Document

The Framers wanted to ensure that if their document were amended, it would be a meaningful and arduous process. Article V specifies that for an amendment to be attached to the Constitution, the following steps must be followed:

1. A 2/3's vote in both the House of Representatives and the Senate or a 2/3's vote from the legislatures of "the several states" for Congress to call a national convention to even begin the amending process.
2. If the amendment passes the first step, then it must be ratified or approved by 3/4ths of the state legislative houses.

Although numerous constitutional amendments are introduced in Congress each legislative session, very few have survived step one. For step 2, usually Congress will set a specified period of approximately seven to ten years for state legislative houses to initiate their ratification processes. As in the case of the failed Equal Rights Amendment, Congress set a seven-year time frame for clearance through state legislative houses only to extend it for an additional three years to get the required ¾'s approval. To date, only seventeen amendments have made it through the entire process. The Framers understood that the document was not perfect and that changes would have to be made. But, they envisioned that any changes would be absolutely necessary and driven by sound reasoning. As Madison pointed out, "the mode preferred by the convention seems to be stamped with every mark of propriety. It guards equally against that extreme facility, which would render the Constitution too mutable; and that extreme difficulty, which might perpetuate its discovered faults. It, moreover, equally enables the general and the State governments to originate the amendment of errors, as they may be pointed out by the experience on one side, or the other."[63]

RATIFICATION AND ADOPTION

The Ratification Process

Article VII of the proposed Constitution outlines the process by which the document would receive final ratification. Final approval would be secured by a positive vote from nine of the thirteen states. Why only nine and not thirteen states? The Framers understood that the document was a radical one in which they abolished one government and replaced it with a totally new one based on concepts of governance that had never been tried before in this nation. So, they knew that not every state would be on board. While they would have liked to require a unanimous vote of approval, they agreed that nine affirmatives constituted a majority. They did, however, want the people of each state rather than their elected state assemblymen to cast the vote. Therefore, each state was required to convene an elected convention to consider whether to adopt the document.

Federalists versus Anti-Federalists

Supporters of the Constitution, or the Federalists, gathered their forces together to battle state by state for the ratification of the document. James Madison was their primary political strategist. "He kept up a steady correspondence with allies around the country, gathering intelligence, coordinating campaigns, and offering advice on such crucial matters as the precise timing of the state conventions."[64] The opposition, now known as the Anti-Federalists, used the local media to air their complaints of virtually everything contained in the document. As a rebuttal, Madison called upon two of his closest allies—Alexander Hamilton and John Jay—to respond to the opposition's claims. The resulting *Federalist Papers* are eighty-five articles written primarily by Madison with some from Hamilton and Jay. As soon as an article criticizing the Constitution was published, these three had an immediate response.

The major issue for the Anti-Federalists was that the Constitution did bind the national government to the civil rights and liberties provisions state constitutions guaranteed to its citizens. They wanted a Bill of Rights attached to the document prior to the ratification process. Hamilton came to the rescue by pointing out that "the truth is, after all the declamations we have heard, that the Constitution is itself, in every rational sense, and to every useful purpose, a bill of rights. . . And the purposed Constitution, if adopted, will be the bill of rights of the Union."[65] He went a step further by delineating portions of the Constitution guaranteeing protected rights to include the guarantee of the writ of habeas corpus, prohibitions against bill of attainder and ex-post facto laws. To finally silence the Anti-Federalist criticisms, the Federalists guaranteed that if the Constitution were ratified, the first step of the newly installed government would be to draft and adopt a Bill of Rights guaranteeing to protect civil rights and civil liberties.

The first state to ratify the document was Delaware followed by Pennsylvania, New Jersey, Georgia, and Connecticut. Massachusetts resulted in a close vote to approve the Constitution followed by Maryland, South Carolina and Rhode Island. The biggest battles were in New York with Anti-Federalists and the state's governor, George Clinton, leading the charge and in Virginia where Patrick Henry warned his fellow Virginians that if this document was approved, the national government would impose harsh taxes and strip away protected civil liberties. Henry truly thought that their state alone would sink the Constitution. However, four days before Virginians voted to approve the document, New Hampshire's approval sealed the deal as the ninth state to ratify the document. Eventually, New York approved the document and the stragglers followed suit. This was indeed what the Framers hoped for—a unanimous vote of approval.

CONCLUSIONS

As Ben Franklin so eloquently put it, the Constitution is not perfect, but it is the best to date for this nation. There is a direct connection between the Declaration of Independence and the Constitution. A close examination of both documents reveals that many of grievances lodged against the British monarchy and the Parliament were addressed through provisions in the Constitution and, in particular, the first ten amendments collectively known as the Bill of Rights. As one progresses through the text, the rights and privileges guaranteed in the Bill of Rights and subsequent amendments have an impact on the nation's judicial system (see Chapter 12), civil liberties (see Chapter

13) and civil rights (see Chapter 14), and the involvement of interest groups (see Chapter 8) and political parties (see Chapter 5) as well as citizens in the election process. Articles IV and VI of the Constitution lay down the concept of federalism and seal the relationship between national and state governments as well as the relationship state governments have with their county, local and special district governments (see Chapter 3). Of course, Articles I, II, and III firmly outline the roles of the legislative, executive, and judicial branches of the government as specifically assigned to them in the Preamble of the Constitution—promote the general welfare and provide for the common defense. This document is the appropriate application of both the separation of powers doctrine and the system of checks and balances. This is a living document, the organic law of the state, and, of course, the Supreme Law of the Land.

CHAPTER NOTES

[1] George Klosko, *History of Political Theory: An Introduction*, Vol. 2: Modern Political Theory, (New York, New York: Thomson/Wadsworth, 1995), 274.
[2] *Treasury of Presidential Quotations*, Caroline Thomas Harnsberger, ed., (Chicago, IL: Follett Publishing Company, 1964), 42.
[3] Jack C. Rakove, "Philadelphia Story," *The Wilson Quarterly*, Vol. 11, No. 2, Spring, 1987, 120.
[4] William Ebenstein, *Great Political Thinkers: Plato to the Present*, (New York, New York: Rinehart & Company, Inc., 1951), 76.
[5] Ibid., 77.
[6] *The American Political Dictionary*, Jack C. Plano and Milton Greenberg, eds., 10th ed., (Orlando, Florida: Harcourt Brace and Company, 1997), 12.
[7] Ebenstein, 75.
[8] Klosko, *History of Political Theory*, Vol. 2, 230.
[9] Roger Scruton, *A Dictionary of Political Thought*, (New York, New York: Harper & Row Publishers, 1982), 421.
[10] George Klosko, *History of Political Theory: An Introduction*, Vol. 1: Ancient and Medieval Political Theory, (Mason, Ohio: Cengage Learning, 2002), 49.
[11] Ibid.
[12] Ibid.
[13] Klosko, *History of Political Theory*, Vol. 2, 296.
[14] Ibid.
[15] Ibid., 106.
[16] Ibid., 108.
[17] *The American Political Dictionary*, 9.
[18] William J. Duiker and Jackson J. Spievogel, *World History*, 3rd ed., (Belmont, California: Wadsworth/Thomson Learning, 2001), 99.
[19] Klosko, *History of Political Theory*, Vol. 1, 4.
[20] *The HarperCollins Dictionary of American Government and Politics*, Jay M. Shafritz, ed., (New York, New York: HarperCollins Publishers, Inc., 1992), 174.
[21] Klosko, *History of Political Theory*, Vol. 2, 202.
[22] Duiker and Spievogel, 327.
[23] Eric T. Kasper, "The Influence of Magna Carta in Limiting Executive Power in the War on Terror," *Political Science Quarterly*, Vol. 126, No. 4, Winter, 2011-2012, 547.
[24] *The American Political Dictionary*, 2.
[25] Ibid., 34.
[26] *The HarperCollins Dictionary of American Government and Politics*, 141.
[27] C. Herman Pritchett, *The American Constitutional System*, 2nd ed., (New York, New York: McGraw-Hill Book Company, 1976), 3.
[28] *The American Political Dictionary*, 13.
[29] Ibid.
[30] Alexis de Tocqueville, *Democracy in America*, George Lawrence translator and J. P. Mayer, ed., (Garden City, New York: Doubleday and Company ,Inc. 1969), 724.
[31] "Thomas Paine Calls for a Break With England, 1776," *Major Problems in American Constitutional History*, Vol. 1: The Colonial Era Through Reconstruction, Kermit L. Hall, ed., (Lexington, Massachusetts: D. C. Heath and Company, 1992), 71-74.
[32] Klosko, *History of Political Theory*, Vol. 2, 202.

33William Hogeland, "Suicide Pact: 56 Men Put Their Lives on the Line by Signing the Declaration of Independence," *American History*, Vol. 48, No. 3, August, 2013, 32.
34Ibid.
35Ibid., 37.
36Pritchett, 8.
37Peter Onuf, "It Is Not A Union," *The Wilson Quarterly*, Vol. 11, No. 2, Spring, 1977, 101.
38Pritchett, 8-9.
39John Jay, "No. 5: Perils of American Discord," *The Enduring Federalist*, Charles Beard, ed., 2nd ed., (New York, New York: Frederick Ungar Publishing Co., 1964), 50-51.
40Pritchett, 3.
41Onuf, 101.
42Rakove, 109.
43Ibid., 105.
44Steven A. Peterson and Thomas Rasmussen, *State and Local Politics*, (New York, New York: McGraw-Hill, 1994), 24.
45John Jay, "No. 2: The True Basis of a Federal Union," *The Enduring Federalist*, Charles Beard, ed, 2nd ed., (New York, New York: Frederick Ungar Publishing Co, 1964), 39.
46James Madison, "No. 51: Internal Checks of the New Constitution," *The Enduring Federalist*, Charles Beard, ed., 2nd ed., (New York, New York: Frederick Ungar Publishing Co., 1964), 225.
47John C. Miller, *The Federalist Era: 1789-1801*, (New York, New York: Harper and Row Publishers, 1960), 35.
48*The American Political Dictionary*, 18.
49Ibid., 24.
50James Madison, "No. 14: The New Form of Government Adapted to Large Country," *The Enduring Federalist*, Charles Beard, ed., 2nd ed., (New York, New York: Frederick Ungar Publishing Co., 1964), 86.
51Alexis de Tocqueville, *Democracy in America*, 232.
52*The HarperCollins Dictionary of American Government and Politics*, 519-520.
53James Madison, "No. 47: Separation of Powers Within the Federal Government," *The Enduring Federalist*, Charles Beard, ed., 2nd ed., (New York, New York: Frederick Ungar Publishing Co., 1964), 211.
54*The American Political Dictionary*, 50.
55*The HarperCollins Dictionary of American Government and Politics*, 519-520.
56*Treasury of Presidential Quotations*, 259.
57Alexander Hamilton, "No. 69: Powers of the President," *The Enduring Federalist*, Charles Beard, ed., 2nd ed., (New York, New York: Frederick Ungar Publishing Co, 1964), 290.
58*Treasury of Presidential Quotations*, 255.
59Ibid., 350.
60Ibid., 351.
61*The HarperCollins Dictionary of American Government and Politics*, 102.
62James Madison, "No. 42: Powers Over Foreign and Interstate Affairs," *The Enduring Federalist*, Charles Beard, ed., 2nd ed., (New York, New York: Frederick Ungar Publishing Co., 1964), 182-183.
63James Madison, "No. 43: Miscellaneous Powers," *The Enduring Federalist*, Charles Beard, ex., 2nd ed., (New York, New York: Frederick Ungar Publishing Co., 1964), 191.
64A. E. Dick Howard, "Making It Work," *The Wilson Quarterly*, Vol. 111, No. 2, Spring, 1987, 122.
65Alexander Hamilton, "No. 84: Why The Constitution Needs No Bill of Rights," *The Enduring Federalist*, Charles Beard, ed., 2nd ed., (New York, New York: Frederick Ungar Publishing Co., 1964), 364.

SUGGESTED READING

Beard, Charles, H. *The Enduring Federalist*. Garden City, N.Y.: Doubleday and Co., Inc., 1948.

Collier, Christopher, and Collier, James Lincoln. *Decision in Philadelphia.* New York: Random House, 1986.

Klosko, George, *History of Political Theory: An Introduction, Vol. 1, Ancient and Medieval Political Theory*, Mason, Ohio: Cengage Learning, 2002.

Klosko, George, *History of Political Theory: An Introduction, Vol. 2: Modern Political Theory*, New York, New York: Thomson/Wadsworth, 1995. 975.

CHARLESTON MERCURY

EXTRA:

Passed unanimously at 1.15 o'clock, P. M., December 20th, 1860.

AN ORDINANCE

To dissolve the Union between the State of South Carolina and other States united with her under the compact entitled "The Constitution of the United States of America."

We, the People of the State of South Carolina, in Convention assembled, do declare and ordain, and it is hereby declared and ordained,

That the Ordinance adopted by us in Convention, on the twenty-third day of May, in the year of our Lord one thousand seven hundred and eighty-eight, whereby the Constitution of the United States of America was ratified, and also all Acts and parts of Acts of the General Assembly of this State, ratifying amendments of the said Constitution, are hereby repealed; and that the union now subsisting between South Carolina and other States, under the name of "The United States of America," is hereby dissolved.

THE UNION IS DISSOLVED!

Chapter Three

FEDERALISM

Intergovernmental relations (IGR) are "the complex network of interrelationships among governments, i.e., political, fiscal, programmatic, and administrative processes by which higher units of government share revenues and other resources with lower units of government, generally accompanied by special conditions that lower units must satisfy as prerequisites to receiving the assistance."[1] All nation states have levels of government from national to local communities, and each level is interrelated and interdependent upon each other, regardless of the formally outlined structure. For the United States, the structure is called federalism, a unique relationship between all levels of government that gives each some degree of independence from each other but definitely binds them together through the United States Constitution. The relationship has never been a smooth one. Even the Framers wondered whether this hybrid combination of the unitary and confederative systems coined federalism would actually work. In *Federalist #46* titled "Relative Strength of the Federal and State Governments," James Madison wrote:

> I proceed to inquire whether the federal government or the State governments will have the advantage with regard to the predilection and support of the people. Not-withstanding the different modes in which they are appointed, we must consider both of them as substantially dependent on the great body of citizens of the United States. . . . . The federal and state governments are in fact but different agents and trustees of the people, constituted with different powers, and designed for different purposes.[2]

Alexis de Tocqueville expressed the same sentiments in his *Democracy in America*:

> Among the inherent defects of every federal system, the most obvious of all is the complication of the means it employs. This system necessarily brings two sovereignties face to face. The lawgiver may succeed in making the operations of these two sovereignties as simple and

balanced as possible and may enclose them both within precisely defined spheres of action, but he cannot contrive that they shall be but one or prevent their touching somewhere.[3]

Under the day-to-day grind of governing, each part of the federal system does its job from the White House to the mayor's house. However, the inherent weaknesses in the system are tragically apparent whenever a national disaster or a usually violent weather episode hits the American shores. For example, the wrath and aftermath of Katrina brought undo hardships upon the people of the Gulf Coast, particularly, New Orleans. Historically, residents along the Gulf Coast area are well aware of the typical hurricane season—the beginning of June to usually the end of September. Every year, the National Hurricane Center announces the predicted number of storms, the category levels, and a list of alternative male and female names for each storm. Hurricanes can range from the least potentially dangerous Category 1 to the extremely damaging Category 5 with its 175 plus mile per hour winds—"the big one." Despite a cadre of sophisticated weather equipment and well-trained meteorologists, predicting the path of where a hurricane will strike is extremely difficult. Far too often, Mother Nature has the final say on where a hurricane will eventually make landfall. The 2005 hurricane season was anything but typical. The number of hurricanes exceeded the chosen names from A to Z. Officials resorted to using the Greek alphabet of Alpha, Beta, Gamma, etc. And on August 29, 2005, the rare "big one" named Katrina headed, as predicted it would, straight for the approximately 455,000 residents of New Orleans, Louisiana. When Katrina hit, New Orleans was already 10 feet below sea level surrounded by its well-known levee system. Frankly, "Katrina knocked one of the nation's largest cities back to the Stone Age—no electricity, no phone system, no water, no sanitation, no commerce," no way out, and no immediate substantial help on the way from any level of government.[4]

As Katrina's high winds and storm surges tore apart New Orleans and it levees, as well as areas stretching from Louisiana to Mississippi, it also severely and painfully exposed the inability of government at all levels from city hall to the White House to alleviate the suffering of the victims of Katrina's wrath. Those who had the time, the personal transportation, and the financial means did leave the area before the storm hit. However, the majority of the area's poor, sick, and elderly simply did not have a way out without some form of public assistance. Like the majority of our nation's cities, city leaders in New Orleans did not have a full-scale evacuation plan in place. For days on end, Americans across the country watched the tragedy of the Gulf Coast unfold with report after report of starving, thirst, and residents of New Orleans sitting on expressway overpasses in stifling heat waiting for someone to rescue them. Thousands of people were sitting on top of their roofs waving white pieces of cloth and holding signs hoping to attract the attention of an occasional helicopter hovering overhead to take them to safety. News footage showed stranded people using makeshift boats to ferry themselves and those they could rescue to the Superdome. Eventually, the high winds tore a hole in the Superdome's roof, rendering an already unbearable situation impossible. "In the local hospitals, doctors and nurses trapped with thousands of patients had to decide who got medicine and who got hooked up to life-saving ventilators in hot, dark wards as supplies of water, food and medicine dwindled. By the end of the first week, doctors were forced to decide between intravenously feeding themselves or their patients."[5] To add insult to injury, another major hurricane Rita would tear into the same area and coastline areas of East Texas approximately one month later.

As those 2005 Katrina winds and rain tore apart the Gulf Coast, the façade of a com eral system crumbled before our very eyes as city leaders were at odds with state and fede and agencies. This is not the first and, unfortunately, will not be the last episode of fede worst. November 22, 2013, marked the 50th anniversary of the assassination of Presid... Kennedy. As the Americans were glued to their television sets watching the tragic events in Dallas, behind the scenes were the on-going struggles between the federal agencies of the Secret Service, the Central Intelligence Agency (CIA), the Federal Bureau of Investigation (FBI), Texas state law enforcement agencies including the Texas Rangers, and the local Dallas police department over which level of government had jurisdiction over the investigation and the capture of Lee Harvey Oswald. On January 28, 2014, the city of Atlanta, Georgia was hit with an unusually fierce snowstorm. It is not that the South never sees snow but it only comes once and while, bringing just enough of the "white stuff" to close down schools and businesses, shut down all highway overpasses, build a lope-sided snowman, and have a few snowball fights. However, this snowstorm resulted in "tens of thousands of people, including children on school buses, stranded on icy, wreck-strewn roads."[6] While stranded, people slept in their cars, tried to walk home or go wherever they could find shelter. Georgia's Governor Nathan Deal blamed Atlanta Mayor Kasim Reed for not taking the looming snow storm seriously. The mayor blamed the governor's office for not supplying the metropolitan and outlying areas with heavy snow moving equipment, failing to spray the deicing chemicals on the city's highways and interstates before the snow began to fall, and for not closing down the icy overpasses before commuters were struck in traffic, sliding off the roads, or becoming victims of automobile accidents. The local media pointed the finger at the school districts who early released their students at the same time resulting in both parents trying to get to schools to pick up their children and buses trying to get students home, being stuck in the traffic congestion lasting hours into the next day. Both the mayor and the governor tried to blame the National Weather Service for underestimating the fury of the storm and its location. The Weather Service, in turn, blamed city and state officials for not taking their forecasts seriously. While elected officials were pointing countless fingers and accusations at each other, the city of Atlanta was at a standstill!

At least on paper, the concept of federalism gives the national government the superior or upper hand over state and local governing authorities and, of course, the people. The **Supremacy Clause** of Article VI of the United States Constitution clearly states "this Constitution, and the laws of the United States which shall be made in pursuance thereof; . . . shall be the supreme law of the land; and the judges in every State shall be bound thereby, anything in the Constitution or laws of any State to the contrary notwithstanding." In practice, however, the relationships between the national, state and local governments have never been a solid one. The history of this nation sees far too often periods of close cooperation between them followed by episodes of clashes pitting them against each other in their struggles for control and power. Unfortunately, in the middle of their struggles are the American people who as a whole have always been fickle about the role government should play in their daily lives. Under normal circumstances, they fear the intrusion of the "big brother" muscle of the national government having a say on what they can and cannot do. Yet, whenever a natural disaster, such as a hurricane or a snow storm or a threat to national security like the destruction of the Twin Towers at the World Trade Center or the bombing at the Boston Marathon, they demand federal attention and assistance particularly when they see that their state and local governments are incapable of meeting their needs.

Chapter Three

Before a joint session of Congress, newly inaugurated President Barack Obama delivered his first State-of-the-Union message. After the speech, Louisiana's Republican Governor Bobby Jindal delivered his party's official response to Obama's speech. Jindal criticized the president's proposed stimulus package of federal funds to states, local communities, and businesses designed to jumpstart the slumping economy. He drew upon traditional Republican positions of less government, less regulatory oversight from Washington, and the fear of the big muscle of the federal government becoming too intrusive into the lives of Americans. He told the audience "there has never been a challenge that the American people, with as little interference as possible by the federal government, cannot handle."[7] Jindal perhaps regretted those words when in April 2010, an offshore deep drilling platform owned by British Petroleum (BP) exploded, the pipe line stretching miles below sea level broke, and billions of barrels of thick crude oil seeped quickly into the Gulf of Mexico off the coast of Louisiana. Jindal placed the blame for not quickly stopping the mass of black crude heading for Louisiana's shoreline directly on the federal government and, in particular, the Environmental Protection Agency (EPA). During a public press conference, the Governor said "the administration [Obama] has not provided enough equipment, including booms, skinners, vacuums and barges, and that it stood in the way of his proposal to erect artificial barrier islands" that would have prevented the oil from reaching the shoreline.[8] Jindal's remarks before and after the oil spill illustrate the re-occurring frustrations many have voiced about the federal system. Should the federal government have the power to force state governments to follow its dictates? Does the constitutional responsibility of government to promote the general welfare of the American people fall upon just the national government, the state governments, or is this a shared responsibility placed upon the backs of all levels of government? Is this the relationship the Framers envisioned for this nation? Just who is in charge, the state or the national government? Should the role of the national government be proactive and take charge of a natural disaster or a crisis or should the national government initially stand aside and allow state governments to be the first responders with the national government serving only as a backup plan?

This relationship we commonly call federalism is indeed a fragile one that is not clearly defined in the Constitution that mandates its existence. Not even the collective wisdom of the Framers could clearly delineate under all conceivable situations what actually belongs exclusively to the national government or to the states or to be shared by both. In *Federalist #45*, James Madison attempted to clarify the confusion: "the powers delegated by the proposed Constitution to the federal government are few and defined. Those which are to remain in the State governments are numerous and indefinite. The former will be exercised principally on external objects, as war, peace, negotiation and foreign commerce; with which last the power of taxation will, for the most part, be connected. The powers reserved to the several States will extend to all objects which, in the ordinary course of affairs; concern the lives, liberties and properties of the people, and the internal order, improvement and prosperity of the state."[9] In theory, Madison envisioned a national government that would be more focused on the external affairs and the day-to-day operations of running a nation while the state governments would be in charge of meeting the local or regional needs of the residents within their boundaries. However, the lines of responsibility have become intertwined with each other, making it almost impossible to separate them. This chapter explores and analyzes the concept of federalism and its impact upon both the national and fifty state governments.

TYPES OF INTERGOVERNMENTAL RELATIONSHIPS

In the majority of the world's nation states, the interrelationship enjoyed between national governments and their states usually conform to either a unitary or confederative relationship. In these configurations one level of government has complete authority over the other. The **unitary system** is "one in which principal power within the political system lies at the level of a national or central government rather than at the level of some smaller unit, such as a state or province."[10] Usually, the national government possesses the authority to create and, if necessary, abolish sub-government units. States and other sub-government units basically serve as administrative agents to their national governments. Under this format, power and governing authority flows from top to bottom. More than 90 percent of all modern nation states use this format. The advantages of the unitary system are (1) uniformity of public policy enforcement and (2) a centralized government. The primary disadvantage to this system is that sub-governments lack both the authority and the resources to adequately address immediate emergencies and regional demands.

In contrast, power flows from bottom to top under a confederative format. A **confederation** is "a loose collection of states in which principal power lies at the level of the individual states rather than at the level of the central or national government."[11] Created by its own sub-governing units, the national government has very narrowly defined governing authority and functions as assigned to it by the sub-governing entities. Although the national government may be empowered to create legislative acts, the individual sub-governing units must decide whether to implement those acts upon those within their boundaries. Usually, the national government is denied the power to tax and must rely upon funding from their sub–governing units. The national government may have the authority to declare war, but the national government does not have its own standing army. Therefore, it is dependent upon the sub-governing units to supply the needed manpower and weaponry. The individual units or states have the option of whether to participate with the understanding that the national government does not have the authoritarian muscle to force compliance. The relationship is indeed a very loose one. According to the enabling documents, a state or sub-governing unit may opt at any time to withdraw from the confederacy. And, the national government simply lacks the authority and the military power to force that state to remain a member. The United Nations is basically a confederative association of nation states. As evidenced by several international crises, the official response by the United Nations is oftentimes a weak one since the organization does not have the authority to compel compliance, cooperation, or even obedience from its member nations.

The **federal system** is a combination of the best features of both the unitary and confederative formats. In this configuration, governing authority and power flows simultaneously from top to bottom. **Federalism** is "the mode of political organization that unites separate polities within an overarching political system by distributing power among general and constituent governments in a manner designed to protect the existence and authority of both."[12] It is a system of shared governance. All levels of government whether it is a school district, water or utility district, a city council, a county government or a state government, have the legitimate authority to actually govern the people within respective jurisdictions.

Chapter Three

Why A Federal System?

After winning a long fight for their independence from Britain, the former colonies initially selected a confederative governing system under the **Articles of Confederation**. Unfortunately, the weaknesses of confederative system doomed its longevity. The framers opted to change their governing structure. Through the Constitution, the Framers basically dismantled a confederative government and replaced it with the federal model. As adopted in 1789, the Constitution "created a national government with sovereign powers of its own—powers that once belong exclusively to state governments. The proud sovereignty of the states was radically undermined; the 'state's rights' which remained, although robust in the Founding Period, bore scant resemblance to the autonomy enjoyed by the states under the Articles."[13] As detailed in Chapter 2, the Framers desired to create a government based on the concepts of separation of powers and checks and balances as well as establishing a workable and viable governing relationship between the national government and the individual states. This task was not an easy one:

> The Constitutional place of the states in the federal system is determined by four elements: the provisions in the federal and state constitutions that either limit or guarantee the powers of the states vis-a-vis the federal government; the provisions in the federal constitution that give the states a role in the composition of the national government; the subsequent interpretations of both sets of provisions by the courts (particularly the United States Supreme Court); and the unwritten constitutional traditions that evolved informally and only later become formally recognized through the first three, directly or indirectly.[14]

However, the Framers saw several benefits to a federal system including:

> the prevention of abuse of power because no single group is likely to gain control of government at the state and local levels; the encouragement of innovation by testing new ideas at the local level; the creation of many centers of power to resolve conflict and to handle administrative burdens; the stimulation of competition among levels of government that encourages policy innovation; and as James Madison predicted, the prevention of abuse of power because it is nearly impossible for a single group to gain control of government at all levels.[15]

Actually, there are two distinct levels of federalism in the United States. The relationship and lines of authority between the national government and her individual state governments were cemented through vertical federalism whereas horizontal federalism establishes a constitutionally mandated mutual and, hopefully, beneficial harmonious relationship between the states.

Constitutionally Mandated Intergovernmental Relationships—Vertical Federalism

Vertical federalism is the governing authority that flows up and down between the national and state governments. Vertical intergovernmental relations "take place when the national government interacts with the states or localities or when the states interact with localities."[16] This is the concept

Not all citizens are treated fairly in a federated system. The distribution of goods and services required by families for a healthy and meaningful existence usually comes from the state. But what happens if the state either refuses to provide such services or, worse yet, decides to distribute them unequally? Does this occur in America? Can you cite some examples?

of shared governance whereby all levels of government have some governing authority, including the authority to make laws or in the case of local government, ordinances, implement them, enforce them through the application of appropriate sanctions, and govern under the watchful eye of the Constitution. "In the American federal system, sharing of functions by all planes of government is and always has been the norm."[17] The essential piece of vertical federalism, **Article VI** of the constitution, cements the relationship between the states and the national government, and mandates without any doubt that all levels of government must comply with the spirit and meaning of the Constitution.

Enumerated powers also referred to as **delegated powers** are "those rights and responsibilities of the U.S. government specifically provided for and listed in the Constitution."[18] To address weaknesses in the Articles of Confederation, the Framers took those specific powers originally given to the states and reassigned them to the national government. In **Article I,** the United States Congress is granted the exclusive authority to levy and collect taxes for the national government, borrow money, regulate interstate commerce, coin and establish the value of money, raise an army, establish post offices, establish the laws of naturalization, issue patents and copyrights, and declare war. These enumerated powers give the national government its muscle to exercise considerable control over all levels of government. The enumerated power to regulate interstate commerce, for example, has been used quite frequently to force state governments, business owners, and citizens to obey congressional enactments. In *Gibbons v Ogden* (1824), the United States Supreme Court "first put forth a broad interpretation of the commerce clause by defining interstate commerce to include all navigable waters even those within a state."[19] Subsequent Court decisions have liberally expanded the national government's interstate commerce jurisdiction as anything that has crossed or will eventually cross a state boundary line. The federal courts, Congress and the executive branch have used their power over interstate commerce to compel state compliance of congressional acts ranging from civil rights, desegregation, environmental regulations, welfare programs, work safety regulations, minimum wage laws, and highway speed limits.

The Framers also realized that they could not enumerate or list all of powers the national government would need to adjust to changing circumstances. Consequently, they added to Article I, Section 8 of the Constitution the statement that Congress can "make all Laws which shall be **necessary and proper** for carrying into execution the foregoing powers vested by this Constitution in the government of the United States, or in any department or office thereof." This clause is the **implied powers doctrine,** commonly referred to as the **necessary and proper clause** or the **elastic clause**. The implied powers doctrine gives considerable leverage to the national government to enact legislation addressing the concerns that oftentimes should be the privy of state governments. Once again, the U.S. Supreme Court has historically upheld the national government's use of its implied powers. From the beginning, the **Anti-Federalists** expressed their displeasure of the implied powers doctrine emphasizing that this clause along with the Supremacy Clause (Article VI) gave the national government far too much power over the states:

> How far the clause in the 8th section of the 1st article may operate to do away all idea of confederated states, and to effect an entire consolidation of the whole into one general government, it is impossible to say . . . But what is meant is, that the legislature of the United States are vested with the great and uncontroulable [uncontrollable] powers, of laying and collecting taxes, duties, imposts, and excises; of regulating trade, raising and supporting armies, organizing, arming, and disciplining the militia, instituting courts, and other general powers. And are by this clause invested with the power of making all laws proper and necessary, for carrying all these into execution; and they may so exercise this power as entirely to annihilate all state governments, and reduce this country to one single government. And if they may do it, it is pretty certain they will; for it will be found that the power retained by the individual states, small as it is, will be a clog upon the wheels of government of the United States; the latter therefore will be naturally included to remove it out of the way. Besides, it is a truth confirmed by the unerring experience of the ages, that every man, every body of men, invested with power, are ever disposed to increase it, and to acquire a superiority over every thing that stands in their way. This disposition, which is implanted in human nature, will operate in the federal legislature to lessen and ultimately to subvert the state authority, and having such advantages, will most certainly succeed, if the federal government succeeds at all. It must be very evident then, that what this constitution wants of being a complete consolidation of the several parts of the union into one complete government, possessed of perfect legislative, judicial, and executive powers, to all intents and purposes, it will be necessarily acquire in its exercise and operation.[20]

Although the national government has never taken any steps to "annihilate all state governments," it has from time to time interjected itself into policy areas that constitutionally and traditionally belong to the states. However, the Constitution does charge the national government with the task "to promote the general welfare" of the American people. The national government's involvement into matters such as education, transportation, civil rights, environment, etc., have taken place when state governments have demonstrated over a considerable period of time their inability to address these concerns.

Several enumerated powers are held **concurrently** by both national and all sub-government levels. For example, all governing authorities have the power to levy and collect taxes. However, each level of government must tax a different commodity and/or tax only a specified portion of the tax item such as state and federal income tax programs. Traditionally, the primary tax revenue stream for the national government is individual and corporate incomes. The majority of the states have a state income tax program combined with other sources of revenue. A state without a state income tax, Texas, relies heavily upon sales taxes and other regressive tax programs. Counties and cities have concurrent jurisdiction to tax property. Without the power to generate revenue from its residents, sub-government units would not be able to provide essential basic services. Also, the national and state governments concurrently have the power to establish judicial courts, make and enforce laws, and exercise eminent domain.

The Constitution would not have been ratified without granting some authority to the states. **Reserved powers** are granted to the states through the **Tenth Amendment**: "Those powers not delegated to the United States by the Constitution, nor prohibited by it to the States, are reserved to the States, respectively, or to the People." However, the amendment does not enumerate those powers nor does it clearly define the boundaries for the execution of those powers. State authority has evolved over time to encompass four broad areas: policing, taxing, propriety authority, and eminent domain. **Police power** is "the authority to promote and safeguard the health, morals, safety and welfare of the people."[21] Consequently, all state and local authorities have their own law enforcement agencies operating under state laws and local ordinances to keep the peace. However, national law enforcement agencies such as the Federal Bureau of Investigation (FBI) do have jurisdiction when the criminal activity violates a federal law or involves crossing state boundary lines to commit a crime. State laws and local ordinances are subjected to judicial review by the federal courts when challenged on grounds of constitutionality. Actions taken by law enforcement officers also can be challenged before federal courts if their methods of enforcement violate protected constitutional rights. The **proprietary function** is "a governmental activity involving business-type operations ordinarily carried on by private companies . . . to include such activities as supplying electricity and gas, recreational facilities, garbage collection, transportation, etc."[22] This delegated power gives states and local governments the authority to provide necessary infrastructure and essential services to their citizens. Granted to all levels of government, the power of **eminent domain** enables government to take private lands for public use as long as the property owner is justifiably compensated for loss of the property.

Section 9, of **Article I** of the Constitution places certain restrictions on both the national and state governments. The **Writ of Habeas Corpus** cannot be suspended except in cases of rebellion and insurrection. President Abraham Lincoln did suspend Habeas Corpus throughout the Civil War. All levels of government are constitutionally forbidden to issue bills of attainder, enact ex post facto laws, grant titles of nobility, and tax exports. **Section 10** of **Article I** specifically prohibits state governments from entering into treaties, granting Letters of Marque (documents issued by a nation allowing a private citizen to seize the citizens or goods of another nation), coining money, levying taxes on imports without prior congressional approval, maintaining an army or navy, forming interstate compacts with each other without prior congressional approval, and declaring war.

Constitutionally Mandated Intergovernmental Relationships—Horizontal Federalism

Horizontal federalism is "state-to-state interactions and relations."[23] The Framers were concerned about the ability of the states to cooperate with each other since the Articles of Confederation encouraged rivalry rather than cooperation. The Framers inserted **Article IV** or the **Full Faith and Credit Clause** to insure that the states would indeed work together. According to Section 1 of Article IV, "Full Faith and Credit shall be given in each State to the Public Acts, Records, and Judicial Proceedings of every other state." Furthermore, the Framers stressed the need for uniform acceptance by adding "and the Congress may by general Law prescribe the Manner in which such Acts, Records and Proceedings shall be proved, and the Effect thereof." Consequently, the majority of legal documents, including property deeds and birth and death certifications, are legal in all of the states regardless of the state originating the documents. Whereas all states recognize marriage licenses and divorce decrees of traditional man-to-woman marriages, the question still remains whether the national government can mandate that states recognize but not necessarily perform same-sex marriages and/or recognize same-sex divorce decrees.

As stated in Section 2, "the Citizen of each State shall be entitled to all the Privileges and Immunities of Citizens of the Several States." This provision clearly places the individual as a citizen of his/her country above residency in a state. Citizens are guaranteed freedom of movement from state to state and residency in any state under the jurisdiction of the United States government. Individual states cannot put any additional requirements, such as educational attainment or income level for a person, to move to another state. Also, the requirement that states recognize and uphold individual rights and privileges as detailed in the Bill of Rights were strengthened with the passage of the Fourteenth Amendment's guarantee of equal protection and due process of the law for all citizens. The federal courts, in particular the Supreme Court, has dealt with numerous cases involving a state law or local ordinance that failed to provide equal protection and due process. In ***Fullilove v Klutznik*** (1980) the Supreme Court ruled "Congress has the authority to use quotas to remedy past discrimination in government public works programs, reasoning that the 14th Amendment's requirement of equal protection means that groups historically denied this right may be given special treatment."[24] Also, in ***Goesaert v Cleary*** (1948), the Court ruled any state laws denying women the right to practice certain occupations usually held by men to be an unconstitutional violation of the Fourteenth Amendment's equal protection clause. States, however, do exercise limited authority to treat newcomers differently. For example, state agencies are not required to honor professional and occupational licenses issued by other states. A licensed attorney in New Jersey cannot practice law in California until he/she has successfully passed the California Bar Exam. The same standards apply to teachers, hairdressers, plumbers, electricians, etc. Also, public colleges and universities can charge a higher out-of-state tuition fee to those students who do not meet local residency requirements. States can set different residency requirements for voting, filing for public office, qualifications for public office, etc. Section 2 also states that "A Person charged in any State with Treason, Felony, or other Crime, who shall flee from Justice, and found in another State, shall on Demand of the executive Authority of the State from which he fled, to be delivered up, to be removed to the State having Jurisdiction of the Crime." Therefore, the Constitution mandates that states actively participate in **interstate rendition** that is, "the return of a fugitive from justice by a state upon the demand of the executive authority of the state in which the crime was committed."[25]

The Framers addressed the practice of states arguing with each other over state boundary lines and the ownership of unsettled territories such as the Northwest Territories with a provision in Article III. This Article gives original jurisdiction to the federal courts in all cases involving "controversies between two or more States, between a State and Citizens of another state; between Citizens of different states; between Citizens of the same State claiming lands under Grants of different States." Obviously, the Framers had little faith that the individual states would successfully settle or judge fairly in disputes between each other.

FEDERALISM AND THE FEDERAL COURTS

As detailed in Chapter 12, the Judiciary Act of 1789 granted judicial review to the federal courts. Although all levels of government can pass laws, statutes or ordinances, those legislative acts that do not conform to the spirit and meaning of the United States Constitution can be judged by a panel of federal judges as unconstitutional acts. The United States Supreme Court is the court of last resort, meaning no subsequent appeal is possible. In exercising this authority, it is the federal courts that play a vitally crucial role in defining the appropriate relationship between the national and state governments.

The United States Supreme Court, however, has had periods of advocating a strong national government or **nation-centered federalism** offset by decisions that favored state laws. Immediately following the adoption of the Constitution, the newly formed Supreme Court rendered decisions in favor of a strong national government over state matters. In **McCullough v Maryland (1819)**, the questions before the justices involved whether the national government had the authority to use eminent domain over the state of Maryland to construct a branch office of the National Bank as part of the implementation of a national banking law; and secondly, whether the state of Maryland had the right to levy and collect a property tax on the now-held federal property. This case challenged the necessary and proper clause of Article I, Section 8. Issuing a ruling that strengthened the national government's power over the states, the Supreme Court under the guidance of Chief Justice John Marshall ruled "after the most deliberate consideration, it is the unanimous and decided opinion of this Court, that the act to incorporate the Bank of the United States, is a law made in pursuance of the Constitution and is part of the supreme law of the land."[26] Additionally, Marshall stressed the power of the national government over the states by noting that their decision was based on a firm "conviction that the states have no power, by taxation or otherwise, to retard, impede, burden, or in any manner control, the operations of the constitutional laws enacted by Congress to carry into execution the powers vested in the general government. This is, we think, the unavoidable consequence of that supremacy which the Constitution has declared."[27]

Once again, Chief Justice Marshall's Court favored the national government over the states in **Cohen v Virginia (1821)** by defending the federal court's right to review judicial decisions issued by state courts. Cohen centered on the arrest and subsequent conviction of Cohen for illegally selling Washington, D.C., issued lottery tickets in Virginia. The Virginia state legislature had recently passed a law prohibiting the sale of any lottery tickets within the state. After losing his case at the state level, Cohen decided to file his complaint with the U.S. Supreme Court. Unfortunately for Cohen, the Supreme Court upheld the lower court ruling. Yet, just by hearing the case the Supreme

Court opened the door for the federal courts to review the judgments issued by state courts. In writing the majority opinion, Marshall addressed this issue:

> The American States, as well as the American people, have believed a close and firm Union to be essential to their liberty and to their happiness. They have been taught by experience, that this Union cannot exist without a government for the whole; and they have been taught by the same experience that this government would be a mere shadow, that must disappoint all their hopes, unless invested with large portions of that sovereignty, which belongs to independent States. Under the influence of this opinion, and thus instructed by experience, the American people, in the conventions of their respective States adopted the present Constitution. If it could be doubted, whether from its nature, it was not supreme in all cases where it is empowered to act, that doubt would be removed by the declaration, that 'this constitution, and the laws of the United States, . . . shall be the supreme law of the land, and the judges in every State shall be bound thereby; anything in the constitution or laws of any state to the contrary notwithstanding.' This is the authoritative language of the American people; and . . . of the American States. It marks, with lines too strong to be mistaken, the characteristic distinction between the government of the Union, and those of the States. The general government, through limited as to its objects, is supreme with respect to those objects. This principle is part of the Constitution; and if there be any who can deny its necessity, none can deny its authority.[28]

In **Gibbons v Ogden (1824)**, the Supreme Court tackled the question of whether the states or the national government had the authority to control shipping on the Hudson River. The Court's final decision dealt a blow to the states by once again favoring the national government over the states. The Marshall Court ruled that "this power [regulation of interstate commerce], like all others bested in Congress, is complete in itself, may be exercised to its upmost extent, and acknowledges no limitations other than are prescribed in the Constitution."[29] Chief Justice Marshall used this case to define the Court's interpretation of "interstate" commerce:

> The words are 'Congress shall have the power to regulate commerce with foreign Nations, and among the several states, and with the Indian tribes' . . . The subject to be regulated is commerce; and our Constitution . . . one of enumeration, and not of definition, to ascertain the extent of the power, it becomes necessary to settle the meaning of the word . . . Commerce, undoubtedly, is traffic, but it [is] something more—it is intercourse. It describes the commercial intercourse between nations, and parts of nations, in all its branches, and is regulated by prescribing rules for carrying on that intercourse . . . The power over commerce including navigation, was one of the primary objects for which the people of America adopted their government, and must have been contemplated in forming it. . . . The word used in this Constitution, then, comprehends, and have been always understood to comprehend, navigation within its meaning; and a power to regulate navigation is expressly granted, as if that term had been added to the word 'commerce'. To what commerce does then power extend? The Constitution informs us, to commerce 'with foreign nations, and among the

several states and with the Indian tribes'. It has, we believe, been universally admitted, that these words comprehend every species of commercial intercourse between the United States and foreign nations . . . The subject to which the power is next applied, is to commerce 'among the several states'. The word 'among' means intermingled with . . . Commerce among the states cannot stop at the external boundary line of each state . . . The grant of this power carries with it the whole subject, leaving nothing for the state to act upon.[30]

Therefore, the Court's ruling gave the national government the constitutional authority to oversee all commercial activity that crosses any state boundary line, leaving the states with just the authority of commerce traveling within their state boundary lines, commonly known as **intrastate commerce**. In 1887, Congress created the **Interstate Commerce Commission (ICC)** to provide federal regulatory oversight for all surface transportation systems including trains, trucks, buses, freight forwarders and express companies as well as all in-land waterway and coastal shipping with the primary goal of eliminating rate discrimination by mandating fair rates. In 1906, the ICC's authority was expanded to include automobile transportation. The ICC was abolished in 1995 but its regulatory functions were reassigned to the Surface Transportation Board.

The Supreme Court shifted its strong national government position to a more pro-state position in the early nineteenth century. However, the Court shifted back to a pro-national government stance during the Great Depression as the national government expanded its authority over the states with the implementation of New Deal legislation. Consequently from the 1930s to the mid-1990s, "the expansion of the federal role has been greatest, for example, in matters involving individual rights, civil rights, voting rights, and legislative apportionment. It has not been as extensive in programmatic areas that affect state and local finances or directly, such as welfare and education."[31] The shifting between pro-national and pro-state positions is illustrated in two Supreme Court decisions. Initially in ***National League of Cities v Usery* (1976)**, the Court ruled that the Tenth Amendment prohibited the national government from setting wages and maximum working hour requirements for state employees. However, in ***Garcia v San Antonio Metropolitan Transit Authority* (1985)**, the Court reversed its *Usery* decision by ruling that a federal mandate requiring that state public employees must be paid at least the minimum wage and be granted overtime as detailed in the Fair Labor Standards Act did not violate any constitutional provision. In ***South Carolina v Baker* (1988)**, the Court ruled that Congress could tax interest earned from individual savings accounts and dividends on state and locally issued bonds.

An advocate of returning more governing authority to the states, President Ronald Reagan established in 1987 a thirteen-person commission to study whether services traditionally provided by the federal government could be either privatized or reassigned to the states. He also appointed jurists to federal benches who supported his position. In particular, his appointment of Antonin Scalia in 1986 followed by George H. W. Bush's selection of Clarence Thomas to Supreme Court moved the Court to a more conservative panel favorable to a less intrusive role for the national government into matters traditionally reserved to the states. Consequently "not since before the New Deal-era constitution revolution in 1937, have the states received such protection in the U.S. Supreme Court from allegedly burdensome federal statutes."[32] A pro-state decision was handed down by the Court in ***United States v Lopez* (1995)** when the justices "struck down as exceeding congressional authority under the commerce clause, a federal law that made it a crime to carry a gun within 1,000 feet of a school. The Court declared that the law had nothing to do with commerce and intruded upon the police power of the states."[33] In ***Plintz v United States* (1997)**, the Court once again backed state governments by declaring unconstitutional a provision of the Brady Bill requiring local law enforcement officials to conduct background checks before issuing handguns as an unfunded mandate and an unconstitutional intrusion upon state governing bodies. The current Court under the guidance of Chief Justice John Roberts has taken a case-by-case approach in determining whether the national government has overstepped its authority with state and local governing bodies.

STATES' RIGHTS V NATIONAL POWER

The nagging question of how much authority the national government can exercise over state and other governing authorities was debated from the very founding of this country and was a hot topic of debate during the Constitutional Convention in Philadelphia. However, the brewing and contentious political battle over the abolition of slavery drew the battle lines between the North and South over the national government's attempt to politically and economically control the southern states. Slavery was indeed abolished, but the arguments of states' rights over the national government persist today. Whenever the muscle of the national government is feared to be too instructive, state governors fight back. In the 1960s, it was Governor Ross Barnett of Mississippi that openly defied his own National Guard units who under the direct order of President John Kennedy were charged with protecting James Meredith, as he became the first African-American student admitted to the University of Mississippi. It was Lester Maddox of Georgia who hailed an ax in the air to symbolically cut the state's ties with the national government over mandated desegregation of the state's public schools. In 1994, an angry group of Texas ranchers and landowners openly challenged the Environmental Protection Agency's (EPA) mandate to protect the breeding grounds of the Golden Warbler over individual property rights. Several state governors unsuccessfully sued the national government over the Affordable Care Act as the majority of the nation's Republican governors have openly defied the Obama administration by not accepting increased Medicaid fund-

Integration at Ole Mississippi University James Meredith walking on the campus of the University of Mississippi accompanied by U. S. marshals. October 1, 1962.

ing and supporting Obamacare registration efforts. A former governor himself, President George W. Bush faced criticism from a multitude of state governors over his mandated federal education program, No Child Left Behind. The term **states' rights** is defined as the "opposition to increasing the national government's power at the expense of the states."[34] Historically, those who have advocated states' rights over national authority include Thomas Jefferson, John C. Calhoun, the Supreme Court from 1920-1937, Presidents Ronald Reagan and George W. Bush and Republican presidential candidate Mitt Romney.

John C. Calhoun (1782-1850) was undoubtedly the most ardent advocate of states' rights. A former vice president and renowned senator from South Carolina, Calhoun believed in the **compact theory** of government whereby governments were created by and existed for the benefit of the people. If that government failed to provide for its people, then the people had the right to abolish that government and begin anew. In his *Discourses of the American Constitution*, Calhoun argued that the American government was "federal and not national because it is a government of a community of States, not the government of a single State or nation."[35] Seeing the Constitution as merely an intergovernmental agreement, Calhoun wrote that "the sovereignty of the States, in the fullest sense of the term, is declared to be the essential principle of the Union; and it is not only asserted as a incontestable right, but also claimed as an absolute political necessity in order to protect the minority against the majority."[36] Accordingly, these sovereign states envisioned creating a national government with limited power over the states. States' rights advocates see the national government as merely an agent serving the needs of the state governments similar to the confederative system created under the Articles of Confederation. They stressed that those powers not enumerated specifically to the national government are exclusively reserved to the states. Also, the national government has absolutely no right to use any of its enumerated and implied powers to interfere in state governance.

Calhoun developed three options that both states and the American people could take to halt the intrusive nature of the national government into state affairs. First, Calhoun shifted the placement of people in their relationship with the national government. Those advocating a strong national government, see both the national and state governments having direct authority over people with each level of government enacting and enforcing legislation independently of each other. Calhoun on the other hand, believed in the concept of **interposition** whereby "a state may place itself between its citizens and the national government so as to prevent the enforcement of national law upon its citizens."[37] He placed the states as the middlemen or buffer zones to shield the people living in their states from, as he perceived, harmful national mandates. Calhoun believed that "the states have the right 'to interpose' when the Federal government is guilty of a usurpation, because, as there is not common judge over them, they, as the parties to the compact, have to determine for themselves whether it has been violated."[38] Basically, he argued that Congress could pass any law it wanted, including the abolition of slavery; however, it was up to each state's legislative house to approve any congressional act before it could be implemented and enforced within their states. Second, Calhoun's concept of **concurrent majority** was based on the belief that "democratic decisions should be made only with the concurrence of all major segments of society."[39] Subsequently, national laws are binding only if a majority of the nation's citizens concurred with these enactments. Calhoun wrote that "government of the concurrent majority . . . excludes the possibility of oppression by giving to each interest or portion, or order—where there are established classes—the means of protecting itself by its negative against the measures calculated to advance the peculiar interests of others at its expense."⁴⁰ Once again, if Congress voted to abolish slavery, it could do so only after a national referendum election indicated that a majority of the American people agreed to it. He also had measures to protect American citizens living in frontier areas not under the protection of statehood. Calhoun believed that "each sectional majority or large interest that was not territorially based has the constitutional power to an absolute veto over any action of the federal government that, while representing the national majority, threatened the welfare of the minority."⁴¹ Third, the last option available to the states would be **nullification** whereby a state or states could see no other avenue available but to declare the relationship between themselves and the national government null and void. This would free the states from their contractual agreement through the Constitution to establish their own sovereignty as an independent nation absolutely separated from the union. Calhoun's arguments of an over intrusive national government into state affairs would prove to be one of the justifications the southern states used to secede from the union and set the stage for the American Civil War.

The issue of whether a state could successfully secede from the union was settled with the Supreme Court's ruling in ***Texas v White* (1869)**. The Court's decision reinforced the sentiments of a strong national government advocated by Alexander Hamilton, George Washington and James Madison:

> The Union of the States never was a purely artificial and arbitrary relation. It began among the Colonies and grew out of common origin, mutual sympathies, kindred principles, similar interests, and geographical relations. It was confirmed and strengthened by the necessities of war, and received definite form, character, and sanction, from the Articles of Confederation. By these the Union was solemnly declared to 'be perpetual.' And, when these Articles were found to be inadequate to the exigencies of the country, the Constitution was ordained 'to form a more perfect union.' But the perpetuity and indissolubility of the Union by no means implies the loss of distinct and individual existence, or of the right of self-government by the States. On the contrary, it may be not unreasonably said, that the preservation of the States, and the maintenance of their governments, are as much within the design and care of the Constitution, as the preservation of the Union and the maintenance of the National Government. *The Constitution, in all of its provisions, looks to be an indestructible Union composed of indestructible States.*⁴²

In a subsequent ruling in ***Coyle v Smith* (1911)**, the Court reinforced the equality of the states in the eyes of the national government. The ruling "established the principle that all states are admitted to the union on an equal footing. Congress may not enforce conditions that would undermine the equality of the states."⁴³ However, the Court has yet to rule that states cannot decide to split into separate states such as West Virginia from Virginia.

States' rights arguments are essential to gaining an understanding of the fragile relationship between the states and the national government. The Tea Party movement was to a degree founded on the principle of state supremacy over the national government particularly on issues such as health care, welfare programs, gun control, etc. In Texas, there is the Republic of Texas group that believes that Texas was imperialistically taken into the United States. They advocate that Texas is still an independent nation under the Republic of Texas established in 1836 after gaining its independence from Mexico. Throughout the South, southern conservative Democrats and many Republicans preach the same tune—the fear of an overly intrusive national government—Big Brother—meddling into matters that by constitutional decree should be addressed in state legislative houses, not the Capitol on Hill.

THE CHANGING FACES OF FEDERALISM

Whether state interests overshadow national interests or vice versa, the course of federalism swings back and forth. It does not, however, change in precise cycles where, for example, every fifty years the states are in the driver's seat only to see the national government turn the swing to its side for another fifty years, and so forth. Oftentimes the change is driven by the political ideology on Capitol Hill, in the White House, or both. The pattern shows that "in conservative periods, the roles of state governments have been enhanced, whereas in liberal or pro-government periods, the role of the national government has grown."[44] Currently, the gridlock in Washington, particularly in 2013, involves a Republican/conservative majority in the House of Representatives against a Democratic/liberal Senate and a Democratic/liberal president. The Republicans want less government control from Washington while the Democrats want a strong presence for the federal government into state affairs. One of the historically guiding factors opening the door for the might of the national government is when the states have failed to manage their own affairs; or have demonstrated their inability to handle their own problems; or they simply ask for federal assistance. In its preamble, the United States Constitution tasks the national government with the responsibility to promote the general welfare of the people of the United States. To accomplish this, the national government has been from time to time motivated to take the upper hand over the states, not in response to period cycles or political shifts in power, but in response to particular problems and crises threatening the general welfare of the American people.

From the inception of the Constitution to 1932, the relationship between the states and the national government was one of **dual federalism** whereby "autonomous national, subnational, and local governments all pursued their own interests independently" of each other.[45] Dual federalism is also known as **layered cake federalism** since its approach to intergovernmental relationships resembles a traditional layer cake with the national government as the top tier and subsequent tiers belonging to sub-government units ranging from the states to the lowest possible governing unit. The layers are separated and protected from interference from each other by thick layers of icing. The United States Supreme Court respected this relationship with only rare occasions when the Court extended the role of the national government over the states. For example, the need for a national banking system was evidenced by the individual states' inability to control their own evolving banking industries, thus crippling national business development. In most states, banks were operating without the guidelines of state charters, charging inconsistent interest rates, and operating under unfair practices detrimental to the nation's economy. In ***McCullough v Maryland (1819)***, the Supreme Court upheld the national government's authority to create a national banking system. The prevailing belief of the time was that the national government had no constitutional right to intervene into a function "reserved" to the individual states. Even during the height of the Progressive Era with its cadre of social reforms, the states remained in the preeminent role. It was state governments, not the national government, that was "left to take action regarding such problems as care of dependent children. Federal domestic programs in the late 1920s were so limited that state spending was double federal spending. States also were dominant over cities as policy makers, spending about three times as much money as local governments."[46]

The 1929 collapse of the Stock Market and the tragedy of the Great Depression of the 1930s changed the relationship from dual to cooperative federalism. The states were totally unprepared to handle Depression-era problems particularly in dealing with millions of unemployed, widespread hunger, and homelessness. **Cooperative federalism** is "the notion that the national, state and local governments are interacting agents, jointly working to solve common problems, rather than being conflicting, sometimes hostile competitors pursuing similar or more likely conflicting ends.[47] The New Deal programs created by President Franklin Roosevelt were dependent upon cooperation between the national government and state and local governments to provide much needed employment opportunities, food, housing and economic development, in hopes of preventing another catastrophic economic downturn similar to the Great Depression. Cooperative federalism is also known as **marble cake federalism**. Cooperative federalism brought billions of federal dollars to state and local governments for much needed infrastructure improvements, economic development, job creation programs and incentives, and social service programs. Cooperative federalism ended in 1964.

The hallmarks of Lyndon Johnson's presidency were the Great Society programs and his declared War on Poverty. He believed that with the adoption of his programs he could improve the quality of life for all Americans. The Johnson era ushered in a reconfiguration of federalism known as **creative federalism**, that is "characterized by joint planning and decision making among all levels of government (as well as the private sector), in the management of intergovernmental programs."[48] Particularly for social programs, the success of creative federalism was dependent upon "relationships between Washington and many other independent centers of decision in state and local governments, in new public bodies, in universities, in professional organizations and in business. Creative federalism includes a deliberate policy of encouraging the growth of institutions that will be independent of and, in part, antagonistic to federal government power. Almost every part of every new program transfers federal funds to some outside agency."[49] Johnson was convinced that the only way to address this nation's problems was to use the talents of a multi-leveled think tank of experts from all walks of life. During the 1960s, landmark legislation dealing with civil rights, equality of accommodations, voting rights, affirmative action, desegregation, abolition of restrictive covenants, equal employment opportunities, etc., were passed and signed into law. The implementation and enforcement phases of these new laws were legislatively given to the individual states. Initially, state governments particularly in the southern states were unwilling and very uncooperative. It was creative federalism that gave the national government its leverage to encourage and, oftentimes, force states into compliance by cementing the flow of ample and much needed federal grant money to the new federal mandates. To continue receiving money for low-income housing (Section 8), highway and roadway projects, public education, and so on, the states had to enforce the federal laws. Non-compliance would mean either a reduction in federal monetary allocations or, at worst, elimination of federal dollars. Creative federalism dealt another severe blow to the states. Under numerous programs, any agency, city or county government could apply and

Signing of the Voting Rights Act
President Lyndon B. Johnson moves to shake hands with
Dr. Martin Luther King while others look on.
LBJ Library photo by
Yoichi Okamoto, 08/06/1965.

receive a federal grant without prior approval from their governor's office. And if awarded, the money went directly to the grant recipient. "As a result, by 1980 about 30 percent of all federal aid bypassed state governments, compared to 8 percent in 1960."⁵⁰ Consequently, governors and state legislative houses lost some of their control over their own sub-government units. Governors wanted to assume the role of "gatekeeper" over federal monies. For example, a city's mayor wanted to apply for a federal grant for a low-income housing project. City leaders would have to have the permission from their state governor to even begin the application process. If granted permission to proceed, the grant application would have to be filed with the state governor's office, which could either approve or disapprove sending it to Washington for consideration. And if the grant were awarded, the federal money would come to the governor's desk first for subsequent allocation to the local governing body. The fear in Washington was that any state governor could either keep the money for the state treasury or use if for something else.

A former governor, Ronald Reagan, entered the White House with firm the resolve to reverse the direction of intergovernmental relationships. Once again, the essence of federalism shifted back to the states. He was particularly critical of the numerous federal mandates attached to federal grants viewing them as intrusions upon the ability of states and local governments to govern for themselves and as a blatant violation of the Constitution's Tenth Amendment. Sounding like John C. Calhoun, Reagan told a national audience "it is my intention to curb the size and influence of the Federal establishment and to demand recognition of the distinction between the powers granted to the Federal Government and those reserved to the states or to the people. All of us need to be reminded that the Federal Government did not create the states; the states created the Federal Government."⁵¹ Coined **New Federalism**, Reagan's primary goal of his reconfigured brand of federalism was "to make states' rights the effective policy of the land by reducing the role of the national government in state and local affairs by slowing the flow of federal dollars to states and municipalities as part of a national strategy to discourage their dependency on the federal government, and by returning to state and local officers more control over how money should be spent."⁵² Reagan, however, had an ulterior motive. For him, New Federalism was also a tool to reduce the national deficit by shifting the financial burden for state/local infrastructure projects from the federal purse to state/local pocketbooks.

The credit for New Federalism actually belongs to President Richard Nixon. In a radio message delivered on Labor Day in 1972, Nixon warned workers "when Government tampers too much with the lives of individuals, when it unnecessarily butts into the free collective bargaining process, it cripples the private enterprise system on which the welfare of the worker depends."[53] During his tenure in the White House, Nixon consolidated numerous federal agencies overseeing state/local grant programs into ten regional councils. Federal regulations were simplified and streamlined to allow state and local governments more autonomy in the decision-making process. Reagan went a step further by consolidating fifty-seven categorical grant programs into nine broad block grants. Another sixty categorical grants were eliminated in 1981.

Once again, to reduce the federal deficit, Reagan planned to give state governments full administrative and financial responsibility for two of the nation's costliest federal programs—food stamps and Aid to Families with Dependent Children plus another forty-one smaller programs. In return, the federal government would assume control over the Medicaid program. This creative swap was stalled in Congress when state governors complained about their lack of funds to run the programs. With pressure from discontented Democrats and minority groups, Reagan abandoned New Federalism by the start of his second term of office. However, he did accomplish the easing of federal intrusion into state business by issuing **Executive Order 12612,** which eliminated and/or relaxed numerous federal regulations dealing with social service programs. However, New Federalism was only marginally successful as Congress gradually reinstated and added new federal regulations and mandates.

The course of federalism shifted once again with the election of Bill Clinton. Serving as a governor during the Reagan presidency, Clinton understood a governor's frustration of trying to solve poverty, crime, and unemployment without ample financial assistance from the national government. Yet, like Reagan, Clinton was unprepared to give states and local governing bodies a federal blank check. He created a new brand of federalism—**Constrained Empathetic Federalism** based on the creation of **empowerment zones** whereby non-federal resources are combined with modest federal-cash outlays. Clinton requested congressional funding for six urban and three rural zones. Initially, the federal government would fund the majority of the costs with the understanding that once a zone achieved its targeted economic development, the financial burden would shift to the empowerment zone, alleviating the federal government's financial commitment.

The pendulum swung again when George W. Bush entered the presidency with his intention of reconfiguring Reagan's New Federalism into his **pragmatic federalism**. Initially, he formed a special committee to evaluate which federal programs would fare better under federal or state/local control. However, pragmatic federalism never really took root. After the attacks on the World Trade Center, the Bush administration's focus was more on firming up national security and the war on terrorism. Although he was not yet ready to coin a new term for federalism, President Obama has adopted Franklin Roosevelt's New Deal policies to address the nation's economic upheaval. Initially, Obama agreed to Bush's federal rescue of the automobile industry and continued fueling money into major businesses and financial institutions to reverse declining economic trends. In another package closely akin to Roosevelt's Works Progress Administration, Obama allocated federal dollars to state and local governments to address needed infrastructure projects but, at the same time, put the unemployed back to work. Regardless of what direction the federal/state pendulum swings, it is a truism that states and local communities do not have the financial resources needed to stand alone in addressing their state's problems. The federal government has and will always be called upon to provide financial assistance to sub-government units.

FEDERAL GRANT PROGRAMS

The federal government's adventure into providing financial assistance to the states actually began in 1785 with the passage of the **Northwest Land Ordinance Act** that gave federal lands for public education in the Western territories. A grant is "a form of gift that entails certain obligations on the part of the grantee and expectations on the part of the grantor."[54] The "gift" has strings attached to it that the recipient must fulfill or the recipient will be subjected to a sanction, fine, or denied the privilege of receiving another "gift." Federal dollars have helped to build the nation's interstate and intrastate highway systems, the Intercontinental Railroad, canals, etc. Sporadic in the beginning, the flow of federal funds via grants began to significantly increase in the 1950s. Federal grant programs are designed to give much needed federal dollars to state and local governments to offset the costs of providing for the "general welfare" of the American people. The relationship between the national and state/local governments reminds one of the tales of Robin Hood and his men of Sherwood Forest of taking from the rich and giving to the poor. Giving state and local governments federal money enables these governing bodies to provide better services to their residents, as well as to experiment with new approaches to solve decades-old urban problems. The generosity of the federal government is staggering. In 1990, the federal government gave $135,325,000,000 in federal grants-in-aid to state and local governments. By 2011, the allocation increased to an estimated $625,211,000,000.[55]

Collectively, **grants-in-aid** are "federal payments to states or federal or state payments to local governments for specified purposes and are usually subject to supervision and review by the granting government or agency in accordance with prescribed standards and requirements."[56] There are several types of grant programs including categorical, project, formula, and block. A categorical grant was a federal payment to a state or local government for a specific purpose. These grants were awarded for social service programs, educational projects, highway construction, building airports, etc. Interested parties applied and competed with each other for the federal funds. Usually categorical grants had a matching requirement whereby the recipient was required to contribute some its own money towards the project. Matching agreements could range from 10 to 50 percent of the total costs, insuring that the recipient would be anxious to complete the project since its own money was now committed to it. The two basic types of categorical grants were project and formula. Favored in the 1960s, project grants were used to build the majority of the nation's public housing projects. The money was allocated to state and local governments on an as-need-basis, as demonstrated through the application process. Under the **formula grant program**, Congress allocates money to states and local governments based on a predetermined formula. Constituting approximately 80 percent of all federal grants, categorical grants were preferred by Congress since they had an influential role in determining how the money would be spent. In ensure compliance to grant specifications, the federal government reserved the right to conduct periodic on-site inspections and audits. Perhaps the only major weakness in the program was the confusion over which agency to apply with and the overwhelming number of duplicated projects. Whereas categorical grants were designed for specific projects, block grants are given for prescribed broader activities ranging from health care to education. These grants have fewer federal guidelines and regulations over other grant programs, giving the recipient more flexibility in using the money. Presidents George H.W. Bush, George W. Bush and Barack Obama and most state governors prefer block grants.

Introduced by President Nixon in 1972, the cornerstone of the Robin Hood approach was the **General Revenue Fund** whereby through **revenue sharing** federal money would be provided without a cadre of burdensome strings and mandates from the federal government. Funding allocations were based on a formula that took into account an area's population, income level, tax effort, etc. Urban areas with a high percentage of below poverty-level residents would receive a larger allocation over a predominately higher income area. Revenue sharing was gradually phased out beginning in 1980 when President Carter eliminated state governments from the program. In 1986, the entire program was eliminated since the Reagan administration believed that "legislators and bureaucrats should not collect taxpayers' money from each state only to turn around and send that same money back to the states."[57]

Federal grants have always been controversial. On the positive side, the ample flow of federal dollars to resource-starved sub-government units has enabled the federal government to force grant recipients to implement federally mandated nondiscriminatory laws and workforce regulations. Grants have strengthened the relationship between the national governments and sub-government units. The national government provides the funding, overall regulations, and program goals and objectives as determined through congressional legislation. In turn, the states and/or sub-government units administer the programs, deliver the services, and implement federal mandates. However, federal grant programs have their drawbacks. A list of complaints from attendees at a National Governor's Conference held in the 1970s ring true today:

- There is a lack of coordination among federal departments or agencies limiting the effectiveness of programs in addressing problems that the programs were designed to solve.
- The increased administrative burden on the states is oftentimes overwhelming.
- The federal executive branch has exceeded its proper authority in some areas, encroaching on matters which are in the proper jurisdiction of the states.
- Federal regulations are prescriptive in methodology rather than oriented toward end results.
- Excess reporting and paperwork requirements must be met by state/local governments participating in federal programs.
- Funding and program implementation can be held up by lengthy approval processes, absence of program guidelines, and other administrative practices that lead to serious dislocations and inequities at the state/local level.
- Lack of federal coordination and consistency in implementing direct cost determination procedures creates continuing administrative confusion for the states.[58]

A lingering complaint about all federal grant programs is the practice of the national government forcing recipients to comply with a laundry list of federal laws and regulations by attaching strings or mandates to the grants. Noncompliance can be disastrous. There are four major categories of mandates. First a **direct order** is a congressional law or regulation that must be enforced or grant recipients can be held accountable to civil or criminal penalties. For example, all federal grant recipients must comply with all of the provisions of the Equal Employment Opportunity Act, the Occupational Safety and Health Act, the Americans with Disabilities Act, Title VII of the Civil Rights Act, all subsequent civil rights laws, the Fair Labor Standards Act, and the Environmental Protection Act. Failure to comply carries a very stiff price. Second, **crossing cutting regulations** apply to every grant program including, if necessary, an environmental impact statement. Many grants contain **crossover sanctions** whereby state and local governments will lose their federal funding for noncompliance. Finally, a **partial and out-right pre-emption mandate** occurs when a state or local government fails to establish its own requirements thereby leaving the door open for the federal agency overseeing the project to have partial or complete jurisdiction over the project. Congress supports mandates as the only means of forcing state and local governments to follow its dictates or face losing billings of dollars in federal funding.

Both Congress and state legislative houses are guilty of applying unfunded mandates to their sub-governing units. An **unfunded mandate** is "one level of government requiring another to offer and pay for a program as a matter of law or as a prerequisite to partial or full funding for either the program in question or other programs."[59] For example, a state legislative house passes a law requiring that all public school districts reduce their average classroom size in the elementary and pre-school levels to ensure more quality time between teachers and students. However, the legislature does not give the school districts the additional revenue to build additional classrooms or to hire more teachers. In 1994, the Republican Party under the leadership of Speaker of the House Newt Gingrich issued its "Contract with America" that included a push for Congress to eliminate all federal unfunded mandates. In 1995, President Clinton signed into law a bill requiring the Congressional Budget Office to provide at least the cost of the proposed legislative mandate prior to the bill's approval. However, very few state legislative houses have follow suit.

While the pros and cons of federal grants programs are being continuously debated, the reality is state and local governments are dependent upon federal funding. They cannot shrink from their responsibilities to their citizens. Local governments cannot simply delegate this burden to the next lowest governing unit because there is no level below them. Emergency situations such as a hurricane in the Gulf Coast, wildfires in California, an oil spell heading for Louisiana or a snow storm in Atlanta, Georgia must be properly handled. Once again, the states and definitely local governments simply do not have the funds or the resources to handle these situations by themselves.

Rising Interstate Conflicts

As evidence by the Articles of Confederation, states had numerous conflicts with each other over everything from the route of canals to state boundary lines. To correct this, the Framers envisioned that the **interstate compact**, defined as an agreement between two or more states requiring congressional approval, would fix the problem. These agreements over the years have been used to settle transportation disputes, river boundary changes, and interstate commerce issues. However, the Framers certainly did not anticipate the commercial and business rivalries of today. States openly compete with each other over sports franchises, sites for national political conventions, and business relocations. States market themselves by emphasizing their positives and downplaying their negatives. Recently, Texas Governor Rick Perry hit the road with his campaign to bring more business to Texas by hailing the state's favorable business climate to include low taxes. His commercials flooded the airwaves in both California and New York, prompting both governors to issue their own commercials condemning Perry's actions and highlighting the negatives of Texas, including its rising poverty and dropout rates. The best known sectional rivalries are between East versus West, and "sunbelt" versus "frost belt" or "rustbelt" states.

THE FUTURE OF FEDERALISM

The concepts of vertical and horizontal federalism are based on shared governance between the various levels of governing units. The Framers wanted a balanced government with national and state governments working side by side to address the nation's problems. Basically, "federalism has been praised because:

(1) it permits a flexible policy that can be adopted to individual circumstances, and therefore, reduces conflict between levels of government;
(2) it disperses power widely and thus, in its pluralism it minimizes the risk of tyranny;
(3) it encourages public participation in governance, and hence, makes office holders more accountable and more responsive to the needs of the people;
(4) likewise, a more decentralized system tends to be a more equitable distribution of benefits and burdens;
(5) it improves efficiency (by reducing the delays and red tape usually associated with a central bureaucracy), and encourages experimentation and innovation at subnational levels of government."[60]

On the other hand, critics of federalism point out that:

(1) "it protects the interests of a local majority, often at the expense of racial and other minorities;
(2) it permits states to thwart the efforts of the national government to achieve uniform standards and equal treatment across all states and this leads to inequalities;
(3) in asking states and localities to rely more on themselves it gives advantages to rich states and disadvantages to poor states."[61]

Unfortunately, no model of government is perfect nor is the relationship between governing units going to be smooth and efficient. Despite its flaws, the American brand of federalism has proven over time to be the best plan to include all levels of government into the decision-making and public policy processes. By themselves, each level of government is limited in its ability to meet even the day-to-day needs of the American people. A disaster like a hurricane or a wildfire awakens us to the realization that government is indeed limited. However, when all levels of government from the White House to City Hall put their heads together, dismiss their jealousies towards each other, stop pointing accusatory fingers at each other, and pool their resources, they can fulfill the Framers charge in that preamble to the Constitution to "promote the general welfare" of the American people.

CHAPTER NOTES

[1] *The HarperCollins Dictionary of America Government and Politics*, Jay M. Shafritz, ed., (New York, New York: HarperCollins Publishers, Inc., 1992), 301.

[2] James Madison, "No. 46: Relative Strength of the Federal and State Governments," *The Enduring Federalist,* Charles Beard, ed., 2nd ed., (New York, New York: Frederick Ungar Publishing Co., 1964), 203.

[3] Alexis de Tocqueville, *Democracy in America*, Translated by George Lawrence, J. P. Mayer, ed., (Garden City, New York: Doubleday & Company, Inc., 1969), 164.

[4] Ray Bragg, "Storm of the Century," *San Antonio Express-News* (Sunday, September 11, 2005), 4N.

[5] Ibid.

[6] "Blame Game Delicately Played in Georgia By Governor, Mayor," *San Antonio Express-News* (Friday, January 31, 2014), A8.

[7] Leonard Pitts, "Big, Bad Government? Sure, Until They Need It," *San Antonio Express-News* (Saturday, May 29, 2010), 9B.

[8] Karen Tumulty and Steven Mufson, "Officials Fueling Over Oil Cleanup," *San Antonio Express-News* (Tuesday, May 25, 2010), 1A.

[9] James Madison, "No. 45: Federal Powers Not Dangerous to the States," *The Enduring Federalist*, Charles Beard, ed., 2nd ed., (New York, New York: Frederick Ungar Publishing Company, 1964), 202.

[10] D. Grier Stephenson, Jr., Robert J. Bresler, Robert J. Frederich, and Joseph J. Karlesky, *American Government*, 2nd ed., (New York, New York: HarperCollins, 1992), 59.

[11] Ibid.

[12] Daniel J. Elazar, *American Federalism: A View from the States*, 3rd ed., (New York, New York: Harper & Row Publishers, 1984), 2.

[13] Russell L. Hanson, "Intergovernmental Relations," *Politics in America States: A Comparative Analysis*, Virginia Gray, Herbert Jacob, and Robert A. Albritton eds., 5th ed., (Illinois: Scott, Foresman/Little Brown, 1990), 41.

[14] Elazar, 41-42.

[15] David C. Saffell and Hary Basehart, *State and Local Government: Politics and Public Policies*, 8th ed., (New York, New York: McGraw Hill, 2005), 63.

[16] Richard Bingham ad David Hedge, *State and Local Government in a Changing Society*, 2nd ed., (New York, New York: Harper and Row Publishers, 1984), 31.

[17] Elazar, 31.

[18] *The HarperCollins Dictionary of American Government and Politics*, 206.

[19] Ibid., 254.

[20] Michael Kammen, *The Origins of the America Constitution: A Documentary History*, (New York, New York: Viking Penguin, Inc., 1986), 306-308.

[21] Jack C. Plano and Milton Greenberg, *The American Political Dictionary*, 10th ed., (Orlando, Florida: Harcourt Brace & Company, 1997), 47.

[22] Ibid., 453.

[23] *The HarperCollins Dictionary of America Government and Politics*, 226.

[24] Ibid., 245.

25 Plano and Greenberg, 44.
26 Ralph A. Rossum and G. Alan Tarr, *American Constitutional Law: Cases and Interpretation*, (New York, New York: St. Martin's Press, Inc., 1983), 120.
27 Ibid., 122.
28 Ibid., 215.
29 Saffell and Basehart, 42.
30 Rossum and Tarr, 261 and 264.
31 Richard P. Nathan, "The Role of States in American Federalism," *The State of Stats*, Carl E. Van Horn, ed., (Washington, D.C.: Congressional Quarterly, 1989), 23.
32 Steven G. Calabresi, "Federalism and the Rehnquist Court: A Normative Defense," *The Annals Of the American Academy of Political and Social Science*, Vol. 574, March, 2001, 25.
33 Plano and Greenberg, 57.
34 Ibid., 51.
35 *John C. Calhoun: A Disquisition on Government and Selections from the Discourses*, C. Gordon Post, ed., (New York, New York: Bobbs-Merrill, 1953), 86.
36 Hermann E. von Hoist, *John C. Calhoun: American Statesman Series*, Arthur M. Schlesinger, Jr., ed., (New York, New York: Chelsea House, 1980), 78-79.
37 Plano and Greenberg, 44.
38 von Holst, 79.
39 Plano and Greenberg, 6.
40 *John C. Calhoun: A Disquisition on Government and Selections from the Discourses*, 30.
41 Steven A. Peterson and Thomas H. Rasmussen, *State and Local Politics*, (New York, New York: McGraw-Hill, 1994), 28.
42 "*Texas v White*: The Constitutionality of Reconstruction-1869," *Documents of Texas History*, 2nd ed., Ernest Wallace, David M. Vigness and George B. Ward, eds., (Austin, Texas: State House Press, 1994), 208-209.
43 Plano and Greenberg, 55.
44 Nathan, 17.
45 Malcom L. Goggin, "Federal-State Relations: New Federalism in Theory and Practice," *Perspectives on American and Texas Politics: A Collection of Essays*, Donald S. Lutz and Kent L. Tedin, eds., (Dubuque, Iowa: Kendall/Hunt, 1989), 187.
46 Saffell and Basehart, 43.
47 *The HarperCollins Dictionary of American Government and Politics*, 226.
48 Ibid., 226.
49 David B. Robertson and Dennis R. Judd, *The Development of American Public Policy: The Structure of Public Restraint*, (Glenview, Illinois: Scott, Foresman and Company, 1989), 145.
50 Saffell and Basehart, 45.
51 Goggin, 194.
52 Ibid., 183-184.
53 "Richard Nixon: Labor Day Radio Address-1972," *The Rise of Conservative America: 1945-2000: A Brief History With Documents*, Ronald Story and Bruce Laurie, eds., (Boston, Massachusetts: Bedford/St. Martins, 2008), 91.
54 *The HarperCollins Dictionary of American Government and Politics*, 226.

[55] U.S. Bureau of the Census, *Statistical Abstract of the United States: 2012*, 131st ed., (Washington, D.C.: 2011), Table 431, 268.
[56] *The HarperCollins Dictionary of American Government and Politics*, 262.
[57] Peterson and Rasmussen, 39.
[58] Bingham and Hedge, 45.
[59] *The HarperCollins Dictionary of America Government and Politics*, 352.
[60] Goggin, 186.
[61] Ibid.

SUGGESTED READINGS

Daniel J. Elazar, *American Federalism: A View from the States*, New York, New York: Harper and Row Publishers, 1984.

David C. Saffell and Harry Basehart, *State and Local Government: Politics and Public Policies*, 8th ed., New York, New York: McGraw-Hill, 2005.

John C. Calhoun: A Disquisition on Government and Selections from the Discourses, C. Gordon Post, ed., New York, New York: Bobbs-Merrill, 1953.

Politics in the American States: A Comparative Analysis, Virginia Gray and Russell L. Hanson, eds., Illinois: Scott, Foresman/Little Brown, 1990.

Chapter Four

PUBLIC OPINION, POLITICAL CULTURE, AND POLITICAL SOCIALIZATION

Consider the following scenario. Pollsters visit your college, among a number of other colleges and universities in the United States, and ask each student for his/her thoughts on the cost of higher education in the United States. Perhaps 65 percent say that education costs too much, 30 percent believe that the cost is fair, and 5 percent have no opinion. ("No opinion" is referred to as "**latent opinion**" when the response is given because the individual has not yet fully formed a judgment.) Suppose the pollsters then analyze the data and find:
- (1) that while all the male students believe that the cost is too high, only a simple majority (50 percent plus 1) of the female students believes so,
- (2) that responses to the cost question also varied according to the age, race, ethnicity, and political party affiliations of those polled.

These findings, the **distributions** (65 percent, 30 percent, 5 percent) and the other distributions or percentages of responses based on gender, age, race, etc., are commonly referred to as "public opinion."

Public opinion is so closely related to political culture and political socialization that it is sometimes difficult to talk about it, or about either of them, without reference to the other two. However, each will be considered in this chapter, and the connections among them should become rather apparent.

PUBLIC OPINION

Public opinion has been formally defined as "an aggregate of individual views, attitudes or beliefs shared by a portion of a community."[1] As this definition suggests, there may be more than one public and more than one opinion. In the community of college students the 65 percent who expressed the view that a college diploma is too "pricey" is one public; the attitudes of male students who concurred on one side or the other is a second public; female students who shared the same position is a third, and so on.

The Importance of Public Opinion

Limited Range Importance

Knowledge about how people feel about specific issues may be of importance to relatively few individuals such as to politicians who want to be elected or re-elected. Armed with the information obtained from the fictitious poll described above, for example, candidates seeking to win the college-age vote in a presidential election would probably make some effort to argue for a reduction in tuition.

The extent of that effort would be partially dependent upon how important or **salient** students say the issue is, that is, whether the cost of tuition is more or less important to them than perhaps the issues of abortion or the economy. In part, the extent of the candidates' efforts to woo students will also be based on how strong or **intense** they say the tuition issue is to them. The greater the intensity, the more burning the issue, the less likely a smart candidate will be to ignore it.

When issues are both salient and intense, they are taken very seriously by politicians. Both Presidents Richard M. Nixon and Lyndon B. Johnson cut their political careers short because of the convictions expressed by the public. High negative ratings in public opinion polls contributed to the resignation of the former and caused the latter to reject a bid for a second term in office. In both instances young voters helped to generate the hostile political climate that brought these presidents down, and the opinions of young people have, therefore, continued to carry some weight. In the 1992 presidential campaign, voters between the ages of 18 and 24 were successfully courted by Bill Clinton and, probably because 37 percent of those young voters turned out at the polls for that election, they have been pursued by both parties ever since. No candidate pursued and organized voters more successfully (largely through YouTube, Facebook and, in 2012, Twitter) than Barack Obama did in the 2008 election. This internet courtship paid off. Obama won 66 percent of voters between the ages of 18 and 29 in 2008 and 60 percent in 2012.[2]

Candidates and politicians seeking to ascertain the public mood on various issues generally rely heavily on public opinion polls. Those polls throughout the 2012 election campaign revealed two significant findings about the public mood.

1. A big majority of voters said the economy was the most important issue of the election.
2. Most voters continue to blame George W. Bush rather than Barack Obama for the country's economic problems.[3]

The use of polls by candidates and by incumbent politicians is currently so widespread that it is a bit surprising to discover that the practice is a relatively recent one. Scientific public opinion polls first appeared in the 1930s. Table 4.1 cites some of the opinions about government held by Americans during that early period. The first politician to use such data was Governor Thomas E. Dewey in his unsuccessful bid for the Republican presidential nomination in 1940, and, twenty years later John F. Kennedy became the first candidate to actually hire a pollster.

> **TABLE 4.1**
>
> **PUBLIC OPINION POLL DATA, CIRCA NEW DEAL ERA**
>
> Three-fourths believed "the government should see to it that any man who wants to work has a job."
> *Fortune*: July 1935
>
> Eight out of ten members of the public favored "an amendment to the Constitution prohibiting child labor."
> Gallop: March 28, 1936
>
> Six out of ten approved minimum wage regulations.
> Gallop: June 6, 1937
>
> Eight out of ten felt the Federal Government should "provide free medical care for those unable to pay."
> Gallop: June 14, 1937
>
> Seven out of ten approved Government regulation of the stock exchanges.
> Gallop: October 17, 1937
>
> Seven out of ten thought "the Federal Government should give money to the states to help local schools."
> Gallop: March 26, 1938
>
> Seven out of ten thought "it is the government's responsibility to pay the living expenses of needy people who are out of work."
> Gallop: April 5, 1939
>
> Source: Cited in Lloyd A. Fred and Hadley Cantril, *The Political Beliefs of Americans: A Study of Public Opinion* (New York: Simon and Schuster, 1968), 10.

These public opinion findings of discontent among the electorate are obtained in a number of different ways in addition to polls, such as the Gallup and exit polls mentioned above. They are also acquired by quantifying the frequency of large-scale political protests, demonstrations, and riots, such as those that took place in the 1960s over civil rights and the conflict in Vietnam; the growing numbers of negative articles and reports about the government in the media; and the decline in legitimate political participation, such as in voting, paying taxes, or volunteering for military service. All of these actions and negative expressions are reliable measures of public opinion.

Public Opinion and Democracy

Because American democracy embraces the notion that government rule should be in the public interest, it is necessary for official decision-makers to know both what that interest is and whether it is being satisfied. That doesn't necessarily mean that the government will always act on its knowledge. Neither the Equal Rights Amendment nor stricter gun control, both of which are, and have been, favored by a majority of Americans, have become public policies. Nevertheless, keeping a finger on the pulse of public opinion is an important technique for monitoring—to put it in systems analysis terms—levels of "support."

It was noted in the introductory chapter of this text that an increase of public support shows a high degree of citizen satisfaction and acceptance of the government and the regime and suggests the continuing stability and persistence of a democratic system. The withdrawal of support by an extremely large number of individuals is, on the other hand, suggestive of the loss of a government's or a regime's legitimacy and may portend a government's fall in an upcoming election.

Such predictions were made during the second term of the Bush administration when the failure to provide adequate relief to the victims of Hurricane Katrina, the upwardly spiraling rise in gasoline prices and the persistence of fighting in Iraq all contributed to George W. Bush's plummeting public approval levels. By May 2006, his approval rating in the polls was down to 31 percent (Nixon and Carter were the only presidents that rated lower in the polls) and political pundits were already beginning to speculate that the Democrats would win seats in—if not control of—Congress during the 2006 mid-term elections and would win the presidency in 2008. They were correct on both counts.

Public Opinion and Political Culture

Political culture is defined as "a people's predominant beliefs, attitudes, values, ideals, sentiments, and evaluations about the political system of its country, and the role of the self in that system."[6] The term "predominant" in the definition just quoted is one key to differentiating public opinion from political culture. Public opinion, as defined at the beginning of this chapter, refers to the beliefs or opinions that are "shared by a portion of a community." These beliefs may or may not be the same as those that prevail or "predominate" in the population as a whole. Another difference between the two concepts is that public opinion tends to be much more volatile and transitory in nature.

AMERICAN POLITICAL CULTURE

American political culture refers to the widely shared and enduring beliefs, attitudes, feelings and emotions, and values, etc., about government and about politics and about the role of citizens in the United States. These include: beliefs in freedom, liberty, equality, justice, citizen participation, and limited government; feelings of pride and respect for national heroes and martyrs such as George Washington, Susan B. Anthony, the "unknown soldier" buried in Arlington Cemetery, Neil Armstrong, Malcolm X, and Martin Luther King; emotional attachments to symbols including the U.S. flag, the Statue of Liberty, the White House, the bald eagle, and the three Charters of Freedom; and values such as peace, security, and prosperity.

All of these components of American political culture, which systems analysts refer to as the country's "domestic environment," transcend, for the most part, the ethnic, racial, religious, social, political, geographical, educational, and gender diversity of the population in this country. There are "subcultures" in the United States to be sure, but the long list of shared beliefs, feelings, attachments, and values given above itemizes just some of the things that unite the "majority" of Americans. Many of these items, as the next two statements made by eminent statesmen show, have united us for centuries.

A Few Selected Descriptions of U.S. Political Culture

Benjamin Franklin

Born in America in 1706, and a participant in the deliberations for both independence from England in 1776 and the new Constitution in 1787, Franklin recognized early on that a unique national spirit, character, and culture prevailed in America. He expressed these sentiments often and considered them to be valid reasons for the colonies to separate from England. Some of the special qualities that were uniquely American were later put forth in a humorous letter, written in 1784 to his daughter Sarah Bache, in which he described the reasons for his dismay about the choice of the Bald Eagle as the national symbol of the country. The eagle, he explained,

> is a Bird of bad moral Character; he does not get his living honestly; . . . too lazy to fish for himself, he watches the Labour of the Fishing-Hawk; and, when that diligent Bird has at length taken a Fish . . . the Bald Eagle pursues him, and takes it from him. With all this Injustice . . . . he is generally poor, and often very lousy. Besides, he is a rank Coward; the little KingBird, not bigger than a Sparrow, attacks him boldly and drives him out of the District. He is therefore by no means a proper emblem for the brave and honest [Americans] who have driven all the Kingbirds from our Country . . . .

A more suitable selection, one more representative of those unique American values Franklin suggested, was the turkey,

> a much more respectable Bird, and withal a true original Native of America . . . . He is, . . . a Bird of Courage, and would not hesitate to attack a Grenadier of the British Guards, who should presume to invade his FarmYard with a **red** Coat on.[7]

Alexis de Tocqueville

This Frenchmen, a nobleman and an assistant magistrate at Versailles, visited America in 1831 and kept a record of the trip including his conversations with John Quincy Adams, Sam Houston, Daniel Webster, and President Andrew Jackson. His notes, which filled the pages of many journals, were published in 1835 under the title *Democracy in America*. Like Franklin, he too recognized and wrote about the qualities that distinguish Americans.

Of all the aspects of American political culture, and Tocqueville uses the term "political character" rather than culture, he was perhaps most struck by the strong emphasis placed on "equality." This is the first thing he comments upon in the introduction to the book.

> Amongst the novel objects that attracted my attention during my stay in the United States, nothing struck me more forcibly than the general equality of condition among the people. I readily discovered the prodigious influence which this primary fact exercises on the whole course of society; it gives a peculiar direction to **public opinion** [emphasis added,] and a peculiar tenor to the laws; it imparts new maxims to the governing authorities, and peculiar habits to the governed.

Equality in Europe, he adds by way of comparison, has not "reached the extreme limit which it seems to have attained in the United States...."[8]

Gabriel Almond and Sidney Verba

The expression "political culture" was popularized over a hundred years after Tocqueville's journals were published by these renowned political scientists in a groundbreaking book entitled *The Civic Culture* (1963). In this work, now considered to be a classic in political science, the authors, among many other things, describe the U.S. political culture and compare American "feelings toward government and politics" with those in four other countries. Americans were found to have the most pride in their government and political institutions.

> Eighty-five percent of the American respondents cited some feature of the American government or political tradition—the Constitution, political freedom, democracy, and the like—as compared with 46 percent for the British, 7 percent for the Germans, 3 percent for the Italians, and 30 percent for the Mexicans.[9]

In addition, Americans more strongly favored political participation and had more confidence in their ability to influence government and its laws. That, of course, was in the early 1960s. In a follow-up work, *The Civic Culture Revisited*, edited by Almond and Verba and published in 1980, American political culture was described as being "under stress." Americans, having experienced both the Vietnam War and Watergate, were found to be "more cynical about politicians, less confident in political institutions, and more politically sophisticated...."[10] It was concluded, however, that these "changes in American political culture during the late 1960s and early 1970s were produced by short-term issues and events rather than fundamental changes in American society."[11]

In other words, while political culture is not changeless, it is very tenacious. The American values and beliefs identified so long ago by Franklin and Tocqueville have endured and, as one author explains, "have given us a common identity in the midst of incredible diversity... [and] have made us one people."[12] In fact, a core of fundamental cultural beliefs and values tends to be handed down or transmitted from one generation to the next relatively intact not only in the United States but in every country. It is this persistence of political values over time that makes the process by which they are transmitted an interesting one to so many students of American government today.

The Source of Political Culture

It has been said that the most basic question that can be asked about political culture is "where does it come from?"[13] The answer is probably already clear. Political culture is bequeathed (taught), and it is inherited (learned). The process by which this transferal or transmission takes place is called "political socialization."

POLITICAL SOCIALIZATION

Political socialization is defined in two ways. It is sometimes defined, as suggested above, as the process by which political cultures are passed on over the generations. The actual teaching and learning parts of the process, however, are not a collective one. It is one that takes place individual by individual and citizen by citizen in every local community in every state in every country. The child in eighteenth century America who listened to adults speak about the tyrant King George III was being socialized. So too is the twenty-first century college student whose tuition costs increase each semester because of cutbacks in government funding.

When the focus shifts away from the political culture in general and turns to the individuals—children or adults—that are being taught and are acquiring the political values and beliefs that predominate in the community and/or in the country, political socialization is defined in a second way. It is defined as the process by which individual political outlooks are acquired.

The two aspects and the two definitions of socialization are—like the chicken and the egg—closely related; the accumulation of individual beliefs in a country constitutes its political culture, and the political culture in turn shapes the beliefs acquired by the individual. Having already spent some time examining the first component, political culture, the second—the acquisition of individual political outlooks—will be explored in the remainder of this chapter.

Political Socialization and the Individual

In 1959 Herbert H. Hyman published the first major work on the subject of political socialization. His book, entitled *Political Socialization: A Study in the Psychology of Political Behavior*, set down a fundamental point to remember about when and how individuals are politically socialized: they are socialized over the entire span of their lifetimes by a wide variety of structures or sources Hyman called "agencies of socialization." Today these "agencies" are more commonly referred to as "agents."

Agents of Socialization

An agent of socialization is any formal or informal group or structure that intentionally or unintentionally sends out a political message. This description is so broad that virtually everyone at some point probably qualifies as an agent. But while there are many, some of them, including those discussed below, are considered to be more important than others.

The Family. "Foremost among agencies of socialization into politics," Hyman wrote over fifty years ago, "is the family."[14] Given the current realities of everyday life, the notion of what a "family" is should probably be expanded to include any and all of the infant's and young child's primary caregivers. But Hyman's premise—which is that those that have the initial contacts and/or spend extended time with the child ("proximity") have the best opportunity to pass on fundamental beliefs and values—remains the same.

There is a certain common sense logic being employed by Hyman and those that agree with him. They begin with the assumption that since parents generally succeed in transmitting their own religious and social beliefs to their offspring, (Young children, for example, usually belong to the same faith and root for the same sports teams as the adult members of the family) then the same should hold true for political beliefs and values.

While this assumption is a reasonable one, supporting empirical evidence only partially confirms it. The family does not seem to transmit specific political positions (on abortion or legalizing drugs, for example), but it does seem to excel at passing on general orientations, such as partisan values. That is to say that a child whose parents are Democrats or Republicans is likely to follow suit. This is especially the case when both of the parents and/or others in the family are members of the same political party, are strongly committed to it, and regularly engage in political conversations and express their beliefs in the child's presence.

In addition to party affiliation, general attitudes about authority and government are often passed on from the adults to the young children in a family. For example, David Easton, who has been referred to earlier in this text in connection with both his definition of politics and with the systems analysis approach, reports the following conversation with his three-and-a-half year old son that took place as the two were looking for a place to park their car.

Child. "There's somewhere."
Father. "I can't park there."
Child. "Why?"
Father. "It's not allowed."
Child. "Who say so?"
Father. "I'll get a ticket."
Child. "Uh."
Father. "A policeman will stop me."
Child. "Oh."[15]

Easton goes on to explain that this "laconic" conversation was significant, because the child "learned if not his first political lesson at least the beginning of an important one. He was being introduced to the notion that his father is not omnipotent, that there is a power external to the family to which even his father has to submit, and that somehow the policeman represents this power."[16] In short, the child was being exposed to the ideas that politics both touches his daily life and that he is expected to obey the laws passed by the government.

These are certainly among the predominant views held today, and over the centuries, by most Americans. If a child, such as young Easton, does not happen to learn them from the family, another agent of socialization, the school, is expected to pick up the slack and deliver the message in an even more direct way.

The School.

> [Teachers] use very great endeavor and diligence to put into the heads of their children while they yet be tender and pliant, good opinions and profitable for the conservation of their weal public. Which when they be once rooted in children do remain with them all their life after, and be wondrous profitable for the defense and maintenance of the state of the commonwealth, which never decayeth but through vices rising of evil opinions.
>
> Sir Thomas More, *Utopia*, 1516

Schools, from kindergarten through college, make it their business to teach citizenship, patriotism, and obedience to authority. They have done so from the earliest days of the American republic when the curriculum included "civic training." By 1915, the term "civics" was regularly used to designate those high school courses that were expressly developed to teach students about citizenship and about political institutions and processes.[17]

Although "civics" is no longer a requirement in most educational institutions, memories of many readers' earliest school days probably include the efforts made by their teachers to instill patriotic values. These attempts usually started at the beginning of the day with the singing of the national anthem and the recitation of the pledge of allegiance and continued later on with instruction in American history and government. Lessons in these subjects, especially in the early grades, frequently centered around national holidays (Thanksgiving, Veterans Day, Presidents Day) and national heroes and heroines. (Is there anyone who did not hear about George Washington Carver and the peanut or Betsy Ross and the flag?)

Perhaps because teachers, as More put it, "use very great endeavor and diligence to put [patriotic ideas] into the heads of their children while they yet be tender and pliant," empirical studies have shown that they have been largely successful in instilling patriotic attitudes to even the youngest students. One of the most fascinating of the early studies, conducted by Easton and Dennis in 1961 and 1962, surveyed the feelings of 12,052 children in grades 2-8 about the president. An analysis of their findings showed that

> from the earliest grade the child sees the President as on a commanding height, far above adults as well as children. The President flies in on angel's wings, smiling, beneficent, powerful, almost beyond the realm of mere mortals . . . . He is seemingly a storehouse of inexhaustible virtues—wisdom, benevolence, power, trustworthiness, and exemplary leadership.[18]

"In all of our testing and interviewing," the researchers observed, "we were unable to find a child who did not express the highest esteem for the President. The descriptions of him were universally so approving that we must describe them as a form of idealization."[19] A little more than a decade later, after the Watergate scandal and the resignation of President Nixon, another researcher concluded that although children had negative judgments about Nixon they "still idealized the presidential role in the abstract."[20]

The ability to transmit feelings of patriotism and other political orientations is facilitated in that children in the United States, and in almost every other country, are required by law to attend school daily while it is in session. For many of them that means that more of their waking hours are spent there than at home. It is because so much of a child's life is spent in school that countries that have experienced a change in regime (the Soviet Union, Nazi Germany, Communist China, Cuba) have used this agent in a deliberate effort to "resocialize" children and to encourage loyalty to the new order.

Peers. While family and schools are apparently the most important agents of political socialization during childhood, by adolescence, and throughout the adult years, the individual's personal experiences play a larger and more significant role. These experiences, often in the form of peer pressure or influences from the peer environment, may either affirm or lead to the adjustment of existing political beliefs.

Peers are those who in some way, such as age, rank or position, share equal status. One's peers include friends, colleagues, and neighbors, as well as other individuals who may be known more casually, those, for instance, who attend the same place of worship, or belong to the same volunteer organization, or social or sports club.

The more overlap or agreement there is in the beliefs held by an individual's different peer groups, the stronger the potential to exert influence. Similarly, the more time that is spent with any one group of peers (proximity), the greater its impact is likely to be. Peer impact on some preferences such as the music an individual listens to or the type of clothes she/he wears can be immediately appreciated by taking a look at how the majority of students in the reader's American government course are attired the next time the class meets or by browsing through some friends' CD collections. Though less obvious to see at a glance, peers also have the potential to affect each others' political beliefs and behavior.

Schools as an Agency of Resocialization in Fascist Germany

Shortly after Hitler came to power in 1933 the National Socialist Party (the Nazis) assumed immediate control over the educational system and devoted itself to two goals: to remove all vestiges of democratic principles and to replace them with fascist doctrines. Speaking in May 1933, the German Minister of the Interior, issued many decrees for the redirection of education; "the schools," he was quoted as saying, "must be politicized and become centers for the political training of youth so that there will result an undivided political will as the basis of a strong and permanent nation; everything that menaces this national-political foundation must be excluded." And what was to be taught?

History and those subjects that are essential for national survival are the most important, for the task of the Revolution is to develop the highest patriotism and fanatical enthusiasm for the nation. The school should instill national pride; it should paint great discoverers as national heroes, who love their people and show this love through devotion and sacrifice. Nationalism and a feeling of national uprightness and righteousness should be combined without hesitation . . . .The greatest revolutions in history occurred as a result . . . of fanatical, hysterical passion. Finally, no boy or girl should leave school without realizing the significance of racial or blood purity. An education conducted from the point of view of race and nation must culminate in military service, the crown of the normal education of the average German.

Source: I. L. Kandel, *The Making of Nazis* (New York: Bureau of Publications Teachers College, Columbia University, 1934), 40-41, and 45.

Public Opinion, Political Culture, and Political Socialization

The pledge of allegiance is a typical scene in most schools across the nation. In this way children learn the political values of the country and develop pride in their heritage. Such values and commitment are a necessary ingredient to an orderly and just society.

The extent of peer influence on the attitudes of college students during the politically turbulent years of the late 1960s and early 1970s was documented by a Columbia University professor and two graduate student researchers whose offices and laboratories had been occupied by student demonstrators. Using a variety of measures, including the New Left Scale, interviews, and survey questionnaires, they found that conservative freshmen students took on the political values of their peers and were radicalized during their first year at Columbia. When asked why they had changed their political beliefs, about one-half of a sample of students reported that their friends, rather than any other alternative—parents, political participation, communications media, books, or teachers—had influenced their political attitudes.[21]

The socialization/radicalization process at Columbia and throughout the country resulted in a "peer counterculture," one that was against the war in Vietnam, the deceptive practices of the national government, the profit-at-all-costs motivation of big businesses and corporations, existing college curricula (which was found to be largely irrelevant), and racial and sexual inequality. The media helped to disseminate all of these views to a generation of young people, two of whom were George W. Bush and Bill Clinton. It is an interesting exercise to ponder the possible effects that those views may have had on the policy decisions of the Clinton and Bush administrations.

Mass Communication Media. The mass communication media—magazines, newspapers, television, cable, radio, and increasingly the information superhighway—primarily report topical political information, that is, facts and opinions about current political events and issues that help to shape the political attitudes and behavior of adults. When the political messages delivered by the media are fictionalized and presented in the form of cartoons and comic books, it serves primarily as an agent of childhood political socialization.

The Media and Children. Many children spend at least some of their after school hours and their weekend mornings in front of the television set watching cartoon programs. Aside from the violent content of many of these programs, there are some, which intentionally or not, also teach basic political values. Over the years cartoon programs such as "G.I. Joe," "He-Man," "She-Ra," "Rambo," "The Gobots," "Voltran," "Trans-Formers," and "The Defenders of the Earth" have xpert on the subject has pointed out, a view of the world in terms of "good empires," a view in which the United States is always the good country and

- have only peaceful intentions;
- my, the world would remain at peace;
- ...can) rarely strikes first;
- the enemy attack that prompts the hero to respond with force; and
- the hero always acts in self-defense to insure freedom and uphold his moral convictions.[22]

There are a number of political messages that these cartoons convey but foremost among them is the value of "patriotism." Whether the media should teach this and other basic political values in a less biased fashion remains an ongoing subject of debate.

The Media and Adults. Except for when the news that it reports is cataclysmic in nature, the media does not usually play a significant role in changing the "predominant" political beliefs that adult Americans have long-held. More often, it helps to shape their opinions about political personalities and, according to some, in the case of Michael Moore's controversial movie about George W. Bush—*Fahrenheit 9/11*—to reaffirm their pre-existing beliefs. The media does, however, help to change attitudes about "specific" events or issues, and it has done so in this country ever since Thomas Paine's little pamphlet, *Common Sense*, swayed public opinion against King George III and toward independence in 1776. In more recent times it has been the reporting of newspaper columnists and television newscasters that has informed the public and shaped its opinions about particular issues, sometimes in rather unexpected ways. During the 1996 presidential campaign the *New York Times*, based on the results of a survey conducted by the Pew Research Center for the People and the Press, reported that 40 percent of young people (under age 30) and 25 percent of Americans over all said that they had learned something about the 1996 presidential campaign from late-night television comedy. Television comedy continued to shape public opinion in the 2008 campaign. As one media expert explained, "while the McCain-Palin campaign and the news media were simultaneously attempting to 'define' Sarah Palin for the voting public, *Saturday Night Live* (SNL) took this nationally unknown politician and, through its satirical commentary on news footage, cemented a largely negative and damning public perception of the candidate. In the process, SNL demonstrated that entertainment television, more than other forms of political communication . . . can produce perhaps the most effective interpretation of all."[23] However, other forms of political communication, such as YouTube, were beginning to emerge as well. In fact, "many in the press have dubbed the 2008 election "The YouTube Election" to note the significance that this new outlet of communication (which did not exist in 2004) had on the campaign."[24] By 2012, President Obama chose to communicate with voters via Twitter, Town Hall Meetings, a Google "hangout," and LinkedIn discussions.

The Significance of Political Socialization

Individual by individual the major agents of socialization, family, schools, peers, and the media, transmit the predominate political beliefs, attitudes, and values from one generation to the next. The significance of understanding this never-ending process is twofold: it provides some concrete insights into what makes Americans tick politically, and it is used, as Tocqueville and Almond and Verba did, as a measure for comparing the United States with other countries.

Comparisons can help both scholars and citizens in the U.S. to understand the similarities that unite and the differences that separate them from those in other countries with different political cultures. Americans were reminded of this during the Russian run-off presidential election between President Boris N. Yeltsin and his Communist rival, Gennadi A. Zyuganov, which was held in June 1996.

Watching the conventions, seeing the campaign advertisements and posters, and listening to the speeches from a distance, some U.S. observers did not realize how superficial the trappings of American style democracy actually are in Russia. However, one of Boris Yeltsin's senior aides, Viktor Ilyushin, attempted to set the record straight. From the first meeting he had with foreign election specialists who were attempting to coach the Russians in campaigning techniques he realized, as he told a U.S. reporter, "that it was unlikely we could get many useful tips from our foreign colleagues. Because this is Russia. This is not Germany, not the United States, not Italy. Here we have the Russian people, Russian traditions, Russian habits and a Russian president. Elections in Russia will always take place in the Russian way."[23] This was just another way of saying that as long as Russians socialize Russians, the political culture will not be easily changed. It is as durable for them as it is for Americans.

In informing us about the durability of the beliefs and attitudes that are acquired over a lifetime, socialization theories and concepts provide an explanation for why Americans today distrust national government and executive leadership and why they believe in liberty and freedom and equality. These are among the two-hundred-year old legacies from their colonial past. The durability of beliefs also helps explain why the U.S. political system persists in spite of the many assaults upon it. It persists in the face of communist scares (1950s), youth movements that call for its destruction (1960s and 1970s), domestic and international terrorist attacks that are designed to alter its policies and dilute its legitimacy (beginning with the downing of Pan Am flight 103 over Lockerbie Scotland on December 21, 1988), and militia or paramilitary groups such as the Freemen and the Vipers that try to undermine its institutions (1990s). The system persists because the majority of Americans have been sufficiently socialized. They have been taught and they have learned to support it in good times when it's easy do so and in bad times when it is not and to support it when the system meets their demands and on the occasions (as long as they are not too frequent) when it does not. Easton calls this type of unequivocal support "**diffuse**" support.

CONCLUSION

In discussing public opinion, political culture, and political socialization we have come full circle. These concepts, to use a popular analogy, are like a doughnut—there is no beginning, there is no middle, and there is no end. It's okay then to pick up a round confection and to bite into it anywhere. And so it is with the concepts covered in this chapter. Public opinion consists of political attitudes and beliefs; the predominant political attitudes and beliefs shared by a population is called its political culture; political culture is transmitted to each individual through the process of political socialization; and political socialization helps to shape political attitudes and beliefs and to transmit political cultures.

For political scientists the importance of understanding these concepts and processes is that they provide at least some tentative answers to some of the important political questions that have been asked ever since Western politics began back in ancient Greece. Questions about

> the political orientations and behaviors of individuals: about who votes and who does not, about who participates in political life and who does not, about what accounts for citizen loyalty, obedience and patriotism and partisanship, liberalism and, conservatism, etc. and questions about political systems: about what accounts for democracy, authoritarianism, regime stability and instability, revolutions, peaceful change, development, legitimacy, etc.

It is because public opinion and political culture and socialization concepts provide some answers to these eternal questions that they may aptly be described as "mega-concepts."[24] They are among the most powerful explanatory concepts in the discipline of political science.

CHAPTER NOTES

[1] Jack C. Plano, and Milton Greenberg, *The American Political Dictionary*, 7th ed. (New York: Holt, Rinehart and Winston, 1985), 171-172.

[2] *Newsweek Commerative Issue* n.d. 69..

[3] Jackie Calmes and Megan Thee-Brenan, "Electorate Reverts to a Partisan Divide as Obama's Support Narrows," *The New York Times*, 7 November 2012, 5.

[4] Joannie M. Schrof, David Fischer, Kenan Pollack, Beth Brophy and Linda Kulman, "Speak Up! You Can be Heard!," *U.S. News & World Report*, 19 February 1996, 42.

[5] Jackie Calmes and Megan Thee, "Voter Polls Find Obama Built a Broad Coalition," *The New York Times*, 5 November 2008, sec. P, 9.

[6] Larry Diamond, "Political Culture and Democracy," chap. in *Political Culture and Democracy in Developing Countries* (Boulder, Colorado: Lynne Rienner Publishers, Inc., 1994), 7.

[7] Benjamin Franklin, "Letter to Mrs. Sarah Bache, January 26, 1784," in *The Writings of Benjamin Franklin*, Volume IX, 1783-1788, ed. Albert Henry Smyth, (New York: The Macmillan Company, 1907), 166-167.

[8] Alexis de Tocqueville, *Democracy in America*, edited with an Introduction by Andrew Hacker (New York: Washington Square Press, Inc., 1964), 3.

[9] Gabriel A. Almond and Sidney Verba, *The Civic Culture: Political Attitudes and Democracy in Five Nations* (Princeton, New Jersey: Princeton University Press, 1963), 102.

[10] Alan I. Abramowitz, "The United States: Political Culture under Stress," in *The Civic Culture Revisited*, eds. Gabriel A. Almond and Sidney Verba (Boston, Massachusetts: Little, Brown and Company, 1980), 270.

[11] Ibid., 206.

[12] Frances Moore Lappe, *Rediscovering America's Values* (New York: Ballantine Books, 1989), 3.

[13] Larry Diamond, "Causes and Effects," chap. in *Political Culture & Democracy in Developing Countries* (Boulder, Colorado: Lynne Rienner Publishers, 1994), 229.

[14] Herbert H. Hyman, *Political Socialization: A Study in the Psychology of Political Behavior* (New York: The Free Press, 1959), 51.

[15] David Easton and Jack Dennis, *Children in the Political System: Origins of Political Legitimacy* (New York: McGraw-Hill Book Company, 1969), 3

[16] Ibid., 3 and 4.
[17] Kenneth P. Langton and M. Kent Jennings, "Political Socialization and the High School Civics Curriculum in the United States," in *Socialization to Politics: A Reader*, ed. Jack Dennis (New York: John Wiley & Sons, 1973), 365-366.
[18] Easton and Dennis, 171 and 178.
[19] Ibid., 177.
[20] Fred I. Greenstein, "The Benevolent Leader Revisited: Children's Images of Political Leaders In Three Democracies," *The American Political Science Review* 69 (December 1975): 1397.
[21] Alice Ross Gold, Richard Christie and Lucy Norman Friedman, *Fists and Flowers: A Social Psychological Interpretation of Student Dissent* (New York: Academic Press, Inc., 1976), 99-100, 138 and 149.
[22] Petra Hesse, *The World is a Dangerous Place: Images of the Enemy on Children's Television* (Cambridge, Massachusetts: Center for Psychological Studies in the Nuclear Age, 1989), video cassette.
[23] Michael Specter, "The Election Shows Russia is Russia," *The New York Times*, 7 July 1996, sec. 4, 1 and 4.
[24] Lucian W. Pye, "Political Culture Revisited," *Political Psychology* 12 (September 1991) 487-508.

SUGGESTED READINGS

Asher, Herbert. *Polling and the Public: What Every Citizen Should Know*. Washington, D.C.: CQPress, 2011.

Dennis, Jack, ed. *Socialization to Politics: A Reader*. New York: John Wiley & Sons, 1973.

Greenstein, Fred I. *Children and Politics*. New Haven, Conn.: Yale University Press, 1985.

Jacobson, Gary C., *A Divider, Not a Uniter: George W. Bush and the American People*. New York: Pearson Longman, 2007.

Milburn, Michael A. *Persuasion and Politics: The Social Psychology of Public Opinion*. Belmont, Calif.: Wadsworth, Inc., 1991.

Renshon, Stanley Allen, ed. *Handbook of Political Socialization: Theory and Research*. New York: The Free Press, 1977.

Sigel, Roberta S., and Marily B. Hoskin. *The Political Involvement of Adolescents*. New Brunswick, New Jersey: Rutgers University Press, 1981.

Will, George F. *The Leveling Wind: Politics, the Culture and Other News*, 1990-1994. New York: Viking, 1994.

Woshinsky, Oliver H. *Culture and Politics: An Introduction to Mass and Elite Political Behavior*. Englewood Cliffs, New Jersey: 1995.

Chapter Five

POLITICAL PARTIES

The value of political parties in the American political process has been debated since George Washington assumed the presidency. In his famous farewell address, Washington emphasized that by their very nature political parties divide rather than unite people. He pointed out that "the spirit of party serves always to distract the public councils, and enfeeble the public administration. It agitates the community with ill-founded jealousies and false alarms; kindles the animosity of one part against another; foments occasional riot and insurrection."[1] Washington had a valid point as witnessed time and time again at both the Republican and Democratic national conventions as speaker after speaker criticizes and defiles the opposition party while at the same time highlighting the virtues and accomplishments of their own political party. John Adams lamented about the inability of political parties to work with each other with the spirit of harmony and compromise needed to address the nation's problems. "I have always called our Constitution a game of leap frog.... neither party will ever be strong, while they adhere to their austere, exclusive maxims. Neither party will ever be able to pursue the true interest, honor, and dignity of the nation. I lament the narrow, selfish spirit of the leaders of both parties, but can do no good to either. They are incorrigible."[2] Adams's comments ring true today as Americans witness the daily battles between Congressional Democrats and Republicans over every single piece of legislation. With congressional approval ratings at an all-time low, the interparty gridlock between Democrats and Republicans coupled with the heated bickering within the rank and file of Congressional Republicans is a daily topic of the evening news. Thomas Jefferson went a step further: "If I could not go to heaven but with a party, I would not go there at all."[3]

On the other hand, there are those who support the party system and believe that without it, our nation's pursuit of democratic principles and values would be seriously jeopardized. In a speech delivered in 1923, President Warren G. Harding underscored the value and importance of political parties:

> I believe in political parties. These were the essential agencies of the popular government which made us what we are. We were never perfect, but under our party system, we wrought a development under representative democracy unmatched in all proclaimed liberty and attending human advancement. We achieve under the party system where parties were committed to policies, and party loyalty was a mark of honor and an inspiration toward accomplishment.[4]

Both interest groups and political parties bring together under their respective umbrellas those possessing similar ideological persuasions and issue positions. As a whole, interest groups have a narrower prospective than their political party counterparts. For example, the Sierra Club's agenda is advocacy for the protection and preservation of the environment. Labor unions promote the interests of the nation's workers with emphasis on wages, benefits, and working conditions. The various Chambers of Commerce actively support business development and advocate legislative actions favorable to a profitable business climate. On the other hand, political parties place as many diverse groups as possible under their broader umbrellas. The Democratic Party's base supports the majority of the nation's blue-collar workers, Hispanics, African Americans, women, lower- to lower-middle income Americans and those carrying the liberal banner. Under the Republican umbrella are business-owners, upper-middle and upper-income groups, and those who uphold to more conservative viewpoints. There are growing numbers of individuals who simply do not want to carry the Democrat or Republican label. They prefer to be called independents. The fabric that binds the majority of the American electorate to either of the two major political parties is tied to each party's unique political philosophy that molds their issue positions. The issues will be the same—poverty, national security, the economy, taxes, government regulation, etc. However, the Democratic and the Republican Party, as well as the occasional third party movements, will take different positions on those issues. While the majority of the American electorate rarely watches a party's national convention or read their party's platforms, they generally recognize the liberal camp as affiliating themselves with the Democratic Party and conservatives with the Republican Party. This chapter examines the broad political philosophies that guide each party's issue positions.

The political scene can involve one or more major parties with numerous minor or third parties. However, regardless of the number of political parties, these organizations play essential roles in the election process from the recruitment of candidates for public office to the turning out the vote on Election Day. It is these organizations that galvanize their supporters behind their candidates and also bind the candidates to the party label. In the American party system, it is the state and local organizations that register the voters, stage and, oftentimes, fund their party's primary elections, assistant in candidate fund raising, etc. While candidates use their party to get themselves on a general election ballot, these candidates overlook the important bond one must have with his/her party and the work party members from top to bottom do to help that candidate win on election night. Once elected, one cannot successfully drive any piece of legislation through a legislative house nor can any president be successful without the support of his/her political party. It is a team effort! This chapter delves into the organizational structure of American political parties and the roles each level plays not only in the election process but also in the development and implementation of public policy.

THE ANATOMY OF A POLITICAL PARTY

British political philosopher and himself a member of the House of Commons, Edmund, described a political party as "a body of men united, for promoting by their joint endeavors the national interest, upon some particular principle in which they all agreed."[5] Therefore, a **political party** is "an organization whose members are sufficiently homogeneous to band together for the overt purpose of winning elections which entitles them to exercise government power, in order to enjoy the influence, prerequisites, and advantages of authority."[6] Basically, political parties "consist of three inter-related components: the **party in the electorate**, those who identify with the party; the **party in government**, those who are appointed or elected to office as members of a political party; and the formal **party organization**, the party 'professionals' who run the party at the national, state, and local levels."[7] Each function is vital to a party's survival. For example, the influence of any political party will be short lived if the party's candidates do not win their elections since the ultimate goal of any political party is to have a meaningful if not commanding role in the formulation and implementation of public policy initiatives.

In fulfilling its **party in the electorate role**, political parties must:

- Develop a solid political philosophy that attracts individuals to affiliate themselves to the party for hopefully, the long rather than the short-term.
- Constantly recruit and support their candidates for public office.
- Oversee the internal selection process of candidates to represent their party in the general election.
- Analyze, develop and articulate the issues and the party's position on addressing them.
- Provide a venue for its members to criticize government and the officials in charge of operating that government in a non-violent and legal atmosphere.
- Develop and maintain intraparty loyalty among their rank and file membership.

Once elected to office as the **party in government**, the number one priority is to actually assume control of the government. Basically,

> in the efforts to secure control of the machinery of government, American political parties have assumed the responsibility for organizing the governments, for recruiting leaders and staffing the bureaucracies, for getting out the voters, and for welding together alliances of disparate interests in support of party tickets and programs. Although these functions are not directly concerned with public policy, they do have a rather substantial impact on policy outcomes in the government. Through their officeholders the parties become major participants in conflict resolution, policy leadership, and policy adoption and administration. Though the control and discipline of their members of the legislatures is limited, the parties are a major influence on voting in these policymaking bodies. Thus party outputs in the areas of recruiting and staffing the policymaking machinery have significant bearing on policy outcomes.[8]

After securing their respective party nominations, both President Obama and Mitt Romney formed a committee to start the screening process of individuals to fill their Cabinet, White House staff, bureaucratic chiefs and judicial positions. It is imperative that an in-coming president has as many key positions as possible filled and ready to go to work as he/she is taking the official oath of office. The party in government is effective if its leadership maintains the loyalty and the commitment of its elected officials to design and implement policy directives along the philosophical positions of his/her party. This oftentimes, places the lawmaker in an uneasy position as his/her party's policy preferences may well conflict with the needs of his/her constituents. For example, a bedrock issue of the Republican Party is reducing the national deficit without raising taxes. To accomplish this, the budget ax has become the operating tool. A handful of Republicans in the House of Representatives are trying to regenerate the Base Realignment and Closure Commission (BRCC) to consider closing more military bases. A representative from a community whose livelihood is very dependent upon military installations has a very tough choice to make. Should you side with your party's leadership goal of fiscal responsibility and anger your constituents or do you side with your constituents at the expense of support from your party's leadership?

Cohesive **party organization** can only be achieved if a political party has a strong talented and committed staff of professionals at every level of the party's organizational structure. Among the rank and file, membership in any political party is voluntary. Those who align themselves with one party may very well switch their allegiances if they believe their party has strayed from the course or adopted a position that they simply cannot support. Internal fighting within a political party deters it from achieving its goals and objectives. It is the responsibility of the leadership to keep the party on its course. The Republican Party leadership in the House has been and probably will continue to be at loggerheads with a faction within their own ranks—the Tea Party. The inability of this handful of Tea Party Republicans to compromise with members of their own party over the debt ceiling and federal budget led to a disastrous government shutdown. Regardless of their personal political affiliations, the majority of Americans lost confidence in Congress, the Republican Party, and, in particular, the leadership of the Republican Party. Regardless of the issue at hand, it is the inner core leadership of a party's organization that must keep the party together.

Historical Development of Political Parties

The concept of the modern political party actually emerged during the English Civil War between the cavaliers who supported the ill-fated Charles I and the Puritans (later known as the Roundheads) under Oliver Cromwell. Thomas Osborne, the Earl of Danbury, founded the Tory Party (the pro-king faction) while Anthony Ashley-Cooper, the Earl of Shaftesbury, founded the opposition faction known as the Whig Party (the anti-king faction). By 1675, both had drawn their political ideological lines with the Tories opting for a conservative approach and the Whigs the liberal side of the political spectrum. The Whigs are credited with the development of the first political party platform. Their stated issue positions included a strong stand for Protestantism over particularly Catholicism, religious toleration, guarantees of personal liberties, promotion of commerce and business development, and the supremacy of Parliament over the monarchy. The rise of political parties in England was directly tied to the changing tide of the political fortunes of the entrenched enfranchised privileged few members of the aristocracy who were ruled under the absolutism of the divine right theory of kings to the rise of democratic governments that enabled the rising middle-class urbanites to finally enjoy the same political and personal freedoms that for so long belonged only to the aristocracy. Once only available to the privileged few, the invention of the printing press coupled with an increased emphasis on universal education, enabled the "common man" to read the writings of John Lock, Jean Jacques Rousseau, and Charles de Montesquieu. In particular, these three political philosophers stressed that governments were created by the people and empowered by the people to protect the people's natural or inalienable rights. Kings were not the sons of God; but the servants of the people who entrusted their kings to rule for the people under the people's directives.

> As democratic ideas corroded the old foundations of authority, members of the old governing elite reached out to legitimize their positions under the new notions by appealing for popular support. That appeal compelled deference to popular views but it also required the development of organization to communicate with and to manage the electorate. Thus members of a parliamentary body, who earlier occupied their seats as an incident to the ownership of property or as a prerequisite of class position, had to defer to the people—or to those who had the suffrage—and to create electoral organizations to rally voters to their support.[9]

It was the political party that drew the masses together under one umbrella and gave them the leadership they needed to pursue their common issue positions guided and crafted by their cohesive bond to a particular political philosophy, a lesson soon to be known in newly formed United States.

Party Systems

The strong two-party system in the United States is unique since the majority of nation states use the **multiparty system** defined as "an electoral system based on proportional representation that often requires a coalition of several parties to form a majority to run the government."[10] The political landscape in Norway and Sweden involves at least four to five political parties embracing the entire political spectrum from socialists and communists to middle-of-the-road agrarian and centrists to the traditional dichotomy of liberals versus conservatives. There are at least six major political parties in France while German politics is dominated by two major and three minor political parties. Lacking even one major political party, Italian politics revolves around a multiplicity of minor political parties. Consequently, in France, Germany and Italy, the leadership of these various political parties must form coalitions among each other in hopes of winning an election. Once in office, the leadership of the winning coalition stays in power only as long as they are able to fulfill the promises and concessions made to their coalition partners. In Italy, the strength of the coalition usually falls apart within a few months, meaning that the prime minister has lost "the confidence" of his parliament and must call for new elections, leading to the development of another fragile coalition government. These countries have a **conflictual party system** whereby "the legislature is dominated by parties that are far apart on issues or highly antagonistic toward each other and the political system."[11] Although they have a multitude of political parties, both Norway and Sweden follow a **consensual party system** in which "the parties commanding most of the legislative seats are not too far apart on policies and have a reasonable amount of trust in each other and in the political system."[12] In a multiparty system, citizens have a wide range of party alternatives and issue positions to determine their voting preferences. Nations such as North Korea, Cuba, and Vietnam use the one-party or **exclusive governing party** format. With a tight top-down structure, the party leadership "recognizes no legitimate interest aggregation by groups within the party nor does it permit any free activity by social groups, citizens or other government agencies."[13] The one-party system was used in the former Soviet Union before 1985, the majority of the Eastern European nations before 1989, and China.

The American political party system is basically a two-party system with minor or third parties surfacing from time to time. The two-party system fits nicely into the dichotomous relationship of the American political landscape. Beginning with the emergence of the Federalist and Jefferson-Republican Parties, the pattern follow that whatever position one party takes on an issue, the other party will take the opposite viewpoint. Since the election of Franklin Roosevelt to the presidency in 1936, the Republican Party holds to conservative viewpoints while the Democrats favor the liberal side of the political spectrum. For example, on the environment, Republicans support less government regulation while Democrats favor stronger federal regulatory oversight. The Republican Party supports legislation favorable to the business community while Democrats pursue legislation addressing worker issues such as increasing the minimum wage, work safety laws, etc. For voters, it is a simple choice. The two-party system is essential to the organizational structure of legislative houses at both the national and state level. The party that wins the majority of the seats in the House of Representatives controls of the leadership of that body. The Speaker of the House is a member of the majority party. Although the vice president is the presiding officer of the United States Senate, the actual operation of the Senate's business is controlled by the Senate Majority Leader, a member of the majority party. Committee assignments are based on the majority/minority concept. The chairperson and vice chairperson of a committee are usually the members of the majority party that have served on that committee the longest among the majority party's membership. If the election results in the once minority party becoming the majority party, the chair and vice chair positions

American women had to campaign for the right to vote in the early 1900s.

shift to those individuals from that party who have served the longest and second longest on that particular committee. The composition of the committee membership also falls under the majority/minority concept. For example, in the 2014 Congress, a committee composed of 15 members will have at least eight Republicans and seven Democrats because the Republicans hold the majority of the total congressional seats.

THE POLITICAL SPECTRUM

The guiding principles behind a political party are the philosophical approaches taken in both the selection of and the positions taken on the issues. Political scientists have developed a straight-line **political spectrum** on which they place the political philosophical positions or the ideological perspectives groups follow. An **ideology** is "a comprehensive system of political beliefs about the nature of people and society."[14] The right of the line is reserved for conservative ideological positions while the left is for the more liberal approaches. The middle position is reserved for those ideological positions that are not staunchly conservative or liberal but more middle-of-the-road or moderate. A brief overview or the prevailing political philosophies indicates the underlying principles behind these positions.

Conservatism—The Right of the Spectrum

Conservatism is "the political outlook which springs from a desire to conserve existing things, held to be either good in themselves, are at least safe, familiar and the objects of trust and affection."[15] Basically, a true conservative is the defender of the status quo against any major changes to existing policies. Conservatives adhere to **incrementalism** defined as "a doctrine holding that change in a political system occurs only by small steps, each of which should be carefully evaluated before proceeding to the next step."[16] President Woodrow Wilson, a Democrat, defined conservatism as "the policy of 'make no change and consult your grandmother when in doubt.'"[17]
Conservatism rests on six major positions:

- First, conservatives generally have a religious bent. They believe a "divine intent rules society, as well as conscience."
- Second, there is an attachment to traditional life, in spite of its variety and apparent disorder.
- Third, conservatives believe "civilized society requires orders and classes." Thus society cannot be leveled. Though all people are equal morally, they must be unequal in social terms.
- Fourth, there is a close relationship between freedom and private property. The former is made possible only by the existence of the latter, and so conservatives support the existing distribution of property, even with its inequalities.
- Fifth, conservatives have a belief in **prescription** (the action of laying down authoritative rules or directions) and distrust of reason. Consequently, reason is not an adequate guide to human conduct.

- Six, though conservatives are willing to countenance a measure of reform, they distrust more substantial change subscribing to the belief that "innovation is a devouring conflagration more often than it is a touch of progress."[18]

Basically, a true conservative supports upholding the existing social and political order. While acknowledging society's inherent inequalities based on wealth, political power, etc., conservatives embrace a class system based on wealth and, in some societies, lineage. Considered to be the father of conservative political thought, Edmund Burke based his beliefs on "a few simple generalizations: that the present state of things is the sum total of all past developments; that is too complex to understand; that meddling with it is therefore dangerous; and that arrangements that work well enough are best left alone."[19] Several members of the Republican side of the House of Representatives embrace Burke's observations particularly over issues of Obamacare, immigration reform, etc. Opposition over Obama's reform of the health-care system centered on the beliefs from Republicans that although the private-provider health-care program had its problems, it surely should not be radically replaced with an entirely new approach. They envisioned instead a more studied deliberative approach to gradually address the problems of the health-care system without radically changing the entire program. The same attitude pervades any discussion of immigration reform. Let's take this issue one step at a time and, if necessary, make gradual changes to address the issue.

Just right of conservatism, **cultural conservatism** is based on "support for traditional western Judeo-Christian values not just as a matter of comfort and faith, but out of a firm belief that the secular, the economic, and the political success of the western world is rooted in this value."[20] Further to the right, the New Right or the Religious Right, places its emphasis more on religious rather than cultural values. The agenda of the Religious Right sees an extremely limited role for government across the board particularly in policy areas involving the economy, welfare programs, the environment, etc. Its membership takes very strong anti-communist and anti-socialist positions. The Religious Right upholds traditional moral values including strong pro-life positions and advocacy for prayer in the public schools. A person adhering to the conservative position on the spectrum would uphold the free enterprise system, capitalism, a strong military, less government regulation, private property ownership and rights, cultural conservatism, and a strong sense of moral and religious values.

Moderates—The Center of the Spectrum

A **moderate** or **centrist** is "an individual or political group advocating a moderate approach to the political decision making and to the solution of social problems."[21] A moderate upholds:

- A desire for conciliation or compromise rather than confrontation.
- A preference for reform over revolution. Moderates want policy options that correctly assess a problem and offer timely and reasonable responses to fix it.
- Political transformations gradually occurring without violence against existing governing institutions.
- Tolerance towards views which do not match the consensus, but are voiced in a non-violent manner.[22]

The majority of the American electorate shares political viewpoints that place them in the middle. In many respects, the **mainstream** or the middle of the spectrum is more advantageous simply because it does not attract those whose political positions align themselves with the extremes of the traditional left (liberal) or right (conservative).

Liberalism—The Left of the Spectrum

While conservatives dread change, liberals embrace it. Initially, **liberalism** was "a political doctrine that espouses freedom of the individual from interference by the state, toleration by the state in matters of morality and religion, laissez-faire economic policies, and a belief in natural rights that exist independent of government."[23] As a political perspective, liberalism is a by-product of the Enlightenment through the writings of John Locke, Charles de Montesquieu, Jean Jacques Rousseau, Jeremy Bentham, John Mill, John Stuart Mill, Baruch Spinoza and Immanuel Kant. In his *Spirit of the Laws*, Montesquieu defines **liberty** as "in a state, that is, in a society where there are laws, liberty can consist only in having the power to do what one should want to do and in no way being constrained to do what one should not want to do."[24] Furthermore, he differentiates between **positive liberty** whereby one is forced to be free and **negative liberty** which is "that tranquility of spirit which comes from the opinion each one has of his security, and in order for him to have this liberty, the government must be such that one citizen cannot fear another citizen."[25] Basically, no government can force someone to vote (positive liberty), however, government must provide unstrained accessibility to the voting process so someone can make an individual choice whether or not to vote (negative liberty). Liberalism is based on the following concepts:

- The belief in the supreme value of the individual, his freedoms and his rights. Liberals embrace the concept of **individualism** defined as "the political, economic and social concept that places primary emphasis on the worth, freedom and well-being of the individual rather than on the group, society or nation."[26]
- The belief that every individual has natural rights, i.e., life, liberty and property, which exists independently of government. It is the responsibility of government to protect everyone's individual rights from interference from others (civil rights) and from the arbitrary actions of government (civil liberties).
- The belief of the supreme value of freedom by limiting the power of government and preventing it from inhibiting one from exercising his/her freedoms. John Locke wrote in his *Second Treatise of Government*, that "the liberty of man in society is to be under no other legislative power but that established by consent in the commonwealth, nor under the domination of any will, or restraint of any law, but what the legislative shall enact, according to the trust put in it."[27]
- Tacit consent and the social contract. According to John Locke, **tacit consent** means that an individual who enjoys some benefit from living in a certain nation consents to obey the law of that country, therefore, giving his/her consent for the existence of that government. "Locke emphasizes that possessing property in a country constitutes consent to its government. Because it is impossible to remove one's land from a country, accepting ownership of land requires membership in a society and so consent to obey its laws."[28] The

social contract theory underscores that once absolutely free individuals living in isolation from each other come together to form a community that out of necessity for public order, subsequently create a governing body that establishes the rules for the exercise of certain basic fundamental rights. If the government, in turn, fails to protect those rights, then the people have the right to abolish the governing contract and begin anew.

Located slightly left of the liberal position on the spectrum, the **New Left** movement in the United States during the 1960s and 70s initially began on college campuses across the nation as students staged angry protests against the established political, social and economic order throughout the nation. The New Left was fueled by the convergence of three major political and social movements—the unpopularity of the Vietnam War, and both the civil rights and woman's liberation movements. Although there was no meaningful cohesive massive convergence of the three camps, what emerged was an agenda of common themes, i.e., anti-Vietnam War, advocacy against racial and gender discrimination, promotion of women's issues to include equal pay and abortion rights, and sincere empathy towards the economic deprivation of the nation's poor.

Sandwiched between liberals and the far left, **libertarians** believe "in freeing people not merely from the constraints of traditional political institutions, but also from the inner constraints imposed by their mistaken attribution of power to ineffectual things."29 Written in 1972, the Statement of Principles from the American Libertarian Party states that:

> We, the members of the Libertarian Party, challenge the cult of the omnipotent state, and defend the rights of the individual. We hold that each individual has the right to exercise sole dominion over his own life, and has the right to live his life in whatever manner he chooses so long as he does not forcibly interfere with the equal right of others to live their lives in whatever manner they choose. . . We . . . hold that the sole function of government is the protection of the rights of each individual: namely, (1) the right to life—and accordingly we support laws prohibiting the initiation of physical force against others; (2) the right to liberty of speech and action—and accordingly we oppose all attempts by government to abridge the freedom of speech and press, as well as government censorship in any form; and (3) the right to property—and accordingly we oppose all government interference with private property, such as confiscation, nationalization, and eminent domain, and support laws which prohibit robbery, trespass, fraud and misrepresentation. Since government has only one legitimate function, the protection of individual rights, we opposed all interference by government in the areas of voluntary and contractual relations among individuals. Men should not be forced to sacrifice their lives and property for the benefit of others. They should be left free by government to deal with one another as free traders in a free market; and the resultant economic system, the only one compatible with the protection of man's rights, is laissez-faire capitalism.30

Table I lists several of the bottom line issues embraced by the Libertarian Party.

Those under the far left umbrella include democratic socialists, Marian socialists, communists, and anarchists. Evolving into both a social and economic movement in Europe in the middle of the nineteenth century, **socialism** is "a doctrine that advocates economic collectivism through governmental or industrial group ownership of the means of production and distribution of goods."³¹ Whereby, **communism** also known as **Marxism-Leninism** envisions an end to formalized structured government by the developed of collectivistic societies. Communism, in theory, espouses the doctrines of historical inevitability, economic determinism, labor value, and the 'inner contradictions' of capitalism, class conflict, capitalist colonialism and imperialism, world wars resulting from competition for markets, and the destruction of the bourgeoisie, the dictatorship of the proletariat, the socialist revolution, and the final 'withering away' of the state."³² The primary advocates of both socialist and communist doctrines are Karl Marx and Friedrich Engles who collectively wrote *The Communist Manifest*. Furthermore, Marx detailed his concept of socialism in *Capital*. A Russian revolutionary, Vladimir Lenin laid out his plan for the 1917 Bolshevik Revolution and the plans for a new Russia through a series of essays entitled collectively as *The Little Lenin Library*. An **anarchist** holds that "government is an unnecessary evil and should be replaced by voluntary cooperation among individuals and groups."³³ Several anarchist groups advocate violent revolution as the only means of eliminating "the state as an instrument used by the propertied classes to dominate and exploit the people."³⁴

Ideological Versus Issue Base Parties

As evidenced primarily in European politics, it is the particular political ideological prospective articulated by the party leadership that draws one to affiliate with either a conservative- or liberal-oriented party. From the voter's perspective, the candidate and/or the candidate's personal issue positions are overshadowed by the party's guiding philosophical positions. The term *Weltanschauung* oftentimes is used to describe the overall embracing power of ideologically based political parties that permeates "virtually all social relationships and thus a politics of limitless scope and total involvement."³⁵ However, in American politics, the focus of the voter's attention is more on the candidate than his/her political party. While many Americans label themselves as either liberals or conservatives, few can actually articulate the overriding political philosophies associated with liberalism or conservatism. Philosophically, one is apt to say that there is very little difference between a mainstream Republican and a moderate Democrat. American political parties, therefore, are more pragmatic and less ideological. "The American parties are relatively non-ideological parties of the political center. Since their mission is the organization of majorities, they cannot be deflected by the wishes of small ideological minorities. To organize the stable majorities that undergird the American polity, the parties must often compromise, soften, or smooth over the issues that divide Americans. As competitive parties in the heterogeneous American society, they must be pragmatic, brokerage parties, appealing for votes wherever those votes may be and regardless of the ultimate inconsistency of the appeal."³⁶ In a 1939 radio address, President Franklin Roosevelt commented "a radical is a man with both feet firmly planted in the air. A conservative is a man with two perfectly good legs, who, however, has never learned to walk forward. A reactionary is a somnambulist walking backwards. A liberal is a man who uses his legs and his hands at the behest . . . of his head."³⁷

Chapter Five

AMERICAN POLITICAL PARTIES

Development

Winning the support of every elector, George Washington assumed the presidency in 1789. He was the first and only person to win the presidency without a political party nomination, endorsement, or label. Serving in his cabinet were two of his closest allies and personal friends—Thomas Jefferson as Secretary of State and Alexander Hamilton as Secretary of the Treasury. The friendship between the two quickly deteriorated as Hamilton launched his plan for a centralized banking system and the national government's assumption of the debts owned by the states from the Revolutionary War. A member of Congress, James Madison was so irked by the Hamilton's debt proposal that he resigned from Congress. Jefferson was definitely opposed to the centralized banking plan. Consequently, Hamilton and Jefferson were at loggerheads and "engaged in such fierce controversies over the proper course to pursue that Washington could not mollify them, hard though he tried."[38] Washington favored Hamilton's plans but lacked the means to secure support even among his own supposed supporters in Congress. For Hamilton, the only way for a president to ensure continual support for a president's policies was to have some form of collective leverage, like a political party. As the leader of a political party, Washington could remind other party members that his successes or failures were their successes or failures.

Consequently, Hamilton and his supporters formed the Federalist Party while Jefferson's group gathered under the banner of the Jeffersonian Republicans also known as the Democratic/Republicans. The base support for the Federalist Party came from the northern industrial and shipping business community. They favored Hamilton's pro-business positions particularly on low taxes, a strong central government, and opposition to the French Revolution. "In effect the Federalist party could lay claim to representing 'the wealth and talents' of the conservative classes in the United States. . . . He [Hamilton] and Washington resented popular agitations at home, as they abhorred such agitation in France and they thought that the 'democratic societies' springing up in towns and country districts ought to be suppressed before they got out of bounds."[39] Jefferson's party gathered their support base from agricultural interests particularly in the South. Jefferson supported the democratic zeal of the French revolution, openly opposed any notion of a strong central government, and basically became the standard bearer of the common man.

Although the Federalist Party will meet its demise by 1815, the impact of its twelve years in power was significant. "They organized a new government, set precedents that have never been broken, established a sound financial system, obtained the withdrawal of the British from the Northwest, eliminated the Spanish threat to the Southwest, and prevented the United States from becoming involved in a general European war."[40] Meanwhile, Jefferson's party successfully elected him to two presidential terms under a cohesive party platform of "frugal government, reduced national debt, smaller national defense, 'free commerce with all nations' but 'political connections with none,' freedom of religion, press, and speech."[41] Jefferson also introduced a new campaign technique—the grassroots approach of taking the candidate's message directly to the people. By 1828, the Jeffersonian-Republicans would split into two separate political parties, namely, the National Republicans and the Jacksonian Democrats. The National Republicans would regroup by 1832 as the Whigs. The Whig Party met its demise by 1848. With the election of Jackson in

1828, the Democratic Party dominated American politics until 1860 by holding the White House for all but eight years, controlling the Senate for twenty-six years and the House for twenty-four years.

The Democratic Party dramatically lost its political domination in 1860 as the party's membership was severely divided over slavery. While Abraham Lincoln had the solid support of the Republican Party behind him, the Democrats split into two factions. The northern faction nominated Senator Stephen A. Douglas, Lincoln's perennial political foe while the southern Democrats nominated incumbent vice president, John C. Breckenridge, a pro-slavery advocate from Kentucky. Former Whig Party members joined forces with the remnants of the Know-Nothing Party to form the Constitutional Union Party. This group nominated John Bell of Tennessee for the presidency. On election night, Lincoln took advantage of the split in the Democratic Party's base and won the election by losing the popular vote but carrying a large number of electoral votes primarily from the northern states. Beginning with this election, the Republicans became the dominant political force in Washington until 1932 by occupying the White House for fifty-six years and controlling the House for fifty years and the Senate for sixty years. But Republican domination began to decline with the 1929 Stock Market Crash. Its hold on Washington politics ended with the election of Franklin Roosevelt in 1932. The Democrats would hold onto the White House consecutively until the election of Republican Dwight Eisenhower in 1952. Since then control of both the White House and Congress has had periodic spurts of power holds between the two parties.

The Modern Republican Party

Emerging as a third party movement, the Republican Party's base was a mixture of supporters from failed third parties—the Whigs, Know-Nothings, Free Soilers and disgruntled anti-slavery Democrats. The party's first run at the White House was in 1856 with John C. Frémont as its presidential candidate. Although he lost the race, Frémont was able to garner approximately one-third of the popular vote and carried eleven states. Initially, the party favored the trans-continental railroad and other infrastructure improvements, homestead protection laws, protective tariffs, and took a strong anti-slavery position. Many credit Woodrow Wilson for changing the philosophical positions of both political parties. A Democrat, Wilson believed that the words in the Preamble to the United States Constitution definitively charged the federal government with the tasks to "insure domestic tranquility, provide for the common defense, and promote the general welfare." Therefore, in times of a national emergency, a threat to the nation's security, and a decline in the general welfare of the American people, it was the responsibility of the federal government to come to the aid of its people. Consequently, the Democrats endorsed a more liberal approach and the Republicans choose the more conservative roadway to address the nation's problems. The dichotomy was firmly established with the Republicans taking the conservative positions and the Democrats the liberal route.

Beginning in 1945, the Republican Party began to solidify its conservative base on the domestic front by denouncing the continuation of New Deal policies that ushered in the welfare state and in particular "to dismantle liberalism's social programs and the progressive tax policies that paid for them."[42] On foreign policy, "the advent of the cold war between the United States and the Soviet Union, moreover, led to the end of conservatism's traditional association with isolationism and suspicion of a strong military establishment. Fear of Soviet-style communism—atheistic, totalitarian, socialist, and heavily armed—turned conservatism into a force for an aggressive foreign policy aimed at collapsing communism on a worldwide scale."[43]

The **2012 Republican Platform** entitled "We Believe in America" states their primary conservative-leaning political perspectives in the preamble of the document:

> The pursuit of opportunity has defined American from our very beginning. This is a land of opportunity. The American Dream is a dream of equal opportunity for all. And the Republican Party is the party of opportunity. . . . This platform affirms that America has always been a place of grand dreams and even grander realities; and so it will be again, if we return government to its proper rule, making it smaller and smarter. If we restructure government's most important domestic programs to avoid their fiscal collapse. If we keep taxation, litigation, and regulation to a minimum. If we celebrate success, entrepreneurship, and innovation. If we lift up the middle class. If we hand over to the next generation a legacy of growth and prosperity, rather than entitlements and indebtedness."[44]

A more detailed examination of the document details the GOP's policy positions:

- We offer our Republican vision of a free people using their God-given talents, combined with hard work, self-reliance, ethnical conduct, and the pursuit of opportunity to achieve great things for themselves and the greater community.
- Republicans will pursue free market policies that are the surest way to boost employment and create job growth and economic prosperity for all.
- We will reform the tax code to allow business to generate enough capital to grow and create jobs for our families, friends and neighbors all across America.
- Extend the 2001 and 2003 tax relief packages—commonly known as the Bush tax cuts—pending reform of the tax code, to keep tax rates from rising on interest, dividends and capital gains.
- Any value added tax or national sales tax must be tied to the simultaneous repeal of the 16th Amendment, which established the federal income tax.
- We call for a Constitutional amendment requiring a super-majority for any tax-increase, with exceptions for only war and national emergencies, and imposing a cap limiting spending to the historical average percentage of the GDP so that future Congresses cannot balance the budget by raising taxes.
- A Republican president will insist on full parity in trade with China and stand ready to impose countervailing duties if China fails to amend its currency policies.
- We affirm our support for a Constitutional amendment defining marriage as the union of one man to one woman.
- We oppose the National Popular Vote Interstate Compact or any other scheme to abolish or distort the procedures of the Electoral College.
- We support State laws that require proof of citizenship at the time of voter registration to protect our electoral system against a significant and growing form of voter fraud.
- We support the public display of the Ten Commandments as a reflection of our history and of our country's Judeo-Christian heritage, and we affirm the right of students to engage in

prayer at public school events in public schools and other public facilities to accommodate religious freedom in the public square.
- We uphold the right of individuals to keep and bear arms.
- We support a human life amendment to the Constitution and endorse legislation to make clear that the 14th Amendment's protections apply to unborn children.
- The Republican Party is committed to domestic energy independence.
- Call for a moratorium on the development of any new major and costly regulations until a Republican Administration reviews existing rules to ensure that they have a sound basis in science and will be cost-effective.
- The appointment of constitutionalist jurists, who will interpret the law as it was originally intended rather than make it.
- On immigration, oppose any form of amnesty for those who, by intentionally violating the law, disadvantage those who have obeyed it. We support the mandatory use of the Systematic Alien Verification for Entitlements program.
- We support English as the nation's official language, a unifying force essential for the education and economic advancement of—not only immigrant communities—but also our nation as a whole.
- We support the repeal of Obamacare.
- We are committed to aggressively pursuing tort reform legislation to help avoid the practice of defensive medicine, to keep healthcare costs low, and to improve healthcare quality.
- We support consumer choice in education to include home schooling, and local innovations like single-sex classes, full day school hours, and year-round schools.
- We support a national registry for convicted child murderers. We oppose parole for dangerous or repeat felons.
- Support a strong national defense as the pathway to peace, economic prosperity and the protection of those yearning to be free.
- We give unequivocal support of Israel.[45]

The Modern Democratic Party

On the other hand, entitled "Moving America Forward," the **Democratic National Platform of 2012**'s preamble emphasizes the differences between the Republican and Democratic vision for the future by stressing that "this election is not simply a choice between two candidates or two political parties, but between two fundamentally different paths for our country and our families."[46] The preamble highlights the accomplishments of Obama's first term of office and lays out the general path for the next four-years:

> Democrats see a young country continually made stronger by the greatest diversity of talent and ingenuity in the world, and a nation of people drawn to our shores from every corner of the globe. We believe American can succeed because the American people have never failed and there is nothing that together we cannot accomplish. . . . restoring the basic values that made our country great, and restoring for everyone who works hard and plays by the rules the opportunity to find a job that pays the bills, turn an idea into a profitable business, care

for your family, afford a home you call your own and health care you can count on, retire with dignity and respect, and most of all give your children the kind of education that allows them to dream. . . These values are why we enacted historic health care reform that provides economic security for families and enacted sweeping financial reform legislation that will prevent the recklessness that cost so many their jobs, homes, and savings. They're why we rescued the auto industry and revived our manufacturing supply chain. They're why we helped American families who are working multiple jobs and struggle to pay the bills save a little extra money through tax cuts, lower health care costs, and affordable student loans. . . . The problems we are facing right now have been more than a decade in the making. We are the party of inclusion and respect differences of perspective and belief. And so, even when we disagree, we work together to move this country forward. But what is holding our nation back is a stalemate in Washington between two fundamentally different views of which direction American should take."[47]

To address these issues, the Democrats proposed the following:

- Commitment to rebuilding the middle class with the extension of middle-class tax, providing assessable, affordable, high quality health care, stabilizing the housing market and hard-hit communities, protecting social security and Medicare, providing greater access to higher education and technical training and making college more affordable and assessable.
- Efforts to put Americans back to work through relief for the long-term unemployed, a ban on hiring discrimination against the unemployed, expanded universal work training and job search assistance.
- Cutting waste and reducing the deficit by cutting taxes for every working family by providing $3,600 in tax relief to the typical family during Obama's first term and extending the middle-class cuts for the 98 percent of American families who make less than $250,000 a year without any additional tax increases.
- To reduce the national deficit while at the same time making investments in education, research, infrastructure and clean energy, the president has asked for the wealthiest taxpayers to pay their fair share and opposed efforts to give additional tax cuts to the wealthiest Americans at the expense of the middle class and investments in our future.
- Emphasis on sustainable energy-independent future to include wind, solar, biofuels, geothermal, hydropower, nuclear, oil, clean coal and natural gas.
- Ending insourcing by cutting tax breaks for companies that are shipping jobs overseas and for special interests and offer tax breaks to companies investing in the United States.
- We support long-term investments in our infrastructure to include roads, bridges, rail and public transit systems, airports, ports, and sewers critical to economic growth.
- Raise the minimum wage and index it to inflation.
- Help small businesses with tax breaks and loan incentives.
- Reforms for Wall Street to hold them accountable and bring new transparency to financial markets.
- Support campaign finance reform to include revealing donors to the public.
- Support of the Dream Act.

- Support of troops, military families and veterans tax credits such as the Returning Heroes Tax Credit and the Wounded Warrior Tax Credit to give companies incentives to hire veterans and the post 9/11 GI Bill to provide opportunities for military personnel, veterans and their families.
- Support tribal sovereignty with the HEARTH Act to promote tribal self-determination and create jobs in Indian Country.
- Renewed commitment to civil rights and equal pay for women.
- Pro-choice position.
- Support of gay marriage.
- Reenergizing the Voting Rights Act.
- Commitment to protecting the environment of our natural resources while creating jobs, preserving habitats, and ensuring that future generations can enjoy our nation's outdoor heritage.
- Responsibly ending the war in Iraq, defeating Al-Qaeda and ending the war in Afghanistan.
- Prevent nuclear proliferation particularly in Iran.
- Strengthen United States commitment to NATO and the United Nations.
- Strengthen alliances, expand partnerships with international institution and with European nations, Australia, New Zealand, the Philippines, South Korea and Thailand with the understanding that the United States cannot do it alone.
- Continue to establish cooperative relationships with an emphasis that China must reduce tensions on the Korean Peninsula, uphold international standards and rules of the road to include trade, protection of the environment, human rights, etc.
- Continue to seek peace in the Middle East and in particular, between Israel and Palestine.
- Promote global prosperity and development by addressing the global financial crisis, promoting free and fair trade, advancing global development, combating HIV/AIDS and other diseases, ensure food security, and responding to human rights violations.
- Maintain a strong military.[48]

As evidenced in their platforms, both political parties articulate their bottom-line issues and the policy responses they would initiate to address those issues.

American Third Party Movements

By definition, a **third party** is "usually composed of independents and dissidents from the major parties in a two-party system that typically is based on a protest movement and that may rally sufficient voter support to affect the outcome of a state or national election."[49] The entrenched two-party system does not openly embrace the existence of third parties. The American political scene has seen these movements spring up from time to time, but they simply do not survive in the long term for several reasons. First, state legislative houses are controlled by one or both of the two major parties. These bodies have enacted state laws that make it extremely difficult for third party and independent candidates to even secure a place on the ballot. For example, Carole Keeton Strayhorn, a Republican officeholder in Texas, wanted to run against incumbent Republican governor Rick Perry. As an independent candidate, she had to obtain thousands of signatures of registered voters who did not already have a party affiliation. Second, third party movements oftentimes are formed around a specific individual who lacks the political clout within one of the two parties to even secure a nomination for an elective office. For example, Ross Perot, a billionaire businessman decided to make a run for the White House. He did not have any political experience, never held an elective office, nor did he have any long-lasting ties to either the Democratic or Republican Party. He opted to form his own political party—the Reform Party. He placed on all fifty state ballots but, obviously, did not win the election. Consequently, the Reform Party no longer exists. Third, the positions taken by third party movements are usually incorporated into either the Republican or Democratic Party. Ralph Nader usually runs for the White House as a member of the Green Party, a pro-environment group. Yet, the Democratic Party already has strong positions and a proven track record of advocacy for environmental issues. The Democratic Party definitely has more clout and more presence at the ballot box than the Green Party. Fourth, third party candidates simply cannot raise the money needed to launch a competitive election for any national office. Federal campaign finance laws give campaign funds to candidates from the two major parties after they have secured their party's nomination. Third party candidates must secure a certain percentage of the popular vote to even qualify for funding. They receive their public money after the election. Table I lists the various third party movements that have arisen on the national scene

Factions Within the American Party Organization

The success and longevity of any major political party depends on how the party leadership handles various factions under the party's wide umbrella. A **faction** is "a political group or clique that functions within a larger group, such as a government, party or organization."[50] In his *Federalist #14*, James Madison warned about the danger factions posed to national unity. In *Federalist #109*, he defined factions as "a number of citizens, whether amounting to a majority or a minority of the whole, who are united and actuated by some common impulse of passion or of interest, adverse to the rights of other citizens, or to the permanent and aggregated interests of the community."[51] Both the Democratic and Republican Parties have encountered factional interests who challenge the party's leadership. Factions within these parties are oftentimes sanctioned groups known as caucuses. For example, the Hispanic Caucus of the Democratic Party helps the party leadership tackle such issues as immigration reform and voter registration to ensure that these issues are included into the party's platform and issue positions. Factions can be beneficial by keeping the party in touch with all of its various diverse members. However, a faction can prove just as Madison stressed, detrimental to survival of the political party. In determining the course of action to take with internal factions, party leadership members must:

> Consider the element of discontinuity in factionalism. . . . The groups lack continuity in name—as exists under a party system—and they also lack continuity in the make-up of their inner core of professional politicians or leaders. Naturally, they also lack continuity in voter support that, under the two-party conditions, provides a relatively stable following of voters for each party's candidates whoever they may be. . . . Loose factions lack the collective spirit of party organization, which at its best imposes a sense of duty and imparts a spirit of responsibility to the inner core of leaders of the organization.[52]

Table I   **Third Parties in American Politics**

Name of the Party	Year	Major Issue Positions and Outcome
American Independent Party	1968	Strict adherence to Constitution; opposed liberalism; free trade; pro-life positions; strong support of 2nd Amendment; founded by George Wallace; ran Wallace for president in 1968; national presence ended with attempted assassination of Wallace.
Anti-Mason Party	1830s	Nation's original third party. Promote abolition of secret organizations such as the Masons. Ran William Wirt for president. Party Dissolved.
Constitutional Union	1860	Defended Constitution and unity of the federal government. Unsuccessfully ran John Bell for presidency.
Free Soil Party	1848	Opposed extension of slavery into the territories; Supported national internal improvement programs, moderate tariffs and enactment of homestead laws. Unsuccessfully ran Martin Van Buren for president. Party dissolved. Party Issues incorporated into Republican Party.
Know-Nothing Party	1840s	Anti-immigration; prohibit Catholics and foreign-born from holding elective office; English as the official language. Changed its name to the American Party. Its platform issues were adopted by the Republican Party. Party dissolved.
Libertarian Party	1972	Promote laws protecting individual rights; anticensorship; protection of privacy; promote the right to bear arms; all-voluntary military; anti-government involvement in economy; abolition of all tariffs; end all social/welfare programs; support repeal of compulsory education. Party active in state and local elections.
Populist Party	1891	Silver rather than gold standard for American currency; deny property ownership to aliens; confiscation of public lands given to railroads; balanced budgets; free public education; reform the prison system; worker protection laws; eight-hour work day; abolishing the Electoral College. Ran James Weaver for president in 1892 and Terry Roosevelt in 1912. Issues adopted by the Democrats and Roosevelt returned to the Republican Party. Party dissolved.
Progressive Party	1912	Founded by Theodore Roosevelt. Promote direct primaries for nomination of state and national offices; abolish Electoral College; prohibit child labor; worker benefits such as higher wages and workers compensation; tariffs against foreign-made products; protect the environment, Unsuccessfully ran Roosevelt for president. Party dissolved. Roosevelt returned to Republican Party.

Socialist Party	1912	Support collective ownership of transportation and communication and all other large industries; shorter workday for all workers; absolute freedom of speech; abolition of monopoly ownerships; equal suffrage for men and women; abolish Electoral College; end judicial review; abolish all federal courts; call convention for revision of the constitution. Ran Eugene V. Debbs in 1912 for presidency. Party still active.
Southern Democratic Party	1860	Support right of states to withdraw from the union; institution of slavery; implementation and enforcement of state fugitive slave laws. Unsuccessfully ran John C. Breckinridge for president. Party dissolved.
States Rights Democratic Party	1948	Founded by Sen. Strom Thurmond; promote states' rights; anti-civil rights and anti-segregation position; ran Strom Thurmond for president. Party dissolved.
The Grange	1867	Advocated for farmers and ranchers for regulatory action against railroads, banks and insurance companies. Declined in the 1890s as the Farmers Alliance adopted their issues. The Alliance in turn also advocated for the poor, improvements in education, and prohibition of alcoholic beverages. Its platform issues were adopted by the Democratic party. Party dissolved.
The Green Party	1996	Predominately pro-environment; support peace and disarmament of nuclear weapons; support independence for Puerto Rico; support expansion and protection of civil rights; support single-payer health care; reform of prison and justice system. Jill Stein and Cheri Honkala ran respectively for president and vice president in 2012; more successful at winning state elections in selective states. Platform issues similar to those of the Democratic Party
The Reform Party	1995	Supports fiscal responsibility and accountability; fair taxation politics; "American first" position; affordable and accessible healthcare based on decisions between doctor and patience; energy independence. Founded by Ross Perot. Ran Perot for president. Active in state elections in selective states.
Whig Party	1834	Opposed Andrew Jackson's policies; promoted industrial and business interests in Northeast; promoted higher tariffs and subsidies for shipping; establishing relations with China and Japan; party dissolved; 1848 Millard Fillmore elected vice president as Whig candidate who became president with death of Taylor but lost White House in 1856; issues incorporated into Republican Party.

Currently, the Tea Party Movement is a faction operating within the Republican Party. The Tea Party could not survive on its own as a viable and long lasting third party movement. Consequently, the membership believes that their issue positions fit under the conservative umbrella of the Republican Party. The preamble to their platform states "the Tea Party is an all-inclusive American grassroots movement with the belief that everyone is created equal and deserves an equal opportunity to thrive in these United States."[53] Major positions include elimination of the national debt through fiscally conservative policies at all levels of government, elimination of deficit spending, protection of free markets, adherence to the Constitution, promotion of civic responsibility, reduction of the overall size of government, and maintenance of local independence. Several of Tea Party members have been elected under the Republican banner to both the U.S. House and Senate as well as to several state legislative positions. Tea Party members are adamant about their issues in drastically eliminating and hopefully abolishing tax programs such as the income tax, and reducing the federal budget by eliminating all government-sponsored social programs such as food stamps, Medicaid, etc. They simply do not want to compromise on their issue positions. This stance has put them at odds with the House Republican leadership. Members of each respective political party in these legislative houses agree to disagree with each other but ultimately when they do reach a consensus on any political directive it is through discussion, debate, and compromise. The unwillingness of the Tea Party faction to accept compromise has led to very public displays of frustrating confrontations within the Republican Party. Speaker of the House John Boehner (R-Ohio) has publically voiced his displeasure with the group, and to date has not been able to foster a good relationship with them.

Organizational Structure of American Political Parties

Usually one thinks that political parties are structured like the modern corporation with the top of hierarchy controlling the entire structure. The top of the structure is supposedly controlled by the national party organization with the national chairperson and the national committee charged with overseeing the day-to-day operation of the national organization and establishing policy and procedures for state, county and local party units. The lowest rung of the party ladder is reserved for the local precincts also known in several states as the wards. Local precincts or wards are managed through a chairperson elected by their own precinct party members. This top to down structure implies that the parties operate under a centralized structure with the national committee controlling all party activities with state and local organizations having little or no autonomy. In practice, however, the pyramid is inverted because the most important and essential component of any political party is the local precinct, the lowest rung of the party ladder. In practice, American political parties are decentralized organizations. "Decentralization of power is by all odds the most important single characteristic of the American major party; more than anything else this trait distinguishes it from all others. Indeed once this truth is understood, nearly everything else about American parties is greatly illuminated. . . The American major party is, to repeat the definition, a loose confederation of state and local bosses for limited purposes."[54] Basically, the national party organization focuses once every four years on the presidential election and rarely gets directly involved in congressional races and even less so in state gubernatorial and legislative contests. The lack of a tight cohesive organizational relationship between the various levels of the nation's two

Chapter Five

...tical parties can best be described as **stratarchy**, whereby each level acts independently of ...[55] A closer look at the duties and responsibilities assigned to each level within the party ...es an insight into its internal operations.

The National Party Organization

Perhaps the most prestigious assignment for any local party member is a seat on the Democratic National Committee (DNC) or the Republican National Committee (RNC). Initially the membership of each party's core leadership team consisted of just the national chairperson elected from the entire party membership, and one man and one woman from each of the fifty states. Today, the membership of the RNC National Committee is approximately 150 while the DNC has over 300 committee members. The DNC places two (one man and one woman from each state) as well as "two hundred additional members allocated to the states on the same basis as delegates are apportioned to the national convention; and a number of delegates representing such organizations as the Democratic Governors' Conference, the U.S. Congress, the National Finance Council, the Conference of Democratic Mayors, the National Federation of Democratic Women, the Democratic County Officials Conference, the State Legislative Leader's Caucus, and the Young Democrats of America."[56] Obviously, both political parties use these plum positions on their national committees to recognize those who have either devoted a considerable amount of personal time to the party's activities or have donated considerable campaign contributions to both the parties and their candidates. Although the national committees officially elect their respective chairpersons, the selection is actually made by the president whose party controls the White House. The 2016 Democratic National Convention will be to a large extent controlled by President Obama's team, even though Obama cannot seek a third term. For the party out of power, the national committee does indeed select its national chairperson. Although the primary duty of the national chairperson is to be the chief fundraiser, other responsibilities include recruiting candidates, conducting campaign strategy training programs for candidates and their campaign staffers, conducting issue and voter research, and when called upon, assisting their respective party's presidential candidate's campaign efforts.

Organizational Chart

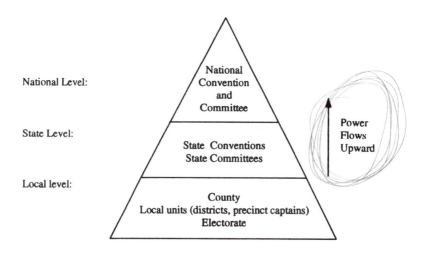

Increasing the membership of the national committee oftentimes compromises the effectiveness of the body. Meeting infrequently, the primary responsibilities of these committees are confined to policy making, selecting the site of their respective national conventions, and establishing the criteria for the selection of convention delegates. While both political parties have millions of either direct card-carrying members and/or those who periodically attach themselves to one of the parties, it is ironic that the internal operations of these large organizations are actually run by a few high ranking party members or an oligarchy. As seen in interest groups as well as political parties, the **Iron Law of Oligarchy** underscores that "in every organization, whether it be a political party, a professional union, or any other association of the kind, the aristocratic tendency manifests itself very clearly. The mechanism of the organization, while conferring a solidity of structure, induces serious changes in the organized mass, completely inverting the respective position of the leaders and the led. As a result of organization, every party or professional union becomes divided into a minority of directors and a majority of the directed."[57]

Furthermore, there is a serious "disconnect" between the national committee and the party membership as well as a lack of coordination and cooperation between the national organization and state and local party units. National organizations rarely get involved in state and local elections unless the candidate's election fortune has or could have national implications. For example, in 2006 a special election was held for the redrawn 23rd U.S. Congressional district. This election pitted incumbent Congressman Henry Bonilla (R-Texas) against former Congressman Ciro Rodriguez (D-Texas). Initially, Bonilla had a large lead over six other candidates including Rodriguez. As the polls tightened, the DNC took an interest in the election. The DNC contributed funds to the Rodriguez campaign and President Bill Clinton made campaign appearances on behalf of Rodriguez. On election night, Rodriguez won! National party organizations have taken a back seat as the election campaign itself has shifted elections from party-centered to candidate-centered events. Initially political parties took the center stage in planning the campaign strategy from start to finish. Today, the primary responsibility of the campaign falls upon each individual candidate who must now raise his/her own money, hire their own campaign staff, and plot for themselves the course of their campaigns from the primaries to the general elections.

The major event for these national committees is indeed their national conventions held once every four years. The convention is composed of delegates from all fifty states and U.S. territories who meet to nominate their candidates for both president and vice president, as well as to draft and approve their national party platform. One of the most important committees, the **platform committee**'s job is to craft a document that embraces the overall political philosophy of the party while at the same time, incorporates into the document the important issue positions and concerns gathered during each state's party convention, which, in turn, originated in part at the district convention attended by representatives from each precinct. A **platform** is "a statement of principles and objectives espoused by a party or a candidate that is used during a campaign to win support from voters."[58] Once officially nominated, it is the responsibility of the party's candidates to incorporate party platform issues into his/her campaign effort. Once elected, it is the responsibility of the party's candidates, especially the president, to ensure his/her policy choices and decisions mirror in part the positions articulated in the party platform. President Dwight D. Eisenhower once commented that "there may be some cynics who think that a Platform is just a list of platitudes to lure the naïve voter—a sort of façade behind which candidates sneak into power and then do as they please. I am f those."⁵⁹ Once officially adopted at the national convention, state party organizations their own issue concerns into the nation party's overall philosophy. Resolutions made ventions held in off-presidential years are entertained at the next national convention.

A major event for both national conventions is the highly anticipated **keynote address** delivered by each party's presidential nominee. While not covering these conventions from gavel to gavel, all of the media networks televise or record this speech. The pre-speech media hype focuses on the verbiage of the speech, how well it is anticipated that the nominee will deliver the speech, and how well the audience will react to the speech. In the text of the speeches, the nominees officially accept their party's nomination and layouts his/her own agenda for the upcoming general election. The speech will be interrupted numerous times with clapping and cheering. At the end of speech, the candidate, his/her family members, elected officials and key members of the national committee gather together to watch the balloons drop, the posters wave, the confetti fly, and the convention members cheer on their candidate for the November election. This is prime time television exposure for both the party and its candidates.

However, the media usually devotes no coverage to the internal wheeling and dealing between the national committee members, state party leadership and the candidates. For example, the official seating of the convention's delegates falls upon the shoulders of the **credentials committee** who prior to the convention set the process for certifying a state's official delegation. Each state's party organization sends both officially elected pledged and unpledged delegates. **Pledged delegates** are chosen specifically to cast their vote for a particular candidate. Each state party organization has different criteria as to whether a delegate is pledged throughout the presidential and vice presidential selection or released to vote their own preferences after a certain number of ballots. **Unpledged** or **independent delegates** are not required to cast their votes as their state parties wish, regardless of the number of ballots. Every national party convention has had its credentialing issues. During the 2008 presidential election convention cycle, the DNC debated whether to credential delegates from several states whose state organizations refused to follow the DNC's primary election timeline and subsequently moved their own state primaries from Super Tuesday to another date. If not credentialed, these state delegates would not have been officially admitted into the convention nor would they be able to cast votes for presidential and vice presidential nominees. In the end, the questionable state delegations were properly credentialed and did vote. At times, the United States Supreme Court has been tasked with negotiating party credentialing issues. In 1891, for example, the Court ruled in ***Democratic Party v Lafollette*** that a state's party leadership could not force the DNC's credentials committee to accept a delegation that was selected in clear violation of DNC rules. In ***Cousins v Wigoda* (1975)**, the Court ruled that only the credentials committee of a national political party has the authority to settle credential disputes between rival state delegations.

Both the DNC and RNC have faced criticisms that their traditional ways of "doing business" are more exclusive than inclusive and not in touch with their voting bases. In other words, the 'good ole boy' wheeling and dealing between a few well-entrenched elites actually control the party organization from top to bottom, leaving the rank-and-file party membership to believe that their parties only needed them to cast their votes on election day for the party's slate of candidates. Particularly, for the Democrats, the 1968 national convention was a tragic eye-opening internationally covered event. Amid the anti-war protests against Vietnam and the rising civil rights and feminist movements, the DNC selected Chicago, Illinois as the site for the national convention. Despite

Kay Bailey Hutchison (R-TX) was one of the keynote speakers at the 2000 Republican National Convention. Convention speeches lavish praise and extol the virtues of the candidate. Prominent party leaders usually make an appearance to solidify party support.
Photo credit:
Sen. Hutchison's website,
http://www.hutchison.senate.gov/

assurances from Chicago officials that no violence outside of the convention center would occur, convention security forces harassed, beat, tear-gassed, and arrested scores of protesters outside of the facility. Meanwhile, on the convention floor, angry delegates lashed out at DNC officials for their backdoor politicking that many believed had predetermined the outcome of platform issues and the selection of candidates. The convention was anything but peaceful, and many left with ill feelings about the future of the Democratic Party. DNC Chairperson Fred Harris responded to the outcries by appointing Senator George McGovern to head a special investigation into DNC practices. Filed in 1971, the McGovern Commission recommended a return to grassroots politics to broaden the delegate pool, and the inclusion of minorities and women. The report recommended that state party officials could no longer demand that their delegates nominate and actually vote for their "favorite son or daughter" candidates who in the end would not even have a chance to win the prized presidential or vice presidential nomination. Also, the report recommended that at least 75 percent of a state's delegation had to be chosen at their state conventions specifically from their congressional districts or even smaller units such as districts or precincts. The RNC also reexamined their convention format and delegate selection processes. Since then both parties have continued efforts to ensure that their delegation selection process does include a broad representation reflective of the entire party membership with particular emphasis on minorities, women, and younger party supporters.

The State Party Organizations

The U.S. Constitution makes no mention of either interest groups or political parties and no subsequent amendments recognize their existence, nor detail any responsibilities and operational procedures that could guide them. The Framers did not ignore that sooner or later both interest groups and political parties would develop. They simply left it up to the states through their individual legislative houses to set the overall ground rules for the establishment and operation of both interest groups and political parties as well as establishing election procedures and rules pertinent to their individual states. Consequently, each state has its own election code, methods of selecting their slates of electors for the Electoral College, types of ballots, candidate qualifications, election certification, criteria for third party or independent candidates to gain a position on the ballot, etc. For example, in Texas the elections for statewide offices are held in non-presidential election years. Many states, however, use the presidential election cycle to select all statewide, county and local officeholders.

Usually, both political parties have an elected or appointed state executive committee composed of a chairperson, vice chairperson, and other members. For the party in power of the governorship, the state chairperson is basically a ceremonial position since the governor serves as the official head or his/her political party. The basic functions of any state executive committee include canvassing state-wide election results, certifying a candidate's qualifications for office in primary and general elections, receiving candidate filing forms, in some states collecting candidate filing fees, overseeing the site location and coordinating the upcoming state convention, establishing the selection process for the state credentials and platform committees, and setting the guidelines for the selection of delegates for the national party conventions. The state chairperson is the party's "cheerleader" in that he or she promotes party unity and party platform issues at both the county and precinct levels and encourages all party leadership to continue their grassroots efforts by encouraging people to register and vote on election day, raising money for candidates and working within the framework of both the state and national party organizations. Many state legislative houses have given state party organizations the authority to oversee and, in some instances, to take punitive sanctions against local party units who violate party rules and practices.

County/District Organizations

The county party leadership is vested in an executive committee composed of all the precinct chairs for that particular county. In larger counties, state laws may divide it into proportionately equal districts. Usually, the county chairpersons are popularly elected to either two- or four-year terms of office. County/district organizations are primarily responsible for preparing the election ballot, receiving filing forms for countywide elective positions, collecting the appropriate filing fees, and determining the ballot order for the candidates. The ballot order can be an alphabetical listing by office or a random drawing of numbers with the lowest number getting the top of the ballot position. The county/district is also responsible for canvassing the returns for the primary elections and arranging for the county/district conventions.

Precincts

The workhorse of these two major political parties is the **election precinct** or **precinct**. In some states, precincts are called **wards**. The chairperson for precincts is either selected by placement on the primary ballot or nominated and elected from the floor at the precinct convention. Normally held the evening of the party primary elections, precinct conventions are open to all individuals who voted in their party's primary elections. The primary duties of the precinct chair include mobilization of voter turnout, selecting election judges and poll watchers for the primary and general elections, arranging for the precinct convention, and serving on the county executive team.

In every way, the precinct is the core of a party's grassroots political presence. It is the primary duty of the precinct chairperson to canvass the residents within his/her precinct or ward and to separate the party die-hards from those vacillating between party loyalties and those who are not even registered to vote. It is the chairperson who coordinates voter registration drives, a who need mail-in ballots and arranges rides to the polls on election days. Chairperson coffees in their homes for candidates running on the lower-end of the ballot so the can establish a physical presence within the community and, hopefully, encourage the atten a campaign contribution into the jar. Chairpersons oftentimes arrange for candidate forums and debates. It is also the chairperson who gathers the volunteers to distribute campaign literature, post signs, etc. One could call the precinct or ward chairperson the cheerleader-in-chief for the party.

CONCLUSIONS

In *Democracy in America*, Alexis de Tocqueville concluded that the primary goal of American political parties is to gather once every four years to elect a president. During the election, political parties take center stage. However, once the election has come and gone, the parties fade into the shadows only to reemerge four-years later.

> Moreover, in the United States as elsewhere, parties feel the need to rally around one man in order more easily to make themselves understood by the crowd. Generally, therefore, they use the Presidential candidate's name as a symbol; in him they personify their theories. Hence the parties have a great interest in winning the election, not so much in order to make their doctrines triumph by the President-elect's help, as to show, by his election, that their doctrines have gained a majority.
>
> Long before the appointed day arrives, the election becomes the greatest, and one might say the only, affair occupying men's minds. At this time, the factions redouble their ardor; then every forced passion that imagination can create in a happy and peaceful country spreads excitement in broad daylight.
>
> The President, for his part, is absorbed in the task of defending himself. He no longer rules in the interest of the state, but in that of his own reelection; he prostrates himself before the majority, and often, instead of resisting their passions as duty requires, he hastens to anticipate their caprices.
>
> As the election draw near, intrigues grow more active and agitation is more lively and widespread. The citizens divide up into several camps, each of which takes its name from its candidate. The whole nation gets into a feverish state, the election is the daily theme of comment in the newspapers and private conversation, the object is every action and the subject of every thought, and the sole interest for the moment.
>
> It is true that as soon as fortune has pronounced, the ardor is dissipated, everything calms down, and the river which momentarily overflowed its banks falls back to its bed. But was it not astonishing that such a storm could have arisen?[60]

De Tocqueville's observations of American political parties in action in the 1800s are quite similar to what we witness every four years. The media covers the highlights of the national convention. The cameras are focused on the candidates making their speeches, the confetti and the balloons falling from the ceilings, etc. Once the convention lights are turned off, the candidates abandon their respective parties as they hit the campaign road. Candidates speak about what they would do if elected. Both the candidates and the media have marginalized the importance of political parties in the American electoral and governing process. Nightly news reports center on what the candidate did today, who he/she spoke to, and what they said. Rarely are the activities of the political parties mentioned. But, political parties wield their powerful influence on the public policy process behind "closed doors" for they are the driving force behind the advocacy of issues, the development of the responses, and the electability of candidates to public office. The candidates need their respective political parties to help them get elected, and once in office, they need the party to remind their fellow elected officials that one's legislative successes or failures are everyone's successes or failures! As James K. Polk lamented "we have a country as well as party to obey."[61]

CHAPTER NOTES

[1] *A Treasury of Presidential Quotations*, Caroline Thomas Harnsberger, ed., (Chicago, Illinois: Follett Publishing Company, 1964), 235.
[2] Ibid., 235-236.
[3] Ibid., 236.
[4] Ibid., 238.
[5] George Sabine, *A History of Political Theory*, 3rd ed., (New York, New York: Holt, Reinhart, Winston, Inc., 1961), 611.
[6] William Goodman, *The Two-Party System in the United States*, 3rd ed., (Princeton, New Jersey: D. Van Nostrand Company, Inc., 1964), 6.
[7] Susan Welch, John Gruhl, Michael Steinman, John Comer and Susan M. Rigdon, *American Government*, 5th ed., (Minneapolis/St. Paul, Wisconsin: West Publishing Company, 1994), 146.
[8] Thomas W. Madron and Carl P. Chelf, *Political Parties in the United States*, (Boston, Massachusetts: Holbrook Press, 1974), 302-303.
[9] V. O. Key, Jr., *Politics, Parties, and Pressure Groups*, 4th ed., (New York, New York: Thomas Y. Crowell Company, 1958), 220.
[10] Jack C. Plano and Milton Greenberg, *The American Political Dictionary*, 10th ed., (Orlando, Florida: Harcourt Brace and Company, 1997), 88.
[11] Gabriel A. Almond, G. Bingham Powell, Jr., Kaare Strom and Russell Dalton, *Comparative Politics Today: A World View*, 8th ed., (New York, New York: Pearson Longman, 2004), 90.
[12] Ibid.
[13] Ibid., 92.
[14] *The HarperCollins Dictionary of American Government and Politics*, Jay M. Shafritz, ed., (New York, New York: HarperCollins Publishers, 1992), 286.
[15] Roger Scruton, *A Dictionary of Political Thought*, (New York, New York: Harper & Row Publishers, 1982), 90.
[16] Plano and Greenberg, 13.
[17] *A Treasury of Presidential Quotations*, 42.
[18] George Klosko, *History of Political Theory: An Introduction*, Vol. 2: Modern Political Theory, (Belmont, California: Wadsworth Group/Thomson Learning, 1995), 266-267.
[19] Ian Adams and R. W. Dyson, *Fifty Major Political Thinkers*, (New York, New York: Routledge, 2003), 90-91.
[20] *The HarperCollins Dictionary of American Government and Politics*, 139.
[21] Plano and Greenberg, 5.
[22] Scruton, 302.
[23] *The HarperCollins Dictionary of American Government and Politics*, 335.
[24] Klosko, 200.
[25] Ibid.
[26] Plano and Greenberg, 14.
[27] Adams and Dyson, 63.
[28] Klosko, 111.
[29] Scruton, 271.

[30] http://www/presidency.ucsb.edu
[31] Plano and Greenberg, 26.
[32] Ibid., 5.
[33] Ibid., 2
[34] Ibid.
[35] Frank J. Sorauf, *Political Parties in America*, (Boston, Massachusetts: Little Brown and Company, 1968), 381.
[36] Ibid., 380.
[37] *A Treasury of Presidential Quotations*, 239.
[38] Charles A. Beard and Mary R. Bread, *A Basic History of the United States*, 1st ed., (Philadelphia, Pennsylvania: The Blakeston Company, 1944), 165.
[39] Ibid., 166.
[40] Harry K. Carman, Harold C. Syrett and Bernard W. Wishy, *A History of the American People*, Vol. 1 to 1877, 3rd ed., (New York, New York: Alfred A. Knopf, 1967), 271.
[41] James MacGregor Burns, *The Deadlock of Democracy: Four Party Politics in America*, 2nd ed., (Englewood Cliffs, New Jersey: Prentice-Hall, Inc., 1967), 32-33.
[42] *The Rise of Conservatism in American, 1945-2000: A Brief History with Documents*, Ronald Story and Bruce Laurie, ed., (Boston, Massachusetts: Bedford/St. Martin's: 2008), 1.
[43] Ibid.
[44] http://www.gobconvention2012.com
[45] Ibid.
[46] http://www.democrats.org
[47] Ibid.
[48] Ibid.
[49] *The HarperCollins Dictionary of American Government and Politics*, 417.
[50] Plano and Greenberg, 88.
[51] Sorauf, 18-19.
[52] Ibid.
[53] http://www.teaparty-platform.com
[54] Sorauf, 108.
[55] L. Sandy Maisel, *Parties and Elections in America: The Electoral Process*, 2nd ed., (New York, New York: McGraw-Hill, Inc., 1993), 54.
[56] William J. Keefe and Marc K. Hetherington, *Parties, Politics and Public Policy in America*, 9th ed., (Washington, D.C.: CQ Press, 2003), 16.
[57] *The HarperCollins Dictionary of America Government and Politics*, 305.
[58] Plano and Greenberg, 95.
[59] *A Treasury of Presidential Quotations*, 244.
[60] Alexis de Tocqueville, *Democracy in America*, translated by Gorge Lawrence, J. P. Mayer, eds., (Garden City, New York: Doubleday & Company, Inc., 1969), 135.
[61] *Treasury of Presidential Quotations*, 236.

SUGGESTED READINGS

Key, V.O., Jr., *Politics, Parties and Pressure Groups*, 4th ed., New York, New York: Thomas Y. Crowell, Company, 1958.

Klosko, George, *History of Political Theory: An Introduction*, Vol. 2: Modern Political Theory, Belmont, California: Wadsworth Group/Thomson Learning, 1995.

Maisel, L. Sandy, *Parties and Elections in America: The Electoral Process*, 2nd, ed., New York, New York: McGraw-Hill, Inc., 1993.

Sorauf, Frank J., *Political Parties in America*, Boston, Mass.: Little Brown and Company, 1968.

Chapter Six

CAMPAIGNS AND ELECTIONS

To an extent not seen in the last one hundred years, corporations and wealthy investors, with a clear economic self-interest in the election outcome, poured money into the campaigns of 2012. This deluge of big money is the result of two game-changing events. The first is the Supreme Court's 5-4 decision in *Citizens United vs. Federal Election Commission,* which overturned provisions of the McCain-Feingold campaign finance act that had prohibited corporations and unions from making expenditures to influence the outcome of electoral contests. The other game changer is the amending of the tax code to allow creation of 501(c) political action committees to which donors can contribute anonymously. The tax exception is intended to go to organizations that make less than half of their expenditures for political purposes. Many of these groups claim that their funds are going to "educational" purposes, an umbrella term that includes many activities that are clearly political in design and intent.

While the first game changer, the January 2010 *Citizens United* Supreme Court decision, left intact the 103-year-old ban on direct donations by corporations to candidates, it overturned a 1947 law and two earlier high court rulings that barred corporations and unions from spending money directly from their treasuries on ads that advocate electing or defeating candidates for president or Congress, but that are produced independently and not coordinated with a candidate's campaign. The decision also overturned a provision in the McCain-Feingold Act that since 2002 had barred issue-oriented ads paid for by unions or corporations 30 days before a primary and 60 days before a general election. What the Court did leave intact is the McCain-Feingold provision that anyone spending money on political ads must disclose the names of contributors. With this decision, the Supreme Court sent a wave of corporate and union money flooding into the 2012 campaign, but it did so with the promise that the public would know, almost instantly, who was paying for them. The Internet held the promise of such prompt disclosure, thereby enabling the electorate to make informed decisions. What the high court did not foresee was the second campaign game changer underway: new loopholes in tax laws that would not only further allow corporations and the wealthy to spend huge sums on campaign ads but would also allow them to avoid the full disclosure on which the Supreme Court was counting.

Perhaps the most opaque political players since pre-Watergate days of anonymous cash contributions to candidates are a group of tax-exempt non-profit organizations organized under 501(c) of the tax code. Depending on the type of group, the various 501(c) organizations have different limitations on the amount of political activity in which they may participate. The focus in the election cycle of 2010 has been on 501(c)(4) social welfare organizations, 501(c)(5) labor organizations, and 501(c)(6) trade associations and chambers of commerce. All three are able to engage in political activities as long as these activities are not their "primary purpose." At the same time, donors to these groups need not be disclosed. Consequently, 501(c) organizations may engage in political campaigns on behalf of or in opposition to candidates for public office and do an unlimited amount of lobbying as long as such activities do not constitute the organization's primary activity. In the 2012 election, this meant that these groups could spend millions of dollars on campaign ads without having their name disclosed.

In 2012, special interest money continued to flow even after the election. Though President Barack Obama had directed his Presidential Inaugural Committee to decline donations from lobbyists, the inaugural festivities on Monday, January 21, the third anniversary of the *Citizens United* decision, were bankrolled by several of the nation's most powerful corporate lobbying forces, which collectively spent at least $158.6 million on lobbying since the president first took office. Chief among corporate inaugural donors were: AT&T Inc., Microsoft Corp., energy giant Southern Company, biotechnology firm Genentech, and health plan manager Centene Corp. Together, more than 300 registered lobbyists worked on the five companies' behalf to influence legislation and government policy, according to their federal filings covering January through September 2012.[1]

THE CHANGING FACE OF AMERICAN CAMPAIGNS AND ELECTIONS

There is perhaps no area of American politics that has undergone as much change as the electoral system. In 1789, George Washington was elected unanimously by the electoral college. There were no political parties, and the mass media consisted of only a few newspapers with limited readership. The whole concept of campaigning would be largely foreign in such a system in which the president would be selected indirectly by electoral college delegates themselves indirectly selected by their various state legislatures. Senators, too, were selected by these state legislatures. Only members of the House of Representatives would be directly elected and then only by white men, and in twelve states only white men with property.

Today, candidates not only campaign for over 450,000 elected positions at the local, state, and national levels, they campaign, at least in most states, for their party's nomination for these offices. It is not uncommon for campaigns to run over a year or longer.

After their creation at the turn of the nineteenth century, political parties conducted all phases of the campaigns for office. They nominated their candidates; they funded the campaigns; and the parties were the principal communications link between the candidates and the voters. The parties held campaign rallies and worked behind the scenes to line-up support in the big urban centers of

Tea Party gathering in Freedom Plaza (just off the Mall) Washington D.C. March 15, 2010. Credit: RTNews

America. On election day, it was the party precinct workers who walked door-to-door getting out the vote. Party competition appears to have been the key in stimulating voter turnout. Competition between alternative parties gave citizens an incentive to vote and politicians an incentive to reach them and get their vote.[2] It was the competitive organizing activities of the Jeffersonian Republicans and the Federalists that first led to the democratic impulse to extend the franchise and the number of offices directly elected.

How different campaigns are run today! Beginning with the anti-party reforms of the Progressive Era, the parties' roles in campaigns have been greatly diminished. The civil service, direct primary, and nonpartisan elections have transformed the political landscape. Candidates are now nominated by voters casting ballots in primary elections in forty-two states. To win public support, candidates must turn to high-tech politics. Candidates need to be able to construct a meaningful message and take it to the public. Candidates pay enormous sums of money to conduct focus groups and public opinion polls to find out what issues most concern the American public. Once they get their message, the candidates need to communicate it to the most people at the least cost. Enter the mass media. Party organizations working door-to-door are simply no match for the slick and sophisticated technology of political advertisements, or for that matter a thirty-second soundbite on the evening news. The nomination secured, the candidate then moves on to the general election, where even more voters are involved and the mass media, therefore, all the more important.

All of this modern campaigning costs money and large amounts of it. A typical day on the presidential campaign trail involves moving more than 100 people, including the candidate, his staff, dozens of reporters, and security through stops in as many as six states per day. Working behind the scenes, the campaigns create virtual traveling towns, setting up hotel rooms, banquet halls, lighting, food, telephone lines, and plane flights, every day, seven days a week. The costs add up quickly. Renting a Boeing 727 goes for about $8,000 an hour. Setting up the lights at an event can cost as much as $25,000. When a campaign is in full swing, it is not unheard of to spend more than $200,000 a day. The political parties, while still important in fund-raising, cannot possibly raise all the money needed for the high-tech politics of polling, media events, and advertising so central to modern campaigns. Candidates today are entrepreneurs who increasingly have turned to the private sector for the resources necessary to run an effective campaign and win. Such resources may come from the candidate's own wealth, interest groups, corporations, or other individual donors. The way in which we finance campaigns places the candidate in a more central role. On election day, for most offices, a party label stands beside the candidate's name. But this label disguises the great number of changes that have fundamentally altered the electoral system of the United States, transforming it from a party-based to a candidate and media-centered system.

NOMINATING THE CANDIDATES

Historical Background

When the Constitution was being written, it was assumed by the framers that George Washington would be selected to be the first president of the new United States. In addition, it was largely assumed that the supporters of the new Constitution, the Federalists as they were called, would win most of the seats in the House and Senate, for to be anything other than Federalist was to be a traitor to the new government. Beyond these minimal assumptions, little else was known. The Constitution is completely silent on the subject of elections, choosing to leave it to each state to organize and control the elections. There was little thought given to how the nomination of future candidates would be conducted.

George Washington, upon becoming president, appointed Alexander Hamilton as Secretary of the Treasury and Thomas Jefferson as Secretary of State. Because Hamilton and Jefferson held divergent views on everything from foreign policy to a national bank to internal improvements, Jefferson soon quit the cabinet and began to organize the first political party, the Jeffersonian Republicans. Jefferson based his party in Congress, drawing together members who shared his political viewpoint. Hamilton, similarly, had his group of devotees in the House and Senate.

With the differences in political ideas apparent, the beginnings of party organization underway, democratic forces running strong, and Washington expressing no desire to seek a third term, the question soon arose how each party would nominate a candidate for the highest office of the presidency. By 1800, both the Federalists under Hamilton and the Republicans under Jefferson had established congressional caucuses that would nominate their party's candidate. These congressional caucuses were made up of men in the House and Senate sharing either the Federalist or Republican views.

The Caucus System

As the early 1800s progressed and party organization grew stronger and more complex, state party organizations began to develop state caucuses. These state party caucuses chose delegates that would participate in a national party convention, which would then nominate the party's presidential candidate. These national conventions quickly replaced the congressional caucuses as vehicles for nominating candidates. By 1830, the nomination process had become extremely complex with candidates having to be nominated at a variety of geographical levels, from the smallest electoral unit up to the national convention itself. The process began with local meetings, or caucuses, of party supporters to choose delegates to attend a larger subsequent meeting, usually at the county level. Most of the delegates selected in these local caucuses openly supported one of the presidential candidates seeking the party nomination. The process finally culminated in a state party convention with delegates selecting other delegates to the national party convention that will formally nominate the party's presidential candidate.

Today, one or both parties in fourteen states employ caucuses to select delegates to attend presidential nominating conventions. The Iowa caucuses, which are the first held, are similar to those in other states. The campaign in Iowa starts several months before the caucuses are actually held. In the election year 2008, presidential candidates spent over 1,000 days campaigning in Iowa. In early February, the party caucuses are held in private homes, schools, and churches. All who consider themselves party members can attend. They debate and vote on the candidates. The candidates receiving the most votes win delegates to later county and then state conventions. The number of delegates is proportional to the vote that the candidate received at the caucuses. The candidate must get at least 15 percent of the caucus vote in order to receive any delegates.

While Iowa is a small state and chooses only a handful of delegates to the party conventions, it is important as a bell weather of public opinion. The media widely cover these caucuses, looking to identify frontrunners in each of the two major parties. The winners of the Iowa caucuses attract not only media coverage but also the large donations that will allow them to continue to successfully campaign in the other state caucuses and primaries. Iowa is viewed as the state that jump-started Obama's campaign in 2008 and set him on track to win the nomination and the presidency. He ended up winning the Iowa caucus, with John Edwards coming in second and Hillary Clinton a close third.

The Primary System

Because there is no national legislation governing the selection of delegates to a national party convention, and because pressures for greater democracy and participation continued to grow throughout the early twentieth century, some states began to develop an alternative to the state caucus. In 1903, in response to reform movements seeking to end party controlled selection processes, the state of Wisconsin passed the first statewide primary law. Within only ten years, many states followed Wisconsin's lead.

In a presidential primary election, every presidential candidate who chooses to enter the state primary lists a slate of convention delegates who may, at least in some states, have promised to support his candidacy at the party's national nominating convention. Voters in that state then can choose between competing slates of national party convention delegates. In the presidential preferential primary, voters choose delegates who have not agreed to support any particular candidate.

A state primary may be either **open** or **closed**. A primary is considered closed when each voter must declare a choice of party before voting, either when registering or actually at the voting place itself. Party members in these closed primaries may only choose among those candidates on their party's ballot. The primary election is closed, then, to members of other parties. In the open primary, on the other hand, the voter receives ballots for all the parties and chooses which party election they want to vote in, right there in the voting booth on election day. A few states even have **blanket** primaries in which voters may choose candidates for various offices off different party ballots.

Whether their delegates are chosen in state **caucuses** as in Iowa or in primaries as in California, the convention system quickly worked to extend the number of people involved in the electoral process. In addition, the democratic forces that encouraged the creation of the primary system also led to more intense party competition along with efforts to extend the franchise, dropping the property qualifications for voting by 1840. Campaigns became festive affairs. For example, tens of thousands of men and women attended the Whig Party festival in Nashville in 1840. They carried torches, donned uniforms, chanted party slogans, and whipped themselves into a virtual frenzy of party sympathy.

The Entitlement Revolution

In the 1960s, new groups emerged on the scene, seeking greater representation in the American party system. In particular, the Civil Rights Movement began to make demands on the Democratic Party organization for greater representation and recognition. At the 1964 Democratic national convention, the Mississippi Freedom Democratic Party filed a challenge against an all white Mississippi delegation that had been selected through the Mississippi caucus system. The Mississippi Freedom Democratic Party charged that the Mississippi caucus system had systematically excluded blacks from registering to vote and from participating in the state party meetings.

The conflict at the 1964 Democratic national convention resulted in the 1968 Democratic convention requiring state parties to ensure that voters in each state, regardless of race, color, creed, or national origin, be given the fullest opportunity to participate in party affairs. Furthermore, in July 1967, a Special Equal Rights Committee established by the Democratic National Committee adopted unanimously a resolution urging the 1968 convention to replace any state delegation "not broadly representative of the Democrats of the state with a rival representative delegation."[3] This resolution led to the seating of the Mississippi Freedom Democratic Party delegates at the 1968 Democratic national convention held in Chicago.

The call for equal opportunity for black participation was matched by an even wider call for fuller participation on the part of all rank and file voters. It was not only the caucus system that was challenged; reformers began to look at the primary system as well. Before 1968, the primaries were nothing more than what Harry Truman called "eye wash." In fact, the election of 1952 proved Truman right. In that election year, Democratic Senator Kefauver sought to be the Democratic nominee. Kefauver, however, had angered and alienated the Democratic party organization with his Senate investigation of organized crime and subsequent embarrassment of Democrats in Illinois and Florida. Kefauver's standing was much higher with the American public who had watched the televised hearings. It was estimated that an average of 69.7 percent of American television sets in New York were watching the hearings, twice the number who watched the World Series game in October 1950.[4] The hearings were carried by television stations in twenty states.

At least in part because of this media attention, Senator Kefauver was able to win large victories in the primaries. He received over 257 delegates chosen in the various state primary elections; he needed 616 delegates to win the Democratic nomination. At the Democratic convention, after four ballots, Kefauver lost the nomination to Adlai Stevenson who was the choice of the Democratic party organization but who had entered no primaries. Stevenson went on to be solidly defeated by Eisenhower in the general election, suggesting to many that primary voters might be better judges of candidates than those in the party organization.

In 1960, another Democrat, John F. Kennedy, used the primary system to challenge party leaders and secure the nomination. Kennedy was viewed by his party as a weak presidential hopeful. He was Catholic, and never had voters elected a non-Protestant to the White House. Kennedy was also seen as young and fairly inexperienced. It was not until he won the primary of West Virginia, a largely Protestant state, that Kennedy was seen as potentially electable.

Then came 1968. On November 30, 1967, a little-known Senator from Minnesota, Eugene McCarthy, announced his intention to challenge the incumbent president, Lyndon Johnson, for the Democratic party nomination. In the state of New Hampshire, the White House made an all-out effort to mobilize public support behind the incumbent president. The effort was not very successful with Johnson receiving less than 50 percent of the vote and McCarthy garnering 41.9 percent. Then on March 16, another insurgent candidate, Robert Kennedy, entered the race for the Democratic nomination. On March 31, Lyndon Johnson announced that he was pulling out of the race. His vice president and heir apparent, Hubert Humphrey, delayed his formal declaration of intent to seek the nomination until April 27, after all the final deadlines for the primaries had passed.

At the Democratic convention that year in Chicago, Humphrey won the nomination on the first ballot with 67 percent of the delegate vote. Even in fifteen primary states, 53 percent of the delegates voted for Humphrey abandoning the wishes of the voters in their state. In 1968, most states used some form of appointment in delegate selection. Either the Governor, the state party committee, or other state committees appointed all or some of the state's delegates to the party's national convention.

As in 1952, the candidate chosen by the Democratic national convention went on to be defeated in the general election. In the aftermath of defeat, the McGovern-Fraser Commission was organized by the Democratic Party to reform the delegate selection process to make it more representative of the rank-and-file voters in the party. The results were the extended use of the primary system and a more open and inclusive process in the states that continued to use the caucus system. The Republican Party has moved in a similar direction although less emphasis has been placed on making the delegate population demographically representative of the Republican voters. Once selected, by either state caucus or state primary, the delegates attend their party's national nominating convention in the summer before the November general election. Originally, the party conventions actually determined the nominee of the party. Today, the conventions merely ratify the decisions made in the state caucuses and primaries. The conventions have become extravagant media events that are used by the parties to whip up enthusiasm for the nominee and the party platform.

The most widely watched part of the convention is the last night when the keynote speaker gives an address reviewing the history of the party and promising a bright future for it. A party spokesperson who reviews the candidate's background and experience then places each candidate in nomination. The roll call of the states follows, formally nominating the party's presidential nominee. The presidential and vice presidential candidates give their acceptance speeches to much cheering. Those who fought for the nomination are often welcomed on stage in a show of party unity.

Special Interests and the Nominating Conventions

While the delegate selection process has become more open to the rank-and-file members of the parties, the party conventions themselves provide special privileges to the party leadership and the interest groups that support them. For example, one tradition at the national party conventions is the parties thrown for Members of Congress by special interest groups and corporations with business pending before Congress. Special interests sponsor these events to honor Members, who in many cases have direct influence over legislation affecting their industries.

Members of Congress take special advantage of the rules surrounding conventions, which exempt them from the federal ban on gift taking. A 1995 law forbids Members of Congress from taking gifts worth more than $50 from interest group lobbyists. However, Congress left the door open during the conventions by exempting themselves from the rule during special events. Members are not even required to disclose sponsors of their events and how much the sponsors gave.

Additionally, in the wake of the new ban on "soft money" enacted as part of the 2002 McCain-Feingold law (to be discussed later in this chapter), which prevents the national political parties from accepting unlimited contributions from special interests, corporate cash has instead been pouring into the coffers of the nonprofit host committees for the Democratic and Republican conventions. Despite McCain-Feingold, these donations are still completely unlimited.

As a candidate in 2008, Barack Obama vowed to squelch the role of special interests in financing the party conventions. So, he barred corporations and lobbyists from contributing money to the Democrats 2012 national convention in Charlotte, North Carolina. Organizers, however, found ways to skirt the rules and give corporations and lobbyists a presence at the nominating convention. Despite the ban on corporate money, for example, convention officials encouraged corporate executives to write personal checks and suggested that corporations could participate by donating goods and services to the convention, and by giving up to $100,000 through a corporate foundation. They also quietly explained to lobbyists that while they could not make contributions, they could help raise money from their clients by soliciting personal checks from executives or in-kind contributions from corporations. Lobbyists who complied then received perks like premium credentials and hotel rooms.[5]

Independent and Third-Party Nominees

Recent elections have seen strong independent candidates emerge: Ross Perot in 1992 and 1996 and Ralph Nader in 2000, 2004, and 2008. It is not easy for independent and third-party candidates to get on the ballot. State laws control access to the ballot, and Democratic and Republican

Ross Perot, May 2, 1980
Photo credit: UTSA's Institute of Texan Cultures

legislators and governors make those laws. Unsurprisingly, the candidates of the Democratic and Republican Parties are automatically placed on the ballot in all fifty states. Independent candidates, on the other hand, must demonstrate significant support to get on the ballot through petitions signed by voters.

Nominations for Congress and State Offices

Today, most candidates for major national and state offices are nominated through the primary election system. Thirty-seven states use primary elections to nominate candidates for all state and national offices. Primaries play at least some role in the nomination process in several other states.

Because partisan redistricting (discussed later in this chapter) has ensured that fewer general elections for the U.S. House of Representatives are meaningfully competitive, the primary election of the dominant party is often the most important race in many districts and money is now a key factor in determining primary election outcomes. An analysis of Federal Election Commission (FEC) campaign finance data for the 2012 primary elections shows that money played a key role in determining election outcomes and that most campaign contributions came from a small number of large donors. In the primary elections, the vast majority of campaign contributions come from a small number of large donors. FEC data indicate that while only 0.27 percent of voting-age Americans made a contribution to a candidate of $200 or more, these large donations accounted for 82 percent of individual contributions received by primary candidates. More than a quarter (31 percent) of the contributions came at or above the $2,000 level, while only 0.04 percent of voting-age Americans made a $2,000 contribution.

Many powerful incumbents have accumulated large war chests of campaign money which then further hinders electoral competition in the primary elections. Fully three quarters (76 percent) of 2006 congressional primary races featured only one candidate seeking his or her party's nomination, providing voters with no real choice on primary election day.[6] One reason for this is that large financial advantages of incumbents discourage meaningful competition. Normally, incumbents in Congress have an enormous financial advantage over their challengers. This is one of the reasons why congressmen's re-election rates are so high. During the 2012 election cycle, on average, incumbents in the U.S. House of Representatives enjoyed a fund-raising advantage of over one million dollars more than their challengers.

Voting turnout in primary elections tends to be relatively low, usually with less than one quarter of eligible voters participating. Still, almost 40 million citizens cast ballots in the Democratic and Republican primaries of 2012. Another half a million participated in state caucuses. The nomination process almost certainly requires candidates to reach millions of voters across the fifty states. This has certain consequences for campaigning. First, the process takes time. Technically the selection process begins in February with the Iowa state caucuses. These are followed by the New Hampshire primaries. Even though only a very few delegates are selected in the small states of Iowa and New Hampshire, an exorbitant amount of media coverage and public attention attaches to them. The candidates victorious in these states will gain momentum from the early recognition as "winners."

In truth, the selection process begins way before February. Competitive candidates must raise huge sums of money to establish themselves as serious contenders. In 2012, Mitt Romney was viewed as the likely Republican candidate way before Iowa and New Hampshire. This was because he had financial reserves unmatched by the other Republican hopefuls. Besides raising cash, the candidates test the waters before the actual selection process begins.

The second upshot of this lengthy, complex nomination process is that candidates win the nomination largely on the basis of the resources they can bring, on their own, to the campaign. The national party organization will usually refrain from backing one of their party's hopefuls over the others. There is little incentive for the party to play favorites so early in the game when so much is still uncertain. As a result, candidates are on their own to mobilize the money they need from individuals and interest groups willing to support their campaigns. Recent elections have yielded candidates who run against their party as anti-establishment "outsiders." Even incumbents Ronald Reagan and George Bush ran against their party, critical of what they called the "Washington insiders." Then, once victorious, such candidates are not likely to feel great loyalty to the party organization and, instead, may feel indebted to individual donors and powerful interest groups that may have been instrumental in their victory.

THE GENERAL ELECTIONS

By national law all 435 seats in the House of Representatives and one-third of the seats in the United States Senate must be filled every two years in the general election, held the first Tuesday after the first Monday in November of an even numbered year. In the years when a president is elected as well, the election is called a presidential election. In the years when no president is to be elected, the elections are called off-year congressional, or midterm, elections.

House Elections

Single-Member Plurality Elections

There is a series of steps involved in electing the House of Representatives that begins long before the November election of an even numbered year. The first step actually occurs every ten years: the United States Census. As mandated by the United States Constitution, every ten years an attempt is made to get an accurate count of every person residing in this country, legal and illegal (at least according to 1992 court decisions). Since 1911, the number of seats in the House has been set at 435; so, after the census, the total number of people living in the U.S. is divided by the number of seats, 435. Following the 2010 census, this will yield a number, 710,767, which is the number of people to be represented by each member of the House. The 435 seats are then apportioned to each of the states on the basis of its state population. For example, a state with the population of 1.4 million would be given two seats in the House. After the 2010 census, California was allotted 53 and Alaska 1. Washington D.C. has no seats in the House because it is not a state. After the state is told how many seats it has in the House, it must divide its state population into that number of congressional districts, each with approximately 711,000 people. This reshuffling that occurs every ten years is known as **reapportionment**.

In November, the nation votes as 435 separate congressional districts. Each district chooses one single member on the basis of which candidate gets the most votes, a plurality (not necessarily a majority). These elections are called **single-member plurality elections**.

The Framers of the American Constitution chose the single-member system to insure that the pluralist nature of American society would be represented at the national level. Rather than adopting the European system of multi-member proportional representation in which the national popular vote is represented proportionally in a national legislature, the American system allows each small district to produce a leader to represent the dominant interest in that district. The result of such a system is that the members of the House of Representatives are usually selected because they are perceived as serving *that* district. A House member is not intended nor expected to represent the interests of the nation as a whole. As a result, voters may decide to vote for one party for the House and a different party for the presidency. In the seventeen elections between 1952-2008, voters split their vote and opted for unified control only eight times. For the past 50 years, not too long after one party achieves unified control, Americans almost reflexively put the other in charge of at least one branch of government. Such was the case in 2010, when voters returned the House of Representatives to Republican control.

An additional upshot of the single-member plurality system is that a party's share of the popular vote need not necessarily be reflected in the number of seats that party has in the House. In fact, Republicans have won a smaller percentage of seats than votes in every House election since 1954. Why? One reason is that in single-member plurality elections, the candidate who gets even one more vote than the other candidate or candidates wins the election. So, if in 275 districts the Democrats win by a small margin of 51 percent to the Republicans 49 percent and in the remaining 160 districts the Republican candidates win with 90 percent to the Democrats 10 percent, more votes across all 435 districts will have been cast for the various Republicans but the final House delegation will consist of 275 Democrats and only 160 Republicans.

A second reason why party representation in the House may not mirror the popular vote is that some of the congressional districts have been gerrymandered by some of the state legislatures that are responsible for the drawing of district lines. Gerrymandering is the drawing of state district lines to benefit the political chances of one party's candidates over the other party's. Using lists of registered voters, which include the voter's party affiliation and place of residence, the political party that controls a state legislature could be tempted to draw the district lines so that their registered voters are a majority in as many districts as possible, while the opposing party's registered voters are lumped in the remaining few districts.

The result of such gerrymandering is that the opposition party will carry only the few districts where they have been isolated. Gerrymandering effectively wastes the opposition party's votes, since the party only needs a plurality. Although gerrymandering, historically, has been done by both parties, the Democrats have been in control of most of the state legislatures for most of this century and, as a result, Republicans have born the brunt of gerrymandering. In 1986, the Supreme Court heard a case that challenged gerrymandered congressional districts in Indiana. The Court ruled for the first time that redistricting for the political benefit of one group over another can be challenged on constitutional grounds.[7]

Criticisms of the Single-Member System

Many say that the American system is the worst ever invented.[8] Mathematicians first began to take the problems with plurality seriously in the years leading up to the French Revolution. In the 1770s, Jean-Charles Borda showed that pluralities pick the most popular candidate only in two-person

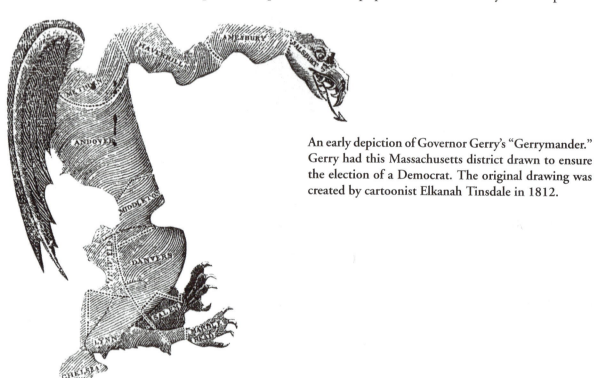

An early depiction of Governor Gerry's "Gerrymander." Gerry had this Massachusetts district drawn to ensure the election of a Democrat. The original drawing was created by cartoonist Elkanah Tinsdale in 1812.

races. In elections involving three or more candidates, the one with the plurality might easily lose when matched up against each of the other candidates one on one.

Plurality systems, used in most U.S. elections, hand victory to the candidate with the most votes even if that candidate falls short of a majority and even if the candidate is the person the majority likes least. The current system, then, can fail to reflect the wishes of most of the people much of the time.

Some are calling for a new system, approval voting. **Approval voting** allows everyone to cast one vote per candidate. A liberal voter in the 1980 New York Senate race could have, in this system, voted for Holtzman and Javits. The candidate approved of by most voters wins. Approval voting has its own problems, however. It tends to produce bland, mediocre winners who lack the sharp edges that may turn voters off.

An alternative solution would be **cumulative voting**, in which voters can pile up several votes for a single candidate they feel strongly about. Each voter would have as many votes as candidates running and distribute those votes among the candidates or give them all to one candidate. Many feel that this would give minorities more say in American elections, without creating race-based districts. Any group that has sufficient cohesion to vote as a bloc could greatly affect the outcome of an election. Cumulative voting has been around for over one hundred years and is widely used in the private sector to elect corporate boards of directors. It is also a system championed by C. Lani Guinier who was Clinton's nominee to head the civil rights branch of the Justice Department. Her nomination was withdrawn after her legal writings were criticized as *radical*.

The problem with all of these alternative plans is that since 1967, federal law has required that all states use single-member congressional districts. The law, passed in 1967, was designed to prevent minority votes from being diluted in at-large elections in Southern states. Ironically, scholars like Guinier now argue the rule actually works to impede minority representation. New legislation would be needed if change is to be made. A Washington based activist group, the Center for Voting and Democracy, has helped draft legislation recently introduced in Congress by Democratic Representative Cynthia McKinney of Georgia, an African American whose district prompted the Supreme Court ruling rejecting the use of race in drawing district lines. Her bill would permit states to experiment with alternative voting schemes.

Many who study the American system see it as the worst of all worlds. Indeed, the United States is the only democracy that gives the plurality winner all the power. And the system does so not just at the House level but at the electoral college level as well (discussed below). Robert Richie, the director of the Center for Voting and Democracy, says that "the current system is just a disaster for most voters and it's getting worse and worse."[9]

Senate Elections

Even though senators are elected by a statewide popular vote, their elections are just as likely to produce a split government, with one party in control of the Senate and another in control of the White House. One reason is that, similar to the House, a voter may perceive his or her state's two senators to be representatives of his or her state, not the entire nation. Voters are less likely to think about national issues like foreign affairs and international trade than they are to think foremost of what a candidate can do for their state.

As in the House, incumbent members seeking re-election enjoy a significant advantage. Incumbents are known to use their office to deliver valuable goods and services to their districts, in the case of House members, and states, in the case of senators. Incumbents are prone to support pork-barrel legislation, laws that deliver the *bacon* to the district or state. Challengers have a much more difficult time of it. They can make promises, but they lack a record of delivery.

A second reason that Senate elections may produce a majority party different from that which controls the presidency is that Senate elections are staggered. Only one-third of the United States Senate is up for election in any two-year election. This results in exactly what the framers of the Constitution intended: a Senate that does not reflect the temporary passions of the moment. While the framers expected the House to be the repository of majority opinion, they designed the Senate to be a bastion to preserve the rights of minority viewpoints. While the majority may sweep the House and presidency, the Senate resists such popular tides. The result has often been divided government.

PRESIDENTIAL ELECTIONS

In contrast to both the House and Senate, the election of the president entails a two-step process.

The Electoral College

The Framers of the Constitution agreed that the president, being so singularly important, should be indirectly selected rather than directly elected by the voters. They further agreed that there would be a national body, the electoral college, that would select the president every four years. Agreement broke down, however, on the question of exactly how the states would be represented in this electoral college. Would small states have less representation or the same level of representation as the more populous states?

The final compromise created a formula for establishing representation in the electoral college. Each state gets a number of electoral college delegates, and, therefore, votes for president equal to the number of representatives that state has in the House plus an additional two for its two Senators. This formula pleases the large states because they will have a greater number of seats in the college. But it also pleases the smaller states in that a state, no matter how small its population, will have three electoral college delegates. Because the Twenty-third Amendment awards Washington, D.C. three electoral college votes, the total number in the electoral college comes to 538.

Each state legislature is designated by the Constitution to select the method of selection for electors to the electoral college. All states have written laws designating the political parties as the institutions that will in some way select the electors. The most common ways are party convention or state party committee. For example, in Kentucky, state statute says that each political party shall choose the method by which they select electors. Both the Democrats and Republicans have selected the party convention. At the party convention, each party selects the number of electors each state is constitutionally guaranteed. Only party faithfuls will be chosen, and they will only vote for the presidential candidate from their party. In Florida, the governor officially chooses the electors. However, he must choose only those electors selected by the parties' state executive committee.

Then on election day in November of a presidential year, state populations vote. Although the names of the presidential candidates appear on the ballot, voters are actually not casting a vote for a candidate. Rather, the voter is casting his or her ballot for the candidate's slate of electors. Each state's popular vote is then counted. The candidate that wins the plurality of the popular votes "carries" the state and wins all of its electoral votes. This means that all of that candidate's slate is elected to the Electoral College. (There are two exceptions. In Maine two and in Nebraska three of the electoral votes are awarded by congressional district. The presidential candidate who carries each district wins a single electoral vote, and the statewide winner gets two additional electoral votes.)

In short, on the first Tuesday in November, all that has transpired is the election of the 538 members of the electoral college. While the assumption is that these delegates will keep faith with the popular vote in their state, the electoral college delegates do not actually cast their ballots for president until December. At that time, the winning state slates travel to their various state capitals and cast their votes. Occasionally electors have broken from the popular vote. In 1988, for example, Margaret Leach, chosen as a Democratic elector by the voters in West Virginia, abandoned Michael Dukakis and voted instead for his running mate, Senator Lloyd Bentsen.[10] Usually, however, electors vote along the lines of their state's popular vote.

A candidate must receive a majority vote of the Electoral College to become president. If none of the candidates receive these 270 votes, the presidential election is thrown to the House of Representatives. There each state delegation casts one vote, choosing between the top three candidates with the most electoral college votes. This has only happened twice, once in 1800 and again in 1824, both before the establishment of a stable two-party system.

The electoral college has several troubling aspects. The most worrisome is the possibility that the candidate who wins the most popular votes may not be elected president. This could happen if a candidate wins some states by a very large margin and loses by very narrow margins in the others. For example, if a candidate wins in the thirteen largest states with 51 percent of the vote and loses in the remaining states with only 10 percent of the vote, that candidate will become president although the other candidate would have received a greater number of popular votes. This has happened in three elections. In 1824, John Quincy Adams received fewer popular votes than Andrew Jackson. In that election, no candidate received a majority vote in the Electoral College, and the House went on to choose Adams over Jackson. In 1876, Rutherford Hayes received fewer popular votes than his opponent, Samuel Tildon, but still won the presidency with 50.1 percent of the Electoral College. In 1888, Grover Cleveland received 48.6 percent of the popular vote to Benjamin Harrison's 47.8 percent. Cleveland nevertheless lost to Harrison in the Electoral College by a vote of 168 to 233. Most recently, in the election of 2000, George W. Bush won the presidency with 271 votes in the Electoral College even though he had fewer popular votes than his opponent Al Gore.

A second undemocratic feature of the Electoral College is that not all states require their electors to cast their votes for the candidate who won the state's popular vote. The **faithless elector** is one who casts his or her vote for a personal choice, even a candidate who was not on the ballot. While the Framers of the American Constitution wanted the Electoral College delegates to be independent, from today's perspective the faithless elector is problematic.

Another troublesome aspect of the Electoral College is that it punishes third parties and their candidates. It is very difficult for a new, fledgling party to get more votes in any state than either of the two, well-established parties. It is not enough for a candidate to get votes; he has to get the most votes to get any representation in the Electoral College.

This trend breeds a psychology among voters that they are throwing away their votes in voting for a third party candidate. Even more disturbing is that third parties widely across the nation, say Ross Perot's candidacy in 1992, are the most punished. Parties that have a strong regional base, being concentrated in only certain states, like George Wallace's candidacy in 1968, have a much better chance of at least carrying a state or two and thereby receiving electoral college representation. Some might argue that in choosing a president for the *nation*, regional parties might be better discouraged than those that have a fairly wide national appeal.

Abolish the Electoral College?

Given these significant issues, some have called for the abolishment of the electoral college. There have been numerous proposals to revert to a direct, majoritarian popular vote. That none of these proposals has ever come close to adoption suggests that the electoral college does have its advantages.

To begin with, the original intent of the framers was to design a strong national government but one that allowed for state representation at the national level. In fact, there is very little evidence that the Constitution was concerned with the representation of individuals; rather, the Constitution is concerned with the representation of the dominant interest in each congressional district, in the case of the House of Representatives, and each state, in the case of the Senate and electoral college. Placed in this light, the electoral college today continues to function effectively just as the framers intended.

Another advantage of the electoral college is that it strengthens the mandate of the president. In our two-party system, most presidents have won with a fairly narrow margin of victory in the popular vote. Even in *landslides* like 1984, the president may win with only about 57 percent of the vote. The electoral college takes very narrow state margins of victory and turns them into state unanimity in the electoral college. Such amplification of the popular vote is especially important in elections like 1992 when the winning candidate may not have even won a majority of the popular vote. In 1992, Clinton received only 43 percent of the popular vote and in 2000, George Bush received fewer popular votes than Al Gore. The electoral college system, however, allowed both Clinton and Bush to say they had received a majority because, at least at the electoral college level, that was the case.

Finally, the electoral college, as noted above, strengthens the two-party system. A change in the electoral college would require a constitutional amendment. Because every existing amendment to the Constitution has been proposed by two-thirds of the House and two-thirds of the Senate, the Democrats and Republicans in Congress would have to vote to break their own lock on the presidency. This is not likely.

Table 6.1: Allocation of Electoral Votes based on the 2010 Census

Total: 538;   Majority Needed to Elect: 270

ALABAMA - 9	MONTANA - 3
ALASKA - 3	NEBRASKA - 5
ARIZONA - 11	NEVADA - 6
ARKANSAS - 6	NEW HAMPSHIRE - 4
CALIFORNIA - 55	NEW JERSEY - 14
COLORADO - 9	NEW MEXICO - 5
CONNECTICUT - 7	NEW YORK - 29
DELAWARE - 3	NORTH CAROLINA - 15
DISTRICT OF COLUMBIA - 3	NORTH DAKOTA - 3
FLORIDA - 29	OHIO - 18
GEORGIA - 16	OKLAHOMA - 7
HAWAII - 4	OREGON - 7
IDAHO - 4	PENNSYLVANIA - 20
ILLINOIS - 20	RHODE ISLAND - 4
INDIANA - 11	SOUTH CAROLINA - 9
IOWA - 6	SOUTH DAKOTA - 3
KANSAS - 6	TENNESSEE - 11
KENTUCKY - 8	TEXAS - 38
LOUISIANA - 8	UTAH - 6
MAINE - 4	VERMONT - 3
MARYLAND - 10	VIRGINIA - 13
MASSACHUSETTS - 11	WASHINGTON - 12
MICHIGAN - 16	WEST VIRGINIA - 5
MINNESOTA - 10	WISCONSIN - 10
MISSISSIPPI - 6	WYOMING - 3
MISSOURI - 10	

Source: National Archives and Records Administration—U.S. Federal Election Commission
Last Update: 2/23/10

CAMPAIGNING IN THE GENERAL ELECTION

The Political Context

The most important structural feature of a general election is whether an incumbent is seeking re-election or whether it is an open election in which there is no incumbent running. Incumbents enjoy an enormous advantage at all levels but especially in House and Senate elections. House incumbents have historically been almost impossible to defeat. The average rate of re-election for members of the House since 1964 has been 93.3 percent, and, over the last decade, it has been 96 percent. In the Senate, the average since 1964 has been 81.6 percent. Even in 2010, when anti-government sentiment hit a fever pitch, incumbents still did well with a re-election rate of 86 percent. Though the percentage was relatively low compared to previous years, there was no massive anti-incumbent movement ready to kick the establishment out of Congress. The median percent of the vote won by incumbents (65 percent) was in line with the historical average (68 percent). Additionally, the percent of races with no incumbent running in the general election was 10 percent, a pretty mundane figure. This refutes the notion that many incumbents decided not to run or lost in the primaries. Incumbents enjoy such an advantage, at least in part, because of their ability to attract greater campaign contributions. Money is extremely important in modern campaigns.

Financing Campaigns

How Much Campaigns Cost

The total cost of the 2012 election was $6 billion, making it the costliest election in history and surpassing the $5 billion spent in 2008. The increase was largely driven by rapidly increased spending among "super PACs" and outside groups that can raise unlimited amounts of money from donors. Spending by outside groups reached to more than $970 million for the 2012 cycle. These estimates could substantially understate the total amount of money spent in 2012 for while super PACs, political committees that sprang into being after the Supreme Court's 2010 *Citizens United* ruling, spent at least $539.4 million, hundreds of millions of dollars more were spent below the radar by groups that do not register with the Federal Election Commission and purport to focus on educational, not political, activities. Such groups spent at least another $203 million in the last two months of the campaign, a window during which federal law requires formal disclosure of any expenditures that mention a candidate, and they spent even more earlier in the campaign cycle on "issue ads" that are not subject to disclosure. The biggest expansion of outside spending was in the battle for the House and Senate. Between 2008 and 2012, independent expenditures in the House and Senate races increased from $46 million to $445 million, a tenfold increase that does not include issue ads that were run in support of incumbent congressmen even before the official campaign seasons started.

Regulating Campaign Finance

The way in which campaigns are financed in this country has changed dramatically over the last twenty-five years primarily because of changes in national campaign finance laws. Congress began to regulate campaign finance as early as the 1920s through a variety of federal corrupt practices acts. The first, passed in 1925, limited primary and general election expenses for congressional candidates. Then in the 1930s, Congress prohibited, by law, corporate and bank contributions. Then the Hatch Act (Political Activities Act) was passed in 1939 in another attempt to control political influence buying. The Hatch Act forbade contributions by government employees and individuals and companies receiving government funds, for example in the form of government contracts. In 1943, Congress went on to outlaw labor union contributions.

These early laws provided no avenue for enforcement. How could Congress know whether its laws had been violated? There was no effective way to make candidates fully disclose where they got their money or where they were spending it for that matter. The Watergate scandal of 1972 and the investigations that followed made it clear that abuse of the campaign finance system was rampant. It was discovered that large amounts of money had been illegally funneled to Nixon's committee to re-elect the president (CREEP). Congress acted quickly to prevent continued abuse of the system.

The Federal Election Campaign Act (FECA) of 1971 essentially replaced all past laws and instituted major reform. The law requires all candidates to fully disclose all contributions and expenditures in excess of $100. The effectiveness of this law was soon apparent. In 1968 before disclosure was strictly demanded, candidates reported spending $8.5 million. Only four years later, in 1972, the candidates reported to the FECA that they had spent $88.9 million.[11] The 1971 law also tried to limit the amount that each individual could spend of his own money in running for office. In *Buckley v. Valeo* the Supreme Court declared that provision of the law unconstitutional.[12]

In closing one loophole, that having to do with disclosing campaign finance information, the 1971 law opened another. The FECA said that it was permissible for corporations and labor unions to set up "separate, segregated funds . . . that could be used for a political purpose." This led to the creation of a large number of **PACs (political action committees)** that could now channel corporate, labor, and other interest group money to candidates. For a PAC to be legal, the money must be raised from at least fifty volunteer donors and must be contributed to at least five candidates in the federal election. Each corporation or each union is limited to one PAC.

In 1974, Congress amended the Federal Election Campaign Act. These amendments created the Federal Election Commission (FEC) to enforce compliance with the requirements of the act. Presidential candidates would be provided with public financing for the primaries and general elections if they agreed to limit their campaign expenditures to the amount prescribed by the law. In addition, the law limited individuals to campaign contributions of no more than $1,000 per candidate and a total of $25,000 in contributions in one year. Groups and PACs could contribute up to $5,000 per candidate in any election, primary and general.

The FECA was again amended in 1976 in response to the provisions ruled unconstitutional by *Buckley v. Valeo*, and again in 1979 to allow parties to spend unlimited amounts of hard money on activities like increasing voter turnout and registration. In 1979, the Federal Election Commission ruled that political parties could spend unregulated or "soft" money for non-federal administrative and party building activities. Later, this money was used for candidate related issue ads, which led to a substantial increase in soft money contributions and expenditures in elections. This in turn created pressures leading to passage of the Bipartisan Campaign Reform Act ("BCRA").

The Bipartisan Campaign Reform Act of 2002

In 2002, Congress approved the first major overhaul of the nation's campaign finance system in a quarter century, breaking a nearly decade-long impasse that thwarted efforts to reduce the influence of big money in American politics. The Bipartisan Campaign Reform Act (also known as McCain-Feingold) bans unrestricted soft money to the political parties, restricts end-of-the-campaign advertising by outside groups, and raises limits on direct cash contributions to $2000 to a candidate, $5000 to a PAC, and $25,000 to a political party. Corporations, unions, and other groups would still be allowed to pay for issue advertisements but not within 60 days before a general election and 30 days before a primary election.

Legal Challenges to BCRA

In January 2010, in *Citizens United vs. Federal Election Commission*, the U.S. Supreme Court struck down a major portion of the McCain-Feingold campaign finance law that prevented union and corporate paid issue ads in the final 30 days of election campaigns. The Court also ruled that corporations can spend as much as they want to support candidates running for Congress or president. The High Court based its opinion on its previously stated position (*Buckley v. Valeo*) that the First Amendment protects political speech and money spent in furtherance of promoting and disseminating political speech. The Court noted that historically and legally, corporations do enjoy First Amendment rights to free speech; and that the federal campaign law criminalizing the corporate act of simply using its lawful monies to disseminate lawful political speech, is in fact an unlawful restraint of protected speech.

New Loopholes in the Wake of the 2002 Campaign Finance Reform

Despite recent attempts to limit the flow of money into politics, campaign spending continues to skyrocket. The money is coming in through a variety of loopholes, some tried and true and some more newly minted.

Soft Money to State Political Parties

The McCain-Feingold reforms permit state party committees to continue to raise soft money and on June 22, 2002, the Federal Election Commission amended the Bipartisan Campaign Reform Act with a series of regulations that permit broader activities by state committees. Additionally, on November 13, 2008, the national Republican Party sued the Federal Election Commission, seeking to overturn prohibitions on unregulated corporate and labor contributions and to make it easier to coordinate spending with federal candidates. The lawsuits came after the defeat of Republican presidential candidate John McCain, a fierce opponent of soft money and one of the authors of the 2002 legislation that banned the parties from raising unlimited money from corporations, unions and wealthy individuals. The RNC lawsuit said the total ban on soft money amounts to a violation of the First Amendment's guarantees of free speech and association.[13]

The 527 Organizations and Independent Expenditures

When the Supreme Court upheld the McCain-Feingold ban on unlimited donations to political parties and other groups, so-called "soft money," it had no illusions about the difficulties faced in trying to reduce the role of money in politics. "Money, like water, will always find an outlet," wrote Justices John Paul Stevens and Sandra Day O'Connor.[14] For despite passage of the new campaign finance law in 2002, soft money is still finding a niche in elections. While the McCain-Feingold legislation approved in 2002 banned the parties from receiving unlimited contributions from unions, corporations, and individuals, the Democratic and Republican national committees together raised over $250 million by May 2004, more than what they collected during the same period in 2000 when soft money was allowed.

Table 6.2

**Top Ten
527/Advocacy Group Receipts and Expenditures**

Committee	Total Receipts	Total Expenditures
ActBlue	$11,648,124	$10,181,470
College Republican National Cmte	$9,172,430	$9,718,040
Citizens United	$8,120,525	$7,903,079
EMILY's List	$7,716,027	$6,104,379
Service Employees International Union	$6,191,200	$7,421,296
Plumbers/Pipefitters Union	$4,700,542	$3,944,237
Gay and Lesbian Victory Fund	$3,792,865	$5,335,287
GOPAC	$3,303,261	$3,340,415
New Conservative Coalition	$3,030,479	$2,744,671
Intl Brotherhood of Electrical Workers	$2,838,540	$3,172,906

This data is based on records released by the Internal Revenue Service on September 26, 2012.

The soft money is now coming in through donations by independent groups, known as the 527s. These tax-exempt groups are organized under section 527 of the Internal Revenue Code to raise and disburse funds to influence the nomination, election, appointment or defeat of candidates for public office. On the face of the definition of what have become known as 527 organizations, they appear to be the same as PACs. And, in effect, a 527 is just a PAC by another name. However, there is one key difference. A 527 organization does not fall within the regulator realm of the Federal Election Commission and therefore is not subject to the same limits as the FEC regulated PACs. Unlike the PACs, the 527s are permitted to accept contributions in any amount from any source. The only requirement is that the 527 must make regular reports of its funding and expenditures to the Internal Revenue Service. Spending by 527 groups approximated $500 million in the 2008 election. The new campaign finance law did not curtail spending.

State regulations on the independent expenditures of these groups are now likely to fall as well. The *Citizens United* case overturned the Supreme Court's earlier decision in the 1990 case, *Austin v. Michigan Chamber of Commerce,* which held that the Michigan Campaign Finance Act, which prohibited corporations from using treasury money to support or oppose candidates in elections, did not violate the First and Fourteenth Amendments. States are left little room to try and control the independent expenditures of these groups.

Many states do not even have laws that effectively regulate independent expenditures. In the 2010 California governor's race, outside groups spent more money through so-called independent expenditure committees than in any past years, spending more than $31.7 million, breaking the record sent in 2006. In California, groups backing Jerry Brown's candidacy spent most of the money, about $25 million worth. The generous giving to the state PACs has also been an important aspect of the 2012 money race. By 2010, a handful of big donors had each contributed, in the realm of $100,000, or more, to Mitt Romney through a network of state political action committees he set up that enable him to avoid federal campaign finance limits. The money, which went to the politicians' "leadership PACs," cannot be used to fuel a presidential run; but it often acts as seed money to help raise a potential candidate's national profile and provide financing to other politicians who can help him later.

Issue-Related Advertisements

The most controversial provisions of the 2002 campaign finance reform had to do with the law's prohibition of issue-related advertisements that refer to a federal politician within 30 days of a primary election and 60 days of a general election. In June 2007, the Supreme Court, in a 5 to 4 decision, ruled that issue ads immediately before federal elections are not banned by the campaign finance reform law. Then in its 2010 landmark *Citizens United* ruling, the Supreme Court held that the federal government could not limit corporations, unions, associations, or individuals from spending money to influence the outcome of elections. This ruling led to the creation of super PACs which cannot make contributions directly to a candidate or campaign but can engage in unlimited spending independently of campaigns. The Center for Public Integrity estimates that the *Citizens* ruling allowed nearly one billion dollars to enter campaign coffers with $933 million coming directly from the companies, unions and individuals who took advantage of *Citizens United* to funnel money into super PACs.

The FEC records show that about two-thirds of all the *Citizens United*-fueled money went to ten super PACs or political nonprofits, nine of which focused exclusively on buying media spots and ads for candidates. Of these ad spots, 89 percent were focused on denouncing the opposing candidate and the prevalence of attack ads throughout the contest made the 2012 election one of the most historically bitter contests, with pundits regularly calling it the "nastiest," "meanest," and even "dirtiest campaign in history."[15]

Analysis of 2012 campaign spending also demonstrates the truth of the widely-held suspicion that little if any firewall separates super PACs from the candidates' actual campaigns. While the Federal Election Commission bans coordination between the super PAC and the actual campaign, these rules were easily skirted through the 2012 contest. In some cases, super PACs even shared mailing addresses and offices with the chosen candidate's own election campaign.[16]

Bundling

Another consequence of the Bipartisan Campaign Reform Act of 2002 limitation upon personal contributions from any one individual ($2400 for each election, with a total of $4800 for a pri-

At the CPAC 2011, former Mass. Gov. Mitt Romney, seeking to build on his momentum as a leading candidate from the 2008 GOP nomination process, took more direct aim at Obama, delivering a speech loaded with stinging criticisms of the administration. Credit: RTTNews

mary and general election) and its prohibition of soft money contributions to political parties is that campaigns have shifted gears into "hard money" contributions. Instead of handing over one $100,000 check to a candidate's party (soft money), the influence peddler now hands a candidate 50 checks from different contributors of $2,000 each (hard money). This is all perfectly legal, and has an enormous effect on buying influence with the candidate or officeholder. This method is called "bundling." Bundling is the fundraising practice of pooling together a large number of contributions from PACs and individuals in order to maximize the political influence of the bundler and the interests they represent. Most often, the bundler is a corporate executive or lobbyist, with expectations of something in return. While there are disclosure requirements for bundling, they only go into effect when a bundler personally hands over checks. Most campaigns get around the disclosure provision by not having the bundler ever touch the checks. Bundling has always existed in various forms, but became organized in a more structured way in the 2000s, spearheaded by the "Bush Pioneers" for George W. Bush's 2000 and 2004 presidential campaigns. During the 2008 campaign, the six leading primary candidates (three Democratic, three Republican) had listed a total of nearly two thousand bundlers.[17]

At the CPAC 2011, Texas Rep. Ron Paul, who launched a well financed but ultimately unsuccessful insurgent campaign for the 2008 presidential nomination, ultimately won the CPAC straw poll in a result that mirrored the 2010 results. Paul won the support of 30 percent of the attendees as their first choice for the presidential nominee, with Mitt Romney coming in second with 23 percent. Gingrich secured just 5 percent with Pawlenty at 4 percent, Palin at 3 percent and Huckabee at 2 percent. Paul, in his speech to the convention, hit on his familiar themes of limited government and restricting foreign aid. Credit: RTTNews

Effects of the American Campaign Finance System

The Incumbency Advantage

Ninety percent of House incumbents and 91 percent of the Senators who ran for re-election in 2012 were returned to office, with most of them befitting from a huge fundraising advantage over their challengers. House incumbents had a more than 7-to-1 financial advantage over their challengers. Incumbents have an even greater advantage in special-interest PAC fundraising, raising eight times the amount given to challengers. As Table 6.3 reveals, incumbents continued to enjoy a financial advantage in 2012.

Table 6.3

**Incumbent Advantage
Raised for Campaign
2012 Election Cycle**

	Senate	House
Incumbent	$11,802,711	$1,616,034
Challenger	$1,377,312	$266,676
Open Seat	$2,853,915	$477,283
Total	$2,983,246	$665,000

Based on data released by the FEC on January 22, 2013.

Selling Access and Influence

Americans have long worried that campaign contributions are a way for powerful individuals and groups to buy access to policy makers and to influence the policy making process. Concern with such influence peddling reached a crescendo immediately following the 1996 presidential election. President Clinton and the Democratic National Committee were heavily criticized for a series of 103 coffee klatches in the White House Map Room that were held for business executives and other supporters who had given over $27 million to the Democratic National Committee in 1995 and 1996. Revelations of these coffee klatches were soon followed by stories of well-healed donors who had spent the night at the White House apparently as a thank you for generous campaign contributions. The total amount of money contributed by those invited for the overnights is still not known but a partial guest list included Hollywood moguls Steven Spielberg and Lew Wasserman, who gave $300,000 and $335,000 to the Democratic National Committee. All total, close to nine hundred campaign contributors stayed overnight at the White House, many sleeping in the Lincoln Bedroom. Charles Lewis, executive director of Citizens for Public Integrity, an independent watchdog group with expertise in campaign finance, said: "Those numbers are staggering. It should be alarming to the American people that the president of the United States was using the national symbol of our democracy as a way station for fat-cat donors like a Holiday Inn or Motel 6."[18]

There is also evidence that campaign contributions allow powerful groups to influence public policy making. For example, both the coal and oil industries have mobilized vast resources to influence energy policy in the United States. Even though it has become very clear in recent years that American energy policy is at a crossroads, with experts agreeing that a shift in our energy and consumption is necessary to avert catastrophe brought on by global warming, there has been strong resistance to a major move away from a coal-fired electricity and oil-based economy to one based on alternative sources of renewable energy. In 2012, the estimated spending on television ads promoting coal and more oil and gas drilling or criticizing clean energy exceeded $153 million, nearly four times the $41 million spent by clean-energy advocates.[19]

Weakening the Role of the Political Parties

As noted above, after the passage of the Bipartisan Campaign Reform Act, many of the soft money-funded activities previously undertaken by political parties were taken over by various groups. The *Citizens* decision then further fueled the rise of these nonprofit political action groups, such as Republican strategist Karl Rove's Crossroads GPS, that has poured millions into campaigns. Business groups, unions, and interest groups spent upwards of $400 million in 2010, including at least $128 million by groups that are not required to publicly disclose their donors. Anonymous outside interests have gone from being a relatively minor source of funding for campaign-season television ads to being the dominant player in 2010. In the 2006 midterm election, the Democratic and Republican Party committees accounted for 82 percent of all outside spending on express advocacy; outside groups accounted for only 18 percent. In 2010, the numbers flipped dramatically, with outside groups spending more money on independent expenditures than did the party committees—59 percent to 41 percent. In 2010, the two largest campaign contributors to Democratic candidates were ActBlue, which gave a total of $23,885,958, and Service Employees International Union, which gave $6,934,290. The two biggest contributors to the Republican candidates were AT&T Inc with $3,708,490 and Elliott Management with $3,121,969.

A Weakening of the Public Finance System

As campaign money flows in from individuals, corporations, and interest groups, the public financing system is faltering. The public financing program offers presidential candidates a monthly taxpayer-financed match of up to $250 for each private contribution they raise during the primary season, up to total grants of approximately $18.6 million. To qualify, candidates must raise at least $5,000 in each of twenty states and abide by other requirements, including overall, state-by-state, and personal spending limits. In 2012, almost all of the major candidates opted out of public financing in the primaries, freeing them to spend unlimited amounts. In the 2008 general election, Barack Obama was the first Democrat in history to forgo the taxpayer-financed system that encourages small donations by matching them with federal funds, freeing him to exceed the $45 million spending cap that comes with the public money.

Increased Number of Personally Wealthy Candidates

The faltering of the public finance system is related to another effect of campaign finance laws is that candidates who are either personally wealthy or who can appeal to many small donors by mass mailings and television will have an advantage. A candidate with only modest means and little television appeal will find it much more difficult to raise the money needed to finance a campaign. Recent campaigns have seen very wealthy candidates spend considerable amounts of their own money running for office. In 2012, presidential candidate Mitt Romney's fortune was estimated by the media to be upwards of $250 million. Most believe that is a very low estimate given that his fortune derives in large part from his founding in 1984 of Bain Capital. Bain Capital made billions of dollars during the years when Mitt Romney ran the private equity firm.

Raising Campaign Money: A Distraction

Candidates are now forced to spend considerably greater amounts of time raising money. Particularly in congressional campaigns, which have no public funding, candidates must meet with many groups and many individuals to raise the money for a campaign. Insofar as many candidates for Congress are incumbent members of Congress themselves, these fund raising activities constitute a significant distraction from legislative duties. Additionally, because fund raising activities are so demanding on a politician's time and energy, candidates are increasingly finding it more efficient to stay in the nation's capital, working the fund raising party circuit. This means that trips home to their districts or states are made less frequently and constituents have, as a result, fewer opportunities to see their representatives. Such a focus on fund raising inside the belt of Washington, D.C., may work to insulate the politicians from the very constituents they seek to serve.

Abuse and Scandals: The Case of Enron

In just 15 years, Enron grew from nowhere to be America's seventh largest company, employing 21,000 staff in more than 40 countries. The firm's success, however, turned out to be an elaborate scam. Enron lied about its profits and stands accused of a range of shady dealings, including concealing debts so that they did not show up in the company's accounts. Enron executives lied about the profitability of the company and encouraged their employees to buy stock even as they themselves sold their stock knowing that it was inflated and would soon fall, which it did. While the executives sold their stock at its high, walking away with millions in stock profits, the Enron employees lost billions because their pensions were heavily invested in Enron's own stock. In December 2002, the company filed bankruptcy taking with it the lifetime savings of its employees and other investors.

A chorus of outraged investors, employees, pension holders, and politicians are demanding to know why Enron's failings were not spotted earlier. As the investigation unfolded in 2003, two principle culprits have been identified: a corrupt campaign finance system and an intricate web of relationships built up between the business community and politicians.

The Enron scandal has illustrated how widely the taint of large campaign contributions has spread. Enron spent a total of $5.8 million on federal elections over the past 12 years, 73 percent of the money going to Republicans. The company's donations went to 71 out of the 100 senators and 188 out of the 435 House members.

While hefty campaign contributions were forging a close working relationship between the Bush administration and Enron, other ties were also being developed. Fourteen top Bush administration officials held stock in Enron. Karl Rove, the president's senior adviser, listed more than $250,000 worth of Enron stock. Peter Fisher, the undersecretary of commerce who received more than a half-dozen phone calls from Enron executives in the months before the company's collapse, owned equities in the company as well. Additionally, Enron alumni fill prominent positions in the current Bush administration. The CEO of Enron, Kenneth Lay, worked for the Bush administration screening potential appointees to the Federal Regulatory Commission. President Bush's most prominent economic advisor, Larry Lindsey, and his point man on trade issues, Robert Zoelick, both served as Enron advisors. Secretary of the Army Thomas White was an Enron executive before joining the

Six

So much influence did Enron wield with the Bush administration that Kenneth L. Curtis Herbert Jr., chairman of the Federal Energy Regulatory Commission, that he reappointed if he changed his views on electricity regulation. Mr. Herbert did not, and not.

The question at the center of the U. S. political stage now is what Enron got in return for its investment in politics. It appears that the campaign donations and close personal ties between Enron and government worked to insulate Enron from government attempts to regulate business dealings and allowed Enron to falsely conceal some of its debts. In 2002, Enron executives held a total of six meetings with Vice President Dick Cheney and his staff, who were responsible for the drawing up of one of the administration's most important initiatives, the energy plan, which advocates expansion and deregulation of U. S. production, including the opening up of the Arctic National Wildlife Refuge for oil drilling.

Enron is not unique in the annals of lobbyist interests prevailing over the public interest. From contracts for unneeded weapons to a banana trade war, the decisions often tend to come out in favor of the big campaign contributors. What makes the Enron case different is the drama of the huge implosion in full view of thousands of victimized employees and investors. As one journalist has written: "Enron's woes aren't really a scandal at all—instead they're a magnifying glass allowing us to see clearly exactly how government and business operate today."[20]

Money and Campaigns: Prognosis for the Future

Two features of the American political landscape virtually ensure that money will play an ever-growing role in U.S. campaigns and elections. The first is the Supreme Court's heightened commitment in recent years to the Buckley V. Valeo finding that campaign money, both the giving and spending of, is a form of speech and, therefore, protected by the First Amendment to the Constitution. The current Supreme Court has five members who tend to vote as a conservative block on campaign finance issues, blocking government attempts to restrict campaign contributions. President Obama has added two liberals to the Court, Sonia Sotomayor and Elena Kagan, but together with Justices Ginsberg and Breyer, they are a minority of four. It is likely that for the foreseeable future the Court will not support any major attempt to limit money in politics.

While the current make-up of the Supreme Court suggests that new attempts to limit money in elections are not likely to pass muster with the Court, a second feature undermines the enforcement of the already existing laws. At present, there is no agency to provide effective oversight of campaign contributions. The Federal Election Commission (FEC) is the regulatory body established by the Federal Election Campaign Act of 1974 that is responsible for enforcing campaign finance laws. Common Cause and other citizen groups have long been critical of its effectiveness and willingness to perform the job it was created to do. Rather than providing swift rulings and forcefully policing the campaign finance system, they argue, the FEC is a failing agency that is built for gridlock and often held captive by the very elected officials that it is meant to police.

This alleged cooptation of the FEC is said to be the result of the party leadership in Congress seating FEC commissioners who are loyal to the party that appoints them. Even the structure of the commission makes it difficult to act. The FEC has three Democratic appointees and three Republican appointees who vote on official agency actions. A 3-3-tie vote results in no action by the commission, effectively giving each party veto power over any potential FEC enforcement action. Additionally, the FEC is largely toothless since it has few actual powers of enforcement. The FEC cannot, on its own, sanction groups it believes have violated the law. It can only negotiate for a payment of civil penalties by candidates or political groups. The commission has the power neither to seek court injunctions to halt illegal activity while it is occurring nor to conduct random audits of campaigns. Perhaps nothing illustrates the FEC's failings better than the first seven months of 2008, when, in the midst of the most expensive election cycle in history, the country lacked a functioning FEC because the nominees were stopped in the gridlock of the Senate.[21]

CAMPAIGN STRATEGIES AND TACTICS

Polling

A good place for any candidate to begin his campaign is with an identification of the electorate's concerns. To do this, candidates have in modern times increasingly turned to pollsters and political consultants. According to year-end research tabulated by the Center for Responsive Politics, Obama spent more than $35 million on "Polling/Surveys/Research" and Hillary Clinton spent another $40 million in these areas.[22]

Well-funded candidates may begin with focus groups. These groups usually consist of ten to twenty people selected because they are representative of certain groups that a candidate particularly wants to target in his campaign. These small focus groups, questioned at great length and depth, provide a way to identify the values and issue preferences of likely voters. Often a candidate's campaign consultants will then formulate "soundbites" on the basis of statements made in these focus group sessions. For example, in 2012, the Romney campaign discovered that Walmart Moms, women with children 18 or younger who shop at Walmart at least once per month, make up 27 percent of all registered female voters and about 14 percent of all American voters. Focus groups revealed that while most of these moms voted for Obama in 2008, by November of 2010 they were voting Republican and proving key in helping Republicans take over the House. The Romney campaign then actively sought their support in 2012.[23]

While focus groups are most useful in the early stages of the campaign, helping candidates identify issues of concern, other types of polls become more important as the campaign moves forward. A trend poll, for example, may be used to determine how well the candidate is doing and in what parts of the nation or state or district. In early October, tracking polls, using quick phone interviews of people on a daily basis, are used to make critical decisions about where the candidate should go and what he should try to convey.

Making the News

While polling helps the candidate tailor his message to the interests of the public, the candidate must also tailor his message to the needs of the news organizations. News values emphasize the dramatic, the conflict-laden, and the brief. Television, in particular, sees no value in airing long-winded statements by the candidates. Furthermore, most Americans have little interest in hearing them. Even newspaper readers are unlikely to read beyond the first paragraph of a story. As a result, candidates need to learn to speak in soundbites which are easily understood. They should be no longer than thirty seconds and preferably as short as ten seconds in length.

Candidate control of the soundbite is particularly important. If the candidate fails to set the *lead* for the story, the journalist may do so and may do so in a manner much less sympathetic to the candidate than the candidate would be to himself. One study has found that while visuals of the candidate are being aired, the news commentators voice overs are not as positive as the visuals themselves.[24]

Candidates also need to be concerned with news deadlines. It does little good for a candidate to make a major policy statement at 8:00 in the evening, too late for the national evening news, too stale for the next morning's breaking news. In fact, it may not be worth the candidate's trouble to make a policy statement at all. Given the media's preoccupation with image and the horserace aspects of a campaign, the candidate might be better to talk in generalities with good visuals running in the background.

The Tabloids

In 1992, the Twentieth Century Fund studied television coverage of that year's presidential campaign. They discovered the ascension of what they called the "new news." The new news consists of network morning shows, call-in talk shows, often with studio audiences, and other shows like *Larry King Live*, *MTV*, and *Oprah*. These tabloid shows allow the candidates to bypass the established press.[25]

In 2012, several tabloid stories surfaced. For example, Texas Governor Rick Perry, who ran for the Republican nomination for the presidency in 2012, was forced to play defense against a report that his family's hunting grounds were known by a racist name.

Advertising

Studies of recent campaigns have found that most voters get their campaign information not from the news but rather from advertisements.[26] As will be discussed in Chapter 7, the increased sophistication of broadcast technology coupled with the use of multimodal techniques (for example, use of visuals and music) have enhanced the power of advertisements in molding public opinion.

Today, House candidates spend about 25 percent of their campaign budgets on advertising, and Senate candidates spend about 35 percent of theirs.[27] In the 2012 presidential election, candidates spent an estimated $9.8 billion on television advertising. If one watched every single ad that the presidential candidates ran before the Iowa caucuses alone, it would have taken more than 15 days.[28]

Party strategists have begun to look beyond television and radio audiences to a whole new generation of Web surfers. In 2012, Barack Obama's re-election campaign spent record amounts of money for online advertising. In just the first few months of 2012, his campaign bought nearly $16.4 million worth of online ads.[29] The 2003 McCain-Feingold campaign finance reform law placed sharp limits on using campaign donations to pay for broadcast TV and radio ads, especially in the two months before an election. But the law was silent on the use of large checks from corporations, unions, and wealthy individuals, contributions known as "soft money," to finance Internet ads.

Arguably, the online channel is more efficient than other forms of media, primarily television. There is as much, if not more, video inventory available online, and at much lower cost, including in-banner and in-stream video impressions that can be geo-targeted as well as targeted to specific demographic audiences. For example, in 2008, the Obama campaign ran an "Obama for President" billboard in the Xbox 360 racing game *Burnout Paradise* in an effort to reach young voters. An additional advantage of online advertising is that political advertising online will not sell out, and candidates' ads do not run back-to-back against each other like they do on television. Furthermore, viewers cannot skip ads online, and if they are interested in learning more, they have only to click to the candidate's website where the candidate has an opportunity to immediately engage them.

Internet and High Tech Campaigning

In addition to online ads, campaigns are increasingly using e-mail to communicate with activists and raise money. In 2004, blogs, which are personal, frequently updated Web pages that typically contain short essays on a particular topic, played a significant role. During the 2004 presidential campaign, Howard Dean blazed the trail of electronic campaigning through his use of these Web blogs and aggressive use of online fundraising helped transform the obscure former Vermont governor into a frontrunner for the Democratic nomination.

The importance of the Internet in American campaigns is likely to grow in the future. More than 121 million American adults now use the Internet, according to Nielsen/Netratings. Additionally, Web users are more likely to vote and to show an interest in politics.[30] Today, every candidate has a blog and new blogs are being added daily. They are becoming an alternative news universe, giving everyone with a PC and a Web connection access to the sorts of political gossip that was once available only to reporters on the campaign press bus.

By 2008 it became apparent that political information and political advertisements could now be made available on mobile phones. Broadband video was in 80-million phones and YouTube went mobile by the end of the 2009. In 2010, congressional candidates tried out these new virtual ways to reach voters. The office of former Republican presidential candidate and Arizona Senator, John McCain, announced a revamp of the McCain 2010 campaign website, with special mention of their new online video strategy—a "Video Supporter Wall" that would attempt to use the power of video to create a dialogue with the voters of Arizona.

The Mechanics of Elections

The presidential election of 2000 will no doubt go down in history as one of the strangest. While it was the most expensive campaign in history, costing an almost unimaginable $1 billion, it produced no clear victor.

Hanging Chads, Pregnant Chads

In 2000, thousands of potentially valid votes were lost because ballot designs were confusing, counting methods were inconsistent, and, in some cases, election officials never looked at ballots that were rejected by machines. On more than 1700 ballots in Florida, the voters' choice for president was clear, but the ballot was rejected nonetheless. In an additional 5000 cases in Florida, voters' mistakes, apparently caused by confusing ballot design, made it impossible to determine the voters' intent.

The confusion surrounding the 2000 election outcome highlights an important but often ignored aspect of the American electoral process: state law and local policies determine the mechanics of elections, even national presidential elections. The Constitution gives the power to regulate elections to the states as part of the federal structure. In some parts of the country, votes are cast on automatic voting machines; in other places, paper ballots are used. Still other jurisdictions require voters to bubble in their choice. Finally, many voters vote by punching their vote on the punch cards that were the center of the controversy in the state of Florida in 2000.

Since 2002, federal law has encouraged the use of paperless voting systems, especially for people with disabilities. In 2008 electronic voting was widespread, and so were the problems. According to an analysis of 1,700 incident reports from the nation's largest voter hotline, machines often failed to turn on, voter databases omitted names, and touch screens did not properly record votes.[31] The voting machine issues and the confusion they caused among poll workers compounded the delays faced by untold thousands of voters. Additionally, there were inaccurate voter registration records, not enough early voting sites, and planning that did not accommodate high turnout. The voting machinery used simply exacerbated these very issues. In Atlanta, all 15 voting machines in a polling place stopped working; in Georgia, as a whole, there was a shortage of e-poll book laptops; in New York City, there was only one poll book for hundreds of voters. And in Maryland poll workers could not get their electronic voting systems up and running at all. Across the country, machinery malfunctions were a common complaint with numerous reports of lights and buttons not working on machines and machines that kept rebooting or did not work with other computers in the network. In 14 states, voters reported "vote flipping," where the machines selected another candidate other than their pick. Clearly, the faulty mechanics of American elections are not a thing of the past.

POLITICAL PARTICIPATION IN ELECTIONS: THE WAXING AND WANING OF THE AMERICAN ELECTORATE

The Waxing of the American Electorate

At the time the Constitution was ratified, the right to vote was limited to taxpayers or property owners. By the administration of President Andrew Jackson (1829-1837), almost all of the states had extended the right to vote to all white males. Then after the Civil War and the Fifteenth Amendment, African Americans were given the constitutional right to vote. The Southern states, however, continued to find ways to disenfranchise Southern African Americans. Between 1915 and 1944, the Supreme Court overturned some of the most discriminatory of the rules: the poll tax (requiring payment to vote) and the grandfather clause (you could vote if your grandfather had had the right to vote). Still, a small proportion of Southern African Americans actually registered and voted.

It was not until the passage of the Voting Rights Act in 1965 that African-American participation in Southern elections would increase dramatically. This law suspended literacy tests and authorized the appointment of federal examiners who could order the registration of African Americans in states and counties where fewer than 50 percent of the voting-age population registered or had voted in the previous presidential election. The law also included criminal penalties for interfering with the right to vote. Additional efforts by Jesse Jackson have helped increase the voter registration among African Americans.

Though women were allowed to vote in some state elections, it was not until the Nineteenth Amendment in 1920 that women's suffrage was extended across the entire nation, doubling the size of the electorate. Then, the Twenty-sixth Amendment, ratified in 1971, gave the right to vote to eighteen-year-olds. Given these changes, the United States now has the widest voting rights of any country in the world.

The Waning of the American Electorate

Given this history of safeguarding and extending the right to vote, one would think that participation in elections would have risen over time. In fact, a smaller percentage of people vote today than in the latter part of the nineteenth century. Some argue that this decline is more apparent than real. Until the early twentieth century, voter fraud, for example, ballot-box stuffing, was common.[30] Also, the Australian ballot was introduced at the turn of the century. This ballot was to be cast in secret in private booths. This change also helped to reduce fraudulent voting.

Voter fraud, however, cannot explain the recent decline in voting turnout. Despite great enthusiasm and predictions of higher voter turnout, the 2010 turnout was 41.5 percent of registered voters, only a slight improvement from the 2006 midterms, when just over 40 percent of voters headed to the polls. Perhaps more worrisome is that only 20.9 percent of young people ages 18 to 29 who had registered to vote actually turned out and voted in the midterm elections. A recent study by the Institute for Democracy and Electoral Assistance found that in national elections since World War II, the United States ranks 103rd in voter participation out of 131 democracies.[32]

Explaining Turnout

While there are many reasons for not voting, one that appears common to all nonvoters is that politics offers few rewards and may exact some hardships. One must register to vote, read a long ballot and make sense of it, leave work to go vote, and even wait in lines to vote. All of this to cast a ballot that will surely not, in and of itself, effect the outcome of an election.

The people most likely to vote, then, tend to be people that have ways to reduce the costs of participating and/or increase the perceived benefits. Clear party differences, education, and family socialization of civic duty are all factors that can work to reduce the burden of voting. In countries with strong parties with clear ideological differences, voters may have an easier time making sense of the choices offered to them. The American parties are weak in comparison, often expressing similar policy positions. In such a weak party system environment, it is little wonder that many voters fail to perceive the significance of casting a ballot for one candidate over the other. While strong parties are one way to reduce the costs of voting, education is certainly another. People who are educated are in a much better position to process the ballot and understand the relevance of the choices being offered. Finally, coming from a family that has instilled a strong sense of civic duty is important as a motivating force.

Family socialization experiences may also work to clarify the rewards of voting. Some children grow up in an environment that stresses the importance of voting and the significance of the right to vote. Additionally, wealth and property ownership are tied to a person's ability to perceive that they have an immediate stake in the outcome of elections. People who own homes, have children in the school system, and who are paying income taxes are more likely to see that elections are important to their lifestyle and well being.

An additional reason for low voter turnout may be the lack of competition in congressional elections. The average victory margin in U.S. House races is 40 percent, meaning winners on average won more than 70 percent of the votes cast in their race. Fewer than 1 in 10 races are won by competitive margins of less than 10 percent. Second, 77 percent of House races are won in a landslide, defined as winning by at least 20 percent. Third, on the average 97 percent of incumbents are re-elected, and two-thirds of them won their last two elections in landslides.

The non-competitiveness of congressional elections has contributed to an ongoing decline in voter participation. The states with the least competitive elections, heavily centered in the South, also have the lowest voter turnout. Obviously when powerful incumbents are faced with little or no challenge, they will not conduct the kind of energetic campaigns that might get voters to the polls.

The non-competitiveness of American electoral politics is due to several of the electoral features discussed in this chapter. The winner-take-all quality of single-member plurality elections amplifies the electoral power of the winner while discouraging voters of the opposition party in the district. Additionally, partisan methods of redistricting after every census allow state legislators to draw safe districts. The manner in which legislative districts are drawn is the single most powerful factor in who wins and loses legislative elections. In essence, the state legislators are choosing their constituents before the constituents choose them.

Increasing Turnout

From the above discussion it should be clear that turnout can be increased by reducing the cost, or the burden, of voting. In the United States the entire burden of registering to vote falls on the citizens. In most European nations, on the other hand, registration is done for you automatically by the government. Some states have moved to make registration easier. In some, people may register on the same day and at the same time as they vote. In 1993, Congress also took steps to simplify registration. The motor-voter bill requires states to allow people to register to vote when applying for a driver's license, at various state offices, and by mail. Of course, easing registration will not necessarily increase turnout. Voting itself may impose burdens. Elections, for example, are held on Tuesdays, a work day for most. In recent elections, a greater number of Americans used absentee ballots, which allowed the voter to fill out the ballot and mail it in by a certain date. Some states are also trying to reduce the "costs" of voting by providing an early voting period that includes the weekend.[33]

Turnout will also increase if more people see the benefits that flow from their participation. People who perceive an immediate stake in the outcome of an election are more likely to vote. Such a perception is more likely to develop as people increase their level of political literacy. Advertising campaigns to get out the vote, for example MTV's *Rock the Vote* campaign, may increase the perception that elections are important. Revitalized political parties, with clear platforms and re-invigorated methods to mobilize voters, could certainly also contribute to a renewed voter enthusiasm with the electoral process.

THE VOTERS: EXPLAINING VOTE CHOICE

In casting their ballots, voters are influenced by both long and short-term factors. A particular election does not exist in a vacuum. Voters bring with them a set of personal characteristics and a history of experiences with past candidates and issues. The current campaign then plays upon the stage of pre-existing ties. These predispositions, for many voters, are summarized by their partisan identification, a long-term attachment to one of the political parties. This party identification may be thought of as an anchor sunk in the past. A current campaign with its short-term forces of candidates and current issues may produce waves and swells that either may or may not be able to dislodge the partisan anchor.

Long-Term Forces: Group and Party Identification

Party identification is a general, long-term, psychological attachment to a political party. Early studies in the 1940s and 1950s found that most people expressed a long-term attachment to one or the other of the two political parties. Researchers found, furthermore, that these attachments were very stable over time, so stable that one could actually describe a social group profile for each party. What this means is that each of the parties was a coalition of groups that had, for relatively long periods, been tied to it. For example, upper-middle class Protestant voters have tended to call themselves Republican since the late 1800s, while Catholics, Jews, and other newer immigrant groups have disproportionately been tied to the Democratic Party. Loyalty to a party was, then, cemented by a larger group tie to the party, a tie passed down from one generation to another.

The early studies of voting behavior also found that this group identification with a party was an important determinant of the vote. About 40 percent of voters, in these early polls, would say that they had made up their mind for whom they would vote before the election campaign even began; and this intention was usually consistent with their party identification. Furthermore, on election day voters in the 1950s tended to cast a vote consistent with their long-term partisan identification, and over 60 percent even voted a straight ticket, remaining loyal to their party across national, state, and local offices.[34]

Today, the long-term ties to the political parties seem to be weakening. Today, only 30 percent said that they had made up their minds before the campaign began and 44 percent said they would not decide until after the debates. Voters also exhibit greater volatility, often defecting from partisanship when casting their ballots. Since the middle of the 1960s, over 60 percent split their ticket, switching their votes from party to party.[35]

The greater amount of indecision evidenced in recent elections should not lead to the assumption that party identification is no longer an important determinant of vote choice for many individuals and groups in the electorate. In recent elections, the pattern of votes, along with other evidence about the political leanings of young voters, suggests that a significant generational shift in political allegiance is occurring. This pattern has been building for several years and is underscored among voters in 2008. Among voters ages 18-29, a 19-point gap now separates Democratic Party affiliation (45 percent) and Republican affiliation (26 percent). In 2000, party affiliation was split nearly evenly among the young. The party gap among young voters has expanded over the last four years. Since 2004, Democratic identification among voters under age 30 has increased 8 points, while Republican identification has fallen by 9 points. The percentage of young voters declining to identify with either of the two major parties remained stable at 29 percent.[36]

While party identification is a strong determinant of the vote, there is always some defection from this partisan identification. These defections, together with the vote decision of those who express no partisan predisposition (about 25 percent of the population) can be explained by short-term forces associated with a current campaign, its candidates, and issues.

Short-Term Forces: Issues and Candidate Image

Issues

Issues can be important determinants of vote choice. Some people may make a prospective vote decision, identifying the candidates' positions and determining which candidate is likely to serve the interests of the voters. Other members of the electorate may vote retrospectively, evaluating the current office holders and voting to reward or punish that office holder on the basis of his/her record in office. In general, studies have found that retrospective voting is much less demanding and, therefore, more likely to be the way in which voters use issues in voting.

Of all the issues that are likely to drive short-term electoral forces as well as defections from partisanship, the state of the economy is by far the most important. Studies have shown, however, that the voter's *perception* of the economy as a whole may be more important than the *actual* state of the voter's own pocketbook or for that matter the *actual* state of the economy itself.

The most important campaign issue in 2012 was the troubled economy. According to one survey, 78 percent of voters in 2012 reported that economic issues such as jobs and taxes were the issue most important in choosing for whom to vote. Second most important were social issues such as abortion or same-sex marriage, 14 percent. Foreign policy issues such as the war in Afghanistan and the war on terrorism were seen as much less important with only 8 percent selecting this as most important.[37]

Candidate Image

Studies have consistently found that candidate image is more important than the issue positions of the candidates. While character issues have always been important in American campaigns, they seem to be becoming more central to the vote decision. In recent elections, character issues have been extremely important: Clinton's alleged extramarital affairs, his avoidance, while a college student, of the draft during the Vietnam War, his visit to the Soviet Union, and use of marijuana. Character issues need not always be negative. Leadership, honesty, and decisiveness are also characteristics that voters consider in selecting a candidate. Arthur Miller, in fact, found that along with concern about the deficit, the candidate's level of *caring* were the two strongest predictors of the vote.[38]

THE 2010 MIDTERM ELECTIONS: A RETURN TO DIVIDED GOVERNMENT

Democrats barnstormed into Congress in huge numbers in both 2006 and 2008. By 2010, however, frustration over the economy and fear that an activist government was over-reaching with legislation in areas from health care to the regulation of Wall Street fueled a crop of candidates vowing to bring a renewed model of small-government conservatism to Washington. The most visible and vocal driver of this anger and frustration was the Tea Party, a movement that has no central leadership but is rather composed of a loose affiliation of national and local groups. With the strength of the Tea Party movement behind them and riding a wave of voter frustration over the economy and the federal government itself, the Republican Party sailed into the majority in the House of Representatives and picked up six seats in the Senate, including the Illinois seat once held by President Barack Obama. The Republican gains in 2010 are on a scale not seen since the end of the New Deal.

Once again, the American voters have opted for divided government. In fact, in the past half-century, voters have opted for divided government over 60 percent of the time. Some have argued that Americans rest easier when the purse and sword are in different hands.[39] After all, the Framers tried to craft a constitution that gave politicians proper incentives to check each other. "Ambition [would] counteract ambition," as James Madison saw it, with congressmen keeping presidents honest and vice-versa. Since 1952, voters seem to sense that when different parties hold the legislature and the executive, the Madisonian system works better. From 1900 to 1952, unified government was the norm in Washington. During those years, the same party controlled the presidency and at least one branch of Congress 22 times, while Republicans and Democrats split power only four times. But since 1952, the unified party control seen after the 2008 election is more rare. Voters split control in 17 elections between 1952-2008 and opted for unified control only eight times. The election of 2010 follows this trend with American voters once again separating the purse and the sword by deliberately splitting our tickets. In 2010, more than 20 percent of American voters sided with Madison by purposefully trying to divide and balance power by voting Republican because a Democrat held the White House.[40]

THE 2012 PRESIDENTIAL ELECTION

President Barack Obama's re-election victory exposed tectonic demographic shifts in American society that are reordering the U.S. political landscape. The 2012 presidential election likely will be remembered as marking the end of long-standing coalitions, as voters regroup in cultural, ethnic and economic patterns that challenge both parties—but especially Republicans. Older voters and white working-class voters, once core elements of the Democratic Party, have drifted into the Republican column. Rural and small-town voters, whose grandparents backed the Democrat Franklin Roosevelt and the New Deal, are now reliably Republican. But in cities and sprawling suburbs, a rapidly growing force of Latinos, Asian-Americans, African-Americans and higher-income whites united to give President Obama a winning coalition.

The party coalitions now evidence age, gender, and racial divides. Younger voters are voting Democratic in large numbers while the oldest voters in the electorate have been moving solidly into Republican ranks. Millennial voters, those under 30, favored Obama by a 61 percent to 37 percent margin, while the Silent Generation, those over 70, favored Romney by 54 percent to 41 percent. The 20-point generational gap in support of Obama (61 percent among Millennials versus 41 percent among Silents) is almost identical to the 21-point generation gap in the 2008 national election exit polls, when 66 percent of younger voters and 45 percent of older voters backed Obama. While the younger voters are more liberal on both economic and social issues, older Americans have held relatively conservative views on social issues and the role of government for most of their lives. Their growing unease, and even anger, about the direction of the country in recent years has moved them further toward the Republican Party.[41]

The parties are also divided along gender and racial lines. President Obama's campaign focused heavily on women's issues in 2012 and it paid off on election night, resulting in an 18-point gender gap that largely contributed to the president's re-election. According to CNN exit polls, women made up about 54 percent of the electorate and 55 percent of them voted for Obama, while only 44 percent voted for Mitt Romney. Men preferred Romney by a margin of 52 to 45 percent. In total, the gender gap added up to 18 percentage points, a significantly wider margin than the 12-point gender gap in the 2008 election.[42] The party coalitions also remain racially divided with Democrats enjoying a huge advantage among African Americans and a somewhat smaller advantage among Hispanic voters and Republicans having a 6 percent advantage over Democrats among white voters.

While the support of younger voters for Democrats suggests the Democratic Party is likely to enjoy an electoral advantage at least for the near future, the Republicans continued control of the House and a historically high number of governorships and state legislatures illustrates that neither party can claim a clear ascendancy in the electorate. Furthermore, the number of people who call themselves independent is more numerous than at any point in the last 70 years suggesting an electorate that may still largely be up for grabs. And with a narrow popular vote victory, 51 percent Obama and 47.3 percent Romney, the country is still facing the likelihood of partisan polarization and gridlock. In 2012, President Obama's core constituencies—blacks, Hispanics, young voters, and women—delivered again for both the president and the Democratic Party. Still, 2012 was a markedly different election. Gone was the optimistic tone of hope so prevalent in the 2008 election. The road ahead in the second term is paved with tough choices, amid worsening fiscal conditions. The scorched-earth quality of the negative ad campaign, fueled by unprecedented spending by super PACs has left the country divided and uneasy about the ability of government to solve the major problems facing the nation.

CONCLUSION

Democracies rest on elections and popular participation in them. This is because true and peaceful competition that takes place in the electoral arena is a way for a society to reach decisions. At the same time such participation works to channel support for the democratically elected institutions of government. In the end, the stability of democratic regimes rests on mass support.

Some are coming to question the health and vitality of American electoral politics and, therefore, of the American form of government itself. As we saw at the beginning of this chapter, campaigns are increasingly expensive, and driven by advertising and poll technology. Yet substantive media coverage of campaigns and elections is declining, and congressional races are almost completely dominated by the incumbents who can use the vast resources of their office to discourage meaningful opposition. True competition is disappearing at a rapid rate.

As competition in the electoral arena declines, political conflict spills over to other arenas. Lowi and Ginsberg argue that unelected institutions are now at the epicenter of political conflict: the criminal justice system and courts and the mass media.[43] Between the early 1970s and the present, there has been a tenfold increase in the number of indictments brought by federal prosecutors against national, state, and local officials. In addition, there have been numerous investigations that have not resulted in indictments. The prominence of the courts has also been heightened by the great number of major policy issues that are being fought out in the courts. Abortion, women's rights, civil rights, and a host of environmental issues are currently being debated by judges and juries. The media, as well, have become prominent players in this nonelectoral politics. Today, investigative reporters are eager to publicize and expose official misconduct.

Not only has conflict spilled outside the electoral arena, the conflict has also intensified. We have had over two solid decades of divided government marked by intense battles between the legislative and executive branches. Perhaps because the partisan battles of today are not being fully decided through the elections that enjoy such low voter turnout, conflict continues to be fought out in acrimonious struggles between the branches of government. Neither Congress nor the president will concede defeat, both claiming to be the majority party. In the end, however, the question is whether democratic politics can remain robust in an atmosphere of weak political parties, candidate-centered media campaigns, and special interest group financing of campaigns.

CHAPTER NOTES

[1] Dave Levinthal, "Obama Inauguration Sponsors Spent Millions Influencing Government," The Center for Public Integrity, http://www.huffingtonpost.com/the-center-for-public-integrity/obama-inauguration-sponso_b_2504754.html.

[2] Stanley Kelley, Jr., Richard E. Ayres, and William G. Bowen, "Registration and Voting: Puttin First Things First," *American Political Science Review* 61 (June 1967): 359-70.

[3] William Crotty, *Party Reform* (New York Longman, 1983), 13-25.

[4] Ibid.

[5] Matea Gold, "Democrats Give Special Interests a Role at Convention," *Los Angeles Times*, April 5, 2012, http://articles.latimes.com/2012/apr/05/nation/la-na-convention-money-20120406.

[6] U.S. Pirg, "The Wealth Primary: The Role of Big Money in the 2006 Congressional Primaries," http://uspirg.org, Nov. 1, 2006.

[7] *Davis v. Bandemer*, 478 U.S. 109 (1986).

[8] Donald Saari, "Vetoing the Way We Vote," *Los Angeles Times*, 16 August 1995, A1.

[9] Ibid.

[10] Michael Nelson, ed., *Congressional Quarterly Guide to the Presidency* (Washington, D.C.: Congressional Quarterly Press, 1989), 1427.

[11] *Federal Election Commission*, "The First Ten Years: 1975-1985," Washington, D.C. Federal Election Commission, 14 April 1985, 1.

[12] *Buckley v. Valeo*, 424 U.S. 1(1976).

[13] The Associated Press, "Republican Party Challenges 'Soft Money' Laws," http://msnbc.msn.com/id/27699900, November 13, 2008

[14] Charles Lane, "Supreme Court Upholds McCain-Feingold Campaign Law," *The Washington Post*, December 11, 2003.

[15] Laura Gottesdiener, "The Top 10 Biggest Beneficiaries of 'Citizens United' in the 2012 Election," AlterNet, http://www.huffingtonpost.com/2013/01/21/citizens-united_n_2519178.html?utm_hp_ref=politics

[16] Ibid.

[17] David D. Kirkpatrick, "Use of Bundlers Raises New Risks for Campaigns," *The New York Times*, August 31, 2007, A1.

[18] "Up to 900 Donors Stayed Overnight at White House," *Los Angeles Times*, 9 Feb. 1997, A33.

[19] Eric Lipton and Clifford Krauss, "Fossil Fuel Industry Ads Dominate TV Campaign," *The New York Times*, September 13, 2012, http://www.nytimes.com/2012/09/14/us/politics/fossil-fuel-industry-opens-wallet-to-defeat-obama.html?pagewanted=all&_r=0.

[20] Julian Borger & David Teacher, "As Enron Scandal Spreads, U.S. Starts to Question Cash for Influence Culture," *The Guardian*, Jan. 16, 2002.

[21] Common Cause, "FEC Reform," http://www.commoncause.org/site/pp.esp?c, 2008.

[22] Ann N. Cigler, Marion R. Just, and Timothy E. Cook, "Local News, Network News and the 1992 Presidential Campaign," paper presented at the annual meeting of the American Political Science Association, Washington, D.C., September 1993, 9.

[23] Jessica Rettig, "Walmart Moms Could Swing 2012 Elections," Ken Walsh's Washington, November 2, 2012, http://www.usnews.com/news/blogs/Ken-Walshs-Washington/2011/11/02/walmart-moms-could-swing-2012-elections.

[24] Sam Stein, "Obama Has Spent More on Polling," *The Huffington Post*, http://www.huffingtonpost.com, February 5, 2008.

[25] The Twentieth Century Fund, 1-800-President (New York Twentieth Century Fund Press, 1993), 31.

[26] Montague Kern, *30-Second Politics: Political Advertising in the Eighties* (New York: Praeger, 1989), 57.

[27] Sara Fritz and Dwight Morris, "Burden of TV Election Ads Exaggerated, Study Finds," *Los Angeles Times*, 18 March 1991, A1, A14.

[28] Cotton Delo, "Super PACs Could Drive Total 2012 Election Spending to $9.8 Billion," AdAge blogs, March 7, 2012, http://adage.com/article/campaign-trail/total-2012-election-spending-hit-9-8b/233155/

[29] CNN, "2012 Campaign Online Ad Spending," eM&P, June 3, 2012, http://www.emandp.com/post/single/2012_campaign_online_ad_spending.

[30] Nick Anderson, "Political Attack Ads Already Popping Up on the Web," *LA Times*, March 30, 2004, A15.

[31] Steven Rosenfeld, "Machine Problems Worsened 2008 Voting Woes," www.alternet.org?democracy/107034/machine_problems_worsened_2008_voting_woes, November 13, 2008.

[32] "Dubious Democracy," http://www.fairvote.org/2002/overview.htm

[33] Kay Lehman Schlozman, Sidney Verba, and Henry Brady, "Participation's Not a Paradox: The View from American Activists," *British Journal of Political Science* 25 (January, 1995), 1-36.

[34] Norman H. Nie, Sidney Verba, and John R. Petrocik, *The Changing American Voter* (Cambridge, MA: Harvard University Press, 1976), 29.

[35] Nie, Verba, and Petrocik, *Changing American Voter*, 52.

[36] Scott Keeter, "Young Voters in the 2008 Election," PEW Center Research Publications, http://pewresearch.org, November 13, 2008.

[37] "Economic Issue Drive Voting Decisions," Center for Marketing and Opinion Research, 2012, http://www.cmoresearch.com/pressreleases/2012_04_02.php.

[38] Miller, "Economic, Character, and Social Issues," 317.

[39] Gene Healy, "Three Cheers for Divided Government, " *The Washington Examiner.com*, November 3, 2009, http://washingtonexaminer.com/node/152036.

[40] Gallup, "Independent Voters Favor GOP in 2010 Election Tracking," *Gallup*, July 1, 2010, http://www.gallup.com/poll/141086/independent-voters-favor-gop-2010-election-tracking.aspx.

[41] Pew Research Center, "The Generation Gap and the 2012 Election," November 3, 2011, http://www.people-press.org/2011/11/03/the-generation-gap-and-the-2012-election-3/.

[42] Laura Bassett, "Gender Gap in 2012 Election Aided Obama Win," Huffington Post, November 7, 2012, http://www.huffingtonpost.com/2012/11/07/gender-gap-2012-election-obama_n_2086004.html.

[43] Lowi and Ginsberg, *American Government*, 571.

SUGGESTED READINGS

Abramson, Paul R., John Aldrich, and David W. Rohde. *Change and Continuity in the 2000 Election.* Washington, D.C.: CQ Press, 2002.

Ackerman, Brice and Ian Avers. *Voting and Dollars.* New Haven, CT: Yale University Press, 2004.

Browning, Graeme. *Electronic Democracy.* New York: Cyberage, 2002.

Ginsberg, Benjamin and Martin Shefter, *Politics by Other Means: Institutional Conflict and the Declining Significance of Elections in America.* New York: Norton, 1999.

Hellemann, John and Mark Halpetin. *Game Change: Obama and the Clintons, McCain and Palin, and the Race of a Lifetime.* New York: Harper, 2010.

Nelson, Michael, ed. *The Elections of 2008.* Washington, D.C.: Congressional Quarterly Press, 2009.

Raymond, Allen and Ian Spiegelman. *How to Rig an Election.* New York: Simon and Schuster, 2008.

Web Sites

Center for Voting and Democracy, www.fairvote.org.
The Color of Money, www.colorofmoney.org.
Common Cause. www.commoncause.org.
CQ Moneyline. www.moneyline.cq.com/pml/home.do.
Federal Election Commission Webpage. www.fec.gov.
JibJab, www.jibjab.com.
OpenSecrets. www.opensecrets.org.
Voter Information Services, www.vis.org.

Chapter Seven

THE MEDIA

The opening decade of the new millennium has seen two trends in the mass media that appear to run in opposing directions. On the one hand, there has been a remarkable consolidation in the ownership of the traditional mass forms of communication with a concomitant reduction in both the number and variety of voices heard. On the other hand, the recent invention of new digital technologies challenges this monopolistic control of information and promises to offer a greater access to a greater number of people and groups.

Newspapers, television and radio stations, and magazine and book publishing companies are now owned by a very few corporations. In 1983, fifty corporations controlled the vast majority of all news media outlets in the United States. In 2008, five corporations, Time Warner, Disney, Murdoch's News Corporation, Bertelsmann of Germany, and Viacom (formerly CBS), control most of the media industry in the United States. General Electric's NBC is a close sixth. Radio stations in the United States have seen the greatest consolidation in the past 10 years. Clear Channel Communications, Cumulus Media Inc., Disney, Emmis, Entercom Communications, and Viacom combined own 18 percent of all radio stations in the United States. Measuring by number of stations, however, is misleading. It is the audience share of these giants that is more telling. Of the 287 possible radio markets, the top six media companies together account for reaching 100 percent of the listening audience. Clear Channel Communications Inc. alone has grown from owning 173 stations in 1997 to owning 1,207 stations, reaching 201 out of the 287 markets in the United States.[1]

The consolidation of ownership has worked to the disadvantage of women and minorities. Today, women comprise 51 percent of the U.S. population, but own a total of only 80 stations, or 5.87 percent of all full-power commercial television stations. Minorities comprise 34 percent of the U.S. population but own a total of 43 stations, or 3.15 of all full-power commercial television stations. Hispanics/Latinos comprise 15 percent of the U.S. population but own only a total of 17, or 1.25 percent, of all stations. Asian Americans, comprising 4.5 percent of the U.S. population, own a total of 13, or .95, of all TV stations. The bottom line is that Non-Hispanic White owners control 1,116 stations, or 81.9 percent. Large publicly traded corporations such as ABC/Disney, control the remaining 203, or 14.9, percent of all stations.

While corporate ownership now extends to include the new media like the Internet market, with more than one in four Internet users in this country now logging in with AOL Time-Warner, a whole new universe of digital technologies is now challenging corporate control of the mass media. The first decade of the new millennium saw the end of the era in which consumers received news and entertainment from only a limited number of sources. People are increasingly turning to social networking sites and blogs to not only get political information but also to discuss it. The opportunities to access and communicate information appear infinite. Technorati, an Internet search engine, currently tracks over 112.8 million blogs and over 250 million pieces of tagged social media. Since Technorati focuses almost exclusively on the English language blogosphere, these numbers do not include the millions of other blogs worldwide.

The young may be the greatest consumers of online information, but the new Internet technology is transforming the way campaigns and elections are conducted for all of us. The United States has entered a new age of digital technology, and there will be no going back. The elections of 2008 mark a fundamental shift in how campaigns are conducted in the United States. The most reliable place to find the most current campaign footage is no longer CNN or the broadcast networks but rather one of over ten dozen websites that carry campaign clips ready for public consumption. The Web officially became, in 2008, a vast repository, overflowing with electronic campaign excerpts. In 2008, 61 percent of a sample of registered voters said they had gone to the Internet cruising for political information in the previous week, and 50 percent had swapped political e-mails with someone. Within the previous twenty-four hours, 53 percent had talked to someone about a candidate through a social networking site.[2]

Partly due to its relatively low costs, the Internet facilitates the diversification of communication channels. This is politically important because it expands the range of voices that can express themselves. Until recently, the traditional mass media enjoyed enormous social power based on their unrivaled ability to deliver huge quantities of information to large numbers of people in short time-spans. Their power was further enhanced by the fact that the reception of this information is often passive and rarely involves thought and learning. Now, however, the new technologies compete with the traditional media and, unlike the traditional media, they can be used synchronously or asynchronously, offering users the chance to debate as well as the time to think and deliberate.

This chapter explores these changes as well as their effects. The great expansion in opportunities to communicate political information does not necessarily ensure that citizens will receive pluralist content, for the new digital technologies carry with them the risk of segmenting the American public into narrow special audiences talking to themselves and not hearing contrary voices. Digital technologies are not mass media in the traditional sense. They allow people to pick and choose what they see and hear. The main risk of this audience segmentation is that, in an extreme case, it destroys the common ground on which we base our shared working, living and co-operating.

Young people are the main, and most creative, users of new digital technologies and future generations will use technology in ways we cannot even think about today. Their imaginative uses, however, might turn out quite different from those that we expect. What is clear is that the day of corporate-dominated news dissemination has passed. The consequences of this passing, however, are yet to be seen. We live in an exciting time.

DEMOCRACY AND THE MASS MEDIA

In a democracy, communications must move in two directions: from government to citizens and from citizens to their government. In the United States, a technologically complex nation of over 300 million people, communication in either of these directions would be virtually impossible without mass forms of communication.

The Structure of the Mass Media

The term **mass media** covers the seven major channels of communication that carry messages to a mass audience.

Books

Over forty thousand books are published each year in the United States. While most of them are designed for entertainment, many others focus on public policy and government. In 2010, George W. Bush's memoir *Decision Points,* sold 775,000 copies during its first week on sale. The last nonfiction author to match that scale was Bill Clinton with his autobiography *My Life,* which sold 900,000 hardback copies during its first week. Clinton is one of six former presidents who have landed at the top of *The New York Times* bestseller list for nonfiction since the list began in 1942. Barack Obama earned the honor before taking office, and his *Dreams of My Father* remained on the bestseller list for 156 weeks.

Magazines

Close to ten thousand magazines are published each year in the United States, and the average American reads at least two a week. Again, many of these are solely for entertainment. Still, many others are specifically designed to address matters of political interest. *Time, Newsweek*, and *U.S. News and World Report* have a combined circulation of over 10 million readers. In addition, there are numerous magazines targeted at readers with particular ideological perspectives, for example, *Nation, New Republic,* and *The National Review.* Finally, there are many professional journals like the *American Political Science Review.*

Newspapers

Approximately 10,000 newspapers are regularly published in this country, with 1,500 in daily circulation. Both newspaper circulation and readership have recently declined dramatically as more people are turning to online sources for their news. Back in 1970, newspapers sold roughly one newspaper per household every day in America. In 2008, daily newspaper sales equaled only half the households.

Television

At one time, the three networks—ABC, NBC, and CBS—and their affiliates controlled the medium of television. Today, however, the networks are part of a much larger and more competitive market. The arrival of cable and satellite television has greatly increased the number of stations available to many in the United States. During the economic recession the number of homes that had cable declined to the 1990 level. But alternative delivery systems' (ADS) penetration grew markedly in 2010, reaching 28.7 percent of TV households, an all-time high. Direct broadcast satellite, the largest component of ADS, is at 28.4 percent, up from 27.6 percent in Nov. 2007. Whether broadcast, cable, or satellite, television remains the medium most used and relied upon by the American public. The average household spends seven hours a day in front of the television set, and the average individual spends three hours a day watching TV. Americans say that they are most likely to get the news from television, and they tend to feel that television news is the most credible.

Radio

There are over ten thousand radio stations, divided between the AM and FM bands. The average American listens to the radio two-and-a-half hours a day. Today, talk radio programs like that of

Obama At Podium
Televised coverage of President Obama's White House Press Conference, August 7, 2009. Credit: RTTNews

conservative Rush Limbaugh have become potent forces in the world of politics. Politicians and candidates use talk radio to interact with the American public. Ideologues on the left and the right compete for talk radio time to disseminate their particular views on the issues of the day.

Records

Each year more than seven million records, tapes, and compact discs are sold in the United States. While CDs are primarily produced and consumed for enjoyment, many of the most popular songs have overtly political themes and messages. Rock concerts and rock artists often raise funds for politically charged causes such as AIDs, environment, world hunger, and so forth.

Motion Pictures

Twelve thousand theaters across the country show approximately 250 films a year. Many of these movies deal with political subjects, for example, Al Gore's *An Inconvenient Truth*, the 2005 hit, *Thank You for Smoking*, and in 2006, *Who Killed the Electric Car?*

The Internet

In recent years, the traditional news outlets have failed to expand their audiences despite the high level of interest in the war in Iraq and the financial crisis of 2008-2009, which has led to an increase in the amount of time Americans spend on the news. With other media trends flat, the steady growth in the audience for online news stands out. As of 2011, there are over 250 million Internet users in the United States, and Internet news, once largely the province of young, white males, now attracts a growing number of minorities. The percentage of African Americans who regularly go online for news has grown from 16 percent in 2000 to 58 percent in 2009. The Internet population has also broadened to include more older Americans. Nearly three-quarters of Americans in their 50s and early 60s say they go online, up from 45 percent in 2000. Education continues to be the biggest single factor driving online news use, largely due to the continuing gap in Internet access. Fully 91 percent of college graduates regularly use the web for news, compared with just 36 percent of those who do not finish high school. Both men and women over age 40 without a degree are the least likely to go online for news with any regularity.[3]

Social Media

The political landscape has been radically altered by the social media's pervasive influence on public discourse. It was only ten years ago that people thought Vice President Al Gore was weird for texting his wife, Tipper. By 2011, every politician checks e-mail on a Smartphone and monitors what the media and voters are saying on social media platforms. In the midterm elections of 2010, a large majority of the members of Congress were on Facebook and a smaller majority used Twitter, YouTube and Flickr.

Social media, like *Facebook* and *Twitter*, empower one-on-one local engagement. A political campaign relying on social networks can decentralize its message and reach individual voters directly.

While tweets and updates may not sway Independents in of themselves, building strong online communities of supporters can translate into electoral success. The Republican National Committee's Women Site is just one example of how the Republican Party has used social network community to rally groups. The Democrats are using Facebook to broadcast posts from Barack Obama; some of these posts have received thousands of comments. The Democrats have also recently employed a mobile phone strategy. The OFA iPhone application lets party supporters find people living in their immediate vicinity to contact and to try and get them out to vote. In addition, the application provides canvassing tips. The Democrats have also used text messaging to activate mobile phone users and have them place calls to potential voters.

The social media are mostly the domain of younger Internet users and while young adults (18-24) are, as a group, less interested in political activities, they are far more likely than any other group to use blogs and social networking sites to engage in political discussions. A new report by Pew Internet and American Life Project has found that 34 percent of young adults make political use of social networking sites and 34 percent post political material on the Internet. What will be interesting to watch, the Pew study points out, is how these younger users will use these existing networks as they get older. It will also be interesting to see if these developments will mean that socio-economic status will become less of an indicator of civic engagement, or if these new technologies will create new barriers of entry for those with a lower income and education level.[4]

Government Regulation of the Media

Thomas Jefferson wrote that "Our liberty depends on freedom of the press, and that cannot be limited without being lost."[5] Jefferson would be pleased with the amount of freedom enjoyed by the press today. Unlike journalists in many European and most African and Asian countries, journalists in the United States do not need a license to practice their trade. Stories do not have to be cleared with the government before publication and, in fact, the courts of this country have consistently ruled that there can be no prior restraint of the media.

The following sight is sure to bring a smile to the face of any protestor or candidate running for public office. Media attention is the one indispensable ingredient to success. The media can make or break candidates and causes.

The First Amendment does indeed give the media considerable freedom from governmental interference. Still, this freedom is not complete. There are very real constraints on the content of mass communications. One of the most important of these constraints takes the form of government regulation of three aspects of media operation.

Technical and Ownership Regulation

In the early years of radio, there was chaos. Stations would often broadcast on similar frequencies, thereby jamming each others' signals. The broadcasters petitioned the government to make some sense out of the cacophony. The result was that Congress passed the Federal Radio Act of 1927, which declared public ownership of the airwaves. The argument was that there was only a scarce number of airwaves, and these needed to be regulated in the interest of the American public. Accordingly, the law requires that private broadcasters obtain a license in order to use these airwaves.

Later, in 1934, Congress passed the Federal Communications Act, which created the Federal Communications Commission (FCC). The FCC has seven members, chosen by the president, with no more than four members being from the same political party. The members of the FCC serve a fixed term of seven years. They may not be removed by the president and can only be removed through impeachment by the House and conviction by the Senate. This makes the FCC an independent regulatory agency.

The FCC regulates all interstate and international communication by radio, television, cable, and satellite. The FCC is also charged by Congress to regulate the ownership of the mass media. In the 1940s, the FCC actively fought the concentration of media ownership. For example, an owner was limited to one of any type of broadcast medium, FM station, AM station, or TV station, in a single community.

In the 1950s the FCC loosened its ownership rules somewhat to allow a single owner to own up to seven AM, seven FM, and seven television stations across the nation. By the 1980s the number of television stations had more than quadrupled, and the number of radio stations had tripled. The FCC responded by further relaxing its ownership limits, allowing an owner to control up to twelve of each type of broadcast medium. The technological developments of the 1990s have continued to make the 1930s structure of communications regulation obsolete. In 1996, Congress overwhelmingly approved a major telecommunications act that seeks to replace government regulation with competition. The act removes the long-standing barriers between sectors of the telecommunications industry. For example, the new legislation abolishes the local phone monopolies and allows local companies to compete in offering long distance services.

On June 2, 2003, the Federal Communications commission relaxed decades-old restraints on the broadcast industry. In a bitter split along party lines, the Republican majority of the FCC, led by Chairman Michael K. Powell, voted 3 to 2 to relax rules that prevented TV stations from merging with local newspapers and restricted how many stations one company could own, both nationally and locally. The new rules repealed a 28-year-old ban on cross-ownership of TV stations and newspapers in all but the smallest media markets and one person or company would be able to own three TV stations up from two. This broad revision of ownership rules would clear the way for further consolidation by the biggest media conglomerates, enhancing the economic prospects of companies such as News Corp., Viacom Inc., and Tribune Co., parent of the *Los Angeles Times*.

In Los Angeles, for example, Tribune would be permitted to continue its ownership of both the *Los Angeles Times* and KTLA Channel 5. Without the FCC's action, the company would have been required to divest itself of one of those properties by 2006, when the station's broadcast license comes up for renewal. Also under the new rules, broadcasters would be permitted to own stations reaching 45 percent of the nation's viewers, up from 35 percent. Taken together, the new rules would allow a single company to own the following media outlets in Los Angeles: the *Los Angeles Times*, KTLA, KCBS Channel 2, KCOP Channel 13, Time Warner Cable, KIIS-FM, KROQ-FM, KNX-AM, KFWB-AM, and KABC-AM. Then in late 2007, despite staunch opposition from both Congress and media watchdog groups, the FCC voted 3-2 to further relax its rules against businesses consolidating ownership of media outlets in a given region. The 3-2 vote was strictly along party lines, with FCC Chair Kevin Martin and commissioners Robert McDowell and Deborah Tate, all Republicans, supporting the rule change.

In January 2009, President Obama, a Democrat, selected Julius Genachowski as the new head of the FCC and the partisan make-up of the FCC was thereby altered. Soon after, the FCC took up the issue of Internet regulation, and in December 2010, a divided Federal Communications Commission approved new "net neutrality" rules by a vote of 3 to 2. Once again the decision was divided along party lines, but this time it was with two Democratic commissioners and the Democratic chairman Julius Genachowski voting in favor of the rules. The FCC's two Republican commissioners voted against the rules. **Net neutrality** is the concept that as providers of this ever-important public resource, they must maintain a neutral, hands-off policy of allowing that information to flow unmolested. The rules prohibit Internet providers such as telephone and cable companies from discriminating against Internet services, such as those that come from their rivals. But the new rules give broadband providers flexibility to exercise what the FCC calls "reasonable management" of data to deal with problems of network congestion and unwanted traffic, including junk emails. Internet companies will also be allowed to charge more for higher speed access in some cases. The rules for wireless companies are similar to those for broadband companies when it comes to prohibiting the blockage of content and services. Wireless companies, however, were given more leeway to manage data traffic because wireless systems have more bandwidth constraints. The new rules are likely to be challenged by the courts and by members of the incoming 113th Congress.

Regulation of Content

The First Amendment bars congressional interference with the press. But because broadcast channels are scarce, or at least were scarce until the arrival of cable and satellite technology, Congress has argued a right and need to regulate the content of the broadcast media. This congressional duty to regulate does not extend to the theoretically unlimited world of news print.

There are two principal restraints on broadcast content in effect today. First, the FCC requires a station that gives or sells air time to a candidate for any public office make an equal amount of time, under the same conditions, available to other candidates for that same office. This is called the **equal time provision**. Congress passed the law requiring the FCC to monitor compliance with this provision because it wanted to ensure a level and fair playing field for political debate in the United States. Congress, however, has never extended the equal opportunities rule to news coverage.

Roosevelt was an outstanding media president.

In 1949 the FCC created a second rule, the **fairness doctrine**, which required that stations provide opportunities for the expression of conflicting views on issues. Like the equal-time provision, the fairness doctrine was never applied to news coverage. In 1987, the FCC repealed the fairness doctrine because the growth of cable television made it unnecessary. Recent efforts on the part of Congress to enact the fairness doctrine into law have failed. Similarly, efforts to regulate the Internet have met with staunch opposition. Congress is currently considering regulating certain types of speech, for example obscenity, on the Internet.

There are three other legal restraints that place limitations on the content of both the print and broadcast media. Libel laws preclude the media's printing or airing of a story that unjustly and falsely damages a person's reputation. Obscenity laws limit the media's right to show obscene materials. Finally, there are laws limiting the media's access to classified information about intelligence operations.

In addition to the legal restraints, media content, especially in regard to the coverage of war, is also constrained by government pressure. During the Spanish-American War of 1898 and throughout World Wars I and II, journalists considered themselves part of the war effort. Beginning with the Korean and then Vietnam Wars, the press took an increasingly independent and critical view of the military. When the Vietnam War ended, many in the military blamed the press for "losing Vietnam." In 1983, the Pentagon barred all journalists from the initial invasion of Grenada. During this same period, the Reagan administration threatened to prosecute reporters for violating espionage laws.[6] Then in 1989, the Pentagon selected a dozen reporters to cover the invasion of Panama but restricted them to an airport until nearly all the fighting was over. Then during the first Persian Gulf War, the Pentagon accredited pools of journalists who had to first pass a military security review and who could then only interview military personnel with an escort present. News organizations filed suit charging the military with violating the First Amendment. Before the lawsuit against Gulf War press restrictions could come before a judge, however, Desert Storm ended. For the war in Iraq in 2003, the U.S. military devised new press rules. About 500 reporters (one-fifth of them from foreign countries) were placed, or "embedded," in military units. These embedded journalists have been given greater access to operational combat missions.[7]

Political Functions of the Mass Media

Entertainment

The news media in the United States are different from the media in other countries in that they are almost all private, for-profit corporate enterprises. This means that one of their principal functions is to make money for those who own them. These profits are tied to the media's ability to sell off their space, in the case of newspapers, or time, in the case of radio and television, to corporate advertisers called sponsors. Advertising revenues are directly related to the size of the audience, usually measured in terms of newspaper circulation or reader/viewer ratings. The ratings game, the need to attract large audiences, will even affect the content of the news and public affairs programs. The dramatic and sensational, the conflicted and the sordid, are more likely to attract large audiences.

Surveillance

Surveillance involves the press's role in the definition of what constitutes "news." The media are the gatekeepers, determining what the public sees, reads, and hears. It is the job of a journalist to sort through the enormous number of stories that might be considered as news and winnow them down, giving the audience a distilled, condensed version of reality.

Interpretation

But the news is nothing as simple as reality, or even parts of reality. The news is a story about reality told by a storyteller, a journalist. The media place events and people in a context, probing motives, causes, and effects. It is quite common for a newspaper or TV news program to run a segment that offers analysis and interpretation. In addition, there are whole programs devoted to such interpretative news reporting, for example, *60 Minutes*, *Nightline*, and *20/20*.

Watchdog

Traditionally, the American press has accepted responsibility for protecting the public from corrupt, incompetent, or deceitful politicians. In 2004, for example, the press reported the abuses of prisoners by U.S. soldiers in Iraq. Graphic photos of naked Iraqi prisoners forced into humiliating sexual poses were aired on national television news. Congress, forced by the airing of these photos to respond, launched hearings to discover why U.S. troops had behaved in such an illegal and horrible manner.

Socialization

The media are the principal purveyors of American culture, influencing particularly the young and recent immigrants. Studies have shown that children pick up most of their political information and many of their most basic values from the mass media.[8] Children who have the most exposure to mass communications tend to be better informed and have more political opinions than those who have less exposure.[9]

Persuasion and Propaganda

The mass media have long been looked at as vehicles to be used to persuade and mobilize mass publics. Governments, public officials, candidates, and interest groups have all, at one time or another, attempted to turn media coverage to their advantage. Advertisements and public information programs are examples of modern forms of propaganda. But all political campaigns involve propaganda designed to persuade and mobilize support.

Agenda Setting

Many believe that the media's power to persuade and change opinions is greatly overrated. They suggest instead that the media's primary power is the power to influence what the public thinks about rather than what they think. Issues prominently featured in the media, for example, become the issues that citizens think are most important. In 1990, on the twentieth anniversary of Earth Day, the television news featured many stories on the environment. Studies have shown that such coverage led many in the public to focus on environmental issues as a top priority. Certainly the media's coverage of Barack Obama's 2008 campaign for the presidency helped to jettison the issue of health care onto the national political agenda.

THE INCREASED IMPORTANCE OF THE MODERN MASS MEDIA

The press has become the political intermediary in the American political system. This role has grown out of two modern, parallel developments. The first is the pervasiveness of the American media that has in turn led to the public's and politicians' increased reliance upon the press. The second is the movement of the press into an increasingly autonomous position, largely free from political controls.[10]

A Pervasive News Media

The media are more pervasive today than ever before. The types of media, however, that Americans use on a regular basis have changed radically in the last ten years. Newspaper circulation has been in decline for many years, but the drop accelerated in 2007 and even more rapidly through the recent recession. In just four years, nearly a dozen metro dailies have shut down. This includes the *Baltimore Examiner* and the *Cincinnati Post*. And according to the aptly named NewsPaperDeath-

Watch.com, many of the remaining papers are switching to a hybrid print/online format. In some cases, they have gone online-only. In 2009, CNN listed digital publishing as one of the Top 10 Tech Trends. The article also mentioned Twitter and other micro-blogs as a huge threat to the newspaper business. The article noted, "[Twitter] lets authors post short bursts of information, which become searchable the moment someone clicks 'send.'"[11] When it comes to news, a daily paper simply cannot compete with the up-to-the-second Internet. And of course, there is the added incentive that the Internet is free,

The audience for network television news programs also has shrunk over the last quarter-century. To get a sense of the extent of decline over time, consider 1980, the year that CNN began, and *U.S News & World Report* asked "Is TV News Growing Too Powerful?" For the month of November of that year, total viewership of the network news programs was 52.1 million. If one compares November-to-November data, nightly network news viewership has fallen 53 percent, since 1980. In 2008, the cable channels came closer than ever to surpassing the networks. On election night, the big three broadcast networks attracted an average of 32.9 million viewers between 8 p.m. and 11 p.m. That was down 9 percent from election night 2004. The big three cable news channels, by contrast, attracted 27.2 million viewers on average during that period, up 58 percent from 2004. The networks are not only challenged by cable news. Another challenge for the evening network newscasts is that of attracting younger viewers. In 2008, they made no progress on this front. The median age of nightly news viewers was 61.3 years for all three evening newscasts in 2008, according to data provided by Magna Global USA, a media-buying firm. That was virtually unchanged from 2004 when the median age was roughly 60 years of age.[12]

More Americans get their news today from the Internet than from newspapers or radio, and three-fourths say they hear of news via e-mail or updates on social media sites, according to a new report. Sixty-one percent of Americans said they get at least some of their news online, according to a survey by the Pew Internet and American Life Project. That is compared with 54 percent who said they listen to a radio news program and 50 percent who said they read a national or local print newspaper. Almost all respondents, 92 percent, said they get their news from more than one platform. "In the digital era, news has become omnipresent. Americans access it in multiple formats on multiple platforms on myriad devices," reads the report, based on a survey conducted in 2010. "The days of loyalty to a particular news organization on a particular piece of technology in a particular form are gone."[13]

An Autonomous Press

The American press had its early beginnings as a partisan tool first of the American revolutionaries and then of the first political parties. Over the course of two centuries, however, the press has been transformed into a fiercely independent, autonomous profession, or as some call it, a "fourth estate."

Phase I: The Early Partisan Press

The first continuous newspaper in the United States was published in Boston by two brothers, John and Duncan Campbell.[14] The single-sheet Boston *Newsletter* began publication on April 24,

1704. By 1750, there were thirteen regular newspapers being printed in the colonies and gradually four-page papers replaced the single sheet.

The spread of the colonial press was actively encouraged by the government. In fact, these early papers were under the control of the British colonial government. Most papers carried on their mastheads "By Authority" and received a subsidy for publishing the proceedings of the colonial governments. Besides these subsidies, the papers were also sustained through lucrative government printing contracts. A final aspect of government control was to be found in the fact that the papers could be prosecuted for seditious libel if they included content seen as offensive to the colonial authorities.

During the Revolutionary War, the newspapers actively distanced themselves from the British colonial governments. The Stamp Act that had placed a tax on newspapers greatly angered the press, and as their anger made its way onto the pages of the papers, the press became the engine that would drive opinion against the British.

The press became further politicized during the fight over ratification of the new Constitution of 1787. The supporters of the Constitution sought to mobilize opinion through *The Federalist Papers* while the opponents of the new Constitution argued their case in the *Letters of a Federal Farmer*. This period of history is early evidence of the critical role the press plays in linking government and public opinion.

After the Constitution was ratified, the press remained partisan and politicized. Alexander Hamilton encouraged John Fenno, an ardent Federalist, to come to the nation's capital and establish a newspaper to serve as a voice for the administration of President Washington. Hamilton's encour-

Ronald Reagan was one of the best with the media.

agement of Fenno came primarily through the promise of government printing jobs. In response, the Jeffersonian Republicans cultivated Philip Freneau, urging him to publish a Republican journal, luring him with the promise of a government position, personal loans, and government printing contracts.

During the Jacksonian period, increased and intensified competition within and between the political parties led to an even greater party reliance on the press to mobilize electoral support. As the parties continued to subsidize and support the press through government printing contracts and patronage appointments, the number of newspapers burgeoned to over 12,000, with one copy for every fifteen people. Largely because of their financial dependence on the parties, the press remained intensely partisan during this period. The U.S. Census listed only 5 percent of all newspapers as "neutral" or "independent."

Phase II: The Penny Press and Yellow Journalism

After the Civil War, rapid breakthroughs in printing and communication technologies worked to give the press greater financial independence, thereby freeing it from its earlier partisan control. The high-speed rotary press meant lower costs and lower subscription rates. In addition, the invention of the telegraph carried with it the ability to disseminate information between cities at low cost. Growing numbers of people in the urban centers of the country provided a ready audience for the cheaper newspapers. When the suffrage was extended in the 1800s to nonproperty owning white males, this audience was not only ready but eager as well for political news. Finally, the commercialization and industrialization of America created a merchant class eager to reach mass audiences by way of advertising. The press was no longer dependent on the political parties. In the end, politicians themselves began to relinquish their partisan hold on the press as they found other ways to communicate with the public, in particular, strong party organizations geared to mass mobilization.

Together these developments worked to create a penny press with mass readership and much greater independence from partisan control. The editors of these newspapers often engaged in **yellow journalism**, focusing on sensationalism and scandal. Also during this period, an elite set of newspapers, including for example the *New York Times*, was developing. These newspapers were beginning to define their work as a profession, and the journalists working for these papers adopted a libertarian theory of the press.

The libertarian theory argued that journalists must print "the truth." It is not, according to libertarian theory, the job of the journalist to express his own viewpoint. Rather, the journalist is merely a conduit for the views of others. For example, it was not uncommon in the first half of the eighteenth century to find newspapers expounding the political philosophy of the owner of the newspaper. The press moguls of the nineteenth century, men like William Randolph Hearst and Joseph Pulitzer, had great influence on American government and society.

The libertarian theory of the press worked to the advantage of sitting presidents as well. During the period from 1870 through the middle of the 1960s, presidents in particular had greater access to press coverage and used the press as a bully pulpit to shape public opinion. It was generally accepted that in exchange for press access to politicians, certain topics would be off limits to the press corps. The private behavior of politicians and behind-the-scenes partisan machinations, for example, were taboo. Even John F. Kennedy's Addison's disease, for example, was left undiscussed in the press.[15]

Phase III: Investigative Journalism

In the middle of the 1960s, people began to see that big business was dominating many of the economic markets in the United States. It was little wonder that journalists soon began to look at the marketplace of ideas and recognize that this market too was dominated by established politicians often at the expense of other views. By the 1960s the prohibitive cost of starting a newspaper meant that the only way to get into the newspaper business was to buy out an existing one. Broadcasting further challenged the libertarian theory's assumption of an unlimited number of outlets for the expression of ideas. The technology of broadcasting made unlimited access impossible at the same time that it called for government regulation.

The Vietnam War, Watergate, and the Kerner Commission's criticism of media coverage of race relations worked to further call into question just how open a marketplace the press had ever been to any views other than those of the political establishment of public officials and established leaders. As a result, journalists began to articulate a new professional code of social responsibility. The professional press corps began to argue that the American public has a right to know the full story. If the full story does not spring from the mouth of officials, journalists have the responsibility to go behind the scenes and unearth the full story.

The result was the advocacy journalism of the late 1960s. Reporters felt justified in using journalism for what they perceived to be morally just causes: fighting corruption in government, disclosing environmental degradation, and unearthing examples of racial inequity. By the 1970s, advocacy journalism had given way to a new stage of adversarial journalism with the journalists actively challenging statements made by officials. The press acts as the opposition. The press's tradition of yellow journalism muckraking, the new technology of television, and the press's increasing access to alternative sources of information allowed the press to assume this role. In addition, the investigative, inside story made good sense economically; such stories filled with conflict and titillation built audiences that could then be sold to corporate advertisers.

Phase IV: Conglomerate Ownership of the Press

Today the news media are big business. The nine most influential national news organizations—ABC, CBS, NBC, *the New York Times, the Washington Post, the Wall Street Journal, the Los Angeles Times, Newsweek,* and *Time*—are all owned by corporations that rank among the five hundred largest in the United States.[16] Even more dramatic than the size of these media companies is the trend toward even greater concentration and at a very rapid rate. In 1981, a majority of the business in newspapers, radio, television, magazines, books, and movies was controlled by forty-six corporations. By 2007, ownership has become further consolidated into nine conglomerates. (AOL-Time Warner, Disney, Bertelsmann, Viacom, News Corporation, TCI, General Electric-NBC, Sony, and Seagram.)[17]

The trend towards increased concentration of media ownership is most evident with newspapers. Between 1960 and 1985, newspaper chains, that is, companies that own more than two daily newspapers in different cities, increased their share of total daily newspaper circulation from 46 to 77 percent.[18] Gannett Company, for example, owns *USA Today* as well as eighty-seven other dailies, and Knight-Ridder owns twenty-nine daily newspapers.

Ownership of radio and television stations is less concentrated but apparently only for the moment. The year 1995-1996 alone saw a number of huge conglomerate media mergers involving broadcasting. On July 30, 1995, the largest entertainment company in the world was created when Walt Disney Company agreed to buy Capital Cities/ABC Inc. for $19 billion in cash and stock. This second largest merger in U.S. history (after the $25 billion acquisition of RJR Nabisco by Kohlberg Kravis Roberts & Company in 1989) brings together the number one television distributor and network and the nation's premier producer of movies, creating a powerhouse with combined sales of $20.7 billion. On August 29, 1995, Time Warner announced its intention to buy Turner Broadcasting, which owns CNN, a merger that would create the largest media company in the world, a conglomerate with revenues of more than $18.7 billion. On August 1, 1995, CBS announced its intended merger with Westinghouse Electric Corporation. This merger at a cost of $5.4 billion will create the biggest TV, radio empire, with control over fifteen television stations and thirty-nine radio stations that reach over one-third of the country's listeners and viewers. Then on June 20, 1996, Westinghouse announced its imminent buy out of Infinity Broadcasting Corporation, bringing to Westinghouse an additional eighty-three radio stations. The government maintains that diversity of voices in the media is protected because of the proliferation of new technologies, from the Internet to satellites. As a result, Congress has further deregulated the telecommunications industry, and beginning in 1996, cable, radio, and television corporations underwent an even more radical wave of consolidation. Then, on January 10, 2000, American Online and the Time Warner conglomerate announced that they would merge into a $350-billion media empire.

Media concentration appears to be accelerating. In September of 2003, the Federal Communications Commission allowed Univision Communications Inc.'s $3.25 billion acquisition of radio chain Hispanic Broadcasting Corp. Univision now controls two-thirds of the nearly $2.8 billion spent on advertising on Spanish-language television and radio. On October 7, 2003, General Electric merged its NBC assets with Vivendi Universal's entertainment operations, including movie studio Universal Pictures and the TV unit that owns three cable channels and produces the "Law and Order" franchise. NBC Universal, as the new company is called, posted sales of more than $13 billion in 2003. Then in 2006, Walt Disney announced that it would buy Pixar for $7.4 billion and newspaper publisher McClatchy acquired rival Knight-Ridder for $6.1 billion. Overall, there were 138 media mergers in the United States worth $48.1 billion in 2006 and 372 mergers in 2007, including Rupert Murdoch's purchase of *The Wall Street Journal*. In 2009, after nine months of negotiations, Comcast, the United States' largest cable operator, acquired NBCUniversal in a deal valued at around $30 billion. The mergers are also getting much bigger, and media experts expect many more mergers, particularly since the "old" media companies are seeking to reinvent themselves in order to cash in on the growing number of viewers/listeners/readers/ who are flocking to online media sites like the ones owned by Google, for example YouTube, and Yahoo. In short, the media are now huge corporate entities largely independent of political control. Their status as business enterprises will, no doubt, affect the news gathering process.

Phase V: Atomization of the Media

Despite the growing concentration of media ownership, a contrary trend, an atomization of the media, has also developed in recent years. Whereas concentration has led to a national media, atomization has fragmented the influence of this national media. The major newspapers and networks have lost their dominance, while other media, some not even considered news organizations, have started to play a greater role in American politics.

This trend is partly the result of technological changes. First, the national networks began to lose viewers to the local news stations. The local stations are now linked together via satellite and can thereby share coverage of national and international affairs. Next, the traditional stations lost viewers to the cable television, which because of their number can offer more, specialized programming. The offerings of cable television have become more focused. This "narrow casting" appeals to small segments of the audience in contrast to the networks' more generalized attempts to appeal to a mass audience. For example, C-SPAN provides live coverage of Congress and allows viewers to see and hear Congress at work.

There are other cable stations that cater to various racial and ethnic groups. A cable system in Los Angeles and New York is targeted to the Jewish population. A cable channel in California broadcasts in Chinese, one in Hawaii broadcasts in Japanese, and one in Connecticut and Massachusetts broadcasts in Portuguese. Stations in New York provide programs in Greek, Hindi, Korean, and Russian.

The Internet has led to additional news sites. Major newspapers can now be read on-line, as can several political magazines. Often these on-line services are at the forefront of the news. During the 2010 campaign, Web logs, or "blogs," played a critical role. Free Republic and the DailyKos are two of the ideologically driven Web logs that managed to attract hundreds of thousands of readers and helped shape the presidential campaign and contributed to a powerful grassroots mobilization of voters.

The trend toward atomization of the media is also a reflection of the increasing partisan polarization of the American electorate following the 2000, 2004, 2008, and 2012 elections. This polarization is clearly reflected in the viewing habits of Americans. Since 2000, the number of people who regularly watch the Fox News Channel has increased by nearly half from 17 percent to 25 percent and the gains have been greatest among political conservatives. At the same time, CNN, Fox's principal rival, has a more Democrat-leaning audience than in the past. A nationwide poll, conducted in April and May, 2004, has found that the audiences for Rush Limbaugh's radio show and Bill O'Reilly's TV program on Fox are overwhelmingly conservative and Republican. By contrast, audiences for some other news sources notable NPR, the NewsHour, and magazines like the *New Yorker*, the *Atlantic*, and *Harper's* tilt liberal and Democratic.[19]

The line between information and entertainment has been blurred. The trend toward atomization has worked to make politics more accessible to more people, but it has also made the news less factual. The newspapers and network news must compete with the more sensational coverage and so they too have become more focused on scandal, personalities, and entertainment-driven stories. Accuracy has suffered in the process. In an effort to attract viewers on election night in 2000, the networks prematurely predicted the victor in Florida to be Al Gore, then had to retract it and give the state to Bush, and then retract that and admit the race was too close to call. The public is largely

THE NEWS GATHERING PROCESS

There are three main sets of factors that affect news decisions.

Personal Background and Values

Sociologist Herbert Gans has found that media personnel tend to be drawn disproportionately from middle and upper middle class backgrounds.[20] Today there are still very few minorities in the journalistic professions. It is perhaps not surprising that reporters tend to have values that correspond to their socioeconomic backgrounds. Studies have found that journalists tend to have a positive orientation to private business, emphasize individualism, and take moderate positions on political and social matters.[21] While some have suggested that journalists tend to be liberal, no such consistent ideological bias has ever been documented. Rather than being consistently liberal or Democratic, journalists might better be thought of as Progressive, reform-oriented, almost anti-partisan in approach.

It may be more difficult for the voices of women and minority groups to be heard because, as noted in the beginning of this chapter, the ownership of mass media by only a handful of huge conglomerates, has worked to reduce ownership by women and minorities. In the landmark 2003 decision *Prometheus v. FCC*, the Third Circuit chastised the FCC for ignoring the issue of female and minority ownership of mass media outlets. Following the decision, however, the FCC has done almost nothing to address the issue. Consequently, from October 2006 to October 2007, the number of minority-owned commercial TV stations decreased by 8.5 percent. In the same time period, the number of African-American-owned stations decreased by nearly 70 percent. Finally, it should be noted that there has been no improvement in the level of minority broadcast television ownership since 1998, even as the total universe of stations has increased by approximately 13 percent.

The state of female and minority ownership in the broadcast sector is even more shocking when compared to other industries. Women own 28 percent of all non-farm businesses but currently own less than 6 percent of commercial broadcast television stations. Minorities own 18 percent of all non-farm businesses, but own approximately 3 percent of commercial broadcast television stations. While female and minority ownership has been advancing slowly in other sectors since the late 1990s, it has gotten progressively worse in the broadcast industry. The level of minority ownership in the general non-farm sector rose 23 percent from 1997 to 2002. However, from 1998 to 2007, the level of minority broadcast TV ownership dropped.[22]

Professional Values

Since the beginning of the 1900s, journalists have increasingly taken themselves seriously as professionals. The result has been the creation of journalistic societies, trade journals, and even a code of ethics to be followed. Reporters today follow certain standards of decency, refusing, for example, to print, say, or quote racial epithets. In addition, reporters depend on documentary practices such as reliance on reliable sources. Finally, since Watergate, journalists see themselves as social critics, crusaders for justice, ombudsmen for the disadvantaged. The post-Watergate generation of journalists takes a participatory stance. In Carl Bernstein's words: "The job of the press is not to follow Ronald Reagan's or George Bush's agenda, but to make its *own* decisions about what's important for the country."[23]

Organizational Factors

Perhaps more important than either personal background or professional considerations are the economic imperatives of the modern mass media. The news media, as noted above, are now part of larger conglomerates. These conglomerates often include non-media companies, and they are usually run by business executives that have little or no background in the media. The governing imperative of such conglomerates is to make a profit. To make a profit both newspapers and broadcasting must build an audience. This audience can then be sold to corporate advertisers, or sponsors.

Advertising is big business. Despite its lowest ratings in history, the broadcast industry experienced a banner year in 2008. Advertisers paid $45 billion to the networks and broadcast stations and an additional $3.7 billion to cable networks. Social network advertising revenues have also grown enormously in recent years. In 2010, mobile social networking alone reached revenues of $421 million, marking a 50 percent increase overall. It is projected that advertising on social network sites will breakthrough the $1 billion revenue mark by 2013.[24]

THE CONTENT OF THE NEWS: INFORMATIONAL BIASES

The Bias Debate

The media's growing importance has led to an increased concern over possible bias in media coverage of current events and people in the news. Left-wing critics claim that the press is simply a tool of "the establishment." Michael Parenti, for example, sees corporate ownership of the mass media as inevitably leading journalists in a pro-capitalist, pro-corporate posture.[25] These critics see all forms of mass communication as bolstering the establishment line. Even films are viewed as reinforcing capitalist dogma. There is an equal number of media critics on the right. They see the media as the tool of anti-government, anti-American "liberals." Journalists are viewed as advocates of a pro-welfare spending, anti-business, liberal agenda.

What critics on the left and right have failed to realize is the overriding influence of the economic pressures on the increasingly competitive mass media. A continually biased program is unlikely to attract a large audience. To ensure profits, the media must entertain the audience. The pressure to entertain and make money is far more determinant of media content than ideological purity. Both the networks and newspapers are experiencing stiffer competition—the networks from cable and the newspapers from human-interest tabloids. This increased competition in a field already driven by the profit motive works to produce a number of biases in media content.

Informational Biases

Infotainment

As discussed above, the first priority of the media is to build an audience. This means that even political matters will be played as "stories." The news tends to personalize, concentrating on individuals rather than institutions or process. For example, stories on the president commonly focus on some personal habit or trait of the person holding the office. Similarly, statistical data is often glossed over in favor of an illustration using an individual's story. For example, a jump in unemployment may be illustrated by an interview with someone standing in an unemployment line.

The media also attempt to build audiences through a focus on the dramatic, the visual, the exceptional. Violence is a central element of the news because it tends to be so visual. Change is emphasized over continuity, and news stories often follow certain intuitively understandable schema: good versus bad, rich versus poor.

Several authors have recently noted that audiences for news programs are built and maintained when the content of the news is brought to the lowest common denominator. Responding to the merger of Capital Cities/ABC with Disney, author Brian Stonehill, director of the Media Studies Program at Pomona College, argues that "the juvenile sets the tone for the culture, and the escapism of fun and games wins a shutout over the business of information."[26]

Negativity

An outgrowth of the media's need to entertain as well as its professional adherence to a watch-dog role, is a tendency to accentuate the negative aspects of American life. Journalists are intent upon publicizing the missteps of political leaders. The media's preference for "bad news" can be seen, for example, in the fact that the negative coverage of presidential candidates has risen steadily in recent decades and now exceeds the positive coverage.

In 2012, both President Obama and Governor Romney received overwhelmingly negative treatment in the press over the entire course of the general election campaign. Just 19 percent of stories about Obama were "favorable" in tone versus 30 percent that were "unfavorable." For Romney the ratio was 15 percent favorable to 38 percent unfavorable. Compared to social media like Facebook and Twitter, though, much of the news was outright friendly. Statements about Obama on Twitter were negative by a 2-1 margin and 4-1 margin for Romney. "Every week studied on Twitter was as negative as the worst week each candidate had in the mainstream press," the study concluded.[27]

COVERAGE OF CAMPAIGNS

The informational biases built into the mass media can all be seen in the media's coverage of political campaigns. An agenda dominated by problems, divisive issues, and the "negative" dominates campaign coverage. Reporters seek to find the story behind the official story. A former editor of *The Washington Post* has said of reporters: "[They] want to be important players in the political process, not passive bystanders. They want to mix it up with the candidates, join the debate and defend the Republic as surrogates of the masses."²⁸ As a result, campaign coverage tends to follow a fairly set formula.

The Horserace

The media's proclivity toward the personal, the dramatic, and the divisive has led campaigns to be covered primarily as horseraces between competing sets of candidates. During the 2000 election, 71 percent of network television stories were horse race-style features and in 2012, almost 9 out of 10 stories were about the horse race, according to the Pew News Coverage Index study.²⁹

This fixation on the horserace may stem from the fact that many journalists were once campaign insiders. For example, ABC's Jeff Greenfield, George Stephanopoules, and George Will, NBC's Ken Bode, CBS's Diane Sawyer, PBS's Bill Moyer and David Gergen, and *The New York Times's* William Safire were all campaign insiders before they were journalists. It is little wonder that these journalists see campaigns in terms of strategy and winning.³⁰

Gaffes

In Washington, an off-the-cuff remark is referred to as a gaffe. A gaffe has been defined as the trouble a politician get into when he or she says what is actually being thought. The media often amplify the initial gaffe by repeatedly covering it, and the politician unwittingly further amplifies it by repeatedly apologizing over it. The end result is that such mistakes trap candidates in a spiral of controversy, getting them in ever deeper trouble.

There were an abundant number of slips of the tongue and embarrassing moments during the course of the 2012 campaign. If there were an Olympics for political gaffes, Republican nominee Mitt Romney would be a gold medalist. At the height of the primary season, he said, "I like being able to fire people…" Romney then followed that misstep with another, this time in an interview on CNN: "I'm not concerned about the very poor. I'm in this race because I care about Americans. I'm not concerned about the very poor. We have a safety net there. If it needs repair, I'll fix it." The debates provided yet another forum for his gaffes. While discussing discretionary spending, Romney said that the government should not be in the business of public television, including funding PBS. Instead, television should be privately funded, he insisted. But his point got lost when he added, "I don't want to kill Big Bird; I love Big Bird." The phrase ricocheted around Twitter and Facebook, and eventually became the subject of an Obama attack ad. He did not fare any better in the second debate when, while discussing his time as Massachusetts governor, Romney said that he did not have enough female job candidates for state office, and so he asked assistants to bring him "binders of women." This comment was followed by the inevitable Twitter hashtags, tumblr blogs and t-shirt carrying the line.³¹

Coverage of the Incumbent

Incumbents running for re-election enjoy a number of advantages over their challengers, including a greater amount of media attention. Because the incumbent is in a position of power, the press corps is more likely to cover his or her actions. It is not unusual, for example, for the press to become almost fixated on a president's eating habits, holiday travels, and golf game, in addition to his discharge of the affairs of state. A recent study has found, however, that such abundant coverage is not always a good thing. Apparently journalists believe that because incumbents enjoy an advantage in terms of the amount of coverage, the press corps must balance this advantage by scrutinizing more carefully his or her actions. Such intense scrutiny leads to more negative coverage. Media coverage of the incumbents running in the 2010 midterms was overwhelmingly negative. The Republicans received 31 percent positive coverage and 69 percent negative. For the Democrats, the comments were 32 percent positive and 68 percent negative.[32]

COVERAGE OF THE PRESIDENT

All the informational biases discussed above lead the news media to fixate on the presidency. The president is one individual while the Congress is made up of 535 individuals. The presidency is dramatic; the Supreme Court is less so. In foreign affairs, the president is virtually the sole actor, and foreign affairs often involve a crisis likely to dominate the news agenda. Finally, that the president has sole responsibility for nuclear weapons, together with assassinations and assassination attempts, has heightened the press's interest in the health and well-being of the president.

This focus on the presidency is also stimulated by the White House itself. White House correspondents, numbering close to seventy-five, cover the White House as a regular beat and rely on information they receive from the president's own staff, information carefully crafted by the staff to control the direction of the story. The most frequent form such control takes is the press release, a prepared text distributed to reporters in the hopes that they will use it verbatim. A daily news briefing at 11:30 A.M. enables reporters to question the president's press secretary about these news releases and get film footage for the nightly television news. To no small extent, the correspondents are the captives of the White House press releases.

Such intense scrutiny may set the president up for eventual negative coverage as his performance falls short of heightened expectations. One study found that 76 percent of all references to President Bush by network news reporters was negative.[33] Similarly, President Obama received mainly bad press after his first 100 days in office, reversing his previous run of positive news coverage, according to a study by researchers at George Mason and Chapman Universities. The study found that every major policy of the administration received more criticism than praise from the press.[34]

COVERAGE OF CONGRESS

Most reporters in Washington are accredited to sit in the House and Senate press galleries, but only about four hundred cover Congress exclusively. Most news about Congress comes from the numerous press releases issued by the members of Congress. In addition, C-Span now covers Congress live.

In general, Congress tends to receive less coverage than does the president, because of the informational biases of the media discussed above. Congress does not walk. Congress does not talk. Consequently, it is difficult to personalize the institution in the same way that the office of the presidency can be personalized. One study has found that over 60 percent of the *CBS Evening News* shows opened with a story that featured the president.[35] In addition, coverage of Congress has actually declined in recent decades. One study found that congressional stories on the network news dropped by two-thirds between the 1970s and 1980s.[36]

When the Congress can be made more personal and dramatic, it is more likely to get on the news. After the Republicans in the House censured President Obama for not being open and transparent enough, particularly regarding healthcare reform, C-SPAN proposed to the then-presumptive House Speaker John Boehner an increase in the number and scope of press cameras in the House chamber.

THE POLITICIANS RESPOND: THE MANAGEMENT OF NEWS COVERAGE

Shorter Campaign Speeches

Candidates' and politicians' speeches are getting shorter and shorter. In the nineteenth century, hour-long speeches were the norm. Today, candidates deliver stump speeches in less than seventeen minutes. Politicians know that whatever they say is likely to be reduced to only a few seconds on the evening news. To control these few seconds of air time, candidates speak in soundbites, tricky little statements that are most likely to fill the media's need for drama and brevity. In 2008, Barack Obama's "Yes we can" was so often repeated that a song was made out of it and made available on iTunes. While these sound bites are an important part of a communications strategy, consumers now have many more sources for news and information about the candidates and the campaign. Concerns about the length of the sound bite seem anachronistic in the age of digital technology. From the candidates' homepages to YouTube, the full text of a speech or the latest commercial is just a click away. Voters can get not only news more easily, they can also make it themselves with access to a blog, video camera and an Internet connection. While the Internet allows sound bites to be transformed into whole speeches with a click of a mouse, it also enables us to access information sources we support and ignore those we oppose, and it makes it easier for rumors to spread and survive. Ironically, 20 years ago, political observers were lamenting the brevity of candidates' speeches; today there is so much political discourse available as to potentially numb the electorate rather than deprive it.

Spin Control

Politicians have not been willing to sit by idly, leaving journalists in control of the news agenda. A group of political consultants, "spin doctors," have begun to play a central role in determining strategy, first at the presidential campaign level and then in more and more state and local races. These consultants attempt to tailor the politician's message to the needs of the news organizations for drama, personalization, and brevity. Increasingly, these consultants stage media events, situations that are simply too newsworthy for the media to pass up.

In 2010, the federal government hired a New Orleans man for $18,000 to appraise whether news stories about its actions in the Gulf oil spill were positive or negative for the Obama administration, which was keenly sensitive to comparisons between its response and former President George W. Bush's much-maligned reaction to Hurricane Katrina. The government also spent $10,000 for just over three minutes of video sent to the networks showing a routine offshore rig inspection. And, in what appeared to be an attempt to ward off negative criticism, it awarded a $216,625 no-bid contract for a survey of seabirds to an environmental group that had criticized what it called the "extreme anti-conservation record" of Sarah Palin, a possible 2012 rival to President Barack Obama.[37]

Presidential Debates

Candidates ideally would like to get as much free media coverage that they can control as possible. The presidential debates that have been regular features of presidential campaigns since 1960 offer the perfect setting for a candidate to warehouse his ideas with fairly little intervention on the part of journalists. In general, the political challenger has the most to gain from a debate. The challenger needs the attention, has little to lose, and gains the appearance of being presidential because of being on the same stage with the president himself. The incumbent president, on the other hand, has little to gain and may lose by making a mistake or appearing unprepared.

The debates are usually only an hour and a half in length, and usually no more than three debates are televised. The candidates can, however, extend the reach and importance of the debates by getting the news media to continue to discuss what occurred in the debates and perhaps show film footage from the debates repeatedly. Presidential debates have, therefore, also begun to turn on the production of effective, catchy soundbites. Traditional debate in the pre-radio age tended to focus, for a sustained period, on a single issue and tended to involve the real interchange of views. For example, the 1948 Dewey-Stassen debate was on the Mundt-Nixon bill outlawing the Communist Party. While radio did not kill such serious debate outright, it did insofar as the audience for radio expected to be entertained, expected messages to be brief, and expected to change the channel if any of their expectations were not met. Debates, in other words, had to be briefer and more entertaining. In 1856, Charles Sumner's eighty page *Crimes Against Kansas* speech was reprinted in its entirety, and almost one million copies were sold to people who actually read it! Barack Obama's broadcast campaign messages in 2008 and 2012, on the other hand, would not in their entirety even begin to approach that length. Today, in a ninety minute debate each candidate will actually speak for less than thirty minutes.

One of the most important features of presidential debates is exclusivity. For the nation's scores of third-party presidential candidates, the debates are the political equivalent of not getting asked to the high school prom. While Pat Buchanan, Ralph Nader, and other third-party candidates sought to fight back through lawsuits and the Internet, they should not have taken their exclusion personally. Third-party candidates have been getting the debate brush-off since 1960, when Congress modified a 1934 law that required any broadcast station staging a debate to welcome all candidates. Congress suspended that rule to let Richard Nixon and John F. Kennedy square off by themselves in the first televised debates.

A special nonprofit commission selected by the Republican and Democratic hierarchy now controls the task of selecting who appears in the presidential debates. Not surprisingly, the bipartisan

Commission on Presidential Debates, established in 1987, has set the bar higher than the current third-party candidates can jump, mandating they score at least 15 percent in nationwide polls. Only Ralph Nader came close in 2000 with 5 percent.

Political Advertisements

While politicians can never hope to control completely either the content or slant of their *free* news coverage, they can turn to paid political advertisements over which they can exert complete control over the message. Political advertisements have a long history in this country, but they have become increasingly central components of modern campaigns.

The new importance of political advertising has six sources. First, the primary election system used to choose nominees for public office requiring candidates to appeal directly to thousands, even millions, of voters. In the case of presidential primaries, candidates must reach voters in each of the thirty-eight separate states that employ primary elections. Second, advertisements now represent the biggest campaign expenditure in most campaigns. In 1952, only 30 percent of overall funds were so spent. In 2012, candidates bought over $1 billion in air time; that is eight times as much, after inflation, as was spent in 1972.[38]

A third factor working to increase the importance of advertisements is that there are legal limits on how much candidates for certain public offices can spend on their campaigns. Such limits lead candidates to place a premium on reaching the most voters at the lowest possible cost. A fourth source of the centrality of advertisements in modern campaigns is found in the legal limits placed on how much money the Democratic and Republican National Committees and interest groups can donate to a candidate's campaign. However, one way around these limits is for interest groups and political parties to make and air an advertisement on behalf of the candidate. Such independent spending is not limited by federal campaign finance laws, and the Supreme Court in July 1996 ruled that parties and groups may spend unlimited amounts on behalf of candidates. The Bipartisan Campaign Reform Act (BCRA) of 2002 prohibited any corporate expenditure on issue ads mentioning the names of candidates during the period 30 days before a Federal primary and 60 days before a Federal general election. The FEC then ruled that any ad mentioning a candidate in the pre-election period was prohibited by BCRA. In 2007, however, the Supreme Court ruled the prohibition unconstitutional as applied to a Wisconsin Right to Life group. The group had aired ads in 2004 urging voters to contact Wisconsin Senators Feingold and Kohl to oppose a Senate filibuster. The ads did not specifically support or oppose the election of Senator Feingold, who was up for reelection that year, but it clearly stated a candidate's name. The decision in the case, *Federal Election Commission v. Wisconsin Right to Life, Inc.* led to an increase in issue advertising during the 2008 election.

The changing structure of the advertisements themselves may account for their increased importance. Today's television advertisements employ the rich multimodal properties of television. These advertisements use montage, music, and symbolism to create an entire mood. The soft focus, long shots, and slow music are the grammar of this mood. In addition, the increasing negativity built into modern advertisements has made them more powerful campaign tools. Not only have studies shown that people tend to remember negative messages better than positive ones, but also negative ads are dramatic, personal, conflict-laden, in short, news worthy. The news media often pick up soundbites taken from the advertisements and replay them on the evening news. The news media thereby amplify and legitimize the negativity of the original advertisement, and they do so for free!

Negative political ads hit a new low during the election of 2012. One ad, from Priorities USA Action, an outside group supporting President Obama, featured former Missouri steelworker Joe Soptic saying, "When Mitt Romney and Bain closed the plant, I lost my health care." The ad suggests that Soptic's wife died of cancer because he lost his insurance after Romney's company, Bain Capital, closed the plant. "There was nothing they could do for her, and she passed away in 22 days," the man continues in the ad. "I do not think that Mitt Romney realizes what he's done to anyone." What it failed to mention was that Soptic's wife died five years after he lost his job, and she had her own insurance for part of that time. Conservative strategist Frank Luntz, president and CEO of Luntz Global, LLC, conducted various focus groups on the effectiveness of political ads, and found that the 2012 ads are different in one key way. "It's one thing to be negative," he observes. "It's another thing to demonize your opponent."39

Political advertisements may also carry subliminal messages that covertly influence viewers' attitudes. In 2008, an anti-Obama video produced by the McCain campaign contained an eight-minute montage of sometimes-contradictory statements about the Iraq war made by Senator Barack Obama. At the very beginning, the title, "The Obama Iraq Documentary," flashes into place in a blaze of orange. For a single frame, a tiny fraction of a second, Obama's face is framed by the following prominent letters: "a l q D." While many editing programs do allow randomized letter placement, for a brief moment, letters that the brain may want to play with and try and spell something that makes sense with, frame Obama's face. If you type "al qD" into Google, you get this response: "Did you mean: al qaeda."

Finally, political advertisements may have become more important because they may be more informative than the news itself. In the month leading up to the 2006 mid-term elections, local television news viewers got considerably more information about campaigns from paid political advertisements than from news coverage. Local newscasts in seven Midwest markets aired 4 minutes, 24 seconds of paid political ads during the typical 30-minute broadcast while dedicating an average of 1 minute, 43 seconds to election news coverage. The analysis also shows that most of the news coverage of elections on early and late-evening broadcasts was devoted to campaign strategy and polling, which outpaced reporting on policy issues by a margin of more than three to one (65 percent to 17 percent).40

THE EFFECTS OF THE MASS MEDIA

What People Remember and Know

Since the late 1980s, the emergence of 24-hour cable news as a dominant news source and the explosive growth of the Internet have led to major changes in the American public's news habits. But a new nationwide survey finds that the digital revolution and attendant changes in news audience behaviors have had little impact on how much Americans know about national and international affairs. On average, today's citizens are about as able to name their leaders, and are about as aware of major news events, as was the public nearly 20 years ago.[41] In 1989, for example, 74 percent could come up with the name of the vice president; today, it is somewhat fewer who can do so (69 percent). In 2010, 43 percent said they did not know what Obama's religion is and 34 percent of Republicans thought President Obama is Muslim.[42]

Influencing Public Opinion

Documenting the effects of mass media on specific attitudes is difficult. Studies have found that prolonged, sustained media coverage on a single topic, especially in a crisis like war, can significantly influence mass opinions.[43] The same study found that of all the people expressing opinions on the news, for example the president, members of Congress, network commentators had the greatest influence on the audience. Other studies have found that even a single story can influence attitude change.[44]

Setting the Political Agenda

Evidence suggests that media coverage does heighten the audience's concern with certain topics over others. For example, studies have found that news coverage of crime has led to increased, in fact unrealistic, concern on the part of the mass public. Furthermore, the less knowledgeable a viewer is about political affairs, the more influenced he is by the agenda of the press.[45]

Cynicism, Alienation, and Declining Efficacy

The press's role in setting the political agenda also means that the increasingly sensational and negative topics covered in the news will dominate the public's agenda as well. Years ago, Michael J. Robinson attempted to document that the CBS documentary "The Selling of the Pentagon" produced antimilitary attitudes in the program's audience.[46] A more recent study has shown that the media attentive are more likely to pick up negative views of the economy.[47]

Other studies have found that those most attentive to the news experience reduced levels of political efficacy with feelings of political powerlessness and mistrust. One study concluded that "the presentation of news in a manner that conveys a high degree of political conflict or criticism leads to a sense of distrust and inefficacy among newspaper readers."[48]

Behavior

There is little consistent evidence that mass forms of communication can alter behavior. Recent studies attempting to link violence on television with violence in young adults have failed to find a clear causal relationship. What the mass media appear to be able to do is channel the behavior of people already predisposed to behave in a particular way. For example, news coverage and political advertisements may work to reinforce an individual's pre-existing partisan views, thereby further encouraging that individual to vote for the favored candidate. Another study has found a relationship between teenage suicide rates in troubled youths and media coverage of teenage suicide.[49]

CONCLUSION

This chapter has focused primarily on the role of the mass media in transmitting images and information to the citizenry of this country. The media are equally important transmitters of the citizens' views to those in government. Throughout history, journalists have suggested policy concerns and offered solutions to pressing problems. In doing so, the mass media have worked to bring issues of public concern to those in government. Today, the media have developed sophisticated methods to tap mass sentiments. Beginning in the 1800s, newspapers conducted straw polls to measure public opinion. These polls usually questioned subscribers but made no scientific attempt to get a random sample. By the middle of the twentieth century, the media began to conduct scientific polls and develop their own survey research divisions. Newspapers and broadcasters even team up to do extensive polling together. Virtually every day, the results of one major poll or another are published. During the 2012 campaign, CNN and *USA Today* reported a fresh poll daily from September 30 through the November election.

Recent developments suggest that the media link between governed and government will only become a more direct one in the future. The 2012 campaign organized supporters and reached voters who no longer rely primarily on information from newspapers and television. YouTube now provides people a continual stream of political information, and cell phone text messages remind them to vote.

Not all consequences of the new technology are likely to be benign, for while American elections have always included a certain amount of deceptive practices, the advent of Internet technology allows for a more widespread and effective dissemination of misinformation. In 2008, for example, robo calls told people their polling places had been changed. According to the National Network for Election Reform, registered voters in Virginia, Colorado, and New Mexico reported receiving phone calls in the days before the election claiming that their registrations were cancelled and that if they tried to vote they would be arrested. Domain names with prospective and actual vice-presidential nominees' names also popped up on the Internet, leading to sites with unexpected information. For example, Obama-Biden.org and Obama-Biden.com diverted people to the website of the American Issues Project, an extremely anti-Obama organization.

At the moment, most states do not have adequate or any legislation that addresses the concerns inherent in such deceptive practices, and candidates have not done a good job of protecting themselves by proactively registering typo domains.[50] What remains to be seen is whether the new forms of media will work to create an electronic democracy with fully informed and participating citizens. Today's audience is now at once better informed, more skeptical and, from reading blogs, sometimes trafficking in rumors or suspect information.

CHAPTER NOTES

[1] "Media Giants: Who Owns What?" www.thinkandask.com/news/mediagiants.html.

[2] Patt Morrison, "A Case of Elective Compulsive Disorder," *Los Angeles Times,* October 30, 2008, A23). The candidates recognize the importance of these new forms of communication.

[3] The Pew Research Center, "News Audiences Increasingly Politicize," http://people-press.org, June 8, 2004, p.4.

[4] Frederic Lardinois, "Social Media is Slowly Changing the Demographics of Political Engagement," *ReadWriteWeb*, September 1, 2009, http://www.readwriteweb.com/archives/social_media_is_slowly_changing_the_demographics_o.php

[5] Quoted in Robert Kurz, "Congress and the Media: Forces in the Struggle Over Foreign Policy," in *The Media in Foreign Policy*, ed. Simon Serfaty (New York: St. Martin's, 1990), 77.

[6] Jay Peterzell, "Can the CIA Spook the Press?" *Columbia Journalism Review* (July/ August 1986): 18-19.

[7] Jason DeParle, "17 News Executives Criticize U.S. for Censorship of Gulf Coverage," *New York Times*, 3 July 1991, 1.

[8] Sidney Kraus and Dennis Davis, *The Effects of Mass Communication on Political Behavior* (University Park: Pennsylvania State University Press, 1980), 127.

[9] Doris Graber, *Mass Media and American Politics* (Washington, D.C.: Congressional Quarterly Press, 1980), 127.

[10] Richard Davis, *The Press and American Politics* (New York: Longman, 1992), 6.

[11] Alexander Moschina, "The 'Must Own' Tech Stock for 2011," *Investment U*, January 8, 2011, http://www.investmentu.com/2011/January/the-mcclatchy-company-newspaper-publishing-company.html.

[12] Pew Project for Excellence in Journalism, "The State of the News Media," 2009, http://www.stateofthemedia.org/2009/narrative_networktv_charts_and_tables.php?media=6&cat=92009).

[13] Doug Gross, "Survey: More Americans Get News from Internet than Newspapers or Radio," *CNN Tech*, March 1, 2010, http://articles.cnn.com/2010-03-01/tech/social.network.news_1_social-networking-sites-social-media-social-experience?_s=PM:TECH.

[14] Alfred McLung Lee, *The Daily Newspaper in America* (New York: Macmillan, 1937), 17.

[15] James MacGregor Burns, *John Kennedy: A Political Profile* (New York: Harcourt, Brace, 1960).

[16] Mark Hertsgaard, *On Bended Knee: The Press and the Reagan Presidency* (New York: Schocken Books, 1989), 77.

[17] Ask Questions.org, "A New Bridge to the Media," http://www.askquestions.org, Nov. 21, 2005.

[18] Hertsgaard, *On Bended Knee*, 78.

[19] The Pew Research Center, "News Audiences Increasingly Politicized," p.2.

[20] Herbert J. Gans, *Deciding What's News* (New York: Pantheon, 1979).

[21] Michael Parenti, *Inventing Reality* (1985).

[22] Out of the Picture 2007: Minority & Female TV Station Ownership in the United States," http://www.freepress.net/files/otp2007.pdf, October, 2007.

[23] Carl Bernstein quoted in *Vanity Fair*, March, 1989, 106.

[24] "Report: Social Network Ad Revenue to Double in 2010: *MobileMarketingWatch*, March 25, 2010, http://www.mobilemarketingwatch.com/report-social-network-ad-revenue-to-double-in-2010-reaching-revenues-of-421m-5851/.

[25] Parenti, *Inventing Reality*.

[26] "The Mickey Moused Media," *Los Angeles Times*, 1 August 1995, B9.

[27] Benjy Sarlin, "Pew Study: 2012 Campaign Coverage Overwhelmingly Negative For Both Sides," TPM, November 2, 2012, http://2012.talkingpointsmemo.com/2012/11/pew-study-2012-campaign-coverage-overwhelmingly-negative-for-both-sides.php.

[28] Richard Harwood, "The Press Should Set The Agenda," Washington Post, 26 September 1988, sec. 4, 3.

[29] Kevin Drum, "Campaign Coverage 2012: It's All About the Horse Race, Baby," *Mother Jones*, November 19, 2012, http://www.motherjones.com/kevin-drum/2012/11/campaign-coverage-2012-its-all-about-horserace-baby.

[30] Kathleen Jamieson, *Dirty Politics* (New York: Oxford University Press, 1992), 181-2.

[31] Keli Goff, "The Top Campaign Gaffes of 2012," Loop 21, June 2012, http://www.loop21.com/politics/top-political-campaign-gaffes-2012.

[32] Howard Kurtz, "Networks Diss Dems, Favor Tea Party," *The Daily Beast*, October 20, 2010, http://www.thedailybeast.com/blogs-and-stories/2010-10-20/media-bias-in-politics-tv-networks-favor-tea-party/

[33] Karen J. Callaghan, Frauke Schnell, Robert M. Entman, *Framing American Politics,* Pittsburgh: University of Pittsburgh Press, 2005.

[34] Meredith Jessup, "Obama Paid $18K to Monitor "Negative' Coverage of Oil Spill," *The Blaze*, September 13, 2010, http://www.theblaze.com/stories/obama-administration-hired-media-guru-to-monitor-negative-coverage-of-oil-spill-response.

[35] Michael Robinson and Margaret Sheehan, *Over the Wire and on TV* (New York: Russell Sage, 1983).

[36] S. Robert Lichter and Daniel Amundson, "Less News is Worse News: Television News Coverage of Congress, 1972-92," in *Congress, the Press, and the Public*, eds. Thomas Mann and Norman Ornstein (Washington, D.C.: American Enterprise Institute, 1994), 131-40.

[37] Nikki Schwab, "Media Coverage of Obama Grows More Negative," *U.S. News Politics*, September 14, 2009, http://www.usnews.com/news/washington-whispers/articles/2009/09/14/media-coverage-of-obama-grows-more-negative.html?PageNr=2.

[38] "Mad Money: TV Ads in the 2012 Presidential Campaign," *The Washington Post*, http://www.washingtonpost.com/wp-srv/special/politics/track-presidential-campaign-ads-2012/.

[39] Nancy Cordes, "Negative Presidential Campaign Ads Going to Extremes," CBS *This Morning*, August 10, 2012, http://www.cbsnews.com/8301-505267_162-57490682/negative-presidential-campaign-ads-going-to-new-extremes/.

[40] Dennis Chaptman, "Study: Political Ad Time Trumps Election Coverage on the Tube," http://11news.wisc.edu, Nov. 21, 2006.

[41] The PEW Research Center for the People and the Press, "Public Knowledge of Current Affairs Changed by News and Information Revolution," http://people-press.org/report/319, April 15, 2007.

[42] Chris Good, Barbour on Muslim Rumors: People Know Little About Obama," *The Atlantic*, September 8, 2010, http://www.theatlantic.com/politics/archive/2010/09/barbour-on-muslim-rumors-people-know-little-about-obama/62629/.

[43] Benjamin Page, Robert Y. Shapiro, and Glen R. Dempsey, "What Moves Public Opinion?" *American Political Science Review* 81 (March 1987): 31.

[44] David L. Jordan, "Newspaper Effects on Policy Preferences," *Public Opinion Quarterly* 57 (Summer 1993): 191-204.

[45] Shanto Iyengar and Donald R. Kinder, *News That Matters: Television and American Opinion* (Chicago: University of Chicago Press, 1987), 33.

[46] Michael J. Robinson, "Public Affairs Television and the Growth of Video Malaise," *American Political Science Review* 70 (1976): 425-30.

[47] David E. Harrington, "Economic News on Television: the Determinants of Coverage," *Public Opinion Quarterly* 53 (Spring 1989): 17-40.

[48] Arthur Miller, Edie Goldenberg, and Lutz Ebring, "Type-Set Politics," *American Political Science Review* 73 (1979): 77.

[49] Madelyn Gould and David Shaffer "The Impact of Suicide in TV Movies," *New England Journal of Medicine* 315 (11 September 1986): 685-94.

[50] Common Cause, "Deceptive Practices 2.0," http://www.commoncause.org/deceptive_practices_report.pdf)

SUGGESTED READINGS

Alterman, Eric. *What Liberal Media? The Truth About Bias and the News.* New York: Basic Books, 2004.

Anderson, David M. and Michael Cornfield, eds. *The Civic Web: Online Politics And Democratic Values.* Lanham, MD,: Rowman & Littlefield, 2003.

Bagdikian, Ben. *The New Media Monopoly.* Boston: Beacon Press, 2004.

Campbell, Richard, Christopher Martin, and Bettina Fabos. *Media and Culture.* New York: St. Martin's Press, 2009.

Chester, Jeff. *Digital Destiny: New Media and the Future of Democracy.* New York: New Press, 2008.

Fenton, Tom. *Bad News: The Decline of Reporting, the Business of News, and the Danger to Us All.* New York: Harper Collins, 2005.

Graber, Doris A. *Mass Media and American Politics.* Washington, D.C.: CQ Press, 2002.

Hamilton, James T. *All the News That's Fit to Sell.* Princeton, NJ: Princeton University Press, 2004.

Jenkins, Henry. *Convergence Culture: Where Old and New Media Collide.* New York: New York University Press, 2008.

Schaeffer, Todd and Thomas Birkland. *Encyclopedia of Media and Politics.* Washington, D.C.: CQ Press, 2007.

Weaver, David, et al. *The American Journalist in the 21st Century: U.S. News People at the Dawn of a New Millennium.* New York: Eribaum, 2006.

West, Darrell M. *Air Wars: Television Advertising in Election Campaigns, 1952-2008,* 5th ed. Washington, D.C.: CQ Press, 2009.

Web Sites

Accuracy in the Media, www.aim.org.
Federal Communications Commission, www.fcc.gov.
Journalism.org, www.journalism.org.
Newseum, www.newseum.org.
Claremont Institute. www.townhall.com.
TotalNEWS. www.totalnews.com.

Chapter Eight

INTEREST GROUPS

Estimating the power of an interest group is not easy. One might think that an interest group with 4.5 million members would be less powerful than one that speaks for a majority of the population. If one did think that, one would be wrong. Take the case of the National Rifle Association and the women's movement. In 2012, nearly 1,000 anti-women laws were passed in this country. From attempts to defund Planned Parenthood to the reauthorization of the Violence Against Women Act being stalled in Congress to candidates like Todd Akin, who claimed there are cases of "legitimate rape," women find themselves fighting for rights they thought they had long won. The National Rifle Association, on the other hand, scored numerous victories despite 2012 breaking the record for the most mass shootings in a single year.

There are a number of factors that go into making one group more powerful than the next. To begin with, it helps to have the Constitution on your side. The Equal Rights Amendment for women was never ratified. The Second Amendment, on the other hand, was proposed and ratified in the 1700s. A second factor that helps the NRA is mission unity. The NRA has only one goal, legalized gun ownership. The same cannot be said for women who have groups like the National Women's Political Caucus and the League of Women Voters but who do not share a common mission. Perhaps because women have a varied set of goals, women tend not to be single-issue voters. In 2012, women tended to prioritize economic issues over the more strictly women's issues of abortion and birth control. The NRA has built its reputation on being able to turnout single-issue gun voters. Related to this issue of mission unity is the fact that women tend not to be identity voters; they do not vote for women candidates simply because they are women. Gun advocates do turnout to vote for candidates for no other reason than they have a record of voting against gun control legislation.

Some interest groups are lucky to benefit from being organized on an issue that is, quite simply, popular. Even after the recent history of gun violence in this country—the shootings at Columbine

High School, the shooting of Congresswoman Gabby Giffords, the Aurora, Colorado massacre that left 12 dead and 58 wounded, and the December 2012 shooting at Sandy Hook Elementary School that left 20 children and 6 adults dead—polling suggests that Americans favor more gun rights not less. This support for guns is no doubt related to an additional factor aiding the NRA, strong political allies. The NRA has vocal allies in both the Democratic and Republican Parties. Women do not enjoy such a great number of friends in high places. Even though there are now a greater number of women in Congress and state government positions, they are still under represented.

A final advantage that the NRA enjoys over women's groups is the myth that it is extremely powerful. In 2012, many of the candidates supported by the NRA did not win and many of the candidates whom they opposed, went on to win. Women's groups were, in fact, way more successful. In 2012, Planned Parenthood alone spent $5 million more than the NRA and won 98 percent of the races they supported. Still, the fact is that many politicians fear the power of the NRA in a way they do not fear women's groups.

The year 2013 is shaping up to be the year of the battle over gun control. With women making greater gains in Congress and the Connecticut massacre fresh in the public's collective conscience, 2013 could see a real power shift for both the NRA and women's groups. If women can capitalize on their 2012 electoral successes and mobilize some of the factors the NRA has in the past, they could become a force with which to be reckoned.[1]

DEFINING INTEREST GROUPS

An **interest group** is an organization of people and or companies with specific policy goals, entering the policy process at several points. The key here is that an interest group is an *organization*. There are many people with many interests throughout the United States; but many, if not most, fail to organize with others to pursue their goals. In addition, many of the groups that do go on to get organized pursue private or social purposes. Groups only become political interest groups when they try to affect policies of local, state, and federal governments.

Interest Groups versus Political Parties

Political parties and interest groups are often easily confused because they both seek to influence policy; they are, however, distinct. Political parties nominate candidates for office and seek to gain office by aggregating groups into a coalition. In doing this, political parties often try to mute their policy positions to appeal to as many differing groups as possible. Interest groups, on the other hand, seek to articulate the specific viewpoint of the group. While it is true that some groups have a wider set of concerns than others, every interest group is concerned with representing the position or positions of the group. Usually, the interest group stands little to win from muting its position.

The Roles of Interest Groups

While political parties do mainly one thing, nominate candidates and run them for office, interest groups play several roles.

Representation

Perhaps the most important role performed by an interest group is representing the interests of its members. The Tobacco Institute promotes the interests of cigarette companies, and the Human Rights Campaign Fund works to advance the cause of gay and lesbian rights.

Political Participation

Interest groups provide people with an avenue to participate in politics. Many people feel that their vote is not very important. Still, these people may see strength in numbers and interest groups as the vehicle to express this strength. & power

Education

Interest groups expend a great deal of effort on educating their members, the general public, and government officials. It is quite common to see spokespersons for interest groups interviewed on television news programs or talk shows. Groups may also advertise both on television and in the newspapers. Interest groups may even try direct-mail campaigns to explain their viewpoints and mobilize support.

Agenda Building

By educating their members, the general public, and public officials, interest groups are seeking to set the agenda of issues that are to be actively debated by policy makers. In 2008, most politicians, voters, and analysts alike assumed that the 2008 presidential campaign, like the midterm elections in 2006, would continue to be a referendum on Iraq and little else. But interest groups representing major corporations, labor unions, and interest groups representing the public became so strong that reformation of the health-care system began to drown out the other issues. A group calling itself Better Health Care Together demanded that the presidential candidates of both parties commit themselves to health-care reform and jettisoned this issue to the fore of the campaign.

Hyperpluralism!

Program Monitoring

Interest groups are not only concerned about what laws are passed; they are also concerned with the implementation of policy. Interest groups monitor how the government administers the programs that affect them. Sometimes the law may even require federal agencies to work with interest groups to ensure that their interests are taken into account. Clearly interest groups play several important roles in American politics. They shape policy outcomes through representation of their members, providing an avenue of participation, education, agenda setting, and the monitoring of government programs. Still, some groups may be more effective at fulfilling these roles than other groups. Some citizens may never see their interests represented. Some groups may mislead rather than educate officials and the public. Other groups may work to distort national priorities and

...ams to benefit their interests at the expense of the nation as a whole. To understand the inequities and inefficiencies of interest group politics, it is necessary to understand that some groups simply get better organized than others.

WHO IS ORGANIZED?

There is an astounding number of interest groups in the United States. *The Encyclopedia of Associations*, a voluntary government publication of national interest groups, lists over twenty-five thousand organizations working to affect public policy. The number of groups is matched by their incredible diversity. Everyone from the National Cricket Growers to the Flying Physicians is listed in the numerous volumes of the *Encyclopedia*. The multiplicity and obscurity of the groups disguise, however, some typical membership patterns.

Economic Interest Groups

Business Groups

Business groups are the most common type of interest group. Business groups account for approximately 20 percent of the organized interest groups in Washington. If one adds in lobbyists and law firms hired to represent business interests, business interests constitute up to 70 percent of all groups housed in the national capital.²

There are three distinct types of business organizations. The organization with the broadest membership is the peak business association. Peak associations attempt to speak for the entire business community. The Chamber of Commerce, for example, represents an assortment of local chambers of commerce and other groups. The National Association of Manufacturers (NAM) represents more than ten thousand manufacturing firms, and the Business Roundtable represents the country's two hundred largest corporations.

Businesses may also attempt to advance their interests through trade associations. These organizations represent companies in the same line of business. Mobil, Shell, and Texaco, for example, belong to the U.S. Petroleum Association.

Finally, many businesses try to influence public policy on an individual basis. Most large companies have offices in Washington or hire Washington lobbying firms to work with government officials in the making and implementation of policy.

While the Republican Party has traditionally favored business, in recent years the Democrats have also worked in the interests of the business community. The pro-business stance of the two parties reflects business's increasing financial contributions to both parties. In 2012, Wall Street invested more heavily in Mr. Romney, a former financier who had pledged to repeal the financial regulations initiated during President Obama's first term, than in any presidential candidate in history. Employees of financial firms gave more than $18 million dollars to the Romney campaign through the end of September 2012 and tens of millions more to the super PACs that supported him. Insurance companies, doctors and law, accounting and real estate firms gave less to the Obama campaign and the Democratic National Committee than they did in 2008 but other big business donors stepped in. The technology industry donated about $14 million to the president and the Democrats, substantially more than in 2008.³

Organized Labor

Unions try to influence government policy across a wide array of issues. The minimum wage, safety regulations, health care, and civil rights issues are all of importance to the workers of America. The most important voice of organized labor is the AFL-CIO, which includes the Teamsters 1.4 million members, the American Federation of State, County, and Municipal Employees' 1.2 million members, the United Food and Commercial Workers International Union's 1 million workers, and the United Auto Workers 840,000 members.

Public sector unions have grown in membership, while membership in their private-sector counterparts has flagged. In 2010 there were more public-sector employees (7.9 million) than private-sector workers (7.4 million) in unions, the first time in the history of the United States that this has happened. Public-sector unions have a distinct advantage over private ones in that they elect the very politicians with whom they negotiate their employment contracts.

The public's perception of these public sector unions has become very negative in recent years as overgenerous contracts, lavish pensions, and benefits and early retirement have put states in dire fiscal straits. It is predicted that the pension funds of eight states—California, Connecticut, Indiana, New Jersey, Hawaii, Louisiana, Oklahoma, and Illinois—will go broke by the end of fiscal year 2020. At the national level, the Obama administration has been even more generous with unions. Amid savage private-sector job cuts, one-third of the funds from the 2009 stimulus bill went to state and local governments, mainly to rescue public-sector employees. An executive order strongly encouraged government agencies to use construction companies with unionized workforces for any federal construction project over $25 million. Additionally, when the Obama administration bailed out Chrysler and GM, their unions won special favors, and he imposed tariffs on imports of Chinese tires at a union's request.

The approval of labor unions has decreased across a very wide demographic cross section of America, including in union-oriented households. According to the Pew survey, today, 42 percent

Unionism in America grew out of the strife between low-paid workers and the greed of capitalism. The struggle for unionization was long and bitter but was eventually won when the government recognized the right of workers to organize. Eugene Debbs is shown here addressing railroad workers. He and other union officials were jailed for disobeying a court injunction against the Pullman Strike of 1894.

of respondents currently have an unfavorable opinion of labor unions. In January of 2007, that number was just 31 percent. Conversely, 41 percent of respondents currently have a favorable view of organized labor, when in 2007, 58 percent favored unions. This amounts to a significant downward swing of opinion in just three years. In households categorized as union-oriented, the decline in union favor was not quite so drastic, yet the ratings do show a similar decline. In 2007, 77 percent of those union-oriented households had favorable opinions of organized labor. By 2010 that percentage has crept downward to 74 percent. Across political lines the picture is even more vivid. In 2007, 47 percent of Republicans spoke favorably of labor unions. By 2010 that number has declined to a paltry 29 percent. On the other side of the aisle, Democrats who favored labor unions numbered 70 percent in 2007. Today that number has declined to only 56 percent. Among Independents, the decline fell from 54 percent favoring labor unions in 2007 to 38 percent today.[4]

Agriculture

There are two types of organizations representing agricultural groups. General farm interest groups, the biggest of which is the American Farm Bureau Federation, seek to represent the interests shared by most farmers. For example, the American Farm Bureau speaks for the interests of large farms while the National Farmers Organization and the National Farmers Union represent the interests of the smaller farmer.

A newer type of agricultural group is found in those that have organized around specific commodities. Today, almost every crop and type of livestock has a corresponding group. Pigs have the National Swine Improvement Federation. Lettuce greens have the National Leafy Greens Council.

Professional Associations

Professional associations represent occupations that usually involve extensive education and formal training and perhaps government licensing. The American Medical Association (AMA) and the American Bar Association (ABA) are two prominent examples of professional associations.

Citizen Groups

Unlike economic interest groups, citizen groups, often called **public interest groups**, work to promote their vision of the public good. Citizen groups exist for almost every issue but the most visible have been in the area of consumer protection and environmental policy making. Some groups advance broad agendas. For example, People for the American Way is a liberal interest group that pushes its position on issues from school prayer to abortion to censorship of the arts. Other citizen groups are single-issue groups that are organized around one specific issue, like abortion, saving the whales, or drunk driving.

Women's Groups

There are many groups organized to advocate women's equality. The National Organization for Women (NOW) is the largest of these groups with 250,000 members and chapters in all of the fifty states. In recent years the women's movement has divided between groups pushing an ideological agenda, such as NOW, which continues to focus on the issue of abortion, and more pragmatic groups, such as the National Women's Political Caucus, which seeks to elect women to public office regardless of their stands on specific issues. Another group, EMILY, is an organization that recruits, trains, and endorses pro-choice Democratic women candidates and then works to fund and elect them to public office. The organization holds seminars for candidates, campaign managers, and journalists. It has successfully elected women to the Senate and House. In 2012, EMILY was one of the largest contributors to the Democratic Party.

Religious Groups

Religious groups have become increasingly well organized. Conservative Christian groups have had a particularly large impact on American elections and politics. Christian groups were the major force behind the presidential candidacy of Pat Robertson in 1988. Following his inability to capture the Republican nomination, Robertson converted a mailing list of two million names into the Christian Coalition. The Coalition has sought to gain control of the Republican Party, and today has gained dominance, or at least leverage, in twenty state parties.[5]

In the 2008 campaign, religious groups again played a prominent role, although they were often placed in a negative light. Obama was forced to sever ties with his fiery pastor of 20 years, Reverend Jeremiah Wright, for sermons that were deemed racist, anti-American and at times downright bizarre. McCain, in turn, was forced to return the endorsements of John Hagee, the pastor of a huge Texas church. Focus on the family founder, James Dobson, also played a role in the 2008 campaign by first saying he would not vote for McCain "under any circumstances" and then later reversing himself by calling McCain's choice of Sarah Palin as a running mate "God's answer" to a prayer. Even after the election, contention over a religious figure continued to dog President Obama. The president-elect's selection of Rick Warren to give the inaugural invocation spurred anger among liberal groups and gay activists. They were critical of Warren's opposition to abortion and gay marriage and were unhappy that Obama gave him a prominent role in his inauguration.

In 2010, there was a significant overlap between the Tea Party, made up mostly of Republicans, and the religious right, with members of the Tea Party supporting a Christian conservative agenda. A recent survey has found that nearly half of those who identify with the Tea Party believe that the Bible is the literal word of God, and a similar proportion thinks that public officials do not pay enough attention to religion. They are more likely than the population as a whole to view America as a Christian nation and are less likely than the general public to support same-sex marriage, abortion rights, or a compromise on immigration reform that would allow people who are in the United States illegally to become citizens.[6]

Gays and Lesbians

After World War II, the first gay rights groups organized to share information and fight police repression. During the 1960s, the gay rights movement became better organized and more visible. By 1972, gay rights issues were being addressed by politicians, and by 1973 the American Psychiatric Association removed homosexuality from its list of mental disorders. The election of Bill Clinton in

1992 was a crucial turning point for gay rights. He ended the federal policy treating homosexuals as security risks and invited gay activists to the White House for the first time.

Lesbian, gay, bisexual, and transgender (LGBT) groups actively organized in 2010 to work for the repeal of the Defense of Marriage Act and laws barring discrimination in employment and easing the path toward gay adoption. These groups are largely credited with the historic repeal of the military's "Don't Ask, Don't Tell" Policy in December 2010. In 2013, President Obama in his second inaugural address made history by referring to "our gay brothers and sisters."

The Elderly

Today, 12 percent of the nation's population is over sixty-five. Several groups, sometimes called the "gray lobby," represent their interests. Founded in 1958 to provide insurance for the elderly, the American Association of Retired Persons (AARP), with thirty-three million members, is the largest and of its most powerful interest groups. The AARP, through an active mail drive, attracts eight thousand new members every day. For only $10, anyone over fifty can join and gain access to the bounty of benefits provided by the organization, everything from auto and home insurance to car rentals.

With 1,800 employees and eighteen lobbyists, the AARP has become a potent political force. The goals of the AARP are primarily to preserve and expand government benefits to the elderly, which total about $14 billion each month.[7] Although programs for the elderly represent one-third of the budget, politicians are reluctant to touch them. Mindful of their political clout, President Clinton got the AARP to support his health-care reform by including long-term nursing home care. In 2003, the support of AARP's 35 million members helped the Republicans win passage of controversial Medicare legislation.

Several groups have formed to try to stem the power of the gray lobby. Groups such as Americans for Generational Equity and Children's Defense Fund are, however, smaller and less influential than AARP.

Environmental Groups

In the United States, a wide range of organizations sometimes called non-governmental organizations or NGOs represents the organized environmental movement. The largest and most influential environmental organizations are the so called Group of Ten: Environmental Defense Fund, National Wildlife Federation, National Audubon Society, Defenders of Wildlife, The Wilderness Society, Natural Resources Defense Council, World Wide Fund for Nature, Friends of the Earth, Sierra Club, and Izaak Walton League.

According to research conducted by the Urban Institute, an economic and social policy research group, the number of nonprofit organizations dedicated to conservation and the environment rose faster than the number of nonprofit groups overall since 1995, growing by 4.6 percent per year compared to 2.8 percent per year for all nonprofits. In fact, the environmental movement has expanded in the number of organizations, members, and total revenue almost every year since 1960. The study further shows that while there is a core group of prominent national organizations, more interestingly, there is a larger, more rapidly growing group of regional, local and other specialized groups fighting for environmental causes.[8]

As public awareness and the environmental sciences have improved in recent years, environmental issues have broadened to include key concepts such as "sustainability" and also new emerging concerns such as ozone depletion, acid rain, global warming, and biogenetic pollution. Today, environmental movements often interact or are linked with other social movements such as the animal rights, anti-nuclear weapons and/or nuclear power, peace, poverty, hunger, and human rights movements.

Single-Issue Groups

Single-issue groups are distinguished by their concern for a single issue and their reluctance to compromise. The abortion issue has generated a number of single-issue groups. The National Right to Life Committee is supporting a constitutional amendment to ban all abortions. The committee works to elect candidates that favor such an amendment and defeat those who do not. The same-sex marriage issue has also generated single-issue groups. For example, in 2010, Fight Back New York formed to support New York lawmakers who favor gay marriage while the National Organization for Marriage (NOM) was instrumental in overturning same-sex marriage in California and Maine.

Foreign Governments

Foreign governments, foreign corporations, and citizens of foreign countries are also represented in Washington. Governments of the largest U.S. trading partners, such as Japan, South Korea, Canada, and the European Union (EU) countries, maintain large research and lobbying staffs. Even smaller nations, such as those in Central America, engage lobbyists when legislation affecting their interests is under consideration by the Congress.

The Cayman Islands in 2009 spent more than $7.8 million, solely for promoting the islands to American tourists. The seven sovereign nations that form the United Arab Emirates in all spent a total of $5.3 million in 2009 lobbying the U.S. government and a small, war-torn African country, the Republic of Congo, became the third largest spender ($3.9 million) on Washington influence, petitioning the U.S. government over the past two years to help it fend off efforts to collect debts incurred by previous regimes.[9]

The Internet

Web activism is perhaps the newest addition to organizational efforts to influence government and policy making. For example, a recent online rally was held against the Stop Piracy Act, or SOPA, being debated by Congress. Opponents of the bill say it would diminish Internet freedom, online privacy, and the free and fair use of copyrighted material. Anonymous has joined ranks with the mainstream users organizing to kill the legislation through more traditional interest group organization and methods. Users of the popular social news website Reddit have called for direct action against lawmakers who support SOPA, as well as PIPA (Preventing Real Online Threats to Economic Creativity and Theft of Intellectual Property Act), a similar piece of legislation that has been introduced in the Senate. The Reddit community has not gone the route of illegal hacks against politicians, instead using its online power to organize large numbers of people to punish pro-censorship lawmakers by publicizing their "failures" and by trying to defeat their bids for re-election. Specifically, Reddit targeted Congressman Paul Ryan who ran for the vice presidency in 2012.

On January 18, 2012, widespread online protests against SOPA and PIPA were held including an English Wikipedia blackout. Several senators who sponsored PIPA announced their withdrawal of support and on January 20, Senate Majority Leader Harry Reid announced that a vote on PIPA would be postponed. The power of the online activist community is growing with its numbers and ability to organize. From Cairo to London to Singapore to Washington, through Twitter, Facebook, and other online forums, web activism is making itself known.[10]

Government Interest Groups

Because the federal government in Washington controls most of the financial resources of the country and because the federal government gives grants of money to states and localities, state and local governments organize to lobby for these funds. In addition, the National Governors' Association, the National Association of Counties, and the National League of Cities all work to influence national policy on a wide array of issues affecting their levels of government.

In spending more than $19.5 million in the first three months of 2010, cities, states, municipalities and territories lobbied the federal government in hope of greater returns in federal aid. Puerto Rico, Pennsylvania, Miami-Dade County, Los Angeles County and Riverside County in California, respectively, ranked in 2009 as the top five state and local governments in lobbying spending. In the first three months of 2010, after President Barack Obama called on Congress to approve $50 billion in emergency assistance to local and state governments to help avoid sharp cuts in core services such as policing and fire protection, these five topped the charts again, spending a combined $1,175,000 on federal lobbying.[11]

COMMON FEATURES OF INTEREST GROUPS

While there are thousands of interest groups in the United States and while they come in all types and sizes, they share certain organizational features. First, every group must have a leadership and decision-making structure. The complexity of this structure will differ by group, but at a fundamental level, the group will need a staff including a public relations office, or a lobbying office, preferably in Washington, D.C. Second, the group must build a financial structure capable of sustaining the organization and funding group activities. Most groups require members to pay dues, and they often solicit additional funds through mailings and fundraising activities. Third, all groups must attract members to pay the dues and engage in group activities.

To attract such a membership, groups can offer three kinds of incentives. **Solidary incentives** involve the pleasure that members get from joining the group. Such incentives may include companionship and status. Parent-Teacher Associations and the Rotary Club are good examples of groups based principally on the provision of solidary incentives. **Material incentives** include anything that might make the group financially attractive to a member. The American Association of Retired Persons, for example, offers a grocery list of low-cost insurance, low-cost travel, and discounts in a variety of stores. These material incentives can only be obtained by people who join the group. The

Unfortunately, some issues are not easily resolved. To dramatize their cause against "acid rain," members of Green Peace, an environmental group, hung banners from smokestacks in four different European countries to protest factory emissions.

third type of incentive is the **purposive incentive**, the goals of the group. Some groups can attract members on the basis of passionate feelings about the group cause. Groups that rely primarily on their goals to attract members tend to be smaller groups where the purpose of the group involves a clear economic self interest. Groups with more amorphous purposes, for example, peace or solving world hunger, may have more difficulty arousing passion in their members for reasons discussed in the next section.

BIASES IN INTEREST GROUP FORMATION AND MAINTENANCE

The tremendous number and diversity of interest groups in the United States may disguise some inherent biases in the universe of interest group politics. The fact is that not all interests get organized and represented by groups. Neither are all groups that are organized equal in strength and influence. There are serious obstacles in the way of both interest group formation and interest group maintenance.

Obstacles to Interest Group Formation

The main obstacle to interest group organization is the problem of getting people to actually join the group, pay the dues, go to meetings and, in short, do the work. Many people may share a particular concern or interest; few will actually join the group. The reason that so few join the group is that all interest groups provide what economists call *collective goods*, benefits that will go not only to members of the group but nonmembers as well. Why go the full nine yards and work for the group when one can receive the benefits without expending the effort? In other words, interest groups are plagued by the age-old problem of free-riders, people who take the collective good without paying for it or working for it.

Some groups are faced with a greater free-rider problem than others. In 1965, in his book *The Logic of Collective Action,* Mancur Olson argued that interests shared by a larger number of people have a harder time getting organized than those shared by only a few people.[12] The reason, according to Olson, is that the larger the number of people sharing an interest the more likely each individual is to make the rational calculation that his or her effort is not needed and that someone will do the work of obtaining the collective good. For example, many people are concerned with a cleaner environment; yet, many refuse to donate time or money to the cause, not because they do not care but rather because they figure with so many other people out there concerned with the environment, there must surely be others who will do the work. Everyone will receive the benefits from a cleaner environment, but only a few will do the work. In a small group, however, members are more likely to see that if they fail to do the work, maybe no one will do the work. Consequently, maybe the collective good will not be obtained at all.

Additionally, when an interest is shared by a large number of people, it may often be the case that each individual member's share of the collective good is quite small. For example, a group called Heal the Bay works to clean up the Santa Monica Bay in southern California. While everyone would like a cleaner bay, each person's share of the bay is quite small, with many not living right on the coast or swimming in the bay regularly. On the other hand, in a small group the benefits may be very large. Say that one hundred people allegedly harmed by breast implants sue the manufacturer and receive thirty million dollars in damages. Quite obviously, the incentive to organize becomes stronger as the member's share of the collective good becomes larger.

The result of this collective good, free-rider problem is that many groups, particularly the larger ones, have a hard time tapping their potential membership. In the end, once organized, the groups may appear illegitimate and unrepresentative in that they have tapped such a small percentage of the population that should be concerned with the issue. Politicians tend to address issues only when they perceive the public to be fully aroused about and organized to pursue that issue. If a group has managed to organize only a bare fraction of those who should be sympathetic to the cause, politicians are likely to take a wait-and-see attitude.

What is important is that groups have a large *market share*, the number of members actually in the group compared to its potential membership. For years the American Medical Association (AMA) enrolled a very large percentage (more than 70 percent) of the nation's doctors as members. As its membership declined, however, so did the influence of the AMA.

Overcoming the Obstacles Through Interest Group Maintenance

After the publication of Olson's book, groups began to make serious efforts to attract and maintain their membership. One of the best ways for groups to attract members and keep them active in the group is to offer selective benefits, or one might think of them as noncollective goods, to only those who actually join the group. Such selective benefits can take any or all of three forms: material, solidary, and expressive benefits.

Material benefits are goods and services that come from belonging to a group. For example, the very well organized American Association for Retired Persons offers members a cornucopia of cheap travel rates, insurance benefits, and a monthly magazine. Similarly, the National sociation's $25 annual membership fee entitles one to a magazine subscription, a shooter's eligibility to apply for a low-interest credit card. Fundraisers for public television often offer coffee mugs to those who make a contribution of a certain amount. Of course, selective benefits need not be material. Groups may also entice members with the **solidary benefits** of fun, camaraderie, and status. Other groups may offer **expressive benefits**, those derived from working for an interest group whose cause they see as just and right.

Selective goods are, however, expensive to provide. In each of the next 15 years, another 3 million Americans will reach age 50. Each one will get an invitation to join perhaps the most muscular political organization in the country, the American Association of Retired People (AARP). In May 2000, the organization unveiled a campaign to capture the loyalty of a generation of baby boomers with a series of selective goods. Not merely cruise discounts, but a new telephone hotline to put members in touch with experts who can help find a nursing home for a parent who has just suffered a stroke, or furnish a list of college scholarships for a high school senior. Not just auto rental coupons, but big savings on eye exams and glasses, perhaps even laser surgery. Not just motel promotions, but cut-rate subscriptions to AOL and savings on financial software programs and magazines. The provision of all these selective goods is expensive.

This provision siphons off money that the group might have otherwise used for political purposes like lobbying or campaign funding. Smaller groups, with less of a free-rider problem, are, therefore, at an advantage in that they do not have to spend money on these selective goods. In addition, business and trade groups, which often tend to be small, have the additional advantage in that their members have a clear economic self-interest. Such a clear self-interest may work to get the group organized making the provision of selective goods unnecessary.

Interest Group Bias

Although there are tens of thousands of interest groups organized in the United States, the interests of all the people are not equally represented. Studies have consistently shown that the affluent, the better educated, those with a clear self-interest, are far more likely to join groups, participate at high levels, and remain with the group. There are, of course, significant examples of poor, uneducated people getting organized. Cesar Chavez successfully organized farm workers into the United Farm Workers Union. Still, such cases are more the exception than the rule. As this chapter has discussed, groups with a large potential membership and groups that are organized around issues that may not be clearly related to the members' economic self-interest may face additional problems both in organization formation and maintenance. These groups are quite often those that attempt to speak for the poor, the consumers, the environment, and the disenfranchised.

While donations are still crucial (and are often abused, as the recent revelations about "soft money" excesses in recent presidential elections show), they are not the only keys to the kingdom. These days, interest organizations are valued more for the votes they can deliver. Most powerful groups have large numbers of geographically dispersed and politically active members who focus their energies on a narrow range of issues. In other words, they know their convictions and vote them. In this era of low voter turnout, that kind of commitment can mean the difference between victory and defeat in close elections, which translates into real heft on the legislative front. Few things are more important to a Congressman than getting reelected.

Many powerful groups were propelled there on the strength of their long-established grassroots networks. Kings of the town hall meeting are the American Association of Retired Persons; the National Federation of Independent Business, better known as the small-business lobby; the National Rifle Association; the Christian Coalition; and the National Right to Life Committee. This is not to say that money does not talk at all anymore. The AFL-CIO garnered great grades for both its grassroots and its campaign fundraising.

In contrast, groups with huge memberships that also have an intense self-interest in government payouts are the National Education Association and AFSCME, the American Federation of State, County, and Municipal Employees, whose members rely on government for their paychecks. More to the point are the Veterans of Foreign Wars and the American Legion, whose members not only get veterans' benefits but also have a patriotic pull on politicians. The lesson: It takes both time and more than a modicum of support from politicians in both political parties for an interest group to gain any real standing in the hidebound world of Washington.[13]

THE PROLIFERATION OF INTEREST GROUPS

Americans have long worried about this bias in interest group organization and activity. Even at the time of the writing of the Constitution, it was clear that divisions among the citizenry were inevitable, sown into the very fabric of a free society. Writing in 1787, James Madison warned that these "factions" could prove dangerous to the larger public interest as they attempted to control policy making on their own behalf. For Madison, tyranny by either a majority or minority was problematic.

According to Madison, only two solutions exist to cure the "mischief of faction." One is to do away with the very freedom that spawns the conflict between groups. This solution Madison rejected because it would destroy the foundation of the American experiment in self-government. The other solution would be encourage and nurture the factious nature of American society. Madison's vision was of a large, diverse nation with so many differences of opinion that domination by any one group would be unlikely. A group that might form on the basis of agreement on one issue would probably be internally divided by differences of opinion on other issues.

> Take in a greater variety of parties and interest [and] you will make it less probable that a majority of the whole will have a common motive to invade the rights of other citizens . . . [Hence the advantage] enjoyed by a large over a small republic.[14]

Madison's constitutional theory was that a government must actually encourage the proliferation of interest groups to prevent tyranny by any one group. This theory is today called pluralism. The theory suggests that all interests are and should be free to pursue their goals through bargaining and compromising, accommodating the interests of other groups. Madison's solution may be seen at work today. Since the founding of this nation, groups have proliferated at a phenomenal rate. Today, the bias in favor of the wealthy, the educated, and the professional is somewhat mitigated by the recent expansion in the number of interest groups found in this country. Tyranny by any one group is made less likely in such an environment rich with interest group organization and activity. While this proliferation is partly a result of what Madison called a large republic, the seeds of the proliferation are also to be found in more modern developments.

Sources of Interest Group Proliferation

Increased Government Regulation

Before the Second World War, the national government played a relatively limited role in American life. After the war, the federal government began to regulate various sectors of the economy and society. In the 1970s, the reach of government regulation had extended to almost every nook and cranny of the country's life. In the 1940s and 1950s, laws were passed regulating the eight-hour work day, child labor, and minimum wages. In the 1960s, with President Lyndon Johnson's War on Poverty, additional laws were passed to regulate race relations. Such government regulations have a powerful politicizing effect, often igniting interest group organization and activity.

The greatest expansion in government regulation came in the 1970s when the national government moved into the areas of automobiles, oil, gas, education, and health care. A *New York Times* report notes that these regulations spawned increased interest group activity in all the regulated areas.¹⁵ The first groups to organize were usually the affected industries, organizing to fight the regulations. But just as a pebble tossed into a pond sets off concentric circles, so did government regulation spawn growing interest group activity. New groups, often called **clientele groups**, soon sprang up to encourage the regulation and to influence the distribution of the benefits of regulation. A clientele group is a group or segment of society whose interests are directly affected or promoted by a government agency. The first clientele department was the Department of Agriculture established by Congress in 1862 to promote the interests of farmers.

Recently, despite serious concerns that U.S. chemical plants could be targets for terrorists, the chemical industry has successfully blocked legislation that would mandate more stringent security rules for chemical manufacturers and others. Following the September 11 attacks, the Environmental Protection Agency warned that 123 chemical plants across the country each contained enough toxic chemicals to kill or injure one million people, if terrorists attacked the facility, and that another 750 facilities could threaten more than 100,000 people. Due in part to the generous campaign donations from the chemical plants, neither Congress nor the White House, nor any federal agency, has been successful in closing this large hole in homeland security.

Court decisions and presidential actions may also stimulate interest group organizations. For example, when the Supreme Court stepped into the abortion controversy in 1973 with *Roe v. Wade*, pro-life groups were quick to organize. Then, the *Webster* case set off the pro-choice groups. Other issues, such as school prayer, flag burning, and the death penalty, have set off a similar pattern of group proliferation. Most recently, the health-care debate in Congress set off a virtual stampede of interest groups and prompted more than $200 million in advocacy ads, breaking records for lobbying. In 2009, companies and trade groups hired more than 4,500 lobbyists to influence health reform, amounting to about eight lobbyists for each member of Congress, according to the Center for Public Integrity.¹⁶

Postindustrial Changes and Public Interest Groups

The spread of affluence and education in the United States has led to a society that is capable of thinking of more than mere subsistence issues, a society that some have called postindustrial. On the other hand, countries plagued with constant poverty and endless wars are societies that may not spawn interest groups concerned with saving whales. In addition, agrarian, preindustrial nations are not faced with the technological complexities that would breed groups such as Mothers Against Drunk Drivers and consumer safety groups concerned with breast implants.

Postindustrial changes in the United States have generated a large number of interests, particularly among occupational and professional groups in the areas of science and technology. For example, genetic engineering associations have sprung up in the wake of recent DNA discoveries. The excesses and errors of technology have also increased the number of groups in American society. Today there are dozens of groups organized to protect animal rights, including People for Ethical Treatment of Animals (PETA), Progressive Animal Welfare Society (PAWS), Committee to Abolish Sport Hunting (CASH), and the Animal Rights Network (ARN). Postindustrial affluence has freed discretionary income and channeled it towards these new causes.

Great numbers of new groups that have sprung up particularly in the affluent, professional, and college-educated sector of American society have led some to label this a "New Politics" movement.[17] The members fueling this New Politics had formative experiences rooted in the civil rights movement and the Vietnam War. Today, new politics issues include environmental protection, women's rights, nuclear disarmament, and gay rights.

A major result of the New Politics movement is the creation of "public interest" groups. These groups are not based on the economic self-interest of the members. Rather, the benefits to their members are largely ideological. Today, many public interest groups are important players in Washington politics. Most are environmental and consumer groups, but there are other groups that work on corporate accountability, good government, and poverty issues. Common Cause, the Sierra Club, the Environmental Defense Fund, and Greenpeace are all examples of public interest groups.[18]

Interest Group Friendly Laws and Actions

An additional stimulus to the New Politics groups, and group proliferation in general, has been the wide array of environmental and consumer laws that has opened up avenues for group participation in the policy-making process. Such legislative invitations to group participation have not always been the norm. Early in the twentieth century workers often found it hard to organize because business and industry used government-backed injunctions to prevent labor strikes. By the 1930s, prohibition of such injunctions in private labor disputes and the rights of collective bargaining were established and union formation flourished with government approval and protection. Recent campaign finance laws (discussed below) have also contributed to group proliferation.[19]

Government often intervenes directly in group creation. Since the 1960s, for example, the federal government has been especially active in providing start-up funds for groups. Interest group scholar Jack Walker found that nine citizens' groups out of ten received some outside funding in the initial stages of development.[20] For example, the Center for Substance Abuse and Prevention (CSAP), which is part of the Department of Health and Human Services, gives grants to hundreds of nonprofit groups, financing after-school and summer youth programs, counseling for pregnant women, drug-free work place programs, and good nutrition workshops.

Cheaper Forms of Communication

After World War II great technological changes produced a variety of communication forms that would allow groups to reach their members more easily and facilitate their communication with government officials. Bulk mail rates and special phone rates reduced the costs of communication. These were followed by the FAX machine and the personal computer. Today, individuals and groups can communicate directly with public officials through the Internet and E-mail. Not only is such communication direct, it is immediate.

There are now also numerous computer mailing list companies that allow groups to target potential members. These companies assemble a bank of information about people including subscription lists, information put on warranty cards, and membership lists of other groups. A group trying to get laws to censor sex and violence in rock lyrics and videos, for example, might buy from such a company a subscription list of conservative readers of the magazine *National Review*. These people then can be contacted through the mail. These letters are personally addressed and the group message specifically tailored to the individual receiving the letter.

The Rise of Single-Issue Groups

The recent proliferation of interest groups has been fueled largely by a new type of group that first began to emerge in the 1970s: single-issue groups. These groups have three characteristics. First, they are concerned with only one issue. Second, their members are people new to politics. Finally, the group either will not or cannot compromise on the issue. The pro-life and pro-choice groups, Mothers Against Drunk Drivers, and the anti-nuclear proliferation groups are all examples of single-issue groups.

INTEREST GROUP METHODS AND STRATEGIES

Interest groups use four principal methods in their effort to influence policy making: electioneering, lobbying, mobilizing public opinion, and litigating.

Electioneering and Political Action Committees

Whenever and wherever people seek to influence decision making, the following is always good advice: get friends in the right places. Interest groups work very hard at doing exactly that. Given that in the United States 450,000 government officials get into office through elections, interest groups must affect election outcomes. There are many ways for groups and individuals to affect elections. They can man the phone banks on election eve; they can go door-to-door with campaign literature; they can vote. But the principal way in which interest groups affect elections today is through money. And the candidates are more than willing to play the game by taking it.

The Creation of Political Action Committees

The United States is the only country that expects its candidates for public office to raise virtually all the money necessary to run for office. Even in presidential elections, where there is public financing available, the candidates still work to raise additional millions of dollars. As campaign costs have escalated, candidates have had to mine as many sources of money as possible. Interest groups are one of those sources, and a lucrative one at that.

Before the early 1970s, national laws made it illegal for banks, corporations, labor unions, and businesses with government contracts to make campaign donations. While one result of these laws was to keep these groups at bay, the other result was that the laws allowed wealthy individuals to be the primary, if not sole, source of campaign money. So, in the 1970s Congress passed several laws to prevent "fat cat" donors from "buying" the loyalty of elected officials through the financing of their campaigns. The 1971 Federal Election Campaign Act limits individuals to $1,000 cash contribution per candidate. The law also, however, allows interest groups, including corporations, businesses, and labor unions, to set up **political action committees** (PACs), organizations that solicit campaign contributions from group members and channel those funds to candidates' campaigns. PACs are now the primary avenue by which interest groups contribute to federal election campaigns.

Federal campaign finance law limits PACs to cash contributions of no more than $5,000 per election, per candidate for national office. Under the law, primary, general, run-off, and special elections are all considered to be separate elections. As a result, a PAC may contribute $5,000 to each. In addition, the Supreme Court in the 1976 case of *Buckley v. Valeo* struck down as unconstitutional any attempt to deny individuals or groups the right to spend "on behalf of" a candidate. The Court argued that such spending was a form of "speech" and therefore protected by the First Amendment. The result is that PACs can spend unlimited amounts of money on in-kind services.[21]

The number of PACs exploded in the 1970s. Today, nearly 5,000 PACs are active in the electoral process.[22] Corporate PACs give the most money, followed in order by PACs representing trade, health associations, and labor.[23]

Super PACS

In 2002, Congress tried to limit the growing influence of Political Action Committees in the McCain-Feingold Bipartisan Campaign Reform Act. But a Supreme Court decision of January 21, 2010, *Citizens United v. Federal Election Commission*, overturned a portion of the law that prohibited corporations and unions from funding, through their general fund, any "electioneering communications" for 30 days before a primary or 60 days before a general election. They also overruled a 1990 decision that limited corporate spending in support or opposition of a candidate.

The *Citizens* case has led to the creation of super PACs. Technically known as independent expenditure-only committees, Super PACs may raise unlimited sums of money from corporations, unions, associations, and individuals and then spend unlimited sums to overtly advocate for or against political candidates. As is the case for traditional PACS, Super PACs must report their donors to the Federal Election Commission on either a monthly or quarterly basis (their choice). Unlike traditional PACs, however, Super PACs are prohibited from donating money directly to political candidates. As of January 14, 2013, 1,283 groups organized as Super PACs have reported total receipts of $833,888,714 and total independent expenditures of $641,832,249 in the 2012 cycle. Restore Our Future, a Super Pac supporting Mitt Romney, raised the most money in 2012, a total of $153,841,706. President Obama, on the other hand, enjoyed the $79,063,478 support of the Priorities USA Action Super Pac.[24]

The Effects of PACs and Campaign Contributions

PAC contributions benefit some candidates over others. Interest groups are pragmatic organizations. Given the high re-election rates in Congress, PACs favor the incumbents running for re-election. House incumbents collect nearly 13 times more money from PACs than the challengers receive.[25] Furthermore, more than half of the money raised by House incumbents comes from PACs.[26]

Incumbents feel the effects of PACs in other ways as well. A second effect of the privately financed campaign system in the United States is that politicians are distracted from their job of governing, with their energies siphoned off by having to raise the inordinate amounts of money needed to run an effective campaign. Candidates become entrepreneurs raising, in some cases, tens of thousands of dollars in a day's round of PAC cocktail parties, lunches, and dinners. A related problem is that incumbents running for re-election can raise money more efficiently by staying in Washington and working the PAC circuit of fund raisers. As a result, incumbents are spending less time at home with their constituents.

It might be expected that a third effect of PACs is that influence is being bought. While there is little evidence that PAC contributions actually buy the votes of politicians, there is evidence that PAC money can, and does, buy access. A member of Congress or one of the congressional staff is not likely to turn a deaf ear to a representative of an interest group that has donated generously to his or her campaign. The so-called Keating Five is a case in point. In this case, five senators, Alan Cranston (D-Calif.), Dennis DeConcini (D-Ariz.), John Glenn (D-Ohio), John McCain (R-Ariz.), and Donald Riegle (D-Mich.), came under the scrutiny of the Senate Ethics Committee. There were charges that these senators had sought to pressure the Federal Home Loan Bank Board to give lenient regulatory treatment to Lincoln Savings and Loan Association, headed by Charles Keating, a wealthy political contributor. The bank later failed, at a cost to government of more than $2 billion.[27] Buying access to politicians seems to be the main point of electioneering.

Senator Edward Kennedy once remarked that we "have the best Congress money can buy."[28] In the 2007-2008 electoral cycle, Wall Street's biggest banks were the top givers to the presidential campaigns of both Obama and McCain. Goldman Sachs was the corporate leader with its employees and their families giving nearly $1.5 million to the presidential candidates, 71 percent to Democrats. Employees of the other major banks, Citigroup, Morgan Stanley, Lehman Brothers, JP Morgan Chase, and others, also made major campaign contributions.[29] Sheila Krumholz, executive director of the Center for Responsive Politics said, in 2008, "No matter who becomes our next president, Wall Street will have an indebted friend in the White House."[30] She was right. Even before he officially took office, President Barack Obama used all of his persuasive powers to convince Congress to release the remaining $350 billion to bailout the banks after the mortgage failure crisis.

Campaign donations do, then, appear to buy access to politicians and to policy-making. The campaign donations allow the donor to catch the politician's ear. This, then, leads to a second interest group method, lobbying.

Direct, or Inside, Lobbying

Once an interest group has access through campaign donations, the group will try to influence what those elected politicians do. Interest groups do this through **lobbying**, pressuring through the provision of information, often highly technical in nature. Most politicians are inexpert in many of the policy areas they govern. They come to rely on the expert advice provided by interest groups.

The phrase *to lobby* originated in seventeenth-century England where people seeking to influence the government stopped members of the Parliament in a large lobby off the floor of the House of Commons. Perhaps because of this, lobbying is usually associated even in this country with Congress. But interest groups also lobby the executive branch of government. Executive branch lobbying focuses on senior staff aides in the White House and the various federal agencies. Even the president is lobbied and encourages lobbying activities through the Office of Public Liaison, an office whose express purpose is to communicate with interest groups.

The Federal Regulation of Lobbying Act defines a **lobbyist** as "any person who shall engage himself or pay any consideration for the purpose of attempting to influence the passage or defeat of any legislation of the Congress of the United States." In 2012, the oil and gas industry spent $104,118,544 on their lobbying efforts.[31]

There are different types of lobbyists. Some groups send one of their own members to Washington to lobby on the group's behalf. Such amateur lobbyists are often unfamiliar with the intricate workings of the Washington establishment and may find it difficult to gain access to the critical centers of power. A second type of lobbyist, the staff lobbyist, is a paid professional who works full time for a particular interest group.

Finally, groups may hire a third type of lobbyist who has Washington experience, particularly lawyers, former members of Congress, or former employees of executive branch agencies and departments. Government officials often leave office and become lobbyists. Federal law does prohibit members of Congress and executive branch officials from lobbying on matters they worked on while in government for one year after leaving office. Even so, 272 former members of Congress have registered as lobbyists since 1996 and 43 percent of members of Congress who left office since 1998 have become lobbyists.[32] Interest groups frequently hire former executive branch officials, as well. These professional lobbyists can cultivate their close working relationships with government policy makers. Interest group lobbyists bring pressure on government officials in a variety of ways.

Providing Information

Interest groups spend a considerable amount of time engaged in what is called **direct lobbying**. One study of Washington lobbyists found that 98 percent use direct contact with government officials to express their group's views.[33] Information is the key to direct lobbying. A lobbyist will, of course, try to present information that supports the interest group's position on an issue. Still, over the long term, lobbyists cannot afford to be perceived by policy makers as biased or untrustworthy. A lobbyist's access to a politician is only as good as the expert information he or she can provide. Lobbyists must maintain daily contact with politicians, providing them with information and data. Corporate groups, in particular, often have hundreds, even thousands, of personnel all equipped to provide mounds of information on a minute's notice.[34]

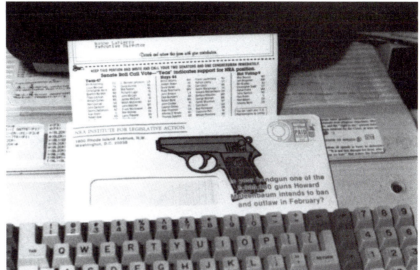

A PAC for the NRA sends letters to its constituents to update them on the voting behavior of their legislators. Notice the letter identifying which legislators supported NRA's position on a critical piece of legislation. Members are urged to write to their House and Senate legislators.

Recently, interest groups have taken to virtual lobbying through use of the Internet and other social networking sites. In the battle over the Employee Free Choice Act (EFCA), which would make it easier for workers to join a union, the Chamber of Commerce has worked on an anti-EFCA social media effort, expanding a virtual march on Washington that was created the last time the bill went to Congress in 2007. It allows users to register for the march as avatars and send an automatic letter to their elected officials through a Facebook application. Participants in the "march" – generally businesses around the country opposed to unions – created avatars that appeared on a specially designed Web site on the appointed day, timed to coincide with a vote on the bill and with e-mail correspondence to members of Congress from the avatars.

The Effects of Direct Lobbying

Lobbying often leads to the development of a close relationship between the interest group, the congressional committee involved in the policy area important to the group, and members of a bureaucratic department or agency responsible for the implementation of those policies. Such a tight relationship is referred to as an **iron triangle**, with three points: the interest group, the congressional committee, and the bureaucratic department or agency. These three points are mutually supporting. A committee member takes campaign donations from an interest group and is then lobbied by that group. The interest group also seeks out the bureaucracy as an ally who then can bring additional pressure on the congressional committee members. Remember also that there is often an exchange of personnel among the three points of the triangle. Many defeated or retired members of Congress join or form Washington law firms that are filled with lobbyists. A study has found that 43 percent of the House and Senate members who left government to join private life since 1998 have registered to lobby.[35] According to a 2010 report by the *New York Times*, more than 125 former congressional personnel, from aides on the banking committees to elected officials, are now working on behalf of financial companies, using their expertise and connections to influence legislation that is meant to regulate the financial industry. Visa has the most lobbyists with ties to Washington, 37, followed by Goldman Sachs, Prudential Financial, and Citigroup.[36]

The point is that the interest of the interest group becomes the interest of the congressional committee members and bureaucrats. The relationship is referred to as *iron* because other than the three major players, everyone else is left out. The unorganized, those without lobbyists on Capitol Hill, those who lack expertise, are largely on the list of uninvited. In addition, presidents who come in with their own agenda for change may soon be faced with recalcitrant iron triangles. The president, in such cases, is usually the new boy in town, whereas the incumbent members of Congress, lobbyists, and career bureaucrats may have been part of the Washington establishment for twenty years or more. There is little reason to think that they will be willing to see or do things the president's way.

An example of an iron triangle is the military-industrial complex. This is a complex of relationships among manufacturers, the Department of Defense, and the Armed Services Committees in Congress. Even back in the 1940s, more than 1,400 officers, including 261 at the rank of general or its equivalent in the navy, had left the armed forces for employment by one of the hundred leading defense contractors.[37] Many see the military-industrial complex at work today. Even at a time when the government is seeking to slash programs to reduce the huge federal deficit and the United States has withdrawn from Iraq, the Department of Defense launched a pre-emptive campaign to try and maintain their grip on the federal budget, proposing a $450 billion increase in defense spending over five years. In 2010, the Department of Defense did not get all it wanted, but it did secure an 8 percent increase in its budget.

Regulating Lobbying

Lobbying is a form of speech and, therefore, protected by the First Amendment to the Constitution. In 1946, Congress passed the Federal Regulation of Lobbying Act, which requires groups and individuals seeking to influence legislation to register with the secretary of the Senate and the clerk of the House and to file quarterly financial reports. In 1954, in the case of *United States v. Harriss*,

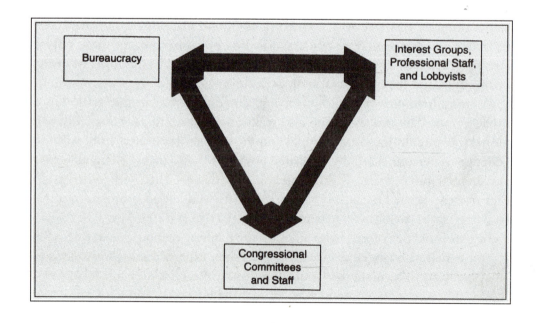

President Obama has an agenda to end the economic recession. Back on the phone, the President tries to persuade a Republican Senator to vote for the stimulus bill.
Feb. 4, 2009
Credit: White House Photo by Pete Souza

the Supreme Court upheld the 1946 law but limited its application to only lobbying involving direct contacts with members of Congress.[38] Not only was the 1946 law limited in its application, it was also very difficult to enforce.

In 2007, Congress passed the Lobbying Transparency and Accountability Act that requires registered lobbyists to report lobbying activities quarterly, as opposed to semiannually. These reports must include the disclosure of funds that lobbyists donate to candidates personally, as well as funds raised from clients, which are then "bundled" and given to politicians as larger contributions. Disclosure reports must be submitted to the Secretary of the Senate no later than 20 days after the end of the quarterly period. The reports must be made available electronically with free access to the public over the Internet, as well.

The regulations discussed above are limited in several respects. The registration and reporting requirements do not extend to grassroots organizations. Nor is there any enforcement organization to make sure there is compliance with the law. Congressional officials who suspect violations may refer them to the Justice Department for action. Fines for breaking the law may be as high as $50,000.

The Newest Trend in Lobbying: Supreme Court Nominations

A recent consensus exists among judicial scholars that judicial power is expanding and this expansion of judicial power has, in turn, politicized the process through which judicial appointments are made. Interest groups now actively seek to influence the Senate's confirmation of nominees to the

U.S. Supreme Court. A new analysis of the role of interest groups and their television advertising campaigns by the Brennan Center for Justice at the NYU School of Law concludes that while the spending levels have not as yet reached the stratosphere, interest group spending on television ads and other lobbying tools can have a potent effect on who becomes a judge in America. For example, President Bush's nomination of Samuel Alito to the Supreme Court in 2006 set off the most hard fought battle, with interest group spending reaching into the millions.[39]

Attempts to influence judicial appointments are likely to increase in the future. Under the Internal Revenue Code, tax-exempt organizations such as social welfare organizations under section 501(c)(4), labor, agricultural, or horticultural organizations under section 501(c)(5), and business leagues under section 501(c)(6) may engage in unlimited lobbying and are allowed to try to influence the nomination or confirmation of a potential justice to the federal court, including the Supreme Court. As discussed earlier in this Chapter, these groups now play a significant role in politics.

Grassroots, or Outside, Lobbying: Going Public

Going public is a strategy that attempts to mobilize the widest and most favorable climate of public opinion. Whereas direct lobbying involves contact between a lobbyist and a politician, this grassroots lobbying uses rank-and-file members and other supporters to bring pressure on government. Such an outside strategy may include education campaigns, demonstrations, letter writing, and any other strategy that attempts to mobilize a large number of people to bring pressure on policy makers.

One way interest groups try to mobilize public opinion is by educating the public about issues. A group may send speakers armed with pamphlets to address gatherings of policy makers and other groups. A media campaign may prove even more effective. The pro-life groups have made considerable inroads into mass public opinion on abortion through their emotionally charged advertisements. In general, the great expense of media campaigns limits their widespread use to only those interest groups that have significant financial resources. The corporate sector appears to have the advantage here. Even as early as the 1930s, some were identifying a *new lobby* of public relations professionals.[40] The 1970s, however, saw a rapid rise in the sophisticated use of advertising to sway public opinion. The oil companies, particular Mobil and Chevron, began airing advertisements that were directed at soothing the sentiment of the American public. These advertisements were not designed to sell gasoline but rather to create a more sympathetic picture of corporations. Microsoft is another corporation that has always seen public and media relations as an integral part of their success. Over the years, their need to communicate has increased with their size and the controversy surrounding their dominant position in software markets.

Interest groups may try to obtain free media coverage. Protests, sit-ins, and demonstrations are often specifically tailored for the evening news. In 2008 and 2009, about 200 gays and lesbians, upset over the California voter-approved ban on gay marriage, marched from East Los Angeles to the downtown Catholic Cathedral of Our Lady of the Angels. Other protests occurred across the state, and clergy announced that they would continue to conduct wedding ceremonies for same-sex couples, even though county clerks had stopped issuing marriage licenses. Protest groups seeking amplification of their cause through the mass media should be aware, however, that they are dealing with a two-edged sword: they get media coverage, but it is negative. The early women's movement in the 1960s tried to attract media attention by burning their bras. Much of the resulting media

coverage painted the early feminists as masculine man-haters. An additional problem
attention is that it tends to be short-lived. It is difficult to keep a protest going long
the government to recognize the issue and act on it. The civil rights movement sh
movements can be kept alive, but it takes enormous organizational skills and charisma

Litigating

Interest groups can also pursue the method of legal advocacy, trying to achieve goals through litigation. Interest groups can use the courts to affect public policy in any of three ways. First, the group may bring a suit on behalf of the group itself. Second, the group can finance suits brought by other individuals. In fact, groups sometimes actively seek test cases where they can challenge the constitutionality of existing laws or the ways in which they have been implemented. For example, in the 1950s, the National Association for the Advancement of Colored People was looking for a test case to challenge the racially segregated southern school system. Thurgood Marshall, a young attorney working for the NAACP, successfully litigated the case on behalf of the Browns. Finally, a group may also participate in the litigation process by petitioning the court for the right to file an *amicus curiae* ("friend of the court") brief that lays out arguments why the court should rule in favor of one of the parties to the case. A 1989 abortion case drew a record 78 such briefs. They were evenly divided between those who favored or opposed the right to abortion. In February 2003, however, that previous record was broken when over sixty groups filed friend-of-the-court briefs in defense of the University of Michigan's use of race-based affirmative action in their admissions policy. The public interest groups spawned by the New Politics movement have been particularly active in the litigation process. The controversy over the completion of a dam being built by the Tennessee Valley Authority (TVA) is an example of New Politics litigation. The dam would have ruined the habitat for a small fish known as the snail darter. The Endangered Species Act at that time prohibited federal agencies from engaging in any actions that would "jeopardize the continued existence of an endangered or threatened species or . . . result in the adverse modification or destruction of [the species'] critical habitat." In *TVA v. Hill*, the Supreme Court held that the act made it an unqualified duty for agencies to refrain from taking actions that would harm the threatened or endangered species.[41]

Businesses and corporations have responded to the strong public interest movement by mobilizing their own forces. The 1970s and 1980s saw a massive increase in the number of businesses lobbying offices in Washington, and many trade associations head quartered elsewhere moved to Washington or opened branch offices there.[42] The number of registered lobbyists representing business interests in Washington, D.C. grew even larger during the first term of George W. Bush's administration, doubling from 16,342 in 2000 to 34,785 in 2005.[43] The result has been that many of the early victories of public interest groups have been overturned or muted by Congress or other court decisions. In the case of the TVA dam, after the Supreme Court decision, Congress amended the Endangered Species Act to soften the language and allow agencies like the TVA to weigh the costs of protecting a species against the benefits to be gained from proceeding with certain kinds of projects.

Chapter Eight

Bribery

While there may be only a fine line between campaign donations and bribery, the line is nonetheless drawn by the legal code. Bribery involves the giving of cash gifts, worth over a certain amount, in exchange for a politician's promise to act in a certain way. The history of the United States has been punctuated with scandals involving interest groups bribing politicians. On July 29, 2008, Senator Ted Stevens was indicted by a federal grand jury on seven counts of failing to report gifts received from VECO Corporation and its CEO Bill Allen on his Senate financial disclosure forms and was formally charged with violation of provisions of the Ethics in Government Act. Stevens, seeking to clear his name before the November election, pleaded not guilty and asserted his right to a speedy trial. The trial began on September 25, 2008 in Washington, D.C., and on October 27, 2008, barely a week before the election, Stevens was found guilty on all seven counts. He went on to lose his re-election bid on November 4, 2008.

Bribery is probably not as widespread as many fear. It is a risky strategy for an interest group to pursue. As a result, it is mostly used to sustain a friendship rather than convert an enemy. In addition, bribery works best when the issue involved is fairly narrow, for example, involving a government contract. The bigger the issue, the more participants are likely to be involved and the more media coverage devoted to it. Bribery fares poorly in such an open arena of policy making.

Prospects for Reform

Even if the problem of illegal bribery is not overwhelming, when coupled with the legal system of campaign finance and PACs, perhaps some reform is needed. Some sectors of the interest group community do enjoy advantages over others. Such advantages may impede the equal opportunity of all groups to be heard in the political system. The Madisonian design, in other words, has not worked perfectly.

Allowing those who have the clearest self-interest and the resources to communicate and amplify their message may lead to inefficient and even bad policy-making. The Savings and Loan debacle of the 1980s and 1990s is a case in point. At the insistence of the Savings and Loans, President Bush and key members of Congress, all of whom had taken hefty contributions from the S&L industry, worked to deregulate the Savings and Loans. The industry was freed up to take depositors' money and invest it in high risk enterprises, like commercial real estate and junk bonds. When the Savings and Loans in many cases lost the money, the national government moved in to insure the deposits. The cost to taxpayers to date is in the billions. To avoid such costly mistakes, some are calling for public financing of congressional elections. Other plans have suggested reducing the amounts that can be given to candidates.

CONCLUSION

James Madison recognized that in a free and diverse nation, groups would inevitably form and attempt to impress their will on others. He called what we now know as interest groups, factions, and defined them as groups "whether amounting to a majority or minority of the whole, who are united and actuated by some common impulse of passion, or interest, adverse to the rights of other citizens, or to the permanent and aggregate interest of the community."⁴⁴ Madison believed that the only solution to the tendency of factions to impose their will on the greater society is a large republic that encourages a greater diversity of opinion thereby making despotism at the hands of any one group difficult if not impossible.

Madison's idea of forming a republic to keep interest groups from becoming too powerful has not turned out exactly as planned. The reality of the American political landscape is that interest groups have always better represented those with the greatest resources, and the least wealthy have suffered because of their failure to organize. The challenge of democracy is to provide the freedom that will allow all members of the society to participate in policy making and to find new ways to harness the power of interest groups for the greater national interest.

CHAPTER NOTES

[1] Mike Young, "NRA Lobby Has More Political Power Than Women, With Far Fewer Numbers," *Policymic*, December 2012, http://www.policymic.com/articles/21065/nra-lobby-has-more-political-power-than-women-with-far-fewer-numbers.

[2] John T. Tierney and Kay Lehman Scholzman, "Congress and Organized Interests," in *Congressional Politics*, ed. Christopher J. Deering (Chicago: Dorsey Press, 1989), 198.

[3] Nicholas Confessore and Jo Craven McGinty, "Obama, Romney and Their Parties on Track to raise $2 Billion," *The New York Times*, October 25, 2012, http://www.nytimes.com/2012/10/26/us/politics/obama-and-romney-raise-1-billion-each.html.

[4] "Labor and the Left," The Economist, October 27, 2010, http://www.economist.com/blogs/democracyinamerica/2010/10/unions_america

[5] Sidney Blumenthal, "Christian Soldiers," *New Yorker*, July 18, 1994, p. 36.

[6] Andy Sullivan, "Many Tea Partiers Part of Religious Right," *Reuters*, October 5, 2010, http://www.reuters.com/article/idUSTRE6943IQ20101005

[7] "Grays on the Go," *Time*, February 22, 1988, p. 69.

[8] Kenny Luna, "Number of Environmental NGO's Growing By Leaps and Bounds," *Treehugger*, December 5, 2008, http://www.treehugger.com/files/2008/12/number-of-environmental-groups-growing-rapidly.php

[9] Anupama Narayanswamy, "International Influence: Agents of Foreign Clients Report Thousands of Lobbying Contracts, Millions in Fees," *Sunlight Foundation*, December 31, 2010, http://reporting.sunlightfoundation.com/2010/top-players-2009/

[10] Jeb Boone, "Has the Internet Become an Interest Group?" *Globalpost*, January 5, 2012, http://www.globalpost.com/dispatch/news/regions/americas/united-states/120104/sopa-reddit-paul-ryan-web-activism

[11] Summer Lollie, "State and Local Governments Aggressively Lobby the Federal Government," *OpenSecretsblog*, July 2, 2010, http://www.opensecrets.org/news/2010/07/state-and-local-governments-agressi.html

[12] Mancur Olson, *The Logic of Collective Action* (Cambridge: Harvard University Press, 1965).

[13] Jeffrey H. Birnbaum, "Washington's Power 25," http://money.cnn.com Dec. 8, 2006.

[14] James Madison, *Federalist Paper No. 10* in *The Federalist Papers*, ed. Clinton Rossiter (New York: New American Library, 1961), 83.

[15] John Herbers, "Special Interests Gaining Power as Voter Disillusionment Grows," *New York Times*, 14 Nov. 1978, 1.

[16] Dan Eggen, "Expecting Final Push on Health-Care Reform, Interest Groups Rally for Big Finish," *The Washington Post*, February 28, 2010, http://www.washingtonpost.com/wp-dyn/content/article/2010/02/27/AR2010022703253.html

[17] Theodore J. Lowi and Benjamin Ginsberg, *American Government*, 3d ed. (New York: W.W. Norton, 1994).

[18] Andrew McFarland, *Common Cause* (Chatham, N.J.: Chatham House, 1984).

[19] Allan J. Cigler and Burdett A. Loomis, *Interest Group Politics* (Washington, D.C.: Congressional Quarterly Press, 1991).

[20] Jack L. Walker, "The Origins and Maintenance of Interest Groups in America," *American Political Science Review* 77 (June 1983): 390-406.

[21] Richard E. Cohen, "NRA Draws Bead on Incumbents," *National Journal*, 19 September 1992, 2134.

[22] Federal Election Commission, *FEC Releases 1992 Year-End Pac Count*, 23 January 1993, 1.

[23] Federal Election Commission, *PAC Activity Rebounds in 1991-92 Election Cycle-Unusual Nature of Contests Seen as Reason* 29 April 1993, 9.

[24] "Super Pacs," OpenSecrets.org, http://www.opensecrets.org/pacs/superpacs.php.

[25] "Political Action Committees," http://ap.grolier.com,2005.

[26] Frank Sorauf, *Inside Campaign Finance* (New Haven, Conn.: Yale University Press, 1992), 71.

[27] Nathaniel C. Nash, "Savings Unit Donations Criticized," *New York Times*, 29 June 29 1990, D4.

[28] Theodore J. Lowi and Benjamin Ginsberg, *American Politics*, 4th ed. (New York: W.W. Norton, 1996), 497.

[29] OpenSecrets, "Lobbying Data Base," http://www.opensecrets.org/lobby/index.php

[30] Blog4Presidents, "U.S. Election Will Cost $5.3 Billion," http://blog.4president.org/2008/2008/10/us-election-will-cost-53-billion-most-expensive-in-history.html

[31] "Oil and Gas," OpenSecrets.org, http://www.opensecrets.org/lobby/indusclient.php?id=E01.

[32] Knight Ridder News, "Exiting Congressmen Cash in Years of Service for High-Paying Jobs," http://billingsgazette.com, Dec. 26, 2004.

[33] Key Lehman Schlozman, and John T. Tierney, *Organized Interest and American Democracy* (New York: Harper and Row, 1986), 50.

[34] John E. Chubb, *Interest Groups and the Bureaucracy* (Stanford, Ca.: Stanford University Press, 1983), 144.

[35] Jeffrey H. Bimbaum, "Hill a Steppingstone to K Street for Some," *The Washington Post*, July 27, 2005, http://www.washingtonpost.com/wp-dyn/content/article/2005/07/26/AR2005072601562.html

[36] Cassandra LaRussa, "Congressmen Become Lobbyists," *OpenSectretsblog*, April 14, 2010, http://www.opensecrets.org/news/2010/04/congressmen-become-lobbyists-charli.html

[37] *U.S. Congress, House of Representatives, 96th Congress, 1st Session, Report of the Subcommittee for Special Investigations of the Committee on the Armed Services* (Washington, D.C.: Government Printing Office, 1960), 7.

[38] *United States v. Harriss*, 347 U.S. 612 (1954).

[39] Brennan Center, "Three Nominations Reveal Contrasting Influence of Interest Groups in High Court Nomination Process," http://www.bennancenter.org/content/resource/three_nominations_reveal_contrast

[40] *Pendelton-Herring, Group Representation Before Congress* (New York: McGraw Hill, 1936).

[41] *TVA v. Hill*, 437 U.S. 153 (1978).

[42] *Boston University School of Management, Public Affairs Offices and Their Functions* (Boston: Boston University School of Management, 1981), 8.

[43] Jeffrey Bimbaum, "The Road to Riches is Called K Street," *The Washington Post*, June 22, 2005, http://www.washingtonpost.com/wp-dyn/content/article/2005/06/21/AR2005062101632.html

[44] James Madison, *Federalist #10* in *The Federalist Papers*, ed. Clinton Rossiter (New York: New American Library, 1961).

SUGGESTED READINGS

Ainesworth, Scott H. and Kenneth A. Shepsle. *Analyzing Interest Groups.* New York: W. W. Norton, 2003.

Baumgartner, Frank, Jeffrey Berry, Beth L. Leech, David C. Kimball, and Mary Hojnacki. *Lobbying and Policy Change: Who Wins, Who Loses and Why.* Chicago: University of Chicago Press, 2009.

Berry, Jeffrey M. *The Interest Group Society*, 3rd ed. New York: Longman, 1997.

Birnbaum, Jeffrey. *The Lobbyists: How Influence Peddlers Work Their Way in Washington.* New York: Random House, 1992.

Cigler, Alan J. and Burdett A. Loomis, eds. *Interest Group Politics,* 7th ed. Washington. D.C.: CQ Press, 2007.

Kaiser, Robert. *So Damn Much Money: The Triumph of Lobbying and the Corrosion of American Government.* New York: Vintage, 2010.

Lowery David and Holly Brasher. *Organized Interests and American Government.* New York: McGraw-Hill, 2004.

Lowi, Theodore J. *The End of Liberalism.: The Second Republic of the United States.* 2nd ed. New York: Norton, 1979.

Olson, Mancur. *The Logic of Collective Action.* Cambridge, MA: Harvard University Press, 1965.

Rozell, Mark J., Clyde Wilcox, and David Madland. *Interest Groups in American Campaigns: The New Face of Electioneering.* Washington, D.C.: CQ Press, 2005.

Strolovitch, Dara. *Affirmative Advocacy: Race, Class and Gender in Interest Group Politics.* Chicago: University of Chicago Press, 2007.

Truman, David B. *The Governmental Process: Political Interests and Public Opinion*, 2nd ed. New York: Knopf, 1971.

Web Sites

Center for Responsive Politics. www.opensecrets.org.
Federal Election Commission. www.fec.gov.
Institute for Global Communications. www.igc.apc.org
Internet Public Library Association. www.ipl.org/ref/AON.
Political Advocacy Groups: A Directory of U.S. Lobbyists. www.vancouver.wsu.edu/fac/kfountain/.
MoveOn, www.moveon.org.
Senate Office of Public Records. http://sopr.senate.gov.
U.S. Public Interest Research Group (PIRG). www.uspirg.org.

Chapter Nine

THE CONGRESS

The 112th Congress that ended its term in December 2012 will go down in history as the least productive and most dysfunctional Congress in two generations.[1] From the debt-ceiling debacle to the fiscal cliff to the inability to pass appropriations bills, the legislative branch was in a state of perpetual gridlock. Gridlock has been an issue in Congress many times in America's past, but even to causal observers of politics, it seems like it has become far more of an issue in recent years. Reflecting our political culture as a whole, Congress, and especially the House of Representatives, has become more politically polarized on both sides of the aisle than it has in recent memory. Both parties have largely purged themselves of the middle ground, "moderate" Republicans and "Blue Dog" Democrats, and become far more represented by the most heavily ideological wings of their respective parties. This is one of the reasons that compromise has become such a dirty word in Washington on both sides of the political aisle.

There are many factors at play in the recent gridlock of Congress. One of the most important is the political impact of redrawing the House district lines following the 2010 Census. The vast majority of 2012 House candidates came from districts where they faced no real threat to their re-election. In 1992, there were 103 members of the House of Representatives elected from what might be called swing districts: those in which the margin in the presidential race was within five percentage points of the national result. In 2012, however, there were only 35 such congressional districts, barely a third of the total 20 years ago. In comparison to the number of swing districts, the number of landslide districts, those in which the presidential vote margin deviated by at least 20 percentage points from the national result, has roughly doubled. In 1992, there were 123 such districts (65 of them strongly Democratic and 58 strongly Republican). Today, there are 242 of them (of these, 117 favor Democrats and 125 Republicans).

The bottom line is that today most members of the House come from hyper partisan districts where they face essentially no threat of losing their seat to the other party. Given the fact that incumbent re-election rates for the House typically run in the 90 percent range, this portends entering an era where the political makeup of the House is likely to only change at the margins and in which both political parties are likely to become more polarized as time goes on.

There is a second cause for the current gridlock in Congress. Going all the way back to the earliest days of the republic, "You scratch my back, and I'll scratch yours" was the operating rule in congressional lawmaking. One member of Congress gets a road or a monument for his or her state in exchange for a vote on the bill in question. Until the 1990s, earmarks, often referred to as "pork," were mostly used by leaders in Congress to fashion coalitions by enticing members to support bills that carried political risk. Then, in 1995, when the Republicans took control of the House, earmarks began to be viewed as a way to secure re-election by delivering goodies to their districts and states. A frenzy of spending ensued with Congress doubling the amount spent in earmarks to more than $14 billion by 1998. Critiques lambasted the Congress for wasteful spending. and in 2010 Congress banned the use of earmarks. Without such enticements, voting in favor of politically divisive issues such as the fiscal cliff deal promised nothing but grief at home and nothing positive in return.

Historically, earmarks have helped House and Senate leaders win support from that politically challenging middle ground. Without them, congressional leadership is unable to forge a consensus on difficult policy, spending and tax issues and is increasingly unable to negotiate with the White House from a position of strength. The unintended consequence of the ban on earmarks may be that Congress is ceding its constitutionally derived law making power to the president for, in the absence of congressional action, the executive branch is left free to shape a federal response to the challenging issues facing the nation. President Obama has used executive orders to set the federal agenda on an array of important issues ranging from immigration to gun control. As this book goes to press, many are calling for restoring earmarks in the hope of restoring the balance of power between Congress and the executive branch and giving back to elected officials an important tool to help them do the people's work.[2]

THE ORIGIN AND POWERS OF CONGRESS

The Constitution and the Great Compromise

Perhaps because the framers of the Constitution believed that Congress would be the most powerful branch of the national government, the most contentious issue at the constitutional convention concerned the question of how the states would be represented in this national legislature. The small states, which had the most to fear from union, wanted equal representation in a one chamber legislature; this was put forth as the New Jersey Plan. The more populous states, on the other hand, supported the Virginia Plan that proposed a two chamber legislature. One of its chambers, the lower chamber, would have state representation on the basis of state population; this chamber would then select an upper chamber.

The final Connecticut Compromise created a **bicameral**, meaning two chamber, national legislature. The House of Representatives, the lower chamber, is apportioned to the states on the basis of state population. The United States Senate, the upper chamber, has equal state representation with each state having two senators, originally to be selected by their various state legislatures. While the House members serve only a two-year term and all seats are elected in every two-year election, the senators serve a six-year term, and only one third of the Senate is selected in any two-year election.

The Powers of the House and Senate

The Expressed Powers

The first seventeen clauses of Article I, section 8, specify most of the **enumerated powers** of Congress, powers expressly given to the national legislature by the Constitution. The most important of the domestic powers listed are the rights of Congress to collect taxes, to spend money, and to regulate commerce. The most important foreign policy power is the power to declare war. Other sections of the Constitution give Congress a wide range of additional powers. Article 1, section 5 gives Congress the power to establish rules for its own members. Article 1, section 7 gives it the power to override a presidential veto. Congress is also given the power to define the appellate jurisdiction of the Supreme Court (Article III, section 1), regulate relations between the states (Article I, section 10 and Article IV), and propose amendments to the Constitution (Article V). In addition, amendments to the Constitution have provided additional congressional power. The Twelfth Amendment, for example, requires Congress to certify the election of the president and vice president or to choose these officers if no candidate has received a majority of the electoral college vote. Congress may levy an income tax under the Sixteenth Amendment.

The House and Senate do have some responsibilities that they discharge on their own. Only the House of Representatives can originate revenue bills. Early colonial Americans had been sensitive about the issue of taxation without representation. As a result, the framers believed that money matters should be passed first by the House, the chamber that has representation on the basis of population, and only after that would the Senate address the issue. According to Article I, section 2 the House has the power to impeach a federal judge, the president, or vice president. To **impeach** means to bring up on charges, calling for a trial in the Senate. If two-thirds of the senators vote to convict, the federal official is then removed from office.

The Senate has the power to advise the president when he is appointing federal judges, ambassadors, and cabinet positions. In addition, the Senate can either vote to confirm or reject these appointments. The Senate also has the power to ratify or reject treaties negotiated by a president with a foreign nation.

The Implicit Power

Under Article I, section 8, the **elastic clause**, Congress has the power "to make all Laws which shall be necessary and proper to carrying into Execution the foregoing powers [of Article I], and all other Powers vested by this Constitution in the Government of the United States, or in any Department

The impeachment trial of President Andrew Johnson, who became president with the assassination of Abraham Lincoln, took place in the Senate.

or Officer thereof." The open ended quality of the elastic clause has allowed Congress to define and redefine its powers over time and thereby alter the balance of power Congress shares with the president.

The Ebb and Flow of Congressional Powers

Because the framers of the Constitution feared tyranny emanating from any source, executive or legislative, they pitted Congress and the president against each other. For the first one hundred years, Congress clearly was the more dominant institution. Congress chose to use the powers outlined in Article I, section 8 and further extended its power by defining other activities as within its scope under the elastic clause. Even in foreign affairs, Congress exercised its muscle. The War of 1812 was planned and directed by Congress. After the Civil War, when President Andrew Johnson tried to interfere with congressional plans for Reconstruction, he was summarily impeached, though missed conviction in the Senate by one vote.

By the 1960s, however, congressional dominance was declining. The presidency became the stronger of the two branches. Franklin Roosevelt's "New Deal," Harry Truman's "Fair Deal," John F. Kennedy's "New Frontier," and Lyndon Johnson's "Great Society" had transformed American politics, placing the president in the center of the legislative process. Similarly, in foreign affairs, presidential initiative and direction took the country into both World Wars and then later wars in Korea and Vietnam.

The strength of either the presidency or the Congress as an institution is at least partly the result of the institution's ties to important groups in the American electorate. Until the administration of Franklin Roosevelt, people were more likely to see Congress as their representative institution. But Roosevelt's New Deal mobilized organized labor, farmers, African Americans, and key sectors of American industry and tied their loyalty to the executive branch of government. Such electoral support was and continues to be empowering to the branch that can best mobilize it.

Events of the later 1960s and 1970s set the stage for a reassertion of congressional power. Groups that had not found the executive branch hospitable to their claims, now turned to the legislative branch to defend their interests. Environmental and consumer groups, along with civil rights and women's groups, pressed their claims upon Congress and, in doing so, provided a base for the reassertion of congressional power. It was inevitable that conflict would grow between the executive and legislative branches of government; and grow it did beginning during the Johnson administration.[3]

The most dramatic illustration of this growing tension was the congressional Watergate investigation that eventually led to the resignation of President Richard Nixon. But the tension between the branches has evidenced itself in other ways as well. Increasingly, Congress passed legislation mandating clear and specific action by the president, for example, the Wars Powers Act and the Endangered Species Act. Congress has also moved to increase its budgetary powers through the Budget and Impoundment Control Act of 1974 and the creation of the Congressional Budget Office (CBO).

More recently, Congress has asserted its power through the Iran-Contra investigation of President Reagan and the Whitewater investigation of President Clinton. Between January 2009 and August 2010, the Republican members of the Oversight Committee had sent forty-six letters to the Democratic Chairman of the committee or its subcommittee chairs requesting hearings, additional witnesses at hearings, or subpoenas of important documents related to significant investigations of the Obama administration.

Differences Between the House and Senate

House	Senate
Larger (435 members)	Smaller (100 members)
Shorter term of office (2 years)	Longer term of office (6 years)
Less flexible rules	More flexible rules
Narrower constituency	Broader, more varied, constituency
Policy specialists	Policy generalists
Power less evenly distributed	Power more evenly distributed
Less prestige	More prestige
More expeditious in floor debate	Less expeditious in floor debate
Less reliance on staff	More reliance on staff
Less press and media coverage, but floor proceedings televised	More press and media coverage

The Era of Divided Government

By the end of the 1980s, divided government had become the norm in American politics, certainly at the national level and often in the state governments as well. Since 1975, the president's party has controlled the House of Representatives for only six years (1977-1980, 1993-1994) and the Senate for only ten years (1977-1986, 1993-1994). In such a state of divided government, it is hard to see either the president or Congress as the more powerful. A better understanding of the workings of the national government would be to see that any policy making is likely to be incremental, as Congress and the president inch their way toward common ground. Such common ground is largely to be found in symbolic politics.[4] Control of the deficit through budgetary ceilings and caps on spending is a way for both branches of government to appear to be doing something without really making substantive policy decisions.

The 107th Congress, elected in 2000, faced tremendous obstacles to its work due to the extremely small majority held by the Republicans in the House and the Democrats in the Senate. In the House consensus on legislative issues was possible because some twenty to thirty Democrats, calling themselves "Blue Dog Democrats," said that they were willing to work with the Bush administration. But, harmony in the Senate was much harder to achieve. Republican Senator Trent Lott, unseated as majority leader when Senator Jeffords defected and threw Senate control to the Democrats, had been quoted after the November 2000 election as making snide comments about newly elected Democratic Senator Hillary Clinton. If passing legislation in such a deeply divided Congress was difficult, it was virtually impossible to build the two-thirds majority needed to override a presidential veto. The Democrats' control of both the House and Senate during the final years of the Bush presidency continued to make policy making difficult.

With the election of 2008, Democrats captured the presidency and large majorities in both chambers of Congress. This unified Democratic control was, however, short-lived, as the 2010-midterm elections brought Republicans back in control of the House of Representatives. This return to divided government is likely to lead to legislative gridlock. Political scientist, Sarah Binder, measured both the size of the policy agenda and the number of agenda items that failed to be addressed with any enacted law. Divide the latter by the former and you have a measure of gridlock. She found that gridlock increases under divided government by roughly 11 percent.[5] The 2012 election again created a divided government and if we use the past half-century as our guide, we can expect divided control of government to increase the frequency of stalemate by roughly 11 percent.

REPRESENTATION IN CONGRESS

Theories of Representation

While Article I, section 8, outlines the specific powers of Congress, the essence of all congressional powers is the quality of congressional representation. The United States Congress was created by the framers to be the branch of the federal government that represented the population. The question is what does *representation* mean? There are different theories as to what constitutes representation.

The Instructed-Delegate View of Representation

Some believe that legislators are duty bound to mirror the views of a majority of their constituents. The argument is that members of Congress are delegates with specific instructions from their voters at home on how to vote on critical issues. Delegates are not supposed to vote the party-line; nor are they to vote their conscience. For a member of Congress to be a delegate of his constituents, the constituents would have to hold well-formed views on the issues. In addition, they would have to have a clear-cut policy preference. Neither condition is likely to be found in reality. On many issues voters may not have enough information to formulate an opinion. On many other issues, there may be no majority opinion.

The Trustee View of Representation

Edmund Burke argued that legislators must be free to vote as they see best.[6] Burke saw the legislator as a **trustee**, to do what he/she believed to be in the best interest of the society. Members, according to this theory, are expected to pursue the broad interests of the larger society and vote against the narrow interests of the constituents if these are in conflict with the needs of the greater society.

The Politico View of Representation

Studies have found that most members of Congress are neither pure delegates nor pure trustees.[7] Members of Congress try to combine both the delegate and trustee perspectives into a pragmatic mix, the so-called **politico** approach. Members from marginal districts, those in which the election was close, may tend to see themselves as obligated to vote as their constituents intend. Legislators from safer districts may feel more free to express their conscience. In addition, there may be times when the wishes of the voters are unclear or contradictory or cases in which constituents have no

Several southern states elected African-American senators and representatives to Congress after African Americans gained voting rights in 1870.

opinion; in such areas, the member may feel the need to act more as a trustee than a delegate. In any district, however, there are likely to be some issues on which constituents have pronounced opinions on which representatives feel they enjoy little latitude in supporting their constituents' preferences. For example, representatives from wheat, cotton, or tobacco districts will not be able to exercise great discretion on farm issues. Likewise, members from oil rich states can hardly risk being anything other than the advocates of the oil industries.

The Quality of Congressional Representation

When acting as either a delegate or a trustee, a member's ability to represent his or her district or state largely depends on two factors: descriptive representation and ties to a constituency.

Descriptive Representation

There are some who believe that the quality of representation in the United States Congress is dependent upon how descriptively representative the Congress is. The argument is that a legislature should be demographically similar to the general population.[8] If a high quality of representation really does hinge on descriptive representation, the Congress of the United States faces serious problems. The people we elect to Congress are not a cross section of American society. While nearly one-third of all workers in the United States are employed in blue collar jobs, most members are professionals, drawn primarily from business and legal backgrounds.[9] Only 22 percent of American families earn over $50,000 a year, yet 100 percent of the members of Congress earn over that amount. In 2009, annual congressional salaries were $174,000.00 In fact, 30 percent of the House and 40 percent of the Senate have assets of over a million dollars. Over the years Congress has become more diverse and the 113th session of Congress is the most diverse in our country's history, including more minorities, women, religions, sexual orientations, and backgrounds than ever. Included in the new members is the first Buddhist to be elected to the Senate, as well as the first Hindu member and openly bi-sexual woman to the House. With such a broad range of Congress members, the likelihood that a wider range of Americans will actually be heard and represented only increases. A record number of women now represent their states in the U.S. Senate, with a total of 20 women in the 100-seat chamber. House Democrats became the first caucus in the history of either chamber not to have a majority of white men.

There is reason to believe that the descriptive characteristics of the members of Congress may affect the legislative process. The Congressional Black Caucus was formed in 1969 when the thirteen black members of the U.S. House of Representatives joined together to strengthen their efforts to address the legislative concerns of black and minority citizens. Today, the forty-two members of the Congressional Black Caucus represent many of the largest and most populated urban centers in the country, together with some of the most expansive and rural congressional districts in the nation. These members, now as in the past, have been called upon to work as advocates for America's varied constituent interests and the CBC has been involved in legislative initiatives ranging from full employment to welfare reform, South African apartheid and international human rights, from minority business development to expanded educational opportunities. Most noteworthy is the CBC alternative budget, which the Caucus has produced continually for over 16 years. Historically, the CBC alternative budget policies depart significantly from administration budget recommendations as the Caucus seeks to preserve a national commitment to fair treatment for urban and rural America, the elderly, students, small businessmen and women, middle and low income wage earners, the economically disadvantaged and a new world order. There is also a more informal Congressional Hispanic Caucus that includes members of Congress of Hispanic descent. The Caucus is dedicated to voicing and advancing issues affecting Hispanic Americans in the United States.[10]

Constituent Ties

Evidence suggests that members of Congress do not need to look like their constituents to feel the pressure to serve those who live in their state or district. Members claim that they spend significant amounts of time and energy on addressing the individual level and state or district level needs of their constituents. When a member of Congress works on the statewide or district wide needs, it is often called **pork barrel**. When a member of Congress attempts to serve individual needs of a particular constituent it is commonly called **casework**.

Pork Barrel Legislation. Members of Congress cannot afford to systematically neglect constituency pressure emanating from groups within their district or state. Representatives from districts with defense industries, and perhaps thousands of jobs tied to those industries, are likely to feel the pressure to support defense spending that may end up funding a lucrative contract with one or more of these firms. A Senator from Florida knows that a vote for an increase in social security payments is a vote for the elderly, so many of whom live in his state.

Pork barrel legislation is very common in the United States Congress. Some have argued that pork barrel bills are the only ones that members of Congress take seriously because they are seen as so important to the members' chances for re-election. Often, controversial bills can only achieve passage by being filled with pet projects that mobilize the support of members of Congress and maybe even the president himself.

In 2005, Congress passed a $286.4 billion highway bill. In addition to funding the interstate highway system and other federal transportation programs, it set a new record for pork-barrel spending, earmarking $24 billion for a staggering 6,376 pet projects, spread among virtually every congressional district in the land. The enormous bill—1,752 pages long—passed 412 to 8 in the House and 91 to 4 in the Senate. The bill funneled upward of $941 million to 119 earmarked projects in Alaska, including $223 million for a mile-long bridge linking an island with 50 residents to the town of Ketchikan on the mainland. The bill also funded horse riding facilities in Virginia ($600,000), a snowmobile trail in Vermont ($5.9 million), parking for New York's Harlem Hospital ($8 million), a bicycle and pedestrian trail in Tennessee ($532,000), a daycare center and park-and-ride facility in Illinois ($1.25 million), dust control mitigation for rural Arkansas ($3 million), The National Packard Museum in Ohio ($2.75 million) and a historical trolley project in Washington ($200,000).[11]

In 2006, Congress passed the $16 billion Foreign Operations Bill, which pays for everything from the Peace Corps to the aerial fumigation of Colombian coca. The 3,320-page bill includes $100,000 for goat-meat research in Texas, $549,000 for "Future Foods" development in Illinois, $569,000 for "Cool Season Legume Research" in Idaho and Washington, $63,000 for a program to combat noxious weeds in the desert Southwest, and $175,000 for obesity research in Texas. It was the biggest single piece of pork-barrel legislation in American history.[12] The cost of such earmarks has tripled in the last 12 years, to more than $64 billion annually, and some lawmakers treat their share of the pork as personal accounts to dole out to constituents and campaign contributors.

On January 5, 2007, in the first one hundred hours of the 110th session of Congress, the new Democratic majority in the House of Representative imposed substantial new restrictions on earmarking. The new rules do not end the practice of packing legislation with pork but they do force legislators to attach their names to the pet items they slip into spending or tax bills and to certify that they have no personal financial stake in their earmarks.[13] Then in December of 2010, Congress announced a moratorium on earmarks. At this writing, it is unclear whether this moratorium will effectively stop the flood of earmarks that have routinely been part of all major pieces of legislation.

Casework. There is fairly consistent communication between constituents and congressional offices. Even in the 1970s, the House and Senate post office handled nearly 100 million pieces of incoming mail.[14] Today, with the Internet, members are even more accessible to the mass public. House members claim that over a quarter of their time and nearly two-thirds of their staff members' time is devoted to working on the needs of individual constituents.[15]

Casework can take several forms. **Patronage** is a direct form of casework in which the member of Congress runs interference with a federal administrative agency seeking favorable treatment for a constituent or constituents. Patronage may even take the form of securing a government job for a constituent.

Casework can also take the form of a **private bill**, a proposal to grant some kind of relief or special privilege to the person named in the bill. Approximately 75 percent of the private bills introduced into Congress are concerned with helping foreign nationals who are unable to get permanent visas in this country.[16]

Congressional Elections

The process of electing members of Congress is decentralized. Congressional elections are controlled by individual state governments, which must, however, conform to the U. S. Constitution and national statute. The Constitution states that representatives are to be elected every second year by popular ballot, and the number of seats awarded to each state be established by a decennial census. Each state has at least one representative, with most congressional districts having close to seven hundred thousand residents. Today, each state's two senators are elected by their state's voters for a six-year term. Only one-third of the senators are elected in any two-year election.

Congressional Reapportionment

By far the most complicated aspects of congressional elections are the issues of **reapportionment** (the allocation of seats in the House to each state after each census) and **redistricting** (the redrawing of the boundaries of the districts within each state).

Congress sets the number of seats in the House, and the number of seats in the House has grown with the country. The Constitution set the number of representatives at 65 from 1787 until the first Census of 1790, when it was increased to 105. The House has had 435 seats since 1913. Reapportionment is the process of dividing these 435 memberships, or seats, in the House of Representatives among the 50 states based on the population figures collected during the census that is conducted every ten years on the decade.

The first decennial census was conducted in 1790 and has been taken every ten years as mandated by Article I, Section 2 of the U.S. Constitution. Since the first census, conducted by Thomas Jefferson, the decennial count has been the basis for our representative form of government as envisioned by our nation's Founding Fathers. In 1790, each member of the House of Representatives represented about 34,000 residents. Today, the House has more than quadrupled in size, and each member represents about 20 times as many constituents.

In 1962, in the case *Baker v Carr*, the Supreme Court held that reapportionment must not violate the Fourteenth Amendment principle that no state can deny to any person "the equal protection of the laws." Then in the 1964 case of *Wesberry v Sanders* the Court held that reapportionment must not violate the "one person, one vote" principle embodied in Article I, Section 2, of the Constitution, which requires that members of Congress be chosen "by the People of the several States." Prior to *Wesberry*, severe malapportionment had resulted in some districts containing two or three times the populations of other districts in the same state, thereby diluting the vote in the more populous districts. After the Census is completed, states must redistrict, divide their state populations into congressional districts. Each state decides for itself who will draw its district lines, which has led to a few different models: state legislature, political commissions and independent commissions. This is called **redistricting**.

Redistricting and Gerrymandering

While the one person, one vote principle has dealt with the issue of district size successfully, the issue of how to draw the district boundaries has not yet been completely resolved. It is usually the job of each state legislature to divide its state's population into the number of congressional districts apportioned to it following the census. Many districts have been gerrymandered. A district is said to be gerrymandered when the dominant party in the state legislature alters its shape substantially in order to maximize its electoral strength at the expense of the legislature's minority party. Either concentrating the opposition party's voters in as few districts as possible or dispersing them thinly across many districts can achieve this.

In 1986, the Supreme Court heard the *Davis v Bandemer* case that challenged gerrymandered congressional districts in Indiana. The Court ruled for the first time that redistricting for the political benefit of one group could be challenged on constitutional grounds. The Court has gone on to declare as unconstitutional districts that are uneven in population or that violate norms of size and shape to maximize the advantage of one party.

Despite the Supreme Court's attempts to control gerrymandering, it continues to plague the drawing of congressional district lines. Following the 2000 census, after a protracted legislative struggle, the Republicans in Texas succeeded in drawing districts that benefit candidates of their party. Under the districting plan, the city of Austin, Texas is split three ways into a district that runs from North Austin to Houston, a district that runs from Southeast Austin to the Rio Grande, and a district that lumps San Marcos, South Austin, West Austin, New Braunfels, and Northern San Antonio together. After the 2008 election, unsurprisingly, Republicans won 20 of the 32 Texas congressional seats.

Racial Gerrymandering and "Minority-Majority" Districts

In the early 1990s, the Supreme Court actually began to encourage a type of gerrymandering that made possible the election of a minority representative from what is termed a "minority-majority" area. Under the mandate of the Voting Rights Act of 1965, the Justice Department issued directives to states after the 1990 census instructing them to create congressional districts that would maximize the voting power of minority groups, that is, create districts in which the minority voters were the majority. In 1995, these "minority-majority" districts were challenged, and the Supreme Court took the position that when race is the dominant factor in the drawing of congressional district lines, the districts are unconstitutional.

Then in 2001, the Supreme Court further confused the issue of racial gerrymandering by ruling 5-4 that an oddly shaped, mostly black congressional district in North Carolina is constitutional. The Court determined that the North Carolina state legislature did not act improperly in its redrawing of the 12th district due to its intention to create a heavily Democratic voting district. In essence, the high court said the fact that blacks vote 90 percent Democratic was a coincidence and not evidence of a racially motivated effort.[17]

Candidates for Congress

Candidates for congressional seats are largely self-selected. They are likely to be people who have been active in local politics. Because congressional campaigns are expensive, candidates also must have access to substantial resources. The average cost of winning a Senate seat is now over $5 million and a House seat over one million.

Most candidates for Congress must win the nomination of their party through a direct primary, in which voters identified with their party choose among their party's candidates, picking the one they would like to see run against the opposing party in the general election. Because voter turnout tends to be very low in primary elections, those who do vote tend to be more ideological than those who stay home. As a result, Democratic candidates often take more liberal positions and Republican candidates more conservative positions, trying to appeal to the ideologues in their party. Later, in the general election when turnout is higher, these same candidates may have to moderate their views to attract the votes of independents, voters from the other party, and moderate voters in their own party.

The Costs of Congressional Campaigns

Over 90 percent of House of Representatives races and 95 percent of Senate races that were decided on Nov. 6, 2012, the candidate who spent the most money ended up winning, according to a post-election analysis by the nonpartisan Center for Responsive Politics. Continuing a trend seen election cycle after election cycle, the biggest spender was victorious in 397 of 426 decided House races and 30 of 32 settled Senate races. While the overwhelming majority of the races featured incumbents running for re-election, money was also decisive when newcomers squared off. In 2012, in 58 of the 74 contests in which power changed hands, the winning candidates rode enormous waves of cash, outspending their opponent.[18]

The average cost of winning a House race in 2012 was nearly $1.4 million, based on pre-election finance reports, and almost $6.5 million for a Senate seat. The most expensive Senate race in 2012 was the Kaine-Allen race in Virginia where the candidates alone spent $79.2 million. The costliest House race in 2012 was in the 18th District of Florida. The Republican Allen West and the Democrat Patrick Murphy together spent $23.6 million.[19]

The Advantages of Incumbency

The most important feature of any congressional election is the incumbency effect. The incumbency effect refers to the fact that since World War II, almost 95 percent of incumbent members of Congress have sought to be re-elected, and among those who seek re-election, more than 95 percent of them are re-elected. In 2008, 95 percent of House incumbents and 93 percent of Senate incumbents won re-election. Even in 2010, when anti-government sentiment hit a fever pitch, incumbents still did well with a re-election rate of 86 percent. In 2012, 23 House incumbents were defeated and only one incumbent was defeated in the Senate. There are several reasons why incumbents have an advantage over their challengers.

Visibility. Not only are incumbent members of Congress able to support pork barrel legislation and do casework, they are also positioned to be able to claim credit and advertise their constituent service. Senators and House members spend a significant amount of time and resources on cultivating media attention. The job of congressional press secretaries is to make sure the press is at media events and that copies of congressmen's and congresswomen's speeches are disseminated to the press. Today, members of Congress are increasingly developing direct lines to their local media markets, often bypassing the national press completely. These local news organizations are hungry for such direct news from Capital Hill and are likely to run the story unedited, guaranteeing favorable coverage of the members.

Members of Congress also make themselves visible through their free use of the postal system, the **franking privilege**. In recent years, members of Congress have sent out nearly 400 million pieces of mail.[20] In one year alone, members of Congress spend about $1.5 million on stamps, all at

To What Extent Does the House Mirror Society?

	Number in the House if it were representative of American society at large	Number in the 109th Congress	Number in the 110th Congress	Number in the 111th Congress	Number in the 112th Congress	Number in the 113th Congress
Men	184	367	365	357	362	374
Women	226	68	70	78	73	81
Black	52	42	42	39	44	42
Hispanic	30	24	21	31	23	29
Poor	65	0	0	0	0	0
Lawyers	2	237	239	238	248	231
Under 45	300	140	140	140	141	140

taxpayers' expense. These mailings quite commonly are used to remind the members' constituents of all the pork he/she is responsible for delivering to his/her constituents.

The Role of Gerrymandering in House Incumbency

Pork barrel, casework, and visibility are not the only explanations for the high rate of incumbent re-election. The way in which the House district lines are drawn may also work to the benefit of the incumbents. As discussed above, districts may be gerrymandered. In 1986, in the case of *Davis v. Bandemer,* the Supreme Court ruled that redistricting for the political benefit of one group could be unconstitutional. However, since that case, specific instances of gerrymandering have been difficult to prove in court and the practice continues.

The 2012 House elections were in no small part determined by gerrymandering. Democrats outpolled Republicans in the total number of votes cast for congressional candidates. Still, Republicans won more seats. This happened because Republican-controlled redistricting after the 2010 Census packed Democratic voters into a handful of imaginatively shaped districts around Pennsylvania's urban centers and created many more districts in the rest of the state. The overwhelming Democratic margins in the two heavily African-American Philadelphia districts did not require constructing oddly shaped districts, but carving up the rest of the state to minimize districts that Democrats might win required politically driven line drawing. Similarly, Obama won Ohio by two points, and Democratic Senator Sherrod Brown won by five, but Democrats emerged with just four of Ohio's 16 House seats. In Wisconsin, Obama prevailed by seven points, and Democratic Senate candidate Tammy Baldwin by five, but their party finished with just three of the state's eight House seats. In Virginia, Obama and Democratic U.S. Senate candidate Tim Kaine were clear victors, but Democrats won just three of the commonwealth's 11 House seats. Obama carried Florida and Democratic Senator Bill Nelson won by 13 points, but Democrats will hold only 10 of that State's 27 House seats.

Campaign Finance and Incumbency

For many years, researchers overlooked the role of campaign contributions in the re-election of incumbents. This was because studies have consistently found that there is no relationship between money spent on a campaign and winning the election. The big spender does not always win. In fact, incumbents win even when they spend less than their challengers. Because over 90 percent of incumbents will win re-election, they usually win whether they spend more or less than their opponent.

The problem with such studies is that they have focused on campaign *spending*. What they should look at is the relationship between money *raised* and winning, not money *spent* and winning. Incumbents enjoy an enormous advantage not enjoyed by their challengers: PAC money. Political action committees gave 83 percent of their donations to House incumbents during the 2007-2008 election cycle, compared to a mere $24.4 million to the challengers.[21] In 2010, Senate incumbents raised, on average, $9.4 million as compared to $519,000 raised, on average, by their challengers.[22]

Even though incumbents raise more money than challengers, they do not necessarily spend all the money. Any unused campaign money goes into a **war chest**; this money can then be used for the following campaign or given to the incumbent's political party upon his retirement from Congress. Many incumbents have amassed significant war chests, so significant, in fact, that they may scare an opponent off. A significant number of congressional incumbents run unopposed, at least partly because their war chests are so daunting to a challenger. Obviously, if one runs unopposed, one will win. It is the money raised and amassed in huge war chests, but not necessarily spent, that may scare potential challengers out of the arena.

In 2006, despite the record expense to elect Congress, nearly one quarter of House races—111 in all—involved an incumbent with zero financial opposition. One senator, Richard Lugar (R-Ind.), faced no financial opposition, in 36 House races, the winning candidate ran completely unopposed, and another 5 winning candidates faced challengers who either spent no money or filed no reports with the FEC. One scholar has noted that "Congress may have changed hands, but overall this election was not competitive," Krumholz said. "Incumbents overwhelmed their opponents—or simply ran unopposed—because they had a huge cash advantage."[23]

The Issue of Term Limits

The enormous advantages enjoyed by incumbents have led many to call for mandatory term limits. Term limits are popular. Today, 78 percent of voters favor establishing term limits for Congress. That is nearly five times as many as oppose limiting the number of terms members can serve (16 percent).[24] Twenty-three states tried to limit the terms of their delegation to Congress, with the general formula being three terms [six years] in the U.S. House and two terms [twelve years] in the U.S. Senate. As they pertain to Congress, however, these laws are no longer enforceable because of lawsuits filed by term limits foes including ousted Speaker of the House, Tom Foley. In *U.S. Term Limits Inc. vs. Thornton*, the Supreme Court, by a vote of 5 to 4, declared that a state has no power to impose limits on the number of terms for which its members of the U. S. Congress are eligible either by amending its own constitution or state law. Because the Constitution explicitly addresses qualifications for both the House and Senate, the Court reasoned that the only way to change terms of office would be through the amendment process.

THE ORGANIZATIONAL STRUCTURES OF CONGRESS

Power in Congress is heavily decentralized. What limited leadership there is, comes in four forms: the party system, the committee system, the staff, and the caucuses.

The Formal Leadership of Congress: The Political Parties

Leadership in the House

Every two years, at the beginning of a new Congress, the members of each party gather to elect their House leaders. This gathering is usually referred to as the caucus, or conference. The elected leader of the majority party becomes the **Speaker of the House**. House leadership is primarily exercised by the speaker. He presides over meetings in the House. He appoints members to joint

House Republicans surround the President after the meeting on the stimulus bill. Every House Republican eventually voted against the bill. Jan. 27, 2009. Credit: White House Photo by Pete Souza

committees and conference committees. He schedules legislation for floor action. He decides points of order and interprets the rules with the aid of the House parliamentarian. He refers bills and resolutions to the appropriate standing committees in the House. In 1975, the speaker's powers were enlarged by the House Democratic caucus, which gave its party's speaker the power to appoint the Democratic Steering Committee, which determines new committee assignments for House Democrats. A speaker may fully participate in floor debate, and he may vote, although in recent years, the speaker has only voted to break a tie.

After the speaker is selected, the House majority caucus then elects a **majority leader**. The majority leader is the spokesperson for the majority party in the House and generally acts as the speaker's first lieutenant. The majority leader also conducts most of the substantive and procedural floor debate.

The minority party goes through roughly the same process, selecting a **minority leader.** Like the majority leader, the minority leader is primarily responsible for maintaining party cohesion and acting as the party's spokesperson. The minority leader also speaks on behalf of the president if the president is of that party.

The formal leadership of each party also includes assistants known as **whips**. The whips assist the party leaders by transmitting information from the leaders to party members and by getting party members onto the floor when a vote is being called. Even before the vote is taken, the whips will have conducted polls of their party's members and communicated members' intentions to the leaders. Today, both the Republican and Democratic whips are elected by their party's caucus.

Next in line in importance for each party is its **Committee on Committees** whose tasks are to assign newly elected legislators to committees and deal with the requests of incumbent members for transfers from one committee to another. Members usually receive the assignments they want; and they usually request assignment on a committee related to the dominant interests in their districts.

Finally, every committee and subcommittee is chaired by a member of the majority party. In general, the most senior member, the one with the longest continuous service on that committee, is the chair. This is also true in the Senate.

Leadership in the Senate

The two highest-ranking leaders in the Senate are defined by the Constitution and are largely ceremonial. Under the Constitution, the vice president is the president of the Senate but rarely attends meetings of the Senate and may vote only to break a tie. The Constitution also allows the Senate to elect a **president pro tempore** to preside over the Senate in the vice president's absence. The president pro tem is a member of the majority party and usually is the member with the longest continuous service in the Senate.

Representative John Boehner is the third representative from the state of Ohio to serve as Speaker of the House of Representatives. He has served Ohio's 8th congressional district since 1991. The 8th district sits on the west side of Ohio, bordering Indiana. It includes several rural and suburban areas near Cincinnati and Dayton and a small portion of Dayton itself. John Boehner served as the Republican House Minority Leader from 2007 until the election of 2010 gave the Republicans control of the House. Boehner was then elected Speaker. Credit: RTTNews

Harry Reid And Nancy Pelosi at a press conference following health care reform summit in Washington. February 25, 2010   Credit: RTTNews

The real leadership power in the Senate is exercised, as in the House, by the **majority floor leader**, the **minority floor leader**, and the whips, all elected by party caucus. These leaders have powers similar to their counterparts in the House. They schedule debate, make committee assignments, select members to the conference committees, mobilize the party vote, and act as their party's spokesperson. The Democratic leaders are more powerful than the Republican leaders in the Senate. This is because the Democratic floor leader is also the chairperson of all the following: the Democratic Conference (caucus), the Steering Committee (makes committee assignments), and the Policy Committee (schedules legislation for floor action).

The Role of Money in Choosing Congressional Leadership

The leadership positions in Congress are often determined primarily by the ability to raise campaign money. For example, Representative John Boehner, who was elected by the Republicans to be Speaker of the House following the 2010-midterm elections, is known for his ability to raise campaign money and use it to help other Republicans get elected and thereby amass support from them. In 1995, he started Freedom Project, a Political Action Committee, to raise money and provide direct financial assistance to Republican candidates in federal elections. In the latest election cycle, the PAC raised more than $2.7 million and doled out more than half of that to dozens of other congressional candidates in $5,000 increments that included numerous multiple-donations

PARTY LEADERS IN THE 113th CONGRESS, 2011-2012

Position	Incumbent	Party/State	Leader Since
House			
Speaker	John Boehner	R., Ohio	Jan. 2011
Majority leader	Eric Cantor	R., Va.	Jan. 2011
Majority whip	Kevin McCarthy	R., Ca.	Jan. 2011
Chairperson of Republican Conference	Cathy McMorris Rodgers	R., Wash	Jan. 2013
Minority leader	Nancy Pelosi	D., Ca.	Jan. 2011
Minority whip	Steny Hoyer	D., Maryland	Jan. 2011
Chairperson of the Democratic Caucus	Xavier Becerra	D., Calif.	Jan. 2013
Senate			
President	Joe Biden	D., Del.	Jan. 2009
President *pro tempore*	Patrick Leahy	D., Vermont	Jan. 2013
Majority floor leader	Harry Reid	D., Nev.	Jan. 2007
Chairman of the Republican Conference	John Thune	R., S. Dakota	Jan. 2013
Minority floor leader	Mitch McConnell	R., Ky.	Jan. 2007
Chairperson of the Democratic Caucus	Harry Reid	D., Nev.	Jan. 2005
Majority Whip	Richard Durbin	D., Il.	Jan. 2007
Minority Whip	John Cornyn	R., Texas	Jan. 2013

to some, according to the Federal Election Commission. His bid to become Speaker was successful largely because he garnered the support of those like Representative David Hobson who Boehner helped get elected and then helped get on the Appropriations Committee and into other leadership positions in Congress.[25]

Party Discipline

A vote on which 90 percent or more of the members of one party take a particular position while at least 90 percent of the members of the other party take the opposing position is called a **party vote**. In the early 1900s, party votes accounted for nearly one-half of all votes in Congress. Today, they are very rare. Much more common is a weaker form of party voting in which the majority of a party votes one way, and the majority of the other party votes the other way. Such voting has increased in recent years.

Party discipline increased during the first administration of George W. Bush because the Republicans controlled the House and Senate as well as the White House. Party discipline was also strong in the first two years of the Obama presidency when Democrats controlled all three institutions. The 111th Congress (2009-2010) began with a burst of legislative productivity, as Democrats enacted a $787 billion economic stimulus package at the start of 2009, then a landmark health-care law and a sweeping overhaul of Wall Street rules. In the final days of the session, the Democrats forced through a historic social change by lifting the ban on gay men and lesbians serving openly in the military, a major foreign policy achievement in approving the New Start arms control treaty with Russia, and an $858 billion tax-cut package.

Most of the legislative victories of the Democratic-controlled 111th Congress were secured on party-line or near-party-line votes. Party-line voting often sets the controlling party up for electoral losses in the next election. When the 2010 voters became angry with government big spending, it was the Democrats who bore the brunt of that anger and were ousted from Congress. The Democratic Party paid a devastating price for its accomplishments, losing control of the House and six Senate seats in 2010. Party-line voting may also cause partisan animosity that can bring the Congress to a grinding halt as the two parties battle each other over major pieces of legislation. In the immediate aftermath of the 2010-midterm elections, it became clear that much of the 112th session would be spent fighting over what was done in the 111th. The congressional spending and budget process completely collapsed at the end of 2010 for the first time in a quarter-century and Congress did not fulfill its most basic responsibility, allocating money to federal agencies. This lapse set up a spending fight early in the current Congress over financing the government while House Republicans tried to carry out their plan to cut $100 billion in domestic spending.

Standing Committees of the House and Senate

House	Senate
Agriculture	Agriculture, Nutrition and Forestry
Appropriations	Appropriations
Armed Services	Armed Services
Budget	Banking, Housing, and Urban Affairs
Education and the Workforce	Budget
Energy and Commerce	Commerce, Science and Transportation
Ethics	Energy and Natural Resources
Financial Services	Environment and Publics Works
Foreign Affairs	Finance
Homeland Security	Foreign Relations
House Administration	Health, Education, Labor, and Pensions
Judiciary	Homeland Security & Government Affairs
Natural Resources	Judiciary
Oversight and Government Reform	Rules and Administration
Rules	Small Business & Entrepreneurship
Science, Space and Technology	Veterans' Affairs
Small Business	
Transportation and Infrastructure	
Veterans' Affairs	
Ways and Means	

THE COMMITTEE AND SUBCOMMITTEE SYSTEM

The Work of Committees: Legislation and Oversight

In any institution as large as the United States Congress, a division of labor is necessary. Because most members of Congress have backgrounds in law or business, they cannot be expected to be experts on all the wide variety of issues on which they are asked to vote. Every year, thousands of bills are introduced into Congress. As a result, members must specialize in one or two issue areas of particular importance to their districts or states. They will then sit on committees and subcommittees dealing with these issue areas.

Most of the actual work of legislating is done by the committees and subcommittees within Congress. Committees usually control the fate of bills, particularly in three ways. First, the committee controls the scheduling of hearings and formal action on a bill and decides which of its subcommittees will act on the bill. A committee can hold up action on the bill and thereby virtually kill its chances to be considered by the entire chamber and passed into law. The only way to remove a bill from a House committee is through a **discharge petition**, signed by 218 members of the House. Such petitions are rare, with only twenty-one succeeding between 1909 and 2008.[26] The most recent successful discharge petition was the Bipartisan Campaign Reform Act. Beginning in 1997, several attempts were made to bring it to the floor via the discharge petition. It finally passed in 2002, and the Senate passed it 60-40. Committees control the fate of a bill in a second way: they mark-up the bill. To mark-up means to alter the bill, essentially rewriting it. It is this marked-up version of the bill that will be submitted for consideration to the entire chamber, either House or Senate.

Committees exercise a third form of control over legislation: the committee vote, while not binding on the chamber, almost always determines the chamber's final vote. Committees and subcommittees make a formal report on proposed legislation. These reports are available from the Government Printing Office. The committee's decisions can be reversed on the floor of the chamber, but this is highly unlikely. The whole point of a committee system is to allow for specialization and the effective division of labor.

The work of committees does not end when the bill goes to the entire chamber for consideration. Members of the committee act as floor managers of the bill, offering advice to other members and lining up support. Finally if there are any differences between the version of the bill passed by the House and the version passed by the Senate, it is the committee members who will be asked to serve on a conference committee whose duty it is to adjust the legislation into a compromise that, if the bill is to be passed, must be acceptable to a majority in both chambers.

Even after the legislation is passed into law, the work of the committees and subcommittees is not finished. Committee members remain active in their role of oversight, the process of monitoring the bureaucracy in its administration of policy. Oversight is accomplished primarily through committee hearings. At these hearings, agency heads, even cabinet secretaries, testify concerning their progress, or lack thereof, in administering the law and carrying out the will of Congress. Committee members and their staff question agency officials, probing particular areas that may seem problematic. If the committee feels the agency is not complying with either the letter or the spirit of the law, it may seek to cut the agency's budget to secure compliance with congressional intent.

The Committee System in the Era of Divided Government

Congress's oversight function has become especially visible in the modern era of divided government. In the 28 years since the Watergate scandal erupted, the same party has simultaneously controlled the White House and both Houses of Congress for only 12 years: during Jimmy Carter's one-term presidency, during the first 2 years of Clinton's first term, from 2002-2006, and from 2009-10.

The result has been to set off what amounts to guerrilla warfare between the executive and legislative branches. In 1973, the Senate established the Select Committee on Campaign Activities to investigate the misdeeds of the 1972 presidential campaign, otherwise known as the Watergate scandal. This was followed the next year by the House Judiciary Committee's hearings on the impeachment of President Nixon for his attempt to cover up the scandal. Shortly after the Judiciary Committee recommended these articles of impeachment, the president resigned.

After the Republicans lost control of Congress following the midterm elections of 2006, there was a flurry of congressional investigations of George W. Bush's executive branch. In their first two months on the job, Democrats held an astounding 81 hearings on the war in Iraq. Foremost among these hearings were the inquiries into conditions at Walter Reed Army Medical Center. Apart from the war, questions concerning FBI domestic surveillance under the Patriot Act also provoked a string of hearings and demands on Capitol Hill for revising the law to protect civil liberties. There was also an investigation into the firing of eight federal prosecutors, allegedly for partisan political purposes, which prompted widespread calls for the resignation of Attorney General Alberto Gonzales and subpoena threats for presidential advisors Harriet Miers and Karl Rove.

Not surprisingly, when the Republicans regained control of the House in 2011, many began to call for investigations of the Obama administration. On January 3, the first day of the new session of Congress, Rep. Darrell Issa, Chairman of the House Oversight Committee, launched investigations on everything from WikiLeaks to Fannie Mae to corruption in Afghanistan. The outline of the Committee's hearing topics also included investigation of how regulation impacts job creation, recalls at the Food and Drug Administration and the failure of the Financial Crisis Inquiry Commission to agree on the causes of the market meltdown.[27]

Types of Congressional Committees

Standing Committees

The standing committee is the most important type of committee in Congress. These are permanent committees that specialize in a particular policy area. For example, the Banking, Finance, and Urban Affairs Committee in the House and the Banking, Housing, and Urban Affairs Committee in the Senate specialize in legislation dealing primarily with the banking industry.

Party leaders determine which members serve on each committee. The majority party always has a majority of members on each committee. The majority party names the chair of each committee based on seniority, power, loyalty, and other criteria. Committee chairs have substantial power: they schedule hearings and votes and can easily kill a bill if they choose. The senior committee member from the minority party is called the ranking member. Members of Congress try to get good committee assignments. Most members want to be on powerful committees, such as the

Ways and Means Committee (which deals with taxes and revenue), or on a committee that covers issues important to their constituents. Getting a good committee assignment can make reelection easier for members. Typically, seventeen to twenty House members sit on each of these committees, with members sitting on an average of two standing committees. Members who serve on either the Appropriations, Rules, or Ways and Means Committee, however, can only serve on that one committee. Senators sit on two standing committees and one minor committee (either the Rules and Administration Committee or the Veterans Affairs Committee).

Select Committees

A select committee is a temporary committee created by Congress to fill a certain purpose. After they report to their chamber, they are disbanded. Select committees are often investigative committees, for example, those dealing with Watergate, Iran-Contra, and Whitewater. The Select Committee on Energy Independence & Global Warming, tasked with finding solutions that address the energy, economic and national security challenges associated with our dependence on foreign oil and increasing carbon pollution, held 80 hearings between March 2007 and December 2010, exploring American energy resources, clean technologies, climate change and the risks associated with it.

Joint Committees

A joint committee is *joint* in several respects. It is created by the House and Senate, and it is made up of members from both chambers and from both political parties. Joint committees may be either temporary or permanent, but they always deal with very specific policy areas, such as economic policy or taxation.

Conference Committees

The conference committee is both a joint committee and a temporary committee. It is created by the House and Senate to work out a compromise in the case in which the House and Senate pass different versions of a bill. While only about 15 to 25 percent of all bills go to conference committee, almost all the most important and controversial ones will.

The House Rules Committee

The House Rules Committee is a uniquely powerful committee. It serves as a gatekeeper, structuring floor action. The Rules Committee sets the time limit on debate and decides whether and in what ways the bill can be amended from the floor.

Committee Membership

One of the first things newly elected members of Congress do upon arriving in Washington is to write to their parties' congressional leadership and the other members of their state delegation, indicating their committee preferences. Members seek to get on committees that will achieve three goals: re-election, influence in Congress, and the opportunity to make policy in areas they think are important.[28] Party leaders generally honor these requests because they want their party members to serve their constituents and thereby win re-election.

Each party in each chamber has its own particular way of making committee assignments. In the House, for example, the Democrats have the Steering and Policy Committee while the Republicans have their Committee on Committees. While these committees do have the authority to assign their party members to the committees and subcommittees, every committee must reflect the party balance of the entire chamber and every chair of every committee will be from the majority party in that chamber. In other words, if the Senate has, say, 60 Republicans and 40 Democrats, every committee and subcommittee in the Senate will have approximately 60 percent Republicans and 40 percent Democrats, and every chair will be a Republican.

Committee and Subcommittee Chairs

Until the 1970s, there was a simple rule for picking committee chairs: the seniority system. This system assigned the chair position to the committee member of the majority party who had the longest continued service on that committee. In the early 1970s, in the wake of the Watergate scandal, Congress faced a revolt staged by younger, newly elected members. Both parties moved to permit their party members to vote on committee chairs. Until 2002, however, seniority still remained the rule, although there were always significant exceptions.

Then after the 2002 election, the Republican leadership in the House announced that they would not be following the seniority principle in assigning the new committee chairs. Majority Leader Tom DeLay and Speaker Dennis Hastert chose the new chairs on the basis of who demonstrated fundraising ability and party loyalty.

There have been a series of reforms to somewhat reduce the power of the chairs. Chairs of a generation ago could bully members and bottle up legislation and succeed in killing it all together. Today's chairs are less able to control their committees decision-making processes.[29] They still are primarily responsible for scheduling their committees' hearings, hiring staff, appointing subcommittees, and managing committee bills once they are brought to the floor of the chamber.

The Staff System

More than 38,660 people are employed by the United States Congress. The average Senate office employs about thirty staff members but twice that number work for senators from the more populous states. House members employ about fifteen staff members.[30] These staffers handle constituent communications and deal with the details of legislative and administrative actions. Increasingly, staffers are responsible for formulating proposals, organizing hearings, dealing with interest group lobbyists, and advising the members for whom they work.

Besides their personal staff, Congress employs more than three thousand committee staffers. These employees are permanent and stay from one session of Congress to the next. Key pieces of important legislation have been proposed or altered by these committee staff members. Senator Robert Morgan (D-N.C.) has said, "this country is basically run by the legislative staffs of the Senate and House of Representatives."[31]

President Obama leaves the White House with his legislative affairs director Phil Shiliro en route to the U.S. Capitol to meet with the Republican caucuses.   Jan. 27, 2009   Credit: White House Photo by Pete Souza

Congress has also created four different support institutions to enable Congress to oversee the actions of the executive branch, its administrative agencies, and the president himself. The Congressional Research Service does research on policy proposals. The General Accountability Office is Congress' financial watchdog over the bureaucracy, checking the departments and agencies to make sure they are spending the money appropriated by Congress in the way in which Congress meant it to be spent. The Office of Technology Assessment provides Congress with analyses of scientific or technical issues. The Congressional Budget Office assesses the economic implications and probable costs of proposed federal programs. Finally, a section of the Library of Congress acts as an information and fact-finding center for legislators and their staff members. It provides a computer based record of the content and status of major bills that can be accessed by members and their staff.

The Caucuses

Caucuses are groups of senators or representatives who share certain opinions, interests, or social characteristics. Some of the most important caucuses are the Congressional Black Caucus, the Congressional Caucus for Women's Issues, and the Hispanic Caucus. These three have actively sought to advance the interests of the groups they represent through the promotion of legislation and lobbying administrative agencies for favorable treatment. The Congressional Black Caucus now includes over forty members and has dramatically increased its role in the policy-making process.

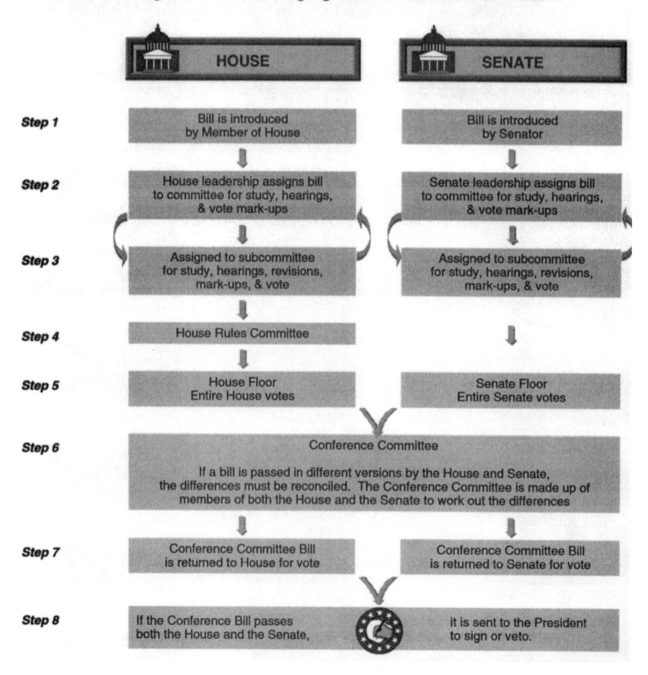

There are also ideological caucuses such as the Blue Dog Caucus (conservative Democrats), Congressional Progressive Caucus (liberal Democrats), Republican Study Committee (conservative Republicans), and the new Tea Party Caucus that includes 52 members of Congress.

THE LEGISLATIVE PROCESS

For a bill to become law, it must pass through a series of steps in both the House and the Senate and be passed by a majority of both chambers in identical form. While flow charts may make the legislative process appear to be neat and tidy, the reality is far more complex and far messier. A bill may be introduced in one chamber, work its way through that chamber and then be taken up by the other chamber of Congress. Or a bill might be working its way through the two chambers simultaneously, though not necessarily at exactly the same stage in both. It is also not necessarily the case that the version of the bill in the Senate will be the same as the version in the House. In general, however, the steps discussed below must be completed within one two-year session of Congress. All sessions run from January of an odd year through December of the following even year.

Step One: The Bill is Introduced

The formal legislative process begins when a member of Congress introduces a bill. But before a bill can be introduced, a problem must be identified and a solution formulated. In short, the issue must get on the congressional agenda. An issue can exist for a time without becoming a *political* issue.

Issues get on the legislative agenda in a variety of ways. Certainly a sudden crisis can propel an issue to the forefront, for example, the terrorist attacks on September 11, 2001. Sustained media coverage of an issue can also work the issue into the collective congressional consciousness. Presidents can also bring an issue to the fore, as President Bush did with the issue of Iraq. Interest groups are quite often instrumental in politicizing an issue, for example, Mothers Against Drunk Driving.

Of course, members of Congress themselves may be instrumental in advancing an issue to the legislative agenda, particularly in two situations. When the president is of one party and the other party controls both chambers of Congress, initiation of legislation is very likely to come from Congress itself. When the Republicans took control of the House after the 2010 elections, they quickly unveiled their "Pledge to America," an ambitious plan that would roll back spending to 2008 spending levels and would put in place strict budget caps. The other situation that tends to encourage congressional initiation of legislation is when one or more members of Congress are seeking to be nominated as a candidate for the presidency. In 2008, Senator Hillary Clinton, considered the frontrunner for the Democratic nomination, was eager to lead the legislative process.

Step Two: The Bill is Assigned to Committee

After a bill is introduced, in the House by a House member and in the Senate by a senator, it will be assigned to a committee that has jurisdiction over that policy area. The speaker of the House and the majority leader in the Senate are responsible for this assignation. While it is often very clear which committee should receive the bill, there are some cases when it is less than clear. In these situations the leaders can use their discretion to send the bill to a committee that will be friendly to it or to a committee that may be more hostile to the bill.

Once assigned to committee, the bill then will be further assigned to one of the committee's appropriate subcommittees. The subcommittee will do three things with the bill. First, the staffers of the committee members will conduct research on the issue, and the subcommittee may choose to hold hearings on the issue. The committee members will want to hear from people with expertise in the issue area. This group will likely include interest group lobbyists and bureaucrats from the executive branch department or agency involved in the issue area. These people will be asked to testify at the hearing.

When the subcommittee feels that it has sufficient information, it will hold meetings called **mark-up sessions**. The original bill will be marked-up, altered to reflect the information Congress gleaned from the hearing process. Finally, the subcommittee will vote on the bill. If passed, the bill will be sent by the subcommittee to its full committee. The full committee may accept the recommendation of its subcommittee or choose to hold its own hearings and prepare its own bill. It should be noted, however, that many bills will *die* in committee, with little or no consideration given to it. Many pieces are symbolic in that members of Congress introduce them to please some group in their constituency but expect nothing to be done on the bill. In a typical session of Congress, 95 percent of the roughly eight thousand bills introduced die in committee. In those cases when the committee has acted on the bill, the bill is ready to go to the floor of the chamber.

In the House, before the bill goes to the floor, it must go the House Rules Committee. The Rules Committee attaches a rule to the bill that will govern the floor debate in the House. The Rules Committee specifies the length of debate and decides whether amendments can be added from the floor and, if so, of what type.

Before the bill can go to the floor, in both the House and Senate, it must be placed on the calendar. The majority and minority leaders, after consultation with committee chairs, the White House, and the leaders from the other chamber, place the bill on the calendar. Some bills are given an early date while others stay on the calendar from one session to the next.

Step Three: Floor Action

Debate in the House of Representatives is structured by the Rules Committee and the speaker of the House. The speaker can decide whether to grant recognition to a member. The time allotted by the Rules Committee for debate is usually controlled by the bill's sponsor and by its leading opponent. These two are usually the chairman of the committee to which the bill was assigned and the ranking minority member on that committee.

Debate on the floor of the Senate can only be structured by unanimous consent agreements to set the starting time and length of debate. If a senator wants to stop a bill from being passed, he or she may start a **filibuster**, speaking for as long as the member wants. The number of filibusters has risen dramatically in recent years, leading some to complain that there has been a trivialization of the filibuster. By simply raising an anonymous objection, senators can trigger the need for a 60-vote supermajority for virtually every piece of legislation. In the last two congressional terms (2006-2008, 2008-2010), Republicans have brought 275 filibusters. This is by far the highest number in congressional history, and more than twice the amount in the previous two terms. Republicans have routinely filibustered not only the final vote on a bill but the initial motion to even debate it, as well as amendments and votes on conference committees. Even bipartisan measures like the Food Safety Bill are routinely filibustered and delayed. Breaking each of these filibusters adds days or weeks to every bill. These filibusters are the reason there was no budget passed at the end of 2010, and why as many as 125 nominees to executive branch positions and 48 judicial nominations were never brought to a vote.[32] In January 2013, Senate Majority Leader Harry Reid and Senate Minority Leader Mitch McConnell failed to reach an agreement that would have reformed the filibuster process and instead agreed to only the most minor changes.[33]

If there is a filibuster, it can be ended under Senate Rule 22, debate may be ended through **cloture**. Sixteen senators must propose closing off debate. Then, after a two-day waiting period, sixty senators must vote for cloture for the debate to be ended. After cloture, each senator may speak for a maximum of one hour on a bill before a vote is taken.

The Senate of the United States is purposefully structured to allow intense minorities to block legislation. Whereas the House is the repository of majoritarianism, the Senate is the protector of the minority. The filibuster is only one of several techniques that allow for this minority veto. Under Senate rules, members are able to propose unlimited amendments to a bill. Each amendment must be voted on before the bill can come to a final vote. The introduction of new amendments can only be blocked by unanimous consent.

When debate is finished, a vote may be called. If a majority of the House votes for a bill, it is passed by the House. A majority vote in the Senate similarly passes the bill in that chamber. If there are any differences between the version passed by the House and the version passed by the Senate, then the bill is sent to a conference committee.

Step Four: The Conference Committee

It is often the case that a bill passed by the House will differ in significant ways from that passed by the Senate. In such cases, a conference committee is composed of the senior members of the committees and subcommittees that had had responsibility for the bills. The job of the conference committee is to work out a compromise version of the bill. When the bill gets out of conference, the House-Senate conference report must be approved on the floor of each chamber. Usually such approval is given readily. The bill can then be voted on. If it is passed by a majority of the House and a majority of the Senate, the bill then goes to the president.

It should be noted that the members of a conference committee are often chosen because they have strong ties to the interest groups impacted by the proposed bill. For example, in 2010, lobbyists for the financial services industry enjoyed longstanding ties to the members of Congress who were named to the conference committee on financial reform legislation. At least 56 of the industry lobbyists had previously served on the personal staffs of the 43 members of Congress named to the conference committee. The financial services industry's links to the Senate's representatives on the panel were particularly extensive. Collectively, 41 industry lobbyists had once worked on the legislative staffs of the committee's 12 senators. And each senator once employed at least one current lobbyist.[34]

Senator Susan Collins (R-ME) meets with President in the Oval Office. Collins was one of three Republican Senators who eventually voted for the stimulus bill. Feb 4, 2009. White House Photo by Pete Souza

Step Five: The President

When a president receives the bill, he may do any of three things with it. In the most usual situation he will sign the bill, in which case it becomes law. He may, on the other hand, choose to let the bill sit for ten days, excluding Sunday. On the tenth day, the bill becomes law without his signature. A president may choose to follow this course when he is presented with a bill that he does not approve of but for political purposes is willing to go along with Congress.

The third thing the president can do is **veto** the bill. The veto is the president's constitutional right to reject a piece of legislation passed by Congress. To veto a bill, the president must return it to the chamber in which it originated within ten days with his objections to the bill. Congress can try to override the president's veto, but such an override requires a two-thirds vote in both chambers. Overrides are very rare.

If Congress adjourns during this ten-day period in which the president may act, and the president has taken no action, the bill is considered **pocket vetoed**. A pocket veto cannot be overridden by Congress for the simple reason that Congress has adjourned.

For a brief period, the president also enjoyed the power of the **line item veto**. In 1996 President Clinton signed into law a bill passed by Congress authorizing the item veto that allows a president five calendar days following Congress' passage of a bill to notify Congress of his decision to "rescind" an item. This item veto applies to discretionary spending, new direct spending, and items of limited tax benefit. Congress has thirty days to override the president's item veto by a simple majority vote. In April 1997 U. S. District Court Judge Thomas P. Jackson declared the item veto authority unconstitutional because it violates the separation of powers.

Step Six: Oversight

Once Congress has passed a bill and the president has either signed it or allowed it to become law, the law must be put into effect. In the executive branch there are departments and agencies specifically responsible for executing the laws of the land. Members of Congress and their committees must oversee how these departments and agencies carry out the policies passed into law by Congress. This is the **oversight** function of Congress.

Congressional supervision of the executive branch bureaucracy takes several forms. First, no agency or department may exist (except for a few presidential offices and special commissions) without congressional approval. It is Congress that passes the **enabling legislation** that creates these agencies and empowers them. During the presidency of George Washington, Congress created three departments: Treasury, State, and War. Today, the bureaucracy has grown to over eighteen hundred departments, agencies, commissions, and government corporations, with a budget of over one and a half trillion dollars, and employing over five million people. While Congress cannot control all aspects of personnel selection, the Senate does have the constitutional power to advise and to consent to (or refuse to consent to) presidential nominations of top agency and department personnel.

The vast size of the bureaucracy does make oversight difficult. In addition, the legislative process itself complicates effective oversight. Congress tends to pass laws that are general outlines for policy development. Congress cannot anticipate all the possible applications of the law and so leaves much for the bureaucracy to fill in. On a typical weekday, agencies issue more than a hundred pages of new regulations. Determining how good a job a particular agency is doing will not be an easy job.

Congress also exercises oversight through its control of the budget. No money may be spent unless it has first been authorized and appropriated by Congress. **Authorization legislation** originates in a legislative committee and states the maximum amount of money an agency may spend on a given program. This authorization may be permanent, it may be fixed for a number of years, or it may be annual. Once funds have been authorized by Congress, they also must be appropriated. **Appropriations** are usually made annually and originate from the House Appropriations Committee and its various subcommittees. The Appropriations Committee may, and often does, appropriate less than was authorized.

Congress' oversight function does not stop once the money has been appropriated to the department or agency. In fact, Congress can actively participate in the activities of the bureaucracy. A congressional committee may obtain the right to pass on certain agency decisions. This is called **committee clearance**, and though the agency is not legally bound by the committee's decision, few agencies would risk angering the committee that largely controls its budget.

Perhaps the most visible and dramatic form of congressional oversight of the bureaucracy is the **investigation**. This investigative power of Congress is not mentioned in the Constitution but has been seen as implicit in the legislative powers of Congress. The Supreme Court has consistently upheld wide investigative powers.³⁵ As part of this investigative power, Congress may also hold committee hearings and investigations and gives these committees the power to subpoena witnesses, take oaths, cross-examine, compel testimony, and bring criminal charges for contempt and perjury. The most formal oversight methods include conducting a hearing or requesting a report on specific agency practices.

Oversight may also be done more informally, through day-to-day contact between committee members and administrators in the executive branch. Congress has a large number of staff members working on oversight issues, as well as several specialized oversight offices, the congressional Budget Office, the Office of Technology Assessment, the Government Accounting Office, and the congressional Research Service of the Library of Congress.

Since the Republicans took control of the House in 2011, they have placed a heavy emphasis on oversight. Republican Congressman Dan Lungren, the chairman of the House Administration Committee, has said that Congress has the obligation to oversee the executive branch, ensuring that the FBI, the Drug Enforcement Agency and the Justice Department are carrying out the laws passed by Congress. He has gone on to insist that each agency list its priorities to help Congress shrink the federal budget. Political scientist Mark Sandelow has written that for all the hearings and investigations, the real power for congressional oversight is in its purse. In the end, it is Congress that determines the budget for the federal government.³⁶

CONCLUSIONS

The midterm elections of 2010 ended a brief two-year period of unified government under Democratic control. In 2011, the Republicans took control of the U.S. House of Representatives, beginning an era of divided government in Washington that will test the unity of both parties. As Congress began a new session in January 2013 and President Obama readied to start his second term, gridlock has continued. The elections of 2012 ushered in a more partisan and less experienced set of lawmakers. In the House, the parties retrenched toward partisan corners, with regional divisions sharpened. The 87-member, ardently conservative class elected in 2010 was returned mostly intact, bolstered by a big new class of Republican freshmen. After a cycle that saw a 20-year high of seats without incumbents seeking reelection, at least one-third of the 113th Congress will feature House members with less than three years of experience. Similarly, the Senate is both more partisan and less experienced with twelve new senators. As senior members and committee leaders are departing, a large pool of relatively new members are left to try and reach the consensus that is required to pass legislation.

Compromise is needed in an era of divided government. Not only does a Democrat occupy the White House but Democrats also still control the other chamber of Congress. The Senate will make every effort to thwart the Republican's ambitious legislative agenda. It opened for business in 2011 with the Democrats' majority down from the 60 votes their party enjoyed following the 2008 election to just 53, making it harder to enact legislation President Obama seeks. But 53 votes still give the Democrats more than enough clout to block the Republicans from keeping their campaign promises, including the one most central to their electoral victories, to repeal Obama health care. The United States has now entered its run-up to the 2012 congressional and presidential elections.

With campaigns but a short time away, President Obama and congressional Republicans are set to square off over the extremely important questions regarding the size of government and the amount of taxpayer dollars it takes to run that government and its programs.

CHAPTER NOTES

[1] Scott Frisch and Sean Kelly, "Lack of Earmarks Makes Congress harder to Lead," *Roll Call*, January 21, 2012, http://www.rollcall.com/news/frisch_and_kelly_lack_of_earmarks_makes_congress_harder_to_lead-220811-1.html?pos=oplyh).

[2] Roger Gwinn, "The Case for Restoring the Earmark Ban," *The Ferguson Group Blog*, January 18, 2013, http://thefergusongroup.typepad.com/grants/2013/01/the-case-for-ending-the-earmark-ban.html.

[3] Theodore J. Lowi and Benjamin Ginsberg, *American Government*, 4th ed. (New York: W. W. Norton, 1996), 198.

[4] Lowi and Ginsberg, *American Government*, 749.

[5] Sarah A. Binder, *Stalemate: Causes and Consequences of Legislative Gridlock*, Washington, D.C.: Brookings Institution Press, 2003.

[6] Edmund Burke, *Burke's Politics*, ed. Ross J. H. Hoffman and Paul Levick (New York: A.A. Knopf, 1949).

[7] Roger Davidson, *The Role of Congressmen* (New York: Pegasus, 1977), 117.

[8] Hanna Fenichel Pitkin, *The Concept of Representation* (Berkeley: University of California Press, 1967), 60-91.

[9] Norman J. Ornstein, Thomas E. Mann, and Michael J. Malbin, eds., *Vital Statistics on Congress, 1993-94* (Washington, D.C.: Congressional Quarterly Press, 1994), 58-61.

[10] Discoverthenetworks, "Congressional Black Caucus," http://www.discoverthenetworks.org/groupProfile.asp?grpid=7126, 2008.

[11] "The 105th Congress: A Study in Sameness," 19 January 1997, sec. 4, 5E.

[12] "Highway Bill Larded with Hometown Projects," *Champaign-Urbana News-Gazette*, March 30, 1999, p. A5.

[13] Lizette Alvarez, "Congress on Record Course For 'Pork' with Alaska in a Class of Its Own," *New York Times*, November 19, 1999, p. A28.

[14] *Congressional Quarterly, Guide to the Congress of the United States*, 2d ed. (Washington, D.C.: Congressional Quarterly Press, 1976), 588.

[15] John S. Saloma, *Congress and the New Politics* (Boston: Little, Brown, 1969), 184-85.

[16] *Congressional Quarterly Guide*, 229-310.

[17] NewsMax.com, "Supreme Court Upholds Racial Gerrymandering," http://www.adversity.net/special/gerrymander_1.htm, April 19, 2001.

[18] Deirdre Walsh, "Congressional Races Set Records for Spending," *CNN Politics*, Nov., 2012, http://www.cnn.com/2012/10/31/politics/house-preview/index.html.

[19] Russ Britt, "The Costliest Races in House and Senate," *Wall Street Journal Market Watch*, Nov. 5, 2012. www.marketwatch.com/story/the-costliest-races-in-the-House-and-Senate2012-11-057pagenumber=z

[20] *Congressional Quarterly Guide*, 588.

[21] "Campaign Notes, Report Says Incumbents Get Most PAC Money," New York Times, Jan. 18, 2009.

[22] Dave Gilson, "The Price of Admission to the House and Senate," *Mother Jones*, September/October 2010, http://motherjones.com/politics/2010/09/incumbent-campaign-fundraising-advantage-congress

[23] Sheila Krumholz, "2006 Election Analysis: Incumbents Linked to Corruption Lose, but Money Still Wins," www.opensecrets.org, Nov. 8, 2006.

[24] Diana Blanton, Fox News Poll: 78 Percent Favor Term Limits for Congress," *FoxNews.com*, September 3, 2010, http://www.foxnews.com/politics/2010/09/03/fox-news-poll-percent-favor-term-limits-congress KPBS, "GOP Representative Darrell Issa to Chair Oversight and Reform Committee," December 2010, Daylife,http://www.daylife.com/article/08Q86TBbKMbfK?q=Darrell+Issa

[25] Joe Cogliano, "Boehner Readies for Speaker Role," *Dayton Business Journal*, October 29, 2010, http://www.bizjournals.com/dayton/print-edition/2010/10/29/boehner-readies-for-speaker-role.html

[26] *Congressional Quarterly*, Guide, 426.

[27] Jake Sherman, "Democrats Tap Top Obama Lawyer to Counter Darrell Issa," *Politico*, January 3, 2011, http://www.politico.com/news/stories/0111/46981.html

[28] Richard F. Fenno, Jr., *Congressmen in Committees* (Boston: Little, Brown, 1973), 1.

[29] Christopher J. Deering and Steven S. Smith, *Committees in Congress,* 3rd ed. (Washington, D.C.: Congressional Quarterly Press, 1997).

[30] The Tax Foundation, *Tax Features*, March, 1992, 6.

[31] Congressional Record, quoted in Lowi and Ginsberg, *American Politics,* 180.

[32] Ross Douthata, "Reform and the Filibuster," *The New York Times*, January 2, 2011, http://www.nytimes.com/2011/01/03/opinion/03mon1.html.

[33] Scott Lemieux, "What Killed the Filibuster?" *The American Prospect*, January 25, 2013, http://prospect.org/article/what-killed-filibuster-reform.

[34] Open Secrets, " Financial Reform Conference Committee Offers Industry Lobbyists a Chance to Reunite with Former Bosses," *OpenSecretsblog*, June 11, 2010, http://www.opensecrets.org/news/2010/06/financial-reform-conference-committ.html.

[35] Edward S. Corwin, *The Constitution and What It Means Today*, 13th ed. (Princeton, N.J.: Princeton University Press, 1973), 151.

[36] Kitty Felde and Justin Ho, "The Word for the New Congress: Oversight," *Southern California Public Radio*, January 5, 2011.

SUGGESTED READINGS

Bell, Lauren Cohen. *Master the U.S. Congress: A Simulation for Students.* Belmont, CA: Wadsworth, 2004.

Congressional Quarterly, *CQ's Politics in America.* Washington, D.C.: CQ Press, 2008.

Davidson, Roger, Walter Olesvek, and Frances Lee. *Congress and Its Members*, 11th ed. Washington D.C.: CQ Press, 2008.

Dodd, Larewnce C. and Bruce Oppenheimer, eds. *Congress Reconsidered,* 9th ed. Washington, D.C.: CQ Press, 2008.

Dodson, Debra L. *The Impact of Women in Congress.* New York: Oxford University Press, 2006.

Fiorina, Morris. *Congress: Keystone of the Washington Establishment.* 2nd ed. New Haven, CT: Yale University Press, 1989.

Hamilton, Lee. *How Congress Works.* Bloomington: Indiana University Press, 2004.

Jacobson, Gary C. T*he Politics of Congressional Elections*, 7th ed. New York: Longman, 2009.

Koger, Gregory. *Filibustering: A Political Hsitory of Obstruction in the House and Senate.* Chicago: University of Chicago Press, 2010.

Mann, Thomas E., and Norman J. Ornstein. *The Broken Branch: How Congress is Failing America and How to Get It Back on Track.* New York: Oxford University Press, 2006.

Palmer, Barbara, and Denise Simon. *Breaking the Political Glass Ceiling: Women and Congressional Elections.* 2nd ed. New York: Routledge, 2008.

Sinclair, Barbara. *Unorthodox Lawmaking: New Legislative Processes in the U.S. Congress*, 3rd ed. Washington, D.C.: CQ Press, 2008.

Smith, Stephen S., Jason M. Roberts, and Ryan V. Vander Wielen. *The American Congress.* New York: Cambridge University Press, 2007.

Web Sites

The Center on Congress at Indiana University. http://congress.indiana.edu.
Congress. www.congress.org.
Cook Political Report. www.cookpolitical.com.
Federal Register. www.access.gpo.gov.
Federal World. www.fedworld.gov.
General Services Administration. www.gsa.gov.
Library of Congress: Thomas. http://thomas.loc.gov.
National Committee for an Effective Congress. www.ourcampaigns.com.
Roll Call. www.rollcal.com.
The Sunlight Foundation and Taxpayers for Common Sense. http://earmarkwatch.org.
U.S. Government Gateway Site. www.usa.gov.
U.S. House of Representatives. www.house.gov.
U.S. Office of Management and Budget. www.omb.gov.
U.S. Senate. www.senate.gov.
The U.S. Government Printing Office Access on the Web. www.gpoaccess.gov

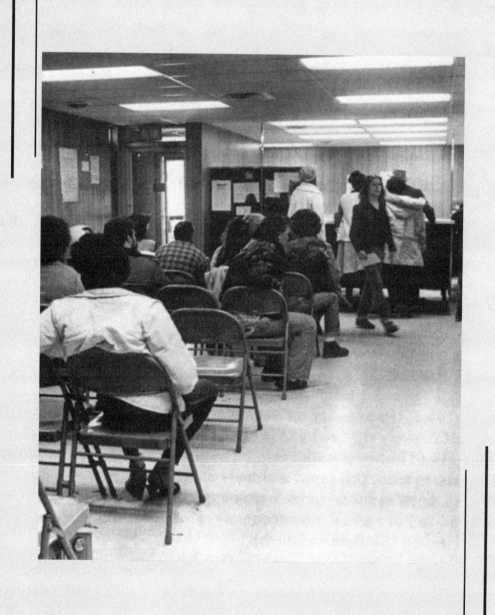

Chapter Ten

THE BUREAUCRACY

An explosion on the BP operated Deepwater Horizon oil rig killed eleven crew members on April 20, 2010, sparking the greatest environmental disaster in United States history. In combination with the Texas City Refinery Explosion and the Prudohoe Bay Oil Spill, this marked the third serious incident involving BP in the United States in five years. Scientific estimates put the amount of oil that was being discharged from the broken well at above 1,470,000 U.S.gallons per day! There are over four hundred different species of animals living in the area affected by the spill and 464 sea turtles and 60 were found dead.. On July 15, 2010, BP finally succeeded in stopping the flow of oil from the wellhead, after spilling 190 million gallons of oil into the gulf over a three-month period.

The BP oil disaster has shined a spotlight on an offshore drilling regulatory agency, the Minerals Management Service (MMS). MMS was created in 1982 to lease tracts to private oil companies for exploration, collect the government's share of oil and gas revenue, and regulate the industry. The agency was, therefore, directed to regulate the oil industry but to also share in the profits flowing from the oil dwells that it licensed. This built-in conflict would hamstring the agency for decades, with the agency being riddled with scandals over ethical problems, improper handling of royalties, and lax oversight of an industry with which it kept too-friendly ties.

The BP disaster reveals clearly that MMS faced three problems common to government regulatory bodies. First, there is the knowledge problem. MMS inspectors are guided in their work simply by a handbook of "potential incidents of noncompliance." With just five short paragraphs of regulations to guide it on how to conduct an investigation, the MMS never had a clear picture of its mandate. Additionally, while MMS knew that it was supposed to ensure the safety of oil drilling and existing wells, it had fewer than 60 inspectors to cover nearly 4,000 offshore facilities in the Gulf of Mexico. And the inspectors that MMS did have were underpaid, compared with similar jobs in the industry, and received mostly on-the-job training. This lack of expertise left MMS largely reliant on the oil industry, which it was supposed to regulate, to document and accurately report on operations, production, and royalties. According to American Petroleum Institute records, MMS ended up adopting at least 78 industry-generated standards as federal regulations.[1]

The second problem common to many government regulatory bodies is that of regulatory capture. Directed by law to "meet the nation's energy needs," MMS pursued that mission by declaring itself publicly and formally as industry's partner. Charged with collecting royalties from companies for the right to produce oil and gas from federally controlled land and water, officials at MMS routinely referred to the companies under their watch as "clients," "customers" and especially "partners." As the relationship became more intertwined, regulatory intensity subsided. MMS officials waived hundreds of environmental reviews and did not aggressively pursue companies for equipment failures. They also participated in studies financed and dominated by industry, more as collaborator than regulator. In the face of industry opposition, MMS abandoned proposals that would have increased costs but might have improved safety. Such lax regulation paid off; the Minerals Management Service brought in an average of $13 billion a year to the U.S. treasury.[2]

Many regulatory bodies have fallen prey to a third problem, corruption. An eye-opening series of reports in fall 2008 by the Department of the Interior's Inspector General disclosed a stunning level of corruption at MMS and coziness with industry officials that included a "culture of substance abuse and promiscuity" at the agency. The agency also runs the Royalty-in-Kind program out of its Denver office, through which it takes delivery of oil and gas from energy firms in lieu of cash payments, and then sells it to refiners. The Inspector General concluded that officials in the MMS Royalty-in-Kind program "frequently consumed alcohol at industry functions, had used cocaine and marijuana, and had sexual relationships with oil and gas company representatives." The Inspector General also found that one-third of Royalty-in-Kind officials were taking bribes and gifts, and noted that former MMS officials received contracts from their friends still in the department.[3]

While MMS's bad behavior was unusually egregious, there are many other recent disasters that, if not caused by, were certainly abetted by inept government regulation. Mining regulators allowed operators like Massey Energy to flout safety rules that led to the massive explosion that killed at least 25 West Virginia coal miners. Financial regulators let A.I.G. write more than half a trillion dollars of credit-default protection without sounding an alarm. The S.E.C. failed to spot the frauds at Enron and WorldCom, turned a blind eye as Bernie Madoff's Ponzi scheme defrauded thousands of investors of billions of dollars, decided to let Wall Street investment banks take on obscene amounts of leverage, and ignored myriad signs of fraud and recklessness in the subprime-mortgage market.

These failures were not accidents. They were the all too predictable result of the deregulationary fervor that has gripped Washington in recent years, pushing the message that most regulation is unnecessary at best and downright harmful at worst.[4] Beginning in the 1980s, regulation became delegitimatized, seen as little more than the tool of Washington busybodies. The regulators themselves became skeptical of their duties. Many are political appointees who come and go with each new presidency. This makes it hard for them to develop expertise and also makes it hard for them to develop loyalty to the agency and long-term commitment to its goals. The end result is that we have the worst of both worlds: too little supervision encourages corporate recklessness, while the mere existence of these agencies encourages the public's complacent belief that the government is protecting their interests.

How we, as a nation, think about regulators, and how they think of themselves, has a profound impact on the work they do. The political scientist Daniel Carpenter, in *Reputation and Power*, argues that a key to the success of the Food and Drug Administration has been its staffers' dedication to protecting and enhancing its reputation for competence and vigilance. That reputation, in turn, has made the companies that the F.D.A. regulates more willing to respect its authority. But the success of the F.D.A appears to be more the exception than the rule. In most other cases, as the idea of regulation has come to seem less legitimate, regulators have become less effective and companies have felt more free to ignore them.[5]

The social psychologist Tom Tyler has shown that acceptance of a law's legitimacy is the key factor in getting people to obey it.[6] So reforming the system is less about writing a host of new rules than it is about elevating the status of regulation and regulators.[7] Paying regulators competitive salaries (as is done, for instance, in Singapore, which has one of the world's least corrupt, and most efficient, bureaucracies) would attract talent and reduce the temptations of corruption. Offering regulators the kind of reputational rewards that, say, soldiers or firefighters get will make it easier for them to develop a similar sense of common purpose. The BP disaster, along with several others in 2010, suggests that it may be time to consider such an investment in the bureaucracy and its regulatory bodies.

THE DEVELOPMENT OF THE BUREAUCRATIC STATE

Constitutional Beginnings

The Constitution does not specify the structure of the federal bureaucracy. The seeds of the modern administrative state, however, can be found in Article II, section 2, paragraph 2. The president is told that he may appoint, with the advice and consent of the Senate, "ambassadors, other public ministers and consuls, judges of the Supreme Court, and all other officers of the United States whose appointments are not herein otherwise provided for, and which shall be established by law." The Constitution, then, gave both Congress and the president authority to devise and operate a bureaucracy. Congress has the power by law to create new agencies, and the president has the power to appoint (subject to Senate confirmation) the heads of the agencies.

The first Congress that met in 1789 created a simple bureaucratic structure consisting of three executive departments: the Department of State, the Department of War, and the Department of the Treasury. The first Congress also established the positions of the attorney general and postmaster general. The attorney general is the government's chief legal official, and in 1870 when Congress created the Department of Justice, the attorney general became the head of that department. The postmaster general is in charge of the Post Office.

All in all, the early bureaucracy was quite small. The original Department of State had only nine employees. Even by 1816, the federal bureaucracy employed fewer than five thousand people. The federal bureaucracy, however, grew rapidly thereafter. For the most part, the growth of the bureaucracy stems from the deep-rooted American belief that problems have solutions and progress can be made.

President Lyndon Johnson took on new commitments with programs of the Great Society.

The Progressive Movement

In the early 1900s, a philosophy of political reform, Progressivism, began to call into question the dominant economic theory of the nineteenth century, laissez-faire. The theory of **laissez-faire** dictated a minimal role for the government in economic management. Business was viewed as largely autonomous, and government action was to be discouraged as obtrusive and unnecessary.

By the end of the nineteenth century it had become apparent that the laissez-faire, hands-off approach had allowed the emergence of huge oligopolies, dominating whole fields such as railroads. Gradually, people began to see the need for government involvement in at least parts of the economy. The question was which of the institutions of government would be responsible for protecting the marketplace from its own ogopolistic tendencies.

The answer given by the Progressives of the early twentieth century was the creation of the modern administrative state. Congress moved to create new bureaucratic agencies enabled to regulate specific industries. The Federal Trade Commission (FTC) was created in 1914 to protect consumers from unfair business practices especially in advertising and labeling. The Food and Drug Administration (FDA) was created in 1906 to regulate the purity and safety of foods and pharmaceuticals.

The New Deal and Social Welfare Legislation

The economic depression of the 1930s reaffirmed the nation's belief that government action was essential to economic stability and the financial security of individuals. The enormous effects of economic cycles on the population of the United States convinced most that any needed government intervention would have to come from the federal level of government. State governments were simply not equipped to deal with national economic cycles. As a result, it fell to Franklin

Roosevelt and his New Deal legislative program to expand the scope of government action into areas of unemployment, electrical production, housing, and bank regulation. The Railroad Retirement Act of 1934 was the first federal attempt at an extensive security program. In 1935, the Social Security Act created a fund into which workers pay so that they will have income upon retirement. Today, Social Security pays over 56 million Americans every month with the average person receiving about $13,184 per year.[8]

World War II

By the 1940s, the federal government's role in regulating the economy was largely accepted as necessary. What was less clearly established was a permanent infrastructure of an administrative state. The New Deal involved many emergency boards and did not work to create a more permanent set of regulatory bodies.

World War II would lead to the creation of a permanent administrative state. During the war, the national government hired thousands of people. When the war ended, many of these people were absorbed into the civilian bureaucracy.

The Great Society and the Entitlements Revolution

By the end of the administration of President Lyndon Johnson, the size of the bureaucracy would reach its postwar peak, with 2.9 million civilian employees and an additional 3.6 million military personnel. In the 1950s, new problems had spawned new agencies to solve them. For example, in 1953, Congress created the Department of Health, Education, and Welfare (renamed the Department of Health and Human Services in 1979) to administer the nation's health, education, and assistance programs. Other departments and agencies were spawned in the 1960s when new interest groups began to press their claims on government. For example, Ralph Nader, a consumer activist, drew the public's attention to faulty automobile designs that posed a threat to the consumer. Congress responded in 1966 with the creation of the National Safety Agency (later renamed the Highway Traffic Safety Administration).

The programs of Lyndon Johnson's Great Society were a natural outgrowth of the public's growing sense that the government was responsible for the social welfare of the people. The government took on new commitments in the areas of aid to minorities and the poor. As a result, more and more groups began to see themselves as entitled to government protection. As the programs and their clientele groups grew in number, so did the bureaucratic agencies of the federal government.

Lobbying by Administrators

The budgets and staffs of bureaucratic departments and agencies have continued to grow as a result of activist bureaucrats seeking to defend their budgets and expand their authority. These administrators have often reinvented themselves to assure their continued existence. For example, after the collapse of the Soviet Union, the Department of Defense began to pressure Congress for budgets to do research on worldwide environmental degradation.[9] Similarly the Central Intelligence Agency (CIA) has recently defended their continued existence as necessary to the fight against the international drug trade. As a result, the national bureaucracy and federal spending has kept pace with the growth of the economy and society.

Ronald Reagan and Deregulation

America's acceptance of bureaucratic regulation developed slowly and never fully eclipsed a basic American dislike of government. Laissez-faire is deeply embedded in the very capitalist fabric of the American economy. Perhaps, then, it is unsurprising that as the bureaucratic state grew, uneasiness with it grew as well. By 1980, the American public was expressing disgust with the bureaucracy and government intervention. This disgust coalesced in support of Ronald Reagan in 1980 and then again in 1984.

President Reagan became the spokesperson for the belief that the national government was too involved in regulation, interfering in what should be the natural working of the business markets. Conservatives championed deregulation as a way to return unhampered efficiency to the marketplace.

Considerable deregulation was accomplished in the late 1970s and 1980s, most notably in the airline, trucking, financial services, and telecommunications industries.[10] In each of these areas, the government began to loosen the regulatory ties that were now seen as placing American industries in a less competitive posture in the now global economy. Some deregulation did lead to greater benefits for consumers. For example, in the case of the airlines, the Civil Aeronautics Board (CAB) had been determining fares and controlling access to routes. Some argued that such regulations actually reduced competition between airlines, thereby adversely affecting consumers.

Not all the deregulatory efforts, however, have proved so beneficial to the American economy or to American consumers. Some deregulation has led to horrific results. Savings and loans had been regulated by the national government up through 1988. The reasoning behind such regulation was that money is deposited in a savings and loan on the depositor's full faith that that money will be safe and will be returned on demand with interest. Many depositors come from the population of fixed income elderly retirees, seeking a secure investment.

The economic depression of the 1930s made it amply clear that such security may require some government regulation. As a result, the savings and loans came to be regulated in three ways. First, the savings and loans were told that they must keep a certain amount of the depositors' money "on deposit" in case depositors wish to withdraw funds. Second, the savings and loans were limited with the types of investments they could make with the depositors' money. Specifically, they were limited to making home loans, seen as the most secure because the home acts as collateral for the loan, can be repossessed and resold through foreclosure proceedings, and the depositors' money thereby recouped. Finally, the government insured the deposits just in case the savings and loans did lose the depositors' money in bad home loans.

The savings and loans ran profitably under such regulations until the 1970s when a number of competitors for depositors' money entered the picture. These new investment banking houses, free from government regulation, could promise the depositors greater interest on their money. As the financial market became more competitive, the savings and loans asked the government to ease the regulations and thereby allow them to compete more effectively with the investment banking houses.

Between 1980 and 1983, Congress approved a number of changes that significantly deregulated the savings and loans industry. In brief, Congress allowed the savings and loans to keep a Congress increased the insurance on deposits from $40,000 to $100,000.

While these changes began to reshape the savings and loans industry, the Reagan administration refused to allow the Federal Home Loan Bank Board, which was in charge of supervising the system, to hire the bank examiners it believed it needed to monitor the health of the system. As the real estate market began to slide, the savings and loans began to have trouble. Eventually, they were plunged into insolvency, and taxpayers had to cover the insured deposits to the tune of hundreds of billions of dollars.

More recently, energy companies were deregulated, and again disaster followed. When energy companies were deregulated, the belief was that a deregulated market would send cheaper and more reliable supplies of electricity coursing into homes and offices across the nation. What happened instead was that Enron Corporation, the vast energy trader at the center of the new freewheeling U.S. power markets, collapsed amid a blizzard of questionable financial deals. California, the first big state to deregulate its electricity market, watched its experiment in deregulation turn into a disaster, with intermittent blackouts and retail power rates as much as 40 percent higher than they were the year before. For the consumer, energy deregulation has been anything but good news. Unlike the deregulated telecommunications market, where fierce competition brought down prices while guaranteeing a reasonable level of reliability, the deregulated power market provided no real benefits and many costs. Consumers have been at the mercy of wholesale forces they often cannot understand and have few real options to switch service providers.

Many blame the catastrophic deregulation of energy companies on the campaign finance system. In the 2000 election cycle, the oil and gas sector contributed $15.4 million in contributions to the national party committees; electric utilities contributed $10.1 million more. Enron, alone, gave more the $1.4 million. Many believe that the Enron contributions exempted the company from oversight by the government agencies charged with protecting the interests of the employees, retirees, and shareholders. In other words, some say, the company paid the cop on the beat to take a nap.

Such debacles have fueled support of government regulations. Farmers continue to pressure for government subsidies administered by the Department of Agriculture. Labor unions want the protection offered to workers by the Occupational Safety and Health Administration. Defense contractors lobby for the lucrative government contracts of the Defense Department. In short, many Americans very much want the protections provided by the modern bureaucratic state. In light of such support, it is unlikely that any significant reduction in the size of the bureaucracy is likely in the near future.

Privatization of the Bureaucracy

As noted above, Congress, for over two decades, has been engaged in a bipartisan effort to shrink the size of government. But today, although fewer people appear on federal payrolls, more people than ever work for the U.S. government.

This seeming paradox has been achieved by hiring private contractors to perform many of the tasks previously performed by federal employees. The war in Iraq turned the spotlight on this shift.

Government contractors are working in Iraq as prison interrogators, bomb defusers, and armed bodyguards for U.S. officials. They have landed lucrative contracts to rebuild infrastructure and to feed American troops. Paul Johnson, beheaded in June 2004 by Islamic militants in Iraq, worked as an engineer for Lockheed Martin. The four Americans whose bodies were mutilated by a mob in Fallouja worked for Blackwater Security, a "strategic support" firm that, among other things, was responsible for protecting U.S. administrator L. Paul Bremer III. More than one hundred other contract employees, including about forty Haliburton employees, have lost their lives while driving trucks, cooking dinner, or cleaning up damaged oil wells. It was a government contractor who issued student visas to two Sept. 11 hijackers and notified a Florida flight school of the issuance six months after they crashed their planes into the World Trade Center. In 2005, the United States spent $275 billion, more than 10 percent of the federal budget, buying goods and services from private contractors, often through contracts never fully opened to competitive bidding.

Nobody knows exactly how many contractors the government employs. Paul Light of the Brookings Institution estimates that the federal budget funds a "shadow government" of nearly 6 million contractors, about half of them in defense. That means contractors outnumber civil servants and military personnel by a ratio of 2 to 1.[11]

How did this privatization of the federal bureaucracy occur? President Ronald Reagan who sought to downsize what he saw as a bloated federal workforce launched the privatization. His mission has been embraced by every subsequent administration and, in 1998, was codified by Congress with the Federal Activities Inventory Reform Act. This law requires government agencies and departments to publish an annual accounting of which tasks under their auspices "are not inherently governmental functions" and could, therefore, be put out to private bid.

There are several concerns about the privatization of the federal workforce. First, these private contractors are driven solely by profit not the pursuance of the public good. Second, private contractors are not necessarily more efficient. In Iraq much of the $21 billion spent on reconstruction goes to high-priced foreign contractors rather than low-cost local labor. For example, non-Iraqi contractors charged $25 million to repaint 20 police stations, a job the government of Basra claims could have been done by local forms for $5 million. Finally, how should this growing army of workers be managed? Most of the contracts are not subject to competitive bidding and once they get the contract, the government is so dependent on them that it is virtually impossible to end the contract. These and other concerns will continue to fuel the debate about a privatized bureaucracy.

Budget Cuts and the Size of the Bureaucracy

In recent years, most change in the size of the bureaucracy has stemmed from budget cuts. The 105th session of Congress, controlled by Republicans, attempted to enact such cuts, some of which would be quite steep. The Environmental Protection Agency (EPA) was one of the hardest hit when Congress reduced its antipollution inspection programs.[12] These budget cuts, however, have been met with an outcry from the public and organized interest groups. Congress has been forced, in many cases, to reinstate the funds. The 105th Congress, in the end, retreated from its attempt to reduce the size of the EPA.

Budget cuts and attempts at deregulation have not significantly reduced the size of the federal bureaucracy. In fact, while federal employment has remained fairly stable, employment among federal contractors and consultants and in state and local governments has increased. In addition, the power of the federal bureaucracy has continued to grow in terms of its ability to make discretionary policy decisions. The number of regulations issued and the amount of money spent have risen much faster than the number of employees who write these regulations and spend the money. While the number of regulations dipped between 1980 and 1990, they have risen between 1990 and the present.

THE EXPANDING FUNCTIONS OF THE BUREAUCRATIC STATE

As the bureaucracy has grown in response to public demand for a greater number of services, so have its functions expanded. Today, the functions of the federal bureaucracy fall into four main categories. It is not uncommon for a federal department or agency to perform more than one of these functions, or even all of these functions.

National Maintenance

After the Constitution was ratified, Congress moved to create the beginnings of a bureaucratic state that could perform the basic functions essential to maintaining the country. Originally, three departments were created: the Treasury Department to collect tax revenue, the State Department to conduct relations with other countries, and the Department of War to defend the country militarily. Congress also created the Post Office to allow for communication across a fairly vast expanse of land. As long as the functions of the federal government were linked to national maintenance, the bureaucracy's growth occurred when the nation grew. So as new western territories were settled, Congress was moved to create the Interior Department in 1849 to manage these new territories.

Clientele Services

Toward the middle of the nineteenth century particular groups began to seek government services. Farmers, labor, and business were the first to press their claims. They were soon followed, however, by the poor, racial minorities, women, and veterans, to name only a few. Today, many of the departments at the federal level are specifically designed to serve the clientele needs of these groups: the Departments of Agriculture, Labor, Health and Human Services, Housing and Urban Development, Education, and Veterans Affairs.

Regulation

The federal government early on moved to regulate the economy. Prices of goods and services, the amount of competition in the marketplace, and the kinds of information that must be disclosed to consumers were all regulated by the national bureaucracy. In the 1960s, government regulation was extended into other areas. Congress has created agencies to regulate the quality of our air and water, our workplaces, and the safety of the goods we buy.

Income Redistribution

The fourth function of the federal bureaucracy is its most recent: the government's attempt to redistribute resources between groups in our society. Most redistributive efforts involve direct payments to individuals and groups. For example, Aid to Families with Dependent Children for many years involved cash subsidies paid to needy families. Similarly, the Social Security system makes cash payments to the elderly.

While many people think of these redistributive efforts as primarily going to the less privileged members of society, redistribution often goes to the wealthy as well. For example, the Department of Agriculture subsidizes farmers, many of whom are large corporate farmers. The Department of Defense gives lucrative government contracts to large corporations. Finally, Social Security payments go to the wealthy elderly as well as the poor elderly.

THE ORGANIZATION OF THE FEDERAL BUREAUCRACY

The federal bureaucracy includes four types of organizations: cabinet departments, independent agencies, regulatory agencies or commissions, and government corporations.

Cabinet Departments

Executive departments were the first bureaucratic organizations created by Congress, and they are now the biggest units of the executive branch bureaucracy. Today, there are fifteen departments, and they meet most of the federal government's responsibilities. These departments are headed by a single individual who, while appointed by the president with the "advice and consent" of the Senate, may be removed by the president acting alone.

The fourteen secretaries and the attorney general, who heads the Department of Justice, make up what has become known as the **cabinet**. In theory, the cabinet is meant to be the president's closest set of advisers. Historically, however, presidents have made little use of their cabinets, preferring instead to rely on the White House staff. Such a preference for the White House staff stems from the fact that the departments are created by Congress, funded by Congress, and overseen by Congress. The White House staff is more under the control of the president himself.

Each of the executive departments is quite large. As a result, the departments are further divided into many agencies, bureaus, and offices. For example, the Department of the Treasury oversees the U.S. Mint, the Bureau of Alcohol, Tobacco, and Firearms, the Secret Service, and the Internal Revenue Service.

The Fifteenth Department: The Department of Homeland Security

The creation of the department of Homeland Security is the most significant transformation of the U.S. government in over a half-century. The mission of the department is to prevent terrorist attacks within the United States, reduce America's vulnerability to terrorism, and minimize the damage and recover from attacks that do occur. The department has a clear organizational structure with four divisions: border and transportation security, emergency preparedness and response, chemical, biological, radiological, and nuclear countermeasures, and information analysis and infrastructure protection.

Independent Agencies

Independent agencies are not part of any executive department and their heads lack cabinet status. Independent agencies may be headed by a single individual or by a commission. These agencies have been created by Congress to perform a particular function. Some, like the Small Business Administration, provide a service; others (discussed in the next section), like the Environmental Protection Agency, perform a regulatory function. These agencies also vary in how closely they are tied to the president. Some, like the Central Intelligence Agency, are very directly under the influence of the president. Others, like NASA (National Aeronautics and Space Administration), are much less so.

Regulatory Agencies or Commissions

Even though the **regulatory agencies** are the second most important type of organization within the federal bureaucracy, after the cabinet departments, they are fairly recent creations of Congress. As noted earlier in this chapter, the national government did not begin to regulate economic and social affairs until the Progressive period of the late nineteenth century. The first independent regulatory commission, the Interstate Commerce Commission, was established in 1887.

All regulatory agencies perform the same basic function: they try to promote the public interest by writing and enforcing rules that regulate a sector of the economy or specific type of activity. The rules made by these agencies have the force of law.

Regulatory agencies may be either of two kinds. Some are actually bureaus housed within one of the 15 departments. For example, the Food and Drug Administration is part of the Department

A disappointed office seeker assassinated President Garfield. Civil service positions began to replace the "spoils system."

of Health and Human Services. The Occupational Safety and Health Administration (OSHA) is housed within the Department of Labor. On the other hand, there are regulatory agencies that are independent of any department. The Federal Communications Commission (FCC), the Federal Aviation Agency (FAA), and the International Trade Commission (ITC) are all independent regulatory bodies.

Regulatory agencies and commissions tend to be much smaller than the fourteen departments. Also, the regulatory bodies are headed by a small number of commissioners (usually an odd number) appointed for a fixed term by the president with the consent of the Senate. The heads of the regulatory agencies are more removed from presidential control than are the heads of the departments because they serve staggered fixed terms. When a president comes into office, he will have to deal with commissioners appointed by a previous president. He will be able to appoint new commissioners only as vacancies open up.

While the regulatory agencies tend to be largely beyond the purview of the president, they are not independent of all types of political pressure. Client groups actively lobby the regulatory agencies to issue rules that are in their favor. For example, for most of its history, the Interstate Commerce Commission was closely tied to the interests of the railroad and trucking industries.

Government Corporations

Finally, Congress has created a small number of **government corporations** that provide public services that could be provided by the private sector. Government corporations are government-owned businesses that sell a service or a product to the public and thereby generate their own revenues. For example, the Postal Service, the Tennessee Valley Authority (TVA), and the Federal Deposit Insurance Corporation (FDIC) all charge for the service they provide whether it be stamps, electricity, or depositors' insurance. Some government corporations are headed by an individual; others have a plural leadership.

WHO ARE THE BUREAUCRATS?

The national bureaucracy employs about 3 million civilian employees, accounting for 2.3 percent of the entire United States work force.[13] Most of these workers are today hired through the civil service process. Such was not always the case.

A Bureaucracy of Gentlemen

In the early years of the nation's history, service in the bureaucracy was considered the special purview of an elite class. Government office was seen as a prize to be awarded to men of experience, education, and wisdom. Presidents from the two major political parties, the Federalists and the Democratic-Republicans, appointed men drawn largely from these elite ranks.

The Spoils System

The **spoils system**, the practice of hiring and firing federal workers on the basis of party loyalty, was introduced in 1829 by Andrew Jackson. Under the spoils system, the "spoils" of government jobs were doled out by the victorious candidate to loyal campaign workers, friends, and even relatives. Such patronage following an election resulted in almost a complete turnover in government jobs.

By the early 1880s, the public was fairly cynical about the integrity and efficiency of a bureaucracy built upon party loyalty and nepotism. Public office was seen as the path to self-enrichment and corruption flourished. Finally, when President James Garfield was assassinated by a disgruntled campaign worker who was not awarded a job by Garfield, it became clear that a system based on merit was preferable to the spoils system.

The Civil Service

In 1883 Congress passed the **Pendleton Act**, which created the Civil Service Commission (now called the Office of Personnel Management). This commission makes sure that bureaucratic positions are filled on the basis of merit, not partisanship or cronyism.

In the beginning, only 10 percent of federal jobs were covered by the civil service system. Today, over 80 percent of federal employees fall within the purview of the civil service. Of these, approximately 60 percent are hired through the General Classification System, and another 25 percent are covered by the Postal Service System. Federal positions not covered by the civil service, those at the highest level of the bureaucracy, are appointed by the president with the advice and consent of the Senate.[14]

The line between civil servants and presidential appointees has been somewhat muted by the Civil Service Reform Act of 1978. This act creates the Senior Executive Service (SES), consisting of civil servants, today numbering about eight thousand, who have reached the highest level in their particular career path. The purpose of the SES is to allow these career bureaucrats to move into other positions that are usually reserved for appointees of the president. Individuals who join the ranks of the SES can be moved from one job to another by the sitting president.

Changes in the Demographic Composition of the Bureaucracy

Beginning as a "government by gentlemen," the bureaucracy has been slow to reflect the diversity of the expanding nation.[15] In the early 1970s, Congress moved to require the federal government to follow affirmative action guidelines in hiring. As a result of such guidelines, women now make up 50 percent of the federal work force and racial minorities make up an additional 26 percent. Still, at the highest level of the civil service, minorities are underrepresented.[16]

Presidential Appointees

While most of the bureaucratic positions are filled through the civil service, presidents may nominate a second category of bureaucrats called political appointees. To fill these positions, the president and his advisers solicit suggestions from politicians, businesspeople, and interest groups. Appointments to these positions offer the president a way to pay off political debts, reward campaign contributors, or reward voting blocs, for example women or African Americans, within his party. Often, the appointee may have strong ties to the interest groups whose interests he or she may be in charge of overseeing. President Obama's pick for interior secretary, Sen. Ken Salazar, was welcomed by industry groups reassured by his support for expanded offshore drilling, and his selection for agriculture secretary, former Iowa governor Tom Vilsack, was cheered by groups representing big agricultural interests, who praised him for his support of biotechnology and subsidies for corn-based ethanol.

WHERE ARE THE BUREAUCRATS?

Most of the national government's workers are employed outside Washington. Fewer than 350,000 (or about 12 percent) of career civilian employees work in the Washington area. The vast majority are scattered throughout the country and the world. In fact, nearly 20,000 federal civilian employees work in territories belonging to the United States, and another 100,000 in foreign nations. California, Texas, Florida, and several other states each house more than 100,000 civilian employees. Congress has every incentive to try to spread the jobs around. These jobs are "pork" for the members districts and states, "pork" that might help gain them re-election.

Many people believe that the welfare state now employs the greatest number of civilian employees. In reality, less than 15 percent of bureaucrats work in welfare agencies such as the Social Security Administration. The Department of Veterans Affairs employs twice the number of workers than these welfare agencies and nearly one-third of the civilian bureaucrats work for the army, the navy, the air force, or some other defense related agency.

WHAT BUREAUCRACIES DO

Bureaucracies implement policy. They take congressional, presidential, and sometimes even judicial pronouncements and develop procedures and rules to implement the policy goals outlined, often vaguely, in these pronouncements. In implementing policy, the bureaucracy comes to manage the day-to-day routines of government: training the armed services, delivering the mail, and building the country's roads. The sections that follow discuss the many ways in which the bureaucracy implements policy.

Policy Development

Members of the executive branch are often very involved in the development and drafting of legislation. Sometimes the initiative for such involvement may come from the bureaucracy, at other times from Congress. For example, Congress routinely asks agencies to respond to countless official and unofficial inquiries, some of which may lead to new legislation. Furthermore, congressional hearings on proposed legislation usually include members of the bureaucracy. Such expert testimony from the bureaucrats has considerable influence on congressional decision making.

All government agencies devote a considerable amount of their time and resources to research, and collecting and analyzing mounds of data. Some agencies, in fact, have such data collection as their principal task. The Bureau of Labor Statistics, for example, collects and publishes information about the economy while the Centers for Disease Control compile public health statistics.

Rule Administration

Cabinet departments, regulatory agencies, and government corporations are all creatures of Congress. Because the Constitution is silent as to the question of how the president shall faithfully execute the laws of the land, Congress has had to fill in the gaps. It is Congress that creates the different agencies and departments through enabling legislation that directly empowers the bureaucracy. Such enabling legislation cannot possibly describe every specific situation or contingency. As a result, Congress often leaves the bureaucracy with significant administrative discretion. Particularly in the areas of domestic and international security, Congress has afforded agencies enormous latitude.

Rule administration is the core function of the national bureaucracy. Departments and agencies carry out the policies of the Congress, the president, and even the courts. For example, the Environmental Protection Agency (EPA) is responsible for administering the multitude of laws passed by Congress to clean up the nation's air and water.

Rule Making and Regulation

The bureaucracy has a number of ways to carry out policy. The most common is through rule making. The bureaucracy issues regulations that are simply rules that govern the operation of government programs. These rules are the way in which the bureaucracy fleshes out the more general guidelines laid down by Congress in laws.

Regulations have the effect of law. For example, Congress passed the Nutrition Labeling and Education Act. The Food and Drug Administration (FDA) then needed to formulate rules to implement the law. The FDA has mandated that labels specifically list the nutritional content of food products. Because bureaucratic rules have the force of law, an agency must follow very detailed procedures in issuing these rules. For example, the agency must propose the rule by publishing it and giving all interested parties an opportunity to comment on the regulation.

Rule Adjudication

Many federal agencies are responsible for determining if the rules they administer have been broken, a process known as **rule adjudication**. Acting like a court, the agency provides the affected parties the opportunity to present arguments and evidence in a more-or-less formal hearing. In addition, more than twenty-five federal agencies employ administrative law judges to help them determine whether defendants have violated any relevant rules. Today, more than twenty-five federal agencies employ a combined total of nearly 1300 administrative law judges. As a greater number of federal agencies have gained responsibility for regulating economic activity, rule adjudication has grown in importance.[17]

Litigation

The most serious disputes between an agency and those affected by its decisions may end up in federal court. The courts have the authority to review all agency rules and decisions brought before them. In general, any party adversely affected by an agency decision has standing to bring suit. The 1970 Clean Air Act, for example, authorized three different types of suits: challenges to environmental protection agency rules and regulations, citizen suits seeking the performance of duties by the EPA, and enforcement suits against polluters.[18]

According to some sources, the 2010 health-care bill may end up creating at least 159 new commissions and boards. By creating new federally enforceable rights and obligations, layers of complex federal regulations, and dozens of new programs and agencies, the Health Care Reform Law is likely to generate a flood of litigation. To implement the legislation, federal bureaucrats will necessarily generate thousands of pages of regulations. Under the Administrative Procedure Act, trial lawyers—as well as attorneys for industry, the medical profession, and countless interest groups—will challenge not only the substance of the regulations, but also the procedures used to generate them.[19]

Program Evaluation

Congress, the civil service, and the president usually all require agencies to keep fairly detailed records of their various programs and to evaluate them on an ongoing basis. Both Congress and the president may also rely on outside consultants, analysts, and scholars for program evaluation. For example, the Department of Education spends upwards of $100 million per year on program evaluation and program data collection.[20]

THE POLITICAL RESOURCES OF THE FEDERAL BUREAUCRACY

Authority

The bureaucracy possesses authority because Congress passed legislation granting it and because other players recognize it by obeying its decisions.

Administrative Discretion

The power of a department or agency does not simply hinge on congressional delegations of power. Congress gives agencies great latitude to make policy; this is called **administrative discretion**. For example, Congress charges agencies with protecting the "public interest" but leaves them free to determine what specific policies will best serve the public. At times, Congress may be able to define the problem but may not be able to define a particular solution. Congress, then, leaves it to the bureaucracy to fill in the specifics. In 1988, the Department of Health and Human Services issued regulations that forbade family planning clinics that receive federal money to provide "counseling concerning the use of abortion as a method of family planning." When President Clinton came into office, his HHS secretary, Donna Schalala, used her administrative discretion to rescind this so-called gag rule.[21] Because Congress commonly gives only broad and vague directives to the bureaucracy, critics, like Theodore Lowi, charge that Congress delegates too much power to appointed administrators. Agencies also establish their power through exercising discretion in rule making.[22]

Rule Making

Agencies exercise their administrative discretion through rule making. **Rule making** is the bureaucracy's issuance of regulations that govern the operation of government programs. The power to issue these rules or regulations flows from the power of the bureaucracy to implement the programs and policies enacted into law by Congress. Because these regulations are authorized by Congress, they have the full effect of law. For example, after Congress enacted the Nutrition Labeling and Education Act, the FDA proposed rules requiring manufacturers of vitamins and dietary supplements to substantiate the health claims they make for their products on their labels.[23]

Expertise

When Congress grants power to a particular bureau or agency, it usually does so by way of a fairly broad and general grant of authority. Congress expects that bureaucrats, specialists in a particular area, will use their expertise in applying the laws in specific cases. Agencies gain considerable power, then, from the expertise of their employees. This expertise also allows the bureaucrats to be a considerable source for the development of policy proposals and the lobbying for them. Studies have found that many of the bills introduced into Congress have actually been drafted by members of the bureaucracy.

The fact that bureaucrats are hired, and can only be fired, through the civil service process contributes to their level of expertise. Most civil servants spend their entire career within one agency, gaining considerable expertise over the course of many years. Few members of Congress will ever develop this level of knowledge in one particular policy area. This gives the members of the federal bureaucracy a significant advantage in pressing their claims upon the legislative branch of government.

The expertise of the bureaucrats gives them a significant amount of independence from the political appointees who are their superiors. After all, the typical career bureaucrat will remain in the agency long after political superiors have been replaced. Their job security may allow the bureaucrats to resist the dictates of their bosses. Such bureaucratic resistance tends to frustrate not only the political appointee technically at the helm of the department but also the president who appointed him. Hear the frustration in President Richard Nixon:

> We have no discipline in this bureaucracy. We never fire anybody. We never reprimand anybody. We never demote anybody. We always promote the sons-of-bitches [who] kick us in the ass.[24]

Clientele Support

The groups and organizations affected by an agency's actions form its **clientele**. Many of the departments and agencies in the executive branch are specifically what political scientists call **clientele agencies**. These are agencies specifically designed by law to foster and promote the interests of certain groups.[25] For example, the Department of Labor and Commerce was created by Congress in 1903 "to foster, promote, and develop the foreign and domestic commerce, the mining, the manufacturing, the shipping, and fishing industries, and the transportation facilities of the United States."[26]

The power of an agency depends heavily on the power of its clientele. An agency that is actively supported by large, well-organized, and well-funded groups is much more likely to achieve its goals than is an agency with little or weak support. Interest groups can help the agency by bringing pressure on Congress and the president, for bigger budgets, greater powers, or new duties. As a result, congressional committees and subcommittees may become very important parts of an agency's clientele.

There tends to be regular communication between the agency, the clientele groups, and committee members in Congress. This routinized communication makes the agency a lobbyist on the group's behalf and the group a lobbyist on the agency's behalf. The result is the development of very close relationships between congressional committee members, clientele groups, and agencies. Such cozy relationships are often referred to as **iron triangles**.[27] These relationships tend to work to reinforce a particular program against drastic change or abolition at the hands of a hostile president.[28] Iron triangles make clientele agencies the hardest to change or coordinate. Generally, these agencies are able to resist external demands by vigorously defending their own prerogatives. Because of this resistance to change, Congress and the president have frequently been forced to create a new clientele agency rather than to try to convince an existing one to implement programs that the agency opposes.

HOW BUREAUCRACIES MAKE DECISIONS

Political scientists have offered two alternative models to describe bureaucratic decision making.

The Rational-Comprehensive Model

The rational-comprehensive model of bureaucratic decision making suggests that bureaucrats follow a sequence of four steps:

1. Clear specification and prioritization of the goals to achieve along with their underlying values.
2. Identification of all alternative methods for achieving those goals.
3. Identification and evaluation, according to formal rules, of all the various outcomes likely to result from each method.
4. In each step, reliance upon information and analysis.

Bureaucratic policy implementation often does not conform to an ideal, rational process in which a problem is identified, various solutions weighed in terms of their costs and benefits, and the most effective, cheapest solution settled upon. Indeed, studies of how policy actually gets made in the federal bureaucracy suggest that the rational-comprehensive model may be far from reality.

The Incremental Model of Bureaucratic Decision-Making

In his classic article "The Science of Muddling Through," Charles Lindblom argues that a more prevalent model of bureaucratic decision making is the incremental model.[29] Bureaucrats work under the constraints of time and limited resources. Under such conditions, it may not be possible to research all the possible solutions to a problem. In the end, Lindblom suggests bureaucrats seek a solution in the modification of an already existing policy. In incrementally altering the status quo, policy making inches along one step at a time.

Incrementalism exhibits the following characteristics:

1. The problem itself may not be clearly defined. For example, take the problem of poverty. What is the problem to be solved? Feeding and housing people, preparing them for a job, or actually getting them a job? Often a problem is multi-faceted, and solving one aspect may make another aspect all the worse. For example, the provision of housing and food may work to discourage a poor person from seeking to get a job.

2. For a variety of reasons, only certain solutions are identified for serious consideration. First, policymakers may not know what to do about a particular problem. Second, it is often difficult to imagine doing things differently than the way you are currently doing them. As a result, radically different approaches to a problem are rarely considered. Finally, limited time and resources may make identification and analysis of all possible solutions unfeasible.

3. The values needed to assess the various solutions are unclear and unranked.

4. Policymakers tend to stop their analysis of solutions when they find one that is "good enough."

Incrementalism leads to a form of decision-making best described as just "muddling through." Rational, comprehensive, scientific analysis of a wide assortment of alternative policies is either not feasible or impossible. As a result, decision-makers make do with "good enough" as they make incremental changes to the status quo.

BUREAUCRATIC ACCOUNTABILITY

Big government, at least in the abstract, is unpopular with the public. The size of the federal bureaucracy is often equated with waste, remoteness, and incompetence. In the last twenty years, a period of "deregulation," more than 250 new federal agencies or bureaus have been created; fewer than two dozen have been disbanded. The government holds title to 400,000 buildings and rents 50,000 additional buildings. Many people believe that the national government has become an octopus, uncontrolled, uncontrollable, and largely unaccountable.

Presidential Control over the Bureaucracy

Presidents have never found it easy to exercise control over the bureaucracy, and civil service and other reforms have further insulated most government workers from the partisan politics inherent in both Congress and the presidency. An incoming president can appoint fewer than 1 percent of all executive branch employees, that is approximately three thousand people out of a bureaucracy that numbers in the millions.[30]

While it is true that the president nominates those who will fill the top policy-making positions in government, these appointments must be made with the advice and consent of the Senate. Additionally, most of these appointees are not personal friends of the president, nor do they tend to be drawn from the ranks of loyal campaign workers. Instead, most come from the sectors for which they will be responsible. For example, the top officials in the Department of Defense tend to have military backgrounds or experience in the defense industries. The Federal Communications Commission (FCC) has often included people from the communications industry.

The American system of separated powers and checks and balances further exacerbates a president's ability to control the direction of the bureaucracy. The party winning a presidential election does not necessarily gain control of the national government. The president has limited time, limited political resources, and limited influence over the millions of decisions made by thousands of bureaucrats each day.

A president with a very clear agenda and a loyal White House staff may still be able to influence the direction of bureaucratic policymaking. During his two terms in office, Ronald Reagan and his White House staff gained effective control over the bureaucracy. The administration required that all major regulations of departments and agencies be approved by the Office of Management and Budget (OMB), which is part of the Executive Office of the President.

Congressional Control over the Bureaucracy

Congress, with an institutional staff of more than forty thousand, is more readily equipped to oversee the federal bureaucracy. It is Congress that creates the agencies, determines their organization and duties, and funds the budgets. In addition, Congress oversees the activities of the bureaucrats in appropriations hearings, special investigations, and congressional hearings. Finally, it is the Senate that confirms presidential appointments of high, cabinet-level officials.

Congress can significantly influence agency behavior by the statutes that it enacts. In the past, Congress has passed broad statutes that left much to the bureaucrats' discretions. Since the 1960s, however, Congress has attempted to restrict such agency discretion. Until 1983, Congress made increasing use of the **legislative veto**, a law that grants broad power to the executive branch but reserves for Congress the power to block the exercise of power in particular cases.

In 1983, in the *Chadha* case, the Supreme Court declared the legislative veto unconstitutional, ruling that the legislative veto violated the constitutional requirement of separation of powers among the branches of the federal government.[31] Even after the *Chadha* decision, Congress has continued to pass laws containing legislative vetoes. Congress has also rewritten some of the laws so as to require both Houses of Congress and a signature by the president.

Congress has also recently moved to tighten the financial reins on the bureaucracy. No money may be spent by the bureaucracy unless it has first been authorized and appropriated by Congress. In the past, many programs enjoyed permanent authorization. Today, most programs are permanently funded, for example Social Security and the hiring of military personnel. Increasingly, however, there has been a trend toward annual authorizations that enable Congress to strengthen its oversight of executive agencies and their spending. After the military procurement abuses of the 1980s, for example, Congress made Defense Department budgets for military equipment subject to annual authorizations.

Even after the funds have been authorized by Congress, they cannot be spent unless they are also appropriated by Congress. The House Appropriations Committee and its various subcommittees control appropriations. Because appropriations may be, and often are, for less than the amount authorized, Congress can at this second stage further control the budgets of the various bureaucratic departments and agencies.

The most visible and dramatic form of congressional oversight is the investigation. While the power to investigate is not mentioned in the Constitution, it is implicit in Congress' power to legislate. Congress may subpoena a person, compelling that person to come testify before Congress. If the person refuses, Congress may charge him or her with contempt and either vote to send the person to jail or refer the matter to a court for further action.

While it is apparent that Congress does exercise oversight over the executive bureaucracy, none of this is to say that Congress exerts significant control, only that it exerts more control than the president. Many charge that members of Congress actually benefit from the red tape associated with the national bureaucracy, gaining popularity and prestige from running interference with the bureaucracy and interceding on behalf of their constituents. In addition, many point to the fact that members of Congress, ever eager for re-election, avoid conflict by delegating sweeping authority to the agencies and bureaus.

Iron Triangles and Issue Networks

One reason that presidents and Congress often find it difficult to control bureaucracies is that the agencies have strong ties to interest groups, on the one hand, and to particular committees and subcommittees in Congress, on the other. As discussed in Chapter Eight, when agencies, groups, and committees come to depend on each other for support and information, they form what political scientists refer to as **iron triangles** or **subgovernments**.

The decisions reached by members of the iron triangle may not be easily controlled, or interfered with, by the president or Congress as a whole. As pointed out in Chapter Nine, Congress often defers to the decisions reached at the committee or subcommittee stage. Especially when an issue has little press coverage and, therefore, low visibility, decisions reached by the members of the iron triangle are likely to be final.

There is mounting evidence that the concept of iron triangles is overly simplistic, especially when applied to issue areas of higher visibility and greater conflict. In the modern period, as the number of interest groups and policy experts has expanded, congressional committees and bureaucratic agencies may be bombarded with competing demands from multiple sides of an issue. These relationships may be better characterized as fluid **issue networks**. Whether these relationships are iron or fluid, they still work to make congressional or presidential oversight over the bureaucracy difficult.³²

REFORM AND REORGANIZATION

Some are calling for a complete overhaul of the civil service system. In an era in which term limits for elected government officials are gaining in popularity, perhaps it is not surprising that some are calling for term limits for career civil servants. Limiting their tenure is seen as a way to break up the iron triangles and bring new blood and breathe new life into the system.

These calls for reform are only the latest in a long string of efforts to rein in the federal bureaucracy. In 1946, Congress passed the **Administrative Procedures Act (APA)**, which requires that citizens have the opportunity to be heard concerning proposed rules or regulations to be issued by the executive branch bureaucracy. The APA also allowed citizens to appeal adverse decisions by the bureaucracy to the federal courts.

The increasing power of the federal executive branch also has led to concerns about the public's access to information. The **Freedom of Information Act** (FOIA), passed in 1967 and strengthened in 1974, was designed to address these problems. FOIA requires that government agencies make information "promptly available" to any person who asks for it. Some types of information are exempt: information that would compromise national security, law enforcement, personal privacy, or trade secrets.

Congress has also moved to open government meetings to the public. The **Sunshine Act** requires government agencies headed by commissions or boards to be open to the public. A similar law, the **Federal Advisory Committee Act**, applies this openness requirement to meetings involving executive officials and private citizens.

Congress has tried to make it easier for the bureaucracy to be held accountable through the 1989 **Whistle-Blower Protection Act**. This law says that agencies may not punish an employee who reports fraud, waste, corruption, or abuse on the part of their agency. This law also creates the Office of Special Counsel to help enforce the act. However, to date, very few employees have chosen to exercise their right to "blow the whistle" on their employer.

The Clinton administration attempted to study the question of how a government agency might be more responsive to the citizens they serve. The National Performance Review led by former Vice President Al Gore conducted an extensive survey of government agencies to try to discover which agencies are efficient and responsive and which are not. In his speech accepting the Democratic nomination for president, Barack Obama issued a call for government reform that echoed President Clinton's wide-ranging effort to reform the federal bureaucracy. He pledged to "go through the federal budget, line by line, eliminating programs that no longer work and making the ones we do need work better and cost less—because we cannot meet 21st century challenges with a 20th century bureaucracy."³³

BENEFITS OF BUREAUCRACY

For all the complaining about big government, there are real and clear benefits of bureaucracy.

Managing Complexity

Life in modern America is complex. Government programs are increasingly sophisticated. Members of Congress are generalists usually not well equipped to deal with all the subtleties that new situations can entail. The tax code of the United States, for example, is nearly three thousand pages long. Only a well-staffed office of accountants can cope with such legal complexity.

Stability and Predictability

The stability and predictability of the federal bureaucracy allow citizens to more effectively grapple with their government. In addition, some communities, like the business community, rely on a certain amount of consistency in government rules, regulations, and programs. Constant reform would leave many in confusion.

CONCLUSION

Americans appear to have a love-hate relationship with their bureaucracy. On the one hand, the twentieth century saw the size and scope of the executive branch bureaucracy grow dramatically. This growth appears to be an inevitable consequence of the growing technological complexity of modern America, and Americans are the first to say they want the services meted out by the various departments and agencies of the federal government. The Department of Agriculture performs vital services for farmers. The Departments of Education, Labor, Veterans' Affairs, and Commerce all have their clientele. The public as a whole admits the absolute necessity of a Food and Drug Administration to protect the safety of our foods and pharmaceutical drugs.

Still, Americans complain that the bureaucracy is inefficient and cold, unresponsive to even the most incessant demands. Most often Americans complain of bureaucratic red tape and waste. These problems are inherent in government institutions serving a population as large as that of the United States.

CHAPTER NOTES

[1] Juliet Eilperin and Scott Higham, "How the Minerals Management Service's Partnership with Industry Led to Failure," *The Washington Post*, April 24, 2010, http://www.washingtonpost.com/wp-dyn/content/article/2010/08/24/AR2010082406754.html

²The Center for Public Integrity, " Scandal, Incompetence at Mineral Management Service," Fall 2008, http://www.publicintegrity.org/investigations/broken_government/articles/entry/1022.

³Ibid.

⁴James Surowiecki, "The Regulation Crisis," *The New Yorker,* June 14, 2010, http://www.newyorker.com/talk/financial/2010/06/14/100614ta_talk_surowieckA

⁵Daniel Carpenter, *Reputation and Power*, New Jersey: Princeton University Press, 2010.

⁶T.R. Tyler, *Why People Obey the Law*, New Jersey: Princeton University Press, 2006.

⁷Geoffrey Brennan and Philip Petit, *The Economy of Esteem*, Oxford: Oxford University Press, 2004.

⁸U.S. Bureau of the Census, Statistical Abstract of the U.S., 2007 (Washington, D.C.: Government Printing Office, 2007).

⁹Philip Shabecoff, "Senator Urges Military Resources Be Turned to Environmental Battle," *New York Times*, 29 June 1990, A1.

¹⁰Martha Derthwick, and Paul J. Quirk, *The Politics of Deregulation* (Washington, D.C.: Congressional Quarterly Press, 1985).

¹¹Paul C. Light, "Fact Sheet on the New True Size of Government," Center for Public Service, Sept. 5, 2003, http://www.brookings.edu.

¹²John H. Cushman, Jr., "E.P.A. Is Canceling Pollution Testing Across the Nation," *New York Times*, 25 Nov.1995, 1.

¹³U.S. Bureau of the Census, Statistical Abstract of the United States, 1992 (Washington, D.C.: U.S. Government Printing Office, 1992), 331-381.

¹⁴U.S. Bureau of the Census, Statistical Abstract of the United States, 1995, 115th ed. (Washington, D.C.: Bureau of the Census, 1995), 350.

¹⁵Frederick C. Mosher, *Democracy and the Public Service*, 2d ed. (New York: Oxford University Press, 1982) 58-60.

¹⁶U.S. Bureau of the Census, Statistical Abstract, 1992, 332-33.

¹⁷Ann Crittenden, "Quotas for Good Old Boys," *Wall Street Journal*, 14 June 1995, 1.

¹⁸R. Shep Melnick, *Regulation and the Courts* (Washington, D.C.: Brookings Institute, 1989), 55.

¹⁹Curt Levey, "Health-Care Reform Could Create a Litigation Explosion," *The Wall Street Journal.Opinion Journal*, February 10, 2010, http://online.wsj.com/article/SB10001424052748704541004575011390617073222.html

²⁰U.S. Department of Education, "New Directions for Program Evaluation at the U.S. Department of Education," *ED.gov*, 2004, http://www2.ed.gov/news/pressreleases/2002/04/evaluation.htm.

²¹Marrion Burros, "F.D.A. Is Again Proposing to Regulate Vitamins and Supplements," *New York Times*, 15 June 1993, A25.

²²Theodore J. Lowi, *The End of Liberalism*, 2d ed. (New York: W. W. Norton, 1979).

²³Michael W. Spicer and Larry D. Terry, "Administrative Interpretation of Statutes," *Public Administration Review* 56 (January/February, 1996): 36-47.

²⁴Richard Nixon to John Ehrlichman, presidential transcript published in *Washington Star News*, 20 July 1974, A1.

²⁵Theodore J. Lowi and Benjamin Ginsberg, *American Government*, 3d ed. (New York: W. W. Norton, 1994), 274.

²⁶15 USC 1501.

²⁷Lowi, 276.

²⁸Martin Shapiro, "The Presidency and the Federal Courts," in *Politics and the Oval Office*, ed. Arnold Meltser (San Francisco: Institute for Contemporary Studies, 1981), Chapter 8.

²⁹Charles Lindblom, "The Science of Muddling Through," *Public Administration Review* 19 (Spring 1959): 19.

³⁰Patricia Wallace Ingraham, *The Foundation of Merit* (Baltimore: John Hopkins University Press, 1995), 9.

³¹*Immigration and Naturalization Service v. Chadha*, 462 U. S. 919 (1983).

³²Hugh Heclo, "Issues Networks and the Executive Establishment,": in *The New American Political System* ed. Anthony King (Washington, D. C.: American Enterprise Institute, 1978), 87-124.

³³Robert Brodsky, "Obama Calls for End of '20th Century Bureaucracy,'" *Government executive.com*, August 29, 2008, http://www.govexec.com/dailyfed/0808/082908ts1.htm.

SUGGESTED READINGS

Aberbach, Joel D., and Mark A. Peterson, eds. *Institutions of American Democracy: The Executive Branch* (Institutions of American Democracy Series). New York: Oxford University Press, 2006.

Downs, Anthony. *Inside Bureaucracy.* Boston: Little, Brown, 1967.

Goodsell, Charles T. *The Case for Bureaucracy: A Public Administration Polemic,* 4th ed. Washington, D.C.: CQ Press, 2003.

Gormley, William T. and Steven J Balla. *Bureaucracy and Democracy: Accountability and Performance,* 2nd ed. Washington, D.C.: CQ Press, 2004.

Heclo, Hugh. *A Government of Strangers: Executive Politics in Washington.* Washington, D.C.: Brookings Institution, 1977.

Johnson, Ronald N. and Gary D. Libecap. *The Federal Civil Service and the Problem of Bureaucracy.* Chicago: University of Chicago Press, 1994.

Kettl, Donald F. and James W. Fesler. *The Politics of the Administrative Process,* 4th ed. Washington, D.C.: CQ Press, 2009.

Light, Paul C. *A Government Ill Executed: The Decline of the Federal Service and How to Reverse it.* Cambridge, MA: Harvard University Press, 2008.

Maxwell, Bruce. *Insider's Guide to Finding a Job in Washington.* Washington, D.C.:CQ Press, 2000.

Meier, Kenneth. *Politics and the Bureaucracy: Policy-Making in the Fourth Branch of Government,* 5th ed. Fort Worth, Texas: Harcourt-Brace, 2006.

Nelson, William. *The Roots of the American Bureaucracy, 1830 – 1900.* Washington, D.C.: Beard Books, 2006.

Pressman, Jeffrey L and Aaron Wildavsky. *Implementation,* 3rd ed. Berkeley: University of California Press, 1984.

Reich, Robert. *Locked in the Cabinet.* New York: Knopf, 1997.

Stivers, Camilla, ed. *Democracy, Bureaucracy, and the Study of Administration.* Boulder, CO: Westview Press, 2001.

Verkuil, Paul. *Outsourcing Sovereignty: Why Privatization of Government Functions Threatens Democracy and What We Can Do About It.* New York: Cambridge University Press, 2007.

Wood, Dan B. *Bureaucratic Dynamics: The Role of Bureaucracy in a Democracy.* Boulder, CO: Westview, 1994.

Web Sites

Department of Homeland Security, www.dhs.gov.
Fed World Information Network. www.fedworld.gov.
FirstGov. www.firstgov.gov.
Library of Congress, www.loc.gov.
National Archives and Records Administration. www.nara.gov.
Project on Government Oversight, www.pogo.org
The Reason Foundation, www.reason.org/areas/topic/privatization.
U.S. Government. www.firstgov.gov.

Chapter Eleven

THE PRESIDENCY AND LEADERSHIP

"For better or for worse, who gets to be President of the United States makes a difference for our future."
James David Barber,
The Presidential Character, 1992

Write to: President Barack Obama
Office of the President
The White House
1600 Pennsylvania Avenue
Washington, D.C. 20500

Salutation: Dear Mr. President:

Complimentary close: Sincerely yours,

Telephone: 202-456-1414
FAX: 202-456-2461
E-mail: www.whitehousegov/webmail

There are two major perspectives or ways of conceptualizing the U.S. presidency. It is, first of all, often conceptualized as a job. Like most other salaried executive positions (George W. Bush was the first president to receive a $400,000.00 salary.), it comes with a "job description" that sets forth the personal qualifications that the individual seeking the position must meet and provides a statement of the formal responsibilities the person selected for the job is expected to fulfill. The job description for the presidency is found in Article II of the Constitution.

Another way of thinking about the presidency places less emphasis on what a president is constitutionally required to do and more on who he is and how that affects what he does. The focus in this second, "non-constitutional," perspective is on the personal qualities of presidents and presidential leadership rather than on the institution of the presidency.

Neither of the two perspectives provides a complete picture. To understand what many consider to be the most important job and the most powerful person in the world today, this chapter then will examine both points of view.

THE PRESIDENCY

Qualifications: Formal and Informal

Article II of the Constitution establishes a minimum age of thirty-five to serve as president, but the average age has been fifty-five. The youngest president to date was Theodore Roosevelt, who was forty-two when he was inaugurated in 1901. The oldest was Ronald Reagan, who was sixty-nine when he began his first term (January 1981) and seventy-three when he began his second term (January 1985). If John McCain had won the 2008 election, he would have become, at age 72, the oldest first term president in history. Other qualifications for those seeking the office of the presidency include residency in the U.S. for at least fourteen years and "natural born" citizenship (Sec. 1, Clause 5). These are the "formal" or "legal" criteria that the framers of the Constitution believed would secure mature, experienced, and loyal Americans to fill the office of the presidency.

Although race, religion, and gender are not among the specified requirements, until the 2008 election, only white males have held the office, and the majority of these have been Anglo-Saxon, Protestants. In addition, most of the forty-four U.S. presidents began their terms with prior government experience as a governor, a senator, a representative, or as a vice president. Most, if not wealthy themselves, have had access to those who were wealthy and willing to help finance their election campaigns. Because these are "informal" qualifications, potential candidates are not legally bound by them. Thus, journalist Patrick Buchanan, who has never held an elected or appointive government position; former State Department official Alan Keyes, who is an African American; Senator Arlen Specter, who is Jewish; and Hillary Clinton have been among the serious contenders competing for the presidential nomination. Former Presidents William Jefferson Clinton and James Earl Carter, who were both Southern Baptists, also broke away from the historical tradition.

Getting Elected: The Electoral College

In addition to personal qualifications, the Executive Article of the Constitution also sets forth the procedure by which a president and vice president are to be elected (Section 1, Clause 3). Since the framers considered and then rejected the idea that the people would directly vote for president, the responsibility for the selection was to be that of their representatives, the electors, or, as they are more commonly and collectively referred to, the electoral college.

The procedure by which electors were to be chosen was left up to the individual states (Section 1, Clause 2). Some opted for having their legislature appoint the electors. Others relied on popular elections that were either statewide or by district. Some used a mixed system that required actions on the part of both the legislature and the voters. Whatever the method, the number of electors for each state was to equal the total number of its senators and representatives.

When the electors' joint ballot for president and vice president resulted in a tie between Thomas Jefferson and Aaron Burr in 1800, the selection process was modified in 1804 by the Twelfth Amendment to provide for a separate ballot for the president and for the vice president. This continues to be the way presidents are selected today.

Voters cast their ballots on Election Day for electors, even though their names may not appear on the ballot, rather than for a particular presidential candidate. The electors then cast their votes in their respective state capitols in December and select the president. All states, with the exception of Maine and Nebraska (which divide the Electoral College vote according to who wins in each congressional district), follow a winner-takes-all rule. This means that all of a states' electoral votes, except for that of an occasional **faithless elector** (one who follows personal choice rather than the wishes of state voters), go to the candidate who received the most votes in that state. The winner-takes-all rule also means that it is possible for a candidate to win the popular vote but lose the election. This actually occurred in 1824, in 1876, in 1888 and in 2000, and the results of the imaginary presidential election described below demonstrates how that happened.

In this imaginary election there are only three states, "Yours," which has a population of 50,000 and 50 electors; "Mine," which has a population of 35,000 and 35 electors; and "Theirs," which has a population of 20,000 and 20 electors. Using these numbers, assume that every person in each of these states votes for either the Democratic or Republican candidate as follows:

STATE	VOTE FOR DEMOCRAT	VOTE FOR REPUBLICAN	DEMOCRAT ELECTORAL VOTE	REPUBLICAN ELECTORAL VOTE
YOURS	40,000	10,000	50	0
MINE	15,000	20,000	0	35
THEIRS	9,000	11,000	0	20
TOTALS	64,000	41,000	50	55

The results of this election show that although the Democratic candidate with 64,000 votes was the people's choice, the electoral college—following the winner-take-all rule—selected the Republican candidate with his 41,000 votes. In actual elections a candidate must win a majority of at least 270 of the present total of 538 electoral votes.

Voters in large states with large numbers of electors generally prefer this system to a direct election. Candidates spend a lot of time and make many campaign promises to voters in those large states to secure those important electoral votes. After all, a win in the eleven largest states is all that is needed to obtain the needed majority. As one journalist bluntly put it, "Winning by a single vote in New York is worth more than winning by millions of votes in a dozen western states put together."[1]

It was not much more than a single vote that determined the outcome of the 2000 presidential election. After five weeks of intense legal disputes over the ballot count and partial recounts in the State of Florida, George Walker Bush was ultimately declared the winner of that state's twenty-five electors by only 537 votes. Those electoral votes brought his total to 271, just one more than is required to win the presidency. (Al Gore won 267.) Bush did not, however, win the national popular vote—Al Gore received 50,158,094 votes to Bush's 49,820,518 votes. Considering the numbers, it is not surprising that critics of the presidential election system (including former First Lady and Secretary of State, Senator Hillary Rodham Clinton) immediately began to call for reform of what they consider to be an inherently undemocratic process.

A number of possible alternative methods, such as the district plan, the automatic plan, the proportional plan, and the direct-vote plan—which were discussed in an earlier chapter—have been suggested. However, to change the existing procedure would require a constitutional amendment and without the support of the large states it is unlikely that such an amendment would presently get the necessary three-fourths of the state legislatures to ratify it. At least for now, those seeking to occupy the oval office will have to plan their campaign strategies within the parameters set down in Article II and the Twelfth Amendment of the Constitution.

Presidential Powers and Duties: Given and Assumed

Powers Given

The first words of Article II give the president executive power, the power to carry out or administer the laws that Congress passes, and the duty to see that they are faithfully executed. Section 2, Clauses 1 and 2 of the Article list several additional powers the framers decided should be given to the president. These include the power to make treaties, "**with the Advice and Consent of the Senate,**" to appoint Supreme Court justices, to appoint and receive Ambassadors, and to grant pardons to individuals convicted of federal offenses. They also include the responsibility of informing the Congress about the "State of the Union," and the powers—such as commissioning officers—associated with his role as "**Commander in Chief of the Army and Navy of the United States, and of the Militia [National Guard] of the several States.**"

In sum the list of given, or constitutional, presidential powers includes the power to:

- administer federal laws
- make treaties
- appoint federal officials
- receive ambassadors from foreign countries
- grant pardons
- inform the Congress about the state of the union
- serve as commander in chief

Powers Assumed

Looking at this limited list of formal powers, it becomes obvious that, however much the framers tried to limit them, the powers of the presidency have vastly increased over time. They have increased because Congress has gradually given the executive more to do (to submit an annual budget, for example), because the American people now expect him to take the legislative initiative in diverse matters such as health care and the environment, and because other world leaders often turn to him for economic or military assistance and guidance. They have also increased because so many of the men who have occupied the office have taken advantage of the opportunities, both domestic pressures and foreign crises, to do so by exercising what we have come to call their **emergency powers**.

The evolution of presidential power began immediately. It was George Washington (1789-1797) who, by issuing the 1794 Proclamation of Neutrality in the war between England and France, expanded the range of presidential decision-making into the area of foreign policy. This was an area that the framers expected to fall under congressional direction. It was Thomas Jefferson (1801-1809) who seized the opportunity to double the size of the country by purchasing Louisiana before getting congressional approval. It was Andrew Jackson (1829-1837) who went over the heads of the members of Congress, appealed directly to the people, and then, with their support, expanded the power of the president deep into the legislative process. Jackson was the first president to veto legislation not because he thought it was unconstitutional but because he did not like the policy.

With these early assumptions of foreign and legislative powers the stage was set for other presidents to follow suit and to increase them still further. James Polk (1845-1849) popularized the doctrine of "manifest destiny," which enabled him to declare war on Mexico and to add a half million square miles to the United States; Abraham Lincoln (1861-1865) bypassed both Congress and the Constitution and assumed enormous emergency powers during the Civil War; William McKinley (1897-1901) applied Polk's doctrine outside the country to acquire new economic markets for the U.S. (the beginning of American imperialism); and Theodore Roosevelt (1901-1909), who got Columbia to cede Panama and Panama to cede the Canal Zone to the U.S., intervened in Santo Domingo and Cuba and reformed the practices of big business and industry (railroads, mining, and meat) with a vengeance.

Roosevelt, the first president of the twentieth century and sometimes referred to as the first modern president, adhered to the philosophy that unless the Constitution explicitly stated that he couldn't do something, he could and would if he thought it was necessary. He expressed these sentiments candidly in a letter explaining that,

> while President I have **been** President, emphatically: I have used every ounce of power there was in the office and I have not cared a rap for the criticisms of those who spoke of my "usurpation of power"; for I knew that the talk was all nonsense and that there was no usurpation. I believe that the efficiency of this Government depends upon its possessing a strong central executive, and wherever I could establish a precedent for strength in the executive, . . . I have felt not merely that my action was right in itself, but that in showing the strength of, or in giving strength to, the executive, I was establishing a precedent of value.[2]

He did succeed in setting a precedent for the twentieth century presidents who followed him. In responding to events such as the Depression, World Wars I and II, the rise of Communism, the Cold War, the Korean War, the Vietnam Conflict, Iraq, Afghanistan, and instances of domestic and foreign terrorism, they broke away from what Woodrow Wilson had referred to in the 1880s as "congressional government."[3] Wilson (1913-1921) and Franklin Delano Roosevelt (1933-1945) joined the growing list of presidents who helped to institutionalize presidential power and established its primacy. Political scientist James MacGregor Burns refers to the ascendancy of the institution of the presidency as "presidential government."

Presidential Roles

The evolutionary growth in the power of the presidency, it was observed many years ago by presidential scholar Clinton Rossiter, is reflected in "the staggering number of duties we have laid upon its incumbent."[4] The important presidential roles include both those which are formerly bestowed by the Constitution and some which were implied by the words "**he shall take Care that the Laws be faithfully executed**" (Article II, Section 3) and taken on by those who have held the office. Some of the major roles briefly described below, identified by Rossiter in his book *The American Presidency*, include: chief of state, chief executive, commander in chief, chief diplomat, and chief legislator.

Chief of State

This important role is an essentially "ceremonial" or a "symbolic" one, which is to say that as chief of state the president serves as a "figurehead" rather than as a "working head" of the U.S. government. In this role the president speaks and acts for all Americans in the U.S. and represents them in other countries. "He greets distinguished visitors from all parts of the world, lays wreaths on the tomb of the Unknown Soldier and before the statue of Lincoln, makes proclamations of thanksgiving and commemoration, bestows the Medal of Honor on flustered pilots, holds state dinners for the diplomatic corps and the Supreme Court, lights the nation's Christmas tree, buys the first poppy from the Veterans of Foreign Wars, gives the first crisp banknote to the Red Cross . . . rolls the first egg for the Easter Bunny, and in the course of any month greets a fantastic procession of firemen, athletes, veterans, Boy Scouts, Campfire Girls, boosters, hog callers, exchange students, and heroic school children."[5]

When President Bush delivered a televised address on the morning after the 2001 terrorist attacks in New York and Washington D. C., he was speaking both to all Americans and, in their behalf, to the rest of the world. He therefore used the collective term "we." "The United States of America will," he said, "use all our resources to conquer this enemy. We will rally the world. We will be patient. We'll be focused, and we will be steadfast in our determination."[6] President Obama also used the collective "we" when he visited New York and New Jersey in the aftermath of Hurricane Sandy and observed that when disaster hits "we're reminded that we are bound together and have to look out for each other."[7]

Presidents are also acting as chief of state in their visits to other countries in an effort to demonstrate friendship or discuss issues. Needless to say, this role is extremely demanding on a president's time and energy. But a president who does not fulfill it to the people's satisfaction is not likely to win their enthusiastic approval or their votes.

Chief Executive: The Executive Office of the President, The White House Office, and The Cabinet

That the terms "president" and "chief executive" are so often used interchangeably indicates how closely a president is identified with this particular role. His job to "**take Care that the Laws be faithfully executed**" is a constitutional directive to see to it that acts of Congress, federal court decisions, federal rules and regulations, and treaties are put into effect. In short, the president runs the executive branch of government. He is the "chief administrator." He is the government's equivalent to the Chief Executive Officer (CEO) of a major private corporation.

Like the CEO of a corporation the president is a "personnel manager." He has the power to hire and to fire, that is "to appoint" and "to remove from office." Instead of having to seek the approval of a corporate executive board, he appoints government personnel including Supreme Court justices, ambassadors, members of his cabinet, and members of boards and commissions with the advice and consent of the Senate.

George Washington predicted that "one of the most difficult and delicate parts of [his] Office" would be related to "nominations for appointments."[7] He was correct in that not all appointments do go smoothly. For example, Obama suffered his first political setback in January 2009 when he accepted a request from Governor Bill Richardson of New Mexico that his name be withdrawn from consideration for the Cabinet post of Commerce Secretary. At that time, Richardson was part of an investigation into whether he or his advisors and campaign aides had exchanged state contracts for political contributions. In putting together a new Cabinet at the beginning of his second term, the president's prospective nominee for Secretary of State, Susan Rice, withdrew her name for consideration because of Republican opposition. His nomination of Chuck Hagel for Secretary of Defense, the president was told, was not likely to be an easy confirmation.

Presidents routinely appoint thousands of lesser officials, about two thousand out of the approximate total of three million civilian civil service employees, without any problems at all. While these appointments do not require the approval of the Senate, it has become customary in a practice known as **senatorial courtesy** for the president to yield some of the choices of agency heads and federal judges to the senators in his party. They generally select individuals from their respective states who might then feel that they owe their primary loyalties to the senators who chose them rather than to the president.

As burdensome as personnel matters may sometimes be, it has long been recognized that the presidency, just as a large corporation, cannot be run as a one-man shop. While he, as are all CEOs, is solely "responsible" for executing policy, he alone cannot see to it that the laws of Congress are carried out. "The President," according to the findings of a 1937 presidential committee report that is usually referred to as the Brownlow Report, "needs help."[8] After all, it concluded, things had changed in the executive office since the turn of the twentieth century when presidents could get by much of the time with just a few hours of work.

Stephen Hess, a researcher at the Brookings Institution and staff member in the Eisenhower and Nixon White House, explains that prior to World War I, Woodrow Wilson only worked for three or four hours a day. The remainder of his time was spent "happily and quietly, sitting around with his family."[9] The War, and later the Great Depression of the 1930s, changed all of that. The government began to grow, and it grew rather haphazardly.

The Executive Office of the President (EOP) It was both to cope with new responsibilities and to bring some order to the administration of policy that the Brownlow Report recommended that the executive branch be reorganized and enlarged to include an "Executive Office of the President (EOP)." That recommendation was gratefully accepted by President Franklin Delano Roosevelt, who explained:

> that no enterprise can operate effectively if set up as is the Government today. There are over 100 separate departments, boards, commissions, corporations, authorities, agencies and activities through which the work of the Government is being carried on. Neither the President nor the Congress can exercise effective supervision and direction over such a chaos of establishments, nor can overlapping, duplication, and contradictory policies be avoided.[10]

So it was that the EOP was established in 1939 by **Executive Order** (a presidential order that has the force of law) number 8248. The Executive Office has changed over time. Under Roosevelt it consisted of six administrative assistants, a National Resources Planning Board, the Liaison Office for Personnel Management, and the Office of Government Reports. As of now, the EOP consists of approximately forty thousand key federal executives and military leaders of which the top eight thousand, who hold policy and supporting positions, are presidential appointments. These forty thousand individuals staff positions in: The White House Office, The Office of the Vice President, Agencies of the Executive Office of the President, Presidential Advisory Organizations, The Executive Departments, Independent Agencies, and Quasi-Official Organizations.

When political writers and commentators speak of the "institutionalized" presidency, they are referring to the numerous and diverse offices, agencies, organizations, departments, and councils which constitute the EOP. The magnitude of this office provides an accurate reflection of the vast and growing responsibilities of a modern president and serves to remind us that while the final decision-making responsibility is his, much of the day to day preliminary work is by necessity carried out by the thousands of others who advise him.

The White House Office (WHO). Among the thousands of individuals in the EOP who assist the president are those in the White House Office. They are physically and often emotionally the closest to the president. The WHO consists of people—the number has varied from president to president—who provide such services as housekeeping, secretarial support, legal counseling, medical care, speech-writing, communication with the media and with the Congress, and a myriad of other functions needed to run the White House and assist the chief executive.

Frequently, the president's top assistants and advisors are his longtime acquaintances or close friends. The appointment of individuals with whom he has had a personal relationship has an "up" side—they are people who the president knows and whose judgments he trusts—but it sometimes has a "down" side as well—friends may be too protective and in the process of keeping the president "safe" inadvertently isolate him from people and information that he should have access to. It is said that this was the case in Richard M. Nixon's White House Office and contributed to his downfall.

Upon assuming office in 1969, Nixon appointed two of his California friends, which were dubbed by at least one political scientist as the "California mafia."[11] H.R. (Bob) Haldeman became Chief of Staff (the director of the White House Office) and John Erlichman was made Assistant to the President for Domestic Affairs. Because they knew the president and recognized that he was very much a loner, they organized and managed the White House with an eye to providing the seclusion that Nixon seemed to desire. In allowing them to centralize power, historian Arthur M. Schlesinger, Jr. suggests Nixon had made a fatal error. "He rarely saw most of his so-called personal assistants. If an aide telephoned the President on a domestic matter, his call was switched to Haldeman's office. If he sent the President a memorandum, Haldeman decided whether or not the President would see it. 'Rather than the President telling someone to do something,' Haldeman explained in 1971, 'I'll tell the guy. If he wants to find out something from somebody, I'll do it.' The result," Schlesinger concludes, "was the enthronement of unreality . . . . The White House became a world of its own, cut off from Washington and the nation."[12] In his role as Chief Executive, Nixon became a model of what not to do.

The Cabinet. The Constitution of 1789 makes no mention of a cabinet. The framers had specifically rejected the formation of such an advisory council. However, the wording of Section 2 of Article II makes it clear that the president could ask for the opinions of the "**principle Officer in each of the executive Departments.**" With this instruction, it didn't take very long for a presidential cabinet to evolve. George Washington got the ball rolling in 1789 by inviting his attorney general and the secretaries of state, treasury and war to meet with him. Today the cabinet is one of the entrenched bodies in the Executive Office of the President, and its secretaries are among the first appointments made by a president-elect.

This is not to say that the cabinet, as a collective group, necessarily plays an essential role in advising the chief executive. As in all things, presidents run the gamut in their opinions of its utility. Some have found that within a short period after they appoint members of the cabinet, their appointees, such as those that head Agriculture, Labor, and Veterans Affairs, become stronger advocates for the departments they head rather than for the executive branch of government or for the general population. Nixon, who demanded the complete loyalty of his advisors, not surprisingly rebuffed his cabinet secretaries with the observation that "no [president] in his right mind submits

The President confers with senior advisors in the Oval Office.
Feb. 4, 2009. White House Photo by Pete Souza

anything to his cabinet."¹³ While President Obama has not rebuffed his cabinet he has followed most of his predecessors and seldom meets with his full cabinet.

The Obama cabinet consists of fifteen **"principle officers of the executive departments."** In making some of these appointments, including that of the Secretary of Defense, the Secretary of State, the Chairman of the Joint Chiefs of Staff, and the Executive Secretary of the National Security Council, the president's role as chief executive overlaps with that of his role of commander in chief.

Commander in Chief

It was the objective of the framers to place the military protection and the safety of the country in the hands of the national government rather than in those of the individual states. It was also their objective to place control over the military into the hands of a civilian. The Constitution in designating the president as **"Commander in Chief of the Army and Navy of the United States, and of the Militia [National Guard]"** accomplishes both of those objectives.

Still another objective, to ensure that the president was not an out-of-control warmonger, was accomplished by checking his power and leaving it to Congress to **"declare war** (Article I, Section 8, Clause 11)." Thus, as Madison wrote to Jefferson in 1798, "the constitution supposes, what the History of all Govts demonstrates, that the Ex. is the branch of power most interested in war, & most prone to it. It has accordingly with studied care vested the question of war in the Legisl."¹⁴

Although widely debated in *The Federalist Papers* (See Nos. 24-27 and 41) the framers did not specify in the Constitution just how much control the president was to have over the armed forces or how much direction he was supposed to provide, if any, in peacetime or, for that matter, in wartime. Apparently they didn't believe it would be very much—certainly not nearly as much as that of the British king. In the 69th *Federalist* Hamilton notes that while the king commands the military and naval forces, declares war and raises and regulates fleets and armies, the American president has only the "right to command the military and naval forces of the nation."

Since the Constitution is not much more specific than this, presidents have used their own discretion, sometimes acting in concert with the Congress, sometimes manipulating it, and sometimes bypassing that legislative body altogether. President James K. Polk (1845-1849) deliberately deployed U.S. troops in territory that was claimed by Texas and Mexico to provoke an attack by Mexico and to obtain congressional "recognition" of a state of war. Lincoln in waging the Civil War suspended the writ of **habeas corpus** (an order to bring a prisoner before a judge and explain why that individual is being held), instituted naval blockades of ports in the South, purchased military supplies, and enlarged the army and navy without congressional approval. "As commander-in-chief of the army and navy," he said, "in time of war I suppose I have a right to take any measure which may best subdue the enemy."[15]

Franklin Delano Roosevelt apparently agreed with Lincoln's supposition because he too stretched his role as commander in chief to the limits during World War II. Reminiscent of Lincoln, F.D.R. made it clear to the legislature on one occasion that "in the event that Congress should fail to act, and act adequately, I [FDR] shall accept the responsibility, and I will act."[16]

And act he did. His administration seized and ran industries deemed to be vital for the war effort, restricted consumer access to vital war materials such as gasoline, created scores of war-related defense agencies, and ordered the internment of about one hundred thousand Japanese Americans.

Harry Truman (1945-1953), who knew that there were eighty-seven historical instances in which American presidents had unilaterally sent military forces into combat, followed suit and, without consulting Congress, ordered troops into Korea. In more recent times, John F. Kennedy (1961-1963) orchestrated the invasion of Cuba; Lyndon B. Johnson (1963-1969) sent twenty-two thousand troops into the Dominican Republic and greatly expanded U.S. involvement in the war in Vietnam; Richard M. Nixon (1969-1974) ordered the invasion and the bombing of Cambodia; Jimmy Carter (1977-1981) sent troops into Iran to rescue American hostages; Ronald Reagan (1981-1989) invaded Grenada and Libya; George H. W. Bush (1989-1993) sent troops into Panama and Saudi Arabia; Bill Clinton (1993-2000) deployed U.S. forces to the Iraqi border, to Haiti, and to Kosovo, ordered the bombing of Serbian targets in Bosnia and Kosovo, and sent two aircraft carriers to the waters off Taiwan and George W. Bush (2001-2009) announced a new "preemptive" military strategy against enemies of the United States and ordered troops to Iraq and President Obama increased the number of troops in Afghanistan.[17]

The War Powers Resolution, passed by Congress in 1973, was an attempt to make it more difficult for presidents to initiate and to carry out these types of actions without congressional approval. The resolution requires that the president:

- consult, where possible, with the Congress before introducing U.S. forces into hostilities,

- submit a report to Congress, within forty-eight hours after introducing forces, explaining his actions,
- shall terminate the use of armed forces within sixty days unless Congress, declares war, or extends the sixty-day period, or there is an armed attack upon the United States.

Between 1973 when the Resolution was passed and 1995, there were thirty occasions where presidents had committed troops abroad. An analysis of their compliance to the provisions of the Resolution shows that it had been very low (No president had ever acknowledged the constitutionality of the resolution.) and that Congress had largely backed off from enforcing it.[18] It is not surprising then that Congress approved House Joint Resolution 114, which formally recognizes a president's right to act unilaterally, on October 16, 2002. The Resolution only requires that a president notify Congress, either before he orders an attack or within forty-eight hours, as to why a military action was (or needed to be) taken. It was Resolution 114, proposed by President George W. Bush, which gave him the power to use military force in Iraq without having to first ask Congress for a declaration of war. Clearly we are still in an era of what Schlesinger called "presidential war," an era where presidents in their role as commander in chief are able to use military force to carry out their foreign policy objectives.

Chief Diplomat

Foreign policy objectives are carried out through diplomacy, as well as through the use of military force. The president, who heads the diplomatic corps, is the country's chief diplomat. The framers gave him this job because they understood that "the structural characteristics of the Presidency—unity, secrecy, decision, dispatch, superior sources of information—were . . . especially advantageous to the conduct of diplomacy."[19] In his role of chief diplomat the president may appoint diplomatic personnel and envoys, receive ambassadors, recognize foreign governments, negotiate treaties, make executive agreements, and hold summit meetings.

Appointing Diplomatic Personnel and Envoys. The Constitution (Article II, Section 2, Clause 2) states that the president "**shall appoint Ambassadors, [and] other public Ministers and Consuls.**" With approximately 190 sovereign countries in the world, the appointments are so numerous that a president generally is only able to personally select candidates for the top posts and leaves to his advisors to choose the remainder. Sometimes they fill the less important posts with senior foreign service officers who may already have extensive diplomatic experience.

Once selected, the Constitution states that it is then up to the Senate to confirm or deny confirmation to these presidential designees. The Senate, however, plays no confirmation role when a president decides to send a personal envoy, such as his wife, to a foreign country.

Receiving Ambassadors. In fulfilling his duties as chief diplomat the president not only appoints and sends ambassadors to represent the United States abroad he is instructed in Section 3 of Article II that it is also his duty to "**receive Ambassadors and other public Ministers**" from foreign governments. Every country has a certain protocol, or rules of etiquette to be followed, that it adheres to when formally receiving an ambassador.

> ### THOMAS JEFFERSON AS AMBASSADOR TO FRANCE AND AS CHIEF DIPLOMAT OF THE UNITED STATES
>
> Thomas Jefferson replaced Benjamin Franklin as the American Minister to France in 1784. He was a good one, in that he accomplished his main mission of negotiating credit and new markets for America. Jefferson was charmed by the French aristocracy but considerably less enchanted by some of their non-democratic diplomatic procedures.
>
> David Humphreys, a secretary of the American commission, observed Jefferson's first meeting with King Louis XVI and later described one of these procedures. As he watched the ceremony in which Jefferson presented his credentials to the "rather fat" King who was "attended by one hundred Swiss guards," he observed the "somewhat ridiculous . . . rituals of bowing and hat removing, noting that every time Jefferson mentioned the name of either King or Queen in his prepared paper he took off his hat and the King and all his courtiers did the same."
>
> When he became president, Jefferson, as his "rules for foreign ministers" indicate, would have none of this. Among his rules were the following three:
>
> 1. the Executive Government would consider every Minister "as the representative of his nation, and equal to every other, without distinction of grade,"
>
> 2. "no titles being admitted here, those of foreigners have no precedence,"
>
> 3. "at dinners in public or private, and on all occasions of social intercourse, a perfect equality exists between the persons composing the company, whether foreign or domestic, titled or untitled, in or out of office."
>
> Needless to say, many foreign ministers were outraged by these rules.

Sources: Fawn M. Brodie, *Thomas Jefferson: An Intimate History* (Toronto, Canada: Bantam Books, Inc. 1975) 245; Claude G. Bowers, *Jefferson in Power: The Death Struggle of the Federalists* (Boston, Massachusetts: Houghton Mifflin Company, 1964), 37.

Recognizing Foreign Governments. There is nothing in the Constitution that explicitly gives a president the authority to grant recognition to the government of a foreign country. However, presidents, beginning with George Washington who received the French ambassador Edmond Genet, have done so based on the assumption that this is an **inherent power**, one that is inferred by the constitutional directive that the president appoints and receives ambassadors. In other words, when any country, including the United States, sends or receives the credentials of an official representative, the recognition of the legitimacy of that official's government is implied.

It is also implied that when a president withdraws or refuses to receive an ambassador, the recognition of a foreign government has been terminated or denied. Cuba, Iran, and the Republic of China (Taiwan) are among the countries that have had their legal recognition terminated by the United States.

Negotiating Treaties. As chief diplomat, the Constitution (Article II, Section 2, Clause 2) empowers the president to make treaties. Although a president does not do so without assistance, he has the exclusive authority to negotiate a treaty with another country. While the Constitution does call for the Senate to play an advisory role at some time either before or during the negotiations, they have been asked to do so only sporadically.

Presidents have generally accepted the constitutional instruction to secure Senatorial consent. So upon concluding negotiations, the document is presented to the Senate where it is either accepted "as is" by two-thirds of the membership, or it is modified. A modified treaty, such as the "Strategic Arms Limitation Treaty" (SALT II) to which the Senate attached twenty-three conditions, must then be returned to the president who may accept or reject the changes made by the Senate or withdraw the treaty from consideration. President Carter, who negotiated SALT II, opted to withdraw it.

Entering into Executive Agreements. An **executive agreement** is an understanding that is reached between the president and a foreign head of state or by their designees. These agreements have been used by contemporary presidents on such matters as "trade agreements, the annexation of territory, military commitments, and arms control pacts."[20] All of this and yet the Constitution makes no mention of them. As in the case of recognizing ambassadors, entering into an executive agreement is an inherent power.

Executive agreements can take the form of written statements, or they can be verbal agreements. In either instance, they have the same legal standing as treaties—they are binding on the parties who enter them. Unlike a treaty, an executive agreement does not require either the advice or the consent of the Senate. It has therefore been used with increasing frequency by presidents who want to circumvent the confirmation process because they deem the likelihood of having a treaty ratified to be somewhat remote or because they want to keep their conduct of foreign policy a secret from Congress. (Frequencies are given in Table 11.1.) Nixon, for example, entered a "secret" agreement with the president of South Vietnam in 1973, assuring him that the U.S. would provide full military support should North Vietnam invade the South. They did in 1975. By then Nixon was out of the White House, and the commitment was not met.

The Congress has tried, without much success, to limit the use of executive agreements. In 1953 an amendment (the Bricker Amendment) to establish a congressional review of executive agreements was introduced but never came to a vote in the Senate; and the Case Act (1972), which

Table 11.1
Treaties and Executive Agreements, 1789-1998

Period	Treaties	Executive Agreements
1789-1839	60	27
1839-1889	215	238
1889-1939	524	917
1940-1970	310	5,653
1971-1977	110	2,062
1978-1983	114	1,999
1984-1988	65	1,890
1989-1993	84	1,606
1994-1998	147	1,372

Source: Robert E. DiClerico, *The American President* (Upper Saddle River, New Jersey: Prentice Hall, 2000), 50.

requires the president to inform Congress within sixty days of all executive agreements entered into, has been successfully circumvented by presidents who choose to define their understandings with foreign governments as something other than an executive agreement.

Holding Summit Meetings. Summit meetings, still another example of an inherent power, are a form of personal diplomacy. They are the private, face-to-face meetings that take place between two or more leaders of the world's superpowers.

Little actual negotiation takes place at these meetings. Most of that is handled between lower-level diplomats before the summit even begins. These meetings, about such things as military, economic, and environmental concerns, give world leaders an opportunity to get to know one another. Ronald Reagan and Mikhail Gorbachev, Bill Clinton and Yizhak Rabin, and George W. Bush and Tony Blair are examples of the close relationships that sometimes develop. In addition, because they receive a lot of media attention, summits provide an excellent forum for leaders to promote themselves and their policies to the international community and the voters back home. President Obama used both G-20 summits in April 2010 and June 2012 to express his views on restoring global economic growth and to discuss financial concerns about the Greek economy. He also held a Nuclear Security Summit (April 2010) to discuss how to keep nuclear weapons away from terrorist groups and to tighten sanctions on Iran for its nuclear ambitions and, in 2012, he met with Russian President Vladimir Putin to express American concerns about Russia supplying arms to Syria.

Clearly, in conjunction with the other diplomatic powers discussed in this section, summit meetings have enabled presidents to steal much of the foreign policy thunder out from under the Congress. As if that was not enough, he has in his role of chief legislator also taken from them considerable legislative responsibilities.

Chief Legislator (Presidential/Congressional Relations)

What the framers wanted was for the Congress to propose and pass legislation and for the president to execute it. They also wanted to provide a check on legislative power and so they included the following instruction among the listed duties of the president: **"he shall from time to time give to the Congress Information of the State of the Union, and recommend to their Consideration such Measures as he shall judge necessary and expedient** (Article II, Section 3). This directive, in conjunction with the use of the veto and the responsibility to see to it that the laws are executed, has allowed for an immense expansion in the role that presidents were originally expected to play in the legislative process. Today, as the saying goes, "the president proposes and the Congress disposes."

Presidents as Legislators. The expansion in the legislative role of the president has occurred gradually. While some presidents have sought an active role in this area, others have seen their legislative role as being a passive one. There is a long run of nineteenth and early twentieth century presidents who, as inheritors of the old Whig beliefs (The Whig party was the successor to the Federalists [1832] and the predecessor of the Republicans [1860].), either had no desire—or resisted the temptation—to take the legislative initiative away from Congress.

Among those who adhered to the Whig philosophy of a presidency subservient to the Congress are: William Henry Harrison (1841), Zachary Taylor (1849-1850), Franklin Pierce (1853-1857),

James Buchanan (1857-1861), Ulysses S. Grant (1869-1877), Benjamin Harrison (1889-1893), William McKinley (1897-1901), William H. Taft (1909-1913), Warren G. Harding (1921-1923), Calvin Coolidge (1923-1929), Herbert Hoover (1929-1933), and, more recently, Dwight D. Eisenhower (1953-1961). Each of these presidents conformed, with varying degrees, to the theory "that the presidency is limited strictly to following the Congress and adhering to the letter of the Constitution, that it could reasonably suggest fields in which legislation was required but no legislative program itself . . . ."[21]

This point of view gradually began to change after Theodore Roosevelt, who sent numerous legislative proposals over to the Congress, came into office in 1901. The pace of the change accelerated, and the legislative leadership of the president became more firmly established under Woodrow Wilson (1913-1921). It was Wilson who first submitted his recommendations and then went to the Congress in person to advocate in favor of them. Harry Truman (1945-1953) went even further than Wilson. He was the first president to submit to the Congress a whole legislative program, as opposed to individual proposals, at the beginning of each session.

A president today initiates as well as executes legislation. He sets forth a broad legislative agenda for Congress in his annual State of the Union address in January; he sends proposals for legislation to the Congress; he occasionally twists a few arms in trying to secure the passage of bills that he favors; and he vetoes any legislation that Congress sends to him for his signature that is not to his liking.

The Veto. The veto is one way a president has to say "I forbid"—which is what the Latin translation of the word veto means—the passage of a bill into law. Thus "the character of the veto power," as Taft once said, "is purely legislative."[22]

The procedures for two types of vetoes are set forth in Article I, Section 7, Clause 2 of the Constitution. The first way is for the president to return a bill without his signature and with his stated objections to the house in which it originated. The house at that point can either amend the bill and try again, or it can attempt to override the presidential veto. An override requires passage by a two-thirds majority of both congressional houses. The statistics in the table below reveal how rarely that majority is obtained. So a presidential veto virtually assures that the legislation will never be passed into law. For that reason sometimes even the threat of a veto is sufficient to cause Congress to make changes in legislation before they send it on to the president. Clearly that is what George W. Bush had in mind when he threatened to veto a reconstruction package for Iraq if part of it was made a loan.[23]

A second way that a president has to veto legislation, known as a **pocket veto**, is to hold on to it—not necessarily in his pocket—and if the Congress adjourns within ten working days after he has received it, the bill is automatically killed. It follows that pocket vetoes most often occur at the end of a legislative session when the Congress adjourns.

Whichever procedure a president uses, the veto applies to an entire bill. This "all or nothing" selection permits the Congress to attach a **rider**, an extraneous amendment that a president does not support, to a bill that he supports. So at times a president may either sign legislation, even when it has provisions that he does not particularly approve of, rather than see the whole bill go down in defeat, or he may veto legislation that he favors because he refuses to accept the rider.

TABLE 11.2
PRESIDENTIAL VETOES AND OVERRIDES, 1932-2009

PRESIDENT	NUMBER OF BILLS VETOED (Regular and Pocket Vetoes)	NUMBER OF TIMES OVERRIDDEN
Roosevelt	635	9
Truman	250	12
Eisenhower	181	2
Kennedy	21	0
Johnson	30	0
Nixon	43	7
Ford	66	12
Carter	31	2
Reagan	78	9
Bush	46	1
Clinton	36	2
G. W. Bush	5	0

Source: Robert E. DiClerico, *The American President* (Upper Saddle River, N.J.: Prentice Hall, 2000), 95; Updated by the authors.

Clinton, for example, vetoed two welfare reform bills (on December 6, 1995 and on January 9, 1996) because the Congress had coupled them with extreme changes in the Medicaid system, which he believed were "wrongheaded cuts" to which he would just not accede.[24] When the Medicaid provisions were decoupled from welfare reform in a third bill, Clinton announced on July 31, 1996, that he would endorse it. However, there were certain stipulations in the bill, such as excluding "legal" immigrants from getting most of the federal benefits and a cut of $24 billion dollars in the allotment of federal funds for food stamps, that he still did not condone.

The Federal Budget and Impoundment. The Constitution does not place the budget under the purview of the president. He has been brought into the process through his role as chief executive; by his power to veto spending bills; by the passage of the Budget and Accounting Act of 1921, which required the president to submit an Executive Budget (the Budget of the United States Government) to the Congress; and by the creation of the "OMB" the **Office of Management and Budget** (known from 1921 through 1971 as the Bureau of the Budget), one of the most important agencies assisting the president in the Executive Office of the President.

It is through the OMB that the president proposes funds for the programs and bureaucratic agencies that he supports. The OMB budgets money very much the way private corporations and citizens do. There is just so much available to allocate, and tradeoffs are often required. G. W. Bush recognized that tradeoffs would probably have to be made to fully fund the U. S. war against terrorism and, to make sure that Congress knew it too, he threatened to veto any bill that required "unnecessary" spending.

In making tradeoffs a president plays a part in the shaping of the federal budget and fulfilling his role as chief legislator. Every one of his executive agencies must clear any policy recommendation it wishes to present to the Congress with the OMB. Budgeting and policy making are, in a word, inseparable.

In addition to vetoing the budget or an appropriations bill, presidents also have the prerogative to just say no—that is, to refuse to spend the money that has already been appropriated by Congress. This power of refusal is called **impoundment**. A president might want to impound funds to save money, or he might want to impound funds as matter of policy because he believes, for example, that too much is being spent on defense, or on space exploration, or on the environment, or on any other program. Congress, under the authority of the Budget and Impoundment Control Act of 1974, has the final say on whether a president can delay or withhold spending.

Presidential Persuasion. Before resorting to the use of such techniques as the veto and impounding funds, a president can try to secure congressional support for his legislation by using persuasion. There are several "tools and tactics" that a president may opt for. Among those listed by DiClerico are:

- Status Conferral: flattering legislators by calling them on the telephone to thank them for their support, writing a personal letter, taking a picture with them, and so on.
- Legislative Assistance: offering to assist members of Congress to get their own legislation passed perhaps by agreeing to sign their bill when it reaches his desk.
- Programs, Projects, and Patronage: in exchange for support, a president may offer a representative such things as federal judgeships, federal contracts, and economic assistance for his/her district.
- Campaign Assistance: campaigning on behalf of the member or seeing that the party treasury gives generous support to the congressperson's campaign.
- Appeal to the Public: bringing pressure to bear on the Congress as a whole by taking his case directly to the American people.

Clearly a president has a wide range of options to choose from in his efforts to fulfill his role as chief legislator. However, while the options are available to all of them, not every president is equally successful.[25]

Success may be measured in a number of ways. It can be measured by the number of times his veto has been overturned [See table 11.2.], the number of executive orders he issues, the volume of legislation he proposes, and the number of those proposals that are made to fulfill campaign promises.

Success can also be measured by public perceptions as reflected in the almost daily polls reported in the media and in the opinions of experts on the presidency. One authority on the subject, who suggests that it is a great oversimplification to give all the credit for legislative success to any one individual or to any one branch of the government, nevertheless names just four men for contributing to the image of the president as a strong legislator. The four, "credited with achieving landmark legislation and giving new direction to national policy," are: Theodore Roosevelt, Woodrow Wilson, Franklin D. Roosevelt, and Lyndon B. Johnson.[26]

Other Roles. The five presidential roles that have been the focus of the first part of this chapter have all been roles that the Constitution specified, however vaguely, were to be filled by the president of the United States. The responsibilities, and even the number of roles a president plays, have grown in number since 1789. Today, for example, a major role of the president is that of a politician. He is the head of his political party, and, as such, he is a **spin doctor** (gives the media favorable interpretations of his party's actions), a political campaigner for himself and for others running for election or re-election on the party ticket, and a major fundraiser.

Presidential Roles v. The Whole Picture

Just as medical students are expected to learn, to name and to describe the functions of various parts of the human anatomy and auto-tech students are expected to learn the parts and the workings of the components that make up a car, students of American government are expected to learn to identify the major presidential roles and to be aware of the responsibilities and the powers of the office of the president. However, learning just these things is not enough, for each of the examples above it can be said that the whole is larger than the sum of its parts.

Probably nobody expressed this sentiment about the presidency better than Clinton Rossiter who, after a lengthy and "piecemeal analysis of the Presidency" and its many roles, confessed:

> I feel something like a professor of nutritional science who has just ticked off the ingredients of a wonderful stew. The members of the audience may be clear in their minds about the items in the pot, but they have not the slightest notion of what the final product looks like or tastes like or will feel like in their stomachs. The Presidency, too, is a wonderful stew whose unique flavor cannot be accounted for simply by making a list of ingredients. It is a whole greater than and different from the sum of its parts, an office whose power and prestige are something more than the arithmetical total of all its functions. The President is not one kind of official during one part of the day, another kind during another part—administrator in the morning, legislator at lunch, king in the afternoon, commander before dinner, and politician at odd moments that come his weary way. He is all these things all the time, and any one of his functions feeds upon and into all the others. He is a more exalted Chief of State because he is also Voice of the People, a more forceful Chief Diplomat because he commands the armed forces personally, a more effective Chief Legislator because the political system forces him to be Chief of Party, a more artful Manager of the Prosperity because he is Chief Executive.[27]

To get the whole picture of the presidency then one has to get beyond the roles that presidents play and take a closer look at the actors or players. This "non-constitutional" look at presidents focuses primarily on the leadership qualities of the men who have occupied the Oval Office.

LEADERSHIP AND LEADERS

One of the most daunting tasks facing anyone, including political scientists and other experts who write on the subject of leadership, is to define the term. So discouraging is it that some authors don't even make an attempt, and it is difficult to fault them. After all, as James MacGregor Burns, the author of the Pulitzer Prize winning book, *Leadership*, discovered, there were—as far back as 1978—at least 130 definitions of the word.[28]

In addition to an abundance of definitions there are also many different types of political leadership. Burns devotes a full chapter each to "Intellectual Leadership," "Reform Leadership," "Revolutionary Leadership," "Opinion Leadership," "Group Leadership," "Party Leadership," "Legislative Leadership," and "Executive Leadership." Other scholars have identified additional types so the list is seemingly an inexhaustible one.

The definitional and conceptual problems are not going to be resolved here. But an awareness of them should serve to remind the reader that any response to the question "What is leadership?" is both selective and tentative.

What is Leadership?

Leadership may be best understood by its absence. Imagine for example what would happen in a work situation where the boss informs the staff that she/he has something important to do and is, for the first time ever, leaving the office for the morning so that the workers will be entirely on their own. Before leaving, however, the boss tells them that while he/she is gone, they are to come up with some new ideas for increasing the company's sales and that their failure to do so will result in a decrease in their wages. What would happen? What feelings would these workers experience? Empirical studies have shown that most people who suddenly find themselves in circumstances where there is a "leadership vacuum"—a situation in which there is no one to answer their questions or provide instructions—often experience feelings of considerable anxiety.[29] It is because they are apprehensive, psychologically uncomfortable or uneasy that eventually one or more of the individuals in the leaderless group will be likely to step up, fill the vacuum, and act as the leader. "Leadership," as it has been observed, "is a necessary phenomenon in every form of social life."[30] At its most fundamental level, leadership is the ability to make others feel safe and secure by providing them with direction and guidance. This definition implies three things:

> (1) It implies that leadership is a relationship. Leaders require followers—those who are to be directed and guided. Leadership, in short, implies followership;
> (2) It implies that the ability to provide leadership is a special quality that an individual possesses. It has not yet been determined whether this quality is inborn or inherited, whether it is something that can be learned, or whether it is some combination of the two;
> (3) It implies that not every individual who holds a position such as "boss" or "President of the United States" can provide direction and guidance. Such people are formal or nominal "heads" as opposed to "leaders."

Leadership and Headship

"Headship" according to Barbara Kellerman is a distinct type of leadership; it is **leadership by position**. "Leadership" is the term she reserves for the **relationship between leaders and followers**. As she explains it:

headship is associated with the "rights and duties of an office or status in a hierarchical structure, whether a formal organization or an informally stratified collectivity.... Leadership too, is associated with the one who shapes the actions of others. But the focus here is not on role, or position, but on the special relationship between leader and followers. Leaders, in contrast to heads, are accorded their authority spontaneously by group members who, it [sic] turn, follow because they **want** to rather than because they **must**.[31]

Every U.S. president is a leader or head simply because of his formal or constitutional position. But not every president is a leader in terms of his ability to inspire others to follow him. Some presidents have been notable failures in their attempts to provide the direction the American public has come to expect. Among the more recent presidents who have not measured up according to Robert Shogan, in his political bestseller on presidential leadership from 1948 to 1988 (from Truman to Bush) are Jimmy Carter (1977-1981) and George H. W. Bush (1989-1993.)[32]

Leadership Failures: Two Case Studies

Shogan argues that there are three key leadership qualities that ultimately determine whether a president will be a failure or a success in providing direction and guidance to his constituents. These interacting qualities are: ideology, values, and character. Ideology refers to a president's beliefs and his strategy for achieving his political objectives. Values are roughly equated with morality. They consist of private and public principles that guide a president's behavior. Character alludes to a president's temperament and inclinations.[33] Weakness in any of the three qualities might doom a presidency.

The Case of Jimmy Carter

Ideology. James Earl Carter, the thirty-ninth president of the United States, never fully articulated either his political beliefs or a strategy to achieve them for the American public. As a candidate, Carter defined himself predominantly as an "outsider." "This was equivalent to defining himself by what he was not. He was not from Washington, he was not a member of Congress, he was not a liberal, he was not a spokesman for any of the major interest groups in his party."[34] His biographer, Betty Glad, reached the same conclusion as Shogan had a decade earlier. "Where Carter differed in essence from his opponents," she observed, "was in his eagerness to appeal to everyone and in his refusal to connect his various individual stands in terms of some philosophic framework that would place him somewhere on the traditional spectrum of social and political values."[35]

Values. Jimmy Carter, a Southern Baptist, a born-again Christian, a lifelong faithful churchgoer, a Sunday School teacher, a peacemaker, an advocate for the poor, was and is a moral man. There has never been even the slightest hint of immoral behavior in his private or public life. Shogan reports hearing Carter tell a crowd of people in Concord, Massachusetts during the 1976 campaign that "There's a lot of things I will never do to get elected.... I will never tell a lie, make a misleading statement, or betray a trust. If I should ever betray a trust, don't support me."[36] He was never publicly accused of doing any of those things.

President Jimmy Carter and Rosalynn Carter at the Inaugural Ball. January 20, 1977.
Photo credit: Jimmy Carter Library

Given his strong moral and religious commitments, it is hardly surprising that Carter chose to publish his presidential memoirs under the title *Keeping Faith* or, as he reminisces in that work, that his inaugural speech focused "on those concerns that embodied [his] most important values—human rights, environmental quality, nuclear arms control, and the search for justice and peace."[37]

Character. Among Carter's often mentioned character or personality traits are his: intelligence, charm, perseverance, flexibility in choosing political strategies and rhetorical appeals, ambition, a tendency to exaggerate his record, single-minded determination, goodness, shyness, self-absorption and insecurity.[38] Some of these qualities, such as flexibility and single-mindedness, seem to be somewhat inconsistent with one another and probably reflect observations of Carter's behavior at different times or in different situations.

Of all the descriptions of the former president's character the most positive was that made by one of his speech-writers, James Fallows. The Carter that Fallows knew

> is unusually patient, less vindictive than the political norm, blessed with a sense of perspective about the chanciness of life and the transience of its glories and pursuits. [Fallows] left his service feeling that when moral choices faced him, he would resolve them fairly; that when questions of life and death, of nuclear war and human destruction were laid upon his desk, he would act on them calmly, with self-knowledge, free of interior demons that might tempt him to act rashly or to prove at terrible cost that he was a man . . . .[39]

If he "had to choose one politician to sit at the Pearly Gates and pass judgment on [his] soul," Fallows continued, "Jimmy Carter would be the one."[40]

Given this glowing testament, it is at first a bit difficult to understand why Carter's presidency failed, why he became the first incumbent president since Hoover lost to FDR in 1933 not to win re-election. To be sure external events, such as the fall of the Shah of Iran, the energy crisis, high inflation, and the seizure of the U.S. embassy in Iran coupled with the taking of American hostages, all contributed to Carter's downfall.

However, as Shogan is quick to point out, other presidents managed to survive such difficult circumstances whereas Carter could not. He could not because he never clearly stated his ideological position. The public did not know what Carter stood for or wanted; there was no vision to rally public support when there were problems. Carter faltered because values and character, without ideology, are not sufficient.

The Case of George Herbert Walker Bush

Ideology. George Herbert Walker Bush, the forty-first president of the United States, inherited a conservative mantle from his predecessor Ronald Reagan—one of the most ideological presidents in recent history—and did not embrace or hold on to it. To be sure, Bush had at times during his political career taken rather strong conservative positions. In the period that he was a member of the House of Representatives, he voted with the conservatives 83 percent of the time; he endorsed conservative Barry Goldwater rather than moderate Nelson Rockefeller during the 1964 Republican presidential primaries; he opposed the 1964 Civil Rights Act, Medicare, and the nuclear test-ban treaty; and he rejected the endorsement of the liberal Ripon Society during his own 1968 Senate campaign.[41]

George Bush had a record as a moderate as well. After moving to the political right in 1964, he had by 1966 moved far enough to the left to win the support of a respectable number of liberal Democrats. When he sought the presidency in 1980 and needed conservative support, Bush took a step away from his "excessive" liberalism and "tried to present himself as a moderate alternative to Reagan. The combined burden was not easy to carry."[42] When asked during that presidential campaign whether he thought of himself as a conservative or a moderate, Bush could only reply "I don't want to be perceived as either."[43]

However, as one newspaper later reported:

when Mr. Reagan chose him as his running mate . . . that sort of talk was quickly shelved. Mr. Bush quickly took on the ideological coloration of the Reagan Administration; not once during its whole eight years did he distance himself from any of its policies in any significant way. George Bush the Planned Parenthood advocate became George Bush the foe of abortion, for example.[44]

George Bush was apparently ideologically adrift long before he ever became president.

Values. Bush, as was Carter, was perceived as being a moral man, and his presidency too was unmarked by personal scandal. However, it was not as much moral propriety as it was loyalty that was the dominant value that guided Bush's actions.

President Bush meets with the Emir of Kuwait, Jabir Al-Ahmad Al Jabir Al-Sabah in the Office of the White House to discuss the situation in the Gulf. September 28, 1990. Photo credit: George Bush Presidential Library

Loyalty was the operative word: loyalty to family and to friends, loyalty to his Vice President Dan Quayle who he kept on the ticket in 1992 in spite of advice not to do so, loyalty to Nixon, loyalty to Reagan, loyalty to the Republican Party, and loyalty to the Central Intelligence Agency. "I make friends," Bush stated, "I believe in staying in touch with people. And I learn from them. Loyalty goes two ways, to them and from them. I pride myself on that."[45]

The loyalty was usually returned. Glad tells how Richard Nixon ordered his assistant John Erlichman to purge the politicians from his cabinet and then added "except George Bush. He'd do anything for the cause."[46] Bush did stand by him. He was one of the few individuals who accepted Nixon's proclamations of innocence right up to the last few hours before Nixon resigned from office.

Character. By temperament George Bush was congenial, optimistic, energetic, enthusiastic, and, as most presidents are prone to be, ambitious. He was also, although he disliked the characterization, a "patrician," a man of "breeding and cultivation" who was reared from birth to be self-reliant, self-disciplined, and self-contained. These admiral qualities were countered by others that were far less positive. Bush was perceived by many to be a "preppie" and a "wimp." This

perception was rooted partly in his proclivity to avoid conflicts within the organizations in which he worked and partly in his patterns of speech. When he talked of getting into "deep doo doo," Bush sounded like a New England prep school boy. Aggressive language was a way of countering that image. His remark after his debate with Geraldine Ferraro [the democratic vice presidential candidate] in 1984—that "we kicked ass" last night—was one such episode . . . . The wimp charge was put to rest at this time by these devices.[47]

His wealthy upbringing also led to the charge, which was never really put to rest, that Bush was out of touch with the concerns and the problems of average Americans. His complacency about the faltering economy and his behavior during the 1992 election campaign did not do much to counter the charges of his indifference and his inability to empathize. On a stop at Orlando, Florida he was, for example, damaged by his expressions of astonishment over the electronic price scanners that are used at supermarket checkouts.[48] After all, not too many average citizens could identify with the president's surprise over technology that has been used in supermarkets and department stores for approximately two decades. The president, some thought, didn't seem to have a clue about how average citizens lived their daily lives.

There were other more serious criticisms of the president. Of these Bush was probably most severely reproached for not keeping his 1988 "read my lips—no new taxes" campaign pledge, and for not attempting to deal more definitively with the potential threat of further military incursions by Saddam Hussein, the Iraqi leader who invaded Kuwait at the end of the Gulf War. However, he might have withstood the heavy criticism he received about those decisions and been re-elected. Bush, just as Carter, was done in not so much by what he did as by what he didn't do.

What George Bush didn't do was to provide leadership. He asked Americans to "stay the course" and re-elect him for another four years, but he never told them exactly what the course was or would be. He never fully explained where it was that he wanted to take the country and how he planned to get there. Nor did he appear to think it was necessary to do so. In his autobiography, Bush wrote that the essence of presidential leadership was to have "faith in the system . . . confidence in the people . . . [and] optimis[m] about the future of the country . . . ."[49] He seems to have been unaware that voters, like tourists thinking about taking an ocean voyage, are not very likely to book passage on ship where the captain is known to navigate solely on the basis of his faith, confidence, and optimism rather than on a course that has been carefully chartered. So George Bush lost his bid for re-election in 1992.

Presidential Types

George W. Bush is a Republican, and Jimmy Carter is a Democrat. Although their party affiliations differ, as presidents, they nevertheless had something in common. Both of them had reputations as being moral men and both were unable to provide the direction and guidance that their constituents wanted. These personal qualities, in addition to others that they shared, enable scholars to speak of them, and any other presidents who have the corresponding attributes, as being the same "type."

It is as convenient to lump presidents together according to types as it is to categorize anyone else. It is much simpler to describe a friend as being the "intellectual" type than to provide a long list of "intellectual" behaviors (spends hours and hours doing homework, doing research at the library, writing poetry, reading *The Decline and Fall of the Roman Empire*, watching public television, etc.).

In addition to convenience, typing individuals (be they presidents or friends) also facilitates the making of accurate predictions about them. For example, one can reasonably predict that intellectual types will get good grades in school and that presidents who are typed as being ineffective leaders will—all things being equal—be less likely to get re-elected than those who do provide direction. There is nothing mystical about making these predications—the forecasts are simply based on what experience and observation have taught.

Barber's Presidential Typology

One of the best known presidential "**typologies**" in the discipline of political science is one that was developed by political psychologist James David Barber and published in his extraordinary book (Carter called it the best book on the presidency that he ever read.) entitled *The Presidential Character: Predicting Performance in the White House.*[50] This work, as its title implies, uses "character" or "the way [a] president orients himself toward life" as the basis for determining whether he will successfully perform or fulfill his leadership role. It is, as Barber says, a book that is "meant to help citizens and those who advise them cut through the confusion and get at some clear criteria for choosing Presidents."[51]

There are two criteria or "baselines" used to classify presidents. They are "activity" and "affect."

1. Activity: A president is typed by his level of activity, his energy, or how much time he spends on the job. Those who devote a lot of time are typed as "active," and those who do not are typed as "passive." Activity levels vary from president to president. "Lyndon Johnson," Barber reports, "went at his day like a human cyclone, coming to rest long after the sun went down. Calvin Coolidge often slept eleven hours a night and still needed a nap in the middle of the day. In between, the Presidents array themselves on the high or low side of the activity line."[52]

2. Affect: This baseline differentiates presidents according to how they (not the media or the voters) feel about what they do, that is whether they seem to enjoy doing the job. Those who seem to be having fun are typed as "positive" while those who are not are classified as "negative." Franklin Roosevelt, Barber says, was happy in the job—Richard Nixon was not.

These two criteria when mixed and matched in every conceivable combination, as the matrix below shows, produce an array of four different types. In other words, when there are two baselines each having two options (activity: active/passive and affect: positive/negative) the result is a 2 X 2 matrix that yields the following four presidential types.

		AFFECT	
		Positive	Negative
ACTIVITY	Active	Active Positive	Active Negative
	Passive	Passive Positive	Passive Negative

Every president beginning with George Washington can be classified as one of these four types; however, the last edition of Barber's work, the fourth edition, concentrates on the character of the fifteen presidents from Taft through Bush (#41). They are typed as follows:

		AFFECT	
		Positive	Negative
ACTIVITY	Active	<u>Active Positive</u> FDR Truman Kennedy Ford Carter Bush (George H. W.)	<u>Active Negative</u> Wilson Hoover LBJ Nixon
	Passive	<u>Passive Positive</u> Taft Harding Reagan	<u>Passive Negative</u> Coolidge Eisenhower

It is interesting that Barber's research revealed that each of our first four presidents fit into a different category: Washington was a passive-negative type; Adams was an active-negative; Jefferson was an active-positive; Madison was a passive-positive.[53] These men, as well as the fifteen presidents in the matrix above, were typed according to their levels of energy and enjoyment, but they also had, Barber found, other characteristics in common.

Active Positive: The Presidents Who Want to Achieve Results

There is a congruence, a consistency, between being very active and the enjoyment of it, indicating relatively high self-esteem and relative success in relating to the environment. The man shows an orientation toward productiveness as a value, and an ability to use his styles flexibly, adaptively, suiting the dance to the music. He sees himself as developing over time toward relatively well defined personal goals—growing toward his image of himself as he might yet be. There is an emphasis on rational mastery, and on using the brain to move the feet. This may get him into trouble; he may fail to take account of the irrational in politics. Not everyone he deals with sees things his way, and he may find it hard to understand why.

Active-Negative: The Presidents Who Want Power

The contradiction here is between relatively intense effort and relatively low emotional reward for that effort. The activity has a compulsive quality, as if the man were trying to make up for something or to escape from anxiety into hard work. He seems ambitious, striving upward and seeking power. His stance toward the environment is aggressive and he has a persistent problem in managing his aggressive feelings. His self-image is vague and discontinuous. Life is a hard struggle to achieve and hold power, hampered by the condemnations of a perfectionistic conscience. Active-negative types pour energy into the political system, but it is an energy distorted from within.

Passive-Positive: The Presidents Who Want Love

This is the receptive, compliant other-directed character whose life is a search for affection as a reward for being agreeable and cooperative rather than personally assertive. The contradiction is between low self-esteem (on grounds of being unlovable, unattractive) and a superficial optimism. A hopeful attitude helps dispel doubt and elicits encouragement from others. Passive-positive types help soften the harsh edges of politics. Their dependence and the fragility of their hopes and enjoyments make disappointment in politics likely.

Passive-Negative: The Presidents Who Emphasize their Civic Virtue

The factors [passive and negative] are consistent—but how are we to account for the man's **political** role-taking? Why is someone who does little in politics and enjoys it less there at all? The answer lies in the passive-negative's character-rooted orientation toward doing **dutiful** service; this compensates for low self-esteem based on a sense of uselessness. Passive-negative types are in politics because they think they ought to be. They may be well adapted to certain nonpolitical roles, but they lack the experience and flexibility to perform effectively as political leaders. Their tendency is to withdraw, to escape from the conflict and uncertainty of politics by emphasizing vague principles (especially prohibitions) and

Prime Minister of Israel, Yitzhak Rabin, President Clinton, and Yasser Arafat, chairman of the Palestine Liberation Organization, shaking hands in an electrifying ceremony. September 1993.
Photo credits: Clinton Presidential Materials Project

procedural arrangements. They become guardians of the right and proper way, above the sordid politicking of lesser men.[54]

Clinton Typed

Barber never typed the forty-second president, Bill Clinton. However others have used his typology to categorize the president and one of them, political psychologist Fred Greenstein, expressed the widely held view that Clinton's "outward characteristics seem almost to have been custom-made to illustrate . . . the active-positive character type."[55]

Activity: Energy Expended Doing the Job

Virtually anyone who followed the 1992 election campaign would have found it easy to classify Clinton—who spent up to eighteen hours a day shaking hands, kissing babies, and talking, talking, talking—as an active rather than a passive politician. Had there been any lingering doubts, his first year in the White House would have certainly laid them to rest.

Just a week and a half after his inauguration on January 20, 1993, it was observed that "Clinton is rattling the country," "activist government is here again," and Americans were warned to fasten their seat belts.[56] Those seat belts remained fastened through the middle of his first year in office when his pace at the time was described by a columnist as being "frenetic":

> after a whirlwind first stretch that has lasted seven long months, President Clinton has finally gone on vacation today. He has left Washington weary; even worse, much of his support is exhausted. Not for two generations has a new President sought to do so much, so fast and so directly.[57]

A four-day vacation, termed an exercise in "exhaustive relaxation," which Clinton took at the end of his first year, led another reporter to remark that Bush (#41) was simply "frenetic" while Clinton is a "whirlwind."[58] On his second day of so-called rest and relaxation, for example, Clinton went horseback riding, jogged on the beach, played volleyball, posed for photographs, signed autographs, flew to Pasadena to attend a black-tie birthday celebration, partied until the early hours (It was said that he was the last to leave.) and ordered pizza from room service at 3:00 A.M.[59] The long days and the high levels of energy expended at work and at play never stopped. In President Clinton's penultimate year in office, 1999, he held a news conference in which he responded to the media's observation that because he was a lame duck president he was probably winding down. Clinton stated that he still didn't mind hard work and long hours and, he observed,

> I don't feel myself winding down. I feel myself keying up. I want to do more. I want to try to make sure that I give the American people as much as I can every day. So I've got plenty of energy and I'll do whatever I'm asked to do.[60]

Clinton kept his word. On January 20, 2001, the morning of his last day in office, Clinton was busy at his desk in the Oval Office working on presidential pardons.

Affect: Enjoyment of the Job

It is reasonable to wonder how much fun the president was having during his long, hard work days. It seems that he was enjoying himself immensely. At least those that observed him on a daily basis, the press, thought so.

One of the classic stories from the early days of the Clinton administration, so illustrative of his enthusiasm for the job that it has been repeated more than once, centers on the president's appearance on a network television "town hall" hosted by Ted Koppel. A newspaper reporter who was there to witness the episode explains it this way. After receiving instructions from Koppel to "zip" right along in answering questions put to him by the audience

> Mr. Clinton nodded sympathetically, as he is wont to do, and then unleashed two and a half hours worth of highly detailed "first, secondly" and "let me just add this" and "I want to make this very clear" and "Can I say one thing real quick?" and "I would like to amend that answer" answers about his health care plan.

The president was willing, actually "eager," to talk about any health matter—lumbago, massage therapy, chiropractors, malpractice suits, or bulimia.

The president had promised to stay as long as anyone had a question—a promise that alarmed his staff, who envisioned the policy equivalent of the dance-marathon movie, "They Shoot Horses, Don't They?" "Do you want a Xanax?" said Robert Boorstin, a White House health policy aide, jokingly offering a tablet of the anti-anxiety medication to a reporter who planned to stay up as long as the President.

Although his advisor on health care was in the audience to take on any technical questions that the president might have needed assistance with, Clinton never called on him. Long into the night he carried on solo.

As Mr. Koppel looked on bemusedly, the increasingly hoarse President continued to take questions from people in the front rows during commercial breaks, even though his microphone was turned off.... Long after Mr. Koppel, who had a bad cold and kept checking his watch, looked like he was ready to be on his way, Mr. Clinton was still eagerly scanning the crowd for questioners and jumping up from his black leather swivel chair to get a little roving room while he talked.

The television station finally cut the show at 12:15 A.M. but

> the President continued to take questions from people who crowded around the stage for another 20 minutes.... He ignored his advisers... and his personal aides... who surrounded him like sheepdogs and, nipping, tugging and nudging, tried to herd him off the stage.... The President paid no attention to Mr. Koppel and Roone Arledge, the president of ABC News, who were waiting on stage to have their pictures taken with Mr. Clinton and to escort him to a private reception. He paid no attention to the ABC technician who reached under his jacket and took off his microphone. He was busy with a question from a woman....

By 12:30 the president had been coaxed

> over to the edge of the stage, close enough where they could actually pull him backstage without too much effort. But the President was still looking longingly at the crowd, hoping to make a few more points, to win a few more converts. His hoarse voice could be heard fading in and out on dozens of different aspects of the plan....

Finally,

> with one last tug from his advisers, the President was . . . backstage. But it did not stop there. He went up to his health care advisers ... wanting to go over various points he had

made.... The President, who did not get back to his hotel until the wee hours, seemed happy with his all-talk special. "He was having fun," explained [a media adviser].[61]

He was still having fun twelve years later while campaigning for President Obama's reelection with a hoarse voice, a hacking cough and little sleep, Clinton "after talking (and pointing and gesticulating) for three-quarters of an hour before a crowd of 4,000…spent an additional 10 minutes high-fiving his way along a rope line with a big grin."[62]

Clinton is a "positive" president. The enjoyment of being president did not diminish even after his impeachment in December 1998. In a press conference held seven months, almost to the day, after that event, Clinton told the media "I love this job. I love it. Even on the bad days, all of a sudden you can do something good for the country, you can do something good for the future. I have loved doing this."[62] Enthusiasm, such as that demonstrated at the televised town hall meeting and at the news conference, cannot be easily faked. This kind of fervor is an integral part of his being, a part that has its roots deep in his distant past.

The Socialization of an Active-Positive President: William Jefferson Clinton

Hugh Sidey, a writer who observed and wrote about the presidents and the presidency for over fifty years, once explained that his subjects are analogous to "complex geologic formations." By that he meant that "they are created over the years as the various strata are deposited by heritage, by experience. They do not appear overnight at center stage, nudging nations this way and that. They are gentled by mothers, challenged by fathers, inspired by teachers, humbled by failure and assembled finally in the forge of continuous exposure to the world's realities."[63] This is just another way of saying that presidents, just as the rest of the population, are the products of their socialization. (See Chapter 4). Barber put it more succinctly. "The personal past," he said, "foreshadows the Presidential future."[64] That is very obvious in the case of Bill Clinton.

Origins. The baby born in Hope, Arkansas, on August 19, 1946, and named William Jefferson Blythe III was the son of a woman who had been widowed three months earlier. So Bill Clinton never knew his father. He lived with his mother in the home of his maternal grandparents. After his mother remarried in 1950, they set up a new household with Bill's stepdad, Roger Clinton, the name Bill later legally took as his own. Roger Clinton was a sometimes abusive alcoholic. As Bill grew older, he began to take on the role of family protector.

David Maraniss, the author of the Pulitzer Prize winning biography on the president entitled *First In His Class*, explains that it is not unusual for the eldest child of an alcoholic parent to take on the role of protector or "family hero."[65] In this capacity the child may either take charge and assume adult responsibilities or may, instead, serve as the family's "redeemer," bringing to it praise and rewards from the outside world.[66] Bill Clinton did both.

The Redeemer. Clinton was known as a "superachiever" in high school because of the numerous activities he participated in and honors he earned during those years. Among his many accomplishments, Bill played tenor saxophone in the school band and other performance bands, helped organize musical festivals all over Arkansas, was a devoted and active Boy Scout, served as president of his junior class and president of the Key Club and the Beta Club, was a member of the Student Council, the National Honor Society, and a leadership training organization called

DeMolay, was accepted into the American Legion's Boys State, became a delegate to Boys Nation, was a semifinalist in the National Merit Scholarship competition, did volunteer work at a nonprofit treatment and research center in the hospital in which his mother was a nurse, and graduated fourth in a class of 363.[67]

Georgetown University, a Rhodes Scholarship at Oxford, Yale Law School, twelve years as Governor of Arkansas, and two terms as the President of the United States of America were to follow. Bill Clinton, the redeemer, did his family proud.

Predicting Presidential Performance. As the biographical sketch above indicates, Clinton has been a high-energy, enthusiastic person with a penchant for hard work ever since childhood. Knowing this, it would have been possible to predict that he would demonstrate these same attributes as president. As Barber explained,

> The best way to predict a President's character, world view, and style is to see how he constructed them in the first place. Especially in the early stages, life is experimental; consciously or not, a person tries out various ways of defining and maintaining and raising self-esteem. He looks to his environment for clues as to who he is and how well he is doing. These lessons of life slowly sink in: certain self-images and evaluations, certain ways of looking at the world, certain styles of action get confirmed by his experience and he gradually adopts them as his own. If we can see that process of development, we can understand the product.[68]

Clinton acknowledged the importance of his early life in shaping his adult behavior in an interview. "The violence and dysfunction in our home made me a loner, which is contrary to the way people view me, because I'm gregarious, happy, all of that" the president said. "But I had to construct a whole life inside my mind, my own space . . . . I don't believe in psychobabble. You can overdo all that, but I think I have to be acutely aware that I grew up as a peacemaker, always trying to minimize the disruption."[69]

At times, Clinton learned, the best way to achieve harmony and end discord is to compromise, to listen, to accept, and even to borrow the ideas of others. As president, therefore, he has had no problem identifying himself as a "new kind of Democrat," one who could co-opt Republican ideas (the theme of family values and the crime issue) and incorporate liberal and conservative ideas into his policies. As a compromiser, it was also relatively easy for Clinton to back away from some of his policies. For example, in 1994 he backed off from his attempt to overhaul the entire health-care system by providing universal health care because he knew he wouldn't get his proposal through Congress; in its place he substituted smaller initiatives such as the transportability of health insurance from one job to the next and the continuance of health insurance for the newly unemployed, which did pass. Similarly, he signed a welfare reform bill into law in August 1996 even though he recognized that parts of the bill were "deeply flawed" because he believed it was the best he could get at the time and because he concluded that some change was better than no change at all.

These types of compromises could have been a surprise only to people who were unfamiliar with Clinton's early socialization. His presidential actions, including those that resulted in scandal, were entirely in keeping with the personality or character that was first shaped back in Hope, Arkansas.

George W. Bush Typed

George W. Bush's presidential behavior and his past political style place him squarely into the passive-positive category of Barber's framework.

Activity: Energy Expended Doing the Job

George W. Bush is no Bill Clinton. He did not work into the wee hours of the morning. In fact, while Governor of Texas, he admitted that "my wife and I like to go to bed at nine P. M., earlier than our daughters, where we read and watch the news for awhile. But sometimes," he added, "I stay up late and type the girls' theme papers for them if they need help."[70] Nor did George W. Bush have the campaign stamina of his predecessor. When, for example, he was informed that his aides had scheduled two fundraisers and appearances at both a reading center and a baseball game for the same day (not an unusual agenda during a presidential campaign), he, according to one biographer, "went ballistic."

> What you're telling me is that because you guys [messed] up, I got to break my ass all day and won't get home until midnight?" Bush said. "We're going back to Plan A." The reading center and baseball game appearances were canceled, but the governor still didn't return to Austin until 11 P. M., resulting in a tired candidate departing the next day for Iowa.[71]

And so it was that on his very first campaign trip, before he had even officially declared that he was seeking the Republican nomination, Bush felt the need to account for his rather apparent fatigue by explaining to reporters that he

> only got six hours sleep last night . . . . I need more than that."[72]

More often than not, he got it. And he got it in part by keeping his working day short. As reporter John Leland observed in an article comparing Bush's coasting manner ("he raised coasting to a form of personal expression") with Clinton's workaholic frenzied style ("leading the country as if it were the world's biggest aerobics class"), "as governor of Texas, he typically knocked off at 5 p.m. and still managed to schedule a couple hours during the day to exercise, play video games, get a massage or nap. He clipped the time he spent reviewing each scheduled execution from half an hour to 15 minutes. If briefings droned too long . . . Bush would point to his computer's solitaire program . . . . If this man stands for anything," Leland concludes, "it is for working only as hard as he has to."[73]

The schedule did not change radically when Bush became the chief executive. Frank Bruni, who has described the Bush presidency as "no-fuss, no-sweat, look-Ma-no-hands," makes note of the president's need for "restorative breaks" during the work day.[74] Bush acknowledged as much when he told a group of Democrats that he would answer some of their questions "and then I'm going to head home and take a nap."[75]

Affect: Enjoyment of the Job

If the biography of the president entitled *Shrub: The Short But Happy Political Life of George W. Bush* is at all accurate, Bush is enjoying his job.[76] According to his autobiography he certainly enjoyed being a student (Phillips Academy, Andover, Yale, Harvard—Yale fraternity brothers have likened him to the John Belushi character Bluto in the movie *Animal House*); forming his own oil company (Arbusto later renamed Bush Exploration Company); being a manager and general partner of the baseball team, the Texas Rangers; and holding the only other political position to which he was elected, the governorship of Texas.[77]

His memoir includes recollections about some of these pursuits. Bush recalls that "my friends and I found ways to have fun. I have always looked for the lighter side of life, and I did so at Andover."[78] And of the other "major endeavors" of his life Bush philosophizes, "baseball is a pursuit for optimists, just like drilling for oil or running for office. To come to the ballpark every day, you have to believe you can win. To drill another well after a dry hole, you have to believe this one will be successful. To run for office, especially after losing [a congressional race in 1978], you have to believe you can win."[79] Such optimism and sense of fun are trademarks of the "positive" character.

The enjoyment that Bush derives from the job comes from the "people" rather than the "policy-making" side of politics. In other words, he enjoys working a room, shaking hands, kissing babies, and slapping backs but does not enjoy long hours sitting behind a desk immersed in papers and in reading documents. These tasks, as the president explains, are delegated. "I put a lot of faith and trust in my staff. I look for people who are smart and loyal and who share my conservative philosophy. My job is to set the agenda and tone and framework, to lay out the principles by which we operate and make decisions, and then delegate much of the process to them. The final decision **often** [emphasis added] rests with me, but their judgment has a big influence."[80]

Even after the turbulent events that followed the September 11 attacks in the United States, the president maintained his "management" or "C.E.O." style of governing. (George W. Bush is the first U. S. president to hold an M.B.A. degree.) In a televised interview that aired in January 2002, when American troops were fighting in Afghanistan, the president was questioned about his "ease of mind" as compared with Presidents Johnson and Nixon who were "consumed" by Vietnam.[81] Bush explained it this way:

> It goes to show that the war [Vietnam] was not **managed** [emphasis added] properly. The president shouldn't be running the war. The generals run the war. The president sets the strategy. That's the lesson of Vietnam that I brought to this office.[82]

But was he having any fun during this demanding time? Bush said that he was enjoying himself and, true to his type, enthusiastically added that "I really, really like being the president."[83]

The Socialization of a Passive-Positive President: George W. Bush

George W. Bush, 53 years old when he took the oath of office for the presidency, was born on July 6, 1946 in New Haven, Connecticut. Two years after his birth his father, "poppy," graduated from

**George H. W. Bush with his four sons, left to right: Neil, George H., Jeb, George W., and Marvin. 1970.
Photo credit: George Bush Presidential Library**

Yale University and took a job that moved the family first to Odessa, Texas and eventually, after the birth of a second child, Pauline Robinson (nicknamed Robin), twenty miles northwest of Odessa to Midland. It was, George W. Bush's parents believe, Robin's death from leukemia in the spring of 1953 that played a large role in shaping their son's personality and, later in life, his political style. As biographer J. H. Hatfield tells it,

> when he was running for reelection as governor of Texas, George W.'s parents acknowledged that their eldest son's "back-slapping, wisecracking, occasionally teasing style" was developed as a child of seven, when his sister died, and he felt it was his responsibility to try and lift his parents out of their grief.[84]

George W. Bush had to deal with more than the death of his sister. He had to deal with growing up in a household headed by a powerful and politically prominent father. In tracing the Bush legacy one reporter noted that a young adult growing up in such a household tends to either flee or embrace the shadow of the powerful parent.[85] George W. Bush, who doesn't believe in psychoanalyzing himself, is somewhat uncomfortable with the notion that he has embraced and is following in his father's footsteps. As the following comments indicate many Bush observers disagree.

When one steps back from any stage of Mr. Bush's life and examines his biography as a whole, one theme runs through each stage of his life: hero worship of his father, leading to an instinct to follow his father's trail. Many friends think that at some level, a driving force of George W.'s career has been an effort to honor his legacy and please his father, or at least to emulate him. Some acquaintances, though not all, even believe that [his] presidential bid is a culmination of that quest . . . . Some acquaintances believe that Mr. Bush's political career arose from a desire to avenge his father's defeat, although Mr. Bush dismisses the idea . . . "What makes him tick?" asked an old friend of both Bushes. "It's Daddy . . . . Daddy is the motivation—to please his dad."[86]

It is, in part, the "daddy" factor that may explain what has been called (depending on one's point of view) George W.'s "discipline" and "constancy" or his "stubbornness" and "inability to reverse course." For example,

the economic landscape changed, but Bush's faith in tax cuts has not. When he did reverse course, on campaign-finance reform or creating the Department of Homeland Security, he did so brazenly, without explanation or apology, that even caving was portrayed as an act of bold leadership. Above all, he has defended his decision to target Saddam Hussein even when some of the basic premises [weapons of mass destruction] of the war turned out to be wrong. He has continued to argue that he has set Iraq on the path to democracy even when others say its future is so much in doubt.[87]

As two journalists who sought to discover "why Bush doesn't budge" suggested, perhaps it was "the searing lesson of watching his father break a promise not to raise taxes and be fired for it."[88]

Barack H. Obama Typed

At the time this edition is being written, Barack Obama is in his second term of office. The first term was, at times, a difficult four years, in which Republicans won a majority in the House of Representatives and picked up seats in the Senate in the 2010 congressional elections. President Obama, however, remained resilient and during the brief lame duck session immediately following the election pushed Congress to end the military's "don't ask, don't tell policy," pass an $858 billion package of tax cuts and unemployment benefits, and approved the New Start nuclear treaty with Russia. His signature piece of legislation, the Affordable Health Care Act (which five earlier presidents tried and failed to pass) was challenged by congressional Republicans but deemed Constitutional by the Supreme Court in June 2012. This resiliency—what the president called his "persistence"—led Charles Krauthammer, a conservative commentator on Fox News, to label Barack Obama "the new comeback kid."[89] Just like the first comeback kid, Bill Clinton, Barack Obama demonstrates all of the qualities of an active positive president.

346 / Chapter Eleven

From his private study, the president pays courtesy calls to governors hit hard by the economic crisis. Feb. 4, 2009   White House Photo by Pete Souza

Activity: Energy Expended Doing the Job

Although Obama's demeanor is considerably calmer and cooler ("no drama Obama") than that of Bill Clinton, his level of energy is almost identical. Obama, as Clinton did, had many eighteen hour days during his first run for the presidency, which was the longest presidential campaign in American history. The "endless campaign," according to reporters, began on February 10, 2007, when Obama announced his candidacy and ended on election day November 4, 2008. Some pundits suggest that Obama's second campaign began on that day.

Barack Obama, an admitted "night owl," is no stranger to long hours. He has talked about a "painful year" writing his memoirs in which he slept only three or four hours a night. "There are," he later explained, "times when I want to do everything and be everything . . . . I want to have time to read and swim with the kids and not disappoint my voters and do a really careful job on each and everything that I do. And that can sometimes get me into trouble. That's historically been one of my bigger faults. I mean, I was trying to organize Project Vote at the same time as I was writing a book, and there are only so many hours in a day."[90]

His desire to do and be everything has resulted in many more near-sleepless nights during the first two years of his presidential term. A term which, according to biographer Jonathan Alter, began after the November 2008 election but before Obama took the presidential oath of office in January 2010.[91] Alter notes that although "Obama could not yet sign bills, issue executive orders, or sleep in the White House, . . . he was otherwise already discharging many of the functions of office: announcing personnel, receiving daily briefings on national security and the economy, negotiating with Congress, and holding as many as five press conferences a week.[92] In short, Alter states that beginning the day after the 2008 election Obama "made more big decisions than any president-elect in history.[93]

Actions taken during the president's first week in office included, but were not limited to:
- Signing executive orders restricting lobbyists; closing the detention center at Guantanamo Bay (as soon as possible) and lessening governmental secrecy
- Signing the Fair Pay Act for women
- Visiting the major departments
- Presenting to Congress a proposed agenda which included raising money for health care, a middle income tax cut, and limiting tax deductions for charitable contributions for those earning over $250,000.[94]

It wasn't long before legislators began to complain the president was too active and trying to do too much. As one Senator explained, "'Every time I think he's gonna step on the brake, he hits the gas.' TARP, the Recovery Act, equal pay for women, children's health, Afghanistan, bank bailouts, auto bailouts, national service, the new ambitious budget—When would the fire hose get turned off? Not soon."[95] By the end of the presidents' first year he "had fulfilled or made progress on nearly four hundred of five hundred campaign promises.[96]

Affect: Enjoyment of the Job

Clearly it is easier to spend long hours doing a job that is really liked, and Obama has always liked his. In an early presidential interview with one biographer he spoke about even "enjoy[ing]" just the day-to-day work of, you know, framing debates."[97] His upbeat and positive presidential campaign messages of "hope" and "change" and his belief in the creed that he feels "sums up the spirit of a people:

Yes, we can . . . ." are obviously rooted in that enjoyment of political life.
Yes, we can. Yes we can. Yes, we can.
It was a creed written into the founding documents that declared the destiny of a nation.
Yes, we can.
It was whispered by slaves and abolitionists as they blazed a trail toward freedom through the darkest of nights.
Yes, we can.
It was sung by immigrants as they struck out from distant shores and pioneers who pushed westward against an unforgiving wilderness.
Yes, we can.

It was the call of workers who organized, women who reached for the ballot, a president who chose the moon as our new frontier, and a king who took us to the mountain top and pointed the way to the Promised Land.

Yes, we can, to justice and equality.
Yes, we can, to opportunity and prosperity.

> Yes, we can heal this nation.
> Yes, we can repair this world.
> Yes, we can.[98]

These are the words of a "positive" politician. Perhaps the president put it best when he described himself at his first press conference on February 9th 2009. "I am," he said, "the eternal optimist."

The Socialization of an Active-Positive President: Barack H. Obama

Barack Obama was born on August 4, 1961, not quite a generation after the two presidents who preceded him, in Honolulu, Hawaii. His Hawaiian roots and upbringing, friends have said, explain his "unexcitable steadiness," his "peaceful state of mind" and his "acceptance of a variety of ideas and cultures."[99]

The acceptance of different ideas and cultures was also learned from his mother, Ann Soetora. Ann was an anthropologist who traveled widely throughout Africa and Asia, spoke Indonesian, Japanese, French and Urdu and married and divorced two men from two countries (Kenya and Indonesia.)[100] The son born from the first of these marriages, Barack Obama, admired not only his mother's appreciation of cultural diversity, he admired, perhaps even more, her ability to see what is good in people even when they did not meet her expectations. This quality, according to a biographer, is one that Barack shares and "imparts in his political speeches—that all of us are bound together as one, and if we are to prosper as a country and, indeed, as a species, that we must focus on the good we see in others."[101] And so, upon assuming the presidency, Obama…"came to office with what [has been] called the Reasonable Person Theory of Government. If he could simply sit down and talk with other political actors, whether they be Republicans from the House or mullahs from Tehran, he seemed certain he could work something out."[102] His persistent efforts to negotiate and compromise with recalcitrant political opponents was frustrating to many Democrats who may not have realized that the acceptance of ideas other than his own is an integral part of Barack Obama's character.

Obama has written that what is best in him he owes to his mother.[102] He is also keenly aware of his father's influence, attributing to him his own personal ambition and his high expectations of himself. As Obama explained, "every man is trying to live up to his father's expectations or make up for his mistakes. In my case, both things might be true."[103]

If what also seems to be true in the case of Barack Obama, which is that the unique combination of geography and genetics described above has resulted in an active-positive president, then he is well equipped to deal with the many difficult problems (jobs, the economy, the environment, immigration, gun safety, and terrorism) that still confront him. The successful resolution of these issues in his second term remains the challenge of the next four years of the Obama presidency.

Presidential Types and Leadership

The potential that a candidate has to succeed in providing the direction and guidance that voters want varies according to which of the four categories or types of presidential character, identified by Barber, that he fits into.

Active-Negatives

Barber says: "the best prediction . . . is that the relatively grim, intensely striving, onward-and-upward-through-thick-or-thin type is particularly liable—given ultimate political power—to play out the drama to its psychological conclusion."[104] This character type, which is prone to adhere rigidly to a losing policy, is the most likely to bring himself down in defeat. (Richard Nixon and Lyndon Johnson are good examples of this.)

Passive-Negatives

Barber says: "The trouble with the passive-negative type in the Presidency is that he leaves untapped the energizing, initiating, stimulating possibilities of the role. He is a responder; issues are 'brought to his attention'—and there are too damned many of them. Under the flag of legitimacy, the nation unites—and drifts. Presidential dignity is restored at the cost of Presidential leadership."[105]

Passive-Positives

Barber says: "The passive-positive types are political lovers. Considering what politics does to some of them, they do not often wind up as lovers of politics, at least in its rougher aspects. Like the reluctant passive-negatives, they are responders, not initiators or pushers, but they go about their work with a different demeanor, an appearance of affectionate hopefulness. . . . The passive-positive type lives in a marketplace of affection, trading bright hellos for smiles in return. What threatens the fragile structure of that adaptation is conflict and particularly conflict at close quarters . . . . The passive-positive character is built around surfaces: when the surface begins to crack, collapse is imminent."[106]

Active-Positives

Barber says: "Their apparent happiness in what they do—as Presidents—stands out in contrast to the defenses other Presidents cling to. Each has shown in his own way these qualities: . . . . he is fully able to meet the challenges of the job . . . he learns quickly . . . . [he has] a sense of the future as possible . . . [and] a repertoire of habits. The active-positive President uses a variety of styles, moving flexibly among a number of modes of political action. Such a President seems to base his self-definition on ground deeper than the collection of stylistic approaches he has put together over the years. His style is a bag of tools, not a way of life."[107]

Although there are no guarantees, and there have been notable exceptions, such as Carter and Bush senior, of the four types of presidential character identified by Barber, active-positives are likely to provide the most effective political leadership.

CONCLUSION

Two major perspectives or ways of examining the presidency were discussed in this chapter. The presidency was first looked at as a job that is described, somewhat ambiguously, in Article II of the

Constitution. That Article sets down the necessary qualifications for aspirants to the office, and it describes the process by which presidential elections are to be conducted. It also specifies the major presidential powers and duties. Presidential responsibilities are more commonly referred to simply as "roles." These roles, some aspects of which have only been implied in the words "he shall take Care that the Laws be faithfully executed" (Article II, Section 3), include: Chief of State, Chief Executive, Commander in Chief, Chief Diplomat, and Chief Legislator.

A second perspective taken by experts on the subject of the presidency is one that focuses on the person or the personality/character of the individual who does the job rather than on the job itself. From this point of view there is a clear distinction that can be made between leaders (men that have been elected to occupy the oval office and are leaders in name only) and leadership (the personal quality or ability of some of those men to provide direction and guidance). This distinction is sometimes expressed in terms of "headship" v. "leadership."

Leadership, according to Robert Shogan, consists of three interacting qualities: ideology, values, and character. All three, as was shown in the cases of Presidents Carter and George H. W. Bush, are necessary for success. James David Barber places his emphasis primarily on only one of these qualities—character. His contention is that the "active-positive" character type has the best potential as president to provide successful leadership.

It is useful for anyone who reads about and studies the presidency to try to keep in mind that the two perspectives are like the two sides of a coin: virtually impossible to divide and, if separated, without much practical value.

CHAPTER NOTES

[1] Lloyd Robinson, *The Stolen Election: Hayes versus Tilden—1876* (New York: Doubleday & Company, Inc., 1968), 118.

[2] Roosevelt to George Otto Trevelyan, June 19, 1908, *The Letters of Theodore Roosevelt*, ed. Elting E. Morison (Cambridge: Harvard University Press, 1952), vol. 6, 1087; quoted in James MacGregor Burns, *Presidential Government: The Crucible of Leadership* (New York: Avon Books, 1965), 73, n. 29.

[3] Woodrow Wilson, *Congressional Government* (New York: Houghton, Mifflin and Co., 1885.)

[4] Clinton Rossiter, *The American Presidency* (New York: New American Library, 1956), 10.

[5] Ibid, 11.

[6] *The New York Times*, 13 September 2001, 16(A).

[7] Quoted in Arthur Bernon Tourtellot, *The Presidents on the Presidency* (Garden City, N.Y.: Doubleday & Company, Inc., 1964), 137.

[8] President's Committee on Administrative Management, *Administrative Management in the Government of the United States* (Government Printing Office, 1937), 5.

[9] Stephen Hess, *Organizing the Presidency* (Washington, D.C.: The Brookings Institution, 1976), 1-2.

[10] Franklin Delano Roosevelt, "Message on Reorganizing the Executive Branch, January 12, 1937," in Tourtellot, 124.

[11] Fred I. Greenstein, "The Need for an Early Appraisal of the Reagan Presidency, in *The Reagan Presidency: An Early Assessment*, ed. Fred I. Greenstein (Baltimore, Maryland: The Johns Hopkins University Press, 1983), 12.

[12] Arthur M. Schlesinger, Jr., *The Imperial Presidency* (Boston, Massachusetts: Houghton Mifflin Company, 1973), 222-223.

[13] Richard M. Pious, *The Presidency* (Boston, Massachusetts: Allyn and Bacon, 1996), 277.

[14] Schlesinger, 5.

[15] Tourtellot, 328.
[16] Edward S. Corwin, *Presidential Power and the Constitution: Essays*, ed. Richard Loss (Ithaca, New York: Cornell University Press, 1976), 113.
[17] The "National Security Strategy of the United States," October 2002.
[18] Robert E. DiClerico, *The American President*, (Englewood Cliffs, New Jersey: Prentice-Hall, 1995), 38-45.
[19] Schlesinger, 7.
[20] Michael Nelson, ed., *Congressional Quarterly's Guide to the Presidency* (Washington, D.C.: CQ, 1989), 510.
[21] Tourtellot, 185-187.
[22] Ibid., 245.
[23] October 2003.
[24] *The New York Times*, 1 August 1996, 22 (A).
[25] DiClerico, 87-92.
[26] Harold M. Barger, *The Impossible Presidency: Illusions and Realities of Executive Power* (Glenview, Illinois: Scott, Foresman and Company, 1984), 100.
[27] Clinton Rossiter, *The American Presidency*, revised ed. (New York: Harcourt, Brace & World, Inc., 1960), 41.
[28] James MacGregor Burns, *Leadership* (New York: Harper & Row, Publishers, 1978), 2.
[29] See Michael B. Binford, "Decision Making and Participation: An Exercise," *News: For Teachers of Political Science* 41 (Spring 1984): 26-27.
[30] Robert Michels, *Political Parties: A Sociological Study of the Oligarchical Tendencies of Modern Democracy* (New York: The Free Press, 1962), 364. Michels, a sociologist who studied the behavior of political elites, refers to this phenomenon of the need for leadership in all organizations, even the most democratic ones, as the "iron law of oligarchy."
[31] Barbara Kellerman, "Leadership as a Political Act," in *Leadership: Multidisciplinary Perspectives*, ed. Barbara Kellerman (Englewood Cliffs, New Jersey: Prentice-Hall, Inc., 1984), 70-71.
[32] Robert Shogan, *The Riddle of Power: Presidential Leadership from Truman to Bush* (New York: A Dutton Book, 1991).
[33] Ibid., 6-7.
[34] Ibid., 205.
[35] Betty Glad, *Jimmy Carter: In Search of the Great White House* (New York: W.W.Norton & Company, 1980), 312.
[36] Shogan, 198.
[37] Jimmy Carter, *Keeping Faith: Memoirs of a President* (Toronto, Canada: Bantam Books, 1982), 20.
[38] Glad, 488-493; Shogan, 207-211.
[39] James Fallows, quoted in James David Barber, *The Presidential Character: Predicting Performance in the White House* (Englewood Cliffs, New Jersey: Prentice Hall, 1992), 447.
[40] Ibid.
[41] Betty Glad, "How George Bush Lost the Presidential Election of 1992," in *The Clinton Presidency: Campaigning. Governing, & the Psychology of Leadership*, ed. Stanley A. Renshon (Boulder, Colorado: Westview Press, 1995), 33; Shogan, 264.
[42] Shogan, 265.
[43] Ibid., 259.
[44] R.W. Apple Jr., "In His Various Defining Moments, Has Bush Clearly Defined Himself?" *The New York Times*, 23 February 1992, Section 4, 1.
[45] Shogan, 269 and 272.
[46] Sidney Blumenthal, *Pledging Allegiance: The Last Campaign of the Cold War* (New York, HarperCollins, 1993), 62; quoted in Glad, "How George Bush Lost the Election," 31.
[47] Glad, "How George Bush Lost the Election," 25.
[48] Ibid., 22.
[49] George Bush, *Looking Forward: An Autobiography* (New York: Doubleday, 1987), 193.
[50] James David Barber, *The Presidential Character: Predicting Performance in the White House*, 4th ed. (Englewood Cliffs, New Jersey: Prentice Hall, 1992.)
[51] Ibid., 1.

[52] Ibid., 8.
[53] Ibid., 10.
[54] Ibid., 9-10.
[55] Fred I. Greenstein, "Political Style and Political Leadership: The Case of Bill Clinton," 144.
[56] Thomas L. Friedman, "Ready or Not, Clinton Is Rattling the Country," *The New York Times*, 31 January 1993, Sec. 4 (1).
[57] Douglas Jehl, "Weary Clinton Takes Break From His Own Frenetic Style," *The New York Times*, 15 August 1993, 1 (A).
[58] Michael Kelly, "Clinton's 4-Day Holiday: Exhaustive Relaxation," *The New York Times*, 1December 92, 9 (B).
[59] Ibid.
[60] "Excerpts from President Clinton's Wide-Ranging News Conference." *The New York Times*. 22 July 1999, 17 (A).
[61] Maureen Dowd, "On Health, Clinton Finds Heaven Is in the Details," *The New York Times*, 25 September 1993, 1(A) and 8(A).
[62] "Voice Is Strained, but Support on the Trail Unstinting," *The New York Times*, 5 November 2012, 9(A).
[63] Dowd, ibid.
[64] Hugh Sidey, preface to *George Bush: An Intimate Portrait*, by Fitzhugh Green (New York: Hippocrene Books, 1989), xii.
[65] Barber, 11.
[66] David Maraniss, *First in His Class: A Biography of Bill Clinton* (New York: Simon & Schuster, 1995), 38.
[67] Ibid.
[68] Charles F. Allen and Jonathan Portis, *The Life and Career of Bill Clinton: The Comeback Kid* (New York: Carol Publishing Group, 1992), 11-12; George Carpozi, Jr., *Clinton Confidential: The Climb to Power* (Del Mar, California, Emery Dalton Books; 1995), 21-22; Meredith L. Oakley, *On the Make: The Rise of Bill Clinton* (Washington, D.C.: Regnery Publishing, Inc., 1994), 32-33.
[69] Barber, 7.
[70] Todd S. Purdum, "The Incumbent as a Riddle: William Jefferson Clinton," *The New York Times*, 29 August 1996, 13 (B).
[71] J. H. Hatfield, *Fortunate Son: George W. Bush and the Making of an American President* (New York: Soft Skull Press, 2000), 167.
[72] Ibid., 276.
[73] Ibid., 275.
[74] John Leland, "To Loaf or Not to Loaf," *The New York Times Magazine*, 17 December 2000, 26.
[75] Frank Bruni, "Presidency Takes Shape With No Fuss, No Sweat," *The New York Times*, 10 February 2001, 1(A).
[76] Ibid.
[77] Molly Ivins and Lou Dubose, *Shrub: The Short But Happy Political Life of George W. Bush* (New York: Vintage Books, 2000).
[78] Bill Minutaglio, *First Son: George W. Bush and the Bush Family Dynasty* (New York: Times Books, 1999), 95.
[79] George W. Bush, *A Charge to Keep: My Journey to the White House* (New York: Perennial, 2001), 21.
[80] Ibid., 197.
[81] Ibid., 103-4.
[82] NBC. 23 January 2002. "The Bush White House: Inside the Real West Wing." Tom Brokaw.
[83] Ibid.
[84] Ibid.
[85] Hatfield, 22.
[86] Nicholas D. Kristof, "A Father's Footsteps Echo Throughout a Son's Career," *The New York Times*, 11 September 2000, 16 (A).
[87] Ibid., 16 (A).
[88] Nancy Gibbs and John F. Dickerson, "Inside the Mind of George W. Bush: For This President, The Essence of Wisdom Lies In Knowing Whe Change," *Time*, September 6, 2004, p. 28.
[89] Ibid.
[90] Frank Rich, "Let Obama's Reagan Revolution Begin," *The New York Times*, 9 January 2011, 10 (WK).

[91] David Mendell, "Interview with Obama October 2004," in *Obama: From Promise To Power* (New York: Harper Collins Publishers, 2007), 103-104.
[92] Jonathan Alter, *The Promise: President Obama, Year One*, (New York: Simon & Schuster, 2010.)
[93] Ibid.,78.
[94] Ibid., Picture Caption.
[95] Ibid., 112.
[96] Ibid., 137.
[97] Ibid., Picture Caption.
[98] Mendell, 146
[99] Barack Obama, "Excerpts from Speech, January 8, 2008," reprinted in *Newsweek Commemorative Issue*, 67.
[100] Jeff Zeleny, "Obama's Zen State, Well, it's Hawaiian," *The New York Times* 25 December 2008, 14(A).
[101] Amanda Ripley, "A Mother's Story," *Time*, April 21, 2008, p.40.
[102] "4 Years Later, Scarred but Still Confident," *The New York Times*, 6 September, 2012, 15(A).
[103] Mendell, p.27.
[104] Ripley, p.36.
[105] Mendell, pp.39-40.
[106] Barber,122.
[107] Ibid., 193.
[108] Ibid., 195 and 223.
[109] Ibid., 267.

SUGGESTED READINGS

Barber, James David. *The Presidential Character: Predicting Performance in the White House*, 4th ed. Englewood Cliffs, N.J.: Prentice Hall, 1992.

Barger, Harold M. *The Impossible Presidency: Illusions and Realities of Executive Power*. Glenview, Ill.: Scott, Foresman and Company, 1984.

Burns, James MacGregor. *Leadership*. New York: Harper & Row, Publishers, 1978.

_____. *Presidential Government: The Crucible of Leadership*. New York: Avon Books, 1965.

George, Alexander L., and Juliette L. George. *Presidential Personality and Performance*. Boulder: Westview Press, 1998.

Hinckley, Barbara. *The Symbolic Presidency: How Presidents Portray Themselves*. New York: Rutledge, 1990.

Jacobson, Gary C. *A Divider, Not a Uniter: George W. Bush and the American People*. New York: Pearson Education, Inc., 2007.

Pious, Richard M. *The Presidency*. Boston, Mass.: Allyn and Bacon, 1996.

Renshon, Stanley A., ed. *The Clinton Presidency: Campaigning, Governing, & the Psychology of Leadership*. Boulder: Westview Press, 1995.

Rossiter, Clinton. *The American Presidency*. New York: Harcourt, Brace & World, Inc., 1956.

Schlesinger, Arthur M. Jr. *The Imperial Presidency*. Boston, Mass.: Houghton Mifflin Company, 1973.

Wayne, Stephen J. *Personality and Politics: Obama for and against Himself*. Washington, D.C.: CQPress, 2011.

Chapter Twelve

THE FEDERAL COURT SYSTEM

The necessity of a body of rules and regulations to govern the day-to-day operations of a village, city, town, empire or nation state as well as to set the standards for appropriate behavior of any society is as old as civilization itself. A nation without law is a lawless one, riddled with injustices whereby no one can ever feel secure in their surroundings. It is a truism that governments cannot exist without laws; and laws cannot exist without government to implement and enforce them upon the citizenry. As Theodore Roosevelt once commented:

> No nation ever yet retained its freedom for any length of time after losing its respect for the law, after losing the law-abiding spirit, the spirit that really makes orderly liberty. . . . No man is above the law and no man is below it; nor do we ask any man's permission when we require him to obey it. Obedience to the law is demanded as a right; not asked as a favor.[1]

This chapter examines the development of law and the impact law has on the American judicial system, particularly, the federal justice and judicial systems.

During the summer of 2013, all eyes were focused on the nine justices of the Supreme Court who were hearing arguments from both sides of the issue regarding the constitutionality of the federal government's Defense of Marriage Act, as well as a ruling on Presidents Obama's Affordable Care Act. Most Americans view the Supreme Court as the definitive arm of the federal judiciary system. The media only covers the most controversial cases heard by the Court. This overlooks that during its 2010 session alone, there were 9,066 cases filed for the Supreme Court's consideration.[2] Yet, this body of nine is just one of the many federal courts that decide both appellate and original jurisdiction cases. In turn, the caseload before these courts is staggering. For example, the docket for 2010 reveals that 56,097 cases were heard in the Courts of Appeals, 285,215 by U.S. District Courts in civil matters, 78,213 in criminal matters, and U.S. Bankruptcy Courts handled 1,572,597 cases.[3]

Behind the scenes are the numerous individuals employed in the investigation of federal criminal and civil offenses. With over forty agencies assigned under its umbrella, the United States Department of Justice employees approximately 114,451 operating under a $31.2 billion budget for fiscal year 2013.[4] This chapter examines the federal justice system beginning with the investigation and gathering of evidence phase to the final decision rendered by the juries and judges.

LAW—THE GUIDING PRINCIPLE OF JUSTICE

Law is simply "a body of rules enacted by public officials in a legitimate manner and backed by the force of the state."[5] The importance of law cannot be underestimated. A Roman jurist and noted statesman, Cicero (106-43 B.C.) wrote that:

> law is the highest reason, implanted in Nature, which commands what ought to be done and forbids the opposite . . . the origin of justice is to be found in law, for law is it's natural force; it is the mind and reason of the intelligent man, the standards by which justice and injustice are measured.[6]

However, there is no universal or standard body of law applicable to all of mankind. Each society has had to develop its own body of laws. A nation's set of laws is unique to that nation, perhaps the ultimate embodiment of that particular nation's history, social mores and folkways, cultural perspectives, moral values, religious perspectives, and political viewpoints. Throughout many nations in the Middle East, the development of their laws and legal systems is directly tied to Islam for there is no separation of church and state. In the United States, separation of church and state means that while religious values and morals are important to the American people, they are not the driving force in the creation of the laws that rule over them. In addition, the degree of enforcement of law varies from nation state to nation state. For example, the United States imposes the death penalty for heinous criminal acts while many other nations have either abolished the death penalty or never imposed it in the first place.

Laws are only meaningful if all members subject to the laws have a clear understanding of the nature of the laws, the criteria for obedience of those laws, and the penalties for one's disobedience. "Law comprises three basic elements—force, official authority, regularity—the combination which differentiates law from mere custom or morals in a society."[7] The legitimacy of any government, regardless of the political philosophy underlying it, must have the ability to both make and enforce laws. People respect their nation's right to make laws if that government, in turn, makes sure their laws are both necessary and reasonable. Of equal importance, governments must enforce those laws in an equitable, fair, and consistent manner. As evidenced in Chapters 13 and 14, the United States Supreme Court's docket is filled with cases focusing on laws that are claimed to be procedurally and substantially questionable. Justice is not served when laws are vaguely written and enforced unfairly and unequally. The statute in front of the United States Supreme Court building in Washington, D.C., depicts Lady Justice. She wears a blindfold over her eyes to remind everyone that in the eyes of the law, everyone is equal regardless of who you are and what status you hold in society.

Codification of Law

In the ancient world, the growth of villages, towns and cities mandated a higher authority to make and enforce rules upon the citizenry. The Sumerians developed a rudimentary code of laws. The credit for the initial codification of those laws belongs to Babylonian King Hammurabi who compiled a concise listing of over 282 laws. The Babylonian empire had a strict system of justice, oftentimes not equally applied. "A crime against a member of the upper class (a noble) by a member of the lower class (a commoner) was punished more severely than the same offense against a member of the lower class."[8] Well known for its emphasis of "an eye for an eye," the Code's punishments were harsh. For example, according to No. 25: "if fire broke out in a free man's house and a free man, who went to extinguish it, cast his eye on the goods of the owner of the house and has appropriated the goods of the owner of the house, that free man shall be thrown into that fire."[9] Justinian (527-565), Emperor of the Eastern Roman Empire, codified Roman law into the *Corpus Luris Civilis* (Latin for *The Body of Civil Law*).

In 1066, William the Conqueror of Normandy successfully invaded and conquered Great Britain. He soon discovered that British laws were haphazardly applied for the same crime depending upon the shire in which the crime was committed. He codified these laws and standardized the penalties. Kings Henry I and Henry II continued the codification process. Consequently, "the term 'common' law was used for the law developed in the King's Courts and was generally employed in order to distinguish between it and that of the ecclesiastical courts," commonly known as **canon law**.[10] Henry II went a step further requiring judges to put in writing the details of the cases they heard and the rational for their decisions. Thus, the judges began to use **precedents** whereby they would find "a case previously decided that serves as a legal guide for the resolution of subsequent cases" similar to the one currently under their consideration.[11] This practice gives legitimacy to the body of the law, underscores the necessity of laws and, if found guilty, the punishments are equally, fairly and consistently applied. Judicial precedents are based on the Latin term ***stare decisis***, meaning "'let the decision stand'; the legal principle that once a precedent is established, all similar cases should be decided the same way."[12] Henry II also required that his judges travel throughout the countryside trying cases in remote areas rather than holding court in major cities. Thus, Henry is credited with the practice of using traveling or **circuit judges**. A cornerstone of the American judicial system, precedents gives a judge the confidence that the decisions rendered in his/her court are validated by previous court rulings. Judges are less likely to stray from *stare decisis* since an errant or unsubstantiated ruling that clearly violates the protected constitutional rights of the accused can be appealed to a higher state or federal court for review with the possibility of the judge's ruling being overturned.

The application of precedents was vital to the codification of **common law** defined as "law developed in England by judges who made legal decisions in absence of written law. Such decisions served as precedents and became 'common' to all in England. Common law is judge-made, it uses precedent, and it is found in multiple sources."[13] Underscoring the importance of common law to the legitimacy of any judicial system, Associate Justice of the U. S. Supreme Court from 1902 to 1932 Oliver Wendell Homes wrote in his *The Common Law* (1881):

The life of the law has not been logic; it has been experience. The felt necessities of the time, the prevalent moral and political theories, institutions of public policy, avowed or unconscious, even the prejudices which judges share with their fellow men, save had a good deal more to do than syllogism in determining the rules by which men should be governed. The law embodies the story of a nation's development through the many centuries, and it cannot be dealt with as if it contained only axioms and corollaries of a book of mathematics. In order to know what it is, we must know what is has been, and what it tends to become . . . the very considerations which judges rarely mention, and always with an apology, are the secret roots from which the law draws all the juices of life. I mean, of course, considerations of what is expedient for the community concerned.[14]

Closely akin to common law, **equity law** begins where the law ends. Basically, "equity leaves the judge reasonably free to order *preventive* measures—and under some circumstances even *remedial* ones—usually in the form of a writ, such as an *injunction*, or restraining order, designed to afford a remedy not otherwise obtainable, and traditionally given upon a showing of peril."[15] A **writ** is "an order in writing issued by a court ordering the performance of an act or prohibiting some act."[16] For example, judges can order that children be removed from a home pending the conclusion of a divorce and child custody hearings or issue protective orders to prevent alleged spousal abusers from having any contact with the abused party. Judges can also issue an **injunction** defined as "an order issued by a court in an equity proceeding to compel or restrain the performance of an act by an individual or government official. Violation of an injunction constitutes contempt of court, punishable by fine or imprisonment."[17] Federal judges frequently use injunctions to halt a state law or ordinance from taking effect while it is under the Court's review.

Additional bodies of law include **constitutional law** that is the compilation of all court rulings on the meaning of the various words, phrases, and clauses in the United States Constitution."[18] Bureaucratic agencies are tasked with the implementation of congressional acts. Usually the law empowers the agencies to implement new laws but leaves the details of how to administer these laws up to the agencies. Thus, **administrative law** is "that branch of law that creates administrative agencies, establishes their methods of procedures, and determines the scope of judicial review of agency practices and actions."[19]

THE TERMINOLOGY AND PROCESS OF THE JUSTICE SYSTEM

The primary charge of the federal justice system is to enforce laws as prescribed by the United States Congress. These laws fall into two broad categories. **Civil law** "deals with the disagreements between individuals, for example, a dispute over ownership of private property."[20] The parties involved in a civil suit are the **plaintiff** who initiates the grievance and the **defendant**, the person accused of causing harm to either the person of or to the property of the plaintiff. Civil litigation usually involves disputes over contracts, domestic and business relations, destruction of property, medical malpractice, and fraud. In the American judicial system, a conviction in a civil case is based upon the **preponderance of the evidence** defined as "the standard of proof required to prevail at trial. To win, the plaintiff must show that the greater weight or preponderance of the evidence supports his/her version of the facts."[21] The focus of a civil suit is to determine whether the defendant's actions were negligent towards the plaintiff. **Negligence** is "carelessness or the failure to use ordinary care, under the particular circumstances revealed by the evidence in the lawsuit."[22] The plaintiff is seeking a remedy that is the "vindication of a claim of right; a legal procedure by which a right is enforced or the violation of a right is prevented or compensated."[23] The remedy is usually a monetary settlement or a tort granted to the injured party (the plaintiff), a fine paid to the courts by the defendant, or, in some instances, the defendant can be given a prison term plus a fine. **Tort law** is "the law of civil wrongs. It concerns conduct that causes injury and fails to measure up to some standard set by society."[24] If negligence is established, the question arises as to the monetary value of the remedy. Usually, this involves two steps. For example, in January 2014, a plant in West Virginia owned by Freedman Industries suffered a major chemical spill that poured toxic substances into the Elk River, the sole source of water for that area, resulting in over 300,000 residents unable to drink, bathe, or even wish dishes and clothes for several days. The Environmental Protection Agency (EPA) surely wanted to hold the company liable for the damages. The question is not whether the company was responsible for it was their company that polluted that river. The question is how much monetary damages are due to the residents and what will the sanctions levied by the EPA cost the company for its violation of federal water pollution laws. The first step would involve reimbursing the residents for the current damage caused by the chemical spill. What is more difficult to determine is future monetary loss. The adverse impact of a chemical spill could take years or decades to determine. On both the national and state political level, Republican candidates have pushed for the enactment of tort reform citing that companies simply cannot afford to pay large monetary settlements. The Civil Rights Division of the Justice Department can charge and try a person for violations of another's civil rights. Here again, the initial remedy addresses current damage (i.e., physical injuries, identifiable mental issues); however, the hardest question is how much should the defendant pay to the plaintiff for future physical impairment related to the initial injury and/or the possibility of reoccurring or to be discovered issues.

Criminal law is the embodiment of "offenses against the state itself—actions that may be directed against a person but that are deemed to be offensive to society as a whole."[25] A conviction of criminal charges is based on guilt **beyond a reasonable doubt**. In other words, a member of a jury or the judge cannot render a guilty verdict if he/she has any doubt of the person's guilt. A criminal violation is categorized according to the severity of the action. A **felony** is "a serious crime punishable by death or by imprisonment in a penitentiary for a year or more."[26] According to Section 3559, United States Code, Title 18, there are five levels of a federal felony offenses:

- Class A felony—life imprisonment, or if the maximum penalty is death.
- Class B felony—25 years or more.
- Class C felony—less than 25 years but more than 10 years.
- Class D felony—less than 10 years but more than 5 years.
- Class E felony—less than 5 years but more than 1 year.
- All classes carry a maximum fine of $250,000.[27]

A **misdemeanor** is "a minor criminal offense."[28] The U.S. Department of Justice has four levels of misdemeanor offenses:

- Class A misdemeanor—1 year or less but no more than 6 months and a maximum fine of $100,000.
- Class B misdemeanor—6 months or less but no more than 30 days and a possible fine of $5,000.
- Class C misdemeanor—30 days or less but no more than 5 days and a possible fine of $5,000.
- Infraction—5 days or less, or if no imprisonment is authorized, a possible fine of $5,000.[29]

A more detailed overview of the protected constitutional rights of the accused is addressed in Chapter 12—Civil Liberties. However, the proper execution of the investigation of any criminal activity is vital to securing a conviction whether the case is tried in a federal or state court. The most vital component part to the judicial process is the initial investigation of the crime scene to include the gathering of evidence, apprehending and interrogating the suspect(s), and building a solid case against the accused. By the time a case does go to trial, federal agents could have the best of the nation's federal prosecutors, but if the evidence gathered by the investigative teams was flawed or compromised, then the prosecution will lose the case. Unlike a city or state police force, federal investigative agents have the best equipment, the most advanced forensics laboratories in the nation, and the best trained personnel. The likelihood of federal prosecutors not winning a case is marginal in comparison to state legal systems. But occasionally, they do indeed lose a case due to flawed investigative techniques and compromised evidence.

The majority of the problems for any level of law enforcement have centered on both the investigative and pre-trail actions from illegal search warrants, improper wiretapping, illegal interrogation techniques, and coerced confessions. In particular, the legalities of the search warrant and the interrogation process can be problematic. A **search warrant** is "a written document signed by a judge or magistrate, authorizing a law enforcement officer to conduct a search."[30] Under normal circumstances, a search must be conducted with the 4th Amendment to the Constitution in mind, which clearly states that there must be a **probable cause**, that is a "set of facts and circumstances that would induce a reasonably intelligent prudent person to believe a particular person had committed a specific crime or reasonable grounds to make or to believe an accusation."[31] In addition, the evidence recovered through the search should be directly tied to the specific criminal action detailed in the warrant. If evidence has been improperly seized or it is not tied to the charge at hand, then the judge will evoke the **exclusionary rule**, meaning "evidence which is otherwise admissible may not be used in a criminal trial if it is a product of illegal police conduct."[32] To avoid this possibility from happening, the officer seeking a warrant should under normal circumstances prepare an application for a warrant that indicates the reason for the search, the location of the search, and the items sought through the search. Once signed by a federal magistrate, the federal officer can now use the warrant to conduct the search.

But what if the officer believes that by the time he/she obtains the warrant, the evidence sought will have disappeared or have been destroyed? In this situation, law enforcement can conduct an on the spot **warrantless search**. If the owner of the property to a search grants permission, the search can take place without an official warrant. With or without warrant, evidence seized during a search is legal if it is in **plain view**. For example, a Drug Enforcement Agent (DEA) is conducting a search for illegal drugs. In plain view of his sight is an operating Meth Lab. This agent can seize the equipment and charge the defendant with an additional violation since the object in question was indeed in plain sight of the agent. However, if in the course of the search, the agent finds Meth Lab equipment hidden in the back of a closet, then it is questionable whether the additional charges will be upheld in court. Also, there are situations that occur when in the process of a search, an agent will seize items directly linked to the criminal act but were not listed on the warrant. This constitutes a **good faith exception** to seize the evidence. In *Illinois v Krull* (1967), the Supreme Court did rule that the good faith exception did apply to warrantless searches. However, agents must be careful to ensure that the evidence seized is definitely tied to a criminal act or the defendant's legal team will attempt to rule the evidence as inadmissible during pre- and trial proceedings.

Another area of concern is the interrogation of the suspect. **Investigative** questioning can continue without legal representative present. Yet, when the investigative questioning shifts to accusatory questioning, the process must stop immediately if the accused evokes his/her right to legal counsel (**Minnick v Mississippi, 1990**). Any confession obtained through physical or psychological coercion is inadmissible in court. Oftentimes, the accused will agree to confess to the criminal charge before him/her as part of a plea agreement. **Plea bargaining** is "the process through which a defendant pleads guilty to a criminal charge with the expectation of receiving some consideration from the state."[33] While critics charge that plea bargaining is used by defendants as a convenient way to avoid trial or a lengthy prison term by just promising to provide law enforcement additional information, law enforcement sees numerous advantages to it. First, agents have gotten what they wanted in the first place—a confession that taken voluntarily will hold up in court. Second, it surely saves the federal government the time and money of a trial. More importantly, the agreement can lead to the apprehension of an individual that committed a more serious crime. Federal law enforcement has used the **witness protection program** as an effective bargaining chip to gain evidence leading towards the arrest and conviction of leaders of organized crime such as the Mafia and drug cartels. At any time during the interrogation process, federal agents can issue an **arrest warrant**, "a document issued by a judicial officer directing a law enforcement officer to arrest an identified person who has been accused of a specific crime. For an arrest warrant to be issued there must be either a sworn complaint or evidence of probable cause that the person being arrested committed a crime.[34]

The Constitution does mandate that anyone accused of a crime must be informed of the charges against him/her within a reasonable period of time. The initial **appearance** of the accused occurs within a few hours or days following the initial arrest. Usually for misdemeanor offenses, the accused merely enters a plea and the magistrate disposes of the case. A federal magistrate is "a minor judicial officer who holds preliminary hearings in federal criminal cases, issues arrest warrants, sets bail, and, if the parties consent, holds jury and nonjury trials in civil cases or in criminal misdemeanor cases and supervises the selection of jurors in felony cases."[35] For felony charges, a plea at this stage is not allowed. Once the **charging document** detailing the particulars of the charges has been presented, the accused is presented at the **arraignment**, a "hearing before a court having jurisdiction in a criminal case, in which the identity of the defendant is established, the defendant is informed of his/her rights, and the defendant is required to enter a plea."[36] A defendant can avoid a trial by entering in a ***nolo contendere plea***, a "Latin phrase meaning 'I will not contest it.' A plea of 'no contest' in a criminal case means that the defendant does not directly admit guilt but submits to sentencing or other punishment."[37] It is up to the discretion of the judge to either sentence the defendant at that moment or opt to hold a sentencing hearing at a later date. If the defendant enters a not guilty plea, then the judge will determine the disposition of the defendant pending trial by either granting **bail** (a cash payment for release), releasing the defendant on **personal recognizance** based on the lack of a prior criminal record, employment, ties to the community, and not deemed at a flight risk, or **remand** in jail until after the preliminary hearing whereby a judge will determine whether to grant bail or to continue to remand the defendant until and during trial. At this juncture of the process, the defendant is asked whether or not he/she has obtained legal counsel. If the defendant indicates he/she cannot afford to hire a personal attorney, the federal courts will use the **assigned counsel system** whereby the judge will provide an attorney selected from a list of qualified attorneys paid at public cost to represent the defendant. Attorneys whether privately acquired or court appointed, can opt to take the case on ***pro bono public***, a Latin phrase meaning for the public good. Often abbreviated to *pro bono*, it usually stands for work done by lawyers without pay for some charitable or public purpose."[38] With the exception of providing testimony at trial, the role of federal investigative agents has ended.

An intermediate step, a **federal grand jury** is tasked with the chore of reviewing the prosecution's evidence before the trial begins. The notion of a grand jury is a product of English law under King Henry II. The 5th Amendment to the Constitution states that "no person shall be held to answer for a capital, otherwise infamous crime, unless on a presentment or indictment of a grand jury." While states have the option to use a grand jury, the federal judicial system does not have the option. Grand juries are impaneled for a specified period of time, usually three to six months. Composed of at least six members, panelists are drawn from different walks of life. They do not meet daily but will convene periodically or on an as needs basis. The functions of a grand jury have been described as the shield and sword of the judicial system. "Shield refers to the protections the grand jury offers, serving as a buffer between the state and its citizens, preventing the government from using the criminal process against its enemies. Sword refers to the investigatory powers of this body."[39] Grand juries have considerable investigative authority in that they can issue a **subpoena**, "an order of a court, grand jury, legislative body or committee, or any duly authorized administrative agency, compelling the attendance of a person."[40] Furthermore, a *subpoena duces tecum* could be issued requiring the individual to produce specific documents pertinent to the case under consideration. A witness failing to appear can be charged with contempt, resulting in a fine, imprisonment, or both. Grand juries can also grant witnesses immunity from further prosecution if their testimony will lead to possible criminal charges against them. The most generous is **transitional immunity** that provides "absolute protection against prosecution for any event or transaction about which a witness is compelled to give testimony or furnish evidence."[41] After its investigation, the grand jury will render a decision. A **true bill** is "an indictment made and endorsed by a grand jury when it finds that there is sufficient evidence to bring a person to trial."[42] However, if the grand jury determines that the evidence presented is not sufficient enough for a jury trial, they will issue a **no bill** decision. With a no bill decision, the prosecution has the opportunity to gather additional evidence to secure a true bill, or release the defendant.

If a trial does take place, the defendant has the opportunity to ask for a non-jury trial, whereby the evidence against him/her is presented to a judge who then renders his/her decision or proceed to a jury trial. A federal trial jury pool is impaneled for a month with prospective jurors checking usually every Sunday evening to determine whether they need to report the next morning. Since federal court districts can extend over several counties, the federal court system reimburses jurors for the commute and, if selected, for jury service, their hotel/motel and meal expenses if the commute is a certain distance from the federal courthouse. The selection process of a federal trial jury is the same used for state jury service. The jury pool is narrowed by a series of **peremptory challenges** from both the defense and prosecution attorneys to eliminate jurors without stating a specific reason. Additional questions from both sides will continue to eliminate jurors to the required number of usually twelve. Once the jury has been selected, the presiding judge will issue the official charge to the jury members. To ensure a fair and impartial trial, judges may issue a **gag order**, "a judge's order that lawyers and witnesses not discuss the trial with outsiders."[43] A juror that compromises the order will be removed from the panel, which can lead to the defense ordering the judge to declare a mistrial. For high profile cases, federal judges can grant a **change of venue**, which is "the movement of a case from the jurisdiction of one court to that of another court that has the same subject-matter jurisdiction but is in a different geographical location."[44]

After the presentation of the evidence from both the defense and prosecution, the state will rest its case, allowing the judge to charge the jury with the instructions of deliberation. Usually, the judge informs the jury of its sentencing options, if indeed, they find the defendant guilty. The sentence should match the severity of the crime, if not the case could very well be appealed to a higher court. Judges oftentimes will issue a **determinate sentence** that carries "a term of imprisonment that has a specific number of years."[45]

THE FEDERAL JUSTICE SYSTEM

Like state judicial systems, the federal justice system is composed of four primary entities. Unlike state judicial systems, three of the four parts fall under the direction of the U.S. Department of Justice headed by one person—the United States Attorney General. The investigative arm is charged with the apprehension, investigation, and charging of individuals suspected of committing a federal felony or misdemeanor offense. The prosecuting arm of the department involves the U.S. District Attorneys presenting the state's case in court against the accused. The Bureau of Prisons oversees the incarceration and possible parole of those convicted of a criminal offense. The advantage to the federal system is that three of the component parts are all under one umbrella controlled by just one person. As stated in its Strategic Plan for fiscal years 2012-2016, the mission of the Department of Justice is:

> To enforce the law and defend the interests of the United States according to the law, to ensure public safety against threats foreign and domestic, to provide federal leadership in preventing and controlling crime, and to see just punishment for those guilty of unlawful behavior, and to ensure fair and impartial administration of justice for all Americans.[46]

The fourth part is, of course, the federal court system.

The United States Attorney General

Heading the Department of Justice is the United States Attorney General who in addition to administering the department serves as the nation's chief law enforcement officer and lawyer. The position was originally established with the passage of the Judiciary Act of 1789. The duties of the office are to prosecute and conduct all suits filed in the Supreme Court in which the United States government was a party, i.e., constitutionality of congressional laws and executive acts and treaties, and provide legal advice to the President of the United States or to any head of a federal department. The position is filled by a presidential appointment with confirmation by the Senate. Edmund Randolph, a noted statesman and Constitutional Framer from Virginia, first held the position. Other notables include William Pinkney appointed by James Madison; Edwin Stanton appointed by James Buchanan; Harlan Stone appointed by Grover Cleveland; Robert F. Kennedy appointed by his brother John F. Kennedy; John Mitchell of Watergate fame appointed by Richard Nixon; Janet Reno, the first woman to hold the position, appointed by Bill Clinton; and Alberto Gonzales, the first Hispanic Attorney General, appointed by George W. Bush. The first African American to hold the position, Eric Holder, was named acting Attorney General by George W. Bush but the Senate approved him for the permanent position upon nomination by President Barack Obama. The Attorney General can be dismissed by the president at any time and is subject to impeachment by the House of Representative on charges as specified in the Constitution for "treason, bribery, and other high crimes and misdemeanors." Table 1 is an organizational chart of the Department of Justice. All of these agencies report directly to the Attorney General.

The Investigative Arm of the Department of Justice

Although there are several agencies falling under the investigative arm of the Department of Justice, the major ones are the Federal Bureau of Investigation, the U.S. Marshals Service, the United States Drug Enforcement Administration, and the Bureau of Alcohol, Tobacco, Firearms and Explosives. Each agency is assigned specific tasks in enforcing federal laws.

The mention of federal criminal investigations brings to mind only one agency—the **Federal Bureau of Investigation (FBI)**. The agency was created in 1908 by then Attorney General Charles Bonaparte during the Theodore Roosevelt administration. Initially, the agency investigated violations of national banking laws, naturalization issues, antitrust laws, bankruptcy filings, and land fraud schemes. The notoriety of the FBI soared during the 'lawless years" of 1921-1933 with prohibition and the rise of the gangsters, such as Bonnie and Clyde and Al Capone, and the appointment of J. Edgar Hoover as its director, a position he held for forty-eight years. Today, the FBI has a staff of approximately 35,295 employees.[47] The FBI investigates criminal violations involving over two hundred various categories of federal criminal laws and also serves as the nation's primary internal security agency. One of its major duties is to investigate all criminal activities on Native American Reservations.

Table 1

The United States Department of Justice

Established July 1, 1870, the Department of Justice is headed by the Attorney General of the United States. Forty separate component organizations are under the direction of the Attorney General.

Office of the Attorney General

Deputy Attorney General

Associate Attorney General

Solicitor General	Investigative Agencies:	Litigating Divisions:
U.S. Attorneys	Federal Bureau of Investigation	Antitrust
	Drug Enforcement Administration	Civil Rights
	Bureau of Alcohol, Tobacco, Firearms and Explosives	Criminal
		Environment and Natural Resources
		Tax

Offices:	Other Agencies:	Special Programs:
Office of Legal Policy	U.S. Marshals Service	Office of Justice Programs
Office of Legislative Affairs	Bureau of Prisons	Office on Violence Against Women
Office of Public Affairs	National Security Division	Office of Community Oriented Policing Services
Office of Legal Counsel	Executive Office for U.S. Trustees	Office of Policy Information
Office of Tribal Justice	Justice Management Division	Office of Professional Responsibility Advisory Office
Office of the Solicitor General	Executive Office for Immigration Review	Office of Professional Responsibility
	Community Relations Service	
	Office of the Inspector General	
	Community Oriented Policing Services	
	Foreign Claims Settlement	
	Interpol Washington	
	Office of the Pardon Attorney	
	U.S Parole Commission	
	Executive Office for Organized Crime Drug Enforcement Taskforce	

The nation's oldest investigative federal agency is **United States Marshals Service** created with the passage of the Federal Judiciary Act of 1789. Appointed by the president or the Attorney General, there are ninety-four U.S. Marshals assigned to ninety-four district offices across the nation as well as the U.S. territories of Guam, the Mariana Islands, Puerto Rico and the Virgin Islands. Deputy U.S. Marshals are assigned to all federal courts to escort defendants to and from trial, protect judges, prosecutors and witnesses, and conduct courtroom and courthouse security. Outside of the courtroom, U.S. Marshals also conduct domestic and international fugitive investigations. Some are assigned to the federal prison system to secure prisoners and defendants in custody, transport prisoners and defendants to and from the jail to the courthouse, receive prisoners from other federal law enforcement agencies, conduct jail inspections, and protect government witnesses. Collectively, 5,499 individuals were employed by this agency in 2013.[48]

Founded in 1973 by the Nixon administration, the **United States Drug Enforcement Administration (DEA)** is charged with enforcement of the Controlled Substance Act to include the growing, manufacturing, and distribution of controlled substances. Its agents combat drug smuggling into and within the nation by apprehending the traffickers, sellers, and users of controlled substances. It shares some of its duties with both the FBI and Immigration and Customs Enforcement. It is the sole agency responsible for conducting all drug-related investigations abroad. The agency also manages a national drug intelligence program in cooperation with state, local and foreign governments. The agency serves as the nation's liaison with the United States and Interpol on issues related to international drug control programs. As of 2013, the agency employed 9,410 people.[49]

Created in 1972, the Bureau of Alcohol, Tobacco, Firearms and Explosives (ATF) is tasked with the responsibilities of investigating and preventing the unlawful use, manufacturing, and possession of illegal firearms and explosives, as well as acts of arson and bombings. It regulates through federal licensing requirements, the sale, possession and transportation of firearms, ammunition, and explosives via interstate commerce. The agency also investigates illegal trafficking of alcohol and tobacco products. ATF works closely with other federal agencies, state and local law enforcement agencies, and promotes local community awareness programs such as the Project Safe Neighborhoods.

The Litigation Arm of the Department of Justice

The litigation divisions falling under the direction of the Department of Justice include the Antitrust, Civil, Civil Rights, Criminal, Environmental and Natural Resources, and Tax divisions. These cases are prosecuted by the **United States Attorneys**. They also defend the United States government when it is sued in a federal trial court. Each federal judicial court has at least one U.S. Attorney assigned to its district as well as several federal assistant attorneys. Currently, there are ninety-four U.S. Attorneys in all fifty states, the District of Columbia, Guam, the Mariana Islands, Puerto Rico, and the U.S. Virgin Islands. All U.S. Attorneys are presidential appointees serving a four-year term. They too are subject to Senate confirmation. At the end of the president's term, all of these attorneys submit their resignations when the opposition party wins the White House. The president, in turn, may re-appoint them or opt to appoint others to the positions. Regardless, nominees for a U.S. Attorney position must reside in the federal district court he/she will prosecute in and, of course, they all must be licensed attorneys. While one would expect that these attorneys follow the letter of the law, one cannot overlook that these are political appointees that sometimes can fall victim to Washington political intrigue. For example, George W. Bush's administration ran into considerable controversy when his legal team in the White House decided mid-way into Bush's first term of office to fire several of these attorneys for poor job performance, even though they did not have any indication that they were not performing their jobs. It was revealed later than their firings were due to the lack of enthusiasm of prosecuting cases akin to the political agenda of the Bush administration.

The **Solicitor General of the United States** represents the federal government in all litigation presented before the Supreme Court. Approximately two-thirds of the Supreme Court's yearly docket involves the federal government. All such litigation is channeled through this office. The solicitor general reviews to determine which cases the government will take action on as well as the official positions the government will present to the Court. Along with his/her staff, the Solicitor General prepares the appropriate positions, briefs and other required papers filed on behalf of the government to the Supreme Court. The Solicitor General presents the majority of the oral arguments in support of the government's position in cases before the Court or can assign cases to the Assistant to the Solicitor General or to another federal attorney. In addition, it is the Solicitor General's office that reviews all cases decided against the government by lower federal courts to determine whether to initiate the appeal process and, if so, what positions the government will pursue. Also, he/she is responsible for determining whether the government will participate as ***amicus curiae*** (Latin for "friend of the court").

THE FEDERAL COURT SYSTEM

Constitutional Courts

There are two types of federal courts. The Framers of the Constitution created Article I, legislative courts, and Article III, judicial courts. Legislative courts have administrative, quasi-legislative, as well as traditional judicial duties. Justices of legislative courts are appointed by the president with Senate confirmation and serve for specified terms. Courts falling under Article III are trial courts. Judges for Article III courts are also appointed by the president with Senate confirmation but serve under "good behavior," that is, for life terms.

Selection of Judges

Article III, Section 1 of the United States Constitution states that "the judicial power of the United States shall be vested in one Supreme Court, and in such inferior courts as the Congress may from time to time ordain and establish. The judges, both of the Supreme and inferior courts, shall hold their offices during good behavior, and shall, at stated times, receive for their services a compensation which shall not be diminished during the continuance in office." **Article II, Section 2** gives to president the power to appoint judges to federal benches; however, the United States Senate is empowered to conduct the necessary confirmation hearings and to confirm or not confirm the president's nominee.

It seems like such a simple process. The president nominates and the Senate confirms. However, several of President Obama's nominees for non-Supreme Court benches have been lingering for years with no Senate confirmation hearings scheduled. An empty court bench means that cases must be reassigned to other Federal District Courts, causing a lengthy backlog of pending cases.

Some nominees have sailed through the Senate process while others have had an arduous task of receiving a favorable vote. The most controversial to date was the confirmation hearings for Clarence Thomas, an appointee of President W. H. Bush, replacing retiring jurist Thurgood Marshall. Thomas was accused by a former employee, Anita Hill, of sexual harassment. Fearful of reprisals from Thomas, Hill waited years until she secured a "safe" job before leveling accusations against Thomas. The media had a field day with each word of her testimony before the Senate Judiciary Committee making the evening news. She could not press formal charges against him because the statute of limitations had expired; but she did go into great detail about the incident during the confirmation hearings. Thomas eventually won confirmation. A worst fate awaited Robert Bork, a federal judge appointed by Ronald Reagan for a seat on the Supreme Court. The grilling he took from the Senate panel at times turned hostile and Bork did not win confirmation. Why is securing a federal bench so difficult?

Part of the blame can be levied at the Framers. The Constitution lists no specific qualifications for the job. There is absolutely no requirement that a judge to a federal bench have a law degree, legal experience, or prior bench experience. Yet with few exceptions, presidents usually nominate individuals who do have law degrees and have decades of either legal or bench experience. When a bench becomes available, the president's staff shifts through the mounds of applications to find the right person to fit the job. Sometimes, an excellent candidate will withdraw from consideration in anticipation of a rough time in front of the Senate Judiciary Committee.

A presidential nominee can run into immediate trouble if the president bypasses the time-honored tradition of **senatorial courtesy.** Presidents need the support of every senator they can muster. So the tradition holds that before the nominee is formally announced, the president makes a courtesy call to the senator of his party from the nominee's state to gage whether the Senator will back the appointee. Of course, the confirmation process is supposedly an easier one for both the president and his/her nominee if the president's party holds a clear majority of the seats in the Senate.

Today, the judicial philosophy of the nominee is more of a consideration than the judicial expertise of the candidate. For conservatives, the appropriate approach is **judicial self-restraint,** defined as "a self-imposed limitation on judicial decision making. [It is] the tendency of judges to favor a narrow interpretation of the laws and to defer to the policy judgment of the legislative and executive branches."[50] The 2012 Republican platform has a plank position calling for the appointment of "constitutionalist" jurists who will interpret the law as it was originally intended rather than make it. On the other hand, liberals or Democrats prefer federal judges to follow **judicial activism,** whereby "the making of new public policies [is] through the decision of judges. This may take the form of a reversal or modification of a prior court decision, the nullification of a law passed by the legislature, or the overturning of some action of the executive branch."[51] For example, in rendering the decision in ***Brown v the Board of Education*** (1954), the arguments centered on whether the lack of an equal education was a violation of the Fourteenth Amendment's guarantee of equal protection of the law. Using judicial activism, the Court would have heard and ruled on the case even though the word education is not directly tied to the equal protection clause of that amendment. On the other hand, a judicial self-restraint Court would not have even heard the case because the Fourteenth Amendment does not specifically mention educational equality under equal protection of the laws clause. Therefore, this Court would call the issue a political question, that is, "a doctrine enunciated by the Supreme Court holding that certain constitutional issues cannot be decided by the courts but are to be decided by the executive or legislative branches."[52] Members of the Senate Judiciary Committee comb through the nominee's legal background. Every case the nominee may have defended or prosecuted as a lawyer or rendered a decision on as a judge is carefully reviewed for any sign of the nominee's personal approach to judicial decision-making. The activism versus self-restraint argument is the prevailing "two approaches to the judicial decision making in the American political system. Activists hold that a judge should use his/her position to promote desirable social ends. Proponents of self-restraint counter than in deciding cases, a judge should defer to the legislative and executive branches, which are politically responsible to the voters, and not indulge his/her personal philosophy" when making a decision.[53] During the confirmation hearings of Elena Kagan, Sonia Sotomayor, and John Roberts, all three were repeatedly questioned on whether they were activists or restrainers.

However, once confirmed there is no guarantee that the nominee will stick to the same judicial philosophical position that won him/her Senate confirmation. For example, Republican President Dwight Eisenhower appointed two people to the Supreme Court who he believed were conservative and strict or self-restraining judges. Yet, both William Brennan and Earl Warren turned out to be far more on the liberal or activist side than Eisenhower could have ever envisioned. Bryan White, a Democrat, was selected to the bench by John Kennedy. Yet, White voted more frequently on the conservative side of the Court than with his more liberal jurists.

Jurisdiction

Jurisdiction is the "authority vested in a court to hear and decide a case."[54] Each of the three levels of the federal court system has a prescribed list of judicial issues under **original jurisdiction**, defined

President Obama and Sonia Sotomayor at White House Press Conference, August 12, 2009 Credit: RTT News

as "the authority of a court to hear a case in the first instance."⁵⁵ All federal district courts have original jurisdiction over any criminal or civil violations of federal laws. **Appellate jurisdiction** is the "authority of a court to review decisions of an inferior court."⁵⁶ Both the federal appellate courts and the Supreme Court basically hear appeals from lower court decisions or on challenges to state or federal legislative acts. As specified in the Constitution, the Supreme Court has original jurisdiction to settle suits between two or more states. It does share original jurisdiction with federal district courts in cases involving charges against foreign ambassadors or counsels, in cases involving the federal government against a state, and in cases levied by a state against citizens of another state or against aliens.

Federal District Courts

Currently, there are 677 federal district judges including those assigned to the territorial courts. There are ninety-four federal judicial districts with at least one district in each state, as well as a courts assigned to the District of Columbia and Puerto Rico. The president nominates these judges to these courts with Senate confirmation for lifetime terms. The caseload before these courts is staggering. In 2010, there were 285,215 cases filed, 295,909 cases terminated, meaning a decision was reached, and 287,799 cases pending, meaning the case had not been put on the Court's docket.⁵⁷ The cases before the justices included contract issues, real estate property actions including foreclosures, tort actions such as personal injury and medical malpractice, personal property damage, actions under statutes, bankruptcy suits, civil rights litigation, environmental concerns, prisoner petitions, labor law, immigration issues, securities-related issues, social security laws, tax suits, and freedom of information petitions for the release and/or use of government documents.

Federal Appellate Courts

There are twelve Federal Appellate Court geographical districts in the United States plus one circuit court—the Court of Appeals for the Federal Circuit. Each court has three to fifteen permanent or lifetime appointed judges assigned to it. The president with Senate confirmation appoints these positions. The judges can hear cases either in a group of three or *en banc*, defined as a "French term referring to a session of an appellate court in which all the judges of the court participate."⁵⁸

By definition, an **appeal** is "a formal request to a higher court that it review the actions of a lower court."⁵⁹ The term **appellant** refers to "the party usually the losing one, that seeks to overturn the decision of a lower court by appealing to a higher court."⁶⁰ Not every case heard as original jurisdiction in a state or federal court is appealed. For a case to even to be heard by the federal appeals courts, the question before the jurists must a constitutional one, in that, the defendant or the losing party in a lawsuit has to tie their concern directly to a violation of a provision in the U.S. Constitution. For example, a person tried and convicted of robbing a bank is a federal crime. In the process of interrogation, the defendant requested a lawyer, but the request was denied and the questioning continued. This situation is directly tied to the rights and privileges within the Constitution. The defendant's denied request for an attorney to be present during interrogation was a constitutional violation of his/her right to legal representation. The Appellate Court would definitely entertain hearing this case. A defendant tried in a state court can seek a federal appeal without first going through the state appellate process if the issue at hand is seen as a violation of the U.S. Constitution. If it were a violation of the state constitution, then this case would begin the appeals process at the state appellate level. As previously stated, if a decision rendered by the Federal Appellate Court is appealed to the Supreme Court, the Supreme Court can refuse to hear the case, thus making the Federal Appeals Court the court of last resort.

There is no real trial on the appellate level. The convicted individual or, as in the case of a civil matter, the aggrieved party and any of the witnesses that testified at the trial court do not testify or even appear before the appellate court. Each side of the issue has their legal team address the court. On legislative matters, both Federal Appellate Courts and the Supreme Court have the power of judicial review. Appellate judges are only interested in the constitutional question laid before them. They are not concerned, for example, about the particulars of a murder trial or how brutal the offense may have been, the name of the victim, etc. For them, it is the constitutional basis for the appeal that is the one and only issue before the panel. Oftentimes, the same issue is presented before two or more appellate courts. For example, several federal appellate judges have issued rulings on state laws pertaining to same-sex marriage prohibitions. One judge will rule in favor of the laws while another will rule the state laws unconstitutional. Since the appellate judges cannot come to one decision, it will be up to the Supreme Court to make the decision.

If the Appellate Court upholds the lower court's decision, then the aggrieved party can either accept the outcome or try an appeal to the Supreme Court. If the Appeals Court rules in favor of the aggrieved party then, in the case of a criminal conviction, the decision of the lower court is overturned. The resolution of the case then falls upon the original prosecuting agency such as the U.S. Attorney or in a state matter the District Attorney who now must decide whether to retry the individual or allow the appellate ruling to stand. A new trial probably will not take place especially if the evidence used against the defendant has been either ruled unconstitutional or has been compromised.

The Supreme Court

It is an arduous process for a judicial issue to make it through the appeals process and wind up on the Supreme Court's docket. To file an appeal at the appellate or Supreme Court level, the aggrieved party must submit a **brief**, "a document prepared by an attorney for presentation to the court containing arguments and data in support of a case. The brief will embody points of law, precedents, and in a case involving a major social issue, relevant economic, sociological and other scientific evidence."[61] The Court issues a manual that guides one in the preparation of the brief. It cannot be handwritten. In fact, the Supreme Court has accepted only a handful of written briefs with the most famous being for *Gideon v Wainwright*. The briefs are presented to the justices who in turn, depend upon their assigned law clerks to read them. If a law clerk believes this is indeed a case the Court should hear, he/she presents it to their assigned judge. The majority of the Court's seasonal docket is filed through the ***writ of certiorari***, "an order or writ from a higher court demanding that a lower court send up the record of a case for review."[62] This usually happens after four of the nine justices invoked the **rule of four**, meaning that four of the justices want to consider this case for the Court's review.

Once the case is on the Court's docket, legal experts from both sides of the issue prepare their **oral arguments** to be delivered at a precise date for a designated time period. During the oral arguments, the justices will ask questions of the presenters, interrupt them with their own comments, or even consult with each other. For cases argued before the Appellate Courts or the Supreme Court, no decision is rendered immediately after oral arguments have been presented. A final decision could take months or years. Usually during their annual session, which begins in October, the justices reserve either a Wednesday or Friday of each week to discuss the cases that have been presented to them. The Chief Justice presides over the session with each of the justices speaking in order of seniority. This is a closed-door secret meeting. Each justice will cast a vote. If a majority is not reached then the justices may ask for additional information to affirm their decisions. It could take several conferences and several rounds of voting before a final decision is reached.

Table 2

The Justices of the United States Supreme Court

Justice	Appointed by	Date Confirmed
Chief Justice John Roberts	George W. Bush	Sept. 29, 2005
Associate Justice Antonio Scalia	Ronald Reagan	Sept. 26, 1986
Associate Justice Anthony Kennedy	Ronald Reagan	Feb. 18, 1988
Associate Justice Clarence Thomas	George H.W. Bush	Oct. 23, 1991
Associate Justice Ruth Bader Ginsburg	Bill Clinton	Aug. 10, 1993
Associate Justice Stephen G. Breyer	Bill Clinton	Aug. 3, 1994
Associate Justice Samuel Alito, Jr.	George W. Bush	Jan. 31, 2006
Associate Justice Sonia Sotomayor	Barack Obama	Aug. 8, 2009
Associate Justice Elena Kagan	Barack Obama	Aug. 7, 2010

The Power of Judicial Review

In was the intention of the Framers to make the judicial branch an equal partner with the legislative and executive branches. In a 1788 speech, Oliver Ellsworth explained the role of the judicial branch:

> This constitution defines the extent of the powers of the general government. If the general legislative should at any time overleap their limits, the judicial department is a constitutional check. If the United States go beyond their powers, if they make a law which the Constitution does not authorize, it is void; and the judicial power, the national judges, who, to secure their impartiality, are to be made independent, will declare it void.[63]

With the passage of the **Judiciary Act of 1789**, the federal courts at all levels were granted the right of judicial review. Section 25 of the law empowers, in particular, the United States Supreme Court to render:

> a final judgment or decree in any suit, in the highest court of law or equity of a state in which a decision in the suit could be had, where is drawn in question the validity of a treaty

or statute of, or an authority exercised, under the United States, and the decision is against their validity; or where is drawn in question the validity of a statute of, or an authority exercised under, any State, on the ground of their being repugnant to the constitution, treaties, or laws of the United States, and the decision is in favour of such their validity, or where is drawn in question the construction of any clause of the constitution, or of a treaty, or statute of, or commission held under, the United States, and the decision is against the title, right, privilege or exemption, specially set up or claimed by either party, under such clause of said Constitution, treaty, statute, or commission, may be re-examined, and reversed or affirmed in the Supreme Court of the United States, in the same manner and under the same regulations, and the writ shall have the same effect as if the judgment or decree complained of had been rendered or passed in a circuit court, and the proceedings upon the reversal shall also be the same, except the Supreme Court, instead of remanding the cause for a final decision as before provided, may, at their discretion, if the cause shall have been once remanded before, proceed to a final decision of the same, and award execution. **But no other error shall be assigned or regarded as a ground of reversal in any such as aforesaid**, than such as appears on the face of the record, and immediately respects the before-mentioned questions of validity or construction of said constitution, treaties, statutes, commissions, or authorities in dispute . . .[64]

Many congressional and state legislative acts initially have been declared unconstitutional by lower federal courts on the grounds that these laws do indeed conflict with the spirit and meaning of the United States Constitution. Any challenges to these rulings are heard at the federal appellate court level with the possibility of eventually being heard by the Supreme Court. As the court of last resort for constitutional challenges, the Supreme Court can opt to hear the merits of the constitutional issue and render its own decision or merely pass on it, thus making the lower federal court's ruling the final decision on the matter. Table 2 lists a selective number of Supreme Court decisions that have impacted both federal and state criminal and court proceedings in matters ranging from confessions to victims' rights.

While the public eagerly awaits an Appellate or a Supreme Court's final decision, legal experts are more anxious to read the written opinions of the justices related to the decision. These opinions are a part of the precedents judges and lawyers use to render a judgment for cases in the future that mirror the same issues addressed by the higher courts. Legislators and legal experts look towards these opinions to guide them in crafting future legislation to ensure that these bills will not conflict with the Court's rulings. The only way to really overturn a decision made by a federal appellate or Supreme Court is for Congress to pass and the voters to approve an amendment to the Constitution.

These opinions fall into several different categories. For example, in 1947 the Supreme Court ruled 5 to 4 in ***Everson v Board of Education of the Township of Ewing***, that the township's practice of using public tax money to offset the costs of public transportation to both public and private schools for children from low-income families was constitutional. The five justices represent the majority while the four are in the minority. If the Chief Justice of the Supreme Court voted with the majority, the writing of the majority opinion falls upon his/her shoulders or he/she may assign it to another justice of the majority group.

Table 3

Selective List of Supreme Court Cases

Subject Area	Case	Decision
Confessions	*Arizona v Fulminate* (1991)	Coerced confessions do not automatically turnover a conviction.
	Ashcraft v Tennessee (1944)	A confession obtained through psychological coercion is not a voluntary one; inadmissible in court.
	Brown v Mississippi (1936)	A confession obtained by physical coercion is an unconstitutional violation of 14th Amendment's due process clause.
	Harris v New York (1971)	Voluntary statements made prior to a defendant being apprised of constitutional rights can be used at trial to impeach the defendant's credibility.
Constitutional Rights	*Chavez v Martinez* (2003)	Failure of a police officer to apprise suspect of Miranda cannot be used against the officer in civil suit.
	Dickerson v U.S. (2000)	Upheld *Miranda v Arizona*.
	Illinois v Perkins (1990)	A law enforcement officer can pose as a inmate to obtain a confession without apprising inmate of Miranda rights.
Court Proceedings	*Press Enterprises v Superior Court* (1986)	All preliminary hearings must be open to the public.
	Miranda v Arizona (1966)	See under Right to Counsel
	New York v Quarles (1984)	Issues of public safety can justify an officer's failure to provide Miranda Warnings before questioning begins.
Cruel/Unusual Punishment	*Payne v Tennessee* (1991)	The introduction of victim's impact statements during sentencing is not a violation of 8th Amendment.
Death Penalty	*Atkins v Virginia* (2002)	Death penalty cannot be used for defendants with IQ under 70 or less.
	Furman v Georgia (1972)	Death penalty ruled unconstitutional.
	Gregg v Georgia (1976)	Death penalty laws do not necessarily constitute "cruel and unusual" punishment.
	Thompson v Oklahoma (1988)	The death penalty cannot be given to defendants under the age of fifteen.
Due Process	*Brady v Maryland* (1963)	Due process is violated when prosecutors withhold evidence from the defense that might be favorable to the defendant.
	Duncan v Louisiana (1968)	The due process clause of 14th Amendment binds 6th Amendment's right to jury trial to the states.
Evidence	*Jencks v U.S.* (1957)	Prior inconsistent statements made by a witness must be made available to the defense.
	Pennsylvania v Muniz (1990)	Police officers can ask routine questions and video tape responses to those suspected of DWI violations.
	U.S. v Scheffer (1998)	Polygraphs cannot be used in court as evidence.
Exclusionary Rule	*Mapp v Ohio* (1961)	Exclusionary rule applies to both federal and state law enforcement agencies.
Grand Jury	*Hurtado v California* (1884)	States are not required to use the grand jury system for felony charges.
Guilty Pleas	*Boykin v Alabama* (1969)	It is up to the judge to determine if a plea of guilty was knowingly entered and absolutely voluntary.

Independent Counsels	*Morrison v Olson* (1988)	Use of independent counsels is constitutional.
Jury Selection	*Georgia v McCullum* (1992)	The defense cannot exclude jurors based on race.
	Taylor v Louisiana (1972)	Women cannot be excluded from jury duty.
	Witherspoon v Illinois (1968)	Prospective jurors cannot be eliminated due to their views on the death penalty.
Jury Trial	*Baldwin v New York* (1970)	Individuals accused of petty offenses do not have right to a jury trial.
	Ballew v Georgia (1978)	Six is the minimum number for a jury panel.
	Ring v Arizona (2002)	Only juries can decide the critical sentencing issues in a death penalty case.
Prison Conditions	*Ruiz v Estelle* (1980)	Prison overcrowding unconstitutional under 8th Amendment.
Privacy	*Bond v U.S.* (2000)	Passengers on a bus or train have an expectation of privacy when they place their luggage in overhead storage.
Prosecutors	*Berger v U.S.* (1935)	The primary task of a prosecutor's job is the pursuit of justice, not just winning cases.
	Buckley v Fitzsimmons (1993)	Prosecutors have qualified immunity from civil law suits for their actions during criminal investigations.
	Burns v Reed (1993)	Prosecutors have qualified immunity from lawsuits concerning their advice to the police.
	Imbler v Pachtman (1976)	Prosecutors have absolute immunity from civil liability during a criminal prosecution.
	Kalina v Fletcher (1997)	Prosecutors can be sued for making false statements in affidavits.
Rape/Sexual Assault	*Coker v Georgia* (1977)	Rape is not a capital death penalty offense.
Right to Counsel	*Alabama v Shelton* (2002)	Court-appointed counsel must be granted to a defendant facing suspended jail term for minor charge.
	Argersinger v Hamlim (1972)	Non-felony defendants have right to a court-appointed counsel.
	Betts v Brady (1942)	Indigent defendants accused of a noncapital crime are not guaranteed court-appointed counsel.
	Douglas v California (1963)	Indigents have right to court-appointed counsel for their first appeal.
	Hamilton v Alabama (1961)	Counsel is required during arraignment.
	In re Gault (1967)	Juveniles have right to counsel under 6th Amendment.
	Johnson v Zerbst (1938)	Indigent defendants in federal court are guaranteed court-appointed counsel.
	Missick v Mississippi (1990)	Once the defendant has asked for legal representation, interrogation cannot resume until attorney present.
	Miranda v Arizona (1966)	Counsel must be guaranteed when requested by the accused during interrogation; defendant must be apprised of constitutional rights prior to waiving those rights.
	Powell v Alabama (1932)	Court-appointed counsel guaranteed to indigent defendants accused in capital cases.
	Roe v Flores-Ortega (2000)	A lawyer's failure to file an appeal does not constitute ineffective counsel.
	Strickland v Washington (1984)	One's defense attorney can be judged as ineffective only if the court proceedings were unfair and the judgment would have been different.

	Wiggins v Smith (2003)	Lawyer's inability to conduct a complete investigation into client's background does not constitute ineffective defense.
Searches	*Chinnel v California* (1969)	During a search, police can only search the person and the immediate area.
	Florida v J.L. (2000)	Police cannot stop a motorist and conduct a search based solely on an anonymous tip.
	Florida v Jardines (2013)	Ruled using a drug-sniffing dog on a porch to detect drugs in the house unconstitutional violation of 4th Amendment.
	Illinois v Rodriguez (1990)	Good faith exception search is constitutional even though victim allowed entry into apartment she no longer resided in.
	Illinois v Wardlow (2000)	A suspect running from police can be subjected to a stop-and-frisk search.
	Knowles v Iowa (1998)	Just issuing a speeding ticket does not give police right to search the vehicle.
	Maryland v King (2013)	Not a violation of 4th Amendment to use cotton swab to collect DNA from arrested suspected.
	Missouri v McNeely (2013)	Warrant may be required to draw blood by needle to check alcohol levels.
	Payton v Tennessee (1980)	Arrest warrant is required to enter a suspect's private residence with the exception of the suspect's consent or an emergency situation.
	U.S. v Leon (1984)	Upheld a limited use of good faith exception for search warrents.
Self-Defense	*Faretta v California* (1975)	Defendants have the constitutional right to self-defense.
Self-Incrimination	*Kastigar v U.S.* (1972)	Use immunity is not a violation of the 5th Amendment's guarantee of protection from self-incrimination.
Sources	*Brazburg v Hayes* (1972)	Journalists cannot claim confidentiality to sources when subpoenaed before grant juries.
Substantive Due Process	*Lanzetta v New Jersey* (1938)	A law is unconstitutional if the meaning of the law is so vague that "men of common intelligence must necessarily guess as to its meaning."
Victims' Rights	*Booth v Maryland* (1963)	Victim impact statements are unconstitutional in capital cases because statements can result in a arbitrary and capricious application of death penalty.

If the Chief Justice's vote puts him/her into the minority pool, the most senior justice in the majority group selects the justice to write the **majority opinion**. Once completed, the opinion is reviewed by the justices in their respective groups. The body of the opinion details the constitutional issue before the Court and why in this case the five justices were the majority in either upholding the constitutionality of the laws allowing the use of public money for bus fare for students attending private schools. The justice would point out that this was a legal and thus a constitutional application of the child benefit theory (see Chapter 13). The minority justice would choose one of their group to write the **dissenting** or **minority opinion** citing why they did not uphold the constitutionality of the Ewing initiative. Both groups can have a jurist who may have voted either yea or nay but did so for different reasons. This constitutes a **concurring opinion**. An **extended opinion** is "a separate opinion that partly concurs and party dissents from an opinion of the court."[65] Any level of court can be called upon to issue an advisory opinion defined as "an opinion given by a court, though no actual case or controversy is before it, on the constitutional or legal effect of a law."[66] This may be a prudent practice for any lawmaker or legislative or executive body to get before they decide to entertain legislation that will certainly be ruled as unconstitutional by the Court when challenged before it.

Beginning with the landmark decision in *Marbury v Madison* (1803), members of the Supreme Court have defended their use of judicial review. For example, in one of his opinions issued in 1958, Chief Justice Earl Warren wrote:

> We are mindful of the gravity of the issue inevitable raised whenever the constitutionality of an Act of the National Legislature is challenged. . . . [But] we are oath-bound to defend the Constitution. This obligation requires that Congressional enactments be judged by the standards of the Constitution. The Judiciary has the duty of implementing the constitutional safeguards that protect individual rights. . . . The provisions of the Constitution are not time-worn adages or hollow shibboleths. They are vital, living principles that authorize and limit governmental power in our Nation. They are rules of government. When the constitutionality of an Act of Congress is challenged in this Court, we must apply those rules. If we do not, the words of the Constitution become little more than good advice. . . We do well to approach the task cautiously, as all our predecessor have counseled. But the ordeal of judgment cannot be shirked.[67]

The impact of the Court's power of judicial review cannot be understated. Their decisions have had a tremendous impact on the interpretation and extension of civil liberties (see Chapter 13), on the advancement of civil rights and voting privileges (see Chapter 14), on the relationship between federal and state governments (see Chapter 3), on the implementation of federal regulatory laws (see Chapters 10 and 17), on the conduction of elections and political campaigns (see Chapters 5 and 6) and to some extent, on foreign policy (see Chapter 18).

Federal Courts—Territorial Courts

Territorial courts were created as Article I courts by Congress to hear cases of original jurisdiction involving federal law and bankruptcy cases. Article I judgeships were established initially in the Virgin Islands in 1937 and later in Guam in 1950 and the Commonwealth of the Northern Mariana Islands in 1977. The president appoints judges to these benches with confirmation from the Senate for fixed terms of ten years.

Federal Courts—United States Court of Appeals for Veterans Claims

This court was created in 1988 when President Reagan signed into law the Veterans' Judicial Review Act. As a court of record, this Court is part of the federal judiciary and does not fall under the direction of the Department of Veterans Affairs. The court is staffed with seven judges serving fifteen-year terms. Once a judge's term has expired, the judge has the option to remain as a recall-eligible senior judge. This court has exclusive jurisdiction over any decision issued by the Board of Veterans' Appeals filed by a claimant challenging the Board's decision.

Federal Courts—Court of International Trade

Originally established by Congress in 1926 as the Customs Court, its name was changed by Congress to the Court of International Trade. The primary duty of the court is to settle disputes arising over the federal government's tariff laws and any duties levied on imported goods. The court is composed of nine judges appointed to lifetime terms by the president with Senate confirmation. Although its main office is in New York City, there are courts established throughout the nation's principal ports of entry. Although initially an Article I court, it was changed to an Article III court in 1956.

Federal Courts—The Court of Federal Claims

Originally established in 1855, the Article I Court of Federal Claims hears cases filed by private individuals against the federal government involving breaches of contract, injuries caused by the negligent behavior of government employees, claims involving the recovery of other claims such as back pay, tax refunds, eminent domain claims against the federal government, dismissal issues from federal civilian and active military personnel, disputes over patents and copyrights, and land claims brought by Native Americans against the federal government. It also handles claims referred to them by Congress and executive branch departments. The court has sixteen judges appointed for fixed fifteen-year terms by the president with Senate confirmation.

Federal Courts—Court of Appeals for the Federal Circuit

Established by Congress in 1982, the court has the same judicial standing as the federal Courts of Appeals with the exception that its jurisdiction is national rather than geographical. This appellate court was created to consolidate the caseloads from both the former Court of Customers and Patent Appeals with the appellate function of the Court of Claims. The court's appellate jurisdiction extends to issues involving disputes over patents, copyrights and trademarks; appeals from district courts involving contractual matters and Internal Revenue cases in which the United States is the defendant; appeals from the Federal Court of Claims, Court of International Trade, and Court of Veterans Appeals, and any issues involving a review of administrative rulings issued by the Patent and Trademark Office, the International Trade Commission, the Secretary of Commerce, Department of Veterans Affairs, etc. The court is composed of twelve judges nominated by the president with Senate confirmation for life terms. Panels of three judges or en banc can hear their cases.

Federal Courts—United States Court of Appeals for the Armed Forces

As an Article I body, this court was established in 1950 to review military court martial decisions. The primary responsibilities of the court are to review decisions affecting top military personnel and all military court decisions resulting in death penalty sentences. It also is empowered to review other cases upon petition to include bad conduct discharges or military code violations resulting in a lengthy prison term. The court operates under military laws and rules established by Congress. The court is composed of five non-military judges appointed by the president with Senate confirmation for fifteen-year terms.

THE FINAL ARM OF JUSTICE—THE FEDERAL PRISON SYSTEM

If convicted of a federal crime, one will serve their imprisonment in a federal prison overseen by the Bureau of Prisons, a federal agency under the direction of the Attorney General's Office. The number of individuals either incarcerated in a federal minimum or maximum prison or under some form of supervision is staggering. As of September 30, 2010, there were 119,814 convicted federal felons under federal supervision either on probation, supervised release, or parole. During the same period, 6,740 individuals convicted of a wide array of misdemeanor offenses ranging from larceny to drug trafficking offenses were either on probation, supervised release, or parole.[68] A further breakdown of federal offenders under some form of federal supervision reveals that 81.1 percent are males and 18.9 percent females and the majority of those under supervision are white with 58.9 percent followed by African American at 37.5 percent.[69] Of the 89,902 federal felony convictions rendered from October 1, 2009 to September 20, 2010, 77.3 percent were incarcerated while only 29 percent of those convicted of misdemeanors during the same period of time were given prison sentences.[70] As of 2009, the nation's prison population was 1,613,740 with 208,118 in federal facilities and 1,405,622 serving time in state prison systems.[71]

These statistics point to the on-growing debate about what direction the nation's criminal justice system should take regarding its sentencing options and growing prison populations. One side believes in the **just desserts** concept whereby the "punishment for criminal-wrong doing should be proportionate to the severity of the offense."[72] Supporters of this option want both state and national legislative houses to enact strong criminal sanctions for a wide range of offenses. The other side promotes the concept of **rehabilitation**, "the notion that punishment is intended to restore offenders to a constructive role in society; based on the assumption that criminal behavior is a treatable disorder caused by social or psychological ailments."[73] Perhaps the resolution to the prison population is not philosophical but monetary. The cost to maintain both the federal and state prison population, as well as providing the appropriate supervision of those released, is depleting both federal and state budgets. Many states are contemplating de-criminalizing certain offenses from felony to misdemeanor or even eliminating them from the criminal list. U.S. Attorney General Eric Holder is joining many state law enforcement agencies and state attorney generals in the advocating the de-criminalization of certain drug offenses.

CONCLUSIONS

Initially, the Framers envisioned that the legislative branch would be predominant over the executive and that the judiciary would fulfill a supportive role for both. However, once the Framers granted judicial review to the federal courts and mandated life-time terms for federal judges, the federal judiciary now had the muscle to exert itself as a co-equal to both the legislative and executive branches. Today, Americans pay just as much attention to an impending key Supreme Court decision as they do to a presidential speech or policy move. Under the guidance of a series of very capable legal experts, the United States Department of Justice has expanded its jurisdiction and exerts itself as a powerful force in the apprehension and conviction of criminals, protecting of the nation's borders, and stamping out terrorist threats to national security. When called upon, this federal department provides legal expertise and forensic support to state and local law enforcement agencies.

Whether you advocate for an activist or strict constructionist jurist, the judges sitting on an appellate or Supreme Court bench do make and influence the course of this nation's laws. One could credit the Supreme Court with lighting the spark to the Civil Rights Movement of the 1960s. It was the Court's decision in *Brown v the Board of Education of Topeka, Kansas* that began the erosion and eventual demise of the separate but equal doctrine. It has been the courts and not Congress or legislative houses that have taken the "bull by the horns" in securing voting rights for the American people. No longer in a supportive role, the federal judiciary is indeed an equal partner and, at times, the dominant voice in the federal government.

CHAPTER NOTES

[1] *Treasury of Presidential Quotations*, Caroline Thomas Harnsburger, ed., (Chicago, Illinois: Follett Publishing Company, 1964), 167-168.
[2] U.S. Bureau of the Census, *Statistical Abstract of the United States: 2012*, 131st ed., (Washington, D.C., 2011), 209.
[3] Ibid.
[4] Department of Justice, *FY 2013 Agency Financial Report*, I-5 and I-8, http://www.justice,gov/agencies
[5] David W. Neubauer, *America's Courts and the Criminal Justice System*, 8th ed., (Belmont, California: Wadsworth Thomson Learning, 2005), 479.
[6] Henry J. Abraham, *The Judicial Process*, 2nd ed., (New York, New York: Oxford University Press, 1968), 7.
[7] Robert A. Carp, Ronald Stidham and Kenneth L. Manning, *Judicial Process in America*, 6th ed., (Washington, D.C.: CQ press, 2004), 3.
[8] William J. Duiker and Jackson J. Spielvogel, *World History*, 3rd ed., (Belmont, California: Wadsworth Thomson Learning, 2005), 11.
[9] Ibid., 12.
[10] Abraham, 10.
[11] Neubauer, 480.
[12] *The American Political Dictionary*, Jack C. Plano and Milton Greenberg, eds., 10th ed., (Harcourt Brace College Publishers, 1997), 278.
[13] Neubauer, 477.
[14] Abraham, 15.
[15] Ibid., 17.
[16] *The American Political Dictionary*, 284.
[17] Ibid., 265.
[18] Carp, Stidham, and Manning, 8-9.
[19] *The American Political Dictionary*, 248.
[20] Carp, Stidham, and Manning, 7.
[21] Neubauer, 480.
[22] Carp, Stidham, and Manning, 258.
[23] Neubauer, 481.
[24] Carp, Stidham, and Manning, 258.
[25] Ibid., 7.
[26] *The American Political Dictionary*, 263.
[27] U.S. Department of Justice, *Federal Justice Statistics, 2010: Statistical Tables*, (Washington, D.C.: 2013), 42.
[28] *The American Political Dictionary*, 271.
[29] *Federal Justice Statistics, 2010: Statistical Tables*, 42.
[30] Neubauer, 270.
[31] *The HarperCollins Dictionary of American Government and Politics*, Jay M. Shafritz, ed., (New York, New York: HarperCollins Publishers, 1992), 468.
[32] John C. Domino, *Civil Rights and Liberties: Toward the 21st Century*, (New York, New York: Harper Collins Publishers, 1994), 140.
[33] Neubauer, 285.
[34] *The HarperCollins Dictionary of American Government and Politics*, 38-39.

[35] *The American Political Dictionary*, 263.
[36] *The HarperCollins Dictionary of American Government and Politics*, 38.
[37] Ibid., 480.
[38] Ibid., 467.
[39] Neubauer, 277.
[40] *The American Political Dictionary*, 279.
[41] Neubauer, 482.
[42] *The HarperCollins Dictionary of American Government and Politics*, 62.
[43] Neubauer, 478.
[44] *The HarperCollins Dictionary of American Government and Politics*, 100.
[45] Neubauer, 477.
[46] *FY 2013 Agency Financial Report*, 1-1.
[47] Ibid., 1-5.
[48] Ibid.
[49] Ibid.
[50] *The HarperCollins Dictionary of American Government and Politics*, 313.
[51] Ibid., 312.
[52] *The American Political Dictionary*, 274.
[53] Ibid.
[54] Ibid., 267.
[55] Ibid., 272.
[56] Ibid., 250.
[57] *Statistical Abstract of the United States: 2012*, 131st ed., 210.
[58] Neubauer, 478.
[59] *The HarperCollins Dictionary of American Government and Politics*, 30.
[60] Neubauer, 476.
[61] *The American Political Dictionary*, 272.
[62] *The HarperCollins Dictionary of American Government and Politics*, 99.
[63] Charles A. Beard, *The Supreme Court and the Constitution*, (Englecliffs, New Jersey: Prentice-Hall, Inc., 1962), 82.
[64] Michael Kammen, *The Origins of the American Constitution: A Documentary History*, (New York, New York: Viking Penguin, Inc., 1986), 306-308.
[65] *The American Political Dictionary*, 406.
[66] Ibid., 149.
[67] Beard, 10.
[68] *Federal Justice Statistics 2010: Statistical Tables*, 29.
[69] Ibid., 30.
[70] Ibid., 21.
[71] *Statistical Abstract of the United States: 2012*, 217.
[72] Neubauer, 479.
[73] Ibid., 481.

SUGGESTED READINGS

Abraham, Henry J. and Barbara A. Perry, *Freedom and the Court: Civil Rights and Liberties in the United States*, 8th ed., Lawrence, Kansas: University of Kansas, 2003.

Carp, Robert A., Ronald Stidham, and Kenneth L. Manning, *Judicial Process in America*, 6th ed., Washington, D.C.:CQ Press, 2004.

Hensley, Thomas R., Christopher E. Smith and Joyce A. Baugh, *The Changing Supreme Court: Constitutional Rights and Liberties*, Minneapolis/St. Paul, Minnesota: West Publishing, 1997.

Neubauer, David W. *America's Courts and the American Judicial System*, 8th ed., Belmont, California: Thomson Wadsworth, 2005.

O'Brien, David. *Storm Center: The Supreme Court in American Politics*, 3rd ed., New York, New York: W. W. Norton and Company, 1993.

Chapter Thi[rteen]

CIVIL LIBERTIES

While the debate over the context of the new constitution was brewing in Philadelphia, Thomas Jefferson wrote to his dear friend James Madison that "while there were many things about the proposed Constitution that please him, first among the things he did not like was 'the omission of a bill of rights, providing clearly, and without the aid of sophism, for freedom of religion, freedom of the press, . . . and trials by jury in all matters of fact triable by the laws of the land. . . .'"[1] At the end of his letter, Jefferson stressed that a Bill of Rights was absolutely necessary because "it is what the people are entitled to against every government on earth, ... and what no just government should refuse. . . ."[2] Our rights to speak freely, to practice our religious beliefs, to gather with others, to redress our government without fear of imprisonment, to have a fair public trial, and so on are embodied in the Bill of Rights. The Framers guaranteed these rights to **all** citizens by attaching the Bill of Rights to the supreme law of the land—the United States Constitution. "Our nation was founded on the idea that all men are created equal, that they are endowed by their Creator with certain inalienable rights, and that governments are instituted among men to secure the rights nature gives. From the beginning, Americans have believed that if their country was about anything, it was about personal freedom and the rights that helped secure it."[3]

The Framers went a step further to ensure that no level of government could strip citizens of their protected rights. In 1789, the United States Congress passed the **Judiciary Act**, which among many provisions gave the newly created Supreme Court the power of judicial review. The key to understanding the longevity of those unalienable rights called civil liberties rests in part with the Supreme Court's use of judicial review. This chapter focuses on the creation, interpretation, and subsequent preservation of the civil liberties enumerated in the Bill of Rights.

However, the preservation of our civil liberties does not and should not rest wholly upon the shoulders of the nine justices of the Supreme Court. The governed, or citizens, bear an equal burden. The constraints placed upon the governing emphasize that laws are man-made. "Americans are much given to saying with pride—with more pride, perhaps, than understanding—that they

...ve under a government of laws and not a government of men. But laws, of course, are manmade. The Constitution of the United States, the supreme law of the land, was framed by mortal men. Ordinary mortals legislate in Congress, administer the laws in the executive branch of the government, and interpret the laws in the judicial branch. These laws were not delivered to us on tablets from Mount Sinai; they are not self-executing; and there are inevitable conflicts about the application and construction of them."[4] Consequently, this chapter also explores the roles played by ordinary citizens such as Ernesto Miranda, Steven Engle, Dollree Mapp, and Clarence Gideon in reminding the governing of their responsibility to preserve, protect, promote, and defend those precious civil liberties.

The continuing quest to preserve and, in some circumstances, to expand the scope of civil liberties has been oftentimes derailed by events that have seriously threatened the viability of the United States. At the beginning of the Civil War, President Abraham Lincoln issued orders curtailing certain civil liberties such as the *writ of habeas corpus*. President Franklin Roosevelt signed the order that placed American citizens of Japanese extraction into detention camps for the duration of World War II. President George W. Bush was confronted with the same challenge that these two presidents had to face. The tragic international terrorists' attacks of September 11, 2001, placed this nation into a perilous threatened state of emergency. Prompted by the Bush administration, Congress enacted legislature granting more police powers to federal law enforcement agencies that do, to some degree, seriously challenge the scope of American civil liberties. The Preamble of the United States Constitution charges the national government with the tasks to "provide for the common defense" and to "promote the general welfare" of the American people. When the future of the nation is challenged, it is the responsibility of the nation's leaders to do whatever is necessary to protect the American people from threats to their survival, while at the same time trying to avoid the erosion of those precious individual freedoms and civil liberties the Framers gave to us in the Bill of Rights.

THE CONCEPT OF CIVIL LIBERTIES

In 1215, English noblemen gathered in Runnymede to force their king to sign a pledge guaranteeing the preservation of certain privileges and rights to all Englishmen, regardless of rank and bloodline. The **Magna Carta** was the initial quest of Englishmen to end the arbitrary rule of their monarchs who governed under the **divine right theory** of kings. This concept of kingship rested on "the notion that monarchs rule by the will of, indeed in place of God. Since God created this situation, any effort to change it would be considered sinful, because it is through kings that God works his will on men."[5] Subsequently, the writings of John Locke, Jean Jacques Rousseau, and Charles de Montesquieu drew a distinction between alienable and inalienable rights. "Alienable natural rights were those that individuals could have ceded to society, if they wished; inalienable natural rights were so fundamental to human welfare that they were not considered to be in the power of individuals to surrender."[6] Accordingly, Locke's concept of the social contract rested on the belief that men gladly gave up their individual alienable natural rights as a tradeoff for a governing structure that would provide and protect everyone's inalienable rights. In his *Two Treaties on Government*, John Locke joined the ranks of John Stuart Mill and Jean J. Rousseau, who firmly believed that civil liberties were indeed unalienable rights "that belong to individuals by the nature of humanity, and which cannot be taken away without violating that humanity."⁶ For Locke, those fundamental rights were life, liberty and property. Retaining the rights to life and liberty, the Framers opted to borrow from Locke a more expansive notion of property to include more than physical possessions such as land by using the term "pursuit of happiness" to encompass artistic and intellectual expressions. In his *Essay Concerning Human Understanding* (1690), Locke stressed that "as therefore the highest perfection of intellectual nature lies in a careful and constant pursuit of true and solid happiness, so the care of ourselves that we mistake not imaginary for real happiness is the necessary foundation of our liberty."⁸

Although concerned about the protection of individual freedoms, the Framers did not include a Bill of Rights into the original document. "James Madison, for example, argued that since the Constitution was one of strictly enumerated powers, the federal government was necessarily prevented from passing legislation that would trample individual rights."⁹ Besides, the newly formed thirteen states had already written constitutions containing protections of individual rights and freedoms. However, there was no consistency of guaranteed rights in those documents. They were at best "a jarring but exciting combination of ringing declarations of universal principles of a motley collection of common law procedures."¹⁰ Case in point, "two states passed over a free press guarantee; four neglected to ban excessive fines, excessive bail, compulsory self-incrimination, and general search warrants. Five ignored protections for the rights of assemble, petition, counsel, and trial by jury in civil cases. Seven omitted a prohibition of *ex post facto* laws. Nine filed to . . . condemn bills of attainder. Ten said nothing about freedom of speech, while eleven were silent on double jeopardy."¹¹ It was the Anti-Federalists who used the inconsistency of rights in a state's Bill of Rights documents and the omission of a Bill of Rights in the federal document as their major arguments against ratification of the Constitution. "Within hours of the delegates signing the Constitution, George Mason published a pamphlet entitled *Objections to This Constitution of Government*, the central theme of which was that the absence of a 'declaration of rights' made the Constitution unacceptable. Without limitations, Mason believed, the federal government would infringe the basic rights of the citizenry. '[T]he laws of the general government,' Mason warned, 'being paramount to the law and constitution of the several States, the Declaration of Rights in the separate States are no security.'"¹²

Once the Congress convened under the newly adopted Constitution, James Madison led the charge to adopt a Bill of Rights. It is interesting to note that "the first ten amendments to the federal Constitution contain twenty-seven separate rights. Six of these rights, or about 20 percent, first appeared in the Magna Carta. Twenty-one or about 75 percent had their initial formulation in colonial documents written before the 1689 English Bill of Rights. Even more impressive, all but the Ninth Amendment could be found in several of the state constitutions written between 1776 and 1787."¹³ Essentially, the Bill of Rights corrected many of the abuses levied by the British government over its own citizens. Throughout its history, England has a blemished record of denying speedy trials, jury trials, reasonable bail, *writ of Habeas Corpus*, protections from cruel punishment, freedom of religious practices and beliefs, freedom of speech, and so on. The Framers were quick to recognized how important protecting these basic rights were to the successfulness of a democratic government. The permanency of these rights was assured with the adoption of **Article VI (Supremacy Clause)** that declared the Constitution and all subsequent amendments to the document as the supreme law of the land. Any state or local ordinance deemed in conflict with the spirit and meaning of the Constitution would be declared an unconstitutional act. Therefore, the Framers guaranteed to the governed that the governing would not undo what they had created.

However, the Framers were concerned that the absolute and unrestrained individual pursuit of inalienable rights would severely jeopardize the concept of a unified civil society. It was a question of individual liberty defined as "the condition of being free from restrictions or constraints" versus the creation of government restraints on the pursuit of those rights for the protection of society as a whole.[14] The Framers rationalized that "if we were to live in a truly 'civil' society, we must agree to respect the rights of others and subject our activities to reasonable restrictions enacted for the good of society."[15] Reasonable restrictions are the logical and rational curtailments enacted by government upon the absolute unrestrained pursuit of inalienable rights in order to guarantee the protection of those rights to all members of a civil society. Subsequently, religious freedom is not an absolute right. One cannot be arrested because his/her religious beliefs are socially unacceptable. However, one can be arrested when his/her pursuit of their religious beliefs breaks a law or causes damage to another's property or harm to another person. Also, freedom of speech is not an absolute right to say whatever an individual wishes to say. Freedom of speech creases to be a protected right when one's words shifts to fighting words that create a clear and present danger to others.

The phrase "reasonable restrictions" is essential to understanding the relationship of government at all levels to the United States Supreme Court. The Framers never provided a clear-cut guideline for legislating reasonable restrictions on civil liberties. For example, the Second Amendment guarantees the right to bear arms. However, the Framers did not define what constitutes an acceptable weapon or did they explain under what conditions weapons could be legally used. What is reasonable bail? What constitutes a fair trial? Under what conditions can a witness declare protection from prosecution under the Fifth Amendment? Or was the lack of specific definitions and parameters purposeful with the intent of leaving the "details" for future generations of lawmakers and jurists seeking to meet the changing needs of the American people:

> [S]hould we not pay the authors [the Framers] the compliment of believing that they meant no more than they said? What they left unsaid, they left open for us to decide. What then are the judges looking for, if it is not the intent of those who made the Constitution? . . . The Constitution has become something in its own right. It is an integral part of what men do with it. It has long ceased to be more than what other men hoped they would do or intended them to do. The Constitution, together with the Court's work, is not so much pushed by the plans of the past as pulled by the hopes of the future. It is not stuffed, but pregnant with meaning. The intent of the Framers when it is not expressed is only that we, the Congress, the President, and the Court, should be allowed to make good on their best hopes and cash in on their boldest bets. What our forefathers said they said. What they didn't say, they meant to leave to us, and what they said ambiguously, indefinitely, equivocally, or indistinctly, is in so far not said.[16]

Table 13.1

The Bill of Rights

Amendment I - Congress shall make no law respecting an establishment of religion, or prohibiting the free exercise thereof; or abridging the freedom of speech, or of the press; or the right of the people peaceable to assemble, and to petition the Government for a redress of grievances.

Amendment II - A well-regulated militia, being necessary to the security of a free State, the right of the people to keep and bear arms, shall not be infringed.

Amendment III - No soldier shall, in time of peace be quartered in any house, without the consent of the owner, nor in time of war, but in a manner to be prescribed by law.

Amendment IV - The right of the people to be secure in their persons, houses, papers, and effects, against unreasonable searches and seizures, shall not be violated, and no warrants shall issue, but upon probable cause, supported by oath or affirmation, and particularly describing the place to be searched, and the persons or things to be seized.

Amendment V - No person shall be held to answer for a capital, or otherwise infamous crime, unless on a presentment or indictment of a Grand Jury, except in cases arising in the land or naval forces, or in the militia, when in actual service in time of war or public danger; nor shall any person be subject for the same offense to be twice put in jeopardy of life or limb; nor shall be compelled in any criminal case to be a witness against himself, nor be deprived of life, liberty, or property, without due process of law; nor shall private property be taken for public use, without just compensation.

Amendment VI - In criminal prosecutions, the accused shall enjoy the right to a speedy and public trial, by an impartial jury of the State and district wherein the crime shall have been committed, which district shall have been previously ascertained by law, and to be informed of the nature and cause of the accusation; to be confronted with the witnesses against him; to have compulsory process for obtaining witnesses in his favor, and to have the assistance of counsel for his defense.

Amendment VII - In Suits at common law, where the value in controversy shall exceed twenty dollars, the right of trial by jury shall be preserved, and no fact tried by a jury, shall be otherwise reexamined in any Court of the United States, than according to the rules of the common law.

Amendment VIII - Excessive bail shall not be required, nor excessive fines imposed, nor cruel and unusual punishments inflicted.

Amendment XI - The enumeration in the Constitution, of certain rights, shall not be construed to deny or disparage others retained by the people.

Amendment X - The powers not delegated to the United States by the Constitution, nor prohibited by it to the States, are reserved to the States respectively, or to the people.

Amendment Pertaining to Application of Civil Liberties:

Amendment XIV - All persons born or naturalized in the United States, and subject to the jurisdiction thereof, are citizens of the United States and of the State wherein they reside. No state shall make or enforce any laws which shall abridge the privileges or immunities of citizens of the United States; nor shall any State deprive any person of life, liberty, or property, without due process of law; nor deny to any person within its jurisdiction the equal protection of the laws.

In 1789, the United States Congress passed the **Judiciary Act**, the enabling legislation establishing the court system outlined in Article III of the Constitution. Among its provisions was the concept of **judicial review**. Basically, judicial review "authorizes the Supreme Court to hold unconstitutional, and hence, unenforceable any law, any official action based upon a law, any other action by a public official it deems-upon careful reflection and in line with the inherent tradition of the law and judicial restraint-to be in conflict with the Constitution."[17] Far too often, the lack of specifics in the Bill of Rights has produced problems for lawmakers. Too often Congress and state legislative houses have passed what they considered to be reasonable laws only to have the federal courts and the court of last resort, the Supreme Court, declare their legislative actions as unreasonable restraints upon protected civil rights and liberties, and thus unconstitutional. The Framers correctly anticipated that as the composition of the Supreme Court membership changes, so can their decisions. For example, the death penalty was ruled in 1972 as an unconstitutional violation of the Eighth Amendment only to be reinstated as constitutional by the Court in 1976.

The initial question confronting the United States Supreme Court was whether certain provisions of the Bill of Rights were enforceable upon just the national government or applicable to all levels of government. In *Barron v Baltimore* (1833), Chief Justice John Marshall ruled that the first ten amendments to the United States Constitution were enforceable only on the actions of the national government. Marshall believed that "the Constitution was ordained and established by the people of the United States for themselves, for their own government, and not for the government of the individual states.... The powers they conferred on this government were to be exercised by itself; and the limitations on power, if expressed in general terms are ... necessarily applicable to the government created by the instrument. They are limitations of power granted in the instrument itself: not of distinct governments framed by different persons and for different reasons."[18]

The passage of the Fourteenth Amendment with its provisions of equal protection and due process paved the path for the United States Supreme Court to reverse its original decision outlined in *Barron*. In *Gitlow v New York* (1925), Gitlow challenged the ruling of the New York State Supreme Court that declared his use of the *Communist Manifesto* in classroom lectures as subversive and unconstitutionally protected speech. The United States Supreme Court's ruling in this case is significant for two reasons. First, the Court applied the phrase "**clear and present danger**" used initially in its ruling in *Schenck v United States* (1919), as its litmus test for determining the fine line between protected and unprotected speech. Second, and most importantly, the Court clearly expressed its desire to apply the Bill of Rights to the states through the Fourteenth Amendment. The justices rationalized that "for present purposes we may and do assume that freedom of speech and of the press which are protected by the First Amendment from abridgment by Congress are among the fundamental personal rights and liberties protected by the due process clause of the Fourteenth Amendment from impairment by the states."[19]

However, the United States Supreme Court did not and has not yet ruled that the entire Bill of Rights is applicable to all levels of government, particularly the states. Since the *Gitlow* case, the United States Supreme Court has used a piece-meal and often confusing practice of **selective incorporation**. In other words, justices *selectively* apply the due process clause of the Fourteenth Amendment to the states when the constitutional issue tied to the Bill of Rights appeals to the Court's interests. The Court has incorporated the First Amendment's establishment clause (usually referred to as the separation of church and state doctrine) to the states as well as issues involving cruel and unusual punishment, right to counsel, and double jeopardy, among others. "Those provisions that remain unincorporated are: 1) grand jury indictments (Fifth Amendment), 2) trial by jury in civil cases (Seventh Amendment), 3) the excessive bail and fines prohibitions (Eighth Amendment), 4) the right to bear arms (Second Amendment), and 5) the safeguard against involuntary quartering of troops in private homes (Third Amendment)."[20] Historically, liberal jurists favor expanding incorporation whereas conservative jurists, including the current Chief Justice of the Supreme Court John Roberts, reframe from expanding the scope of the Court's jurisdiction into state affairs.

Although the Bill of Rights guarantees sweeping civil liberties and rights, one must remember that initially these rights were granted to a small segment of the population. Voting privileges were granted to only white male property owners until the election of Andrew Jackson to the presidency. According to the Constitution, Native Americans are citizens of foreign nations. They were finally granted American citizenship in 1924 and, therefore, were only then granted protected civil rights and liberties. Until the passage of the Thirteenth Amendment to the United States Constitution, African Americans were not citizens with protected rights, they were slaves or indentured servants. Even though recognized as American citizens, women did not have the rights to own property or to vote until the passage of the Nineteenth Amendment. In has taken years of political battles and corrective legislation to provide to all of this nation's citizens the rights and privileges stated in the Constitution and its Bill of Rights.

Due Process

The application of **due process** is a particularly important consideration in any issue concerning civil liberties and civil rights. Due process involves "the procedural safeguards guaranteed to those who would be deprived of life, liberty, or property because they are accused of criminal wrongdoing."[21] The Fifth and Fourteenth Amendments forbid both the national and state governments from denying to any person life, liberty, and property without due process of the law. Today the application of due process extends beyond the criminal court room to issues involving the employment and termination processes, voting rights, and so on. "The concept of due process of law and its application to our federal and state governments is based an extensive reservoir of *constitutionally expressed and implied limitations upon governmental authority*, ultimately determined by the judicial process, and upon those basic notions of fairness and decency which govern, or ought to govern, the relationships between rulers and ruled."[22]

The law involves the concepts of procedural and substantive due process. **Substantive due process** refers "to the *content or subject matter* of a law or ordinance; that is, whether what it deals with what it is trying to accomplish, *contextually* conforms to due process of the law. On the other hand, **procedural due process**-as the most litigated of the two-refers to the manner in which a law, an ordinance, administrative practice, or judicial task is carried out; that is, whether the procedures employed by those who are charge with the application of the law or ordinance violate *procedural* due process, regardless of the substance of the former."[23] Laws must be equally enacted and enforced. Yet, some enactments are so vague in content that people of common intelligence must guess as to their meaning and application. Government cannot hold citizens accountable for obeying laws that provide nebulous enforcement guidelines to law enforcement personnel, judges, juries, and, of course, the citizens themselves. Second, laws must be clearly written whereby all parties understand what the law means. For example, in 1971 the United States Supreme Court heard arguments in *Coates v Cincinnati* that posed both procedural and substantive issues involving a Cincinnati city ordinance. Dennis Coates and several companions were arrested for violating a city ordinance that made it illegal for three or more persons who assembled on any street corner, sidewalk, or vacant lot to display any behavior that was deemed annoying to persons passing by. The United States Supreme Court ruled this ordinance as an unconstitutional act for several reasons. First, the ordinance was both procedurally unenforceable and too vague in content and substance. Without properly defining what constituted "annoying behavior," both citizens and law enforcement personnel were confused as to the differences between acceptable and unacceptable behavior. Like the appreciation of art, the definition of annoying behavior is a subjective one. Individual interpretation of annoying behavior leads to a discriminatory application of the ordinance. Second, the ordinance was a direct violation of the right to assemble as guaranteed by the First Amendment to the United States Constitution. Again, the power of judicial review rescued the citizen from unfair and unconstitutional treatment.

The Importance of the First Amendment

The First Amendment to the United States Constitution addresses the fundamental civil liberties granted to the American people. This amendment states that "Congress shall make no law respecting an establishment of religion, or prohibiting the free exercise thereof; or abridging the freedom of speech, or of the press; or the right of the people peaceably to assemble and to petition the Government for a redress of grievances." An analysis of the interpretation and application of reasonable restrictions clearly illustrates the roles the federal court system, legislative houses, interest groups, and the people have in establishing acceptable limits for exercising these freedoms.

Freedom of Religion

The phrase "Congress shall make no laws respecting the establishment of religion" is called the **establishment clause**. The Framers did not want government to sponsor one religion over others nor to advocate one religious practice over other practices. The Framers justified their actions by emphasizing century old problems the English government had when it sponsored one religion over other religions and the horrible loss of life and property resulting from religious conflicts. The tendency for one religious group to believe that their teachings and practices should take the pre-eminent position over other beliefs and practices has led to religious conflicts and a breakdown of religious tolerance for centuries. "The bitter memories of religious intolerance suffered by American colonists before coming to America can be seen in a statement in 1774 by the First Continental Congress declaring that the Church of England [Anglicanism] was '. . . a religion that has deluged [England] in blood, and dispersed bigotry, persecution, murder, and rebellion through every part of the world.'"[24]

Banished from the Massachusetts colony for his religious beliefs, Roger Williams "steadfastly maintained that religion was something personal, something defined by an individual's relationship with his or her god. It could not—should not be—coerced by anyone, especially kings, magistrates, or the decree of governments. Forcing someone to worship according to the Christian faith was antithetical to Christ's own teachings."[25] Subsequently, the choice of one's religious beliefs and practices would rest with the individual, not government. The Framers opted to separate church or religious issues from government by incorporating the separation of church and state doctrine into the First Amendment. In particular, George Washington and Thomas Jefferson stressed that religious tolerance and diversification of religious beliefs in this country were to be encouraged, not discouraged. In his capacity as the nation's first president, Washington negotiated a treaty primarily written by John Adams and ratified by the United States Senate in 1797 that assured the Muslim-dominated nation of Tripoli that "the Government of the United States is not, in any sense, founded on the Christian religion."[26] After introducing a bill stressing religious tolerance, Jefferson emphasized that the purpose of the legislation was "meant to comprehend, within the mantle of its protection, the Jew and the Gentile, the Christian and the Mahometan, the Hindoo [Hindu] and infidel of every domination" would be free to exercise their religious beliefs without prejudice from the nation's governing bodies.[27] United States Supreme Court Justice Hugo Black once wrote that the First Amendment's Establishment Clause meant that

> neither a state nor the Federal Government can set up a church. Neither can pass laws which aid one religion, aid all religions, or prefer one religion over another. Neither can force nor influence a person to go to or to remain away from church against his will or force him to profess a belief or disbelief in any religion. No person can be punished for entertaining or professing religious beliefs or disbeliefs, for church attendance or nonattendance. No tax in any amount, large or small, can be levied to support any religious activities or institutions, whatever they may be called, or whatever form they may adopt to teach or practice religion. Neither a state or the Federal Government can, openly or secretly, participate in the affairs of any religious organizations or groups and vice versa. In the words of Jefferson, the clause was intended to erect a wall of separation between Church and State."[28]

The United States Supreme Court has become the champion for ensuring that this fragile wall separating church from state remains intact by steadfastly preserving the right of individuals to hold diverse religious beliefs and practices without recrimination. Consequently, "the balance between the promise of the Declaration of Independence, with its evocation of divine origins and destiny, and the practicalities of the Constitution, with its checks on extremism, remains the most brilliant of American successes."[29] The primary religious-based issues addressed by the Supreme Court clearly indicate its historical effort to uphold that balance.

One of the initial questions concerned the use of public funds derived from tax dollars to promote education in public, private, and parochial schools. In 1947, the Supreme Court heard arguments in *Everson v Board of Education of the Township of Ewing*, questioning the constitutionality of a New Jersey state law that provided public funding to qualifying parents to offset the costs of public transportation for their children to and from public and private schools. Everson filed a suit challenging the use of public funds to send children to parochial schools as a violation of the Establishment Clause. In rendering their 5 to 4 decision in favor of the funding program, the justices applied the child benefit theory whereby public funding can be provided to students who attend both public and private or parochial schools as long as it is the child, rather than the school, that benefits from the funding. Justice Black argued that the New Jersey law "does no more than provide a general program to help parents get their children, regardless of their religion, safely and expeditiously to and

Students in public schools have always prayed, especially around test time. But, the Court objects to sponsorship or encouragement of prayer by public-school authorities. The Court has ruled that prayer can not be an attempt on the part of the government to promote religion.

from accredited schools."[30] President Lyndon Johnson applied the same argument when he signed into law the Elementary and Secondary Education Act of 1965. This legislation was the first major infusion of federal money into the nation's private and public schools. The Court's ruling in **Lemon v Kurtzman** (1971) established the guidelines for subsequent religious-based issues. The *Lemon* case addressed two state programs that provided state funding to private schools. Pennsylvania's plan allocated state funds to private schools for instructional salaries, textbooks, and instructional materials used for nonreligious classes. The Rhode Island state legislature provided a 15 percent pay increase to teachers in private schools teaching nonreligious classes. In both cases, the Court ruled 8-1 that these programs were unconstitutional violations of separation of church and state. Writing for the majority of the Court, Chief Justice Warren Burger emphasized that "we need not decide whether these legislative precautions restrict the principal or primary effort of the programs to the point where they do not offend the Religious Clauses, for we conclude that the cumulative impact of the entire relationship arising under the statutes in each State involves excessive government entanglement between government and religion."[31] The resulting **Lemon Test** is a three-part test that determines whether the law's purpose is basically secular; whether the law's primary effect neither advances nor inhibits religion; and whether the law excessively entangles church and state. For example, in **Mitchell v Helms** (2000) the United States Supreme Court upheld a Louisiana law providing public funding for instructional equipment to include computers, maps, books, etc., to both public and private schools as long as it is "in a secular neutral non-ideological way."[32] The Supreme Court also upheld a lower court's ruling in favor of a 1997 Arizona law granting a tax credit up to $500 for donations to parochial and private school scholarship and tuition assistance programs. Once again, the money is donated to a program benefiting students and is not directed to any particular school.

In response to the declining quality of the nation's public school systems, the Republican Party, guided by members of its conservative wing, advocated voucher programs whereby parents could choose to transfer their children from low performing public schools to higher rated public, private, and parochial schools. To offset additional tuition, textbook, and transportation costs, parents would receive taxpayer-funded vouchers. For example, the Ohio state legislature adopted a pilot program for children attending public schools in Cleveland. "The program gave parents $2,250 per child in tuition vouchers to be used in about 50 schools."[33] Declaring that the "Ohio program is entirely neutral with respect to religion," the United States Supreme Court ruled in its 2002 session that the Cleveland voucher program is constitutional.[34] "Justice Sandra Day O'Connor; writing a concurring opinion with the majority of the Supreme Court, said she was 'persuaded that the Cleveland voucher program affords parents of eligible children genuine non-religious options consistent with separation of church and state protections.'"[35]

Perhaps the most controversial religious issue addressed by the United States Supreme Court is prayer in the public school systems. In 1962 and 1963, the United States Supreme Court heard two cases challenging government-sponsored prayer in the classroom. In *Engle v Vitale* (1962), Steve Engle challenged a 1951 decision of the New York State Board of Regents to approve a brief prayer for recital in the public schools. In 1958, the New Hyde Park School District required their students to recite the prayer each day in every class. Engle protested on the grounds that his two children were required to recite the prayer. Engle charged that an official prayer mandated to be recited in the public schools violated both the First Amendment's guarantees of freedom of religion and the separation of church and state doctrine. The United States Supreme Court ruled 8 to 1 in favor of Engle. Justice Black wrote "that by using its public school system to encourage recitation of the Regents' prayer, the State of New York has adopted a practice wholly inconsistent with the Establishment Clause. *There can, of course, be no doubt* that New York's program of daily classroom invocation of God's blessing as prescribed in the Regents' prayer is a religious activity. It is a solemn avowal of divine faith and supplication for the blessing of the Almighty. . . [T]he constitutional prohibition against laws respecting an establishment of religion must at least mean that in this country it is no part of the business of government to compose official prayers for any group of the American people to recite as part of a religious program carried on by government."[36]

The companion case was the *School District of Abington Township v Schempp* (1963). In this case, a Pennsylvania law required the verbal reading of ten verses from the Bible at the beginning of each school day in all public schools. Children could be excused from this exercise with parental consent. The Schempp family objected to the readings because their Unitarian faith did not interpret the meaning of the Bible in the same manner as other religions. They also felt that their children were the subjects of ridicule because they were sent out into the hallway during the readings. Ruling 8 to 1 in favor of Schempp, the United States Supreme Court decided that mandated Biblical readings conducted in a public school setting were indeed an unconstitutional violation of the doctrine of separation of church and state.

In both cases, the United States Supreme Court never ruled that prayer in the public schools was unconstitutional. Since the *Engle* and *Schempp* rulings, the United States Supreme Court has addressed several cases concerning prayer in the nation's public schools. In 1985, for example, the Court heard arguments in *Wallace v Jaffree*. The primary issue focused on the implementation of an 1981 law passed by the Alabama State legislature which stated that "at the commencement of the first class of each day in all grades in all public schools the teacher in charge of the room in which each class is held, may announce that a period of silence not to exceed one minute in duration shall be observed for meditation or voluntary prayer, and during any such period no other activities shall be engaged in."[37] On behalf of his three children, Ishmael Jaffree charged that the Alabama law was an unconstitutional act in violation of the First Amendment's guarantee of religious freedom. Initially, a federal district court judge upheld the Alabama law. However, a federal appellant court overturned the lower court's ruling. In a 6 to 3 decision, the United States Supreme Court upheld the appellant court's decision. Justice Paul Stevens stressed that "the legislation [was] enacted for the sole purpose of expressing the State's endorsement of prayer activities for one minute at the beginning of each school day. The addition of 'or voluntary prayer' indicates that the State intended to characterize prayer as a favored practice. Such an endorsement is not consistent with the establishment principle that the government must pursue a course of complete neutrality toward religion."[38]

In 1992, the United States Supreme Court ruled in **Lee v Weisman** that clergy-led prayer at public school graduation ceremonies is a violation of the separation of church and state doctrine. "That ruling allowed prayer at school graduation ceremonies only if school officials instructed students to keep them non-sectarian and non-proselytizing."[39] The Supreme Court also addressed the issue of student-led prayers at high school football games. Students attending the Santa Fe School District in Texas decided to continue the tradition of a pre-game prayer conducted by a member of the student body over the stadium's public address system. Two parents sought legal action to end public pre-game prayers. The 5th United States Circuit Court of Appeals ruled that student-led prayers were an unconstitutional violation of the First Amendment's Establishment Clause. The United States Supreme Court has consistently upheld the belief that *voluntary* prayer is legal; however, *involuntary* prayer is not!

The current trend is to allow "a moment of silence" or "a moment for self-reflection" to be used in the public school systems. This policy underscores voluntary self reflection without mentioning the word prayer. The constitutionality of a "moment of silence" was upheld by the United States Supreme Court during its 2001 session when the justices declined to address a challenge to a lower court's affirmation of Virginia's "moment of silence law." "For nearly 25 years, Virginia law allowed school districts the choice of holding a moment of silence for 60 seconds. . . But in 2000, the state's legislature and governor changed the law to require that all schools take part in the moment."[40] The Virginia law clearly met the Supreme Court's litmus test since it is "a moment of silence law that is clearly drafted and implemented so as to permit prayer, meditation, and reflection within the prescribed period, without endorsing one alternative over the others . . .[because it does] not favor the child who chooses to pray over the child who chooses to meditate or reflect."[41]

Traditionally, the United States Supreme Court has held that religious practices are constitutional as long as the activity is lawful and does not violate the personal rights or the property of others. The Supreme Court, for example, upheld the use of animal sacrifices as a bona fide religious ceremony in its ruling in *Church of the Lukumi Babbalu Aye v Hialeah* (1993). In *West Virginia State Board of Education v Barnette* (1943), the Supreme Court ruled that the state's law requiring all teachers and pupils in the public schools to participate in a daily flag salute ceremony or face expulsion from school clearly violated the religious rights of members of the Jehovah Witnesses. Writing for the majority, Justice Jackson stated that "to sustain the compulsory flag salute, we are required to say that a Bill of Rights which guards the individual's right to speak his own mind, left it open to public authorities to compel him to utter what is not in his mind."[42] In a wide variety of rulings on complex issues ranging from school prayer to state-funded public/private education voucher programs, the United States Supreme Court has consistently upheld that the "**exercise clause** protects our right to believe or not to believe in any religious doctrine, prohibits all government regulation of religious beliefs; forbids the government from compelling us to worship; prohibits the punishment of religious beliefs that the government believes to be false; and denies to the state the power to grant benefits or place burdens on the basis of religious beliefs or status."[43]

Freedom of Speech

Over the 2012 summer months, a controversial film condemning Islam and its prophet Mohammad produced by an independent American filmmaker was seen in movie theaters throughout the world, resulting in deadly riots and protests throughout the Middle East. Worldwide Islamic leaders and heads of the Arab states called upon President Obama to ban the movie and silence its producer. However, the president upheld to the belief that the right to express one's opinion is a sacred privilege to all Americans. Although we may not like what some people say and do, we do respect their right to express their viewpoints. Addressing the membership of the United Nations, Obama told the gathering that although the movie was indeed inflammatory to the Islamic faith, the filmmaker had the protected right to express his viewpoint. In America, he pointed out:

> We do so because in a diverse society, efforts to restrict speech can become a tool to silence critics, or oppress minorities. We do so because given our power of faith in our lives, and the passion that religious differences can inflame, the strongest weapon against hateful speech is not repression, it is more speech—the voices of tolerance that rally against bigotry and blasphemy, and lift up the values of understanding and mutual respect. Americans have fought the globe to protect the right of all people to express their view.[44]

Any government action slightly resembling censorship is met with sharp criticism. Lawmakers do not want to repeat the backlash the Federalist Party received in 1798 when it ventured into the realm of censorship with the passage of four laws commonly known as the **Alien and Sedition Acts**. The Federalists rationale for suppressing free speech was deeply rooted in the developing revolution in France. They viewed the overthrow of the French monarchy "as the degeneration of legitimate government into mob rule, particularly during the 1793 and 1794 bloody 'Reign of Terror' when counterrevolutionaries lost their lives on the guillotine. Federalist fears deepened as they watched the new French republican government encourage wars of liberation and conquest in Belgium, Switzerland, Holland, and on the Italian peninsula. In 1798 rumors spread about a possible French invasion of America, one that allegedly would be supported by American traitors and a large number of French émigrés that grew to more than 20,000."[45] The **Naturalization Act** extended the immigrant residency requirement for citizenship from five to fourteen years. The president was empowered through both the **Alien Act** and **Alien Enemies Act** to arrest and subsequently expel all aliens deemed to be a threat to the security of the nation. The most objectionable law was the **Sedition Act**, which made it illegal to publish or utter any statements about the government that were 'false, scandalous and malicious' with the 'intent to defame' or to bring Congress or the president into 'contempt or disrepute.'"[46] Several journalists were tried and convicted of violating the Sedition Act. The legality of the Sedition Act was one of the primary issues in the presidential election of 1800 as Republican candidate Thomas Jefferson denied Federalist candidate John Adams a second presidential term of office. Jefferson subsequently repealed the Sedition Act and pardoned those convicted of violating it.

Overall, Supreme Court decisions have expanded the scope of the freedoms of speech and expression from political campaigns to video games. In 1976, the Court ruled in **Buckley v Valeo** that provision of 1974 congressional act limiting how much personal money a candidate could spend on his/her election was unconstitutional. The rationale was that candidates must have every opportunity to reach out to the voting public. The same sentiment guided the Court's 2010 decision in *Citizens United v Federal Elections Commission* when it declared a provision in the Bipartisan Campaign Reform Act barring the airing of political advertisements days before an election day as an unconstitutional violation of free speech. It also struck down an Arizona law that gave state matching campaign funds to candidates who adhered to the state mandated personal campaign spending level as once again, a violation of free speech. In 2011, the Court ruled unconstitutional a California law banning the sale of videos deemed too violent for children.

However, the Court has drawn the line between acceptable and unacceptable exercises of free speech. Simply, we do not have the absolute right to say or to do whatever we want to do. The United States Supreme Court has distinguished protected speech from unconstitutional breaches of freedom of speech. **Pure speech** is "speech without any conduct."[47] A person's words are constitutionally protected as long as those words do not pose a harm to others. The United States Supreme Court distinguished acceptable from unacceptable speech in its ruling in *Schenck v United States* (1919). Schenck had been convicted by a lower court for violating the Espionage Act of 1917 by distributing Socialist-inspired leaflets encouraging men to resist the draft imposed at the height of World War I. Ruling unanimously against Schenck, the United States Supreme Court ruled that his actions created a "clear and present danger" to others. Justice Holmes wrote:

> We admit that in many places and in *ordinary times* the defendants in saying all that was said in the circular would have been within their constitutional rights. *But the character of every act depends upon the circumstances in which it is done.* . . . The most stringent protection of free speech would not protect a man in *falsely* shouting fire in a theatre and causing a panic. It does not even protect a man from an injunction against uttering words that have all the effects of force. . . . *The question in every case is whether the words used are used in such circumstances and are of such a nature as to create a clear and present danger that they will bring about the substantive evils that Congress has a right to prevent.* When a nation is at war many things that might be said in time of peace are such a hindrance to its effort that their utterance will not be endured so long as men fight and that no Court could regard them as being protected by any constitutional right.[48]

Words that present a clear and present danger are unconstitutional. Collectively these words are called **fighting words**. The United States Supreme Court defines fighting words as words that by their very nature inflict injury upon those to whom they are addressed. If an individual's words incite his/her audience to violence, then that individual can be held accountable for the crowd's actions. It is the resulting actions of the words and not necessarily the words themselves that can be deemed unconstitutional. For example, in 2010, the Supreme Court heard arguments against the actions of the Westboro Baptist Church of Kansas. The congregation composed mostly of family members of its pastor, stage anti-gay protests on public property during the funerals of servicemen killed in combat. Their signs reflect their viewpoint that God is punishing America for its support of the gay community by killing its soldiers. Although the words are indeed painful to family members attending the funeral services of their fallen soldiers, the Supreme Court ruled that the

Not all areas of free speech are protected. The Court has ruled that some practices are clearly illegal. Here, Goddard C. Graves, 22, burns his selective service classification card in front of the local draft board office as a protest against the Vietnam War. Although this gesture of symbolic speech is prohibited, a ruling by the Court gave such protection to burning the American flag.

words on the signs and the actions of the protestors do not by themselves lead to violence, and are therefore, protected by the First Amendment.

Symbolic speech is "the use of symbols, rather than words, to convey ideas."[49] The turmoil of Vietnam in the late 60s and early 70s filled the United States Supreme Court's docket with cases involving the use of symbolic speech. In *Tinker v Des Moines School District* (1969), the Supreme Court ruled that the wearing of black armbands as a silent protest against the war by high school students did not present a clear and present danger. Furthermore, the Supreme Court ruled in *Cohen v California* (1971) that the wearing of a jacket bearing an inappropriate four-letter word against the draft was a protected right. However, the Supreme Court does not consider a violation of a law to be a constitutionally protected expression of free speech. In *United States v O'Brien (1968),* the Supreme Court, for example, upheld O'Brien's conviction for burning his draft card in protest against Vietnam. Although O'Brien's protest was constitutionally protected, his actions of destroying government documents (draft cards) were not afforded the same protection.

The burning of the American flag evokes the strong emotions of the American people. However, the United Sates Supreme Court has held the burning of the flag in protest as a protected expression of speech. In *Street v New York* (1969), the United States Supreme Court reversed a lower court's conviction of Street for defacing and burning the flag. Street's defiant actions followed the 1960 ambush shooting of James Meredith in Mississippi. Likewise, during the 1984 Republican National Convention held in Dallas, Texas, Gregory Johnson headed a political protest against President Reagan. Following their march, Johnson set fire to an American flag soaked in kerosene.

The Court stated, "We do not consecrate the flag by punishing its desecration, for in doing so we dilute the freedom that this cherished emblem represents."

No bystanders were physically injured. Johnson was arrested for the desecration of the American flag, convicted of a Class A misdemeanor, sentenced to one year in prison, and fined $2,000. In a close 5 to 4 decision, the Supreme Court ruled in *Texas v Johnson* that Johnson's actions were constitutionally protected under the First Amendment. Stressing that burning the American flag is not under normal circumstances socially acceptable, Justice Brennan wrote: "Our decision is a reaffirmation of the principles of freedom and inclusiveness that the flag but reflects, and of the conviction that our toleration of criticism such as Johnson's is a sign and source of our strength. We do not consecrate the flag by punishing its desecration, for in doing so we dilute the freedom that this cherished emblem represents."[50] In 1989, Congress thought it had afforded the American flag the appropriate protection with the passage of the Federal Flag Protection Act, only to have it declared unconstitutional by the Supreme Court a year later.

The anti-Vietnam War protests of the 60's and 70's resurfaced with the George W. Bush administration's invasion of Iraq. The fear of potential terrorist acts on American soil moved the Federal Bureau of Investigation (FBI) and the Department of Homeland Security to closely monitor the formation and in particular, the tactics used by anti-war groups. In the time of war or threats to national security, the line separating protected from unprotected speech is blurred. Recalling the infiltration tactics used by the Nixon administration during the height of Vietnam, Anthony Romero, executive director of the American Civil Liberties Union, stated "the FBI is dangerously targeting Americans who are engaged in nothing more than lawful protest and dissent. The line between terrorism and legitimate civil disobedience is blurred, and I have a serious concern about whether we're going back to the days of [J. Edgar] Hoover."[51] Of course, this nation can ill-afford a repeat of events that occurred at Kent State University on May 4, 1970. Across the nation, college students were demonstrating against the Vietnam War and, in particular, President Nixon's decision to bomb Cambodia. The governor of Ohio vowed to "use 'every force possible' to maintain order and drive the protestors out of Kent. He called them 'worse than the brown shirts and the communist element, and also the nightriders and the vigilantes. They are the worse type of people we harbor in American.'"⁵² The governor called in the National Guard to break up the protests and bring calm back to the campus. On that fateful day, the guardsmen were supposed to peacefully disperse the crowd from the college's Commons area. After throwing gas canisters at the students, the guardsmen retreated only to have angry students follow them. Suddenly, "28 guardsmen wheeled and fired on students. At 12:55 p.m., 61 shots from M-1 rifles rained down the hill [near the Commons] for 13 seconds.... Four students lay dead in the parking lot, and nine others were wounded."⁵³

Freedom of speech is unconstitutionally protected when its use deliberately harms the character and reputation of another person. **Slander** is verbal malicious attacks against another person. On the other hand, libel is defamation of character in print or by other visual presentations. The reasonable restrictions involving slander and libel revolve around the intent of the initiating party. In 1964, the United States Supreme Court addressed the issue of libel in its decision in *New York Times v Sullivan*. Sullivan, a Montgomery, Alabama police commissioner, was awarded $500,000 in damages by a lower court to settle his lawsuit against the *New York Times* for printing an advertisement containing false statements charging his police force with brutality and discrimination against African Americans. The United States Supreme Court reversed the lower court decision. The *New York Times* was deemed not accountable for several reasons. First, public officials are natural targets for verbal and printed attacks. Second, erroneous statements are often unavoidable. If the media were held accountable for every erroneous statement it made, the courts would be flooded with libel and slander cases. Third, and most importantly, the Supreme Court ruled that "even false statements about official conduct, therefore, enjoy constitutional protection, unless they were made with actual malice; that is with the knowledge that they were false or with a reckless disregard of whether or not they were false."⁵⁴ The mere printing of false statements is not libel unless those statements were printed with a reckless disregard for the truth for the sole purpose of maliciously harming the reputation of an individual.

Obscenity

If art is in the eyes of the beholder, the same standard applies to determining what is or is not obscene. According to the United States Constitution, we do have the freedom to express ourselves in both word and deed. Paintings, motion pictures, advertisements, dance forms, sculpture, and literature are modes of expression. Judging a work as art or as obscenity should be a personal decision. However, too often it is left to the courts to determine what constitutes obscenity and to establish the criteria for reasonable restrictions. In *Roth v United States* (1957), Justice Brennan drew a fine line in distinguishing the difference between constitutionally and unconstitutionally protected creative expression. Writing for the majority, Brennan pointed out that "the First Amendment was not intended to protect every utterance.... All ideas having even the slightest redeeming social importance—unorthodox ideas, controversial ideas, even ideas hateful to the prevailing climate of opinion—have the full protection of the guaranties unless excludable because they encroach upon the limited area of more important interests. But implicit in the history of the First Amendment is the rejection of obscenity as utterly without redeeming social importance... It has been well observed that such utterances are no essential part of any exposition of ideas, and are of such slight

Adult book stores, such as this one, have been the battlefield for many local communities. Although the Supreme Court has ruled that it is unconstitutional to ban them, zoning ordinances restricting them to certain areas is permissible.

social value as a step to truth that any benefit that may be derived from them is clearly outweighed by the social interest in order and morality. . . . We hold that obscenity is not within the area of constitutionally protected speech or press."⁵⁵ Chief Justice Earl Warren believed that precisely defining obscenity was "the Court's most difficult area of adjudication. What is 'obscenity' to some is mere 'realism' to others; what is 'lascivious' in the eyes of one reader is merely 'colorful' in those of another; what is 'lewd' to one parent may well be 'instructive' to another."⁵⁶ In *Miller v California* (1973), the United States Supreme Court ruled that actions or objects could be deemed obscene only if they meet all three of the following criteria:

1. Whether the average person, applying contemporary community standards, would find that the work taken as a whole, appeals to the prurient interest.
2. Whether the work depicts or describes, in a patently offensive way, sexual conduct specifically defined by the applicable state law.
3. Whether the work taken as a whole, lacks serious literary, artistic, political or scientific value.⁵⁷

Reasonable restrictions tell us that the personal possession of obscene materials by an adult is a protected right. However, the sale and distribution of sexually explicit materials to minors are a crime. Child pornography is a crime. Erotic dancing by an adult, however, is a form of expression legally protected by the First Amendment. Basically for the majority of the obscenity cases argued in the nation's courts, the distinction between legal and illegal activities is determined primarily by the age of the participating parties.

Freedom of the Press

A free press is essential to democratic governments. Citizens do have the right to know what their government is or is not doing. The United States Supreme Court has protected the sanctity of the fourth estate, the press. In 1931, the Supreme Court established the boundary line of "**no prior restraint**" in its decision in *Near v Minnesota*. The editor of the *Saturday Press,* Jay Near, was well known for using his paper to express his "anti-Semitic, anti-Catholic, anti-labor, and anti-black viewpoints. In addition, in a series of articles, Near charged that Minneapolis police and prosecutors were in collusion with Jewish gangsters involved in gambling, bootlegging, and racketeering.[58] The county attorney decided to "stop the presses" by accusing Near of being in violation of a Minnesota public nuisance law prohibiting the publishing of materials deemed to be "malicious, scandalous and defamatory."[59] Ruling in favor of Near, the Supreme Court's decision mandated that the only time government can legally bar the press from publishing a story is when such an action poses a real and eminent threat to national security. For example, it would have been a threat to national security for the press to publish in advance the exact date and time of the dropping of nuclear bombs on Japan during World War II or to divulge the schedule for sending scud missiles into Iraq during the Gulf War. It is not a breach of national security to publish information about these activities after the fact.

The concept of no prior restraint was held to close scrutiny when the United States Supreme Court heard arguments in *New York Times v United States* (1971). The case centered on the actions of Daniel Ellsberg, a temporary federal employee who discovered a cache of secret government documents detailing the cover-up by the federal government regarding the United States' initial entry into the Vietnam conflict. Ellsberg was a trusted ally to the paper's reporters since he occasionally provided background information for storylines. Ellsberg voluntarily offered the seized

Dr. Daniel Ellsberg, antiwar activist who was arrested for releasing the secret "Pentagon Papers," holds an impromptu news conference outside a federal building in Boston while his wife, Patricia, waits behind him. Daniel Ellsberg was indicted for espionage, theft, and conspiracy. His case was dismissed on the grounds of government misconduct.

documents to the *New York Times* and the *Washington Post*. After publishing the first excerpts from the documents, both newspapers were placed under federal court ordered injunctions to stop the presses. The federal government claimed that publishing these sensitive documents presented a threat to national security, even though the United States was already heavily involved in the Vietnam conflict. The United States Supreme Court ruled against the federal government's actions. Justice Black credited the papers' bold actions to print the documents by stating, "in my view, far from deserving condemnation for their courageous reporting, the *New York Times*, the *Washington Post*, and other newspapers should be commended for serving the purpose that the Framers saw so clearly. In revealing the workings of government that led to the Vietnam War, the newspapers nobly did precisely that which the Founders [Framers] hoped and trusted they would do."[60] The Supreme Court also decided that the purported threat to national security was non-existent since the event had already happened. Ellsberg, however, still suffered the consequences of his actions by being convicted of stealing government documents. A similar fate may wait for Eric Snowden, an employee of the National Security Agency (NSA) who leaked to the public the internal records of the NSA detailing the agency's monitoring of e-mails, internet connections, and phone calls made by American citizens. The agency justifies its actions by pointing out that preventive rather than reactive actions will halt terrorist attacks against the United States. Snowden and his supporters take the position that the agency's policies violate protected First Amendment rights. Wanted for numerous federal criminal charges including treason, Snowden fled the United States and was granted asylum in Russia.

Although the First Amendment initially extended constitutional protections to the print media, the rise of the electronic media to include television, cable, and internet accessibility has expanded the application of "freedom of the press." Established in 1934, the **Federal Communications Commission (FCC)** sets the programming and broadcasting guidelines for the majority of the nation's television and radio stations. In 1996, Congress passed the **Telecommunications Act** requiring cable stations that did not abide by the FCC's programming guidelines for airing sexually explicit programs only at late-night hours to completely block out their signal to protect children from watching these programs. In a 5 to 4 decision, the United States Supreme Court ruled that the Telecommunications Act was an unconstitutional infringement upon the stations' protected First Amendment rights. In 1997, the Supreme Court ruled that the **Communications Decency Act** was an unconstitutional infringement upon users of the internet. The act banned the electronic transmission of any materials deemed indecent to minors. "This was the first time that the highest court had contemplated the status of the key medium of the next century. Instead of regarding the Net with caution the court usually shows while exploring new frontiers, the justices went out of their way to assure that this most democratic of mediums would receive the highest level of protection. Internet speakers will not be shackled with the regulations that limit content on television and radio; instead, they will enjoy the freedom granted to printed matter."[61]

Assembly and Association

A basic civil liberty granted to all American citizens is the right to associate with others and to assemble or to join their ranks if we so choose to do so. The freedom of association is just as important to a free society as the freedoms of speech, redress, and religion. Our history, however, has been severely tainted by the actions of racial supremacy groups, such as the Klan, skinhead groups, the American Nazi Party, and so on. However, in times that pose a threat to national security, the federal government is empowered by federal legislation to take extraordinary steps to protect its citizens. Particularly in the aftermath of September 11, 2001, outraged citizens demanded that the White House and Congress enact measures empowering federal agencies to investigate the actions of, identify members affiliated with, and even infiltrate the ranks of international terrorist organizations as well as domestic-based interest groups hostile to the American government. However, the Framers never intended for governing authorities at any level to legislate whether citizens could affiliate with certain groups deemed in conflict with our nation's fundamental principles. The rights to protest and redress the government are fundamental constitutionally protected rights. Allowing someone to join the local PTA but arresting a person affiliated with a white supremacist group is unconstitutional. However, individuals can be held legally accountable for actions that violate another's rights to life and property whether their actions were guided by a group's philosophy or advocacy of violence.

In determining whether an action is constitutional, the fine line for the Supreme Court has been the difference between mere advocacy and action. In 1969, the United States Supreme Court heard arguments in *Brandenburg v. Ohio*, a landmark case that set the stage for subsequent rulings in assembly-related cases. Charles Brandenburg, leader of a local Ku Klux Klan (KKK) chapter, invited a television station to film several Klan rallies. The film contained excepts from his speech in which he stated that "if our president, our Congress, our Supreme Court, continues to suppress the white, Caucasian race, it's possible that there might have to be some revengence taken."[62] No violent action resulted from his speech. Brandenburg, however, was arrested and convicted of violating Ohio's Criminal Syndicalism Act, prohibiting the advocacy of terrorism. The United States Supreme Court overturned Brandenburg's conviction because the Ohio statute was designed "to punish mere advocacy and to forbid on pain of criminal punishment, assembly with others merely to advocate the described type of action. Such a statute falls within the condemnation of the First and Fourteenth Amendments."[63]

The price of free society! The Court has ruled that the constitutional right to free speech and assembly apply to all citizens regardless of how offensive their beliefs might be to the majority.

The question of assembly arose once again in 1978 with the emotionally charged case, *Village of Skokie v National Socialist Party*. The National Socialist Party, also known as the American Nazi Party, wanted to hold a public march through the predominately Jewish suburb of Skokie, Illinois. Since the majority of the suburb's residents were either survivors of or had lost relatives in the Nazi concentration camps of World War II, they were furious and petitioned their city council to deny the group a parade permit. Denied the permit, the Nazi Party filed a challenge on the grounds that their First Amendment rights had been violated. The Illinois state courts refused to allow the march on the grounds that it might create a clear and present danger to the residents of Skokie. The United States Supreme Court reversed all lower court rulings on the grounds that a mere presumption of violence is not a valid reason to deny the group's constitutional right to march. This decision was a reasonable restriction accommodating to both parties. Although the Nazi Party decided to bypass Skokie and march through downtown Chicago, they retained their constitutional right to stage a public march as long as they applied for the proper permits. For those who would have been offended by the message of the marchers, their protected rights not to watch the march were preserved!

The rise of teenage gangs has prompted municipal governments across the country to implement curfew laws designed to restrict teenagers' accessibility to gang-related activities. These city ordinances mandate that unsupervised juveniles cannot be allowed on city streets after a predetermined time period. In 1999, the United States Supreme Court essentially gave municipal governments a green light to continue curfew laws. The same court, however, ruled that an anti-gang ordinance crafted by the Chicago, Illinois, city council was unconstitutional. Enacted in 1992, the ordinance allowed the Chicago police to disperse and/or arrest individuals "if they stood or sat around in one place with no apparent purpose in the presence of a suspected gang member."[64] In *Chicago v Morales*, the United States Supreme Court ruled 6 to 3 that this ordinance was a violation of the First Amendment's right to association and assembly. Writing in support of the majority, Justice John Paul Stevens noted that "the ordinance allowed the police to order people to move on without inquiring into their reasons for remaining in one place... It matters not whether the reason that a gang member and his father, for example, loiter near Wrigley Field is to rob an unsuspecting fan or just to get a glimpse of Sammy Sosa leaving the ballpark. Friends, relatives, teachers, counselors, or even total strangers might unwittingly engage in forbidden loitering if they happen to engage in idle conversation with a gang member."[65] The Supreme Court further ruled that the vagueness of the Chicago city ordinance posed both substantive and procedural due process problems by giving the police too much discretion in predetermining the intent of those individuals participating in a sidewalk gathering.

However, the threat to national security posed by September 11 was real and, unfortunately, the reality is that this country is not shielded from another act of terrorism. The Bush administration and Congress responded after September 11 by merging both foreign and domestic federal intelligence agencies under one roof—the Department of Homeland Security. Congress passed the **Patriot Act** in conjunction with several presidential executive orders and additional congressional acts narrowing the scope of protected civil liberties including freedom of speech, association, unreasonable searches, and guarantees to speedy and public trials. In particular, the Patriot Act grants law enforcement expanded rights to wiretapping, tracking e-mails and internet sources, and legalizing conduct that would be otherwise illegal such as surprise searches of suspected terrorists' property as well as the authority to increase security checks at airports and international borders. A similar piece of legislation, the **Smith Act,** was enacted during the Cold War as a result of the Red Scare and McCarthyism. Overtime, the federal courts eventually dismantled provisions of the Smith Act. Recently, a federal judge ruled that the Patriot Act's provision of allowing the NSA to keep records of Americans' phone calls was unconstitutional. The judge ordered the agency to stop recording the calls and to destroy all records of calls made by the lawsuit's plaintiffs. Complaints levied by airline passengers have resulted in the relaxation of security rules at the nation's airports. Librarians have voiced their concerns about federal agencies monitoring the library checkout records of library users. The federal courts are now beginning to dismantle the Patriot Act in the same piecemeal fashion as they used with the Smith Act.

The Right to Bear Arms

Throughout the thirteen original colonies, local residents, particularly in isolated rural areas, had to form local militias to defend themselves from hostile Indian raids. Militia members had to supply their own weaponry. It was common for the flint-locked rifle to be visibly hung above the family fireplace so when the community bell called militia members to action, one could just grab their gun and report for duty. When the relationship between the British government and colonists soured, the British colonial governing bodies decided to punish the colonists by confiscating their weapons. The colonists were outraged. Therefore, the Framers addressed this concern through the Second Amendment to the Constitution that guarantees the right to bear arms.

Since its adoption in 1791, applying reasonable restrictions to the Second Amendment has always been a bone of contention. The mere mention of "gun control" is met with disdain by gun owners and those who don't own a gun but simply do not want any level of government restricting their access to potentially purchase and own a firearm. The right to bear an arm of defense is directly tied to the prevailing belief that one should be able to do whatever is necessary to defend one's life and property from harm. Founded in 1871, the **National Rifle Association** is the most powerful organization supporting gun rights and ownership. The "gun lobby" in Washington and in all fifty state legislative houses constantly monitors any legislation restricting access to firearms. However, reasonable restrictions have been applied to the Second Amendment, for example, the **National Firearms Act** of 1934 banned the sale and use of machine guns and levied a tax on both gun manufacturers and sellers. Following the assassination of President Kennedy, the **Gun Control Act** (1968) restricted gun sales across state lines and tightened license requirements for gun sellers. In 1972, the federal Bureau of Alcohol, Tobacco, Firearms and Explosives (ATF) was created to enforce federal gun and weapon laws. The most controversial legislation was the **Brady Bill** named for Jim Brady, President Reagan's press secretary who was seriously wounded during the attempted assassination of the president. This legislation mandated a five-day waiting period and a detailed background check before anyone could purchase a handgun. The law's ban on assault weapons has expired.

Gun control is now in the forefront once again with the tragic mass murders on the campus of Virginia Tech., at a crowded movie theater in Aurora, Colorado, and the December 14, 2012, slaying of six adults and twenty children in a Newtown, Connecticut elementary school. All of these crimes were committed by a single individual armed with several high-powered weapons.

President Obama called upon Vice President Joe Biden to conduct a series of meetings for pro- and anti-gun control advocates, and law enforcement officials to determine what measures could be taken to avoid a reoccurrence of these tragic events. Based upon their recommendations, President Obama signed twenty-three executive orders strengthening background checks, reinstating the ban on assault weapons, stiffening penalties for gun trafficking, allocating federal funding for mental health initiatives, and providing federal funding to school districts desiring to hire police officers and security guards to patrol their school grounds. Whether these executive orders become congressional acts is questionable as the NRA and gun owners and Second Amendment supporters voice their opposition to further gun control measures.

Protecting the Rights of the Accused

The American judicial system artfully created by the Framers is firmly based on the **adversary system** whereby the accused is innocent until proven guilty. The burden of proof is placed squarely on the shoulders of the prosecution who must establish beyond a **reasonable doubt** that the accused did indeed commit a crime. Regardless of the severity of the crime, the accused has the same protected civil liberties as any other American citizen, until the accused has been declared guilty by a jury of his peers. "The Constitution strongly emphasizes the protection of rights of defendants in the criminal process. The original document contains no fewer than seven provisions specifically addressed to this matter—these are in keeping with the Founder's [Framers] concern to protect minorities (in this case, unpopular defendants) from the tyrannical excesses of an aggrieved or outraged majority . . . . The Bill of Rights places an even greater stress on criminal procedure. Of the twenty-three separate rights enumerated in the first eight amendments, thirteen relate to the treatment of criminal defendants."[66] The protection of the rights of the accused was needed to reverse the historical pattern governments used to abuse its citizens. The history of Europe is tainted by arbitrary arrests, imprisonment without benefit of trial, horrific punishment methods, and so on. The Framers realized that citizens should be protected from criminals. However, even criminals, particularly those *accused* of a criminal action, should be treated in a humane and fair manner.

The initial problem was whether these amendments applied to both the federal and state governments. The states were charged with establishing their own criminal procedures. Article III of the United States Constitution gave the federal court system extremely limited original jurisdiction in both criminal and civil matters. Despite the passage of the Fourteenth Amendment's provision of due process and equal protection, the United States Supreme Court was extremely reluctant to require the states to incorporate protections for the accused as detailed in the Bill of Rights into their state judicial procedures. "In its earliest interpretation of the Fourteenth Amendment, the famous *Slaughterhouse Cases* of 1873, the Supreme Court reaffirmed Marshall's opinion in *Barron* that the guarantees in the Bill of Rights and the Fourteenth Amendment were not construed to apply to the states."[67] However, the Supreme Court opted for selective incorporation of pretrial rights.

The landmark case cementing the states to compliance with the "fundamental rights" guaranteed in the Bill of Rights was ***Palko v Connecticut* (1937)**. Frank Palko was originally indicted and tried on a first-degree murder charge. However, the jury found Palko guilty of a second-degree murder charge and gave him a life sentence without parole possibilities. The state appealed the decision to the Connecticut Supreme Court of Errors. This court subsequently overturned the original decision and ordered a new trial. Palko was tried again on a first-degree murder charge, convicted, and handed the death sentence. Palko petitioned the United States Supreme Court to overturn his latest conviction as a violation of the Fifth Amendment's protection against double jeopardy and the Fourteenth Amendment's guarantee of due process. The Supreme Court ruled against Palko. However, Justice Benjamin Cardozo's "carefully crafted opinion has long been regarded as a catalyst in the nationalization of the rights of the accused, as it established categorically that the states were obligated to the fundamental imperatives of the Bill of Rights through the Fourteenth Amendment. Cardozo distinguished rights that are fundamental—the very essence of a scheme of ordered liberty—from rights that are not quite so fundamental . . . . Fundamental rights must always be applied to the states, whereas, others may be applied to the states only when state action violates the due process clause of the Fourteenth Amendment."[68] Subsequent Supreme Court rulings conform with Cardozo's position.

The Framers firmly believed that no one should be arbitrarily arrested and allowed to waste away in prison without knowing the charges against them. A guaranteed constitutional right, a *writ of Habeas Corpus* is "an order to an incarcerating official to bring a person held in custody before the court to determine if the person is being held lawfully."[69] Basically, the accused is brought before a judge or magistrate within a short time after arrest. The accused and the presiding court official are informed of the charges against the accused by the arresting officer. The accused is then given the opportunity to explain his/her actions. If the presiding court official finds the arresting officer's actions valid, the accused will be held for further confinement or granted bail options. If the arresting officer does not provide a valid reason for the arrest, the presiding court official will release the accused. Article I, Section 9 of the United States Constitution, mandates that the Writ of Habeas Corpus "shall not be suspended, unless when in cases of rebellion or invasion the public safety may require it." Abraham Lincoln suspended the right during the American Civil War, George W. Bush immediately after the attacks of September 11, and the Patriot Act suspends it for individuals accused of or being investigated for terrorist crimes against the United States.

The question of whether accused persons can waive their constitutionally protected rights to self-incrimination even though the accused is unaware of their rights in the first place was addressed by the United States Supreme Court in *Miranda v Arizona* (1966). Ernesto Miranda was arrested and questioned about the kidnapping and rape of an eighteen-year-old girl. During interrogation, Miranda signed a confession with a statement waving his constitutional protection against self-incrimination. However, Miranda did not have any prior knowledge of the United States Constitution, its Bill of Rights, and his protected constitutional rights. Miranda did not even speak English fluently. The arresting officers argued that they assumed Miranda was aware of his protected right to remain silent and voluntarily waived that right. The confession was admitted as evidence during the trial. Miranda was convicted and sentenced to twenty to thirty years in prison. The United States Supreme Court ruled 5 to 4 that Miranda's rights had been violated. Chief Justice Earl Warren "made it clear that the prosecution may not use a statement against the accused elicited during custodial interrogation 'unless it demonstrates the use of effective safeguards to secure' his or her constitutional rights, and they must be made known to the accused. Interrogation could proceed if the accused 'voluntarily, knowingly, and intelligently' makes a waiver of the rights to which he or she is entitled."[70] The Supreme Court mandated that law enforcement personnel must verbally apprise an arrested suspect of the following rights prior to questioning:

1. He must be told he has the right to stay silent.
2. He must be told anything he says may be used against him in court.
3. He must be told he has the right to have an attorney with him before any questioning begins.
4. He must be told that, if he wants an attorney but cannot afford one, an attorney will be provided for him free.
5. If, after being told this, an arrested suspect says he does not want a lawyer and is willing to be questioned, he may be, provided he reached his decision "knowingly and intelligently."
6. If, after being told all his rights, a suspect agrees to be questioned, he can shut off the questions any time after they have started, whether or not he has an attorney with him.[71]

In addition, law enforcement officials must operate on a more than reasonable assumption that the accused understands English. If not, the arresting officers should postpone questioning until an interpreter can be present. Once these warnings are given, the accused may opt to stop answering questions at any time; halt an interrogation until legal representation is present; or voluntarily waive his rights.

The *Miranda* case was revisited by the United States Supreme Court in a case questioning whether a section of a federal anti-crime law, allowing voluntary confessions without benefit of *Miranda* protections, could be used as evidence during a trial. Ruling against the federal government, the Supreme Court reaffirmed the necessity of *Miranda* in a 7 to 2 decision. Chief Justice William Rehnquist commented that "*Miranda* announced a constitutional rule that Congress may not supersede legislatively. We decline to overrule *Miranda* ourselves. *Miranda* has become embedded in routine police practice to the point where the warnings have become part of our national culture."[72]

The Fourth Amendment protects citizens from unreasonable searches and seizures. The English concept that a "man's home is his castle" was first addressed in the Magna Carta. In 1763, William Pitt declared before the British Parliament that "the poorest man may, in his cottage, bid defiance to all the forces of the Crown. It may be frail; its roof may shake; the wind may blow through it; the storm may enter, the rain may enter, but the King of England may not enter; all his force does not cross the threshold of the ruined tenement."[73] Despite the reassuring words of Pitt, the Crown continued to conduct invasive searches through the use of general warrants. These search documents were issued without probable cause, allowing English custom agents to seize whatever they deemed of value to compensate for delinquent taxes. In the American colonies, the **Townshend Acts** of 1767 granted colonial courts the power to use general warrants. At a 1772 Boston Town Meeting, colonists complained that:

"Thus our houses and even our bed chambers, are exposed to be ransacked, our boxes, chests and trunks broke open, ravaged and plundered by wretches, whom no prudent man would venture to employ even as menial servants; whenever they are please to say they suspect there are in the house wares for which the duties have not been paid. Flagrant instances of the wanton exercise of this power have frequently happened in this and other seaport towns. By this we are cut off from that domestic security which renders the lives of the most unhappy in some measure agreeable. Those Officers may under colour of law and the cloak of a general warrant break thro' the sacred rights of the domicil, ransack mens' houses, destroy their securities, carry off their property, and with little danger to themselves commit the most horred murders."[74]

After declaring their independence from England, several of the newly formed states addressed the issue of searches and seizures in their state constitutions. These documents outlawed the use of general warrants, opting instead for courts to issue specific warrants detailing both the items subjected to the search and possible seizure, as well as the rationale for the search. For example, the tenth article of the 1776 Pennsylvania constitution states "that the people have a right to hold themselves, their houses, papers and possessions free from search and seizure, and therefore, warrants without oaths or affirmations first made, affording a sufficient foundation for them, and whereby any officer or messenger may be commanded or required to search suspected places, or to seize any person or persons, his or their property, not particularly described are contrary to that right, and ought not to be granted."[75] Consequently the Framers used the guidelines established in these early state constitutions when they penned the Fourth Amendment to the United States Constitution.

Although Americans fear rising crime and demand swift action against violators, the United States Supreme Court has exercised reasonable restrictions in delineating proper from improper searches and seizures, and the effects a search has on the fate of the accused. "As far back as 1886, in *Boyd v United States*, the Court in effect, tied the Fourth Amendment to the Fifth Amendment's self-incrimination provision, indicating that the two 'run almost into each other.' An unreasonable search and seizure, the Court felt, is in reality a 'compulsory extortion' of evidence that could result in compulsory self-incrimination."[76] The key to understanding the logic of the Supreme Court's rulings rests with the interpretation of probable cause and the application of the exclusionary rule.

Under normal circumstances, police officers should obtain a search warrant issued by a magistrate prior to conducting the search. Officers must demonstrate **probable cause**, that is, a reasonable assumption that a crime has or will be committed. The suspicion of the execution of a criminal act compels the search and possible seizure of evidence. A proper warrant must describe the places to be searched and the items to be seized. The **exclusionary rule** means "that evidence which is otherwise admissible may not be used in a criminal trial if it is a product of illegal police conduct."[77] One of the landmark cases tying probable cause to the exclusionary rule is *Mapp v Ohio* (1961).

In May 1957, three Cleveland police officers arrived at Dollree Mapp's residence after receiving a tip that she was harboring a wanted fugitive. After twice refusing to admit the police without a search warrant, the officers forcibly gained entry, physically assaulted her, and handcuffed her. The search did not produce the sought after fugitive. However, Mapp was arrested and subsequently convicted of possession of the obscene materials the officers seized during their search. The United States Supreme Court overturned Mapp's conviction. Speaking for the majority, Justice Tom C. Clark wrote that "all evidence obtained by searches and seizures in violation of the Constitution is, by that same authority [Amendment Four], inadmissible in a state court and since the Fourth Amendment's right of privacy has been declared enforceable against the States through the Due Process Clause of the Fourteenth, it is enforceable against them by the same sanction of exclusion as is used against the Federal Government."[78] Since its initial ruling, the Supreme Court has revisited several of the issues raised by the *Mapp* case, particularly involving permission to enter, unannounced entries, and searches conducted without a warrant. In a 5-4 decision, the Court ruled that "yes, the so-called knock-and-announce rule is violated when police fail to announce their presence and wait a reasonable amount of time before entering someone's home and what they find once they're inside. But no, that violation isn't sufficiently related to what they find during a search to justify banned drugs, guns or any other evidence that's uncovered from later criminal proceedings."[79] The Court also ruled that police officers after viewing a violent melee through a window did not need a warrant to enter the residence to break up the fight. Chief Justice John Roberts wrote: "the role of a peace officer includes preventing violence and restoring order, not simply rendering first aid to casualties; an officer is not like a boxing (or hockey) referee, poised to stop a bout only if it becomes too one-sided."[80] The question over consent to search without a warrant resulted in a 5-3 decision in favor of the homeowner. Initially, the police were granted permission by one of the residents, only to have the other resident refuse. "A warrantless search of a shared dwelling for evidence over the express refusal of consent by a physically present resident cannot be justified as reasonable."[81]

The Court has heard numerous cases involving searches and seizures conducted outside the protection of a person's home. For example, Steven Dewayne Bond was a passenger on a Greyhound Bus that was stopped at an immigration checkpoint in California. A random squeezing of his luggage convinced agents that Bond was carrying controlled substances. Upon opening the bag, the agents discovered a package of methamphetamines. Bond was subsequently convicted of drug possession. Bond's attorneys argued that the random squeezing of the luggage constituted an illegal search and seizure. The Supreme Court concurred. The Supreme Court dealt another blow to law enforcement ruling that police officers cannot search people and their vehicles after issuing a routine traffic citation. Local police officers in Iowa searched Patrick Knowles' car after he was given a traffic ticket. The search of the vehicle revealed that Knowles was carrying marijuana. Although recognizing the necessity for searching suspects after their arrests for dangerous weapons, the Supreme Court ruled that in this situation, no arrest occurred, therefore, the search was illegal. Therefore, "absent probable cause and/or a warrant, police may not conduct a full-blown search of motorists and their vehicles after pulling them over and ticketing them for speeding or other minor traffic violations."[82] The United States Supreme Court has oftentimes ruled on the side of law enforcement. During its 2004-2005 session, the Court ruled that during routine traffic violation stops, law enforcement could legally use drug-sniffing dogs to detect possible possession of illegal substances. In support of the Court's 6-2 decision, Justice Paul Stevens wrote that "a dog sniff conducted during a concededly lawful traffic stop that reveals no information other than the location of a substance that no individual has any right to possess does not violate the Fourth Amendment."[83]

The right to counsel is guaranteed by the Sixth Amendment. However, not every person accused of a criminal action can afford an attorney nor are they guaranteed that their legal representation will provide an adequate defense. The United States Supreme Court addressed the issue of court appointed legal representation in capital criminal cases in **Powell v Alabama** (1932). Powell and six other African-American youths were arrested, indicted, tried, and given the death penalty for the rape of two Anglo women. The trials began six days after their arrests with two tried at a time in proceedings lasting only a day. The Supreme Court ruled overwhelmingly that all of the defendants were blatantly denied their rights of due process and equal protection of the law. Lacking financial resources, the defendants were provided court-appointed attorneys on the day of their trials. Echoing the sentiments of his fellow justices, Justice Sutherland wrote that "in light of the facts—the ignorance and illiteracy of the defendants, their youth, the circumstances of public hostility, the imprisonment and close surveillance of the defendants by the military forces, the fact that their friends and families were all in other states and communication with them necessarily difficult, and above all, that they stood in deadly peril of their lives—we think the failure of the trial court to give them reasonable time and opportunity to secure counsel was a clear denial of due process."[84]

In *Escobedo v Illinois* (1964), the question before the United Sates Supreme Court was whether legal representation should be present during the interrogation of the defendant by law enforcement officials. Danny Escobedo and three others were arrested for the fatal shooting of his brother-in-law. Initially, Escobedo was released after fourteen and a half hours of questioning without the presence of legal representation. Escobedo was rearrested, and despite the requests of both the defendant and his lawyer, legal representation was not present during that interrogation period. Consequently, Escobedo did make incriminating statements that led to his indictment and conviction. Escobedo petitioned the United States Supreme Court to overturn his conviction on the belief that his Sixth Amendment right to counsel had been violated. "Justice Arthur Goldberg's opinion for the majority stressed the need for counsel when the police action shifts from the investigatory to the accusatory stage, that is, when the focus is directed on the accused and the purpose of interrogation is to elicit a confession."[85] The Supreme Court overturned Escobedo's conviction.

One of the most high profile cases heard by the United States Supreme Court was *Gideon v Wainwright* (1963). Clarence Gideon was arrested for burglarizing a pool hall. Gideon could not afford to hire an attorney. His plea for a court appointed attorney was denied since the Florida courts granted these requests only to defendants accused of capital criminal charges. Gideon pleaded not guilty, conducted his own defense, and, of course, was found guilty. From his prison cell, Gideon submitted to the Court one of the rarely accepted hand-written briefs. The Supreme Court overturned Gideon's conviction. The decision in this case "extended the absolute right of indigents to have counsel assigned in all criminal cases—save those involving certain misdemeanors—by making the Sixth Amendment's requirements of the Assistance of Counsel obligatory upon the states via the due process of the law clause of the Fourteenth Amendment."[86] Gideon was retried and acquitted.

American society is still debating whether the death penalty is a violation of the Eighth Amendment's prohibition against cruel and unusual punishment. After winning independence, the states created penitentiaries as viable substitutes to punish violent criminals. Michigan and Wisconsin abolished the death penalty in the 1840s while other states restricted its use and banned public executions. Today the death penalty is just as controversial as it was in the eighteenth century. The United States Supreme Court has vacillated over the appropriateness of the death penalty. In 1972, the Court ruled in *Furman v Georgia* that the use of the death penalty in this particular case was a violation of the Fourteenth Amendment. "Although the Court never decided that execution was necessarily cruel and unusual punishment, the justices outlawed mandatory death sentences and approved a two stage process for capital cases, with guilt determined first and punishment fixed later by predetermined standards."[87] The *Furman* decision made states reevaluate their capital punishment laws and resulted in a virtual moratorium of the death penalty. The Court reversed its decision against the use of the death penalty in 1976, giving the green light for states to reintroduce the use of capital punishment. The number of executions rose dramatically. Recent death penalty related decisions rendered by both the federal district courts and the Supreme Court indicate a change in

Former Governor George Ryan (R. IL) (left) and Senator Dick Durbin (D. IL) (right) at a news conference. On Saturday, Jan. 11, 2003, Former Gov. George Ryan cleared Illinois' death row, commuting 167 condemned inmates' sentences in the broadest attack at the death penalty in decades. Ryan's decision came three years after he temporarily halted state executions to examine the system's fairness. George Ryan said, "I had to act. Our capital system is haunted by the demon of error—error in determining guilty, and error in determining who among the guilty deserves to die."

prospective once again towards restricting the use of capital punishment. U.S. District Judge Jed Rakoff declared the 1994 Death Penalty Act unconstitutional. The judge's ruling was based on the fact "that the best available evidence indicates that on one hand, innocent people are sentenced to death with materially greater frequency than was previously supposed and that, on the other hand, convincing proof of their innocence often does not emerge until long after the convictions."[88] Although the Supreme Court has not once again declared the death penalty unconstitutional, three of its decisions placed limitations on its use. In a 6-3, the Court ruled that the execution of mentally handicapped inmates was an unconstitutional violation of the Eighth Amendment's prohibition against cruel and unusual punishment. During its 2002 session, the jurists ruled that juries, not judges, must determine whether a convicted murderer should receive the death penalty. Affirming the 7-2 decision, Justice Ruth Bader Ginsburg stated that "the Constitution guarantees a trial by jury, and that right extends to weighing whether a particular killing merits death or life in prison."[89] In 2005, the Supreme Court ruled in a 5-4 decision that the execution of juveniles was indeed cruel and unusual punishment. In support of the majority opinion, Justice Anthony Kennedy wrote: "The . . . national consensus here—the rejection of the juvenile death penalty in the majority of the states; the infrequency of its use even where it remains on the books; and the consistency in the trend toward abolition of the practice—provide sufficient evidence that today our society view juveniles, in the words . . . used respecting the mentally retarded as 'categorically less culpable than the average criminal.' Once the diminished culpability of juveniles is recognized, it is evident that the penological justifications for the death penalty apply to them with lesser force than to adults. The age of 18 is the point where society draws the line for many purposes between childhood and adulthood. It is, we conclude, the age at which the line for death eligibility ought to rest."[90] In 2006, the Supreme Court opened the door for death row inmates to challenge their sentences through DNA testing. Calling for a new trial, Justice Kennedy wrote "that the DNA evidence, combined with other errors in the case, made it quite probably that [Paul Gregory] House could convince jurors of his innocence" of committing a murder that happened twenty years ago.[91]

While the debate continues the death penalty, violent crimes continue to plague the nation's cities. Several states have opted to impose longer prison terms without the possibility of parole in hopes that the knowledge of spending years and years in prison will be an effective deterrent to committing a criminal act. President Clinton introduced the concept of "three strikes and your out" mandating that an individual convicted of a third felony would receive an automatic life prison sentence, regardless of the nature of the crime. Clinton also signed "Aimee's Law" whereby "a murderer, child molester or rapist released before serving 85 percent of his or her sentence, or before his or her jail term passes the national average for the offense, then commits the same crime in a different state, the original jailing state will have to pay for the new investigation and incarceration with its federal crime funds."[92] During its 2004-2005 session, the United States Supreme Court gave judges more latitude in determining sentencing options when it ruled the Sentencing Reform Act unconstitutional. Now, federal judges are able judge on their own without the influence of the United States Congress whether or not the circumstances involved in the commission of a felony merits a stiffer sentence.

The appeals process has also been revisited with several states enacting laws limiting the accessibility of the convicted to the court system. In the past, those convicted of a crime in a state court could seek a direct appeal to a federal court if that individual received the death penalty or could demonstrate that his/her constitutionally protected rights were violated at some point from arrest to conviction. In 1999, the United States Supreme Court ruled 6 to 3 that those convicted of crimes in state courts must initiate their appeals at the state-court level. "Writing for the majority, Justice Sandra Day O'Connor said that as long as a state has given its supreme court the choice to review a case, federal courts should require state inmates make use of the available process to give the state court a chance to exercise its discretionary jurisdiction."[93] The inmate still has the option to begin the appeal process at the federal court level only if the state court refuses to hear the case. United States Supreme Court justices further restricted the appeals process to death row inmates. The issue involved a provision of the Anti-Terrorism and Effective Death Penalty Act that shorten the time between conviction and execution. In a 5 to 4 decision, Justice O'Connor stated that "the law requires a hands-off approach by federal judges unless a state court clearly is wrong about some Supreme Court precedent or unreasonably applies that principle to the facts of the prisoner's case."[94] The Supreme Court sent a clear message that defense attorneys can use the federal courts only if the state court system has clearly violated the constitutional rights of the accused. "This decision makes clear that the *writ of habeas corpus* is not to be used as a device to go judge-shopping, running the same marginal claims past multiple sets of judges."[95]

The Sixth Amendment to the United States Constitution entitles those accused of committing a criminal offense to be judged by a jury of one's peers. The majority of the nation's state and federal courts select nine to twelve members from a panel of potential jurors. These individuals are charged with weighing the evidence and, subsequently, rendering a verdict of guilt or innocence. The concept of the jury system emerged in England after the Norman invasion. Determining the method of proving one's guilt or innocence has taken numerous avenues. Prior to the arrival of William the Conqueror, "under Saxon law, if you could carry several pounds of glowing red-hot iron in your bare hands for nine steps or walk barefoot over nine red-hot plowshares without getting any blisters, you were not guilty. . . In Britain, Africa and parts of Asia, plunging your arm into boiling water, oil or lead without the usual results proved your innocence. Water was also knowledgeable stuff. The innocent sank; the guilty floated and could be fished and dealt with."[96] In some instances, the Saxons dismissed the hot irons and opted for a rudimentary jury composed of twelve people. The practice of the twelve-member jury is credited to Morgan of Glamorgan, Prince of Wales. In 725 A.D., he wrote: "For as Christ and his Twelve Apostles were finally to judge the world, so human tribunals should be composed of the king and twelve wise men."[97] The jury system, however, has posed serious questions as to whether a panel of nine to twelve can be a truly fair and impartial group capable of rendering a decision based solely on the evidence presented during the trial without injecting their own biases and emotions into their deliberations.

The rulings of the United States Supreme Court have upheld and preserved the rights of the accused. Both state and federal courts have been more inclined to grant **changes of venue** for high profile cases to ensure a fair trial for the accused. For example, the federal trial of those accused of the tragic bombing of the federal building in Oklahoma City was moved to another federal district court. The judge believed that finding a fair and impartial jury in the Oklahoma district was an impossible task.

Protection of Property and Privacy

In *Democracy in America,* Alexis de Tocqueville observed that "in no other country in the world is the love of property keener or more alert than in the United States and nowhere else does the majority display less inclination toward doctrines which in any way threaten the way property is owned."[98] Once again, the Framers desired to reverse the historical patterns of governments using arbitrary measures to seize private property for political purposes. The Articles of Confederation failed miserably to protect the rights of property owners to transact their business without undo interference from individual state governments. It was the business community and property owners that compelled the Framers to meet in Philadelphia in the first place. Consequently, the Framers created a document that specifically granted constitutional protections for the right to own, use, rent, invest, and contract for property with the minimal interjection of government. After all, the free enterprise system is based on the concept of private property ownership.

Article I, Section 10 of the United States Constitution prohibits the states from passing any laws that impair the obligation of contracts. Known as the **Contract Clause,** this provision was designed to prevent state governments from passing laws that would expand a debtor's right not to pay an obligation or to back out of a contractual agreement. However, the Constitution did not give property owners the exclusive right to do whatever they wanted to do with their property. Property ownership and property rights evoke the classic struggle of the individual or private needs against the collective good of the community or public needs. It has been the task of state and federal courts under the guidance of the United States Supreme Court that have selectively applied the concept of reasonable restrictions to property issues.

The United States Supreme Court began gradually to restrict the exclusiveness of the contract clause in the 1880s by subjecting contracts to reasonable police powers designed to protect the health, safety, welfare, and, in some instances, the morals of the public. In ***Home Building and Loan Association v Blaisdell*** (1934), the Supreme Court ruled that contracts between two or more parties could be modified by state laws to prevent social and economic catastrophe. Subsequent rulings have upheld federal regulations ranging from worker safety standards to the proper disposal of hazardous substances by property and business owners. City and county ordinances can determine whether a home owner can paint his residence a certain color or fix the site location of sexually explicit businesses and establishments selling liquor, and so on. These actions are constitutional as long as these restrictions are not unreasonable applications of police powers.

The Framers also recognized the necessity for government to seize or to use private property for the collective benefit of the community or the nation. The United States Constitution specifically grants the power of **eminent domain** to the federal government. However, the property owner must receive just compensation for the loss of his/her property. The states and other subgovernmental units received the right of eminent domain through the Fourteenth Amendment. The use of reasonable restrictions is key to understanding the scope of eminent domain. Governments need privately held lands to build additional government buildings, public schools and hospitals, to expand the nation's transportation systems and airways, and so on. But, the rights of property owners must be recognized and justly compensated for their losses. During its 2006 session, the Supreme Court ruled that governments could use eminent domain to condemn lower valued residential property as blighted or a slum in order to allow a private business to develop the land into higher valued residential property such as townhouses. Not supportive of the Court's ruling, property owners across the nation pushed their state legislative houses to enact laws restricting the use of eminent domain for private gain.

Privacy issues are tied directly to the Fourth Amendment's protection from unreasonable searches and seizures particularly when law enforcement enters a private residence. In *Boyd v United States* (1886), the United States Supreme Court decided that "the Fourth and Fourteenth Amendments extend to all invasions on the part of the [federal] government and its employees of the sanctity of a man's home and the privacies of life. It is not the breaking of his doors and the rummaging of his drawers that constitutes the essence of the offense, but it is the invasion of his indefeasible right of personal security, personal liberty, and private property."[99] However, the Supreme Court did not address this issue seriously until technological advancements gave law enforcement the capability to use wiretapping and sophisticated surveillance tools to enhance their efforts to apprehend potential lawbreakers. In *Olmstead v United States* (1928), the Supreme Court applied reasonable restrictions to the right to privacy and gave law enforcement a boost by ruling that wiretapping was not a breach of the Fourth Amendment. At the height of the Prohibition Era, Ray Olmstead and several of his cohorts were convicted of violating the National Prohibition Act for their bootlegging activities. The federal government introduced wiretapped conversations between the defendants as their primary incriminating evidence. The Supreme Court justified its ruling against Olmstead with the rationalization that "if a person installs a telephone for the purpose of projecting his or her voice outside of the home, then the person gives up an expectation of privacy in the conversation."[100]

However, the United States Supreme Court did not give law enforcement the green light to spy on American citizens at will. In *Silverman v United States* (1961), the Supreme Court ruled that law enforcement eavesdropping on conversations in private residences through the pipes of a heating system was an unconstitutional violation of the Fourth Amendment. The use of electronic listening and recording devices in public telephone booths drew the ire of the Supreme Court. In *Katz v United States* (1967), Justice Potter Stewart wrote "that when a person enters such a booth, closes the door behind him, and pays a toll to make a call, he is entitled to assume that the words he utters into the mouthpiece will not be broadcasted to the world."[101] Corrective legislation was passed with the 1968 Omnibus Crime Control and Safe Streets Act, which granted limited use of wiretapping and bugging devices for investigative purposes. This legislation allowed warrantless use of listening devices for forty-eight hours for emerging investigations involving organized crime or threats to national security. Although subsequent legislation has expanded the use of listening devices, the courts do weigh the absence of a warrant when judging admissibility of evidence against the accused.

Privacy issues extend to a wide variety of subjects from drug testing, alternative lifestyles, reproductive freedom, and so on. However, the increased use of drugs has prompted businesses and insurance companies to push for drug-free working environments through random drug testing. Although the use of drugs is extremely detrimental to the survival of our society, some Americans believe that random blood sampling and supervised urination is a gross violation of one's dignity and an invasion of privacy. It's a basic question of protecting the rights of the individual to privacy or the intrusion into a person's lifestyle to preserve the safety of the public. In a series of decisions, the United States Supreme Court did rule that testing for drugs or alcohol by penetrating the skin is a search under the Fourth Amendment (*Terry v Ohio*, 1968), as well as the use of breathalyzer tests on suspected drunken drivers (*California v Trombetta*, 1984). Despite the cries of civil libertarians, the Rehnquist Court ruled 6-3 in favor of mandatory drug testing in *Skinner v Railway Labor Executives Association* (1989).

The United States Supreme Court could be confronted by extremely complicated privacy issues caused by advanced high-tech computer systems and breakthroughs in genetic testing. Computer hackers are capable now of accessing information about an individual's buying habits, credit history, and medical problems. How can the average citizen protect his privacy when potentially damaging information is only an access code away? Who do you sue? The person who accessed the data in the first place or the company that gathered it and made it so readily available? Advanced genetic testing has the capability to chart a person's medical history through generational genetic patterns. Should the right to know whether you have a defective gene that will eventually give you cancer be held in strict confidence, or should it be publicly revealed to potential insurance carriers and employers? Could this information create a new form of discrimination whereby healthy individuals will be denied employment, long-term loans, and health insurance because their medical profile indicates a generational genetic pattern of heart disease?

CONCLUSIONS

The Framers seized the moment to craft a document suitable to a democratic government by advancing the causes of freedom, individualism, and equality. "That Constitution erected a fortification for freedom. It furnishes safeguards against ourselves, against our passions and extravagances. It set forth in a Bill of Rights those 'inalienable rights,' which no Congress, no government, no majority of the people could invade or violate."[102] The Framers also created a federal court system charged with the heavy burden of defending this document from those desiring to weaken it or to deny protected rights to others. With judicial review, the Supreme Court has become the definitive authority and ultimate defender of the Constitution and the Bill of Rights. However, the preservation of freedom, individualism, and equality has not been an easy task to accomplish. "There remains intense controversy over the definition, scope, and application of these values. For one thing, in particular circumstances these values may and do collide and conflict with each other. Individualism, for example, may conflict with what many might think is necessary to safeguard the 'public interest' or to promote the 'general welfare.' Then again, suppose these values are denied by government itself (and others) to particular individuals. How and to what extent should government intervene to rectify the damage that has been done? And might such intervention itself be viewed as an encroachment upon these very values, e.g., individual freedom? These questions continue to pose a dilemma for American politics and politicians."[103]

CHAPTER NOTES

[1] "The Bill of Rights: Amendments I-X," Milton R. Konvitz, ed., *An American Primer,* Daniel J. Boorstin, ed., (Chicago, Illinois: The University of Chicago Press, 1966), 171.

[2] Ibid., 172.

[3] Gary L. McDowell, "Rights Without Roots," *The Wilson Quarterly*, (Vol. XV, No. 1, Winter, 1991), 71.

[4] Alan Barth, *The Rights of Free Men: An Essential Guide to Civil Liberties*, James E. Clayton, ed., (New York: Alfred A. Knopf, 1987), 111-112.

[5] Jay M. Shafritz, *HarperCollins Dictionary of American Government and Politics*, (New York, New York: HarperCollins Publishers, Inc. 1992), 186.

[6] James H. Hutson, "A Nauseous Project," *The Wilson Quarterly*, Vol. 15, No. 1, Winter, 1991, 63.

[7] Leon W. Blevins, *Texas Government in National Perspective*, (N. J.: Prentice-Hall, 1987), 221.

[8] Robert Darnton, "The Pursuit of Happiness," *The Wilson Quarterly*, Vol. 19, No. 4, Autumn, 1995, 48.

[9] Kermit L. Hall, "Framing the Bill of Rights," *By and For the People: Constitutional Rights in American History*, Kermit L. Hall, ed., (Ill.: Harlan-Davidson, Inc., 1991), 17.

[10] Huston, "A Nauseous Project," 62.

[11] Ibid.

[12] Hall, 18.

[13] Ibid. 17.

[14] John C. Domino, *Civil Rights and Liberties: Toward the 21st Century*, (New York: HarperCollins College Publishers, Inc., 1994), 1.

[15] Ibid., 2.

[16] Paul Brest, "The Intentions of the Adopters in the Eyes of the Beholder," *The Bill of Rights: Original Meaning and Current Understanding*, Eugene W. Hickok, ed., (Charlottesville, Virginia: University Press of Virginia, 1991), 23.

[17] Henry J. Abraham and Barbara A. Perry, *Freedom & The Court: Civil Rights and Liberties in the United States,* 8th ed., (Lawrence, Kansas: The University Press of Kansas, 2003), 3-4.

[18] Lucius J. Barker and Twiley W. Barker, Jr., *Civil Liberties and the Constitution*, 6th ed., (Englewood Cliffs, N. J.: Prentice-Hall, 1990), 13.

[19] Ibid.

[20] Kermit L. Hall, "Introduction," *By and For the People: Constitutional Rights in American History*, Kermit L. Hall, ed. (Ill.: Harlan-Davidson, Inc., 1991), 8.

[21] Domino, 132.

[22] Abraham, 109.

[23] Ibid.

[24] Thomas R. Hensley, Christopher E. Smith and Joyce A. Baugh, *The Changing Supreme Court: Constitutional Rights and Liberties* (St. Paul, Minnesota: West Publishing, Co., 1997), 132.

[25] "Liberty for the Soul," *American History*, (Vol. 42, No. 1, April, 2007), 27.

[26] John Meacham, "God and the Founders", Newsweek, April 10, 2006, 54.

[27] Ibid.

[28] Hensley, 141.

29 Meacham, 54.
30 Hensley, 139-140.
31 Ibid., 152.
32 Anjetta McQueen, "Religious Schools Get Public Aid," *San Antonio Express-News* (Thursday, June 29, 2000), 12A.
33 Gary Martin, "High Court Oks School Vouchers," *San Antonio Express-News*, (Friday, June 28, 2002), 12A.
34 Martin, "High Court Oks School Vouchers," 1A.
35 Ibid., 12A.
36 Abraham, 310.
37 Hensley, 162.
38 Ibid., 163.
39 J. Michael Parker and Cecilia Balli, "Justices to Tackle Football Prayers," *San Antonio Express-News* (Tuesday, November 16, 1999), 1A.
40 Mark Helm, "Silent Nod Given to 'Silence' Law," *San Antonio Express-News*, (Tuesday, October, 30, 2001), 10A.
41 Hensley, 164.
42 Ibid., 206.
43 Domino, 87-88.
44 "Obama Defends Right to Free Speech in U.S. Talk," *San Antonio Express-News*, (Wednesday, September 26, 2012), 2A.
45 Larry Gragg, "Order vs. Liberty," *American History* (Vol. XXIII, No. 4, October, 1998), 26.
46 Ibid.
47 Susan Welch, John Gruhl, Michael Steinman, John Comer, and Susan M. Rigdon, *American Government*, 5th ed., (St. Paul, Minn.: West Publishing Co., 1994), 450.
48 Abraham, 178.
49 Welch, 454.
50 Domino, 47.
51 Eric Lichtblau, "FBI Keeps Tabs on War Protests," *San Antonio Express-News* (Sunday, November 23, 2003), 10A.
52 Charles Phillips, "A Day To Remember: May 4, 1970," *American History*, (Vol. 39, No. 2, June, 2004), 18.
53 Ibid.
54 Ralph A. Rossum and G. Alan Tarr, *American Constitutional Law: Cases and Interpretations*, (New York: St. Martin's Press, 1983), 383.
55 Hensley, 381.
56 Abraham, 231.
57 Domino, 67.
58 Hensley, 326.
59 Ibid.
60 Rossum, 418.
61 Steven Levy, "On the Net Anything Goes," *Newsweek*, July 7, 1997, 28.
52 Rossum, 397.
63 Ibid., 398.
64 Aaron Epstein, "Anti-Gang Loitering Ordinance Rejected," *San Antonio Express-News* (Friday, June 11, 1999), 1A.
65 Ibid., 1A and 20A.
66 Rossum, 469.
67 Domino, 133-134.
68 Ibid., 138.
69 Hensley, 895.
70 Barker, 263.
71 Abraham, 142.
72 Mark Helm, "Miranda Warning: Court Upholds 'The Right to Remain Silent,'" *San Antonio Express-News* (Tuesday, June 27, 2000), 1A.
73 Leonard W. Levy, "Origins of the Fourth Amendment," *Political Science Quarterly*, (Vol. 114, No. 1, Spring, 1999), 80.
74 Ibid., 92.
75 Ibid., 93.

[76] Barker, 249.
[77] Domino, 140.
[78] Abraham, 69.
[79] Stephen Henderson, "Court Comes Down on Cops' Side," *San Antonio Express-News*, (Friday, June 16, 2006), 1A.
[80] Gina Holland, "Justices Say Cops Can Enter Homes to Stop Violence," *San Antonio Express-News*, (Tuesday, May 23, 2006), 4A.
[81] David G. Savage, "Court Slams A Door on Cops," *San Antonio Express-News*, (Thursday, March 23, 2006), 1A.
[82] Ibid., 159.
[83] Jan Crawford Greenburg, "High Court Expands Police Right to Search," *San Antonio Express-News*, (Tuesday, January 25, 2005), 1A.
[84] Rossum, 522.
[85] Barker, 268.
[86] Abraham, 138.
[87] Domino, 98.
[88] Delvin Barrett, "Federal Death Penalty Halted," *San Antonio Express-News*, (Tuesday, July 2, 2002), 3A.
[89] Anne Gearan, "Justices Give Jury Last Say On Executions," *San Antonio Express-News*, (Tuesday, June 25, 2002), 6A.
[90] Marco Robbins, "Justices Rule Teen Killers Can't Be Put To Death," *San Antonio Express-News*, (Wednesday, March 2, 2005), 6A.
[91] Stephen Henderson, "Killers Get New Way to Avoid Needle," *San Antonio Express-News*, (Tuesday, June 13, 2006), 6A.
[92] Jesse J. Holland, "Crime Package Approved; Will Turn Up Heat on States," *San Antonio Express-News* (Thursday, October 12, 2000), 6A.
[93] Linda Greenhouse, "Court Limits Inmate Appeals," *San Antonio Express-News* (June 8, 1999), 1A and 6A.
[94] Richard Carelli, "Justices Make Death Row Appeals Tougher," *San Antonio Express-News* (Wednesday, April 19, 2000), 6A.
[95] Ibid.
[96] Barbara Holland, "You Swear That You Will Well and Truly Try?", *Smithsonian*, (Vol. 25, No. 12, March, 1995), 110.
[97] Ibid., 108.
[98] Alexis de Tocqueville, *Democracy in America*, J. P. Mayer, ed., (Gordon City, New York: Doubleday and Co., Inc., 1969), 638-639.
[99] Domino, 190.
[100] Ibid.
[101] Barker, 569.
[102] Barth, 122.
[103] Barker, 10.

SUGGESTED READINGS

Abraham Henry J., and Barbara A. Perry, *Freedom & the Court: Civil Rights & Liberties in the United States*, 8th ed., Lawrence, Kansas: University Press of Kansas, 2003.

Barth, Alan. *The Rights of Free Men: An Essential Guide to Civil Liberties*. James E. Clayton, ed. New York: Alfred A. Knopf, 1987.

Domino, John C. *Civil Rights and Liberties: Toward the 21st Century*. New York: Harper Collins College Publishers, Inc., 1994.

Hall, Kermit L. ed. *By and For the People: Constitutional Rights in American History*. Arlington Heights, Ill.: Harlan Davidson, Inc., 1991.

Hensley, Thomas R., Christopher E. Smith and Joyce A. Baugh, *The Changing Supreme Court: Constitutional Rights and Liberties*, St. Paul, Minnesota: West Publishing Co., 1997.

Rossum, Ralph A., and G. Alan Tarr. *American Constitutional Law: Cases and Interpretations*. New York: St. Martin's Press, 1983.

Signing of the Civil Rights Act of 1964.

Chapter Fourteen

CIVIL RIGHTS

On August 29, 2013, President Barack Obama, our nation's first African-American president, addressed the nation at the same location that Dr. Martin L. King, Jr., delivered his "I Have A Dream" speech fifty years ago. To the thousands of people gathered around the reflecting pool near the Lincoln Memorial, his words echoed the challenges still ahead. Acknowledging fifty years of progress towards racial equality, President Obama stressed that "to dismiss the magnitude of this progress, to suggest as some sometimes do that little has changed, that dishonors the courage and the sacrifice of those who paid the price to march in those years. But we would dishonor those heroes as well to suggest that the work of this nation is somehow complete. The arc of the moral universe may bend towards justice, but it doesn't bend on its own. To secure the gains this country has made requires constant vigilance, not complacency."[1] Sadly, vigilance and non-complacency alone will not end the incidents of racism, prejudice, and discrimination that have haunted this nation since its founding.

Nor can we ever forget the faces of those who have been the victims of racially motivated hatred and violence. On September 15, 1963, four young African-American girls in Birmingham, Alabama, decided to make a last minute visit to their deserted church's basement lounge after Sunday school. A dynamite bomb planted outside the church by members of the Ku Klux Klan (KKK) exploded killing 11-year-old Denise McNair, 14-year-olds Cynthia Wesley, Carole Robertson and Addie Mae Collins, and injuring twenty others. Although the Federal Bureau of Investigation (FBI) quickly identified four Klansmen as the likely suspects, it took 39 years before the final suspect was tried and convicted of the bombing. Basically, "the killers of the girls hid for decades inside a brittle silence that cracked only when they boasted among kin and people they believed held the same hatred."[2]

In the early hours of June 2, 1998, James Byrd left a family gathering to begin his walk to his home in Jasper, Texas. As he walked along a dark road, three white ex-cons with ties to an in-prison white supremacy group, stopped and offered Byrd, an African American, a ride. Accustomed to hitch hiking, Byrd willingly accepted their offer and got into the bed of their truck. Byrd never made it home that night. Instead, the three men beat him unconscious, chained him to the tailgate of the truck, and dragged him to his death. The three were captured, charged, and subsequently convicted of first-degree murder. Two received the death penalty. On Friday, April 28, 2000, an Anglo male randomly opened fire in several suburban Pittsburgh, Pennsylvania communities. "The gunman fatally shot a person of Indian descent at an Indian grocery store, two employees at a Chinese restaurant and a black [African American] man at a martial arts school. A Jewish woman who lived next door to the suspect's parents was found dead in her home."[3] He also shot out the glass doors of a nearby synagogue and painted the outside walls with swastikas. With the exception of one of the victims, the suspect did not know these people nor did they do anything to provoke him. They were simply at the wrong place at the wrong time. These killings were racially motivated by the suspect's hatred of minorities. Although incidents of this caliber are extremely isolated tragedies, what happened at that church in Birmingham, on that dirt road in Jasper, and on those streets in Pittsburgh reminded all of us that racism still haunts a nation that was founded, in part, on the sacredly revered Declaration of Independence that boldly proclaims that "all men are created equal." Yet, nothing is further from the truth. For thousands of years, the history of humanity has been continuously marred by periods of horrific and, far too often, deadly indignities leveled by individuals upon their fellow human beings. For over two hundred years, United States lawmakers from George Washington to Barack Obama have struggled to erase the blemishes of previous conditions of servitude, racial hatred, and gender discrimination only to be confronted by a new wave of racism, sexism, and intolerance.

For many Americans, the civil rights movement of the 1960's and 70's did awaken the social consciousness of this nation to the destructiveness of racism. Yet, the awakening failed to solve the problems. The obvious shortcomings and failures of the public policy process to address racial discrimination are seen in the faces of those the laws were supposed to help. Far too often minorities feel that the scales of justice move too slowly to bring those accused of civil rights violations to justice. For example, in 1966, the bullet-riddled body of Ben Chester White, an African-American farmhand, was found in Pretty Creek, near Natchez, Mississippi. Three known Klansmen were arrested with one actually confessing to the murder. All three were acquitted in state courts. In 2003, the federal government reopened the case, charging 72-year-old Ernest Avants, the only defendant still living, with the crime. The federal government discovered a loophole. "For years his [Avants] acquittal of state murder charges in the 1960s had shielded him from new prosecution. But White's body was found on federal land, in a national forest, enough to get around double jeopardy and give federal prosecutors jurisdiction."[4] Another tragic case was the 1964 slayings of James Chaney, 21, an African American from Mississippi and his two white companions from New York. They were three young men traveling through the Deep South trying to register potential African-American voters. Although more than a dozen well-known Klan members were involved in the slayings, only a few were actually charged, tried and convicted. "One of the men who was convicted, Sam Bowers—the Neshoba County Klan's Imperial Wizard—later said that he was 'quite delighted to have been the main instigator of the entire affair,' meaning the real instigator [Edgar Ray] Killen, 'walk out of the courtroom a free man.'"[5] Although Killen was never charged with the crimes in the state courts, he was tried on federal-civil rights violations in 1967, but acquitted by an all-white jury. In 2005, the state of Mississippi officially charged 79-year-old Killen with three counts of murder. It took 40 plus years to bring the man responsible for these murders to justice. The frustrations and disappointments experienced by this nation's minority group populations are further fueled by the perception that their lawmakers and their government also move too slowly to enact the proper corrective legislation with enough governmental muscle to end racial discrimination. The lofty words of the Declaration of Independence and the Constitution declaring equality for all are meaningless to those confronted with racial hatred, poverty, inadequate educational opportunities, and the stark realization that the American dream of riches and success belongs to someone else.

Any discussion of civil rights must also encompass the struggles of American women to gain an equitable footing with their male counterparts. Incidences of gender-based discrimination are just as offensive as racial discrimination. Charges of sexual harassment are prevalent. Both Senators Kirsten Gillibrand (D-NY) and Claire McCaskill (D-Mo.) have been the catalysts behind corrective legislator to expedite prosecutions of sexual assault and sexual harassment charges filed by female military personnel against their male counterparts. While the Secretary of Defense Chuck Hagel has opened the door for women to serve in combat, there is an historical tract record of "documented cases of retaliation against assault victims, failure to provide legal and medical support for them and dismissal from the service after they reported the abuse. The Pentagon estimates there were 26,000 sexual assaults in the military last year [2012], but just over 300 cases were prosecuted."[6] Women are still struggling with wage disparity issues as their male counterparts continue to earn more than they do in comparable positions. Although few disputed the need to reform the welfare state, national women's organizations were adamantly opposed to the rhetoric of welfare reform that openly attacked, belittled, and blamed low income single parent women for the faults of the welfare system.

While women and minorities are seeking redress through the courts and legislative houses, some Americans believe that an over zealous government has gone too far by arbitrarily granting special treatment for minorities and women to the detriment of its Anglo male citizens. Although the majority of all Americans support the concepts and philosophy of civil rights and are themselves law-abiding citizens, a small group of white supremacists and militants have become extremely vocal and, in some cases, violent in venting their anger against politicians, lawmakers, and government. The fear that government is systematically stripping away their rights while giving preferential treatment to minorities, women, and immigrants has materialized into white backlash attacks against affirmative action, civil rights laws, and immigration policies. Both sides have valid arguments; however, the rhetoric of the debate has become hostile, laden with racial slurs and charges of racism from both sides.

The challenge before government at all levels is to protect and uphold the rights and privileges of all its citizens. On June 14, 1997, President Bill Clinton introduced his plan to end racial strife in a speech delivered at the University of California—San Diego. Entitled "One America in the 21st Century: The President's Initiative on Race," the president's plan had five goals: "to articulate the President's vision of a just, unified America; to inform the nation about the facts surrounding race in this country; to promote a constructive dialogue and work through the difficult issues of race; to encourage leadership at the federal, state, and local community levels to help bridge racial divides; and to identify policy and program recommendations and solutions to critical areas such as education and economic opportunity."[6] On paper, this seemed to be a simple charge for a country founded on the democratic principles of equality and freedom. However, racial tolerance, gender equality, and political and social acceptability have eluded this country for over 200 years.

Men and women of diverse races, nationalities, and beliefs have and will in all likelihood continue to battle against racial and gender discrimination, physical and verbal abuses, and threats just to gain the right to have a job at a decent and fair wage, to hold and purchase property, to receive an equitable educational opportunity, and to participate in the full spectrum of the political process. Their struggles will continue because we as a nation have finally realized that equality is one of the most difficult public policy issues confronting this country. The inability of this nation's people to achieve racial and gender equality is deeply rooted in the historical, political, and cultural development of this nation. Of course, government has and probably will continue to pass laws mandating equality laden with sanctions to be leveled against those who choose not to comply with the laws. However, laws cannot change attitudes no matter how hard lawmakers try. This chapter focuses on the development and theories of racism and prejudice and the struggles of those targeted with the slurs and the repercussions of racism. This chapter also examines the actions government has taken to address the issues of racism and gender discrimination in this country.

Civil Rights and Racism

Civil rights are collectively known as "the acts of government intended to protect disadvantaged classes of persons or minority groups from arbitrary, unreasonable, or discriminatory treatment."[7] Government at all levels has the authority to pass laws and statutes designed to protect citizens against prejudicial and discriminatory actions caused by other citizens. Basically, these laws protect us from each other. Essentially a learned behavior, **prejudice** is "a feeling or act of any individual or any group in which a prejudgment about someone else or another group is made on the basis of emotion rather than reason."[8] **Discrimination** is an action precipitated by prejudice against an individual or group.

There are two forms of discrimination. The most obvious form is **de jure discrimination** whereby a *purposeful action* adversely impacts one group over another group. The creation of "all white" communities across this country was accomplished through a series of government ordinances backed by personal threats and reprisals to keep minority groups out of certain cities and towns. However, **de facto discrimination** is an *undeliberate action* adversely impacting one group over another group. For example, white flight to the suburbs created racially segregated neighborhoods, located primarily in economically depressed and deteriorating central business districts. No laws or deliberate actions were taken to force Anglo residents to leave their inner city neighborhoods. These individuals simply possessed the resources and the desire to relocate. The question of whether the adverse action was a result of de facto or de jure discrimination usually arises over a multiplicity of issues ranging from legislative redistricting and reapportionment issues to public school financing problems.

Before delving into the theories of racism, it is important to understand the vital role the United States Supreme Court has taken in promoting and protecting civil rights as the means of eradicating the damages wrought by prejudice, discrimination, and racism. "When the race controversy attained a degree of no longer an ignorable public concern at the highest governmental level in the late 1940s, it was the judicial branch of the government, with the Supreme Court at its apex, which led the other branches in tackling the problem. While it probably did not lead eagerly or joyously, a people's rightful claims could no longer be ignored merely because the political, in particular, the legislative branch refused then to become involved beyond the most cursory of levels, and in fact consistently passed the problems on to the Court. It is an intriguing question how much strife might have been spared and how much understanding might have been engendered had the elective branches of the government provided the decisive leadership with which they are charged and, as subsequent events proved, of which they are capable when pressed."[10] For example, the 1960s civil rights movement actually began when the Supreme Court completely dismantled the nearly century-old concept of separate but equal in its landmark ruling in *Brown v the Board of Education of Topeka, Kansas* (1954). The pattern appears to be that once the federal judicial bench renders a decision concerning civil rights, it then becomes the responsibility of the legislative and executive branches to enact the much needed corrective legislation.

Unfortunately, the only public policy options normally open to lawmakers are the alleviative, preventive, and punitive. (These policy options are discussed in detail in Chapter 15.) The civil rights acts were designed to prevent incidences of racial discrimination from spreading by penalizing violators with both civil and criminal sanctions. The suffering of those adversely impacted by acts of discrimination is alleviated by civil monetary determinations as well as criminal sanctions, particularly acts that violate a person's civil rights. **Affirmative actions** are the formalized efforts on the part of government to remedy previous incidences of past discrimination particularly in the employment and political processes. The purpose of affirmative action is two fold. First, it alleviates those adversely impacted by racial discrimination by sanctioning actions to reverse previous conditions of discrimination in the workplace. Second, affirmative action like civil rights laws prevents further damage by providing punitive sanctions against violators. The curative approach is not a viable option at this point due to the deeply rooted attitudes of racism and discrimination that have been and continue to be instilled through the cultural and social development of all population groups.

Theories of Racism

For centuries, humanity has been emboiled in a great debate over whether equality is achievable in multicultural societies. Colonized by immigrants, the United States population is a mixture of people hailing from various countries who brought their cultural values, folkways, and mores to America's shores. Americans oftentimes try to convince themselves that their multicultural society is a melting pot of diversity that speaks with one voice. This nation's continual struggle to achieve racial and cultural equality reveals a country that speaks with many voices, oftentimes in conflict with each other. Europe has experienced its own struggles with multiculturalism. "Only fifty years ago, a collection of distinct nations that were mostly linguistically and culturally homogenous, Europe has become a multicultural stew, one that has grown all the faster with the collapse of the Soviet Union, the removal of trade barriers and blurring of national borders, and the desire of the poor in Asia, Africa and the Middle East to seek a better life. Increasingly, those who say they have done their best to adapt socially and culturally in their adopted countries complain they're kept at arm's length by the majority, tolerated at best, marginalized, mocked and attacked at worst."[10] Not every European openly embraces the concept of multiculturalism. Even the ancient Greeks clearly divided their societies by granting citizens a full spectrum of political, social, and economic privileges while denying those same rights to noncitizens. Slaves fared worse. An advocate of equality, Aristotle "on the other hand was sure that all men possessed reason, but thought that the distinguishing mark of slaves was that they possessed only so much of the power of reason as to enable them to understand their masters, without being able to reason for themselves; and he concluded that manual workers ought not to participate in government on the grounds that their lives denied them the opportunity to cultivate the qualities essential to wisdom."[12] Embedded in Aristotle's words are four of the prevailing rationalizations for racism: nativism, the superior/inferior concept, the economic theory of racism, and the concept of racial separation. An examination of each concept reveals the basis for racism in America.

The concept of **nativism** is based on the belief that only those born on their country's soil should reap the benefits of their birthrights. The first generation of English colonists born in America quickly established themselves as the natives of this country. The original immigrants now became the **host culture** for subsequent immigrants. For example, the United States Constitution recognizes the lofty status of the native culture by declaring that only a native-born person can be president. Alexis de Tocqueville observed this distinct separation between the native-born and others by noting that in the United States "the first that attracts attention, and the first in enlightenment, power, and happiness is the white man, the European, man 'par excellence,' below him come the Negro [African American] and the Indian."[13] When he wrote *Democracy in America* in 1835, the majority of the nation's African American and Native American population groups were not recognized as citizens. Eventually, the host or native culture becomes very protective of its superior position, seeing any intrusion of an outside culture as a threat to their livelihood and survival.

The concept of nativism surfaced in the 1790s as Americans began their quest to preserve and protect their culture by advocating English-only and pressing for anti-immigration laws. "In the flush of their newfound freedom, the Americans began to view all foreigners—even those from England—as possible carriers of anti-republican beliefs that might threaten the new nation. They tended to suspect that the Catholics might be monarchist subversives and that anyone French might attempt to ferment the kind of unrest that had led to the French Revolution."[14] The cries against increased immigration were coupled with violence, racial slurs, and harassment towards immigrants, particularly the Irish and Catholics.

Around 1850 a national organization called the Secret Order of the Star Spangled Banner was formed in New York. Renamed the Order of United Americans, lodges were formed in every state, with approximately 960 organizations in New York alone. "Only native-born male citizens of the Protestant faith, born of Protestant parents, reared under Protestant influence and not united in marriage with a Roman Catholic, could actually join a lodge."[15] The nativist movement developed into the **Know-Nothings,** a third political party movement launched in 1854. In their first campaign effort, "they elected more than a hundred Congressmen, eight governors and thousands of local officials, including the mayors of Boston, Philadelphia and Chicago. They won control of state legislatures in a half dozen states, from New Hampshire to California, and made a strong showing in a dozen more from New York to Louisiana."[16] In 1856, the party ran Millard Filmore for president. His electoral defeat was the swan song for the Know-Nothing movement. However, the party's primary anti-immigrant policy continues to play a key role in American politics. Today, the debate on immigration reform echoes the same concerns expressed in the 1790's as congressional proposals include efforts "to restrict immigration, limit the rights of immigrants, and increase the length of time needed to become a naturalized citizen."[17] In the 2010 mid-term elections, several candidates advocated amending the Constitution to remove the portion of the Fourteenth Amendment, which automatically gives citizenship rights to those born on American soil.

Closely related to nativism, the **superior/inferior** explanation for racism is based on the belief that one group or culture is genetically, intellectually, and culturally more superior than any other group. Thus, the superior group becomes the natural choice to rule over the inferiors. Adolph Hitler viewed the Germanic race as the genetically superior race. His desire to create an Aryan nation served as his justification for his horrific actions against Jews during the 1930s and 1940s. In *Mein Kampf*, Hitler envisioned a new world order dominated by the Aryan or Germanic race whereby races would be divided into three groups: "the culture-creating or Aryan race; the culture-bearing races which can borrow and adopt but cannot create; and the culture-destroying race, namely, the Jews."[18] The culture-creating race is destined to rule over the genetically inferior races. In addition, advocates of this theory believe that members of certain white "races" are destined to rule not only over the nonwhite races but over the other white races as well. Under this more specific version of the doctrine of white supremacy, "the tall, blond, blue-eyed peoples of northern and western Europe were the modern remnants of a talented race called the Nordics (or Teutons), who were descended from the ancient Aryans of India. The Nordics were said to have a special talent for political organization that enabled their members to form representative governments and create just laws; hence, the Nordic portion of the White race was destined to rule over all races, including the shorter 'alpine' and the darker-skinned 'Mediterranean' portion of the White race."[19]

The superior/inferior concept of racism is often justified as a benevolent action to protect a perceived inferior race from self-destruction. In 1732, prominent slaver John Barbat wrote "that the slave's conditions in his own country were so appalling that it was a kindness to ship him to the West Indies and more considerate masters, not to mention the inestimable advantage they may reap of becoming Christians, and saving their souls."[20] This is basically the same rationale used by the Spanish conquistadors and missionaries for the enslavement of Native American tribes in Central and Latin America. The white South African apartheid policies were based on the notion that black Africans were historically and genetically too inferior to survive on their own. Armed with the lofty challenge of saving souls and protecting those incapable of protecting themselves, the self-proclaimed superior races have been able to conquer and, subsequently, control the fortunes of those deemed inferior.

In his book, *Jim Crow America*, Jim Conrad states that racism is purely an economic issue, not a culturally or genetically based concept. For example, in the United States it was the overwhelming desire for land, natural resources, and gold that compelled Anglo Americans to use whatever means available to them to acquire these precious treasures. Native American tribes were the initial targets because they possessed vast rich fertile land holdings. The discovery of gold on Indian land just intensified the greed factor. In 1863, representatives from the federal government met with Nez Perces tribal leaders to negotiate the purchase of approximately 90 percent of their reservation lands located in the territory that would become the states of Washington, Oregon and Idaho. Signed by only a handful of the tribal leaders, the federal government "agreed to pay the Nez Perces $265,000 for the ceded land. In his report to the Commissioner of Indian Affairs in Washington, Superintendent Calvin Hale announced the signing of the treaty as a great victory for the government: 'The amount thus relinquished is very nearly six million of acres, and is obtained at a cost not exceeding eight cents per acre . . . In the tract of country there is much that is exceedingly valuable, by reason of its gold and silver mines, whilst many of its valleys, and much of its uplands, will be found desirable and necessary for agricultural and grazing purposes.'"[21]

Once these groups become economically depressed and totally dependent upon their benefactors, Native Americans, slaves, Hispanics, and immigrants alike were denied accessibility to the two tools that could liberate them—education and voting rights. Minorities, in particular, were constantly reminded of their inferior status by a series of laws known as **Jim Crow**, which successfully built a wall of separation between them and Anglo Americans. According to Conrad, racial explanations are overshadowed by the prevailing economic issue. "The issue comes down to pennies, then, and so it has been since the time when slave traders marched into Africa, handed out a few bottles of rum, and walked off with a hundred or so human commodities. The profit was enormous . . . . Twenty-five cents in the hands of two white men is twenty-five cents less in the hands of a African-American laundress. Magnify that in terms of the economic process intensively at work in all Southern states, and almost as sharply operative in the north, and you can put an arrow through the heart of Jim Crow.[22] The economic theory also fuels anti-immigrant sentiments. When the economy slumps and job security is questionable, some Americans see the flow of immigrants as a threat to their own economic viability. Another traditional economic argument for halting immigration is the belief that immigrants keep the wage system depressed by accepting jobs that pay at or below minimum wage levels.

Another perspective of racism is **separation**. Immigrants, for example, usually lived among members of their own culture, forming their own cities within a city such as China Town, Little Italy, and so on. Within their own neighborhoods, they felt more secure in speaking their own language and adhering to their own traditions and beliefs. Separation was further encouraged with the denial of interracial and intercultural marriages. The creation of cluster neighborhoods or zones was enforced by invisible lines and barriers backed by social, economic, and political laws, customs, and mores on the part of all parties involved. Immigrant groups themselves were just as eager to avoid intrusions into their cultures just as much as the host Anglo cultures wanted to protect their own lifestyles and livelihoods. However, separation from other cultures creates isolation and can lead to the fear of other cultures. "The minute society separates people from each other by color or class, it sets in motion diverse economic, psychological, and cultural processes. Society builds two antithetical cultures side by side. They can be different economies and different cultures separated by a railroad track or a picket fence, and one can then pit one culture against the other and make each group hate and misunderstand the other."[23] Once races and cultures have been separated from each other for generations, it is easy to see why the feelings of prejudice, mistrust, and suspicion would develop. In part, the desire of lawmakers to integrate the various races has been only marginally successful in this country because of a long history of cultural and racial separations.

Oftentimes, fear of a real or potential threat to national security can result in racist policies or actions levied at a particular ethnic or cultural group that played no active role in planning or executing the threat. For example, the Japanese attack on Pearl Harbor in Hawaii in December 1941, set shock waves throughout the United States that perhaps the Japanese government had already convinced Japanese sympathizers and/or already placed military personnel among the Pacific coastline to launch an actual invasion of the United States. Perceiving this as a viable threat to national security, federal officials decided to intern Japanese immigrants and Japanese-American-born citizens living on the West Coast into internment camps for the duration of the war against

Japan. In total, 120,000 people of Japanese descent of which 65 percent were American citizens were resettled into barbed-wired detention facilities surrounded by search-lights and armed guards. Japanese-Americans did serve in the war effort with distinction, but they were not assigned to the Japanese front. The United States government finally issued an official apology for the internments, and a provision of the 1988 Civil Liberties Act paid each detainee or his/her family member $20,000 each in reparations. Asking for $148,000,000 to cover lost property, the federal government paid only $37,000,000 to the detainees.[24] Immediately following the terrorist attacks on the World Trade Center, numerous physical and property-related crimes against Muslim Americans were reported.

Racism in America

Of course, we cannot overlook the obvious. All people, regardless of their own racial and cultural identity, harbor to some extent prejudices against others. These acquired habits have become as much a part of our own roots and traditions as patriotism and nationalism are to every American. It should be clearly understood that not every Anglo American is a racist nor is every member of a minority group a victim of racial discrimination and hatred. Regardless of their individual racial backgrounds, the majority of the American people have learned to transcend past discriminatory practices by coming to terms with their own prejudices. However, there are some individuals who harbor intense hatred towards others. Their vocal and sometimes violent displays of their hatred divide rather than unite the American people.

The increase in the number of racially motivated crimes has created a new category of criminal offenses—hate crimes. The Hate Crimes Statistics Act defines hate crimes as "crimes that manifest evidence of prejudice based on race, gender, or gender identity, religion, disability, sexual orientation, or ethnicity."[25] Both federal and state government tract officially reported hate-motivated criminal activities. Statistics released by the Federal Bureau of Investigation (FBI) indicated that in 2012 there were 5,790 single-bias incidents. Of these, 48.3 percent were motivated by racial bias, 19.6 percent by sexual-orientation bias, 19.0 percent by religious bias, and 11.5 percent by ethnicity/national origin bias. Bias against disabilities accounted for 1.6 percent of single-bias incidents. Of the 3,968 hate crime offenses classified as crimes against persons in 2012, simple assaults accounted for 39.6 percent, intimidation for 37.5 percent, and aggravated assault for 21.5 percent. Ten murders and 15 forcible rapes were reported as hate crimes. Of the 5,331 known offenders, 54.6 percent were white and 23.3 percent were black. The race was unknown for 11.5 percent, and other races accounted for the remaining known offenders."[26] These figures illustrate only the reported incidents whereby an individual violated the rights and property of others purely on the grounds of hatred. The increase in the number of hate crimes has prompted state and national lawmakers to introduce hate-crime bills.

Several law enforcement units have been practicing their own form of racial discrimination known as **racial profiling**. This practice is based on the assumption that criminals possess certain common traits and characteristics that separate them from the law-abiding citizen. Armed with a profile of those most likely to commit a crime, law enforcement officers in several states have been stopping innocent drivers, subjecting them to vehicle searches, and, in some instances, harassing them simply because they possess physical characteristics associated with the criminal element. The 9th U.S. Circuit Court of Appeals overturned the United States Border Patrol's use of racial profiling against Hispanics. The justices defended their decision by pointing out that "stops based on race or ethnic appearance send the underlying message to all our citizens that those who are not white [Anglo] are judged by the color of their skin alone. Such stops also send a clear message that those who are not white [Anglo] enjoy a lesser degree of constitutional protection—that they are in effect assumed to be potential criminals first and individuals second."[27] In 2013, the United States Supreme Court dealt a near fatal blow to Arizona's tough immigration enforcement law by ruling it as racial profiling, and thus unconstitutional. Known as Senate Bill 1070, the Court struck down the provisions requiring that all immigrants carry on their person at all times their immigration papers, making it a criminal offense for an illegal immigrant to seek work or hold a job, and allowing law enforcement to arrest any suspected illegal immigrant without a search warrant. The Court did uphold the right of state and local law enforcement to demand proof of citizenship and/or immigration status when an individual is stopped for other matters, such as a traffic violation with the understanding that the Court would revisit this if it is being used in a discriminatory manner.

An examination of the struggles of Native Americans, Hispanics, African Americans, women, and immigrants to achieve the same civil rights granted by the Framers initially to only white male citizens reveals that this country has yet to reverse racism and discrimination. There is much left to be done. At the 1848 Seneca Falls Convention, Frederick Douglass reminded the audience of the ultimate goal of civil rights when he declared that "right is of no sex, truth is of no color."[28]

Native Americans

No racial group has suffered more humiliation, destruction, abuse, and discrimination from the "white man's" ways than the American Indian. Where once hundreds of thousands of Indians inhabited this land, today there are only "562 distinct tribes with federal recognition, and scores of others recognized only locally or not at all."[29] Basically, Native Americans fell victim to the economic theory of racism justified by the superior-inferior concept. North American Indians became a target from the very beginning of the colonial experience since they possessed what American settlers desired most—rich fertile lands. The arrival of the first English colonists to the shores of the James River in 1607 initiated this over 400-year-old relationship as the settlers carved out of the virgin forests the Jamestown colony. Predictably, Native Americans viewed the white man's encroachment into their lands as a threat to their culture, livelihood, and, ultimately, their survival. Consequently, the settlers were subjected to continuous attacks from members of the Powhatan chiefdom, a confederative alliance consisting of nearly 30 different tribes. After seven years of attacks and counterattacks, the colonists captured Pocahontas, daughter of the chief. Both sides unofficially agreed to end the warfare. However, "hostilities persisted until a peace settlement in 1632. But colonial expansion continued, gobbling up Powhatan land. Opechancanough [Pocahontas' uncle] retaliated again in 1644 in a final spasm of attacks, killing more than 500 colonists."[30] Since few Native Americans were agriculturalists, the white man's way of developing the land destroyed it for the Native American's nomadic hunting lifestyle. Native American tribes initially sought to negotiate with Anglo-American settlers as they saw more and more of their lands taken from them with each new wave of colonists. Tribal leaders quickly realized that the only viable option left for Native Americans was to fight to keep what was theirs.

The initial public policy response from the British government was to relocate various tribes first west to the Mississippi and then to lands further beyond. The negotiation process began in earnest at the end of the French and Indian War, fought between 1754 and 1761. Pontiac, an Ottawa chief, convinced the tribal leaders of the Hurons, Potawattomis, Chippewas, Delawares, Kickapoos, Shawnees, and other tribes to join forces to drive the English out of America. Confronted with the might of the British military, Pontiac sued for peace by signing the Proclamation of 1763, which declared that: (1)all land west of the crest of the Appalachian mountains was "Indian Country"; (2) any settlers west of the Appalachian who had not acquired a legal title to their land from the Indians must return to the colonies; and (3) all future land purchases from the Indians must be conducted in public meetings attended by representatives of the king.[31] As anticipated, colonists openly violated the treaty by establishing more settlements in "Indian Country." After winning independence, the nearly formed United States government continued the practice of signing nation-to-nation treaties with tribal leaders. The framers, however, did not draw a distinction between treaties negotiated between Native American tribes and sovereign foreign nations when they elevated all treaties as "the supreme law of the land" in Article VI, Section 2, of the United States Constitution.

The question of whether Native American tribes were separate sovereign nations was addressed by the United States Supreme Court under Chief Justice John Marshall. Between 1823 and 1832, the Court developed the federal trust doctrine by its decisions in *Johnson v McIntosh, Cherokee Nation v Georgia,* and *Worcester v Georgia*. These three cases are collectively known as the **Marshall Trilogy**. Basically, Marshall's rulings held that "the federal government and the Indian nations are inextricably bound together as trustee to obligee. . . .He also ruled that treaties are a granting of rights from the Indians to the federal government, not the other way around, and all rights not granted by the Indians are presumed to be reserved by the Indians."[33] In other words, expansion into lands held by Native American tribes was supposed to be a negotiated legal process whereby the fundamental rights of the tribes were to be respected. However, treaties between the United States government and the Iroquois, Delawares, Wyandots, Chippewas, Ottawas, Shawnees, Cherokees, Choctaws, Chickasaws, Seminoles, Cheyenne, and Navajo were openly violated by the zeal of **manifest destiny**, the belief that the Anglo-American's destiny was to own all of the land between the Atlantic and Pacific Oceans. Uprooting whole tribes from their sacred ancestral lands and forcing them to walk hundreds of miles to reach far western territories only served to accelerate the tension and mistrust between the United States government and Native American tribal leaders. The Jackson administration signed approximately ninety-four treaties demanding tribal relocations. The **Trail of Tears** resulted in the forced relocation of the Cherokees, Choctaws, Creeks, Chickasaws, and Seminoles from East of the Mississippi to Indian territory on the opposite side of the river simply because gold was discovered in Georgia in 1829. The Seminoles, in particular, posed serious problems for the government's relocation schemes. In retaliation of the **Indian Removal Act** (1830), the Seminoles launched their own war against the United States known as the Second Seminole War. Eventually, "the United States removed 3,800 Seminoles to Indian Territory, but at a terrible price. The war lasted for an interminable seven years, 1,500 American soldiers died, and the cost has been estimated at between $20,000,000 to $60,000,000—significantly more than the United States paid for the entire Louisiana Purchase only fifty-two years earlier.[33]

Native Americans began to fight back with violent attacks against settlers. Realizing that a peaceful settlement was impossible, the federal government gave its army the green light, in effect, to exterminate those tribes who refused to relocate. Lawmakers justified their actions by portraying Indians as savage killers bent on brutally attacking and scalping innocent settlers whose only desire was to carve out a better life for themselves and their families by moving West. In 1862, the United States Army was ordered to begin the extermination of the Mescalero Apaches. Granted leniency, approximately 400 tribe members were located to Bosque Redondo, a remote area in the New Mexico territory. The Navajos were next. "Well over half the estimated 12,000 Navajos eventually were rounded up. They first went to Fort Canby, near present-day Window Rock, Arizona, where many died of exposure and dysentery. Survivors were sent off in groups to march 300 miles to Bosque Redondo. . . Some who could not keep up the pace, including the elderly, children and pregnant women, were shot by soldiers. . . In all, nearly 3,000 Navajos died at Bosque Redondo."[34] The slaughter of Indians during the Plains War ensued. On January 29, 1863, the United States calvary under the leadership of Col. Patrick O'Connor attacked a Shoshone tribe at Bear Creek, near present day Salt Lake City, Utah. Tribe after tribe saw its mighty braves, women, and children killed by bullets, diseases, and starvation. The Battle of Bear River was "much more grim than better-known Indian massacres at Sand Creek in Colorado Territory, where 133 Cheyennes were killed by troopers on Nov. 28, 1864, and at Wounded Knee, S. D., where soldiers slaughtered 153 Sioux on Dec. 28, 1890."[35]

Placed on reservations, Native Americans became the victims to the whims of lawmakers as they vacillated between policies advocating **cultural assimilation** and **separation**. Assimilation meant that reservation Indians were to become "civilized" by adopting to the white man's society and culture. "The Bureau of Indian Affairs (BIA) agents, who supervised the reservations, tried to root-out Native American ways and replace them with white dress and hairstyles, the English language, and the Christian religion."[36] In the 1930s, the federal government, however, reversed its

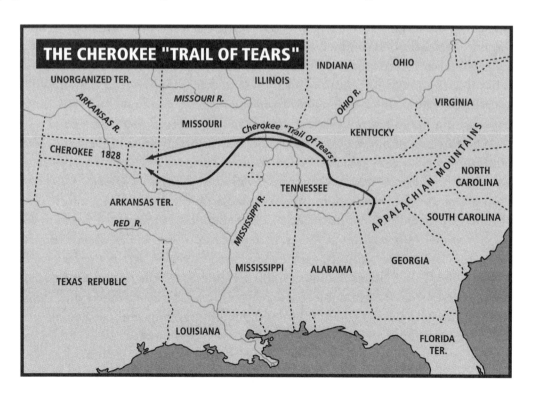

assimilation policy by urging a return to tribal identities. But, irreversible damage had been done as Native Americans did not know who they were or where they belonged in American society.

One of the primary issues for Native Americans is reclaiming ownership of or at least royalties from their ancestral lands. In 1887, the United States Congress passed the **Dawes Severalty Act** as a concerted effort to break up large reservation holdings that bond Native Americans to their tribes. "Rather than allotting reservation lands to tribal groups, the act allowed the president [of the United States] to distribute these lands to individuals. Private property, the framers of the bill reasoned, would undermine communal norms and tribal identity and encourage Indians to settle down and farm as white men did."[37] However, the land redistribution scheme merely took Indian lands held supposedly in trust by the Bureau of Indian Affairs from public oversight to private ownership. "Within 20 years of the Dawes Act, Native Americans had lost 60 percent of their lands. The federal government held the profits from land sales 'in trust' and used them for 'civilizing' missions."[38]

Recent federal legislation coupled with favorable federal court rulings have given Native Americans more control over their lands and, subsequently, their own futures. In particular, the federal courts have rendered favorable decisions in cases involving treaty violations by the federal government. The Oneida Indian Nation has been battling in court since 1920 seeking compensation from the state of New York over 250,000 acres located between Utica and Syracuse, land the tribe claims that was stolen from them. "The federal government first signed a treaty reserving some 270,000 acres for the Oneidas in 1794, after tribe members fought British troops and reportedly lugged 600 bushels of corn hundreds of miles to George Washington's starving troops at Valley Forge. Congress, however, specified that all future purchases of Indian lands could proceed only with federal consent. The Oneidas signed some 27 treaties with New York State over the years, but only one of the state's treaties received federal approval. Eventually, the Oneidas' lands in the state dwindled to a single 32-acre tract."[39] In 1985, the United States Supreme Court ruled that the initial 1794 treaty was a binding document. The Blackfeet are also challenging the BIA's withholding of trust money from the sale or lease of Indian lands dating back to 1820. Through numerous treaties, Native Americans were supposed to receive just compensation for the seizure of their lands. Through treaty agreements, Native American tribes were given the land that was initially deemed unfit for cultivation and settlement. Today, it is estimated that these lands hold 40 percent of the nation's coal reserves, 65 percent of the nation's uranium supply, ample veins of gold, silver, cadmium, platinum and manganese, large untapped pockets of natural gas and oil, acre after acre of uncut prime timber, and 20 percent of the nation's fresh water.[40]

The United States Census Bureau estimates that American Indian and Alaskan Native populations will "increase by more than half from now to 2060, from 3.9 million to 6.3 million, with their share of the total population edging up from 1.2 percent to 1.5 percent."[41] With few exceptions, the majority of the nation's Native Americans, particularly those living on reservations, live at or below the poverty level. Educational and gainful employment opportunities are limited. Of the 833,337 associates degrees awarded in 2010, only 1.2 percent of those diplomas were awarded to American Indians and Alaskan Natives. During the same period, American Indians and Alaskan Natives were awarded only 0.8 percent of all Bachelors, 0.6 percent of Masters and 0.7 percent of first professional degrees.[42] Table 14.1 illustrates some of the important events that have had both a positive and negative impact on Native Americans.

Table 14.1

Significant Events for Native Americans

Date	Event
1778	The newly formed United States negotiates its first treaty with an Indian nation promising future statehood to the Delawares.
1787-1789	The United States Constitution gives the federal government the exclusive authority to regulate trade and commerce with Indian tribes.
1809	Treaty of Fort Wayne secures 2.5 million acres from Indians for Anglo-American settlement in Ohio and Indiana.
1813-1814	The Creek Wars end with treaty agreements relinquishing all lands held by the Creeks in the Southeast to the American government.
1817-1818	First Seminole War.
1820-1824	Kickapoos resist removal from Illinois territory.
1824	Bureau of Indian Affairs established under the War Department.
1830	Congress passes the Indian Removal Act.
1835-1842	Second Seminole War.
1853-1856	United States government obtains 174 million acres of Indian lands through treaties.
1854	United States Indian Affairs Commission ends the Indian Removal Policy.
1855-1858	Third Seminole War.
1861-1863	Mangas Colorados and Cochise lead Apache uprising.
1862	Smallpox kills 200,000 Indians in the Northwest Coast.
1863-1866	Navajo Wars in New Mexico and Arizona.
1866	United States Congress declares Indian land as right-of-way for construction of the Trans-Continental Railroad.
1876-1877	Sioux Wars waged by Sioux, Cheyenne and Arapaho under Sitting Bull and Crazy Horse.
1881-1886	Apache resistance under Geronimo.
1885	The last great herd of buffalo are exterminated.
1887	Congress passes the General Allotment Act or the Dawes Act.

1924	Congress grants citizenship to Native Americans.
1926	National Council of American Indians is formed.
1928	Charles Curtis, Kansas Indian and United States Senator, is elected vice president under Herbert Hoover.
1934	Congress passes United States Indian Reorganization Act, reversing United States practice of land allotment by establishing tribal self government and landholding.
1965	Congress passes Voting Rights Act ensuring suffrage to all Native Americans.
1968	Passage of the American Indian Civil Rights Act extending civil liberties outlined in the Bill of Rights to Indians living on reservations.
1969-1971	Members of Red Power movement occupy Alcatraz Island to call attention to the plight of Native Americans.
1973	Members of American Indian Movement and 200 armed Oglala Sioux occupy site of Wounded Knee Massacre on Pine Ridge Reservation in South Dakota for 71 days.
1978	Congress passes American Indian Freedom of Religion Act.
1988	Congress passes Indian Gaming Regulatory Act, allowing Indians to operate casinos on their reservations under guidelines established by the states.
1990	Congress passes Native American Graves Protection and Repatriation Act.
1999	President Bill Clinton becomes the first president to visit an Indian reservation since President Franklin Roosevelt included a stop at a Cherokee reservation while on vacation in North Carolina in 1936.
2004	National Museum of the American Indian opens in Washington, D.C.

African Americans

The economic prosperity of the pre-Civil War South was the result to a large degree by the backbreaking toil of African-American slaves and their descendents who worked in the fields from sun up to sun down either bent over picking cotton, wielding a machete cutting sugar cane, or standing in ankle-deep water planting and harvesting rice. Most Southerners rationalized the exploitation, brutality, injustice, and degradation of slaves with the "old assumptions of Anglo-Saxon superiority and innate African inferiority, white supremacy, and Negro [African American] subordination."[43] The institution of slavery completely controlled the fate of the slave from birth to death. Slaves were part of their owner's properties just like the house, the fields, and the furniture. Frederick Douglass once remarked that "whatever of comfort is necessary for him [the slave] for his body or soul that is inconsistent with his being property, is carefully wrested from him, not only by public opinion but by the laws of the country . . . . He [the slave] is deprived of education. God gave him an intellect; the slaveholder declares it shall not be cultivated."[44] The denial of education, even the simplest forms of reading and writing, reinforced the concept of the superior/inferior relationship by making the slave more dependent upon his master and, thus, less likely to be disobedient or to run away.

Slavery was first introduced to the colonies in 1619 when a few Black Africans were brought to the new world to harvest Jamestown's tobacco crop. "Within a decade after South Carolina's 1691 adoption of a comprehensive slave code, other Colonies had laws defining and regulating human chattel."[45] Aided by a lucrative cross-Atlantic slave trading industry, the slave system grew rapidly. "By the eve of the [American] Revolution, slave-holding was deeply rooted in all of those Colonies, with New York City, among colonial cities, standing second only Charleston, S.C., in its population of slaves."[46] The emerging slave system was economically attractive to both the agricultural interests in the South and the developing textile industries in the North. Although many plantation owners and farmers opposed the institution of slavery on moral grounds, economic reality prevented the abolition of the system, opting instead to ban the exportation of new slaves into the country by 1808. "By as early as 1815, cotton was America's most valuable export, and the worth of the people who harvested the product grew apace with cotton's steadily growing value. 'By the eve of the Civil War, the dollar value of slaves was greater than the dollar value of all of America's banks, railroads, and manufacturing combined.'"[47] Unable to halt the spread of slavery in the traditional Southern states, the abolitionist movement convinced Congress to limit the spread of slavery into new territories seeking statehood with the passage of the **Missouri Compromise** in 1820.

The fate of the Missouri Compromise was determined by the United States Supreme Court's decision in *Dred Scott v Sanford* (1857). First, the Court invalidated the Missouri Compromise of 1820 as an unconstitutional intrusion into state affairs. Second, it ruled that Dred Scott, a slave, did not have the right to sue the government because he was not a citizen of the country. Third, Scott was still considered to be a slave since the Court affirmed that slaves were the property of their owners, and only their owners could release them from their bondage.

The man who would eventually abolish slavery echoed superior/inferior sentiments against slaves in a speech delivered in 1858 at a Republican Party function. Abraham Lincoln stated: "I will say then that I am not, nor ever have been in favor of bringing about in any way the social and political equality of the white [Anglo] and black [African American] races, [applause]—that

The Supreme Court decided that Dred Scott was not a citizen of the United States.

I am not nor ever have been in favor of making voters or jurors of Negroes [African Americans], nor of qualifying them to hold office, nor to intermarry with white [Anglo] people, and I will say in addition to this that there is a physical difference between black [African American] and white [Anglo] races which I believe will forever forbid the two races living together on the terms of social and political equality. And inasmuch as they cannot so live, while they do remain together, there must be the position of superior and inferior, and I as much as any other man, am in favor of having the superior position assigned to the white [Anglo] race."[48] During the Civil War, free African Americans living in the Northern states were initially denied the right to join the military effort. "The hardest problem for black [African American] men was not in being brave, it was in getting a chance to fight at all. At every step, they were confronted with racial scorn and fear, created by the long existence of slavery itself."[49] In 1862, Congress passed the Militia Act, enabling African Americans to join the warfront. However, African Americans received less than half of the standard soldier pay and were denied any officer and command positions. At the end of the war, "some 180,000 black [African-American] solders served in the Union Army, about 10 percent of its total strength; 2,800 were killed in battle, 34,000 died of disease in the field, and twenty-one were awarded the Medal of Honor for bravery."[50]

The end of the Civil War brought limited social, economic, and political relief to former slaves. Economic viability was difficult, if not immediately impossible. Few knew how to read or write. Few had ventured far from their plantations. Once emancipated, few knew how to survive on their own. During the final months of the Civil War, General William Sherman attempted to entice southern African Americans to join the union cause by offering to each family forty-acres of prime farmland in Georgia and South Carolina. He also promised to lend them Army mules. Congress also allocated approximately 850,000 acres of southern soil to the Freedman's Bureau. In turn, the Bureau was supposed to help former slaves make the transition from slavery to freedom by giving them land. Few received any land since President Andrew Johnson used his executive muscle to allow former Confederates to quickly reclaim their properties. In 1865, the United States Congress finally outlawed slavery with the passage of the **Thirteenth Amendment**. Former slaves were granted citizenship with the passage of the **Fourteenth Amendment** and voting privileges with the **Fifteenth Amendment**. The **Civil Rights Act of 1866** granted former slaves the rights to own property, file lawsuits, and make contractual agreements. Initially, the Republican-dominated Congress used these three constitutional amendments and the Civil Rights Act to punish defeated members of the **Confederate States of America**. Known as the **Radical Republicans**, these individuals desired to topple the Southern aristocracy by placing former slaves into policy-making roles. Across the South, former Confederate officials, soldiers, and any one who supported the Southern cause lost their rights to vote and to run for elective office. Consequently, citizenship and voting privileges enabled former slaves to now run for public office. "Every session of the Virginia General Assembly from 1869 to 1891 contained black [African American] members. Between 1876 and 1894 North Carolinians elected fifty-two blacks [African Americans] to the lower house of their state legislature, and between 1878 and 1902, forty-seven blacks [African Americans] served in the South Carolina General Assembly . . . . Southern states elected two blacks [African Americans] to the U. S. House of Representatives after Reconstruction, the same number elected during Reconstruction. Every Congress but one between 1869 and 1901 had at least one black [African American] member from the South."[51]

"Yet despite these enactments, despite the mandates of Amendment Fourteen, and despite the language of the Fifteenth Amendment of 1870 which on its face seemed to assure to blacks [African Americans] the privilege of the ballot, neither the myth of white supremacy nor the fact of color prejudice was wiped out."[52] The Southern states struck back at the federal government by enacting a series of legislative acts and city ordinances known as black codes or **Jim Crow laws** that denied freedoms and political rights to African Americans. Punitive sanctions were levied against both African Americans and whites providing assistance to freedmen.

National lawmakers soon realized "that you cannot change the mores of a people by law, and since the social segregation of the races is the most deep-seated and pervasive of the Southern mores, it is evident that he who attempts to change it by law runs risks of incalculable gravity."[53] Jim Crow laws began to have an impact on African-American accessibility to the ballot box, blocking full political participation. The **grandfather clause** required passing a **literacy test** for those potential voters whose grandfathers could not vote before 1867. Variations of the grandfather clause were incorporated into the state constitutions of South Carolina, Louisiana, North Carolina, Alabama, Virginia, Georgia, and Oklahoma. The **poll tax**, a state mandated voting fee, was enacted in Florida, Tennessee, Arkansas, and Texas. The Democratic Party's **white only primary** effectively eliminated African-American participation, since in most general races, the opposition party did not run a candidate. This tactic was adopted in South Carolina, Arkansas, Georgia, Florida, Tennessee, Alabama, Mississippi, Kentucky, Texas, Louisiana, Oklahoma, Virginia, and North Carolina.

Jim Crow laws also socially separated Anglos from African Americans. Immediately following the election of 1884, "the rumor, when it struck, was deemed as vile as any that had ever hit the nation's capitol. A 'colored man' [African American], people were whispering, had attended a White House function. Grover Cleveland swiftly responded. 'It so happens,' the President assured the nation, 'that I have never in my official position, either when sleeping or walking, alive or dead, on my head or my heels, dined, lunched, or supped or invited to a wedding reception any colored [African-American] man, woman, or child.'"[54] The mean-spiritedness of Jim Crow pervaded legislative houses across this nation. The Virginia state legislature passed a 1912 ordinance mandating segregated residential districts. The law made it "unlawful for any colored [African-American] person to move into a white district, or a white [Anglo] person to move into a colored [African-American] district. This act [did] not preclude persons of either race employed as servants by persons of the other race from residing on the premises of the employer."[55] In the Southern states, the segregation of the races was conducted under the **separate but equal** policy. "They [African Americans] were either excluded from railway cars, omnibuses, stage coaches, and steamboats or assigned to special 'Jim Crow' sections; they sat, when permitted, in secluded and remote corners of theaters and lecture halls; they could not enter most hotels, restaurants, and resorts, except as servants; they prayed in 'Negro [African-American] pews' in white [Anglo] churches, and if partaking of the sacrament of the Lord's supper, they waited until the whites [Anglos] had been served the bread and wine. Moreover, they were often educated in segregated schools, punished in segregated prisons, nursed in segregated hospitals, and buried in segregated cemeteries."[56] Almost all the Southern states passed laws requiring railroad stations to have separate waiting rooms and segregated cars. Public facilities had separate drinking fountains, restrooms, swimming pools, and parks. "There was nothing particularly secretive about either public or private discrimination; it was simply a way of life."[57] These tactics effectively created African-American ghettos and slum areas whereby African Americans were kept economically, socially, and politically depressed. In smaller towns, an invisible line successfully separated African Americans from Anglos. The term "living on the wrong side of the tracks" indicated the societal status of the resident. Both the white and black communities felt the adverse impact of Jim Crow. Civil rights advocate James Meredith stressed that "you can't forget that whites in the South were as unfree as any black. White supremacy was official and legal—it was enforced by judges and the law people—and a white that failed to acknowledge and carry out the mandate of white supremacy was as subject to persecution as any black."[58]

Ironically, the United States Supreme Court upheld Jim Crow laws in hearing a case that originated in Louisiana. Originally a French colony, Louisiana was far more liberal in its treatment of African Americans than her sister states. "New Orleans began experimenting with integrated public schools—the only Southern city to do so. Blacks [African Americans] served with whites [Anglos] on juries and public boards. New Orleans had an integrated police department with a color-blind municipal pay scale... Between the years 1868 and 1896, racial intermarriage was made legal, and Louisiana elected 32 black [African-American] state senators and 95 state representatives. It had the only black [African-American] governor in U.S. history before the late 1980's."[59] With the end of Reconstruction, the power of the Radical Republicans in the South began to erode as former Confederates, armed with their voting rights, reestablished the Democratic Party power base in the South. In 1890, the Louisiana legislature passed the **Separate Car Act,** mandating separate accommodations for Anglo and African-American patrons. "Under its terms any railway company that did not provide separate coaches for blacks [African Americans] and whites [Anglos] could be fined $500. Except for nurses attending children of the other race, individual whites [Anglos] and blacks [African Americans] would be forbidden to ride together or risk a $25 fine or 20 days in jail."[60] Opposition groups decided to test the validity of the law. Homer Plessy, who was one-eighth African American, was purposely selected by the East Louisiana Railroad to sit in the "white" section of the railway car headed from New Orleans to Covington. Railroad officials believed the uproar of Plessy's arrest would convince the courts that the law was unconstitutional. When ordered to give up his seat, Plessy refused and was arrested. Plessy sued, believing that the Louisiana law violated the Thirteenth and Fourteenth Amendments to the United States Constitution. The United States Supreme Court's 1896 ruling in *Plessy v Ferguson* resulted in a 7 to 0 vote against Plessy. In defense of its decision, the Court maintained that "a statute that made a legal distinction between the races on the basis of color did not destroy the legal equality of the races or create a condition of slavery; it merely reflected the social distinctions based on color that existed in society. Furthermore, while the object of the Fourteenth Amendment was to enforce the absolute legal and political equality of the two races, it was not intended to abolish distinctions based upon color or enforce social equality and the 'commingling' of the two races upon terms unsatisfactory to either."[61] This ruling gave state legislative houses the ability to continue passing laws separating the races, providing the segregated accommodations or services were basically in principle equal. The United States Supreme Court also struck down the **Civil Rights Act of 1875**, prohibiting private discrimination in accommodations, transportation, and public places of amusement. The Court's decision was based on the premise that the Fourteenth Amendment applied to state or public actions, not to private activities.

African Americans were "kept in their place" through the intimidation of the **Ku Klux Klan** (**KKK**). The Klan emerged in the South during the Reconstruction era. Garbed in white robes and hoods, Klansmen used a variety of scare tactics against defiant African Americans and whites [Anglos] sympathetic to the plight of African Americans. Burning crosses, public tar and featherings, floggings, and lynchings were used throughout the South to remind African Americans of their inferior status. The steadfastness of the Klan was openly challenged by President Grant with the passage of the Enforcement Act of 1871. Hoping to put the Klan out of business, this law "allowed persons deprived of their rights under the Constitution to bring suit in federal courts (rather than state courts). It defined conspiracy to deprive citizens of the equal protection of the laws or prevent citizens of the equal protection of the laws or prevent citizens from voting, and it permitted the prosecution of such conspiracies in federal courts."[62] It also empowered the president to suspend the writ of habeas corpus. By October 1871, Grant suspended habeas corpus in nine counties in South Carolina and sent federal marshals and troops to arrest Klan members and other marauders and hold them for federal prosecution. Subsequently, "political violence in South Carolina and across the South decline dramatically, and soon the KKK virtually disappeared from southern life, not to be seen again until the 20th century."[63] While the Klan may have been crippled, the actions of southern state legislative houses and their courts continued to level legal sanctions against African Americans. Thurgood Marshall once commented that "even in Mississippi a Negro [African American] will get a trial longer than 42 minutes, if he is fortunate enough to be brought to trial."[64] In some southern communities, African Americans could be arrested for petty offenses, such as not stepping off the sidewalk to make way for an Anglo pedestrian. Far too often, "justice" for African Americans was a lynch mob, not a jury of twelve impartial men and women. "In the past two decades of the nineteenth century more than 2,500 blacks [African Americans] were lynched in the South. Another thousand or so were murdered in this way in the first decade and a half of the new century."[65] It was the efforts of the **Association of Southern Women for the Prevention of Lynching** that finally gained public support of state laws prohibiting lynching. During its 2002 term, the United States Supreme Court heard arguments in a case concerning the Klan's continued practice of burning crosses as a means of intimidating African Americans. Known for his quiet demeanor

The Ku Klux Klan was politically strong in the South. Action was directed at African Americans and white sympathizers.

on the bench, Justice Clarence Thomas, the Court's only African-American member, decried that "this [the Klan's activities] was a reign of terror, and the cross was a symbol of that reign of terror. Isn't that significantly greater than intimidation or a threat? . . . We had almost 100 years of lynching and activity in the South by the Knights of Camellia and the Ku Klux Klan. It was intended to cause fear and to terrorize a population."[66]

Jim Crow also meant that African Americans were prohibited from moving into white neighborhoods by the restrictive covenant, redlining, and steering techniques. A **restrictive covenant** was a provision in a mortgage contract that forbade the buyer from eventually selling the house to a member of a minority race. If such a sale occurred, the property could revert back to the original owner. Another ploy was to increase the selling price of the property based upon the interested party's race, placing the sale price at a prohibitive cost. **Steering** was the practice of just showing properties to minorities located in solely minority residential areas, thus keeping them away from already segregated white [Anglo] neighborhoods. **Redlining** was the tactic used by financial institutions to deny loans to individuals wanting to purchase property in a racially changing neighborhood. The loan would either be denied outright or the interest rate would be substantially increased to discourage the potential borrower.

African Americans began to challenge Jim Crow laws and acts of discrimination by forming community and nationally based organizations. In 1909 a well-known African-American scholar, W.E.B. DuBois, founded the **National Association for the Advancement of Colored Persons** (NAACP). Groups leading the charge for equality for African Americans included the Congress of Racial Equality (CORE), and the Southern Christian Leadership Conference (SCLC), founded by the late Dr. Martin L. King, Jr., in 1956. The modern civil rights movement drew national attention to the adverse discriminatory practices of Jim Crow when Mrs. Rosa Parks [an African American] was arrested for refusing to give up her seat on a Montgomery, Alabama bus to a white [Anglo] person; four African-American students at the North Carolina Agricultural and Technical College sat peacefully at a lunch counter at Woolworth's while employees refused to serve them and bystanders hurled racial insults and food at them; and Dr. Martin L. King, Jr., led protesters in peaceful, nonviolent demonstrations throughout the South. When asked why she refused to give up her seat, Rosa Parks said "my feet were hurting, and I didn't know why I refused to stand up when they told me. But the real reason of my not standing up was I felt that I had a right to be treated as any other passenger. We had endured that kind of treatment for too long."[67] Honored as the "Mother of the Civil Rights Movement," Mrs. Parks continued her fight for equal treatment.

A new term began to emerge from the protesters—**integration**. "One cannot be close to the problem very long without hearing that word. *Integration* is what the Negro [African American] has not got. He is on the outside, and he wants to be on the inside. He is not allowed to play or live or work as others and he wants to play, live, and work as others. He occupies a negative position, and desires the positive. The principle of integration (and its opposite, non-integration) cuts a pattern through the nation just as widespread but far more complex than the transportation system over which the trains roll, planes fly, farm wagons crawl, and people walk."[68] The demand for inclusion from a group excluded from the political, social, and cultural environment of mainstream America for over two hundred years could no longer be ignored or dismissed. One by one the repressive practices of Jim Crow began to be challenged and successfully overturned by the federal courts. The actions of the United State Supreme Court awakened the United States Congress to pass a series of civil rights acts, which provided voting rights and desegregation of public accommodations and public schools to correct past abuses. The first major civil rights bill since Reconstruction, the **Civil Rights Act of 1957**, created the United States Commission on Civil Rights and the Civil Rights Section of the Justice Department. The federal government was now empowered to obtain injunctions to halt illegal voting activities. The **Civil Rights Act of 1960** authorized federal appointed voter referees to conduct voter registration drives and to monitor federal elections in areas with historical patterns of voting problems. The **Civil Rights Act of 1964** prohibited discrimination in public accommodations and employment practices. Discriminatory housing practices to include restrictive convenants, redlining and steering were prohibited with the passage of the **Civil Rights Act of 1968**.

The United States Supreme Court began to curtail discriminatory voting practices as early as 1927. In *Nixon v Herndon*, the Supreme Court invalidated the Texas White Primary Law of 1924, which mandated that "in no event shall a Negro [African American] be eligible to participate in a Democratic primary election in the State of Texas, and should a Negro [African American] vote in a Democratic primary election, such ballot shall be void and election officials shall not count the same."[69] Defiantly, the Texas Democratic Party continued the white-only primary by declaring the party a private club capable of establishing its own membership criteria. The United States Supreme Court finally dealt the fatal blow to this practice by ruling in *Smith v Allwright* (1944) that the Texas Democratic Party was not a private club but an agent of the state, subject to state and federal mandates. As a state agency, the party could no longer deny voting privileges to any qualified voter for any election.

The poll tax was outlawed with the passage of the **Twenty-fourth Amendment** to the United States Constitution. In *Guinn v United States* (1915), the United States Supreme Court invalidated Oklahoma's grandfather clause as a direct violation of the Fifteenth Amendment. The literacy test was dismantled in a piecemeal fashion. The **Civil Rights Act of 1964** required states to accept a sixth grade education as meeting voter literacy and testing requirements. Minor errors on the test or voter registration card, such as abbreviations, could not be used to deny voting privileges. The **Voting Rights Act of 1965** suspended the use of discriminatory literacy tests. A 1970 amendment to the Voting Rights Act completely eliminated the literacy requirement.

Jim Crow also extended to the military. During World War II, for example, African Americans were denied officer and leadership roles. Supervised by Anglo officers, African-American soldiers were far too often segregated into their own camps, barracks, mess halls, and even latrines. "More than a million blacks [African Americans] served in that war, of the more than 16 million U.S. military personnel. Most were assigned to construction, transportation, service or support units."[70] On July 26, 1948, President Harry Truman issued **Executive Order No. 9981**, which desegregated the military by mandating "equality of treatment and opportunity for all persons in the armed forces without regard to race, color, religion or national origin."[71]

The demise of the "separate but equal" doctrine began with the certainly separate but definitely unequal conditions in public schools and colleges across the nation. For example, Herman Sweatt, an African-American mail carrier from Houston, Texas, wanted to attend the University of Texas Law School. Sweatt was denied admission because of his race. His only option was to attend the Texas State University for Negroes, an academically inferior school when compared to the University of Texas. In *Sweatt v Painter* (1950), the United States Supreme Court ruled that

Sweatt should not be forced to attend a racially separated inferior school. "By ruling that the term *equal* applied not only to tangible factors, such as university buildings, books, and faculty, but to intangible qualities such as institutional reputation and opportunity to interact with a cross-section of the legal profession, the Court made it more difficult for states to maintain and justify separate but equal or 'dual' school systems."[72] A similar ruling was made that same year in ***McLaurin v Oklahoma State Regents***. The University of Oklahoma did not have a separate graduate school for African Americans. The university would admit African Americans on a segregated basis, meaning that African Americans sat in totally segregated classes and facilities from white students. The Court ruled against the university's policy.

In 1954, the United States Supreme Court handed down its "separate but equal" shattering ruling in ***Brown v the Board of Education of Topeka, Kansas***. Eight-year-old Linda Brown was refused admittance to an all-white public school located just five blocks from her home because of her race. Instead, she was forced to attend an African-American school located twenty-one blocks from her home. The *Brown* suit was one of four filed by African-American families confronted with similar situations in South Carolina, Virginia, and Delaware. Basically, African-American children were forced to attend poorly equipped, inadequately staffed, and seriously underfunded African-American public schools. The question before the Court was whether the Fourteenth Amendment's equal protection clause extended to public schools. The United States Supreme Court ruled unanimously with Brown concluding that *"in the field of public education the doctrine of 'separate but equal' has no place. Separate educational facilities are inherently unequal . . . The plaintiffs and others similarly situated for whom the actions have been brought are, by reason of the segregation complained of, deprived of the equal protection of the laws guaranteed by the Fourteenth*

The mule-drawn wagon bearing the body of Dr. Martin Luther King, Jr. moves up Auburn Avenue toward downtown Atlanta after funeral services for the slain civil rights leader. Winner of the Nobel Peace Prize and a staunch supporter of nonviolence, Dr. Martin Luther King, Jr. was assassinated in Memphis, Tennessee, on April 4, 1968

Amendment.[73] The *Brown* decision dismantled the philosophical basis of Jim Crow. However, public schools, colleges, and universities reluctantly and defiantly opened their doors to African-American students. Orval Faubus, governor of Arkansas, openly defied desegregation of Little Rock's four high schools by closing them down for the entire 1958-59 academic year, leaving approximately 3,700 public school students to make their own arrangements. To counter the governor's actions, federal authorities decided to force desegregation by enrolling nine African-American students into Little Rock's Central High School. With the assistance of the United States Army, the nine were finally admitted into the door of the high school. Their school year, however, was not a pleasant experience. "The nine students were bombarded with racial hatred. The U.S. Department of Justice had assigned a bodyguard to each of them, but white [Anglo] students still harassed them. They were body-slammed into lockers, attacked in gym class, tripped in the hallways, and push down stairs. And the name calling was incessant. So were the death threats."[74] By 1960, the federal government realized that it had to assume a more forceful role in desegregating public schools and facilities. "In Louisiana, Mississippi, Alabama, Georgia, and South Carolina there has been no change at all. In Florida, Arkansas, Tennessee, North Carolina and Virginia, only an occasional school district has allowed white [Anglo] and colored [African American] children to sit in the same classrooms. Texas, Oklahoma, Missouri, Kentucky, West Virginia, Maryland, Delaware, and the District of Columbia range, however, from extensive to complete desegregation of schools."[75] Consequently, the enforcement of desegregation was accomplished through court mandated busing and federal threats of denial of federal money to schools participating in discriminatory practices. Subsequent court decisions and legislative acts mandated desegregation of all public facilities and accommodations. The now outlawed practices of separate but equal proved to be very costly to the South, both in budgetary dollars and public image as the rest of the country began to see the impact of their discriminatory practices. One observer noted that Jim Crow laws "compels the South to have to buy two of everything, two schools, two toilets, two communities, two worlds."[76]

The victories won by civil rights leaders in the 1960s should not be underestimated. Civil rights activists were murdered for their efforts to register African Americans to vote in the Deep South. Martin L. King, Jr., Malcolm X, Medger Evers, and many others were slain because their quest for African-American equality was viewed by some as too revolutionary for mainstream America. The Civil Rights Movement of the 60s has resulted in more African Americans registering, voting, and running for public office. Although not the first African American to make a bid for the White House, electing Barack Obama to the Oval Office took the collective will power of the "rainbow coalition" that Dr. Martin Luther King, Jr., so passionately sought. On the evening of both of his successful elections to the presidency, Obama faced a multitude of American citizens—black, brown, white—all celebrating as one. Commemorating the 50th anniversary of King's speech, speaker after speaker recalled the struggles confronted by King and his followers and the price they paid for the enactment of laws outlawing discriminatory practices, protecting voting rights, and giving African Americans accessibility to social, economic, and political mobility. However, as each speaker painfully noted that "but for all that progress, sizable gaps remain between white and black America in areas of wealth, income, poverty and economic opportunity."[77] The 2012 poverty rates indicate that 4,201,000 or 37.9 percent of African Americans have incomes below the poverty level in comparison to 9,979,000 or 18.5 percent of whites [Anglos].[78] Table 14.2 is a selective listing of significant events and achievements for African Americans.

Table 14.2

Significant Events for African Americans

Date	Event
1619	The first African slaves arrive in Virginia.
1831	William Lloyd Garrison begins publishing *The Liberator*, an abolitionist newspaper. Nat Turner leads rebellion in Virginia, resulting in the deaths of 57 white men, women, and children. Turner was executed for his role.
1833	Lewis Tappan, Theodore Weld and William Garrison establish the American Anti-Slavery Society, a national organization opposing slavery.
1851	Sojourner Truth gives her "Ain't I A Woman?" speech at the women's rights convention held in Akron, Ohio. Myrtilla Miner opens the first school to train African-American women to be teachers.
1852	Harriet Beecher Stowe publishes *Uncle Tom's Cabin*.
1855	In *Missouri v Celia, a Slave,* an African-American woman is declared to be property without the right to defend herself against her master's continuous acts of rape. She was eventually executed for murdering her master. Fighting breaks out in Kansas, known as "Bloody Kansas."
1857	The U.S. Supreme Court rules in *Dred Scott v Sanford* that slaves are not citizens; therefore, they do not have the right to sue. This case nullifies the Missouri Compromise.
1862	Mary Jane Patterson is the first African-American woman to receive a full baccalaureate degree from Oberlin College.
1863	Lincoln issues his Gettysburg Address to include the Emancipation Proclamation.
1865	Congress passes the 13th Amendment abolishing slavery. Lee surrenders. Lincoln is assassinated. The Freedmen's Bureau is founded to assist newly freed slaves. Black codes enacted across the southern states.
1866	The 14th Amendment granting citizenship to former male slaves is passed by Congress. The Civil Rights Bill of 1866 is passed over President Johnson's veto. The Ku Klux Klan is organized.
1867	African Americans vote in Southern elections.
1870	The 15th Amendment, expanding voting rights to former male slaves, is officially ratified.
1875	Civil Rights Act of 1875, guaranteeing desegregated public facilities, passes Congress. This law will be ruled as unconstitutional by the Supreme Court in the *Civil Rights Cases*, 1883.
1896	The National Association of Colored Women, founded by Margaret Murray Washington, unites several African-American women's groups under one organization. Mary Church Terrell serves as its first president. In *Plessy v Ferguson,* the Supreme Court upholds the separate but equal doctrine.
1909	The National Association for the Advancement of Colored Persons (NAACP) is formed with W. E. B. Dubois as its first president.

1935	Mary McLeod Bethune organizes the National Council of Negro Women as a lobbying group for African-American women. Key agenda items focus on fighting job discrimination, racism & sexism.
1939	Marian Anderson gives a concert at the Lincoln Memorial.
1954	*Brown v Board of Education of Topeka, Kansas.*
1955	Montgomery Bus Boycott in response to Rosa Parks being arrested for refusing to give up her bus seat to a white person. The boycott is staged from December 5, 1955 to December 21, 1956. The Interstate Commerce Commission bans segregation on interstate travel. Emmett Till is killed on August 28.
1956	Tallahassee Bus Boycott begins on May 27. The boycott ends in March 1958. Autherine Lucy is admitted to the University of Alabama. The Southern Manifesto is presented. The Supreme Court upholds the use of busing for desegregation of public schools.
1957	Southern Christian Leadership Conference is formed. Protests begin at the Little Rock Central High School. The protests end in May 1959. The first civil rights bill since 1875 passes through Congress.
1960	Greensboro sit-in occurs on February 1, followed by sit-ins and boycotts all over the South and in some Northern cities. Civil Rights Act of 1960 signed.
1961	Freedom Rides occur during the summer. Federal courts order Hunter and Holmes to be admitted to the University of Georgia.
1962	James Meredith enters the University of Mississippi. John Kennedy federalizes Mississippi State Troopers to protect Meredith. Los Angeles riots occur on April 27 followed by the Ole Mississippi riots in October.
1963	University of Alabama desegregation crisis occurs as George Wallace attempts to block federal troops sent by the president. John Kennedy meets with civil rights leaders for the March on Washington, August 28. Medgar Evers and John Kennedy are killed.
1964	Title VII of the Civil Rights Act barring employment discrimination by private employers, employment agencies, and unions is enacted. Martin L. King, Jr., awarded Nobel Prize. The 24th Amendment to the U.S. Constitution, banning the poll tax, is ratified. Race riots occur in New York, New Jersey, Chicago, and Philadelphia. Goodman, Schwerner, and Chaney killed on June 24.
1965	Lyndon Johnson enacts Executive Order 11246 calling for the federal government to take affirmative action in overcoming employment discrimination. Voting Rights Act signed into law. Malcolm X is killed. Race riots in Watts.
1968	Martin L. King, Jr., and Robert Kennedy are assassinated. Riots at the Democratic Convention.
1971	Shirley Chisholm (D-NY) is the first African-American woman elected to the U.S. Congress.
1972	Barbara Jordan (D-TX) becomes the first African American elected to U.S. Congress from a southern state.
1984	The nonpartisan National Political Congress of Black Women is founded by Shirley Chisholm to address women's rights issues and to encourage political participation.

1988	Rev. Barbara Harris becomes the first female African-American bishop of the Episcopal Church.
1990	The number of African-American women elected to office increased from 131 in 1970 to 1,950 in 1990.
1992	Carol Moseley-Braun (D-Ill). becomes the first African-American woman elected to the U.S. Senate.
2000	Colin S. Powell becomes the first African American to serve as the nation's Secretary of State and Condoleezza Rice becomes the first woman and African American to serve as the National Security Advisor.
2005	Condoleezza Rice becomes the first African-American woman to serve as the nation's Secretary of State.
2009	Barack Obama is inaugurated as the nation's 44th President of the United States, becoming the first African American to hold the office; Eric Holder becomes the nation's first African-American Attorney General.

The Hispanic Experience

Other victims of discrimination, racial hatred, prejudice, and stereotyping are Hispanics, Americans of Mexican and Spanish descent. When most Americans voice their concerns over illegal immigration, their attention is focused to the Mexican national crossing the Rio Grande in the Southwestern states or the international border into California. Anti-immigration advocates fail to mention that other nationalities have come to this country illegally. In addition, we should not forget that "the Spanish Mexicans of the Southwest are not truly an immigrant group, for they are in their traditional home."[79] Hispanics are the fastest growing minority group in the United States. "While Hispanics made up less than 15 percent of the population in 2005, the Census Bureau predicts they will be a quarter of the country by 2050. The Hispanic population is expected to jump from 42 million to over 100 million, making up nearly half of the nation's total projected growth during that time."[80] Despite their booming population, Hispanics have been victimized by the very same philosophy of Anglo superiority that was used against African Americans. The "Hispanic" community also suffers from stereotyping that fails to recognize the cultural diversity of those called "Hispanics." "The label Latino or Hispanic covers people who come from two dozen countries and who can claim mixtures of Spanish, Portuguese, Indian, African, Italian, German and Italian ancestry."[81] Basically the Hispanic community is composed of three culturally, socially, and politically diverse groups who live in different areas of the country. "Mexican-Americans, who make up almost two-thirds of the Hispanics in the United States, are concentrated in the Southwest. Cuban-Americans live primarily in South Florida. Puerto Rican Americans have settled mostly in the Northeast, particularly in New York City and New Jersey."[82] Politically, Mexican-Americans promote liberal Democratic candidates while Cuban-Americans are known to cast a bloc vote for conservative Republican candidates.

The growing distrust between Hispanics and Anglo Americans began in earnest with the colonization of Texas. Unable to settle Texas with families from Spain and Mexico, both governments opened up the region to Anglo Americans through a land grant program known as the empresario system. Initially welcomed into the region, Anglo Americans soon began to take advantage of their hosts by openly defying the Mexican government. The aftermath of the inevitable Texas Revolution made the already fragile relationship deteriorate further as Hispanics encountered "the wrath of Anglos, who considered them a conquered people and an alien race and who persecuted them with impunity."[83] Although there are several explanations for the racial tensions between Hispanics and Anglos, the economic theory of racism was evident in the settlement of the Southwestern states and California. Like the Native American tribes, Spanish and Mexican landowners held a precious commodity Anglo Americans wanted—vast landholdings. Anglo American settlers guided by a government bent on achieving its manifest destiny cast an envious and greedy eye upon those vast parcels of land that were granted by the Spanish monarchy to the economic elites or Creoles. Gradually, Anglo Americans used a variety of schemes to seize these lands.

Meanwhile, the non-economic elite Hispanics, known as **Mestizos,** became the primary labor force in building the nation's railroads, working in the mines extracting precious natural resources, toiling in the fields picking agricultural crops, or riding fence on cattle ranches. Relegated to a life of picking fruits and vegetables, herding cattle or laboring at unskilled or semiskilled jobs at exceptionally low wages, Hispanic workers were needed for their muscles, not their minds. Testifying before the House Immigration and Naturalization Committee in 1920, then Congressman John Nance Garner from Uvalde, Texas, stated: "I believe I am within the bounds of truth when I say that the Mexican man is the superior laborer when it comes to grubbing land… And I may add that the prices that they charge are much less than the same labor would be from either the Negro [African American] or the white man and for the same time they do … a third more—they produce a third more results from their labor then either the Negro [African American] or white man would do."[84] Unfortunately, Hispanics were subjected to the same Jim Crow laws and acts of wanton discrimination as those levied against African Americans. "For roughly 75 years after the end of the war between Mexico and the United States, Mexican Americans in the Southwest contended with segregation in the public schools, segregation and discrimination in public facilities such as restaurants, movie theaters, swimming pools, and barbershops; primary election procedures that prevented them from exercising their right to vote; and discrimination in housing. They also suffered discrimination in the administration of justice that prevented them from serving on juries and treated violence against them as so common as to pass almost unnoticed."[85]

The story of the farmer laborer or **compensino** in the Southwest and California is a tragic one. The movement of Mexican labor into the United States picked up stream during World War I. "In California, the demand for workers in the citrus, melon, tomato, and other industries increased sharply, encouraging Mexicans to come across the border to perform these necessary tasks. The other southwestern states were similarly affected. Workers were needed in Texas to tend the cotton, spinach, and onion crops and in Arizona, New Mexico, and Colorado to raise vegetables, forage crops, and sugar beets."[86] Since these are not yearly crops, the term "seasonal" or "migratory" workers was used to describe this Mexican labor force. At the turn of the twentieth century, approximately 85 percent of Hispanics living in Texas were employed as farm workers, ranch hands, and tenant farmers. Tenant farmers worked the landowner's fields from sun up to sun down in return for extremely low wages, a one-room shack, and a small plot of land to grow their own vegetables. The future of tenant farmers rested squarely upon the shoulders of the landowner, who could at any time raise rents, restrict planting, or relocate and remove the tenant from his property. Whether stationary or migratory, the farm workers of today toil in the fields picking and harvesting crops in the same bent over position assumed by their fathers and grandfathers. Living conditions are in some instances akin to third world poverty. Job security is just as nonexistent as health care and education. Severe weather destroys both crops and jobs. In the mid 1960s, the late César Chávez began organizing campesinos into the **United Farm Workers Union (UFW)**. This organization brought national attention to the living and working conditions of farm workers in Texas and California by its series of protests and strikes over the picking of lettuce and grapes. "In the 1970s, they [the campesinos] still faced lamentable working conditions. Most fields lacked restrooms, and since modesty compelled women to delay their bodily functions for hours, they suffered from disproportionately high levels of kidney infections. Wages remained as low as $2 or $3 for a typical day of field labor. Diseases such as typhoid, typhus, dysentery, and leprosy afflicted farm workers to a degree unknown to other Texans. Infant mortality rates among the compesinos in South Texas were among the highest in the United States at that time, and the life expectancy for field hands hovered around forty-nine."[87]

The success of the United Farm Workers Union has helped to produce corrective legislation designed to improve the lifestyle of farm workers. They can apply for unemployment and workers compensation benefits. Their children can attend schools offering half day class schedules to accommodate those students who must spend a portion of their day working along side their parents. State health laws mandate that growers provide clean drinking water and field restrooms. Although the wage scale has gradually increased, farm workers still are not fairly compensated for a hard day's work. "Picking a 50-pound bag of onions earns a farm worker $1.20 (market price is $6 per bag)... The rate for harvesting a 10-gallon bucket of jalapeno peppers is $1. When they work watermelon, cantaloupe, lettuce and cabbage fields, they can earn minimum wage. Clearing a large field of weeds might pay $500. UFW leaders say a 'respectable wage' would be $8 an hour."[88] Farm workers still do not have collective bargaining rights, life insurance, health care, or protection against hazardous pesticides and chemicals. Growing up in migrant farm labor camps, Chávez knew first hand the problems confronting Hispanic farm workers. Although he dedicated his life to organizing workers and conducting voter registration drives, Chávez strongly believed that political empowerment alone could not fully uplift Hispanics from their plight. In a 1973 interview, Chávez stated:

> But political power alone is not enough. Although I've been at it for some twenty years, all the time and the money and effort haven't brought about any significant change whatsoever. Effective political power is never going to come, particularly to minority groups unless they have economic power. And however poor they are, even the poor people can organize economic power.
>
> Political power by itself, as we've tried to fathom it and to fashion it, is like having a car that doesn't have any motor in it. It is like striking a match that goes out. Economic power is like having a generator to keep that bulb burning all the time. So we have to develop economic power to assure a continuation of political power.... As a continuation of our struggle, I think we can develop economic power and put it into the hands of the people so they can have more control over their own lives, and then begin to change the system. We want radical change. Nothing short of radical change is going to have an impact on

our lives or our problems. We want sufficient power to control our own destinies. This is our struggle. It is a lifetime job. The work for social change and against social injustice is never ended.[89]

The untimely death of Chávez has left a leadership void in the Hispanic community. "Many Hispanics regard[ed] Chávez as akin to Mohandas Gandhi in India and Martin Luther King Jr., in the United States because of his belief nonviolent protests lead to social change."[90] On November 28, 2000, the Hispanic community lost another hero—United States Congressman Henry B. Gonzalez. He too devoted his life's work to the Hispanic community. Although more Hispanics are being elected to state and national legislative houses, there has been no one to rise to the occasion as a viable replacement for Chávez or Gonzalez.

The Hispanic community has been in some respects adversely impacted by illegal immigration of Mexican nationals to the United States. In the Southwestern border states, it is still a daily task for Immigration and Naturalization Service agents to round up illegals who crossed over the border or swam across the Rio Grande and send them back home. Mexican nationals are also buying their way into the United States by hiring a coyote to smuggle them across the border. The trip can prove to be deadly. Far too often illegals are crammed into un-air conditioned vehicles, semi-tracker trailers, and railroad cars. Fearful of being captured by border guards, coyotes will often abandon the vehicle or the railroad car, leaving the illegals locked inside. If the border agents do not find them soon enough, illegal immigrants usually die of heat-related illnesses or starvation. The simple solution would be to hire more agents and seal up the border. But, the issue of illegal immigration and the exploration of possible solutions is far more complicated and more difficult to solve. In part, the number of illegals from Mexico is directly tied to the Mexican economy. Although Mexico is improving its economic footing, the wealth is still distributed to a very small percentage of Mexico's people. Mired in third and fourth world poverty, Mexican nationals see even a below minimum wage job in the United States as their only means to feed, clothe, and educate their children.

There are, however, several misnomers and misconceptions about Mexican immigration into this country. First, the advocates of anti-immigration laws always point a finger at the Hispanic community as the source of this country's immigration woes. While immigrants were entering this country in the thousands from Europe, relatively few Mexican nationals entered the country as permanent residents for nearly fifty years after the signing of the Treaty of Guadalupe Hidalgo, ending the Mexican War. "For one period, in fact, between 1886 and 1893, there are no official records of immigration from Mexico into the United States."[91] The increase flow of immigrants has been seen in periods of economic upheavals and political discords in Mexico. For example, "in the latter years of the nineteen century and extending into 1910 were the distressful conditions many faced under the dictatorship of President Profirio Diaz. The rural poor were forcibly removed from their common lands by ambitious land barons and faced a dismal life of peonage on the rural estates. . . . The Mexican Revolution which broke out in 1910 and lasted until 1920 also became a catalyst for migration. Mexicans fled to the United States to escape the horrors of war or reprisals from the feuding factions."[92] Second, the United States government has not always cast a negative eye at the Mexican national worker. For example, the United States experienced a dramatic decrease in cheap farm laborers during and immediately after World War II. The United

States government contracted with the Mexican government to bring agricultural workers into the United States. The **Bracero program** allowed farm workers to enter the country under the following conditions: "free transportation and food; guarantees concerning wages, working conditions, and housing; and the right of Mexican officials to make inspections and to investigate workers' complaints."[93] The program ended in 1964 as growers sought ways to bypass the program by hiring illegal Mexican nationals at wages far below those offered through the Bracero contracts. Third, not every person crossing the border is a Mexican national. Since Mexico is the only Central and Latin American country sharing a border with the United States, it has become the "pathway" to the United States for many from Central American countries such as Honduras, Guatemala, El Salvador, Costa Rica, and Nicaragua.

Fourth, illegal immigration, particularly from Mexico, has resulted in "white fear," a new concept of the economic theory of racism. **White fear** is the feeling "of becoming a member of the new minority as the existing minority becomes a majority within the social community."[94] The potential loss of economic viability, and social and political clout fuels the fires of those advocating stronger anti-immigration laws. Expressing their fears that the continuous flow of both legal and illegal Mexican immigrants across the Rio Grande will eventually take jobs away from American workers and depress the wage market, white fear advocates created a system of political and economic barriers against Hispanic citizens. Particularly in the Southwestern states, Hispanics were kept from developing any political muscle to flex at city, state, or national legislative houses. Redistricting plans ensured that Hispanics were grossly under-represented in legislative houses while at-large city council elections precluded the election of Hispanic candidates. While statistics do not support their claims against Mexican nationals, the cries of white fear accelerate whenever the American economy slumps or job security becomes questionable. Basically, "as long as there was a shortage of cheap labor, the 'Mexicans' were welcomed and praised as cooperative, uncomplaining workers; but when economic times were bad, 'American' officials wanted the 'Mexicans' to go 'home.'"[95] The Mexican nationals' threat to American job security is in itself a misnomer since the majority of Mexican nationals and other Hispanic immigrants are seasonal workers toiling at jobs few Americans want to work.

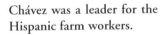

Chávez was a leader for the Hispanic farm workers.

Table 14.3

Significant Events for Hispanic Americans

Date	Event
1845	Texas is admitted into the United States.
1846	The United States declares war on Mexico.
1848	The Treaty of Guadalupe Hidalgo ends the war with Mexico. The United States purchases Mexican territories held in the Southwest for $15 million with the promise of respecting the property rights of Mexicans living now in the U. S. and allowing them to become citizens.
1897	Mexican-American Miguel A. Otero is appointed governor of New Mexico.
1910	The Mexican Revolution brings Mexican nationals to the U. S. for safety and employment. Mexican immigrants become a source of cheap farm labor in the Southwest.
1918-21	More than 50,000 Mexican nationals are recruited to combat a labor shortage in the Southwest.
1924	The Immigration Act of 1924 establishes guidelines for the admission of Mexican workers, collecting a head tax on each. More than 89,000 enter the U. S. on permanent visas while others enter illegally to avoid the fees.
1928	The *Confederacion de Uniones Obreras Mexicanas* (CUOM) is formed to organize all Mexican workers in the U. S. to fight for wage parity and an end to racial discrimination. Octaviano Larrazola (NM) is the first Mexican American elected to the U. S. Senate.
1929	The League of United Latin American Citizens (LULAC) forms in Corpus Christi, Texas, to help Mexican Americans assume their rightful places as U. S. citizens and to fight discriminatory practices.
1931	Female Mexican-American garment workers in Los Angeles, California, are unionized by labor organizer Rose Pesotta.
1939	El Congreso del Pueblo de Habla Espanola (The Spanish Speaking People's Congress) is founded by Lusia Moreno. This working-class organization aims to secure basic rights for all Spanish-speaking people in the U. S. by forming a unified labor movement to combat poverty and discrimination. Mexican Americans in Beeville, Texas, desegregate the local high school.
1942	The bracero program begins, allowing Mexican nationals to work in the Southwest as a source of cheap agriculture labor. The program ends in 1964. Approximately, 300,000 Mexican-American men served in WWII with 17 awarded the Congressional Medal of Honor.
1946	LULAC supports a class-action suit by Gonzalo Mendez against several school districts in California. The Federal District Court rules that segregation in these school districts is unconstitutional. Andres Morales becomes the first Mexican American to be elected to a city council in California since the 19th century.
1947	The Community Service Organization (CSO) is established in Los Angeles to encourage voter registration and grass-roots political support for Mexican Americans.

1953-58	The U. S. Immigration Service arrests and deports over 3.8 million persons of Mexican descent during Operation Wetback. Many U. S. citizens are deported unfairly.
1961	Henry B. Gonzalez (D-Tex) is the first Mexican American elected to the U. S. House of Representatives from Texas. He retired from the House in 1998.
1962	César Chávez organizes the National Farm Workers Association (NFWA) in Delano, California.
1965	César Chávez and the NFWA begin a grape boycott, targeting Schenley Industries and the Di Giorgio Corporation.
1967	Corky Gonzales writes the epic poem "I Am Joaquin." The Mexican-American Legal Defense and Education Fund (MALDF) is formed. The Brown Berets are established in Los Angeles, California.
1974	Willie Velasquez forms the Southwest Voter Registration and Education Project. MANA, the Mexican-American Women's National Association, is established as a feminist activist organization. By 1990, MANA chapters operate in 16 states.
1975	The 1965 Voting Rights Act is extended to the Southwest.
1992	Lucille Roybal-Allard (D-CA) becomes the first Mexican-American woman elected to the U. S. House of Representatives.

Beginning with the election of Ronald Reagan, anti-immigration advocates joined forces with the conservative wing of the Republican Party and gained the upper-hand in promoting immigration reform legislation. A series of 1997 immigration laws made it more difficult for both foreigners to seek political asylum and legal immigrants to bring immediate family members into the country. Particularly after September 11, 2001, the federal government was granted more authority to deport immigrants who arrived without proper documentation. All job applicants are required to provide proof of work eligibility and citizenship status. Beginning in January 2004, the Bush administration made it more expensive to become a legal worker or a citizen by increasing the fees to apply for citizenship; to apply, replace, or renew a permanent residency card, also known as a green card; to petition to bring in a fiancé or family member into the country; and all had to be fingerprinted. A key element of the Bush administration was to discourage illegal immigration while at the same time, provide foreign nationals the opportunity to work legally in the United States under a guest worker program similar to the Bracero program. An ill-fated attempt introduced by Senators John McCain (R-Arizona) and Edward Kennedy (D-Massachusetts) would have allowed workers who have illegally worked in the country for six years or more, to apply for green cards and eventually gain citizenship. Anti-immigration advocates successfully got Congress to approve the building of a fence along the Mexico/United States border. However, the Obama administration canceled the fence project due to budget deficits.

Since the founding of this nation, it has been the responsibility of the federal government to enact and enforce immigration laws. Between 1880 and 1908, Chinese and Japanese immigration was restricted. Passed over President Wilson's veto, a 1917 law required immigrants to pass a literacy test before they could be admitted into the country. In 1921, Congress limited European immigration in any one year to 3 percent of the number of each nationality admitted into the United

States in 1910. The National Origins Act of 1927 limited European immigration to 150,000 per year. Subsequent legislation banned Asian immigrants. The Supreme Court has consistently held that immigration-related issues rest with the federal and not state governments. "A 1986 federal law forbids states from enacting stricter criminal or civil penalties for illegal immigration than those adopted by Congress.[96] In a 2006 decision, the United States Supreme Court signaled that federal law, not state laws, guide the nation's immigration and deportation policies. In an 8-1 decision the Court ruled in favor of an immigrant who had violated a South Dakota law making it a deportable offense to possess illegal substances. "The issue before the Supreme Court was the interpretation of the federal Immigration and Nationality Act, which says immigrants found guilty of aggravated felonies are subject to deportation. Conduct that's felony under state law but a misdemeanor under the Controlled Substance Act isn't a felony for purposes of immigration."[97] However, it has been the inability of Congress to pass immigration reform measures, coupled with the changing pattern of illegal immigration from the traditional border states to regions from the Midwest, Rocky Mountains to New England and the increased drug-related gang war violence in Mexico that has moved state legislative houses to enact their own versions of immigration reform only to see their legislative issues ruled unconstitutional or unenforceable by the federal courts.

A measure supported by the Obama administration, the Dream Act failed to win congressional approval. Introduced in 2001, this law would have provided an easier path towards citizenship for illegal immigrants who were brought into the United States as children. To qualify, the applicant had to submit to a background check from Homeland Security and have a clean criminal record. Once approved, the applicant would be granted a ten-year conditional residency permit with the understanding that during that period, they would at least complete two years of college or join the United States military. While the law would have applied to all illegal children, the Hispanic community in particular would have reaped the benefits. Although they supported Obama's reelection to the White House, the Hispanic community continues to express their displeasure with the Obama administration's failure to press Congress for immigration reform, in particular the passage of the Dream Act. Senator Marc Rubio (R-Fla.) also pledged to offer his own plan for immigration reform but failed to win over his Republican colleagues to support his effort. Obama did initiate the Deferred Action for Childhood Arrivals in 2012. "Under the policy, people younger than 31 can apply for a two-year deferral of any deportation if they can prove they came to the United States before the age of 16, have lived here for the past five years, have not been convicted of select crimes and are not a threat to national security. Applicants must have a high school diploma or GED, be currently enrolled in school or have been honorably discharged from the military."[98] However, this program does not lead to permanent citizenship. Applicants must pay an application fee of approximately $465 plus be subjected to background checks and provide financial, medical and employment records. Also, there is no appeal if one's application is denied. Perhaps the zeal for immigration reform got put on the back burner as both congressional members and the president's team focused more on reviving the American economy.

The key to Hispanic empowerment does begin within the political arena. In the 1970s, a small group of students from St. Mary's University in San Antonio, Texas, led by Jose Angel Gutierrez founded a third political party movement dedicated to the causes of the Hispanic community. **La Raza Unida** (LRU) began in the South Texas Rio Grande Valley, a predominately agricultural area stretching south of San Antonio to the Mexican border. The majority of the region's Hispanic population are farm workers who toil in the fields picking fruits and vegetables, earning at or below minimum wages. The party began at the lowest political level by winning positions on the Crystal City, Texas, city council and school board. La Raza ceased to be a viable third party as the organization's political agenda was adopted by the Democrats, which usually garner at least two-thirds or better of the Hispanic vote in local, state and national election efforts. Founded in 1968, the National Council of La Raza provides a cadre of lobbyists to promote Hispanic issue concerns in state and national legislative houses. Hispanic organizations such as the **League of United Latin American Citizens** (LULAC) and the **Mexican-American Legal Defense and Educational Fund** (MALDF) keep the social, economic, and political needs of the Hispanic community alive by conducting voter registration drives, recruiting and supporting Hispanic candidates, and lobbying legislative and executive houses across the country. Outdated discriminatory redistricting plans have been successfully challenged in federal courts, and the corrective legislation embodied in the Voting Rights Act and subsequent amendments have provided bilingual ballots and materials. In 1968, the late Willie Velasquez, another graduate of St. Mary's University, founded the **Southwest Voter Registration Project** (SVRP) and organized voter registration drives throughout Southwest Texas, California, Arizona, and New Mexico. However, the United States Supreme Court ruled in 2013 that Section 5 of the Voting Rights Act was unconstitutional. In particular, Section 5 was the backbone of the legislation since it required many state legislative houses and city/local officials to submit their electoral redistricting plans for pre-clearance by the U.S. Justice Department if there was an historical pattern of voter irregularities and gerrymandering of representational district designed to deny minorities' equal representation.

No Hispanic had ever served in a cabinet level position until President Ronald Reagan appointed Lauro Cavazos as Secretary of Education and President Clinton appointed Henry Cisneros and Frederico Pena to his team. President George W. Bush appointed several Hispanics to high ranking positions including Alberto Gonzales to attorney general. Hispanic empowerment is also hampered by a lack of cooperation among Hispanics. "Even activists acknowledge that Hispanic potential has been sapped by the group's overall political apathy and its inability to knit together Mexican-Americans, Cuban-Americans, Puerto Ricans, and other factions . . . . Hispanics don't have any issues they can come together on . . . . The only things they really have in common are that they tend to be Catholic, speak Spanish, have generally the same skin color, and have some of the same cultural values. Other than that they are very different and distinct groups."[99] Hispanic political clout, however, is beginning to exert its presence. Traditionally, Hispanics joined the ranks of African-American voters in their solid support of Democratic candidates. The Democratic Party continues to draw a large percentage of the Hispanic vote due to the party's positions on immigration, education, the economy, and health care. The Hispanic vote cannot be taken for granted. The increase in Hispanic voting clout "should serve as a cautionary note to anyone in political life that campaigning in this community is a lot more than speaking Spanish."[100] The Hispanic community, however, must begin to exert more of a solid presence in the political arena and actively recruit and, subsequently, elect more Hispanic candidates to public office to ensure that the quest so eloquently voiced by the late Cesar Chávez will not fall upon deaf ears.

Gender Issues

In 1776, Abigail Adams warned her husband John Adams to: "Remember the Ladies, and be more generous and favorable to them than your ancestors. Do not put such unlimited powers into the hands of the Husbands. Remember all Men would be tyrants if they could. If particular care and attention is not paid to the Ladies, we are determined to ferment a Rebellion, and will not hold ourselves bound by any Laws in which we have no voice, or Representation."[101] Unfortunately, the framers chose to ignore her warnings, opting instead to deny women basic rights guaranteed to men through the United States Constitution. In 1995, women across this nation celebrated the seventy-fifth anniversary of the passage of the **Nineteenth Amendment** to the United States Constitution, granting women suffrage rights. While civil rights struggles have been focused primarily on minority groups, we cannot overlook the tremendous and arduous task women of this nation faced to not only vote but to own property, apply for credit, get an education, earn a decent wage, and even serve on a jury. These basic rights should have been guaranteed to all American citizens, male and female, when the framers pinned both the Constitution and the Bill of Rights.

For centuries, however, gender-based discrimination fueled by paternalistic attitudes has kept women in subservient roles. It was women of all creeds and colors who worked side by side their male counterparts to build this nation. Yet, they realized from the very beginning that they had very few civil rights that fell under the protection of the Bill of Rights, no meaningful voice in the political arena, and only a marginal role in society. In 1872, ardent feminist Victoria Woodhull decided to take on incumbent President Ulysses S. Grant and Horace Greeley for the race for the White House. The first woman to run for the presidency, Woodhull's time was "a much more difficult one for women, who then had almost no rights to property or person. If a married woman worked, her wages were given directly to her husband. She could not dispose of her property upon death. If she divorced, she automatically forfeited custody of her children. Women could not enter universities, law schools or medical schools. They could not vote. Most significantly, women had no control over their own bodies: There were no laws to protect them from physical abuse at the hands of their husbands or fathers, although some states stipulated the size of the objects that might be used to inflict discipline.... Men were allowed all means of sexual license, but a woman who committed adultery was subject to a jail sentence."[102] Although improvements have been made, women not only in the United States but across the globe are still battling against those historical and cultural barriers that continue to keep them in a subservient role, usually one step behind their male counterparts.

The **paternalistic attitude** of male superiority over women is supported by the myth that women are just too fragile mentally and physically to survive the rigors of life by themselves. Women need a "knight in shining armor" to protect them from harm and unpleasantness. The Southern plantation system went a step further by placing women on pedestals. Frail and fragile like a treasured piece of fine bone china, women became the objects of worship, requiring the constant watchful protective eye of their husbands and fathers. The frontier experience with its encouragement of rugged individualism played right into the hands of paternalism by creating the "macho" male role. In 1873, Supreme Court Justice Joseph Bradley wrote:

> Man is, or should be, woman's protector and defender. The natural and proper timidity and delicacy which belongs to the female sex evidently unfits it for many of the occupations of civil live. The constitution of the family organization, which is founded in the divine ordinance, as well as in the nature of things, indicates the domestic sphere as that which properly belongs to the domain and functions of womanhood. The harmony . . . of interests and views which belong, or should belong, to the family institution is repugnant to the idea of woman adopting a distinct and independent career from that of her husband. . . . The paramount destiny and mission of woman are to fulfill the noble and benign offices of wife and mother.[103]

Paternalistic attitudes toward women resulted in repressive laws, social barriers, restrictive employment opportunities, and denial of education. Oddly, single women had more rights and freedoms than married women. "The very being of woman was suspended during marriage or at least incorporated into that of her husband, under whose wing she maintained her legal status."[104] State legislative houses passed laws prohibiting women from selling or borrowing against her own private property without her husband's permission. Women could not on their own enter into contracts, apply for loans and credit, witness a will, sue, or serve on a jury. The Texas Constitution once contained an amendment barring women from purchasing a refrigerator without prior approval from their spouses.

With very few exceptions, women did not venture forth into the world of politics until the beginning of the Abolitionist movement in the 1830s. However, antislavery organizations did not openly embrace or offer leadership roles to women. A disgusted Sarah Grimke wrote the president of the Boston Female Anti-Slavery Society that "all history attests that man has subjugated woman to his will, used her as a means to promote his selfish gratifications, to minister to his sensual pleasure, to be instrumental in promoting his comfort; but never has he desired to promote her to the rank she was created to fill. He has done all he could to debase and enslave her mind; and now he looks triumphantly on the ruin he has wrought, and says, the being he has thus deeply injured is his inferior."[105] The plight of women prompted Lucretia Mott and Elizabeth Cady Stanton to organize the first Women's Rights Convention held at Seneca Falls, New York, in 1848. Their penning of the **Declaration of Sentiments and Resolutions** declaring women equal to men set the stage for the Women's Suffrage Movement. Stanton was adamant about gaining the right to vote for women. She argued "to have drunkards, idiots, horse racing rum-selling rowdies, ignorant foreigners, and silly boys fully recognized [with voting privileges], while we ourselves are thrust out from all the rights that belong to citizens, is too grossly insulting to be longer quietly submitted to. The right is ours. We must have it."[106] The United States Supreme Court gave the emerging movement a chance to vent its frustrations when the Court ruled in *Minor v Happersat* (1875) that the Fourteenth Amendment to the United States Constitution did not give women the right to vote. The quest for a constitutional amendment to reverse the Court's decision solidified an emerging feminist movement to the cause of suffrage.

Ardent feminists, Elizabeth Cady Stanton and Susan B. Anthony, founded *The Revolution*, a weekly newspaper focusing on feminist issues. Stanton and Anthony also formed the **National American Women Suffrage Association** while Lucy Stone organized the **American Woman Suffrage Association**. Francis Perkins Gilman took on the economic issues confronting women. The incidents of the mistreatment of workers, particularly women, were too frequent to be ignored. "Far from gaining in personal freedom, women were increasingly the victims of the factories and workshops; competition no doubt drove their employers to exploit their defenseless positions on the labour market just as the need for subsistence, the absence of special qualifications, and the lack of alternatives drove innumerable young women into the factories and garment-making shops."[107] Women garment workers joined women of all classes in massive demonstrations as the New York Women's Trade Union League staged strikes in 1909.

Of course, women's organizations were confronted with the task of uniting the majority of nation's men and women behind "the cause." Author of *Uncle Tom's Cabin,* Harriet Beecher Stowe and her sister Catharine Beecher were the leading voices opposing woman's suffrage. In an 1869 article, they commented:

> Let us suppose that our friends have gained the ballot and the powers of office: Are they any real beneficent measures for our sex, which they would enforce by law and penalties, that fathers, brothers, and husbands would not grant to a united petition of our sex, or even to a majority of the wise and good? Would these not confer what the wives, mothers, and sisters deemed best for themselves and the children they train, very much sooner than they would give power and office to our sex to enforce these advantages by law? Would it not be a wiser thing to ask for what we need, before trying so circuitous and dangerous a method? God has give to man the physical power, so that all that woman may gain, either by petitions or by ballot, will be the gift of love or of duty; and the ballot never will be accorded till benevolent and conscientious men are the majority—a millennial point far beyond our present kin.[108]

Lacking cohesive leadership, women's organizations needed a board-base issue to draw the various factions together. The **Temperance Movement** in the 1900s helped to solidified women behind the desire to rid the nation of alcohol. Their efforts resulted in the passage of the **Eighteenth Amendment** and the Prohibition Era. Meanwhile, a new suffrage leadership was emerging under Dr. Anna Howard Shaw, Carrie Chapman Catt, and Alice Paul, founder of the Congressional Union, which later became the **Woman's Party**. Although several states allowed women to vote in statewide and local elections, women did not have voting rights in national elections. Both Paul and Chapman organized daily marches and protests in front of the White House to jar a reluctant President Woodrow Wilson to assert pressure for the passage of a woman's suffrage amendment. Women's organizations began lobbying Wilson immediately after he took office in 1913. In his 1916 re-election effort, Wilson advocated giving women the right to vote. However, once re-elected, he changed his mind. Members of the National Woman's Party met with Wilson on January 9, 1917, only to be rebuffed in their efforts. "The next morning the White House picketing began. The press described the pickets as 'Silent Sentinels.' Nearly every day, rain or shine, whenever Congress was in session, they were there. They stood essentially motionless, holding large purple, white, and gold banners. 'How long must women wait?' some banners asked. 'President Wilson, what will you do for woman suffrage?'"[109] To break the monotony of daily protests, Alice Paul had "theme days" whereby the messages on the banners would be changed on a daily basis. Finally Wilson caved in. Approved by Congress in 1919, the **Nineteenth Amendment** was ratified by the required number of states by August 1920.

The suffrage movement involved a complex array of political, social, and economic issues. Women were scorned, publicly and socially humiliated, arrested, jailed and even killed in their struggle to reverse the stranglehold of paternalism. Conditions in the jails were horrible. "The cells at the workhouse in Occoquan, Virginia, were small, dark and rat-infested. Bedding hadn't been cleaned in almost a year; the staff handled it only with rubber gloves. The suffragists held contests to see who had the most mealworms in her food. For extended periods the women were allowed no visitors or legal counsel. All mail was censored . . . Dorothy Day, 20, the future founder of the Catholic Worker Movement, had her arms twisted and was violently thrown against a iron bench. Dora Lewis, 55, was knocked unconscious. Lucy Burns, identified as a Woman's Party leader, was beaten and left handcuffed to her cell bars with her hands above her head."[110] Alice Paul was arrested for protesting in front of the White House. Staging a protest hunger strike, Paul was forced-fed simply because the White House feared the repercussions her death would have on the American public and, ultimately, political careers. "Hoping to discredit her by having her diagnosed as mentally ill, the warden moved her to the psychopathic ward, where the screams of patients and a flashlight shined in her face every hour, kept her awake."[111] Once they were released from prison, the women continued their fight to gain social, economic, legal, and political equality with their male counterparts.

With the exception of the war years of the 1920s and 1940s, employment opportunities for women were limited to a few low paying positions usually available to just single women. In most states, female public school teachers had to resign their positions when they married. In the 1920s, women gained in the job market by replacing men who were fighting overseas. However, the Depression Era reversed this trend as women were deliberately fired to open up job opportunities for unemployed men. World War II again gave women a chance for employment as they replaced men in industrial and manufacturing positions. Today, the economic necessity of the two-household income has substantially increased the number of females in the workforce.

Despite countless litigations and legislative acts correcting previous adverse actions, women are still confronted by a multiplicity of job-related discriminatory practices. The **pay equity** issue addresses the problem that women earn less than their male counterparts employed in comparable positions. Women, as a whole, earn less since they hold the majority of clerical and secretarial positions, collectively known as **pink collar** jobs. Across the board, men earn more than women. The trends clearly show that within each racial/ethnic group, women are now earning the majority of college-level degrees versus their male counterparts. However, the wage disparity gap still favors men. A man with only a high school diploma will earn approximately $35,468 per year compared to $24,304 for a woman with that same high school diploma employed in a comparable job. A woman with a bachelor's degree employed in a similar position to her male counterpart with the same education earns only $43,589 per year while he brings home $69,479. The professional category includes doctors, lawyers, engineers, scientists, etc. Once again, women earn on an average $89,897 per year while men in comparable positions with the same degree credentials earn an average of $150,310.[112] Whether they are Anglo, African American, or Hispanic, women in all of these categories earn less than men. Although job promotability and mobility opportunities for women have increased substantially, women are still victims of the **glass ceiling**, which prohibits them from becoming the CEO or president of the firm. A military career for women is still a controversial issue. Initially women entered the military in hopes of building a career by moving up the promotional ladder. However, the majority of them were traditionally confined to non-combat duties such as nursing and official clerical duties. The majority of the command positions were held by men, particularly those assigned to combat commanding roles. Forced through congressional acts, presidential decrees and orders by the Secretary of Defense, military academies reluctantly opened their doors to female cadets. Secretary of Defense Chuck Hagel has cleared the way for women to serve in combat. Yet, these sweeping changes have been tarnished by the on-going sexual assault and sexual harassment charges made by women against their male trainers and commanders.

The woman's movement, like other social movements, has failed to maintain a consistent and cohesive battlefront. In the 1920s, "the newly political liberated womanhood of America made no move to disturb the social order; they arranged themselves instead along lines already marked out by the structure and economic interests of a society dominated by men. What was more surprising, and disappointing to those who had hoped for real alterations among the roles in American society, was the limping and limited manner in which women attempted to move into positions occupied by men throughout industry or the professions. Leaders of the suffrage movement did not see their duty now as that of inspiring a diffused and dispersed multitude of followers . . . ."[113] True to form, the woman's movement declined after winning the suffrage battle only to re-emerge in the 1960s under new leadership and new issues—reproductive freedom and women's liberation. The feminist movement achieved its goal when the Supreme Court upheld reproductive freedom of choice in *Roe v Wade* (1973). The women's movement began to decline in the 1980s, only to re-emerge in the 1990s with the issue of electing more women to public office. In the 1992 "Year of the Woman," women did succeed in increasing their numbers in state and national elective offices. In 2007, Senator Hillary Clinton (D-NY) made an unsuccessful bid for the presidency. Even as an unannounced candidate, she is the front-runner for the 2016 Democrat presidential nomination. Throughout its history, Texas has had only two female governors and no female lieutenant governors. Times might be changing. In the 2014 statewide elections, state Senator Wendy Davis (D) is running for governor and Leticia Van de Putte (D) is seeking the lieutenant governor's position.

The feminist movement has yet to address the problems confronting the average woman and those women who are undereducated and living in poverty. The separate sisters—"women in minority groups; women in 'traditional' women's jobs; women who stay at home to raise children; elderly, rural, some poor and younger women—acknowledge their debt to feminism's early battles. But they charge that the feminist movement has failed to broaden its base and remains made up largely of white, highly educated women who have not adequately addressed the issues that matter to them: child care rather than lesbian and abortion rights, economic survival rather than political equality, the sticky floor rather than the glass ceiling."[114] In addition, women's organizations like minority groups have not established a consistent proactive record. They join to battle an issue and then disperse. For example, their lack of cohesive vigilance has enabled state legislative houses to pass anti-abortion legislation that is successfully and legally chipping away at the provisions of *Roe v Wade*. Their success hinges on pursuing a proactive diverse array of issues that will unite women of diverse races and incomes rather than just reacting to a problem.

Table 14.4

Significant Events for American Women

Date	Event
1848	The first women's rights convention is held in Seneca Falls, New York on July 19 and 20. A *Declaration of Sentiments and Resolutions*, setting the agenda for the women's movement, was adopted.
1851	Sojourner Truth gives her speech "Ain't I a Woman?" at the women's rights convention in Akron, Ohio.
1866	The American Equal Rights Association is founded. This is the first organization in the United States advocating national suffrage rights for women.
1868	Sorosis, the first professional club for women, is founded. The Working Women's Protective Union in New York is founded by middle- and upper-class women to lobby for laws protecting women workers. Elizabeth Cady Stanton and Susan B. Anthony begin publishing *The Revolution*, a women's periodical.
1869	Women shoe stitchers from six states form the Daughters of St. Crispin, the first national women's labor organization. The first woman suffrage law in the United States passes in the territory of Wyoming. Susan B. Anthony and Elizabeth Cady Stanton form the National Woman Suffrage Association as Lucy Stone establishes the American Woman Suffrage Association.
1870	For the first time in the history of jurisprudence, women serve on juries in the Wyoming Territory. Iowa becomes the first state to admit a woman to the bar.
1872	Congress passes an equal pay law for women federal employees. Susan B. Anthony is arrested, tried, found guilty, and fined $100 for registering and voting in the presidential election.
1874	The United States Supreme Court rules in *Bradwell v Illinois* that states can restrict women from any professional career "to preserve family harmony and uphold the law of the Creator." The Woman's Christian Temperance Union is founded by Annie Wittenmyer.
1875	The Supreme Court rules in *Minor v Happersett* that the 14th Amendment does not give women the right to vote.
1884	Belva Lockwood, presidential candidate of the National Equal Rights Party, becomes the first woman to receive votes in a presidential election.
1917	Jeanette Rankin of Montana becomes the first woman elected to the U. S. Congress. In January, suffragists begin a silent vigil in front of the White House.
1919	The House of Representatives and the Senate pass the woman suffrage amendment.
1920	On August 26, the 19th Amendment to the Constitution is ratified, giving American women citizens the right to vote.
1924	Nellie Tayloe Ross of Wyoming becomes the first woman elected governor of a state.
1926	Bertha Knight Landes is the first woman elected mayor of a sizable U. S. city (Seattle).
1933	Frances Perkins becomes the first woman to serve on a president's cabinet.

1948	Margaret Chase Smith (R-Maine) becomes the first woman elected to the U. S. Senate in her own right. In 1964, she is the first woman to run for the presidency in the primaries of a major political party.
1963	The Equal Pay Act, establishing equal pay for men and women performing the same job duties, passes Congress.
1964	Pasty Mink (D-Hawaii) becomes the first Asian-American woman elected to the U. S. Congress.
1966	The National Organization for Women (NOW) is founded as a civil rights organization for women.
1970	Betty Freidan organizes the first Women's Equality Day, August 26, to mark the 50th anniversary of women's right to vote. The Equal Rights Amendment is reintroduced into Congress.
1973	The Supreme Court rules in *Roe v Wade* that women have a right to an abortion. This overturns 46 state laws banning the procedure.
1974	The Equal Credit Opportunity Act prohibits sex discrimination in all consumer credit practices. Ella Grasso (Connecticut) becomes the first woman to win election as governor in her own right.
1975	The Supreme Court rules in *Taylor v Louisiana* that states cannot prohibit women from serving on juries.
1981	Sandra Day O'Connor becomes the first woman appointed to the U. S. Supreme Court. In 1993, Ruth Bader Ginsburg was appointed to the bench.
1982	The Equal Rights Amendment fails to secure ratification. Over 900 women hold positions as state legislators, compared with 344 a decade ago.
1984	Geraldine Ferraro (D) becomes the first woman vice presidential candidate of a major political party.
1986	The U. S. Supreme Court declares sexual harassment as a form of illegal employment discrimination.
1992	The Year of the Woman results in 24 women elected to the House of Representatives and 6 to the Senate, including Lucille Roybal-Allard (D-CA), the first Mexican-American woman in the House; Nydia Velazquez (D-NY), the first Puerto Rican woman elected to the House; Carol Moseley-Braun (D-IL), the first black woman elected to the Senate; Barbara Boxer and Dianne Feinstein (D-CA), the first two women elected to the Senate from the same state. Janet Reno becomes the first U.S. woman attorney general.
1997	Madeleine Albright is appointed Secretary of State, becoming the first woman to hold that position.
2005	President Bush names Condoleezza Rice as his Secretary of State.
2007	Nancy Pelosi (D-CA) becomes the first woman Speaker of the House of Representatives.
2008	Senator Hillary Clinton (D-New York) makes an unsuccessful bid for the Democratic presidential nomination but is appointed as Secretary of State in the Obama White House.
2009	President Obama successfully appoints Sonia Sotomayor, the first Hispanic woman to the United States Supreme Court.
2010	President Obama successfully appoints Elena Kagan, a Jewish woman, to the United States Supreme Court.

The LGBT Community

Just based upon their sexual orientation, homosexuals were denied a wide range of privileges enjoyed by the "straight" community. Homosexuals in partner relationships were faced with the reality that their relationships had no legal standing. In other words, their relationships defied the traditional definition of a couple as being one of a man with a woman. Anyone in the military suspected of or openly declaring their homosexuality was discharged, regardless of their military performance records. Many state legislative houses passed laws and constitutional amendments defining marriage as between a natural born man and a natural born woman. In 1996, Congress passed the Defense of Marriage Act (DOMA) that mirrored state laws. Basically, these laws simply did not recognize gay and lesbian relationships. If one partner was employed, he/she could not qualify their partners for dependent health-care coverage and other fringe benefits. If one of the partners was hospitalized, the other partner could not be considered as the legal guardian capable of making necessary and, in some instances, life-saving decisions for his/her partner. Guy and lesbian partners were denied death benefits at both the state and federal level including social security.

Gradually, public opinion has changed. During his first term of office, President Clinton addressed the issue of discriminatory practices against homosexuals in the military. Although lacking definitive evidence that one's homosexual orientation was detrimental to a successful military career, the military systematically eliminated gays and lesbians from its ranks through blatant harassment, early discharges, and threats of court-martials. President Clinton offered a compromise policy of "don't ask, don't tell" as a means of eliminating harassment and allowing gays and lesbians to successfully pursue a long-term career in the military. Candidate Barack Obama vowed to rescind the policy altogether pointing out that one's sexual orientation should not be an issue of whether an individual could fulfill their military obligations. Once in the White House, he did move Congress to overturn it.

Several state legislative houses were pressed to change their laws regarding gay and lesbian partnerships. Currently, twenty-one states have either legalized gay marriage and/or civil unions with full or partial legal rights. During its 2013 session, the United States Supreme Court heard arguments against the constitutionality of DOMA. The pro-gay community argued that denial of federal survivorship benefits of a legally married gay or lesbian couple while granting the same benefits to a traditional marriage of man to woman was disparate treatment. The Supreme Court agreed and basically ruled that DOMA was indeed unconstitutional.

Disabled Americans

Unfortunately, disabled Americans have been the targets of discriminatory practices that have denied them social acceptance, personal mobility, and economic viability. Some have disabilities so severe that they cannot care for themselves, much less hold a job. Historically, care for the disabled fell upon individual family members and private charities and institutions. State and local governments provide few, if any, means of assistance. The national government did not provide substantial support for disabled Americans until 1920 with the passage of the **Vocational Rehabilitation Act**. The **Social Security Act** provided federal income-support for the disabled. It was not until 1948 that a special presidential commission was established to explore the problems confronted by the disabled.

For the disabled, normal errands can be extremely frustrating, oftentimes, impossible to achieve. Although corrective legislation has been passed at federal, state, and local levels, the laws are only marginally successful in addressing disability concerns. The United States Constitution prohibits any level of government from passing **ex post facto** laws. Once passed, legislation is enforceable for present actions, not for actions that occurred before the law was passed. For example, the **Architectural Barriers Act** (1970), the **Rehabilitation Act** (1973), and the **Americans with Disabilities Act (ADA)** (1990) require that all new public buildings must be handicapped accessible. These laws, however, cannot mandate that buildings constructed prior to the legislation must be reconfigured to accommodate the disabled. The legislation can only strongly encourage owners of existing public buildings to provide *reasonable but affordable* accommodations. Transportation issues were initially addressed with the passage of the **Urban Mass Transportation Act** in 1970. This act required that state and local governments must ensure that their transportation systems are handicapped accessible.

Title VII of the **Civil Rights Act of 1964** initially barred employment discrimination based on race, color, national origin, religion, and sex. Subsequent legislation has expanded the parameters to include age (individuals over the age of 40), Vietnam era veterans, and the handicapped. "The aim of the civil rights legislation is to prohibit any considerations of disability-related characteristics unless they can be shown to affect ability to perform the job."[115] The law prohibits employers from using any action that treats disabled employees differently from non-disabled employees. "**Disparate treatment** refers to actions in which employers treat people with disabilities differently. **Disparate impact** results when the standards for employment have the effect of excluding people with disabilities on the basis of standards or tests that are not directly related to determining the skills or experience necessary to perform the job."[116]

The major flaw of the ADA law is the legislation's inability to clearly define what constitutes a disability and to set clear-cut direction for reasonable accommodations for the disabled. "In defining the disabled population, the act not only includes anyone with a physical or mental impairment that substantially limits one or more of the major life activities but also includes anyone with a record of having such an impairment or anyone who is perceived as having such an impairment."[117] The issue of reasonable accommodations is oftentimes confusing to employers. For example, what reasonable accommodations should an employer provide to employees who suffer from mental impairments, chronic illnesses, or a bad back? How reasonable should employers be?

While lawmakers and jurists argue over what constitutes a disability, disabled Americans are earning far less than their non-disabled counterparts. In order to lead productive lives, disabled Americans must be able to earn the same paycheck as the non-disabled. Of course, no legislation can change the negative attitudes and stereotypes that are used against the disabled.

CONCLUSION

The public policy process has tried to respond to the needs of minority population groups and women by removing many of the political, economic, and social barriers that kept the doors of success locked for so long. Corrective legislation is, of course, part of the solution. However, the leadership of minority and women's organizations must fulfill their obligations by actively pursuing an all inclusive agenda in the political arena. Lawmakers favorable to minority and women's issues cannot continue to promote legislation in hostile political environments without the full support of the groups they are trying to help. Low voter turnout among minority and female population groups feeds right into the hands of those legislators seeking to hold the line and, in some instances, roll back the clock on civil rights and liberties for minorities and women. These groups cannot afford compliancy.

Frederick Douglass once wrote that the "so-called race problem cannot be solved by keeping the Negro [African American] poor, degraded, ignorant and half-starved . . . It cannot be solved by keeping the wages of the laborer back by fraud . . . It cannot be done by ballot-box stuffing . . . or by confusing Negro [African American] voters by cunning devices. It can, however, be done, and very easily done . . . Let the white [Anglo] people of the North and the South conquer their prejudices . . . Time and strength are not equal to the task before me. But could I be heard by this great nation, I would call to mind the sublime and glorious truths with which, at its birth, it saluted a listening world . . . Put away your race prejudice. Banish the idea that one class must rule over another. Recognize... that the rights of the humblest citizen are as worthy of protection as are those of the highest, and . . . your Republic will stand and flourish forever."[118] Although speaking on behalf of the African-American community, Douglass' words apply to all who have suffered from discrimination and prejudice. The United States Constitution and the Bill of Rights protects the civil rights of all Americans, not just a few. The framers charged the nation's leaders with the task of preserving these civil rights for generations to come. As previously mentioned, presidents and governors can compel legislative houses to pass laws ranging from banning discrimination and to outlawing hate motivated crimes. However, Douglass' challenge transcends laws. All Americans regardless of their race, gender or sexual orientation, must practice what Douglass preached—put away your prejudices.

CHAPTER NOTES

[1] "Obama Cites His Own Dream for America," *San Antonio Express-News* (Thursday, August 29, 2013), A6.

[2] Rick Bragg, "Justice At Last," *San Antonio Express-News* (Thursday, May 23, 2002), 10A.

[3] Todd Spangler, "Race Tied to Fatal Shooting," *San Antonio Express-News* (Saturday, April 29, 2000), 1A.

[4] Rick Bragg, "Klansman Faces Trial in '66 Mississippi Slaying", *San Antonio Express-News* (Sunday, January 26, 2003), 14A.

[5] Tim Pagdett, "Long Wait for Justice", *Time* (January 17, 2005), 53.

[6] Gary Martin, "Votes Delayed But Lobbying Continues," *San Antonio Express-News* (Sunday, November 24, 2013), A18.

[7] Judith A. Winston, "One America in the 21st Century: The President's Initiative on Race," *The National Voter* (The League of Women Voters, March/April 1998), (6-7), 6.

[8] John C. Domino, *Civil Rights and Liberties: Toward the 21st Century*, (New York: HarperCollins Publishers, 1994), 2.

[9] Leon C. Blevins, *Texas Government in National Perspective*, (New Jersey: Prentice-Hall, 1987), 255-256.

[10] Henry J. Abraham and Barbara A. Perry, *Freedom & the Court: Civil Rights & Liberties in the United States*, 8th ed., (Lawrence, Kansas: The University Press of Kansas, 2003), 367-368.

[11] Kevin Cullen, "Europe Scowls At Immigrants," *San Antonio Express-News* (Friday, December 29, 2000), 26A.

[12] J. R. Poole, *The Pursuit of Equality in American History*, (Los Angeles, Calif.: University of California Press, 1978), 6-7.

[13] Alexis de Tocqueville, *Democracy in America*, Translated by George Lawrence, J. P. Mayer, ed. (Garden City, New York: Doubleday and Company, Inc., 1969), 317.

[14] Dale McLemore and Harriet D. Romo, *Racial and Ethnic Relations in America*, 7th ed., (Boston, Massachusetts: Pearson Education, Inc., 2005), 47-48.

[15] Robert Wernick, "The Rise and Fall of a Fervid Third Party," *The Smithsonian* (November, 1996), 152.

[16] Ibid., 154.

[17] McLemore, 115.

[18] George H. Sabine, *The History of Political Thought*, 3d ed. (New York: Holt, Reinhart and Winston, 1961), 906.

[19] McLemore, 117-118.

[20] Joseph E. Harris, *Africans and Their History*, 2nd ed. (New York: New American Library Penguin, Inc., 1987), 18.

[21] David Vachon, "Chief Joseph Refuses to Sell Tribal Lands", *Old News*, March, 2004, 1.

[22] Conrad, 27-28.

[23] Ibid., 94.

[24] Christine M. Keiser, "A First-Class U.S. Citizen," *American History*, Vol. 44, No. 2, June, 2009, 23.

[25] "Special Report: Hate Crime Victimization, 2003-2011," U.S. Department of Justice Programs, March, 2013, 1.

[26] "FBI Releases 2012 Hate Crime Statistics," Federal Bureau of Investigation, Nov. 25, 2013 (www.fbi.gov)

[27] Henry Weinstein, "Court Bars Racial Profiling on Border," *San Antonio Express-News* (Wed., April 12, 2000), 19A.

[28] Richard Conniff, "Frederick Douglass Always Knew He Was Meant to be Free," *The Smithsonian*, (February, 1995), 116.

[29] Thomas Hayden, "Modern Life," *U.S. News & World Report* (October 4, 2004), 46.

[30] Bill Baskervill, "Indians Say 'No Thanks,'" *San Antonio Express-News* (Thursday November 23, 2000), 3AA.

[31] McLemore, 291.

[32] Paul VanDevelder, "What Do We Owe the Indians?" *American History*, Vol. 44, No. 2, June, 2009, 35.

[33] Floyd B. Largent, Jr., "The Florida Quadmire," *American History*, Vol. XXXIV, No. 4, October, 1999, 42.

[34] Anthony Dellafora, "Center May Preserve Story of 'Long Walk,'" *Dallas Morning News* (Sunday, March 8, 1998), 45A.

[35] "U.S. May Soon Admit Battle Was Massacre," *The Express-News*, (Sunday, March 11, 1990), 6A.

[36] Susan B. Welch, John Gruhl, Michael Steinman, John Comer, and Susan M. Rigdon, *American Government*, 5th ed. (St. Paul, Minn.: West Publishing Co., 1994), 505.

[37] Gary B. Nash and Julie Roy Jeffrey, *The American People: Creating A Nation and A Society*, 5th ed., (New York, New York: Addison-Wesley Educational Publishers, Inc., 2001), 546.

38 Ibid.
39 David Whitman, "A Court Fight Truly Off the Reservation," *U.S. News & World Report* (April 5, 1999), 42.
40 VanDevelder, "What Do We Owe the Indians?" 32.
41 "U.S. Census Bureau Projections Show A Slower Growing, Older, More Diverse Nation A Half Century From Now," U.S. Bureau of the Census, December 12, 2012 (http://www.census.gov/newsroom/releases)
42 "The Condition of Education 2012 (NES 2012-045), U.S. Department of Education, National Center for Education Statistics: 2012, Indicator 47 (http://nces.ed.gov.fastfacts/display)
43 C. Van Woodward, *The Strange Career of Jim Crow*, 3rd. ed. (New York: Oxford University Press, 1974), 11.
44 Conrad, 109.
45 Jay Tolson, "The Complex Story of Slavery", *U.S. News & World Report*, February 14, 2005, 66.
46 Ibid., 66-67.
47 Ibid., 67.
48 Woodward, 21.
49 Jack Fincher, "The Hard Fight Was Getting Into the Fight At All," *Smithsonian*, Vol. 21, No. 7, October, 1990, 46.
50 Ibid.
51 Woodward, 54.
52 Abraham, 374.
53 Woodward, 104.
54 "A Farewell to 'Mr. Civil Rights'," *U. S. News & World Report*, (February 8, 1993), 10.
55 Conrad, 98.
56 Woodward, 18-19.
57 Abraham, 375.
58 Carolyn Kleiner Butler, "Down In Mississippi", *Smithsonian*, Vol. 35, No. 11, February, 2005, 24.
59 Keith Weldon Medley, "The Sad Story Of How 'Separate But Equal' Was Born," *Smithsonian*, Vol. 24, No. 11, February, 1994, 106.
60 Ibid., 108-109.
61 Domino, 226.
62 H. W. Brands, "Grant Takes On The Klan," *American History*, Vol. 47, No. 5, Dec. 2012, 46.
63 Ibid.
64 David Uhler, "Jim Crow Was A Loser in Korean War," *San Antonio Express-News* (Sunday, June 4, 2000), 1A.
65 Paul Finkleman, "Race and the Constitution," *By and For the People: Constitutional Rights in American History*, Kermit L. Hall, ed., (Illinois: Harland Davidson, Inc., 1990), 155.
66 Gregg Holland, "Quiet Justice Speaks Out on Cross Burning", *San Antonio Express-News* (Thursday, December 12, 2002), 4A.
67 Bree Fowler, "'Mother of the Civil Rights Movement' Dies", *San Antonio Express-News*, (Tuesday, October 25, 2005), 1A.
68 Conrad, 156.
69 Abraham, 420.
70 Uhler, 1A.
71 Ibid.
72 Domino, 227.
73 Abraham, 396.
74 Scott Parks, "The Little Rock Nine: School Integration Battle Changed Lines Of Players in Central High Drama," *Dallas Morning News* (Sunday, September 21, 1997), 45A and 56A.
75 Alan Barth, *The Rights of Free Men: An Essential Guide to Civil Liberties*, James E. Clayton, ed., (New York: Alfred A. Knopf, 1987), 172.
76 Conrad, 207.
77 Dan Balz, "The Agenda Remains Unfinished," *San Antonio Express-News*, (Sunday, August 25, 2013), A25.
78 "Poverty Status of People By Age, Race and Hispanic Origin: 1959-2012," U. S. Census Bureau (www.Census.gov)
79 McLemore, 227.
80 Will Sullivan, "A Population's Assimilation," *U.S. News & World Report*, April 23, 2007, 34.

[81] Mark Helm, "Diversity Among Hispanics Make For Political Disunity," *San Antonio Express-News* (Tuesday, October 13, 1998), 1A.

[82] Ibid.

[83] Arnold DeLeon, "Los Tejanos: An Overview of Their History," *The Texas Heritage*, Ben Procter and Archie McDonald, eds., 1st ed., (Ill.: Harlan Davidson, Inc., 1980), 134.

[84] Arnold DeLeon, *Mexican-Americans in Texas: A Brief History*, (Ill.: Harlan Davidson, Inc., 1991), 67.

[85] McLemore, 243.

[86] Ibid., 236-237.

[87] DeLeon, *Mexican-Americans in Texas: A Brief History*, 134.

[88] Hector Saldana, "United They Stand," *San Antonio Express-News* (Sunday, March, 31, 2002), 5J.

[89] "An Interview," *Voice of Diversity: Perspectives on American Political Ideals and Institutions*, Pat Andrews, ed., (Guilford, Conn.: The Dushkin Publishing Group, Inc., 1995), 164-165.

[90] Mark Helm, "Soldiers Blazed The Trail to Political Prominence," *San Antonio Express-News* (Sunday, October 11, 1998), 17A.

[91] McLemore, 223.

[92] DeLeon, *Mexican-Americans in Texas: A Brief History*, 66.

[93] McLemore, 238-239.

[94] Blevins, 259.

[95] McLemore, 238.

[96] Erick Schelzig, "States Immigration Laws May Not Pass Court Test," *San Antonio Express-News*, (Sunday, August 20, 2006) 8A.

[97] Pete Yost, "High Court Slaps Leash on Booting Immigrants," *San Antonio Express-News*, (Wednesday, December 6, 2006), 7A.

[98] "Deferred Deportation Plan to Begin," *San Antonio Express-News* (Sunday, August 12, 2012), A5.

[99] Tim Lopes, "Hispanic Muscle Going Unflexed," *The Houston Chronicle*, (Sunday, April 16, 1995), 6A.

[100] Gary Martin, "Latino Vote Bloc Hard to Pin Down," *San Antonio Express-News*, (Friday, October 4, 2002, 18A.

[101] Paula Petrek, "Women and The Bill of Rights," *By and For the People: Constitutional Rights in American History*, Kermit L. Hall, ed., (Ill.: Harlan Davidson, Inc., 1991), 133.

[102] Barbara Goldsmith, "The Woman Who Set America on Its Ear," *Parade Magazine, The San Antonio Express-News* (Sunday, March 8, 1998), 14-15.

[103] Domino, 252.

[104] Paula Petrek, 134.

[105] Poole, 301.

[106] Rynder, 25.

[107] Ibid., 307.

[108] "Catharine Beecher and Harriet Beecher Stowe on Why Women Should Not Seek the Vote," *Major Problems in American Women's History*, Mary Beth Norton and Ruth M. Alexander, ed., 2nd ed., (Lexington, Mass.: D.C. Heath and Company, 1996), 169.

[109] "The Object at Hand," *Smithsonian*, Vol. 23, No. 12, March, 1993, 30.

[110] Ibid., 32.

[111] Ibid.

[112] U.S. Bureau of the Census, *Statistical Abstract of the United States: 2012*, 131st. ed., Washington, D.C., 2011, Table. 232, 152.

[113] Poole, 309-310.

[114] "Separating the Sisters," *U. S. News & World Report*, (March 28, 1994), 49.

[115] Nancy R. Mudrick, "Employment Discrimination Laws for Disability: Utilization And Outcome," *The Annals of the American Academy of Political and Social Science*, Vol. 549, January, 1997, 55.

[116] Ibid., 56.

[117] Marjorie L. Baldwin, "Can the ADA Achieve Its Employment Goal?", *The Annals of the American Academy of Political and Social Science*, Vol. 549, January, 1997, 40-41.

[118] Coniff, 127.

SUGGESTED READINGS

Abraham, Henry J., and Barbara A. Perry, *Freedom & the Court: Civil Rights & Liberties in the United States,* 8th ed., Lawrence, Kansas: University Press of Kansas, 2003.

Barth, Alan. *The Rights of Free Men: An Essential Guide to Civil Liberties.* James E. Clayton, ed. New York: Alfred A. Knopf, 1987.

Conrad, Earl. *Jim Crow America.* 2d ed. New York: Duell, Sloan, and Peace, 1947.

Domino, John C. *Civil Rights and Liberties: Toward the 21st Century.* New York: HarperCollins Publishers, 1994.

McLemore S. Dale, and Harriet D. Romo, *Racial and Ethical Relations in America,* 7th Ed., Boston, Mass.: Pearson Education Inc. 2005.

Tocqueville, Alexis de. *Democracy in America.* Translated by George Lawrence, J. P. Mayer, eds. Garden City, N. Y.: Doubleday and Company, Inc., 1969.

Woodward, C. Van. *The Strange Career of Jim Crow.* 3rd ed. New York: Oxford University

Conrad, Earl. *Jim Crow America.* 2d ed. New York: Duell, Sloan, and Peace, 1947.

Chapter Fifteen

PUBLIC POLICY

On October 1, 2013, millions of uninsured Americans gathered around their computers in anticipation of officially signing up for the nation's new health insurance plan through the newly established website—HealthCare.gov. They had done their homework by plowing through numerous health care plans to find the health-care coverage that they felt would meet their medical needs. For far too many, this was their first chance to have health care they could afford. The Obama administration spent four hard years of work and millions of federal dollars to ensure that the "official launch" of the signup period would go without a hitch. Although millions of uninsured and under-insured Americans were ready to click onto the website, the website was not. It simply could not handle the overwhelming number of inquiries that poured in. Within a few hours, HealthCare.gov crashed. It took nearly two months for a cadre of software engineers and programmers to fix it.

In his 2008 bid for the White House, Barack Obama promised to change the nation's health care system to ensure that the millions of Americans without any health insurance would have the opportunity to receive quality medical coverage at a minimal or, in some instances, no cost at all. For candidate Obama, health care was a personal issue. He toured the country telling uninsured and under-insured Americans about how his cancer-stricken mother had to not only deal with her terminal illness, but with the mounting number of doctor and hospital bills pilling up on the kitchen table. Although employed, she did not have employer-offered medical insurance nor could she afford to pay the premium for self-insurance. He vowed that if elected, he would make sure that no American regardless of his/her income level or pre-existing illness would ever have to face the problems confronted by his mother. In his inaugural address, President Obama emphasized his commitment to accomplish his election promise. He also urged lawmakers from both sides of the aisle to pass the Patient Protection and Affordable Care Act through Congress. In his February 24, 2009 speech delivered to a joint session of Congress, President Obama told both lawmakers and millions of Americans that "let there be no doubt: Health care reform cannot wait, it must not wait, and it will not wait another year."¹ After a year of debate in both Houses with numerous Republican-driven attempts to kill the measure, including over 160 amendments accepted in the House mark-up session alone, the bill finally passed both Houses and an President Obama signed the massive 2,500 plus page legislation into law on March 23, 2010.

Commonly known as the Affordable Care Act (ACA) or Obamacare, the legislation ran into partisan politics from the very beginning. Democrats hailed it as the cure for the nation's rising health-care costs incurred through the Medicaid and Medicare programs. On the other hand, Republicans decried the bill as the federal government's move to take health care from the private sector to the public sector, labeling it as "socialized" medicine. The ACA does mandate that all businesses employing more than 50 employees must either provide health insurance to them or pay a hefty fine to the federal government. Self-employed, as well as millions of uninsured Americans, would also be fined if they did not purchase health insurance through the ACA insurance exchange network. As true in all group insurance plans, the cost to the individual drops as the number of enrollees increase. Democrats emphasized that the only way to drive down health-care costs was to change the emphasis of health care from reactionary to preventive. They argued that an individual with health insurance is more likely to use it for annual checkups and exams thus catching a potentially serious illness early. Early prevention is, of course, a less expensive option. Not to be deterred, the law's opponents tried every means possible to turn public opinion against the measure. President Obama and his team went on the defensive with a series of "damage control" tactics including the president stumping across the country in his campaign-mode style. In August 2011, the 11th Circuit Court of Appeals ruled parts of the ACA unconstitutional. Obama's Justice Department fought back and the decision was reversed by the United States Court of Appeals. The opposition now turned to the United States Supreme Court as twenty-six states filed a petition before the Court challenging the legality of the law.

Meanwhile, President Obama was seeking a second term of office. The primary issues of the campaign were obvious—the economy and Obamacare. Republican hopeful Mitt Romney hammered away at the pitfalls of the health-care law and vowed that if elected, his first act would be to repeal it. Obama, on the other hand, pointed out that his health-care program in many respects mirrored the one Romney himself designed and successfully implemented in Massachusetts when Romney served as the state's governor. Admitting that his own health-care program was wrong for Massachusetts, Romney spoke at podiums across the country bearing signs "Repeal & Replace Obamacare." At one campaign stop Romney told the audience, "if we want to get rid of Obamacare, we're going to have to replace President Obama. This is my mission. That is our work."² Meanwhile, the United States Supreme Court announced its verdict on the ACA on June 28, 2012. Ruling 5-4, the Court upheld the constitutionally of the health-care law and its mandates. Although the majority ruled that "the government could not, under the Constitution's commerce clause, require most Americans to buy insurance," it also ruled that "the insurance mandate is constitutional as a tax."³ Despite the Court's ruling, the Republican opposition continued its efforts to undo the Affordable Care Act. Some levied their frustrations at Chief Justice Roberts. "The decision stunned legal observers on both sides and made Roberts the focus of heated invective from conservative activists and some Republican members of Congress, who derided him as a 'traitor.' Rep. Louis Gohmert, R-Texas, talked about the possibility of removing Roberts and other justices from the bench."⁴

While the debate over the ACA continued on Capitol Hill and on talk-radio and internet sites across the nation, the Obama administration began the initial implementation of the program. Texas Senator Ted Cruz has made the demise of Obamacare his personal mission. On September 25, 2013, Cruz held the United States Senate at bay by staging a 21-hour filibuster decrying the ACA. Spaced between his criticisms of the president's plan, Cruz read passages from Dr. Seuss's children's book *Green Ham and Eggs*. Failing at the filibuster, Cruz blamed his fellow Republicans for passage of the bill in the first place, conducted a nationwide anti-Obamacare petition drive to repeal it, introduced numerous amendments to defund it, and went on a nationwide speaking tour to convince Americans to petition their lawmakers to defund and repeal the law. On October 1 through the 16, 2013, the federal government shut down simply because lawmakers in the House and the Senate could not agree upon a short-term budget deal to prevent the federal government from defaulting on its financial obligations. While federal workers were furloughed and government services were at a standstill, Conservative Tea Party members of the Republican Party continued their efforts to rid the nation of Obamacare. Once the government re-opened, House Republicans conducted hearings, drilling both the software engineers and Secretary of Health and Human Services Kathleen Sebelius about the website collapse.

The Affordable Care Act has survived forty-six plus Republican attempts to defund and/or abolish it. It has survived numerous legal battles. It has survived Tea Party-led criticism especially from Senator Ted Cruz. It has survived a hostile assault during the 2012 presidential election. But the premier legislative effort of Obama's eight-year presidency nearly suffered a fatal blow when that website collapsed.

It would be easy to place the blame for the program's rocky enrollment kick-off on just a computer-programming blunder or to level it upon a consistent and, oftentimes, hostile assault on the law led by certain members of the Republican Party. Yet, one cannot overlook the fact that while public policy is itself a product of politics, the blame for policy failures cannot be solely contributed to "politics as usual." The primary cause of poorly written and ineffective public policies is the inability of both legislative houses and members of executive branches alike to follow the public policy process from start to finish. The majority of this nation's laws and city ordinances suffer from crippling design flaws that may ultimately result in policy failures.

Most lawmakers propose legislation with good intentions in mind. For example, the New Deal legislation of Franklin Roosevelt's administration that produced the modern welfare state was founded on the principles of government helping those in financial need. The Great Depression, caused by the 1929 crash of the stock market, put millions of hardworking Americans and their families out of work and one step away from starvation and potentially irreversible financial ruin. State and local governments, as well as private charities, simply did not have the resources to meet the needs of the destitute. Roosevelt reasoned that a compassionate government should without question address the needs of its people.

However, good intentions do not necessarily produce skillfully crafted and successfully implemented public policies. In the 1980s and 1990s, it became clearly evident that the welfare state created by President Franklin Roosevelt had deteriorated to the point that politicians from all political parties advocated reforming it with the ultimate goal of actually eliminating the bulk of its income support programs. A bureaucratic nightmare, the welfare system produced an economically disadvantaged underclass that became almost totally dependent upon the "system" for survival.

The hardworking and over-tax-burdened middle class resented a welfare system that continuously needed more tax dollars to fund its programs, while failing to deliver on its lofty promise to eliminate poverty. Public opinion shifted from favoring a benevolent government intent on providing for everyone faced with adverse economic hardships to one that provided for only those who were not only truly desperate but willing to work for their share of the dole. The welfare system, as originally conceived, broke down. However, the welfare reform package finally enacted during the Clinton administration has not adequately addressed the needs of the nation's poor. Just establishing stiffer eligibility requirements and time limits for services does not mean that former recipients of government-sponsored income support programs have raised their income levels to the point that they no longer need government assistance. In some instances, the poor are in a worse situation because of welfare reform.

In the 1970s, Americans were awakened to the state of their deteriorating environment. Lawmakers responded by enacting corrective legislation covering an array of environmental concerns from cleaner air and water to protection of endangered plants and wildlife. Once again, good intentions did not produce effective policies. Business and industry see environmental laws laden with costly impact statements, threats of litigation, fines and penalties as cost prohibitive and unnecessary impediments to the economic viability of the free market system. On the other hand, environmentalists believe that the existing laws are just halfhearted attempts to address a potentially irreversible problem. They criticize the government for doing too little too late to save our planet. Public opinion is also divided. The average American citizen is concerned about the environment. All agree that something must be done to ensure a cleaner environment or the future of this planet may be in serious jeopardy. However, these same citizens are fearful that the expense of producing environmentally safe consumer products will be cost prohibitive. They are also concerned as to the extent of the personal sacrifices they may be asked to make to preserve the environment. Both sides are not pleased with the existing laws.

After the tragic September 11, 2001, terrorists' attacks on the World Trade Center, the pressure was on the George W. Bush administration to reevaluate existing domestic and foreign security agencies to guarantee to the American public that this type of terrorist attack would not happen on American soil again. The Bush administration consolidated the domestic-oriented Federal Bureau of Investigation with the foreign-oriented Central Intelligence Agency under one roof—a cabinet-level Department of Homeland Security. Congress swiftly passed the Patriot Act giving federal agencies more authority over surveillance, including the monitoring of telephone and internet communications. A list of potential terrorists and terrorist sympathizers was drawn up to prevent these individuals from entering the country. Security at the airports was tightened to include personal body scans, x-raying luggage, and restricting carry-on items. Just when Americans were beginning to feel "secure" again, on April 15, 2013, the Tsarnaev brothers ignited bombs during the Boston Marathon leaving three dead and approximately 264 injured. Among the questions posed by the citizens and lawmakers was that with all of these new surveillance laws and security-empowered federal agencies, how could a terrorist attack on American soil happen again? What went wrong?

This chapter explores the public policy process from the inception of the concept to its final evaluation as a means of discovering exactly what goes wrong with the majority of the public policy initiatives created by the legislative and executive branches at all levels of government from the national to the city/county level. In actuality, the "process" of public policy is a series of steps that must be equally weighed in importance. Overlooking just one step can condemn a potentially successful legislative action to failure before it is even written. Public policy is more than a legislative act. The final product is the embodiment of the prevailing political, economic, social, and cultural philosophies of the time. The answers to who makes public policy begins with the average citizen and ends on the desk of the president to await its fate. While the wheeling and dealing between party leaders, legislators, and the president continues, the average citizen must pay close attention to their actions because the outcome of their decisions impacts everyone. "Public polices in a modern, complex society are indeed ubiquitous. They confer advantages and disadvantages, cause pleasure, irritation, and pain, and collectively have important consequences for our well-being and happiness. They constitute a significant portion of our environment. This being so, we should know something about public policies, including how they are formed, budgeted, implemented and evaluated."[5] Eventually, the prudent student of government will conclude that "politics is about policy. The decisions that government makes are the end result of a complex process. Many potential issues never get discussed seriously by political leaders; and policy is not necessarily determined even for those issues on which serious debate takes place. Even after policies have been announced, the politics of the policy process continues, as efforts may be made to shape implementation of the program."[6] The creation of the policy is often more important than the policy itself. The success or failure of a policy initiative hinges more on how it was created, budgeted, implemented, and evaluated than the problem or issue the policy was intended to address. The process of creating public policy extends to all items of domestic and foreign policy issues and considerations. This chapter explores how to create a policy masterpiece while avoiding a policy disaster.

PUBLIC POLICY DEVELOPMENT

The term **policy** is defined as "a relatively stable, purposive course of action followed by an actor or set of actors in dealing with a problem or matter of concern."[7] Policy, therefore, is not just a statement concerning a problem or issue. It is a purposeful action designed to reach a defined goal or objective. Policy originates in both the private and public sectors with one major exception. Created by governmental bodies, **public policy** can be defined as "an officially expressed intention backed by a sanction, which can be a reward or punishment."[8] Governing institutions at all levels make public policy. Laws, edits, rules, and ordinances are public policy initiatives created by governing bodies in response to the demands of the citizens for authoritative action deemed necessary to address a public concern, issue, or need. Consequently, "public policy has an authoritative, legally coercive quality that the policies of private organizations do not have."[9] If citizens obey and follow the policy directives of their government, they are rewarded for their obedience. Contrary, citizens who disobey the laws of their government will be punished by a sanction, fine, imprisonment, or any combination thereof.

The development of public policy at any level of government is based upon four fundamental principles. First, public policy initiatives created in a democratic government are the products of conflict and accommodation. As evidenced by the day to day bickering between legislative and executive leaders, "all forms of political organization have a bias in favor of the exploitation of some kinds of conflicts and the suppression of others because organization is the mobilization of bias.

Some issues are organized into politics while others are organized out."[10] The result, the policy directive, is a compromise between various factions and key governmental actors. Regardless of the issues before a legislative house, "there is opposition to virtually every policy proposal, and agreement is reached only after bargains have been struck and compromises have been agreed on."[11] In particular, the 2013 congressional session has resulted in the most publically aired political bickering in decades. Labeled as a "doing nothing" Congress, both Democrats and Republicans have been locked in heated grudge matches. Whereas the arguments were usually ideologically based, members of Congress from both sides of the aisle are personally attacking each other. The Tea Party faction of the Republican Party has pinned the Republican leadership into a corner where compromise is no longer an acceptable option. The Republican Party is basically divided into two diametrically opposed factions that may agree on ideological positions but differ greatly on the tactics used to achieve those positions. The on-going battles between the two parties over everything from the budget, Obamacare, and presidential appointments have left the American public frustrated and angry. The 2013 government shut-down did very little to instill public confidence in the nation's lawmaking body. Regardless of the setting, political bickering is a given in the creation of public policy. It is an extremely high stakes game with every interested party desiring to be a winner, not a loser. Second, public policy is a series of policy outputs and outcomes. "**Policy outputs** are the things actually done by agencies in pursuance of policy decisions and statements."[12] For example, the policy establishing the income tax was supposed to create a progressive tax program whereby everyone would pay their proportionate share of taxes. Those with higher incomes would pay a higher amount of tax in comparison to those with lower incomes. However, subsequent policy initiatives and practices have resulted in a regressive income tax plan. By allowing deductions for a wide-range of expenditures and investments, taxpayers in the highest income brackets are actually paying a considerable lower percentage of their income toward their tax obligations than those whose earnings are in the lower income brackets.

Policy outcomes are" the consequences for society, intended or unintended, that stem from deliberate governmental action or inaction."[13] For example, the civil rights acts were enacted to ban discriminatory actions against minorities, particularly African Americans, in all areas including employment, voting, housing, education, and public accommodations. The implementation of these laws lead to profound and oftentimes violent upheavals to the political, social, and cultural traditions embraced by American society. Laws designed to eliminate discrimination by encouraging desegregation often resulted in sit-ins, race riots, violent protests, and race-related killings that further eroded the fragile relationship between the Anglo and African-American communities. The resulting lesson painfully learned by lawmakers and jurists alike was that legislative acts alone cannot change longstanding attitudes and beliefs.

Third, there is a distinct difference between decision-making and policy-making. **Decision-making** "involves making a discrete choice from among two or more alternatives," whereas, **policy-making** "typically encompasses a flow and pattern of action that extends over time and includes many decisions, some routine and some not so routine."[14] Decisions are made on a daily basis, often without the benefit of a deliberation process. To be effective, policy decisions must be treated as purposeful deliberative actions resulting from an intense and often lengthy planning process. Quick decisions on the part of lawmakers can have disastrous policy results.

Taxpayers had lofty desires for the space program. America won the race to place a man on the moon. Watching the lift-off of the first American in space. (L-R) Vice President Johnson, Arthur Schlesinger, Adm. Arleigh Burke, President Kennedy and Mrs. Kennedy,
White House, Office of the President's Secretary. May 5, 1961..
Photo credit: Cecil Stoughton, White House/ JFK Library

Fourth, the taxpayer demands that lawmakers create policies that are both cost-effective and successful in achieving intended goals and objectives, subsequently, "the need is to design realistic goals that embrace a balance between efficiency and effectiveness."[15] Efficiency and effectiveness are often diametrically opposed to each other. For example, the national space program is an expensive project. Americans expect the space program to launch space shuttles, build space stations, and explore the galaxy at the cheapest cost possible. Far too often taxpayers' expectations are lofty desires that cannot be fulfilled by lawmakers. There can be a balance between efficiency, effectiveness, and cost. However, in the case of the space program and other government programs, the quality and quantity of the service is questionable when the budget alone guides the policy decision process.

Who Makes Public Policy?

There is a multiplicity of key actors in the public policy process. Each actor plays an essential role in the creation, implementation, and evaluation of a policy directive. The interplay between the actors is politics at its best and worst.

Public opinion does play a vital role in determining the scope and response of policy issues and outcomes. Basically, public opinion is collectively "those public perspectives or viewpoints on policy issues that public officials consider or take into account in making decisions."[16] Elected officials do listen to public opinion. Input from concerned citizens is essential to a democratic government. Citizens express their concerns through public opinion polls and, most importantly, the ballot box. Despite the oftentimes fickleness of public opinion, it is a truism in politics that those "elected public officials who totally ignore public opinion and do not include it among their criteria for decisions, should any be so foolish, are likely to find themselves out of luck at election time."[17] However, public opinion is hard for lawmakers to gage on a long-term basis since it is so unpredictable. Surveys reveal that public opinion can change from staunchly supporting a policy decision to hostility against it. The public unrealistically wants immediate actions from their lawmakers that miraculously address their concerns. A disappointed public can turn government on its backside without mercy. The Democrats were able to hold onto their majority status in both the House and the Senate and win the White House in 2008 due to a large extent on the unpopularity of the Bush presidency's policies in both Iraq and Afghanistan as well as the failure of his administration to successfully address an already declining economy. In 2010, the Democrats lost the majority in the House and are clinging to a slight majority in the Senate. The 2012 election cycle gave Obama a second term, but the Republicans maintained their majority in the House and the Democrats kept control of the Senate. The 2014 mid-term election cycle could well be a barometer for the 2016 presidential elections. Obviously, the success or failure of Obamacare will be a hotly debated issue in both election contests and will play a key role in voter preferences. What is promised in the heat of a campaign must be *successfully* delivered. Basically, "the American public does not seem to feel that the government copes very well at all. Congress has been portrayed as unproductive and spineless, unwilling to tackle the tough problems that require discipline or sacrifice."[18]

Interest groups play an extremely important role in the policy process. The 1960s saw the rapid rise of liberal citizen groups advocating a wide range of issue positions from anti-war protests to voting rights, equal opportunity, and environmental concerns. Today, a wide range of citizen or social movement groups have impacted public policy decisions in "defense and foreign affairs; health care policy pertaining to AIDS and abortion; environmental protection; and the rights of various groups including women, gays, the handicapped, the homeless, and racial and ethnic minorities."[19] The Framers were concerned that interest groups would eventually fragment and destroy the collective spirit of community and nationalism. In actuality, the growth of interest groups has strengthened the democratic nature of the political system. "The rise of liberal citizen groups was largely responsible for catalyzing an explosion in the growth of all interest groups. Efforts to limit the impact of liberal citizen groups failed, and the policy-making process became more open and more participatory."[20] Openness and transparency demanded that lawmakers change their approach towards interest groups. "Policymaking moved away from the closed subgovernments, each involving a relatively stable and restricted group of lobbyists and key government officials to much broader policymaking communities. Policymaking in earlier years is typically described as a product of consensual negotiations between a small number of back-scratching participants."[21] Once confined to closed-door meetings, congressional hearings are now fully open to the public through the watchful eyes of the media. Cable television networks now offer continuous daily broadcasts of congressional committee hearings. The media has helped to keep those once closed doors wide open to the public. Currently aligned with the Conservative wing of the Republican Party, the Tea Party Movement's agenda includes a provision that whenever a law is introduced into one of the legislative houses, the full text of the law is placed on the internet so citizens can read a proposed legislative act in its entirety before a congressional vote is cast. They simply want more transparency in government.

The past fifty years have also witnessed a change in the tactics traditionally used by social movement groups. The 1960s style of haphazardly organized protest movements, massive rallies, sit-ins, and, sometimes, violent displays of behavior have been replaced by well-organized "going public" media campaigns; professionally trained lobbyists sitting side by side those representing economic and business interests; well-financed and highly visible political action committees capable of raising large sums of money for candidates garnering the groups' public endorsements; a cadre of well-prepared attorneys poised to use litigation through the courts whenever the legislative side of government fails to push their causes; and a well-organized structure of locally-based chapters guided by a strong national organization capable of mobilizing its membership on a very short notice. Today, citizen or social movement interest groups resemble a corporate structure.

It has also become more difficult for lawmakers to successfully fulfill the requests of social movement groups since many of these organizations are apt to pursue narrowly defined ideological issues such as abortion, school prayer, environmental concerns, and so on. The traditional public policy approach rested on the belief that consensus is a compromised product of conflict and accommodation with each participant able to claim a partial victory. Unfortunately, lawmakers find compromise oftentimes impossible when working with groups that take an "all or nothing" approach. "Democracy requires adequate representation of interests as well as institutions capable of addressing difficult policy problems. For policy makers who must balance the demand for representation with the need for results, the key is thinking creatively about how to build coalitions and structure negotiations between large groups of actors."[27] Far too often, the agenda items of social movements are in direct conflict with the business and economic interests of this country, placing lawmakers in a perilously difficult and often impossible position of trying to broker a compromise.

There are noticeable pros and cons to interest group involvement in the public policy arena. "On the positive side, interest group politics create a dynamism, often through conflict, that draws out diversity in policy proposals, a diversity producing innovation and social change. Interest groups also provide access for the public to effect government decision-making . . . . On the negative side, interest groups fighting for their special goals can fragment the policy process. This struggle reduces the leadership's capacity to direct citizen demands toward an effective solution, promoting instead a compromise that may partially satisfy each group but not resolve the initial issue."[23]

Political parties exert their influence directly on public policy issues by electing lawmakers. It is the elected official's primary responsibility to his/her political party to actively pursue the agenda outlined in their party's platform. The leadership of legislative houses is controlled by the political parties. Loyalty to one's political party and its agenda can mean a key committee assignment for a legislator. Unlike interest groups, political parties are board-based umbrella organizations pursuing a multiplicity of diverse policy items. "Generally, parties have a broader range of policy concerns than do interest groups; hence, they act more as brokers than as advocates for particular interests in policy formation."[24] The credibility of a political party rests solely with the ability of its elected party members to enact public policy on behalf of their party.

Since both the president and members of Congress are popularly elected representatives of their respective political parties, the roles they play in the development of public policy are paramount throughout the process. As lawmakers, they must take on issues concerning the few and transform them into policies potentially benefiting the many. The framers compounded the complexity of this task by creating a two-house (bicameral) legislature charged with different focuses. The House of Representatives was designed to serve regional needs. Members of the House are obligated to pursue issues beneficial to his/her constituents. A congressperson voting against a legislative act potentially beneficial to his/her constituents could pay a career-ending price on election day. In contrast, senators are focused more on the needs of the nation as a whole. However, they too must ensure that what benefits the whole will to some degree benefit the state they represent. Basically, "representatives tend to be known as subject matter 'specialists' while senators tend to be 'generalists.' If the Senate has been the nation's great forum, a representative said, then the House has been its workshop."[25] Sometimes enacting what is morally and ethically correct conflicts with what is politically correct. Members of Congress are also members of their respective political parties and their ideological positions. It is a duty of congressional party leaders to constantly remind members of their party loyalties wherever a key vote is on the floor.

Since the executive is constitutionally bound to work with the legislature, the president oftentimes finds himself in the middle of the congressional fray. In 1936, President Franklin Roosevelt, a Democrat, remarked on a comment made by his Republican cousin: "Theodore Roosevelt said, 'Sometimes I wish I could be president and Congress too.' Well, I suppose if the truth be told, he is not the only president that has had that idea."[26] Franklin Roosevelt was merely echoing the frustrations all presidents have had in their dealings with the legislative branch. Executive-legislative relationships do shape the course of public policy. Legislatively successful presidents have developed a strong positive working relationship with their Congresses. Of course, the relationship is far smoother if the president's political party holds the majority of the seats in both houses. Nevertheless, presidents do exercise influence at all levels of the legislative process to include the ultimate threat and/or use of the veto.

Beginning with George Washington, every resident of the Oval Office wants future generations to know his particular impact on American history. "It has been a habit of presidents to try to write their own history, to establish themselves as a legitimate embodiment of America's past and shaper of America's future."[27] A president's legacy is seen through the legislation passed during his administration. Therefore, it is imperative that the president and his White House staff play an important role in the development and eventual implementation of public policy. Presidents officially inform Congress about their policy agendas through their yearly delivery of the State of the Union message. Realizing they have only four, or if lucky eight, years in office, presidents are prone to promise too much in the beginning, only to see their lofty expectations reduced by Congress into piecemeal legislative victories. Richard Nixon appeared to be totally prepared for the reality of Washington, D.C. However, "for a man with a perfect resume to become president—military officer, congressman, senator, vice-president for eight years—it was surprising how much Nixon's views on policy making changed in the first two years of his administration."[28] Initially, Nixon advocated complete and expedient elimination of the Great Society programs that were the cornerstone of the Johnson administration. He quickly found himself at odds with his staff over the appropriate approach his administration should take with Congress. "Thus, the administration's initial problem was not deciding what its policies were, instead it was converting campaign policy positions to the 'bullet proof' presidential messages and detailed draft legislation that can achieve major changes in public policy."²⁹ Nixon quickly found out what every president has discovered, that Congress is reluctant to approve quick sweeping changes advocated by the White House. Instead, they prefer to take several small steps rather than one large leap. After pressure from congressional Republicans and the White House staff, a staff person noted that "a consensus emerged that the president [Nixon] should launch relatively few initiatives, because we could not afford many; we needed to be bold, but we needed to get results; and we needed to communicate a focused approach."³⁰

However, the congressional incremental approach can be extremely frustrating for presidents. For example, in 1946, President Harry Truman was determined that he would desegregate all branches of the military's officer corps. Truman was facing pressure from civil rights organizations to fulfill his campaign promises. "Harry Truman was crude and ineloquent, but he made tough decisions and got them mostly right (a view that stands up well)."³¹ Bypassing Congress and his own party's congressional leadership, Truman took the initiative by issuing an executive order. Truman's action changed the leadership core of the nation's military branches. Traditionally, African Americans and other minority military personnel were limited to non-leadership roles. Truman's desegregation plan provided the impetus for minorities to strive for officer positions. Colin Powell was able to become the first African American to be named the Chairman of the Joint Chiefs of Staff, and ultimately, Secretary of State in part because Harry Truman could not wait for Congress to drag its collective feet. With or without the blessings of Congress, presidents can and do exert a tremendous impact on the direction of this nation's domestic and foreign policy initiatives.

The media has a direct role in public policy by bringing sensitive issues to the public's attention, and playing a key role in shaping public opinion. The key for government agencies and elected officials is to learn how use the media to their advantage. "President Bill Clinton, for one, showed extraordinary talent at using direct televised presidential addresses and nationally televised 'town meetings' to reach citizens in the studio audience and nationwide audiences who witnessed and identified with this direct interaction. . . . some commentators have observed that part of President Clinton's skill in influencing (and some would say misleading) public opinion about his sexual affairs later aggravated his legal and constitutional problems—and as with his State of the Union address during his trial, helped him survive those challenges."³²

Traditionally, **bureaucrats** were viewed as mere implementors of public policy with little impact on the development of policy directives. This perspective has changed dramatically. "Although it was once common doctrine in political science that administrative agencies only carried into effect, more or less automatically, policies determined by the 'political' branches of government, now it is axiomatic that politics and administration are blended, and that administrative agencies are often significantly involved in the formation of public policies. This is particularly apparent, given the concept of policy as encompassing what government actually does over time concerning a problem or situation."³³ Consequently, bureaucracies do shape public policy. Bureaucratic agencies begin their influence at the initial stages of policy development. Lawmakers are not experts on every policy issue. They rely upon bureaucratic agencies to provide research and testimony before committee hearings. Their input can determine the course of action Congress will eventually take on a policy issue. However, federal agencies will also flex their muscles to block unfavorable legislation by actively lobbying members of Congress and soliciting the support of key interest groups. In addition, bureaucracies can make or break policy initiatives simply by the manner in which agencies implement a new policy directive. Bureaucrats can control the fate of any law since the majority of the congressional legislation leaves implementation schemes totally in the hands of the responsible federal agency.

Many federal, state, and local laws have been overturned by the federal courts. The **judiciary** does make public policy whenever it declares a law unconstitutional. **Article VI** of the United States Constitution called the **Supremacy Clause** has been interpreted to allow the United States federal courts to rule any law passed at any level of government as unconstitutional when that law conflicts with the spirit and meaning of the United States Constitution. The power of **judicial review** has compelled government at all levels to reconsider its course of public policy options. A judge's gavel makes public policy!

The Supreme Court's 1954 ruling in *Brown v Board of Education of Topeka, Kansas*, began the modern civil rights movement. The United States Congress and state legislative houses began to pass laws reversing over one hundred years of discriminatory practices aimed at minorities. The *Roe v Wade* (1973) decision overturned about forty-six state laws prohibiting elective abortion procedures. In 2005, the Supreme Court handed down two significant rulings involving criminal procedures used by state courts nationwide. First, the Court declared the federal sentencing guidelines established by Congress two decades ago as unconstitutional. Basically, "the Supreme Court said making the guidelines mandatory violated a defendant's Sixth Amendment right to a jury trial because they call for judges to make factual decisions that affect prison time. Under the ruling [of the Supreme Court] the guidelines are now only advisory; federal judges are free to sentence convicted criminals

President Reagan holds a National Security Council meeting on the Persian Gulf with National Security Advisor Colin Powell in the Oval Office. April 18, 1988.

as they see fit, but they may be subject to reversal if appeals courts find them 'unreasonable.'"[34] The Supreme Court also ruled that the application of the death penalty to defendants under the age of eighteen is a violation of the Eighth Amendment's prohibition against cruel and unusual punishment. As the nation's court-of-last-resort, there can be no appeals of the body's decisions.

In summary, the key actors in the public policy process are the public, interest groups, political parties, the media, the bureaucracy, the courts, and elected officials. All of these actors play a key role in shaping public policy. All public policy is a byproduct of conflict, consensus, accommodation, and compromise among these essential policy actors.

What is the Purpose of Public Policy?

Governments enact public policy in response to the public's demand to address an on-going or new concern, issue or problem. Far too often the initial approach taken by government to address the nation's on-going pressing issues failed to accomplish its stated goals and objectives. Hopefully, corrective public policy will present a new alternative or change from the traditional approach. Also, government may not have had to respond to this policy concern before. The framers did not address such issues as the environment, air traffic, radio and television programming issues, and so on. In the early 1800s, the environment was not an issue, much less a potential threat to the survival of mankind.

Through public policy, government at any level must be able to enforce legislative acts either through sanctions, fines, or imprisonment for noncompliance. "Consequently, it must be clearly understood that all public policies are coercive, even when they are motivated by the best and most beneficent of intentions . . . . For us, the coercive element in public policy should instill not absolute opposition but a healthy respect for the risks as well as the good that may be inherent in any public policy."[35] In other words, public policy through its enforcement mechanisms, modifies our behavior and, in some cases, changes our perspectives. Few of us like to drive the posted speed limit. But we definitely modify our driving habits to the mandated speed when we see the police car in front of us since we all want to avoid a costly ticket.

The primary purpose of law enforcement is to serve as a visible deterrent to crime. Criminal statutes and civil fines and penalties are attached to each criminal activity to warn an individual of the consequences of his/her criminal actions. The problem confronting law enforcement is the same problem faced by the Environmental Protection Agency, the Immigration Service, Internal Revenue Service, and any other government agency charged with enforcing a government policy. Basically, how can government ensure that the penalties for noncompliance are severe enough to mandate compliance and deter a would be violator? As we will discover, government at all levels has failed to find the absolute deterrent penalty.

Governments can use a variety of tools besides laws to force behavior modifications. The direct approach is through contracting and licensing. **Government contracts** contain mandates that the recipient must enact or face losing the contract. A federal housing contract, for example, will specify the types of approved building materials, construction methods, inspection criteria, and so forth to include compliance with federal laws, such as the Equal Employment Opportunity Act, Occupational Safety and Health Act, Americans with Disabilities Act, and wage and labor laws. To enforce these requirements, each segment of the construction project must be open to inspection

President Bush signing the Americans With Disabilities Act in the Rose Garden of the White House.
July 26, 1990. Photo credit: George Bush Presidential Library

by federal agents before the next phase can begin. Noncompliance means loss of existing and, perhaps, future contracts. The contract mandates ensure that taxpayer money will produce a properly constructed product at the best possible price.

A **license** is "a privilege granted by government to do something that it otherwise considers to be illegal."[36] A license compels behavior modification by forcing the recipient to comply with industry or professional standards. Noncompliance can mean revoking the license and denying the recipient to practice his/her own profession. The threat of removing the license should ensure proper professional conduct. Teachers, doctors, lawyers, and even plumbers and hairdressers must be licensed by their state governments to practice their trades.

Particularly in the foreign policy arena, nations such as the United States, are more apt to use sanctions rather than full-scale warfare as a viable option to force weaker nations to comply with their demands. **Sanctions** are "the penalties meted out as consequences of illegal conduct."[37] Sanctions can range from economic restrictions on exports and imports, suspension of diplomatic ties, to limited military intervention. For example, the United States government severed all diplomatic ties with Cuba following Castro's rise to power in 1959. In addition, the United States issued an economic embargo prohibiting any shipments of cigars and sugar from the island nation into American ports. Sanctions, however, must be used with caution. "In absence of an international executive to enforce the law, the imposition of sanctions depends upon the degree of consensus in the international community and on the willingness of each member of the state system to accept responsibility to uphold the law. To be effective in specific cases, sanctions must create more hardship for the offending state than is created for the states applying the sanctions."[38] Severe sanctions can be an effective short-term plan to modify the offending nation's behavior as long as the entire international community abides by them. Gulf War I was fought by the international community against Iraq's invasion of Kuwait. Suffering a humiliating defeat, Iraq was placed under severe sanctions levied by the United Nations. The Iraqi government could only sell a predetermined amount of oil with the understanding that the generated revenues could be used only for food and medical necessities. The Iraqi government tried every conceivable way to circumvent the sanctions while at the same time, showing media coverage of the adverse impact the imposed sanctions were having on the Iraqi people. Years of economic sanctions did not produce the anticipated goal of crippling the Iraqi government.

Indirectly, every citizen's spending habits are governmentally controlled through taxing, banking, and pricing policies. The on-going tensions in the oil-rich Middle East plays havoc with the price of gasoline at the pump. For example, political tensions and regional government instability throughout the Middle East heightened after Saddam Hussain's invasion of Kuwait and President George H.W. Bush's military initiative to liberate it. In the United States, the price of a gallon of regular grade gasoline quickly rose to over four dollars in some areas of the country. The rapid increase in the price of gasoline forced drivers to use their vehicles less frequently than when gasoline prices were lower. Drivers began to conserve fuel opting for either carpooling or using public transportation. Once the prices went down, drivers reverted back to their old ways.

An economic stimulus involves the manipulation of interest rates. An increase in mortgage and consumer loan rates will force people to think twice before purchasing a new home or automobile. Conversely, government can encourage increased consumer buying by just lowering the prime interest rate, decreasing taxes, or increasing IRS deduction amounts. The Carter administration attempted to lure Americans into saving more money by increasing the interest rates on savings and checking accounts.

Government can modify our use of certain products and public services by charging us a fee. **User fees** or charges or "specified sums that consumers of a government service pay to receive that service."[39] The United States Park Service assesses a higher user fee for those individuals utilizing the nation's parks. The Service wanted to provide additional protection to wildlife and parklands by reducing the number of visitors and campers to these sites. Park rangers used to charge a fee for each vehicle that entered a park, regardless of the number of individuals in the vehicle. The new regulations stipulate that each person in the vehicle will pay a fee to use the parks. The per-person fee has accomplished its intended purpose of reducing the number of visitors. User fees provide governments at all levels with the mechanisms to control the use of the service while at the same time providing additional revenue for the maintenance and delivery of that service.

The Public Policy Process

The development of public policy is "analogous to biological natural section. In what we have called the policy primeval soup, many ideas float around, encountering new ideas, and forming combinations and recombinations . . . . Through the imposition of criteria by which some ideas are selected out for survival while others are discarded, order is developed from chaos, pattern from randomness. These criteria include technical feasibility, congruence with values of community members, and the anticipation of culture constraints, including a budget constraint, public acceptability, and politician's receptivity."[40] The **process** of developing the policy is the key to creating effective policy initiatives. The task confronting lawmakers is a difficult one. However, "legislators and other policy formulators can go a long way toward assuring effective policy implementation if they see that a statute incorporates a sound technical theory, provides precise and clearly ranked objectives, and structures the implementation process in a wide number of ways so as to maximize the probability of target group compliance. In addition, they can take positive steps to appoint skillful and supportive implementing officials, to provide adequate appropriations and to monitor carefully the behavior of implementing agencies throughout the long implementation process, and to be aware of the effects of changing socio-economic conditions and of new legislation (even in supposedly unrelated areas) on the original statute."[41] Lawmakers can make good laws if they are totally committed to the process from the start to the finish. The process involves eight crucial steps. Each step is vital to the success of the policy initiative and must be afforded equal attention. If one step is marginally treated or overlooked, the policy initiative, no matter how necessary, will usuallyy fail. Bad ineffective public policy is the result of poor planning. The process begins with the difficult task of identifying the problem and ends with an evaluation of the resulting policy initiative.

Problem Identification

The first step confronting lawmakers is to identify the problem. A **policy problem** is "a condition or situation that produces needs or dissatisfaction among people and for which relief or redress by governmental action is sought."[42] Not all issues and concerns expressed by the general public will become policy problems requiring government action. For too often, city halls are faced with the ire of one citizen who wants council to pass an ordinance addressing his one particular concern, a concern that may not be an issue for anyone else. For example, Mrs. Brown claims that her trash cans are being periodically damaged by city trash crews. She calls her councilperson demanding that city leaders pass an ordinance fining garbage workers for abusing garbage containers. Of course, she is the only one making this request. City Council members simply cannot do this because identified "public problems are those affecting a substantial number of people and having broad effects, including consequences for persons not directly involved. Such occurrences as dirty air, unwholesome food, the practice of abortion, urban traffic congestion, crowded prisons, and global warming are conditions that may become public problems if they produce sufficient anxiety, discontent, or dissatisfaction to cause many people to seek governmental remedies."[43]

Generally, public policy problems fall into one of two categories, namely foreign and domestic, however, foreign policy decisions can positively and negatively impact domestic considerations and vice versa. For example, President Jimmy Carter decided to punish the former Soviet Union over its invasion of Afghanistan by cancelling wheat shipments to the Soviets. The Soviet Union had been experiencing severe grain shortages caused by over ten years of crop failures. The United States Department of Agriculture purchased wheat from American farmers only to ship it free to the Soviets. Cash-strapped farmers were relieved that their surplus grain stored in silos had finally found a buyer. The subsequent grain embargo cost farmers dearly and created a domestic policy embarrassment for the Carter administration. This breakdown in the wall of separation between domestic and foreign policy has produced "**intermestic issues**," that is, "those issues (such as trade, finance, pollution, energy, terrorism, human rights, etc.) which overlapped the foreign and domestic policy boundaries."[44] Lawmakers are confronted with the realization that their actions on internal or domestic issues effect foreign policy matters and vice versa. Consequently, the public policy arena has become more complex.

There is also a noticeable difference between substantive and procedural problems. "**Procedural problems** relate to how government is organized, and how it conducts its operations and activities. **Substantive problems** are concerned with the actual consequences of human activity, whether it involves free speech, the sale of used cars or environmental pollution."[45] Each problem area demands unique policy directives to address the issues and concerns.

Too often legislation treats what the problem causes without actually solving the problem. "The effort to define a problem by identifying the causes of broad conditions rests on a certain conception of cause. In this conception, any problem has deep or primary causes that can be found if one only looks hard enough and does careful research.... Once 'the' cause is identified, policy should seek to eliminate it, modify it, reduce it, suppress it, or neutralize it, thereby eliminating or reducing the problem."[46] The contributing factors or **causal factors** should be the targets of legislative action if lawmakers want to solve the problem. The solution to crime is not just arresting more people and building more jails. Today, the United States has a record number of prisons; court dockets are teeming with new criminal cases; more people are being arrested; and convicts are serving longer sentences without parole. The crime rate is declining for some offenses. However, crime has not been eliminated. The actual criminal act is the end result stemming from a multiplicity of complex causal factors. The solution to crime rests, in part, with adequately identifying the causal factors that motivate a person to commit a crime.

Oftentimes, lawmakers believe they have identified the correct casual factors only to find out that they have wasted their energies by focusing on something that is closely associated with the problem but is not the cause of the problem in the first place. For example in the fourteenth and seventeenth centuries, the Bubonic Plague, or Black Death, killed thousands of people in Europe and England. Initially, lawmakers were convinced that the disease was being spread by rats. The public policy decision was to kill the rats and destroy the homes and personal belongings of the dead. The Plague, however, remained. Lawmakers overlooked the actual cause of the disease. True, rats and their fleas spread the disease to humans, but the real culpit was the living style of the citizens. Residents threw trash out into the streets, and personal waste was pitched into open sewers. The rats and their fleas were thriving in the debris. The solution to curing the disease was to eliminate the cause by encouraging healthier personal habits and proper sanitation procedures. Through corrective legislation backed by sanctions, personal and sanitation habits improved as the rats, their fleas, and the disease disappeared.

Another consideration is the distinct difference between a crisis situation and a problem. The policy responses are significantly different for both situations. A crisis situation demands an immediate short-term response from government. In the case of an advancing hurricane, prudent evacuation plans must be executed to remove people, their pets, and livestock from rising waters. Temporary housing, food, and clothing for the displaced, heavy equipment to clear roadways and restore public utilities, clean drinking water, medical services, and so on are the prudent and necessary responses required to address the crisis. The same short-term crisis responses would apply to any natural or man-made disaster. The long-term problem, however, involves an in-depth analysis of what caused the problem in the first place. In the case of a hurricane, the long-term solution rests with tactics to minimize property loss and eliminate loss of life when the next storm comes ashore. In the case of New Orleans, the federal Army Corps of Engineers was deemed responsible for the collapse of the levees that failed to hold back the surge of wind-swept water generated by the fury of Katrina. The Corps task is to rebuild those levees to ensure that they will hold up against a Category 5 hurricane storm surge. Along the Gulf Coast and interior flood-prone areas, such as San Antonio, Texas, the emphasis has been on flood control projects. Although expensive undertakings, underground drainage systems take flood waters away from central business districts to rural areas, thus minimizing both loss of life and property damage. City ordinances have been passed prohibiting flooded out residents from rebuilding their homes in flood-plain areas. Turning traditionally flooding personal properties into public parklands means less costly rescues, property damage and, of course, loss of life. In the case of the wildfires that raged in California, Colorado, Texas, and Utah part of the long-term problem is to clear-out dying bush in forest areas caused by long-term droughts. A prudent in-depth analysis can produce successful long-term solutions. However, when lawmakers treat problems as crises, unfortunately the problems will never be adequately addressed or solved.

Lawmakers must also avoid the trap of allowing public opinion to turn a problem into a crisis. Public outcry is not necessarily a crisis situation. The senseless tragic bombing of a federal building in Oklahoma City, Oklahoma, was caused by two individuals marginally associated with a paramilitary anti-government group. Likewise, James Byrd, an African American, was dragged to his death by three men advocating the racial hatred espoused by the Klu Klux Klan. The existence of these anti-government and racial hatred groups is a problem, but not a crisis. Although the ideological foundations of these groups are objectionable to the majority of the American people, the United States Constitution does guarantee the right of association. The document does not distinguish between acceptable and unacceptable groups. This nation's lawmakers can not overreact by passing legislation forbidding association with racially objectionable groups. The rational approach is to hold individuals legally accountable when their actions, whether they be guided by their affiliation to a racial supremacy group, caused harm to individuals or their property.

Agenda Building

Once the causal factors have been identified, an agenda, or action plan, must be developed. The agenda is the embodiment of the philosophical and technical approaches to an identified policy issue. For example, Democrat and Republican lawmakers agree that the nation's health care system is in critical condition; Americans are paying too much of their hard earned income into tax programs; the minimum wage needs to be increased; and the national debt is too high. Each political party, however, has different philosophical approaches to these issues. Consequently, each party follows a different agenda.

An effective agenda should attack all the identified causal factors at the same time. Doctors have realized that bombarding one side of a cancerous tumor with heavy doses of radiation and chemotherapy will halt the growth of the tumor on just the treated side while the untreated side continues to grow. The same holds true for public policy. By treating and curing just one symptom, policy makers allow the other symptoms to grow stronger. The drug policies passed during the Reagan administration desired to end the importation of drugs into the country. Instead of focusing on all international drug sources, the agenda focused primarily on Columbia. Columbian drug trafficking was substantially slowed. However, the flow of drugs continued as other international drug operatives assumed the Columbian share of the market.

> "In the issue of death and injuries resulting from drunk driving, both our laws and our cultural beliefs place responsibility with the drunk driver. There are certainly alternative ways of viewing the problem: we could blame vehicle design (for materials and structure more likely to injure or kill in a crash); highway design (for curves likely to cause accidents); lack of ambulance service or nearby hospitals; lax enforcement of drunk-driving penalties by police; or even availability of alcoholic beverages . . . Even when there is a strong statistical and logical link between substance and a problem—such as between alcohol and car accidents, handguns and homicides, tobacco and cancer deaths, or cocaine and overdose deaths—there is still a range of places to locate control and impose sanctions . . . . In the case of alcohol, we have traditionally seen drinkers as the cause and limited sanctions to them, although sellers have more recently been made to bear the costs. In lung cancer deaths, we have blamed the smoker primarily, but to the extent that people have sought to place blame elsewhere, they have gone after cigarette manufacturers, not sellers or tobacco growers. With handgun homicides, we have limited blame to the user of guns, rather than imposing sanctions on either the seller or manufacturers."[47]

Regardless of the issue, the answer to solving the problem rests with identifying all of the factors that caused the problem in the first place and holding each factor equally accountable for its actions. Again, the good intentions of lawmakers fail to achieve anticipated results when they overlook that effective public policy must attack the problem from all sides.

Action plans must contain well defined goals and objectives to ensure that all of the involved parties have a clear understanding of the intent of the policy directive. A **goal** is the end result of an action. For example, the ultimate goal of the Medicare program is to ensure that elderly and permanently disabled citizens are provided with government-sponsored health care. **Objectives**, on the other hand, are the strategies used to obtain the desired goals. Clearly defined and precise goals and objectives are an essential ingredient to the successful implementation of a policy directive just as a set of blueprints is to a homebuilder. "Statutory objectives that are precise and clearly ranked in importance serve as an indispensable aid in program evaluation, as unambiguous directives to implementing officials, and as a resource available to supporters of those objectives both inside and outside the implementing agencies."[48]

Action plans must also include measurable and attainable goals and objectives. Far too often, lawmakers attempt to sell their ideas as wondrous miracle cures. How many times have voters heard their leaders pledge that their proposed policy or program will completely eradicate a problem, only to see the policy fall disastrously short of its objectives. For example, President Lyndon Johnson's War on Poverty program was designed to eliminate poverty. Johnson's pledge was a lofty, unreasonable, and unattainable goal. Lawmakers should be honest and realistic with their constituents. An anticrime package designed to achieve a 5 percent reduction in crime each year over a five-year period has a better chance of seeing this goal achieved and/or exceeded over a policy with the lofty goal of eliminating all crime within a five-year period.

Formulation of Policy

The formulation process involves more than just designing the programs and the policy responses needed to address agenda items. Lawmakers must first determine the policy approach, and the type of policy option, as well as whether the responsibility for the resulting programs should be assigned to the public or private sector. Usually, lawmakers opt for one of four policy approaches: punitive, alleviative, preventive, and, the rarely used, curative. The selection of the policy approach will fluctuate depending upon the prevailing political philosophy of lawmakers, public opinion, the severity of the deprivation and/or damage, and the status of the nation's economy.

The **punitive approach** rests upon the premise that the problem arose from self-inflicted causal factors. For example, there is a belief that poverty is usually a self-inflicted result of an individual's failure to achieve economic viability. Guided by the concepts of Social Darwinism and the free market theory, the belief holds that poverty is "the product of moral or character deficiencies in the individual. If people were poor, it was their own fault" and, subsequently, their responsibility alone to rise above their economic deprivation.[49] The punitive approach recognizes their economic needs while, at the same time, punishing the poor for their misfortunes. For social service programs, the usual approach has been an attempt to distinguish the deserving from the undeserving poor. Means-tested programs require applicants to demonstrate that they are indeed deserving of the benefits of the government program. The same approach has been used in a wide range of policy issues including environmental concerns. The majority of the environmental laws are designed to identify and punish violators. Few environmental laws award businesses, industries, and individuals for not polluting. The punitive approach is a reactionary response to an existing problem. The primary objective of the punitive approach is to *punish* violators, not *solve* problems.

The **alleviative approach** seeks to relieve the suffering caused by the policy problem without adequately addressing the problem itself. For example, the New Deal programs were designed as temporary measures to relieve the suffering of economic deprivation caused by the Great Depression. The Roosevelt administration believed that temporary federally funded social programs would stop the suffering while the economy recovered on its own. "The designers of the Social Security Act in 1935 assumed that needs-tested public assistance would wither away as younger workers became fully covered by social insurance—an expectation that was shattered by changing demographics, steadily expanding welfare rolls, and more generous benefits during the postwar period."[50] Unable and, in most respects, unwilling to face the actual causes of poverty and eventually attempt to cure it, lawmakers opted for the easy way out. Relieving or alleviating the suffering of the effected parties is an excellent short-term policy alternative that should never be used as a long-term policy commitment. The same observation can be made for the majority of the social service programs enacted by the federal government. Building more prisons merely alleviates the suffering criminals inflict upon society. Providing the homeless with overnight temporary shelters and three square meals a day simply alleviates the suffering of hunger. Merely easing the pain does not cure the disease. In addition, the alleviative approach is extremely costly to taxpayers who demand that their dollars actually eliminate the policy problem.

The most significant reform enacted in 1935 was the Social Security Act.

The third option is the **preventive strategy**. This alternative adverts actually curing the problem by just preventing it from getting worse. The farm price subsidy programs were designed to prevent farmers and food processors from losing more money. The program was based on the assumption that by controlling the supply of the product, the price of the product would be stabilized. The Social Security program was designed to prevent retired workers from falling into poverty by creating a self-funded insurance program for workers. Medicare and medigap insurance programs were designed to prevent senior citizens from falling below the poverty level due to medical expenses. Social preventive policy schemes have successfully built a safety net from the ills of poverty for retired workers, the elderly, and disabled Americans while successfully avoiding the task of curing the potential income deprivations confronting these citizens. Again, the preventive strategy should be treated as a short-term response that realistically will not meet the long-term goal of eliminating the problem.

The most difficult and, subsequently, the least used policy option is the **curative approach**. The primary objective of this option is to eliminate or cure the problem. The bulk of today's problems can be solved eventually or, at least, dramatically reduced in scope and adverse impact. It is possible, for example, to eliminate some types of crime and to successfully protect the environment from future pollution. However, the ultimate success of the curative approach is dependent upon several factors. First, this approach can be used only after a deliberative assessment has been made that correctly identifies the factors that created the problem in the first place. Second, the curative approach mandates a long-term policy commitment. Crime cannot be solved in a five, ten, or even a twenty year period. Long-term solutions also need non-partisan support. This is exceptionally difficult to achieve in a democratic environment whereby periodic elections can unseat incumbent administrations. Reasonable goals are essential to the acceptance and ultimate success of any curative policy initiative.

LBJ and Harry Truman (day of Medicare Bill Signing). July 30, 1965

Most lawmakers opt for a combination of the punitive, alleviative, and preventive approaches. For example, the Clean Water Act is designed to prevent future pollution to our nation's water supply by mandating quality standards while using the alleviative option to relieve the suffering and damage caused by previous incidences of water pollution. The punitive approach to the Clean Water Act includes a series of criminal and civil sanctions to be levied on those who participate in pollution activities. The curative approach, however, is seldom used.

Decision-makers must also select the type of policy required to meet anticipated goals and objectives. Domestic policy alternatives include distributive, redistributive, and regulatory options. **Distributive policies** are "governmental actions that convey tangible benefits to individuals, groups or corporations."[51] The most commonly used form of distributive policy is the subsidy. **Subsidies** are "simply government grants of cash and other commodities."[52] However, subsidies must be used correctly to achieve anticipated results. Initially, the gift of the subsidy is given with few strings or conditions attached. For example, the Department of Agriculture gives Farmer Brown a cash payment for not planting turnips. The recipient continues to receive the subsidy to the point that Farmer Brown becomes financially dependent upon receiving the yearly payment. Once dependency is established, government can now begin to add more stringent conditions to the gift. The coercive arm of government will now threaten to reduce and/or actually revoke the gift if Farmer Brown fails to meet the new conditions. The dependency factor usually results in compliance! Subsidies can range from agricultural payments to partial or full payments to low income individuals to offset rent expenses. The United States government uses a wide range of subsidies such as cash payments, military arms and equipment, and humanitarian aid in cementing its relationships with foreign countries.

On the other hand, a **redistributive policy** is "a conscious attempt by the government to manipulate the allocation of wealth, property, rights, or some other value among broad classes or groups in society."[53] Those policies are often called Robin Hood programs since the wealth of the affluent is given to the economically disadvantaged. The federal grant programs of the 1960s and 1970s were designed to reallocate federal tax revenues to the poorer states under the premise that the wealthier states could afford their own infrastructure programs. Consequently, economically strapped states, such as Arkansas, received large federal cash outlays to rebuild its highways, bridges, airports, and so on. The welfare system is another example of redistributive policy. The popularity of redistributive policies is directly tied to the economy. When the economy is in a healthy growth pattern, the wealthier states rarely balk about these initiatives. However, a depressed economy renders Robin Hood schemes exceptionally unpopular.

Finally, lawmakers may opt to use regulatory actions to address a domestic issue or problem. **Regulatory actions** are "governmental actions that extend government control over particular behavior of private individuals or businesses."[54] Initiated in 1887 with the creation of the Interstate Commerce Commission, the federal government has used regulatory actions to exert its influence into virtually every segment of the economy from banking to the environment. To insure regulatory compliance, each act is accompanied by a series of punishing civil, criminal, and monetary sanctions. As evidenced in our discussion of environmental issues, businesses, corporations, farmers, and ranchers, as well as property owners, have come to resent the federal mandates attached to federal regulatory legislation. Lawmakers should realize by now that regulatory policies laden with costly mandates followed by extremely punitive sanctions do not lead to effective public policy that is openly embraced by the regulated party.

In addressing foreign policy concerns, lawmakers generally mold their policy decisions into one of three policy options. The decision may involve a **crisis policy response**. This option is used when "the perception of a threat to national security cuts across normal channels of decisions."[55] Due to the sensitivity and the potential threat to national security, crisis issues are centered in the executive branch of the government. As evidenced by the Cuban Missile Crisis, President Kennedy involved only a few key members of his cabinet in formulating his response to the presence of Soviet missiles in Cuba. Although the executive branch has more latitude in foreign policy concerns, both the legislative and executive branches are involved in the formulation of foreign policy issues. **Strategic defense policy** is "oriented toward foreign policy and international politics, and it involves the units and uses of military force, their strength, and their deployment."[56] The initial decision to send troops rests with the president. The continual deployment of those troops will involve congressional action, particularly when the time limits under the War Powers Act have expired. The formulation of the policy response involves more than just sending troops into hostile territories. For example, the deployment of troops into Bosnia was only one piece of a complex American foreign policy initiative aimed at ending the civil war in former Yugoslavia. Congress assumes a larger role in foreign policy when the issue requires the use of a **structural defense policy**. This option is "oriented toward foreign policy and international politics, and it involves decisions about the procurement, allocation, and organization of men, money, and material that constitute the military forces."[57]

Lawmakers must consider which sector of the economy, namely, public or private, will be responsible for the implementation of the program. Traditionally, government services and policies have been the sole responsibility of government or the public sector. Each new major piece of legislation led to the creation of another federal agency and the hiring of more government employees. The outcry to cut the federal deficit, reduce spending, and balance the budget has led lawmakers to consider another option. The current move is towards privatization that reassigns some functional areas from the public or government sector to the private sector through contracting. Technically, **privatization** is "a general effort to relieve the disincentives toward efficiency in public organizations by subjecting them to the incentives of the private market."[58] Privatization has gained supporters who believe this scheme will save the government money in personnel and equipment costs, while at the same time, relieving government of the burdens of providing a service to the public. Enthusiastic proponents would like "to privatize the full gamut of public assets and services, including many forms of public provisions such as public schools, national parks, public-transport infrastructure, and prisons, whose origins and rationale fall comfortably within the gambit of the classical liberal state. In privatization they believe they have found a sovereign remedy against all ailments to the body politic, good for stimulating economic growth, improving the efficiency of services, slimming down the state, and expanding individual freedom, including the opportunities to disadvantaged minorities, too."[59] Despite lofty expectations, privatization should be used sparingly and with extreme discretion. The drawbacks of privatization include loss of control over that functional area. Government will bear the responsibility and the blame when things go wrong whether the problem is handled by the public or private sector. The troubled website HealthCare.gov, was not designed by Secretary Sebelius. Tony Trenkle, the chief information officer at the Centers for Medicare and Medicaid Services, "supervised the spending of $2 billion a year on information technology products and services, including the development of the website" by a private contractor.[60] However, it was Sebelius and not Trenkle nor the private contractor that had to take the bulk "of the heat" from Congress for the website collapse. During her testimony, she told the congressional panel that "she was accountable for what she described as 'a miserable five weeks' and the 'excruciatingly awful' debut of the insurance website."[61] Second, government can not privatize all functions due to the sensitivity of the function. For example, local governments would be very foolish and irresponsible to contract to the private sector all of its law enforcement functions.

The actual formulation of public policy also involves all the key actors. Once an idea evolves into a proposed piece of legislation, all potentially effected parties are set for action. "As the formulation process moves toward the decision stage, some proposals will be rejected, others accepted, still others modified; differences will be narrowed; bargains will be struck, until ultimately, in some instances, the final policy decision will be only a formality. In other instances, the question will be in doubt until the votes are counted or the decision is announced."[62] The formulation phase is the most politically heightened step in the process of developing public policy.

Budgeting

The proper preparation of a budget is a crucial step in the development of public policy initiatives. A **budget** is a "technical document in the form of a detailed balance sheet that identifies expenditures and revenues for all government activities."[63] The budget is the embodiment of the national government's prevailing fiscal policies. Basically, **fiscal policy** is "public policy that concerns taxes, government spending, public debt, and management of government money."[64] The preparation of a budget entails the estimation of expected expenditures and calls upon the skillful talents of budget makers to find the funding sources needed to pay for these items. For example, state governments are using everything from lotteries, casino gambling, horse racing, state income taxes, and a full array of fines, fees, and special taxes to fund their activities. The budget is also a political document, indicating in dollar amounts to specified budget categories the prevailing political ideologies of lawmakers. "If politics is regarded as conflict over whose preferences are to prevail in the determination of policy, then the budget records the outcomes of this struggle."[65]

Agenda items must reflect budgetary reality. Attainable goals and objectives must be affordable. An improperly budgeted program is doomed for several reasons. First, lawmakers may grossly underestimate the cost of the program. Usually this happens on long-term projects. The cost projections for each year should be increased to adjust for increases in salaries, equipment, materials, maintenance, and customary expenses. "Financial resources are perhaps particularly problematic in labor-intensive service delivery programs and in regulatory programs with a high scientific or technological component, where implementing agencies often lack the funds to engage in the research and development necessary to examine critically the information presented by target groups and, in some cases, to develop alternative technologies."[66] A poorly funded program means that targeted service areas will shrink considerably, rendering the program a failure. Second, lawmakers are extremely skeptical of appropriating large sums of money for an unproven project. The program must look good enough on paper and promise long lasting results to garner full budgetary treatment. Third, the voters can influence the budgeting process. Voters always want top quality services while at the same time demanding budgetary cuts.

A priority in the budgeting process is whether to **dedicate** or **earmark** funds to certain budgetary items. States more often than the national government use dedicated budgetary strategies to fund highways, public education, and so on. Dedicating does ensure that the money will be used for its intended purpose. However, once revenue is dedicated it cannot be transferred to another budget item or used to offset an unexpected crisis.

A sometimes ominous term associated with the budgeting process is porkbarreling. **Porkbarrel politics** is "the use of political influence by members of Congress to secure government funds and projects for their constituents."[67] A congressperson's job includes fighting for federal funds for projects and needs within his/her legislative district.

Taxation has become the traditional means for governments to acquire revenue. A **tax** is a "compulsory contribution for a public purpose rather than for the personnel benefit of an individual."[68] Tax dollars are returned to the citizens in the form of public services. Citizens constantly demand increases in services. However, the majority of Americans are weary of paying taxes and do not support too many politicians and lawmakers advocating tax increases. In developing a tax program, lawmakers must select a plan that will provide a reliable ample source of revenue with a minimal affect on the taxpayers' pocketbooks.

There are several key factors that lawmakers must consider in considering the type of tax they wish to levy on citizens. First, **elasticity** is "an economic criterion applied to a tax which refers to the tax's ability to generate increased revenue as economic growth or inflation increases."[69] A highly **elastic tax** will expand and/or contract proportionally with economic growth or stagnation. Elastic taxes are reliable and predictable sources of revenue. The income tax is the best example of an elastic tax. As a person's income increases, his/her tax burden increases. A tax is tagged as **inelastic** when it does not generate increased revenues in proportion to economic growth. Sales taxes are inelastic taxes. The sales tax rate is fixed. It does not matter what the individual's income level is, the amount of tax is fixed on the item. An individual whose income is $100,000 will pay the same amount of tax on an item of clothing as an individual earning $10,000 who purchases the same item.

Lawmakers must take into account the potential **reliability** of the tax as a source of revenue. A tax that meets its anticipated level of revenue is a better program than a tax that is highly unpredictable in revenue returns. "Sales, property and income taxes are reliable because experts can predict with only a small margin of error future economic growth and activity upon which taxes are based. Severance taxes on energy production can be unreliable because the income they generate is affected by rapidly changing and unpredictable international political forces."[70]

Tax accuracy and reliability go hand in hand. Governments must have adequate revenue sources to accurately predict income generation. Revenue may be lost if the measurement tool to assess tax values is inadequate or antiquated. Accurate tax sources are essential to economic security. The Internal Revenue Service depends upon employers accurately submitting W-2 wage information to both the IRS and the employee. The "honor system" is an extremely unreliable revenue reporting source as some taxpayers purposefully would not report their current earnings.

How much money a tax will ultimately produce is called the **tax yield**. The cost of administering the tax program and eventually collecting the tax can effect the yield of the tax. "Taxes that return substantial sums of money at minimal costs are preferred to taxes that require large outlays for moderate revenues."[71] The easiest taxes to administer and collect are income and sales taxes. These taxes produce a higher yield over property taxes. Property taxes are costly to administer because property must be assessed for its tax value on a regular basis.

The **tax effort** is "a measure of whether, given a state's economic situation, it is taxing above or below its capacity to raise revenue."[72] In other words, states with strong track records of economic growth have the potential to raise ample revenues at average tax rates, if willing to do so.

The **visibility** of a tax is an important political consideration for lawmakers. Although very reliable revenue sources, income and property taxes are highly visible. The taypayer receives an income tax form and a property tax bill in the mail. To add salt to the wound, taxpayers are constantly reminded to pay those taxes on time or face costly late charges, fines, imprisonment, or loss of property. On the other hand, sales taxes are low visibility taxes since the majority of consumers do not keep records of sales tax expenditures. Politicians usually prefer low visibility tax programs.

The **application** of the tax program is another major consideration for budget makers. The primary categories for budget expenses are operating costs and capital expenditures. **Operating expenses** are yearly expenses needed to run government. These items would include salaries, benefits, equipment, rent, utilities, supplies, and so on. **Capital expenses** are multi-year or amortized expenses. A new mainframe computer system or a new building is an expense allocated over five, ten, or thirty year periods. It is essential that reliable revenue sources be used to fund operating expenses.

There are four types of taxes government may levy upon its citizens. A **progressive tax** is "one that increases the tax burden for upper-income people while reducing it for lower-income people."[73] Income, property, and corporate taxes are progressive tax programs. The national government relies heavily on income and corporate taxes; whereas, most state, county, and city governments rely on property taxes. In contrast, a **regressive tax** "increases the tax burden for lower-income people while reducing it for upper-income people."[74] Sales, excise, and energy taxes are regressive taxes since they place a heavier burden on individuals whose incomes are in the middle to lower brackets than those in the upper income levels. The national government uses a wide variety of regressive tax programs such as taxes on cigarettes, alcohol, and so on. Advocated by President Ronald Reagan, **proportional taxes** impose equal tax burdens regardless of one's income level. Reagan believed in a flat tax rate on income with no deductions. Subsequently, a 5 percent tax rate would produce the same tax burden regardless if one's income was $10,000 or $100,000 per year. Finally, the tax system can follow a **benefit principle system**. "Under this principle, those who reap more benefits from government services should shoulder more of the tax burden than people who do not avail themselves of service opportunities to the same degree."[75] Municipal governments impose a wide range of user fees to offset the costs of maintaining their roads and public transportation systems.

Tax equity or the fairness of the tax is another major consideration for lawmakers. As long as the taxpayer believes the tax is fairly applied and justifiable, he/she will pay the tax. However, this country separated itself from England in part over inequitable taxes imposed on the colonists. The principle of fairness in taxation cannot be overlooked by lawmakers seeking re-election.

The selection of the budget strategy is also vital to the planning process. There are several budgetary strategies available to budget makers. The **incremental process** has been the traditional budgetary approach. It is virtually an automatic process whereby federal agencies receive marginal budget increases or decreases with each new budget cycle. Federal agencies merely submit their budget requests with a built-in increase. Without much review, budget makers would normally accept the budget request. However, there are several potentially severe drawbacks to using the incremental system. "There is little attempt to evaluate program results or compare across different program areas in a given fiscal year. Such systematic evaluation would require a number of factors not readily available to most state (or federal) agencies: clear agreement on programmic objectives, reliable methods of measuring progress towards those objectives, and personnel skilled in methods of policy analysis."[76] Second, the incremental system encourages federal agencies to inflate their budget requests and to spend all of their allocated money during the fiscal year. "Typically, administrators ask for more money than they actually need, believing that those appropriating the money will automatically cut budgetary requests. Also they tend to spend all funds that are allocated for a specific time, such as a fiscal year, because to return funds can lead to a reduction of funds during the next budgetary period."[86] Experimental budgetary strategies include the **planning program budgeting (PPB)** concept with a cost benefit analysis feature. The focus is on programs, not line item allocations. "Agencies were obliged by PPB to define each activity's objectives and to indicate how the budget amounts related to the objectives, how to accomplish the objectives in alternative ways, and whether the objectives were being accomplished."[87] The cost benefit is a built-in feature. **Zero-based budgeting** is similar to PPB. It is a program based strategy. However, each agency's budget has to be totally rewritten with each budgetary cycle starting from zero. Agencies submit their budgetary requests every year as if they were just beginning their operations. Zero-based budgeting has lost some of its appeal since it is a very complicated process for all parties involved.

Political Implications

Regardless of the policy issue, all lawmakers must consider the potential political implications of their actions. Each legislative action will provide benefits to one group and hardships to another. One of the fundamental keys is to hurt those who cannot politically hurt you. For example, Democrats and Republicans ran their 1994 and 1996 election campaigns on the need for welfare reform. By pointing out the failure of the program plus examples of fraud and abuse, politicians scored with the middle class voter at the expense of those lower income groups most likely to be welfare recipients. Why? Voter statistics indicate that the poor usually do not vote in large enough numbers to be an electoral threat. A well-crafted public policy initiative adversely hurts those groups who are too politically weak to hurt lawmakers.

All presidents have been keenly aware that their foreign policy decisions are often more visible and potentially harmful to their political careers. Few Americans are concerned about foreign aid packages or the shipment of grains to foreign countries. Once a president commits American forces to a foreign soil, the American public pays close attention. A failing war effort will ruin the re-election opportunities for an otherwise popular president. For example, Lyndon Johnson decided not to seek re-election based primarily on his administration's failure to bring the Vietnam War to a successful conclusion. He knew he would not win the election. Perhaps the election of 1980 would have had a different outcome if President Jimmy Carter's mission to rescue the hostages in the American embassy in Iran had been successful.

The political implications for a congressperson are long lasting since each vote becomes public record. The congressperson's opposition will not let the public forget those votes perhaps cast years ago that run against the grain of current public opinion. Interest groups and political action committees do review congressional voting records to ensure that both endorsed candidates and individuals requesting endorsement have been true to the bottom line issues of their groups. Far too often incumbent candidates must justify their actions for voting for or against controversial legislative items such as abortion, school prayer, gun control, and so on.

Adoption/selling

A policy must be sellable to the recipient and, if required, the group targeted to fund the program. Politicians must package their programs by emphasizing the good benefits and downplaying any potential negatives. Poor salesmanship can destroy a perfectly well designed program. At a glance, the Affordable Care Act should have garnered nationwide support, particularly among the millions without any health insurance coverage. Obama explained to all Americans that once implemented, this legislation would make it "against the law for insurance companies to deny you coverage or charge you more because of pre-existing medical condition like diabetes, high blood pressure or asthma. And they could no longer drop you from coverage just because you got sick or got into an accident. What's more, insurance companies could no longer imposed an annual cap on your health benefits. They could not deny you coverage simply because you made a mistake on your paperwork. Most plans must now cover preventive services like cholesterol and cancer screenings, at no out-of-pocket cost. And, being a woman is no longer a pre-existing condition."[79] However, the Obama administration severely underestimated the potency and determination of the bill's critics. As evidenced during the 2012 presidential primary season, every Republican running for his/her party's nomination called Obamacare socialized medicine. Nothing could be further from the truth. The federal government is only providing an access to an exchange of many privately owned insurance carriers following the coverage detailed in ACA. Despite their best efforts, the Obama administration did not effectively remove the stigma of socialized medicine from the ACA. Another problem was the lag time between the signing of the legislation and the implementation of the program. It took four years before anyone could sign up for the insurance coverage. This gave the opposition four years of continuous efforts to discredit every provision of the legislation. The Obama administration spent the majority of those years responding to critics and defending its signature program. A frustrated President Obama told the American people "my main message today is we're not going back. If I've got to fight another three years to make sure this law works, that's what I'll do. . . . We need to make sure that folks refocus on what's at stake here. Go back. Take a look at what's actually going on. It can make a difference in your lives and the lives of your families. I'm going to need some help in spreading the word."[80]

Public opinion and support for public policy actions are a series of peaks and valleys. On the 2000 campaign trail, George W. Bush advocated sharing the nation's budgetary surplus with taxpayers by lowering income tax rates and providing a one time tax refund to every American taxpayer. The perceivably overtaxed American voter was elated that meaningful tax relief could become a reality. After the 2000 election, the Bush administration followed through on its promise. The Bush tax rebate did not garner the anticipated overwhelming support from the American taxpayer for several reasons. First, candidate Bush made a lofty promise of a tax rebate without revealing how much would be refunded nor which taxpayers would qualify for the rebate. After the election, the Bush administration stated that all single taxpayers would receive $300 while married couples who filed a joint return would receive a $600 rebate. In actuality, the majority of the nation's taxpayers received less than what was promised. Many taxpayers received no rebate. Individuals who owed outstanding taxes were excluded as well as the poorest Americans whose incomes fell below taxable income scales. Therefore, the tax rebate and the proposed reduction in income tax rates for all Americans was perceived as just another tax break for the nation's wealthy. Second, the Bush administration was convinced that tax rebates would be used to buy new goods and services that would generate economic growth. Unfortunately, the maximum refund amount of $300 was not enough of a stimulus to prompt Americans to buy higher end consumer goods. The majority of individuals who received rebates used the money to pay outstanding debts. Third, the inability of the Bush administration to properly sell their tax rebate program soured many Americans against additional tax rebates and tax reductions. "In fact, four in five think cuts generally benefit someone else. . . The public also is decidedly more sympathetic to congressional candidates who place a higher priority on balancing the budget than they do on cutting taxes—with three-fourths preferring the budget-balancers and only a fourth supporting the tax-cutters."[81] It is remarkable that a policy effort designed to give tax dollars back to taxpayers actually resulted in taxpayers wanting their tax dollars to be used to balance the budget! In reality, those tax rebates coupled with the

Bush administration's commitment in Iraq are, in part, responsible for the nation's current budget deficit problems.

The selling process is an ongoing process extending throughout the life-cycle of the public policy initiative. Supporters of both foreign and domestic policy directives must not forget that "a statute, no matter how well it structures implementation, is not a sufficient condition for assuring target group compliance with its objectives. Assuring sufficient compliance to actually achieve those objectives normally takes at least three to five, and often ten to twenty, years. During this period, there are constant pressures for even supportive agency officials to lose their commitment, for supportive constituency groups and sovereigns to fail to maintain active political support, and for the entire process to be gradually undermined by changing socioeconomic forces."[82] Lawmakers must not overlook that targeted groups adversely affected by a policy directive will gain the upper hand in the battle for public opinion support if left unchecked. "There is a general tendency for organized constituency support for a wide variety of programs— including environmental and consumer protection, as well as efforts to aid the poor—to decline over time, while opposition from target groups to the costs imposed on them remains constant or actually increases. This shift in the balance of constituency support for such programs gradually becomes reflected in a shift in support among members of the legislature as a whole and the committees in the relevant subsystem(s).[83] Candidates espousing the negatives of an existing policy effort, once elected, will introduce measures to reform or dismantle that policy effort. Particularly in foreign policy, the waxing and waning of public support and subsequent congressional actions has resulted in the United States flip flopping in its relations with foreign countries. These governments are confused and, far too often, become suspicious of the everchanging policies of the United States government. Consistency in foreign policy is extremely difficult to achieve.

Implementation

Despite the well advertised policy flops, governments can and do successfully implement many of its public policy initiatives. Successful implementation ensures that policies will achieve their anticipated results well within their budgetary constraints. Paul Sabatier and David Mazmanian believe that policies can be successful if the following conditions are met:

1. The program is based on a sound theory relating changes in target group behavior to the achievement of the desired end-state (objectives).
2. The statute (or other basic policy decision) contains unambiguous policy directives and structures the implementation process so as to maximize the likelihood that target groups will perform as desired.
3. The leaders of the implementing agencies possess substantial managerial and political skill and are committed to statutory goals.
4. The program is actively supported by organized constituency groups and by a few key legislators (or the chief executive) throughout the implementation process, with the courts being neutral or supportive.

5. The relative priority of statutory objectives is not significantly undermined over time by the emergency of conflicting public policies or by changes in relevant socioeconomic conditions that undermine the statute's "technical" theory or political support.[92]

A successfully implemented policy directive is not achieved by accident or through sheer luck. It takes a staff committed to executing all the required steps according to the designated time table by using all the necessary tools including budget, personnel, and equipment. Lawmakers can certainly help the implementation process by first clearly delineating the levels of responsibility and, most importantly, the measurements of accountability to be followed by the agency designated to oversee the implementation of the policy directive. Bureaucrats can make or break a good policy simply by the manner in which they phase in the implementation process. "Any new program requires implementing officials who are not merely neutral but also sufficiently committed and persistent to develop new regulations and standard operating procedures and to enforce them in the face of resistance from target groups and from public officials reluctant to make mandated changes."[93] Far too often legislatively created programs have failed due to the lackluster and haphazard actions of bureaucratic agencies.

Second, successful programs correctly anticipate the demand for the service and adequately allocate resources to meet the demand. Resources include personnel, equipment, site location, and revenue. For example, opening a new facility to handle food distribution to a low income group with one clerk in a building located in a higher income neighborhood is missing the targeted service group. This is poor allocation of resources and a waste of money.

Third, long-term policy initiatives are multiple year phased in projects. Each phase must be implemented to produce anticipated goals and objectives. It can take as long as ten to twenty years before even a well-crafted policy can fulfill its goals and objectives. Unfortunately, "an overemphasis on pragmatism can produce a focus on immediate results rather than long term or enduring programs."[94] Impatience on the part of the average American citizen can ruin a perfectly designed long-term plan. The tendency is to implement one or two phases and use a half implemented program as the sole measurement of the success or failure of the entire program. Also, a change in administrations and party leadership could conceivably prevent a program from achieving full implementation. A newly elected Democrat president is unlikely to continue to carry out policies initiated by a Republican president and vice versa.

Evaluation

The final stage of the policy process is a complete and honest evaluation of the policy and resulting programs. Essentially, "governments cannot make rational policy choices unless they can evaluate whether programs attain their objectives. Without evaluation, they cannot know which programs are successful, which administrative practices work, and even which groups of employees are competent."[87] Every program should be effectively evaluated to determine its successes or failures. "At a minimum, policy evaluation requires that we know what we want to accomplish with a given policy (policy objectives), how we are trying to do it (programs), and what, if anything, we have accomplished toward attainment of the objectives (impacts or outcomes, and the relation of the policy thereto). And, in measuring accomplishments, we need to determine not only that some change in real-life conditions has occurred, such as a reduction in the unemployment rate, but also that it was due to policy actions and not to other factors, such as private economic decisions."[88]

Regardless of the policy issue, congressional investigation after investigation focusing more on accusatory finger pointing than on actually analysis in a non-confrontational and non-partisan manner the ineffectiveness of policy choices and the ultimate decision making process is not an effective evaluation tool. Government at all levels can learn from its mistakes by conducting a meaningful evaluation of the actions they took, and the steps they should have taken to properly address the issue or the problem. If a meaningful evaluation does not take place, then it will be government as usual—responding to a crisis after crisis rather than preventing the crisis from happening in the first place.

CONCLUSION

The planning process is a series of eight steps beginning with problem identification and culminating with an in-depth evaluation process. As previously stated, each step is equally vital to the development of cost effective, administratively effective, and goal achievable public policy initiatives. It takes a well thought out action plan to create good public policy. As we examine public policy issues, we should remember how the planning process was applied in addressing these concerns.

CHAPTER NOTES

[1] "Key Moments in the History of the Affordable Care Act," *San Antonio Express-News*, (Friday, June 29, 2012), A15.
[2] Richard S. Dunham, "Parties Mobilize for November Election," *San Antonio Express-News*, Friday, June 29, 2012), A13.
[3] "Roberts Likens Himself to an 'Umpire' in Ruling," *San Antonio Express-News*, Friday, June 29, 2012), A13.
[4] Ibid.
[5] James E. Anderson, *Public Policymaking: An Introduction*, 5th ed., (Boston, Mass.: Houghton Mifflin Company, 2003), 1.
[6] Steven A. Peterson and Thomas H. Rassmussen, *State and Local Politics*, (New York: McGraw-Hill, Inc., 1994), 199.
[7] Anderson, 5th ed., 2.
[8] Theodore J. Lowi and Benjamin Ginsburg, *American Government: Freedom and Power*, 4th ed., (New York: W. W. Norton & Co., 1996), 607.
[9] Anderson, 5th ed., 5.
[10] Ibid., 95.
[11] David C. Saffell, *State and Local Government: Politics and Public Policies*, 4th ed., (New York: McGraw-Hill, Inc., 1990), 239.
[12] Anderson, 5th ed., 248.
[13] Ibid., 249.
[14] Ibid., 14.
[15] Gerry Riposa and Nelson Dometrius, "Studying Public Policy," *Texas Public Policy*, Gerry Riposa, ed., (Dubuque, Iowa: Kendall/Hunt Publishers, 1987), p. 11.
[16] Anderson, 5th ed., 130.

[17] Ibid., 132.
[18] Jeffrey M. Berry, "Citizen Groups and the Changing Nature of Interest Group Politics in America," *The Annals, The American Academy of Political and Social Science*, (Newbury Park, Calif.: Sage Publications, 1993), Vol. 528, July, 1993, 41.
[19] Thomas R. Rochon and Daniel A. Mazmanian, "Social Movements and the Policy Process," *The Annals*, The American Academy of Political and Social Science (Newbury Park, California: Sage Publications, 1993), Vol. 528, July, 1993, 76.
[20] Barry, 31.
[21] Ibid., 34.
[22] Ibid., 41.
[23] Riposa, 9.
[24] Anderson, 5th ed., 60.
[25] Walter K. Olezek, *Congressional Procedures and the Policy Process*, 3rd ed., (Washington, D.C., The Congressional Quarterly, 1989), 25-26.
[26] *Treasury of Presidential Quotations*, Caroline Thomas Hornsberger, ed., (Chicago, Illinois: Follett Publishing Co., 1964), 263.
[27] Michael Barone, "The Politics of Negation," *U.S. News & World Report*, February 20, 2006, 40.
[28] Edward L. Harper, "Domestic Policy Making in the Nixon Administration: An Evolving Process," *Presidential Studies Quarterly*, (New York, New York: The Center for the Study of the Presidency, 1996), Vol. XXVI, No. 1, Winter, 1996, 41.
[29] Ibid.
[30] Ibid., 47.
[31] Barone, "The Politics of Negation," 40.
[32] James L. Garnett, "Administrative Communication (Or How To Make All the Rest Work): The Concept of Its Professional Centrality", *Public Administration: Concepts and Cases*, Richard Stillman, II, ed., 8th ed., (Boston: Mass.: Houghton Mifflin Company, 2005), 260.
[33] Anderson, 5th ed., 52-53.
[34] Hope Yen, "Ruling on Sentences Has Judges Scratching Their Heads", *San Antonio Express-News*, (Friday, January 28, 2005), 12A.
[35] Theodore J. Lowi and Benjamin Ginsburg, *American Government: Freedom and Power*, 3rd ed., (New York: W. W. Norton & Co., 1994), 620.
[36] Lowi, 611.
[37] Jack O. Plano and Roy Olton, *The International Relations Dictionary*, (New York, New York: Holt, Reinholt and Winston, Inc., 1969), 265.
[38] Ibid.
[39] Jay M. Shafritz, *The HarperCollins Dictionary of American Government and Politics*, (New York, New York: HarperCollins Publishers, Inc., 1992), 590.
[40] Peterson, 190-91.
[41] Paul Sabatier and Daniel Mazmanian, "The Conditions of Effective Implementation: A guide to Accomplishing Policy Objectives", *Public Administration: Concepts and Cases*, Richard Stillman, II., ed., 4th ed., (Princeton, New Jersey: Houghton Mifflin Company, 1988), 387.
[42] Anderson, 55-56.
[43] Ibid., 81.
[44] Richard Maidment, and Anthony McGrew, *The American Political Process*, (Beverly Hills, Calif.: Sage Publications, Inc., 1981), 135.
[45] James E. Anderson, *Public Policy Making*, (New York: Paeger Publishers,1975), 57.
[46] Deborah A. Stone, *Public Paradox and Political Reason*, (New York: HarperCollins College Publishers, 1988), 147.
[47] Stone, 162-163.
[48] Sabatier and Mazmanian, 380.
[49] Randall W. Bland, Alfred B. Sullivan, Robert E. Biles, Charles P. Elliott, Jr., and Beryle E. Pettus, *Texas Government Today*, 5th ed., (Pacific Grove, Calif.: Brooks/Cole Publishing Co., 1992), 432.

50 Sar A. Levitan, "How the Welfare System Promotes Economics Security," *Political Science Quarterly*, (New York: The Academy of Political Science), Vol. 100, No. 3, Fall, 1985, 453.

51 Randall B. Ripley, and Grace A. Franklin, *Congress, the Bureaucracy and Public Policy*, (Homewood, Ill.: The Dorsey Press, 1976), 16.

52 Theodore J. Lowi, and Benjamin Ginsburg, *American Government: Freedom and Power*, 4th ed., (New York: W. W. Norton & Co., 1996), 610.

53 Ripley, 18.

54 Ibid.

55 Ibid., 19.

56 Ibid.

57 Ibid.

58 Robert W. Bailey, "Uses and Misuses of Privatization," *Prospects for Privatization*, Steve H. Hanke, ed., (New York: The Academy of Political Science, 1987), Proceedings, Vol. 36, No. 3, 138.

59 Paul Starr, "The Limits of Privatization," *Prospects for Privatization*, Steve H. Hanke, ed., (New York: The Academy of Political Science, 1987), Proceedings, Vol. 36, No. 3, 124.

60 "Citing Hundreds of Problems, Sebelius Rejects Delays to ACA," *San Antonio Express-News*, (Thursday, November 7, 2013), A9.

61 Ibid.

62 Anderson, 5th ed., 119.

63 Bland, 329.

64 Ibid, 332.

65 Aaron Wildansky, "Budgeting as a Political Process," *Public Administration: Concepts and Cases*, Richard J. Stillman, II, ed., 4th ed., (Princeton, N.J.: Houghton Mifflin Company, 1988), 346.

66 Sabatier and Mazmanian, 381.

67 Grier D. Stephenson, Jr., Robert J. Bresler, Robert J. Friedrich, and Joseph J. Karlesky, *American Government*, 2d ed., (New York: HarperCollins Publishers, 1992), G15.

68 Eugene W. Jones, Joe E. Ericson, Lyle C. Brown, and Robert S. Trotter, Jr., *Practicing Texas Politics*, 8th ed., (New York: Houghton Mifflin Co., 1992), 433.

69 Nelson C. Dometrius, "Government Revenues and Expenditure Policy," *Texas Public Policy*, (Dubuque, Iowa: Kendall/Hunt Publishing Co., 1987), 33.

70 Ibid., 34.

71 Ann O'M. Bowman, and Richard C. Kearney, *State and Local Government*, (Boston: Houghton Mifflin Co., 1990), 374.

72 Susan B. Hansen, "The Politics of State Taxing and Spending," *Politics in the American States: A Comparative Analysis*, Virginia Gray, Herbert Jacob and Robert Albritton, eds., 5th ed., (New York: HarperCollins Publishers, Inc., 1990), 348.

73 John J. Harrigan and David C. Nice, *Politics and Policy in States and Communities*, 8th ed., (New York, New York: Pearson Education, 2004), 306.

74 Ibid.

75 Bowman, 374.

76 Hansen, 362.

77 Leon W. Blevins, *Texas Government in National Perspective*, (New Jersey: Prentice-Hall, Inc., 1987), 317.

78 Harrigan and Nice, 257.

79 Kathleen Sebelius, "Another View: Affordable Care Act will Bring a Healthy New Year," *San Antonio Express-News*, (Wednesday, January 1, 2014), A15.

80 "Obama: The Health Care Law Is Working," *San Antonio Express-News*, (December 4, 2013), A12.

81 Will Lester, "Tax Rebates Haven't Sold 4 in 5 Americans on Cuts," *San Antonio Express-News* (Wednesday, April 3, 2002), 12A.

82 Sabatier and Mazmanian, 383.

83 Ibid, 384.

84 Ibid., 379.

[85] Ibid., 381.
[86] Nelson C. Dometrius, "The Texas Policy Environment," *Texas Public Policy*, Gerry Riposa, ed., (Dubuque, Iowa: Kendall/Hunt Publishers, 1987), 18.
[87] Harrigan and Nice, 254.
[88] Anderson, 1st ed., 134-135.

SUGGESTED READINGS

Anderson, James E., *Public Policymaking: An Introduction*, 5th edition, Boston, Mass.: Houghton Mifflin Company, 2003.

Harrigan, John B. and David C. Nice, *Politics and Policy in States and Communities,* 8th edition, New York, New York: Pearson Education, 2004.

Mainment, Richard, and Anthony McGrew. *The American Political Process*, Beverly Hills, Calif.: Sage Publications, Inc., 1981.

Peterson, Steven A., and Thomas H. Rassmussen. *State and Local Politics*. New York: McGraw-Hill, Inc., 1994.

Saffell, David C. and Harry Basehart, *State and Local Government: Politics and Public Policies,* 8th edition, Boston, Mass.: McGraw-Hill Companies, 2005.

Stillman, Richard J. II., ed., *Public Administration: Concepts and Cases*, 8th edition, Boston, Mass.: Houghton Mifflin Company, 2005.

Stone, Deborah A. *Public Policy Making*. New York: Praeger Publishers, 1975.

Chapter Sixteen

SOCIAL SERVICES

In 1964, President Lyndon Johnson launched his War on Poverty program, a plan designed to not only reduce but possibly eliminate poverty. The ushering in of 2014 marks the fiftieth anniversary of this bold anti-poverty program. Although strides have been made, the reality is that poverty still stirs deep emotions on both sides of the political spectrum and troubles the consciousness of every American. It is ironic that a nation so blessed with natural resources, ingenuity, and wealth still has millions of its citizens living below the nation's poverty level, roaming the streets during the day with absolutely no place to call home, or living in fear that they are just one step away from falling into the dismal black hole we call poverty. The United States Census Bureau estimates that 49.7 million Americans or 16 percent of the nation's population were living below the poverty line in 2010.[1] The good news is that the unemployment rate is shrinking from its double digit highs at the beginning of the recession in 2007 to approximately 7 percent in 2014. The bad news is that this dip is attributable in part to the millions of Americans who have exhausted their unemployment benefits and/or simply have given up trying to find employment. While this nation has had a number of recessions, this latest one "marks the first period in 20 years in which employment as a percentage of the population in the U.S. has fallen below the rate in countries like the U.K., Germany and the Netherlands."[2] Wages have not kept up with the cost of living. "The average real weekly earnings of a typical blue collar worker are lower today than in 1964."[3] The nation's education system has not been able to keep up with technological advances. There is a direct connection between one's educational attainments to the marketable skills required of the job market. Less education and marginal knowledge of advanced technology closes the doors to those higher paying job opportunities. Despite Medicare and Medicaid, there are still approximately 48 million Americans without health insurance. It is hoped that Obamacare or the Affordable Care Act will drastically reduce that number in the near future. The safety net of government-sponsored programs has protected many more from falling into poverty. Latest Census Bureau statistics paint a very bleak picture:

If it weren't for Social Security payments, the poverty rate would rise to 54.1 percent for people 65 and older and 24.4 percent for all age groups.
• without refundable tax credits such as the earned income tax credit, child poverty would rise from 18.1 percent to 24.4 percent.
• without food stamps, the overall poverty rate would increase from 16.1 percent to 17.6 percent.[4]

The reality is that poverty has always been with us. It has and will continue to plague this nation and baffle our elected officials from George Washington to Barack Obama as each has pondered how to marginalize it or as Lyndon Johnson hoped fifty years ago, actually eliminate it. Despite the efforts of state legislative houses and Capitol Hill, the poor have yet to find the right road leading them to a better life and economic security. Where did we go wrong? Why does the American Dream of promised riches and success continue to elude millions of Americans? These tough questions have yet to be answered.

In the late 1980s, heavily overburdened state legislative houses began to question the ability of the welfare state created by Franklin Roosevelt's think tank to meet the needs of the impoverished, while at the same time pleasing taxpayers whose hard earned dollars fund the system. Politicians and lawmakers agreed that the welfare system needed major repair work simply because it was not working. The all too simple solution was to turn a blind eye to the millions of Americans in financial need by slashing billions of federal dollars from welfare programs that had been providing a safety net against the harshness of poverty since 1935. Yet, this option is not a viable solution. Governments merely washing their hands of welfare programs will not miraculously erase poverty or eliminate the suffering and deprivation. In 1996, a reluctant President Clinton signed a sweeping welfare reform law that significantly changed the welfare system. Initially, it appeared that the reform package was fulfilling its expectations. The number of welfare recipients declined as a healthy economy produced more job opportunities for the nation's poor.

However, as people around the world were celebrating the arrival of a new century, the American economy was beginning to show signs of weakening. Without prejudice, every community in the nation experienced loss of jobs, rising unemployment, increased applications for welfare benefits, businesses either filing for bankruptcy or shutting their doors, and homeowners fearful of losing their homes. "Small and medium-size cities in the Midwest, already suffering from an ailing auto industry, were hit the hardest, with unemployment rates doubling or tripling in cities throughout Michigan, Ohio, Indiana, and Illinois."[5] The effects of the recession began to hit hard by 2007 as 37,276,000 Americans, representing 12.5 percent of the nation's population, lived below the poverty level.[6] By the end of 2009, 43,569,000 Americans, representing 14.3 percent of the nation's population, lived below the poverty level.[7] In 2010, 14,825,000 working age individuals, representing 9.6 percent of the nation's civilian labor force, was unemployed.[8] It is estimated that 6.5 million jobs were lost during this recession.[9] In addition, annual median household incomes declined dramatically from 2005-2007. By the end of 2008, it was estimated that one in ten homeowners were either notified of foreclosure or were on the brink of losing their home. The hardest hit states were Nevada, Louisiana, Mississippi, Florida, Ohio, Indiana and Michigan.[10] Furthermore, "from 2007 to 2009, the number of families in homeless shelters—households with at least one adult and one minor child—leapt to 170,000 from 131,000."[11] The 2010 mid-term elections shifted the balance of power in the House of Representatives from Democrat to Republican control. Since then, every budget battle has focused on Republican efforts in the House to reduce federal funding and balance the budget by slashing spending on income-support programs for the poor. Their 2012 plan included "cutting $23.5 billion from Medicaid and children's health care, $4.2 billion from hospitals that serve the poor and uninsured, and $33.7 billion from supplemental nutrition aid."[12] If this had passed both Houses, the Congressional Budget Office projected that "20 million children would face reduced food and nutrition support, almost 300,000 would be knocked off the federal school lunch program, and at least 300,000 would lose access to the State Children's Health Insurance Program."[13]

While this nation's leaders are so critical of the failures of other countries to address their poverty-related issues, our lawmakers have failed for over two hundred years to adequately come to grips with the human side of this nation's poverty-related problems. The politics of poverty directly affects millions of faces from all races, ages, and genders that oftentimes fare worse under the new programs and funding options crafted in congressional and executive committee rooms. It is this human face of poverty that this nation cannot morally or consciously ignore. We, as citizens, must also remember that poverty involves more than just statistics on a chart or a dollar figure on a budget line. For every number on a chart, bell-curve, or bar graph there is a face of a man, woman, or child who, with few exceptions, found themselves impoverished through no direct fault of their own.

The solution to poverty lies in an extremely complex and painfully difficult re-examination of the American social and economic consciousness. The Framers of the Constitution recognized government's burdensome responsibility of meeting the needs of **all** of its citizens whether rich or poor by charging government with the task of providing for and promoting the general welfare. While liberals and conservatives continue to argue over the proper philosophical approaches to solving poverty, and congressional Democrats and Republicans hurl insults at each other, the sad reality is that the number of poverty-stricken Americans continues to increase as the gap between rich and poor widens. In addition, millions of Americans are employed at minimum or below minimum wage jobs without the benefits of life insurance, pension plans, and health-care coverage for themselves or their family members. Rock bottom poor roam the streets, seeking shelter at night in crowded shelters or the parks and alleys of our nation's streets. As it tore apart the city of New Orleans and portions of the Gulf Coast, hurricane Katrina also exposed the depth of decades-old chronic poverty. "'I hope we realize that the people of New Orleans weren't just abandoned during the hurricane,' then-Sen. Barack Obama said . . . on the floor of the Senate. 'They were abandoned long-ago—to murder and mayhem in the streets, to substandard schools, to dilapidated housing, to inadequate health care, to a pervasive sense of hopelessness.'"[14] Unfortunately, it took a Category 5 hurricane to remind us that America does indeed have a poverty problem. In reality, the United States is a rich nation for the privileged few and a poor one for millions. Poverty does not discriminate in its choice of victims, nor is anyone completely safe from its stranglehold.

This chapter examines the depth of poverty confronting this nation as well as the difficult tasks faced by lawmakers to address the underlying causal factors that lead to poverty and economic deprivation. Basically, since the founding of this country, lawmakers have attempted to address only the **immediate** needs of the poor. The resulting legislative actions have only marginally alleviated the suffering of many, but not all of the poor, and have failed miserably to solve the problems of poverty. This chapter explores the policy actions pursued by all levels of government in their valiant but unsuccessful attempts to fulfill their obligations and challenges of promoting the general welfare. Of course, no discussion of the issue of poverty would be complete without exploring the current health-care crisis confronting not only the poor of this nation but all Americans.

THE VOCABULARY OF POVERTY

Poverty is "the state of condition of being poor by lacking the means of providing material needs or comforts."[15] One of the major problems confronting lawmakers is the actual determination of the number of people who are actually living in poverty. "The current formula was created by President Lyndon Johnson to keep score in his 'war on poverty' and has remained unchanged since 1965."[16] The number will fluctuate depending upon the measurement tool or factor used to determine economic deprivation. For years, policy makers have used a loose definition of the **poverty level** or **threshold** to determine actual numbers as well as benefit eligibility. "Based on the assumption that poor families spend one-third of their income on food, the United States Social Security Administration sets an official poverty line at three times the amount of income needed

Table 16.1

Weighted Average Poverty Thresholds by Size of Unit: 1990-2012
(in dollars)

Size of Family Unit	1990	2000	2012
One Person (unrelated individual)	$6,652	$8,791	$11,722
Under 65 Years	6,800	8,959	11,945
65 Years and Over	6,268	8,259	11,011
Two Persons	8,509	11,239	14,960
Householder Under 65 Years	8,794	11,590	15,452
Householder 65 Years and Older	7,905	10,419	13,891
Three Persons	10,419	13,738	18,287
Four Persons	13,359	17,603	23,497
Five Persons	15,792	20,819	27,815
Six Persons	17,839	23,528	31,485
Seven Persons	20,241	26,754	35,811
Eight Persons	22,582	29,701	39,872
Nine Or More Persons	26,848	35,060	47,536

Source: U.S. Census Bureau, January 18, 2013, *http://www.census.gov/main*.

to eat according to a modest food plan."[17] This numerical figure is adjusted annually for inflation. Poverty levels are established for a wide range of variables. Table 16.1 details the poverty thresholds for an individual to nine or more family members from 1990 to 2012. In 2012, the poverty levels were $11,011 for an individual over the age of 65; $18,287 for a family of three; and $23,497 for a family of four. The highest range was $47,536 for a family of nine or more persons. Each year the income levels are only marginally increased. For example, the poverty level for a family of three increased only $4,549 between 2000 and 2012.

Both liberals and conservatives believe that the current method of determining the poverty level needs to be changed to reflect a more realistic measurement tool of deprivation. "Conservative critics of the official definition point out that it [the poverty level] is based on cash income and does not count family assets or 'in-kind' (non-cash) benefits from government such as food stamps, medical care, and public housing. If poverty rate calculations include these factors, the 'net poverty' rate is lower than the official rate; fewer people are considered poor."[18] On the other hand, liberals contend that "taxes, work expenses, child care costs, and medical expenses paid by consumers from their own pocket should be deducted from cash income."[19] By using these factors, the number of individuals living below the poverty level would increase. "Economists have long criticized the official poverty rate as inadequate. Based on a half-century-old government formula, the official rate continues to assume the average family spends one-third of its income on food. Those costs have actually shrunk to a much smaller share, more like one-seventh."[20]

Poverty levels can also be determined in absolute and relative terms. **Absolute poverty** is defined as "the minimum subsistence income needed to survive deprivation."[21] This determination is based on the cost of a modest income outlay for food, shelter, and clothing. The federal government currently measures poverty in absolute terms, using food as the primary factor. **Relative poverty** compares an individual's income to the nation's overall standard of living. This elastic approach takes into account the ups and downs of the nation's economic growth and prosperity. As the standard

Many of the homeless manage to eke out only a miserable existence.

of living increases, the gap between rich and poor widens, producing an increase in the number of persons whose incomes fall below the poverty level. An adverse economic situation would shrink the gap between rich and poor, resulting in a reduction in the total number of people living below the poverty level.

There are several subcategories of impoverishment. The **working poor** are usually undereducated high school dropouts who are either employed full time or part-time at minimum or below minimum wage positions. Their salaries do not generate enough income to place them above the poverty level. Some of these are holding two or more part-time jobs at the same time. For the nation's working poor "every little setback is a crisis to them; unkindness or fear immobilizes them. Depression, low self-esteem and hopelessness all combine to make them exceptionably fragile. Supporting two kids on the minimum wage requires a lot of togetherness, not to mention sheer stamina. Fighting one's way through the welfare bureaucracy to get the help to which one is entitled is a challenge for someone with a college degree with a lot of self-confidence; try doing it after an eight-hour workday with no transportation, especially if your English isn't good and you are terrified of authority. (Offices open 9 to 5, with long waiting periods, endless forms and proof of income and assets required.) 'Catch-22' is not a trite phrase for poor Americans—it's a way of life."[22] The only benefits part-time workers receive is social security and worker's compensation since healthcare and maybe pension benefits are mandatory only if employees work over 37.5 hours per week for a total of 2080 hours per year. A full time minimum wage job will guarantee health care and life insurance benefits for the worker. However, the cost of dependent care is usually totally or partially the responsibility of the worker.

In the 1990s, a new subcategory of the working poor emerged under the label of **hyperpoor**. These individuals have annual incomes that total less than half of the official poverty level. Many of the nation's mentally and physically handicapped Americans fall into this category. In addition, the hyperpoor include those individuals who are not technically homeless but who must rely upon family members and friends to augment their costs for food and housing. Oftentimes, undereducated and unskilled legal and illegal immigrants fall into this category. For example, in South Texas, individuals who lack the skills to hold regular jobs, gather early every morning at a designated site whereby small building, paving, and construction contractors and farmers can seek a crew of laborers for a day's work. These individuals, known as **day laborers**, are paid a small wage in cash after their employer drops them off at the pickup site after the day's tasks are completed.

The **nonworking poor** include those individuals receiving unemployment compensation, the unemployed without benefits, the homeless, the totally disabled/mentally ill, and the elderly whose incomes fall below the poverty level. An accurate accounting of the nonworking poor is difficult to determine. The unemployment rate, for example, is supposed to indicate the total number of jobless Americans. However, the unemployment rate is an unreliable measuring tool since it only accounts for the unemployed who are currently receiving some form of unemployment compensation. It cannot account for those individuals whose benefits have been depleted even though they are still unemployed or for those who did not qualify for unemployment compensation.

The **feminization of poverty** recognizes the increase in the number of single-parent families headed by a female whose income falls below the poverty level. Since the 1960s, there has been a dramatic steady increase in the number of female-headed households. This rise in matriarchal families is attributed to the increase in the number of divorces, separations, out-of-wedlock pregnancies, and for non-traditional independent living styles. Usually these women are too undereducated and underskilled for the higher paying job market. Consequently, they are employed at the lowest ranking positions at minimum wage or slightly higher without immediate opportunity for promotion or advancement. Stereotypically, the feminization of poverty is seen as a minority out-of-wedlock teenager who drops out of high school, never to return again. This generalization overlooks that the ranks of poor women with dependent children includes those who completed high school and married shortly afterward. After years of marriage, these women now find themselves divorced without marketable job skills beyond low paying service-sector positions, struggling to support their children on a paltry sum of child support from their ex-husbands. Basically, "the U.S. labor market has always failed women who have little formal education and sporadic job experiences. Low-income women are still segregated into low-paying occupations, despite the vast improvements for college-educated women."[23] As single parents, these women must oftentimes make the difficult decision between meeting the needs of their children and their employment-related responsibilities. "Employers, especially those who employ low-wage workers, will not tolerate workers who come in late because a school bus did not show up, miss days because there was no child care or a kid was sick, or worry about their children at 3 p.m. instead of doing their work."[24] In 2012, the median family income of married couples with only one wage earner was $50,881 compared to $30,686 for female householders with no husband present.[25]

Another subcategory of poverty distinguishes the permanently or persistently poor from the marginally or temporarily poor. The determination is based on an individual's income level over a ten-year span. A person is considered **permanently** or **persistently** poor when his/her income has been below the poverty level for eight years or longer within the ten-year period. Individuals whose incomes are below the poverty level for less than two years within the same ten-year span, are **temporarily** or **marginally** poor. Of course, each group has a different set of needs to overcome their financial deprivations. The persistently poor require long-term housing, extensive job training and educational programs, food, and other financial assistance. The temporarily poor need short-term assistance such as unemployment compensation, health-care benefits, and perhaps food stamps and shelter while seeking another job. However, most social programs crafted at both the national and state levels tend to be "one size fits all" plans that truly do not meet the unique needs of both groups.

A Profile of America's Poor

The concept of the American Dream is based on the belief that anyone in the United States can become a rich person if he/she gets an education, works hard and takes advantage of any and every opportunity to improve one's economic status. In reality, the rags to riches story happens to only a very few. The majority work hard and try their best to climb up that corporate ladder, only to see the American Dream happening to someone else. Table 16.2 illustrates the changes in aggregate income from 2000 to 2012. The lowest one-fifth of the nation's population shares only 3.8 percent of wealth while those in the highest one fifth hold 48.9 percent of the nation's total wealth. Consequently, 80 percent of Americans hold only 51 percent of the wealth while 20 percent of the nation's total population control over 48.9 percent of the nation's total income.

Table 16.2 Share of Aggregate Income 2000-2012				
Income Bracket	2000 Income	Percent of Total	2012 Income	Percent of Total
Lowest Fifth	$14,122	3.6%	$15,534	3.8%
Second Fifth	32,289	8.9%	38,184	9.2%
Third Fifth	50,747	14.8%	62,464	15.1%
Fourth Fifth	74,791	23.0%	95,474	23.0%
Fifth Fifth	156,916	49.8%	202,599	48.9%
Top Five Percent	278,063	22.1%	352,338	21.3%

Source: *Statistical Abstract of the United States: 2012*, 131st ed., (Washington, D.C.: United States Census Bureau, 2009), Table 694, page 454 and Tables F-2- Share of Aggregate Income Received by Each Fifty and Top 5 Percent of Families, All Races: 1947-2012 and F-3 Mean Income Received by Each Fifth and Top 5 Percent of Families, All Races: 1966-2012, http://www.census.gov/main)

Basically, lower- and middle-class Americans continue to find themselves with less and less income for basic necessities such as rent, clothing, food, transportation, day care, and health-care costs. A major contributing factor is the disparity in wage treatment. From 1997 to 2006, the minimum wage was stuck at $5.15 per hour. Corrective legislation gradually raised the rate to $7.25 by 2009. If the worker has a full-time job, his/her yearly salary before taxes and benefits are deducted is $15,080. Over the past decade the job market has shifted from the traditional hiring of primarily full time workers to a part-time workforce. In his 2014 State of the Union message, President Obama asked Congress to increase minimum wage to at least $9 per hour.

The gap between rich and poor is further widened by this nation's dependency upon state and federal income taxes and regressive tax programs that place a heavier tax burden upon middle and lower income groups. Sales, property, and excise taxes, as well as user fees, consume a greater chunk of the paychecks earned by the average American worker than those whose wages place them into the upper income brackets. One of the hot-bed issues of the 2012 presidential campaign was tax fairness. Democrat candidate President Barack Obama wanted to shift the tax burden from the middle to upper income class. The campaign was, in many respects, a class-based warfare with the Democrats emerging as the champion of the middle and lower income classes and the Republicans strongly supporting the current lower tax rates for the wealthiest Americans while the Tea Party wing of the Republican Party wanted no tax increases whatsoever for anyone. In particular, one of the perpetual indictments wrongly levied against the nation's poor is that they do not pay their fair share in taxes that, in turn, help to fund the social service programs that they ultimately will need to use. Statistics, however, help to dispel the myth. For example, a family of three (defined by the Census Bureau as two wage earners with one school age child owning their own home and living in a city where taxes apply) with a gross family income of $25,000 paid an average of $2,750 or 11.0 percent of their total income towards state and local taxes. For families with gross family incomes of $150,000, their yearly state and local tax burden was $12,165 or 8.1 percent of their total incomes.[26] These figures do not include federal income tax obligations. If tax burdens were included in the computation of the poverty level, the number of impoverished and needy in this nation would increase substantially.

Poor and lower-middle income Americans are confronted with the task of finding affordable housing. The majority of the nation's poor are forced to live in rental properties, relying on government subsidized housing to offset the costs. Finding affordable livable housing is becoming extremely difficult. For too many Americans, the dream of owning a new or even a pre-owned home is cost prohibitive. The nation's latest economic downturn was in part fueled by the rise in the number of single-family home foreclosures. An inflated real estate market coupled with low mortgage interest rates was attractive to those seeking to purchase a home. However, as the economy soured and unemployment rose, many homeowners simply could not make the monthly mortgage payments. At the same time, home values declined, leaving the homeowner with the option of selling a house at less than what they owed on the home. In other words, the homeowner was upside down on the mortgage loan. For many the only option was to allow the mortgage loan to default resulting in a foreclosure, leaving the former homeowner with a ruined credit rating and slim chances of purchasing a home in the near future.

The impoverished and homeless of this nation are further adversely affected by the stereotypical myths about poverty that far too often cloud the perceptions of lawmakers and the general public. The myth portrays the poor as shiftless, lazy, able-bodied men and women who simply refuse to fend for themselves, opting instead for a life of dependency upon the government's generosity. The homeless are seen as filthy unkept winos and bums who roam the streets panhandling for money to fund their addictive habits. The media has for the past fifty years helped to create the image of impoverishment. In the 1960s, the poor were portrayed as rural Anglos living in the mountainous isolated areas of Appalachia. Pictures documented the poor as living in one-room shacks without electricity or indoor plumbing. The stereotype changed in the 1980s as the poor were portrayed as primarily African Americans living in rundown urban areas called the ghettoes. Stereotypes help to shield Americans from the reality and complexity of poverty. The majority of Americans are actually in denial about homelessness, impoverishment, and poverty. **Denial** is defined as "the inability to recognize a problem in the face of compelling evidence."[27] The majority of Americans are in denial as to the historical depth of our nation's poverty problem. Far too often seen as a third-world country's problem, Americans simply can not continue to ignore the fact that even before this current economic recession, this nation's poverty level is "the highest in the developed world and more than twice as high as in most other industrialized countries, which all strike a more generous social contract with their weakest citizens. Even if the real number is lower that 37 million [in the United States], that's a nation of poor people the size of Canada or Morocco living inside the United States."[28] Across the board, census statistics shatter the myths and reveal the reality that poverty strikes the very young and old of this nation in every hamlet from the East to West Coast and definitely cuts across all racial barriers.

The fate of our nation's children is directly tied to their parent's income status. In 2012, 16,073,000 or 21.8 percent of all children under the age of eighteen were living in poverty conditions.[31] A 2010 breakdown reveals that 12.4 percent of White (Anglo), 38.2 percent of Black (African American), 35.0 percent of Hispanic and 13.6 of Asian children live under the poverty level.[32] Regardless of their racial orientation, all of these children are at risk for constant illnesses and poor diet. "Hungry children are more than four times as likely to suffer from frequent colds, ear infections, and headaches. Hungry children miss school because of sickness more often, and they go to the doctor almost twice as often."[33] Nutritionists have proven that hunger does have a direct affect on a child's ability to retain knowledge. These at-risk children are likely to become tomorrow's high school dropouts, saddled with the same dismal employment opportunities and substandard wage earnings that keep their parents mired in poverty.

Tragically, far too many children born in poverty do not live to reach adulthood. "Poor diet is closely related to low birth weight, which is a factor in the deaths of infants during their first twelve months. Twenty-three other developed nations have lower infant-mortality rates than the United States."[34] Children raised in poverty as also more apt to become victims of criminal activities and gang-related deaths than children raised outside of poverty's grasp. In the ghettoes and low-income neighborhoods across this nation, "high crime rates are the norm, as are underground economies fueled by drugs, prostitution, and African-American markets in goods of all kinds. Most disturbing is the daily body count of young African-American men who are victims of drug wars, gang killings, and the hunger for material possessions so perverse that children kill each other over $100 sneakers and $20 drug debts."[35] The children born and reared in poverty have become the forgotten faces of the cruel reality of economic deprivation and social isolation found in the deteriorating neighborhoods of our nation's cities.

The two primary keys to removing oneself from the shackles of endless poverty are education and economic viability. The two go hand and hand. Unfortunately, this nation is confronted with a consistently high number of teenagers who opt not to complete their high school educations. High dropout rates coupled with low test scores in reading, mathematics and English have resulted in state legislative houses assuming a more pro-active role in the administration of traditionally locally controlled public school districts. As the governor of Texas, George W. Bush demanded more accountability from the state's public schools. A cornerstone of his presidency, Bush pledged that the reforms he implemented in Texas were well suited for all of the nation's public schools. He vowed that his plan would indeed leave "no child left behind." However, standardized testing scores in mathematics, reading and English reveal that many children, particularly minority children, are being left further and further behind the learning curve. "Despite concerted efforts by educators, the test-score gaps are so large that, on average, African-American and Hispanic students in high school can read and do arithmetic at the average level of Anglos in junior high school. The gaps between African Americans and whites are showing very few signs of closing."[36]

Poverty also affects the nation's elderly. In 2012, 3,926,000 or 9.1 percent of the nation's total population over the age of sixty-five had incomes below the poverty level despite the fact that they were either employed, receiving a work-related pension, social security, and/or an additional form of government-sponsored assistance.[37] These figures would be substantially higher if senior citizens were not receiving Social Security and Medicare benefits. However, lawmakers are concerned that the present Social Security system will not be able to meet the income needs of an expanding senior population with potential life expectancies into their eighties and nineties.

A category of poverty that cannot be overlooked is this nation's homeless population. As previously stated, an accurate accounting of the homeless is virtually impossible. Usually, estimates include those who are living in the streets or in shelters. The numbers vary depending on how one defines the parameters of "homeless." Another factor is the nomadic lifestyle of the homeless. According to the National Alliance to End Homelessness, in 2011, approximately 636,017 were homeless. Additionally, "the national rate of homelessness was 21 homeless people per 10,000 people in the general population. The rate for veterans was 31 homeless veterans per 10,000 veterans in the general population."[38] On a positive note, "the chronically homeless population has decreased by 13 percent since 2007" due to an increase in permanent supportive housing such as San Antonio's Haven for Hope.[39] Additionally,

- permanent supportive housing beds increased from 188,636 in 2007 to 266,968 in 2011.
- a majority of homeless people counted were in emergency shelters or transitional housing programs.
- nearly 4 out of 10 were unsheltered, living on the streets, or in cars, abandoned buildings and other structures not suited for human inhabitation.
- the unsheltered population increased by 2 percent from 239,759 in 2009 to 243,701 in 2011.
- the total number of individuals in homeless families decreased by 1 percent nationally, but increased by 20 percent or more in eleven states.
- homelessness increased in twenty-four states and the District of Columbia.[40]

Among the ranks of the homeless are veterans and the elderly. "In 2010, there was an estimated 76,000 veterans with no place to stay."[41] Although many of the homeless would qualify for food stamps, they simply cannot use them effectively. Without shelter, they cannot carry or store a large amount of perishable food items or can goods. Only a handful of restaurants and fast-food chains will accept food stamps. In 1996, Congress attached a work requirement for food stamp recipients. According to the law, "able-bodied adults without children are required to work for at least 20 hours a week to get food stamps for more than three months out of a three-year period."[42] The majority of the homeless are either too physically or mentally impaired to hold a job or lack employable skills. These individuals are caught in a "Catch 22" situation with no viable solution in sight.

The average American citizen is perplexed about the plight of the homeless. "On one hand, many people want to reach out and help these destitute and troubled men, women, and children; on the other, they are frustrated because, despite so many public and private efforts, nothing has eliminated or even decreased homelessness."[43] Once tolerant city councils are passing ordinances removing homeless persons from their makeshift housing in parks and under expressway underpasses; arresting panhandlers for loitering; and charging winos with public drunkenness. The city council in Asheville, North Carolina enacted an ordinance "barring aggressive panhandling with fines of up to $500 and up to 20 days in jail for people with at least five prior misdemeanors. . . . Orlando [Florida] barred people from sitting or lying on downtown sidewalks, with violators fined

$500 and sent to jail for 60 days. Panhandling was restricted to 'blue boxes' drawn on downtown sidewalks."[44] Patterned after a facility in Florida, several major cities have opted to address their homeless issues by constructing a self-contained homeless community known as Haven for Hope. These facilities provide protected separate housing for both single individuals and families. The centers include health and dental clinics, day care facilities, education and job training centers, etc. The Havens for Hope actually accomplish two major goals. First, they provide necessary services needed to alleviate the adverse impact of being homeless. Second, they provide the means of removing the homeless from the streets. With the goal of ending veteran homelessness by 2015, the Obama administration has been working with the Department of Veterans Affairs to provide federal funding for veteran-specific homeless shelters across the country. For example, the Valor Home in Akron, Ohio, provides accommodations for approximately thirty residents.

Statistics reveal that the poverty stricken are either very young or very old. The majority of the children living in poverty are being raised in single-parent female-headed households. We also know that poverty adversely affects more Anglo individuals and families than other racial groups, although a larger percentage of ethnic minorities live in impoverished conditions. Studies indicate that homelessness can strike anyone at any time, particularly those surviving from paycheck to paycheck. Nor can one overlook the possibility of being unemployed. The economic downturn beginning in 2008 changed the traditional stereotype of the unemployed from the blue-collar factory worker to the white-collar manager. The safety net programs of the traditional welfare system have kept millions from becoming mired in poverty. This is the real picture of poverty. The faces of those living in poverty are not just skid row bums, hobos, and winos. They are, in reality, a cross section of American society.

The Philosophy and Politics of Poverty

The latest round of welfare reform initiatives enjoyed widespread bipartisan support with the Democrat and Republican Parties making it a major campaign issue since the rise of Ronald Reagan in the 1980s. However, their zeal for reform revealed that both political parties were, and still are, sharply divided over the philosophical nature of the concept of welfare and welfare reform. In 1996, lawmakers argued over every aspect of the welfare system from methodical approaches to funding options. The resulting package of reform measures received mixed reviews as critics on both sides of the political spectrum level criticisms and complaints while vowing to enact corrective legislation to address identified program weaknesses. Against the backdrop of a sagging economy, Democrats continued their traditional cry to increase government funding for social service programs as President George W. Bush advocated the traditional conservative Republican complaint that the government spends far too much money on welfare programs. During the campaign, President Barack Obama pledged he would revisit the welfare package enacted in 1996 with the intent of expanding the programs offered to the nation's poor. Although the economy is beginning to recover at a frustrating snail's pace, the Obama administration's focus has been on using federal funds to jumpstart the economy to a faster pace and not on new initiatives to address the nation's poor.

Republican Party leaders openly advocate the traditional conservative belief that economic deprivation is the inevitable result of an individual's failure and, in some cases, laziness to avail one's self of the free market's promise of economic viability and riches. They strongly believe that the

American Dream of economic success is like the brass ring at the carnival. The ring can be grabbed by anyone who possesses the talent, determination, and desire to grab it. It's the individual who makes the choice between success and failure, not the economy or any other outside factor. Conservatives concede that the competitive nature of capitalism will naturally award the brass ring to only a select few because they possess a higher level of competitive skills over others. This competitive edge is often explained by Charles Darwin's concept of the survival of the fittest. Subsequently, "life's circumstances will always put some people into poverty, but the people with initiative will overcome their poverty."[45] Most conservatives, therefore, believe that government should play an extremely limited role in aiding the impoverished with benefits limited to the deserving poor, to the physically and mentally impaired, or to those of advanced age unable to compete and survive.

Extreme conservatives uphold that all welfare programs have failed miserably because the impoverished themselves are just too culturally and intellectually deficient to use government-sponsored programs and benefits to lift themselves out of their poverty. In *The Unheavenly City*, Edward C. Banfield argued that economic deprivation is an inwardly acquired trait that eventually evolves into a culture of poverty. Therefore:

> extreme present-orientedness, not lack of income or wealth, is the principal cause of poverty in the sense of the 'culture of poverty.' Most of those caught up in this culture are unable and unwilling to plan for the future, to sacrifice immediate gratifications in favor of future ones, or to accept the disciplines that are required in order to get and to spend. Their inabilities are probably culturally given in most cases.[46]

It followed, according to this line of reasoning, that the welfare state created by Franklin Roosevelt merely sustained the culture of poverty by making benefit recipients dependent upon the government for their survival.

The election of Ronald Reagan to the White House gave anti-welfare conservative Republicans the opportunity to lay the philosophical groundwork that produced the welfare reform legislation passed by the 104th Congress. A strong advocate of the competitiveness of the free market feature of capitalism, Reagan continuously blamed the welfare system for instilling dependency by robbing benefit recipients of their dignity and self-reliancy. "At the heart of President Reagan's opposition to federal welfare initiatives lies the suspicion that the poor are morally different from the nonpoor—that they do not share the values and aspirations of working Americans, that they do not respond to the incentives and opportunities of the market in the same way as the more prosperous do."[47] Republican-led legislative acts at state and national levels are designed to redirect the poor back to the conservative concept of the proper work ethic by tightening benefit eligibility requirements, limiting benefits, and requiring recipients to work, while at the same time slashing federal budgetary dollars traditionally allocated for social service programs.

The liberal perspective is that:

> those who are living in poverty have not individually created their poverty any more than those who are prosperous have individually produced their wealth. The fine line between success and failure represents one of the most sensitive and complex unsolved phenomena

of the era of space, conglomerates and megalopolises. The future . . . of this nation may well rest upon the effectiveness with which the political and economic leadership recognizes and provides for the needs of the less fortunate.[48]

The Democratic Party became the standard bearer for the liberal perspective with the election of Woodrow Wilson to the presidency. Every Democratic president since has to some degree promoted government sponsored programs to meet the needs of impoverished and lower-income Americans with programs ranging from federally insured student loans to food stamps and Medicaid.

Liberals base their position on three major premises. First, they believe that the historical pattern of economic prosperity followed by devastating recessions, high inflation, and depressions have placed the American worker in constant economic peril. It's the fickleness of the economy and the inability of government to respond to economic upheavals that cause poverty and deprivation. Second, statistics support the liberal contention that far too many hard working Americans are losing economically as the rich become richer and the poor only become poorer. Liberals believe that government has the obligation to assist workers in reversing this trend. They stress that without the intervention of government, "the gap between rich and poor would tend to widen in an advanced economy, generating more unacceptable disparities and straining the fabric of an open, free, and democratic society."[49] Third, liberals believe that economic, social, and political equality for all Americans can be realized only through the efforts of the government. Consequently, the safety net created by President Franklin Roosevelt was designed "not only to seek to prevent extreme deprivation among the most disadvantaged, but also to attempt to cushion the impact of economic misfortune and uncertainty on the more advantaged and affluent members of society. The resulting 'safety net' has been remarkably successful in shielding diverse segments of the population from the full brunt of the vagaries and hardships implicit in a free market economy."[50] Affirmative action legislation helped to open the economic doors to disadvantaged Americans, particularly minorities and women. The Voting Rights Act passed during Lyndon Johnson's term in the White House extended voting privileges to the disenfranchised. The liberal perspective underscores inclusion and equal opportunities to the have nots in their struggles to become haves.

The welfare system and the never ending quest to reform it involves a wide range of interested parties. Of course, welfare recipients are extremely concerned that the elimination of benefits will just deepen rather than help them to overcome their suffering. After all, they are the ones in the "economic bubble" whereby any hint of an economic downslide could cost them their jobs. Requiring welfare recipients to work in order to keep their benefits only works if the jobs they are qualified for are available to them. However, the poor are, in most instances, the silent voices in the public policy process simply because they really do not participate. Few vote or even voice their concerns at public meetings or congressional hearings. The poor do not have the powerful advocates and lobbyists that other interest groups use to affect the public policy process. Yet, their survival may very well hinge on the actions of others who have very little first hand knowledge of the plight of the poor beyond statistical and budgetary reports. The poor were not consulted about the direction and scope of welfare reform.

The elderly have voiced their concerns about the future of Social Security, Medicare, and health-care reform. They want assurances from the national government that the Social Security system is financially sound for themselves and for future generations. Health-care reform has seniors worried as the federal government threatens to cut billions from Medicare programs. They fear that cuts in Medicare coverage will lead to inadequate health care. The lobbyists representing the **American Association of Retired Persons (AARP)** are constantly watching legislative actions at both the state and national level. Talks about health-care reform have disabled veterans worried that their federally funded health-care benefits will be severely cut or eliminated, thereby, leaving the majority of them without any form of health-care coverage. Women's organizations play an important role as they see welfare and health-care reform adversely affecting low-income women and children. They are fearful that any additional reform efforts will result in "a whole new world of hurt coming. A world where you scare people. You confuse them. You threaten to take their benefits and make them scared for their children. And its OK to do this because they are just lazy welfare moms anyway."[56] Far too often, lawmakers and politicians alike from both political parties have used demeaning rhetoric towards the recipients of public assistance programs, particularly women.

The providers of public welfare and health-care assistance are equally concerned whenever lawmakers threaten to reform the system. For example, extreme cuts in the food stamp program can adversely impact the nation's farmers and ranchers. It is their food products that are eventually sold in the nation's supermarkets to both cash and food stamp carrying patrons. Any discussion of health-care reform is closely watched by the owners of the nation's drug companies and health-care providers. Cuts in Medicare and Medicaid are keenly watched by the **American Medical Association (AMA)**, the **American Hospital Association (AHA)**, and other health-care-based interest groups. State and federal cost containment efforts mean less money for health-care providers. Health-care providers are worried that reform means a drastic and tragic loss of quality health care for their patients. The elderly, the impoverished, the children, the disabled veterans, the care providers, the farmers, and so on are the key players involved in the legislative battles over welfare and health-care reform. They have a vested interest either personally or professionally in any legislation involving public assistance and health-care interests. Often at odds with each other, the push for reform has the recipients and the providers of health care and social services on the same side as they desire to see that any reform measure adequately protects their interests.

The Historical Development of the Welfare State

Throughout the history of humankind, civilizations have always recognized their responsibility to address the needs of the deserving poor while at the same time holding an unpleasant distaste for those deemed to be undeserving of their charitable efforts.

> Most people in all cultures enjoy the feeling of helping others, and most cultures consider charity a community or religious duty or a measure of good character. But a distaste for freeloaders also characterizes many cultures. The violator may appear to not really need the help, or to use the help in a bad way, or to not work hard. The giver then feels taken in and may become hostile and resentful. But if the recipient is truly needy and unable to help himself or herself—a child, for example, or a handicapped person—the giver no longer feels exploited or concerned about freeloading. Those mixed feelings about giving and sharing have surrounded aid to the needy for centuries in most cultures.[52]

The distinction between the deserving and undeserving poor has pervaded every public policy initiative addressing this nation's poor since its founding. "The first American settlers understood the relationship between work, survival and dependence. The original colonists came from a broad cross section of English society that included many of England's wandering homeless, vagrants, bona fide criminals, lunatics, and misfits of all sorts."[53] Public sympathy was extended to the aged, the sick, the disabled, and the temporarily impoverished due to economic downturns and job loss. It was a community responsibility to help those in true need. The able-bodied, however, received harsh treatment. "As Cotton Mather put it, 'For those who indulge in idleness, the express command of God unto us is, that we should let them starve.'"[54] The English poor laws served as a foundation for the colonial response to poverty and homelessness. Although programs varied from colony to colony, "there were four basic responses to poverty: auctioning off the poor ('selling' them to the lowest bidder, who agreed to care for and maintain them with public funds), contracting the poor (placing them in private homes at public expense), outdoor relief (basic assistance given outside the confines of a public institution), and the poorhouse (public institutions, also known as indoor relief)."[55]

After the Revolutionary War, the newly created states usually opted for outdoor relief assistance aimed primarily to assist long-term community residents confronted with a serious injury, illness, or death of the breadwinner. Pensions were established for war widows and orphans. Local tax dollars supported relief programs as the national government played practically no major role in social service programs. To offset costs, local authorities used several options including "'**binding out**' (indenturing the poor to families needing laborers or servants), '**farming out**' (requiring men to work for wages that were in turn used for their support), and arrangements similar to modern foster care whereby indigents were placed in homes where they received care or where their children were apprenticed to craftsmen to learn trades."[56] Charges of fraud and abuse, as well as the growing belief that outdoor relief programs were undermining the fabric of American society, led to a new alternative—the poorhouse or **almshouse**.

The poorhouses took the poor, the mentally ill, and the criminal element off the streets. It was believed that "institutional life would not only protect the individual from corrupting influences but also allow the individual to reform."[57] Although popular in the 1820s and 1830s, poorhouses soon became just as distasteful as outdoor relief. Despite reform efforts, poorhouses were targeted by Progressive reformers for their deplorable conditions. Report after report revealed that "graft, corruption, and brutality were common; alcohol was smuggled in; inmates came and went; filth and disorder prevailed; criminals, alcoholics, women, mothers, children, and infants were mixed together. Mortality rates were high."[58] There were no state regulatory laws governing the operation of orphanages and poorhouses. There were, with few exceptions, no requirements for periodic on-sight inspections. Poorhouses and orphanages received little monetary support from state treasuries. Dependent upon private donations, orphanages and poorhouses farmed out their residents as laborers for farmers, ranchers, and businessmen and as servants for private residences. Workers' earnings went directly to the orphanage or the poorhouse to help offset operational costs. The only viable options to the poorhouse were shelters provided through religious or private charity groups, outdoor relief, or an innovative form of the poorhouse called the **settlement house**.

Settlement houses were community centers located in the poor districts of major cities. These centers would provide guidance, services, and basic skills training to anyone living within the neighborhood. Settlement workers were usually recent college graduates from middle and upper class families who lived in the settlement houses. "The settlement house movement unabashedly promoted bourgeois values and habits—instructing the poor in everything from art appreciation and home economics to the importance of establishing savings accounts. To children in poverty, it offered recreation, books, clubs, as well as a sense of the history of American democratic institutions. It approached thousands of the urban poor, particularly children and teenagers, with a message of inclusion in the larger world beyond the slums."[59] Similar to those operating in London, the first American settlement house, known as the **Neighborhood Guild**, was opened by Dr. Stanton Coit in the Lower East Side of New York in 1886. By the turn of the century nearly a hundred settlement houses had been opened throughout the United States. The most notable centers were Jane Addams' **Hull House** in Chicago (1889), Robert A. Woods's South End House in Boston (1892), and Lillian Wald's Henry Street Settlement in New York (1893). Settlement houses were only marginally successful since their reliance upon private donations could not keep up with the cost of maintaining the houses much less meeting the demands of the ever increasing number of impoverished Americans.

The states were extremely ill-prepared for the economic deprivation caused by the crash of the Stock Market in 1929. Millions of hardworking Americans were suddenly unemployed. Their savings were gone since banks were not required to insure their deposits. The city streets were soon crowded with Depression Era homeless. Private charity-sponsored soup kitchens and breadlines could not feed all the hungry. As state coffers dwindled, governors began to turn toward the federal government for assistance and, most importantly, money. The United States Congress enacted the **New Deal** proposals of President Franklin Roosevelt, which included work programs under the **Civilian Conservation Corps**, the **Works Progress Administration**, the **Emergency Relief Administration**, and the **National Youth Corps**. These programs were jointly funded by the national and state governments with the bulk of the funding coming from Washington, D.C.

The current welfare system began in earnest when the United States Congress passed the **Social Security Act of 1935**. This landmark piece of legislation established two major insurance programs geared towards protecting the elderly and the unemployed from slipping into poverty. The **Old Age Insurance** program created a self-funded insurance plan providing pensions and benefits for the elderly and disabled; the **Unemployment Insurance** program assisted workers temporarily laid off their jobs. The Social Security Act also created several public assistance programs including **Old Age Assistance**, **Aid to the Blind**, and **Aid to Dependent Children** (later changed to **Aid to Families with Dependent Children**). The bulk of the New Deal policies were designed as alleviative and preventive actions, that is, temporary public assistance to relieve the suffering while protecting millions more from falling into poverty. These temporary fixes almost became permanent fixtures.

The nation's next major assault on poverty occurred when President Lyndon Johnson introduced his **War on Poverty** program in the 1960s. In a speech delivered on May 22, 1964 at the University of Michigan, President Johnson not only declared war on poverty but introduced his concept of the **Great Society**:

"The Great Society rests on abundance and liberty for all. It demands an end to poverty and racial injustice, to which we are totally committed to in our time. But that is just the beginning. The Great Society is a place where every child can find knowledge to enrich his mind and to enlarge his talents. It is a place where leisure is a welcome chance to build and reflect; not a feared cause of boredom and restlessness. It is a place where the city of man serves not only the needs of the body and the demands of commerce but the desire for beauty and the hunger for community. It is a place where man can renew contact with nature. It is a place which honors creation for its own sake and for what it adds to the understanding of the race. It is a place where men are more concerned with the quality of their goals than the quantity of their goods."[60]

The Johnson administration opted for a curative approach to solving poverty by retaining several of the alleviative and preventive plans created by New Deal initiatives and creating a wide variety of programs designed to address and, hopefully, eliminate poverty. The whole program was based on the belief that poverty could be eliminated by providing the poor with the essential tools needed to lift themselves out of their economic deprivation. An inadequate educational opportunity and the lack of proper job training programs were viewed as two of the primary reasons why many Americans were confronted with a lifetime of at or below minimum wage jobs with extremely limited opportunities for advancement.

The **Economic Opportunity Act of 1965** established the Office of Economic Opportunity designed to coordinate all federal initiatives with state and local governments. The War on Poverty was this nation's first major assault designed to eliminate poverty. The package of antipoverty measures also included programs to enhance the quality of life for the needy through such initiatives as the **Model Cities** program. Federal dollars were allocated for the construction of low-income housing units throughout the nation's economically depressed inner cities. Revitalization plans were encouraged as a means of revamping depressed central business districts in hopes of attracting higher paying job opportunities to inner cities.

Jane Addams in Chicago working at Hull House.

The architects of the New Deal and the War on Poverty programs established the pattern for all subsequent social service initiatives. First, the federal government and state legislative houses realized that the complexity of poverty with its ever increasing numbers of impoverished Americans was beyond the limited abilities of the states to handle totally on their own. The horror story of states scrambling to meet immediate needs of the Depression Era unemployed could not be repeated again. Consequently, the federal government would create the policy response and target a specific service group for benefit coverage. While this provided nationally based responses to national issues and problems, the federal government's role deprived the states of their rights to create their own programs. Consequently, few state lawmakers have created innovative public assistance programs independent of the federal government.

Second, program funding was either totally or partially provided by the federal government. Leaving the states off-the-hook, the federal government allowed the states to become totally dependent upon federal funding to assist their state's impoverished. State legislatures could create budgets with the lowest allocations possible for social service programs knowing that the federal government would foot the bill.

Third, the states would continue to receive federal funding only if they complied with the minimal requirements set by the federal government. For example, each state was required to create a separate state agency to administer each federal program. The federal government assumed the majority of the responsibility for funding the program while leaving the administrative chores to the individual states. However, the creation of a multiplicity of state agencies merely complements the

FDR at the Grand Coulee Dam in Washington. October 2, 1937

Grand Coulee Dam on the Columbia River in Washington, which created a 150-mile long lake. Together with the Bonneville Dam (also on the Columbia), the Grand Coulee gave the Pacific Northwest the cheapest electricity in the nation and created the potential for significant economic and population growth. TheBonneville and Grand Coulee Dams made the state of Washington the largest per capita recipient of New Deal funds. The benefits of this dam building program, in terms of economic development and population growth, did not come to fruition until the post-World War II years.

fragmentary and decentralized organization of state governments creating duplication of services, mounds of red tape, and little accountability on the part of state agencies.

Fourth, the federal government permitted the states to set their own eligibility requirements, benefit amounts, service delivery options, and punitive sanctions for abuse as long as the states followed the minimal eligibility and benefit standards set by the federal government. Consequently, the majority of state programs use the punitive public policy approach by just tightening the eligibility requirements every year to guarantee that only the truly deserving receive assistance. Each year, stiffer penalties are attached to each program to guard against fraud and abuse. Unfortunately, the zeal to attached punitive sanctions has cast a suspicious eye on anyone seeking government assistance. Statistics reveal a discrepancy between those in economic need and those receiving government-sponsored assistance. Many needy Americans simply do not apply for assistance because of the stigmatized image associated with "welfare."

Finally, benefit allocations vary from state to state. States can opt to pay only the minimal benefit amount, which is usually totally funded by the federal government, or they can add-on their own allocation to the minimum. "In general, programs tend to be most generous in states with wealth, strong labor unions, high voter turnout by poor people, and liberal political beliefs or cultures. The generous states are found disproportionately in the Northeast, Midwest, and Pacific regions, and the least generous states tend to be in the South, Southwest, and Rocky Mountain regions."[61]

The Programs of the Welfare State Entitlements:
Social Security and Unemployment Compensation

Initially, both **Social Security** and **unemployment compensation** were marketed as temporary programs. Today, they are viewed by some as absolute guaranteed rights for American workers. Millions of retired American citizens believe that they "toiled for years to send Uncle Sam a mountain of dollar bills. These taxes went into individual accounts with their names and Social Security numbers emblazoned on them; now, seniors are simply withdrawing what is rightfully their own."[62] Yet, "Social Security has never been an insurance program, it has never been a contract that we make with ourselves to fund our own retirement, and our tax money is not set aside in a trust fund, as advertised. Nor are our benefits tied to how much we paid in taxes. Most people get back many times what they put in, even after interest is accounted for. To be precise, Social Security is an intergenerational transfer of money from workers to non-workers. Kind of like welfare. Exactly like welfare."[63] The United States Supreme Court settled the issue by its 1960 ruling in *Flemming v Nestor* that Social Security is not a guaranteed right. Justice John Harlan noted that Social Security was "designed to function into the indefinite future, and its specific provisions rests on predictions as to expected economic conditions, which must inevitably prove less than wholly accurate, and on judgments and preferences as to the proper allocation of the nation's resources which evolving economic and social conditions will of necessity in some cases modify."[64]

Social Security is funded through payroll taxes paid by employees and employers. Workers are eligible to receive benefits as early as age 55 if they are deemed unemployable due to permanent disabilities. The benefit amount is based on the individual worker's work history, including length of employment as well as salary history. Those retirees that worked the majority of their adult lives at higher paying jobs will receive a higher benefit amount over those who worked just as long but at lower paying jobs. In 2010, retired workers received an average monthly benefit of $1,176, retired workers with wives $1,930, disabled workers $1,068 and widows and widowers $1,134.[65] Usually Social Security recipients receive a yearly cost of living adjustment ranging between 2 to 3 percent. However, the monthly benefits plus a marginal yearly adjustment simply leave little disposable income for expenses beyond the essentials of food, shelter and clothing. Therefore, the monthly benefits for the average retired worker are not enough to maintain a comfortable lifestyle. Many elderly receive just enough in benefits to put them into the **safety net**, just one perilous step away from poverty.

Initially, seniors were subjected to an earnings penalty that required the government to deduct $1 in Social Security benefits for every $3 dollars earned by seniors under the age of 70. It was estimated that "more than 800,000 lost part or all of their benefits because of the earnings limit."[66] Once the Social Security recipient turned 70, he or she could earn as much as they could without any reductions in benefits. In 2000, President Clinton signed legislation removing the earnings penalty. Now seniors regardless of their age, can continue to work full or part-time jobs without the fear of losing their full Social Security benefits. If Social Security was a true pension program, retirees would receive benefits equal only to what they initially paid into the plan. Social Security, however, guarantees benefits for the life of the retired worker with survivor benefits for their female spouses of 50 percent of the original benefit. Consequently, there is a point where Social Security ceases to be a pension and becomes an entitlement or public assistance payment. **Entitlements** are "benefits provided by government to which recipients have a legally enforceable right."[67] Social Security, Medicare, veteran's benefits, and military retirement are entitlement programs.

The survival of Social Security has lawmakers searching for remedies to keep the program soluble and intact. Currently, the total amount of employee/employer contributions is sufficient to provide benefits for today's retirees. Yet, statistics do indicate an alarming increase in the number of retirees living longer with an offsetting decrease in wage earners. "The Social Security system faces rising gaps between revenues and promised benefits starting in 2017 and an exhaustion of trust fund assets in 2041."[68] Proposals to save Social Security include reducing annual cost-of-living adjustments (COLAs), reducing benefits for high-income beneficiaries, increasing the Social Security payroll tax, increasing the amount of earnings subject to the payroll tax, taxing Social Security like a private pension program, establishing individual accounts, allowing workers to invest a portion of their potential Social Security benefits, and, if all else fails, reducing or actually cutting benefits.

Unemployment compensation was designed to be a temporary entitlement benefit for temporarily displaced workers. Mandated by the federal government, the states determine eligibility requirements, benefit allocations, and benefit time frames. Not every unemployed worker automatically receives unemployment benefits. In most states, individuals who have been involuntarily separated from their employment through no fault of their own will receive full benefits. However, in several states, voluntary separations and terminations by employee actions result in reduced payments or no benefits at all. Recipients are required to continue to search for work or lose their benefits. Generally, it is extremely difficult for unemployed recipients to make financial ends meet. This is particularly problematic for the higher-end of the salary scale employee who loses his/her job.

Public Assistance Programs

The bulk of state and federal public assistance programs are means-tested plans providing in-kind services or cash transfer benefits. **Means-tested eligibility** is based upon the applicant's documented inability to provide for his/herself the desired benefit because of depressed income levels. Basic welfare and Supplemental Security Income (SSI) are two of the cash-transfer programs available to the needy. Each program is available to those who meet the qualifications. For example, the federally funded **Supplemental Security Income** program was designed to provide cash payments to lower income elderly, the blind, disabled adults, and children. To qualify, recipients must have incomes below 185 percent of the poverty level. **In-kind programs** are means-tested services providing "assistance that has a cash value even though it is not received in cash."[69] Subsidized public housing and day care, Medicare, the special supplemental program for Women, Infants, and Children (WIC), food stamps, and legal services are examples of in-kind assistance programs.

Originally introduced in 1964 to the American public as the Food Stamp Program, the Supplemental Nutrition Assistance Program is designed to provide an in-kind exchange of coupons for food items to offset nutritional deficiencies and hunger among America's needy. Administered by the Department of Agriculture through state and county public assistance agencies, the program is totally funded by the national government to include two-thirds of state and county administrative costs. The stamps are supposed to be used to buy staple products, not items that cannot be consumed such as paper products, household cleaners, and so on.

The Census Bureau defines **food secure** as "a household [that] had access at all times to enough food for an active healthy life for all household members, with no need for recourse to socially unacceptable food sources or extraordinary coping behaviors to meet their basic food needs. **Food insecure** households had limited or uncertain ability to acquire acceptable foods in socially acceptable ways. Food insecure households with hunger were those with one or more household members who were hungry at least sometime during the period due to inadequate resources for food."[70] Food stamps have become for many Americans a household necessity simply because their paychecks cannot be stretched enough to cover rent, day care, utilities, and medical costs, plus monthly food costs. It is estimated that 50 percent of a low-income wage-earner's paycheck goes for rent or the mortgage payment. Since the onset of the nation's current economic downturn, the number of food stamp participants has increased substantially. "In fiscal year 2011, about 44.7 million people living in 21.1 million U.S. households participated in SNAP on average per month. . . . Most SNAP participants were children or the elderly."[71] The SNAP program provides an average monthly benefit of only $281; however, "forty-one percent of SNAP households received the maximum benefit for their family size—$668 for a family of four."[72] Unfortunately, many Americans who are in need of food stamps opt not to participate in the program either because of the complicated application process or they are too embarrassed to ask for government assistance. With the passage of the Elementary and Secondary Education Act during the Johnson Administration, the federal government has funded school lunch subsidiary programs providing a free lunch to children whose parents simply cannot afford to provide them with one. The program was expanded to include breakfast which in 2010 provided a free or reduced cost meal to 12,000,000 children at a cost of $2,895,000,000.[73] Without these federally-funded meal programs, these children would probably receive only one meal per day. The Obama Administration has urged that both the Departments of Agriculture and Education push public and private schools to offer nutritious fat-free meals and restrict vending machines to selling only healthy products as a way to offset the growing number of obese children. Since the free lunch and breakfast programs are only available during the normal school year term, many community organizations, and public and private schools, as well as higher educational institutions, have used federal grant money for summer school programs. These programs provide school-age children with additional educational opportunities, nutritious meals, and for their working parents, free child care services.

As with any federally-funded assistance program, critics point out that SNAP is too costly for the government to fund and is riddled with abuse and fraud. Basically, SNAP provides recipients with a coupon book. This does allow the recipient to receive cash back when the grocery bill is less than the face value of the coupons. Some have been charged with selling their stamps to someone else or exchanging the coupons for items not covered under the program. Some states like Texas have addressed this problem by using a pre-approved line-of-credit card that can be used for only approved grocery purchases. However, the majority of program recipients do not abuse the program nor do they participate in fraud. For those who simply do not participate in the program or do not meet eligibility requirements, cities and community organizations across the nation have established food banks whose shelves are stocked through private donations. Community-based voluntary food programs also include meals-on-wheels that deliver hot prepared meals to qualifying elderly and disabled individuals.

The **Special Supplemental Program for Women, Infants and Children,** commonly known as **WIC,** was created to provide nutritional food staples to pregnant women, breastfeeding mothers, mothers up to six months after giving birth, and children under the age of five. Funded by the federal government, this program is administered by the Food and Nutrition Service of the Department of Agriculture with assistance from state and county public agencies. Recipients receive vouchers for food items including milk, iron-fortified infant formula, cheese, eggs, fruit juice, cereals, peanut butter, and beans. The WIC program provides immunizations and prenatal care for free or at a nominal fee. The WIC program has been very successful in reducing health-care costs by treating infants with low birth weights. Additionally funded federal programs include Head Start, Summer Food Service Program, Elderly Nutrition Program, Emergency Food Assistance Program (TEFAP), Commodity Distribution Program, Food Distribution on Indian Reservations (FDPIR), and the Hunger and Food Insecurity program.

The Reform Bandwagon

The political climate of the 1980s and 1990s compelled state legislative houses across this country to enact their own welfare reform initiatives. With few exceptions, state lawmakers took a punitive approach by placing time limits on benefits, requiring recipients to seek work, stiffening eligibility requirements, and placing stronger punitive measures to curb abuse. Although an advocate of welfare reform, President Clinton reluctantly signed into law the **Personal Responsibility and Work Opportunity Act** on July 31, 1996. His signature ushered in the long-awaited package of welfare reform initiatives destined to revamp the system established over 50 years ago. In some respects, this legislation merely duplicated many of the punitive measures already adopted by several states. The legislation's major provisions include:

A) Limiting lifetime welfare benefits to five years.
B) Requiring the head of household to find work within two years or the entire family will lose its benefits.
C) Mandating that at least half of all single parents in any state be employed or involved in work-related activities such as school or job training. However, the new federal law prevents state governments from penalizing women on welfare who are unable to secure day care for their children under six years of age.
D) Limiting all childless adults between 18 and 50 years of age to three months of food stamps during a three-year period. Workers who have exhausted their three month supply of food stamps can apply for an additional three months if they are laid off their jobs during the three-year period.
E) Requiring unwed teenage mothers to live with their parents and attend school to receive benefits. Furthermore, the law does give the states the latitude to deny benefits to teenage mothers who do not meet the new requirements and to children born while the mother is receiving benefits.
F) Prohibiting food stamps and cash aid to anyone convicted of felony drug charges. However, pregnant women and adults in drug programs are exempt.
G) Prohibiting future legal immigrants from receiving Medicaid benefits during their first five years of residency in the United States.

The federal government did soften the punitiveness of the reform package by inserting provisions for exemptions; establishing funding requirements on the states designed to prevent states from eliminating all of their social service programs; and providing additional federal funds to offset potential economic crises such as recessions and periods of high unemployment. Each state is allowed hardship exemptions up to 20 percent of their current welfare cases. This provision ensures a continuation of benefits for the elderly and disabled citizens. The states are also prohibited from dramatically slashing their state budgetary allocations for social service programs. States must maintain their social service budgets at 80 percent of their 1994 levels or face severe reductions in their federal funding. The federal law does provide additional federal funding to states with high unemployment rates or fast-growing populations.

Welfare Reform – Is It Working?

The success of any welfare reform package is tied directly to the nation's economic ups and downs. Initially, one could declare welfare reform a success. Statistically, more poverty-level Americans were removed from the public dole. More were finding employment. But, the question of whether the poor were truly benefiting from welfare reform still plagued lawmakers. Were the income gains of the poor meaningful enough to ensure that they were, as promised, never again to seek public assistance for their daily survival? Were the job opportunities viable ones that would eventually lead to salary increases and possible promotions? Was the economy strong enough in the long run to ensure that the poor were no longer the likely victims of economic downturns?

The initial setting for welfare reform could not have occurred at a better time. The United States economy was booming. The service sector generated an ample number of positions for those with marginal and limited job skills. However, these jobs are usually at minimum or slightly above minimum wage with very little opportunities for advancement. A minimum wage salary simply will not provide enough income to cover the costs of rising rents, gasoline, food, day care, clothing and of course, health care. For welfare reform, true success meant that a former recipient of benefits was able to earn enough to safely say that they had left 'the system' behind. The economic downturn beginning in 2006 has meant a statistical reversal as more and more Americans lost their jobs, their homes, and their credit ratings. As previously pointed out, 2010 saw a steady rise in the poverty rate to the point that it has now surpassed the 1960 rate, which was at that time the highest since the Great Depression. As states are wrestling with their own budget deficits by cutting their contributions to social service programs, more Americans are turning to their local food banks for support.

"More than half of the people seeking emergency food were members of families; two-thirds of the adults were employed. More than one-third of the homeless are families with children. That may be fueled partially by welfare-reform efforts in states, which have placed people in jobs generally paying less than $10,000 a year."[74] Food banks are having a difficult time keeping up with the demand.

Basically, this latest attempt to revamp the welfare system has failed once again to adequately address the needs of the nation's poor. Relying solely upon the take home pay of a low paying job simply does not provide enough income to adequately cover the costs of food, shelter, clothing, day care, and health insurance to this nation's lower-income citizens. If the original intent of welfare reform was to reduce the number of people on public assistance, one can say the program was initially a success. But, if the original intent of welfare reform was to provide the poverty-stricken with the tools to achieve the self-sufficiency required to obtain the income necessary to be above the poverty level over the long term, then the program has been a failure. As previously mentioned, any economic down turn is devastating to this nation's poor. "What if, for poor families, this truly is as good as it gets?"[75]

Health-care Reform

Vowing to revamp the nation's health-care system, candidate Barack Obama told millions of Americans about his personal experience with the existing health-care system as he watched his terminally ill mother suffer through the last stages of breast cancer while at the same time battling with insurance companies, doctors, and hospitals over whether certain procedures were covered, and working through the mounds of forms, bureaucratic red tape, and the ever-growing pile of unpaid medical and drug bills. On March 23, 2010, President Obama signed into law a highly partisan and very controversial sweeping health-care package aimed to meet his goals of a) providing insurance to nation's uninsured; b) reducing rising health-care costs; c) shifting the emphasis of health care from reactionary to preventive; and d) correcting deficiencies in the prescription drug legislation passed during the Bush administration.

Currently, the United States is still the only highly industrialized nation in the world without a universal coverage national health-care plan. The anticipation of 48 million uninsured Americans actually becoming insured was "put on hold" as the October 1, 2013, enrollment kickoff did not happen. With so many entering into the official website, the software crashed. Eventually and gradually, the software has been repaired and many are receiving health-care coverage for the first time. For so many, the price is what the law said it is—the Affordable Care Act. For example, "a middle-age woman, never before insured, learned that a large tax credit would enable her to purchase a $300 per-month health plan for just $25 per month."[76] Whatever it is called, the Obama administration had to wrestle with the reality that "the cost of private health insurance is increasing at an annual rate of 12 percent. Individuals were paying more out-of-pocket costs and receiving fewer benefits."[77] Without substantial health-care reform, "within a decade, an aging America will spend one of every five dollars on health care . . . The nation's total health care bill by 2015: more than $4 trillion. Consumers will foot about half the bill, the government the rest. . . Overall, the analysts forecast a 7.2 percent annual increase in health care costs over the coming decade."[78] The premise behind ACA is the same with any group insurance plan. The more enrollees you have in the plan, the less costly it is for each enrollee. Also, it is hoped that the federal government can reduce costs in both the Medicaid and Medicare programs by shifting the health care industry's emphasis from reactionary more costly procedures to the less expensive preventive health care option.

In addition to the ADA, the three basic publicly funded programs are Medicaid, Medicare and the Children's Health Insurance Program. A jointly funded federal and state program, **Medicaid**, was created in 1965 as part of the War on Poverty. Medicaid was designed as a preventive health-care system whereby a child with a cold would receive the medication necessary to prevent that cold from developing into a potentially life-threatening illness mandating more costly health-care services. Medicaid is an in-kind program with the payment given directly to the provider of the service. Medicaid spending consists of direct payments issued for outpatient and inpatient care services, hospital care, nursing home services, and long-term care facilities. Since the patients receive no direct cash payments, charges of fraud, overpricing, and unnecessary medical treatments must be rightfully levied at the health-care providers. Initially, the program provided benefits to only those receiving AFDC (Aid to Families with Dependent Children) or SSI benefits. Congress extended Medicaid coverage in 1972 by adding benefits for nursing home and intermediate care facilities for the treatment of the mentally ill. Coverage for prenatal, obstetrics, and follow up medical care for one year for pregnant women was added in 1986. By 1988, states were required to extend Medicaid coverage for one year after families became ineligible for AFDC benefits to allow time for personal economic recoveries. Congress also lowered the original eligibility requirements to include children up to age six. In 1990, Congress extended coverage to include children up to age eighteen. The 1996 welfare reform legislation officially changed the name of AFDC to the Temporary Assistance to Needy Families (TANF). The cost of Medicaid alone in part moved the Obama administration to launch Obamacare. In 2009, Medicaid enrollment hit an all-time high of 47,469,000 Americans, representing 15.6 percent of the nation's total population. Approximately, 19,919,000 enrollees have incomes below the poverty level while the remaining 27,500,000 earn incomes that qualify them for the program simply because they cannot afford to purchase their own health care coverage.[79] The costs of the program are staggering. In 2010, Medicaid providers were paid $254,180,000,000 for Part A hospital insurance benefits, $204,855,000,000 for Part B supplementary medical insurance benefits, and an additional $63,525,000,000 for Part D supplementary medical insurance benefits.[80] The costs of this program are shared between federal and state governments. To help the states ease their Medicaid burden, President George W. Bush signed into law in 2008 a Medicaid reform package that enabled the states to charge recipients premiums and higher co-payments for doctor's visits, hospital care, and prescription medications. The legislation also gave the states the latitude to drop coverage for those who opted not to pay the additional fees. States can opt not to participate in Medicaid, but the cost to the states to bear the total cost of providing health care for their needy would be staggering.

Although Medicaid provides insurance coverage to the nation's poor, it does not cover children raised in families whose incomes are too high to qualify for Medicaid coverage but are still too low to afford the premiums for dependent care coverage. Enacted by Congress in 1997 and extended in 2009 with the passage of the Children's Health Insurance Program Reauthorization Act (CHIP) low-cost health insurance was provided through a federal/state partnership with the federal government bearing the financial costs of the plan. Although many of the nation's children still are without health-care coverage, 7,718,400 were enrolled in the program in 2010, an increase of over 4 million since 2000. In 2010, the federal government paid an estimated $7,913,000 in plan reimbursements back to participating state governments.[81]

Medicare was supposed to be the nation's health-care plan extending coverage to all Americans. The ensuing battle between conservatives against the plan and the liberal camp promoting it resulted in a program that basically provides coverage only to the nation's elderly. Liberals originally hoped that over time, coverage would be expanded in a incremental fashion with children first, followed by pregnant women and other groups until the goal of universal coverage was achieved. "All Medicare enthusiasts took for granted that the rhetoric of enactment should emphasize the expansion of access, not the regulation and overhaul of United States medicine. The clear aim was to reduce the risks of financial disaster for the elderly and their families, and the clear understanding was that Congress would demand a largely hands-off posture towards doctors and hospitals providing the care that Medicare would provide."[82] Coverage is automatically granted to all persons over 65 who had paid Social Security taxes during their working lives and to their spouses. Funded totally by the federal government, the Medicare plan is administered by the Social Security Administration. The program provides two plans of health coverage. Part A, commonly known as HI, provides mandatory hospitalization coverage. Part B permits participants to purchase through beneficiary premiums and general tax revenues coverage for doctor's fees and other medical expenses to include prescription drugs. Basically, a program that started out as a universal health-care plan has become a very limited plan geared primarily for retired workers over age sixty-five. Not all of the nation's seniors receive coverage.

The Bush administration launched its health-care reform package by focusing on Plan B of the original Medicare legislation. Passed in 2003, the Medicare Prescription Drug Improvement and Modernization Act was hailed as "the most sweeping change to Medicare since its founding in 1965," with the primary purpose of bringing "the accelerating costs of prescription drugs under control."[83] A controversial piece of legislation, Republican leaders were able to gradually garner the support of the American Association of Retired Persons (AARP) into its camp. AARP leadership felt that although the bill had major flaws, it was a baby step in the right direction to addressing the rising costs of medical care and prescription drugs. However, many rank and file AARP members were outraged, resorting to canceling their memberships and tearing up their AARP cards. The major provisions of the legislation included increasing the premium of the Part B Medicare Plan on a sliding scale whereby those with incomes over $200,000 would pay 80 percent of their premiums; raising the deductible to $110 and providing a tax shelter for those individuals with high-deductible health insurance. The plan, however, still maintained that the private sector and not the public sector would provide the insurance plans and coverage options to participants.

The most controversial section of the legislation dealt with prescription drugs. On paper, the new approach seemed to be simple. The drug portion of Medicare is known as Plan D. "In addition to a monthly premium, seniors must pay for the first $250 in annual costs for covered drugs, the standard deductible. When the year's drug costs reach $251, plan participants start paying out-of-pocket 25 percent of the cost [of the medications] until their contributions hit $2,250. Then comes the infamous 'doughnut hole' in which Part D enrollees are responsible for the entire cost of drugs between $2,251 and $5,100. Above that, catastrophic coverage must kick in, whereby seniors shall out just a small portion (5 percent of the cost or a co-pay of a few dollars) of their annual drug costs."[84] One of the problems is that the cycle begins anew every January 1. Seniors can opt to stay with their current Medicare managed plan, their company retirement plan or opt for a private insurance carrier that offers a medical plan with prescription drug coverage. Basically, "the government is subsidizing dozens of private insurers to offer then own plans (many are offering more than one), which have to meet or exceed the federal government's drug benefit standard. The plans will either be stand-alone prescription drugs plans (PDPs) to supplement Medicare's existing medical coverage or will be part of a more comprehensive Medicare private health plan like a health maintenance or preferred provider organization."[85] Regardless of the plan they picked, seniors found out quickly that their annual drug costs fell into the doughnut hole when they went to the pharmacy to pick up their medications thinking they only had to pay a co-pay but instead had to pay the full amount. Unable to pay the full costs of the prescriptions, seniors were once again facing the choice that this reform package was supposed to fix. They were counting the number of pills they could afford, regardless of the medical necessity of taking the full amount of pills for the prescribed period of time. This situation basically leaves the elderly with only two choices. First, they can purchase medigap insurance to supplement their Medicare coverage. Supplemental insurance usually pays 80 percent or better of the costs not covered by Medicare once the policyholder's expenses exceed the standard deductible amounts. Second, those unable to purchase medigap plans must just limit their health-care options to what they can afford with Medicare. The Obama health care law partially fixes the doughnut problem with an initial $150 rebate and providing a 50 percent discount on prescriptions purchased in the doughnut hole range.

Another area of concern is the claims of fraudulent use of both Medicaid and Medicare by health-care providers and drug companies. In particular, the Obama administration wants to reign in Medicare fraud claims of over-charging for basic medical services, billing errors, billing for unnecessary equipment and procedures, or billing for services never rendered. It is estimated that Medicare loses $60 to $90 billion a year that if recaptured would help to fund Obama's health-care initiatives.[86]

Supporters of the Obama health-care reform effort point out that this is the first time the federal government has developed a comprehensive approach to addressing this nation's health-care issues. Since the New Deal legislation, health care has been reformed in a incremental fashion. The Johnson administration implemented Medicare for the qualifying elderly and Medicaid for the poor. In 1996, the Clinton administration supported the passage of legislation allowing already covered workers to obtain immediate health-care coverage after a change of jobs even if they had a pre-existing illness. It also mandated that new employees had to receive health-care coverage within twelve months of hire. Furthermore, the measure included tax-deductible medical savings accounts primarily for the self-employed and those employed by small companies unable to offer group plans. Whether Obama is successful is seeing the entire reform package implemented is still in limbo.

CONCLUSION

Can the federal government and state legislative houses turn a blind eye to this nation's poor, old, disabled and sick? The answer is a resounding no. Should government and society as a whole provide the incentives and avenues for the impoverished to be less dependent upon the dole and gain self-sufficiency and economic security? Yes, of course. For too long government at all levels has taken the path of providing assistance that just attempts to ease the suffering and prevent it from becoming worse. However, the suffering has not been eased enough. The recent economic downturn has only meant that more people are poor, homeless, and jobless. The fear of becoming poor has not abated, nor has the costs of maintaining the welfare system decreased at all. We are still a frustrated nation! Morally, we cannot stand by and do nothing for starving, impoverished, elderly, and disabled citizens. Financially, we cannot afford to provide for all of their needs. The heart stretches out but the wallet cannot keep up with the pace. Politically, partisan politics levels the blame of the party in power for not fixing the problems and decries the party that tries to fix them. We simply do not have an answer to address the reasons behind chronic poverty and homelessness.

CHAPTER NOTES

[1] "49.7 Million Americans in Poverty, Census Bureau Says," *Business on NBC News*, November 14, 2012, http://www/nbcnews.com.business.
[2] Rana Foroohar, "The Truth About the Poverty Cricis," *Time*, September 26, 2011, 24.
[3] Ibid.
[4] "49.7 Million Americans in Poverty, Census Bureau Says."
[5] Stephen Ohlemacher, "Economy Slid in 2005-2007," *San Antonio Express-News*, (Tuesday, December 9, 2008), 3A.
[6] *Statistical Abstract of the United States: 2010*, 129th ed., Table 695, 456.
[7] U.S. Census Bureau, *Statistical Abstract of the United States: 2012*, 131st ed., (Washington, D.C., 2011), Table 711, 464.
[8] Ibid., Table 594, 382.
[9] "49.7 Million Americans in Poverty, Census Bureau Says."
[10] Alan Zibel, "1 in Texas Homeowners in Trouble," *San Antonio Express-News*, (Saturday, December 6, 2008), 1A.
[11] Michael Luo, "80% Increase in Homelessness Seen," *San Antonio Express-News*, (Sunday, September 12, 2010), 11A.
[12] "House Oks Plan That Slashes Social Services," *San Antonio Express-News* (Friday, May 11, 2012), A11.
[13] Ibid.
[14] Jonathan Alter, "The Other America: An Enduring Shame," *Newsweek*, September 19, 2005, 42.
[15] *The American Heritage Dictionary of the English Language: New College Edition,* (Boston: Houghton Mifflin Co., 1982), 1027.
[16] Louis Uchitelle, "Census Bureau May Raise Poverty Level," *San Antonio Express-News* (Monday, October 18, 1999), 7A.
[17] John J. Harrigan and David C. Nice, *Politics and Policy in States and Communities,* 8th ed., (New York, New York: Pearson Education, Inc., 2004), 332.

[18] Randall Bland, Alfred B. Sullivan, Robert E. Biles, Charles P. Elloitt, Jr., and Beryl E. Pettus, *Texas Government Today*, 5th ed. (Pacific Grove, Calif.: Brooks/Cole Publishing Co., 1992), 431.
[19] "Committee to Recommend Broader Definition of Poverty," *The Dallas Morning News*, (Sunday, April 30, 1995), 4A.
[20] "49.7 Million Americans in Poverty, Census Bureau Says."
[21] Harrigan, 332.
[22] Molly Ivins, "The Working Poor Have Names, Faces," *San Antonio Express-News* (Monday, January 3, 2000), 5B.
[23] Randy Albelda, "Fallacies of Welfare-To-Work Policies," *The Annals*, The American Academy of Political and Social Science, Vol. 577, September, 2001, 66-78, 72.
[24] Ibid., 72-73.
[25] "*F-7-Type of Family, All Races by Median and Mean Income*, 1947-2012, U.S. Census Bureau, http://www.census.gov/main.
[26] *Statistical Abstract of the United States: 2012*, 131st ed., Table 447, 284.
[27] Alter, 44.
[28] Alice S. Baum and Donald W. Burnes, *A Nation in Denial: The Truth About the Homeless*, (Boulder, Colorado: Westview Press, 1993), 3.
[29] "Table 3-People in Poverty By Selected Characteristics: 2011 and 2012," *Current Population Survey, 2012-2013 Annual Social and Economic Supplements*, U.S. Census Bureau, http://www.census.gov.
[30] Ibid.
[31] Ibid.
[32] "Poverty in the United States Frequently Asked Questions," *National Poverty Center*, University of Michigan, http://www.npc.unmich.edu/poverty.
[33] "Portrait of a Poor City: The Facts of Life," *San Antonio Light*, (Sunday, August 18, 1991), 6.
[34] Ibid.
[35] Baum, 45.
[36] Sam Dillion, "Studies See Little Progress for No Child Left Behind," *San Antonio Express-News*, (Monday, November 20, 2006), 4A.
[37] "Table 3-People in Poverty By Selected Characteristics: 2011-2012".
[38] "*State of Homelessness in American 2012*," National Alliance to End Homelessness, 2012, http://www.endhomelessness.org.
[39] Ibid.
[40] Ibid.
[41] "Shelter for Homeless Veterans Expects A Waiting List," *San Antonio Express-News* (Sunday, July 14, 2013), A9.
[42] Philip Brasher, "Advocates Allege Homeless Unfairly Denied Food Stamps," *San Antonio Express-News* (Wednesday, November 24, 1999) 7A.
[43] Ibid., 11.
[44] Robert Tanner, "Cities Pushing Back At Pushy Panhandlers," *San Antonio Express-News* (Sunday, December 22, 2002), 22A.
[45] Harrigan, 337.
[46] Edward C. Banfield, *The Unheavenly City*, (Boston: Little, Brown, and Company, 1970), 125-126.
[47] Sar A. Levitan, "How the Welfare System Promotes Economic Security," *Political Science Quarterly*, (The Academy of Political and Social Science, Vol. 26, No. 3, Fall, 1985, 449.
[48] Edward J. Harpham, "Welfare Reform in Perspective," *Texas At the Crossroads: People, Politics and Policy*, Anthony Champagne and Edward J. Harpham, eds., (College Station, Texas: Texas A & M University Press, 1987), 283.
[49] Levitan, 453.
[50] Ibid., 447-448.
[51] Helen O'Neill, "Welfare Well Drying Up," *Houston Chronicle*, (Sunday, June 9, 1996), (4A-5A), 5A.
[52] Linda Gordon, "Who Deserves Help? Who Must Provide," *The Annals*, The American Academy of Political and Social Science, Vol. 577, September 2001, 12-24, 14.
[53] Baum, 92.
[54] Joel F. Handler, *The Poverty of Welfare Reform*, (New Haven, Conn.: Yale University Press, 1995), 12.
[55] Ibid.
[56] Baum, 92.
[57] Handler, 14.
[58] Ibid., 16.
[59] Howard Hysock, Fighting Poverty the Old-Fashioned Way," *The Wilson Quarterly*, Vol. XIV, No. 2, Spring, 1990, 78-9l, 80.
[60] "Lyndon Baines Johnson, President of the United States, 1963-1969: The Great Society," *Documents of Texas History*, Ernest Wallace, David M. Vigness and George B. Ward, eds. (Austin, TX: State House Press, 1994), 289-290.
[61] Harrigan, 342.

[62] Susan Dentzer, "You're Not As Entitled as You Think," *U.S. News & World Report,* (March 20, 1995), 67.
[63] Joel Achenbach, "Why Poorer Classes Foot The Social Security Bill," *San Light* (Sunday, June 2, 1990) L1.
[64] Michael Barone, "Future Shock," *U.S. News & World Report*, June 13, 2005, 38.
[65] *Statistical Abstract of the United States: 2012*, 131st ed., Table 545, 355.
[66] "'Earnings Penalty' Removal Endorsed," *San Antonio Express-News* (Sunday, February 20, 2000) 13A.
[67] Jack C. Plano and Milton Greenburg, *The American Political Dictionary* (Orlando, Florida: Harcourt, Brace and Jananovich College Publishers, 1993), 489.
[68] Barone, 38.
[69] Harrigan, 347.
[70] *Statistical Abstract of the United States: 2010*, 129th ed., Table 209, 135.
[71] "Characteristics of Supplemental Nutrition Assistance Program – Households, Fiscal Year 2011 Summary," *United States Department of Agriculture Food and Nutrition Service*, November, 2012, www.fns.usda.gov.ora.
[72] Ibid.
[73] Ibid.
[74] Richard Wolf, "Survey Pegs Part of Crisis on Wages," *San Antonio Express-News* (Thursday, December 16, 1999) 17A.
[75] Goodman, 5B.
[76] "Health Website Getter Better Reviews," *San Antonio Express-News* (Tuesday, December 3, 2013), 1A.
[77] Robert Pear, "Panel Says Health Care Is In Critical Condition," *San Antonio Express-News* (November 20, 2002),6A.
[78] "No Cure Seen for Rising Medical Bills," *San Antonio Express-News* (Wednesday, February 22, 2006), 2A.
[79] *Statistical Abstract of the United States: 2012*, 131st ed., Table 148, 107.
[80] Ibid., Table 149, 108.
[81] Ibid., Table 145, 106.
[82] Ted Marmar and Julie Beglin, "Medicare and It Grew...and Grew...and Grew...," *San Antonio Express-News*, (June 25, 1995), 21.
[83] Travis E. Poling and Gary Martin, 'Medicare Rewrite Is Not A Cure-All," *San Antonio Express-News*, (Friday, December 26, 2003), 1A.
[84] Katherine Hobson, "How The Plan Works," *U.S. News & World Report*, (November 7, 2005), 74.
[85] Ibid., 72.
[86] Kelli Kennedy, "Feds Now Are Targeting Medicare Scammers," *San Antonio Express-News*, (Saturday, July 17, 2010), 9A.

SUGGESTED READINGS

Banfield, Edward C. *The Unheavenly City*. Boston, Mass.: Little, Brown and Co., 1970.

Baum, Alice S., And Donald W. Burnes, *A Nation in Denial: The Truth About Homelessness*. Boulder: Westview Press, 1993.

Handler, Joel F. *The Poverty of Welfare Reform*. New Haven, Conn.: Yale Univ. Press, 1995.

Heidenheimer, Arnold, Hugh Helco, and Carolyn Teich Adams, *Comparative Public Policy: The Politics of Social Choice in America, Europe, and Japan*, 3d ed., New York: St. Martin's Press, 1990.

Web Sites:

www.medicare.gov
www.cms.hhs.gov/home/medicaid.asp
www.aarp.org/health/insurance
www.fns.usda.gov/fsp - USDA Food Stamp Program
aspe.hhs.gov/poverty/08poverty.shtml - poverty guidelines
www.census.gov
www.hud.gov/homes - HUD homes

Chapter Seventeen

THE ENVIRONMENT

When the colonists first landed in the New World, they stepped upon the shores of their new homeland awe-strucked by the sight before them. Here was a land rich beyond their expectations. Abounding with the richness of natural resources, America offered millions of acres of virgin forests and wilderness teeming with a vast array of plants and wildlife. Rivers and streams were crystal clear, revealing plentiful stocks of fish. All of this beauty was crowned by clear blue skies. To Native Americans, the earth was the center of their universe. They worshiped and praised her lands and seas. They honored her creatures, plants, mountains, forests, and rivers. They revered her moon, sun, stars, and skies. They feared her anger that was so often vented in violent storms, harsh winters, and dry summers. They treasured the land. "The Indians stressed the web of life, the interconnectedness of land and man and creature."[1] Unfortunately, the European mindset viewed natural resources quite differently from Native Americans. "Chief Luther Standing Bear of the Oglala Sioux put it this way: 'Only to the white [Anglo] man was nature a wilderness and only to him was the land 'infested' with 'wild' animals and 'savage' people. To us it was tame. Earth was bountiful and we were surrounded with the blessing of the Great Mystery."[2] The beauty of this land was soon jeopardized with the continuous flow of new settlers bringing technological advancements to the emerging agricultural and industrial sectors of the New World. "Successive generations of immigrants have come to this country in search of economic opportunity. They arrived from Ireland and Germany in 1850, from Italy and Russia in 1920, and from Haiti and Mexico in 1990. Their hard work transformed abundant natural resources into a cornucopia of material wealth but at a cost of declining environmental quality. We have depleted the fertility of our soils, cut down primeval forests, and used water supplies faster than they can be replenished. Our fields produce meat, milk, and vegetables, but the nation's streams are polluted when fertilizer, pesticide, and animal waste residues run off the land. Factories convert raw materials into appliances, plastic products, and paper, but they also dump waste materials into the air and water."[3] Today, over one hundred years of industrialization with its all too familiar smokestacks have made this country materially wealthy beyond one's expectations but environmentally damaged almost beyond the hopes of repair.

The legacy of the twentieth century will include the tragic vocabulary of environmental damage: ozone alerts, smog, pollution, acid rain, deforestation, endangered species, and hazardous wastes. The challenge before the new millennium is to finally solve the puzzle of how man and nature can co-exist without destroying each other.

The task is even more daunting when one realizes that environmental damage is not just an American problem. It is an international concern that affects every single country, rich and poor alike. A 2007 report issued by the Intergovernmental Panel on Climate Change (IPCC) underscored that due to global warming "animal and plant life in the Arctic and Antarctic is undergoing substantial change. Rising sea levels elsewhere are damaging coastal wetlands. Warmer waters are bleaching and killing coral reefs, pushing marine species toward the poles and reducing fish populations in African lakes."[4] The human side of environmental damage is overwhelming. Across the globe, "more than 3 million die every year from the effects of air pollution, and 2.2 million people die from contaminated water."[5] Experts predict that the world's population will reach approximately 9,284,000,000 people by 2050, an increase of 2.4 billion over 2010 population figures with approximately 86.2 percent of the anticipated growth occurring in less developed countries.[6] Although certainly not a third world country, China is a primary example of a nation trying to "catch up" to her industrial giant sisters. The transition from a primary agricultural society to an industrial one has allowed the Chinese to successfully compete in world wide markets. The emerging Chinese middle-class is now demanding higher-end consumer goods and services to include American-style homes built from wood and concrete and luxury automobiles. China does not have vast forests or a thriving lumber industry to support a housing boom. Consequently, home building materials, especially to construct a traditional American-style house, must be imported primarily from the United States. Building contractors in China are willing to pay premium prices for American building materials, especially lumber and concrete, placing a considerable strain on inventories in the commercial and residential building material businesses. Of course, this has had a domino effect on new home prices in the United States as scarcity of building materials means higher costs to the home buyer. The Chinese thirst for oil, and gasoline has driven up world-market prices. However, there is a considerable downside. "Pollution is pervasive in China, as anyone who have visited the smog-chocked cities can attest. On the World Bank's list of 20 cities with the worst air, 16 are Chinese."[7] The Chinese are well aware of their air pollution problems. Once awarded to host the 2008 Olympics in Beijing, the Chinese government began an earnest effort to curb air pollution in its major city by restricting travel by personal automobiles to a Monday/Wednesday/Friday or Tuesday/Thursday/Saturday diving option with no use of gasoline-driven transportation on Sunday. Even as the games were underway, international commentators were highlighting the sports news with air pollution updates especially during the marathon runs.

Confronted with its own laundry list of environmental concerns, American lawmakers and citizens alike are still searching for the solution that will enable industry to provide us with the goods and services we are dependent upon without causing further damage to the air we breathe and the water we drink. To date, this quest has proven to be extremely difficult to accomplish. The desire to strike a balance between the constitutionally protected rights of property owners and the preservation of the environment evokes strong sentiments and hotly contested debates that sharply divide public opinion. On the one hand, property owners should be able to use and dispose of their property as they choose without undo interference from government. On the other hand, the desire to preserve society and its quality of life does depend upon the maintenance of an ecosystem free of pollution and contamination whereby plants and wildlife can successfully coexist with humankind. In every legislative house at *all* levels of government, there are constant battles between environmentalists and property owners over everything. The issue whether to cut trees to make way for a new mall or business park can wreak havoc at a city council meeting. Part of the problem rests with us, average American citizens. "Although Americans express a general desire to protect their environment, they are reluctant to sacrifice their standard of living to slow the rate of natural resource use and to reduce pollution. As they implement federal environmental rules, state and local governments have been careful to protect local economic interests from being harmed seriously by environmental interests."[8] Despite countless environmental laws riddled with severe sanctions against violators, the United States lags substantially behind other nations in its efforts to address environmental concerns. A 2008 study conducted by LinkedbyAir with the assistance of Yale and Columbia universities evaluated nations on their environmental performances. The top ten nations deemed as improving their environmental damage track records were Sweden, Switzerland, Norway, Lithuania, Latvia, Finland, France, New Zealand, Costa Rica, and Denmark. The United States was 66th![9] Nor does it appear that the United States is making a concerted effort to improve its rating. Major environmental disasters such as the 2010 BP (British Petroleum) oil rig explosion in the Gulf of Mexico that killed over 35 rig workers, cost BP billions of dollars and brought manslaughter charges against several BP managers; a major fertilizer plant explosion in 2013 that nearly leveled the small community of West Texas; and the 2014 dangerous chemical spill into the main water supply for nine counties in West Virginia adversely impacting 300,000 residents who must drink bottled water and not use any tap water for anything, including washing clothes and bathing, only point out that this nation has a long way to go in addressing its environmental problems. This chapter examines both the policy options available to lawmakers as well as future policy choices against the backdrop of an American society struggling to face the reality of the damage their actions have done to the quality of their environment.

Environmental issues and policy considerations are still in the infancy stage when compared to centuries-old poverty-related issues. Environmental politics did not emerge in the United States until the early 1970s when the country's consciousness was awakened to accept the truth that their century-old wanton and abusive habits had produced an extensive array of severe and, in some instances, irreversible damage. All the nation's waterways were to varying degrees polluted with run-offs from pesticides, fertilizers, chemicals, and industrial and municipal wastes. Rural residents were urged to boil their drinking water to ward off the ingestion of harmful substances. Lead-based paint, which had been the only paint base available for decades, was now labeled as a contributing cause of respiratory diseases, moderate to severe learning disabilities among children, and cancer. The once clear blue skies were suddenly noticed for their grayish and brownish hues caused by the spewing of polluting byproducts from the smokestacks of the nation's major industrial areas. The nation's coastal areas were hit with severe oil spills that spoiled tourist and resort areas and killed countless numbers of animals and marine life. Forests and wetlands became the victims of progress as bulldozers and dredgers drained swamplands and chopped whole stands of trees to make way for business and residential construction projects. Ozone alerts began to warn people with chronic respiratory ailments to remain indoors due to dangerously high levels of smog and air pollution. It was discovered during the 1970s that farm workers were the victims of deadly skin cancers acquired through years of hand-harvesting fruits and vegetables heavily sprayed with pesticides. The examples are too numerous to mention within the scope of this chapter. Consequently, this chapter focuses on the extent of the environmental damage to our nation's air, water, coastal areas, wetlands, wildlife, forests, and the problems associated with the disposal of nuclear, hazardous, and solid waste materials.

This chapter also presents a balanced approach by examining both sides of the issue. Traditionally, business and industry have fought regulatory laws that pose a threat to their livelihood. Environmental laws are, with few exceptions, laden with severe punitive actions against violators. Business leaders feel that they have been unfairly targeted and unduly punished for using acceptable traditional industrial production methods that have only now been deemed harmful to the environment. They have a valid argument that cannot be ignored by lawmakers. Antipollution devices are expensive. The increased cost of producing a product is passed onto the American consumer who is always searching for the best product at the cheapest price possible. Yes, these laws are expensive to implement. Irate property owners, business leaders, and anti-big government groups are constantly lobbying Congress to relax environmental restrictions and reduce punitive fines. Environmental groups also have a vital concern. Environmental damage must be curtailed or the future of this planet is in serious jeopardy. In *The Human Home*, British writer J. A. Walker wrote: "How are Americans to restore the environment to its proper position as an essentially political issue, over which reasonable people will disagree . . . ? How can we regain the attitude of those earlier ages which saw the natural world as pointing to the divine without itself being divine? How can we cherish our environment without making a fetish of it?"[10] Thus, the mission of environmental advocates is a noble one—protect the balance between humankind and nature. This chapter explores the role that lobbyists/advocates on each side of the environmental issue play in the creation and subsequent implementation of environmental legislation.

FEDERAL AND STATE ROLES IN ENVIRONMENT POLICIES

The reserved powers clause of the Tenth Amendment delegated to the states those governing powers not specifically granted to the national government. Consequently, the states were initially responsible for addressing environmental concerns. The national government played only a marginal role. Historically, government at all levels did not involve themselves with environmental issues with the exception of a natural disaster. For example, the Johnstown Flood of 1889 gained national attention as over 2,200 residents of several small Pennsylvania towns were tragically swept away after the collapse of a man-made earthen dam. The tragedy, however, did not result in any corrective legislative actions from Congress nor were actions taken against those responsible for operating the dam. The cries of the nation's earliest environmentalists fell upon deaf ears. Former United States Minister to Turkey, George Perkins Marsh, wrote *Man and Nature* in 1864, a novel depicting the destructiveness of deforestation. Marsh believed that "man is everywhere a disturbing agent. Wherever he plants his foot, the harmonies of nature are turned to discords . . . It is certain that a desolation, like that which has overwhelmed many once beautiful and fertile regions of Europe, awaits an important part of the territory of the United States . . . unless prompt measures are taken to check the action of destructive causes already in operation."[11] Marsh's words were instrumental in motivating a group of bird watchers to form the **American Forestry Association (AFA)**, an interest group promoting conservation of the nation's forests. An avid naturalist, John Muir once commented that "pollution, defilement, squalor are words that never would have been created had man lived conformably to Nature. Birds, insects, bears die as cleanly and are disposed of as beautifully . . . The woods are full of dead and dying trees, yet needed for their beauty to complete the beauty of the living. . . . How beautiful is all Death!"[12] In 1892, Muir founded the Sierra Club "to lead city people into the mountains, where he hoped that they would learn to see granite peaks and glacial valleys as he did."[13] A realist, "Muir believed that the retreats where he and others felt such strong emotion were worth defending against the forces of technology and economic development."[14] Consequently, the Sierra Club would evolve into the preeminent political force devoted to the protection of the environment. It was individuals, not national, state, or local governments, that took the early steps to rein in the destruction of the environment. Whether it be George Marsh, John Muir, Al Gore, Teddy Roosevelt, Rachel Carson, Bill Clinton, or Barack Obama, it should be noted that "nearly every aspect of environmentalism since the founding of the AFA has demonstrated the same pattern: a charismatic and influential individual who discerns a problem and formulates a public concern; a group that forms itself around him/her or around his/her ideas and exerts educational pressure on the Congress; legislation that creates some new kind of reserve—national park, national forest, national monument, national wildlife sanctuary or wilderness area; and finally, an increasingly specific body of regulatory law for the protection of what has been set aside."[15]

The first notable piece of federal legislation concerning the environment was the **Refuse Act** passed in 1899. This legislation required that potential dumpers of waste materials into navigable rivers had to obtain a permit from the Army Corps of Engineers prior to dumping. Due to sixteen years of constant pressure from the AFA, Congress finally responded with the passage of the **General**

Theodore Roosevelt meets with conservationist John Muir in the Yosemite Valley. Roosevelt succeeded in making preservation of America's natural resources an important issue.

Revision Act in 1891, granting the President of the United States the authority to promote the general welfare by setting aside forest lands for preserves and parks. Presidents Benjamin Harrison, Grover Cleveland and Teddy Roosevelt did exercise this right by "putting 43 million acres of forest, mainly in the west out of reach of the loggers."[16] Another pioneer environmentalist, George Bird Grinnell, was a boyhood friend of Teddy Roosevelt. Owner of *Forest and Stream*, Grinnell "carried on an impassioned campaign against market hunters, poachers and women who wore feathers on their hats.[17] With the backing of the Audubon Societies, Grinnell was instrumental in moving Congress to pass the **Park Protection Act** of 1894, prohibiting hunting in national parks. As the nation's first "environmental president" Roosevelt believed that "the Nation behaves well if it treats the national resources as assets which it must turn over to the next generation increased, and not impaired in value."[18] In 1903, Roosevelt established the nation's first wildlife sanctuary, Pelican Island. In 1905, he founded the **United States Forestry Service**. In 1906, Roosevelt signed into law the **Antiquities Act**. The initial intent of the legislation was to protect archeological sites in the Southwest from grave robbers. This legislation, however, empowered the President of the United States to set aside for federal protection any monument or sites, including forests, considered to be precious or threatened. When Roosevelt took office, the nation's only national park was Yellowstone. By 1916, however, there were thirteen. "The **National Park Act** [1916] gave these reserves their stated purpose, public enjoyment, public use *without impairment*, and created the National Park Service to carry it out."[19] In 1908, Roosevelt hosted an environmental conference attended by state governors, environmentalists and business leaders. He told the gathering:

> Indeed, the growth of this Nation by leaps and bounds makes one of the most striking and important chapters in the history of the world. Its growth has been due to the rapid development, and alas that it should be said! to the rapid destruction, of our natural resources. Nature has supplied to us in the United States, and still supplies to us, more kinds of resources in a more lavish degree than has ever been the case at any other time or with any other people. Our position in the world has been attained by the extent and thoroughness of the control we have achieved over nature.... The wise use of all of our natural resources, which are our national resources as well, is the great material question of today.... In the past we have admitted the right of the individual to injure the future of the Republic for his own present profit. In fact there has been a good deal of a demand for unrestricted individualism, for the right of the individual to injure the future of all of us for his own temporary and immediate profit. The time has come for a change. As a people we have the right and the duty, second to none other but the right and duty of obeying the moral law, of requiring and doing justice, to protect ourselves and our children against the wasteful development of our natural resources.[20]

When Teddy Roosevelt left office, the zeal for environmentalism went underground. With the exception of the New Deal's Civilian Conservation Corps and the Works Progress Administration in the 1930s, no major environmental legislation was passed until the 1960s.

The issue of environmental quality surfaced in the early 1960s as public awareness began to focus less on the economy and more on the quality of the environment. This shift in values occurred in part because a "period of sustained prosperity following World II brought about a fundamental intergenerational shift in value priorities within Western societies. Citizens became less preoccupied with basic material needs and began to place a higher priority on the quality of their lives. This value shift appears to have been most pronounced among people in white-collar and service occupations—a growing segment of all Western populations . . . . Post-materialists place particularly high value on protection of the environment and a life-style that is high-quality but simple."²¹ Policymakers also realized that the states lacked the initiative and the resources to address emerging environmental concerns. "They [the states] could not afford to develop the technical expertise on pollution issues; they had no jurisdiction over pollution generated in other states upstream or upwind; and polluting industries could threaten to move their operations elsewhere to escape compliance with strict environmental rules."²² Consequently, the individual states needed the muscle of the federal government to establish the guidelines for legislative and, if necessary, legal action to halt environmental damage.

Rachel Carson gave the emerging environmental movement a shot in the arm when her book, *Silent Spring*, was published in 1962. In her novel, the earth and all of humankind is destroyed not by an invading army from outer space but by the wanton use of synthetic chemicals such as DDT, heptachlor, aldrin, and chlordane. Carson weaves her tale of environmental doom around her thesis that:

> the unique speed of human actions, combined with the introduction of synthetic chemicals for insect control, would accelerate the occurrence of resistance mutations to such a degree that invincible insects would swagger across the Earth. Industrial alchemists would then fashion ever-stronger portions in a frantic attempt to stop the superbugs. Armed with mutated immunity the superbugs would defy the new poisons; as farmers grew desperate, pesticides would be sprayed indiscriminately. The superbugs would escape unharmed, but indiscriminate spraying would wipe out the crops, flowers, and "friendly" insects farmers hoped to encourage. The battle would end in less than a human generation, with favored species vanquished at every turn. Once the earthworm, a key friendly species, fell extinct from excess spraying of poisons, the food chain of songbirds would be destroyed forever. The next year would come a silent spring.²³

Placing the blame for the ruin of earth squarely on the backs of all mankind, Carson declares that "the 'control of nature' is a phrase conceived in arrogance, born of the Neanderthal Age of biology and philosophy, when it was supposed that nature exists for the convenience of man."²⁴ *Silent Spring* did for the environmental movement what *The Jungle* did in promoting a stunned national government to move against the meat packing industry with the passage of the **Pure Food and Drug Act**. The federal government responded by passing laws placing controls and bans on DDT, other pesticides, and herbicides.

The United States Congress was jarred into action. In 1963, it passed the **Clean Air Act** giving the federal government a powerful, and to date, permanent role over state and local governments in the creation, implementation, and enforcement of environmental public policy issues. Another pioneering environmentalist, Howard Zahnister, executive director of the Wilderness Society, saw fifteen years of work finally result in the 1964 passage of the **Wilderness Act**. This legislation defined **wilderness** "as an area where the earth and its community of life are untrammeled by man, where man himself is a visitor who does not remain."²⁵ Congress declared approximately 9.1 million acres as wilderness now falling under the protection of the federal government.

The environmental issue became a volatile political concern in the 1970s. Both presidential candidates, Edmund Muskie(D) and Richard Nixon(R), campaigned for rapid and severe federal responses to clean up environmental damage, punish violators, and protect the environment from further damage. During his tenure in the White House, President Nixon was instrumental in convincing Congress to pass "a remarkable series of acts, including the revised Clean Air Act of 1970; the sweeping National Environmental Policy Act of 1970, which created the Environmental Protection Agency and the Council on Environmental Quality and required environmental impact statements for all construction projects affecting land owned by the federal government; the Federal Water Pollution Control Act of 1972; and the Endangered Species Act of 1973."[26] Regardless of political philosophy and party loyalties, every presidential candidate since has advocated protection of the environment. For example, President Jimmy Carter stated that "most of the environmental damage which now occurs can be prevented. The additional cost of responsible surface mining, or preventing oil spills, or cleaning auto and power plant emissions is low, compared to the costs to society and future generations if we fail to act . . . . To maintain environmental quality, and to improve the quality of life for our people is an essential goal, and in its pursuit, we must act responsibly . . . . It makes little sense, if we are concerned about the quality of life, to talk about having to choose between employment and the environment or between enough energy and environmental quality."[27] Reminding the American public of their responsibility to the environment, Carter underscored that "in developing a national energy policy, the government should not try to do the job alone. . . . With the energy crisis, as with other crises, we have met as a nation, government, industry and the public must all do our part."[28] Support for preventive legislation gained public endorsement. "In a survey conducted by the *New York Times* in 1989, an astonishing 80 percent of those polled agreed with the proposition that 'Protecting the environment is so important that requirements and standards cannot be too high, and continuing environmental improvements must be made regardless of cost.'"[29]

Environmental issues were certainly a leading campaign topic during the 2000 presidential elections. Vice President Al Gore had already demonstrated his pledge to promote pro-environmental legislation if he were to be elected to the White House. Then candidate George W. Bush echoed his own commitment to a cleaner environment despite the fact that his vice presidential candidate Dick Cheney was the immediate past president of Halliburton, one of the nation's leading oil and gas producers. Bush promised that if elected he would, along with other environmental actions, seek regulations on carbon dioxide emissions from power plants. His proposal included declaring sulfur dioxide, nitrogen oxide, mercury and carbon dioxide as pollutants subject to regulation by the Environmental Protection Agency (EPA). After assuming the office, President Bush reversed his campaign promise by telling Congress that he would not require the EPA to regulate carbon dioxide emissions from power plants. In addition, the Bush administration withdrew United States participation in the **Kyoto Agreement**. Much to the ire of environmentalists, the Bush administration made a concerted effort to weaken the investigative arm of federal and state environmental agencies, relax environmental standards, and either weaken or actually eliminate legislatively mandated sanctions against polluters. Citing the cost of unnecessary and overburdening restrictions on business and industry, Bush promoted an industry-wide voluntary approach to federal regulations, particularly environmental laws. Meanwhile, Al Gore continued his efforts to promote environmental awareness to include global warming. In 2007, he testified before a joint congressional hearing about the extent of existing and future environmental damage and offered his proposals to include reducing carbon dioxide and other warming gasses by 90 percent in 2050, banning construction of coal-burning power plants that lacked the technology to both capture and store greenhouse gases, imposing stricter fuel efficiency standards for cars and trucks, imposing a tax on carbon emissions, enacting an international climate change treaty, banning incandescent light bulbs, mandating de facto compliance with the Kyoto Protocol, and creating tax breaks and other incentives for those producing or selling electricity.[30] For his efforts, Gore was awarded a Nobel Peace Prize and won an Academy Award for the short-subject film made based on his book *An Inconvenient Truth*.

In his 2008 presidential race, Barack Obama detailed his plans for the environment to include:
- A cap-and-trade system to cut carbon dioxide emissions to 80 percent below 1990 levels;
- Raising efficiency standards to 52 miles per gallon by 2026;
- Goal of renewable energy generating 25 percent of United States electricity by 2025;
- Proposing having at least 60 billion gallons of biofuels in the nation's supply by 2030;
- Advocacy of coal-to-liquid fuels if they emit 20 percent less carbon than conventional gas;
- And stressing that although nuclear power is not optimal, it can be used as an energy source.[31]

The economic recession severely hit the nation's major automobile and truck manufacturers. Auto giants to include General Motors and Chrysler sought federal assistance to keep their companies afloat. President Obama insisted that any reorganization plan and/or federal bailout request for the auto industry had to include meaningful initiatives to build more fuel efficient and environmentally friendly vehicles. In 2009, the White House issued a series of federally-back rules covering gasoline mileage standards and additional curbs on vehicle emissions. In his re-election bid, Obama reemphasized his commitment to promote renewable energy as well as to further reduce carbon emissions. On the campaign trail, President Obama stated:

> So we have a choice to make. We can remain one of the world's leading importers of foreign oil, or we can make the investments that allow us to become the world's leading exporter of renewable energy. We can let climate change continue to go unchecked, or we can help stop it. We can let the jobs of tomorrow be created abroad, or we can create those jobs right here in America and lay the foundation for lasting prosperity. . . . We've been talking about climate change in Washington for years and energy independence and efficiency for years. . . . But no matter how many scientists testified about greenhouse gases, no matter how much evidence that they're threatening our weather patterns, nothing happened with global warming until now."[32]

April 20 is celebrated as Earth Day to remind us of what has been done and what legislation still needs to be enacted to protect this environment. Table 17.1 details the major pieces of environmental legislation passed by Congress. The majority of the legislation passed at both the national and state levels is designed with a ten- or twenty-year life cycle, whereby the initiating governing level must decide whether to extend the legislation for another life cycle. Against this backdrop, environmentalists can never rest easy that public opinion, office seekers, and lawmakers will be on their side whenever these legislative items are before Congress.

The Air We Breathe

The survival of the earth's inhabitants is very dependent upon the quality of the air they breathe. **Air** is basically a "mixture of nitrogen (78.084 percent), oxygen (20.948 percent), argon (0.934 percent), carbon dioxide (0.032 percent), and traces of neon, helium, krypton, hydrogen, xenon, methane, and vitreous oxide."[33] Each element performs an essential function: nitrogen, oxygen, and carbon dioxide are essential for the survival of plant and animal life; oxygen is a basic element necessary for higher forms of life; carbon dioxide plays a key role in photosynthesis and food production; ozone, a byproduct of oxygen, protects life forms from dangerous ultraviolet light; and so on. Even the slightest contamination of these elements jeopardizes the quality of the air all forms of life breathe.

Air pollution is defined "as a group of chemical compounds that are in the wrong place or in the wrong concentration at the wrong time."[34] Air pollution is caused by the release of **suspended particulates** such as ash, smoke, dust, soot, and liquid droplets into the air by the burning of fuels, agricultural practices, and industrial processes. Sulfur dioxide (SO_2) is a particularly harmful substance created by the release of sulfur-based fuels from the burning of coal and oil. On the other hand, carbon monoxide (CO) is released when fuels such as gasoline are not burned completely.

Air pollution also consists of toxic air pollutants that are released into the air during the manufacturing processes used by refineries, chemical plants, and dry cleaners. Toxins are also produced by the burning of lead-based gasoline. The combination of all of these components of air pollution may form into smog, haze, or acid rain. **Smog** occurs when "nitrogen oxides (Nox) produced by burning fuel and volatile organic compounds (VOCs) escape to the atmosphere."[35] Producing a hazy dirty brown cloud, smog is the end product of the mixing of over one hundred various compounds with sunlight and heat. **Ozone** is a primary ingredient of smog. Many of the nation's major cities have ozone alert days urging residents to prevent further damage by not gassing up the car or mowing the lawn during alert hours while at the same time warning those with respiratory ailments and allergies to remain indoors. Similar to smog, **haze** refers to "wide-scale, low-level pollution that obstructs visibility."[36] In the 1970s, scientists discovered that the average American was unknowingly contributing to the nation's air pollution problems simply by using everyday products containing **chlorofluorocarbons** or **CFCs**. Now regarded as one of the worst ozone-depleting chemicals, CFCs belong to "a family of inert, nontoxic and easily liquefied chemicals used in refrigeration, air conditioning, packaging, and insulation or as solvents or aerosol propellants."[37] In particular, primary manufacturers such as DuPont used CFCs for the production of housing insulation products, and Freon, the chemical used for practically every air conditioning system from home use to vehicles. A 1974 report indicated that CFCs were responsible for adding chlorine to the stratosphere, further eroding the ozone layer. Consequently, "the United States banned CFCs as aerosol propellants in all nonessential applications (ranging from hair sprays to deodorants to furniture polish). U.S. production of CFCs dropped by 95 percent."[38] However, the production of CFCs for industrial use continued. It was the response of the international community that gradually but finally ended CFC production in developed countries by 1996. It began with the Vienna Convention on the Protection of the Ozone Layer in 1985 whereby over twenty-eight nations agreed to find a reasonable CFC substitute by 1990. In 1987, the Montreal Protocol signed by 125 nations "froze the production of CFCs by European Community members at mid-1989 levels and called for 50 percent reductions in emissions by 1999.

Table 17.1

Selective List of Federal Environmental Laws

Air Pollution Control Act (1955) - Provided federal funding for air-pollution control research projects.

Air Quality Act (1967) - Created nationwide federal air quality regions and set acceptable pollution levels for each region. Required that all state and local governments must develop their own standards for air-quality or follow federal mandates.

Antiquities Act (1906) – Authorized the President of the United States to set aside by proclamation sites to include national monuments and parcels of land that are objects of historical and scientific interests.

Asbestos Hazard Emergency Response Act (1986) – required the EPA to conduct inspection and removal of asbestos-containing materials from the nation's public schools.

Atomic Energy Acts (1946 and 1954) – created the nation's civilian nuclear energy programs.

Clean Air Act (1963) - Provided federal funding and assistance to local and state governments in their efforts to establish air pollution control programs.

Clean Air Act Amendments (1965) - Set federal pollution standards for automobile exhaust emissions.

Clean Air Act Amendments (1970) - Empowered the Environmental Protection Agency to establish national air pollution standards; restricted the discharge of major pollutants into the lower atmosphere; mandated that automobile manufacturers reduce emissions of nitrogen oxide, hydrocarbon, and carbon monoxide by 90 percent.

Clean Air Act Amendments (1990) - Established formulas for the development of anti-polluting gasoline fuels for use in the nation's smoggiest cities; mandated further emissions reductions of carbon monoxide and exhaust emissions by year 2003; placed additional restrictions on toxic pollutants.

Clean Water Act (1972) – also known as the **Federal Water Pollution Control Act Amendments of 1972**, the federal government's major program overseeing the quality of all surface water.

Clean Water Act (1974) (known as the Safe Water Drinking Act) - Set federal safe drinking water standards for all water suppliers servicing more than 25 people.

Coastal Zone Management Act (1972) – created the Office of Ocean and Coastal Resource Management to give federal grants to states for the development of their plans to preserve coastal areas and estuarine sanctuaries.

Comprehensive Environmental Response, Compensation, and Liability Act (1980) - Established the federal-level Superfund to clean up toxic waste sites.

Endangered Species Act (1973) - Empowered the Departments of Interior and Commerce to purchase land and water for the sole purpose of protecting, restoring, and propagating endangered species; established an identification and listing system for endangered and threatened species.

Energy Policy and Conservation Act (1975) – created the nation's Strategic Petroleum Reserve to offset future oil and gas shortages in emergency situations.

Federal Hazardous Liquid Pipeline Safety Act (1979) - Set federal guidelines for the transportation of hazardous liquids by pipelines.

Federal Insecticide, Fungicide and Rodenticide Act (1947) – authorized the registration and labeling of pesticides used as agricultural chemicals.

Federal Land Policy and Management Act (1976) – empowered the Bureau of Land Management to oversee the leasing of federally held lands for livestock grazing.

Federal Natural Gas Pipeline Safety Act - Set federal guidelines for the transportation of natural and other gases by pipelines.

Federal Water Pollution Control Act (1948) - Established federal standards for the treatment of municipal wastes prior to discharge. (Revised in 1965 and 1967)

Federal Water Pollution Control Act Amendments (1972) - Mandated national water quality standards and goals for the rehabilitation of polluted waters into safe water sources for recreational and fishing purposes.

Fish Conservation and Management Act (1976) - Restricted foreign fishing in U. S. territorial waters.

General Revision Act (1891) – Authorized the President of the United States to establish forest reserves on public land.

Lacey Act (1900) - Outlawed interstate exportation or importation of wildlife harvested or possessed in violation of federal laws.

Marine Mammal Protection Act (1972) - Prohibited the killing and importation of whales and nearly all marine mammals.

Migratory Bird Conservation Act (1929) - Empowered the federal government to purchase land for waterfowl refuges.

Migratory Bird Hunting Stamp Act (1934) - Required hunters over age 16 to purchase a stamp or license before hunting migratory waterfowl.

Migratory Bird Treaty Act (1918) - Prohibited the hunting or injury of wild birds migrating between the United States, Britain, and Mexico.

National Energy Act (1978) – deregulated the pricing of natural gas; encouraged alternative energy sources such as solar and geothermal; granted tax credits for home insulation; and encouraged conservation efforts in home-related products and motor vehicles

National Environmental Policy Act (1969) - Mandated the establishing of the Council for Environmental Quality, and the Environmental Protection Agency.

National Forest Management Act (1976) – established stricter guidelines for the harvesting and selling of timber and placed limits on clear-cutting of forests.

National Park Act (1916) – Stated that the purpose of national parks was to guarantee public enjoyment and public use without impairment. This legislation established the National Park Service.

National Wildlife Refuge System Improvement Act (1997) – underscored the need for wildlife protection and the creation of programs supporting wildlife-dependent recreation.

Nuclear Waste Policy Act (1982) – mandated the construction of federally-supervised permanent disposal sites for nuclear waste.

Oil Pollution Act (1990) – passed immediately after the Exxon *Valdez* oil spill; required all oil companies to create and submit oil spill contingency plans and to train their employees on containment efforts.

Park Protection Act (1894) – Prohibited hunting in national parks.

Pittman-Robertson Act (1937) - Allocated revenue for state wildlife conservation efforts from the collection of excise taxes on rifles, shotguns, ammunition, and archery equipment.

Refuse Act (1899) - Mandated issuance of a permit for dumping of refuse into any navigable waterway.

Resource Conservation and Recovery Act (1976) - Granted federal control over hazardous wastes; prohibited the creation of new dumping sites without prior permission; mandated the upgrade of existing open dumps to sanitary landfills or face closure.

Solid Waste Disposal Act (1965) - Provided federal assistance to state and local governments for the establishment of guidelines for solid waste disposal activities.

Surface Mining Control and Reclamation Act (1977) – placed strict guidelines for strip mining projects to include the restoration of areas subject to strip mining.

Toxic Substances Control Act (1976) – empowered the EPA to identify, register, evaluate and regulate all commercially used chemicals that posed an "unreasonable risk."

Water Quality Act (1965) - Set federal standards for the discharge of harmful substances into water sources.

Wilderness Act (1964) – Authorized a "hands-off" protection for special areas carved out of the national forest, national park and Bureau of Land Management lands.

The treaty permitted developing countries to increase CFC use for ten more years, allowing the former USSR to continue production through 1990."[39] A 1990 amendment to the Montreal Protocol banned the complete use of CFCs by 2000 with a subsequent amendment pushing the date back to 1996. The global elimination of CFCs has been so successful that scientists now predict that "ozone levels could recover to their 1979 levels by 2050."[40]

Another type of air pollution, **acid rain**, is a "complex chemical and atmospheric phenomenon that occurs when emissions of sulfur and nitrogen compounds and other substances are transformed by chemical processes in the atmosphere, often far from the original source, and then deposited on earth in either a wet or dry form. The wet form, properly called 'acid rain,' can fall as rain, snow, or fog. The dry forms are acidic gases and particulates."[41] Acid rain was a contributing factor to a cooling of relations between the United States and Canada during the Reagan administration. The Canadian government threatened to stall a lucrative trade agreement unless the United States took measures to curtail acid rain pollution. Created in the United States, the polluting effects of acid rain were crossing into Canada destroying crops and deteriorating buildings and national monuments, as well as polluting Canadian air.

The various elements that create air pollution are harmful to human beings. Ozone pollution causes respiratory ailments including shortness of breath, premature aging of the lungs, eye irritation, nasal congestion, and asthma, as well as reduced resistance to infections. Eye and throat irritation, cancer, and bronchitis are directly linked to long-term exposure to particulate matter. Both sulfur dioxide and nitrogen dioxide cause respiratory tract infections and damage to both the lung tissue and immune system. Carbon monoxide severely impairs, often with fatal results, the blood's ability to carry oxygen. It can also cause severe damage to the nervous, cardiovascular, and pulmonary systems. Brain damage and mental retardation can be caused by exposure to lead.

Traditionally throughout the hot summer months, farmers, ranchers, and homeowners, particularly in the Southwest and Western sections of the country, cast a hopeful eye at any cloud that could bring much needed rain to rescue their crops, their livestock, and their lawns from withering and dieing. State and local governments have resorted to cloud seeding as a means of jump-starting the rain making process. Weather experts usually point to the El Nino and El Nina weather cycles as the primary culprits for prolonged periods of drought conditions followed by short-lived monsoon like flooding. Scientists, however, have recently cast a suspicious eye towards air pollution as a likely contributor to drought conditions. A study "for the first time, seems to provide direct evidence that tiny particles in industrial pollution cause physical changes in clouds that prevent water from condensing into raindrops and snowflakes."[42] Although the report concedes that definitely pinpointing the source of the pollution that caused the lack of meaningful precipitation is extremely difficult due to changing wind currents, scientists strongly believe that "it is a physical, rather than a chemical process that blocks formation of rain and snow. Industrial plants spew particles formed by fuel combustion that are much smaller than the water droplets normally found in clouds. The small pollution particles inhibit the cloud's water droplets from coalescing into large drops to create rain. Smaller water droplets also are slower to freeze, reducing the ice particles in clouds. In types of clouds that are short-lived, the lack of larger droplets reduces, or even eliminates, the precipitation."[43]

Initially, the federal government believed that air pollution and its subsequent cleanup were the responsibility of the states. Opting for a marginal role, the United States Congress passed the **Air Pollution Control Act** of 1955. This law enabled the federal government to provide funding to those states conducting research on air pollution. The **Clean Air Act** of 1963 provided a $95 million grant-in-aid program to assist state governments in setting their own air quality standards. In 1965, the United States Congress mandated federal emissions standards for hydrocarbons and carbon monoxide for new motor vehicles. The federal regulations were issued in 1966 for the 1968 model year. Congress was still "reluctant to give any real regulatory power to federal officials, however, even though the states were doing relatively little and many air pollution problems transcended state boundaries."[44] The **Air Quality Act** of 1967 went a step further by authorizing the creation of approximately 247 metropolitan air quality regions for the sole purpose of establishing their own air quality standards and developing plans to meet their anticipated goals. For the first time, the United States Congress used a punitive policy approach by authorizing the then Department of Health, Education, and Welfare to force noncomplying states to use federal standards or face lose of federal funds. However, this law proved to be very ineffective. "By 1970, no state had put into place a complete set of standards for any pollutant and the federal government had designated less than one-third of the metropolitan air quality regions that had been projected."[45]

In his State of the Union message delivered in 1970, President Richard Nixon decided to "get tough" with the states by proclaiming both the need for comprehensive federal air quality standards and expanded federal authority to implement the actions required to meet those standards. The **Clean Air Act** of 1970 aimed "to protect and enhance the quality of the nation's air resources so as to promote the public health and welfare and the productive capacity of its population."[46] This law empowered the newly created **Environmental Protection Agency (EPA)** to establish **national ambient air quality standards (NAAQS)** for ozone, carbon monoxide, sulfur dioxide, particulate matter, nitrogen dioxide, and lead. Areas would be designated as **attainment** if air quality met federal standards. Areas failing to meet the standards for one or more NAAQS would be designated as **nonattainment**. Once the EPA announced the standards, states had nine months to develop their implementation plans. In turn, the EPA was to ensure that each plan included monitoring requirements, emission limitations for the six elements, provisions for periodic inspection of sites, and the testing of motor vehicles, as well as a state budgetary commitment to enforce air pollution standards. In addition, motor vehicle emissions of carbon monoxide and hydrocarbons were to be reduced by 90 percent beginning with the 1975 models. Nitrogen oxide emissions were to be cut by 90 percent by 1976. The EPA was granted enforcement power to include leveling fines from up to $10,000 per day for anyone removing a pollution control device to $25,000 per day for each violation of pollution. The investigative tools given to the EPA included injunctions to halt polluting activities pending legal actions. For the first time, citizens could file suits against both the polluter and the EPA for failure to respond to reported incidences of air pollution.

Despite heated debate from all sides of the issue, it was the Nixon administration that garnered public and political support for this legislation. However, the president's aim was to oversee the enactment of legislation that accomplished the goals of both protecting the environment and shielding America's business and industry from unreasonable regulations and penalties. "Part of its motivation [the Nixon administration] was a concern that regulation in some states but not in others, put regulated industries at a competitive disadvantage. Industry representatives also lobbied for one set of federal standards rather than a variety of state provisions. They prevailed on Congress to prohibit the states from imposing more aggressive regulation than provided in the Clean Air Act of 1970."[47] This initial "get tough" policy was further compromised by subsequent amendments to the Clean Air Act that year after year granted waivers to automobile manufacturers that successfully blocked full implementation of the stronger emissions standards. Amendments passed in 1977 did threaten to deny federal funding for highway and sewage treatment projects to those states not in compliance with the Clean Air Act. However, the federal government opted to avoid taking such actions.

Although the Reagan administration sought to weaken it, the George Bush administration did enact a series of amendments to the **Clean Air Act** in 1990. This package included a mandatory production phaseout of chlorofluorocarbons, carbontetrachloride, methyl chloroform, and hydrochlorofluorocarbons, all major contributors to ozone pollution. Vehicle manufacturers were required to reduce harmful emissions and to improve emissions control devices. The gasoline companies were required to produce cleaner burning fuels. Industry was required to reduce emissions levels of both sulfur dioxide and nitrate oxide in an attempt to reduce acid rain levels. The 1990 amendments targeted 250 hazardous pollutants for emissions reductions of 90 percent by 2003. In 1993, diesel engine trucks were added to the list of motor vehicles subjected to emissions control standards.

The air pollution laws passed since 1970 have produced a mixed-bag of results. From 1970 to 1991, "emissions levels of many pollutants have dropped: lead by 96 percent, sulfur dioxide by 28 percent, particulates by 61 percent."[48] However, more Americans are driving personal vehicles, resulting in noticeable increases in ozone, carbon monoxide, and nitrogen oxide emissions levels thus offsetting any decreases. A well-known urban historian, the late Lewis Mumford, once commented that Americans "had adopted the cloverleaf as the national flower."[49] The invention of the automobile enabled Americans to freely travel across the country. However, the automobile's continued success is dependent upon a unique combination of fossil fuels commonly known as gasoline, rubber tires, and miles upon miles of asphalt and concrete roadways. Urban sprawl and highways go hand in hand. "Two million homes are built each year—and with them comes the proliferation of superstores, strip malls, and office parks. Badly planned and not planned, they turn up in the wrong places, allowed by the wrong building and zoning codes. Supported by the infrastructure of the automobile, from highways to sewage lines, and by subsidies for big oil and tax relief for developers, these trophies of highway-fed economic growth consume two million acres of productive farmland a year, according to the American Farmland Trust, and uncounted acres of woods and wetlands."[50] As early as 1991, congressional leaders recognized the necessity of encouraging alternative means of transportation to offset the polluting ways of the personal automobile culture. The **Intermodal Surface Transportation Efficiency Act** allocated $155 billion over a six-year period to "encourage foot power, bike power, mass transit, and other transportation alternatives. Two billion dollars from the act would support transportation-related 'enhancement' projects: fixing up a train station, for instance, or rehabilitating a bridge. . . Further the act mandated an additional billion dollars to Congestion Mitigation Air Quality funds, supporting a broad and vital array of projects ranging from buying alternative-fuel buses to laying light rail lines to organizing ridesharing."[51] Reliable and rapid mass transportation systems do help to reduce the number of commuters using personal vehicles. The majority of the nation's sophisticated mass transportation systems are concentrated in a handful of large metropolitan cities such as New York and Chicago. In most cities, the bus line with its reputation for unreliable service is the mass transportation system. Part of his plan to jump start the nation's economy, President Obama offered billions of dollars in stimulus money to the states not only for infrastructure improvements to upgrade the nation's deteriorating roads and bridges, but to develop alternative transportation options to include both high speed and light rail train systems. In addition, his package of new federally standardized emissions rules would "require each automaker's fleet of cars and light trucks to average 35.5 mpg [miles per gallon] by 2016."[52]

However, the cost of owning and fueling a personal vehicle is becoming more expensive as the price at the pump continues to increase. The solutions are either the development of cheaper but less powerful alternative fuels or the discovery and extraction of new sources of traditional fossil fuels. Experts believe that 40.5 billion barrels of oil can be recovered within the continental United States with an additional 76 billion barrels in nearby offshore sites, such as the Gulf of Mexico, the Alaskan shoreline, etc.[53] Since the Clinton presidency, Congress and environmentalists have been battling over drilling for oil in Alaska's Arctic National Wildlife Refuge. "A 1998 U.S. Geological Survey assessment still used today concluded it's almost certain there are at least 5.6 billion barrels of recoverable oil and possibly as much as 16 billion barrels (a 5 percent likelihood) beneath the refuge's 1.5 million-acre coastal plain."[54] Fearful of the encroachment of oil derricks and tanker trucks, environmentalists want to keep the pristine area preserved for endangered and protected species. Oil companies, on the other hand, believe "there is enough oil in the refuge to supply every drop needed by New Hampshire for 315 years or Maine for 299 years. It's enough oil for the nation's capitol for 1,710 years."[55] The quest to explore and drill at the Arctic National Wildlife Refuge reemerged during the 2012 presidential election. Republican candidate Mitt Romney's environmental issues stressed the need to develop alternative fuels but alongside "exploiting more domestic sources of oil such as Outer Continental Shelf and Arctic National Wildlife Refuge."[56] Another controversial plan is the construction of two pipelines transporting oil extracted from oil sands. The Keystone Pipeline would originate in Hardisty, Canada and wind its way through the United States to its final destination in Houston, Texas. The Trans Mountain project would take oil from Edmonton, Canada to Anacortes, Washington. On the positive side, "the project would give Canada's oil industry something it desperately wants—a wide open conduit between the tar sands and the global market. Direct access to overseas customers could fetch tar sands oil a high price."[57] On the negative side, environmentalists are fearful that "extracting hydrocarbons from the sands releases more carbon dioxide than conventional oil drilling, adding to global warming."[58]

The nation's quest to find more liquid gold hit a tragically significant snag after the BP oil spill in the Gulf of Mexico. Citing safety concerns about off-shore oil drilling projects, President Obama issued a moratorium on all deep water oil projects until new safety regulations could be developed. In particular, the administration wanted offshore operators to develop emergency evacuation plans, blowout prevention measures, and oil spill containment options, etc. However, the outcry from the major oil companies and drilling firms caused the Obama administration to retreat. Consequently, Ken Salazar, Secretary of the Interior, announced that "I have decided that it is now appropriate to lift the suspension on deep-water drilling for those operators that are able to clear the high bar that we have set."[59]

A primary source for the nation's on-going problem with air pollution is industries heavily involved in chemical, oil and gas production, and refining businesses. Corpus Christi, Texas, for example, is well known for its natural beaches along the Gulf of Mexico. While tourism is big business, the city's largest employers are six refineries located all in a row on a 10-mile corridor known as Refinery Row. These six refineries employ 23,000 and pump millions of dollars per year into the local economy. Although these companies have spent millions on devices to control their pollution, "there are days when the pungent smell of rotten eggs, caused by hydrogen sulfide, wafts over neighborhoods. On some occasions when the flares [located on top of the refinery pipelines to burn off excess gas] burn, inky black smoke spreads across the sky, drifting wherever the wind takes it. Residents wake up on some mornings to find their vehicles coated with ash."[60] Once the area's residential properties were prime real estate. Today, these neighborhoods support a dependent minority underclass that simply cannot afford to move elsewhere. Finding a buyer for one's home is not a viable option since given a choice, few would want to live right next door to a polluting oil refinery. Although the area's benzene levels are within the EPA's parameters for compliance, the levels are among the highest in Texas. Work-related accidents in chemical plants are not uncommon. The U.S. Chemical Safety and Hazard Investigation Board reports that "since 1998, an average of five plant workers have been killed every month in the United States by explosions or leaks of chemicals. . . There is at least one chemical accident somewhere in the nation everyday."[61]

In some areas, the quality of the nation's air is questionable. For example in 1997, the Clinton administration instructed the EPA to toughen air quality rules by requiring "states to meet more stringent reductions in smog-causing ozone and in microscopic soot."[62] Through the EPA, the Obama administration has taken a stronger stand on the enforcement of air quality standards. In 2010, the EPA established a greenhouse gas emissions compliance plan for Arizona, Arkansas, Florida, Idaho, Kansas, Oregon and Wyoming. Severe actions were taken against Texas as the EPA in 2010, "declared Texas unfit to regulate its own greenhouse gas emissions and took over carbon dioxide permitting of any new or expanding industrial facilities starting January 2 [2011]."[63]

Global Warming

"The earth's atmosphere works like a greenhouse: It traps solar radiation, making life on earth possible. **Climate change** describes a rise in the earth's temperature caused by an increase in the concentration of certain gases, especially carbon dioxide."[64] Although not alarmists, both climate experts and environmentalists have expressed serious concerns that the future of the earth's greenhouse is being severely compromised to the point that the damage may not be reversible. They warn of **global warming** or the **greenhouse effect** that occurs when "methane, carbon dioxide, and certain other air pollutants increase, trapping heat in the earth's atmosphere and gradually warming it."[65] If their predictions are correct, "the results could be devastating: rising oceans, ferocious hurricanes, and prolonged droughts."[66] So far, the evidence clearly indicates that the earth is, indeed, getting warmer. According to the National Academy of Sciences, "average surface temperatures have climbed about 1.4 degrees Fahrenheit since the 20th century, coinciding with spiking atmospheric levels of carbon dioxide which have ballooned 35 percent over the same period. Levels of methane, a far more potent heat-trapping gas, have jumped 152 percent since the pre-industrial age. . . . Model projections show temperatures jumping anywhere from 2.7 to 10.7 degrees Fahrenheit over the next 100 years."[67] Higher temperatures mean that the polar ice caps are melting. It is predicted that "by the end of this century, Arctic temperatures could reach as high as 130,000 years ago, when the oceans were 13 to 20 feet higher than now."[68] What happens in Greenland and Antarctica does have an impact elsewhere. For example, experts believe that approximately one-third of the coral reefs in the Caribbean waters are dying due to global warming and rising sea temperatures. "The mortality that we're seeing now is of the extremely slow-growing reef-building corals. These are corals that are the foundation of the reef . . . We're talking colonies that were here when Columbus came by have died in the past three to four months. Some of the devastated coral never can be replaced because it only grows the width of a dime per year."[69] The potential demise of the coral reefs means economic ruin for the tourist industries in Puerto Rico and the Virgin Islands.

Realizing that global warming is an international problem involving all nation states, approximately 160 nations, including the United States, signed the 1997 Kyoto Protocol to the 1992 UN Framework Convention on Climate Change. The agreement "set binding reduction targets and assigned emissions caps based on 1990 greenhouse gas emissions. Nations were given a five-year window (2008-2012) in which to achieve its targets. The United States agreed to reduce emissions to 7 percent below 1990 levels by 2010."[70] However, in March 2001, the United States became the only industrialized nation to withdraw from the agreement. The George W. Bush administration faulted the agreement for not placing developing nations on the same time table for emissions reductions as the more advanced or industrial nations. The international environmental community was outraged with Bush, and during his tenure in the White House, whenever he attended an international conference he was met with angry protesters.

The Water We Drink

On paper, the United States had an abundant supply of water, totally 264,129 square miles of water consisting of 86,409 square miles of inland water, 43,185 square miles of coastal waters, and 59,959 square miles of water in the Great Lakes.[71] In reality, the United States has regions with an over abundant supply of water offset by areas that face yearly droughts and water shortages. Also, major rivers and lakes have been used as the dumping sites for industrial and municipal wastes.

Since humans are composed of approximately 80 percent of water, clean and plentiful sources of water are absolutely essential to our survival. Yet, Americans, in particular, rank as the world's largest consumers of water. "The average American family uses more than 300 gallons of water per day at home. Roughly 70 percent of this use occurs indoors. Normally, outdoor water use accounts for 30 percent of households use yet can be much higher in drier parts of the country and in more water-intensive landscapes."[72] Of course, the demand for water increases as the population grows. Unfortunately, Americans have wasted their water resources for far too many years. It is extremely difficult to drive home the need for water conservation particularly when homeowners want beautiful year-round green lawns. Currently, areas throughout the United States are facing severe droughts. Texas has been in a drought for nearly five years, and California's governor has requested residents to reduce their daily water use by 20 to 30 percent as the state is hit by severe and costly wildfires coupled with the lack of substantial rainfall.

However historically, government at *all* levels was extremely reluctant to recognize the damage caused by dumping wastes into the nation's waterways. The federal government did recognize the need for sewage treatment plants by enacting a 1948 law providing federal funds to local communities. It was not until 1965 that Congress mandated that states applying for these federal dollars had to establish clean water standards as a criterion for grant consideration. By the 1970s, incidences of severe water pollution could no longer be ignored. For all practical purposes, Lake Erie was "dead, with garbage and rotting fish regularly washing onto beaches and runoff of fertilizer and raw sewage causing massive algae blooms that starved fish of oxygen. The Cuyahoga River [in

Cleveland, Ohio], which feeds Erie, was so polluted with oil, logs, sewage and every other kind of garbage that it caught fire on June 22, 1969. The Walleye in Erie contained so much toxic mercury that the government banned its consumption. Cormorants were born horribly deformed by pesticides, local populations of peregrine falcons have been driven toward extinction by DDT, and lake trout in Michigan and Huron were wiped out by over-fishing."[73] The majority of the nation's waterways located near heavy and medium-sized industrial plants were heavily polluted. "Before 1972, at least 18,000 communities regularly dumped their untreated raw sewage into rivers and lakes. Food, textile, paper, chemical, metal, and other industries discharged 25 trillion gallons of waste water each year."[74] The federal government's response was the passage of the **Water Pollution Control Act** (also known as the **Clean Water Act**) in 1972. This legislation established guidelines for nationwide water pollution standards.

The Clean Water Act also created the National Pollution Discharge Elimination System (NPDES) whereby all businesses and industries must file for a permit prior to discharging and/or dumping any effluents into a waterway. Municipalities are required to install more sophisticated purification treatment processes into their sewer systems. The Clean Water Act gave the administration and enforcement duties to the EPA, which passed the bulk of the responsibilities onto the states. States were required to establish separate state agencies to handle water pollution problems. In addition, state governments were given the latitude to pass their own water pollution-related legislation as long as state-mandated standards did not undermine federal restrictions and penalties. Federal and state guidelines mandated that all surface water be tested for the presence of harmful substances to include arsenic, lead, toxaphene, and chromium. The Clean Water Act was renewed in 1977, 1987, 1997 and 2007.

One of the major problems associated with water pollution is determining the origination of the pollution and the identity of the polluting party. The Clean Water Act does draw a distinction between nonpoint and point-source pollution. **Point source pollution** is defined as "a pollution source that has a precise, identifiable location, such as a pipe or smokestack."[75] Any business or industrial plant visibly dumping industrial and hazardous wastes into a waterway could be citied for point source pollution. **Non-point source pollution** is "a pollution source that is diffuse, such as urban runoff."[76] A river or stream could be heavily polluted with runoffs from fertilizers and pesticides originating from several farms and ranches located along that waterway. Determining the identity of the guilty party is extremely difficult, if not impossible.

The Clean Water Act has produced some positive results. "From 1972 to 1982, the amount of **biochemical oxygen demand (BOD)** (the amount of oxygen needed by bacteria to breakdown a specific amount of organic matter) declined by 46 percent at municipal sewage treatment plants and by at least 71 percent in industrial discharges."[77] Progress in cleaning up the nation's waterways has met with marginal success. Rivers are classified as either good, threatened or impaired. Bodies of water are declared impaired when they cannot support aquatic life or are unsafe for fishing or swimming. According to the EPA's biennial National Water Quality Inventory Report issued in 2010, of 3,533,205 miles of the nation's rivers and streams, only 26 percent or 934,808 were assessed. The study indicates that 50 percent of the assessed rivers and streams were rated as good with a corresponding 50 percent as impaired and 1 percent as threatened. Once again, of the assessed bodies of water, 55.1 percent were rated as good for fish, shellfish and wildlife protection and propagation, 60 percent for recreation, 93 percent for agricultural use, 40.5 percent for aquatic life harvesting, 75.1 percent for public water supply, 92.8 percent for industrial use, 59.5 percent for other use, 91.2 percent for aesthetic value, and only 10.7 percent for exceptional recreational or ecological significance.[78] The leading causes of impairment were pathogens, sediment, nutrients, organic enrichment (fertilizers) and habitat alterations.

Dams have also been identified as a contributing factor to water pollution. Damming rivers seemed to be the perfect solution to an area's drought conditions particularly in the West and Southwest regions of the United States. The Army Corps of Engineers provided a helping hand in determining the site location and size of the dam. "For nearly a century local water districts and Congress have regarded any Western rivers that flowed to the sea unimpeded as a colossal waste—a waste of water that could be captured for farming and urban development, a waste of potential hydropower, a waste of potential recreation sites that could be created by backing up the great rivers into lakes. To harness the water, federal and state agencies, as well as private developers, have built more than 600 major dams this century [20th]."[79] Damming a river does successfully prevent water from eventually spilling into the ocean. However, it also destroys natural habitat for sea creatures, animals, birds and plants. Damming also provides recreational spots for fishermen and outdoorsmen. However, it destroys the natural runoff patterns for rain. Far too often disastrous floods are caused by the inability of water to runoff naturally from properties. Now the Army Corps of Engineers is leading the charge to tear them down.

Oceans are also heavily polluted. "Throughout the world, important water bodies—especially the oceans—have become virtual waste bins for the tons of plastic products dumped daily by commercial fishermen, military vessels, merchant ships, passenger liners, pleasure boats, offshore oil and gas drilling operations, the plastics industry and sewage treatment plants."[80] While the sun is coming up over the ocean's horizon, it is tragic to realize that the first sight one has in the morning is the fleet of front end loaders making their daily sweep of the trash either thrown on by people or washed up on shore by the evening tide. Because oceans usually fall under international laws, few nations have enacted legislation designed to protect their shorelines from trash and pollution. The victims are the birds and sea creatures who must wade through the piles of garbage.

In 1974, the United States Congress passed the **Safe Water Drinking Act** with the promise of guaranteeing to all Americans a plentiful and healthy supply of drinking water. This legislation set federal standards for all suppliers of drinking water serving more than twenty-five people. The law was amended in 1986 with the provision that water suppliers test for dozens of chemicals and bacterial substances and notify their customers when water supplies did not meet federal standards. The amendments also banned the use of lead pipes in public water systems. In 2006, President Bush signed into law the latest round of amendments to the Safe Drinking Water Act.

Despite federal and state laws, the federal government still cannot guarantee a safe drinking water supply. Far too many communities must boil their water to remove unwanted substances. The renowned **United States Center for Disease Control and Prevention** warned those individuals with weakened immune systems, such as AIDS, and chemotherapy patients to either use bottled or boiled water. Groundwater is still in grave jeopardy of contamination from pesticides, human, animal and industrial wastes, home cleaning products, and gasoline. In addition, municipal governments across the country are confronting costly problems with fixing and or replacing leaking and rupturing water mains and sewer systems. A ruptured sewer main can lead to the introduction of harmful substances, such as pathogens, into the drinking water system. Floods caused by a major storm system or a hurricane will ruin municipal water and sewer systems. In the aftermath of Hurricane Katrina, residents along the Gulf Coast and in Louisiana were warned not to use or come in contact with any of their water supply systems. The flood waters themselves were heavily laden with toxic substances, backed-up sewer waste, gasoline and oil products from the rupture of underground storage tanks, etc. In January 2014, over 300,000 residents in nine counties in West Virginia were ordered not to drink, bathe, or wash clothes or dishes because their tap water was contaminated from a chemical spill in the Elk River. Owned by Freedom Industries, the chemical spill "occurred after a broken water line caused the ground to freeze beneath an aging chemical storage tank, pushing an unidentified object into the bottom of the tank. The resulting puncture allowed 7,500 gallons of 4-methylcyclohexane methanol, a chemical that washes impurities from coal to escape" into the Elk River, the primary source of drinking water in that area.[81] Facing potential lawsuits and fines from the EPA, the company filed for Chapter 11 bankruptcy. City governments can no longer ignore taking "action on the fissures spreading in the 700,000 miles of pipes that deliver water to U.S. homes and businesses. Three generations of water mains are at risk: cast-iron pipes of the 1880s, thinner conduits of the 1920s, and even less sturdy post-World War II tubes. Cost estimates range from the EPA's $151 billion figure to a $1 trillion tally by a coalition of water industry, engineering, and environmental groups. The American Water Works Association (AWWA) projects costs as high as $6,900 per household in some small towns."[82] Several municipalities are taking action to protect their drinking water supplies. Cities such as Dayton, Ohio, and San Antonio, Texas, are using restrictive and/or no-development zoning laws to protect their underground aquifer systems. In Dunedin, Florida, residents angry over the rust in their tap water, pressured city leaders to build a new water treatment plant with membrane-filtration systems.

Oil Spills and Toxic Wastes

On April 12, 2010, the nation's focus was on a deepwater drilling rig named Horizon, owned by the drilling company Trans-ocean and leased to BP. Located in the Gulf of Mexico off the Louisiana coastline, "an explosion rocked the rig, igniting a massive fire. Eleven workers were killed in the inferno, and 17 more were injured. Within two days, while Coast Guard ships were still searching for survivors, the ruined Horizon sank, dragging its equipment and pipes to the bottom of the ocean, 5,000 ft. below."[83] The explosion unleashed a massive oil spill stretching over 2,000 miles that was headed directly towards Louisiana's Barataria Bay. Unable to seal the well head, the oil gushed out at the rate of over 200,000 gallons a day as Gulf Coast residents came to the rescue of oil-soaked birds, turtles, and other marine animals. Work crews used oil dispersants to break up the floating thick crude oil and booms to soak it up before it washed ashore. It took four agonizing months for BP officials and engineers to drill a relief well, plug the broken one with mud and finally seal it. The future of the Louisiana fishing industry is still in limbo as few can assess the future damage this spill has had on marine life, especially shrimp and shellfish. BP has yet to reach a final settlement on the damages caused by the accident. It is estimated that BP will eventually pay out approximately $9.6 billion to Gulf Coast residents who filed settlement claims as well as an additional $17 billion in federal fines. The oil giant has already paid out nearly $42 billion for cleanup and related costs.[84] This spill is definitely the largest to date to hit America's coastline. In 1989, Americans were horrified as the Exxon *Valdez* went aground on Alaska's pristine Prince William Sound, spilling its cargo of crude oil over 900 square miles. The black goo spoiled shorelines, killed millions of marine animals and fish, and destroyed the fishing industry for several seasons. Three more major oil spills occurred that year. The Greek tanker, *World Prodigy*, struck a reef in Narragansett Bay, Rhode Island, dumping 420,000 of No. 2 fuel oil into the waterway. "In Delaware where the Uruguayan tanker, *Presidente Rivera*, ran aground and spilled 300,000 gallons of heavy No. 6 oil, about 70 percent had been cleaned up. The smallest of the spills, which occurred when a barge collided with a cargo ship in the Houston Ship Channel and released 250,000 gallons of heavy crude, was almost completely recovered."[85]

Obviously not every oil spill is preventable, but the majority of them can be avoided. Faced with the reality that only 10 percent of oil spilled is usually recovered, one would assume that the federal government would have taken extraordinary measures to keep disastrous oil spills to the bare minimum. However, interest group politics driven by the major oil producers has successfully prevented the federal government from taking severe punitive criminal and civil actions against violators. For example, then United States Senator Lloyd Bentsen introduced in 1989 a bill requiring all domestically owned oil tankers to use a triple hull structure around the oil storage tanks. Although public opinion sided with Bentsen, particularly after the *Valdez* episode, the legislation was defeated on the grounds that it was a costly unnecessary mandate against both big and small oil firms that would ultimately result in higher prices at the pump. The major oil companies had already served notice that if the bill passed, they would simply bypass the legislation by contracting out to foreign tanker companies to ship their oil. As merely the contracting party, the oil companies could transport their oil more cheaply while at the same time avoiding costly litigation if the tanker spilled its load. Our beaches, marine life, and, in some instances, economic viability is in jeopardy every time one of these tankers enters into America's waters.

The proper identification, storage, and disposal of hazardous, nuclear, and solid and municipal wastes are problems confronting all levels of government. Nuclear energy is a cost-effective method of supplying electricity to homes. Yet, scientists have yet to develop a safe method for the disposal of radioactive materials, much less obsolete nuclear reactors. The Industrial Revolution introduced manufacturing processes that produced toxic byproducts. For over one hundred years, it was an acceptable practice to dump these hazardous substances into waterways and vacant lots. The United States government is just as guilty as the nation's industrial giants. Beginning in the mid-1980s, Congress and the White House began searching for ways to save money. They decided that with the end of the Cold War and the collapse of the Soviet Union, the United States government no longer needed a large standing army supported by thousands of civil servants. The answer was to begin closing down American military bases. However, the Pentagon and lawmakers soon realized that the money they were going to save in closing the bases was small in comparison to the money they were going to be spending to clean up the hazardous materials housed and, unfortunately, dumped on these military bases. In California, McClellan Air Force Base is still in the process of being converted from public to private hands. "Decades of dumping, leaks and spills at the base have left the heavily used aquifer contaminated with chlorinated solvents and fuels that will take more than 30 years to clean up . . . McClellan hasn't fully assessed the extent of its contamination and doesn't expect to have its final cleanup systems in place until 2014. Cleanup is not expected to be finished until 2034. The projected cleanup tab for the 64-year old base is $984 million with $300 already spent."[86]

In addition to military installations, commercial nuclear power plants have their own problems disposing of their high-level radioactive wastes. As of 2010, there were 104 nuclear power plants generating 807,000,000 kWh.[87] The dilemma confronting the EPA is the location of sites for the disposal of radioactive waste materials. The fear of a potential disaster evokes strong emotions from citizens as government officials seek to find dump sites. Oftentimes politics enters into the picture. Although Americans enjoy the benefits of nuclear power, they are extremely fearful of nuclear accidents, particularly when the discussion of a potential site is their neighborhood!

Today, it is known that the disposal of nuclear and industrial byproducts must be properly stored and ultimately disposed of to prevent hazardous spills and contaminations; and individuals must dispose of their solid wastes and trash in a nonpolluting and responsible manner. However, the proper disposal of these materials is extremely costly and demands sacrifices from all participating parties. The federal government took the lead by setting the guidelines for the identification, monitoring, and disposal of solid and industrial waste products in 1976 with the passage of the **Toxic Substance Control Act**. **Solid waste** is defined as "refuse materials composed primarily of solids at normal ambient temperatures."[88] The EPA was empowered through this legislation to establish testing procedures for new chemical substances before they could be sold. The EPA also authorized federal and state authorities to ban the sale of any harmful substances. The law specifically prohibited the sale of toxic polychlorinated biphenyls (PCB) not contained in closed systems. On January 1, 2000, the Clinton administration imposed tighter reporting rules on the use of toxic substances. The old rules required "release reports by companies that manufacture or process more than 25,000 pounds or use more than 10,000 pounds of toxic chemicals a year. The new rules require reports by companies that use 100 pounds a year, or, for some especially dangerous chemicals, 10 pounds a year."[89] The **Resource Conservation and Recovery Act** of 1976 established the process for the disposal of hazardous wastes.

Both federal and state laws prohibit the transportation of any hazardous materials through municipal areas. The risk of a derailment or traffic accident is minimized by redirecting vehicles and railcarriers carrying hazardous substances to rural routes. However, the potentiality of an accident resulting in the release of toxic and harmful substances into rivers, waterways, soil, and the air is still a tragic reality. All parties involved in the storage and disposal of toxic and hazardous materials must record the site with the appropriate county offices as well as file monthly and yearly reports.

The average American throws away tons of garbage every year. **Municipal solid waste** is defined as "solid waste resulting from or incidental to municipal, community, commercial, institutional, and recreational activities including garbage, rubbish, ashes, street cleanings, dead animals, abandoned automobiles, and all other solid waste other than industrial waste."[90] Once it was perfectly acceptable to pile up the trash in landfills and trash dumps, pitch it out the window to the streets below, or simply burn it in the privacy of one's backyard. With every American contributing 4.3 pounds of waste per day, it is estimated that 243,000,000 tons of municipal waste was generated in 2009.[91] Although federal and state laws set guidelines for the disposal of these products, the ultimate responsibility falls squarely upon the shoulders of city and county governments. The laws establish extremely strict regulations covering a wide range of municipal waste activities, including the size of the landfill and the height of the trash piles. Site location is an extremely delicate situation since no one wants a landfill in their backyard. However, the trash can be piled only as high as the federally mandated level allows. Cities can apply for a variance to buy time until a new site can be located. There is just too much trash and too little landfill space to dump it on. In addition, reclamation of landfills is virtually worthless since it is unlikely that anyone would want to build their homes or businesses on a filled-in landfill that may emit harmful vapors and odors.

Communities have adopted volunteer recycling programs for newspapers, paper products, glass, plastics, and aluminum cans. However, converting recycled products into reusable goods is still an expensive venture. Although environmentally aware, the average American consumer is reluctant to purchase higher priced items made from recycled products. Another alternative is incineration, whereby unsorted trash is burned. Although incineration does reduce the need for landfill space, the process of burning mass amounts of trash does pose potential harmful effects to air quality. Site selection proposals for incineration plants produce heated battles between angry residents vehemently opposed to having smokestacks release byproducts from burning trash over their homes and city leaders desperate to find cost effective trash disposal methods. Advanced incineration systems include mass burn combustors, modular combustion systems, refuse-driven fuel combustors, and waste-to-energy plants. Obviously, this nation's major cities are facing an uphill battle unless cost-effective and environmentally safe alternative trash disposal methods are adopted within the immediate future.

Superfund Programs

Since the cost of properly disposing and cleaning up hazardous, solid, and municipal wastes is often too expensive for the violators to bear alone, the **Comprehensive Environmental Response Compensation and Liability Act** established a federally funded Superfund in 1980. Basically, "the federal government imposed taxes on oil and chemical companies and certain other corporations that went directly into a cleanup trust fund, which reached its peak of $3.8 billion in 1996."[92] The special taxes expired in 2006 with Congress taking no action to revive the fund. The EPA, however, continued to identify sites and use the outstanding balance until the funds ran out. The EPA continues to cleanup sites with taxpayer money. The Obama administration wants to reestablish the tax program. The **Emergency Planning and Community Right-to-Know Act** passed in 1986 requires local businesses to notify communities about the types of hazardous substances they use and how these products were being stored, used, and disposed. The **Pollution Prevention Act** (1990) expanded reporting guidelines to include both the amount of waste recycled and the amount of waste not produced because of antipollution devices. The **Community Right-to-Know-More Act** (1991) requires public disclosure of how much of a hazardous chemical is used to produce a particular product.

Forest and Wetland Conservation

The EPA defines **wetlands** as "areas that are inundated or saturated by surface or groundwater often enough or for a long enough period to support vegetation adapted for saturated soils."[93] The wetlands play a fundamental role in maintaining the balance of nature since "among other functions, they reduce flood and storm damage, provide wildlife and fish habitat, help improve water quality by filtering run-off, protect drinking water sources, and provide recreation opportunities."[94] By contrast, **deepwater habitats** are "permanently flooded land lying below the deepwater boundary of wetlands. Deepwater habitats include environments where surface water is permanent and often deep, so that the water, rather than air, is the principal medium within which the dominant organisms live, whether or not they are attached to the substrate."[95] Unfortunately, the wetlands have become the victims of a growing population's demand for residential, recreational, and commercial construction. Initially, both the federal and state governments encouraged the dredging and filling of wetland properties to the point that "about half of the 200 million acres of wetlands in the contiguous 48 states at the time of the European colonization have been lost."[96] The desire of government to protect and preserve wetlands is a classic case of government's charge to promote the "public good" clashing head-on with the treasured rights of private property ownership since over 3/4's of all wetlands is held in private hands.

There are, however, several federal and state laws establishing guidelines for the use and disposition of wetlands property. Section 404 of the Clean Water Act requires the issuance of permits to any interested party involved in the draining and/or filling of wetlands. The U.S. Army Corps of Engineers is the primary agency charged with the issuance of these permits and with periodic inspection of the sites. A provision of the 1990 **Farm Bill** requires that farmers and ranchers receiving U.S. Department of Agriculture benefits and subsidies must protect any wetlands located on their property. In addition, the **Wetlands Reserve Program** provides cash incentives to property owners as a means of encouraging preservation efforts. These legislative enactments, however, have failed to halt the gradual erosion of these precious habitat areas.

With approximately 1.5 million acres, the Florida Everglades is the nation's third largest national park. It is the breeding grounds and habitat for countless species of animal, plant and marine life. However, Florida's booming population has resulted in the dredging of Everglades swamp land for the construction of single- and multi-story dwellings, and the diversion of its water to augment depleting suburban water needs. In addition, the sugar industry has gradually taken Everglades land and converted it into farmland. The Everglades is a natural buffer zone that protects the populated areas from the havoc caused by frequent hurricanes. The erosion of the Everglades has resulted in costlier hurricane damage in both loss of life and property. Conservationists have convinced the Florida's governor to launch a program to rehabilitate the Everglades. The legislature has struck a deal to purchase for $1.75 billion approximately 187,000 acres of former Everglades land from U.S. Sugar Corp.[97] It is hoped that rehabilitation of the area will offer increased protection for endangered and threatened species and provide the needed buffer zone for the Florida coastline.

The nation's forests are also in peril as more and more acres of trees are cut every year. The lumber is used to build homes and businesses. The pulp is processed into the billions of reams of paper and paper products used every day. Forests play an essential role in the maintenance of a healthy clean environment, as well as provide natural habitats for a wide range of plant and animal life. "At the time of white settlement, approximately, 1.1 billion acres of forest thrived in the United States, covering 49 percent of the landscape. From the 1600s to 1920, 370 million acres of forests (34 percent) were cleared, leaving 730 million acres today. Only 10 to 15 percent of today's forests have never been cut."[98] Management of publicly owned forests falls under the jurisdiction of the United States Forest Service. These forests are used for recreation, timber harvest, wildlife habitat, watershed protection, and wilderness and range management. President Bill Clinton used his authority as outlined in the Antiquities Act of 1906 to add another 58,518,000 acres for protection by the federal government.⁹⁹ Through his executive order, these lands are now protected from future road building, private development, oil and gas exploration, and drilling and logging. The Bush administration was taken aback by Clinton's actions and called upon the federal courts to overrule Clinton's midnight hour use of the Antiquities Act. As a candidate, Bush openly advocated the exploration and possible drilling of oil from the Alaskan wilderness as a means of decreasing the nation's dependency upon foreign oil. The 9ᵗʰ Circuit Court of Appeals, however, ruled in favor of President Clinton. The ruling "prohibits virtually all road building in roadless parcels of 5,000 acres or more, acreage that covers a third of America's national forest or 2 percent of the nation's land mass."¹⁰⁰ The ruling includes Alaska's 17-million acre Tongass National Forest.

Endangered Species

Passed in 1973, the **Endangered Species Act (ESA)** is still one of the most controversial of the federally enacted environmental laws. The law empowers the U.S. Fish and Wildlife Service to prohibit the harassing, collection, capture, and hunting of any species determined to be threatened or in danger of extinction. The ESA defines **endangered species** as "one in danger of becoming extinct throughout all or a significant part of its natural range; whereas, a **threatened species** is "one likely to become endangered in the foreseeable future."¹⁰¹ As of 2011, the EPA listed 1,967 species of mammals, bird, reptiles, amphibians, fish, snails, clams, crustaceans, insects, arachnids and plants as either endangered or threatened.¹⁰² However, environmentalists believe the law is not strong enough in protecting species from the encroachment of progress. Viewing it as a reactionary program, they believe that "ideally, the ESA should serve as an emergency room for species on the decline, but only if we also practice preventive medicine by helping healthy populations of wildlife before they get into trouble."¹⁰³ They point to the few successes such as the American Bald Eagle, the alligator, and so on and compare these to the growing list of extinct and so-to-be extinct species.

Opponents believe the law goes too far by placing the value of one animal or bird above economic progress, jobs, and property rights. On the Gulf Coast, fishermen complained that using turtle excluder devices, or break-away nets, would severely hamper the shrimping business, placing smaller trollers out of business. Protecting the habitat of the California gnatcatcher, a small, blue-gray bird, has land developers crying foul. In Texas, the Edwards Underground Recharge Zone is the only breeding habitat for the rare blind catfish. The Fish and Wildlife Service and other environmentally charged federal agencies and the federal court system are still debating how to protect this fish while drought-prone South Texas seeks to meet the water needs of its residents. The list of complaints goes on and on.

Despite the critics, the ESA is "the one legal mechanism in the United States that can force communities to balance conservation with development."¹⁰⁴ The ESA has been successful in slowing the rate of extinction. And, those shrimpers on the Gulf Coast actually improved their catch by using those nets. The logging business in the Pacific Northwest has lost more jobs due to automation and a growing timber industry in the Southeastern part of the United States than to the protection of the spotted owl.

POLICY OPTIONS AND THE POLITICAL CLIMATE

Particularly with environmental issues, policy options are limited. The curative policy approach is not a viable option since existing environmental damage cannot be substantially reversed, much less cured. The alleviative approach can be used to address property or health-related problems caused by previous incidences of environmental damage. However, this option is viable only if the source of the pollution can be identified. For example, an area's residents are experiencing high incidents of lung-related illnesses caused by bacteria in the water supply. Medical experts believe the source of the problem is the one river that runs through this community. However, the water in this river has been contaminated for years as the five to six major industries located on its banks have dumped their industrial byproducts into it. Determining who is responsible for the pollution and ultimately liable for damages is almost impossible. In addition, liability for pollution-related damage is questionable since the majority of the laws have "grandfather" clauses that protect businesses and individuals from litigation for polluting activities that happened before the laws were passed.

Consequently, lawmakers turn to the preventive and punitive approaches. Every environmental law seeks to prevent future damage by punishing those who pollute with strict penalties and with criminal sanctions to deter would-be polluters. "Interestingly, the government of the United States, whose political and legal culture is the most protective of private property rights, takes the most confrontational position towards private polluters of any nation. Its laws are the strictest, giving administrators the least discretion in their dealings with industry."[105] However, the evidence clearly indicates that this nation continues to have a serious environmental problem. It is clear that "the strictness of laws and procedures in the United States has not necessarily produced better results than in other countries that take a more conciliatory stance towards industry."[106] If the laws are strong in verbiage and punitive penalties, why does this nation continue to have an evergrowing environmental problem? The answer rests with an evaluation of (a) the effectiveness of the EPA and other federal agencies; (b) the policy approach used to produce regulations; (c) the lack of incentives to encourage nonpolluting activities; (d) the inability to enforce regulations in a timely and consistent manner; and (e) an often hostile political climate.

Created in 1970 with the passage of the **Environmental Protection Act**, the **Environmental Protection Agency (EPA)** was initially charged with overseeing air and water pollution problems. The role of the EPA has been expanded to include hazardous wastes, pesticides, noise pollution, and, in part, endangered species. The EPA monitors potential environmental damage by requiring all federal agencies to file an **impact statement** detailing any potential harm a project might cause to the environment, as well as proposing solutions to prevent undo environmental damage and potential efforts on the part of a project's sponsors to maintain and hopefully enhance the productivity of the environment. The EPA has the power to make or break a project. If irreversible harm will occur, the EPA should and will cancel a project. Usually, the EPA opts to attach additional requirements or **mandates** to a project in hopes of avoiding environmental damage. The mandates may indirectly lead to the demise of a project simply because they add to project costs. The EPA also reserves the right to inspect all aspects of the construction to ensure compliance.

The EPA has become the enemy to many construction firms, land developers, property owners, state and local governments, environmentalists, and lawmakers and politicians from both sides of the political spectrum. These groups usually have few kind words for the EPA and its impact statements, mandates, and regulations. First, critics believe that the command and control approach used by the EPA is "excessively rigid and insensitive to geographical and technical differences and for being inefficient."[107] Rural areas, for example, are subjected to the same standards as heavily populated urban areas.

The EPA's command and control approach also permits the agency to set the compliance guidelines but turns enforcement over to a myriad of state and federal agencies. This strategy severely compromises the effectiveness of the EPA. First, states may and do pass their own environmental laws. "Generally, the states are not precluded from enforcing criteria more strigent than those required by federal laws, and are given considerable leeway to follow enforcement interpretations which may not be fully consistent with those applied at the federal level."[108] Some states do pass environmental laws that are considerably more strict in scope as well as laden with far more punitive measures than federal sanctions. On the other hand, some states opt for a minimalist approach by barely enforcing federal guidelines. For example, the Texas Commission on Environmental Quality is charged with conducting periodic inspections, assessment of fines and penalties, and investigating reported violations of state environmental laws. The fertilizer plant that exploded in January 2013 in West, Texas is owned by West Fertilizer. A complaint of a heavy ammonia smell was filed with the TCEQ in 2006. Although cited by the TCEQ for a permit violation, little to no follow up was conducted. A contributing factor to the 2013 explosion was heavy concentrations of ammonia! Second, the EPA is not the sole implementator of environmental laws and regulations. The agency shares its authority with a myriad of federal agencies including the Fish and Wildlife Service, the Corps of Engineers, the Interior Department, the National Park Service, and so on. The states have overlapped this fragmented approach by creating numerous state agencies with duplicated functions. A business trying to comply with the various rules often deals with too many agencies, each requiring the submission of duplicated reports, paperwork, and procedures. Although on paper the EPA did set national standards, the individual states have wreaked havoc with them, leaving everyone involved in a state of confusion.

The Science Advisory Board leveled another criticism of the EPA by calling it "a largely 'reactive' agency, insufficiently oriented toward opportunities for the greatest risk reduction . . . . The board also called upon the EPA to pursue a much broader agenda than it has in the past, and to take responsibility for protecting the environment, not just for implementing environmental law by addressing the most serious risks, whether or not agency action is required by law."[110] Basically, the EPA has done very little to prevent damage since it appears to react after the damage has been done!

The policy approach with its emphasis on punitive sanctions is a major point of disagreement to business, industry, and property owners. "The implementation process for environmental laws in the United States is by far the most formalized, rule-oriented, and adversarial—in a word, confrontational."[110] The EPA emerges not as a friend to business but as a sinister rule-laden monster fixated with complicated rules and procedures that are burdensome and often too costly for business to bear. Far too often, environmental issues are decided by judges, not the EPA or its complicated rules. "Regulations are based on collected evidence marshalled by the contending sides and interpreted according to specific procedures that are open to appeals and legal challenges at all stages. The rule-making process is typically long and contentious, often ending in litigation."[111] It can take years of legal action to adjudicate one case. Meanwhile, the accused polluters can continue their polluting ways while the attorneys battle it out in the courts.

The rules themselves are just as reactive. The United States Constitution prohibits the enactment of ex post facto laws. Consequently, laws are enforceable and penalties are binding only for future violations. For example, both federal and state laws mandate that all injection or underground wells and surface pits be plugged and/or filled upon completion of extraction activities. Yet, these laws do not apply to wells drilled before the laws were passed. Natural resource-rich states have thousands of abandoned gas, oil, and water wells left unplugged and pits left unfilled. A small town in Texas lost a whole school bus load of children who drowned when their bus was hit by a truck, pushing the bus into a water-filled abandoned gravel pit. The owner of the pit was not liable since the pit was created before the legislation requiring to fill it was passed.

Perhaps the business community would be more cooperative if the EPA and other environmental agencies would offer incentives to those who voluntarily exceed federally mandated compliance levels. "A factory might be able to reduce its emissions by 70 percent rather than the required 50 percent at little additional cost, but the factory most likely will not do the additional cleanup—its goal is to minimize the cost of product, not to provide a cleaner environment for society."[112] Could not the EPA and other federal and state agencies encourage more conservation through the development of environmentally safe production methods by offering incentives towards research and rewards for results rather than just punishing the violators?

The EPA's enforcement track-record has been described as being mired in lengthy and costly litigation that results in lenient cleanup schedules and few fines. Too often the EPA's targets are small and medium-sized businesses and industries who can not afford the daily fines much less the expensive legal fees to fight a lengthy court room battle with the federal government. Larger firms, however, can afford to tie up the EPA for years while they continue to pollute the environment. Basically, the EPA is "reluctant to enforce standards against large companies with political clout or small profit margins, especially industries crucial to the nation's economic health. To take action against a large industry requires significant political will all the way up to the White House."[113] Although the EPA would have investigated the BP oil spill, President Obama put the investigation on the fast track by taking a very active role in addressing the damage caused by the spill. He initiated a federal-level committee to ensure that those adversely impacted by that spill would be compensated for their current and future losses. He also placed a ban on deep-water drilling projects until the companies involved in off-shore drilling could implement appropriate safety measures to protect both rig workers and the environment from future catastrophic harm. The failure of environmental agencies to take on the giants has ruined their effectiveness, tarnished their reputations, and left small businesses with a justifiable charge of foul play.

The political climate is particularly important in the development and implementation of environmental policies. Public sympathy does support the cause of environmentalists. It would seem reasonable to assume that since public opinion is solidly behind protecting the environment, that lawmakers could easily address this issue. However, like so many other issues, fickle public opinion can change rapidly. The urge to clean up the environment waxes and wanes when the words "sacrifice," "cost," and "accountability" enter into the picture. In general, the American public is not committed to long-term sacrifice without seeing immediate tangible results capable of encouraging them to continue their efforts.

"We associate environmentalism with the burgeoning of grassroots citizen participation in the 1960s throughout the Western countries. As motivating issues, nuclear power and other environmental concerns were second only to the Vietnam War in their power to mobilize middle-class citizens."[114] Today, environmental groups continue to pursue their bottom-line issues. Preeminent groups include the Sierra Club, Wildlife Federation, Environmental Defense Fund, National Resources Defense Council, Greenpeace, and the radial Greens group. Their message advocating a cleaner environment is soundly backed by the visible evidence and statistical data detailing environmental damage. However, the tactics they use often adversely impact their effectiveness. The environmental movement had difficulties "incorporating itself into national politics, largely because its goals and styles did not fit that of traditional party politics."[115] Consequently, environmental groups rely upon protests, demonstrations, and mass arrests to get their point across. Doomsday predictions by environmentalists have led some to label them as extremists who are willing to sacrifice the economic viability of this country to protect the environment from the encroachment of progress. "Environmentalists' perchant for doomsaying is coming back to haunt them. By overstating evidence, by presenting hypotheses as certainties, and predictions as facts to create a sense of urgency, scientist-activists have jeopardized their own creditability."[116]

There is a growing number of individuals who simply believe that environmentalists are wrong about the dangers of global warming, air pollution, etc. Rep. Ann Marie Buerkle (R-NY) stated in a 2010 campaign debate that "'a lot of the global warming myth has been exposed' . . . she added that 'the jury's still out' on whether fossil fuel burning contributes to global warming."[117] Rep. Dan Benishek (R-Michigan) believes global warming is "all baloney. It's all baloney. I think it's just some scheme. I just don't believe it. You know, I'm a scientist, I'm a surgeon, I've done scientific research papers; there's a lot of skepticism."[118] Environmental groups are taking a more proactive role in pursuing their message. The League of Conservation Voters, for example, is conducting a multi-million dollar campaign effort to unseat anti-environmental lawmakers such as Burerkle and Benishek.

Support for or against an issue is oftentimes tied to one's income level. Environmental groups, like the majority of the nation's interest groups, attract advocates from upper- and middle-income classes who view the value of the environment differently from their lower-income counterparts. "The economically secure are more willing to close down polluting factories. They are more willing to ban logging operations in order to preserve wilderness areas and to pay extra for canned goods in order to reduce the cannery's waste emissions into a river."[119] The affluent can afford to make these sacrifices without seriously compromising their social and economic viability. The poor may be sympathetic to environmental concerns; however, they cannot afford to make personal sacrifices. To them, environmentalists and their causes mean factory and business closings and loss of jobs. To the mechanic, factory worker, oil field worker, and so on "their jobs depend upon exploiting environmental resources; their first priority is to maintain a healthy growing economy, and keep factories operating even if emissions pollute the air; feeding one's family and paying the rent are of primary importance; an unpleasant smell in the air is of relatively little concern. Smoke means jobs."[120] It is obvious why the average American factory worker does not embrace the message of environmentalists.

Although the Democratic Party has been more receptive in embracing environmental causes and the cry for stronger federal regulations, the party still must deal with political reality. Among the voting population are those who are adversely affected by strict environmental policies. The Republican Party is well known for its opposition to governmental regulation, particularly environmental laws. Their cries to end the role of big government meddling into the affairs of business, industry, and private property owners win support nationwide. Yet, the Republican Party cannot afford to be too "anti." Both parties are guilty of wanting "to please the voting public by jumping on the 'ecological band wagon' while not alienating the business interests so dominate in the pollution problem and yet so essential to their political successes."[121] The safest course of action for both parties is to pursue a moderate position by avoiding extreme positions on both sides of the issue.

Environmental issues are further complicated by the inclusion of the international community. Policy-makers in the United States must work closely with other countries to ensure a steadfast commitment that protecting the environment is essential to the world's survival, not just the United States. The relationship between United States lawmakers and the international community is a fragile one. Not all nations have the resources that the United States has to deal with environmental concerns. Nor can the United States afford to "lord over" other countries by trying to dominate the policy responses. In addition, the environment, unlike other policy issues such as poverty, transportation, education, and so on, is a problem that the United States cannot address by itself. What happens in the Brazilian rain forest, for example, directly has an impact on environmental efforts in the United States. Effective international environmental policies can only become a reality with a solid and unified front from the international community.

CONCLUSION

In the United States, the collective "we," the industrialists, business people, workers, consumers, politicians, lawmakers, and so on have polluted our communities, our countries, and our planet. We are to blame for polluting the air, watersupply, and waterways. We have allowed our quest for progress and modernization to jeopardize plant and wildlife and to deplete the forests and wetlands. The problem is how can the collective "we" put this wanton destruction to a screeching halt. Obviously, no one is pleased with the current strategy of passing strict regulatory laws backed with costly punitive sanctions. Environmentalists view these enactments as an ineffective tool in combating environmental damage while the opposing camp is embodied in lengthy legal battles as they attempt to ward off both the regulations and the regulators. The current federal and state laws may be strong in verbiage and intent but are weak in implementation, in fair and just enforcement, and in results. No one factor, including the environment itself, is winning the war. The collective "we" can save the environment by not placing the blame on each other but by collectively beginning to make the sacrifices needed to preserve our planet.

CHAPTER NOTES

[1] Wallace Stenger, "It All Began With Conservation," *Smithsonian*, Vol. 21, No. 1, April, 1990, 35.
[2] Ibid.
[3] Steven A. Peterson and Thomas H. Rausmussen, *State and Local Politics*, (New York: McGraw-Hill, Inc., 1994), 241.
[4] "Global Warming's Threat to Species To Be Spelled Out," *San Antonio Express-News* (Sunday, April 1, 2007), 25A.
[5] Joseph B. Verrengia, "Goal Is To Save The Earth And Its People," *San Antonio Express-News* (Sun., Aug. 25, 2002), 18A.
[6] Bureau of the Census, *Statistical Abstract of the United States: 2012*, 131st ed., (Washington, D.C.: 2011), Tables 1329 and 1331, 835.

[7] Jim Yardley, "China Pollution Takes Deadly Toll on Poor," *San Antonio Express-News* (Sunday, September 12, 2004), 26A.
[8] Peterson, 261.
[9] "Green and Not So Green," *Newsweek*, April 14, 2008, 69.
[10] Peter Borelli, "Environmental Philosophy," *Major Problems in American Environmental History*, Carolyn Merchant, ed., (Lexington, Massachusetts: D. C. Heath, 1993), 567.
[11] Stenger, "It All Began With Conservation," 38.
[12] Borelli, "Environmental Philosophy," 560.
[13] Steven Stoll, *U.S. Environmentalism Since 1945: A Brief History with Documents*, (Boston, Massachusetts: Bedford/St. Martin's, 2007), 8.
[14] Ibid.
[15] Stenger, "It All Began With Conservation," 39.
[16] Ibid.
[17] Ibid.
[18] *Treasury of Presidential Quotations*, Caroline Thomas Harsberger, ed., (Chicago: Follett Publishing Co., 1964), 41.
[19] Stenger, "It All Began With Conservation," 40.
[20] "Theodore Roosevelt Publicizes Conservation, 1908," *Major Problems in American Environmental History*, 350-352.
[21] Arnold Heidenheimer, Hugh Helco, and Carolyn Teich Adams, *Comparative Public Policy: The Politics of Social Choice in America, Europe, and Japan*, 3rd ed., (New York, New York: St. Martins Press, 1990), 316.
[22] Peterson, 251.
[23] Gregg Easterbrook, *A Moment On the Earth: The Coming Age of Environmental Optimism*, (New York, New York: Penguin Books, USA, Inc., 1995), 79-80.
[24] Stephen Klaidman, "Muddling Through," *The Wilson Quarterly*, Vol. XV, No. 2, Spring, 1991, 74.
[25] Stenger, "It All Began With Conservation," 43.
[26] Stoll, 19.
[27] *The Presidential Campaign 1976: Jimmy Carter*, Vol. I, Part 1, (Washington, D.C.: United States Government Printing Office, 1978), 662 & 664.
[28] Ibid., 663-664.
[29] Klaidman, 73.
[30] Jeff Nesmith, "Gore Tells Congress 'The Planet Has A Fever,'" *San Antonio Express-News* (Thursday, March 22, 2007), 3A.
[31] Jerry Adler, "Just the Tree of Us," *Newsweek*, April 14, 2008, 43-48.
[32] "Obama Position On The Environment," http://2012.presidential-candidates.org/Obama.Environment.php
[33] Gary C. Bryner, *Blue Skies, Green Politics: The Clean Air Act of 1990*, 1st ed., (Washington, D.C.: CQ Press, 1993), 41.
[34] Ibid., 42.
[35] *The 1993 Information Please Environmental Handbook*, compiled by the World Resource Institute, (New York, New York: Houghton Mifflin Co., 1993), 88.
[36] Bryner, 42.
[37] Ibid.
[38] Susan L. Cutter and William H. Renwick, *Exploitation, Conservation, and Preservation: A Geographic Perspective on Natural Resource Use*, 4th ed., (Hoboken, New Jersey: John Wiley & Sons, Inc., 2004), 281.
[39] Ibid.
[40] Ibid., 282.
[41] Bryner, 187.
[42] Marla Cone, "Study Says Pollutant Suppress Rain, Snowfall," *San Antonio Express-News* (Sunday, March 12, 2000), 8A.
[43] Ibid.
[44] Klaidman, 81.
[45] Ibid.
[46] Ibid., 83.
[47] Ibid., 84.
[48] Ibid.
[49] Jane Holtz Kay, "Moving In The Right Direction," *Preservation*, Vol. 49, No. 3, May/June, 1997, 53.
[50] Kay, 54.
[51] Ibid.
[52] Broder, "U.S. Fuel Efficient Standards Going Up," 1A.
[53] H. Josef Herbert, "Nobody Knows How Much Oil Refuge Holds," *San Antonio Express-News*, (Tuesday, Dec. 20, 2005), 5A.

[54] Ibid.
[55] Ibid.
[56] "Comparing The Presidential Candidates On The Issues," http://2012.candidates-comparison.org
[57] David R. Baker, "Canadians Eyeing More Access By Pipeline To U.S. West Coast," *San Antonio Express-News* (Thursday, April 25, 2013), B1.
[58] Ibid.
[59] Peter Baker and John M. Broder, "Moratorium on Deep-Water Drilling Lifted," *San Antonio Express-News*, (Wednesday, October 13, 2010), 7A.
[60] John Tedesco, "Clearing the Air on Refinery Row," *San Antonio Express-News*, (Saturday, October 7, 2000) 8A.
[61] Marianne Lavelle, "Blasts, But Not From the Past," *U.S. News & World Report*, July 17, 2000, 18.
[62] H. Josef Hebert, "Appeals Court Block on Clean Air Rules," *San Antonio Express- News* (Saturday, Oct. 30, 1999) 11A.
[63] R. G. Ratcliffe, "Texas Loses Say Over Air Quality," *San Antonio Express-News*, (Friday, December 4, 2010), 1A.
[64] Stoll, 17.
[65] Susan Welch, John Gruhl, Michael Steinman, John Comer, and Susan M. Ridgon, *American Government*, 5th ed., (Minneapolis, Minnesota: West Publishing Co., 1994), 615.
[66] Bret Schulte, "Turning Up The Heat", *U.S. News & World Report*, April 10, 2006, 34.
[67] Ibid., 35.
[68] "Concern About Polar Ice Melt, Rising Seas Become More Heated," *San Antonio Express-News*, (Fri, March 24, 2006),1A.
[69] Seth Borenstein, "Hot Water, Disease Kills Coral Reefs That Columbus Saw," *San Antonio Express-News*, (Friday, March 31, 2006), 10A.
[70] Cutter, 202.
[71] *Statistical Abstract of the United States: 2012*, 131st ed., Table 358, 223.
[72] "Water Use Today," *Water Sense*, United States Environmental Protection Agency, http://www.epa.gov/watersense
[73] Peter Annin and Sharon Begley, "Great Lake Effect," *Newsweek*, July 5, 1999, 52.
[74] Welch, 615.
[75] Cutter, 377.
[76] Ibid., 376.
[77] *The 1993 Information Please Environmental Handbook*, 38 & 40.
[78] U.S. Environmental Protection Agency, *The National Water Quality Inventory: Report to Congress for the 2010 Reporting Cycle – National Summary of State Information*, October 13, 2010, 2-3.
[79] Andrew Murr and Sharon Begley, "Dams Are Not Forever," *Newsweek*, November 17, 1997, 70.
[80] Michael Weisskopf, "Plastic Reaps A Grim Harvest In the Oceans of the World," *Smithsonian*, Vol. 18, No. 12, March, 1988, 59.
[81] "Company In West Virginia Spill Files For Bankruptcy," *San Antonio Express-News* (January 18, 2014), A11.
[82] Marianne Lavelle and Joshua Kurlantzick, "The Coming Water Crisis," *U.S. News & World Report*, Aug. 12, 2002, 24.
[83] Bryan Walsh, "The Meaning of the Mess," *Time*, (May 17, 2010), 30.
[84] "Analysis: BP's U.S. Gulf Oil Spill Settlement Challenges May Backfire," *Reuters*, http://www.reuters.com.artcle/2014/01/15
[85] Barbara Rudolph, "Whose Mess Is It?", *Time*, July 10, 1989, 42.
[86] Jerry Needham, "The McClellan Monster," *San Antonio Express-News* (Saturday, October 21, 2000), 15A.
[87] *Statistical Abstract of the United States: 2012*, 131st ed., Table 941, 593.
[88] Susan L. Cutter and William H. Renwick, *Exploration, Conservation, and Preservation: A Geographic Perspective on Natural Resource Use*, 4th ed., (Hoboken, New Jersey: John Wiley & Sons, Inc., 2004), 379.
[89] William C. Mann, "Clinton Airs Tougher Rules for Toxic Pollution," *San Antonio Express-News* (Sun., Oct. 31, 1999), 13A.
[90] Randy Lee Loftis, "Texas Environment: State of Neglect," *The Dallas Morning News* (Sunday, November 24, 1991),3N.
[91] *Statistical Abstract of the United States: 2012*, 131st ed., T*able 377, 231*.
[92] Juliet Eilperin, "EPA Will Push Congress to Reestablish Superfund Tax," *San Antonio Express-News*, (Monday, June 21, 2010), 4A.
[93] Elana Cohen, "Protecting Wetlands: Creating A Sense of Stewardship," *The National Voter*, (Washington, D.C.: League of Women Voters of the United States, June/July, 1996), 15.
[94] Ibid.
[95] *Statistical Abstract of the United States: 2012*, 131st ed., Table 370, 228.
[96] Cohen, 15.
[97] Joel Achenbach, "Florida Strikes Everglades Deal," *San Antonio Express-News* (Wednesday, June 25, 2008), 1A.

⁹⁸*The 1993 Information Please Environmental Handbook*, 176-177.
⁹⁹John Heilpirn, "Court Again Slaps Limits on Use of National Forests," *San Antonio Express-News* (Sun., Dec. 15, 2002), 11AA.
¹⁰⁰Ibid.
¹⁰¹*Statistical Abstract of the United States: 2012*, 131st ed., Table 387, 236.
¹⁰²Ibid.
¹⁰³*The 1993 Information Please Environmental Handbook*, 159.
¹⁰⁴Ibid.
¹⁰⁵Heidenheimer, 310.
¹⁰⁶Ibid.
¹⁰⁷Bryner, 20.
¹⁰⁸J. Gordon Arbuckle, etal., *Environmental Law Handbook*, 111th ed., (Rockville, Md.: Government Institute, Inc., 1991), 8.
¹⁰⁹Bryner, 32.
¹¹⁰Heidenheimer, 323.
¹¹¹Ibid.
¹¹²Peterson, 259.
¹¹³Welch, 614.
¹¹⁴Heidenheimer, 310.
¹¹⁵Ibid.
¹¹⁶"The Doomsday Myths," *U.S. News and World Report*, December 13, 1993, 81.
¹¹⁷"Conservation Group Targets 5 Republicans," *San Antonio Express-News* (Thursday, July 24, 2012), A5.
¹¹⁸Ibid.
¹¹⁹Peterson, 243.
¹²⁰Ibid.
¹²¹"Wilbourn E. Benton, *Texas Politics: Constraints and Opportunities*, 5th ed., (Chicago, Illinois: Nelson-Hill, 1984), 375.

SUGGESTED READINGS

Esterbrook, Gregg, *A Moment on the Earth: The Coming Age of Environmental Optimism*, New York, New York: Penguin Books USA, 1995.

Harrigan, John J., and David C. Nice, *Politics and Policy in States and Communities*, 8th ed., New York, New York: Pearson Education, Inc., 2004.

Heidenheimer, Arnold, Hugh Heclo, and Carolyn Teich Adams. *Comparative Public Policy: The Politics of Social Choice in America, Europe, and Japan*. 3rd ed. New York: St. Martin's Press, 1990.

Klaidman, Stephen. "Muddling Through," *The Wilson Quarterly*. Spring, 1991, Vol. XV, No. 2, pp.73-82.

Peterson, Steven A. and Thomas H. Rausmussen. *State and Local Politics*. New York: McGraw-Hill, Inc., 1994.

Web Sites:

unfccc.int/kyoto_protoco - Kyoto Treaty
environment.about.com
unfccc.int - official site for UN Climate Secretariat

Chapter Eighteen

FOREIGN POLICY

In a letter written to James Monroe in 1796, President George Washington clearly expressed his position on whether the new nation should become involved in world affairs:

> I have always given it as my decided opinion that no nation had a right to intermeddle in the internal concerns of another; that every one had a right to form and adopt whatever government they like best to live under themselves; if this country could, consistently with its engagements, maintain a strict neutrality and thereby preserve peace, it was bound to do so by motives of policy, interest, and every other consideration. . . . Tis our true policy to steer clear of permanent alliances with any portion of the foreign world.[1]

Less than two hundred years later, then Senator John F. Kennedy told an audience in Madison, Wisconsin, that although the United States did not seek it or want it, this country was now the leader of the free world, a role it simply could not abandon:

> Every American is now involved in the world. "The tragic events of . . . turmoil through which we have just passed have made us citizens of the world," said Woodrow Wilson. For a time we tried to dodge this new responsibility, but the world depression, World War II, and the Cold War have finally conveyed his message: "There can be no turning back. Our own fortunes as a nation are involved – whether we would have it so or not.[2]

Whereas few voters in 1789 quizzed George Washington about his foreign policy agenda, the presidential debates of 2012 focused more on foreign policy concerns, with the exception of the declining economy, than on domestic policy issues. Voters of the twenty-first century want to know that their choice for the nation's highest office has at least knowledge of and, at best, expertise in foreign policy. Every resident of the Oval Office beginning with Franklin Roosevelt has spent countless hours on the phone, on a plane or at a conference room table in a foreign country meeting with foreign leaders in hopes of bringing a nonviolent conclusion to a volatile international problem. All nations are faced with the reality that where once one or several nations dominated over the others, today we now live in an international community that is dependent upon each other. On Friday, February 11, 2011, the Egyptian people successfully forced President Hosni Mubarak to resign from the office he held for nearly thirty years. Throughout his tenure, Mubarak was a close ally to the United States and, in many respects, Israel. The international community celebrates with the newly won freedom of the Egyptian people and hoped a new government would fulfill the promise of bringing democracy to the region and, of course, maintain a good relationship with the United States. The newly installed provisional government arrested Mubarak, wrote a new constitution, and held free elections for a new president. A competitive presidential race, Muhammad Morsi, a member of the once outlawed Muslim Brotherhood, was elected to the presidency only to be confronted within a year with the same angry mobs calling for his removal. The Egyptian army eventually removed Morsi from office and arrested him for inciting the riots and plotting against the Egyptian people. Currently, Egypt is being ruled by a military junta who has once again, outlawed the Muslim Brotherhood. Meanwhile the United States Senate is discussing whether to continue to send both humanitarian and military aid to Egypt in protest of the violent and undemocratic removal of Morsi. The regime of Bashar al-Assad in Syria has been embroiled in a two-year plus civil war with no end in sight. World leaders are very concerned the military takeover in Egypt, civil war in Syria, uncertain political unrest in Libya, and the rise of Al-Qaeda in Iraq will be the start of a domino effect of unrest throughout the Middle East region, and the rest of the international community. The drug-related violence in Mexico is having an adverse impact on the American economic recovery as well as creating foreign policy roadblocks hampering a smooth and healthy relationship between the United States and Mexico. Although these practices are centuries old, human rights violations in China are treated delicately by the United States government. The United States economy is in many respects, dependent upon the rising middle-class in China who wants American-made products and building materials. A hardline stance by the United States government could jeopardize this cozy trade and economic partnership. This chapter focuses on the vital role the United States plays in the international arena.

As in the domestic policy arena, the President of the United States may well be the primary spokesperson for this country in foreign affairs but he/she still has to turn to the Senate for approval of treaties and appointments of ambassadors and, of course, key cabinet posts such as the Secretary of State, and to both the House of Representatives and the Senate for the funds to conduct foreign policy initiatives and, if necessary, for approval of a formal declaration of war. Unfortunately, the working relationship between the president and Congress in foreign policy has not always been a cordial one. Far too often, presidents have been frustrated by their inability to sway Congress to their policy choices. Unfortunately over the course of time, presidents have found both constitutionally legal and, at times, potentially illegal means of bypassing Congress. And, Congress has on occasion given the president more latitude than the Constitution grants, only to be placed into the situation of legislatively bringing the presidency back into line. This chapter examines the oftentimes shaky relationship between the executive and legislative branch in foreign policy development.

The media usually shows the president's or his representatives' standing among the worlds' leaders in a friendly setting, shaking hands or casually speaking or joking with each other. Not allowed behind the closed doors, the media cannot show the American people the complicated negotiation process involved in addressing international problems. The development of policy options that preserve the vital interests of the United States, while at the same time meeting the needs of the other foreign leaders gathered at the table, is an extremely complicated and delicate process. Case in point, several representatives of the princely houses of the German provinces met to discuss the possibility of uniting into the nation state of Germany. One of the delegates refused to sit at the conference table because his chair was not the same distance from the other representatives. Unfortunately, the delegate was extremely overweight! The solution was to carve into the table enough room to allow his chair to be the same distance from the others. Once that was accomplished, the representative joined into the negotiations. In particular, the maintenance of longstanding mutual friendships among the various nations is an extremely difficult and delicate process. Everyone at that table must be able to go home with something that benefits their people. Consequently, a focus of this chapter is on the vocabulary and "mechanics" of foreign policy initiatives, as well as a brief regional analysis of the problems confronting the Obama administration in the development of its future foreign policy initiatives.

In the Preamble to the Constitution, the Framers tasked the national government to "provide for the common defense." In other words, the Framers guaranteed the American people that their government would do whatever is necessary to protect their lives, property, and way of life. It is a very daunting and sobering task placed upon the shoulders of the president in his role as the nation's commander-in-chief. Throughout the history of this country, the American people have been very uneasy about warfare in general and in particular about sending American combat forces onto foreign soil. Every president faces the reality that among the troops he sends into combat, many will not return. During the Civil War, President Abraham Lincoln always wore black. Biographers have noted that rarely did he sleep a full eight hours. President Harry Truman had to live with the fact that ultimately it was his decision and his decision alone to drop nuclear bombs on Japanese civilians. President Kennedy was joined by his brother Robert Kennedy and key advisors as they monitored the growing hostile situation between the United States and the Soviet Union during the Cuban Missile Crisis, knowing that the nation was on the brink of a nuclear confrontation. The photograph of Lyndon Johnson slumped over a table with tears in his eyes after listening to a taped recording from his son-in-law Chuck Robb, an officer in Vietnam, detailing a combat mission shows the emotional torment of the president who sent those troops into that battle zone. Particularly in foreign policy, a president must tread carefully.

FOREIGN POLICY TERMINOLOGY

Foreign policy is "a strategy or planned course of action developed by the decision makers of a state vis-à-vis other **states** or **international entities** aimed at achieving specific goals defined in terms of **national interests**."[3] The construct of international entities evolved from the massive empires of Romans and Mongols to smaller territories commonly known as states or nation states. A **nation state** is "a state organized for the government of a nation whose territory is determined by national customs and expectations."[4] Although a group of people may well have the commonality of language and customs, the bringing together of various ethnic groups under one governing

President Lyndon B. Johnson listens to a tape sent by Captain Charles Robb, his son-in-law, from Vietnam. Cabinet Room, White House, Washington, D.C. July 31, 1968.
Photo Credit: LBJ Library photo by Jack Kightlinger

authority has proven to be a very difficult process. The last two groups to form into nation states in Europe were Italy and Germany. While the majority of the European nations had been formed during and immediately after the Middle Ages, it was not until 1871 that unification documents were officially signed in Italy and Germany. What was lacking was the spirit of **nationalism**, that is, "the spirit of belonging together or the corporate will that seeks to preserve the identity of the group by institutionalizing it in the form of a state."[5] Now that the United States combat military forces have left Iraq, the task of the Iraqi government is to convince the Kurds, Sunni, and Shiites that they can peacefully come together as Iraqis under one unified government. The "nations" of Afghanistan and Iraq will never be viable nation states until the various tribes and factions forgo their individual interests and loyalties for the collective general will of the nation.

The ability of a nation state to hold its own over other nation states is dependent upon several factors to include: "1) size, location, climate, and topography of the national territory; 2) the natural resources, sources of energy, and foodstuffs that can be produced; 3) the population, its size, density, age and sex composition, and its per capita relationship to national income; 4) the size and efficiency of the industrial plant; 5) the extent and effectiveness of the transportation system and communications media; 6) the educational system, research facilities, and the number and quality of the scientific and technical elite; 7) the size, training, equipment, and spirit of the military forces; 8) the nature and strength of the nation's political, economic and social system; 9) the quality of its diplomats and diplomacy; and 10) the national character and morale of the people."[6] Only a select few of today's 200 nation states possess all of these factors that enable them to dominate the direction of worldwide international relations. Furthermore, political scientists and economists have developed criteria for categorizing nation states. For the sake of this discussion, let's use the relationship between industry and agriculture. In first world power nation states, industry dominates the economic growth of the nation with agriculture playing a vitally important support role. In second world power nation states, industry and agriculture are equal economic partners. In third world power nation states, agriculture dominates with industry playing a second and, in most instances, a marginal role. In fourth world power nation states, agriculture is the primary economic factor. Since the majority of these nations have been extractive colonial possessions, they have the future capacity for industrialization but need to learn how to retain and subsequently use their own natural resources. There are a few nation states that fall into the fifth world power category whereby they have a difficult time producing enough food to feed their own people and lack the natural resources and the technological skills required for industrial development. Defined as "a condition characterized by economic, social and political backwardness when measured by the standards of the advanced societies," **underdevelopment** means that those nation states falling into the third, fourth and fifth categories also have significantly high infant mortality rates, extreme poverty, a heavy dependence upon subsistence agriculture, high illiteracy rates, extensive use of child labor, a rigid social structure that severely restricts social mobility, and unstable governments.[7]

A nation's foreign policy agenda is based on the pursuit of its **national** or **vital interests**. Basically, all nation states want to preserve their independence to include the right to **self-determination**, that is, "the right of a group of people who consider themselves separate and distinct from others to determine for themselves the state in which they will live and the form of government it will have."[8] If the Framers gathered in Philadelphia had the right to abolish one form of government (confederative) for another (federal), then other nations should have that same right to change both the structure and the political ideology driving that change without interference from the international community. Self-determination underscores the ability to preserve one's culture, religion, customs, and traditions. Akin with self-determination, all nation states seek to exercise their right to **sovereignty**, which is "the independent legal authority over a population in a particular territory, based on the recognized right to self-determination."[9] In other words, all nation states want their governing bodies to exercise "**internal sovereignty** which means the right, without external intervention to determine matters having to do with one's own citizens" and **external sovereignty** which is "the right to conclude binding agreements (treaties) with other states" without interference from other nation states.[10] Both as president of the Constitutional Convention and of the United States, George Washington expressed the same belief that every president has embraced that ". . . . every one had a right to form and adopt whatever government they like best to live under themselves."[11] In particular, many third, fourth and fifth world power nation states must oftentimes rely upon a third party to intervene internally whenever their governments are in peril of being overthrown by a military coup or a powerful group, such as the Taliban in Afghanistan. These nations are more often to be the signees to a first power nation state's treaty rather than be the primary initiator of the document. These countries simply do not have the military might or the diplomatic presence to conduct their own foreign policy.

Every nation state wants to be able to secure its borders and protect its citizens from harm. Regardless of their geographical size and the thickness of their national wallets, all nation states maintain at least a standing army and navy. The dilemma confronting the first power nations is whether every nation should have access to the ultimate weapons of mass destruction—nuclear capability. Today, the international community is closely monitoring the North Korean government's launching of short-range nuclear weapons and Iran's development of its own nuclear program.

Another common national interest is protection of one's economic viability. In part, the Cold War was a struggle over economic philosophies. The Soviet Union wanted to expand its socialist system of state ownership of the means of production throughout the Eastern bloc nations. On the other hand, the United States countered by seeking to convince other nation states that the only viable economic system was capitalism. The expansion of trade routes and the acquisition of natural resources were the driving force behind the colonial aspirations of the British, French, Spanish, Portuguese, Dutch, and other nations.

Basically, the national interests of the United States fall into four board categories:

- Protect our physical security.
- Protect the physical security of our neighbors and major democratic allies.
- Protect our economic security.
- Extend our sphere of influence.[12]

All of the nation's foreign policy decisions are geared towards these four broad objectives.

Since pursuing all of the various national interests at once is virtually impossible, nation states focus their attention on a selective handful of objectives collectively known as the **vital interests**. The others are relegated to secondary considerations. The top priorities vary from nation to nation and hopefully will change to meet new challenges. For example, the United States focused its energy during the Cold War on challenging the Soviet system by encouraging other nation states to adopt democracy and capitalism. Since then the international community has witnessed the breakup of the Soviet Union, the decline of socialist doctrinaire, and the movement on the part of both China and Russia towards a free market or capitalist economic system. Consequently, the focus of United States foreign policy had to change. After September 11, 2001, the nation's focus shifted from a still viable Cold War mentality against Russia and China to international terrorism. In order to remain a player on the international scene, a nation state's foreign policy emphasis must change as events change. If not, the policy direction is stale and ineffective.

Historians will certainly view the destruction of the World Trade Center in New York City, on September 11, 2001, as a turning point in American foreign, as well as domestic policy.©Danny C. Sze Photography

FOREIGN POLICY OPTIONS

In general terms, a nation state can opt to pursue its vital interests in three board policy options, namely, neutrality, isolationism and internationalism. All nation states want physical security, that is, the ability to ward off potential threats of invasion, attacks, or conquest from other nation states. Since gaining its independence through the Peace of Westphalia of 1648, Switzerland has pursued a policy of **neutrality**. Basically, a neutral state takes no part in a war but retains the right to defend its territory against attacks. "Neutral duties include: 1) impartiality; 2) refraining from aiding any belligerent; 3) denying to belligerents the use of neutral territory; and 4) permitting belligerents to interfere with commerce to the extent specified by international law."[13] During World War II, many Europeans fled the advancement of Hitler's army by fleeing to Switzerland and obtaining Swiss citizenship, which protected them from being extradited to Germany. To date, Switzerland has never applied to join the United Nations and only participates in non-political international organizations.

Isolationism is "the policy of curtailing as much as possible a nation's international relations so one's country can exist in peace and harmony by itself in the world."[14] From independence until the 1890's, the United States followed a policy of isolationism as the nation focused internally to expand its borders from the East to the West coast. It sporadically and selectively participated in international incidents. For centuries, both the Japanese and the Chinese were isolationists or closed-door nations until the need to expand their trade routes convinced them to open the doors and establish relations with other nations.

A middle road option, an **alliance,** is "an agreement by [nation] states to support each other militarily in the event of an attack against any member, or to advance their mutual interests."[15] These alliance agreements are based on the Three Musketeers pledge of "one for all and all for one." A nation state would become involved in an international incident or a war only when a member of the pact was attacked or threatened by a non-member. Therefore, a nation state could selectively involve itself in international affairs if called upon to fulfill its obligations as outlined in the alliance. In the fifteenth century, individual associations of merchants throughout Europe joined forces into the **Hanseatic League**. The League members were able to control their own towns and extract trade and business concessions from foreign rulers. They even successfully declared war on the Scandinavian counties, forcing their monarchs to make considerable trade concessions. After the defeat of Napoleon, Tsar Alexander I crafted a unsuccessful **Holy Alliance** agreement between Russia, Prussia, and Austria. "It was an attempt to establish an all-embracing international system on the principles of Christian justice, charity, and peace."[16] The **Quadruple Alliance** formed in 1815 between the governments of Austria, Prussia, Russia, and Great Britain was a successful effort. These rulers agreed to "preserve the territorial boundaries they had set, to insure the perpetual exclusion of [Napoleon] Bonaparte and his dynasty from the French throne, to combat the principles of the Revolution, and to prevent any future revolutionary uprising."[17] The **North Atlantic Treaty Organization (NATO)** was formed in 1949 by the West for the sole purpose of "blocking the threat of Soviet military aggression in Europe through combined conventional forces and by affording Western European states the protection of the American nuclear deterrent."[18] "The signatories bound themselves: (1) to consult together whenever the territorial integrity, independence, or security of any member was threatened; and (2) to consider an armed attack on one as an attack on all, and in case of such an attack each would take such action as it deemed necessary, including the use of armed force."[19] The initial membership included Belgium, Britain, Denmark, France, Germany, Greece, Iceland, Italy, Luxembourg, the Netherlands, Norway, Portugal, Turkey, and the United States. In retaliation, the Soviet Union responded with its own collective security agreement, the **Warsaw Pact** signed by the Eastern bloc countries of Albania, Bulgaria, Czechoslovakia, East Germany, Hungary, Poland, Romania, and the Soviet Union in 1955. In 1956, the Hungarian government launched a short-lived revolution against Soviet domination. Despite pleas for assistance, NATO decided not to send troops into Hungary because it feared Soviet retaliation and the possibility of World War III erupting in Europe. The official excuse was that Hungary was not a member of the NATO alliance, and, therefore, NATO members were obligated to only assist fellow alliance members.

The first American president to visit Europe, Woodrow Wilson came to Paris in 1918 determined to make the world safe for democracy by forming an alliance of the worlds' leaders under the umbrella of the **League of Nations**. The League's constitution, or Covenant, formed Part One of the Versailles Treaty and consisted of twenty-six articles. The League's "purpose, according to the Preamble, was to promote international cooperation, preserve peace, and provide security. This was to be done by accepting obligations not to resort to war, by establishing international law as the role of conduct among governments, and by respecting treaty commitments."[20] Wilson firmly believed that international disputes could be won by words, not guns. The United States Senate saw otherwise by rejecting the Treaty of Versailles and withdrawing United States membership from the League. The League of Nations, however, was the forerunner of the world's ultimate multinational agreement—the **United Nations**. Offered by Roosevelt during the Yalta Conference, the United Nations Charter was drawn up and signed on June 26, 1945, and once ratified by fifty-one nations, became effective on October 24, 1945. The organization's purpose is "to maintain peace and security, to take collective measures for preventing war and aggression, to settle disputes among

Churchill, Franklin D. Roosevelt, and Stalin at the Livadia Palace in Yalta. February 9, 1945
Photo credit: FDR Presidential Library

nations, to develop friendly relations based on the principle of equal rights and self determination, and to promote cooperation in handling international problems."[21]

The opposite of isolationism is **internationalism**, that is, the belief that the course of international events demands that a powerful nation state, such as the United States, must assume an active, and to a large degree, a leadership role in determining the outcome of those events. It's like being the captain of the ship. The direction the ship takes is not determined by the cabin boy but by the captain. Consequently, the nation state is establishing **hegemony**, defined as "the extension by one state of preponderant influence or control over another state or region."[22] Although it is advantageous for one or more nation states to assume the predominate role, they must be careful not to be accused of *ethnocentrism*, the belief that one's own culture is far superior to any other culture. Closely akin to internationalism, **interventionism** is "the coercive interference in the affairs of a state by another group of states to affect the internal and external policies of that state."[23] According to international law, the policy of interventionism is legal under the following conditions: "1) if the intervening state has been granted such a right by treaty; 2) if a state violates an agreement for joint policy determination by acting unilaterally; 3) if intervention is necessary to protect a state's citizens; 4) if it is necessary for self-defense; or 5) if a state violates international law."[24] Since World War II, the United States government has oftentimes used the intervention option. However, there is a fine line between intervention and imperialism. **Imperialism** is "the domination of one state by another, usually for exploitative purposes."[25] Particularly in third power nations, the intervention of the United States into their internal affairs may be welcomed by the incumbent government but verbally resented by its citizens who see the United States as not a benevolent friend but as an imperialistic enemy.

FOREIGN POLICY PROCESS

With few exceptions, the initial step is diplomacy with the hope of preventing a small-scale developing international incident from becoming a full-scale war. During the Nixon administration, Secretary of State Henry Kissinger was the catalyst behind **détente**, "a French word meaning 'the easing of strained relations.'"[26] And in the 1980s, Soviet leader Mikhail Gorbachev introduced **glasnost**, the Russian word for openness. Both policies were designed to ease the tension between the United States and the Soviet Union. Through cultural exchanges, mutual visits to each other's country, the Soviet Union was able to improve the standard of living for its people by gingerly moving its economic philosophy from state-ownership under socialism to the free market of capitalism.

Oftentimes, a third party representative is needed to mediate and broker a deal between the aggrieved parties. For example, the political and religious divide between Arab countries and Israel has been widening ever since the first Jewish settlers arrived in what today is known as Israel. In 1978, President Jimmy Carter invited Egyptian President Anwar Sadat and Israeli Prime Minister Menachem Begin to Camp David, Maryland, site of the presidential retreat. It marked the first time that an Arab leader directly met with and talked to an Israeli government official. Signed in March 1979, the **Camp David Accords** was a landmark agreement between the two leaders whereby Egypt would become the first Arab nation to officially recognize Israel and, in return, Israel would gradually begin withdrawing from the Sinai Peninsula, an area it had occupied since the 1967 Six-

President Reagan, and Vice President Bush meet with Soviet General Secretary Gorbachev on Governor's Island, New York. Mikhail Gorbachev initiated the opening of the Soviet economy and polity (glasnost) during the Reagan years with limited success.
December 7, 1988
Photo credit: Reagan Presidential Library

Day War. Although many serious concerns such as the creation of an independent state of Palestine were not discussed, the bringing together of these two bitter enemies and getting them to the table and agreeing on some concessions was a shot in the arm for United States relations with both Israel and the Arab countries. Carter received a Nobel Peace Prize for his efforts to bring some sense of peace to the Middle East. As a multinational peace keeping force, the United Nations has been successful in defusing external conflicts between two or more nations as well as acting as a neutral arbitrator in ending internal coups, political upheavals, and revolutions.

Agreements are oftentimes signed between world leaders to express their support of or cooperation of a particular issue. World-wide environmental conferences often yield agreements to pursue a cleaner environment, protect endangered species, and promote clean water projects to impoverished nations. There is a wide range of nuclear agreements pledging the signees to reduce their stockpiles and minimize or actually eliminate testing activities. **Bilateral agreements** are between two nation states; whereas, **multi-lateral agreements** bear the signatures of numerous world leaders. Signed in 1945, the **Yalta Agreement** set the parameters for the surrender of Germany. President Franklin Roosevelt, British Prime Minister Winston Churchill and Soviet Marshal Joseph Stalin agreed to an unconditional surrender for Germany, swift trial for high-ranking German Nazi officers for war crimes, reparations from the German government, self-determination for the newly liberated countries in Eastern Europe, and the role Great Britain, the United States and the Soviet Union would play in the newly created United Nations. In return for the concessions he received, Stalin

Carter brought Menachem Begin and Anwar Sadat, leaders of Israel and Egypt, respectively, to the Camp David presidential retreat. After thirteen days of bargaining, the three leaders announced the framework for a negotiating process and a peace treaty. September 7, 1978 Photo credit: Jimmy Carter Library

pledged that the Soviet Union would join the allies in the Pacific front within three months after the end of hostilities in Germany. The war with Japan ended before the Soviets could join the Pacific front. A multi-lateral and multi-national agreement can also lend validity to a unilateral decision. In the case of the Iraq War, the United States could have invaded Iraq on its own. However, the Bush administration wanted a nod of approval from the international community. He sought and got the support of approximately forty nations to include Great Britain, France, and Nicaragua. While it is doubtful that Nicaragua's contribution went beyond having its name on the list, what the Bush administration wanted was to send a clear message to Baghdad that it was not just the United States condemning the Iraqi government but the entire international community.

A **treaty** is "a formal agreement entered into between two or more countries. The treaty process includes negotiation, signing, ratification, exchange of ratifications, publishing and proclamation, and treaty execution."[27] Usually, a treaty is a negotiated settlement between the winners and losers of an armed conflict. Signed in 1783, the **Treaty of Paris** officially ended the American Revolutionary War. The British government recognized the independence of the United States and her claim to the territories west of the Mississippi, north to Canada and south to the Floridas. Treaties can also address mutual defense issues. For example, the **Japanese-American Security Treaty** of 1954 and 1960 is a bilateral defense pact pledging that both parties would respond if the security of Japan was threatened. The treaty gives the United States the authority to maintain military bases on the island with the understanding that military forces can be deployed "1) without prior consultation, to maintain peace and security in the Far East; 2) following consultation, to defend Japan against an armed attack; and 3) at the express request of the Japanese government to help suppress domestic disorders in Japan resulting from the instigation or intervention of an outside power."[28] The treaty fulfills the national interests of both nations. Japan has the assurance that the United States will help to promote the security of their nation. The United States can continue to maintain a military presence in Japan while at the same time solidifying its economic presence in the Far East.

A nation state can be supportive of another's international conflict without committing its own military forces to an armed conflict. In the late 1930s, President Franklin Roosevelt knew that war between Europe and Nazi Germany was inevitable. However, he realized that gaining American support for another European front war so close to the end of World War I was impractical. His administration also realized that the European countries, particularly Great Britain, needed help to offset Nazi Germany's intention to conquer all of Europe, including Great Britain. To avoid a declaration of war from Germany, the Roosevelt administration found a unique way to getting war material to the British. **Lend-lease** enabled the Roosevelt administration to lend much needed military equipment, airplanes, weaponry, and everything short of military personnel to the British with a gentlemen's agreement that the British would eventually reimburse the United States for its generous offer.

At the height of the Cold War, both the United States and the Soviet Union used foreign aid and military assistance packages as a means of "winning friends" within the international community, particularly with third-, fourth- and fifth world nation states. In 2011 the United States government gave approximately $49,593,000,000 in total foreign aid with $31,725,600,000 in economic assistance and $17,867,500,000 in military aid.[29] In his proposed FY 2013 budget for the Department of State and the U.S. Agency for International Development (USAID), Secretary of State John Kerry requested approximately $51.6 billion to include:

- Iraq: $4.8 billion:
  $2.0 billion in assistance, including $1.8 billion to fund police training and military assistance transitioned from the Department of Defense (DOD).
  $2.7 billion in operations funding supports the Embassy and three consulates as well as public outreach.
  This is approximately 10 percent less than in FY-12.
- Afghanistan: $4.6 billion:
  $2.5 billion in assistance for counterterrorism-related programs, economic growth, reconciliation and reintegration, and capacity building to support progress in governance, rule of law, counter-narcotics, agriculture, health and education.
  $2.1 billion supports the expansion of the diplomatic and interagency presence, the extraordinary costs of security in a conflict zone, and public diplomacy programs to build long-lasting bridges with civil society.
- Pakistan: $2.4 billion
  $2.2 billion in assistance to strengthen democratic and civil institutions that provide a bulwark against extremism, and support joint security and counterterrorism efforts, including $800 for the Pakistan Counterinsurgency Capability Fund.
  $197 million supports the U.S. government's civilian presence, as well as programs for engagement with civil society.[30]

On the other hand, embargos and economic sanctions are frequently used to punish a nation state for unacceptable behavior. Economic sanctions are effective in the short run but are not a viable long-term option. For example, the United Nations did impose an economic embargo on Iraq for its production of those mysterious weapons of mass destruction. Initially, the economic sanctions were effective. However, the Iraqi government was able to bypass the stranglehold of the sanctions by negotiating "under the table" deals with those nation states sympathetic to Iraq.

War is defined as "the hostilities between states or within a state or territory undertaken by means of armed force."[31] An official **state of war** "exists in the legal sense when two or more states declare *officially* that a condition of hostilities exists between them."[32] When diplomatic talks are no longer a viable option, the best course of action may be to launch a military strike in hopes of defusing the growing tensions. A **preventive war** option is a limited but powerful military maneuver designed to scare the other side away from hostile action and draw them back to the negotiation table. For example, the Israeli government oftentimes lines up its tanks and positions its heavily armed troops along the Palestinian border as a powerful reminder of what is to come if the Palestinians launch an attack. This tactic goes hand in hand with **psychological warfare** whereby pamphlets or leaflets are dropped from military planes over enemy lines warning the people of an appending attack if they do not convince their government to cease hostile actions. During the Iraq War, the United States military drop millions of leaflets telling the Iraqi people about the virtues of a democratic government and the personal rights they would have if they only would overthrow the Hussein government. Before sending ground troops into combat, the military launched nightly missile barrages and played loud music at night hoping to keep the Iraqi army awake, on edge, and thus too tired to fight.

There are two major categories of armed conflicts. A **limited war** is "an armed conflict fought for objectives less than the total destruction of the enemy and his unconditional surrender."[33] Considering the potentially world-ending destruction caused by nuclear weapons, every military action launched by any nation state after World War II has been limited warfare. At the beginning of the early stages of the Cold War, political scientist Hans J. Morgenthau correctly predicted the pattern of modern warfare. In *Politics Among Nations: The Struggle for Power and Peace*, Mongenthau reasoned that both the United States and the Soviet Union understood fully that they could launch a nuclear attack against each other at any given time. Once one side fired a long-range nuclear warhead, the other side had second-strike capability, that is, the commitment to fight back. If that were to happen, the United States and the Soviet Union could destroy the entire planet. So an all-out nuclear war was off the table. However, both sides still wanted the opportunity to flex their muscles at each other. The answer was selective limited warfare. According to Morgenthau's model, both the Soviet Union and the United States could engage in regional limited wars. For example, the Iran/Iraq War saw the Soviets supplying military personal, weaponry, and air support to Iran while the United States government gave military equipment and warplanes to Iraq. While the international community saw Iranian troops attacking Iraqi forces, it was the Soviet Union and the United States pulling the strings behind the scenes. The same scenario would be used in internal conflicts. For example, during the Iran/Contra Conflict, the United States government supported the Contras in their battle with the Sandinistas who were backed by the Soviets through the Cuban government.

World War I and World War II fall into the category of total war. A **total war** involves "1) participation of entire populations in the war effort; 2) terrorization of civilian populations to destroy their will to fight; 3) the use of modern weapons offering a vast range of destructive power; 4) participation of most nations in the war, with fight carried on globally; 5) gross violations of the international rules of warfare; 6) intense mass emotional attachment to nationalist or ideological ideas or goals that transform the war into a morale crusade for both sides; 7) demands for unconditional surrender; 8) and the political, economic and social reconstruction of the defeated states according to the dictates of the victors."[34] Both wars involved the entire populations of the warring factions and even those who were not directly involved in the hostilities. Particularly with World War II, the advancement of Adolf Hitler into European countries caused massive panic, relocations, and a horrific lost of civilian lives. One source estimates that over six million Soviet citizens were either killed through German military operations or died in German run labor and concentration camps. The Japanese were equally brutal as their military slaughtered non-combatants throughout their acquisition of islands and territories in the Pacific. They also either killed or imprisoned countless members of Japanese resistance forces and Allied troops.

Regardless of whether a nation is involved in a limited or total war, each participating nation state must, or at least should, adhere to the established rules of warfare, that is, "the principles set forth in international law to govern the conduct of nations engaged in hostilities."[35] War is not for the faint of heart. No country places its independence and security on the line or places its citizens in potentially deadly harm with the intention of losing a war. By its very nature, war is inhumane. However, world leaders have come to realize that there is a line in the sand that no nation should violate unless there is no other alternative available to secure victory. The rules of warfare are delineated in a series of documents. The **Declaration of Paris** signed in 1856 abolished privateering. The **Geneva Conventions of 1864 and 1906** mandate the humane treatment for military personnel wounded in battle. The **Hague Convention of 1907** outlaws the use of dum-dum bullets, and poisonous gas, as well as the use of balloons for bombing missions. The **Geneva Conventions of 1929 and 1949** set the guidelines for the treatment of prisoners, sick and wounded military personnel, and the protection of civilian populations held by the enemy. The **London Protocol of 1936** limited the use of submarines against non-combatant merchant ships. The body of international law with its provisions for humane treatment and prohibitions against unwarranted cruelty should also be followed by all parties involved in warfare. At the end of World War II, the top command of both the Japanese and German military and key leaders from both governments were tried, convicted and, in some instances, executed for war crimes. Sixty-seven years later the Japanese government is still apologizing for the Bataan Death March where in April 1942, "78,000 prisoners of war (12,000 American and 66,000 Filipinos) [were] marched by the Japanese 65 miles over six days to a prisoner-of-war camp. As many as 11,000 prisoners died on the march."[36] The German government is still dealing with the horrors of the Holocaust and the millions of people that died in the labor and concentration camps.

The use of nuclear weapons to end the Pacific front of World War II ushered in the ultimate weapon of mass destruction. Whereas nuclear power can be used for appropriate means, such as the generation of electrical power, the first world power nation states are always uneasy when a second- or third world power nation state acquires even the rudimentary components for a nuclear reactor or purchases nuclear warheads. The continued threat of a nuclear war between the United States and the Soviet Union created a **balance of terror** whereby both stock piled nuclear weapons to the point it became a quest to see who had the highest number of the most powerful warheads. Both were on constant alert for a **preemptive strike**, "a first-strike nuclear attack undertaken on the assumption that an enemy state is planning an imminent nuclear attack."[37] To prevent these weapons from getting into the wrong hands, the United States government has negotiated and signed numerous arms limitations agreements. In return for reducing or eliminating its nuclear arsenal, the United States has pledged foreign aid, non-nuclear military support, and funds for infrastructure improvements. Basically, the nuclear-holding nations are using the policy of **deterrence** designed to "discourage other states from pursuing policies unwanted by the deterring state or states."[38]

SECURING THE ECONOMY

All nation states want to preserve and expand their economies. The growth of the bourgeois, commonly known as the middle class, in Europe prompted the search for luxury goods to include silk and spices. Marco Polo's historical journey in 1245-1247 to China established a series of trade routes known collectively as the **Silk Road**. European governments eventually sent explorers including Christopher Columbus, Vasco da Gama, and Bartolomeu Dias to find new trade routes to exchange their finished products for the raw materials and luxuries that they could not produce for themselves. Once industrialization took hold in Europe, the challenge was to find the natural resources and raw materials sorely needed to produce finished goods. Cotton and silk were needed for the British textile mills, gold and silver for the production of coin, and wood to fuel ships transporting finished products into foreign markets. The problem was how to establish both exclusive trade partners and sources of extractive raw materials. The solution was **colonialism**. "Colonies served the imperial powers [Great Britain, Spain, Portugal, France, and eventually the United States] as markets for manufacturers, sources of raw materials and investment opportunities, strategic locations and sources of manpower for national defenses, and as symbols of prestige and great-power status."[39] The British once bragged that the "sun never sat on their empire." Eventually the financial and manpower burden of maintaining colonies became too costly for the first power nation states. Whereas the colonies of the now United States fought a revolution to gain their freedom from their mother colony in 1776, the majority of the third-, fourth- and fifth world power nation states did not receive their independence until the late nineteenth and twentieth centuries.

The United States followed the same pattern of first establishing trade routes and agreements and then acquiring colonial possessions. In 1784, the United States government sent the *Empress of China* to Canton, China, for ginseng, a highly prized herb used for medicinal purposes, tea and silk. By 1854, the United States had annexed the Sandwich Islands or Hawaii, prized for its sandalwood and strategic location as a fuel station for American cargo ships heading for the Far Eastern markets. The Treaty of New Granada in 1846 protected Panama, a possession of New Granada or Columbia and future site of the Panama Canal, from being seized by Great Britain. Because of its strategic location and sugar production capability, Cuba was eyed by France, Great Britain, and the United States. Eventually, the United States would acquire the Philippines, the Marianas, Marshalls and Virgin Islands, and Alaska.

Today the international community gages the strength of their individual economics on the **balance of trade,** which is "a nation's annual net trade surplus or deficit, based on the difference in the value of its total imports and exports."[40] All nation states want a favorable balance of trade whereby they export more goods and services than they import. The United States continues to have an unfavorable balance of trade. An analysis of imports (products entering into the United States) and exports (products leaving the country for foreign markets) from January to September 2012, indicates a trade deficit of $-550,225,500,000; however, there was a noticeable improvement during the same period of 2013 to $-521,400,700,000, an increase of $28,248,000,000 in exports over 2012 figures.[41] The United States continues to have an extremely unfavorable balance of trade with China amounting to $-238,151,000,000 during 2013.[42] All nation states strive for a favorable balance of trade whereby they are exporting more goods and services than they are importing. If an unfavorable balance occurs, then governing bodies will take strides to ensure that domestically made products are cheaper to the consumer than those produced in foreign countries. To ensure this, all nation states have at one time of another turned to a protectionist policy. **Protectionism** is "the theory and practice of utilizing governmental regulation to control or limit the volume or types of imports entering a state."[43] Protectionist trade agreements include tariffs, quotas, exchange controls, and any other options designed to reduce or eliminate competitive imports from entering into a country. During the Great Depression, the United States enacted the **Smoot-Hawley Tariff Act,** imposing high tariffs on agricultural and industrial imports. By making imported products more expensive, the Roosevelt administration wanted American consumers to buy cheaper American-made products and food items. In addition, trade embargos can be used to punish or to compel a nation to reevaluate its course of action. When Fidel Castro assumed power in Cuba in 1956, the United States believed that he would build a government based on democracy. Instead, he opted for a socialist system. In retaliation, the United States government put a trade embargo on the two products that made Cuba famous—sugar and tobacco products, particularly cigars.

To expand its markets, the United States employs a variety of options. Inserting a **most-favored-nation clause** into a trade agreement and extending tariff concessions to participating nations to prevent trade discrimination practices help to reverse an unfavorable trade deficit with another country. The United States government used the **Open Door Policy** to promote trade agreements with both the Chinese and Japanese governments and has continued to establish agreements favorable to American business and industry. The United States, Mexico and Canada signed the **North American Free Trade Agreement (NAFTA)** with the hopes of mutually benefiting from the shipping of goods and services over the three international boundaries. With the global economy, an economic downturn in one country can have a domino effect on the international economic community. Consequently, the United States has joined several international organizations to include the **General Agreement of Tariffs and Trade (GATT)**. With a membership representing approximately 4/5's of the world's trade, the major purposes of the organization include: "1) negotiating the reduction of tariffs and other impediments to trade; 2) developing new trade policies; 3) adjusting trade disputes; and 4) establishing rules to govern the trade policies of its members."[44] To develop third-, fourth-, and some fifth-power nation states into potential trade partners, the industrial nation states have formed organizations such as the **International Development Association (IDA)** and the **International Monetary Fund (IMF)** to provide economic assistance and expertise to these nations.

THE DEVELOPMENT OF AMERICAN FOREIGN POLICY

Constitutional Authority—Is foreign affairs the exclusive prerogative of the president?

Whenever this nation is embroiled in an international incident, the American citizenry naturally turn to their president rather than to Congress for guidance and reassurance that the federal government will indeed do whatever is necessary to fulfill its obligation to "provide for the common defense." The perception is that as the commander-in-chief of the military, the president is completely in charge. But, is he? Did the Framers envision that the executive branch would bear the sole responsibility for foreign affairs? The answer is a resounding no!

The Framers never intended to place the sole responsibility of securing this nation into the hands of the president. "Any latent fears were quickly arrested by assurances from [James] Madison and [James] Wilson that the power of peace and war was not an executive, but legislative function. Given the Framers' conception of the chief executive as little more than an institution to effectuate 'the will of the legislature,' that is, to execute laws and to appoint officers, there was little about the office to fear."[45] The Framers envisioned a shared role between the executive and legislative branches that separated the authority between the two and provided a system of checks and balances to prevent one branch from overstepping its assigned role. A closer look at the president's authority to negotiate treaties, commit American forces to combat situations, and to serve as the nation's commander-in-chief clearly indicates that the president's authority is indeed limited. However, shared governance does not mean that the relationship between the president and Congress is a congenial one.

Commander-in-Chief and Warmaking

Article II, Section 2 of the United States Constitution names the president as the nation's commander-in-chief of the "army, and navy of the United States, and of the militia of the several states, when called into actual service of the United States." Although the Constitution specifically grants the title to the president, it does not specifically delineate the specific duties and responsibilities associated with it. Is it an advisory role? Is it merely a ceremonial role? Or, can the president actually lead American forces into combat situations?

The term commander-in-chief was first used by Charles I of England in 1639 during the First Bishops War. During the civil war between the Royalists Cavaliers under Charles I command and the Parliamentarian Roundheads under Thomas Cromwell, both designated their lead generals as commanders-in-chief. "In 1645, Sir Thomas Fairfax was appointed commander in chief of all of Parliament's forces, 'subject to such orders and directions as he shall receive from both Houses or the committee of Both Kingdoms.'"[46] Basically, the bearer of this lofty title could exercise no independent authority whatsoever and received his orders from within the British government, primarily from the Secretary of War. Holder of the title, the Duke of Wellington once commented "the commander in chief cannot move a Corporal's Guard from one station to another, without a Route countersigned by the Secretary War."[47] At the beginning of the American Revolution, the Continental Congress named George Washington as the commander-in-chief with the clear understanding "that he was to be 'its creature . . . in and every respect. . . .' Instructions drafted by John Adams, R. H. Lee, and Edward Rutledge told Washington 'punctually to observe and follow such orders and directions . . . as you shall receive from this or a future Congress.'"[48] At the Constitutional Convention, the Framers envisioned a similar role for the newly crafted office of the presidency. At the Virginia Ratifying Convention, Framer George Mason pointed out that he had concerns at first about the evolving role of the president as the nation's commander-in-chief:

> The propriety of his being commander in chief, so far as to give orders and have a general superintendency; but he thought it would be dangerous to let him command in person, without any restraint, as he might make bad use of it. He was, then, clearly of opinion that the consent of a majority of both houses of Congress should be required before he could take command in person.[49]

In *Federalist #69*, Alexander Hamilton clarified the role of commander-in-chief by comparing it to the authority granted to both the British monarch and the governor of New York:

> First. The president will have only the occasional command of such part of the militia of the nation as by legislative provision may be called into actual service of the Union. The king of Great Britain and the governor of New York have at all times the entire command of all the militia within their several jurisdictions. In this article, therefore, the power of the President would be inferior to that of either the monarch or the governor. Secondly. The President is to be commander-in-chief of the army and navy of the United States. In this respect his authority would be nominally the same with that of the king of Great Britain, but in substance much inferior to it. It would amount to nothing more than supreme command and direction of the military and naval forces, as first general and admiral of the Confederacy; while that of the British king extends to the declaring of war and to the raising and regulating of fleets and armies,—all which, by the Constitution under consideration, would appertain to the legislature.[50]

Furthermore, the **War Clause of Article I, Section 8** clearly states that only the Congress shall have the power to "declare war [and] grant Letters of Marque and Reprisal and Make Rules concerning captures on Land and Water." Although there was general agreement on vesting executive authority with one person, the Framers debated whether the executive should be given the exclusive authority to declare war. Particularly in Europe, the prerogative of the monarchs to frequently declare war on each other embroiled the entire continent into decades of continuous warfare resulting in severe loss of human life, devastating property damage, and untold misery for noncombatants. The Framers simply did not want their executive to become a divine monarch. However, they also realized that the president in his role as commander-in-chief needed the constitutional footing to immediately call upon the military to repel an invading foreign combatant or to respond to a national emergency without first obtaining congressional approval. Consequently, the compromise was that an official declaration of war could only be declared by a joint session of Congress. However, the president would be empowered to act on his own to repel any internal (insurrection) and external (invasive) sudden attack against the United States. At the Pennsylvania Ratifying Convention, Framer James Wilson defended the Framer's decision:

> This system will not hurry us into war; it is calculated to guard against it. It will not be in the power of a single man, or a single body of men, to include us in such distress; for the important power of declaring war is vested in the legislature at large: this declaration must be made with the concurrence of the House of Representatives: from this circumstance we may draw a certain conclusion that nothing but our interest can draw us into war.[51]

The fine line is the difference between declaring and making war. Congress has officially declared war five times: the War of 1812, the Mexican War, the Spanish-American War, World War I and World War II. Congress has authorized the president to make war, without an official declaration of war, on numerous occasions to include Vietnam, Korea, Gulf War I, Gulf War II, etc. Also, Congress has enabled the president to use extraordinary means of protecting this nation

President Lyndon B. Johnson signs the "Gulf of Tonkin" resolution.
East Room, White House, Washington, D.C.
August 10, 1964
Photo Credit: LBJ Library photo by Cecil Stoughton

from harm such as Franklin Roosevelt's **Executive Order 9066**, mandating that more than 100,000 Americans of Japanese descent be held in relocation centers for the duration of World War II, and Abraham Lincoln's suspension of the *writ of habeas corpus* during the American Civil War. In 1964, President Lyndon Johnson asked and received extraordinary authority to repel attacks from North Vietnam levied at American troops stationed in South Vietnam. With overwhelming congressional support, the **Gulf of Tokin Resolution** empowered the president "as Commander in Chief, to take all necessary measures to repel any armed attack against the forces of the United States and to prevent further aggression."[52] In other words, this resolution gave Johnson the authority to make war without an official congressional declaration of war. However, it was not a blank check. The resolution clearly states in Section 3 "this resolution shall expire when the President shall determine that the peace and security of the area is reasonably assured by international conditions created by the action of the United Nations or otherwise, except that it may be terminated earlier by concurrent resolution of the Congress."[53]

For Lyndon Johnson, Vietnam was his Achilles' heel. Confronted with a rapidly growing hostile anti-war movement at home, Johnson simply could not find a path to victory. He opted not to seek a second term of office. The Nixon administration inherited the failures of Vietnam. For the Nixon administration, the ultimate goal was to find a peaceful honorable means of ending the war without severely damaging America's prestige in the international community. His **Vietnamization Plan** called for the gradual withdrawal of American forces by replacing them with a well-trained and equipped South Vietnamese military. Supposedly intelligence reports revealed that the Cambodian government was aiding the cause of the North Vietnamese by launching air strikes against the South Vietnamese and, of course, American military personnel. Consequently, Nixon used the power granted to the president through the Gulf of Tonkin Resolution to order bombing raids of Cambodian military installations and runways. Inflamed by the growing anti-war movement, an angry Congress struck back in 1970 by repealing the resolution, mandating the end to the bombing raids, and scaling back appropriations for the war effort. In retaliation, Nixon continued the bombing raids in "secret" even as he was withdrawing American troops from South Vietnam.

Congress opted to reign in the presidency with the passage of the 1973 **War Powers Resolution**. "The purpose of the War Powers Resolution was to 'fulfill the intent of the framers of the Constitution' (section 2) by reintroducing a balancing role for Congress."[54] The legislation "does not prohibit the president from sending troops into combat, but it does required the president to notify Congress of the reason for committing combat troops within forty-eight hours of their deployment. The act also specifies that hostilities must end within sixty days unless Congress extends the period; gives the president an additional thirty days to withdraw the troops from hostile territory, although Congress can shorten this period; and requires the president to consult with Congress whenever feasible before sending troops into a hostile situation.[55] Congress can opt to support the president's action by extending the period of the deployment or officially declaring war. If Congress disagrees with the president it can issue "a decision not to support the president during the 60 to 90 days, or passage of a concurrent resolution at any time to direct the president to remove forces engaged in hostilities."[56]

As anticipated, Nixon vetoed it, "calling it 'unconstitutional and dangerous to the best interest of the nation', because it would 'attempt to take away, by a mere legislative act, authorities which the President had properly exercised under the Constitution for almost 200 years.' He particularly objected to the 60-day cutoff provisions and the ability of Congress to force a withdrawal by concurrent resolution."[57] Although Congress overrode his veto, a defiant Nixon vowed he would not follow it. He set the trend, because not one president since Nixon has consistently adhered to the act's provisions. In 2011, President Obama called for a no-fly zone over Libya to protect rebel forces trying to overthrow the Gadhafi government. This was a NATO-backed operation with the United States taking the leading role. A handful of Republicans filed a federal lawsuit challenging Obama's initiative on the grounds that it violated the War Powers Act. The administration filed its response by noting that "U.S. operations do not involve sustained fighting or active exchanges of fire with hostile forces, nor do they involve U.S. ground troops. . . . [They] argued that Obama could initiate the intervention on his own authority as commander in chief because its anticipated nature, scope and duration fell short of a "war" in the constitutional sense."[58] The federal court agreed with President Obama. Basically, the War Powers Resolution is a failure because "first, it does not give Congress any substantial powers to check the president or any substantial new opportunities to participate in foreign policy that it did not already have or could not exercise without the resolution. Second, presidents since 1974 have not regarded themselves as bound by the resolution, at least not in the sense Congress seems to have intended. Indeed, they are able to disregard the provisions with impunity, and they seem to have every incentive to do so."[59]

The Power to Make Treaties

Article II, Section 2 of the United States Constitution states "he [the president] shall have the power, by and with the Advice and Consent of the Senate, to make Treaties, provided two-thirds of the Senators present concur." Of equal importance, **Article I, Section 10** prohibits the individual states from entering into any treaty, alliance or confederation. Consequently, the Framers wanted the treaty making responsibility to rest exclusively with the national government under the guidance of both the executive and legislative branches. Framer Charles Pinckney responded to those wanting the president to have exclusive treaty making authority that "surely there is greater security in vesting these powers as the present Constitution has vested it, than in any other body. Would the gentleman vest it in the President alone? If he would, his assertion that the power we have granted was as dangerous as the power vested by Parliament in the proclamations of Henry VIII, might have been, perhaps, warranted. . . . [The Senate] joined with the president . . . form together a body in which can be best and most safely vested the diplomatic power of the union."[60] In *Federalist #75*, Alexander Hamilton underscored the need for legislative input:

> [Treaties] are contracts with foreign nations, which have the force of law, but derive it from the obligations of good faith. They are not rules prescribed by the sovereign to the subject, but agreements between sovereign and sovereign. . . .the vast importance of the trust, and the operation of treaties as laws, plead strongly for the participation of the whole or a portion of the legislative body in the office of making them. It would be utterly unsafe and improper to entrust that power to an elective magistrate of four years' duration. . . . It must indeed be clear to a demonstration that the joint possession of the power in question, by the President and Senate, would afford a greater prospect of security, than the separate possession of it by either of them."[61]

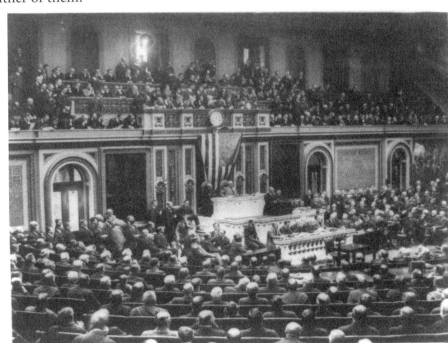

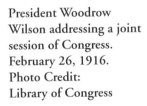

President Woodrow Wilson addressing a joint session of Congress. February 26, 1916. Photo Credit: Library of Congress

While on one hand calling for a shared role between the president and the Senate, the Framers failed to clearly indicate the extent of and the timing of the Senate's responsibility of "advice and consent." President George Washington took the position that the Senate should advise the executive branch on the matters to be addressed in a treaty prior to initiating the treaty negotiation process. He requested to meet with the entire Senate to discuss the conditions of a pending treaty between the United States and several of the southern Indian tribes. Denying the president access to the Senate chamber, the Senate referred the matter to a committee who, in turn, provided the president with scant guidance. By 1794, the process of seeking senatorial advice waned as the Jay Treaty became the first treaty negotiated without prior senatorial involvement.

What is particularly irksome to presidents, the Senate far too often uses its advice role after the treaty has been negotiated and signed by the president or his appointed representative. The executive branch charges that treaties are subjected to unwarranted and numerous amendments initiated by the Senate that oftentimes change the entire focus of a document that took months to negotiate with foreign delegations. In 1901, the Senate added so many amendments to the Hay-Pauncefote Treaty that the British rejected the treaty after initially agreeing to and officially signing it. Also, presidents must face the rare chance that the Senate will reject the entire treaty. President Woodrow Wilson personally headed the American delegation to Paris to negotiate the Treaty of Versailles. Realizing the final document would face intense Senate scrutiny and, perhaps, a few amendments he was totally surprised when the Senate failed to approve it. President Jimmy Carter faced a similar situation when the Senate rejected his original Panama Canal Treaty and the Strategic Arms Limitation II Treaty. Presidents claim that they are subject to embarrassment in front of the international community. Secretary of State Richard Olney commented that "the treaty in getting itself made by the sole act of the executive, without leave of the Senate first hand obtained, had committed the unpardonable sin. It must be either altogether defeated or so altered as to bear an unmistakable Senate stamp. . . . and thus be the means both of humiliating the executive and of showing to the world the greatness of the Senate."[62] Consequently, presidents opt to avoid the Senate's treaty making role by using the executive agreement.

An **executive agreement** is "an international agreement, reached by the president with foreign heads of state that does not require senatorial approval."[63] Initially, presidents were not required to even submit a copy of the agreement to Congress. Executive agreements fall into four categories: "1) those concluded pursuant to a treaty; 2) those concluded to carry out the intention of an act of Congress; 3) those concluded by the president under his constitutional authority and supported or confirmed by Congressional action such as a declaration of war or a joint resolution passed by majority vote; and 4) those concluded by the president according to his constitutional authority and not submitted to or confirmed by the Senate."[64] Category four agreements are commonly known as **pure executive agreements**.

The first executive agreement was the Rush-Bagot Agreement signed by President James Monroe in 1817. Although he subsequently received Senate approval, the agreement provided for the withdrawal of British and American naval forces on the Great Lakes. The propensity of presidents to use the executive agreement over the treaty option is alarming. Thomas Jefferson used an executive agreement to purchase the Louisiana Territory from France in 1803. In 1940, Franklin Roosevelt used an executive agreement to give Great Britain fifty mothballed destroyers. Since Great Britain had already declared war with Germany, this action could have been used by Germany to declare war against the United States for aiding its enemy. In 1963, John Kennedy pledged to Francisco Franco through an executive agreement to provide aid and military support if Spain were to be attacked. This was controversial since Spain had been excluded from NATO because Franco had started a civil war with Hitler's army and openly demonstrated his sympathy for Nazi Germany. The Korean War was initiated and concluded through executive agreements. A steady stream of executive agreements led to the Vietnam War. A frequent user of pure executive agreements, Richard Nixon stated "in short, there have been, and will be in the future, circumstances in which presidents may lawfully authorize actions in the interest of the security of this country, which if undertaken by other persons, or even by the president under different circumstances, would be illegal."[65] The frequent use of and the sensitivity of their content moved a member of the Senate Foreign Relations Committee to remark that "while many crucially important commitments, including base agreements, have been made by executive agreement, trivial agreements [such as] governing the status of three uninhabited coral reefs in the Caribbean; regulating shrimp fishing off the coast of Brazil; and setting rules to prevent collisions at sea, have been transmitted to the Senate as treaties."[66]

Although the United States Supreme Court has upheld the president's right to use executive agreements, Congress has avenues to once again reign in the presidency. The first congressional act to challenge the use of pure executive agreements, the **Case-Zablocki Act (1972)**, required that the Secretary of State transmit to Congress the text of any international agreement with the exception of treaties, no later than sixty days after the agreement has been made. However, the president has the option to withhold any agreements he judges would jeopardize national security. Of course, Congress can use its ultimate power of the purse to block the funding for any initiative they believe to be unjustified to include provisions in executive agreements and treaties.

The President's Foreign Policy Team

Basically, the president's foreign policy team is a two-headed structure with the Secretary of State heading the diplomatic front and the Secretary of War, now Defense, charged with the task of militarily defending the country and protecting its vital security interests. Created in 1789, both positions are presidential appointees subject to Senate confirmation. In 2002, President George W. Bush created the Department of Homeland Security, a cabinet-level position, overseeing the merging of various intelligence agencies. Headed by John Kerry, the State Department oversees all diplomatic initiatives as well as overseeing all United States embassies and consulates. In addition, the State Department supports the Global Health Initiative to include the President's Emergency Plan for AIDS, Feed the Future to combat global human and promote food security programs, humanitarian assistance for victims of natural disasters, crime of conflict and persecution, and efforts to support development investments in the poorest and most unstable nations. The State Department also works closely with the United Nations and numerous nongovernmental bodies (NGOs) in promotion of humanitarian, health-based, education, and economic development programs. Created in 1947 by the National Security Act, the National Security Council (NSC) advises the president on matters of national security to include domestic, foreign, and military. In 2013, $660,037,000,000 was spent on the nation's national defense initiatives. In his 2014 budget plan, Obama is requesting $626,755,000,000 for fiscal year 2014.[67] This figure reflects budget cuts within the Department of Defense to include costs related to the gradual withdrawal of active duty

(L-R) President Lyndon B. Johnson, Sec. Robert McNamara, Gen. Earle Wheeler, and Sec. Dean Rusk.
12:30 P.M. National Security meeting on Vietnam.
Cabinet Room, White House, Washington, D.C.
Photo Credit: LBJ Library photo by Yoichi R. Okamoto

troops from Afghanistan. The nation's largest employer, the Department of Defense has "over 1.4 million men and women on active duty; and 718,000 civilian personnel. . . . Another 1.1 million serve in the National Guard and Reserve forces. More than 2 million military retirees and their family members receive benefits.[68] The Department of Homeland Security includes the inspector general's office, the U.S. Customs and Border Protection, U.S. Immigration and Customs Enforcement, Transportation Security Administration, the U.S. Coast Guard, U.S. Secret Service, Federal Emergency Management Agency (FEMA), and U.S. Citizenship and Immigration Services. The various agencies grouped under the Intelligence Community include the Central Intelligence Agency (CIA), the Federal Bureau of Investigation (FBI), Army and Air Force Intelligence, National Security Agency (NSA), Defense Intelligence Agency (DIA), Drug Enforcement Administration (DEA), and so on. In the aftermath of September 11, 2001, congressional investigations point to lack of cooperation between the CIA and the FBI. Apparently, each agency had minute pieces of a larger puzzle, indicating that a terrorist attack on American soil was in the planning stages. Since the CIA traditionally handles foreign-related issues and the FBI focuses more on domestic criminal activities, they simply did not share their information with each other. Not that the piecing together of this puzzle would have prevented the attacks on the World Trade Center; but it surely would have given the Bush administration a fair warning. Consequently, the Bush administration opted direct oversight of the two agencies through the Department of Homeland Security.

As previously discussed in Chapter 15, the president's foreign policy team will frame their decisions into one of three policy options. The crisis policy response calls upon the president to exercise his emergency powers to act quickly to address a perceived or actual threat to national security. A strategic defense policy calls upon the deployment of military personnel; whereas, the structural defense policy option involves decisions about procurement and the allocation of resources to include manpower and equipment. It is the responsibility of the president's team to present to him the best viable options to include actual and potential costs, possibility of loss of life, and the advantages and disadvantages of each option in reaching the intended goal of the policy decision.

For example, President Johnson met with Pentagon officials and members of his team to include Secretary of Defense Robert McNamara, Secretary of State Dean Rusk, and Chairman of the Joint Chiefs of Staff General Earle Wheeler on the best course of action to follow in Vietnam. The president summarized the options presented to him:

> The options open to us are: one, leave the country, with as little loss as possible; two, maintain present force and lose slowly; three, add 100,000 men, recognizing that may not be enough and adding more next year. The disadvantages of number three option are the risk of escalation, casualties high, and the prospect of a long war without victory. . . . Are we starting something that in two or three years we simply can't finish?[69]

Johnson selected option three. He sent more troops to Vietnam. And as he predicted, the war escalated; the number of casualties dramatically increased; and both the White House and Capitol Hill realized that there was no victory in sight! Unfortunately, these dicey policy decisions are not made with a crystal ball in hand. Particularly in dealing with foreign policy issues, the cost of hasty decisions can be irreversibly damaging to the entire nation. When all is said and done, it is the president that selects the option and bears either the joy of victory or the bitter disappoint of defeat!

Brief Overview of American Foreign Policy

During the nation's formative years, American foreign policy followed an isolationist approach with sporadic and marginal involvement in international affairs. The conflict between Great Britain and France lingered after the end of the American Revolutionary War. Fearful of being entangled into the fray because of France's support to America during the revolution, George Washington issued a **Proclamation of Neutrality** on April 22, 1793. Basically, it was just a statement declaring that "the duty and interest of the United States require that they should . . . pursue a conduct friendly and impartial toward the belligerent powers."[70] By 1794, Congress passed the nation's first neutrality law. "It enjoined American citizens within the United States in four different ways: from accepting commissions to serve a foreign power, from securing the enlistment of others into the armed forces of a belligerent, from launching attacks against a nation with whom their country was at peace, and from arming or equipping private ships for operations against a nation with whom the United States was at peace."[71] Basically, America's foreign policy excursions were more defensive rather than aggressive in nature. For example, Thomas Jefferson received an official declaration of war against the pasha of Tripoli in response to the Barbary pirates attacking American ships in the Mediterranean. The War of 1812 was a defensive measure against the British invasion of the United States. Basically, the nation's focus was on the expansion of the nation's boundary from the Eastern shore of the Atlantic to the Western shore of the Pacific. Jefferson's purchase of the Louisiana territory from France only furthered the zeal of **manifest destiny**.

The only truly bold venture into international affairs was the Monroe Doctrine of 1823. Actually written by John Q. Adams, Monroe's secretary of state, the brief statement warns the members of the Quadruple Alliance that:

we should consider any attempt on their part to extend their system to any portion of this hemisphere as dangerous to our peace and safety. With the existing colonies or dependencies of any European power we have not interfered with and shall not interfere. But with the Governments who have declared their independence and maintained it . . . we could not view any interposition for the purpose of oppressing them, or controlling them in any other manner their destiny, by any European power in any other light than as the manifestation of an unfriendly disposition toward the United States. . . Our only policy in Europe remains the same, which is, not to interfere in the internal concerns of any of its powers . . .[72]

Basically, the Monroe administration warned the European powers not to try to colonize or invade any of the Western Hemisphere nations, and, in return, the United States would not interfere into European affairs.

The ensuring American Civil War, Reconstruction, and the transformation of the United States from a semi-agricultural/industrial economy to an industrial giant kept the United States out of the international arena. However, the growth of industry compelled the nation to seek new markets in foreign waters, natural resources needed to fuel industry's smelting pots, and strategic locations to refuel American cargo ships heading for seaport cities of the Far East. From necessity, American foreign policy shifted from isolationism to colonialism/imperialism and quasi-interventionism. The United States eventually purchased Alaska from the Russians in 1867 and acquired Midway Island in 1867, the Philippine Islands, Johnston Island and Hawaiian Islands in 1898, and Wake Island and American Samoa in 1899. From 1898 to 1915, the United States militarily occupied Cuba, Haiti, the Dominican Republic, and Nicaragua and sent an army expedition into Mexico. In 1903, the United States government gave aid to revolutionaries in Panama in hopes that a victory for them would result in the United States gaining the Isthmus of Panama for a canal.

While the Americans were busy acquiring colonies, Europe was on the brink of war. On June 28, 1914, the Archduke of Austria and his wife were murdered by a Slavic nationalist. In retaliation, Austria-Hungary mobilized to punish Serbia, which was rumored to be the architect of the assassination plot. With the largest army in Europe, Russia called upon France to come to the aid of Serbia. By August 4, 1914, the lines of battle were drawn with the **Triple Entente** of England, France and Russia at war with the **Triple Alliance** of Germany, Austria-Hungary and Italy. In hopes of avoiding the conflict, President Wilson publically announced America's neutrality. As a neutral non-combatant, American merchants carried goods and services to both sides until the British government implemented an unofficial blockade by forcing American vessels into British ports and confiscating their cargo. To halt the continuous flow of American goods into Britain, the Germans freed their submarines to attack and sink any ship near the British Isles. The sinking of the British passenger ship, *The Lusitania*, as well as American ships prompted Congress to approve a formal declaration of war against the Triple Alliance. As a whole, the American public was not solidly behind the war effort. Wilson gained support with his pledge that with the addition of America's military might, a victory would mean the end of all wars. Even before its entry into World War I, the stability of both the Russian monarchy and its government was fragile. After a series of bloody worker or peasant revolts offset by repressive actions on the part of the government, Tsar Nicholas II abdicated and a provisional government was formed. By November 1917, the weak provisional government was overthrown by the Bolsheviks, or the Communists, under the leadership of V. I. Lenin. On March 3, 1918, the Russian government signed the Brest-Litovsk Treaty with Germany, officially withdrawing Russia from the war. After its major offensive into France failed, the Germans surrendered on October 6, 1918. The defeated Germans and her allies agreed to the terms of the **Treaty of Versailles** and Woodrow Wilson's fourteen points, advocating open relations for all nations, freedom of the seas in peace and war, reductions in armaments, and the formation of an international organization known as the **League of Nations** whereby delegates of all member nation states would settle their disputes without warfare.

Germany felt that the punishment levied against them through the Treaty was exceptionally harsh. They were "particularly unhappy with Article 231, the so-called **War Guilt Clause**, which declared Germany (and Austria) responsible for starting the war and ordered Germany to pay reparations for all the damage to which the Allied governments and their people were subjected to as a result of the war 'imposed upon them by the aggression of Germany and her allies.'"[73] The Germans were forced to reduce its army and navy and completely eliminate its air force. Also, the Germans had to return the Alsace and Lorraine back to France. Germany's humiliating defeat and the subsequent collapse of its economy aided the cause of the rising Nazi movement under Adolph Hitler and, in some respects, set the stage for World War II.

For most Americans the euphoria of going "over there" was short lived. World War I was the first time American soldiers fought on European soil. The United States entered the war eighteen months before it officially ended. "Of the 2 million Americans who had served in France, 50,000 had died in combat and 230,000 had been wounded. By comparison, the war claimed 1.8 million Germans, 1.7 million Russians, 1.4 million French, 1.2 million Austro-Hungarians, and nearly 1 million Britons."[74] Consequently, Americans were war weary and wished to isolate themselves from the international community. With the collapse of the stock market in 1929, the nation's attention had to be directed inward as Americans dealt with the harshness of the Great Depression.

President Franklin Roosevelt was well aware of the mounting tensions in Europe with the rise of totalitarian-based **Nazism** in Germany and authoritarian-based **Fascism** in Italy. With the annexation of Austria in 1938, Adolph Hitler began his quest to establish German control over Europe. Meanwhile, the nationalistic aspirations of the Japanese military gradually took over the reins of government from the emperor, rendering the once divine monarch into a puppet. Once the Japanese seized Manchuria in 1931 and made in-roads into China, the command staff of the Japanese army launched a full-scale aggressive plan to dominate the Far East and Asia. By November 1936, the Japanese and the Germans formed an alliance under the terms of the **Anti-Comintern Pact**. Wanting to forestall a German invasion, the Russians signed a nonaggression pact with Hitler in 1939, only to see the Germans eventually invade their country. On September 3, 1939, France and Great Britain declared war on Germany. Roosevelt was caught in a policy quandary. The American people simply did not want to become involved in another war. Therefore, Roosevelt opted to give the French and the British everything short of manpower through his lend-lease program. With the 1941 Japanese attack on Pearl Harbor, Roosevelt had no option left but to ask for an official declaration of war against Japan and its allies Germany and Italy.

Once the United States entered World War II, there was no turning back to the days of neutrality and isolationism. The waning months of the war laid the foundation for the growing tensions between the Socialist Soviet Union and the democratic-capitalistic nations, particularly the United States. Once the gunfire stopped, the ideological warfare with its potential outcome of a nuclear

Jimmy Carter and Giscard d'Estaing at a memorial ceremony for World War II GI's. January 5, 1978. Photo credit: Jimmy Carter Library

confrontation began. The Soviet Union enclosed the Eastern bloc countries to include the eastern portion of Germany, behind an iron curtain under the control of first Lenin then Joseph Stalin. With the horrific destructiveness of the war, both France and Britain were unable to assume the leadership role of confronting the Soviet presence. It was left up to the United States to fill the leadership void. In 1947, President Harry Truman pledged economic and possible military support to protect Greece and Turkey from Soviet intrusion. The **Truman Doctrine** stated "the United States would support free peoples who are resisting attempted subjugation by armed minorities or by outside pressures."[75] The **Marshall Plan** provided economic aid to help those European countries favorable to the United States recover from World War II. In 1949, Truman pledged economic assistance to third world nations. The Russians retaliated by closing off their sector of Berlin to American assistance. Truman responded with the famous **Berlin Lift** whereby American aircraft dropped much needed food and supplies to the "other side." The United States pledged both economic and military support to Latin American countries under the **Rio Pact**. Similar support was guaranteed to Britain, France, Belgium, Netherlands, and Luxembourg through the **Brussels Pact**. The North Atlantic Treaty Organization was signed in 1949. These **collective security agreements** were the cornerstone of Truman's **containment policy** of preventing the Soviet Union from expanding its influence over other countries. Every president since has honored and even extended the collective security agreements initiated by the Truman administration.

Today, the Soviet or Eastern bloc no longer exists. The massive country known as the Soviet Union no longer exists as individual states under the strong arm of Moscow are now independent nation states. The Berlin Wall was dismantled during the Reagan administration. East and West Germany have been reunited as one country. The Russian economy has become more capitalistic and a viable free market partner. However, the White House will continue to be watchful of Russia's actions and policy directives. With a sigh of relief on both sides, the Cold War has ended without the predicted nuclear showdown.

Secretary of State Hillary Clinton hosted an event with the South Korean officials in Washington. July 27, 2009. Credit: RTT News

CURRENT FOREIGN POLICY ISSUES AND CHALLENGES AHEAD

As a presidential candidate, Obama pledged a new approach to languishing foreign policy issues. While since September 11, 2001, the attention has been focused on Iraq, the United States must address pressing concerns in North Korea, Pakistan, Afghanistan, and the continuing conflicts between Israel and Palestine. The nation's relationships with Central and Latin America merit attention as well. Obama has a full plate before him. A closer look at these areas helps us to understand the challenges he faces.

The Far East: North Korea

Initially a tributary of China, Korea fell under the influence of the Japanese and Russians as a result of the Sino-Japanese War in 1894-1895. When the Japanese defeated the Russians in 1905, Korea became part of the Japanese empire until Japan's defeat in World War II. In August 1945, the United States and the Soviet Union decided to create two separate occupation zones at the **38th parallel**. Both sides agreed to hold national elections with the aim of reunifying the country. The fate of Korea and other Asian countries was tied directly to developments in China. The father of modern China, Dr. Sun Yat-sen, led a successful revolution in 1911 that ended the centuries-old monarchial rule of the emperors. However, the newly formed Republic of China was unable to unite the country. While anti-Communist and Nationalist leader Chiang Kai-shek was trying to hold the fragile government together and at the same time fight off Japanese aggression in the southern areas leading to and during World War II, Mao Zedong was gaining support of the peasants in northern China. By 1949, Mao's Communist-inspired peasant army overthrew the Chiang Kai-shek government. China was the beginning of the **domino theory** feared by the Truman administration.

The concept holds that if one country in a particular region falls under the influence of socialism/communism, the other weaker nations will fall into line, just like falling dominos. The Cold War dichotomy in Europe was now in Asia.

Cold War politics created two separate Koreas with North Korea as a socialist/communist nation and South Korea as an anti-socialist/communist country. On June 25, 1950, North Korea invaded South Korea. Truman ordered United States naval and air force support for South Korea as his administration sought and received U.N. resolutions condemning North Korea and pledging U.N. forces under the command of General Douglas MacArthur for South Korea. Unfortunately, the Korean War ended with a cease-fire agreement signed in July 1953. Since the cease-fire, the United States has stationed military forces along the 38th parallel to help the South Koreans prevent another invasion from North Korea. Today, North Korea is a socialist/communist ideological state governed by a quasi-militaristic government headed by their president.

The major issue for the international community is the rapid development of North Korea's nuclear program. The North Koreans contend that it is their right, just like any other nation, to use nuclear power for energy-generation purposes. However, the firing of low- and medium-range nuclear missiles for test purposes has the international community on the edge, fearing that North Korea's possession of nuclear weapons in hands of an unstable leadership could lead to war. On June 12, 2009, the United Nations Security Council voted unanimously to sanction North Korea's actions. The resolution mandates that:

- North Korea not conduct any further nuclear test or any launch using ballistic missile technology.
- North Korea suspend all activities related to its ballistic missile program and re-establish a moratorium on missile launches.
- North Korea return immediately to the six-party talks without precondition.[76]

In addition, North Korea cannot export or receive imports of any arms and weapon-related materials with the exception of small arms and light weapons. The U.N. calls for the inspection of all ships entering and exiting North Korean waters. The problem for the Obama administration is two-fold. Obviously, the North Koreans will not abandon their nuclear ambitions without receiving something in return. In the past, North Korea has asked for and received large-scale food shipments from the United States and other nations. North Korea is confronted with a severely sagging economy and agricultural failures. The United States must also take into account China's concerns that while North Korea's actions are unacceptable, the international community simply cannot punish them so severely that the North Korean government feels that the only choice they have to maintain their popularity at home and prestige abroad is to launch a limited war against South Korea.

Far East: China

The United States' relationship with China continues to be dicey particularly when the topics focus on the economic relationship between the two nations and human rights violations charged against the Chinese government. During the 2012 presidential election, Mitt Romney continuously voiced concerns over trade with China and whether the Chinese government was purposely manipulating its currency values to continue its lop-sided balance of trade with the United States. Basically, "a weaker yuan [China's currency] makes Chinese goods cheaper for American consumers and U.S. goods more expensive in China."[77] This is not the first time the Chinese have been accused of illegal and unfair trade tactics. In 1994, the Clinton administration officially labeled the Chinese as a currency manipulator. In 1989, the repressive policies of the Chinese government drove thousands of student protestors to Tiananmen Square. After weeks of protesting and international news exposure, the Chinese government launched a bloody crackdown resulting in hundreds killed and many more injured and arrested. Since then, the international community has become more aware of and more vocal about China's government-sanctioned human rights violations. However, the official policy position from the White House is to tread cautiously since overstepping its concern about human rights abuses could well jeopardize the extensive investments, business-partnerships, multinational corporations, and trade between the two nations. With the elevation of Xi Jinping to the presidency, China is focusing of changing its image from "simply positioning China as a vanquished, aggrieved inferior [to] reclaiming its rightful place in the world, not just economically but politically and culturally too."[78]

Central and Latin America – Mexico and Cuba

When President George H. W. Bush joined Mexican officials in San Antonio, Texas, to sign the North American Free Trade Agreement, Mexico believed it had finally established itself as a viable trade partner with the United States. The agreement pledged seamless international boundaries between the United States, Mexico and Canada. While Canada and the United States have seamless borders, the border between the United States and Mexico is anything but transparent. From the very beginning, the Teamsters Union and the trucking industry in the United States fought to block Mexican trucks from shipping goods into the United States. The arguments against the Mexican trucking industry have ranged from the quality of the trucks, the qualifications of the drivers, and the concern that the Mexican government would use NAFTA to smuggle in illegal drugs and Mexican nationals. Basically, NAFTA has never been fully implemented.

Illegal immigration from Mexico into the United States has always been a sore spot. When the American economy is sound, there is a need for Mexican workers in primarily agriculture and in some industries. However, immigrant workers, whether legal or illegal, are not wanted when the American economy sours. Initially, the Bush administration wanted to build a fence between the shared border of Mexico and the United States. It soon became evident that a fence will not halt illegal immigration nor will it prevent the Mexico-base drug cartels from smuggling in their wares. The Obama administration canceled the project. It is ironic that when the retail merchants in the border states of Texas, New Mexico, Arizona and California have a slump in Christmas sales, they always rely upon the Mexican nationals coming across the border to shop. The United States government cannot continue to be selective. The George W. Bush administration wanted to implement a guest worker program similar to the Bracero program following World War II, and an amnesty plan to assist illegal workers who have been in this country for years to become citizens. Mexico is the gateway for the majority of those citizens of Central and Latin American countries who want to enter into the United States. If the American government wants to establish solid long-term relations with its neighbors to the South, it must successfully address the immigration issue in a manner that is satisfactory to both sides of the issue. Secretary of State Henry Kissinger once observed that it is personal economic interests that compel a person to leave his/her native country to seek work in the United States. His answer was for the United States to up the ante on economic development and infrastructure foreign aid for Central and Latin America. He argued that the key to illegal immigration is to alleviate the poverty that drives one to cross the Rio Grande, dodge the immigration officers, and survive the heat of the desert just to earn minimum wage or less at a low-end job.

What United States lawmakers cannot ignore is the violence along the Mexican-side of the border that is spilling over to the American side. Nightly news reports cover shootings, kidnappings, and beheadings of both Mexican-nationals and American citizens. Among the list of the missing are three men and a teenager from American-born citizens from New Braunfels, Texas, who simply went to Mexico to visit relatives, never to be heard of again. States along the border region are challenging the traditional role of the federal government to deal with immigration violations and international incidents of criminal acts. The governor of New Mexico wants to repeal a state law allowing persons to apply for drivers' licenses without showing proof of citizenship. The governor of Texas wants American troops to patrol the border. Obviously, part of the solution rests with a more cohesive working relationship between Mexican and American law enforcement agencies to handle the Mexican drug cartels as well as secure the borders from illegal immigration and the transportation of drug-related items.

A good starting point for the Obama administration is Cuba. An ailing Fidel Castro has turned the reigns of the government over to his brother Raul. The Cuban government, in turn, has signaled that they want to, at least, normalize and even enhance its relationship with the United States. The Obama administration has responded by lifting the barriers for family members in the states to visit their Cuban family members; allowing Cuban Americans to send money back home; and lifting some of the trade barriers. Normalizing relations with Cuba could send a strong message to all Central and Latin American nations that the United States does want to be a good neighbor.

The Middle East

The Bush administration focused the majority of its attention on invading Iraq and ending Saddam Hussein's rule over the Iraqi people. On the whole, the invasion was successful particularly with the capture and eventual trial of Hussein. However, the Bush administration did not have a viable "Plan B" for occupying, stabilizing, and, ultimately, governing Iraq. The Bush team's approach to handling the sectarian differences between the Kurds, Sunnis, and Shiites was simply to try to control the violence without really addressing the root causes of the violence. President Obama fulfilled his election promise of withdrawing all active military personnel from Iraq. The on-going challenge for this administration and, more importantly the American people, is to allow the people of Iraq to select their own governing philosophy and structure without undo interference from the United States. The Iraqi people should have the same opportunity as the international community afforded our Framers, as they transitioned from a confederative to a federal form of government. Unfortunately, it will not be a peaceful quick process simply because of the centuries old mistrust between the three factions. And, the final governing structure will not mirror the representative democracy of the United States crafted under the principle of separation of church and state. What will emerge is a governing partnership closely tied to the Muslim religion.

It began in Tunisia, a former French protectorate that gained its independence in 1956 located on the northern coast of Africa. After weeks of persistent protests, the government collapsed, sending its ruler fleeing from the country. The pro-democratic spirit spilled over as massive oftentimes heated, protests hit Jordan, Egypt, and other Middle Eastern countries. Experts believe these protests are fueled in part by a "youth bulge." "About 60 percent of the region's population is under the age of 30. These millions of young people have aspirations that need to be fulfilled, and the regimes in place right now show little ability to do so. The protesters' demands have been dismissed by the regimes as being Islamic fundamentalists or a product of Western inference."[79] But, that is not the case. Initially, the protesters had no desire to overthrow their governments. "What the protesters want in the first place is to be treated as citizens, not subjects.... the No. 1 wish of the young in nine countries was to live a free country."[80] What began as non-violent protests have resulted in bloody repressive actions from traditional autocratic governments unwilling to listen to the protesters' concerns and willing to relax their repressive ways. In Libya, the protests of a few turned into a civil war as an angry mob captured, killed and mutilated Gaddafi. In Egypt, massive protests resulted in the toppling of Mubarak. A civil war is raging in Syria. The massive protests of angry Egyptians with their cries of freedom, democracy and jobs overthrew the incumbent Egyptian government. In 1956, Nasser penned his hope for the Middle East in his *Philosophy of Revolution*. He believed that the key to peace in the region was solidarity, both internal and external. Internally, he advocated that regardless of the form of a national government, the survival of that government hinged on internal sovereignty. When he took office, Egyptians were still holding their allegiance to their tribes and clans, not the national government. If he were standing in the square in Cairo during the celebration of Mubarak's departure, he would have been pleased to hear the crowd chant that they were proud to be Egyptians! Finally, nationalism has come to Egypt and perhaps to the entire Middle East region.

The democratic cries for free elections have failed to materialize in the Middle East, particularly in Egypt. Although officially elected to the presidency, Morsi's ties to the Muslim Brotherhood cost him not only his job but, perhaps, his life. Not new to Egyptian politics, the Muslim Brotherhood was founded by Hassan al-Banna in 1928, as both a religious and political group based on the belief that Islam and it's Sharia law is more than a religious affiliation, it's a way of life. Peaceful demonstrations gave way to violent protests as the Brotherhood became more critical of the Egyptian government. In the 1940s, the Egyptian government officially ordered the dissolution of the Brotherhood. However, the group retaliated by assassinating the Egyptian prime minister. Going underground, the group reemerged in the 1980s vowing to pursue its agenda in a non-violent manner. President Mubarak banned it once again only to see it reemerge in 2003. In 2005, the group won 20 percent of the seats of Egyptian parliamentary elections. However, Mubarak reacted by jailing hundreds of its members and outlawing it. With the overthrow of Mubarak, the Brotherhood reasserted itself and successfully gained seats in the Egyptian legislature, as well as electing Morsi. The overthrow of Morsi by the Egyptian military has signaled once again that the Brotherhood is out of business in Egypt. However, there are branches of the Brotherhood throughout the Middle East and Africa including Sudan, Syria, and Saudi Arabia.

President Obama has already pledged his support for a separate Palestinian state. The United States can be supportive of Israel while at the same time recognizing the need for the Palestinian people to exercise their rights to self-determination and have their own country. Secretary of

President Obama and General David Petreus at a White House Press Conference on June 23, 2010. Gen. David Petraeus, the top U.S. commander in Afghanistan, will succeed Leon Panetta at the helm of the CIA. Petraeus plans to serve through the summer of 2011 in Afghanistan, and will formally retire from the military to take up the CIA Director post in September. Marine Corps Lt. Gen. John Allen, Petraeus' former deputy commander at U.S. Central Command, will succeed Petraeus. Credit: RTTNews

State John Kerry is spearheading a series of talks between the Israeli and Palestinian governments to regenerate the two-state concept. While it probably will not happen in the immediate future, the advocacy of a separate state helps to convince the Arab nations that the United States wants to establish long-term viable relations with both Israel and the Arab world.

International Terrorism and Afghanistan

American intelligence has laid the responsibility for the attacks on the World Trade Center definitively and accurately on the Al Qaeda terrorist organization founded by Osama bin Laden. Unfortunately, Al Qaeda is a worldwide organization composed of ideologically joined but operationally separate independent cells located throughout the world to include first-world power nation states. The hunt for bin Laden focused in the mountainous region between Afghanistan and Pakistan. On May 2, 2011, a special attachment of Navy Seals successfully entered into Pakistan and killed bin Laden. When the news broke, many Americans celebrated his demise across the country particularly at the gates of the White House.

Just eliminating bin Laden has not eliminated Al Qaeda. The rebels trying to oust the Assad government in Syria welcomed anyone who crossed the border into Syria to join their cause. Syrian rebel forces have and will continue to request assistance from the United States. In particular, they would like a no-fly zone similar to the one the United States provided for Libya. Al Qaeda has surfaced in Iraq, particularly in Fallujah and Anbar Providence, Libya, and Iran. However, the

President Obama and Afghan President Hamid Karzai at White House Press Conference on May 12, 2010.
Credit: RTTNews

United States will not support any organization no matter how noble or valid their cause may be, if their ranks include members of Al Qaeda.

The situation in Afghanistan is further complicated by the struggles between the incumbent government of Hamid Karzai and the Taliban. Guided by the traditional Muslim philosophy, the Taliban once ruled over Afghanistan but was ousted. The Taliban has continued their attacks, keeping the ill-equipped Afghanistan military along with American troop support fighting village to village without an end in sight. When he first took office, Obama supported a military surge to oust the Taliban. Yet, every military victory is offset by a defeat. Some have coined the American effort in Afghanistan Obama's Vietnam. They see similarities between the two conflicts: "the president, eager to show his toughness, vows to do what it takes to "win." The nation that we are supposedly rescuing is no nation at all but rather a deeply divided, semi-failed state with an incompetent, corrupt government held to be illegitimate by a large portion of its population. The enemy is well accustomed to resisting foreign invaders and can escape into convenient refuges across the border. There are constraints on America striking those sanctuaries. Meanwhile neighboring countries may see a chance to bog America down in a costly war. Last, there is no easy way out."[81] As long as bin Laden was alive, Americans supported, although reluctantly so, the commitment of American military forces in Afghanistan. However, the support evaporated once bin Laden was dead. Frustrated by the inept Afghan military and lack of leadership from the Karzai government, Obama decided to completely withdraw American forces. However, the Obama administration along with NATO officials want the Karzai government to sign a security agreement giving the United States an opening to send armed troops into Afghanistan if the security of the nation is compromised by either an invasion or an internal insurgency, particularly from the Taliban. Karzai has refused to sign the agreement. American military forces are scheduled to depart by the end of 2014.

CONCLUSIONS

Unlike domestic policy issues, foreign policy decisions impact not only the people back home but also the entire international community. Foreign policy is not benevolent. Every nation state develops its foreign policy responses around its own vital interests. International agreements, compacts, treaties and even wars are geared towards the pursuit of an individual nation state's vital interests. The American people elected George Washington or Barack Obama because they believed that they would protect the best interests of the United States, both at home and abroad.

CHAPTER NOTES

[1] *Treasury of Presidential Quotations*, Caroline Thomas Harnsberger, ed., (Chicago, Illinois: Follett Publishing Company, 1964), 96.
[2] Ibid., 104.
[3] *The International Relations Dictionary*, Jack C. Plano and Roy Olton, eds., (New York, New York: Holt, Reinhart and Winston, Inc., 1969), 127.
[4] Ibid., 313.
[5] Ibid., 120.
[6] Ibid., 58.
[7] Ibid., 45.
[8] Ibid., 121.
[9] Gabriel A. Almond, G. Bingham Powell, Jr., Kaare Strom, and Russell J. Dalton, *Comparative Politics Today: A World View*, 8th ed., (New York, New York: Pearson, Longman, 2004), 12.
[10] Ibid.
[11] Harnsberger, 96.
[12] Susan Welch, JohnGruhl, Michael Steinman, John Comer, and Susan M. Rigdon, *American Government*, 5th ed., (Minneapolis/St. Paul, Wisconsin: West Publishing Co., 1994) 631-632.
[13] Plano and Olton, 262.
[14] *The HarperCollins Dictionary of American Government and Politics*, Jay M. Shafritz, ed., (New York, New York: HarperCollins Publishers, Inc., 1992) 305.
[15] Plano and Olton, 49.
[16] Robert Ergang, *Europe Since Waterloo*, 3rd ed., (Lexington, Massachusetts: D. C. Heath and Company, 1967), 38.
[17] Ibid., 39
[18] Plano and Olton, 292.
[19] Fred W. Wellborn, *Diplomatic History of the United States,* 2nd ed., (Totowa, New Jersey: Littlefield, Adams & Co., 1962), 367.
[20] Richard W. Leopold, *The Growth of American Foreign Policy: A History*, (New York, New York: Alfred A. Knopf, 1962), 374.
[21] Ibid., 629.
[22] Plano and Olton, 216.
[23] Ibid., 62.
[24] Ibid.
[25] Jay M. Shafritz, 289.
[26] Ibid., 177.
[27] *The American Political Dictionary*, Jack C. Plano and Milton Greenberg, eds., 10th ed., (Fort Worth, Texas: Harcourt Brace College Publishers, 1997), 583.
[28] Plano and Olton, 62.
[29] "Ten-Year Country Report", USAID Economic Analysis and Data Services (EDS), (http://gbk.eads.isaoda.net.gov/quert/do)
[30] "State and USAID-FY 2013 Budget," U.S. Department of State, February 13, 2012, (http://www.state.gov/r/pa/ps/2012/02)
[31] Plano and Olton, 77.
[32] Ibid.
[33] Ibid., 64.

34 Ibid., 77.
35 Ibid., 73.
36 Guillermo Contrereas, "Bataan Death March Survivors Hear Apology," *San Antonio Express-News,* (Sunday, May 31, 2009), 1A.
37 Plano and Olton, 68.
38 Ibid., 57.
39 Ibid., 115.
40 Ibid., 15.
41 "U.S. International Trade in Goods and Services, November 2013," Exhibit 5: Exports, and Trade Balance of Goods, U.S. Census Bureau and U.S. Bureau of Economic News, U.S. Department of Commerce (www.census.gov/ft900)
42 Ibid., Exhibit 14: Exports, Imports and Balance of Goods and Services, November 2013, U.S. Census Bureau and U.S. Bureau of Economic News, U.S. Department of Commerce (www.census.gov/ft900)
43 Plano and Olton, 39.
44 Ibid., 30.
45 David Adler, "The Constitution and Presidential Warmaking: The Enduring Debate," *Political Science Quarterly*, Vol. 103, Spring, 1988, 15.
46 Ibid., 9.
47 Ibid.
48 Louis Fisher, *Constitutional Conflicts Between the Congress and the President*, 5th ed., revised, (Lawrence, Kansas: University of Kansas Press, 2007), 250.
49 Adler, "The Constitution and Presidential Warmaking: The Enduring Debate," 12.
50 "The Federalist No. 69", Alexander Hamilton, John Jay and James Madison, *The Federalist,* (New York, New York: The Modern Library, 1937), 448.
51 Adler, "The Constitution and Presidential Warmaking: The Enduring Debate," 5.
52 Virginia Stowitts, Chrstine Schultz, Theresia Stewart, and Karen Sunshine, *The Study Guide and Reader for American Government and Politics in the New Millennium*, 6th ed., (Wheaton, Illinois: Abigail Press, 2007), 279.
53 Ibid., 280.
54 Theodore J. Lowi, "Presidential Power: Restoring the Balance," *Political Science Quarterly*, Vol. 100, No. 2, Summer, 1985, 191.
55 Thomas E. Patterson, *We The People: A Concise Introduction to American Politics,* 8th ed., (New York, New York: McGraw Kill, 2009), 450-451.
56 Fisher, 274.
57 Richard M. Pious, *The Presidency,* (Boston, Massachusetts: Allyn and Bacon, 1996) 459.
58 Charlie Savage and Mark Landler, "White House Stands Firm on Libya Action," *San Antonio Express-News* (Thursday, June 16, 2011), 11A.
59 Lowi, "Presidential Power: Restoring the Balance," 192.
60 Raoul Berger, *Executive Privilege: A Constitutional Myth,* (Boston, Massachusetts: Harvard University Press, 1974), 146.
61 *The Enduring Federalist*, Charles A. Beard, ed., 2nd ed., (New York, New York: Frederick Ungar Publishing Co., 1964), 318-319.
62 Arthur Schlisinger, *The Imperial Presidency*, (Boston, Massachusetts: Houghton Mifflin Co., 1973), 90.
63 Plano and Greenberg, 190.
64 Amy Gilbert, *Executive Agreements and Treaties, 1946-1973: Framework of the Foreign Policy Period,* (New York: New York: Thomas-Newell, 1973), 3.
65 Loch K. Johnson, *The Making of International Agreements: Congress Confronts the Executive*, (New York, New York: New York University Press, 1984), 24.
66 Thomas M. Franck and Edward Weisband, *Foreign Policy By Congress*, (New York, New York: Oxford University Press, 1970), 145.
67 "The Prsident's Budget for Fiscal Year 2014," Table 3.1: Outlays by Superfunction and Function: 1940-2018, Office of Management and Budget, 59 (www.whitehouse,gov.omb/budget)
68 "About the Department of Defense (DOD)," U.S. Department of Defense (http://www.defense.gov/about/)
69 "Conference of July 22 with Pentagon Officials on Committing Large Number of Troops to Vietnam," *Lyndon Johnson and American Liberalism: A Brief Biography with Documents*, Bruce J. Schulman, ed., 2nd ed., (Boston, Massachusetts: Bedford/St. Martins, 2007), 253-255.
70 Leopold, 36.
71 Ibid.

[72] Wayne S. Cole, "Myths Surrounding the Monroe Doctrine," *Myth and the American Experience,* Vol. 1, Nicholas Cords and Patrick Gerster, eds., 2nd ed., (Encino, California: Glencoe Publishing Co., Inc., 1978), 218-219.
[73] William J. Duiker and Jackson J. Spielvogel, *World History,* 3rd ed., (Belmont, California: Wadsworth, 2001), 734.
[74] James West Davidson, William E. Gienapp, Christine Leigh Heyrman, Mark H. Lytle, and Michael B. Stoff, *Nations of Nations: A Narrative History of the American Republic,* (New York, N. Y.: McGraw Hill Publishing Company, 1990), 889.
[75] Wellborn, 364.
[76] Neil MacFarquhar, "N. Korea Faces New Sanctions," *San Antonio Express-News,* (Saturday, June 13, 2009), 1A.
[77] "U.S. Stops Short of Calling China a Currency Manipulator," *San Antonio Express-News* (Wednesday, November 28, 2012), A7.
[78] Hannah Beech, "How China Sees the World," *Time,* June 17, 2013, 29.
[79] Fareed Zakaria, "Why It's Different This Time," *Time,* February 28, 2011, 30.
[80] Ibid., 30-31.
[81] John Berry and Evan Thomas, "Obama's Vietnam," *Newsweek,* February 9, 2009, 30.

•

SUGGESTED READINGS

Charles W. Kegley, Jr., and Eugene R. Wittkopf, *American Foreign Policy: Pattern and Process,* 3rd ed., New York, New York: St. Martins Press, 1987.

Charles W. Kegley, Jr., and Eugene R. Wittkopf, *The Future of American Foreign Policy,* New York, New York: St. Martins Press, 1992.

Frederick H. Hartmann, *American's Foreign Policy in a Changing World,* New York, New York: HarperCollins College Publishers, 2004.

G. John Ikenberry, *American Foreign Policy: Theoretical Essays,* Glenview, Illinois: Scott, Foresman and Company, 1989.

Hans J. Morgenthau, *Politics Among Nations: The Struggle for Power and Peace,* 7th ed., Boston, Massachusetts: McGraw Hill High Education, 2006.

John T. Rourke, *International Politics on the World Stage,* 4th ed., Guilford, Connecticut: Dushkin Publishing Group, Inc., 1993.

Joshua S. Goldstein, *International Relations,* New York, New York: HarperCollings College Publishers, 1994.

Louis Fisher, *Constitutional Conflicts Between Congress and the President,* 5th ed., Lawrence, Kansas: University Press of Kansas, 2007.

Web Sites:

www.archives.gov/presidential-libraries/visit/ - Presidential Libraries
www.Realhistoryarchives.com/collections/conspiracies/irancontra.htm - Iran/Contra
www.library.umass/edu/subject/iraqwar - Iraq War 2003 Links
www.nytimes.com
www.cnn.com
www.fsmitha.com/h2/ch26.htm - Vietnam War
www.pbs.org/wgbh/amex/china/ - Détente
www.gwu.edu/~nsarchiv/nsa/publications/DOC_readers/kissinger/nixzhou/ - Détente

APPENDIX A

Declaration of Independence

Congress, July 4, 1776

When, in the course of human events, it becomes necessary for one people to dissolve the political bonds which have connected them with another, and to assume, among the powers of the earth, the separate and equal station to which the laws of nature and of nature's God entitle them, a decent respect to the opinions of mankind requires that they should declare the causes which impel them to the separation.

We hold these truths to be self-evident: That all men are created equal; that they are endowed by their Creator with certain unalienable rights; that among these are life, liberty and the pursuit of happiness; that, to secure these rights, governments are instituted among men, deriving their just powers from the consent of the governed; that whenever any form of government becomes destructive of these ends, it is the right of the people to alter or to abolish it, and to institute new government, laying its foundation on such principles, and organizing its powers in such form, as to them shall seem most likely to effect their safety and happiness. Prudence, indeed, will dictate that governments long established should not be changed for light and transient causes; and accordingly all experience hath shown that mankind are more disposed to suffer, while evils are sufferable, than to right themselves by abolishing the forms to which they are accustomed. But when a long train of abuses and usurpations, pursuing invariably the same object, evinces a design to reduce them under absolute despotism, it is their right, it is their duty, to throw off such government, and to provide new guards for their future security. Such has been the patient sufferance of these colonies; and such is now the necessity which constrains them to alter their former systems of government. The history of the present King of Great Britain is a history of repeated injuries and usurpations, all having in direct object the establishment of an absolute tyranny over these states. To prove this, let facts be submitted to a candid world.

He has refused his assent to laws, the most wholesome and necessary for the public good.

He has forbidden his governors to pass laws of immediate and pressing importance, unless suspended in their operation till his assent should be obtained; and, when so suspended, he has utterly neglected to attend to them.

He has refused to pass other laws for the accommodation of large districts of people, unless those people would relinquish the right of representation in the legislature, a right inestimable to them, and formidable to tyrants only.

He has called together legislative bodies at places unusual, uncomfortable, and distant from the depository of their public records, for the sole purpose of fatiguing them into compliance with his measures.

He has dissolved representative houses repeatedly, for opposing, with many firmness, his invasions on the rights of the people.

He has refused for a long time, after such dissolutions, to cause others to be elected; whereby the legislative powers, incapable of annihilation, have returned to the people at large for their exercise; the state remaining, in the mean time, exposed to all the dangers of invasions from without and convulsions within.

He has endeavored to prevent the population of these states; for that purpose obstructing the laws for naturalization of foreigners; refusing to pass others to encourage their migrations hither, and raising the conditions of new appropriations of lands.

He has obstructed the administration of justice, by refusing his assent to laws establishing judiciary powers.

He has made judges dependent on his will alone, for the tenure of their offices, and the amount and payment of their salaries.

He has erected a multitude of new offices, and sent hither swarms of officers to harass our people and eat out their substance.

He has kept among us, in times of peace, standing armies, without the consent of our legislatures.

He has affected to render the military independent of, and superior to, the civil power.

He has combined with others to subject us to jurisdiction foreign to our constitution, and unacknowledged by our laws, giving his assent to their acts of pretended legislation:

For quartering large bodies of armed troops among us;

For protecting them, by a mock trial, from punishment for any murder which they should commit on the inhabitants of these states;

For cutting off our trade with all parts of the world;

For imposing taxes on us without our consent;

For depriving us, in many cases, of the benefits of trial by jury;

For transporting us beyond seas, to be tried for pretended offenses;

For abolishing the free system of English laws in a neighboring province, establishing therein an arbitrary government, and enlarging its boundaries, so as to render it at once an example and fit instrument for introducing the same absolute rule into these colonies;

For taking away our charters, abolishing our most valuable laws, and altering fundamentally the forms of our governments;

For suspending our own legislatures, and declaring themselves invested with power to legislate for us in all cases whatsoever.

He has abdicated government here, by declaring us out of his protection and waging war against us.

He has plundered our seas, ravaged our coasts, burned our towns, and destroyed the lives of our people.

He is at this time transporting large armies of foreign mercenaries to complete the works of death, desolation and tyranny already begun with circumstances of cruelty and perfidy scarcely paralleled in the most barbarous ages, and totally unworthy the head of a civilized nation.

He has constrained our fellow-citizens, taken captive on the high seas, to bear arms against their country, to become the executioners of their friends and brethren, or to fall themselves by their hands.

He has excited domestic insurrections among us, and has endeavored to bring on the inhabitants of our frontiers the merciless Indian savages, whose known rule of warfare is an undistinguished destruction of all ages, sexes, and conditions.

In every stage of these oppressions we have petitioned for redress in the most humble terms; our repeated petitions have been answered only by repeated injury. A prince, whose character is thus marked by every act which may define a tyrant, is unfit to be the ruler of a free people.

Nor have we been wanting in our attentions to our British brethren. We have warned them, from time to time, of attempts by their legislature to extend an unwarrantable jurisdiction over us. We have reminded them of the circumstances of our emigration and settlement here. We have appealed to their native justice and magnanimity, and we have conjured them, by the ties of our common kindred, to disavow these usurpations, which would inevitably interrupt our connections and correspondence. They, too, have been deaf to the voice of justice and of consanguinity. We must, therefore, acquiesce in the necessity which denounces our separation, and hold them, as we hold the rest of mankind, enemies in war, in peace friends.

Appendix 1

We, therefore, the representatives of the United States of America, in General Congress assembled, appealing to the Supreme Judge of the world for the rectitude of our intentions, do, in the name and by authority of the good people of these colonies, solemnly publish and declare, that these United Colonies are, and of right ought to be, FREE AND INDEPENDENT STATES; that they are absolved from all allegiance to the British crown, and that all political connection between them and the state of Great Britain is, and ought to be, totally dissolved; and that, as free and independent states, they have full power to levy war, conclude peace, contract alliances, establish commerce, and do all other acts and things which independent states may of right do. And for the support of this declaration, with a firm reliance on the protection of Divine Providence, we mutually pledge to each other our lives, our fortunes, and our sacred honor.

JOHN HANCOCK

BUTTON GWINNETT	THOS. NELSON, JR.	RICHD. STOCKTON
LYMAN HALL	FRANCIS LIGHTFOOT LEE	JNO. WITHERSPOON
GEO. WALTON	CARTER BRAXTON	FRAS. HOPKINSON
WM. HOOPER	ROBT. MORRIS	JOHN HART
JOSEPH HEWES	BENJAMIN RUSH	ABRA. CLARK
JOHN PENN	BENJA. FRANKLIN	JOSIAH BARTLETT
EDWARD RUTLEDGE	JOHN MORTON	WM. WHIPPLE
THOS. HEYWARD, JUNR.	GEO. CLYMER	SAML. ADAMS
THOMAS LYNCH, JUNR.	JAS. SMITH	JOHN ADAMS
ARTHUR MIDDLETON	GEO. TAYLOR	ROBT. TREAT PAINE
SAMUEL CHASE	JAMES WILSON	ELBRIDGE GERRY
WM. PACA	GEO. ROSS	STEP. HOPKINS
THOS. STONE	CAESAR RODNEY	WILLIAM ELLERY
CHARLES CARROLL OF CARROLLTON	GEO READ	ROGER SHERMAN
GEORGE WYTHE	THO. M'KEAN	SAM'EL HUNTINGTON
RICHARD HENRY LEE	WM. FLOYD	WM. WILLIAMS
TH. JEFFERSON	PHIL. LIVINGSTON	OLIVER WOLCOTT
BENJ. HARRISON	FRANS. LEWIS	MATTHEW THORNTON
	LEWIS MORRIS	

APPENDIX B

The Constitution of the United States of America

PREAMBLE

We the people of the United States, in order to form a more perfect union, establish justice, insure domestic tranquility, provide for the common defense, promote the general welfare, and secure the blessings of liberty to ourselves and our posterity, do ordain and establish this Constitution for the United States of America.

ARTICLE I.—THE LEGISLATIVE ARTICLE

Section 1. All legislative powers herein granted shall be vested in a Congress of the United States, which shall consist of a Senate and a House of Representatives.

House of Representatives: Composition, Qualification, Apportionment, Impeachment Power

Section 2. The House of Representatives shall be composed of members chosen every second year by the people of the several States, and the electors in each State shall have the qualifications requisite for electors of the most numerous branch of the State Legislature.

No person shall be a Representative who shall not have attained to the age of twenty-five years, and been seven years a citizen of the United States, and who shall not, when elected, be an inhabitant of that State in which he shall be chosen.

Representatives and direct taxes shall be apportioned among the several States which may be included within this Union, according to their respective numbers, *which shall be determined by adding to the whole number of free persons, including those bound to service for a term of years and excluding Indians not taxed, three-fifths of all other persons.* The actual enumeration shall be made within three years after the first meeting of the Congress of the United States, and within every subsequent term of ten years, in such manner as they shall by law direct. The number of Representatives shall not exceed one for every thirty thousand, but each State shall have at least one Representative; *and until each enumeration shall be made, the State of New Hampshire shall be entitled to choose three, Massachusetts eight, Rhode Island and Providence Plantations one, Connecticut five, New York six, New Jersey four, Pennsylvania eight, Delaware one, Maryland six, Virginia ten, North Carolina five, South Carolina five, and Georgia three.*

When vacancies happen in the representation from any State, the Executive authority thereof shall issue writs of election to fill such vacancies.

The House of Representatives shall choose their Speaker and other officers; and shall have the sole power of impeachment.

Passages no longer in effect are printed in italic type.

Senate Composition: Qualifications, Impeachment Trials

Section 3. The Senate of the United States shall be composed of two Senators from each State, chosen by the legislature thereof, for six years; and each Senator shall have one vote.

Immediately after they shall be assembled in consequence of the first election, they shall be divided as equally as may be into three classes. The seats of the Senators of the first class shall be vacated at the expiration of the second year, of the second class at the expiration of the fourth year, and of the third class at the expiration of the sixth year, so that one-third may be chosen every second year; and if vacancies happen by resignation or otherwise, during the recess of the legislature of any State, the Executive thereof may make temporary appointments until the next meeting of the legislature, which shall then fill such vacancies.

No person shall be a Senator who shall not have attained to the age of thirty years, and been nine years a citizen of the United States, and who shall not, when elected, be an inhabitant of that State for which he shall be chosen.

The Vice President of the United States shall be President of the Senate, but shall have no vote, unless they be equally divided.

The Senate shall choose their other officers, and also a President *pro tempore*, in the absence of the Vice President, or when he shall exercise the office of President of the United States.

The Senate shall have the sole power to try all impeachments. When sitting for that purpose, they shall be on oath or affirmation. When the President of the United States is tried, the Chief Justice shall preside: and no person shall be convicted without the concurrence of two-thirds of the members present.

Judgment in cases of impeachment shall not extend further than to removal from the office, and disqualification to hold and enjoy any office of honor, trust or profit under the United States; but the party convicted shall nevertheless be liable and subject to indictment, trial, judgment and punishment, according to law.

Congressional Elections: Time, Place, Manner

Section 4. The times, places and manner of holding elections for Senators and Representatives shall be prescribed in each State by the legislature thereof; but the Congress may at any time by law make or alter such regulations, except as to the places of choosing Senators.

The Congress shall assemble at least once in every year, and such meeting *shall be on the first Monday in December, unless they shall by law appoint a different day.*

Powers and Duties of the Houses

Section 5. Each house shall be the judge of the elections, returns and qualifications of its own members, and a majority of each shall constitute a quorum to do business; but a smaller number may adjourn from day to day, and may be authorized to compel the attendance of absent members, in such manner, and under such penalties, as each house may provide.

Each house may determine the rules of its proceedings, punish its members for disorderly behavior, and with the concurrence of two-thirds, expel a member.

Each house shall keep a journal of its proceedings, and from time to time publish the same, excepting such parts as may in their judgment require secrecy; and the yeas and nays of the members of either house on any question shall, at the desire of one-fifth of those present, be entered on the journal.

Neither house, during the session of Congress, shall, without the consent of the other, adjourn for more than three days, nor to any other place than that in which the two houses shall be sitting.

Rights of Members

Section 6. The Senators and Representatives shall receive a compensation for their services, to be ascertained by law and paid out of the treasury of the United States. They shall in all cases except treason, felony and breach of the peace, be privileged from arrest during their attendance at the session of their respective houses, and in going to and returning from the same; and for any speech or debate in either house, they shall not be questioned in any other place.

No Senator or Representative shall, during the time for which he was elected, be appointed to any civil office under the authority of the United States, which shall have been created, or the emoluments whereof shall have been increased, during such time; and no person holding any office under the United States shall be a member of either house during his continuance in office.

Legislative Powers: Bills and Resolutions

Section 7. All bills for raising revenue shall originate in the House of Representatives; but the Senate may propose or concur with amendments as on other bills.

Every bill which shall have passed the House of Representatives and the Senate, shall, before it become a law, be presented to the President of the United States; if he approve he shall sign it, but if not he shall return it with objections to that house in which it originated, who shall enter the objections at large on their journal, and proceed to reconsider it. If after such reconsideration two-thirds of that house shall agree to pass the bill, it shall be sent, together with the objections, to the other house, by which it shall likewise be reconsidered, and if approved by two-thirds of that house, it shall become a law. But in all such cases the votes of both houses shall be determined by yeas and nays, and the names of the persons voting for and against the bill shall be entered on the journal of each house respectively. If any bill shall not be returned by the President within ten days (Sundays excepted) after it shall have been presented to him, the same shall be a law, in like manner as if he had signed it, unless the Congress by their adjournment prevent its return, in which case it shall not be a law.

Every order, resolution, or vote to which the concurrence of the Senate and House of Representatives may be necessary (except on a question of adjournment) shall be presented to the President of the United States; and before the same shall take effect, shall be approved by him, or being disapproved by him, shall be repassed by two-thirds of the Senate and House of Representatives, according to the rules and limitations prescribed in the case of a bill.

Powers of Congress

Section 8. The Congress shall have power

To lay and collect taxes, duties, imposts and excises, to pay the debts and provide for the common defense and general welfare of the United States; but all duties, imposts and excises shall be uniform throughout the United States;

To borrow money on the credit of the United States;

To regulate commerce with foreign nations, and among the several States, and with the Indian tribes;

To establish an uniform rule of naturalization, and uniform laws on the subject of bankruptcies throughout the United States;

To coin money, regulate the value thereof, and of foreign coin, and fix the standard of weights and measures;

To provide for the punishment of counterfeiting the securities and current coin of the United States;

To establish post offices and post roads;

To promote the progress of science and useful arts by securing for limited times to authors and inventors the exclusive right to their respective writings and discoveries;

To constitute tribunals inferior to the Supreme Court;

To define and punish piracies and felonies committed on the high seas and offenses against the law of nations;

To declare war, grant letters of marque and reprisal, and make rules concerning captures on land and water;

To raise and support armies, but no appropriation of money to that use shall be for a longer term than two years;

To provide and maintain a navy;

To make rules for the government and regulation of the land and naval forces;

To provide for calling forth the militia to execute the laws of the Union, suppress insurrections, and repel invasions;

To provide for organizing, arming, and disciplining the militia, and for governing such part of them as may be employed in the service of the United States, reserving to the States respectively the appointment of the officers, and the authority of training the militia according to the discipline prescribed by Congress;

To exercise exclusive legislation in all cases whatsoever, over such district (not exceeding ten miles square) as may, by cession of particular States, and the acceptance of Congress, become the seat of the government of the United States, and to exercise like authority over all places purchased by the consent of the legislature of the State, in which the same shall be, for erection of forts, magazines, arsenals, dock-yards, and other needful buildings;—and

To make all laws which shall be necessary and proper for carrying into execution the foregoing powers, and all other powers vested by this Constitution in the government of the United States, or in any department or officer thereof.

Powers Denied to Congress

Section 9. *The migration or importation of such persons as any of the States now existing shall think proper to admit shall not be prohibited by the Congress prior to the year 1808; but a tax or duty may be imposed on such importation, not exceeding $10 for each person.*

The privilege of the writ of habeas corpus shall not be suspended, unless when in cases of rebellion or invasion the public safety may require it.

No bill of attainder or ex post facto law shall be passed.

No capitation, or other direct, tax shall be laid, unless in proportion to the census or enumeration herein before directed to be taken.

No tax or duty shall be laid on articles exported from any State.

No preference shall be given by any regulation of commerce or revenue to the ports of one State over those of another; nor shall vessels bound to, or from, one State, be obliged to enter, clear, or pay duties in another.

No money shall be drawn from the treasury, but in consequence of appropriations made by law; and a regular statement and account of the receipts and expenditures of all public money shall be published from time to time.

No title of nobility shall be granted by the United States; and no person holding any office of profit or trust under them, shall, without the consent of the Congress, accept of any present, emolument, office, or title, of any kind whatever, from any king, prince, or foreign state.

Powers Denied to the States

Section 10. No State shall enter into any treaty, alliance, or confederation; grant letters of marque and reprisal; coin money; emit bills of credit; make anything but gold and silver coin a tender in payment of debts; pass any bill of attainder, ex post facto law, or law impairing the obligation of contracts, or grant any title of nobility.

No State shall, without the consent of the Congress, lay any imposts or duties on imports or exports, except what may be absolutely necessary for executing its inspection laws: and the net produce of all duties and imposts, laid by any State on imports or exports, shall be for the use of the treasury of the United States; and all such laws shall be subject to the revision and control of the Congress.

No State shall, without the consent of Congress, lay any duty of tonnage, keep troops or ships of war in time of peace, enter into any agreement or compact with another State, or with a foreign power, or engage in war, unless actually invaded, or in such imminent danger as will not admit of delay.

ARTICLE II.—THE EXECUTIVE ARTICLE

Nature and Scope of Presidential Power

Section 1. The executive power shall be vested in a President of the United States of America. He shall hold his office during the term of four years, and, together with the Vice President, chosen for the same term, be elected, as follows:

Each State shall appoint, in such manner as the legislature thereof may direct, a number of electors, equal to the whole number of Senators and Representatives to which the State may be entitled in the Congress; but no Senator or Representative, or person holding an office of trust or profit under the United States, shall be appointed an elector.

The electors shall meet in their respective States, and vote by ballot for two persons, of whom one at least shall not be an inhabitant of the same State with themselves. And they shall make a list of all the persons voted for, and of the number of votes for each; which list they shall sign and certify, and transmit sealed to the seat of government of the United States, directed to the President of the Senate. The President of the Senate shall, in the presence of the Senate and House of Representatives, open all the certificates, and the votes shall then be counted. The person having the greatest number of votes shall be the President, if such number be a majority of the whole number of electors appointed; and if there be more than one who have such majority, and have an equal number of votes, then the House of Representatives shall immediately choose by ballot one of them for President; and if no person have a majority, then from the five highest on the list said house shall in like manner choose the President. But in choosing the President the votes shall be taken by States, the representation from each State having one vote; a quorum for this purpose shall consist of a member or members from two-thirds of the States, and a majority of all the States shall be necessary to a choice. In every case, after the choice of the President, the person having the greatest number of votes of the electors shall be the Vice President. But if there should remain two or more who have equal votes, the Senate shall choose from them by ballot the Vice President.

The Congress may determine the time of choosing the electors, and the day on which they shall give their votes; which day shall be the same throughout the United States.

No person except a natural-born citizen, *or a citizen of the United States at the time of the adoption of this Constitution*, shall be eligible to the office of President; neither shall any person be eligible to that office who shall not have attained to the age of thirty-five years, and been fourteen years a resident within the United States.

In case of the removal of the President from office or of his death, resignation, or inability to discharge the powers and duties of the said office, the same shall devolve on the Vice President, and the Congress may by law provide for the case of removal, death, resignation, or inability, both of the President and Vice President, declaring what officer shall then act as President, and such officer shall act accordingly, until the disability be removed, or a President shall be elected.

The President shall, at stated times, receive for his services a compensation, which shall neither be increased nor diminished during the period for which he shall have been elected, and he shall not receive within that period any other emolument from the United States, or any of them.

Before he enter on the execution of his office, he shall take the following oath or affirmation: —"I do solemnly swear (or affirm) that I will faithfully execute the office of President of the United States, and will to the best of my ability preserve, protect, and defend the Constitution of the United States."

Powers and Duties of the President

Section 2. The President shall be the commander in chief of the army and navy of the United States, and of the militia of the several States, when called into the actual service of the United States; he may require the opinion, in writing, of the principal officer in each of the executive departments, upon any subject relating to the duties of their respective offices, and he shall have power to grant reprieves and pardons for offenses against the United States, except in cases of impeachment.

He shall have power, by and with the advice and consent of the Senate, to make treaties, provided two-thirds of the Senators present concur; and he shall nominate, and by and with the advice and consent of the Senate, shall appoint ambassadors, other public ministers and consuls, judges of the Supreme Court, and all other officers of the United States, whose appointments are not herein otherwise provided for, and which shall be established by law: but the Congress may by law vest the appointment of such inferior officers, as they think proper, in the President alone, in the courts of law, or in the heads of departments.

The President shall have power to fill up all vacancies that may happen during the recess of the Senate, by granting commissions which shall expire at the end of their next session.

Section 3. He shall from time to time give to the Congress information of the state of the Union, and recommend to their consideration such measures as he shall judge necessary and expedient; he may, on extraordinary occasions, convene both houses, or either of them, and in case of disagreement between them, with respect to the time of adjournment, he may adjourn them to such time as he shall think proper; he shall receive ambassadors and other public ministers; he shall take care that the laws be faithfully executed, and shall commission all the officers of the United States.

Section 4. The President, Vice President and all civil officers of the United States shall be removed from office on impeachment for, and on conviction of, treason, bribery, or other high crimes and misdemeanor.

ARTICLE III.—THE JUDICIAL ARTICLE

Section 1. The judicial power of the United States shall be vested in one Supreme Court, and in such inferior courts as the Congress may from time to time ordain and establish. The judges, both of the Supreme and inferior courts, shall hold their offices during good behavior, and shall, at stated times, receive for their services a compensation which shall not be diminished during their continuance in office.

Jurisdiction

Section 2. The judicial power shall extend to all cases, in law and equity, arising under this Constitution, the laws of the United States, and treaties made, or which shall be made, under their authority;—to all cases affecting ambassadors, other public ministers and consuls;—to all cases of admiralty and maritime jurisdiction;—to controversies to which the United States shall be a party;—to controversies between two or more States;—*between a state and citizens of another state*;—between citizens of different States;—between citizens of the same State claiming lands under grants of different States, and between a State, or the citizens thereof, and foreign states, citizens or subjects.

In all cases affecting ambassadors, other public ministers and consuls, and those in which a State shall be party, the Supreme Court shall have original jurisdiction. In all the other cases before mentioned, the Supreme Court shall have appellate jurisdiction, both as to law and fact, with such exceptions, and under such regulations, as the Congress shall make.

The trial of all crimes, except in cases of impeachment, shall be by jury; and such trial shall be held in the State where said crimes shall have been committed; but when not committed within any State, the trial shall be at such place or places as the Congress may by law have directed.

Treason

Section 3. Treason against the United States shall consist only in levying war against them, or in adhering to their enemies, giving them aid and comfort. No person shall be convicted of treason unless on the testimony of two witnesses to the same overt act, or on confession in open court.

The Congress shall have power to declare the punishment of treason, but no attainder of treason shall work corruption of blood, or forfeiture except during the life of the person attained.

ARTICLE IV.—INTERSTATE RELATIONS

Full Faith and Credit Clause

Section 1. Full Faith and credit shall be given in each State to the public acts, records, and judicial proceedings of every other State. And the Congress may by general laws prescribe the manner in which such acts, records and proceedings shall be proved, and the effect thereof.

Privileges and Immunities; Interstate Extradition

Section 2. The citizens of each State shall be entitled to all privileges and immunities of citizens in the several States.

A person charged in any State with treason, felony or other crime, who shall flee from justice, and be found in another State, shall on demand of the executive authority of the State from which he fled, be delivered up, to be removed to the State having jurisdiction of the crime.

No person held to service or labor in one State, under the laws thereof, escaping into another, shall, in consequence of any law or regulation therein, be discharged from such service or labor, but shall be delivered up on claim of the party to whom such service or labor may be due.

Admission of States

Section 3. New States may be admitted by the Congress into this Union; but no new State shall be formed or erected within the jurisdiction of any other State; nor any State be formed by the junction of two or more States, or parts of States, without the consent of the legislatures of the States concerned as well as of the Congress.

The Congress shall have power to dispose of and make all needful rules and regulations respecting the territory or other property belonging to the United States; and nothing in this Constitution shall be so construed as to prejudice any claims of the United States, or of any particular State.

Republican Form of Government

Section 4. The United States shall guarantee to every State in this Union a republican form of government, and shall protect each of them against invasion; and on application of the legislature, or of the executive (when the legislature cannot be convened) against domestic violence.

ARTICLE V.—THE AMENDING POWER

The Congress, whenever two-thirds of both houses shall deem it necessary, shall propose amendments to this Constitution, or, on the application of the legislatures of two-thirds of the several States, shall call a convention for proposing amendments, which, in either case, shall be valid to all intents and purposes, as part of this Constitution, when ratified by the legislatures of three-fourths of the several States, or by conventions in three-fourths thereof, as the one or the other mode of ratification may be proposed by the Congress; *provided that no amendment which may be made prior to the year one thousand eight hundred and eight shall in any manner affect the first and fourth clauses in the ninth section of the first article*; and that no State, without its consent, shall be deprived of its equal suffrage in the Senate.

ARTICLE VI.—THE SUPREMACY ACT

All debts contracted and engagements entered into, before the adoption of this Constitution, shall be as valid against the United States under this Constitution, as under the Confederation.

This Constitution, and the laws of the United States which shall be made in pursuance thereof; and all treaties made, or which shall be made, under the authority of the United States, shall be the supreme law of the land; and the judges in every State shall be bound thereby, anything in the Constitution or laws of any State to the contrary notwithstanding.

The Senators and Representatives before mentioned, and the members of the several State legislatures, and all executive and judicial officers, both of the United States and of the several States, shall be bound by oath or affirmation to support this Constitution; but no religious test shall ever be required as a qualification to any office or public trust under the United States.

ARTICLE VII.—RATIFICATION

The ratification of the conventions of nine States shall be sufficient for the establishment of this Constitution between States so ratifying the same.

Done in Convention by the unanimous consent of the States present, the seventeenth day of September in the year of our Lord one thousand seven hundred and eighty-seven and of the Independence of the United States of America the twelfth. In witness whereof we have hereunto subscribed our names.

GEORGE WASHINGTON
President and Deputy from Virginia

New Hampshire
JOHN LANGDON
NICHOLAS GILMAN

Massachusetts
NATHANIEL GORHAM
RUFUS KING

Connecticut
WILLIAM S. JOHNSON FER
ROGER SHERMAN

Virginia
JOHN BLAIR
JAMES MADISON, JR

South Carolina
J. RUTLEDGE
CHARLES G. PINCKNEY
PIERCE BUTLER

New York
ALEXANDER HAMILTON

New Jersey
WILLIAM LIVINGSTON
DAVID BREARLEY
WILLIAM PATERSON
JONATHAN DAYTON

Pennsylvania
BENJAMIN FRANKLIN
THOMAS MIFFLIN
ROBERT MORRIS
GEORGE CLYMER
THOMAS FITZSIMONS
JARED INGERSOLL
JAMES WILSON
GOUVERNEUR MORRIS

Delaware
GEORGE READ
GUNNING BEDFORD, JR.
JOHN DICKINSON
RICHARD BASSETT
JACOB BROOM

Maryland
JAMES MCHENRY
DANIEL OF ST. THOMAS JENI-
DANIEL CARROLL

North Carolina
WILLIAM BLOUNT
RICHARD DOBBS SPRAIGHT
HU WILLIAMSON

Georgia
WILLIAM FEW
ABRAHAM BALDWIN

THE BILL OF RIGHTS

The first ten Amendments (the Bill of Rights) were adopted in 1791.

AMENDMENT I.—RELIGION, SPEECH ASSEMBLY, AND PETITION

Congress shall make no law respecting an establishment of religion, or prohibiting the free exercise thereof; or abridging the freedom of speech, or of the press; or the right of the people peaceably to assemble, and to petition the government for a redress of grievances.

AMENDMENT II.—MILITIA AND THE RIGHT TO BEAR ARMS

A well-regulated militia being necessary to the security of a free State, the right of the people to keep and bear arms shall not be infringed.

AMENDMENT III.—QUARTERING OF SOLDIERS

No soldier shall, in time of peace, be quartered in any house without the consent of the owner, nor in time of war, but in a manner to be prescribed by law.

AMENDMENT IV.—SEARCHES AND SEIZURES

The right of the people to be secure in their persons, houses, papers, and effects, against unreasonable searches and seizures, shall not be violated, and no warrants shall issue but upon probable cause, supported by oath or affirmation, and particularly describing the place to be searched, and the persons or things to be seized.

AMENDMENT V.—GRAND JURIES, SELF-INCRIMINATION, DOUBLE JEOPARDY, DUE PROCESS, AND EMINENT DOMAIN

No person shall be held to answer for a capital, or otherwise infamous crime, unless on a presentment or indictment of a grand jury, except in cases arising in the land or naval forces, or in the militia, when in actual service in time of war or public danger; nor shall any person be subject for the same offense to be twice put in jeopardy of life or limb; nor shall be compelled in any criminal case to be a witness against himself, nor be deprived of life, liberty, or property, without due process of law; nor shall private property be taken for public use without just compensation.

AMENDMENT VI.—CRIMINAL COURT PROCEDURES

In all criminal prosecutions, the accused shall enjoy the right to a speedy and public trial, by an impartial jury of the State and district wherein the crime shall have been committed, which district shall have been previously ascertained by law, and to be informed of the nature and cause of the accusation; to be confronted with the witnesses against him; to have compulsory process for obtaining witnesses in his favor, and to have the assistance of counsel for his defense.

AMENDMENT VII.—TRIAL BY JURY IN COMMON LAW CASES

In suits at common law, where the value in controversy shall exceed twenty dollars, the right of trial by jury shall be preserved, and no fact tried by a jury shall be otherwise reexamined in any court of the United States, than according to the rules of the common law.

AMENDMENT VIII.—BAIL, CRUEL AND UNUSUAL PUNISHMENT

Excessive bail shall not be required, nor excessive fines imposed, nor cruel and unusual punishments inflicted.

AMENDMENT IX.—RIGHTS RETAINED BY THE PEOPLE

The enumeration in the Constitution, of certain rights, shall not be construed to deny or disparage others retained by the people.

AMENDMENT X.—RESERVED POWERS OF THE STATES

The powers not delegated to the United States by the Constitution, nor prohibited by it to the States, are reserved to the States respectively, or to the people.

PRE-CIVIL WAR AMENDMENTS

AMENDMENT XI.—SUITS AGAINST THE STATES
[Adopted 1798]

The judicial power of the United States shall not be construed to extend to any suit in law or equity, commenced or prosecuted against one of the United States by citizens of another State, or by citizens or subjects of any foreign state.

AMENDMENT XII.—ELECTION OF THE PRESIDENT
[Adopted 1804]

The electors shall meet in their respective *States*, and vote by ballot for President and Vice President, one of whom, at least, shall not be an inhabitant of the same State with themselves; they shall name in their ballots the person voted for as President, and in distinct ballots the person voted for as Vice President, and they shall make distinct lists of all persons voted for as President, and of all persons voted for as Vice President, and of the number of votes for each, which lists they shall sign and certify, and transmit sealed to the seat of the government of the United States, directed to the President of the Senate;—the President of the Senate shall, in the presence of the Senate and House of Representatives, open all the certificates and the votes shall then be counted;—the person having the greatest number of votes for President shall be the President, if such number be a majority of the whole number of electors appointed; and if no person have such majority, then from the persons having the highest numbers not exceeding three on the list of those voted for as President, the House of Representatives shall choose immediately, by ballot, the President. But in choosing the President, the votes shall be taken by States, the representation from each State having one vote; a quorum for this purpose shall consist of a member or members from two-thirds of the States, and a majority of all the States shall be necessary to a choice. And if the House of Representatives shall not choose a President whenever the right of choice shall devolve upon them, before *the fourth day of March* next following, then the Vice President shall act as President, as in the case of the death or other constitutional disability of the President.

    The person having the greatest number of votes as Vice President shall be the Vice President, if such a number be a majority of the whole number of electors appointed; and if no person have a majority, then from the two highest numbers on the list the Senate shall choose the Vice President; a quorum for the purpose shall consist of two-thirds of the whole number of Senators, and a majority of the whole number shall be necessary to a choice. But no person constitutionally ineligible to the office of President shall be eligible to that of Vice President of the United States.

CIVIL WAR AMENDMENTS

AMENDMENT XIII.—PROHIBITION OF SLAVERY
[Adopted 1865]

Section 1. Neither slavery nor involuntary servitude, except as a punishment for crime whereof the party shall have been duly convicted, shall exist within the United States, or any place subject to their jurisdiction.

Section 2. Congress shall have power to enforce this article by appropriate legislation.

AMENDMENT XIV.—CITIZENSHIP, DUE PROCESS, AND EQUAL PROTECTION OF THE LAWS
[Adopted 1868]

Section 1. All persons born or naturalized in the United States, and subject to the jurisdiction thereof, are citizens of the United States and of the State wherein they reside. No State shall make or enforce any law which shall abridge **the privileges or immunities** of citizens of the United States; nor shall any State deprive any person of life, liberty, or property, without **due process of law**; nor deny to any person within its jurisdiction the **equal protection of the laws**.

Section 2. Representatives shall be apportioned among the several States according to their respective numbers, counting the whole number of persons in each State, excluding Indians not taxed. But when the right to vote at any election for the choice of Electors for President and Vice President of the United States, Representatives in Congress, the executive and judicial officers of a State, or the members of the legislature thereof, is denied to any of the male inhabitants of such State, being twenty-one years of age and citizens of the United States, or in any way abridged, except for participation in rebellion, or other crime, the basis of representation therein shall be reduced in the proportion which the number of such male citizens shall bear to the whole number of male citizens twenty-one years of age in such State.

Section 3. No person shall be a Senator or Representative in Congress, or Elector of President and Vice President, or hold any office, civil or military, under the United States, or under any State, who, having previously taken an oath, as a member of Congress, or as an officer of the United States, or as a member of any State legislature, or as an executive or judicial officer of any State, to support the Constitution of the United States, shall have engaged in insurrection or rebellion against the same, or given aid or comfort to the enemies thereof. Congress may, by a vote of two-thirds of each house, remove such disability.

Section 4. The validity of the public debt of the United States, authorized by law, including debts incurred for payment of pensions and bounties for services in suppressing insurrection or rebellion, shall not be questioned. But neither the United States nor any State shall assume or pay any debt or obligation incurred in aid of insurrection or rebellion against the United States, or any claim for the loss or emancipation of any slave; but all such debts, obligations and claims shall be held illegal and void.

Section 5. The Congress shall have power to enforce, by appropriate legislation, the provisions of this article.

AMENDMENT XV.—THE RIGHT TO VOTE
[Adopted 1870]

Section 1. The right of citizens of the United State to vote shall not be denied or abridged by the United States or by any State on account of race, color, or previous condition of servitude.

Section 2. The Congress shall have power to enforce this article by appropriate legislation.

AMENDMENT XVI.—INCOME TAXES
[Adopted 1913]

The Congress shall have power to lay and collect taxes on incomes, from whatever source derived, without apportionment among the several States, and without regard to any census or enumeration.

AMENDMENT XVII.—DIRECT ELECTION OF SENATORS
[Adopted 1913]

Section 1. The Senate of the United States shall be composed of two Senators from each State, elected by the people thereof, for six years; and each Senator shall have one vote. The electors in each State shall have the qualifications requisite for electors of (voters for) the most numerous branch of the State legislatures.

Section 2. When vacancies happen in the representation of any State in the Senate, the executive authority of such State shall issue writs of election to fill such vacancies: Provided, that the Legislature of any State may empower the executive thereof to make temporary appointments until the people fill the vacancies by election as the Legislature may direct.

Section 3. This amendment shall not be so construed as to affect the election or term of any Senator chosen before it becomes valid as part of the Constitution.

AMENDMENT XVIII.—PROHIBITION
[Adopted 1919; Repealed 1933]

Section 1. *After one year from the ratification of this article the manufacture, sale, or transportation of intoxicating liquors within, the importation thereof into, or the exportation thereof from the United State and all territory subject to the jurisdiction thereof, for beverage purposes, is hereby prohibited.*

Section 2. *The Congress and the several States shall have concurrent power to enforce this article by appropriate legislation.*

Section 3. *This article shall be inoperative unless it shall have been ratified as an amendment to the Constitution by the legislatures of the several States, as provided by the Constitution, within seven years from the date of the submission thereof to the States by the Congress.*

AMENDMENT XIX.—FOR WOMEN'S SUFFRAGE
[Adopted 1920]

Section 1. The right of citizens of the United States to vote shall not be denied or abridged by the United States or by any State on account of sex.

Section 2. The Congress shall have power to enforce this article by appropriate legislation.

AMENDMENT XX.—THE LAME DUCK AMENDMENT
[Adopted 1933]

Section 1. The terms of the President and Vice President shall end at noon on the 20th day of January, and the terms of the Senators and Representatives at noon on the 3rd day of January, of the years in which such terms would have ended if this article had not been ratified; and the terms of their successors shall then begin.

Section 2. The Congress shall assemble at least once in every year, and such meeting shall begin at noon on the 3rd day of January, unless they shall by law appoint a different day.

Section 3. If, at the time fixed for the beginning of the term of the President, the President-elect shall have died, the Vice President-elect shall become President. If a President shall not have been chosen before the time fixed for the beginning of his term, or if the President-elect shall have failed to qualify, then the Vice President-elect shall act as President until a President shall have qualified; and the Congress may by law provide for the case wherein neither a President-elect nor a Vice President-elect shall have qualified, declaring who shall then act as President, or the manner in which one who is to act shall be selected, and such persons shall act accordingly until a President or Vice President shall have qualified.

Section 4. The Congress may by law provide for the case of the death of any of the persons from whom the House of Representatives may choose a President whenever the right of choice shall have devolved upon them, and for the case of the death of any of the persons from whom the Senate may choose a Vice President whenever the right of choice shall have devolved upon them.

Section 5. Section 1 and 2 shall take effect on the 15th day of October following the ratification of this article.

Section 6. This article shall be inoperative unless it shall have been ratified as an amendment to the Constitution by the Legislatures of three-fourths of the several States within seven years from the date of its submission.

AMENDMENT XXI.—REPEAL OF PROHIBITION
[Adopted 1933]

Section 1. The eighteenth article of amendment to the Constitution of the United States is hereby repealed.

Section 2. The transportation or importation into any State, Territory, or Possession of the United States for delivery of use therein of intoxicating liquors, in violation of the laws thereof, is hereby prohibited.

Section 3. This article shall be inoperative unless it shall have been ratified as an amendment to the Constitution by conventions in the several States, as provided in the Constitution, within seven years from the date of submission thereof to the States by the Congress.

AMENDMENT XXII.—NUMBER OF PRESIDENTIAL TERMS
[Adopted 1951]

Section 1. No person shall be elected to the office of President more than twice, and no person who has held the office of President, or acted as President, for more than two years of a term to which some other person was elected President shall be elected to the office of President more than once. But this article shall not apply to any person holding the office of President when this article was proposed by the Congress, and shall not prevent any person who may be holding the office of President, or acting as President, during the term within which this article becomes operative from holding the office of President or acting as President during the remainder of such term.

Section 2. This article shall be inoperative unless it shall have been ratified as an amendment to the Constitution by the legislatures of three-fourths of the several States within seven years from the date of its submission to the States by the Congress.

AMENDMENT XXIII.—PRESIDENTIAL ELECTORS FOR THE DISTRICT OF COLUMBIA [Adopted 1961]

Section 1. The District constituting the seat of Government of the United States shall appoint in such manner as the Congress may direct:

A number of electors of President and Vice President equal to the whole number of Senators and Representatives in Congress to which the District would be entitled if it were a State, but in no event more than the least populous State; they shall be in addition to those appointed by the States, but they shall be considered for the purposes of the election of President and Vice President, to be electors appointed by a State; and they shall meet in the District and perform such duties as provided by the twelfth article of amendment.

Section 2. The Congress shall have power to enforce this article by appropriate legislation.

AMENDMENT XXIV.—THE ANTI-POLL TAX AMENDMENT
[Adopted 1964]

Section 1. The right of citizens of the United States to vote in any primary or other election for President or Vice President, for electors for President or Vice President, or for Senator or Representative in Congress, shall not be denied or abridged by the United States or any State by reason of failure to pay any poll tax or other tax.

Section 2. The Congress shall have power to enforce this article by appropriate legislation.

AMENDMENT XXV.—PRESIDENTIAL DISABILITY, VICE-PRESIDENTIAL VACANCIES
[Adopted 1967]

Section 1. In case of the removal of the President from office or his death or resignation, the Vice President shall become President.

Section 2. Whenever there is a vacancy in the office of the Vice President, the President shall nominate a Vice President who shall take office upon confirmation by a majority vote of both Houses of Congress.

Section 3. Whenever the President transmits to the President pro tempore of the Senate and the Speaker of the House of Representatives his written declaration that he is unable to discharge the powers and duties of his office, and until he transmits to them a written declaration to the contrary, such powers and duties shall be discharged by the Vice President as Acting President.

Section 4. Whenever the Vice President and a majority of either the principal officers of the executive departments or of such other body as Congress may by law provide, transmit to the President pro tempore of the Senate and the Speaker of the House of Representatives their written declaration that the President is unable to discharge the powers and duties of his office, the Vice President shall immediately assume the powers and duties of the office as Acting President.

Thereafter, when the President transmits to the President pro tempore of the Senate and the Speaker of the House of Representatives his written declaration that no inability exists, he shall resume the powers and duties of his office unless the Vice President and a majority of either the principal officers of the executive department{s} or of such other body as Congress may by law provide, transmit within four days to the President pro tempore of the Senate and the Speaker of the House of Representatives their written declaration that the President is unable to discharge the powers and duties of his office.   Thereupon Congress shall decide the issue, assembling within forty-eight hours for that purpose if not in session.   If the Congress, within twenty-one days after receipt of the latter written declaration, or, if Congress is not in session, within twenty-one days after Congress is required to assemble, determines by two-thirds vote of both Houses that the President is unable to discharge the powers and duties of his office, the Vice President shall continue to discharge the same as Acting President; otherwise, the President shall resume the powers and duties of his office.

AMENDMENT XXVI.—EIGHTEEN-YEAR-OLD VOTE
[Adopted 1971]

Section 1. The right of citizens of the United States, who are eighteen years of age or older, to vote shall not be denied or abridged by the United States or by any State on account of age.

Section 2. The Congress shall have power to enforce this article by appropriate legislation.

AMENDMENT XXVII.—VARYING CONGRESSIONAL COMPENSATION
[Adopted 1992]

No law varying the compensation for the service of the Senators and Representatives shall take effect until an election of Representatives shall have intervened.

APPENDIX C

PRESIDENTIAL ELECTIONS

Year	Name	Party Vote	Popular Vote	Electoral College Vote
1789	George Washington	Federalist		69
1792	George Washington	Federalist		132
1796	John Adams	Federalist		71
	Thomas Jefferson	Democratic-Republican		68
1800	Thomas Jefferson	Democratic-Republican		73
	John Adams	Federalist		65
1804	Thomas Jefferson	Democratic-Republican		162
	Charles C. Pinckney	Federalist		14
1808	James Madison	Democratic-Republican		122
	Charles C. Pinckney	Federalist		47
1812	James Madison	Democratic-Republican		128
	George Clinton	Federalist		89
1816	James Monroe	Dmocratic-Republican		183
	Rufus King	Federalist		34
1820	James Monroe	Democratic-Republican		231
	John Quincy Adams	Democratic-Republican		1
1824	John Quincy Adams	Democratic-Republican	108,740	84
	Andrew Jackson	Democratic-Republican	153,544	99
	William Crawford	Democratic-Republican	46,618	41
	Henry Clay	Democratic-Republican	47,136	37
1828	Andrew Jackson	Democrat	647,286	178
	John Quincy Adams	National Republican	508,064	83
1832	Andrew Jackson	Democrat	687,502	219
	Henry Clay	National Republican	530,189	49
	Electoral votes not cast			2
1836	Martin Van Buren	Democrat	765,483	170
	William Henry Harrison	Whig	550,816	73
	Hugh White	Whig	146,107	26
	Daniel Webster	Whig	41,201	14
	Total for the 3 Whigs		739,795	113
1840	William Henry Harrison	Whig	1,274,624	234
	Martin Van Buren	Democrat	1,127,781	60
1844	James K. Polk	Democrat	1,338,464	170
	Henry Clay	Whig	1,300,097	105
1848	Zachary Taylor	Whig	1,360,967	163
	Lewis Cass	Democrat	1,222,342	127
	Martin Van Buren	Free-Soil	291,263	
1852	Franklin Pierce	Democrat	1,601,117	254
	Winfield Scott	Whig	1,385,453	42
	John P. Hale	Free-Soil	155,825	

Year	Candidate	Party	Popular Vote	Electoral Vote
1856	James Buchanan	Democrat	1,832,955	174
	John Fremont	Republican	1,339,932	114
	Millard Fillmore	Whig-American	871,731	8
1860	Abraham Lincoln	Republican	1,865,593	180
	John C. Breckinridge	Democratic	848,356	72
	Stephen Douglas	Democrat	1,382,713	12
	John Bell	Constitutional Union	592,906	39
1864	Abraham Lincon	Unionist (Republican)	2,206,938	212
	George McClellan	Democrat	1,803,787	21
	Electoral votes not cast			81
1868	Ulysses S. Grant	Republican	3,013,421	214
	Horatio Seymour	Democrat	2,706,829	80
	Electoral votes not cast			23
1872	Ulysses S. Grant	Republican	3,596,745	286
	Horace Greeley	Democrat	2,843,446	
	Thomas Hendricks	Democrat		42
	Benjamin Browns	Democrat		18
	Charles Jenkins	Democrat		2
	David Davis	Democrat		1
1876	Rutherford B. Hays	Republican	4,036,572	185
	Samuel Tilden	Democrat	4,284,020	184
	Peter Cooper	Greenback	81,737	
1880	James A. Garfield	Republican	4,453,295	214
	Winfield S. Hancock	Democrat	4,414,082	155
	James B. Weaver	Greenback-Labor	308,578	
1884	Grover Cleveland	Democrat	4,879,507	219
	James G. Blaine	Republican	4,850,293	182
	Benjamin Butler	Greenback-Labor	175,370	
	John St. John	Prohibition	150,369	
1888	Benjamin Harrison	Republican	5,447,129	233
	Grover Cleveland	Democrat	5,537,857	168
	Clinton Fisk	Prohibition	249,506	
	Anson Streeter	Union Labor	146,935	
1892	Grover Cleveland	Democrat	5,555,426	277
	Benjamin Harrison	Republican	5,182,690	145
	James B. Weaver	People's	1.029,846	22
	John Bidwell	Prohibition	264,133	
1896	William McKinley	Republican	7,102,246	271
	William J. Bryan	Democrat	6,492,559	176
	John Palmer	National Democratic	133,148	
	Joshua Levering	Prohibition	132,007	
1900	William McKinley	Republican	7,218,491	292
	William J. Bryan	Democrat	6,356,734	155
	John C. Wooley	Prohibition	208,914	
	Eugene V. Debs	Socialist	87,814	

Year	Candidate	Party	Popular Vote	Electoral Vote
1904	Theodore Roosevelt	Republican	7,628,461	336
	Alton B. Parker	Democrat	5,084,223	140
	Eugene V. Debs	Socialist	402,283	
	Silas Swallow	Prohibition	258,536	
	Thomas Watson	People's	117,183	
1908	William Howard Taft	Republican	7,675,320	321
	William J. Bryan	Democrat	6,412,294	162
	Eugene V. Debs	Socialist	420,793	
	Eugene Chafin	Prohibition	253,840	
1912	Woodrow Wilson	Democrat	6,296,547	435
	William Howard Taft	Republican	3,486,720	8
	Theodore Roosevelt	Progressive	4,118,571	86
	Eugene V. Debs	Socialist	900,672	
	Eugene Chafin	Prohibition	206,275	
1916	Woodrow Wilson	Democrat	9,127,695	277
	Charles E. Hughes	Republicn	8,533,507	254
	A.L. Benson	Socialist	585,113	
	J. Frank Hanly	Prohibition	220,506	
1920	Warren Harding	Republican	16,143,407	404
	James M. Cox	Democrat	9,130,328	127
	Eugene V. Debs	Socialist	919,799	
	P.P. Christensen	Farmer-Labor	265,411	
	Aaron Watkins	Prohibiton	189,408	
1924	Calvin Coolidge	Republican	15,718,211	382
	John W. Davis	Democrat	8,385,283	136
	Robert La Follette	Progressive	4,831,289	13
1928	Herbert Hoover	Republican	21,391,993	444
	Alfred E. Smith	Democrat	15,016,169	87
	Norman Thomas	Socialist	267,835	
1932	Franklin D. Roosevelt	Democrat	22,809,638	472
	Herbert C. Hoover	Republican	15,758,901	59
	Norman Thomas	Socialist	881,951	
	William Foster	Communist	102,785	
1936	Franklin D. Roosevelt	Democrat	27,752,869	523
	Alfred M. Landon	Republican	16,674,665	8
	William Lemke	Union	882,479	
	Norman Thomas	Socialist	187,720	
1940	Franklin D. Roosevelt	Democrat	27,307,819	449
	Wendell Willkie	Republican	22,321,018	82
1944	Franklin D. Roosevelt	Democrat	25,606,585	432
	Thomas E. Dewey	Republican	22,014,745	99
1948	Harry S. Truman	Democrat	24,179,345	303
	Thomas E. Dewey	Republican	21,991,291	189
	Strom Thurmond	Dixiecrat	1,176,125	39
	Henry Wallace	Progressive	1,157,326	
	Norman Thomas	Socialist	139,572	
	Claude A. Watson	Prohibition	103,900	

Year	Candidate	Party	Popular Vote	Electoral Vote
1952	Dwight D. Eisenhower	Republican	33,936,234	442
	Adlai Stevenson II	Democrat	27,314,992	89
	Vincent Hallinan	Progressive	140,023	
1956	Dwight D. Eisenhower	Republican	35,590,472	457
	Adlai Stevenson II	Democrat	26,022,752	73
	T. Coleman Andrews	States' Rights	111,178	
	Walter B. Jones	Democrat		1
1960	John F. Kennedy	Democrat	34,226,731	303
	Richard M. Nixon	Republican	34,108,157	219
	Harry Byrd	Democrat		15
1964	Lyndon B. Johnson	Democrat	43,129,566	486
	Barry Goldwater	Republican	27,178,188	52
1968	Richard M. Nixon	Republican	31,785,480	301
	Hubert H. Humphrey	Democrat	31,275,166	191
	George Wallace	American Independent	9,906,473	46
1972	Richard M. Nixon	Republican	47,170,179	520
	George McGovern	Democrat	29,171,791	17
	John Hospers	Libertarian		1
1976	Jimmy Carter	Democrat	40,830,763	297
	Gerald R. Ford	Republican	39,147,793	240
	Ronald Reagan	Republican		1
1980	Ronald Reagan	Republican	43,904,153	489
	Jimmy Carter	Democrat	35,483,883	49
	John Anderson	Independent candidacy	5,719,437	
1984	Ronald Reagan	Republican	54,455,074	525
	Walter F. Mondale	Democrat	37,577,137	13
1988	George Bush	Republican	48,881,278	426
	Michael Dukakis	Democrat	41,805,374	111
	Lloyd Bentsen	Democrat		1
1992	Bill Clinton	Democrat	43,727,625	370
	George Bush	Republican	38,165,180	168
	Ross Perot	Independent catdidacy	19,236,411	0
1996	Bill Clinton	Democrat	45,628,667	379
	Bob Dole	Republican	37,869,435	159
	Ross Perot	Independent catdidacy	7,874,283	0
2000	George W. Bush	Republican	49,820,518	271
	Albert Gore Jr.	Democrat	50,158,094	267
	Ralph Nader	Green Party	7,866,284	
2004	George W. Bush	Republican	62,040,610	286
	John Kerry	Democrat	59,028,439	251
	Ralph Nader	Green Party	463,653	
2008	Barack Obama	Democrat	66,882,230	365
	John McCain	Republican	58,343,671	173
2012	Barack Obama	Democrat	60,459,974	332
	Mitt Romney	Republican	57,653,982	206

APPENDIX D

Members of the Supreme Court of the United States

Chief Justices	State App't From	Appointed by President	Service
Jay, John	New York	Washington	1789-1795
Rutledge, John*	South Carolina	Washington	1795-1795
Ellsworth, Oliver	Connecticut	Washington	1796-1799
Marshall, John	Virginia	Adams, John	1801-1835
Taney, Roger Brooke	Maryland	Jackson	1836-1864
Chase, Salmon Portland	Ohio	Lincoln	1864-1873
Waite, Morrison Remick	Ohio	Grant	1874-1888
Fuller, Melville Weston	Illinois	Cleveland	1888-1910
White, Edward Douglass	Louisiana	Taft	1910-1921
Taft, William Howard	Connecticut	Harding	1921-1930
Hughes, Charles Evans	New York	Hoover	1930-1941
Stone, Harlan Fiske	New York	Roosevelt F.	1941-1946
Vinson, Fred Moore	Kentucky	Truman	1946-1953
Warren, Earl	California	Eisenhower	1953-1969
Burger, Warren Earl	Virginia	Nixon	1969-1986
Rehnquist, William H.	Virginia	Reagan	1986-2005
Roberts, John G., Jr.	Maryland	Bush, G. W.	2005-

Associate Justices			
Rutledge, John	South Carolina	Washington	1790-1791
Cushing, William	Massachusetts	Washington	1790-1810
Wilson, James	Pennsylvania	Washington	1789-1798
Blair, John	Virginia	Washington	1789-1796
Iredell, James	North Carolina	Washington	1790-1799
Johnson, Thomas	Maryland	Washington	1791-1793
Paterson, William	New Jersey	Washington	1793-1806
Chase, Samuel	Maryland	Washington	1796-1811
Washington, Bushrod	Virginia	Adams, John	1798-1829
Moore, Alfred	North Carolina	Adams, John	1799-1804
Johnson, William	South Carolina	Jefferson	1804-1834
Livingston, Henry Brockholst	New York	Jefferson	1806-1823
Todd, Thomas	Kentucky	Jefferson	1807-1826
Duvall, Gabriel	Maryland	Madison	1811-1836
Story, Joseph	Massachusetts	Madison	1811-1845
Thompson, Smith	New York	Monroe	1823-1843
Trimble, Robert	Kentucky	Adams, J. Q.	1826-1828

*Acting Chief Justice; Senate refused to confirm appointment.

McLean, John	Ohio	Jackson	1829-1861
Baldwin, Henry	Pennsylvania	Jackson	1830-1844
Wayne, James Moore	Georgia	Jackson	1835-1867
Barbour, Philip Pendleton	Virginia	Jackson	1836-1841
Catron, John	Tennessee	Jackson	1837-1865
McKinley, John	Alabama	Van Buren	1837-1852
Daniel, Peter Vivian	Virginia	Van Buren	1841-1860
Nelson, Samuel	New York	Tyler	1845-1872
Woodbury, Levi	New Hampshire	Polk	1845-1851
Grier, Robert Cooper	Pennsylvania	Polk	1846-1870
Curtis, Benjamin Robbins	Massachusetts	Fillmore	1851-1857
Campbell, John Archibald	Alabama	Pierce	1853-1861
Clifford, Nathan	Maine	Buchanan	1858-1881
Swayne, Noah Haynes	Ohio	Lincoln	1862-1881
Miller, Samuel Freeman	Iowa	Lincoln	1862-1890
Davis, David	Illinois	Lincoln	1862-1877
Field, Stephen Johnson	California	Lincoln	1863-1897
Strong, William	Pennsylvania	Grant	1870-1880
Bradley, Joseph P.	New Jersey	Grant	1870-1892
Hunt, Ward	New York	Grant	1873-1882
Harlan, John Marshall	Kentucky	Hayes	1877-1911
Woods, William Burnham	Georgia	Hayes	1880-1887
Matthews, Stanley	Ohio	Garfield	1881-1889
Gray, Horace	Massachusetts	Arthur	1882-1902
Blatchford, Samuel	New York	Arthur	1882-1893
Lamar, Lucius Quintus C.	Mississippi	Cleveland	1888-1893
Brewer, David Josiah	Kansas	Harrison	1889-1910
Brown, Henry Billings	Michigan	Harrison	1890-1906
Shiras, George, Jr.	Pennsylvania	Harrison	1892-1903
Jackson, Howell Edmunds	Tennessee	Harrison	1893-1895
White, Edward Douglass	Louisiana	Cleveland	1894-1910
Peckham, Rufus Wheeler	New York	Cleveland	1896-1909
McKenna, Joseph	California	McKinley	1898-1925
Holmes, Oliver Wendell	Massachusetts	Roosevelt T.	1902-1932
Day, William Rufus	Ohio	Roosevelt T.	1903-1922
Moody, William Henry	Massachusetts	Roosevelt T.	1906-1910
Lurton, Horace Harmon	Tennessee	Taft	1910-1914
Hughes, Charles Evans	New York	Taft	1910-1916
Van Devanter, Willis	Wyoming	Taft	1910-1937
Lamar, Joseph Rucker	Georgia	Taft	1911-1916
Pitney, Mahlon	New Jersey	Taft	1912-1922
McReynolds, James Clark	Tennessee	Wilson	1914-1941
Brandeis, Louis Dembitz	Massachusetts	Wilson	1916-1939
Clarke, John Hessin	Ohio	Wilson	1916-1922
Sutherland, George	Utah	Harding	1922-1938
Butler, Pierce	Minnesota	Harding	1923-1939
Sanford, Edward Terry	Tennessee	Harding	1923-1930

Stone, Harlan Fiske	New York	Coolidge	1925-1941
Roberts, Owen Josephus	Pennsylvania	Hoover	1930-1945
Cardozo, Benjamin Nathan	New York	Hoover	1932-1938
Black, Hugo Lafayette	Alabama	Roosevelt F.	1937-1971
Reed, Stanley Forman	Kentucky	Roosevelt F.	1938-1957
Frankfurter, Felix	Massachusetts	Roosevelt F.	1939-1962
Douglas, William Orville	Connecticut	Roosevelt F.	1939-1975
Murphy, Frank	Michigan	Roosevelt F.	1940-1949
Byrnes, James Francis	South Carolina	Roosevelt F.	1941-1942
Jackson, Robert Houghwout	New York	Roosevelt F.	1941-1954
Rutledge, Wiley Blount	Iowa	Roosevelt F.	1943-1949
Burton, Harold Hitz	Ohio	Truman	1945-1958
Clark, Tom Campbell	Texas	Truman	1949-1967
Minton, Sherman	Indiana	Truman	1949-1956
Harlan, John Marshall	New York	Eisenhower	1955-1971
Brennan, William J., Jr.	New Jersey	Eisenhower	1956-1990
Whittaker, Charles Evans	Missouri	Eisenhower	1957-1962
Stewart, Potter	Ohio	Eisenhower	1958-1981
White, Byron Raymond	Colorado	Kennedy	1962-1993
Goldberg, Arthur Joseph	Illinois	Kennedy	1962-1965
Fortas, Abe	Tennessee	Johnson L.	1965-1969
Marshall, Thurgood	New York	Johnson L.	1967-1991
Blackmun, Harry A.	Minnesota	Nixon	1970-1994
Powell, Lewis F., Jr.	Virginia	Nixon	1972-1988
Rehnquist, William H.	Arizona	Nixon	1972-1986**
Stevens, John Paul	Illinois	Ford	1975-2010
O'Connor, Sandra Day	Arizona	Reagan	1981-2006
Scalia, Antonin	Virginia	Reagan	1986-
Kennedy, Anthony M.	California	Reagan	1988-
Souter, David H.	New Hampshire	Bush, G. H. W.	1990-2009
Thomas, Clarence	Georgia	Bush, G. H. W.	1991-
Ginsburg, Ruth Bader	New York	Clinton	1993-
Breyer, Stephen G.	Massachusetts	Clinton	1994-
Alito, Samuel A., Jr.	New Jersey	Bush, G. W.	2006-
Sonia Sotomayor	New York	Obama	2009-
Elena Kagan	New York	Obama	2010-

Notes: The acceptance of the appointment and commission by the appointee, as evidenced by the taking of the prescribed oaths, is here implied; otherwise the individual is not carried on this list of the Members of the Court. Examples: Robert Hanson Harrison is not carried, as a letter from President Washington of February 9, 1790 states Harrison declined to serve. Neither is Edwin M. Stanton who died before he could take the necessary steps toward becoming a Member of the Court. *Chief Justice Rutledge is included because he took his oaths, presided over the August Term of 1795, and his name appears on two opinions of the Court for that Term. [The foregoing was taken from a booklet prepared by the Supreme Court of the United States.]

**Elevated.

GLOSSARY

Absolute Poverty - The minimum subsistence income needed to survive deprivation.

Acid Rain - Complex chemical and atmospheric phenomenon that occurs when emissions of sulfur and nitrogen compounds and other substances are transformed by chemical processes in the atmosphere, often far from the original source, and then deposited on earth in either a wet or dry form.

Ad Hoc Committee - A temporary special legislative committee formed to perform a specific task.

Ad Valorum Tax System - Property tax assessment based on the fair market value of the property.

Administrative Law – that branch of law that creates administrative agencies, establishes their methods of procedures, and determines the scope of judicial review of agency practices and actions.

Adversary System - The judicial principle that one is innocent of a criminal act until proven guilty.

Affirmative Action - The formalized effort on the part of government to remedy previous incidences of past discrimination particularly in the employment and political processes.

Aid to the Blind - A financial assistance program created through the New Deal to provided assistance to the nation's blind citizens.

Aid to Dependent Children - A New Deal program designed to provide financial assistance to parents of children whose incomes fall below the poverty level. This program became the primary plan for the welfare system. Its name was changed to **Aid to Families With Dependent Children**.

Air - A mixture of nitrogen, oxygen, argon, carbon dioxide with traces of neon, helium, krypton, hydrogen, xenon, methane, and vitreous oxide.

Air Pollution - A group of chemical compounds that are in the wrong place or in the wrong concentration at the wrong time.

Alien and Sedition Acts - A series of four laws passed during John Adams's administration restricting freedom of press and speech and the rights of immigrants.

Alleviative Approach - A public policy option that seeks to relieve the suffering caused by the policy problem without adequately addressing the problem itself.

Alliance - an agreement by nation states to support each other militarily in the event of an attack against any member, or to advance their mutual interests.

Almshouse - Another term for poorhouse.

Amendatory Veto - A type of veto used by the governors of Montana and Illinois whereby the governor can increase or decrease appropriations made by the legislature without further action from the legislature.

Americans with Disabilities Act (1990) - Federal legislation mandating equal opportunities in employment, housing, and accommodations to disabled persons.

Anarchist – belief that government is an unnecessary evil and should be replaced by voluntary cooperation among individuals and groups.

Annexation - The process by which cities incorporate adjacent land into their municipal boundaries.

Appeal – formal request to a higher court that it review the actions of a lower court.

Appellant – the party, usually the losing one, that seeks to overturn the decision of a lower court by appealing to a higher court.

Appellate Jurisdiction – authority of a court to review decisions of an inferior court.

Apportionment - The process by which the total number of seats in a legislative body is distributed within a state's boundary.

Approach - An orientation, perspective, or way of looking at political phenomena, for example, the traditional or the behavioral approach.

Architectural Barriers Act (1970) - Federal legislation mandating that newly constructed public buildings must be accessible to handicapped persons.

Arraignment – a hearing before a court having jurisdiction in a criminal case in which the identity of the defendant is established, the defendant is informed of his/her rights, and the defendant enters a plea.

Arrest Warrant – document issued by a judicial officer directing a law enforcement officer to arrest an identified person who has been accused of a specific crime.

Article VI - An Article of the United States Constitution mandating that the constitution is the supreme law of the land. See Supremacy Clause.

Articles of Confederation - The first constitution of the United States adopted in 1777.

Association of Southern Women for the Prevention of Lynching - A woman's organization that led the battle to end mob-rule dominated lynchings.

At-Large Election - A city- or county-wide election.

Attorney General - The legal counsel for state governments.

Authority - Legitimate or accepted power in a democracy.

Baker v Carr (1962) - The United States Supreme Court decision mandating that reapportionment of state legislative houses must guarantee the principal of "one man, one vote."

Balanced Budget - Budgetary strategy whereby anticipated revenues equal anticipated expenses.

Balance of Terror - the equilibrium of power among nuclear states stemming from common fear of annihilation in a nuclear war.

Balance of Trade - a nation's annual net trade surplus or deficit, based on the difference in the value of its imports and exports.

Barron v Baltimore (1833) - United States Supreme Court ruled that the Bill of Rights was enforceable only upon the actions of the national government.

Benefit Principle System - Based on the principle that those who reap more benefits from government services should shoulder more of the tax burden than people who do not avail themselves of service opportunities to the same degree.

Beyond a Reasonable Doubt - The criteria for determining guilt or innocence in a criminal case.

Bicameral - A two-house legislature.

Biennial Session - A legislative sessions that meets once every two years.

Bilateral Agreements - agreements signed between two nation states.

Bill - A legislative proposal formally introduced for consideration.

Biochemical Oxygen Demand - The amount of oxygen needed by bacteria to breakdown a specific amount of organic matter.

Block Grants – federal grant programs given for prescribed broader activities ranging from health care to education with fewer federal regulations attached.

Boyd v United States (1886) - The United States Supreme Court tied the Fourth Amendment's protection against unreasonable searches to the Fifth Amendment's protection against self-incrimination.

Bracero Program - A federal government sponsored agreement between the United States and Mexico to hire Mexican nationals as agricultural workers.

Brady Bill - A congressional law mandating that state law enforcement agencies conduct criminal background checks prior to allowing an individual to purchase a handgun.

Brief – a document prepared by an attorney for presentation to the court containing arguments and data in support of a case.

Brown v Board of Education - A 1954 Supreme Court decision that reversed the 1896 *Plessy v Ferguson* decision. The Court, in a unanimous decision, ruled that segregation in public schools was inherently unequal and violated the Fourteenth Amendment and equal protection.

Budget - Technical document in the form of a detailed balance sheet identifying expenditures and revenues.

Bureaucracy - The collective term for government agencies.

Cabinet - The attorney general and the thirteen principle officers of the executive departments that advise the president upon his request.

***California v Trombetta* (1984)** - The United States Supreme Court ruled breathalyzer tests constitute a legal search and are not a violation of protected privacy rights.

Cannon Law – Church or ecclesiastical law.

Capital Expenses - Multi-year or amortized expenses.

Casework - A collective term for the services performed by legislators and congresspersons and their staffs at the request of and on behalf of their constituents.

Cash Transfers - Direct payments to program recipients.

Categorical Grants – federal payments to state or local governments for a specified purpose.

Central Business District (CBO) - The core of a city.

Centrist – an individual or political group advocating a moderate approach to political decision-making and to the solution of social problem.

Cert Conference - Conference at which the Supreme Court justices decide whether to hear a case. Four of the nine justices must agree to hear a case.

Change of Venue - The right of a judge to change the location of a trial to afford the defendant a fair and impartial trial.

Checks and Balances – the notion that constitutional devises can prevent any power within a nation from becoming absolute by being balanced against, or checked by, another source of power within that same nation.

Chief Diplomat - The role of the president in which his job is to appoint diplomatic personnel and envoys, receive ambassadors, recognize foreign governments, negotiate treaties, make executive agreements, and hold summit meetings.

Chief Executive - The role of the president in which his job as the head of the executive branch of the government is, according to the Constitution, to "take Care that the Laws be faithfully executed."

Chief Legislator - The role of the president in which his job consists of setting forth a broad legislative agenda in his annual State of the Union address, sending proposals for legislation to the Congress, making efforts to secure the passage of bills that he favors, and vetoing legislation not to his liking.

Chief of State - The ceremonial or symbolic role of the president in which he serves as a "figurehead" rather than a "working head" of the government.

Child Benefit Theory - The notion that public funding can be provided to students who attend private, public and parochial schools as long as it is the child, rather than the school, that benefits from the funding.

Children's Health Insurance Program (CHIP) - A federally funded health-care plan for children whose parents cannot afford health care even though their incomes are above the poverty level.

Church of the Lukumi Babbalu Aye v Hialeah (1985) - The United States Supreme Court ruled that the church's practice of animal sacrifice was constitutionally protected under the First Amendment's guarantee to religious freedom.

City of Trenton v State of New Jersey (1913) - United States Supreme Court decision upholding Dillon's Rule.

Civil Law – deals with disagreements between individuals.

Civil Rights - Acts of government intended to protect disadvantaged classes of persons or minority groups from arbitrary, unreasonable, or discriminatory treatment.

Civil Rights Acts (1866) - Federal legislation granting former slaves the rights to own property, file lawsuits and make contractual agreements.

Civil Rights Act (1875) - Federal legislation prohibiting private discrimination in accommodations, transportation, and public places of amusement. This law was declared unconstitutional by the United States Supreme Court's ruling in *Plessy v Ferguson.*

Civil Rights Act (1957) - Federal legislation establishing the United States Commission on Civil Rights and the Civil Rights Section of the United States Justice Department.

Civil Rights Act (1960) - Federal legislation authorizing the use of federal voter referees to conduct voter registration drives and to monitor federal elections in areas with historical patterns of voting problems.

Civil Rights Act (1964) - Federal legislation prohibiting discrimination in public accommodations and employment practices. The law also established a sixth grade education as meeting voter literacy and testing requirements.

Civil Rights Act (1968) - Federal legislation prohibiting discrimination in housing practices.

Civilian Conservation Corps. (CCC) - A New Deal program designed to hire the unemployed to work rural areas.

Clear and Present Danger - The criteria established by the United States Supreme Court in *Schenck v United States* (1919) to determine whether or not spoken words or symbolic displays violate the First Amendment's guarantee of freedom of speech.

Coates v Cincinnati (1971) - United States Supreme Court ruling that a city ordinance denying three or more individuals to gather in a public place was an unconstitutional violation of the First Amendment's guarantee to freedom of assembly and association.

Cohen v California (1971) - The United States Supreme Court ruled that the wearing of a jacket bearing an inappropriate word against the draft was a constitutionally protected right to freedom of speech.

Colonialism - the ownership of another territory or state for the sole purpose of exploitation of its people or natural resources.

Commander in Chief - The role of the president in which he serves as the civilian head of U.S. military forces.

Common Law – law developed in England by judges who made legal decisions in absence of written law.

Communism – a political theory that espouses the doctrines of historical inevitability, economic determinism, labor value, and the inner contradictions of capitalism, class conflict, capitalist colonialism and imperialism, world wars resulting from competition for markets, and the destruction of the bourgeoisie, the dictatorship of the proletariat, the socialist revolution and the final withering away of the state.

Compensino - A farm laborer.

Concept - Words or names used to symbolize or represent ideas.

Concurrent Majority - Calhoun's belief that democratic decisions should be made only with the concurrence of all major segments of a society, i.e., national referendum elections.

Concurrent powers - Constitutional powers that are simultaneously shared by the national and state governments, for example, the power to tax. However, in the process of implementing concurrent powers the state does not have the right to thwart national policy.

Concurrent Resolution - A legislative action passed by a simple majority in both Houses that requires the approval of the president or governor.

Confederation - a loose collection of states in which principal power lies at the level of the individual states rather than at the level of the central or national government.

Conference Committee - A special joint legislative committee composed of members from both Houses to reconcile differences over similar pieces of legislation.

Conflictual Party System – a legislature dominated by parties that are far apart on issues or highly antagonistic toward each other and the political system.

Connecticut Compromise - It is also known as the Great Compromise. It was a compromise reached at the constitutional convention between the New Jersey Plan and Virginia Plan. It established a bicameral legislature, the House of Representatives and the Senate. The House of Representatives was based on population; the Senate on equal representation of states.

Consensual Party System – a political party relationship whereby the parties commanding most of the legislative seats are not too far apart on policies and have a reasonable amount of trust in each other and in the political system.

Conservatism – the political outlook which springs from a desire to conserve existing things, held to be either good in themselves, are at least safe, familiar and objects of trust and affection.

Constitution – a fundamental or organic law that establishes the framework of government of a state, assigns the powers and duties of government agencies, and establishes the relationship between the people and their government.

Constitutional Law – compilation of all court rulings on the meaning of the various words, phrases and clauses in the United States Constitution.

Constitutionalism – the political principle of limited government under a written contract.

Containment - U.S. foreign policy designed to physically restrain the Soviet Union in Europe and the ideology of communism throughout the world.

Cooperative Federalism – known as Marble Cake Federalism in which national, state and local governments work together to solve common problems.

Court of Appeal - These courts are the second of the three tiers of the national court system and are designed to hear cases on appeal from the district court.

Cousins v Wigoda (1975) – U.S. Supreme Court ruled that only the credentials committee of a national political party has the authority to settle credential disputes between rival state delegations.

Court of Last Resort – the United States Supreme Court for all appeals.

Creative Federalism – format of intergovernmental relationship characterized by joint planning and decision making among all levels of government as well as the private sector in the management public programs.

Criminal Law - The code that regulates the conduct of individuals, defines crimes and provides punishment for violators.

Crisis Policy Response - A foreign policy option used when the perception of a threat to national security cuts across normal channels of decisions.

Cultural Conservatism – support for traditional western Judeo-Christian values not just as a matter of comfort and faith, but out of a firm belief that the secular, the economic, and the political success of the western world is rooted in this value.

Curative Approach - A public policy option designed to solve an identified problem.

Dayton Accords - Dayton, Ohio, 1996. U. S. brokered peace agreement that attempted to end hostilities between the warring factions in the former Yugoslavia.

Dealignment - Traditional constituents defect from two national political parties.

Decision-making - The choice of an alternative from among a series of alternatives.

Dedicated Revenues - Constitutionally mandated budgetary allocations to a particular budget line item.

De Facto Discrimination - An undeliberate action adversely impacting one group over another group.

De Jure Discrimination - A purposeful action that adversely impacts one group over another group.

Defendant – the person accused of causing harm to either the person of or to the property of the plaintiff.

Democracy – a system of government in which the ultimate political authority is vested in the people.

Democratic Party v Lafollette (1891) – U.S. Supreme Court ruled that a state's party leadership could not force the DNC Credentials Committee to accept a delegation that was selected in clear violation of DNC rules.

Détente - French word meaning the easing of strained relations.

Determinate Sentence – a term of imprisonment that has a specific number of years.

Deterrence - the concept of discouraging other states from pursuing policies unwanted by the deterring state or states.

Direct Democracy - A type of democracy, sometimes referred to as a participatory democracy, in which the people make the political decisions and laws by which they are governed.

Direct Order – a congressional law or regulation that must be enforce or grant recipients can be held accountable to civil and criminal penalties.

Discrimination - Unfavorable action towards people because they are members of a particular racial or ethnic group.

Disparate Impact - Standards used in employment practices that have the effect of excluding people with disabilities on the basis of tests or standards that are not directly related to the skills or experience required to perform the job.

Disparate Treatment - Actions in which employers treat people with disabilities differently from others.

Distributive Policies - Governmental actions that convey tangible benefits to individuals, groups, or corporations.

District Court - They are the first of three tiers of the national court system, and they are designed to function as the trial court.

Districting - The process of drawing boundaries on a map that delineate the geographic areas-the districts-from which representatives will be elected.

Divine Right Theory of Kings - The concept of kingship based on the notion that monarchs rule by the will of, indeed, in place, of God.

Dred Scott v Sanford **(1857)** - United States Supreme Court decision nullifying the Missouri Compromise of 1821 and stipulating that slaves were not citizens of the United States and therefore, could not sue the government in a court of law.

Dual Court System - Network of national and state courts.

Dual Federalism – also known as Layered Cake Federalism – an arrangement whereby autonomous national, subnational, and local governments all pursue their own interests independently of each other.

Due Process - The procedural safeguards guaranteed to those who would be deprived of life, liberty, or property because they are accused of criminal wrongdoing.

Earmarked - Another term for dedicated revenues.

Economic Opportunity Act (1965) - Federal legislation establishing the Office of Economic Opportunity as the coordinator for all federal anti-poverty initiatives with state and local governments.

Elasticity - An economic criterion applied to a tax that refers to the tax's ability to generate increased revenue as economic growth or inflation increases.

Elector - An individual who casts a ballot for the president and the vice president according to the wishes of the majority of state voters. (See "Faithless Elector.")

Elite Theory of Democracy - One of several explanations of who has power in a political community. It holds that power resides primarily with the relatively few people who have the most of one or more of the fundamental values such as wealth, prestige, education, etc.

Emergency Power - An inherent power given to the president to facilitate his ability to act swiftly in times when a national crisis, particularly in the area of foreign affairs, may necessitate an immediate decision or response.

Emergency Relief Administration - A New Deal agency designed to provide food, shelter and clothing to the nation's unemployed during the Great Depression.

Eminent Domain – the authority of government to take private lands for public use as long as the property lower is justifiably compensation for the loss of the property.

Empirical - Knowledge that is derived from and tested by the senses, especially systematic observations.

Endangered Species - One in danger of becoming extinct throughout all or a significant part of its natural range.

Engle v Vitale (1962) - United States Supreme Court decision mandating that involuntary prayer in the public schools was an unconstitutional violation of the First Amendment's guarantee to religious freedom.

Entitlements - Benefits provided by government to which recipients have a legally enforceable right.

Enumerated Powers – also known as delegated powers – those rights and responsibilities of the U.S. government specifically provide for and listed in the Constitution.

Epistemology - A branch of philosophy that examines the origins and nature of human knowledge and the methods that are used to acquire it.

Equity Law – judicial preventive orders in form of a writ such as an injunction or restraining order designed to afford a remedy that otherwise obtainable, and traditionally given upon a showing of peril.

Escobedo v Illinois (1964) - The United States Supreme Court ruled that an individual can request legal counsel when the interrogation process turns from exploratory to accusatory.

Establishment Clause - The First Amendment to the United States Constitution granting religious freedoms and separating church related matters from state or governmental matters.

Ethnocentrism - belief that one's own culture is far superior to any other culture.

Everson v Board of Education of the Township of Ewing (1947) - The United States Supreme Court ruled that giving public tax dollars to low-income parents to offset the cost of children's transportation to and from public and parochial schools was not a violation of the separation of church and state doctrine.

Exclusionary Rule - Evidence that is otherwise admissible may not be used in a criminal trial if it is a product of illegal police conduct.

Exclusive Governing Party Format – recognizes no legitimate interest aggregation by groups within the party nor does it permit any free activity by social groups, citizens or other government agencies.

Executive Agreement - an international agreement, reached by the President of the United States with foreign heads of state that does not require senatorial approval.

Executive Office of the President (EOP) - The numerous offices, agencies, organizations, departments, and councils that provide administrative assistance to the president.

Executive Order - An edict or decree from a president that has the force of law.

Exercise Clause - Another term for Establishment Clause.

External Sovereignty - the right to conclude binding agreements such as treaties with a state or states without interference from other nation states.

Faction – a political group or clique that functions within a larger group, such as a government, party or organization.

Faithless Elector - An individual who follows personal choice, rather than the wishes of state voters, in casting a ballot for the president and the vice president. (See "Elector.")

Federalism - the mode of political organization that unites separate polities within an overarching political system by distributing power among general and constituent governments in a manner designed to protect the existence and authority of both.

Felony - A serious crime punishable by death or imprisonment in a penitentiary for a year or more.

Feminization of Poverty - The increased number of single-parent families headed by a female whose income falls below the poverty level.

Fighting Words - Words that by their very nature inflict injury upon those to whom they are addressed.

Fiscal Policy - Public policy concerning taxes, government spending, public debt, and management of government money.

Food Stamp Program - A federally funded program in the 1960s providing coupons to those whose incomes were below the poverty level to purchase food items.

Foreign Policy - a strategy or planned course of action developed by the decision makers of a state vis a vis other states or international entities aimed at achieving specific goals defined in terms of national interests.

Full Faith and Credit Clause – Article IV of the U.S. Constitution by mandating that "the citizen of each state shall be entitled to all the privileges and immunities of citizens of the several states."

Fullilove v Klutznik **(1980)** – Supreme Court ruled that Congress has the authority to use quotas to remedy past discrimination in government public works programs.

Furman v Georgia **(1972)** - The United States Supreme Court ruled that the death penalty was a violation of the Fourteenth Amendment's guarantee of due process and equal protection of the law.

Gag Order – a judge's order that lawyers and witnesses not discuss the trial with outsiders.

Game Theory - A behavioral approach to the study of politics that focuses on the decision-making process. (See "Approach.")

Gannett v DePasquale **(1979)** - The United States Supreme Court upheld a lower court ruling barring members of the press and the public from pretrial hearings.

Garcia v San Antonio Metropolitan Transit Authority **(1985)** – Supreme Court ruled constitution a federal mandate requiring state public employees must be paid at least the minimum wage and be granted overtime pay as detailed in the Fair Labor Standards Act; overturned Usery decision.

Gatekeeper - An individual or institution who is in a position to control the flow of information.

Gentrification - The process whereby upper-middle income whites (Anglos) move into inner-city neighborhoods and rehabilitate the properties.

Gerrymandering - The purposeful drawing of legislative districts to favor one group or one political party over other groups or political parties.

Gibbons v Ogden - Supreme Court ruling empowering the national government's use of the interstate commerce clause over the states.

Gideon v Wainwright **(1963)** - The United States Supreme Court ruled that all persons accused of committing a crime have a constitutional right to legal counsel.

Gitlow v New York **(1925)** - The Supreme Court was not involved in First Amendment cases until fairly recent times. In 1925, *Gitlow v. New York,* the Court stated that the Fourteenth Amendment made the First Amendment applicable to the states. This was the beginning of the incorporation doctrine of the Supreme Court.

Glass Ceiling - The practice of denying women accessibility to upper management positions.

Global Warming (greenhouse effect) - The effect of increasing amounts of methane, carbon dioxide, and certain air pollutants resulting in trapping heat in the earth's atmosphere and gradually warming it.

Goesaert v Cleary **(1948)** – Supreme Court ruled unconstitutional any state laws denying women the right to practice certain occupations usually held by men.

Government – the formal institutional structure and processes of a society by which policies are developed and implemented in the form of law binding on all.

Grand Jury - A panel charged with reviewing evidence in a case to determine whether or not a case should be forwarded for trial.

Grandfather Clause - A Jim Crow law requiring that individuals whose grandfathers could not vote before 1860 to pass a literacy test as a requirement for voting; ruled unconstitutional by the United States Supreme Court in *Guinn v United States* (1915).

Grant – a form of gift that entails certain obligations on the part of the grantee and expectations on the part of the grantor.

Grants-in-Aid – federal payments to states or federal or state payments to local governments for specified purposes.

Group Theory of Democracy - One of several explanations of who has power in a political community. It holds that power resides primarily with interest groups.

Guinn v United States 1915) - The United States Supreme Court ruled that Oklahoma's use of the grandfather clause to preclude African Americans from voting was an unconstitutional violation of the Fifteenth Amendment of the United States Constitution.

Haze - Wide-scale, low-level pollution that obstructs visibility.

Hegemony - the extension by one state of preponderant influence or control over another state or region.

Health Maintenance Organizations (HMOs) - Prepaid health-care systems emphasizing preventive medical services.

Homeless - A term used to describe those individuals who lack permanent shelter.

Horizontal Federalism - state-to-state interactions and relations.

Housing Act (1937) - Congressional legislation providing for federal funding for the construction of low-income apartments in inner-city areas.

Hyperpoor - A term used to describe those individuals whose annual incomes are less than half of the official poverty level.

Ideology - a comprehensive system of political beliefs about the nature of people and society.

Impact Statement - A report detailing any potential harm a project might cause to the environment, the possible solutions to prevent undo environmental damage, and potential efforts on the part of the project sponsors to maintain and hopefully enhance the productivity of the environment.

Impaired Rivers - A waterway that cannot support aquatic life.

Imperialism - the domination of one state by another, usually for exploitative purposes.

Implied Powers - also known as the Necessary and Proper Clause or the Elastic Clause – as detailed in Article I, Section 8 of the Constitution, Congress shall have the power "to make all laws necessary and proper for carrying into execution the foregoing powers vested by the Constitution in the government of the United States, or in any department or office thereof."

Impoundment - The refusal of a president to release or spend money that has been appropriated by Congress in the federal budget.

Incorporation Doctrine - The Fourteenth Amendment nationalized the Bill of Rights. The Supreme Court began to incorporate the first ten amendments into the Fourteenth so that whatever the national government was forbidden to do, the states could not do either.

Incrementalism – a doctrine holding that change in a political system occurs only by small steps, each of which should be carefully evaluated before proceeding to the next step.

Indian Removal Act (1830) - Federal legislation mandating the forced relocation of Native American tribes from east to west of the Mississippi River.

Indirect Democracy - A type of democracy, sometimes referred to as a representative democracy, in which the people elect others to make political decisions and laws for them. (See "Republic.")

Individualism – the political, economic and social concept that places primary emphasis on the worth, freedom and well-being of the individual rather than on the group, society or nation.

Inelastic Tax - A tax program that does not generate increased revenues in proportion to economic growth.

Infrastructure - The collective term for roads, buildings, sewers, water supply systems, and similar structures essential for a municipality to operate.

Inherited Powers - These are powers the national government inherited from tradition including the British Parliament and early state legislatures.

Initiative - A set of procedures through which residents in a state or local community may propose new legislation or an amendment to the constitution.

In-Kind Programs - Means-tested services providing assistance that has a cash value even though it is not received in cash.

Injunction – an order issued by a court in an equity proceeding to compel or restrain the performance of an act by an individual or government official.

Integration - The practice of desegregating public schools, public accommodations, residential areas, and so on.

Intergovernmental Relations – the complex network of interrelationships among governments, i.e., political, fiscal, programmatic and administrative processes by which higher units of government share revenues and other resources with lower units of government, generally accompanied by special conditions that lower units must satisfy as prerequisites to receiving the assistance.

Interim Committee - A standing committee of a state legislative house that continues to meet when the legislature is not in session.

Intermestic Issues - Those issues such as trade, finance, pollution, energy, terrorism, human rights, etc., which overlap foreign and domestic policy boundaries.

Internal Sovereignty - the right, without external intervention to determine matters having to do with one's own citizens.

Internationalism - belief that the course of international events demands that a power nation assume an active and to a large degree a leadership role in determining the outcome of those events.

Interposition – Calhoun's concept of placing a state as a buffer zone between its citizens and the national government as to prevent the enforcement of national law upon its citizens deemed to be detrimental to the citizens.

Interstate Compact – an agreement between two or more states requiring congressional approval to settle a common interest or concern.

Interstate Rendition – the return of a fugitive from justice by a state upon the demand of the executive authority of the state in which the crime was committed.

Interventionism - the coercive interference in the affairs of a state by another group of states to affect the internal and external policies of that state.

Iron Law of Oligarchy – in every organization, whether it be a political party, a professional union, or any other association of the kind, the aristocratic tendency manifests itself very clearly. The mechanism of the organization, while conferring a solidity of structure, induces serious changes in the organized mass, completely inverting the respective position of the leaders and the led. As a result of organization, every party or processional union becomes divided into a minority of directors and a majority of the directed.

Isolationism - the policy of curtailing as much as possible a nation's international relations so one's country can exist in peace and harmony by itself in the world.

Issue Network - A set of organizations that share expertise in a policy area and interact with each other over time as relevant issues are debated.

Jim Crow - A series of economic, political, and social laws enacted in the southern states to deny African Americans access to employment, social activities, and political rights including voting privileges.

Joint Committee - A legislative committee composed of members from both legislative Houses.

Joint Resolution - A legislative action passed by a majority in both Houses of Congress or a state legislature requiring the president's or governor's signature for approval.

Judicial Court - Article III inferior courts.

Judicial Activism – the making of new public policies through the decision of judges.

Judicial Self-Restraint – a self-imposed limitation on judicial decision making. The tendency of judges to favor a narrow interpretation of the laws and the defer to the policy judgment of the legislative and executive branches.

Judicial Review - The power of the courts to hold unconstitutional and unenforceable any law, any official action based upon a law, any other action by a public official it deems (upon careful reflection and in line with the taught tradition of the law and judicial restraint) to be in conflict with the Constitution.

Judiciary Act of 1789 - First congressional act passed that specifically dealt with its power to create inferior courts.

Jurisdiction – the authority vested in a court to hear and decide cases.

Just Desserts – the punishment for criminal-wrong doing should be proportionate to the severity of the defense.

Katz v United States (1967) - The United States Supreme Court ruled that wiretapping a public phone is a violation of the constitution's guarantee to privacy.

La Raza Unida - A third political party movement dedicated to the concerns of the Hispanic community.

Law – a body of rules enacted by public officials in a legitimate manner and backed by the force of the state.

Leadership - The ability to make others feel safe and secure by providing them with direction and guidance.

Lee v Weisman (1992) - The United States Supreme Court ruled that public schools could use a clergy-led prayer at graduation ceremonies only if the prayer was non-sectarian and non-proselytizing.

Legislative Courts - Article I inferior courts.

Lemon Test - The criteria established by the United States Supreme Court to determine governmental violations of the separation of church and state doctrine.

Lemon v Kurtzman (1971) - The United States Supreme Court established the criteria for judging whether or not government actions or legislative acts violated the separation of church and state doctrine.

Libel - Defamation of character in print or by other visual presentations.

Liberalism – a political doctrine that espouses freedom of the individual from interference by the state, toleration by the state in matters of morality and religion, laissez-faire economic policies, and a belief in natural rights that exist independent of government.

Libertarians – political movement that believes in freeing people not merely from the constraints of traditional political institutions, but also from the inner constraints imposed by their mistaken attribution of power to ineffectual things.

Liberty – in a state, that is, in a society where there are laws, liberty can consist only in having the power to do what one should want to do and in no way being constrained to do what one should not want to do.

License - A privilege granted by government to do something that it otherwise considers to be illegal.

Lieutenant Governor - In forty-two states, the second highest ranking state executive officer.

Limited War - an armed conflict fought for objectives less than the total destruction of the enemy and its unconditional surrender.

Line-item Veto - A governor's authority to disapprove an appropriated amount without vetoing the entire bill. (The United States Congress did grant this authority to the president; however, the United States Supreme Court ruled it as an unconstitutional grant of power.)

Literacy Test - A written or oral examination to determine whether or not an individual possessed the required intelligence to vote.

Magna Carta - A document written in 1215 by English noblemen placing restrictions upon the authority of their king.

Majoritarian Theory of Democracy - One of several explanations of who has power in a political community. It holds that power resides primarily with the people or citizens who take the majority position on a given issue.

Malapportionment - A districting plan whereby legislators from some districts represent more people than legislators from other districts.

Mandates - Legislative orders arising from statutes, court decisions, and administrative orders that demand action from a subordinate government.

Manifest Destiny - The concept that the United States was destined because of its innate superiority to govern the North American continent.

Mapp v Ohio (1961) - The United States Supreme Court established the exclusionary rule whereby evidence obtain in an illegal search is inadmissible in court.

Marbury v Madison - An 1803 Supreme Court decision that established the concept of judicial review.

Matrix - A rectangular array of information.

McCulloch v Maryland (1819) - A landmark Supreme Court decision in 1819 that established both the concepts of national supremacy and implied powers. The Court maintained that the national government had the "implied power" to establish a national bank and that the state governments did not have the right to thwart national policy.

McLaurin v Oklahoma State Regents (1950) - The United States Supreme Court ruled that segregated facilities at public universities was an unconstitutional violation of the Fourteenth Amendment of the United States Constitution.

Means-tested Programs - Eligibility based upon the applicant's documented inability to provide for his/herself the desired benefit because of depressed income levels.

Medicaid - Government-sponsored health-care program for individuals whose incomes fall below the poverty level.

Medicare - Government-sponsored health-care program for individuals over 65 years of age regardless of income level.

Medigap Insurance - Supplemental health-care coverage.

Method - The process by which political knowledge or information is acquired, for example, the scientific method. Methodology is a branch of epistemology. (See "Epistemology.")

Miller v California (1973) - The United States Supreme Court established the criteria for obscenity.

Minor v Happersat (1875) - The United States Supreme Court ruled that the Fourteenth Amendment to the United States Constitution did not give women the right to vote.

Minority Vote Dilution - The process of dividing large minority populations into several legislative districts to prevent them from electing candidates from their own minority group.

Minority Vote Packing - The purposeful drawing of legislative districts whereby large minority population groups are placed into one or two legislative districts.

Misdemeanor - A minor criminal offense.

Mitchell v Helms (2000) - The United States Supreme Court ruled that a Louisiana state law providing public funding for instructional equipment to public and private schools was not a violation of the separation of church and state doctrine.

Model Cities Program - A federal program created in the 1960s to encourage urban areas to provide low-income housing units.

Multi-lateral Agreements - agreements signed by three or more nation states.

Municipal Bonds - A bond program used by governments to fund major capital improvement programs to include roads, drainage, convention facilities, and so on.

Municipal Courts - City courts with limited jurisdiction over traffic-related cases; also known as traffic courts.

Municipal Solid Waste - Solid waste resulting from or incidental to municipal, community, commercial, institutional, and recreational activities including garbage, rubbish, ashes, street cleanings, dead animals, abandoned automobiles, and all other solid waste other than industrial waste.

Multiparty System – an electoral system based on proportional representation that often requires a coalition of several parties to form a majority to run the government.

Nation State - a state organized for the government of a nation whose territory is determined by national customs and expectations.

National Ambient Air Quality Standards (NAAQS) - The attainment levels established by the Environmental Protection Agency for air quality standards.

National Association for the Advancement of Colored Persons (NAACP) - A predominately African-American group founded by W. E. B. Dubois to address social, economic, and political discrimination against African Americans.

National League of Cities v Usery (1976) – Supreme Court ruled that the Tenth Amendment prohibited the national government from setting wages and maximum working hour requirements for state employees.

National Youth Core - A federally fund New Deal program to put unemployed youths to work during the Depression Era.

National Supremacy - It is the concept that the Constitution is supreme to the national government and the national government is supreme to the states. The foundations for national supremacy are found in Article IV of the Constitution in the national supremacy clause.

Nationalism - the spirit of belonging together or the corporate will that seeks to preserve the identity of the group by institutionalizing it in the form of a state.

Nativism - The belief that only those born on their country's soil should reap the benefits of their birthrights.

Near v Minnesota (1931) - The United States Supreme Court established the rule of "no prior restraint" regarding the freedom of the print media to publish news items.

Nebraska Press Association v Stuart (1976) - The United States Supreme Court overturned a gag order issued by a district court as a violation of First Amendment's guarantee to freedom of the press.

Negative Liberty – that tranquility of spirit which comes from the opinion each one has of his security, and in order for him to have this liberty, the government must be such that one citizen cannot fear another citizen.

Negligence – carelessness or the failure to use ordinary care, under the particular circumstances reveled by the evidence in the lawsuit.

Neutrality - the legal status wherein a state takes no part in a war and which establishes certain rights vis a vis the belligerents.

New York Times v Sullivan (1964) - The United States Supreme Court ruled that the *New York Times* was exercising its constitutionally protected right to freedom of the press when it printed a story about a Montgomery, Alabama police commissioner.

New York Times v United States (1971) - The United States Supreme Court ruled that the *New York Times* and the *Washington Post* were constitutionally protected by the First Amendment's guarantee to freedom of the press when they published sensitive data concerning the United States' involvement in Vietnam.

Nixon v Herndon (1927) - The United States Supreme Court ruled that the Texas White Primary Law of 1924 was unconstitutional.

No Prior Restraint - The ability of the print media to publish without government interference.

Nominal Definition - A description that indicates how a concept is to be used.

Non-Working Poor - A term used to describe unemployed individuals whose incomes fall at or below the poverty level.

Nullification – Calhoun's theory that a state or states could declare their association with the social contract as null and void if the national government failed to fulfill its obligations to the state(s) and establish their own independent governments.

Old Age Assistance Program - A New Deal program designed to assist the nation's elderly during the Depression Era.

Old Age Insurance - A program created by the Social Security Act of 1935 providing a self-funded insurance for the nation's elderly and disabled.

Olmstead v United States (1928) - The United States Supreme Court ruled that wiretapping was not a violation of the Fourth Amendment's protection against unreasonable searches and seizures.

Operating Expenses - Yearly expenses needed to run government such as salaries, benefits, equipment, rent, utilities, supplies, etc.

Original Jurisdiction - the authority of a court to hear a case in the first instance.

Outputs - Tangible manifestations of public policies, the things actually done in pursuance of policy decisions and statements.

Ozone - A primary ingredient of smog.

Palko v Connecticut (1937) - United States Supreme Court ruling distinguishing fundamental rights from non-fundamental rights.

Paternalistic Attitude - The belief of male superiority over women.

Pay Equity - The term used to recognize that women earn less than their male counterparts employed in comparable positions.

Personal Responsibility and Work Opportunity Act (1996) - Federal legislation initiating reform of the welfare system.

Pink Collar Job - Collective term applied to secretarial and clerical jobs usually held by women.

Plaintiff - the initiator of a grievance in a legal suit.

Platform – statement of principles and objectives espoused by a party or candidate that is used during a campaign to win support from voters.

Plea Bargaining – process through which a defendant pleads guilty to a criminal charge with the expectation of receiving some consideration from the state.

Plessy v Ferguson - An 1896 Supreme Court decision that provided the constitutional foundations for apartheid in the United States. The Court validated the Jim Crow laws that had been passed after Reconstruction and the concept of "separate but equal" facilities for whites and blacks when it upheld a Louisiana statute that required railroads to provide "equal but separate accommodations for the white and colored races."

Plintz v United States (1997) – Supreme Court declared unconstitutional provision of the federal Brady Bill requiring local law enforcement officials to conduct background checks on individuals wishing to purchase handguns as a unfunded mandate.

Pluralism - The view that competition and subsequent negotiation and bargaining among multiple centers of power is the key to understanding how decisions are made.

Pocket Veto - Upon receiving a bill from Congress the president takes no action and, if Congress adjourns within the following ten working days, the bill is automatically killed.

Point of Service (POS) - A health care program charging members a higher premium and co-payments for using non-HMO approved physicians and health services.

Point-Source Pollution - a pollution source that has a precise, identifiable location, such as a pipe or a smokestack.

Police Power – the authority to promote and safeguard the health, morals, safety and welfare of the people.

Policy - A proposed course of action of a person, group or government within a given environment providing obstacles and opportunities which the policy was supposed to utilize and overcome in an effort to reach a goal or realize an objective or purpose.

Policy Making - A pattern of action, extending over time and involving many decisions, some routine, and some not so routine.

Policy Outcomes - The consequences for society, intended or unintended, that flow from the action or inaction by government.

Political Culture - The predominant political beliefs, attitudes, and values collectively shared by a people at a given time.

Political Party - an organization whose members are sufficiently homogeneous to band together for the overt purpose of winning elections which entitles them to exercise government power, in order to enjoy the influence, prerequisites, and advantages of authority.

Political Question – a doctrine enunciated by the Supreme Court holding that certain constitutional issues cannot be decided by the courts but are to be decided by the executive or legislative branches.

Political Patronage - The hiring and firing of individuals for governmental jobs based on party loyalty and electoral support.

Political Science - The academic discipline devoted to the systematic study of political phenomena.

Political System - A government and its domestic and international environments.

Political Socialization - The process by which an individual acquires political beliefs, attitudes, and values and by which a political culture is passed down from one generation to another over time. (See "Political Culture.")

Politics - Anything related to the making of governmental decisions: the authoritative allocation of values for a society (Easton) or who gets, what, when, how (Lasswell).

Poll Tax - A voting fee; overturned with the passage of the Twentieth Amendment to the United States Constitution.

Porkbarrel Politics - The use of political influence by members of Congress to secure government funds and projects for their constituents.

Poverty - The state or condition of being poor by lacking the means of providing material needs or comforts.

Poverty Level - Based on the assumption that poor families spend one third of their income needed to eat according to a modest food plan.

Powell v Alabama (1932) - The United States Supreme Court ruled that those accused of a crime must be guaranteed their rights of due process and equal protection as guaranteed by the Fourteenth Amendment to the United States Constitution.

Precedent - a case previously decided that serves as a legal guide for the resolution of subsequent cases.

Precinct - Local electoral units.

Preemptive Strike - a first-strike nuclear attack undertaken on the assumption that an enemy state is planning an imminent nuclear attack.

Preferred Provider Organization (PPO) - A health care system where plan members select from a pre-approved list of doctors providing medical services at predetermined fees.

Prejudice - Feeling or act of any individual or any group in which a prejudgment about someone else or another group is made on the basis of emotion rather than reason.
Preponderance of the Evidence – the standard of proof required to prevail a trial.

Prescription – the action of laying down authoritative rules or directions.

Presidential Types - Presidents that share the same personal qualities and are categorized according to these common attributes.

Preventive Approach - A public policy option designed to prevent future damage without adequately solving the problem that caused the damage.

Preventive War - a limited but powerful military maneuver designed to scare the other nation state or states away from a hostile action.

Primary Election - Intraparty election used by political parties to select a candidate to run in the general election.

Privatization - General effort to relieving the disincentives toward efficiency in public organizations by subjecting them to incentives of the private market.

Probable Cause - A reasonable assumption that a crime has or will be committed.

Problem - Condition or situation that produces a human need, deprivation, or dissatisfaction, self identified or identified by others, for which relief is sought.

Procedural Due Process - The manner in which a law, ordinance, an administrative practice, or judicial task is carried out.

Progressive Tax - A tax that increases the tax burden for upper-income people while reducing it for lower-income people.

Proprietary Function – a governmental activity involving business-type operations ordinarily carried on by private companies to include such activities as supply electricity and gas, recreational facilities, garbage collection, etc.

Proportional Representation - Representatives are not necessarily selected from specific geographic regions or districts. Rather, each political party receives representation in proportion to the amount of votes cast. In contrast to the single-member district, this is not a winner-take-all system.

Proportional Taxes - Tax programs that impose equal tax burdens regardless of one's income level.

Protectionism - the theory and practice of utilizing governmental regulation to control or limit the volume or types of imports entering a state.

Public Opinion - The shared views, beliefs, or attitudes of a segment of a population.

Public Policy - An officially expressed intention backed by a sanction, which can be a reward or punishment.

Punitive Approach - A public policy option designed to punish the recipients of the benefit by placing stiff eligibility requirements and sanctions for abuse.

Pure Speech - Speech without any conduct.

Racial Profiling - the practice of law enforcement using stereotypes of the criminal element to determine if individuals should be subjected to searches, seizures, and if necessary, arrests.

Realignment - Shift in constituent base of two national political parties.

Reasonable Restrictions – The logical and rational curtailments enacted by government upon the absolute unrestrained pursuit of unalienable rights to guarantee the protection of those rights to all members of a civil society

Recall - A set of procedures through which residents in a state or local community may remove an elected official from office.

Redistributive Policies - Conscious attempts by government to manipulate the allocation of wealth, property, rights, or some other value among broad classes or groups in society.

Redlining - Practice used by financial institutions to deny loans to individuals desiring to purchase properties located in racially changing neighborhoods.

Referendum - A set of procedures through which residents in a state or local community may indicate their approval or disapproval of existing or proposed legislation and/or changes to their constitution

Regressive Tax - A tax that increases the burden for lower-income people while reducing it for upper-income people.

Regulatory Actions - Government actions that extend government control over particular behavior of private individuals or businesses.

Rehabilitation - the notion that punishment is intended to restore offenders to a constructive role in society; based on the assumption that criminal behavior is a treatable disorder caused by social or psychological ailments.

Relative Poverty - Measurement of the poverty level by comparing an individual's income to the nation's overall standard of living

Representative Democracy (also known as indirect democracy) - form of governance in which the citizens rule through representatives, who are periodically elected in order to keep them accountable.

Republic - a form of government in which sovereign power resides in the electorate and is exercised by elected representatives who are responsible to the people.

Reserved powers - The Tenth Amendment to the Constitution explicitly states that powers not explicitly granted to the national government are reserved to the states.

Resolution - A congressional or legislative action that deals entirely within the prerogatives of one house or the other.

Restrictive Covenant - A provision in a mortgage loan contract forbidding the buyer of a home from eventually selling the house to a minority.

Reynolds v Sims (1964) - United States Supreme Court ruling that redistricting plans for state Senates must guarantee the principle of "one man, one vote".

Reynolds v United States (1879) - The United States Supreme Court upheld a federal law outlawing the practice of polygamy.

Rider - An extraneous amendment attached to a bill by Congress.

Roe v Wade (1973) - The United States Supreme Court ruled that a woman's choice to have an abortion is a protected Constitutional right.

Roth v United States (1957) - The United States Supreme Court ruled that obscenity is not constitutionally protected by the First Amendment's guarantee to freedom of speech.

Ruiz v Estelle (1980) - United States Supreme Court decision ruling that triple bunking in state prisons was an unconstitutional act.

Sanctions - The penalties meted out as consequences of illegal conduct.

Schenck v United States (1919) - The United States Supreme Court decision to apply the term "clear and present danger" to differentiate constitutionally protected from unconstitutionally protected speech.

School District of Abington Township v Schempp (1963) - The United States Supreme Court ruled that the reading of the Bible in a public school constituted an unconstitutional sponsorship of one religious practice over other practices.

Search Warrant – a written document signed by a judge or magistrate, authorizing a law enforcement officer to conduct a search.

Selective Incorporation - The process used by the United States Supreme Court to apply certain rights guaranteed in the Bill of Rights to state actions.

Self-Determination - the right of a group of people who consider themselves separate and distinct from others to determine for themselves the state in which they will live and the form of government it will have.

Senatorial Courtesy - The practice in which a president yields the choice of an agency head or federal judge to a senator in his party.

Separate But Equal - The practice used to segregate public schools, public accommodations, housing, etc., initially upheld by the Supreme Court in *Plessy v Ferguson* (1896); overturned by the United States Supreme Court in *Brown v Board of Education* (1954).

Separate Car Act (1890) – A Louisiana state law mandating that railroads had to provide separate rail cars for Anglos and African-American passengers.

Separation – the belief that each racial or cultural group should live in isolation of other racial and cultural groups.

Separation of Church and State Doctrine - As outlined in the First Amendment, the practice of separating religious issues from governmental control or sponsorship.

Separation of Powers – governing power is distributed among the three branches of government.

Settlement Houses - Community centers located in the poor districts of major cities designed in the 1880s to address the needs of urban poor.

Shaw v Reno **(1993)** - United States Supreme Court decision ruling that racial gerrymandering is unconstitutional.

Silverman v United States **(1961)** - The United States Supreme Court ruled that law enforcement violated Silverman's Fourth Amendment rights when they used the pipes of his heating system to eavesdrop on his conversations.

Single-member district - The political system is divided into districts and the people of that district will select one person to represent them. It is a winner-take-all system.

Slander - Verbal malicious attacks against another person.

Smith Act (1940) - A federal law outlawing the right to organize or associate with any member belonging to any organization advocating the overthrow of any agency or branch of the United States government.

Smith v Allwright **(1944)** - The United States Supreme Court ruled that political parties were agents of state government and therefore, could not deny voting or membership privileges to any qualified voter for any election.

Smog - An air quality problem occurring when nitrogen oxides produced by burning fuels and volatile organic compounds escape into the atmosphere.

Social Security Act (1935) - Federal legislation creating a income support program for the nation's retired citizens funded through payroll taxes.

Socialism – a doctrine that advocates economic collectivism through governmental or industrial group ownership of the means of production and distribution of goods.

Solid Waste - Any garbage, refuse, sludge from a waste treatment plant, water supply, treatment plant or air pollution control facility, and other discarded materials, including solid liquid, semisolid, or contained gaseous material resulting from industrial, municipal, commercial, mining, and agricultural operations.

Sovereignty - the independent legal authority over a population in a particular territory, based on the recognized right to self-determination.

Special Supplemental Program for Women, Infants and Children (WIC) - A federally funded program providing nutritional food staples to pregnant women, breastfeeding mothers, mothers up to six months after giving birth and children under the age of five whose individual or family incomes are at or below the designated poverty level.

Spin Doctor - Serving as a politician and the head of a political party, a president attempts to give the media favorable interpretations (spin) of his own, and his party's actions. This role is also played by his political campaign advisor.

Sprawl - The outward extension of a new low-density residential and commercial development from the core of the city.

Standing Committees - Permanent committees within a legislative house, i.e., Budget Committee, Foreign Relations Committee, and so on.

Standing to sue - A legal reason to be before a court.

State of War - exists in the legal sense when two or more national states officially declare that a condition of hostilities exists between them.

Stare Decisis – let the decision stand.

States' Rights – opposition to increasing the national government's power at the expense of the states.

Statistics - A mathematical method used by some political scientists to analyze data.

Status Quo - Present public policy. What is right now.

Steering - The practice of showing real estate properties to minorities located only in minority neighborhoods thus steering them away from more affluent neighborhoods.

Strategic Defense Policy - Policy response oriented toward foreign policy and international politics involving the use of military force.

Street v New York **(1969)** - The United States Supreme Court ruled that the burning of the American flag was a constitutionally protected right under the First Amendment's guarantee to freedom of speech.

Structural Defense Policy - Policy response oriented toward foreign policy and international politics involving decisions of procurement, allocation, and organization of military forces.

Subsidies - Government grants of cash or other commodities.

Substantive Due Process - The content or subject matter of a law.

Superior/Inferior Theory of Racism – The concept that one group or culture is genetically, intellectually, and culturally more superior than any other group.

Supplemental Security Income (SSI) – A federally funded program providing cash payments to lower income elderly, the blind, and disable adults and children.

Supremacy Clause - Article VI of the United States Constitution mandating that the Constitution is the supreme law of the land.

Supreme Court - The Supreme Court is the only national court that is guaranteed under Article III of the Constitution. Although it serves as a court of original jurisdiction, it is most often the last court of appeal.

Survey - A method used by some political scientists to collect data about the attitudes and beliefs held by a sample of the population.

Sweatt v Painter **(1950)** - The United States Supreme Court ruled that the practice of allowing African Americans to attend racially separated inferior schools was an unconstitutional violation of the Fourteenth Amendment.

Symbolic Speech - Use of symbols, rather than words, to convey ideas.

Systems Analysis - A behavioral approach to the study of politics that focuses on the relationship that exists between a government and its environments. (See "Approach" and "Political System.")

Tax - A compulsory contribution for a public purpose rather than for the personal benefit of an individual.

Tax Equity - Fairness of tax application.

Technique - The specific set of procedures adhered to in the process of acquiring political knowledge.

Temperance Movement - The organized effort to forbid the production, sale, and consumption of alcohol.

Terry v Ohio **(1968)** - The United States Supreme Court ruled that testing for drugs or alcohol by penetrating the skin is not a violation of the Fourth Amendment's protection against unreasonable searches.

Texas v White **(1869)** – Supreme Court ruled that states cannot secede from the union.

Theory - An explanation of some aspect of politics.

Third Party – composed of independents and dissidents from the major parties in a two-arty system that typically is based on a protest movement and that may rally sufficient voter support to affect the outcome of a state or national election.

Threatened Species - A species that is likely to become endangered in the foreseeable future.

Tinker v Des Moines School District **(1969)** - The United States Supreme Court ruled that the wearing of arm bands in protest of the Vietnam War was a protected right to freedom of speech.

Tort Law – the law of civil wrongs.

Total War - an armed conflict involving the participation of the entire population of the combatants with the ultimate aim of total destruction of the enemy with an unconditional surrender.

Trail of Tears - the 1829 forced relocation sponsored by the United States government of the Cherokees, Choctaws, Creeks, Chickasaws and Seminoles from their traditional lands east of the Mississippi to new lands west of the Mississippi.

Transitional Immunity – absolute protection against prosecution for any event or transaction about which a witness is compelled to give testimony or furnish evidence.

Treaty - a formal agreement entered into between two or more countries. The treaty process includes negotiation, signing, ratification, exchange of ratifications, publishing and proclamation, and treaty execution.

True Bill – an indictment made and endorsed by a grand jury when it finds that there is sufficient evidence to bring a person to trial.

Unalienable Rights - Fundamental rights derived from natural law which all people have and which cannot be taken away or transferred.

Unemployment Insurance – A federally funded program providing financial assistance to unemployed workers.

Unfunded Mandate – An order from a higher level of government upon a subordinate level of government to perform a particular task without receiving the additional revenue or resources needed to perform the task.

Unicameral - A one-house legislature.

Unilateral - a foreign policy decision or decree issued by one nation state.

United Farm Workers Union - A labor organization founded by the late César Chávez to address the concerns of migrant farm workers.

Unitary System - one I which principal power within the political system lies at the level of a national or central government rather than at the level of some smaller unit, such as a state or province.

United States v O'Brien (1968) - The United States Supreme Court ruled that the burning of draft cards was an unconstitutional act in violation of the First Amendment's guarantee to freedom of speech.

United States v Lopez (1995) – Supreme Court struck down a federal law making it a crime to carry a gun within 1,000 of a school.

Urban Renewal Program - A federally financed program designed to clear blighted inner city areas and redevelop them with a mixture of commercial and residential properties.

Vertical Federalism - the governing authority that flows up and down between the national and state governments.

Veto - The return of a bill to Congress without a presidential signature and with his stated objections. (See "Pocket Veto.")

Village of Skokie v National Socialist Party (1978) - The United States Supreme Court ruled that the denial of a parade permit to the American Nazi Party violated the organization's constitutionally protected right to assemble.

Vocational Rehabilitation Act (1920) - Federal legislation providing financial assistance to disabled Americans.

Voting Rights Act (1965) - Federal legislation suspending the use of literacy tests to determine voting qualifications.

Wallace v Jaffree (1985) - The United States Supreme Court ruled that Alabama's law requiring a moment for voluntary prayer violated the First Amendment's guarantee to freedom of religious beliefs.

War - the hostilities between states or within a state or territory undertaken by means of armed force.

War on Poverty - The collective term used for President Lyndon Johnson's programs to address poverty-related issues during the 1960s designed to create a **Great Society**.

West Virginia State Board of Education v Barnette (1943) - The United States Supreme Court ruled that the school district's mandatory flag salute violated the religious rights of school children belonging to the Jehovah Witnesses.

Westbury v Sanders (1964) - United States Supreme Court decision mandating that the United States House of Representatives implement the concept of "one man, one vote: in its redistricting plans.

White Fear - Feeling of becoming a member of a new minority as the existing minority becomes a majority within the social community.

White Flight - The movement of white (Anglo) residents from central cities to the suburbs.

White House Office (WHO) - The people who run the White House and assist the chief executive in a variety of functions including speech writing and secretarial services.

White Only Primary - A tactic used by the Democratic Party in southern states to deny African Americans the right to vote in primary elections; overturned by the United States Supreme Court in *Smith v Allwright* (1944) and *Nixon v Hernon* (1924).

Wilderness - An area where the earth and its community of life are untrammeled by man, and where man himself is a visitor who does not remain.

Woman's Party - A third party movement founded by Alice Paul to address the concerns of women.

Working Poor - The term used to describe those individuals who are employed at jobs paying at or below the poverty level.

Works Project Administration (WPA) - A federally funded Depression Era New Deal program providing jobs to the nation's unemployed.

Writ – an order in writing issued by a court ordering the performance of an act or prohibiting some act.

Writ of *Certiorari* - Order by the Supreme Court requiring a lower court to send the records of a case for it to review.

Writ of *Habeas Corpus* - A direct order to the person detaining another and commanding him to produce a body of the person or persons detained.

Writ of Mandamus - a court order directing a public official to fulfill his/her duties or otherwise be in contempt of court.

Index

A

Abington School District v. Schempp (1963), 393
Acid rain, 552
ActBlue, 168
Adams, Abigail, 456
Adams, John, 62, 157, 456
Adams, John Quincy, 599
Addams, Jane, 523, 524
Administration discretion, 298
Administrative law, 358
Administrative Procedures Act (APA) (1946), 304
Adversary system, 406
Advertisements, 203
  political, 209
Affirmative action, 425
Affordable Care Act (ACA), 82, 345, 355, 472, 498, 507
Afghanistan, 578, 579, 608
AFL-CIO, 221
African Americans, 435
Aid to Families with Dependent Children, 523
Aid to the Blind, 523
Air Pollution Control Act (1955), 552
Air Quality Act (1967), 553
Akin, Todd, 217
Alaska, 600
Alienable rights, 384
Alien Act (1798), 395
Alito, Samuel, 240
Alleviative approach, 490
Alliance, 581
Almshouse, 522
Al Qaeda, 608
Amendment,
  Eighteenth, 458
  Eighth, 388, 411
  Fifteenth, 174, 437
  Fifth, 362, 389, 409
  First, 168, 170, 388, 191, 404, 238
  Fourteenth, 78, 368, 388, 403, 427, 437, 439, 443
  Nineteenth, 175, 389, 456, 459
  Ninth, 385
  Second, 217, 405
  Seventeenth, 60
  Tenth, 77, 81, 87, 542
  Thirteenth, 389, 437, 439
  Twelfth, 311, 312
  Twenty-fourth, 442
  Twenty-sixth, 175
American Association of Retired Persons (AARP), 224, 226, 521
American Bar Association (ABA), 222
American Farm Bureau Federation, 222
American Forestry Association (AFA), 543
American Hospital Association (AHA), 521
American Issues Project, 212
American Medical Association (AMA), 222, 228, 521
American Nazi Party, 403, 404
American Political Science Association (APSA), 30
Americans with Disabilities Act (1990), 464, 483
American Woman Suffrage Association, 458
Amicus curiae, 241
Anarchist, 123
Anthony, Susan B., 458
Anti-Comintern Pact, 601
Antiquities Act (1906), 544
Appropriations, 277
Architectural Barriers Act (1970), 464
Arctic National Wildlife Refuge, 555, 170
Aristotle, 4, 26
Armstrong, J. Scott, 40
Arraignment, 361
Article of Confederation, 53–55
AT&T Inc., 168
Attorney General, United States, 363–364
Australian ballot, 175
Avants, Ernest, 422

B

Bain Capital, 168
Baker v. Carr (1962), 257
Balance of trade, 589
Bald eagle, 101
Baldwin, Tammy, 260
Barber, James David, 32, 334
Barnett, Ross, 82
Barron v. Baltimore (1833), 388
Bataan Death March, 588
Begin, Menachem 583, 585
Bell, John, 125
Bentley, Arthur, 37
Berlin Lift, 602
Bertelsmann of Germany, 185
Better Health Care Together, 219
Bicameral, 249
Biden, Joe, 405
Bilateral agreements, 584
Bill of Rights, 385
Binder, Sarah, 252
bin Laden, Osama, 608
Biochemical oxygen demand (BOD), 558
Bipartisan Campaign Reform Act (BCRA), 161, 209, 267
Black Caucus, 271
Black, Hugo, 391
Blackwater Security, 290
Blanket primary, 148
Boehner, John, 133, 207, 264
Bonilla, Henry, 135

Borda, Jean-Charles, 154
Bosnia, 493
Bowers, Sam, 422
Boyd v. United States (1886), 409, 415
Bracero program, 451
Brady Bill, 405
Brandenburg v. Ohio (1969), 403
Brandies, Louis D., 59
Breckenridge, John C., 125
Brest-Litovsk Treaty, 601
Bribery, 242
Bricker Amendment (1953), 322
British Petroleum (BP), 72
Brookings Institution, 290
Brown, Jerry, 164
Brown, Sherrod, 260
Brown v. Board of Education (1954), 368, 80, 425, 443, 482
Brussels Pact, 602
Buchanan, Patrick, 208, 310
Buckley v. Valeo (1976), 161, 234, 395
Budget and Accounting Act (1921), 325
Budget and Impoundment Control Act (1974), 326
Bundling, 164
Bureau of Alcohol, Tobacco, Firearms and Explosives (ATF), 366, 405
Bureau of Prisons, 363, 379
Bureaucracy,
  benefits of, 305
  composition of, 295
  decision-making,
    incremental model of, 301
    rational-comprehensive model of, 300
  development of, 285
  federal,
    organization of, 292
  functions of, 291
  political resources of, 298
  presidential control over, 302
  rule administration of, 297
  size of, 290
Bureaucrats,
  role in policy making, 481
Burger, Warren, 392
Burke, Edmund, 43, 52, 115, 120, 253
Burr, Aaron, 311
Bush, George H.W.,
  Gulf War, 498
  leadership of, 333
  North American Free Trade Agreement, 605
  troops to Panama & Saudi Arabia, 319
Bush, George W., 83, 88
  characteristics of, 342
  civil liberties, 384
  education reforms, 516
  environmental issues, 546
  memoirs, 187
  tax refunds, 499
Business Roundtable, 220
Byrd, James, 421, 488

C

Cabinet, 292, 317
California v. Trombetta (1984), 416
Campaigns,
  advertising in, 172
  congressional nominations, 151
  contributions, 151
  effects of financing, 160
  historical background, 146
  nominating candidates, 146
  nominations for state offices, 151
  strategies, 171
Campbell, John, 196
Camp David Accords, 583
Canon law, 357
Carson, Rachel, 543, 545

Carter, Jimmy, , 310
  Iran hostage crisis, 319, 498
  leadership of, 329
  Panama Canal Treaty, 596
  Soviet grain embargo, 486
Case Act (1972), 322
Casework, 255
Case-Zablocki Act (1972), 597
Castro, Fidel, 590, 606
Catholics, 178
Catt, Carrie Chapman, 459
Caucus, 130, 147, 148
Census, 256
Center for Responsive Politics, 171, 258
Center for Substance Abuse and Prevention (CSAP), 232
Central Intelligence Agency (CIA), 287, 293
Centrist, 120
Chamber of Commerce, 220, 237
Chaney, James, 422
Change of venue, 414
Charging document, 361
Chávez, César, 229, 449
Cheney, Dick, 170
Chicago, convention in, 148
China, 603
Chlorofluorocarbons, 548
Christian Coalition, 223
Circuit judges, 357
Citizens for Public Integrity, 167
Citizens United vs. Federal Election Commission (2010), 143, 162, 396
Civil Aeronautics Board (CAB), 288
Civilian Conservation Corps (CCC), 523
Civil law, 358
Civil liberties, 384
Civil rights, 424
Civil Rights Act (1875), 439
Civil Rights Act (1957), 442
Civil Rights Act (1960), 442

Civil Rights Act (1964), 442
Civil Rights Act (1968), 442
Civil Service Reform Act (1978), 295
Civil service system, 295
Clean Air Act (1963), 545, 553
Clean Air Act (1970), 298, 546, 553
Clean Air Act (1990), 554
Clean Water Act (1972), 558
Clear Channel Communications, 185
Cleveland, Grover, 157
Clientele,
  groups, 231
  services, 291
  support, 300
Clinton, Bill,
  autobiography, 187
  characteristics of, 337
  constrained empathetic federalism, 88
  presidential campaign, 310
  troops to Haiti, 319
  welfare programs, 508
  welform reform of, 474, 530
  Whitewater, 251
Clinton, Hillary,
  as Secretary of State, 597
  as senator, 252
  campaign of 2008, 147, 152, 460
  presidential nomination, 312
Closed primary, 148
Cloture, 274
Coates v. Cincinnati (1971), 390
Cohen v. California (1971), 397
Cohen v Virginia (1821), 79
Cold War, 579, 586, 602
Columbine High School, 217
Commander in chief (president as), 318
Common Cause, 170
Communications Decency Act (1997), 402
Communism, 123

Communist Manifest (Marx and Engles), 123, 388
Community Right-to-Know-More Act (1991), 563
Compensino, 448
Conference committees, 275
Conglomerate ownership, 199
Congress,
  campaign financing, 260
  caucuses of, 271
  committee system of, 267
    membership of, 269
    types of, 268
  expressed powers of, 249
  formal leadership of, 261
  legislative process of, 273
  organizational structure of, 261
  origin of, 248
  powers of, 248
  representation in, 252
    quality of, 254
  staff system of, 270
Congressional Black Caucus, 254
Congressional Budget Office, 271
Congressional Hispanic Caucus, 255
Congressional Research Service, 271
Congressional Union, 459
Congress of Racial Equality (CORE), 441
Connecticut Plan, 60
Conrad, Jim, 427
Conservatism, 119–120
Constitution,
  Article I, 75
  Article VI, 75
  elastic clause, 76
  Full Faith and Credit Clause, 78
  implied powers doctrine, 76
  necessary and proper, 76
  reserved powers, 77

Constitutional law, 358
Constitutional powers (of president), 313
Constitutional Union Party, 125
Constrained Empathetic Federalism, 88
Containment policy, 602
Content analysis, 9
Continental Congress, 52
Contract clause, 414
"Contract with America," 91
Contras, 587
Controlled Substance Act, 366, 454
Cooperative federalism, 86
Council on Environmental Quality, 546
Cousins v Wigoda (1975), 136
Coyle v Smith (1911), 84
Cranston, Alan, 235
Creative federalism, 86
Credentials committee, 136
Criminal law, 359
Crossroads GPS, 168
Cruz, Ted, 473
Cuba, 605
Cuban Missile Crisis, , 493
Cultural assimilation and separation, 432
Cultural conservatism, 120
Cumulus Media Inc., 185
Currency Act, 51

D

Davis v. Bandemer (1986), 257, 260
Davis, Wendy, 460
Dawes Severalty Act (1887), 433
Deal, Nathan, 71
Dean, Howard, 173
Death penalty, 388
Decision Points (Bush), 187
Declaration of Independence, 52
Declaration of Sentiments, 457
DeConcini, Dennis, 235

De facto discrimination, 424
Defendant, 358
Defenders of Wildlife, 224
Defense of Marriage Act (DOMA), 355, 463
Deferred Action for Childhood Arrivals, 454
De jure discrimination, 424
DeLay, Tom, 270
Democracy, 47, 32
  direct, 33
  indirect, 33
Democratic National Committee (DNC), 134
Democratic Party v Lafollette (1891), 136
Department of Health and Human Services, 232, 287
Department of Homeland Security, 404, 231, 292
Deregulation, 289
De Tocqueville, Alexis, 101
Dewey, Thomas, 98
Diaz, President Profirio, 450
Dickinson, John, 53
Disabled Americans, 463
Discharge petition, 267
Disney, 185
Disparate treatment, 464
Distributive policies, 492
Dobson, James, 223
Domestic surveillance, 268
Domino theory, 603
"Don't Ask, Don't Tell," 224
Douglass, Frederick, 435
Douglas, Stephen A., 125
Dream Act, 454, 456
Dual federalism, 85
Due process, 389

E

Earmarks, 248, 256
Earth Day, 547
Easton, David, 22, 29
Economic Opportunity Act (1965), 524

Edwards, John,
  campaign of 2008, 147
Egypt, 583
Eisenhower, Dwight, 125
Elastic clause, 249
Elasticity, 495
Elderly, poverty of, 516
Elections,
  campaigning in, 159
  candidate image in, 181
  issues of, 178
  political participation in, 174
  presidential, 156
    electoral college, 156
  senatorial, 155
  turn-out, 175
  voter party identification, 177
Electoral College, 60, 158, 311
  allocation of votes, 159
Elite theory, 38
Elliott Management, 168
Ellsberg, Daniel, 401
Ellsworth, Oliver, 372
Emergency powers, 313
Emergency Relief Administration, 523
Emmis, 185
Empirical observations, 4
Employee Free Choice Act (EFCA), 237
Endangered Species Act (ESA) (1973), 546, 565
Enforcement Act of 1871, 440
Engles, Friedrich, 123
Engle v. Vitale (1962), 393
Enron, 169–170, 289
Entercom Communications, 185
Entitlements, 527
Enumerated powers, 249
Environmental Defense Fund, 224, 569
Environmental groups, 224
Environmental laws, 549
Environmental Protection Act (1970), 566

Environmental Protection Agency (EPA), 72, 82, 231, 290, 293, 297, 546, 553, 566
Epistemology, 2
Equal Employment Opportunity Act, 483
Equal Rights Amendment, 217
Equity law, 358
Erlichman, John, 317
Escobedo v. Illinois (1964), 411
Espionage Act (1917), 396
Essay Concerning Human Understanding (Locke), 385
Establishment clause, 390
Ethics in Government Act, 242
Evers, Medger, 444
Everson v Board of Education of the Township of Ewing (1947), 373
Exclusionary rule, 360
Executive agreement, 596, 596–597
Executive budget, 325
Executive Office of the President (EOP), 315
Executive Order 9066, 593
Executive Order 12612, 88
Executive orders, 316
Exxon *Valdez*, 560

F

Facebook, 98, 189, 237
Factions, 130
  Tea Party Movement, 133
Fascism, 601
Federal Activities Inventory Reform Act (1998), 290
Federal Advisory Committee Act, 304
Federal Appellate Courts, 370
Federal Aviation Agency (FAA), 294
Federal Bureau of Investigation (FBI), 364, 421

Federal Communications Commission (FCC), 191, 294, 302, 402
Federal Court System,
  Constitutional courts, 367–377
  Federal Appellate Courts, 370
  Federal District Courts, 369-370
  jurisdiction, 369
  selection of judges, 367–368
  Supreme Court, 371–372
Federal Deposit Insurance Corporation (FDIC), 294
Federal Election Campaign Act (FECA) (1971), 161, 234
Federal Election Commission (FEC), 151, 161, 162, 170
Federal Election Commission v. Wisconsin Right to Life, Inc. (2007), 209
Federal Energy Regulatory Commission, 170
Federal grants, 89–91
  block grants, 90
  categorical grant, 89
  formula grants, 89
  mandates, 90
  project grants, 89
  revenue sharing, 90
Federal justice system,
  attorney general, 363–364
  Department of Justice, 364–366
  Federal Bureau of Investigation (FBI), 364
Federal Radio Act (1927), 191
Federal Regulation of Lobbying Act (1946), 238
Federal Regulatory Commission, 169
Federal Trade Commission (FTC) (1914), 286
Federal Water Pollution Control Act of 1972, 546

Federalist Papers, The, 197, 319
Federalists, 323
Felony, 359
Fenno, John, 197
Fiduciary trust, 47
Fight Back New York, 225
Fighting words, 396
Filibuster, 274
Fish and Wildlife Service, 565
Fisher, Peter, 169
Flemming v Nestor (1960), 526
Flickr, 189
Florida, 174, 312
Foley, Tom, 261
Food and Drug Administration (FDA), 286, 297
Food Stamp Program, 528
Foreign Operations Bill, 255
Foreign policy,
  definition of, 577
  terminology, 577–579
Franco, Francisco, 597
Franking privilege, 259
Franklin, Benjamin, 101
Freedom of Information Act (FOIA) (1967), 304
Freedom Project, 264
Freedoms,
  assemble and association, 402
  of religion, 390
  of speech, 395
  of the press, 400
Frémont, John C., 125
Freneau, Philip, 198
Fullilove v Klutznik (1980), 78

G

Gag order, 363
Gallup poll, 99
Game theory, 14
Gans, Herbert, 202
Garcia v San Antonio Metropolitan Transit Authority (1985), 81
Garfield, James, 295
Gay and lesbian rights, 223

Genachowski, Julius, 192
Gender issues, 456
General Agreement of Tariffs and Trade (GATT), 590
General Electric, 185
General Revenue Fund, 90
General Revision Act (1891), 543
Gerrymandering, 154, 257
Gibbons v Ogden (1824), 75, 80
Gideon v. Wainwright (1963), 371, 411
Giffords, Gabby, 218
Gillibrand, Kirsten, 423
Gilman, Francis Perkins, 458
Gingrich, Newt, 91
Gitlow v. New York (1925), 388
Glenn, John, 235
Global warming, 556
Goesaert v Cleary (1948), 78
Gohmert, Louis, 472
Goldman Sachs, 235
Gonzales, Alberto, 268, 455
Gorbachev, Mikhail, 323, 584
Gore, Al, 543, 158
  2000 election, 312
  environmental policies, 546
  National Performance Review, 304
Government, American,
  definition of, 30
  terminology, 28–37
Government contracts, 483
Government corporations, 294
Grandfather clause, 438
Grand jury, federal, 362
Grants-in-aid, 89
Grassroots, 124
Grassroots lobbying, 240
Great Britain, 586
Great Compromise, 60, 248
Great Society, 86, 287, 480
Greenfield, Jeff, 205
Green Party, 130
Greenpeace, 232, 569
Grenada, 193

Gridlock, 247–248
Grimke, Sarah, 457
Guest worker program, 605
Guinn v. United States (1915), 442
Gulf war, 333, 485
Gun Control Act, 405
Gutierrez, Jose Angel, 454

H

Habeas Corpus, Writ of, 77
Hagee, John, 223
Hagel, Chuck, 315, 423, 460
Haldeman, Bob, 317
Haliburton, 290
Hamilton, Alexander, 62, 65, 124, 197
Hammurabi, King, 357
Hanseatic League, 581
Harris, Fred, 137
Harrison, Benjamin, 157
Hastert, Dennis, 270
Hatch Act (1939), 160
Hate Crimes Statistics Act, 429
Hayes, Rutherford, 157
Hay-Pauncefote Treaty, 596
Haze, 548
Health-care package, 531–536
Health-care reform, 520
Hearst, William Randolph, 198
Herbert, Curtis Jr., 170
Highway Traffic Safety Administration, 287
Hitler, Adolph, 106
Hobson, David, 265
Holder, Eric, 364
Holy Alliance, 581
Homes, Oliver Wendell, 357
Homosexual Community, 463
Hoover, J. Edgar, 364
Host culture, 426
House of Burgess, 51
House Rules Committee, 269, 274
Huff, Darrell, 12
Hull House, 523
Human Home, The (Walker), 542
Human rights, 32
Humphrey, Hubert, 149
Hurricane Katrina, 509
Hussein, Saddam, , 333
Hyperpluralism, 38

I

Ideology, 119
Illegal immigration, 605
Illinois v Krull (1967), 361
Impeachment, 249
Impoundment, 325
Inalienable rights, 384
Incremental process, 497
Independent agencies, 293
Independent delegates, 136
Independent groups-527s, 163
Indian Removal Act (1830), 431
Indirect democracy, 48
Inherent powers, 321
Injunction, 358
Integration, 441
Interest groups,
  biases in, 227
  citizen groups, 222
  common features of, 226
  defining, 218
  economic, 220
  government groups, 226
  litigating of, 241
  lobbying, 236
  methods and strategies, 233
  overcoming obstacles of, 228
  political parties versus, 218
  proliferation of, 230
  reform prospects, 242
  roles of, 218
  sources of proliferation, 231
Intergovernmental Panel on Climate Change (IPCC), 540
Intermestic issues, 487
Internal Revenue Service, 496
International Development Association (IDA), 590
International Monetary Fund (IMF), 590
International Trade Commission (ITC), 294
Internet, 186
  campaigning on the, 173
  mass media of the, 189
Interstate Commerce Commission (ICC), 81
Interstate compact, 91
Interstate rendition, 78
Intrastate commerce, 81
Iran, 579
Iraq, , 485
Iron Law of Oligarchy, 135
Iron triangles, 237, 300
Isolationism, 581
Israel, 583
Issa, Darrell, 268

J

Jackson, Andrew, 157, 295, 313
Jackson, Jesse, 175
Japan, 585
Japanese-American Security Treaty, 585
Japanese internments, 429
Jay, John, 54, 65
Jay Treaty, 596
Jefferson, Thomas, 62, 311
  religious tolerance, 391
  use of executive agreement, 596
Jeffords, James, 252
Jim Crow laws, 428, 438
Jindal, Bobby, 72
Johnson, Lyndon, 86, 577
  Great Society, 287
  presidential campaign, 149
  public opinion polls of, 98
  troops into Dominican Republic, 319
  War on Poverty program, 231, 489, 523

Johnson, Paul, 290
Joint committees, 269
Judicial activism, 368
Judicial review 372–373, 388, 482
Judicial self-restraint, 368
Judiciary Act (1789), 364, 372, 388
Jurisdiction, 369

K

Kagan, Elena, 170, 369
Kaine, Tim, 260
Kai-shek, Chiang, 603
Katrina, 70
Katz v. United States (1967), 416
Keating, Charles, 235
Keating Five, 235
Kennedy, Edward, 235
  immigration, 453
Kennedy, John,
  Cuban Missile crisis, 319, 493
  media coverage, 199
  presidential campaign, 149
  use of executive agreement, 597
Kennedy, Robert, 149
Kerry, John, 597, 608
Keyes, Alan, 310
Keynote address, 136
Keystone Pipeline, 555
King, Martin Luther, Jr., 441
Kissinger, Henry, 583, 606
Knox, Henry, 62
Korean War, 597
Krumholz, Sheila, 235
Ku Klux Klan (KKK), 403, 421, 439
Kurds, 578
Kuwait, 485
Kyoto Protocol, 557

L

Laissez-faire, 286, 288
La Raza Unida (LRU), 454
Lasswell, Harold, 29

Latent opinion, 97
Law,
  codification of, 356–357
  terminology of, 358–360
Layered cake federalism, 85
Lay, Kenneth, 169
League of Nations, 582, 601
League of Women Voters, 217
Lee v Weisman (1992), 394
Legislative veto, 302
Lemon test, 392
Lemon v. Kurtzman (1971), 392
Lend-lease, 601
Lenin, Vladimir, 123, 601
Lewis, Charles, 167
Liberalism, 121
Libertarians, 122
Library of Congress, 271
License, 484
Light, Paul, 290
Limbaugh, Rush, 189
Lincoln, Abraham, 77, 125, 313
  civil liberties, 384
Lindsey, Larry, 169
Line item veto, 276
LinkedbyAir, 541
Literacy test, 438
Little Lenin Library, The (Lenin), 123
Lobbying, 236
  grassroots, 240
Lobbying Transparency and Accountability Act, 239
Locke, John, 121, 384, 4
Lockheed Martin, 290
Lott, Trent, 252
Lungren, Dan, 278

M

MacArthur, Douglas, 604
Maddox, Lester, 82
Madison, James, 65, 124, 230, 242
Madoff, Bernie, 284
Magna Carta, 49, 384
Mainstream, 121

Majority,
  floor leader, 264
Malcolm X, 444
Manifest destiny, , 431
Mapp v. Ohio (1961), 409
Marble cake federalism, 86
Marbury v Madison (1803), 377
Mark-up session, 274
Marshall, John, 79, 80
Marshall Plan, 602
Marshall, Thurgood, 241, 440
Marsh, George, 543
Martin, Kevin, 192
Marx, Karl, 123
Matrix, 15
McCain-Feingold, 143, 150
McCain, John, 173, 235
  campaign financing, 162
  immigration, 453
McCarthy, Eugene, 149
McCaskill, Claire, 423
McConnell, Mitch, 275
McCullough v Maryland (1819), 79, 85
McDowell, Robert, 192
McGovern, George, 137
McKinley, William, 313
McLaurin v. Oklahoma State Regents (1950), 443
McNamara, Robert, 599
Media,
  behavior alteration, 211
  biases, 203
    negativity, 204
  campaign coverage, 204
    gaffes, 205
    horserace, 205
    incumbent, 205
  children and the, 107
  congressional coverage, 206
  effects of, 210
  government regulation of, 190
  importance of, 195
  mass communication, 107
  news gathering process, 202
    organizational factors, 203

personal backgrounds, 202
political functions of, 194
politician management, 206
presidential coverage, 206
setting the political agenda, 211
structure of mass, 187
Medicaid, 532–533, 521, 325
Medicare, 520, 521, 533–536
Medicare Prescription Drug Improvement and Modernization Act, 533
Medigap insurance, 534
Meredith, James, 82, 439
Mestizos, 448
Mexico, 605
Micro and Macro approaches, 18
Microsoft, 240
Middle East, 606
Miers, Harriet, 268
Military-industrial complex, 238
Miller v. California (1973), 400
Minerals Management Service (MMS), 283
Minnick v Mississippi (1990), 361
Minority,
  floor leader, 264
Misdemeanor, 359
Mississippi Freedom Democratic Party, 148
Missouri Compromise (1820), 436
Mitchell v Helms (2000), 392
Model Cities, 524
"Moment of silence," 394
Monroe Doctrine, 599
Montreal Protocol, 548
Morsi, Muhammad, 576
Mothers Against Drunk Driver (MADD), 232
Mott, Lucretia, 457
Moyer, Bill, 205
Mubarak, Hosni, 576
Muir, John, 543

Multiculturalism, 425
Multi-lateral agreements, 584
Murdoch's News Corporation, 185
Muskie, Edmund, 546
Muslim Brotherhood, 576
Muslim religion, 606
Myers v United States (1926), 59

N

NAACP 441
Nader, Ralph, 130, 150, 208, 287
National Aeronautics and Space Administration (NASA), 293
National ambient air quality standards (NAAQS), 553
National American Women Suffrage Association, 458
National Association of Counties, 226
National Association of Manufacturers (NAM), 220
National Audubon Society, 224
National Environmental Policy Act of 1970, 546
National Farmers Union, 222
National Firearms Act, 405
National Governors' Association, 226
National interests, 577
National League of Cities, 226
National League of Cities v Usery (1976), 81
National Network for Election Reform, 212
National Organization for Marriage (NOM), 225
National Organization for Women (NOW), 222
National Origins Act, 454
National Resources Defense Council, 569
National Rifle Association (NRA), 217, 229, 405

National Safety Agency (1966), 287
National Security Agency (NSA), 402
National Security Council (NSC), 597
National Socialist Party, 106
National Wildlife Federation, 224
National Women's Political Caucus, 217, 223
Native Americans, 430
Nativism, 426
Nazism, 601
Near v. Minnesota (1931), 400
Negligence, 359
Neighborhood Guild, 523
Nelson, Bill, 260
Net neutrality, 192
Neutrality, 581
New Deal, 86, 286
New Federalism, 87
New Hampshire primary, 152
New Jersey Plan, 60, 248
New Left, 122
"New Politics" movement, 232
New Right, 120
Newtown, Connecticut 405
New York Times v. Sullivan (1971), 399
New York Times v United States (1971), 401
New York Women's Trade Union, 458
Nixon, Richard,
  bombing of Cambodia, 319
  changes in public policy, 480
  environmental action by, 553, 546
  new federalism, 88
  public opinion polls of, 98
  use of executive agreement, 597
  White House office, 317
Nixon v. Hernon (1927), 442
No Child Left Behind, 516

Non-zero sum game, 17
North American Free Trade
    Agreement (NAFTA),
    590, 605
North Atlantic Treaty Organization (NATO), 581, 602
North Korea, 579, 603–604, 604
Northwest Land Ordinance Act, 89
Nutrition Labeling and Education Act, 297

O

Obama, Barack,
  Affordable Care Act, 509
  bank bailout, 235
  best seller, 187
  election of 2008, 147, 207, 444
  environment, 543
  federal bureaucracy reform, 304
  gun control, 395
  health care, 531–536
  on racial equality, 421
  on sexual discrimination, 463
  presidential appointments, 192
Occupational Safety and Health
    Administration (OSH), 294, 483
Office of Management and Budget (OMB), 302, 325
Office of Public Liaison, 236
Office of Special Counsel, 304
Office of Technology Assessment, 271
Ohio's Criminal Syndicalism Act, 403
Old Age Assistance, 523
Olmstead, Ray, 415
Olmstead v. United States (1928), 415
Olney, Richard, 596
Olson, Mancur, 228

Omnibus Crime Control and
    Safe Streets Act (1968), 416
Open Door Policy, 590
Open primary, 148
Oral arguments, 372
O'Reilly, Bill, 201
Oswald, Lee Harvey, 71
Outputs, 476
Ozone, 548

P

Paine, Thomas, 52, 108
Pakistan, 608
Palin, Sarah, 108
Palko v. Connecticut (1937), 406
Panama Canal, 313
Panama Canal Treaty, 596
Parent-Teacher Associations, 226
Park Protection Act, 544
Parks, Rosa, 441
Party-line voting, 266
Patient Protection and Affordable Care Act, 471
Patriot Act, 268, 404, 474
Patronage, 256
Patterson, William, 60
Paul, Alice, 459
Peace of Westphalia of 1648, 581
Pearl Harbor, 601
Pendleton Act (1883), 295
Penny press, 198
People for the American Way, 222
Peremptory challenges, 363
Perot, Ross, 130, 150, 158
Perry, Rick, 91, 129
Personal Responsibility and
    Work Opportunity Act, 529
Pinckney, Charles, 595
Plaintiff, 358
Planned Parenthood, 217
Plato, 4, 26

Plea bargaining, 361
Pledged delegates, 136
"Pledge to America," 273
Plintz v United States (1997), 82
Pluralism, 230
Pluralist theory, 38
Pocket veto, 276
Political Action Committees
    (PACs), 30, 161, 234
  effects of, 235
Political culture, 100
  Alexis de Tocqueville, 101
  Benjamin Franklin, 101
  Gabriel Almond, 102
  Sidney Verba, 102
Political parties,
  anatomy of, 115–118
  caucuses within, 130
  factions in, 130–131
  historical development of, 116
  multiparty system, 117
  national conventions of, 135
  national party organization, 134–136
  platform of, 135
  political spectrum, 119
  role in policy making, 479
  stratarchy of, 134
  two-party system, 118
Political science,
  definition of, 29
Political socialization, 102
  agents of, 103
  fascist Germany, 106
  significance of, 108
Political spectrum, 33
  political left, 34
  political right, 33
Political system, 20
Political techniques,
  limitations of, 12
*Politics Among Nations: The
    Struggle for Power and
    Peace* (Morgenthau), 587
Polk, James, 313
Polling, 171

Poll tax, 438
Pollution, 548
Pollution Prevention Act (1990), 563
Pork-barrel legislation, 156, 255, 495
Postal Service, 294, 295
Poverty,
  feminization of, 512
  levels of, 510, 511
  philosophy of, 518
  politics of, 518
  profile of, 513
Powell, Colin, 481
Powell v. Alabama (1932), 410
Pragmatic federalism, 88
Precinct, 138
Presidente Rivera, 561
President pro tempore, 263
President(s), 309–327
  as chief of state, 314
  cabinet of, 315
  characteristics of, 333
  executive orders of, 316
  impoundment of funds by, 326
  leadership of, 326–343
  personalities of, 334
  powers and duties of, 312
  qualifications for, 310
  roles of, 314
  veto power of, 324
Preventive strategy, 491
Primary system, 147
Priorities USA Action Super Pac, 235
Private bill, 256
Procedural problems, 487
Proclamation of 1763, 431
Proclamation of Neutrality, 599
Progressive movement, 286
Progressive tax, 497
Project Safe Neighborhoods, 366
Prometheus v. FCC (2004), 202
Proportional tax, 497

Public assistance programs, 528
Public opinion, 97–111
  importance of, 98
  role in policy making, 477
Public policy,
  agenda building, 488
  budgeting of, 494
  definition of, 475
  evaluation of, 501
  implementation of, 500
  political implications of, 498
  process of, 485
  who makes, 477
Pulitzer, Joseph, 198
Punitive approach, 490
Pure Food and Drug Act, 545

Q

Quadruple Alliance, 581, 599
Quartering Act, 52
Quayle, Dan, 180, 332

R

Rabin, Yizhak, 323
Racial profiling, 429
Racism,
  of African Americans, 435
  of Native Americans, 430
  theories of, 425
Radical Republicans, 437
Railroad Retirement Act (1934), 287
Randolph, Edmund, 62, 364
Ratification, 64
Reagan, Ronald,
  deregulation viewpoint of, 288
  election of 1980, 288
  Grenada & Libya invasion, 319
  immigration, 453
  privatization, 290
  states's rights, 81, 87
  welfare reform of, 518
Reapportionment, 153
Redistributive policy, 492
Redistricting, 257

Redlining, 441
Reed, Kasim, 71
Reflections on the Revolution in France (Burke), 47
Reform,
  health-care, 531
  welfare, 530
Reform Party, 130
Refuse Act (1899), 543
Regressive tax, 497
Regulatory actions, 493
Regulatory agencies, 293
Rehabilitation Act (1973), 464
Reid, Harry, 226, 275
Religious Right, 120
Reno, Janet, 460
Representative democracy, 48
Republican National Committee (RNC), 134
Republic of Congo, 225
Reserved powers, 542
Resource Conservation and Recovery Act, 562
Restore Our Future Super PAC, 235
Restrictive covenant, 441
Rice, Susan, 315
Riegle, Donald, 235
Rights of Man, The (Paine), 50
Rio Pact, 602
Robb, Chuck, 577
Roberts, John, 82, 369, 472
Rodriguez, Ciro, 135
Roe v. Wade (1973), 231, 460, 482
Romney, Mitt, 164, 472, 555
Roosevelt, Franklin, 86, 123, 125, 287, 314, 319, 473
  civil liberties, 384
  use of executive agreements, 596
Roosevelt, Theodore, 313, 543
Rotary Club, 226
Roth v United States (1957), 399
Rousseau, Jean Jacques, 4
Rove, Karl, 268, 168, 169

Rubio, Marc, 454
Rule adjudication, 297
Rush-Bagot Agreement, 596
Rush, Benjamin, 53
Rusk, Dean, 599
Russell, Bertrand, 35
Russia, 580
Ryan, Paul, 226

S

Sadat, Anwar, 583, 585
Safety net, 527
Safe Water Drinking Act (1974), 559
Safire, William, 12
Salazar, Ken, 296
Salient, 9, 98
Same-sex marriages, 78
Sandy Hook Elementary School, 218
Scalia, Antonin, 81
Schalala, Donna, 299
Schenck v. United States (1919), 388, 396
Scott, Dred, 436
Search warrant, 360
Sebelius, Kathleen, 473
Sedition Acts (1798), 395
Select committees, 269
Selective incorporation, 388
Senate Bill 1070, 430
Senatorial courtesy, 315
Senior Executive Service (SES), 295
"Separate but equal," 438, 442
Separate Car Act (1890), 439
Separation of powers doctrine, 59
Service Employees International Union, 168
Settlement house, 522
Shaw, Anna Howard, 459
Shays, Daniel, 55
Sherman, Robert, 60
Shiites, 578
Sierra Club, 114, 232, 543, 569

Silverman v. United States (1961), 416
Skinhead groups, 403
Skinner v. Railway Labor Executives Association (1989), 416
Slaughterhouse Cases (1873), 406
Small Business Administration, 293
Smith Act, 405
Smith v. Allwright (1944), 442
Smog, 548
Smoot-Hawley Tariff Act, 590
Snowden, Eric, 402
Social contract theory, 47, 122
Socialism, 122
Social Media, 189–190
Social Security Act (1935), 287, 292, 491, 523, 526
Social Security Administration, 510
Soft money, 150, 161, 162, 168
Solicitor General of the United States, 367
Sotomayor, Sonia, 170, 369
South Carolina v Baker (1988), 81
Southern Christian Leadership Conference (SCLC), 441
South Korea, 604
Speaker of the House, 261
Special interest groups, 150
Specter, Arlen, 310
Spin doctor, 207, 327
Spirit of the Laws (Montesquieu), 49
Stalin, Joseph, 602
Stamp Act (1765), 52, 197
Standing committees, 268
Stanton, Elizabeth Cady, 457
Status quo, 34
Steering, 441
Stephanopoules, George, 205
Stevenson, Adlai, 149
Stevens, Ted, 242

Stone, Lucy, 458
Stop Piracy Act, 225
Strategic Arms Limitation Treaty (SALT II), 322
Strayhorn, Carole Keeton, 129
Street v. New York (1969), 397
Subpoena, 362
Subsidies, 492
Substantive problems, 487
Sugar Act, 51
Summit meetings, 323
Sunni, 578
Sunshine Act, 304
Superfund programs, 563
Super PACs, 234
Supplemental Nutrition Assistance Program, 528
Supremacy clause, 71, 385, 482
Supreme Court, 371
Surface Transportation Board, 81
Surveys, 6
Suspended particulates, 548
Sweatt v. Painter (1950), 442
Swing districts, 247
Switzerland, 581
Symbolic speech, 397
Systems analysis, 18

T

Taliban, 579
Tate, Deborah, 192
Tax accuracy, 496
Tax equity, 497
Tax rebate program, 499
Teamsters Union, 221, 605
Tea Party movement, 84, 133, 179, 478
Technorati, 186
Telecommunications Act (1966), 402
Temperance Movement, 458
Tennessee Valley Authority (TVA), 241, 294
Terrorism, 384
Terry v. Ohio (1968), 416

Texas v White (1869), 84
Theories, 27
Third parties, 129, 150
Thomas, Clarence, 81, 441
Tildon, Samuel, 157
Time Warner, 185
Tinker v. Des Moines School District (1969), 397
Tort law, 359
Tory Party, 116
Toxic Substance Control Act (1976), 562
Toxic wastes, 560
Trail of Tears, 431
Transitional immunity, 362
Trans Mountain project, 555
Treaty of Guadalupe Hidalgo, 451
Treaty of Paris, 585
Treaty of Versailles, 582, 596, 601
Trenkle, Tony, 494
Tripoli, 391
Truman Doctrine, 602
Truman, Harry,
    desegregate military branches, 481
    Korea, 319
    primary system views of, 148
Trustee, 253
Tunisia, 607
TVA v. Hill (1978), 241
Twitter, 189
Two Treaties on Government (Locke), 384
Tyler, Tom, 285

U

Unemployment Insurance, 523
Unfunded mandate, 91
United Arab Emirates, 225
United Farm Workers Union, 229, 449
United Nations, 582
United States Drug Enforcement Administration (DEA), 366
United States Forest Service, 564
United States Marshals Service, 365
United States v. Harriss (1954), 238
United States v Lopez (1995), 81
United States v. O'Brien (1968), 397
Urban Institute, 224

V

Valeo, Buckley V., 170
Van de Putte, Leticia, 460
Veto, 276
Viacom, 185
Village of Skokie v National Socialist Party (1978), 404
Vilsack, Tom, 296
Violence Against Women Act, 217
Virginia Plan, 59, 248
Vocational Rehabilitation Act (1920), 463
Voter fraud, 175
Voting Rights Act (1965), 174, 442
Voucher programs, 392

W

Wald, Lillian, 523
Wallace, George, 158
Wallace v Jaffree (1985), 393
Walter Reed Army Medical Center, 268
War chest, 260
War on Poverty, 86, 532, 231, 523, 489
War Powers Act (1973), 319, 493
Warrantless search, 360
Warren, Earl, 377, 407
Warren, Rick, 223

Warsaw Pact, 582
Washington, George, 62, 124, 144, 315
    religious tolerance, 391
Watergate, 161, 199, 251
Ways and Means Committee, 269
Weintraub, Walter, 12
Welfare reform, 508, 530
Welfare state,
    historical development of, 521
    programs of, 526
Wells, H. G., 2
Wesberry v Sanders (1964), 257
Westboro Baptist Church, 396
Wetlands conservation, 563
Wetlands Reserve Program, 564
Wheeler, Earle, 599
Whig Party, 116, 323
Whistle-Blower Protection Act (1989), 304
White, Ben Chester, 422
White House, 206, 315
White only primary, 438
White, Thomas, 169
Whitewater, 251
Wilderness Bill (1964), 545
Wildlife Federation, 569
Will, George, 205
Wilson, Pete, 181
Wilson, Woodrow, 119, 125, 314
Witness protection program, 361
Woman's Party, 459
Women's suffrage, 175
Woods, Robert A., 523
Works Progress Administration (WPA), 523
World Prodigy, 561
World Trade Center, 598
World War II, 287
Wounded Knee, 432
Wright, Jeremiah, 223
Writ, 358
Writ of certiorari, 371

Writ of habeas corpus, 319, 407

Y

Yalta Agreement, 584
Yat-sen, Sun, 603
Yellow journalism, 198
Yeltsin, Boris N., 109
YouTube, 108, 189

Z

Zedong, Mao, 603
Zero-based budgeting, 498
Zero-sum game, 17
Zoelick, Robert, 169
Zyuganov, Gennadi A., 109